Office XP Bible

Edward C. Willett and Steve Cummings

Hungry Minds™

Best-Selling Books • Digital Downloads • e-Books • Answer Networks • e-Newsletters • Branded Web Sites • e-Learning

Indianapolis, IN ✦ Cleveland, OH ✦ New York, NY

Office XP Bible

Published by
Hungry Minds, Inc.
909 Third Avenue
New York, NY 10022
www.hungryminds.com

Library of Congress Control Number: 2001092062

ISBN: 0-7645-3592-7

Printed in the United States of America

10 9 8 7 6 5 4 3 2 1

1B/RU/QX/QR/IN

Distributed in the United States by Hungry
Minds, Inc.

Distributed by CDG Books Canada Inc. for Canada; by
Transworld Publishers Limited in the United
Kingdom; by IDG Norge Books for Norway; by IDG
Sweden Books for Sweden; by IDG Books Australia
Publishing Corporation Pty. Ltd. for Australia and
New Zealand; by TransQuest Publishers Pte Ltd. for
Singapore, Malaysia, Thailand, Indonesia, and Hong
Kong; by Gotop Information Inc. for Taiwan; by ICG
Muse, Inc. for Japan; by Intersoft for South Africa; by
Eyrolles for France; by International Thomson
Publishing for Germany, Austria, and Switzerland; by
Distribuidora Cuspide for Argentina; by LR
International for Brazil; by Galileo Libros for Chile; by
Ediciones ZETA S.C.R. Ltda. for Peru; by WS
Computer Publishing Corporation, Inc., for the
Philippines; by Contemporanea de Ediciones for
Venezuela; by Express Computer Distributors for the
Caribbean and West Indies; by Micronesia Media
Distributor, Inc. for Micronesia; by Chips
Computadoras S.A. de C.V. for Mexico; by Editorial
Norma de Panama S.A. for Panama; by American
Bookshops for Finland.

For general information on Hungry Minds' products
and services please contact our Customer Care
department within the U.S. at 800-762-2974, outside
the U.S. at 317-572-3993 or fax 317-572-4002.

For sales inquiries and reseller information, including
discounts, premium and bulk quantity sales, and
foreign-language translations, please contact our
Customer Care department at 800-434-3422, fax
317-572-4002 or write to Hungry Minds, Inc., Attn:
Customer Care Department, 10475 Crosspoint
Boulevard, Indianapolis, IN 46256.

For information on licensing foreign or domestic
rights, please contact our Sub-Rights Customer Care
department at 212-884-5000.

For information on using Hungry Minds' products
and services in the classroom or for ordering
examination copies, please contact our Educational
Sales department at 800-434-2086 or fax 317-572-4005.

For press review copies, author interviews, or other
publicity information, please contact our Public
Relations department at 317-572-3168 or fax
317-572-4168.

For authorization to photocopy items for corporate,
personal, or educational use, please contact
Copyright Clearance Center, 222 Rosewood Drive,
Danvers, MA 01923, or fax 978-750-4470.

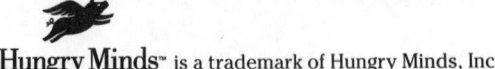

Hungry Minds™ is a trademark of Hungry Minds, Inc.

About the Authors

Edward C. Willett is a freelance writer in Regina, Saskatchewan, Canada. He's the author of several computer books, most recently *Your Official America Online Guide to Internet Safety* also published by Hungry Minds. In addition, he writes a science column for radio and television, children's science books, and fantasy novels for young adults (*Soulworm* and *The Dark Unicorn* from Royal Fireworks Press, and *Andy Nebula: Interstellar Rock Star* from Roussan Publishers). He is also a professional actor and singer.

Steve Cummings is the author of *Microsoft Office 2000 Secrets* and *VBA For Dummies* (both published by Hungry Minds), as well as ten other computer books. He also develops custom Office-based software solutions for health care organizations, retailers, and other businesses.

Contributing writer **Ramesh Chandak** is a graduate with a Fellowship in Advanced Engineering Study from MIT (Cambridge, Massachusetts). He has over 12 years of work experience within the IT industry. Ramesh has worked extensively with Microsoft tools and technologies including Active Server Pages, Visual Basic, and VBA. In addition, he has authored and edited over 33 books and published 25+ technical articles for several leading publishers on client/server application development, databases, multimedia, and Internet technologies. And Ramesh has also authored four Web-based courses and is an avid trainer.

Credits

Contributing Writer
Ramesh Chandak

Acquisitions Editors
Terri Varveris
Jill Byus Schorr

Project Editor
Kevin Kent

Development Editor
Laura Frey

Technical Editor
Karen Weinstein

Copy Editors
Barry Childs-Helton
Dennis Weaver

Editorial Managers
Ami Frank Sullivan
Kyle Looper

Project Coordinator
Regina Snyder

Graphics and Production Specialists
Stephanie D. Jumper
Jill Piscitelli
Heather Pope
Laurie Stevens

Quality Control Technicians
Andy Hollandbeck
Carl Pierce
Dwight Ramsey
Charles Spencer

Proofreading and Indexing
TECHBOOKS Production Services

Cover Image
Kate Shaw

To Ernest Neufeld, publisher of the Weyburn, Saskatchewan, Review, for the invaluable opportunity to learn how to write quickly, write well, and meet impossible deadlines.

Preface

Welcome to the *Office XP Bible*! This is your guide to the latest and greatest version of the immensely popular Microsoft suite of office applications. Within these pages is everything you need to know to make immediate, effective use of Microsoft Word, Microsoft Excel, Microsoft PowerPoint, Microsoft Outlook, Microsoft Access, Microsoft FrontPage, and Microsoft Publisher. You can read about how to use each of these programs separately to help you do your work better, as well as how to use them together to create integrated documents that draw on the strengths of all these programs.

Is This Book for You?

If you use (or will soon be using) Microsoft Office XP, then this book is for you. Beginners should start with the special Quick Start chapters that make up the first part of the book; experienced users can move straight on to the sections devoted to each of the applications or take a brief course in Visual Basic for Applications. Throughout this book you'll find useful tips and step-by-step guides for carrying out the most common Office tasks. Both the excellent index and thorough table of contents can help you find the topics that interest you.

How This Book Is Organized

Office XP Bible comprises 11 parts and an appendix, all of which are described in the following overviews.

Part I: Quick Start

These two chapters tell you just what you need—no more, no less—to start using Office in general, and in particular to start using Word, Excel, and Outlook for their primary purposes: creating documents, creating spreadsheets, and sending and receiving e-mail.

Part II: Getting the Most out of Office

This part covers the Office user interface and other issues concerning the Office suite in general such as the Help system and using Office in conjunction with networks and the Internet.

Part III: Building Great Documents with Office XP

The chapters in this part tell you what you need to know to build great documents in Office, covering topics common to almost all Office applications, such as creating and inserting graphics, sharing information between documents, and printing. This part also covers the important topic of how to protect your precious documents from disaster.

Part IV: Creating Effective Documents with Word

As the flagship of the Office suite, Word is far and away the most widely used application software in the world. Although writing letters and creating other basic documents with Word is easy, this program provides many great features that aren't obvious or that require special steps to achieve the desired results. You'll learn about both the obvious and the less obvious functions of Word in this part.

Part V: Crunching Numbers Efficiently with Excel

Excel is Office's spreadsheet application, and, like Word, it's pretty much the standard in its field. This discussion of Excel shows you how to get the most from this Office application and from your own worksheets.

Part VI: Communicating and Organizing with Outlook

Outlook is Office's application for managing not only messages, such as faxes and e-mail, but also your time, contacts, and commitments. The chapters in this part help you get the most from Outlook — not only from its messaging capabilities, but also from its time- and task-management features.

Part VII: Presenting Your Thoughts Powerfully with PowerPoint

PowerPoint is Office's presentation software. This part demonstrates how to make powerful presentations that communicate your messages clearly and effectively.

Part VIII: Designing Dazzling Publications with Publisher

Publisher is a full-featured desktop-publishing program, perfect for creating everything from newsletters to annual reports. These chapters provide you with a brief introduction to Publisher, which is included in the Office XP Professional Special Edition or in a new PC preinstalled with Office XP Professional with Publisher or the Small Business Edition of Office XP.

Part IX: Creating and Managing a Wonderful Web Site with FrontPage

FrontPage, included in Office XP Developer and Office XP Professional Special Edition, helps you create professional-looking Web pages and manage them effectively. These chapters give an overview of FrontPage and outline how you can use other Office applications to create top-notch Web pages.

Part X: Managing and Manipulating Data with Access

Just as Outlook lets you manage messages and your time, so Access lets you manage data — and use it in other Office applications. This part explains how.

Part XI: Tapping the Programming Power of VBA

Visual Basic for Applications (VBA) gives you greater control of Office applications — even the capability to develop your own specialized Office tools. This part provides a serious introduction to VBA programming.

Appendix

The included appendix points you to Web sites where you'll find more information on Office XP and lots of useful tips, tricks, templates, and so on.

Conventions This Book Uses

We've made finding your way through this massive tome easier by including a variety of signposts that point you to useful information. Look for these icons in the left margin:

Notes highlight something of particular interest about the current topic, or expand on the subject at hand.

These icons clue you in to hot tips, or show you faster, better ways of doing things.

If a process holds some risk of losing data, irrevocably altering a document, or annoying the heck out of you, this icon will warn you of it.

This icon points you to another section of the book where additional information on the current topic can be found.

This icon highlights several of the new features offered by the applications of Office XP.

Menu and keyboard command conventions

When you are directed to use a particular command from a menu, it will appear like this: choose File ➪ New. That tells you to pull down the File menu and click on the New command. If there's another level of menu beyond that, it'll look like this: choose View ➪ Toolbars ➪ Formatting.

Keyboard commands are written like this: press Ctrl+A. That means to press the Ctrl key and continue to hold it down while you press the *A* key.

Typing code and commands

At various places in this book, you find listings of the programming code for macros (technically, VBA procedures) that can make your work more efficient or help you customize your Office applications. In addition, I occasionally suggest entries you should type at various locations. When listed on separate lines, these items appear in a special font, as in the following example:

```
Sub DoNothingProcedure()
    x = x
End Sub
```

Snippets of VBA code or brief commands sometimes appear within a paragraph, in which case they appear in monospace type.

Use the instructions in Chapter 52 to enter macros in the Visual Basic Editor. You should type them into a new module exactly as they appear in the text. Lines that end with an underscore (the _ character) have been broken up so they'll fit on the page. You can type these lines as they are printed—the underscore is VBA's line-continuation character—or you can move up the text from the next line, deleting the underscore to make one longer line.

In a command or line of code that includes paired brackets, the brackets indicate an optional item. If you include that item, leave out the bracket characters when you type the command. Italics indicate an item for which you must supply a name, such as a filename or the name of a macro or command.

What You'll Find in Sidebars

Sidebars provide related information, examples, or additional detail about a topic. Generally the information in sidebars, while interesting, isn't critical to understanding how to use an application, so you can skip them if you like. (Naturally, we'd prefer you didn't — after all, we put a lot of work into writing them!)

Web site with code samples

The longer, more involved code samples in this book can be found at the following Web site: `http://catalog.hungryminds.com/extras/0764535927/`. At that site and at your leisure, you can access and copy these longer code samples for your own trial purposes.

Where Should I Start?

With a such a complete and thoughtfully designed resource (a book as comprehensive as its subject), it may difficult to decide where to begin. Here are a few helpful hints:

✦ **If you're entirely new to Office:** Start with Part I: Quick Start. It will have you using Office's applications in minutes.

✦ **To work with a specific application:** With Word, Excel, PowerPoint, Outlook, Access, or FrontPage, refer to the pertinent parts and chapters in the book.

✦ **To begin teaching yourself VBA:** Part XI provides a thorough introduction to this programming tool.

✦ **To work with a specific topic:** Let the table of contents or the complete index at the back of the book be your guide.

✦ **To find additional sources of information:** Refer to the appendix.

✦ **If all else fails:** Simply turn the page and begin.

Acknowledgments

I would like to thank the team at Hungry Minds for all their hard work in helping to put this manuscript together. Without the efforts of the editors — Terri Varveris, Jill Byus Schorr, Kevin Kent, Barry Childs-Helton, Karen Weinstein, Laura Frey, and Dennis Weaver — and all the others who have touched this book, you wouldn't be holding it now.

Thanks also to my agent, Djana Pearson Morris, and, as always, thanks to my wife, Margaret Anne, for having dared to marry a freelance writer.

—*Edward C. Willett*

Contents at a Glance

Contents

● ●

Part II: Getting the Most out of Office — 39

Part V: Crunching Numbers Efficiently with Excel   525

Chapter 23: Power Customizing Excel 527

Chapter 24: Advanced Navigation and Selection 537

Chapter 38: Saving Time with Templates and Wizards 801

Chapter 39: Sprucing Up Your Presentation with Graphics and Special Effects 817

Chapter 40: Creating and Organizing a Slide Show 831

Part VIII: Designing Dazzling Publications with Publisher   851

Part IX: Creating and Managing a Wonderful Web Site with FrontPage   897

Chapter 43: Designing Web Pages with FrontPage 899

Quick Start

This part provides an overview of Office, discussing how to navigate through Office applications and access their tools and functions. Then it takes a quick dip into each of the three most-used applications in Office — Word, Excel, and Outlook — and explains briefly how to accomplish the tasks they are most often used for: creating a document, creating a spreadsheet, and sending and receiving e-mail.

Welcome to Your New Office!

Welcome to Microsoft Office XP! It's a powerful, complex piece of software, but don't let that worry you; in this chapter (and the ensuing Quick Start chapter), I'll get you up and running in no time, even if you've never used Office before.

Introducing Office Applications: What Do They Do?

You'll explore a lot of different Office applications in this book. Here's a brief list (you may not have all these applications, depending on what version of Office you've purchased):

◆ **Word:** Use this word processor to enter and format text to print or post online.

◆ **Excel:** Use this spreadsheet program to organize numbers into rows and columns, manipulate them, and analyze them for budgeting and planning.

◆ **Outlook:** Use this program to manage electronic messages and your time.

◆ **PowerPoint:** Use this program to communicate your ideas clearly with vivid on-screen or printed presentations.

◆ **Publisher:** Use this desktop publishing software to simplify the task of placing text and graphics exactly where you want them in a document.

◆ **FrontPage:** Use this specialized software to create and manage Web sites.

◆ **Access:** Access makes it easy to collect and analyze data—and to use it in other Office software.

Starting Office Applications

The usual way to start Office applications is with the Start menu: Choose Start ➪ Program, find the application you want to start, and click it. You can also start applications from the Office Shortcut Bar (described in detail later in this chapter).

Tip   You might find it handy to create shortcuts to your most commonly used Office applications on your desktop. To do so, just click and drag the program from the Start ➪ Program menu to the desktop. This doesn't remove it from the Start ➪ Program menu; it just creates a shortcut.

Creating, Saving, and Closing Documents

You can create a new Office document from within an Office application, using the Start menu, or using the Shortcut Bar.

Within any Office application, choose File ➪ New. This brings up different options, depending on the application. Choose the option you want.

Instead of opening an Office application and then creating a new document, you can also create a new document and open the application you need at the same time. To do so, choose Start ➪ New Office Document, or, if you have the Office Shortcut Bar turned on, click the New Office Document button. You'll see the New Office Document dialog box shown in Figure 1-1.

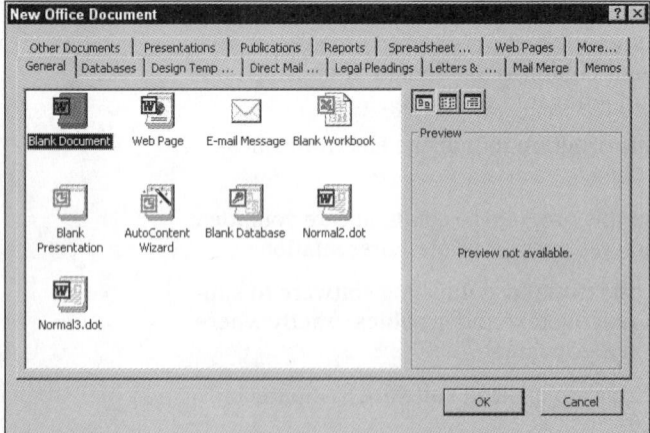

Figure 1-1: The New Office Document dialog box lets you choose which of many different kinds of Office documents you want to create.

Click the tab you want and choose from the options present.

Saving documents

To save a document in any Office application, choose File ⇨ Save or File ⇨ Save As. The first time you choose Save (or any time you choose Save As), the Save As dialog box (see Figure 1-2) appears.

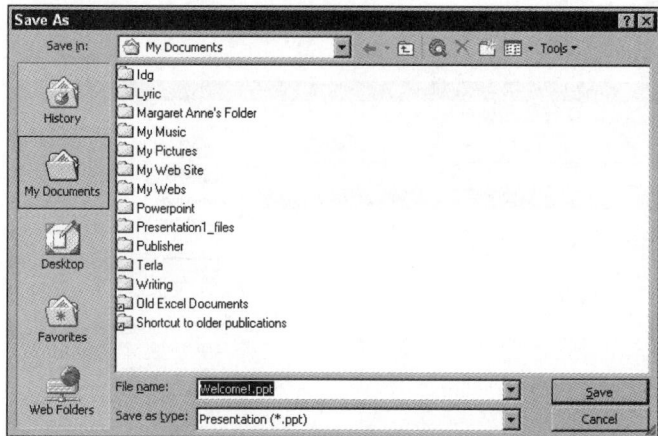

Figure 1-2: The Save As dialog box lets you specify where, in what format, and with what name you want to save your Office document.

Type the name you want to give the document into the "File name" box, and choose the type of file it is in the "Save as type" box, using the pull-down list provided.

After you've saved a document, choosing Save again overwrites the previous version of the document with the current version. To save the new version of a document without overwriting the previous version (or to save it in a different file format), choose File ⇨ Save As; then give the new version a new name or choose a new format for it.

Closing documents

In the upper-right corner of the window that contains your Office document, normally you see two *X*s. Clicking the outermost *X* closes all open documents, and then closes the application. Clicking the inner *X* closes the currently open document but leaves the application running. (Alternatively, choose File ⇨ Close.)

If you haven't saved the current version of the document, Office asks whether you want to save the changes you made. Choose Yes to overwrite any previous version with the current version, No to keep the previous version (and lose any changes in the current version), or Cancel to simply return to the application.

Using Office Search Effectively

Office XP features an enhanced search capability that makes specific documents easier to locate. It even searches through all the messages you've stored in Outlook!

To access Search from any Office application, choose File ➪ Search. This opens the task pane shown in Figure 1-3.

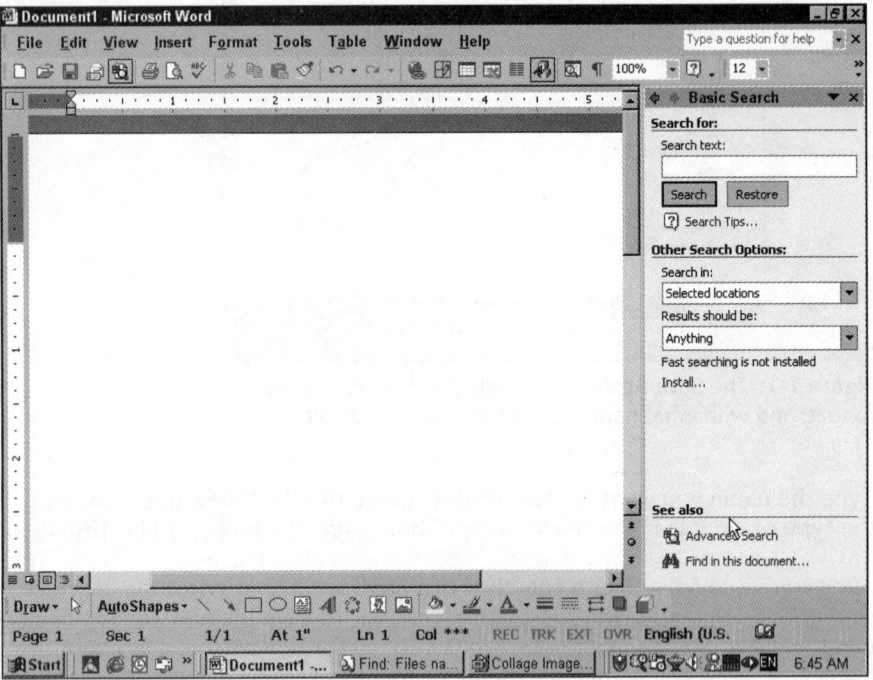

Figure 1-3: The Basic Search task pane helps you find files quickly and easily.

Enter the text you want to look for in the "Search text" box. Search looks for files containing that text in their name, body, or assigned keywords. You can use wildcards: the asterisk (*) can stand for any number of characters (a search for *h*p* would return everything from *hop* to *horsewhip*); the question mark (?) stands for any single character (a search for *h?p* would turn up files containing *hop*, but not *horsewhip*).

Note   Search looks for all forms of a word you enter in the "Search text" box. If you enter **run**, for instance, it also finds files containing *running* and *ran*.

In the "Search in" box , specify where Office should search: My Computer, My Network Places, Web Folders, or Outlook. You can specify certain folders if you want.

Finally, in the "Results should be" box, specify which types of file to search for: Anything, Office Files, Outlook Items, or Web pages. To narrow the search further, specify which types of Office files and which specific Outlook items.

Once results are displayed, rest your pointer on the name of any file to get more information about it, click to open it, right-click to see more actions, or click the Modify button near the bottom of the Search Results task pane to start a new search.

Click Advanced Search at the bottom of the Basic Search task pane to run searches based on document properties, such as author and date modified, and to use logic (that is, And/Or) to include or exclude information.

Tip   If you're searching your Outlook files, and you're working in English, you can ask your search query using natural language — for example, **Find all messages received today.**

Getting Help in Office Applications

Office provides a massive amount of on-screen help, which, considering how complex Office has become, is a very good thing.

To access Help from within an Office application, do one of three things:

✦ If the Office Assistant is turned on, click it and then type a question into its balloon or click one of the topics it suggests.

✦ If the Office Assistant is turned off or hasn't been installed, press F1 or choose the menu item for the current application from the top of the Help menu (for example, Help ➪ Microsoft PowerPoint Help).

✦ New for Office XP, you can type your query into the box labeled "Type a question for help" in the upper-right corner of every application; then press Return or Enter.

Navigating Help

Help offers a simple toolbar at the top of the Help window (see Figure 1-4). At the far left, the Show and Hide buttons determine whether the tabs frame is visible — it's the part that has the Contents, Answer Wizard, and Index tabs. The Back and Forward buttons work like their counterparts in a browser. Clicking the Options button reveals additional choices: Home jumps to the home page defined for the Help topic, Stop and Refresh perform as they do in a browser, and Internet Options displays the same options you find on the Control Panel.

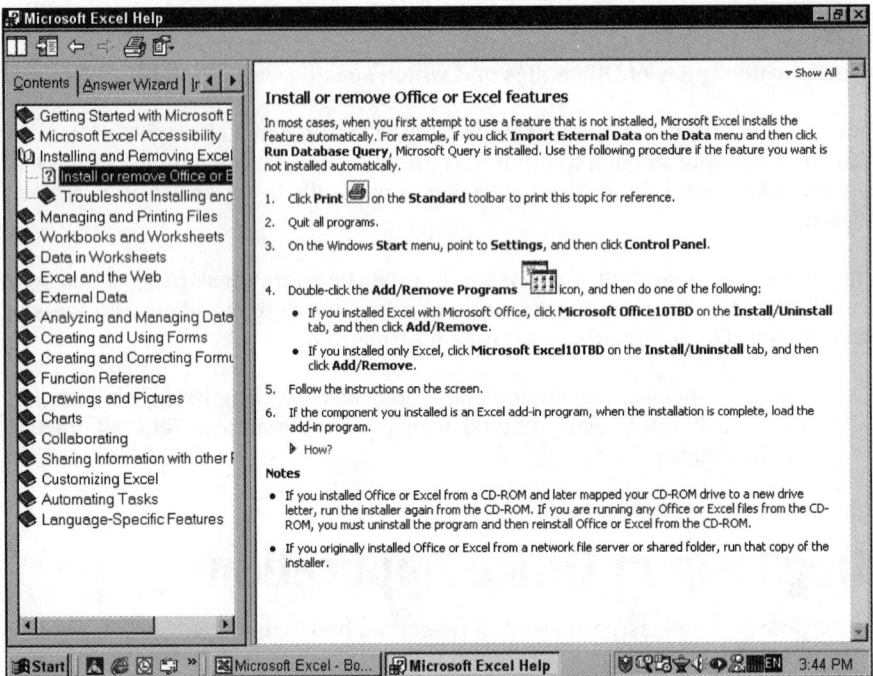

Figure 1-4: HTML Help for Excel

A *topic* is the information contained in the Help window at one time. You may have to scroll to read the entire topic, but you don't have to use any other navigation tools. Click a colored link to see the Help information it refers to. Underlined links take you to other topics. Non-underlined links display a tidbit of information—typically a definition.

When Help tabs are visible, they appear in a separate frame on the left side of the window. You use them to locate Help topics of interest. The three tabs are as follows:

✦ **Contents.** This displays the available Help topics hierarchically. Click any item that displays a plus sign to expand the list.

✦ **Answer Wizard.** Type in a question or just enter a few words describing the subject you want help with. The Help topic deemed most relevant appears in the main part of the window; related topics are listed below your query.

✦ **Index.** The Index tab lists keywords. Type in a term or select one from the list.

Tip

If Help is open with more than one Office application running, you can't switch directly from one application to another. Let's say you're working in Word and want to switch to PowerPoint. If you click PowerPoint's button on the taskbar (or choose its icon using Alt+Tab), you see PowerPoint Help instead of PowerPoint itself. To get to the target application, click its taskbar button again or use Alt+Tab to select its icon again.

Working with the Office Assistant

By now you've undoubtedly crossed paths with the Office Assistant, the animated graphic that steps in to answer your queries and often to offer advice before you ask for it. The Assistant is one of those love-it-or-hate-it affairs. Personally, I find it annoying and distracting, which is why I'm glad Office XP now deactivates the Assistant by default (so you have to turn it on if you want to use it) and instead provides the functions of the Assistant via the "Type a question for help" field.

The Office Assistant offers tips, as soon as you use a program feature it thinks you should know more about, and provides a friendly access point to the Help system via the balloon displayed when you press F1 or click the Assistant. Here, you can select from one of the topics that the Assistant thinks you might be wondering about — based on your most recent actions — or type in a question in ordinary English and choose Search.

Taking control of the Assistant

If the Assistant becomes a nuisance or gets in your way, right-click it and choose Hide. To modify the way the Assistant works more permanently, choose Options in the Assistant's balloon. In the resulting dialog box, click the Gallery tab to preview and select from various Assistant personalities, and click the Options tab to set options.

If, like me, you prefer that F1 activate the full Help system rather than the Assistant, clear the box labeled Respond to F1 Key. Use the settings in the bottom half of the Options tab to control the display of tips. (Notice the box labeled Show the Tip of the Day at Startup. Check here to see a new tip each time you start the current program.)

Tip

You may want to be able to use the Assistant and directly access the full Help system as well. To give yourself this flexibility, first clear the Respond to F1 Key box, Then, in the Tools ➪ Customize dialog box, switch to the Commands tab, select Window and Help in the Categories list, find the Contents and Index command in the list on the right, and drag it to your Help menu.

Shutting off the Assistant

If you regret the fact you activated the Assistant, shut it off by right-clicking it, choosing Options, and then clearing the checkbox labeled Use the Office Assistant. You can revive the Assistant by choosing Help ➪ Show the Office Assistant.

Using Office's Toolbars

If you've used versions of Office before Office 2000, you've probably noticed that there seem to be fewer toolbars at the top of your applications than you might expect.

The usual Standard and Formatting toolbars are still there, but by default they're now on the same level. In addition, they don't display all their buttons all the time — and the buttons they do display change. That's because when you first open an Office application, only the most commonly used commands are visible on the toolbars or menus. However, you can access all other available commands by clicking the Toolbar Options button at the toolbar's right end (see Figure 1-5). (To see all the items available in any menu, hold your mouse pointer over the menu name for a few extra seconds or click the double down arrow at the bottom of the menu.)

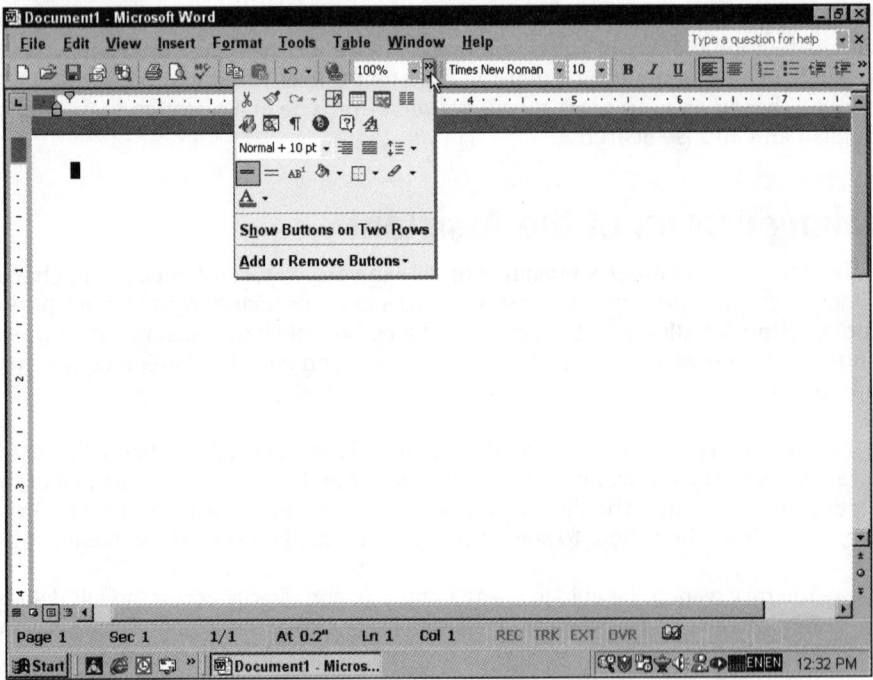

Figure 1-5: Click Toolbar Options to see all the buttons that aren't visible on the short toolbars.

Whenever you use a command, it's automatically made visible on the short toolbar or menu, replacing a button or command that hasn't been used for a while. Eventually the short toolbars and menus display the commands you use most often.

Tip   You can find out what any button does by holding the mouse pointer over the button for a second or two. In Office, the message that appears is called a *ScreenTip*. If you don't see the ScreenTips, turn them on by checking the appropriate box in the Options tab of the Tools ➪ Customize dialog box.

If you'd prefer to have the Standard and Formatting toolbars appear the same way they do in earlier versions of Office, choose Show Buttons on Two Rows from the Toolbar Options menu.

If you don't see the double arrow on the Toolbar Options button, all the toolbar's buttons are already visible. However, on built-in toolbars, the Toolbar Options button always shows a single arrow pointing down, even when all buttons are visible. That's to indicate that you can still access the Add or Remove buttons command.

Cross-Reference The Add or Remove buttons command is covered in detail in Chapter 5.

Will that be hidden, docked, or floating?

Every Office toolbar can either be hidden, docked, or floating. Hidden toolbars can't be seen (duh!), but Figure 1-6 shows both of the other types clearly.

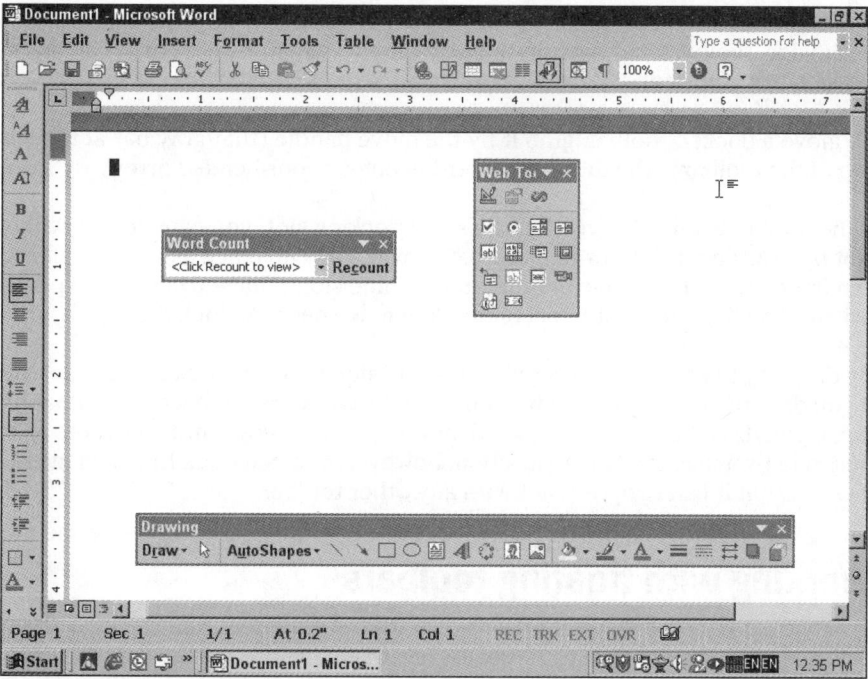

Figure 1-6: This window shows both floating and docked toolbars, including one docked along the left side of the screen.

Displaying and hiding toolbars

To display a hidden toolbar, or to hide one that's visible, right-click anywhere on any toolbar, or choose View ➪ Toolbars, to see the same list.

Office displays some toolbars automatically whenever you enter a certain software mode. In Word, for example, the Outlining toolbar pops up when you enter Outline view. These toolbars don't appear on the toolbar list except when you're using the special mode in question.

Tip   You won't find the menu bar on this toolbar list, so you can't hide it using this technique. In Word and Excel, however, you can use the View ➪ Full Screen command to put the menu bar and all other toolbars out of sight (except for the Full Screen toolbar, which pops up automatically), and then add back just the toolbars you want with the Toolbars tab of the Tools ➪ Customize dialog box. (Although the menu bar is hidden, if you point at the bar across the top of the workspace, it appears.)

Working with docked toolbars

You can dock a toolbar along any of the four edges of the application window. Along each edge, toolbars can occupy as many parallel rows or columns (I call them *docking slots*) as you want.

To move a docked toolbar, grab it by the move handle (that gray bar at the left or top of the toolbar). The mouse pointer becomes a four-headed arrow.

If the toolbar is one of several in the same docking slot, you can move it within its slot by dragging it right or left, or up or down. You can place as many toolbars as can fit end-to-end with one another in the same slot. (Office trims away space from existing toolbars in a slot to accommodate new ones you dock there.)

By dragging the toolbar perpendicular to its slot, you can dock it in a different slot. If you drag the toolbar all the way out into the work area, it becomes a floating toolbar. If you drag it still farther toward another window edge, it docks there as if pulled in by a magnet. One restriction, however: You can dock the main menu bar in any slot, but it can't share a slot with any other toolbar.

Working with floating toolbars

Because a floating toolbar lives in its own discrete window, you can drag that window anywhere you like on the screen — even outside the borders of the Office application you're working with.

Move a floating toolbar by dragging its title bar. Hide a floating toolbar by clicking the Close button (the one with the *X*) at the right of the title bar. Resize a floating toolbar by clicking and dragging one of its edges.

Tip   The quickest way to morph a toolbar from floating to docked, or vice versa, if you've used it as both, is to double-click the toolbar anywhere that isn't directly over a button or the move handle. The toolbar switches to the other form, reappearing where it last was when previously in that form. (This doesn't work on the main menu bar when it's docked, however.)

Using the tear-off submenus

You can convert many Office submenus into toolbars by dragging them away from their menu. You can recognize one of these tear-off submenus by the colored bar at the top. The bar changes color when you point to it.

To tear off a submenu and convert it to a toolbar, drag it by the move handle. It appears in its own floating window at first, but you can dock it like any other toolbar.

Using and Customizing the Office Shortcut Bar

The Office Shortcut Bar is an auxiliary Windows taskbar that gives you a one-click way to start programs or to open documents or folders.

When Office is installed, the Shortcut Bar can be set to load automatically whenever you start Windows. If it isn't already active, you can run it when you please by choosing Start ➪ Programs ➪ Microsoft Office Tools ➪ Microsoft Office Shortcut Bar.

Geography of the Shortcut Bar

Like the Office toolbars, the Shortcut Bar can be docked or floating (see Figure 1-7), and dragged anywhere you want on the screen; the double-clicking Tip just described works on it, too.

Though the Shortcut Bar itself functions as a toolbar, it's really a sort of shell containing a series of subsidiary toolbars. Only one toolbar's buttons are visible at a time. This active toolbar occupies the center of the Shortcut Bar; the other toolbars, if any, are condensed into narrow strips or squares at either side.

The first time you use it, the Shortcut Bar contains only one toolbar, called Office. Several other toolbars come with the program, and you can create new toolbars of your own (see "Customizing the Shortcut Bar" later in the chapter). To show these other toolbars on the Shortcut Bar, right-click the Shortcut Bar background and select them from the list that appears.

The little icon at the top left of the Shortcut Bar is called simply the Shortcut Bar button. Click the Shortcut Bar button to display a menu offering help and other options. Double-click the button to exit the Shortcut Bar.

Like most windows, the Shortcut Bar has a title bar. The title bar is obvious when the Shortcut Bar floats in a separate window. When docked, the title bar is an inconspicuous strip of color next to the Shortcut Bar button at the top or left end of the Shortcut Bar.

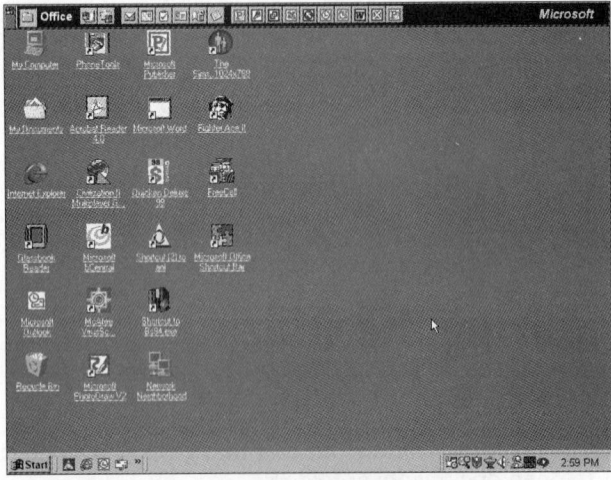

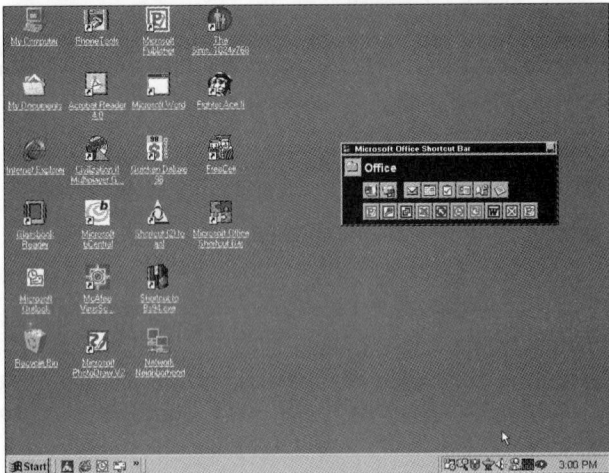

Figure 1-7: The Microsoft Office Shortcut Bar in both its configurations: floating and docked

The background is any part of the Shortcut Bar that doesn't contain a button. Typically, each toolbar has a different color background. Double-clicking the background displays the Customize dialog box, whereas right-clicking it brings up a shortcut menu.

Positioning the Shortcut Bar

Although by default Windows docks the Shortcut Bar along the right edge of the screen, the best location for it is docked at the top or bottom of your screen, because most monitors are wider than they are tall—which gives you room for more buttons.

Turning on Auto Hide

The Shortcut Bar takes up room, so use the Auto Hide feature. With Auto Hide on, the docked Shortcut Bar is invisible until the mouse pointer touches the edge of the screen where it is docked. As soon as you move the pointer away from the Shortcut Bar, it disappears again. The fastest way to turn Auto Hide on is by clicking the Shortcut Bar button and choosing Auto Hide from the pop-up menu.

Note Windows won't let you place two toolbars with Auto Hide enabled (such as the taskbar and the Shortcut Bar) along the same edge of the screen.

Placing the Shortcut Bar in the title bar area

An alternative to Auto Hide is to glue the Shortcut Bar to the top of the screen as a narrow strip as tall as a standard title bar. With this option on, the Shortcut Bar is always visible and immediately available.

To park the Shortcut Bar in the title bar area, first dock it along the top of the screen. Double-click the background to display the Customize dialog box, and, in the View tab, check the box Auto Fit into Title Bar Area.

Application windows hide the Shortcut Bar by default, but you can make it appear in the title bar area by clicking its button on the Windows taskbar. As soon as you click anywhere in your current application, it hides the Shortcut Bar again.

Accessing buttons you can't see

You can stop looking for a secret way to scroll through the buttons on the Shortcut Bar when it's docked — there isn't any. If a toolbar's buttons don't all fit on the screen, the ones you can't see are simply inaccessible. To get to them, you have to haul the Shortcut Bar out into the middle of the screen. It's better to keep your toolbars short and simple.

Refreshing a toolbar to bring the buttons up to date

Each time you start the Shortcut Bar, it reconstructs its toolbars so that buttons representing folders and documents reflect any additions, deletions, or name changes made since the last time you ran the Shortcut Bar. You can have the Shortcut Bar perform this same reconstruction process at your command by right-clicking the Shortcut Bar background and choosing Refresh Icons.

Customizing the Shortcut Bar

You can control most aspects of the Shortcut Bar's layout and function directly with the mouse. For some customization tasks, you need the Customize dialog box, shown in Figure 1-8; click the Shortcut Bar button and choose Customize from the pop-up menu.

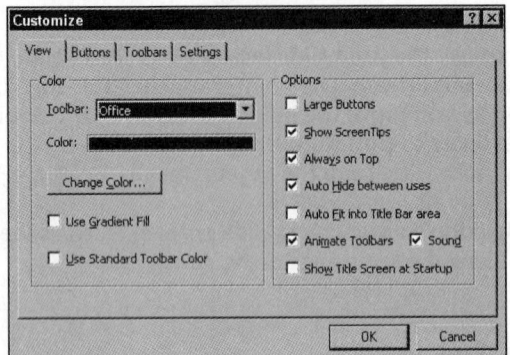

Figure 1-8: The Shortcut Bar's Customize dialog box gives you control.

Creating new toolbars

To create a new toolbar of your own, display the Customize dialog box, select the Toolbars tab, and choose Add Toolbar. In the next dialog box, decide whether you want to create a new folder for this toolbar or add a toolbar representing a folder that already exists on your system. If you create a new folder, you need to type in its name. For an existing folder, choose Browse and select the folder in the usual Windows way.

The folders for toolbars that you create from scratch, as well as for built-in toolbars such as Office, are stored in the Shortcut Bar folder. (The path is `Windows\Application Data\Microsoft\Office\Shortcut Bar`, and it can't be easily changed.)

Reordering toolbars

To change the order of the toolbars on the Shortcut Bar, open the Customize dialog box, switch to the Toolbars tab, and use the arrow buttons to move a selected toolbar up or down in the list.

Adding new buttons to a toolbar

The fastest way to add buttons to a toolbar is to drag them there from My Computer or Explorer. You can't directly drag items such as disks and system folders (such as Control Panel or Printers) from the My Computer folder or from networked computers. The way to add a button for any of these items is to create a Windows shortcut for it first and then drag the shortcut to the Shortcut Bar.

By the way, the Shortcut Bar comes with buttons for the Control Panel and Printers folders — they're just hidden. See the next section.

Hiding and displaying toolbar buttons

Except for the Office toolbar, each toolbar initially displays a button for every file (document, application, or shortcut) in that toolbar's folder. If a toolbar is too cluttered with buttons, you can hide the ones you don't need by right-clicking them and choosing Hide Button.

To display hidden buttons, open the Customize dialog box, select the Buttons tab, be sure the correct toolbar is selected in the Toolbar list, and then, in the Show these Files as Buttons list, check the box for each button you want to display.

Moving toolbar buttons and adding space between them

The fastest way to change the order of the buttons on a toolbar is to hold down Alt while you drag each button to its new location. To add empty space between a pair of buttons, drag the button on the right farther to the right, again while holding down Alt. You can close up the space again by dragging it back to the left. You can accomplish the same tasks with the Buttons tab of the Customize dialog box.

Renaming buttons and toolbars

The quick way to rename the buttons on the Shortcut Bar is to right-click the button and choose Rename. Be forewarned, however, that renaming a button renames the underlying file, folder, or shortcut, too. You can rename an entire toolbar using the same technique. Just be sure to right-click the toolbar's button, given that right-clicking elsewhere on the toolbar won't work. You can also go to the Customize dialog box and rename buttons or toolbars there.

Deleting toolbars

To delete an entire toolbar, open the Customize dialog box and switch to the Toolbars tab. Select the doomed toolbar and click Remove.

Restoring deleted toolbars

Even a removed toolbar, however, isn't necessarily gone forever. If you decide that you want to revive a toolbar that you've previously deleted, add it again with the technique detailed in "Creating new toolbars" earlier in this section. If you created the deleted toolbar from scratch by choosing Create a New, Blank Toolbar in the Add Toolbar dialog box, you can choose this same option. Then type in the name of the toolbar you previously deleted, spelled exactly as it was before. When the Shortcut Bar recognizes your entry as an old toolbar, you get a message asking if you want to restore it.

Alternatively, you can use the Make Toolbar for This Folder choice in the Add Toolbar dialog box. With this approach, you click Browse and navigate to the folder for the dormant toolbar — you'll find it buried in the `Windows\Application Data\ Microsoft\Office\Shortcut Bar` folder.

Caution   You can't revive the deleted default toolbars such as Office, Favorites, Programs, Accessories, and Desktop. Although the Shortcut Bar (sometimes) enables you to add your own toolbars by those names, they don't contain the buttons of the originals. To restore the original toolbars, reinstall the Shortcut Bar; doing so won't delete toolbars you've created.

Deleting buttons

Deleting a toolbar button deletes the underlying file, folder, or shortcut and moves it to the Recycle Bin. Office warns you that this is about to happen and gives you a chance to cancel the operation, but you can still get into trouble if you're not sure whether you're working with a shortcut or the document it represents. I recommend deleting the items that the buttons refer to via My Computer or Explorer instead. The Shortcut Bar automatically detects that they're gone and removes the buttons. (If you insist on deleting buttons via the Shortcut Bar, do so on the Buttons tab of the Customize dialog box.)

Shortcut Bar Tips

Here are some quick tips on using the Shortcut Bar to best advantage.

✦ **Accessing the Windows desktop quickly.** In theory, the Windows desktop is a nice place to store stuff that you use regularly: folders, disk drives, documents, and applications. The problem is, the desktop is inaccessible when you're doing anything productive with Windows. The Shortcut Bar solves this problem: It shows all items on the desktop as buttons when you turn on its Desktop toolbar.

✦ **Avoiding the Programs toolbar.** The prefab Programs toolbar isn't very helpful. It simply duplicates the function of the Start ➪ Programs menu.

✦ **Changing the default folder for Office templates.** Office stores document templates in the Templates folder, located in the main folder where Office is installed. To change the default location where all Office applications look for their templates, use the Shortcut Bar: Open the Customize dialog box and switch to the Settings tab. Select User Templates Location to change the main template folder (or specify a secondary folder for Office templates by selecting Workgroup Templates Location). Choose Modify; browse your system for the new folder.

✦   ✦   ✦

Getting Started with Popular Office Applications

When you know your way around this latest version of Microsoft Office, it's time for a quick introduction to using it. For those who need to get up and running fast, this chapter looks at creating a quick document in Word, creating a quick spreadsheet in Excel, and sending and receiving e-mail in Outlook.

Creating a Quick Document in Word

The moment Word 2002 opens, the insertion point is already located in the document area; Word is ready to receive text. All you have to do to start entering text is start typing.

Editing text

To make changes and corrections to your text, move your insertion point to where you want to make changes by placing the mouse pointer there and clicking. Then, to add a word or phrase, type it in. The existing text moves to the right to make room for it.

To replace a word or phrase, highlight the text you want to replace; then type in the new text. To delete a word or phrase, highlight it and then press Delete. To delete just a few characters, place the insertion point to the left of the characters you want to remove, then press Delete once to delete a single character, or press and hold Delete to delete characters repeatedly. Alternatively, you can place the insertion point immediately to the right of the character you want to delete and press Backspace to delete to the left.

Selecting text

In addition to clicking and dragging, you can select text by holding down the Shift key while moving through the text with the arrow keys. Holding down the Ctrl key at the same time lets you select a word at a time with the left and right arrow keys or a paragraph at a time with the up and down arrow keys.

You can select an entire word by double-clicking anywhere inside it — or an entire paragraph by triple-clicking anywhere inside it. To select an entire line, move the mouse pointer to the left edge of the document until it changes to a right-pointing arrow that points at the line you want to select, and then click. If you want to select an entire document, choose Edit ⇨ Select All (or press Ctrl+A).

Formatting text

The most common tools for formatting text are all available on the Formatting toolbar. Highlight the text you want to format; then click the button of your choice in the toolbar.

When you click the Styles and Formatting button the Styles and Formatting task pane opens, showing you the formatting of the selected text and displaying a list of other styles you can apply to it. The name of each style appears in that particular style. To apply a style, highlight the text you want to apply it to and select the name of the style from the task pane. For a paragraph, table, or list style, just place the insertion point anywhere in the paragraph, table, or list and then apply the style. You can also apply a style from the Style list box (located by default next to the Styles and Formatting button in the Formatting toolbar).

You can choose a font (typeface) from the Font pull-down list of all fonts installed on your system. Each font name appears in the font it names; clicking the name of the font you want changes the highlighted text. Then you can choose the Font Size from the drop-down list next to the Font list. Font sizes, which refer to the height of the capital letters, are given in *points* (1 point = approximately 1/72 inch).

Make text Bold or Italic or Underline it just by clicking the appropriate buttons, and choose Align Left, Align Right, Center or Justify to specify how it is lined up on the page. Single Spacing and Double Spacing let you set the spacing between lines of text.

To create a numbered or bulleted list, click Numbering or Bullets respectively. If you click either before you start typing, every time you press Enter, a number or bullet appears in front of the next item in the list. To stop it, press Backspace to delete the last number or bullet, then resume typing. Click either button after you've highlighted a section of text to turn it into a numbered or bulleted list, adding a new number or bullet to begin each paragraph.

The Decrease Indent and Increase Indent buttons adjust the left indentation for selected text to the left or the right by a set amount.

Click Outside Border to draw a border around a selected word or paragraph. Click the little downward pointing arrow to see a selection of other borders. Clicking Highlight places a transparent color over selected text, similar to drawing over text on paper with a highlighting pen. Click the downward-pointing arrow to select the color. Click the Highlight button before you select text, and you can use your cursor exactly like a highlighting pen, painting a color over any text in your document. Click Font Color to change the color of text; again, click the downward-pointing arrow to choose a color.

Grow Font and Shrink Font increase or decrease the font size of selected text to the next size on the Font Size list. Superscript and Subscript turn selected text into either superscript (as in $E = mc^2$) or subscript (as in H_2O.)

Note   All these formatting options can be combined with each other; many other formatting options are available through the dialog boxes you can access from the Format menu.

Moving around and viewing your document

To move around in Word, you can use the mouse, the scrollbars, the keyboard, the Go To command or the Navigation Tool.

Using the mouse, you can place the pointer wherever you want to start typing and click once. Using the scrollbars, you can click the single arrows at the top or bottom of the vertical scrollbar to move up or down one line at a time, or click the light-colored area above or below the box-shaped slider to move up or down one screen at a time. Dragging the slider moves you smoothly through the document. Use the horizontal scrollbar in the same way to move left or right through documents that are too large to fit on the screen.

The cursor keys on the keyboard move your insertion point up or down one line at a time, or left or right one character at a time. Hold down Ctrl and you can use those keys to move left or right one word at a time, or up and down one paragraph at a time. Home moves you to the beginning of a line, End to the end. Ctrl+Home takes you to the top of the document, Ctrl+End to the end, PgUp one screen up, and PgDn one screen down.

Press Ctrl+G or choose Edit ⇨ Go To when you want to open the Go To dialog box. Enter the page number you want to go to (or a plus or minus sign, followed by the number of pages you want to go forward or back); then click Go To and you're there.

Finally, the three buttons at the bottom of the vertical scrollbar let you browse through your document the way that suits you best. Click the button in the middle, then choose the item you want to browse for: for example, tables. The arrow buttons will then take you to either the previous occurrence of that item or the next.

Word also offers you several ways to view your document. The three you'll use most often are available in the View menu. They are Normal View, Page Layout View and Web Layout View.

Normal View hides page boundaries and special items like headers and footers. It's best if your document is mostly text. Print Layout View (see Figure 2-1) shows you exactly how text, graphics, and other elements will appear when you print your document; it's good if you're using lots of pictures, tables, and so on. Finally, Web Layout View (see Figure 2-2) shows you what your page will look like when viewed with a Web browser, and is best if you're creating a Web page.

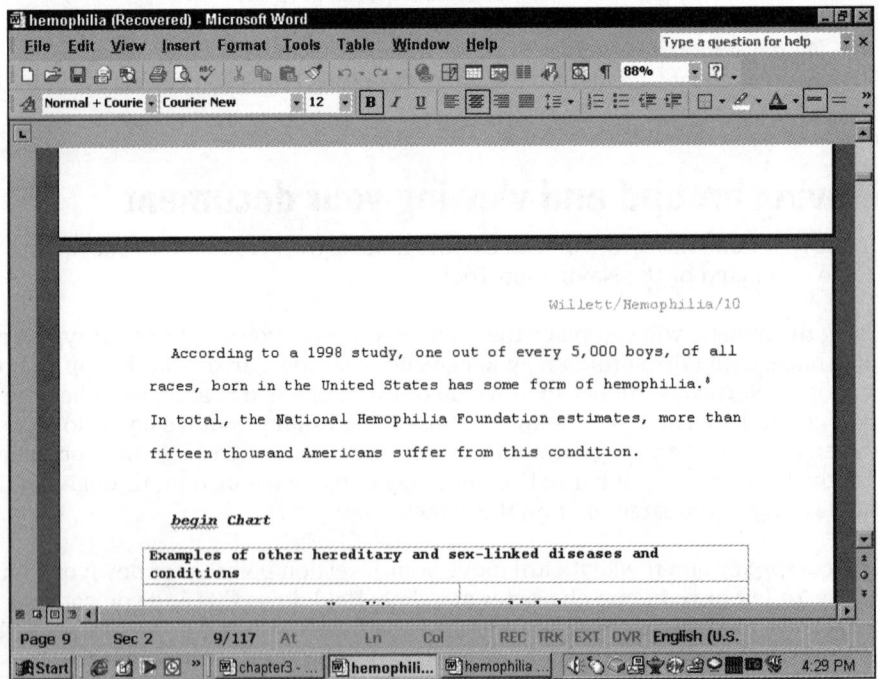

Figure 2-1: Print Layout View gives you a better idea of what your document will look like when printed.

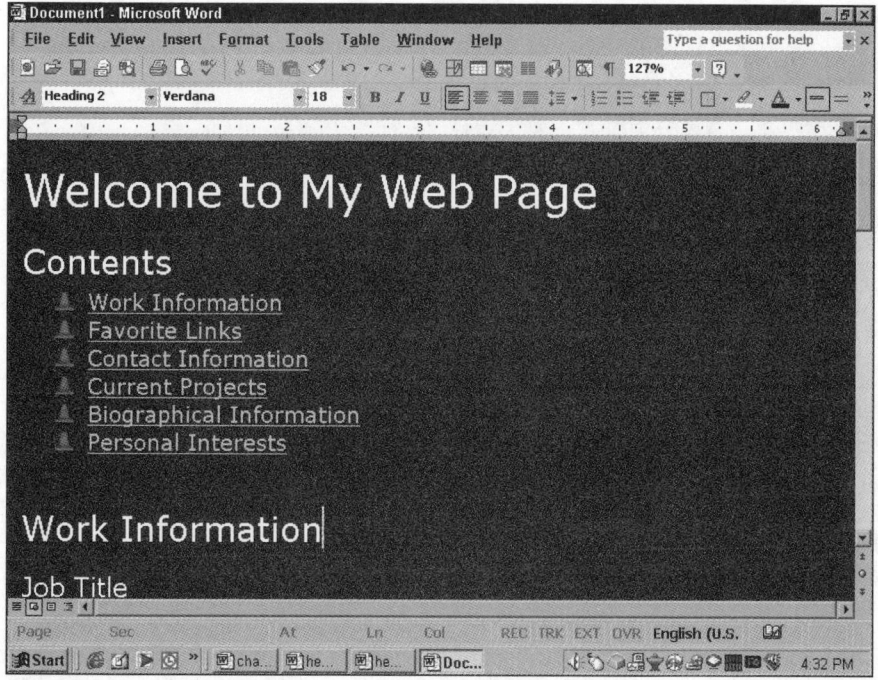

Figure 2-2: Use Web Layout view if you're creating a Web page.

The 3 Ps: Page properties, previewing, and printing

When you're happy with the content and formatting of your document, you're just about ready to print it. Before you do, though, you need to make a few final decisions.

Setting page properties

Choose File ➪ Page Setup to open the dialog box in Figure 2-3.

For most documents, you'll only need to worry about three of the tabs in this dialog box: Margins, Paper Size and Paper Source.

Set top, bottom, right and left margins by entering measurements in the various boxes (or by clicking the arrows to increase or decrease the default measurements). If your printer supports it, you can also add a gutter on the left or top side, if you want to leave extra white space for a binding.

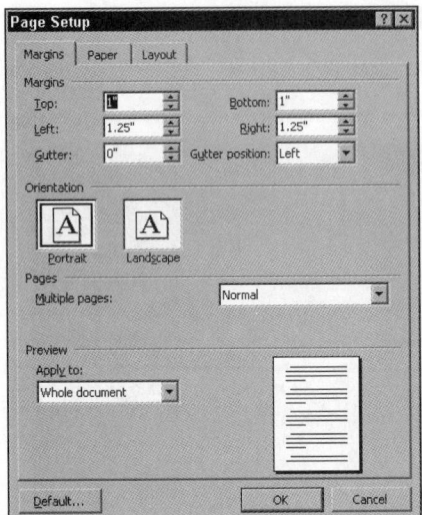

Figure 2-3: Make decisions about the appearance of your document here.

The Paper Size tab lets you choose from a variety of standard paper sizes (letter, legal, A4, and so on) or enter the dimensions of a custom size. You can also choose whether to have your document print across the narrower dimension of the page (*portrait* style) or across the longer dimension (*landscape* style). Finally, the Paper Source tab lets you choose which source of paper available on your printer you want to use: upper tray, lower tray, manual feed, and so on.

Previewing your document

To see exactly what your document will look like once it's printed, choose File ➪ Print Preview. You'll see what looks a bit like a photograph of the first page of your document (see Figure 2-4).

Click the Magnifier button to zoom in for a closer look, or change the size of the preview using the Zoom drop-down list. To see more than one page at a time, click the Multiple Pages button, then drag your mouse through the box that opens to choose how many pages you want to display at once and in what configuration. Navigate through the pages exactly as you would in Normal view, using the scrollbars, the keyboard, the Navigation Tool, Go To, and so on.

You can edit in Print Preview just as though you were in Normal or Print Layout view. (Although the Formatting toolbar isn't visible, you can call it up by choosing View ➪ Toolbars ➪ Formatting.) Or, if you prefer, you can return to Normal or Print Layout view by opening the View menu.

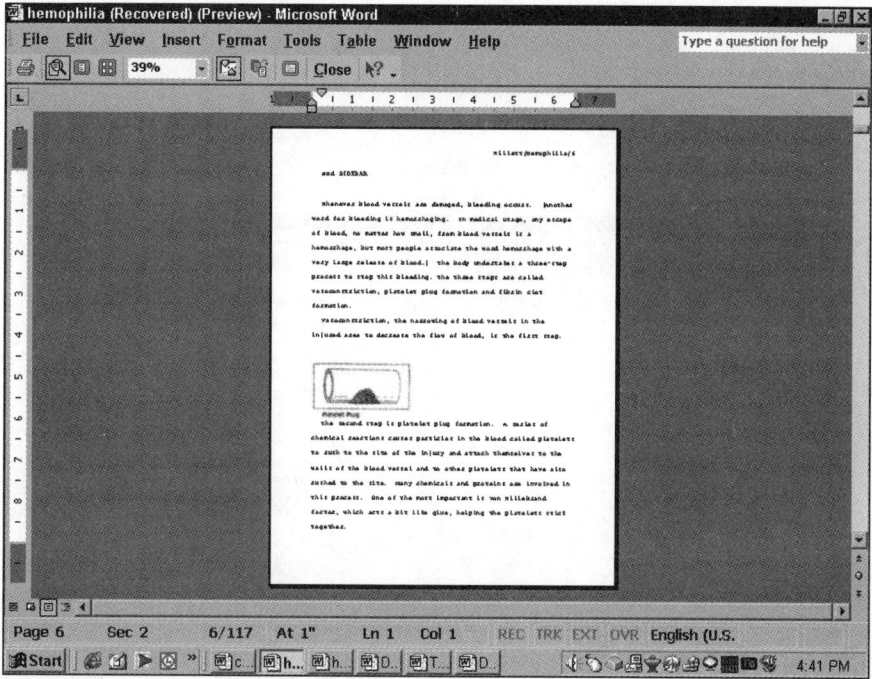

Figure 2-4: Print Preview shows you exactly what your page will look like when it's printed.

Printing

When you're finally one hundred percent satisfied with your document, you're ready to commit it to paper. Click the Print button in the Standard Toolbar to begin printing immediately or choose File ⇨ Print to open the Print dialog box, where you can choose a printer from those installed on your system, set specific properties of that printer, and choose how much of your document to print and the number of copies. You can even choose to print more than one page per sheet of paper or scale your document to fit on a different size of paper than you designed it for: for example, legal-size instead of letter-sized.

When you're satisfied with your choices, click OK, and your document will print.

Creating a Quick Spreadsheet in Excel

In Excel, a *worksheet* is a single spreadsheet; a *workbook* is a collection of worksheets. When you start Excel, it automatically opens a new workbook, called Book1, which contains three worksheets, and by default displays Sheet1 (see Figure 2-5).

Row   Formula bar

Name box

Menu bar   Worksheet

Cell   Column   Toolbars

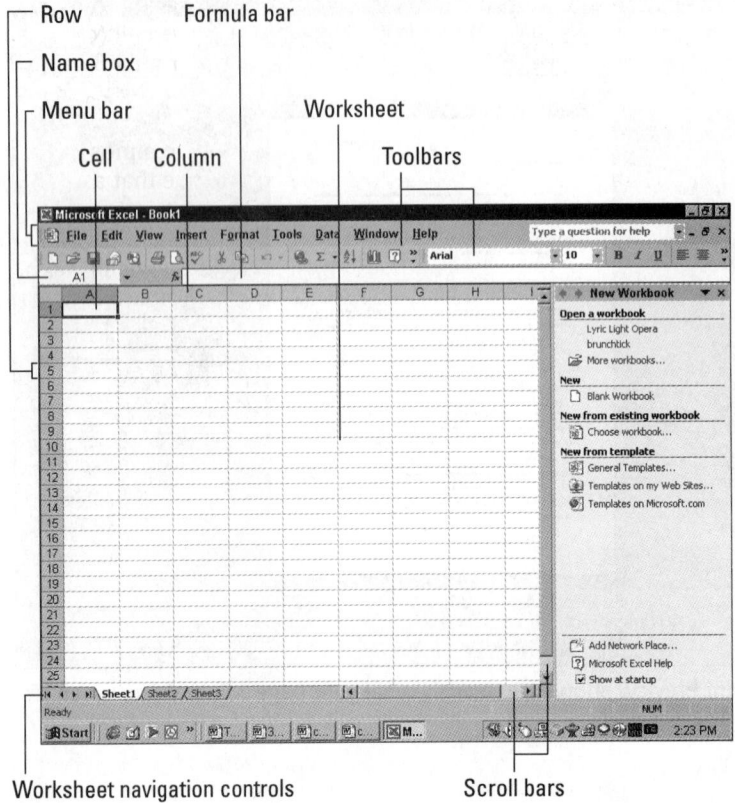

Worksheet navigation controls   Scroll bars

Figure 2-5: This blank worksheet is where you'll enter your own data.

An Excel worksheet has 256 columns, labeled across the top with the letters of the alphabet. When it gets to Z, it starts over with AA, AB, AC, AD, and so on; then BA, BB, BC, all the way up to IV.

Going the other way, a worksheet has 65,536 rows. The place where each column and row meets is called a *cell*. (I'll save you the trouble of doing the math: an Excel worksheet contains 16,777,216 cells.) Each cell is identified by its column and row number, from A1 to IV65536.

The Excel interface also includes the vertical and horizontal *scroll bars,* which you use to move up and down or sideways through your worksheet, and the *worksheet navigation controls* — arrows that take you from worksheet to worksheet in your current workbook. Click the leftmost arrow to go to the first worksheet in the workbook; the middle two arrows move you one worksheet backward or forward through the workbook, and the rightmost arrow takes you to the last worksheet in the workbook. (You can also go directly to any workbook by clicking the appropriate tab.) The Name Box displays the name of the currently active cell (or, as you highlight a range of cells, the dimensions of that range). The Formula Bar is where you enter data and create and apply formulas.

The Menu Bar contains menus of commands that are common to almost all Windows programs — File, Edit, View, Window, Help — plus some that are specific to Excel, such as Data and Chart; the Toolbars contain buttons that activate a variety of features. The Standard and Formatting toolbars appear by default (because they contain the most-used features) but other toolbars appear automatically as you carry out certain tasks. You can choose to display particular toolbars by choosing View ⇨ Toolbars.

Entering and editing data

The simplest way to enter data in Excel is to click the cell into which you want to enter data and type away. You can move from cell to cell with the Tab or Enter keys.

Excel is most commonly used to manage numerical data. By default, Excel displays a maximum of 11 digits in a cell (ten if the number includes a decimal point).

You can enter dates and times as numbers. For dates, use slashes or hyphens to separate the elements. For instance, 12-30 or 12/30 would be interpreted as December 30. If you don't add a year, Excel assumes that it's the current year; if you do want to enter a year, add it with another slash or hyphen. For times, use colons: 3:00 is interpreted as 3 a.m. To tell Excel you want the date to be p.m., type a space (followed by **p** or **pm**) after the time.

Whenever you enter data in a cell, or click a cell that contains data, the contents of the cell are displayed in the formula bar (see Figure 2-6). You can edit data there or double-click the cell containing the data you want to edit and tweak the data directly in the cell.

Whatever you enter in the formula bar appears in the cell and vice versa (assuming you're in edit mode; if you're not, formulas are displayed in the formula bar and formula results in the cell.) Either one acts like the window of a little word processor: you can use the arrow keys to move around, jump to the beginning or end of the data by pressing Home or End, use Delete or Backspace to take out characters, or select data and cut, copy or paste it.

Copying the information from one cell to another is useful when you have a lot of repeating data, or just when you need to reorganize your worksheet. To copy a cell to another location, click the cell you want to copy, then click the Copy button on the Standard toolbar. (The border around the cell will change from a solid line to a moving dotted line.)

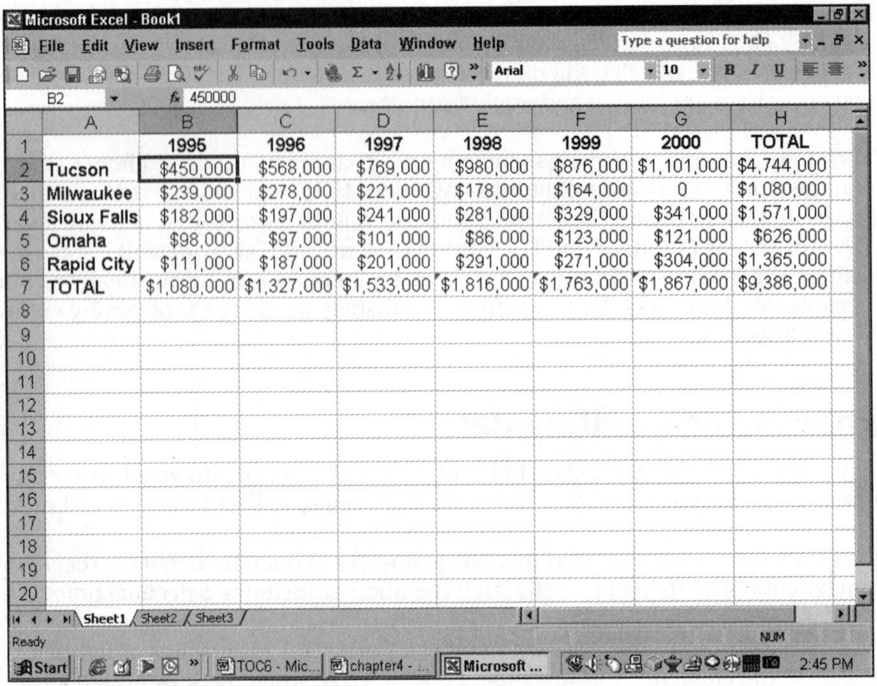

	A	B	C	D	E	F	G	H
1		1995	1996	1997	1998	1999	2000	TOTAL
2	Tucson	$450,000	$568,000	$769,000	$980,000	$876,000	$1,101,000	$4,744,000
3	Milwaukee	$239,000	$278,000	$221,000	$178,000	$164,000	0	$1,080,000
4	Sioux Falls	$182,000	$197,000	$241,000	$281,000	$329,000	$341,000	$1,571,000
5	Omaha	$98,000	$97,000	$101,000	$86,000	$123,000	$121,000	$626,000
6	Rapid City	$111,000	$187,000	$201,000	$291,000	$271,000	$304,000	$1,365,000
7	TOTAL	$1,080,000	$1,327,000	$1,533,000	$1,816,000	$1,763,000	$1,867,000	$9,386,000

Figure 2-6: You can edit data in the formula bar or in the cell itself.

Next, click the cell you want to copy the data to; its border becomes a solid line. Click the Paste button on the Standard toolbar, and the data from the first cell appears in the new cell, complete with formatting. You can paste the same information to as many new cells as you want by clicking additional cells and clicking Paste. You can also copy and paste to and from a range of cells instead of just one.

To move a cell, click anywhere on the border of the active cell (except the fill handle in the bottom right corner), then hold down the mouse button and drag the cell to a new location.

Adding and deleting cells, rows, and columns

To insert a single cell, row or column, right-click the cell located where you want the new cell to appear, and select Insert from the popup menu. In the Insert dialog box, decide whether to shift existing cells rightward or down to make room for the new one. (You can also choose to insert an entire row or column instead of a single cell.) Then click OK.

To delete a cell, follow the same procedure, but choose Delete instead of Insert. In the Delete dialog box, choose whether to shift the remaining cells left or up to fill in the space vacated by the cells you've deleted.

To insert an entire row or column, select a cell anywhere in the row or column currently located where you want the new row or column to appear, then choose Insert ⇨ Rows or Insert ⇨ Columns.

Changing column widths and row heights

Rows change their height automatically to fit your data, but columns don't. To change the width of a column to fit your data, place your mouse pointer on the boundary between its header and the next one to the right, and double-click. You can also drag the header boundaries left or right (or the rows up and down).

Formatting data

The easiest way to format your worksheet attractively is to use AutoFormat, which applies a preset design to whatever range of cells you select. To use AutoFormat, select the range of cells you want to format, select Format ⇨ AutoFormat from the menu, then choose the format you like from the AutoFormat dialog box. To make adjustments or apply only certain elements of the AutoFormat, click Options. When you're satisfied, click OK. The AutoFormat formatting is automatically applied to your selection (see Figure 2-7).

Tip

If you change your mind about AutoFormatting, select the AutoFormatted cells, then choose Format ⇨ AutoFormat, and, in the AutoFormat dialog box, choose the design labeled None. Click OK to remove all formatting. Understand, however, that any formatting you applied before you applied the AutoFormat will not return — you'll be back to square one with a completely unformatted spreadsheet.

Changing fonts

To apply a different font to your data, select the cell or range of cells to which you want to apply the font, then pull down the font list-box from the Formatting toolbar and click the name of the font you want to apply (each font's name is shown in that font).

To change the size of fonts, pull down the Font Size list-box instead. Click the size you want to use. Row heights will automatically adjust to accommodate it.

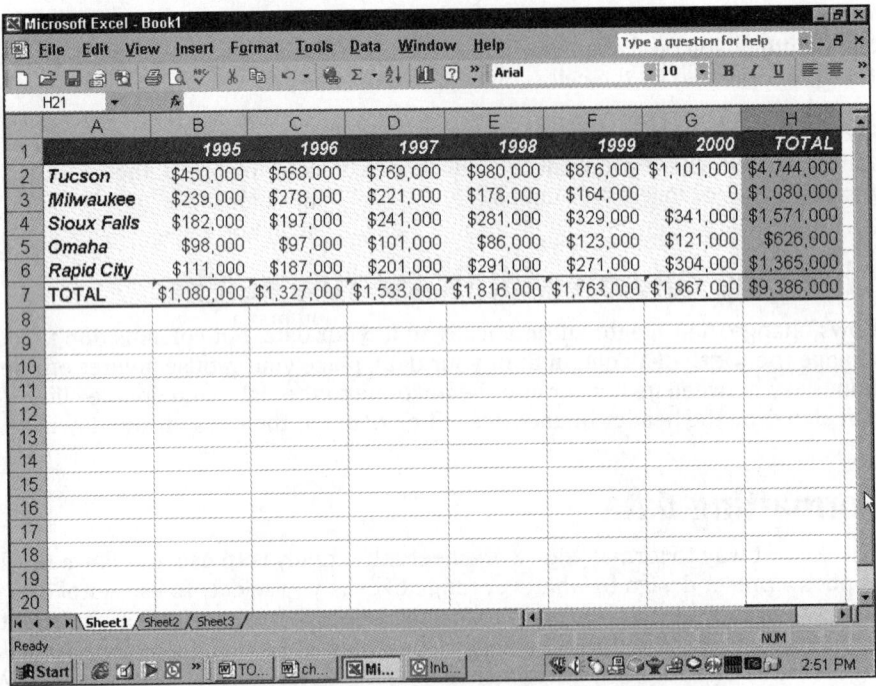

Figure 2-7: Here's what a worksheet looks like with AutoFormat applied.

Other basic formatting

The Excel Formatting toolbar also contains several other basic formatting commands you'll find yourself using quite often, including Bold, Italic and Underline. The Align Left, Center, and Align Right options determine how data is aligned in a cell. Merge and Center merges selected cells into one large cell, and centers data within it (useful for creating labels that go across more than one column).

Caution   When you use Merge and Center, be aware that if more than one of the selected cells contains data, only the data in the upper-left cell will be retained.

Currency Style assumes data in a cell is currency, and displays it accordingly. For example, if you entered 4782 in a cell, then applied Currency Style, Excel would display $4,782.00. Similarly, Percent Style displays data as percentages and Comma Style displays data as a number with every three digits separated by commas. To use other number styles, highlight the cells you want to change, then choose Format ⇨ Cells, and click the Number tab. (You can change many other aspects of cell formatting from this dialog box, as well—simply click the other tabs and explore.)

Increase Decimal and Decrease Decimal add or subtract a decimal place from the end of the data in the selected cells; Increase Indent and Decrease Indent move text or data further from or closer to the left edge of the cell.

Click Borders to apply a border to selected cells; click the down arrow to choose from a number of pre-designed borders. Click Fill Color to fill the selected cells with the color currently displayed on this button, or Font Color to change the characters of the selected data to the currently displayed color. In both cases, click the down arrow to choose from additional colors.

The Standard toolbar also contains two buttons you may use quite often to alter the appearance of your worksheet. Sort Ascending and Sort Descending sort the contents of a selected range by value or (if they contain text) alphabetically.

Navigating in Excel

The scrollbars will scroll you up and down and left and right through your worksheet, but sometimes the keyboard provides more control.

The Home key moves you to the first cell in the current row; Page Down and Page Up move you down and up one screen, respectively. The Arrow Keys move you one cell at a time. Ctrl+Home moves you to the top left cell in the grid (A1); Ctrl+End moves you to the bottom right cell that contains data. End puts you into *End mode* (clicking an arrow key moves you as far as possible, in the direction indicated, within the current block of data). To go to a specific cell, select Edit ⇨ Go To, and type the designation of the cell you want to go to in the Reference field in the Go To dialog box.

Tip

> Go To keeps a list of cells you've used it to access before, so if you need to return to the same cell all the time, all you have to do is double-click it in the list.

Using Excel functions

Excel puts a large collection of common functions at your fingertips. To use them, first select the cell in which you want the results of the function to appear, then choose Insert ⇨ Function to open the Insert Function dialog box (see Figure 2-8).

Type in a rough description of what you want to do in the "Search for a function" box: for example, **Insert a hyperlink**. Click Go, and Excel will search its list of functions and suggest one that might do what you want (in this case, HYPERLINK).

Alternatively, you can select a category (for example, statistical or financial) to see a list of all the functions in that category. You can also choose from Most Recently Used and All. Choose the function you want from the list provided, then click OK to open the Function Arguments dialog box, which requests any additional information needed to make the function work. Click OK a final time to apply the function and display the results in the selected cell.

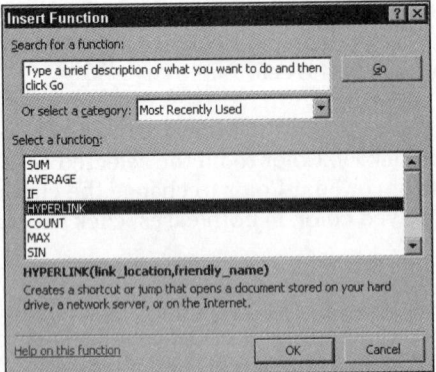

Figure 2-8: The Insert Function dialog box lets you choose from a list of some of the functions Excel supports.

Tip   The most commonly used Excel function, Sum, has been given its own button, labeled AutoSum, on the Standard toolbar. Highlight the cells you want to add together and click the AutoSum button. The total will be displayed either at the bottom of a column or the end of a row, depending on the shape of the selected range.

Setting page properties, previewing, and printing

Before you print, you should set your page properties. Choose File ➪ Page Setup to open the dialog box in Figure 2-9.

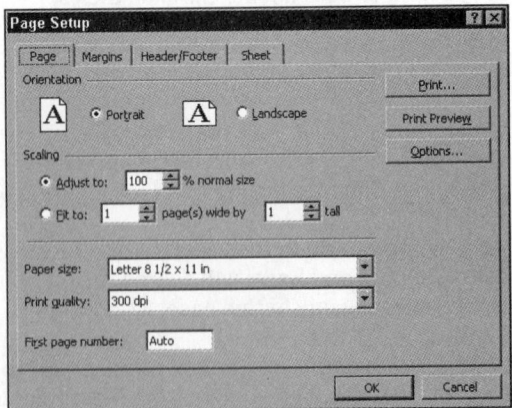

Figure 2-9: Page Setup lets you decide exactly how your data will be printed.

The Page Setup dialog box offers you four tabs. Under Page you can choose between portrait and landscape orientation, select a paper size and print quality, and scale your pages (shrinking or expanding them) to fit your paper. Under Margins, you can set top, bottom, left, and right margins, as well as how far from the top and bottom your headers and footers should appear, and whether to center the printout horizontally or vertically (or both) on the page. Under Header/Footer, enter the text for headers and footers, and under Sheet, select other printing options, such as the range of cells you want to print.

When you're happy with your choices, click Print to open the Print dialog box, described in a moment, or Print Preview to make sure everything is the way you want it (see Figure 2-10). You can also access Print Preview by choosing File ➪ Print Preview.

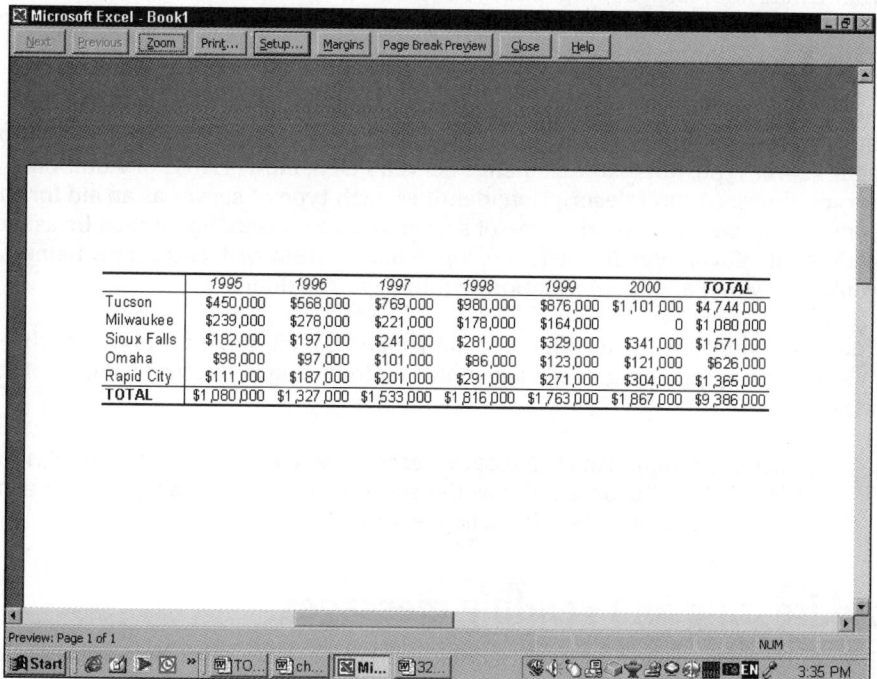

Figure 2-10: Print Preview gives you a sneak peek at your finished document.

You can use the buttons across the top to control Print Preview and fine-tune your printer output. Next and Previous take you to the next or previous page; Zoom toggles you from a full-sized view of the document to a view that shows you the entire page; Setup takes you back to the Page Setup dialog box, and Margins makes the margins appear as lines that you can move with your mouse. Page Break Preview shows you where in your worksheet page breaks currently fall and lets you adjust them. Finally, Close closes Print Preview. If you're ready to proceed to hard copy, click Print.

The Print dialog box gives you a final set of options. Choose the printer you want to use, then decide whether you want to print the entire document or just selected pages. At the bottom, you can also choose whether to print just the selected range of cells, just the active worksheets, or the entire workbook.

Using Outlook to Send and Receive E-Mail

To send and receive e-mail, you first have to have an e-mail account with an Internet service provider. If you, like many people, have more than one account, Outlook lets you use all of them.

To add a new e-mail account to Outlook, first gather the necessary information: your e-mail address, your logon ID, your password, the name of your incoming mail server, and the name of the outgoing mail server. If you're uncertain what any of those are, ask your service provider.

Next, choose Tools ➪ E-mail Accounts; a wizard that will take you step by step through the process of setting up a new e-mail account. You'll be asked to choose your server type: Microsoft Exchange Server, POP3, IMAP, HTTP, or Additional Server Types. (A brief description identifies each type of server as an aid for the confused.) Depending on the type of server you've chosen, you'll then be asked for additional information: for instance, logon name, password, and server name. When you've provided all the information required, you're done!

To make changes to an account, choose Tools ➪ E-mail Accounts and click the "View or change existing e-mail accounts" radio button in the first window of the wizard.

 **Note**   Outlook can even manage messages received via Web-based e-mail services such as HotMail. Just choose HTTP as the server type when creating the new e-mail account and provide the information requested.

Addressing and sending messages

If you're in Inbox view and want to create a new message, click New or press Ctrl+N. If you're in another view, click the drop-down arrow to the right of the New button and choose Mail Message from the menu.

A blank message form opens in Microsoft Word, the default e-mail editor for Outlook (see Figure 2-11). Type the e-mail address of the recipient (or recipients, separated by commas) in the To field, or click To and pick the people you want to send the message to from your Contact list (explained later in this chapter). You can send a copy of the message to additional people by entering their addresses in the Cc ("carbon copy") field.

Tip

You can also send a message to many different people without alerting everyone on the list that it's being sent to more than one recipient. Click the Options button and choose Bcc ("blind carbon copy") from the menu that appears, then enter the e-mail addresses you want to send the message to into the Bcc field that appears below the Cc field.

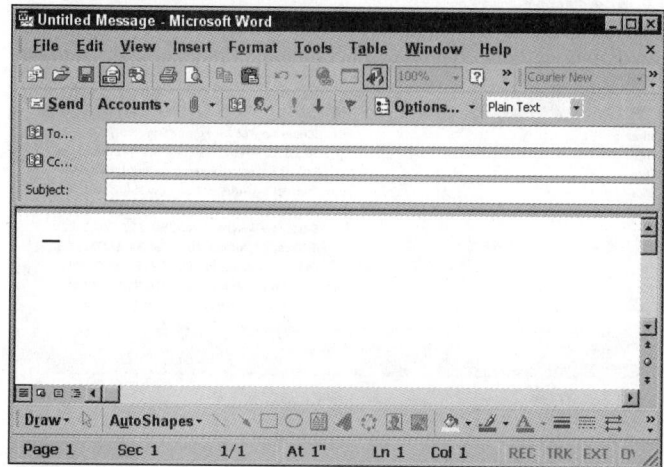

Figure 2-11: Type your message and its address information into this form.

Next, enter a topic in the Subject box and type your message in the main window. You can also attach a file to your e-mail by clicking the Insert File button (the one with the paper clip on it) and browsing your computer for the file you want to send.

Finally, click Send to send the message from your default e-mail account. To send it from a different account, click the Account button and choose the account you wish to use from the list, then click Send.

Note

Outlook offers you a choice of formats to use for e-mail messages: HTML, rich text, or plain text. HTML is for including features normally found on a Web page (different sizes and colors of text, graphics, a background, tables, and so forth). Plain text has the big advantage that everyone can read it, no matter what kind of computer system they're getting their e-mail on. Choose one of the three by choosing Format from the menu bar at the top of the Message form.

Retrieving and reading messages

Click Send/Receive to automatically send any mail in your Outbox and retrieve any mail received by any of your accounts. To retrieve mail from a specific account, choose Tools ➪ Send/Receive and then choose the account from the submenu.

Incoming mail is displayed in the Inbox. By default, Outlook displays a list of messages in a window pane at the top and the text of each message, as you click it, in a pane at the bottom (see Figure 2-12). To display a message in the full window, double-click it.

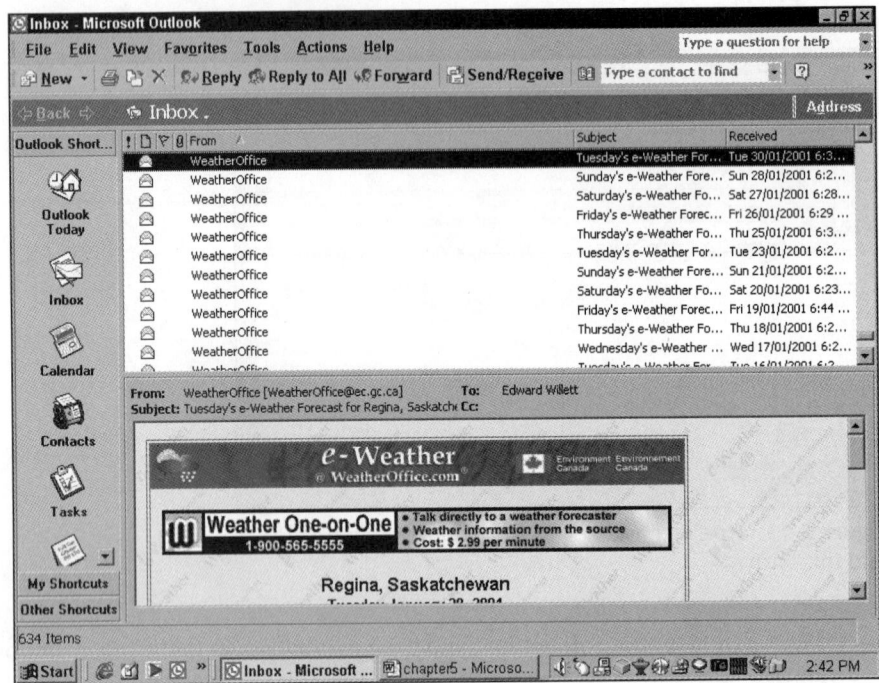

Figure 2-12: Outlook shows you a preview of each message. This message is in HTML format.

To reply to a message, click Reply. A preaddressed form appears, into which you can type your message. Click Send to send it on its way.

Tip

If the message was addressed to other people in addition to yourself, click Reply to All to send the reply to everyone in the original list of addressees.

Saving and managing messages

As noted, new messages are automatically saved in your Inbox. To save a message elsewhere, open it and then choose File ➪ Save As. You can also set up personal folders specifically intended for saving e-mail messages.

To view your personal folders, choose View ➪ Folder List. Outlook opens a new pane that lists current folders (see Figure 2-13). You can add additional folders by right-clicking the folder list and choosing New Folder from the menu that appears.

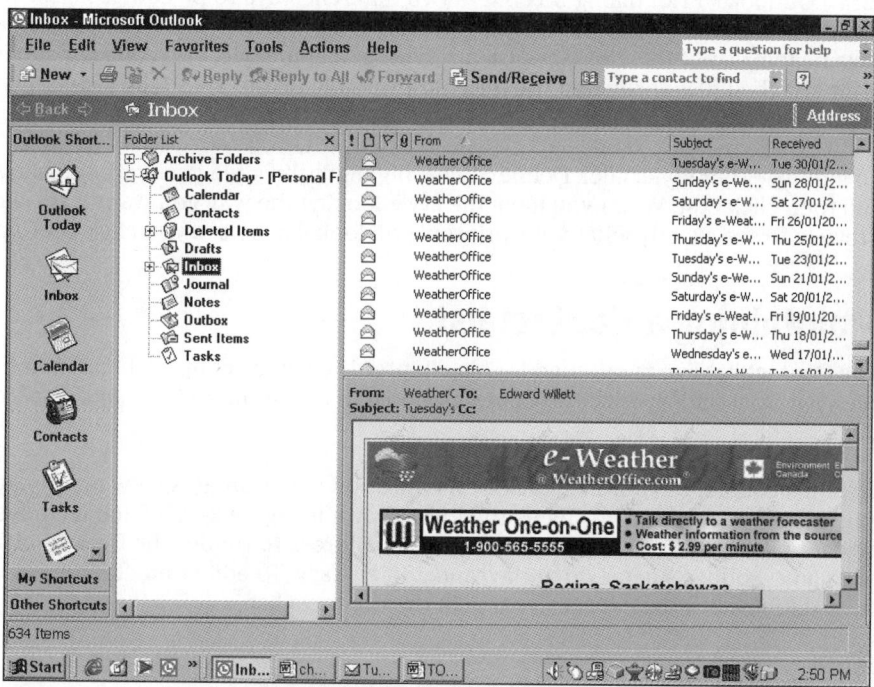

Figure 2-13: Adding additional folders to your Personal Folder list helps you organize your e-mail.

To delete a message, highlight it and press Delete. The message is stored in the Deleted Items folder. By default, it remains there for two months, so you can retrieve it if you need to. You can also trash it whenever you want by opening the Deleted Items folder, highlighting it, and pressing Delete again. You'll be prompted to confirm your decision.

Tip To delete all the items in the Deleted Items folder at once, right-click the folder icon and choose Empty "Deleted Items" Folder from the popup menu.

To save a message from the Inbox into any folder in the Folder list, just click the message and drag it into the chosen folder. You can move messages from folder to folder the same way.

Printing messages

To print a message or messages, highlight them and choose File ➪ Print. (You can highlight multiple messages by holding down Ctrl as you click each message in turn.) Outlook's Print dialog box offers two different ways to print messages: *memo style,* which prints messages as text, and *table style,* which prints a list of the message headings, not the messages themselves. In memo style, you can also choose to print attached files (provided the files are printable text or HTML files, and not program files).

To modify either style, click Define Styles, highlight the style you want to change, and then click Edit. When you have the style looking the way you want it to, click Preview to see exactly what your printout will look like before you click OK to print.

Maintaining a Contact list

The Contact list I've mentioned in this chapter is easy to set up and maintain. To see your Contact list, click the Contacts shortcut in the Outlook bar at the left of the screen.

To add a contact to your list, click New while you're in Contacts view or choose File ➪ New ➪ Contact. This opens the form shown in Figure 2-14, which includes fields for everything from job title and e-mail address to (under the Details tab) nickname, spouse's name, birthday, and anniversary. To edit contact information later, double-click the contact's name in the Contacts list.

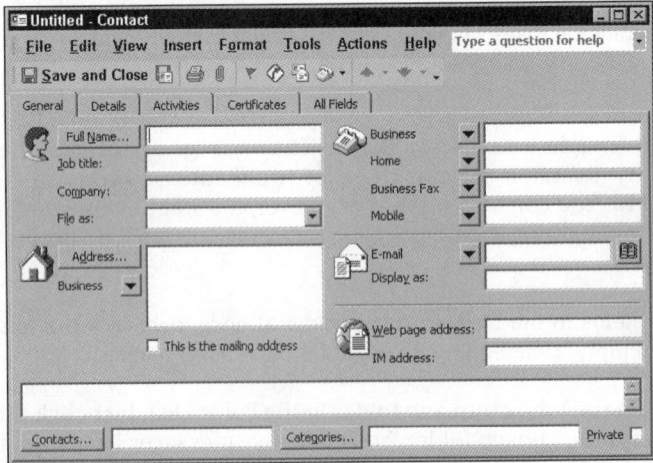

Figure 2-14: If you've got a complete dossier on one of your contacts, Outlook gives you a place to store that information for handy retrieval.

✦   ✦   ✦

Getting the Most out of Office

The focus of this part is to get Office up and running the way you want it to run. You'll learn how to install Office and how to customize its user interface, from toolbars to windows to menus, to suit your personal taste. But often Office is not used by just a single person, but in conjunction with others. To that end, this part also includes information on collaborating with others on Office documents and running Office on a network.

Getting Office Up and Running

E veryone remain calm and keep your hands and feet inside the book at all times. This chapter starts your intensive course in the latest version of Microsoft Office. Throughout this part of the Office XP Bible you discover the benefits of the sweeping changes that apply to all of Office XP — and their pitfalls. You learn techniques for controlling the behavior of all Office applications. And you get connected to a host of sources of Office-related information and software.

Tip   For a complete overview of all the new and improved features in Office XP, see the Office XP Product Guide at `www.microsoft.com/office/xp/xpguide.htm`.

Office Editions

Microsoft makes Office XP available in many editions. Most people pick one of three distinct Office packages: Standard, Professional, or Small Business. In case you want to know how the software you bought compares to the other alternatives, here's a summary of the contents of each Office edition:

✦ **Office XP Standard.** Includes four of the five main Office applications — Word, Excel, PowerPoint, and Outlook — but omits Access.

✦ **Office XP Professional.** Includes all five main Office applications: Word, Excel, PowerPoint, Outlook and Access.

✦ **Office XP Professional Special Edition.** The complete package, but available, according to Microsoft, only for "a limited time to existing Office customers in select worldwide geographies." It includes FrontPage (for creating and managing Web sites), Publisher (a desktop publishing application), and all five core Office applications. Also included are SharePoint Team Services and the new Microsoft IntelliMouse Explorer.

In This Chapter

Choosing an Office XP edition

Installing Office XP

Setting Office options

Using multiple languages with Office

Finding additional Office resources

✦ **Office XP Developer.** This edition includes everything that's in Office XP Professional (except Publisher and Intellimouse Explorer), plus FrontPage, SharePoint Team Services, and other professional tools and resources — everything software developers need to develop their own specialized Office XP-based solutions.

In addition to these four retail editions of Office XP, two editions will be offered to computer makers for preinstallation on new machines: Office XP Small Business, which includes Word, Excel, Outlook, and Publisher, but not Access; and Office XP Professional with Publisher, which includes Word, Excel, Outlook, Publisher, PowerPoint, and Access.

Office Installation

Office is (most likely) already set up on your system, and the installation process itself is straightforward, so I won't detail the steps required to install it. A few comments about installation may help you configure Office optimally, however.

Office Setup should run automatically when you put the first Office CD in the computer. If Office isn't yet installed, you'll be walked through the steps required. Remember, however, that you can run the installer whenever you want to examine or change your current configuration.

If your CD is already in the drive, the easiest way to run it is simply to go to My Computer and double-click the Office CD icon. The Windows installer starts up and displays the Office Setup screen in maintenance mode. To see how Office is currently installed, click the Add or Remove Features radio button; then click Next.

Whether you're installing Office initially or updating an existing setup, the installer's selecting features panel lets you see and change the parts of Office that are available on your computer, and where their files reside. To modify the setting for any component, click the graphic beside the component name and pick from the list of options for that component (see Figure 3-1). As shown in the illustration, the components are organized in hierarchical groups. To work with components individually or as a group, you expand or collapse the hierarchy by clicking the *expand indicators* (small, square boxes that contain a plus or minus sign).

For fastest performance, pick the Run from My Computer choice, which copies the component's files to your hard disk. Selecting the Run from the CD option saves space on your hard disk but drastically slows file operation. Also, it means you must have the Office CDs ready or the feature in question won't work. Use this option only for components that you use quite rarely (or for clip art and other content files that are too large to store on your hard disk). The compromise (that is, on-demand) choice, Installed on First Use, is the topic of the next section.

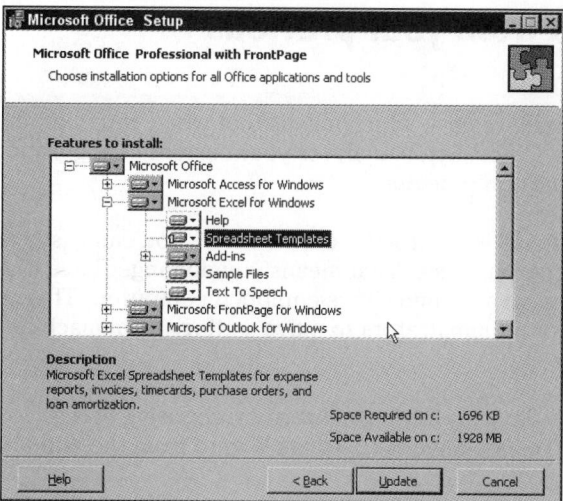

Figure 3-1: Use this panel in Office Setup to select features for installation and control how they're installed.

Using on-demand installation

Selecting Installed on First Use tells the Windows installer to wait before copying the necessary files to your hard disk until the first time you actually use the feature. As a result, you don't waste hard disk space on files you never need. But I find that although you gain time in the initial installation process, you lose more time than you gain when you do activate the feature. The installer has to start up and locate the needed files before it can copy them — and that assumes the Office disc is already in your CD-ROM drive. Bottom-line advice: Select Install on First Use only for components that you're pretty sure you're not going to use.

Manually repairing your Office installation

The Windows installer regularly verifies that your actual Office installation matches the configuration specified during the setup process. If you think something has gone wrong while you're working, however, you can instruct the installer to perform the examination whenever you like. In any Office application, you can choose Help ➪ Detect and Repair. Alternatively, open Office Setup and click Repair Office. With the latter method, you can reinstall Office in its entirety — though you should avoid that option unless the less drastic repair procedure doesn't fix the problem.

Preserving settings from your previous version of Office

Office XP now features *intelligent setup*—which means that when you upgrade to XP from a previous version of Office, Setup analyzes your current configuration and automatically installs the same components.

In addition, you can save your settings directly to a file where you can easily access them and apply them to another machine. That means you no longer have to recreate your settings one-at-a-time on a second Office-equipped computer. (This also makes it quicker and easier for administrators to move settings from machine to machine.)

To save your settings, use the Save My Settings Wizard by choosing Start ⇨ Programs ⇨ Microsoft Office Tools ⇨ Save My Settings Wizard from the Windows taskbar.

Customizing the installation process in an organization

If you manage the installation of Office on other users' PCs, you can use a utility called the Custom Installation Wizard to modify the Windows installer's default settings for the Office setup process. The Custom Installation Wizard is available in the Office Resource Kit (described in "Resources for Office Users," later in this chapter), or you can download it from the Microsoft Web site. Among the installation options it lets you control are the following:

✦ The default path to where Office XP files are installed on the user's hard disk

✦ Whether and how previous versions of Office applications are removed during setup

✦ The installation option for each Office XP component (in network installations, you can designate components to run from a server rather than from the user's hard disk.)

✦ Custom Registry entries

✦ Shortcuts to be automatically created on the Start menu, on the Office Shortcut bar, and in other folders

✦ Outlook and Internet Explorer configuration options

✦ Visual Basic for Applications options (Administrators can now remove VBA from Office installations.)

Caution

Removing Visual Basic for Applications disables a variety of features in Office applications.

Setting Office Options

In every Office application, the Tools ⇨ Options dialog box is the central control panel for controlling a myriad of settings that govern all facets of the program's operations. Figure 3-2 shows the Access version.

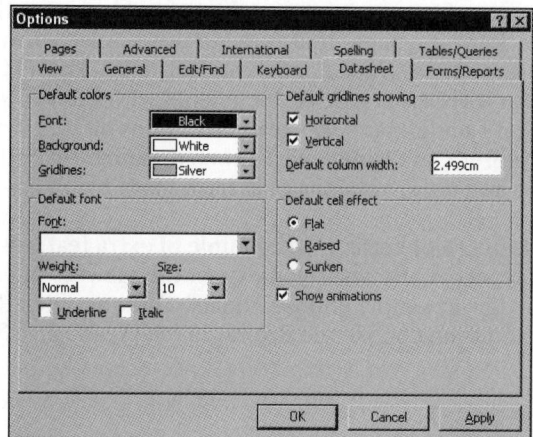

Figure 3-2: The Datasheet tab of Access's Tools ⇨ Options dialog box.

Although I touch on many of the available options in the chapters on the specific Office applications, I don't go through them exhaustively—many are self-explanatory, and many others are useful to relatively few people. For now, I simply recommend that you set aside a few minutes to acquaint yourself with how the Options dialog box is organized in each application and what it has to offer. Page through all the tabs, using the What's This? help tool to explain any choices whose functions aren't clear.

HTML Everywhere, Almost

You can save Office documents, complete with all their formatting, as HTML files—the format used to define Web pages. By default, of course, Office continues to store documents on disk in its proprietary file formats. However, the HTML option gives you an alternative that permits easier exchange of information with others, at least in theory. Because almost everyone has a Web browser, storing documents in HTML format provides nearly universal access to the document content, even for users who don't have their own copies of Office.

Note   Before you get too excited about using HTML as a universal file format, take stock of some real-world limitations. Although the standard version of HTML is certainly gaining better formatting features, it gives you much less control over a document's looks than you have in, say, Word. So when Microsoft tells you that you can save Office documents as HTML files, this doesn't mean that those documents will look the same when you open them in a browser.

What Microsoft has done is add special tags in a more sophisticated language than HTML called XML (Extensible Markup Language) that provide the precise control over layout elements needed to reproduce Office documents faithfully. These XML features enable Office programs to store and retrieve documents with their formatting intact. But some browsers don't understand the new XML codes all that well. The latest version of Internet Explorer can display most Office documents pretty faithfully, but Netscape Navigator and older versions of IE have more trouble.

Office XP has addressed some of these concerns with a couple of extra features. For example, you can specify which type(s) of browser you expect the viewers of your Web page to be using when they view it; simply choose Tools ➪ Options, click the General tab, click Web Options, and then choose the Browsers tab (see Figure 3-3).

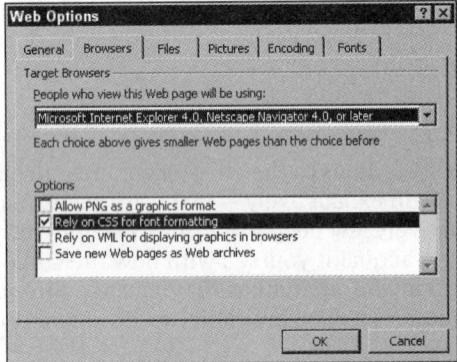

Figure 3-3: The Browsers tab (under Web Options) helps you ensure that the people who want to view your document can view it the way you intended.

In Word, you have an additional option. You can save a document as a *filtered Web page,* which removes the XML tags and allows users to publish their document as a "clean" HTML file.

The International Office

Office has long been available in separate versions for different languages. Office XP continues the standard of vastly improved support for international use begun with Office 2000, offering components with the standard product in more than 80 languages. This relieves headaches for software managers in global organizations, and it's also a boon for individuals who need or want to communicate in more than one language.

Beginning with Office 2000, Microsoft completely separates core software functions from the language-specific portions of the code, which plug into the core as needed. Because Office Professional comes complete with these plug-in language components, you don't need to buy any add-ons — or, worse, a whole different edition of Office — when you want to work in another language, even if you want to change the language in which Office displays its menus and Help system on-screen.

Office XP's support for multiple languages includes the following elements:

✦ Compatibility with Unicode, a standard system for encoding language characters

✦ Fonts for languages such as Chinese and Arabic that don't use European alphabets, and new multilanguage versions of commonly used fonts such as Arial, Courier New, Garamond, and Times New Roman

✦ Proofing tools such as spelling and grammar checkers, as well as their supporting dictionaries, thesauri, AutoCorrect lists, and hyphenation algorithms

✦ Templates and wizards customized for the supported languages

✦ Utilities for editing in (and converting between) various Asian languages

✦ Components for displaying the user interface in any supported language

✦ A translation feature that lets you translate words and phrases between various languages

The Office applications include commands unique to particular languages; the appropriate commands appear automatically on menus and dialog boxes when you enable a given language. As you may expect, Word has the most support for multiple languages among the Office applications, and it is especially rich in language-specific commands. Even more impressively, Word is designed to figure out which language you're typing in — automatically — and this feature usually works.

However, Office is still available in *localized* versions (designed explicitly for specific languages and the date, time, and currency notation in use at a particular locale). That's because the language components provided with English version of Office don't cover every Office feature. Also, some versions of Windows don't let you use all the language features available in Office XP.

Limitations in current versions of Windows

An important caveat: You can only take full advantage of the capability to switch languages freely by running Windows 2000 or (presumably) the upcoming Windows XP. Other versions of Windows, including Windows Me, set some limits. Until you install Windows 2000, then, you may need a localized version of Windows, Office, or both to work with some languages.

One obvious sore spot is support for right-to-left languages such as Farsi, Arabic, and Hebrew. Localized versions of Windows are available for at least some of these languages, and with them, and if you're using Windows 2000 or Windows XP, Office XP supports right-to-left editing. However, you can't use these languages with the English versions of Windows 95, 98, Me, or NT 4.0. You may run into limitations with other languages as well.

Note   If you want to use different languages to label the Office user interface and switch between them, be sure to turn off the Windows Active Desktop first. If you leave Active Desktop on, the user interface appears only in the default language that comes with your version of Windows.

Installing the MultiLanguage Pack

Language-related plug-in components for Office are packaged as the MultiLanguage Pack on a separate set of CDs. To activate the capability to change language settings, install the MultiLanguage Pack by running its own Setup program. After you've installed the pack, the main Windows installer takes over, installing any needed components when you change language settings in Office. Note that your Office CDs don't include files for every supported language — you may have to download files from Microsoft's Web site or order supplemental disks.

Note   Language-specific components that have the same filename in every language are installed in folders named according to Microsoft's locale ID number for the language in question. If you're wondering why you have those folders named 1033, it's because 1033 is the locale ID number for U.S. English. The Help system includes a listing of the locale IDs for the languages Office supports.

If you no longer need to work in a particular language, you should remove its files to free up space on your hard disk. To do so, rerun the Language Pack's Setup program or use the Control Panel's Add/Remove Programs applet to get things started. When the Installer's dialog box appears, click Add or Remove Features to get to the list of installed languages; set the ones you don't want anymore to Not Available.

Turning on language-related features

The control panel for language-related Office features is the Microsoft Office Language Settings dialog box, accessible in Windows via the Start ➪ Programs ➪ Microsoft Office Tools folder. As shown in Figure 3-4, the box has three tabs, User

Interface, Enabled Languages, and About Microsoft Office Language Settings. You'll
use the first two tabs to change language settings; the third tab simply provides
information about which version of the language settings you're using and who it's
licensed to.

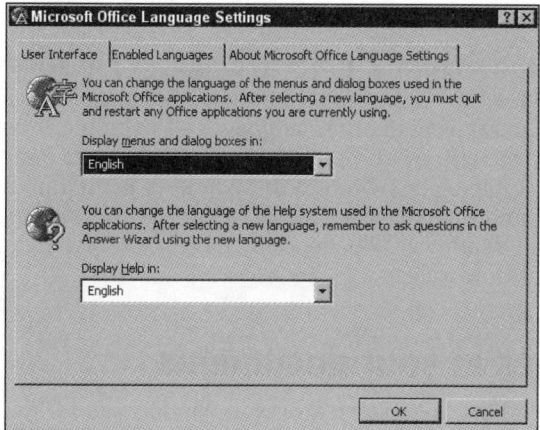

Figure 3-4: Control the Office language settings in
this dialog box.

The settings on the User Interface tab determine the language that Office displays
to the user to label its features (for example, text on menus, in dialog boxes, and in
the Help system). You don't see this tab until you've actually installed language-specific user interface components from the MultiLanguage Pack. When the tab does
appear on-screen, the only choices offered are those of the installed languages.

Use the Enabled Languages tab to specify the languages in which you want to edit
documents. You can have a field day here — all languages supported by Office are
shown, regardless of whether you've installed them on your system. However,
selecting languages you're not actually going to use has a downside: Commands
unique to each selected language appear on the menus and dialog boxes in your
Office apps; they'd serve only to distract if you're not actually using that language.

Turning on keyboard support for other languages in Windows

All Windows versions let you switch among different languages at the operating-sys-
tem level. When you switch to a different *locale* (language), Windows notifies running applications of the change. Of course, many applications pay no attention, but
Office adjusts itself accordingly. The locale setting also determines the layout of
your keyboard (that is, the character Windows "sees" when you press each key).
Although Windows provides a default keyboard layout for each locale, you can
choose any layout you like for any locale.

To add new locales to your Windows 98 or 95 configuration, use the Keyboard applet in the Control Panel. Switch to the Language tab and click Change, then Add, and select a new input language from the lengthy list that presents itself. (In Windows Me, look for a new applet on your Control Panel called Text Input Settings; in Windows 2000, open Regional Settings, and then click Add on the Input Locales tab.)

Adding support for Greek and Eastern European languages in Windows

If you're running Windows 95, 98, or Me and want to compose documents in Russian, Polish, Bulgarian, or a smattering of other languages — including Greek — you must install the Multilanguage Support component. Open the Control Panel, run the Add/Remove Programs applet, and switch to the Windows Setup tab. Check the Multilanguage Support box, and then click Details to select the specific languages you want to work with. In Windows 2000, you only have to be certain you've installed the languages you want to work in.

Using other languages in your documents

After you've installed and enabled the language features in Windows and Office, you can start using them to view and edit documents. You don't have to do anything special to view documents — just open them in the appropriate Office application. Entering new information in a different language requires more work, however.

Editing with alternative keyboard layouts

Often, the language chosen as the active language offers more characters than fit on the standard and shifted keys — this is the norm, for example, with European languages that have accented characters. In such cases, you typically enter accented characters by pressing a two-key sequence that starts with the accent key. In some layouts, still more characters are available when you hold down the right Alt key.

Using the On-Screen Keyboard

Included with Office, the On-Screen Keyboard utility (see Figure 3-5) lets you see the keyboard layout for the language that's currently active in Windows. You can access Visual Keyboard through the Office Language Bar once you've installed Handwriting Recognition. Note that the options available on the Language Bar change with the various languages installed, and the On-Screen Keyboard is not available in all languages.

Cross-Reference   For detailed information on handwriting recognition in Office, see Chapter 4.

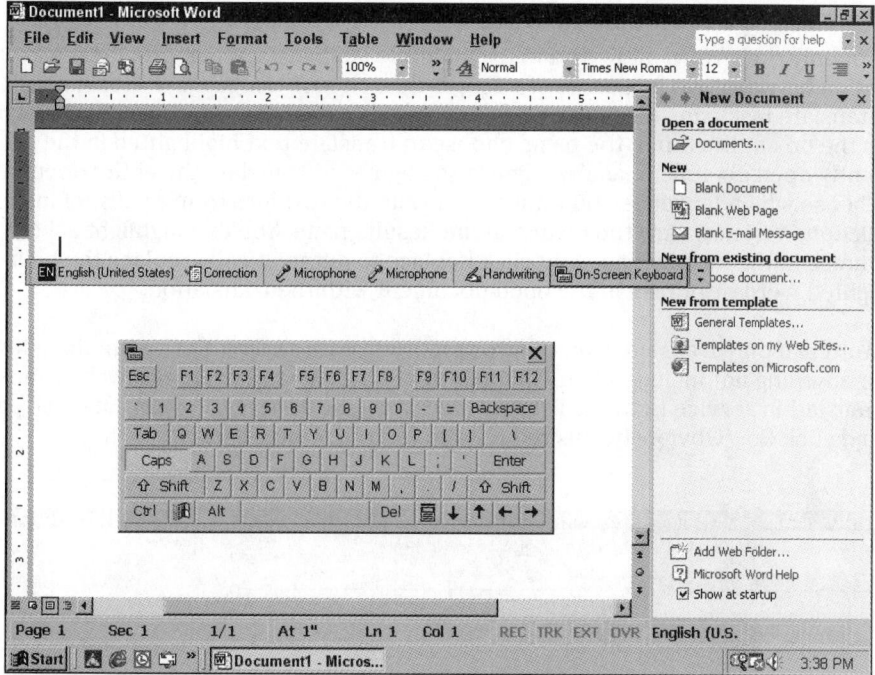

Figure 3-5: The On-Screen Keyboard shows which keys to type to enter the characters available to you in the active keyboard layout.

If you're working with a Windows keyboard layout that differs from the one shown on your real-life keyboard, the On-Screen Keyboard shows you which key you must type to enter any given character into your document, or you can use the mouse to "type" on the On-Screen Keyboard instead of your regular keyboard. Pressing Shift (or clicking the on-screen Shift key) shows you the shifted version of the character set. To use characters that must be entered via a two-key sequence, press or click the key that starts the sequence.

Editing documents in Asian languages

Although you can view documents created in an Asian language when you turn on support for that language, you can't enter new ideographic characters directly. Instead, you need a special tool called an Input Method Editor (IME). Versions of Windows localized for language include the corresponding IME, of course, but only the one for that language. However, the Office MultiLanguage Pack comes with limited IMEs (called *global IMEs*) for Japanese, Korean, and two versions of Chinese (Simplified and Traditional); these work in the English version of Office.

Translating documents in Word

Not only does Word allow you to use multiple languages, it can provide basic translation between two languages. To access this, choose Language ➪ Translate. The Translate task pane (see Figure 3-6) opens. You can enter text you want translated in the box at the top of the pane, choose to translate text highlighted in the currently open document, as I've done in the figure, or translate the entire document. Choose which language you want to translate the text into from the list of installed dictionaries, and view the results in the Results pane. You can highlight a word or phrase in the Results pane and click Replace to automatically replace the highlighted word or phrase in the open document with the translation.

Word can only translate single words or short phrases directly; for anything longer, or anything not included in its dictionaries, you have to turn to the Web. Choose a translation service from the list provided at the bottom of the Translate task pane and click Go. (Obviously, this requires an Internet connection.)

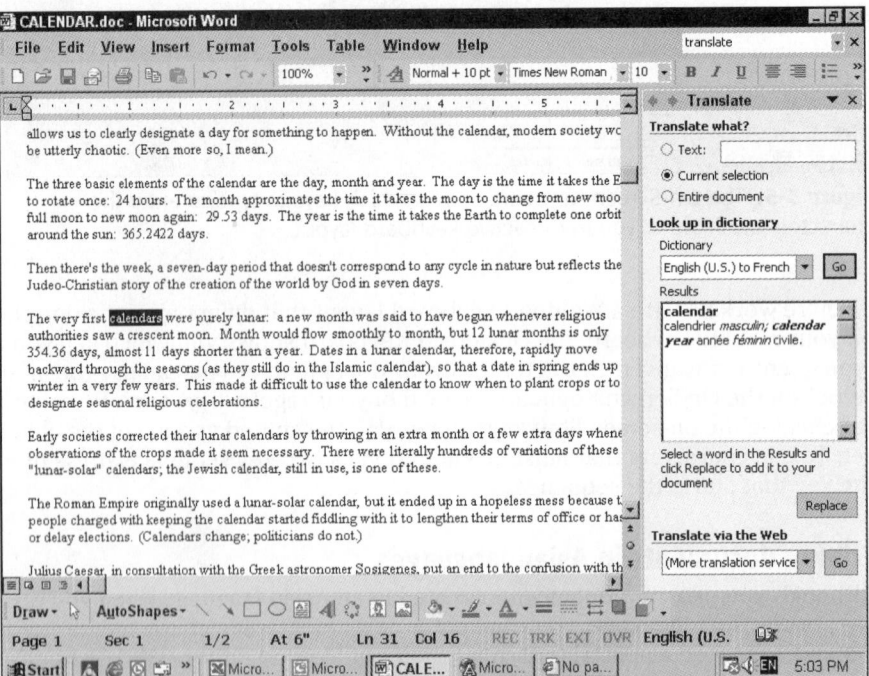

Figure 3-6: Word's new Translate task pane can provide basic translation between installed languages.

Understanding Unicode

The text-handling features of Office support Unicode, an international standard for numerically encoding the characters used in major languages. The Windows Character Map utility shows that conventional Windows fonts can hold only about 200 different characters; Unicode can handle more than 65,000 different characters. Unicode numbers have already been assigned to about 40,000 letters, numerals, ideograms, punctuation marks, and other features unique to particular languages.

You won't see many fonts containing all possible characters. Most Unicode fonts include one or more subsets of characters defined for specific languages. The real point is that Unicode enables fonts and applications throughout the world to use the same code number for each character. Text prepared in any major language can be displayed accurately by other applications and on other computers, as long as the necessary fonts are installed.

About the Unicode font included with Office

If you're curious about the vast range of characters people use to communicate their thoughts in writing, Office XP comes with a complete 40,000-character-or-so Unicode font called Arial Unicode MS. This font's only practical value, however, is in displaying multilanguage text in Unicode-aware applications that don't support font changes. For example, Access allows only one font in each database table. If you happen to have an Access table that lists translations for words from many languages, you need a Unicode font that contains all the characters required to display the table accurately.

Word's Insert ⇨ Symbol dialog box and the Windows Character Map utility (available in most Windows versions at Start ⇨ Programs ⇨ Accessories ⇨ System Tools ⇨ Character Map) both recognize Unicode fonts. When you select a Unicode font, use the Subset box to choose the range of characters you want to see, as shown in Figure 3-7.

Other Unicode fonts

Office also includes a number of Unicode updates for some scalable TrueType fonts that you most likely already have on your system. These big fonts don't contain all the Unicode characters — not by a long shot — but they do offer multiple character sets that cover many non-English languages. Big fonts included with Office include Arial, Arial Black, Arial Bold, Arial Narrow, Bookman Old Style, Courier New, Garamond, Impact, Tahoma, Times New Roman, Trebuchet, and Verdana.

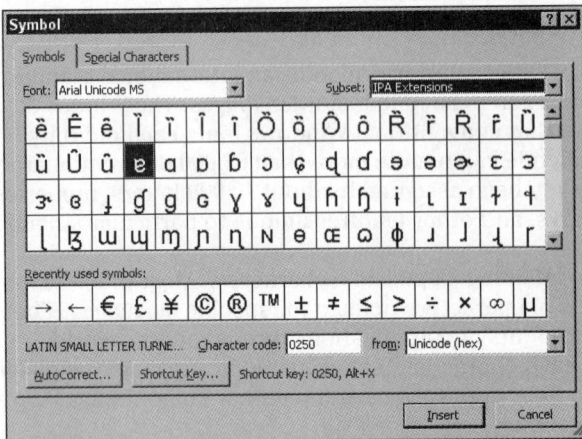

Figure 3-7: Using the Insert ⇨ Symbol dialog box to select and view a subset of Unicode characters

Resources for Office Users

If you can't find the information you need in this book or in the Office Help system, you can turn to many other sources of Office information.

About the Office Resource Kit

Microsoft's Office Resource Kit (ORK) includes a huge collection of information about administering Office XP in organizations, plus a set of supporting software tools. Although Microsoft explicitly intends the ORK for managers (not lowly "end users"), the kit contains loads of details on topics such as custom configuration and file formats. The ORK is available as a separate product on its own CD; you can buy printed documentation as well. But you may also be able to download ORK files from Microsoft's Web site.

Other resources

The Microsoft Web site is packed with material on Office. You can read detailed descriptions of Office technologies, get advanced instruction on VBA programming and database development, find bug reports and answers to technical questions, and download additional templates, sample documents, utilities, and multimedia content. The quickest way to Microsoft's Office Web site is via the Help ⇨ Office on the Web command.

Another source of Office tips and trivia is Woody Leonhard's Woody's Office Watch, a free weekly newsletter via e-mail (subscribe at www.mcc.com.au/wow/).

Elementk Journals at www.elementkjournals.com/ has created a journal for previous versions of Office, so you'll probably eventually find one for Office XP there, too.

And finally, there are books, books, and more books on Office XP to be found at every bookstore. (Look for the ones from Hungry Minds first, of course!)

Cross-Reference
For more suggestions of places to find additional information about Office, see the appendix.

✦   ✦   ✦

Making the User Interface User-Friendly

Achieving the optimal screen view of your work, taking
full control of Office's commands and toolbars, and
moving information into documents smoothly are noble goals
for any Office master-in-training. For this chapter, I assume
that you already know the basics, such as working the menus
and clicking the toolbar buttons. Now I clue you in on some
deeper truths about the Office user interface.

Working with the Screen

Most of this section is devoted to the intricacies of the Zoom
command, which lets you see more or less of your work on
screen as necessary.

Zooming in and out

As someone familiar with Office, you already know about the
Zoom box, where you can select a magnification as a percentage of the document's actual size, or by description (as in
Page Width or selection). Remember, though, that you're not
limited to the options in the drop-down list. You can type in
any whole-number zoom factor within the allowable range (in
Word, from 10 to 500 percent — in Excel, 10 to 400 percent).

Note that once the zoom factor is small enough, Word and
Excel display multiple pages in Page Layout view. In other
words, you don't have to switch to Print Preview (discussed
in Chapter 13) to see several bite-size pages at the same time.

Toggling between Zoom Settings with a Macro

If you're interested in both detail work and the big picture, you typically switch back and forth between two zoom settings. Office doesn't provide a command that lets you toggle the zoom factor, but a macro does the trick.

To create the macro in Word, choose Tools ➪ Macro ➪ Macros, enter **ZoomToggle. ZoomToggle** for the name, and choose Create to start the Visual Basic Editor. Type in the code as it appears here, check it carefully, and then choose File ➪ Exit to save your work and return to Word (see Part XI on Visual Basic for Applications for details on these techniques).

Run the macro by highlighting it in the Tools ➪ Macro ➪ Macros dialog box and choosing Run, or assign it to a keyboard shortcut or toolbar button with the techniques described in Chapter 5.

```
Sub ZoomToggle()
Set objDocVars = ActiveDocument.Variables
With objDocVars

For Each aVar In objDocVars
    If aVar.Name = "StoreZoom1" Then num1 = aVar.Index
    If aVar.Name = "StoreZoom2" Then num2 = aVar.Index
    If aVar.Name = "ToggleFlag" Then num3 = aVar.Index
Next aVar

If num1 = 0 Then
    .Add Name:="StoreZoom1", Value:="0"
End If

If num2 = 0 Then
    .Add Name:="StoreZoom2", Value:="0"
End If

If num3 = 0 Then
    .Add Name:="ToggleFlag", Value:="0"
End If

If .Item("StoreZoom1").Value = 0 Then
    .Item("StoreZoom1").Value = _
        ActiveWindow.View.Zoom.Percentage
    GoTo Out
End If

If .Item("StoreZoom2").Value = 0 Then
    .Item("StoreZoom2").Value = _
        ActiveWindow.View.Zoom.Percentage
```

```
        ActiveWindow.View.Zoom.Percentage = _
            .Item("StoreZoom1").Value
        .Item("ToggleFlag").Value = 2
        GoTo Out
    End If

    If .Item("ToggleFlag").Value = 2 Then
        .Item("StoreZoom1").Value = _
            ActiveWindow.View.Zoom.Percentage
        ActiveWindow.View.Zoom.Percentage = _
            .Item("StoreZoom2").Value
        .Item("ToggleFlag").Value = 1
        GoTo Out
    End If

    If .Item("ToggleFlag").Value = 1 Then
        .Item("StoreZoom2").Value = _
            ActiveWindow.View.Zoom.Percentage
        ActiveWindow.View.Zoom.Percentage = _
            .Item("StoreZoom1").Value
        .Item("ToggleFlag").Value = 2
    End If

    End With

Out:
End Sub
```

In Word, another solution is to flip back and forth between two of the views (usually Normal and Print or Web Layout). Word remembers the zoom setting separately for each view.

Note   In Word, when you choose Page Width in the Zoom box while you're in Page Layout view, the magnification factor that Word sets for you lets you see the edges of the pages and even some of the surface they're resting on, too. In other words, you're zoomed out quite a bit, much more than necessary for most documents. As a result, your text may be hard to read. You can usually set the zoom factor manually to something approaching 100 percent and still see everything of interest on the page with the benefits of Page Layout mode.

Using Full Screen view

The View ➪ Full Screen view, available in Excel and Word, devotes the entire computer screen to the document, hiding other window elements such as the toolbars —

see Figure 4-1. If you prefer the keyboard to the mouse, you may want to spend most of your time in full screen view, where there's less distracting clutter on screen and lots more room for your documents.

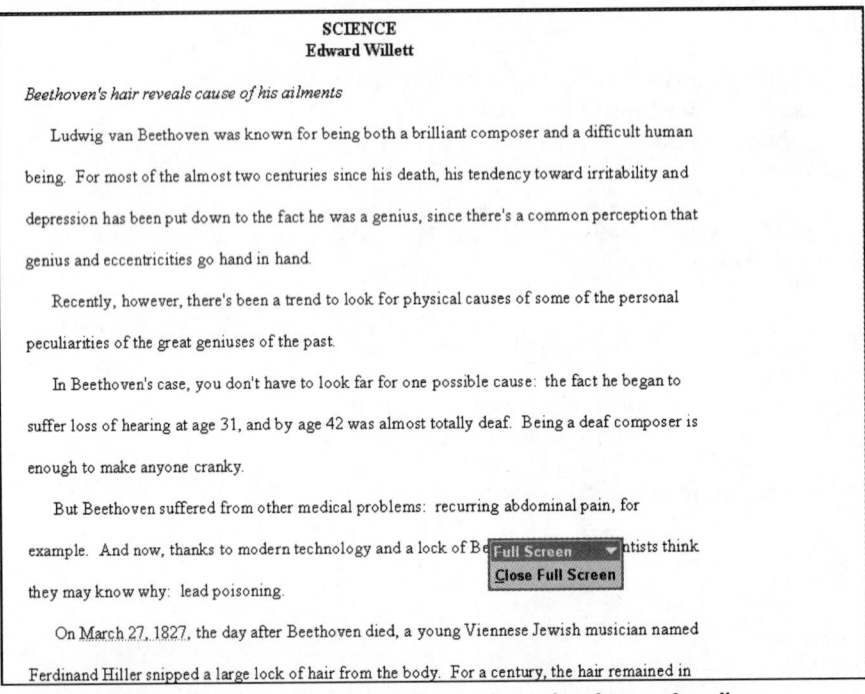

Figure 4-1: Full Screen view in Word frees you from the clutter of toolbars.

Working with document windows

In Word, Excel, and PowerPoint, each open document automatically has one window of its own. You can view different parts of the same document in separate windows by using the Window ➪ New Window command to create additional windows for the document.

Although you can switch between document windows using the application's Window menu, Office XP gives you an alternative technique that's often easier and faster, automatically displaying a separate taskbar item for each document window that's currently open. If you open three workbooks in Excel and create a second window for one of them, you get four separate taskbar items. You can switch to the document you want by clicking its taskbar icon, or by pressing Alt+Tab or Alt+Shift+Tab to cycle through all taskbar items.

Keyboard Secrets

The trade-off for all the freedom a mouse provides, for some people, is a performance hit—they find that taking their hands off the keyboard to pick up the mouse slows them down. (Although even inveterate keyboard users realize that for some tasks using the keyboard would be ridiculously cumbersome, and besides, break-neck speed can lead to emotional stress, physical injury, and more assignments from the boss.)

Still, even if you really prefer the mouse to the keyboard, learning Office's keyboard commands is worthwhile. Everyone uses a different combination of mouse and keyboard commands to accomplish their tasks. The more keyboard commands you know, the more options you have, and the more you can make your Office experience pleasurable and proficient for you.

Cross-Reference When a default keyboard shortcut doesn't exist, or if the existing shortcut doesn't suit you, you can use the techniques discussed in Chapter 5 to create your own.

Recent releases of Office have provided keyboard control over a part of the user interface that was once off limits—the toolbars. Table 4-1 lists the keys you can use to push toolbar buttons without the mouse.

<table>
<tr><td colspan="2" align="center">Table 4-1
Keyboard Control over the Office Toolbars</td></tr>
<tr><td>*To Do This*</td><td>*Press*</td></tr>
<tr><td>Activate the menu bar</td><td>Alt or F10</td></tr>
<tr><td>Select the next button or menu</td><td>Tab or right arrow</td></tr>
<tr><td>Select the previous button or menu</td><td>Shift+Tab or left arrow</td></tr>
<tr><td>Select the next toolbar</td><td>Ctrl+Tab</td></tr>
<tr><td>Select the previous toolbar</td><td>Ctrl+Shift+Tab</td></tr>
<tr><td>Press a selected button or open a selected menu</td><td>Enter (down arrow also works for menus)</td></tr>
<tr><td>Display the toolbar shortcut (right-click) menu</td><td>Shift+F10</td></tr>
</table>

You may notice that as you press Ctrl+Tab, Office activates toolbars in its own order, which may be different from how they appear on your screen.

Tip You can find extensive lists of keyboard shortcuts in the Microsoft Office Help system; do a keyword search for keyboard shortcuts.

Working with Toolbars

After you get the hang of toolbars, they're not hard to work with; Chapter 1 in the Quick Start part of the book provides a quick intro to the topic. One more little tip that didn't fit in that section is in order, though:

When a docked toolbar is too long for all its buttons to fit across the screen in the room available, Office displays a slender button at the far right of the toolbar. This is the More Buttons button, marked with a double arrow pointing to the right. Click this button to see the toolbar's remaining buttons on an attached pop-up menu—see Figure 4-2.

Note   If you don't see the double arrow, then all of the toolbar's buttons are already visible. On built-in toolbars, the More Buttons button always shows a single arrow pointing down. That's to indicate that the More Buttons pop-up menu includes a working Add or Remove buttons command, which is covered in Chapter 5.

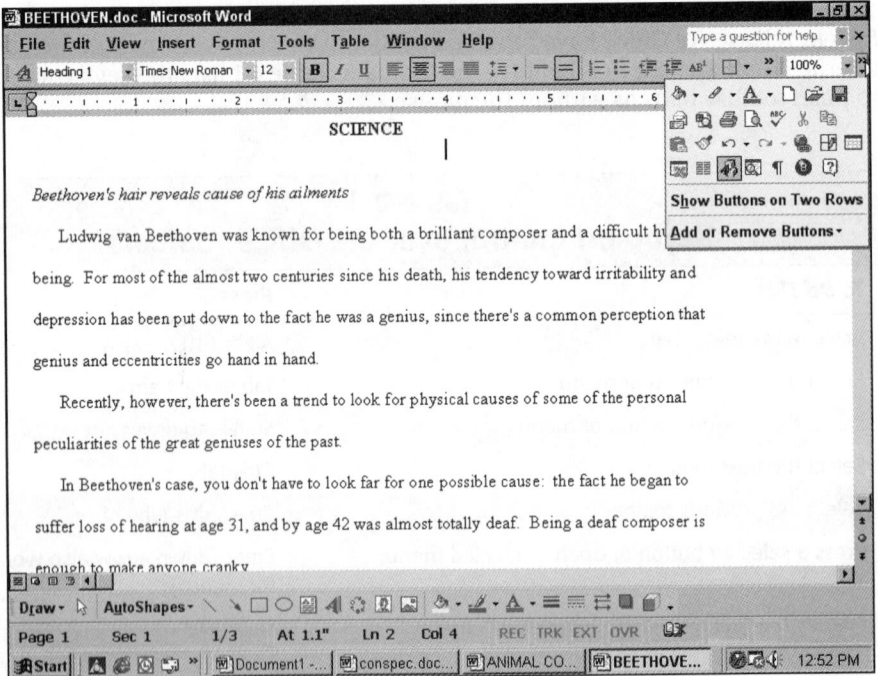

Figure 4-2: Use the More Buttons pop-up menu to access buttons that won't fit on a docked toolbar.

If you click a button on the More Buttons menu, Office carries out the corresponding command. In addition, however, Office updates the visible part of the original toolbar by adding the button you clicked.

Where does Office get room for a button that didn't fit before? If another toolbar is parked in the same row or column, Office subtracts buttons from it and gives that space to the current toolbar. If no other toolbar has space to loan, Office substitutes the button you just clicked for some other button that was visible.

Office is smart enough to keep track of which buttons you click most often, and it swaps out the buttons you haven't clicked recently.

Mouse on Fire

Point and click, drag and drop—everything you can do in Office, you can do with the mouse. Mouse technique is easy to master, but for the uninitiated, the following tips may prove helpful, or at least mildly diverting:

✦ **Remember the power of the shortcut menu.** Right-clicking almost anything produces a *shortcut menu* of choices specific to that item. This is often the fastest way to access commands when you're already using the mouse. (Depending on where you are in Office, Shift+F10 or the special shortcut key on Windows-aware keyboards usually pops up the shortcut menu, too.)

✦ **Watch for Smart Tags.** These new additions to the Office family of on-screen aids are buttons that appear when you need them (or, at least, when Office thinks you need them—such as when you make a mistake in an Excel formula, or when Word automatically corrects something you've done, or when you paste in data from the Clipboard). Clicking the Smart Tag will bring up a small menu that gives you the options you need to fix the error, reverse the action, or whatever else might be appropriate.

✦ **Use mouse clicks in combination with keyboard buttons.** In Windows, clicking a button while you hold down Shift on the keyboard sometimes produces different results than clicking the usual way. This is also true of at least one Office button: the Close button, which normally closes the current document. In Word and Excel, when you hold down Shift and click the Close button, *all* open documents close.

✦ **Take advantage of split buttons.** Many Office buttons such as Font Color and the View button in Access are *split buttons*: Alongside the main part of the button they have a narrow gray bar with a little downward-pointing arrow. Click the main button and Office carries out the corresponding command immediately. Click the narrow bar, and if your aim is true, you get a drop-down panel offering various choices.

✦ **Customize your mouse.** Don't forget that you can use the Mouse applet in the Windows Control Panel to swap the functions of the left and right mouse buttons and to otherwise tinker with the settings of your mouse.

Mouse alternatives

Pointing device is the generic term for any gadget that lets you select options on the screen by pointing at them. The extensive catalog of variations on and alternatives to the standard mouse includes cordless mice, trackballs, touchpads, pointing sticks (both of the latter commonly found on notebook PCs), pen-like styli, and other gizmos too unique to categorize. (Anyone remember Felix the Cat? You never knew what might come next from his bag of tricks — same deal with input devices.)

Chacun à son goût, of course, but be aware that certain pointing devices offer practical benefits as well as their appeal to fashion and ergonomics. In particular, if you like using a mouse more than using the keyboard, I suggest you consider pointing devices with more than two buttons.

A three- or four-button device is a start. The extra buttons can be programmed to act as a double-click or to perform whatever command you use most frequently. Wheeled mice like Microsoft's own Intellimouse are even better — the wheel provides all sorts of benefits (described later in this chapter) and it's *also* a third button.

IntelliMouse and wheeled mice

Microsoft's IntelliMouse may not really be so smart, but it offers (as do other wheeled mice) some genuine benefits when used with Office XP — which was designed with a wheeled mouse in mind.

Pushing the wheel straight down to click is equivalent to using the middle button on an ordinary three-button mouse. You can also roll the wheel to scroll or zoom your document. In more detail, here's what you can do with a wheeled mouse in Office:

✦ Moving the wheel is like clicking the vertical scrollbar arrows — definitely more convenient than having to move the mouse pointer over to the scrollbar and then back again to the document.

✦ To smoothly pan the document without having to keep moving the wheel, drag while holding the wheel button down. The farther up or down the screen you drag from the vertical middle of the work area, the faster the scroll. Cancel this scrolling mode by clicking the mouse or pressing any key.

✦ To zoom in or out on the document, hold down Ctrl and move the wheel.

✦ Expand or collapse outlines in Word by pointing to a heading and then holding down Shift while moving the wheel. Similarly, in Excel, expand an outline by pointing to a summary cell and performing a Shift+forward roll. Collapse the outline by Shift+backward rolling over a cell containing detail.

The IntelliMouse and other wheeled mice usually offer scads of software options for controlling the way they work. Figure 4-3, for instance, shows the dialog box for setting mouse properties on the IntelliMouse.

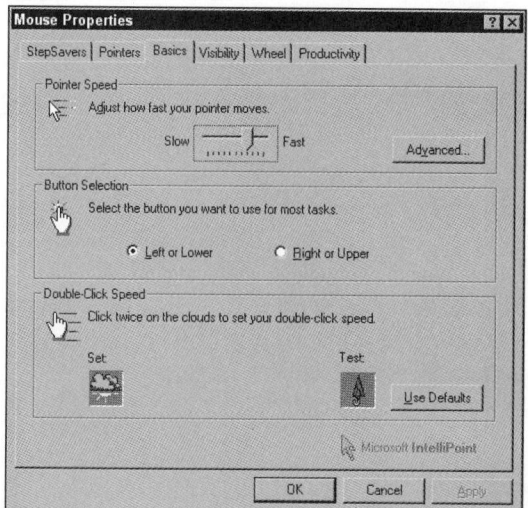

Figure 4-3: Wheeled mice, like the IntelliMouse, let you set a lot of different properties to customize the way you work.

Setting Toolbar and Event Sounds

Whether your toolbars honk, bray, or sigh at you when you fiddle with them depends on an obscure setting on the General tab of the Tools ➪ Options dialog box in Excel or Word. The control in question is named Provide Feedback with Sound. When this box is checked, sound is turned on for all events in all Office applications. Office can give you audible confirmation of many common events such as opening or saving files.

You can turn on sound only if you've installed some required files first. When you select the Provide Feedback with Sound option for the first time, you're asked to point to the Help menu and click Office on the Web to connect to Office Update to download the necessary sounds.

After you've installed Office sounds, you can change the specific sound you hear with each event using the Sounds applet (or Sounds and Multimedia, depending on which version of Office you have) in the Windows Control Panel. Open the Sounds Properties dialog box and scroll down the list until you get to the heading for Office. As shown in Figure 4-4, you can then locate the specific event you want to change and use the available controls to try out other sounds and assign them to the event.

Of course, Office sounds won't do you any good unless you have a sound card and speakers installed in your computer.

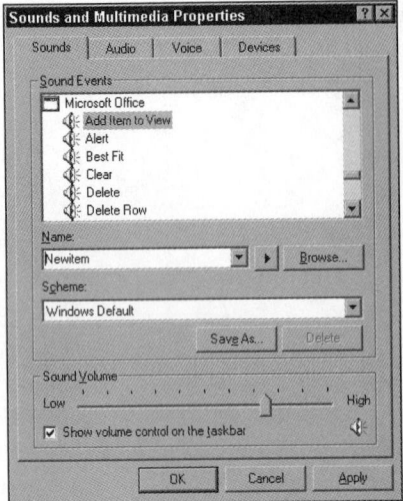

Figure 4-4: Assigning new sounds to Office events in the Windows Control Panel (this is the Windows Me version of this dialog box).

Talking to Office

Office 2000 was supposed to have it, but didn't. Office XP does have it — although it still isn't perfect.

The "it" in question is *speech recognition*, the Office capability to respond to voice commands instead of mouse or keyboard commands, and even to take dictation — if you're willing to put up with a few errors.

Note   I'm sure this is obvious, but just to be clear, you can't use speech recognition unless your computer has a sound card and a microphone installed.

To turn on speech recognition, choose Tools ➪ Speech from the menu of the Office application in which you wish to use it. Doing so opens the Language Bar.

Note   Tools ➪ Speech is the only way to turn on this bar; you won't find it under View ➪ Toolbars or by right-clicking another toolbar. Also, the language toolbar cannot be docked like other toolbars. Try it, and you'll find that it simply floats over top.

Setting speech properties

Before you can use speech recognition, you have to set Speech Properties. You do so in the Speech Properties dialog box (see Figure 4-5), which opens automatically the first time you turn on Speech (or when you choose Tools ⇨ Options from the Language Bar).

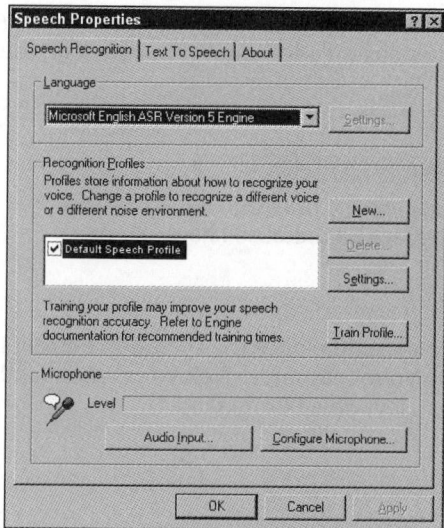

Figure 4-5: Use the Speech Properties dialog box to configure your microphone and other speech-recognition properties.

Click Configure Microphone at the bottom of this dialog box to open a Wizard that will automatically set the level for your microphone. You'll be asked to read a short phrase.

After you've finished the wizard and returned to the Speech Properties dialog box, it's a good idea to think about training your speech profile. (Office lets you set up a number of different speech profiles for different users so the software has a better chance of recognizing the speech of each one.)

Clicking Train Profile opens a wizard that asks you to read a section of text. As you read, the text is highlighted on the screen. If Office doesn't recognize the way you pronounced a word, that word will fail to highlight; just wait a moment and try again from the first un-highlighted word. If Office fails to recognize the word repeatedly, click Skip Word and carry on. You can pause the training process at any time by clicking Pause; to resume training, click Resume.

Tip   Training is always available from the Speech Properties dialog box. The more training you do, the more useful the speech-recognition feature becomes — because it makes fewer mistakes when you issue voice commands or dictation.

The second tab of the Speech Properties dialog box, Text to Speech, lets you pick a default computerized voice for when you want the computer to read text to you; you can choose from a male voice (Michael) or a female voice (Michelle).

To start using speech recognition, click the microphone button on the Language Bar. This turns on your microphone and opens up additional commands on the toolbar (see Figure 4-6).

Figure 4-6: Turning on your microphone expands the Language Bar. (I have two microphone buttons on my Language Bar because I have two microphones installed.)

If you want to use speech recognition for dictation, click the Dictation button; if you want to use it to give voice commands to your computer, click Voice Command (if the microphone is already turned on, just say "Voice Command.")

Using Voice Command

To use Voice Command, speak the name of the command you want to use. For instance, to open the Format menu, say "Format." To change the font from Times New Roman to Arial, say "Font" to open the dialog box and then say "Arial" to change the font.

If you open a menu and not all the commands are visible, say "Expand" or "More buttons." Within a dialog box, you can move from tab to tab by saying the name of the tab and check and uncheck options by saying the name of the option.

You can also use Voice Command for navigation: for instance, say "End" to move to the end of a document, say "Return" to do the equivalent of pressing Return, or say "Escape" to get the normal result of pressing Esc. This form of voice recognition is limited to recognized commands, however; you can't, for example, choose a folder from the Open dialog box by saying the name of the folder.

The Microsoft Help files can assist you in finding more examples of voice commands and how to use them. Search using "speech recognition" as keywords and choose the topic *Things you can do and say with speech recognition*.

Using dictation

Dictation is even more straightforward than Voice Command; just say what you want to say. However, you should be aware of a few tricks while dictating, too. For instance, you have to remember to state your punctuation: "How are you today, Mrs. Smith?" would be dictated as, "Open quote how are you today comma missus Smith question mark close quote." (Office XP's speech recognition is smart enough to turn the spoken "missus" into *Mrs.*)

Tip By default, Office will spell out numbers lower than 20 when inserted, and insert numbers greater than 20 as digits. If you want all numbers to show up as digits, you can do so; just say "Force num" first, and pause briefly before you start dictating digits.

Correcting mistakes

The Language Bar also includes a Correction button. During dictation, clicking the Correction button will cause the computer to read back to you the last word it thinks you said, and open up a short menu of other possibilities. If the correct phrase is in that list, you can click it to replace the error. If the correct phrase isn't in that list, then you'll have to correct the error manually.

Tip That doesn't mean you have to use that nasty old keyboard. You can spell over errors verbally. In Dictation mode, say "Spelling mode," pause slightly, and then spell the word correctly. You can also delete the last thing you said if you say "Scratch that" immediately afterward.

Improving speech recognition

You can improve speech recognition by reading more training exercises, as described earlier; you can also improve it by adding words you use often to the speech-recognition dictionary. To do so, open a document that includes words you want to add to the speech-recognition dictionary; then choose Tools ➪ Learn from Document on the Language Bar to open the Learn from Document dialog box (see Figure 4-7).

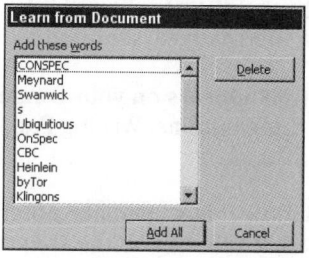

Figure 4-7: Office can add words from the current document to the speech-recognition dictionary.

If the document contains words that aren't in the speech-recognition dictionary, this dialog box finds and lists them. You can then choose which words you don't want to add to the dictionary and click Delete to remove them from the list. After finishing your deletions, click Add All to add all the remaining words to the speech-recognition dictionary.

You can also add individual words to the dictionary as you dictate by choosing Tools ➪ Add/Delete Word(s) from the Language Bar. In the field provided, type in the word you want to add; click Record Pronunciation to record the way you say that word, to help dictation recognize it in the future.

The best way to get used to the foibles of speech recognition is to experiment with it. If you're a slow typist but a quick talker, you may find this feature more helpful than if you're a fast typist. (I can type almost as fast as I can talk, so I haven't found any compelling reason to use it much yet.)

On the other hand, if keyboard and mouse use is difficult for you (or you are at risk of developing a repetitive-strain injury such as carpal tunnel syndrome) speech recognition could make this new version of Office a lifesaver for you.

The Power of the Pen

Office XP offers you yet another way to communicate with it: by handwriting.

These days, hand-held machines equipped with pens are everywhere — in the form of those handheld computers so many people carry, and as specialized business tools, such as the little electronic notepads carried by Federal Express couriers.

Office lets you enter text by using a handwriting input device — such as a graphics tablet, a tablet-PC, or even your mouse (if you have a strong masochistic streak), and converts that handwriting into typed characters — or, in Word and Outlook, even as a graphic preserving the handwritten form.

You can also input handwritten notes you took with a handheld or pocket computer; check the documentation that came with your device.

Handwriting recognition isn't installed by default; you must either install it yourself (using Microsoft Office Setup) or have your network administrator install it for you. (In Setup, you'll find it under Office Shared Features, Alternative User Input.)

After handwriting recognition is installed, a new button appears on your Language Bar — Handwriting. Choosing this button gives you three options: Writing Pad, Write Anywhere, and Drawing Pad.

If you choose Writing Pad, Office opens a special window that's lined like notebook paper. Move your insertion point into the Writing Pad; it will take on the shape of a pen. Now write away, using whatever input device you've got (see Figure 4-8).

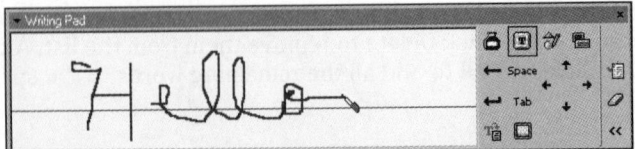

Figure 4-8: The Writing Pad translates your handwriting — even really bad handwriting done with a mouse, as in this figure — into typed text.

The Writing Pad comes with a number of controls. The two buttons at the top left of the little control area let you choose whether you want to insert your text as typed text or as a graphic (this option is available only in Word and Outlook—and it's available in Outlook only if Word is enabled as your default e-mail editor).

Other buttons provide you with spacebar, Backspace, Enter, and Tab keys. If you expand the tool area as I have in Figure 4-8 (by clicking the right-pointing double arrow in the lower-right corner), you also find commands for moving the cursor—as well as an option that calls up a special virtual keyboard that gives you access to all capabilities of all keys on a regular keyboard without having to actually use (or even have) a keyboard. This capability is useful if you're working with a graphic tablet instead of a keyboard. (You can also choose the On-Screen Standard Keyboard from the menu under the Handwriting button on the Language Bar, where you can also find an optional On-Screen Symbol Keyboard for inserting symbols.)

Two other options for entering handwriting are available when you click Handwriting on the Language Bar:

✦ **Write Anywhere:** This option works just like the Writing Pad, except you're not limited to writing inside the pad; you can write anywhere in your document. The same tools appear, without the lined Writing Pad area attached.

✦ **Drawing Pad:** This option allows you to create little sketches that can then be inserted into your document or saved to the Clipboard.

✦   ✦   ✦

Suit Yourself: Customizing Office

◆ ◆ ◆ ◆

In This Chapter

Using macros to
create custom
commands

Customizing toolbars

Customizing menus

Saving custom
toolbars and menus

◆ ◆ ◆ ◆

Out of the box, Office is amazingly powerful. Even so, you're sure to find that in some ways, it doesn't work exactly the way you'd like it to.

If you're like many other people, you use some menu commands and buttons all the time and never touch others. So, why not put your most-needed items where you can get to them quickly? Although Office provides commands for almost all tasks, it can't anticipate the order in which you'll use them. When you repeatedly employ the same set of commands, it makes sense to bundle them into one megacommand, or *macro*.

Fortunately, Office offers a deep level of customization. You can change and rearrange most aspects of the user interface, including the toolbar, menu, and keyboard functions. You can record frequently used command sequences and store them as macros for future use. When ordinary customization methods aren't enough, you can move on to Visual Basic for Applications (VBA), the Office programming language, to create complex custom commands and even complete, specialized applications of your own.

 See Part XI for a detailed look at Visual Basic for Applications in Office XP.

Creating Custom Commands with Macros

To make an Office application do what you want, you must first issue an orderly series of commands. Because your work varies from day to day and document to document, the commands you use vary as well.

However, you probably use certain sequences of commands time and again. This is where macros come in handy. Instead of executing each command in a sequence, you can record the sequence in a macro. Then you can carry out the sequence using the one command that runs the macro.

Note   Although you can record and play back macros without inspecting their contents, you should know that macros and VBA programs are the same. The Office macro recorder is simply a way to convert your actions into VBA code without any effort on your part. If you understand VBA, you can edit a recorded macro or incorporate it into another VBA procedure by switching to the Visual Basic Editor, where you see the macro's underlying VBA code.

When to use macros

The word *macro* means "big." The very term suggests you can accomplish big things with a macro, feats that would otherwise require a succession of individual commands. But macros don't *have* to do big things. Any time you find yourself repeating even two steps, consider condensing the procedure into one macro. You can also use macros to do the following:

✦ Apply predetermined formatting choices to text, tables, or worksheets.

✦ Define keyboard shortcuts for standard menu commands. Office applications generally allow only limited keyboard customization. If you want to use the keyboard to call up a particular dialog box, you may be able to record a macro that does so and then assign it a keyboard shortcut.

✦ Redefine the standard menu and toolbar commands in Word. If you want Word to do something else when you save a file than what it does by default, for example, you could create a macro that replaces the standard Save command.

✦ Use features that aren't available via the standard commands. While this requires VBA programming, it opens up a whole universe of customization possibilities.

You need VBA only if the task you want your macro to perform can't be accomplished via the standard Office commands. If you can do it with the menus and toolbars, you can record it in a macro.

Cross-Reference For a more complete discussion of when to record macros and when to write VBA code, see Chapter 51.

Recording macros

Now comes the bad news: only Word, Excel, and PowerPoint let you record macros. You can create macros of a sort in Access, but they aren't the same VBA-based macros provided by the other three applications. And Outlook doesn't provide any direct macro-making capability. You can use VBA to create custom commands for all Office applications, but that's a different matter.

To record a macro in Word, Excel, or PowerPoint, choose Tools ➪ Macro ➪ Record New Macro. This opens a dialog box in which you can assign a name to the new macro and make other choices, depending on the application you're using. Figure 5-1 shows the Record Macro dialog box for Excel.

The name you choose has to meet certain requirements. The first character must be a letter, and after that you're allowed only letters, numbers, and the underscore character, but no spaces or punctuation marks (for example, Help_Me is acceptable, but Help_Me! is not).

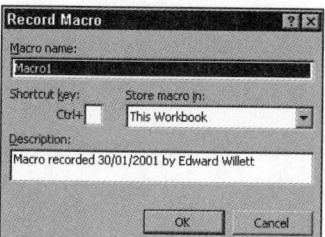

Figure 5-1: Excel's Record Macro dialog box lets you assign a macro name.

To replace a built-in Word command with a custom macro, assign the new macro the same name as the command. You can find the name you need by selecting Word commands from the "Macros in" list on the Macros dialog box (Tools ➪ Macro ➪ Macros). After noting the name exactly, close the dialog box and start recording your macro, giving it the same name as the Word command. Once you've recorded the macro, clicking a button or choosing a menu item for the original command executes the macro instead. In general, when you create a macro of this type you should record the original command as part of the sequence — in other words, the macro should enhance the existing command, not shut it off altogether.

As a simple example, suppose you want Word to display your document at a particular magnification (zoom) percentage every time you switch to Outline view. The name for the command that switches to Outline view is `ViewOutline`. To create this macro, you would do the following:

1. Choose Tools ⇨ Macros ⇨ Record New Macro.

2. Name the new macro **ViewOutline** and then click OK to begin recording the macro.

3. You'll see a little Stop Recording floating toolbar. Move it somewhere it won't get in your way, and then proceed to execute the commands you want to record: choosing View ⇨ Outline, followed by setting the magnification using the Zoom button.

4. When you're finished, click the Stop Recording button on the toolbar.

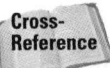 **Cross-Reference**   For an elaboration of this technique that requires VBA coding, see Chapter 15.

Running macros

You can run any macro from the Macros dialog box: Choose Tools ⇨ Macro ⇨ Macros to display it, as shown in Figures 5-2 and 5-3.

 **Note**   This dialog box looks a little different in the various Office applications, but it works essentially the same in all three.

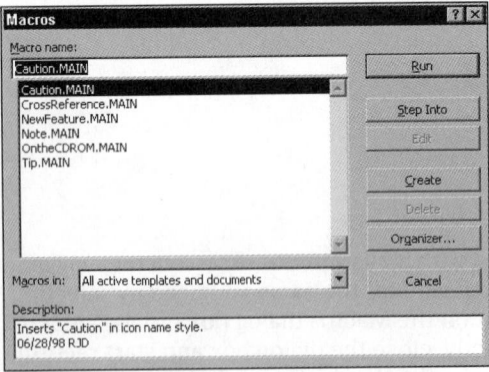

Figure 5-2: The Macros dialog box in Word, displaying macros

To run a macro, select it in the list and choose Run. To delete it, choose Delete. The Step Into, Edit, and Create buttons all take you into the Visual Basic Editor, which is discussed in more detail in Part XI.

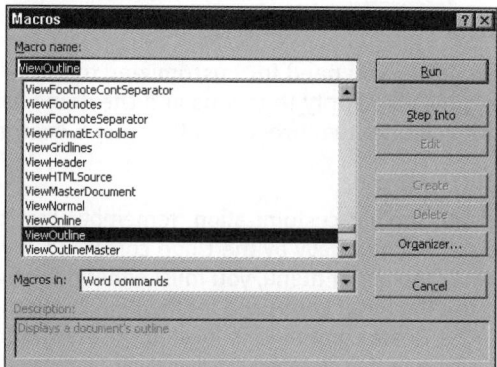

Figure 5-3: The Macros dialog box, showing built-in Word commands

Use the "Macros in" list to select the source for the macros you want to display. In Word, you can choose "All active templates and documents" to see all the currently active macros, or you can pick a single template or document from the list. In Excel and PowerPoint, you can display macros from all open documents (workbooks or presentations, respectively) or any one of the current documents.

Customizing Office Toolbars

All the Office applications share a powerful drag-and-drop system for customizing toolbars, and none of the applications make a distinction between the menu bar and other toolbars.

True, a menu button can be labeled only with text (not a graphical icon), and when clicked, it does something special — listing a bunch of other choices on a drop-down panel. But that doesn't make it fundamentally different from the button that saves the current document to a disk file, for example. In Office XP, the main menu bar is simply another toolbar that by default contains only menu buttons.

That means you can customize toolbars and menu bars using the same techniques. In addition, you can place menus onto toolbars containing graphical buttons, and graphical buttons onto menu bars.

Note   Office doesn't carry this approach to its logical conclusion. You can't display a menu using a graphical button. And while the buttons for the individual items on a menu can include an icon with the text label, Office doesn't provide an option for displaying menu items as icons alone, without text (though you can accomplish this yourself if you like).

Customizing the toolbars

This section covers in detail the techniques you need for customizing toolbars and their buttons. Although these techniques also apply to menus and the items listed on them, enough differences exist between the two processes that menu customization has a separate section later.

Caution   Before you start experimenting with toolbar customization, remember that the changes you make can't be reversed automatically by the Undo command. If you wind up with an unacceptably wacky toolbar or menu, you must either put it right yourself, one button at a time, or use the Reset command for the item in question to restore it to its original state. The Reset command is located on the shortcut menu for the item (see Figure 5-7 later in this chapter).

Putting toolbars where you want them

Any toolbar can appear on the screen in two configurations: docked against an edge of the application window or floating in a separate window that you can move anywhere on the screen. You can dock a toolbar along any edge of the window, and, yes, that includes the two sides.

Cross-Reference   Chapter 4 offers tips on moving toolbars and parking them where you want them.

Displaying and hiding toolbars

The fastest way to display a toolbar that's not currently shown, or to hide one that is visible, is to right-click any toolbar and choose the toolbar you want to display or hide from the shortcut menu.

This shortcut menu lists most of the available toolbars, but not all of them. To display a toolbar that's not on the list, or to toggle more than one toolbar on or off, choose Customize at the bottom of the shortcut menu.

Using the Customize dialog box

The Tools ➪ Customize dialog box, shown in Figure 5-4, is the command center for making changes to the toolbar structure in any Office application. Use it to hide, display, create, rename, or delete toolbars, and to add new buttons.

The list in the Toolbars tab shows almost all the toolbars available in the current application. However, some toolbars appear in the list only when a particular mode of the program is active. In Word, for example, the Print Preview toolbar is listed only when you're doing a print preview. In any case, check or uncheck the box by the name of a toolbar to show or hide it.

That's not all you can do with the Customize dialog box, though.

Creating toolbars from scratch

To add a new toolbar to the current Office application, open the Tools ⇨ Customize dialog box and switch to the Toolbars tab. Choose New and type in a name for the toolbar in the New Toolbar dialog box.

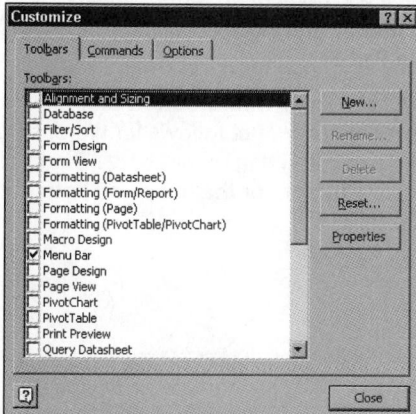

Figure 5-4: The Customize dialog box in Access is typical of the Customize dialog box in all Office applications.

Note   In the Word version of the New Toolbar dialog box, don't neglect that field labeled Make Toolbar Available To. Here you use a drop-down list to choose a template in which to store the new toolbar: Normal.dot (if you want the toolbar to appear in all your documents) or a specific template (if you want the toolbar to show only in documents based on that template).

As soon as you OK the New Toolbar dialog box, the new, tiny, empty toolbar appears. Use the techniques covered later in the chapter to add buttons to it.

Other toolbar options

Excel and Access offer unique toolbar-customization options unavailable in the other programs:

✦ In Excel, choosing Attach on the Toolbars tab of the Tools ⇨ Customize dialog box enables you to save your custom toolbars with the current workbook file so that they are available to others who use the workbook.

✦ In Access, choosing Properties brings up another dialog box that lets you set a variety of options, such as whether the selected toolbar can be docked or altered. (I don't know why Microsoft didn't provide these controls for the other programs, but you can accomplish the same goals via VBA routines.)

Making Two-in-One Toolbars

Push-button access to commands is great, but get carried away and you may wind up with so many toolbars that they crowd out your documents. Still, many of us can't get enough buttons, and with a little VBA programming you can create toolbars that seem to have twice as many buttons as the regular kind. Besides, even if you don't need more toolbars, the VBA procedure discussed here demonstrates how to display and position different toolbars as you need them. (Again, VBA is covered in detail in Part XI.)

The technique actually requires two separate toolbars, each with a button that hides the current toolbar and displays the other one. In the macro code that follows for Word, substitute the names of your two toolbars for `MagicToolbar1` and `MagicToolbar2`. Then, using the techniques described later in this chapter, create a button for the macro on both of the toolbars, placing it in the very first position (the far left).

```
Sub ToolbarSwapper()
For Each cb In CommandBars
   If cb.Name = "MagicToolbar1" Then
      With cb
         .Visible = Not (.Visible)
         If .Visible Then
' Try removing the comments from the next 3 lines
         ' .Position = msoBarTop
         ' .RowIndex = msoBarRowLast
         ' .Left = 0
         Set myControl = .Controls(1)
         myControl.State = msoButtonUp
         End If
      End With
   End If

   If cb.Name = "MagicToolbar2" Then
      With cb
         .Visible = Not (.Visible)
         If .Visible Then
' Try removing the comments from the next 3 lines
         ' .Position = msoBarTop
         ' .RowIndex = msoBarRowLast
         ' .Left = 0
         Set myControl = .Controls(1)
         myControl.State = msoButtonDown
         End If
      End With
   End If
Next

End Sub
```

Working with buttons on toolbars

In this section, I discuss techniques for endowing each toolbar with just the buttons you want it to have. To customize the buttons themselves, see the section "Customizing individual buttons" later in the chapter.

Relocating and deleting buttons

Aside from moving the toolbars themselves, the easiest customizing changes you can make are rearranging and removing buttons. To move a button to a new location, hold down Alt and drag the button to its new home on the same or another toolbar. To copy a button, drag it while holding down Alt+Ctrl. Note that this is consistent with the way Ctrl copies things in Explorer and My Computer. If the Tools ➪ Customize dialog box is open, you can drag buttons around or off toolbars without pressing Alt, or copy them by dragging while holding down only Ctrl.

You can add or remove space (along with that little faux 3-D groove) between two buttons by Alt-dragging the button on the right sideways in either direction (Alt-drag the bottom button of the pair if you're working with a side-docked toolbar). To delete a button, Alt-drag it into the middle of the window, or up onto the title bar, releasing the mouse button when the pointer shows a big black X.

Tip   When space is really tight, you may be able to squeeze in an extra button on some toolbars by narrowing the special buttons that provide drop-down lists. On the Formatting toolbar, for example, the Style, Font, and Font Size buttons are all of this type. To narrow (or widen) a drop-down list button, open the Tools ➪ Customize dialog box and click the button. When you then move the pointer to either edge of the button, it becomes a double-headed arrow. Drag the edge to change the button's width.

Adding buttons the easy way

When any built-in toolbar is docked, clicking the thin Toolbar Options button at the far right drops down a menu offering the Add or Remove Buttons command, as well as any of the toolbar's buttons that aren't currently visible. Pointing at the Add or Remove Buttons command displays a secondary pop-up menu that offers you access to the Customize command or to a display of all the buttons that might be suitable for the toolbar you're working with. Figure 5-5 shows what I mean. Click the buttons on this menu to add or remove them from the toolbar. Deactivated buttons remain on the menu, so you can add them back at any time. This is true even if you removed them by Alt-dragging them off the toolbar.

When a built-in toolbar is floating rather than docked, you access the Add or Remove Buttons command by clicking the little white arrow at the far left of the toolbar's title bar. Custom toolbars you create yourself don't have the Add or Remove Buttons command.

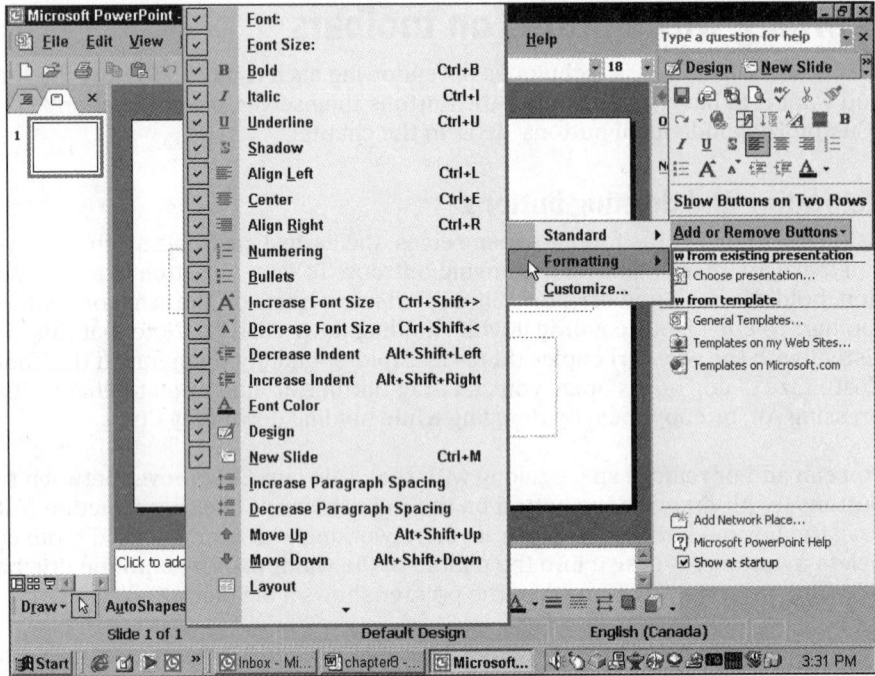

Figure 5-5: Here are the available buttons for PowerPoint's Formatting toolbar.

Adding buttons to toolbars

To place new buttons on your toolbars, start by opening the Tools ➪ Customize dialog box. Switch to the Commands tab, shown in Figure 5-6. The basic procedure for adding a button couldn't be simpler. You just drag the desired item from the Commands list on the right to its destination on any toolbar. The problem is finding the item you want on the list.

Note   Items displayed with an icon in the Commands list become graphical toolbar buttons when you drag them to a toolbar, whereas those without icons are displayed as text-only buttons.

Tip   Unless you get panic attacks when things are out of their proper places, you should take advantage of the empty space on the main menu bar: Cram it full of buttons (take a look at Figure 5-10 later in the chapter).

Using the Commands tab

It pays to acquaint yourself with the way the Commands tab is organized. The key to finding the command or other item you want to put on a toolbar is to know (or, more likely, guess) what category it belongs to.

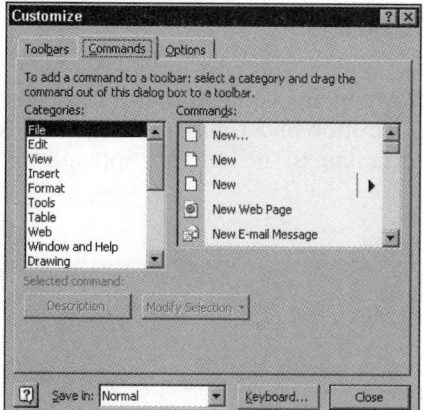

Figure 5-6: The Commands tab of the Tools ⇨ Customize dialog box lets you add buttons to any toolbar.

The left side of the Commands tab lists its commands and other items under Categories, beginning with categories that more or less duplicate the standard menus (File, Edit, and so on) with some variations. When you select one of these categories, the Commands list on the right displays the standard commands found on that menu, along with other related commands.

Below the menu-related categories, the Categories list shows other categories that group together related commands that are not available on the default menus. Then toward the bottom of the list is a category for macros and categories for items that you don't normally think of as commands: in Word, fonts and formatting styles; in Access, database tables, forms, and queries; and in all the Office applications, menus (for details on using the menu categories see "Customizing Office Menus" later in this chapter).

Tip   Word has a category titled "All commands" that puts them all in one very long alphabetical list. When you're not sure what category a command belongs to, don't waste time hunting through the less comprehensive categories.

What does that command do?

Up to this point, I've been assuming that you know the name of the command you want to assign as a toolbar button. But that isn't always the case. Office commands are named inconsistently and sometimes cryptically, so it's easy to be unsure whether a given command will do what you want.

The Commands tab offers some guidance. Select a likely sounding command and choose Description to see a help message describing the command's function. Of course, you can always fall back on trial and error: Place the command on a toolbar and then click the new button and see if it works the way you intended.

Customizing individual buttons

To change the look of a button, start by opening the Tools ➪ Customize dialog box.
You don't need the dialog box itself, but you have to display it to work with the buttons. At this point, pointing your mouse at a button on a toolbar and right-clicking
displays a shortcut menu full of options pertaining to the button's appearance (see
Figure 5-7).

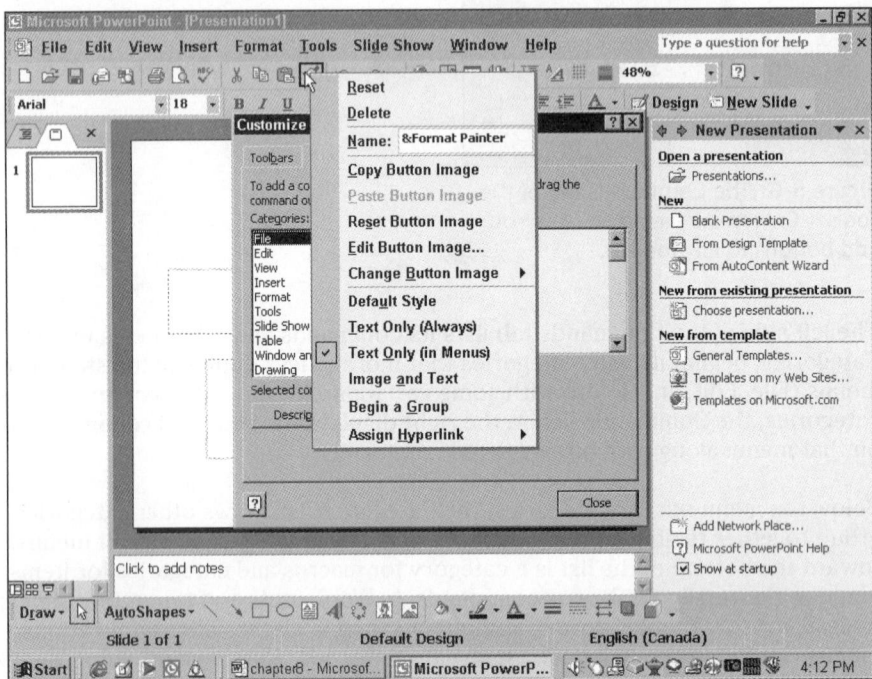

Figure 5-7: This shortcut menu lets you modify a toolbar button's look.

Office can display an icon, text, or both on the surface of any button (except for
menu buttons, which only appear as text). You control this via a set of choices on
the lower part of the shortcut menu:

✦ To display only the icon, or button image, for the command, check Default
Style. Of course, this works only if the button has an associated image; otherwise, you see text.

✦ To display the button with descriptive text only, check one of the Text Only
choices. Which one doesn't matter if you're dealing with a toolbar button, as
opposed to an item on a menu list. The entry at Name on the shortcut menu is
the button's text label.

✦ To display the button with both an image and text, check Image and Text on the shortcut menu. You might want to do this while you're learning to associate the button's image with its function.

Changing or editing button images

To assign one of Office's built-in button images to a button, choose Change Button Image from the shortcut menu. Select a graphic from the pop-up bank of button tops. If none of the supplied button images suits you, you can design a new image from scratch or modify the existing image. Choose Edit Button Image from the shortcut menu to bring up the Button Editor, shown in Figure 5-8.

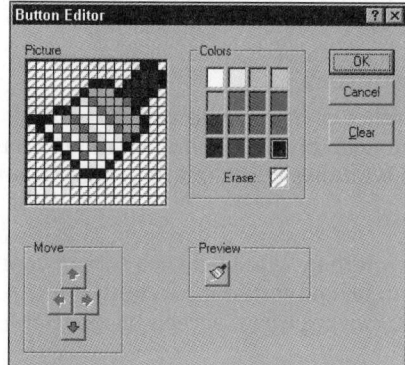

Figure 5-8: Edit the button image in this window.

The Button Editor is a crude painting tool, but it works OK for such small images. The main work area is the grid labeled Picture, where you paint a magnified version of the image. Each of the little squares represents a single pixel in the image and on the screen.

Squares with diagonal gray stripes are empty, meaning the background color shows through in the finished button. Clicking a square toggles it back and forth between empty and the currently selected color. (To remove a color permanently, so it can't be toggled back into action, click the Erase square in the Colors area before clicking in the Picture area.) As you work, the button image appears at actual size in the Preview area.

Choose Clear to erase the entire Picture area and start from scratch. Choose the color you want to use from the Colors palette and start clicking in the Picture area. Those four arrow buttons beneath the Picture move the entire image in case it's not aligned the way you want it.

Copying button images

Office makes it easy to copy images from one button to another. For example, you might be deploying a series of buttons for some related macros and want their images to look alike. For that matter, you might come across a button in Access that perfectly symbolizes a macro you've recorded in Excel. That's no problem, because the button-copying function works across all the Office applications.

To copy a button image to a new button, start from the application that contains the original version. Open the Customize dialog box and right-click the button you admire, choosing Copy Button Image from the shortcut menu. If necessary, switch to the destination application and open its Customize dialog box. Now right-click the button to receive the copied image and choose Paste Button Image. If the copied image requires modifications, edit it by choosing Edit Button Image.

Importing button images from other sources

Because the Paste Button Image command relies on the Windows clipboard, you can feed it any bitmap image. That means you can create a suitable bitmap image from scratch using a paint program such as Windows Paint and then paste it onto a button.

Better yet, you can pilfer graphics from anywhere in Windows via a screen capture program. Anything you see on the screen can be converted into a button image. If you don't have screen capture software, you can capture a screen image to the clipboard by pressing the PrintScreen key.

The key to good results with imported button images is to make them the right size. The button image grid is 16 × 16 pixels. If the image you paste is some other size, Office makes a gallant effort to scale it to fit, but the results generally look terrible. When you capture the image from the screen, it's hard to get the size right at the time. Don't try; instead, capture a larger area, pasting it into Paint or another bitmap editing program. There, you can select the best 16 × 16–pixel area, copying it back to the clipboard for pasting onto the button.

Tip

If you plan to do any serious work with icons, get the right tool for the job—an icon editing and management program.

Displaying ScreenTips for toolbar buttons

ScreenTips are those little message boxes that pop up when you hold the mouse pointer for a second or two over an item. ScreenTips for toolbar buttons should be turned on and probably already are. But if they're not, open the Tools ➪ Customize dialog box, switch to the Options tab, and check the box labeled Show ScreenTips on Toolbars (see Figure 5-9).

No matter which application you use to set this option, it applies throughout Office. In Word, PowerPoint, and Access (but not in Excel) a subsidiary option in the same dialog box tab lets you decide whether each ScreenTip includes the button's keyboard shortcut, if there is one.

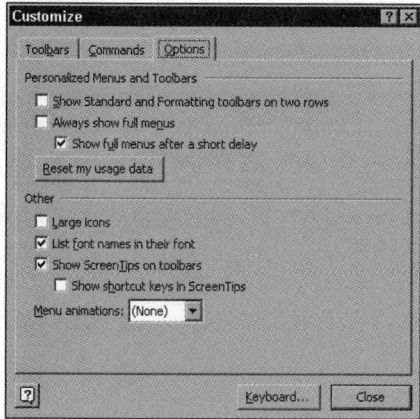

Figure 5-9: The Options tab of the Tools ⇨ Customize dialog box lets you control the display of ScreenTips and menus.

Choosing button names

Although graphical buttons are space-efficient and add zest to your screen, you may prefer that some buttons be labeled only with text. Often you just don't have the time to locate a suitable button image for a command that doesn't already have one or to draw an image of your own. In addition, the text can tell you what the button does, which is certainly nice to know and isn't always obvious from the icon.

Every button has a name, and by default its name is the label you see on the button when you set it to display as text (the available options for button display are discussed at the beginning of the "Customizing individual buttons" section earlier in this chapter). To change the button's name, open the Tools ⇨ Customize dialog box and then right-click the button. In the shortcut menu that appears (refer back to Figure 5-7), edit the entry at Name.

> **Tip**
> If you have a really great visual memory, you can squeeze lots more buttons onto your toolbars by giving them very short names and displaying them as text only. The results may not be pretty, but you'll have one-click access to tons of commands. And if you're willing to do a little work in VBA with the technique described in the text that follows, you can have the ScreenTip display a full description of the command.

Labeling a button with text is also a quick way to create a keyboard shortcut for that command. See "Quick keyboard shortcuts in any Office application" later in this chapter.

Adding More Information to ScreenTips

Normally, the ScreenTip for a button just displays its name, so a default ScreenTip doesn't supplement a short, cryptic button name with further information. However, if you're willing to go to the trouble of writing brief VBA routines, you can define long ScreenTip explanations of each button's function with its `TooltipText` property. Part XI has details on writing VBA modules. Here, I'll just present the code you need for an example routine that defines a custom ScreenTip for an imaginary Excel button:

```
Sub This_Button_Needs_A_ScreenTip()
CommandBars("Mr. GoodBar").Controls(2).TooltipText = _
   "Format cell: centered, bold, currency"
End Sub
```

The `Sub` and `End Sub` statements are just wrappers for the procedure—the statement starting with `CommandBars` performs the work. Analyzing it from left to right, it identifies the toolbar you're working with (in this case a custom toolbar named `Mr. GoodBar`) and then specifies a particular button, the second one on the toolbar in question. Finally, it selects the `TooltipText` property. The text following the equal sign redefines that property.

To prepare your version of this routine, substitute the name of the toolbar that contains your button for the name in quotes. Enter the button's position, counting the first button on the left as 1, in the parentheses after `Controls`. Your new ScreenTip text goes in quotes after the equal sign.

You only have to run this procedure (macro) once. Because Office stores the new ScreenTip with the template or document file you're working with, you can delete the procedure immediately.

Resizing list buttons

You can widen or narrow toolbar controls containing lists, such as the Font button in Word, Excel, and PowerPoint. Right-click over any toolbar and choose Customize to open the Customize dialog box, and then click the control in question. Move the mouse to either end of the control until the pointer becomes a two-headed arrow. You can then drag to change the control's width.

Creating buttons that activate hyperlinks or insert graphics

You can also assign a hyperlink to any button or menu item on any toolbar or menu (I'll refer to toolbar buttons and menu items collectively as "buttons"). The same feature also enables you to create buttons that insert specific pictures into your documents—a good trick for keeping your logo or scanned signature handy.

Begin by opening the Tools ⇨ Customize dialog box. Because assigning a hyperlink to a button deactivates its original function, you probably want to add a new button to the toolbar system. Use the techniques discussed in "Adding buttons to toolbars" earlier in this chapter. With the target button visible, right-click it to display its shortcut menu (refer back to Figure 5-7). Choose Assign Hyperlink and then one of these items:

✦ **Open:** This creates a hyperlink to an Internet site, Web page, or disk file. After you close the Customize dialog box, clicking the button causes the assigned item to appear in the appropriate application or in your browser.

✦ **Insert Picture:** This creates a link to a graphic file (available only in Word, PowerPoint, and Excel). When you click the customized button, the application inserts the specified picture into the current document.

Both commands open the Assign Hyperlink dialog box.

Cross-Reference The dialog box and hyperlinks in general are discussed in detail in Chapter 45.

You can restore a hyperlink button to its original function by choosing Assign Hyperlink ⇨ Remove Link from the button's shortcut menu.

Note You can't convert a menu, submenu, or drop-down list button into a hyperlink.

Customizing Office Menus

Though one-click graphical buttons are fast, menus have their own strengths. They pack lots of commands into very little space, and each command has a descriptive name. Use them for the commands you don't need constantly.

Menus, as noted earlier, are just specialized buttons that display a list of commands. The listed items themselves are usually commands just like the buttons on a toolbar, although they can also be submenus — menu buttons that produce subsidiary lists of commands. At any rate, you use the techniques just described for customizing toolbars, with a few modifications, to customize menus.

The methods covered in "Relocating and deleting buttons" work to move entire menus to other locations on the same toolbar or to any other bar. But in addition, these same techniques let you move a menu itself, or any of its commands, onto another menu. Likewise, a submenu (perhaps one you use all the time) can be moved off its current parent menu and out onto a toolbar to become independent and easier to get at.

Figure 5-10 shows you one example of what you can do: a new menu on the menu bar that contains all the regular menu bar items as submenus.

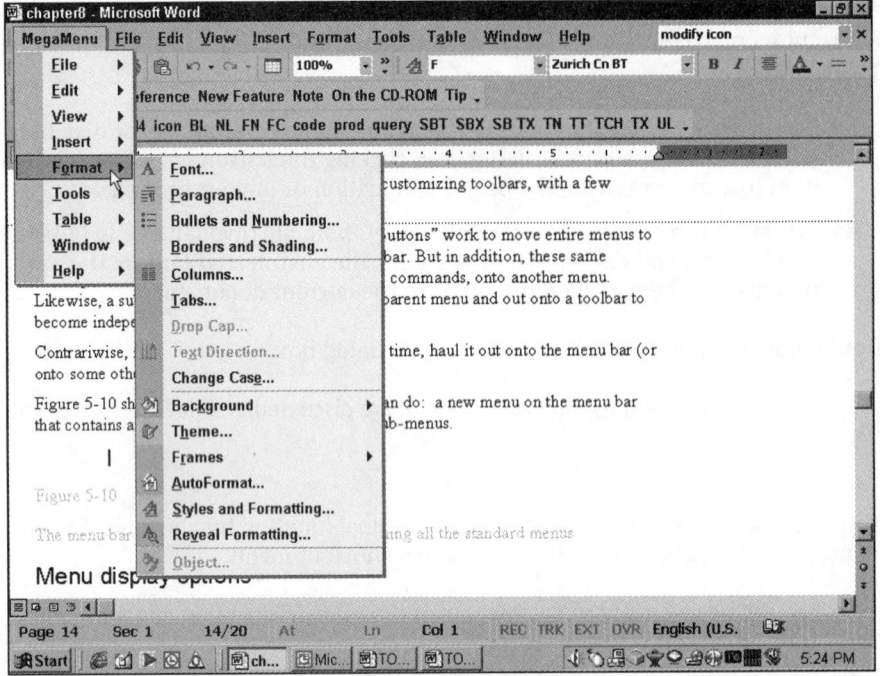

Figure 5-10: Here is the menu bar in Word with a custom menu containing all the standard menus.

Menu display options

To shorten the time you spend hunting for commands, Office applications by default display only the menu commands you've recently used. (You can turn off this feature by choosing the Options tab of the Tools ⇨ Customize dialog box — refer back to Figure 5-9 — and choosing "Always show full menus.") You can still see the entire menu by holding the mouse over the little double-arrow at the bottom of the menu for a few seconds.

Other pertinent settings in the Options tab of the Tools ⇨ Customize dialog box include the following:

✦ **Show full menus after a short delay.** Check this box if you don't want to exert your mouse hand at all to see the complete menu. It appears automatically if you just wait two or three seconds.

✦ **Reset my usage data.** Click here if you want to access the complete set of menu commands again. Office immediately resumes tracking the commands you do use and will soon start hiding the ones you don't.

✦ **Menu animations.** Fond of screen distractions? This setting forces Office to display menus gradually rather than all at once. You can choose Unfold, Slide, or Random.

Note All the menu display settings apply throughout Office, regardless of which application you use to change them.

Moving menus with the mouse

You can move existing menus (the individual menu buttons, not the menu bars they belong to) with the Alt-drag and Alt+Ctrl-drag techniques.

To make a menu into a submenu on another menu, Alt-drag its button over the second menu so the latter opens, displaying its list of items. While still holding down Alt, continue to drag the first menu down the list until you get to the desired position.

To place a submenu on the menu bar or other toolbar, you must open the Tools ➪ Customize dialog box and then drag or Ctrl-drag the submenu to its destination.

Customizing menu items

The Alt-drag technique doesn't work for moving items on menus to new locations, and of course, you can't use it to add new items to menus. To accomplish these goals, you have to open the Tools ➪ Customize dialog box first.

Once the Customize dialog box is open, clicking a menu button displays the entire menu. You can then drag any item (including submenus) to a new position on the menu, onto a different menu, or to a toolbar as an independent item. Note that you must release the mouse button after clicking the main menu button — if you try to drag from the menu button down to the list of menu items, you succeed only in moving the menu to another toolbar or deleting it altogether.

To add a new menu command, find the item in the Commands tab of the dialog box (see "Using the Commands tab" earlier in this chapter). Then drag it into place on the menu you wish to add it to.

To add a 3D groove and a little space between any two menu items, indicating a new group of items, just drag the lower item down a bit. You can remove the groove by dragging the item back up. Right-clicking the item and selecting Begin a Group is an unnecessarily cumbersome alternative (that is, too much hassle).

Note Changes you make to the items on any of the standard menus appear in all copies of that menu, if for some reason you have created more than one. If you want to build two File menus that list different items, don't copy the standard File menu. Instead, create a new menu and rename it (I wouldn't recommend calling it "File"; use a name that won't confuse you).

A command listed on an Office menu can be displayed with a graphical image alongside the item's text, assuming an image is associated with the item. Some of the items on Office's standard menus are set up this way. When a default menu item has an associated graphic, it's the same one that appears on the toolbar button for that command. (However, menu buttons, the ones that open menus or submenus, can't be given images.)

To add a graphic to a menu item, or to replace the graphic it already has, open the Tools ➪ Customize dialog box. Click the menu containing the item, and then right-click the item itself to display the shortcut menu. You can then use the Edit Button Image, Paste Button Image, and Choose Button Image commands to add the image you want.

The image appears in the menu alongside the item text if Default Style or Image and Text are checked in the shortcut menu. To turn off the image display, check either of the Text Only choices.

Note   One difference between menu buttons and other buttons is that Office won't let you assign a graphical button image to a menu button, a submenu item on a menu, or any button that produces a list of items (such as the AutoText button).

Creating new menus

To place a new menu on the menu bar or any other toolbar, start from the Commands tab of the Tools ➪ Customize dialog box. At the bottom of the Categories list, you find two relevant items: Built-in Menus and New Menu:

✦ If you select **Built-in Menus**, the Commands list displays the menus found on the standard menu bar, along with a number of others, depending on the application (many of these are submenus from the standard menus). You can drag the built-in menu of choice onto any toolbar (where it opens with its complete list of commands), and then further customize it there.

✦ If you select **New Menu**, the only choice in the Commands list is New Menu. Dragging this to a toolbar creates a new empty menu, which you can rename anything you like (see the next section) and to which you can add items with the technique covered in the previous section.

Renaming menus

To rename a menu, use the same technique you would for other buttons — with the Tools ➪ Customize dialog box open, right-click the menu to display the shortcut menu and then edit the entry at Name.

Tip   Type an ampersand (&) immediately before the character that should be underlined in the menu name. This character indicates the key that opens the menu with the standard Windows keyboard technique — when you press the key after or while pressing Alt.

Customizing the shortcut menus

In addition to customizing all the regular menus, Word, PowerPoint and Access (but not Excel or Outlook—don't ask me why) let you fiddle around with the context-sensitive shortcut menus that pop up when you click the right mouse button on something in your document.

There are a *lot* of these shortcut menus. Don't plan on a thorough revision of the options Microsoft has provided for you—it'll take you days. However, if a particular shortcut menu cries out for a command that it doesn't possess, you can add it. For example, you might want to add the alignment commands—center, justify, right align, left align—to the shortcut menu that pops up when you right-click on text.

The technique for editing a shortcut menu starts with an awkward first step—you get the feeling that the software designers at Microsoft came up with it at the end of a long day. But hey, it works!

In the Tools ➪ Customize dialog box, switch to the Toolbars tab. Scroll the Toolbars list to find a Shortcut Menus item. Check its box to display a special toolbar intended solely for customizing shortcut menus, as shown in Figure 5-11.

This is awkward because there's no way to know (until you read this book) that you need to turn on a toolbar called Shortcut Menus in order to customize shortcut menus. Every other toolbar actually functions in your applications, and you check its box to display it on the screen after you close the Customize dialog box. But the Shortcut Menus toolbar has no independent life; it exists solely to customize the shortcut menus.

In any event, once the Shortcut Menus toolbar is open, you click one of the special menus on the toolbar, which group together the shortcut menus for the current application in categories. The shortcut menus are submenus of these toolbar menus. When you've found the one you want, click it to display the actual list of menu items. (Remember, you must click and release each menu and submenu button in turn to display the menu lists—you can't drag your way through the hierarchy.)

The rest of the process works just like customizing one of the regular menus. You switch back to the Commands tab in the Customize dialog box and then move items from the list there to the target shortcut menu.

Note By the time you've worked your way through the menu hierarchy, the shortcut menu often covers up the Customize dialog box. Don't be surprised if you have to repeatedly reposition the dialog box, the toolbar, or both before you can access all the tools you need at the same time.

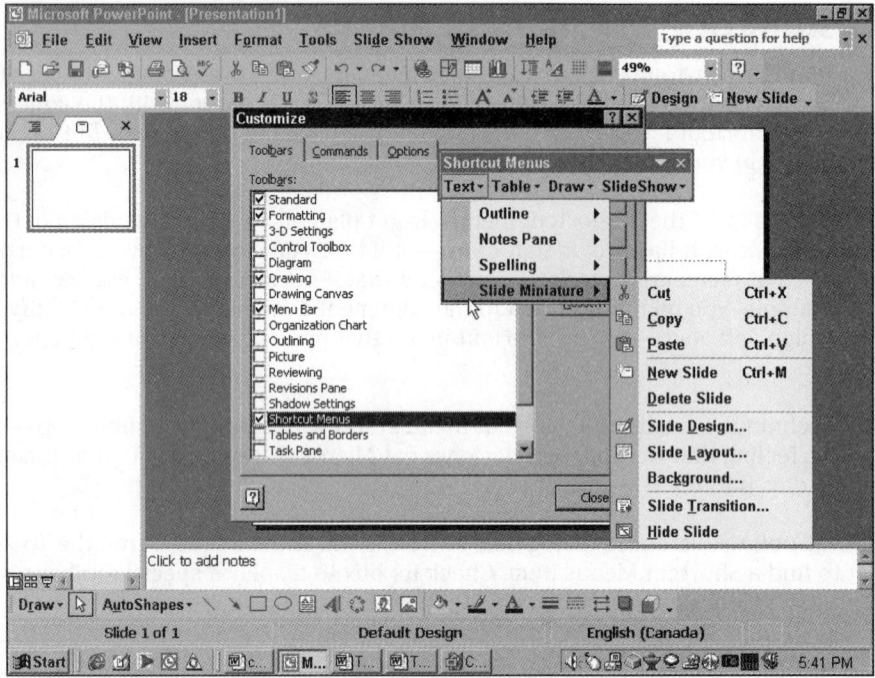

Figure 5-11: Customizing a shortcut menu in PowerPoint

Restoring the original menus

If you customize your menus to the point where even you can't make sense of what you've done, don't fret. Bringing back the original configuration of a built-in menu is easy. Open the Tools ➪ Customize dialog box, right-click the menu you want to restore to its default arrangement, and choose Reset at the very top of the shortcut menu.

Caution   The restoration happens immediately, and there's no going back. Resetting a menu is an all-or-nothing proposition. If you want to preserve customizations of individual menu items, copy them to another menu or toolbar first.

Saving and Reusing Custom Toolbars and Menus

Different custom toolbars, menus, and buttons may be appropriate for different situations or documents. Word and Excel let you store sets of these items so that you can activate the right set when you need it. In Word, you use templates; in Excel, you store them in settings files (.XLB files). The specific techniques required are covered in the parts of the book on the individual Office applications.

Customizing the Keyboard

Office applications may provide you with extensive options for customizing toolbars and menus, but the same can't be said of keyboard modifications. (The exception is Word, which lets you define and redefine keyboard shortcuts with complete abandon.)

Keyboard customization in Excel and Access is much more limited and cumbersome to set up, and it isn't allowed at all in PowerPoint and Outlook. Still, it's worth using the tools that are available.

 **Cross-Reference** For details on customizing the keyboard, see Chapter 15 for the Word options, Chapter 23 for the Excel options, and Chapter 46 for the Access options.

Quick keyboard shortcuts in any Office application

Here's a trick that gives you a quick-and-dirty keyboard shortcut for any command in any Office program. It relies on the standard Windows method for opening menus using the Alt key (first you press Alt, and then the menu shortcut key, or you can press both Alt and the menu key at the same time). Because toolbar buttons and menu buttons are essentially the same, you can "open" a button with an Alt-key menu shortcut as long as you display the button's name:

1. Assign the command to a toolbar button as described in an earlier section of the chapter. If a button for the command already exists, skip this step.

2. Once the button is in place, open the Tools ➪ Customize dialog box (as shown back in Figure 5-6).

3. Right-click the button to display its shortcut menu (refer back to Figure 5-7).

4. Here's the key step. The entry at Name is the label that appears on the button if you display it as text, or if it has no button image. Type an ampersand (&) immediately to the left of the shortcut key (which triggers the command when pressed in combination with Alt).

5. To activate the shortcut, you must display the name on the button. The name will be displayed if Default Style is checked on the shortcut menu only if there is no associated button image. If the button has an image, check Text Only or Image and Text to ensure the name appears on the button.

Choosing the right shortcut key

Choosing the right key for the shortcut created in step 4 can be difficult. Most, if not all, of the built-in commands already have a shortcut key defined in their name. You can accept this default, but it often makes sense to change it.

Ideally, of course, you would prefer a mnemonic letter suggestive of the command, such as F for the Font command. Trouble is, you don't want to duplicate the shortcuts for existing buttons, including the standard menus such as File. (If you do specify a duplicate shortcut key, nothing catastrophic happens — but to use your shortcut, you have to press the shortcut repeatedly until the desired button is selected, and then press Enter.)

The other point to consider when naming a button is that most text labels make the button wider than it would be with an image alone. Try to shorten the name to the minimum text necessary to remind you of the button's function. If you're sure you have the shortcut memorized, change the button's name to the shortcut character alone.

Changing the Color Scheme

You can control the color of items you add to documents — such as text, graphics, or borders — within each Office program. But what about the color of the window itself? To change that, you need the Windows Control Panel.

To change the colors of the work area, open the Display applet in Control Panel (or right-click anywhere on your Windows desktop and choose Display from the pop-up menu) and switch to the Appearance tab. Click in the main work area of the sample window labeled Active Window, so that Window appears in the Item field. Then choose Color to select a new color.

You can also change the ScreenTip color in the same Display Properties dialog box (see "Displaying ScreenTips for toolbar buttons" earlier in this chapter). Select the Tooltip option in the Item drop-down list.

Note

When you assign a text color in Word or Excel, one of the choices is Automatic, hardly a self-explanatory description of color. What Microsoft means is "Windows default window text color." Text assigned to the Automatic color appears in whatever window text color is currently selected in the Appearance tab of the Display applet. To change this color, select Window at Item, and then change the Color (to the right of the Font field).

In PowerPoint and Excel, the Automatic color choice is also available for slide and chart elements, such as text and backgrounds in PowerPoint slides, or bars and lines in Excel charts. In this case, it refers to the default color for the selected element. If you change the defaults, elements assigned to the Automatic color change hue automatically.

✦   ✦   ✦

Office Collaboration: Playing Nice with Others

In most business environments, very few things are done by solitary individuals. Projects are planned, discussed, dissected, and carried out by teams of people working together. If one of the final products of a project is to be an Office document, it's helpful if all members of the team can share information, files, and ideas online — either via the company's internal computer network or (if team members are more far-flung) via the Internet. Office makes it possible!

Accessing the Internet from Office Applications

In the years since the first version of Microsoft Office appeared, we've seen an explosion in the use of the Internet for communication and research worldwide, and of intranets — using the same technology on a smaller scale — for communication and research within corporations. One of the easiest ways to share information with others — and for them to share it with you — is simply to post it to the World Wide Web.

Outlook and FrontPage are obviously designed to give you quick access to the Internet (or an intranet): in Outlook's case, so you can check your e-mail and exchange scheduling information; and in FrontPage's case, so you can maintain your Web site. However, Word, Excel, PowerPoint, and Access also provide instant access through the Web toolbar, which is the same in all four applications (and in Outlook as well).

You open the Web toolbar just as you do any other toolbar, either by right-clicking an existing toolbar and choosing it from the list, or by choosing View ➪ Toolbars ➪ Web.

As you can see in Figure 6-1, the toolbar is essentially identical to what you're probably already familiar with from Internet Explorer.

Figure 6-1: Office's Web toolbar is essentially identical to that of Internet Explorer.

You use the Web toolbar just as you would any browser: to view a Web page, type the URL of the page you want to visit into the address blank and press Enter. Office automatically opens your Web browser and displays the indicated page.

Tip   You can use the Web toolbar to browse Office documents as well as Web pages. If the URL you enter is for an Office document on your own computer or local network, the application in which that document was created opens to display that document.

The Web toolbar provides several other useful buttons, which, from left to right, include the following:

✦ **Back.** This returns you to the previous document you visited, just like the Back button on your browser. If you're using your Web toolbar to browse both Office documents and Web pages, the Back button may also switch you from your browser to another Office application.

✦ **Forward.** Once you've gone backward in the list of sites and documents visited using the Back button, the Forward button should take you forward in that list again.

✦ **Stop.** If it's taking a long time for the site or document you selected to appear, this button is active. Click it to stop the jump to that site.

✦ **Refresh.** This reloads the latest version of the page you're viewing from the network.

✦ **Start Page.** This takes you to whatever page you currently have set to load automatically every time you open your browser.

✦ **Search the Web.** By default, this takes you to a Microsoft site that lets you search the World Wide Web.

✦ **Favorites.** This opens the list of favorite sites you have stored on your computer.

✦ **Go.** This menu includes several of the commands that already appear on the Web toolbar, including Forward, Back, Start Page, and Search the Web. You can also set a new Start Page or Search Page here by calling up the start or search page you want to use, and then choosing Go ⇨ Set Start Page or Go ⇨ Set Search Page. The next time you click Start Page or Search the Web, you'll go to the new sites you've selected. The Open Hyperlink command on this menu opens a dialog box into which you can type a document or folder address or the URL for a Web site; click OK and that document, folder or URL is opened for you. You can also browse for the document you want to folder. Check the Open in new window box to open the document in a new Office window.

✦ **Show Only Web Toolbar.** Click this to hide all other toolbars, leaving only the Web toolbar showing. Click it again to make the other toolbars reappear.

Adding Stuff from the Web to Your Documents

Sometimes, when you're working on a document, you may come across something on the World Wide Web that you'd like to add to your document just as it is. It could be a table of figures, a selection of text, or an image, to name just three possibilities. In Office it's simple to transfer items from the Internet to your document. All you have to do is drag and drop. Here's how:

1. Open Internet Explorer.

2. Open the application into which you want to insert something from the Internet.

3. Resize the windows in which Explorer and your application appear so you can see both of them at once Figure 6-2 shows Internet Explorer and PowerPoint arranged so both are visible at once.

 Tip   If both windows are maximized, you can reduce their size (by clicking the Restore button or right-clicking the title bar and then choosing Restore from the pop-up menu) and move them around to suit you.

4. The next step is to highlight the item on the Web page that you want to transfer to your document. You do this just as you would in Word, by clicking and dragging your mouse pointer over the material you want to highlight.

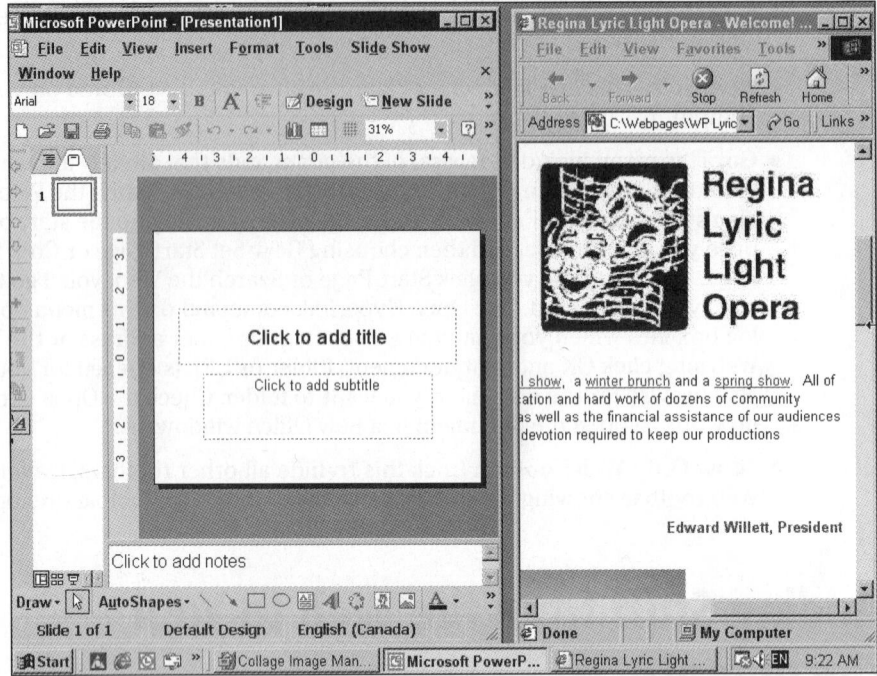

Figure 6-2: The first step to transferring items from the Internet to an Office document is to arrange your browser and Office application windows so both are visible.

5. Now click and drag the selected material to where you want it to appear in your Office document — in this case, because it's placed on a blank PowerPoint slide, anywhere within the boundaries of the slide. Your pointer changes to show you are dragging copied material.

6. Release your mouse button. The material from the Web page appears in your Office document (see Figure 6-3).

Caution

Just because something appears on a Web page does *not* mean it's offered free for anyone to use. Graphics, text, sound files, etc., on the Internet are protected by copyright, just as photographs, books, and CDs are in the non-virtual world. Before using anything from the Internet in a published document or presentation, make sure you have permission from its creator to do so. If you can't obtain that permission, or you aren't sure who owns the rights to the material in question, it's better not to use it at all — and stay on the right side of the law.

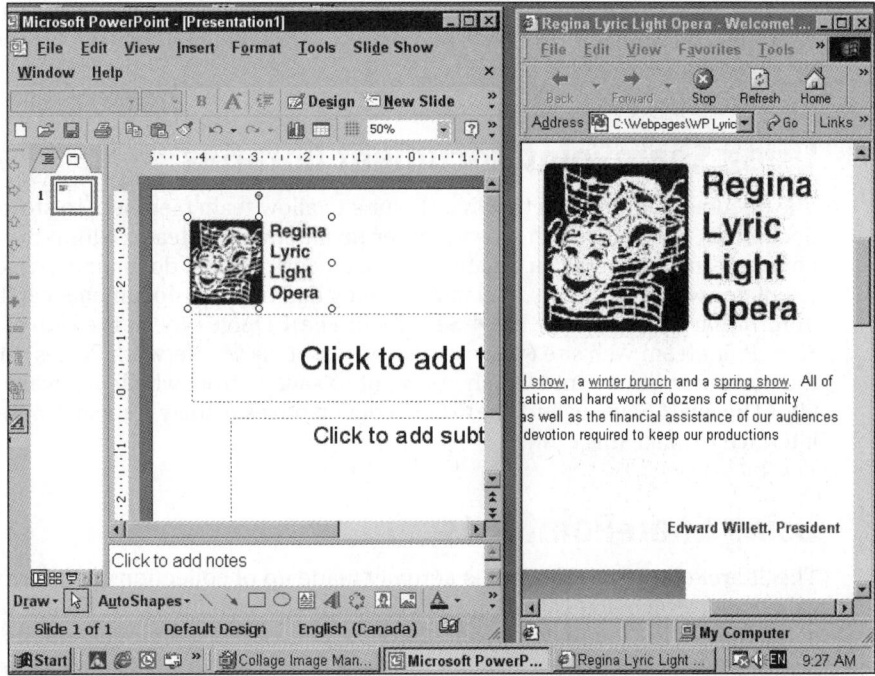

Figure 6-3: The material you want from the Web page is now safely ensconced in your document.

Sharing via SharePoint

SharePoint (or, as Microsoft calls it, the "SharePoint team Web site solution") is a new application designed to help work teams create and use a Web site through which they can collaborate on a variety of projects. Everyone on the team contributes to and utilizes the site in the same way, and the site can be easily managed online via the Web. Microsoft Office XP is specifically designed to work with SharePoint, so team members can access and post material to the team Web site without having to leave the familiar confines of Office and Internet Explorer.

When you set up a SharePoint site, it automatically includes a team home page, a shared document library, general discussion boards, shared contacts, a team calendar, and team tasks. A Settings page lets the team members customize the site to suit themselves.

You can also use FrontPage to customize your SharePoint site; just open the site in your browser and choose Edit. Then you can apply themes and the other formatting amenities FrontPage offers.

Using SharePoint document libraries

The document libraries in the SharePoint site allow team members to store their documents and work on them with other members of the team. Within the document library, team members can create new documents, upload documents, associate templates with documents, and more. Saving and opening documents can be done from within Office; choose File ⇨ Save As or File ⇨ Open, type in the URL of the SharePoint team Web site (you can also access it via My Network Places), and choose the document library into which you want to save or from which you want to open a file. (The File ⇨ Save As and File ⇨ Open dialog boxes display a special Web-page-like interface to make this easier.)

Using SharePoint lists

The SharePoint team Web site is actually made up of collections of information called *lists,* which you can view and edit using the Web interface. SharePoint offers some built-in list templates (team contacts, team events, announcements, and such), or you can create a new list from scratch. You can easily change lists, or export lists to an Office application.

Among the lists are announcements, which are messages team members post to the home page of the site; events, which can be added and edited by team members and exported to Outlook's Calendar (by clicking Export to Outlook while viewing the event listing); tasks, which enable team members to set up tasks for specific people with start and end dates and progress to dates; and team contacts, which enable team members to share contacts with each other. As with events, you can export contacts into Office — either into an Excel spreadsheet (as a group) or into Outlook (individually).

Conducting SharePoint document discussions

You can exchange comments and corrections on documents within Office (more on that later in this chapter), but you can also use a SharePoint team site for that purpose. Open the document, click Discuss on the Internet Explorer toolbar, and then, when the Discussion toolbar opens at the bottom of the window, click Insert Discussion. Discussions aren't displayed within a document online by default, but they can be if you want them to be. (See "Creating Web Discussions," later in this chapter, for more about discussions.)

Note   SharePoint has many more features than I can go into here. Check the Help files and the Microsoft Web site for more details if you expect to use SharePoint to collaborate with others.

Holding Online Meetings

Online meetings let you share data and hold discussions with people at several different sites, just as if they were all in the same conference room, except perhaps for the lack of coffee and doughnuts (maybe in the next version of Office?). There's even a whiteboard!

Online meetings can be held over a corporate intranet or over the Internet. You can start them from any Office application via a built-in utility called Microsoft NetMeeting.

Starting an online meeting

Use the following steps to start an online meeting from an Office application and share an Office document with the other meeting participants:

1. Open the document you want to share.

2. Choose Tools ➪ Online Collaboration ➪ Meet Now.

    The Place a Call dialog box opens.

    If you haven't held an online meeting before, Microsoft NetMeeting asks you to provide information about yourself and choose a directory. If you're not sure which directory to use, check with your system administrator.

3. In the Place a Call dialog box, find the name of the person(s) you want to invite to join the meeting, select the name(s), and click Call.

For the online meeting to happen, the people you are calling have to be running NetMeeting at the same time you are.

The Office application now opens an Online Meeting toolbar (see Figure 6-4), which includes the tools you need for running the meeting.

Figure 6-4: The Online Meeting toolbar includes the tools you need to run (or participate in) an online meeting.

4. To invite another person to join the meeting, click the Call Participant button, just to the right of the list of current participants.

For an explanation of the other buttons on the Online Meeting toolbar, see "Hosting an online meeting," coming up shortly.

Joining an online meeting

If someone else starts an online meeting in Office and invites you to join (and you have NetMeeting running), a Join Meeting dialog box appears. Click Ignore to decline and Accept to join. If you accept, the Online Meeting toolbar appears on your screen, along with the document the host has open. (Only the host has to have the document and the application in which it runs—for example, Word or Excel—installed.)

Hosting an online meeting

If you called the online meeting, then you're the host, which gives you a few more options than ordinary participants have. Here's how it works:

✦ **The host is the only person who can invite new people to join the meeting.** Click the Call Participant button, just to the right of the list of current participants on the Online Meeting toolbar.

✦ **The host is the only person who can remove a participant.** To do so, choose his or her name in the list of participants in the Online Meeting toolbar and then click the Remove Participants button (the second button from the left).

✦ **By default, the host is the only person who can make changes to the document being viewed.** However, you can allow other people to make changes by clicking the Allow Others to Edit button on the Online Meeting toolbar (the third button from the left). When you activate that button, other people in the meeting can take turns controlling the document by double-clicking anywhere in it the first time and simply clicking in it thereafter.

While other people in the meeting are in control, you lose control of your mouse pointer. You can tell who is in control at any given time because their initials appear beside the mouse pointer.

✦ **The host can stop others from editing the document at any time.** To do so, click the Allow Others to Edit button again (if you're in control of the document) or press Esc (if you're not).

✦ **The host is the only one who can activate the Display Chat Window and Display Whiteboard buttons on the Online Meeting toolbar.** These buttons are the fourth and fifth from the left. They activate the Chat window and the whiteboard, described below.

Using the Chat window

The Chat window (see Figure 6-5) is where you talk to other participants in an online meeting. Type your message into the Message field at the bottom of the window, select the recipient, and then click the Send button to the right of the Message field. Your message is displayed and also appears in the Chat windows of all meeting participants to whom you sent the message; they can also post their own messages.

Tip You can vary the way messages are displayed by choosing Options ⇨ Chat Format.

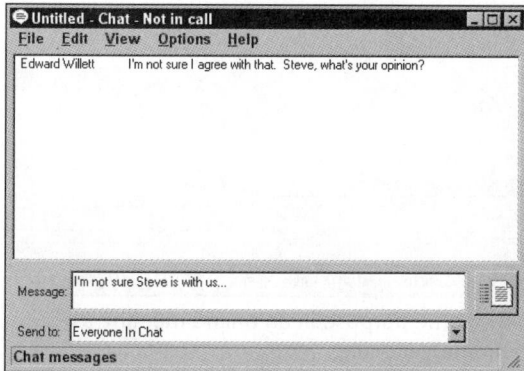

Figure 6-5: Talk to other online participants in the Chat window.

The discussion in the Chat window can be saved and/or printed at any time by choosing the appropriate commands under the File menu, so you can have a permanent record of what was said.

Using the whiteboard

The NetMeeting whiteboard (see Figure 6-6) is very much like a whiteboard in an ordinary conference room, except you have the advantage of computer tools to help you illustrate your points. To completely clear a page, delete a page, or add a new page before or after the current page, click the Edit menu. You can save and print whiteboard pages from the File menu.

Note If you want to set up the whiteboard so that everyone in the meeting can use it simultaneously, make sure that the Allow Others to Edit button is activated.

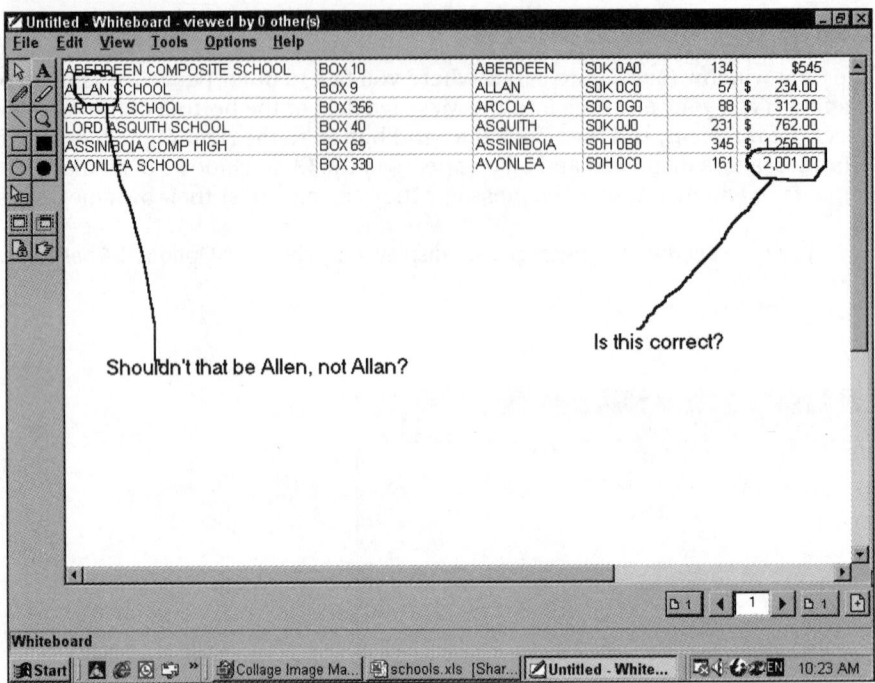

Figure 6-6: The whiteboard serves the same purpose in an online meeting as a real-world whiteboard does in an ordinary meeting.

The whiteboard also provides you with a range of very useful drawing tools:

✦ **Selector.** Click this button, and then click an object in the whiteboard or draw a frame around it to select it.

✦ **Text.** Click this button, and then click anywhere in the whiteboard and start typing. A Font Options button becomes active at the bottom of the whiteboard; you can use it to format your text. That's how the text was typed in Figure 6-6.

✦ **Pen.** Use this tool to draw on the NetMeeting whiteboard just as you would on a real-world whiteboard. In Figure 6-6, the Pen was used to circle potential mistakes and draw lines to them from the text. Choose the color you want the pen to write in from the palette.

✦ **Highlighter.** Use this like a highlighting pen.

✦ **Line.** Use this to draw straight lines.

✦ **Zoom.** Use this to enlarge the whiteboard image.

✦ **Unfilled Rectangle/Unfilled Ellipse.** Use these to draw the outlines of rectangles and ellipses.

✦ **Filled Rectangle/Filled Ellipse.** Use these to draw solid rectangles and ellipses in the active color.

✦ **Eraser.** Click this, and then click any object you want to erase, and away it goes. You can also drag a rectangle around multiple objects to erase them all.

✦ **Select Window.** Click this, and the next window you click is captured to the whiteboard.

✦ **Select Area.** Click this, and then draw a frame around any area of the current screen you want to capture to the whiteboard. That's how the spreadsheet rows were inserted in Figure 6-6.

✦ **Lock Contents.** Click this if you don't want any other participants in the meeting to be able to alter the contents of the whiteboard.

✦ **Remote Pointer.** This is an icon of a pointing finger you can activate and drag around the whiteboard to point out various objects to meeting participants.

✦ **Page Controls.** These controls let you move from page to page on the whiteboard, or directly to the end or beginning of the range of pages.

✦ **Insert New Page.** Click this to add a new page to the whiteboard.

Sending files to other participants

As host, you can send a currently-open Office file to the other participants in an online meeting by choosing File ➪ Send To ➪ Online Meeting Participant in whatever application the file is open in.

Creating Web Discussions

As mentioned earlier, you can hold Web discussions of documents on your SharePoint team Web site, if you have one. You can also carry out discussions of documents published on any Web server that is running Office Server Extensions (check with your network administrator to find out where to publish your documents to enable discussions). You can publish a document to a Web server by choosing File ➪ Save As, and then clicking the Web Folders tool in the Places bar of the Save As dialog box.

The remarks are *threaded;* the response to any remark is nested directly under it, much as you can see in Usenet newsgroups. This makes it much easier to follow the flow of conversation.

Discussions can also be carried out in any frames-capable browser. When Office Server Extensions are installed on a Web server, an Office Server Extensions Home Page becomes available to users. This allows them to search and navigate published documents, and to receive e-mail notifications when published documents are changed or discussed.

Tip
Internet Explorer offers the most integrated experience: It displays a Discussions button on its toolbar and allows inline discussions—discussions that actually appear in the document under discussion.

To start a discussion in Office (this option is available only in Word, Excel and PowerPoint), follow these steps:

1. Choose Tools ➪ Online Collaboration ➪ Web Discussions. This opens the Web Discussions toolbar.

2. Choose Discussions ➪ Options from the Web Discussions toolbar to open the Discussion Options dialog box, shown in Figure 6-7.

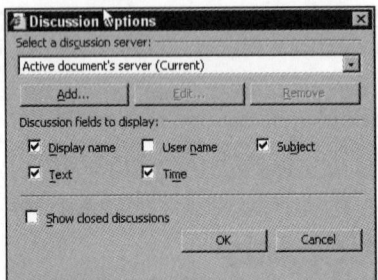

Figure 6-7: Start a Web discussion of the current document from this dialog box.

3. Click Add and enter the name of the discussion server given to you by your network administrator.

   The next time you start a discussion, you can choose the server from the list, and then edit or remove it by clicking those respective buttons.

4. Check the boxes for the discussion fields you want to appear in the discussion window; then click OK.

5. Return to the Web Discussions toolbar; click Insert Discussion About the Document.

6. Under Discussion subject, type a name for the subject of the discussion.

7. Under Discussion text, type your comments and then click OK.

   When you click OK, your comment appears in the discussion pane at the bottom of the window.

8. Choose Discussions from the Web Discussions toolbar again; then choose the type of discussion you want to start.

In Word and in Internet Explorer, you can create a discussion that appears in the document, relating to some particular aspect of it (choose Insert in the Document); in other applications, you have to initiate a general discussion about the document that isn't displayed within it. (If that's the kind of discussion you want to begin, choose Insert about the Document in Word or Explorer.)

After a discussion begins, anyone who has access to the document can add to the discussion by opening the document and choosing Tools ⇨ Online Collaboration ⇨ Web Discussions. They can then use the Web Discussions toolbar buttons (the Web Discussions toolbar can be seen in Figure 6-8) to create new messages, navigate through messages, reply to messages, and edit messages.

Figure 6-8: Use the Web Discussions toolbar to create or reply to discussion items. This is the Word version.

Sharing Office Documents

Many documents represent the combined efforts of several co-authors. Even more commonly, documents are passed around an organization — or to the boss — for review and comment before the final edited version gets distributed. Recognizing the obvious, Microsoft has blessed Office XP with a slew of features that enable groups to share documents on a network and actively collaborate on developing content.

Storing and finding documents on a network

Group collaboration on documents (whether creating or editing) requires opening and saving Office documents where they are accessible to everyone in the group. Office provides plenty of help to that end; the latest wrinkle in this process is SharePoint. Even if your organization has a traditional, non-intranet network, however, you can readily share documents and link them together by placing hyperlinks in them.

If you work on a network, you already know that in Windows, any site accessible on your network appears in file-related dialog boxes just as local disks and folders do.

In Office dialog boxes such as Open and Save As, you open the Network Neighborhood item in the Look In list to navigate to computers on the network and their folders. Once you've opened the right folder, you can store and retrieve documents on another computer exactly as you would those on your own PC.

Cross-Reference For details on how to make sure only the people you want to have access to documents on a network can get at them, see Chapter 14.

Sharing documents on your hard drive with others

Rather than saving your documents to another computer on the network, you may decide to give others access to your documents right where they're stored on your own PC. If you (rather than your network administrator) have control over such things, you can expose any disk or folder to other users on the network. (Tact still demands that you notify the administrator of your plans, of course.)

The first step is to enable network sharing. In the Windows Control Panel, open the Network applet. On the Configuration tab, choose File and Print Sharing, and in the resulting dialog box check the box labeled "I want to be able to give others access to my files."

Once you've enabled sharing in general, if necessary, you must then specify the folders or disks you want to make accessible. Do so in My Computer. For each disk or folder you want to share, select Sharing from its shortcut menu. In the resulting Properties dialog box, choose Shared As to activate sharing for the item and specify which type of access network users can have.

Working with Web documents

Because Office applications can store documents in HTML format without losing content or formatting, you can use either the standard Office file formats or HTML for the documents you place on Web sites. Of course, HTML is the way to go if you expect that the documents will be browsed by people who don't have Office.

Using Web Folders to manage files

Office enables you to open and save files on your organization's Web sites just as you would on your own PC or a network computer. The Web Folders feature is a sort of virtual folder that contains shortcuts to Web sites located on servers on the Web or your intranet.

In My Computer, Explorer, and Office file-related dialog boxes, the Web Folders item appears at the same level as your disk drives — just below the My Computer item itself. The shortcuts it contains are based on Web site URLs, but you can give them sensible names such as "Edna's Web site" or "Protean Polyphonies, Inc."

Figure 6-9 shows the File ⇨ Open dialog box in an Office application with Web Folders selected.

Figure 6-9: When you click the Web Folders button on the Places bar, Office provides file-related dialog boxes that display Web site shortcuts you've created.

Note   In Windows 2000 and Windows Me, Web Folders and Network Neighborhood are both replaced by a new item called My Network Places, which contains shortcuts to Web folders, UNC locations, and computers accessible on your LAN.

Adding shortcuts to Web Folders

Click Add Web Folder to open a wizard that takes you through the steps of either creating a shortcut to an existing Web Folder or to creating a new Web Folder.

Managing files in Web Folders

Opening a Web Folders shortcut gives you access to all the folders and files it contains. Standard file management techniques work for navigating and for moving, renaming, and deleting these items and for creating new folders. In Explorer or My Computer, you can copy files to any folder on the site by dragging them there.

Caution   Just so you're clear: When you work with Web site folders and files that you access from a Web Folders shortcut, you're working with the actual items themselves, directly. If you rename or delete a file, for example, the change affects the actual file on the Web site.

Working with Office documents accessed through Web Folders

Within Office, you can open and save documents to any folder listed in Web Folders. In the appropriate dialog box, Open or Save As, just select the file or type in its name. Remember, however, that opening an HTML file takes you to the application that created it. For example, if you're working in Word and try to open a Web page created in FrontPage, the page opens in FrontPage, not Word. To open it in Word, right-click it and choose Open in Microsoft Word.

If you're using Internet Explorer 5, you can work offline on Office documents stored on a Web site. That way, you can work with the document at top speed, without having to send information back and forth across the network as you edit the file. This technique is especially valuable for saving time if you have a dial-up connection to the Internet.

To work with a document offline, follow these steps:

1. Open Web Folder in an Office file-related dialog box.

2. Navigate to the file and right-click it.

3. Choose Make Available Offline.

   The file is transferred to your computer. From then on, when you open it in Web Folders, you're actually working with the replica stored on your own PC.

When you're through editing the file and want to update the "real" version on the Web site, right-click the file and choose Synchronize. The changes you made offline are incorporated into the file on the Web site. You can also use the Synchronize command to ensure that the replica of the file on your computer contains any changes made to the original version by other users. If you're trying to synchronize a file that you've edited but that others have also changed, you're notified and asked how to deal with any conflicts.

Working with documents on FTP sites

If your company has an intranet, you can retrieve and store Office documents on its FTP sites via the Open and Save As dialog boxes (saving only works if you have access rights, and if the FTP site permits it). You can also browse any FTP site on the Internet that permits anonymous logins, although you may or may not be able to open the files there.

Adding FTP sites to the Open and Save As dialog boxes

In Office, the painful way to access a document on an FTP site is to type its URL in the File Name field of the Open dialog box. Ease the pain by setting up your Office programs with the FTP sites you frequent. After you've added an FTP site, you connect to it by selecting it in the Look In list. After Office makes the connection, you can browse the site's files and folders with standard navigation techniques.

To add an FTP site, drop down the Look In list and choose Add/Modify FTP Locations down toward the bottom. In the dialog box that appears (see Figure 6-10), enter the site name, select a login method, and enter your password. Most sites that allow anonymous login require your e-mail address as the password.

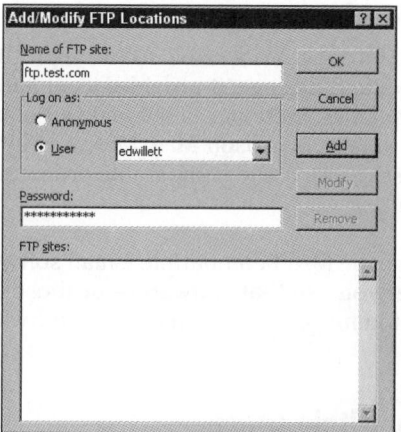

Figure 6-10: Adding an FTP site for access via the Open and Save As dialog boxes

More facts about FTP access

After you add an FTP site, Office remembers the address and login information. From then on, the site appears near the bottom of the Look In list under FTP Locations in the Open and Save As dialog boxes. To connect to the site, just select it from the list.

You can use a system policy to add up to ten FTP sites to the Look In list for multiple users. Using the System Policy Editor (as discussed in Chapter 7), set the following policy:

```
User\Office\Internet\FTP Sites\Add FTP Sites
```

Tip   Include the extension when you save an Office document to an FTP site to ensure that it isn't inadvertently omitted.

Sharing documents via e-mail

As an alternative to sharing your documents directly over a network, consider exchanging them using e-mail. Obviously, this makes sense when the intended recipient isn't accessible on your organization's network. But it also enables you to control more tightly who sees the document and when they get their hands on it.

To share documents using e-mail, you simply need any e-mail program capable of sending binary files as attachments — in other words, any recently released e-mail program works for this purpose. However, if your e-mail software is MAPI- or VIM-compatible, you don't have to attach the files yourself. Instead, you can take advantage of special features that permit you to e-mail your documents directly from within Office.

Understanding MAPI and VIM

MAPI, (Messaging Application Programming Interface) is a 32-bit software protocol that Microsoft introduced with Windows 95 and Exchange. It provides a common conduit between client e-mail applications such as Exchange client and Outlook and the services they connect to, like Exchange server, Microsoft Mail, MSN, and Internet mail servers. VIM (Vendor-Independent Messaging), is the comparable protocol in the 16-bit world and is used by Lotus cc:Mail.

Because you own Office and Windows, you have MAPI-compatible e-mail software in the form of Exchange and Outlook. Whether you use that software — or those capabilities — is another matter; your organization may have adopted e-mail software that isn't based on either MAPI or VIM.

Sending and routing documents from within Office

If Office detects a MAPI- or VIM-compatible e-mail client on your system, the File ➪ Send To menu offers the Mail Recipient and Routing Recipient commands. Use them as follows:

✦ Choose **Mail Recipient** when you want to send the document to one person, or to multiple recipients simultaneously. This is the best choice when you have only one recipient, and it's certainly the simpler approach at send time. But if you're seeking comments from multiple reviewers, you'll get back a separate copy of the document from each of them, which can definitely be an inconvenience.

✦ Choose **Routing Recipient** to specify a series of recipients who should receive the document one at a time. That way, each of them gets to see the comments of the previous reviewers. Only one copy of the document is in circulation, so you get back a single copy containing all the comments and changes. Routing also lets you receive e-mail notification each time the document gets forwarded to a new recipient, and you can have the document automatically returned to you when the last reviewer completes work on it.

Sending a document (without routing it)

You can use one of three versions of the Send To ➪ Mail Recipient command, as follows:

✦ **Send To ➪ Mail Recipient** sends the document in the body of the e-mail.

✦ **Send To ➪ Mail Recipient (for Review)** sends the document as an attachment and fills in the Subject line and body with brief messages asking for the document to be reviewed.

✦ **Send To ➪ Mail Recipient (as Attachment)** attaches the document to a blank message. You may be asked to specify an Exchange profile before the message form appears.

Routing a document

To route a document to a series of recipients, choose File ➪ Send To ➪ Routing Recipient. Again, you may have to specify an Exchange profile before proceeding. At the Routing Slip dialog box, select recipients for the routing list by choosing Address. The order of recipient names in the To list determines the order in which they receive the document. If necessary, change the order by selecting a name and clicking the arrow buttons to the right. Another point: Although you can specify a group alias as the recipient for a routed document, everyone in the group receives the document simultaneously. If that's not what you intend, specify the individual people in the group to whom you want to send the message.

Fill in a subject and any text you want in the message separate from the attached document. At the bottom of the dialog box, specify whether you want the document to be sent to each recipient in sequence or to all of them simultaneously. This latter option is similar to selecting multiple recipients with the Send To ➪ Mail Recipient command. However, it lets you use the special features of the routing command to track the document's status, and in Word, to protect the document from unauthorized changes.

Caution

If you choose the One after another option on the Routing Slip, the document could get held up by a slow reviewer, or just someone who is unexpectedly out of his or her office. If time is of the essence, consider sending the document to everyone on the list at once.

Check Return When Done if you want to get the document back automatically after the last reviewer finishes with it, and check Track Status if you want e-mail notification as it makes its rounds from recipient to recipient.

In Word, the Protect For field at the bottom is important. It determines what in the document recipients can change. Choose from among the following options:

✦ **Comments.** To allow recipients to add comments but prevent them from making any changes in the document's contents.

✦ **Tracked Changes.** To force revision marking to be turned on, which tracks all changes the reviewers make in the document.

✦ **Forms.** When the document is a form that you want the recipients to fill in. They won't be able to alter the form itself.

✦ **(none).** To allow recipients to freely change the document. Their changes won't automatically be tracked, though they can turn on change tracking manually.

To send the document to the first recipient immediately, choose Route. If you prefer, however, you can close the dialog box without sending the document by choosing Add Slip. When you later decide to send the document, choose File ➪ Send To ➪ Next Routing Recipient.

Sending documents that aren't already open

If the Office document you want to send isn't currently open, you can still dispatch it to the intended recipient easily. Start from within an Office Open or Save dialog box — or in My Computer, Explorer, or Outlook's own file manager. Right-click the document and choose Send To ➪ Mail Recipient. Outlook creates an e-mail message containing the document as an attachment. Actually, this works with all types of documents, not just Office ones.

Tip   Although you can attach documents to an Outlook message that's already open, using the Send To command on a document's shortcut menu as just described is often faster. If you send documents by e-mail with any frequency, teach yourself this trick.

Posting documents to Exchange folders

If you don't want to e-mail a document to a large number of recipients, you may have an alternative: You can make it available to anyone who has access to an Exchange public folder. However, posting a document to an Exchange folder only works if your group is using Exchange Server (if you're not running Exchange Server, you can post a document to an Exchange folder on your own computer, but that isn't much good for document sharing).

With the document open, choose File ➪ Send To ➪ Exchange Folder. A list of Exchange folders appears. Specify the destination folder and you're done.

Office Features for Collaborating on Documents

Once you have a handle on the mechanics of sharing Office documents, you and the members of your team can actually work on their contents together.

You don't need a network to take advantage of Office features for working on documents with others — these features are equally appropriate for documents you share via e-mail or on floppy disks. Here's a quick rundown:

✦ Word has several distinct features that support group collaboration on documents. It lets authors and reviewers attach comments to selected text and see those comments by simply holding the mouse pointer over the text. You can have Word display the additions and deletions made by each collaborator in a different color, and compare or merge together different versions of the same document. Finally, different versions of the document can be stored in the same file, each version identified as to when it was saved and by whom. All these features are discussed in Chapter 20.

✦ Excel supplies similar help for groups building worksheets. Comments can be applied to specific cells. A changed cell appears with a border color indicating the person who changed it. The shared-workbook feature allows access to the same workbook by different users, preserving all of their changes in separate versions stored in the same file. See Chapter 28 for more on these features.

✦ PowerPoint's group document features aren't as extensive, but are much better than they used to be. The new Markup feature, similar to the one in Word, shows "call-outs" detailing changes made to the presentation without obscuring the presentation or affecting its layout. The new Revisions Task Pane can display either a list of the changes made by a given reviewer or a graphical representation of the changes. A drop-down menu makes it simple to apply or remove changes the reviewer has made. In common with other Office applications, the reviewing toolbar lets users filter the presentation to view changes by specific reviewers or by all reviewers, step through each change and accept or reject the changes individually, or accept or reject all of the changes at the same time. The Tools ➭ Compare and Merge Presentations command lets you merge all the changes made by reviewers and examine them all at once instead of having to open every version of the presentation one at a time.

✦   ✦   ✦

Running Office on a Network

Networking is a complex and often very technical topic, but it deserves your attention in this era of intranets and workgroup computing. I can't promise that you'll leave this chapter a networking guru, but at least you can get a better sense of what's possible with Office in a networked environment. For detailed information on the technicalities of installing and administering Office on a network, be sure to get Microsoft's Office Resource Kit (ORK); you can find it online at www.microsoft.com/office/ork/.

Installing and Running Office on a Network

In a workgroup setting, Office can be installed on each user's individual computer — locally — or on a network server for shared access. The decision should take into account the following factors:

Where Office Is Installed	Advantages
Local computer	Faster — Office applications perform better when installed on a local computer than when accessed over the network.
	Always available — when the network or the server goes down, the individual user can still run Office.
Network server	Saves disk space on the local computer.
	Provides more convenient support and updates.

Actually, the choice is a little more complicated—you're not locked into one option or the other. You can decide to install some Office components on the local computer and others on the server. If Windows itself is being shared over the network, many of Office's big DLLs and other support files must be placed on the Windows server, even if you install the rest of Office on each local machine.

Installing Office—decisions, decisions

If you plan to share all or part of Office on the network, Office must be set up on each PC through a special network installation process described in the next section. If you plan instead to install Office in its entirety on each PC, you have two choices:

✦ You can use the same installation process required for sharing files over the network but specify that all the Office files be copied to each local computer.

✦ You can always run Setup on each local computer.

Performing a network installation

If you choose to install Office from a network server, you get to decide whether to install Office components on users' computers or have them run on the server. You can make this selection separately for each component. You can also decide which components to install on each computer, depending on the users' needs.

Note Remember that if you set any Office feature(s) to run from the network, then the server must always be online and accessible to users—when the server is down, the feature(s) won't be available. The same is true of any components for which you select the Install on First Use option (see Chapter 3 for more information on the Install on First Use installation option).

Installing Office via the network involves two main steps:

1. **Administrative setup.** Set up the administrative installation point on a network server accessible to all workstations running Office. (Large networks can have more than one administrative installation point.) To do so, specify a folder (that is, a *share*) on an accessible network drive that contains sufficient free disk space. All the Office files are copied to this server during this step.

2. **Client setup.** On each workstation, install Office on that computer by running Setup from the administrative installation point. During this part of the setup process, you can specify the location for the various Office components (server or local computer).

Preparing the installation point and customizing Setup

The key to initiating a shared installation of Office is to run Setup using command-line options. Using the Windows Start ➪ Run command, type the following command in the Open box:

```
[drive letter]:setup /a install.msi
```

Setup asks you to enter your CD Key and organization name (these entries are later supplied automatically during user installation) and then to enter the names of the server and share you created.

After Setup copies all the files from the Office CD to the server, you must then:

✦ Give your users read-only access to the share.

✦ Customize Setup for the installation options and default Office settings you want to specify. You can customize Setup by entering options on the command line, by supplying your settings in the Setup.ini file, or by using the Office Custom Installation Wizard (discussed later in this chapter) included with the Office Resource Kit to create a transform, a special file that controls Setup's behavior.

Running Setup to install Office on user PCs

When you have created and customized the administrative installation point, users can install Office by running Setup from the root folder of the server share. Users can run Setup themselves — using the command-line options, settings file, or transform that you've chosen — or you can run Setup for them through a network login script (or a systems management product such as Microsoft Systems Management Server).

When you're in charge of installing Office on a network, you can decide how much control to give your users during the client setup portion of the installation process. You have four general choices:

✦ **Let your users perform interactive installations at their own workstations.** If you trust your people and they know the drill, you can let them perform an interactive installation, selecting which Office components to install and where.

If they're upgrading from a previous version of Office, Office XP Setup analyzes their current installation and intelligently installs the same components.

✦ **Write a custom script that dictates all installation options when the user runs Setup.** This approach gives you more control over the installation process.

✦ **Write a script that installs Office automatically on a workstation the next time that user logs into the network.** The Office Resource Kit includes the utilities you need for creating such scripts. This approach gives you total control over the installation procedure.

✦ **Use Microsoft Systems Management Server to perform the installation on remote computers.** This out-of-the-box approach is also effective.

Customizing Office for Workgroups: Windows System Policies

To ensure that Office applications behave consistently on all the computers on your network, use Windows system policies. A *system policy* defines the value of a key in the Windows Registry. Office, of course, uses the Registry to store the settings for its many options (for example, those in the Tools ⇨ Options dialog boxes).

Note   System policies can be enabled and enforced only on computers connected to a network whose primary domain controller is a Microsoft Windows NT server or Microsoft Windows 2000 server.

Because system policies change Registry values, you can use them to wrest control of Office from your users. This is handy if you're power-hungry, true, but the real point is to improve efficiency in the group. When Office works the same way on each workstation, a user can work at any computer without encountering unfamiliar toolbars or keyboard shortcuts, and you'll have an easier time giving technical support.

A set of system policies is stored in a *system policy template*, a file kept on the network server. Each time a user logs into the network, Windows automatically downloads the system policy file to the user's computer, which updates the Registry settings accordingly (the file can be set for manual downloading).

Caution   Be aware that because system policies tinker with the Registry, you can really foul things up if you don't know what you're doing. Be sure to back up your Registry files before you try out system policies.

Features you can control with system policies

System policies enable you to exercise control in the following ways:

✦ Disable (or enable) any program command and its corresponding toolbar button.

✦ Disable (or enable) any keyboard shortcut.

✦ Specify a host of application settings, such as most of those in the Tools ⇨ Options dialog box.

Note

System policies can control an Office application's global settings, but not the settings that pertain to a particular document. You can't set document properties, for instance — and in Word, you can't control whether spell-check and grammar checking are active for a particular document.

Network requirements for system policies

On a Windows network, system policies can only be downloaded automatically if Client for Microsoft Networks is the primary network login client and a domain is defined. Likewise, on a NetWare network, the primary login client must be Microsoft Client for NetWare Networks, and a preferred server must be defined. You can download system policies only manually on NETX and VLM networks.

Using the Windows System Policy Editor

Use the System Policy Editor, shown in Figure 7-1, to create or modify a system policy template.

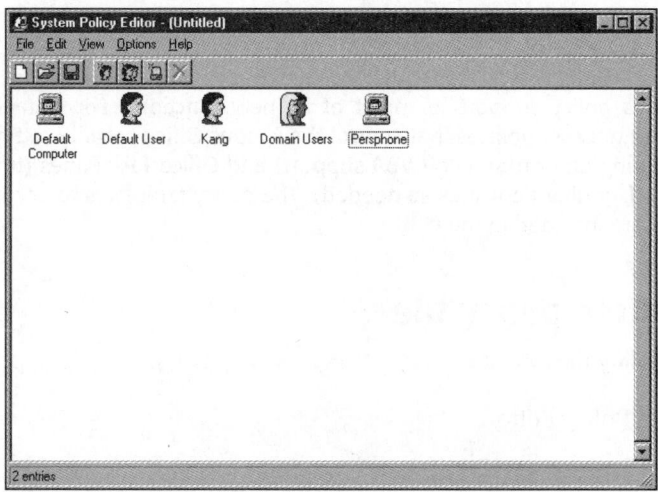

Figure 7-1: Use the System Policy Editor to set options for Office users on a network or shared machine.

You can find the System Policy Editor in the Office XP Resource Kit (if you don't have the ORK, you can download the System Policy Editor and the necessary template files from Microsoft's Web site). Although there is a System Policy Editor included with all versions of Windows, over the last two releases of Office the ORK version has been improved as follows:

✦ **The process of setting policies is easier to understand.** With the ORK version of the Editor, you first decide whether a given setting is to be enforced by the policy or not. If you choose an enforced setting, you then specify its value.

✦ **Policies are more strictly enforced.** If a user changes an option, the setting dictated by the policy is restored whenever the user restarts the application.

✦ **Users' original settings can be restored.** If you clear a policy, each user's previous setting for that option automatically comes back, whether the setting had been customized or was simply the application's default.

✦ **Policies accept environment variables.** Instead of preordaining folder names or filenames or other settings values, you can now assign environment variables to your policies. Because environment variables can be changed readily from the command prompt, you can quickly switch back and forth between different policy settings by running login scripts or batch files that change the environment variables in question. (See "Using environment variables as system policy settings" later in this chapter.)

Another advantage of the System Policy Editor that comes with the Office XP ORK is its predefined template files for Office — with them, you don't have to build new policy files from scratch. The ORK includes separate templates for shared Office settings, the five major applications, Publisher, Clip Gallery, and the Windows Installer.

Note   Office XP provides policy support for most of its new functions. For instance, administrators can now set policies that control the various Office security settings (for example, turning on or turning off VBA support) and Office Task Panes (turning them on or off, adding new links as needed). The policy templates to accomplish these tasks are included in the ORK.

Creating a system policy file

To create a system policy file:

1. Start the System Policy Editor.

2. Choose Options ➪ Policy Template.

    Figure 7-2 shows the resulting Policy Template Options dialog box.

Note   The Policy Template Options dialog box is so narrow that you can't see the template name if the path is more than about 30 characters long.

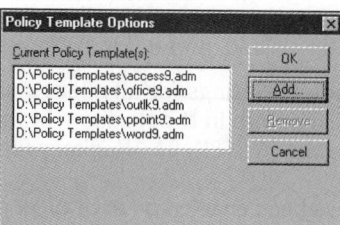

Figure 7-2: The Policy Template Options dialog box

3. Choose Add and then select one or more of the policy template files supplied with the ORK (if they're not already listed).

4. Choose File ➪ New Policy to create the policy document.

5. Choose the computer, group, or user account to which you want to apply the policies in the file (see the next section).

6. Define the individual policy settings you want to control (see "Defining individual system policies").

7. Choose File ➪ Save As; then type the name of your policy folder. For Windows 98 or Windows Me clients, save the policy file as `Config.pol`. For Windows NT 4.0 or Windows 2000 clients, save the policy file as `Ntconfig.pol`.

8. Save the file to the Netlogon folder of the primary domain controller (on NT networks) or the Public folder of the preferred server (for NetWare networks). (Windows 2000 networks require no special positioning of the policy file.)

Tip

You can use the System Policy Editor to change policy settings for the computer you're working on at the moment — even if it's not on a network — to ensure a set of custom settings that persist from session to session, or to assign environment variables to your program options.

Specifying which users or computers a system policy affects

You can set system policies for all client computers, for all users, or for a specific computer, user, or group of users:

✦ **User policies.** These system policies govern the user currently logged into Windows (that is, the person who is going to be running Office when the system policies are activated — not you when you're running the System Policy Editor). These policies are stored in the HKEY_USERS branch of the Registry and the USER.DAT Registry file on disk. You can define user policies for all users or for a single user.

✦ **Group policies.** These policies determine the settings for all members of a particular group and also stored in HKEY_USERS and USER.DAT.

✦ **Computer policies.** These policies control settings for all client computers or for any one computer on the network. They go in the Registry branch HKEY_LOCAL_MACHINE and are kept in the SYSTEM.DAT Registry file.

Note   User policies work only if user profiles have been enabled on each client computer. To use group policies, you must first install groups on each client computer.

Use the icons in the System Policy Editor's main window to specify which users or computers the policy you're defining will control. Initially, the window contains only Default User and Default Computer icons, but you can add icons for specific computers, users, or groups, by choosing Add Computer, Add User, or Add Group from the Edit menu.

Defining individual system policies

When you've created the icons you need, double-click the one for the user(s) or computer(s) you want. As shown in Figure 7-3, the Properties dialog box lets you define the specific policies available.

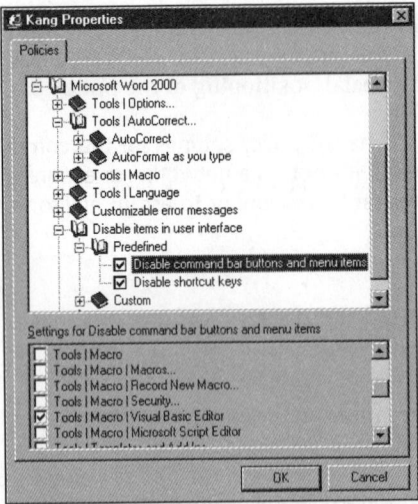

Figure 7-3: Use the Properties dialog box to define specific system policies.

Each system policy in the Properties dialog box has a checkbox that can have one of three settings:

✦ **Checked.** This means that you want your policy setting to be enforced on the user. If you check this box, a subsidiary checkbox or text field becomes available below it, enabling you to enter the setting that you want enforced. When the user logs in, the local Windows Registry changes to match your policy setting.

✦ **Cleared.** The policy and its settings should not be used. If it was previously implemented, then its settings in the Registry are excised, and the settings the user previously had made are restored.

✦ **Grayed (unavailable).** The policy hasn't been changed. All policies are in this state initially. With the checkbox in this state, the Editor makes no modifications to the user's configuration settings, or to any previous changes made by the Editor. You shouldn't change a policy to this state—clear the checkbox instead if you want to allow the user to control the setting.

Details on how system policies work

Each time a user logs in, Windows locates and downloads any system policies that apply to that user, entering the policy settings into the Registry as follows:

✦ If user profiles are enabled, any policies specific for that user are applied first.

✦ If Windows does not find user-specific policies, it applies any policies specified for the Default User (see "Specifying which users or computers a system policy affects," earlier in this chapter).

✦ If group policy support is installed, and if there are no user-specific policies, group policies for all groups the user belongs to are downloaded and applied in order of increasing priority.

✦ If present, computer-specific policies are also applied. If not, Windows applies any policies defined for the Default Computer.

Using environment variables as system policy settings

As noted earlier, Office XP recognizes environment variables as valid system policy settings. To use an environment variable as a system policy setting, place the variable between percent signs in the text field that becomes available when you check the box for the setting itself. Here's an example:

```
%ProjectFolder%
```

As the example implies, one great use for an environment variable is to specify the default file location; you can easily use a different folder for each project. For each project, create a login script or batch file that creates the environment variable you've chosen and sets it to your project folder. Then, when you use the Open command, the script automatically opens the folder for the current project as specified by the environment variable.

Mapping Network Locations within Office

For easy access to a networked computer (or one of its folders), map it so it appears as a drive letter under My Computer and on the Look In list inside Office dialog boxes. Although you can map network drives and folders from Explorer or My Computer, you don't have to leave Office to do it. Instead, in the Open or Save As dialog box, click the Tools button (at the far right of the button strip). When you choose Map Network Drive, the dialog box shown in Figure 7-4 appears. You don't have to leave Office to map a disk drive.

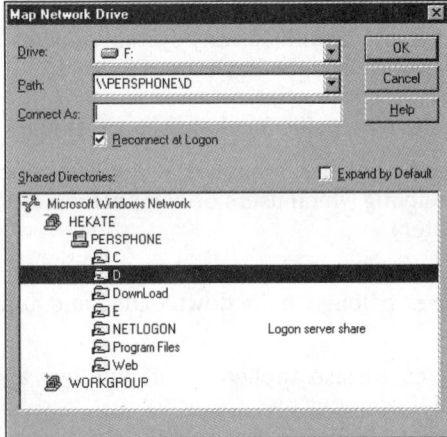

Figure 7-4: The Map Network Drive dialog box

The Drive drop-down list shows the next drive letter available on your computer. You can change this default if you want. In the Path box, enter the path of the drive you want to map, including its computer name, in the following format:

    \\server\share

Here, *server* is the name of the computer and *share* is the name of the disk and folder or directory (this terminology is the official lingo used in the UNC, or Universal Naming Convention, for network computer locations). You can extend the path after share as necessary to identify the proper folder.

If you've previously connected to the folder you're after, you may find it listed in the Path drop-down list. Check the Reconnect at Logon box to map the chosen drive automatically each time you start Windows.

Installing Office Server Extensions

If your organization runs an NT-based Web server, then your users can take advantage of special features for document management and collaboration when you install Office Server Extensions (OSE). These features include the following:

✦ Search and navigation capabilities for documents on OSE-server Web sites

✦ Discussions of Office documents located anywhere on the network—any user on the intranet can participate

✦ Automatic e-mail notification of changes in documents stored on the server

Using the Custom Installation Wizard and Custom Maintenance Wizard

Office XP Office Resource Kit includes two wizards to help you install and maintain your network installation of office. The Custom Installation Wizard (mentioned earlier in this chapter), though available with previous versions of Office, has been improved for Office XP. Among other improvements, it now gives you the ability to remove files at the time of installation (for example, outdated add-ins), set security levels for each application, and customize Outlook in a variety of new ways.

The Custom Maintenance Wizard, meanwhile, lets you maintain and configure Office after it has been installed. Among the options available are the abilities to add or remove files, programs, or components of an installation; to change settings for a given install, and to change Outlook configuration settings—in other words, basically the same capabilities the Custom Installation Wizard gives you at the time of installation.

✦ ✦ ✦

Building Great Documents with Office XP

Although Office consists of several individual applications, they share a lot of features. The focus in this part is on what Office applications have in common. You get a good look at common editing and graphics features; adding active controls to Office documents; and the ways you can move information from one Office document to another. Tricks for effective printing are included, as is a discussion of the various ways Office can protect you — and you can protect yourself — from the heartbreak of document loss or corruption.

The Power of Polished Text

Whether you're creating a simple business letter, a
long, complex report, or a presentation that has to
convince a skeptical audience to support your ideas, your primary tool for communicating your ideas *and* impressing your
audience is almost always your text. You have to choose the
right words, get them into your documents efficiently, spell
them correctly, and then dress them up presentably. That's
what this chapter is about.

Perfect Spelling, Imperfect Grammar

From a writer's perspective, one of the coolest features in
Office is the way Word and PowerPoint unobtrusively but
unmistakably mark misspelled words by underlining them
with little wavy red lines.

On-the-fly spelling checks still aren't available in Excel or
Access. Still, all Office applications do offer spell checking.
And they all share the same dictionaries, so you can be sure
your results are consistent from application to application.

Choose Tools ➪ Spelling to start the process. If Office finds
any spelling errors, you see the Spelling and Grammar dialog
box shown in Figure 8-1 (if you're using Word) or a Spelling
dialog box similar to the one in Figure 8-2 (if you're using
another Office application).

Word's Spelling and Grammar dialog box displays the misspelled word in context, within its entire sentence. You can
accept changes suggested by the spell checker, edit the word
(or for that matter, any part of the sentence), or choose to
ignore the "error," either just this once, or every time it
occurs in the document.

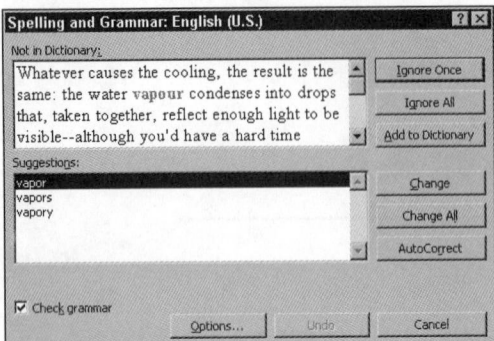

Figure 8-1: Use this dialog box to check spelling and grammar in Word.

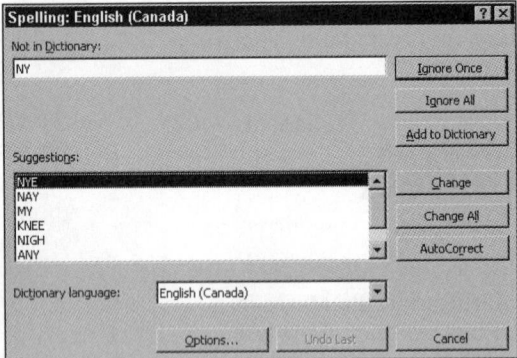

Figure 8-2: The Spelling dialog box, Excel style

What gets checked

Make sure Office checks what you want it to. Keep in mind the following points:

✦ If you select text before you start the spell check, Office checks only the selected text and then asks if you want to check the rest of the document. Take advantage of this technique to avoid being taken to far-off places in the document when all you want to do is check the current word.

✦ In Excel, with nothing selected, almost everything in the current worksheet gets checked: cell values and comments, charts, text boxes, headers and footers, and even buttons. However, formulas and the text that results from them aren't checked, nor are protected worksheets. If you check spelling while you're working in the formula bar, only the formula bar contents get checked.

✦ In Access, you *must* select something — a form, table, or query, or some data within one of those — to check.

✦ In Outlook, the spell checker can be activated only when you're editing an item (a task, journal entry, or contact, for example) and then only when you're working in fields where you enter text in bulk (such as the task description or an e-mail message in a contact item).

Ignoring technicalities

How Ignore and Ignore All work depends on the application:

✦ In Word, choosing Ignore makes the spell checker skip this occurrence of the misspelled word from then on, even if you recheck the document. Choosing Ignore All skips the word everywhere it appears in the document; and again, you won't see it the next time you do a spell check. If you decide you have ignored some words that you really should have corrected, go to the Spelling and Grammar tab of the Tools ⇨ Options dialog box and choose Recheck Document.

✦ In PowerPoint, Ignore and Ignore All are permanent — after you've told the spell checker to ignore a word, you can't get the spell checker to notice that word again in the current document.

✦ In Excel, Ignore and Ignore All affect only the current spell-check operation. The next time you check spelling, the ignored words will again be flagged as misspelled.

✦ In Word and PowerPoint, you can edit your document while the Spelling dialog box is open. If you do, the Ignore button changes to Resume, which you must click to restart the spell check.

Correcting misspellings

If you like one of the suggested spellings, select it and choose Change to make the substitution and move on to the next misspelling.

If you don't like the suggestions, edit the text yourself. Now when you choose Change, Office rechecks your entry (or the whole sentence in Word). If the edited text contains new misspellings, you'll get an appropriate warning. Change All works the same way, but corrects every occurrence of the misspelled word automatically.

Turning off spell checking for specific text

In Word and PowerPoint, you can skip over any text that would otherwise earn poor marks from the spell checker, perhaps because it's full of proper names, technical mumbo jumbo, or foreign language terms. That way, the rest of the document will still be checked.

Making Shutting Off Spell Checking Easy

If you regularly work with goofy spellings, the command to shut off spell checking for specified text deserves a keyboard shortcut or a place on your toolbars. This requires a one-step macro that you can record. Choose Tools ➪ Macro ➪ Record New Macro, assigning the macro to a toolbar or the keyboard. With the macro recorder running, open the Language dialog box and select the option that turns off proofing as described earlier. As soon as you OK the dialog box, stop the macro recorder.

To use the recorded macro, you must first select the text that should not be checked and then click the macro's button or press its keyboard shortcut. In Word, if you want the macro to apply to the current word automatically when no text is selected, create it as follows in the Visual Basic editor (see Part XI):

```
Sub ProofingShutOff()
    If Selection.Type = wdSelectionIP Then
        Selection.Words(1).LanguageID = wdNoProofing ' see below
    Else
        Selection.LanguageID = wdNoProofing
    End If
End Sub
```

To shut off proofing for the paragraph containing the insertion point instead of the current word, substitute the following line for the third line in the preceding macro, the line with the "see below" comment:

```
Selection.Paragraphs(1).Range.LanguageID = wdNoProofing
```

Here's the trick: Select the text and choose Tools ➪ Language ➪ Set Language (in PowerPoint, just Tools ➪ Language) to open the Language dialog box. Then, in Word, check the "Do not check spelling or grammar" box, or, in PowerPoint, select "(no proofing)."

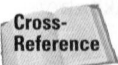
Cross-Reference See "Checking spelling in other languages" later in this chapter for details about the way this dialog box works.

In Word, you can turn off spelling and grammar checking for paragraph styles, too. This way, you can banish the spell checker's red pencil by applying a style.

Managing the spelling dictionaries

Office checks spelling by comparing the words in the document against entries in its dictionaries. These dictionaries are really just lists of correctly spelled words. Office comes with a giant dictionary containing officially approved U.S. English spellings. You can install dictionaries for other languages and variations (such as Canadian English or United Kingdom English), and you can create your own custom spelling dictionaries for special words you use regularly.

Working with custom dictionaries

You probably use lots of words that aren't in the standard spelling dictionary. Maybe you use a lot of specialized jargon in your profession, or maybe you're creating your own slang ("Skatintillating Web page, gladeye!"). If you use such words frequently, you can add them to your custom dictionary to make sure you spell them correctly — or, at least, the same way — each time. You can also obtain prefab custom dictionaries containing common technical terms.

 **Note**   All Office applications use the same custom spelling dictionaries — which you must use Word to activate. Use the Custom Dictionaries dialog box (see Figure 8-3) for this job.

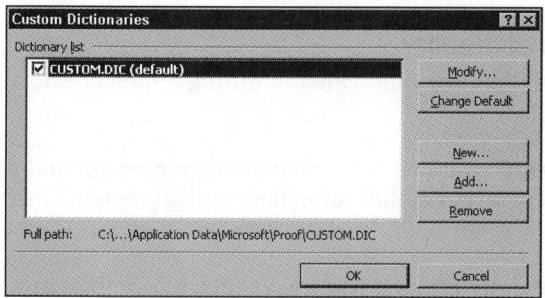

Figure 8-3: The Custom Dictionaries dialog box

If the Spelling and Grammar dialog box is open, choose Options and then Custom Dictionaries to open this dialog box. Otherwise, open the Tools ⇨ Options dialog box, switch to the Spelling and Grammar tab, and choose Custom Dictionaries there.

Activating and deactivating custom dictionaries

Up to ten custom dictionaries can be active simultaneously. Select which custom dictionaries you want activated by checking their boxes in the Custom Dictionaries dialog box.

 **Tip**   If you create documents on a wide range of topics, consider making a separate custom dictionary for each topic. Mix and match the dictionaries depending on which documents you are working on.

Adding and removing custom dictionaries

The Custom Dictionaries dialog box also lets you add more dictionaries to the list (if you already have one somewhere on your hard disk), create new dictionaries from scratch, or retire existing dictionaries from the list. The obvious buttons — Add, New, and Remove — perform these tasks.

When you choose Add, you get a standard Office file dialog box with which you can locate and open the correct dictionary file. By default, dictionary files have the .DIC extension. But that isn't required, so if you're looking for a custom dictionary with a different extension, select All Files at Files of Type.

You can store custom dictionary files anywhere accessible to your system, but they're normally kept with the other proofing tools. On most single-user PCs, that location is `C:\Windows\Application Data\Microsoft\Proof`.

Tip   Because dictionary files are really just ordinary text files, you don't need the New button to create a new custom dictionary. Just use a text editor to create the file, typing a single word on each line (follow each word with a carriage return and line feed pair).

Adding words to a custom dictionary

You can add words to a custom dictionary individually, during a spell check, or in groups, whenever you feel like it.

You must make separate entries in your custom dictionaries for singular and plural forms, as well as for possessives. Also, capitalization makes a difference. The rules work like this:

✦ Enter the word in all-lowercase letters if you want Office to accept it in your documents in lowercase, initial caps, or in all caps.

✦ Enter it with an initial capital letter if Office should accept it capitalized or in all caps.

✦ Enter it with special capitalization (say, with all caps or capitalized like a title, as in `OfficeBible`) if Office should accept it only as written.

Adding words during a spell check

In the Spelling and Grammar dialog box, choose Add to add the highlighted misspelled word to a custom dictionary. In Word and PowerPoint, you can also choose Add from the shortcut menu of a misspelled word marked by the automatic spell checker.

Note   In Word and Outlook, if more than one custom dictionary is active, the new word goes into the dictionary selected at Custom dictionary on the Spelling and Grammar tab of Word's Tools ⇨ Options dialog box. In Excel, Access, and PowerPoint, you can choose which custom dictionary receives added words from a drop-down list in the Spelling dialog box.

Adding or deleting groups of words

From within Office, you have to use Word to freely edit a custom dictionary, whether you want to add a set of new words or remove or edit existing words. In Word's Tools ⇨ Options dialog box, switch to the Spelling tab and choose Custom

Dictionaries. Select the dictionary to which you want to add words and choose Edit. This opens the dictionary in Word. Now you can type your new words, one on each line. You can use the opportunity to delete words you no longer want in the list, or to edit the current entries.

When you finish, save the file without changing its format (remember, it's just an ordinary text file). When you edit a custom dictionary, Word shuts off automatic spell checking, so you have to turn it on yourself after saving the dictionary.

Note If Word isn't already running, a text editor does the trick just as well for editing custom dictionaries. The dictionary files can be edited while you're using Office applications. The Edit button is grayed out and unavailable when you open the Custom Dictionaries dialog box from the Spelling and Grammar dialog box.

Creating an exception dictionary

You can't edit the main spelling dictionary that comes with Office, but you can do the next best thing—you can tell Office to consider specific words as misspelled, even though they're in the main dictionary.

You might want to do this when a word has two or more variant but correct spellings. If you want to be sure that you use one of these spellings consistently, add the spelling you *don't* want to use to the exception dictionary.

For example, say you're writing about winter and relying heavily on the word *grey,* which you prefer to the more modern-looking *gray.* If Office considered both words as properly spelled, you would place *gray* in the exception dictionary. From then on, the spell checker would think *gray* was a misspelling.

As it turns out, in most cases Office has already decided which of the variant spellings should be enforced. (It likes *gray,* not *grey,* for example.) When you want to use the less common variant in this situation, you have to add it to a custom dictionary, in addition to placing the alternative in the exception dictionary.

Another use for the exception dictionary is to catch words that you often misspell correctly, as it were. If you mean *nicer* but often type *ricer* (which passes in Office and is defined by Bookshelf as "a kitchen utensil used for ricing soft foods by extrusion through small holes"), put *ricer* in the exception dictionary.

Okay, enough theory. To create an exception dictionary, use Word or a text editor to list the exception words one per line, just as for custom dictionaries. Save the file as a text file (in Word, choose Text Only at Files of Type in the Save As dialog box). The name and folder location for this file are both critical:

✦ Place it in the same folder as the spell checker and other proofing tools.

✦ The name should be identical to that of the main dictionary for that language, but with the extension .exc. If you're using the U.S. English dictionary, you should call it `mssp2_en.exc`.

Checking spelling in other languages

Chapter 3 discusses the MultiLanguage Pack that comes with some versions of Office.

Using dictionaries for other languages

After you install a dictionary for another language, you can set it up as the default main dictionary for all your Office documents. Alternatively, you can use it to check the spelling of selected text in Word or PowerPoint, or (only in Word) the spelling of specific paragraph styles.

To spell-check a portion of a document using an alternative dictionary, select the text written in that language. If you want to change the default language for all documents in all Office applications, it doesn't matter whether anything is selected. Choose Tools ➪ Language ➪ Set Language to open a dialog box listing all the available languages (in PowerPoint, Tools ➪ Language will do). Figure 8-4 shows the Word version of this box. Pick the language for the selected text and choose OK, or choose Default to change the default main spelling dictionary.

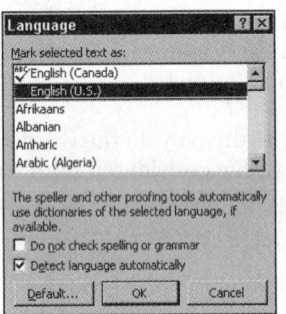

Figure 8-4: Use this dialog box to choose the language for your text, and Office spell checks it with the corresponding dictionary.

Working with language settings in Word

Note that in Word a language setting assigned to selected text works just like other kinds of character formatting except that you can't see it. You can transfer the language setting to other text with the Format Painter. Also, the Reset Character Formatting command (Ctrl+Spacebar) removes it and restores the default language.

Tip   The Language command isn't available in Excel or Access. Instead, use Word or PowerPoint to change the default main dictionary. (In Access, you can also switch to a different dictionary by choosing Options from the Spelling dialog box and picking from the Dictionary list.)

In Word, you don't need the Language dialog box to check spelling in multiple languages. Instead, you can set up paragraph styles for the other languages you use. The spell checker automatically switches to the corresponding dictionaries when it checks these paragraphs. Choose Format ➪ Styles and Formatting, click on New Style, then click Format, and choose Language from the proffered menu.

Word knows whether you have explicitly chosen a language for a given paragraph style. If you have, the style's language setting doesn't change when you set a new default language. But styles that have not been assigned to a specific language always match the default language set in the Language dialog box.

Working with on-the-fly spell checking

In Word and PowerPoint, when the automatic spell checker flags a misspelled word with that wiggly red line, right-clicking the word brings up a spelling shortcut menu. It provides everything you need to fix the problem: a list of suggested corrections and the same Ignore All, Add to Dictionary, and AutoCorrect commands found in the Spelling dialog box.

Tip

In Word, consider enriching the shortcut menu for misspelled words. It lacks the Cut, Copy, Paste, and formatting commands found on the shortcut menu for regular text. Use the techniques for customizing shortcut menus described in Chapter 5 to add any of the missing commands to the Text ⇨ Spelling menu on the Shortcut Menu toolbar.

Spell checking in Word without leaving your document

Thanks to the automatic spell checker, you don't really need the Spelling dialog box in Word. Double-click the icon of a book toward the right end of the status bar to jump to the next word or phrase Word has marked as a spelling or grammatical problem. The Spelling Shortcut menu automatically opens as well.

Turning off automatic spell checking

Why would you want to turn off a tool as useful as automatic spell checking? Perhaps:

✦ You write in a language for which a spelling dictionary isn't available.

✦ Your document is full of technical terms that are marked as misspelled even though they're correct.

✦ You type so fast (or spell so roughly) that the document is riddled with wiggly red underlines, which is tough on your self-esteem.

✦ Your PC is so slow that automatic spell checking slows it to a crawl.

✦ You simply prefer to focus on your ideas, avoid the distraction of wiggly red lines, and check the spelling after you finish the writing.

To shut off the red lines for the current document, or to turn off the whole automatic spell checking system, use the appropriate boxes on the Spelling and Grammar tab (just Spelling in PowerPoint) in the Tools ⇨ Options dialog box. The status of the "Hide spelling errors in this document" box is saved with each document.

Grammar checking in Word

Microsoft has put a lot of effort into improving the Word grammar checker, but the results still leave a lot to be desired. In my experience, it consistently finds errors where there are none, sometimes fails to find glaring mistakes, and (most annoyingly of all) can't tell when you forego "good grammar" to achieve a particular literary effect (not that you could reasonably expect it to, but still it's annoying).

Still, I'm not saying you should shut off the grammar checker altogether. Although it doesn't handle complexities such as subject-verb agreement very well, it can point out some boo-boos, such as too many spaces between words or sentences, with unfailing accuracy. It also does a fair job of pointing out passive constructions, such as the first half of this sentence. (An active construction would be, "It points out passive constructions fairly well.") To customize the grammar checker so that it works within its limits, choose Tools ⇨ Options, select the Spelling and Grammar tab, and then choose Settings to produce the dialog box shown in Figure 8-5.

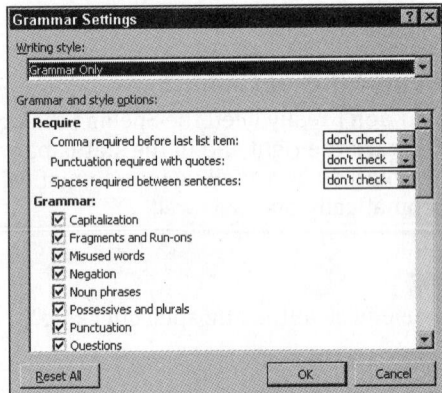

Figure 8-5: Use this dialog box to set options for grammar checking in Word.

In the list at Grammar and Style Options, choose the options that best suit your writing style. You can choose to turn on only grammar rules, or both grammar and style rules, using the Writing style drop-down list at the top of the dialog box.

Working with the Word Thesaurus

Mark Twain said it best in his famous list of rules for writers that require that an author should "Say what he is proposing to say, not merely come near it," and "Use the right word, not its second cousin."

Office offers you some built-in help in achieving these laudable goals in the form of a thesaurus, accessed by choosing Tools ⇨ Language ⇨ Thesaurus (see Figure 8-6). Unfortunately, it's not a great thesaurus — it just doesn't offer a rich enough collection of synonyms. Nevertheless, it's there when you need it, which your dog-eared copy of *Roget's Thesaurus* may not be. Here are some tips for its use:

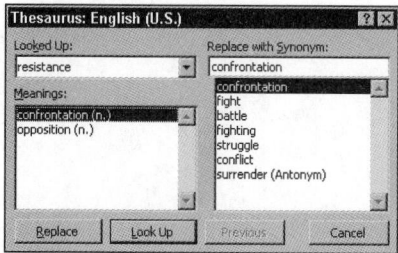

Figure 8-6: The built-in Word thesaurus can help you find (as Mark Twain put it) "the right word, not its second cousin."

✦ You don't have to select a word to look it up in the thesaurus. Word automatically selects the word nearest the insertion point for you.

✦ The keyboard shortcut for the thesaurus is Shift+F7. If you're serious about synonyms, memorize it early. Consider adding the Thesaurus command to the standard Text shortcut menu (see Chapter 5 on customizing shortcut menus) or to the main Tools menu (so you don't have to go through the Language submenu to get to it).

✦ To look up a new word once the Thesaurus dialog box is open, type it into the Replace with Synonym box and then choose Look Up.

✦ To return to a previously looked up word, use the Previous button or select the earlier word from the drop-down list at Looked Up.

✦ To see if the listed synonyms for a suggested synonym for the word you first looked up suits your purposes better, highlight the word in the Replace with Synonym list and then click Look Up.

Using AutoCorrect

AutoCorrect is an umbrella term covering various automatic changes Office can make as you type. It's available in all the Office applications except Outlook. Figure 8-7 shows the AutoCorrect dialog box where you can toggle on or off the various settings. (You can access this dialog box by selecting Tools ⇨ AutoCorrect.) Most of the lower half of the AutoCorrect dialog box is occupied by the *AutoCorrect list*. When you type an entry from the left column into your document, Office substitutes the corresponding entry from the right column.

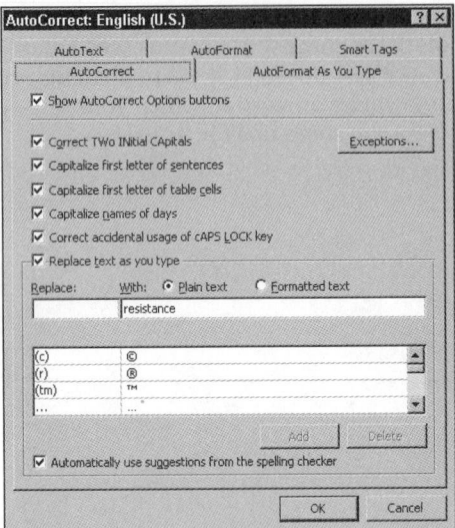

Figure 8-7: Set AutoCorrect options in this dialog box.

AutoCorrect jumps into action the moment you complete a word by typing a space, by typing a punctuation mark, or by pressing Enter. It checks each word against its list, instantly making any indicated substitution. AutoCorrect has two main functions: correcting spelling and usage errors automatically and expanding little shorthand codes (I'll refer to them as abbreviations) into lengthy, complete words or phrases or into special symbols. The default list corrects many common errors such as *adn* for *and*, *isn;t* for *isn't*, *their is* for *there is*, and even *blase* for *blasé*.

Tip   AutoCorrect entries can contain spaces (in other words, AutoCorrect recognizes and replaces more than one word), and in Word, paragraph marks.

To add a new item to the AutoCorrect list, type the misspelling or the abbreviation in the Replace box. The correct spelling—or the word, phrase, or symbol to be substituted for the abbreviation—goes in the With box. If your document already contains the text that belongs in the With box, select it before you open the AutoCorrect dialog box and Office will automatically place it in the With box for you.

Note   Word has several other AutoCorrect-like capabilities not found in the other Office applications, including the ability to use the suggestions of the spell checker to automatically correct misspelled words as soon as you type them (the change is made only if the software is fairly certain that it knows which word you really intended). You can turn this option on or off with the checkbox below the AutoCorrect list.

Cross-Reference   The rest of the special features in Word come under the heading of AutoFormat As You Type (covered in Chapter 17).

Adding special characters to AutoCorrect entries

AutoCorrect is one good way to add special characters that aren't on the keyboard to your documents — but how do you get those special characters into an AutoCorrect item? The easiest way is with the following Word command: Insert ➪ Symbol dialog box (see Figure 8-8).

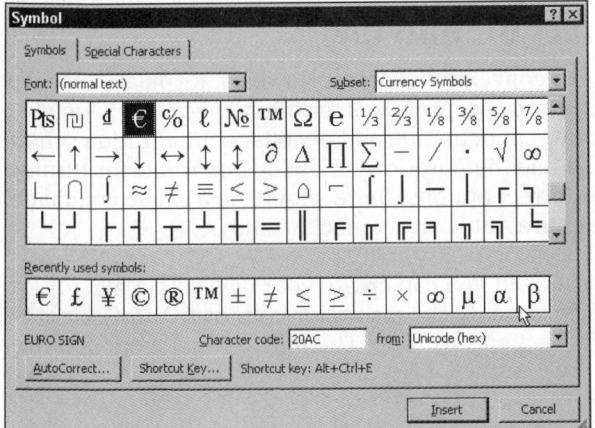

Figure 8-8: The Symbol dialog box in Word

New Feature — This dialog box has been enhanced in Office XP to make the symbols larger and therefore easier to choose from.)

Select the character for which you want to create an AutoCorrect entry. Then choose AutoCorrect to display the AutoCorrect dialog box, with the selected symbol already entered at With. (Note that by default, the Formatted text button is selected.)

This is the way to go if you're creating an AutoCorrect entry for a symbol available only in a special symbol font such as Wingdings. However, if you're creating an AutoCorrect entry for a symbol found in ordinary text fonts, select the Plain Text button in the AutoCorrect dialog box. The entry works throughout Office.

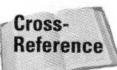

Cross-Reference — See Chapter 17 for further discussion of using formatted text versus plain text for AutoCorrect entries.

If you're creating an AutoCorrect entry that contains more than one symbol, this technique won't work — but you have several alternatives. In Word, you can enter special characters directly into the With field of the AutoCorrect dialog box using the same keyboard shortcuts available in your documents. This includes shortcuts

AutoCorrect works in text boxes, but not in WordArt objects. In Excel, AutoCorrect works on any text you enter into cells, cell comments, embedded charts, text boxes, buttons, and headers and footers. It does not make its substitutions in protected worksheets, formulas, or text that results from a formula.

Expanding abbreviations with AutoCorrect

AutoCorrect does more than correct mistakes in your typing. You can also use it to convert abbreviations into complete words or into symbols that would be hard to enter otherwise.

Suppose, for instance, you work for the Department of Youth, Culture, and Recreation. That takes a lot of typing, which you can avoid by creating an AutoCorrect entry that replaces a shortcut such as *dycr* with the full name. The next time you type *dycr* and a space, Office expands the entry.

Sharing AutoCorrect entries between Office applications

All the Office applications that support AutoCorrect share the same AutoCorrect list. Changes you make to the list in one application immediately (usually) show up in the other programs' AutoCorrect dialog box.

Note — Remember, only Word allows AutoCorrect entries containing formatted text, which it stores in the Normal template. Such entries don't show up in the other programs' AutoCorrect lists.

Caution — In Excel, PowerPoint, or Access, be sure you don't define AutoCorrect entries that match entries containing formatted text in Word. You won't see Word's formatted-text entries on the AutoCorrect list in the other programs, and you won't be warned when you define new entries with matching abbreviations. If you do, the formatted-text entry from the Word list will be replaced.

Using the default AutoCorrect symbol substitutions

The AutoCorrect list that comes with Office includes shorthand codes for symbols you need all the time: trademark symbols, arrows, and the ellipsis. (A true ellipsis is a special one-character mark, not three consecutive periods.) Codes for not-so-useful little faces are provided as well. You can survey these symbol substitutions yourself by selecting Tools ➪ AutoCorrect and scrolling through the AutoCorrect list.

Undoing unwanted AutoCorrect and AutoFormat "corrections"

There's a quick way to reverse any change made by AutoCorrect (or by AutoFormat As You Type): press Ctrl+Z (the keyboard shortcut for the Undo command) as soon as Office has made the substitution. (You can use the Undo button or Edit ➪ Undo if you prefer.) If you meant to type some unusual spelling that happens to be on the AutoCorrect list, Undo gives you back the intentional error (if that's not an oxy-moron) after AutoCorrect has fixed it. Once you've really gotten this concept (that any AutoCorrect or AutoFormat-As-You-Type change can be undone), you'll want to leave most of the AutoCorrect and AutoFormat features on all the time.

Turning off automatic exceptions

If you check the appropriate boxes in the AutoCorrect dialog box, AutoCorrect automatically capitalizes the first word of every sentence and ensures that only one consecutive letter at the beginning of any word is capitalized. AutoCorrect lets you specify exceptions to its rules, because these features don't always give you the results you want. For example, the period that ends an abbreviation shouldn't be seen as the end of a sentence, so an AutoCorrect exception keeps Office from capi-talizing the next word automatically. To add or modify the exception list, click the Exceptions button on the AutoCorrect dialog box.

In Word, if you've turned on automatic corrections via the spell checker, you can tell AutoCorrect to allow specified misspellings to remain without automatic correc-tion. Use the Other Corrections tab of the AutoCorrect Exceptions dialog box to enter words to leave uncorrected. Be careful, because the words in this list are ignored altogether by the spell checker.

Caution   By default, AutoCorrect automatically adds new exceptions based on how you edit your text. Its intentions are good, but it can't tell whether you really typed an abbreviation or decided not to capitalize the next word for some other reason. My advice: Add exceptions manually and turn off the automatic additions feature. To do this, choose Tools ➪ AutoCorrect Options and then click the Exceptions button in the AutoCorrect dialog box. Uncheck the Automatically Add Words to List box in both the First letter and INitial CAps tabs (and in Word, the Other Corrections tab). These are independent settings.

Adding words to the AutoCorrect list during a spelling check

If you repeatedly misspell the same word in the same way, it makes sense to add your habitual boo-boo to the AutoCorrect list. You can do this during a spelling check. Here are two methods:

✦ Using the Spelling and Grammar dialog box, select the correct spelling from the suggestions Word offers, or type it in. Then click the AutoCorrect button.

✦ If you're using automatic spell checking in Word, the shortcut menu that appears when you right-click a misspelled word (one with a wavy red line under it) offers an AutoCorrect choice. Select this, and then select the correct spelling from the suggestions.

Turning AutoCorrect off and on

AutoCorrect is great for most conventional prose. However, if you also use Word to prepare technical manuals, computer programs, or other specialized documents, it can get in the way, "correcting" punctuation and peculiar capitalization schemes when you don't want it to. While the AutoCorrect dialog box is fine for turning on and off the individual AutoCorrect options, there should be a single command that shuts down or revives the entire AutoCorrect mechanism.

Alas, no such command exists, but you can create your own with a macro. Type in the following code. You can customize the macro for your own AutoCorrect needs by changing some of the False items to True. The macro won't work in other Office programs.

```
Sub AutoCorrectShutOff()
    With Autocorrect
        .CorrectInitialCaps = False
        .CorrectSentenceCaps = False
        .CorrectDays = False
        .CorrectCapsLock = False
        .ReplaceText = False
    End With
    With Options
        .AutoFormatAsYouTypeApplyHeadings = False
        .AutoFormatAsYouTypeApplyBorders = False
        .AutoFormatAsYouTypeApplyBulletedLists = False
        .AutoFormatAsYouTypeApplyNumberedLists = False
        .AutoFormatAsYouTypeApplyTables = False
        .AutoFormatAsYouTypeReplaceQuotes = False
        .AutoFormatAsYouTypeReplaceSymbols = False
        .AutoFormatAsYouTypeReplaceOrdinals = False
        .AutoFormatAsYouTypeReplaceFractions = False
        .AutoFormatAsYouTypeReplacePlainTextEmphasis _
            = False
        .AutoFormatAsYouTypeReplaceHyperlinks = False
        .AutoFormatAsYouTypeFormatListItemBeginning = False
        .AutoFormatAsYouTypeDefineStyles = False
    End With
End Sub
```

you have defined yourself. In any application, you can also enter symbol characters in the AutoCorrect dialog box by code number. With Num Lock on, hold down Alt and type the character's four-digit ANSI code as shown in Table 8-2 later in this chapter.

In Word, yet another method (and probably the easiest) is to copy the symbols from a document. Enter the text that AutoCorrect will insert in place of what you actually type in your document, using the Insert Symbol command to place the special characters. Select the text you just entered and choose Tools ➪ AutoCorrect Options. The replacement text will appear in the With field automatically. You can now type in the text to be replaced in the Replace field. If you want to include special symbols in the Replace field, you can do this by typing the text in the document, cutting or copying it to the clipboard, and then pasting it into the field.

Automatic dashes in all Office applications

Consider adding AutoCorrect entries for em and en dashes. True, Word's AutoFormat As You Type converts pairs of hyphens into em or en dashes automatically. But aside from the fact that this feature isn't available in the other Office apps, it has other problems.

AutoFormat's dash substitutions appear only if you type hyphens between two words and then only if you type no more than one space between the words. In fact, they don't appear until after you finish the second word, which can be unnerving. And AutoFormat sometimes refuses to convert the two hyphens at all, if you add them after the fact. A separate problem is that you always get spaces surrounding the en dash. (In my copy of the *Chicago Manual of Style*, en dashes are typeset with no surrounding spaces.)

Word already provides keyboard shortcuts for em and en dashes: Alt+Ctrl+– and Ctrl+–, respectively (both of these shortcuts require the dash or minus sign key on the numeric keypad, not the one in the top row of typewriter keys next to 0). But if you want the convenience of entering them via hyphens, set up the following AutoCorrect entries:

Replace	With
-- (two hyphens)	— (em dash)
—- (em dash+hyphen)	– (en dash)

Note that with these two entries active, you actually type three consecutive hyphens to produce an en dash. AutoCorrect converts the first two hyphens into an em dash. When you type the third hyphen, it converts the whole thing into the en dash.

Using Smart Tags

Among the new features in Office XP are Smart Tags. Office XP can recognize certain kinds of data in your document — for instance, names of people or addresses — and will flag them with a little icon, which in turn opens up a shortcut menu offering you a variety of actions you can perform with that data.

You can fine-tune these Smart Tags in the AutoCorrect dialog box by clicking on the Smart Tags tab, but that's not what I'm focusing on here. Rather, I want to point out that changes made by AutoCorrect are among the types of data Office recognizes and assigns Smart Tags. If you point at a symbol AutoCorrect has inserted — say, © for (c) — you'll see a small blue horizontal line underneath it. Point at that line, and an icon that looks like a blue line with a lightning bolt coming from it will appear, which in turn opens a shortcut menu offering you various AutoCorrect options, including change back to whatever you typed originally and stop automatically correcting that particular usage; it also offers you a link to the main AutoCorrect dialog box.

Understanding Fonts and Typography

Much of the allure of personal computing within the small office stems from its power to create documents that look as though they were produced with the resources of an entire graphics and printing department behind them. That's why it pays to acquaint yourself with the fundamentals of font management, typography, and document design.

Caution   Maybe this is obvious, but it's worth stating anyway: no matter how professional your document may be in appearance, if its full of bad writing, sloppy thinking, misspelled words, and improper grammar, it's not going to help your cause; quite the opposite.

Font mania

Are you frustrated by fonts? You're not alone. Libraries of hundreds of high-quality fonts typesetters once could hardly have imagined are now within the reach of everyone. But keeping track of all those fonts, finding the one that looks right for your document, installing it easily, and accessing its special symbols conveniently are the problems that come along with such an embarrassment of riches.

Managing fonts

Anyone who accumulates more than about 50 fonts needs a system for managing them — and this means you, because with Windows and Office alone you already own about 200 fonts. If you have too many fonts installed at the same time, your Font menu becomes overwhelmingly long, and the performance of your whole system suffers.

The simplest font management system is to simply throw most of them away. Most people aren't graphic designers, and fiddling around with fonts is a great way to waste time while showing off your amateur standing. Choose one font for body text, one font for headings, and no more than five other fonts for spice. Of course, you must also keep the standard Windows fonts: Arial, Times New Roman, Courier New, Symbol, and Marlett, as well as Tahoma and other fonts that Outlook and Office require.

If you're like me, though, you probably love fonts too much to part with a single one. In that case, consider getting some font management software. What you need is a utility that can keep track of your fonts in named groups rather than as individual files, installing and removing these groups as required by your active documents. It will also show you samples of the fonts on-screen before you install them and print sample pages. High-quality shareware font managers abound: do some online research and find the one that suits you the best.

Tip   One good place to look for font managers is ZDNet downloads, at www.zdnet.com/downloads. Search for "font managers" and you'll see a long list of programs, rated from no stars to five stars by the ZDNet staff and by, as PBS might put it, "users like you."

Exploring special characters

Windows fonts offer special characters for every imaginable occasion, and then some. Aside from the ordinary letters, numbers, and punctuation marks found on the keyboard, you can find professional typographic marks; foreign language letters; symbols used in business, math, and science; and loads of hard-to-classify ornaments, dingbats, and doohickeys.

Tables 8-1 and 8-2 list some of the most useful such characters found in standard text fonts and the Symbol font that comes with Windows.

Table 8-1
Special Symbol Characters by Category

Symbol Category	Symbol (* = key to type)	Character Code (if available)	Word Keyboard Shortcut

If a symbol is available only in a special font, the font name appears in parentheses. A symbol marked with an asterisk (*) can be entered by typing the indicated key rather than a character code.

Dashes

	— (em dash)	0151	Alt+Ctrl+— (on numeric keypad)
	– (en dash)	0150	Ctrl+— (on numeric keypad)
	- (nonbreaking hyphen)		Ctrl+_
	(optional hyphen)	Ctrl+ -	

Spaces

	(nonbreaking space)	Ctrl+Shift+Space	
	em space (space the width of the letter m)		By default, em and en spaces are only available via the Insert Symbol command
	-en space (space the width of the letter n)		

Business-Related Symbols

	©	0169	Alt+Ctrl+C
	®	0174	Alt+Ctrl+R
	™	0153	Alt+Ctrl+T
	¢	0162	Ctrl+/,C
	£	0163	
	¤	0164	
	€	0128	Alt+Ctrl+E
	¥	0165	

Symbol Category	Symbol (* = key to type)	Character Code (if available)	Word Keyboard Shortcut

If a symbol is available only in a special font, the font name appears in parentheses.
A symbol marked with an asterisk (*) can be entered by typing the indicated key rather than a character code.

Typographical Marks

Symbol Category	Symbol (* = key to type)	Character Code (if available)	Word Keyboard Shortcut
	… (ellipsis character)	0133	
	¶ (paragraph mark)	0182	
	§ (section mark)	0167	
	• (bullet character)	0149	
	' (open single quotation mark)	0145	
	' (close single quotation mark)	0146	
	" (open double quotation mark)	0147	
	" (close double quotation mark)	0148	
	†	0134	
	‡	0135	

Ligatures (available in expert fonts only)

	ff	V *	
	fi	W *	
	fl	X *	
	ffi	Y *	
	ffl	Z *	

Continued

Table 8-1 (continued)

Symbol Category	Symbol (* = key to type)	Character Code (if available)	Word Keyboard Shortcut

If a symbol is available only in a special font, the font name appears in parentheses. A symbol marked with an asterisk (*) can be entered by typing the indicated key rather than a character code.

Math and Science

Symbol Category	Symbol (* = key to type)	Character Code (if available)	Word Keyboard Shortcut
	× (multiplication sign)	0215	
	÷	0247	
	° (degree symbol)	0176	
	±	0177	
	≤	0163 (Symbol font)	
	≥	0179 (Symbol font)	
	≠	0185 (Symbol font)	
	°	0186	
	¹	0185	
	²	0178	
	³	0179	
	π	p (Symbol font) *	
	∞	0165 (Symbol font)	

Fractions

	¼	0188 (standard or expert fonts)	
	½	0189 (standard or expert fonts)	
	¾	0190 (standard or expert fonts)	
	⅛	0192 (expert fonts only)	
	⅜	0193 (expert fonts only)	
	⅝	0194 (expert fonts only)	

If a symbol is available only in a special font, the font name appears in parentheses.
A symbol marked with an asterisk (*) can be entered by typing the indicated key rather than a character code.

Symbol Category	Symbol (* = key to type)	Character Code (if available)	Word Keyboard Shortcut
Fractions	⅞	0195 (expert fonts only)	
	⅓	0196 (expert fonts only)	
	⅔	0197 (expert fonts only)	
Arrow Characters (available in Symbol font only)	↕	0171	
	↓	0172	
	←	0173	
	↑	0174	
	⇕	0219	
	⇓	0220	
	⇐	0221	
	⇑	0222	
	⇒	0223	

Table 8-2
Non-Keyboard Characters (Normal Text)

Symbol	Character Code	Word Keyboard Shortcut (if available)
'	0130	
ƒ	0131	
"	0132	
...	0133	
†	0134	
‡	0135	
^	0136	Ctrl+^, space
‰	0137	
ˇS	0138	Alt+Ctrl+^, S
‹	0139	
Œ	0140	Ctrl+&, O
'	0145	Ctrl+`, `
'	0146	Ctrl+', '
"	0147	Ctrl+`, "
"	0148	Ctrl+', "
•	0149	
–	0150	Ctrl+– (on the numeric keypad)
—	0151	Alt+Ctrl+– (on the numeric keypad)
~	0152	
™	0153	Alt+Ctrl+T
ˇs	0154	Alt+Ctrl+^, s
›	0155	
œ	0156	Ctrl+&, o
Ÿ	0159	Ctrl+:, Y
¡	0161	Alt+Ctrl+!
¢	0162	Ctrl+/, c
£	0163	
¤	0164	
¥	0165	

Symbol	Code Number	Word Keyboard Shortcut (if available)
¦	0166	
§	0167	
¨	0168	Ctrl+:, space
©	0169	Alt+Ctrl+C
ª	0170	
¬	0172	
-	0173	
®	0174	Alt+Ctrl+R
¯	0175	
°	0176	Ctrl+@, space
±	0177	
2	0178	
3	0179	
´	0180	Ctrl+', space
μ	0181	
¶	0182	
·	0183	
¸	0184	Ctrl+,, space
1	0185	
º	0186	
»	0187	Ctrl+`, >
1/4	0188	
1/2	0189	
3/4	0190	
¿	0191	Alt+Ctrl+?
À	0192	Ctrl+`, A
Á	0193	Ctrl+', A
Â	0194	Ctrl+^, A
Ã	0195	Ctrl+~, A

Continued

Table 8-2 *(continued)*

Symbol	Code Number	Word Keyboard Shortcut (if available)
Ä	0196	Ctrl+:, A
Å	0197	Ctrl+@, A
Æ	0198	Ctrl+&, A
Ç	0199	Ctrl+,, C
È	0200	Ctrl+`, E
É	0201	Ctrl+', E
Ê	0202	Ctrl+^, E
Ë	0203	Ctrl+:, E
Ì	0204	Ctrl+`, I
Í	0205	Ctrl+', I
Î	0206	Ctrl+^, I
Ï	0207	Ctrl+:,
Ð	0208	Ctrl+', D
Ñ	0209	Ctrl+~, N
Ò	0210	Ctrl+`, O
Ó	0211	Ctrl+', O
Ô	0212	Ctrl+^, O
Õ	0213	Ctrl+~, O
Ö	0214	Ctrl+:, O
.	0215	
Ø	0216	Ctrl+/, O
Ù	0217	Ctrl+`, U
Ú	0218	Ctrl+', U
Û	0219	Ctrl+^, U
Ü	0220	Ctrl+:, U
'Y	0221	Ctrl+', Y
Þ	0222	
ß	0223	Ctrl+&, S
à	0224	Ctrl+`, a

Symbol	Code Number	Word Keyboard Shortcut (if available)
á	0225	Ctrl+', a
â	0226	Ctrl+^, a
ã	0227	Ctrl+~, a
ä	0228	Ctrl+:, a
å	0229	Ctrl+@, a
æ	0230	Ctrl+&, a
ç	0231	Ctrl+,, c
è	0232	Ctrl+`, e
é	0233	Ctrl+', e
ê	0234	Ctrl+^, e
ë	0235	Ctrl+:, e
ì	0236	Ctrl+`, I
í	0237	Ctrl+', i
î	0238	Ctrl+^, i
ï	0239	Ctrl+:, I
f	0240	Ctrl+', d
ñ	0241	Ctrl+~, n
ò	0242	Ctrl+`, o
ó	0243	Ctrl+', o
ô	0244	Ctrl+^, o
õ	0245	Ctrl+~, o
ö	0246	Ctrl+:, o
÷	0247	
Ø	0248	Ctrl+/, o
ù	0249	Ctrl+`, u
ú	0250	Ctrl+', u
û	0251	Ctrl+^, u
ü	0252	Ctrl+:, u
'y	0253	Ctrl+', y
þ	0254	
ÿ	0255	Ctrl+:, y

Table 8-3
Techniques for Inserting Special Characters

Method	Pros	Cons	Comments/Tips
Choose Insert ➪ Symbol and select the desired character from the chart in the Symbol dialog box (works in Word and PowerPoint).	Requires no additional software. In Word, you can select symbol characters from a list of descriptions (use the Special Characters tab of the Symbol dialog box), as well as from a chart. Lets you insert characters from different fonts in the same pass.	Not available in Excel, Access, or Outlook. Although you can insert as many characters as you like, the window is so big that it usually covers the insertion point so you can't see that you've actually inserted the correct characters in the correct order. Characters may not show up in files exported to other formats.	
Use the Character Map accessory that comes with Windows (Start ➪ Accessories ➪ Character Map).	Lets you select multiple characters before inserting them, enabling you to edit the sequence before pasting it into your document. Works with all Office (and Windows) applications.	Hard to use because the characters in the chart are *tiny*.	You can only insert characters from one font at a time.
Use AutoCorrect.	Super fast — just type an abbreviation and the desired symbol appears in your document. Works in all the Office applications except Outlook.	You have to set up a separate AutoCorrect abbreviation for each special symbol. You also have to remember all those abbreviations. Works only in Office.	The fastest way to set up an AutoCorrect entry for a special symbol is via Word's Insert ➪ Symbol command.

Method	Pros	Cons	Comments/Tips
Use a Windows utility that works like AutoCorrect.	Your abbreviations will work in all Windows applications. You can organize the entries by category, not just in alphabetical order.	These utilities aren't as sophisticated as AutoCorrect: They can't store formatted text and they don't recognize punctuation as the end of an entry (if a special character falls at the end of a sentence or before a comma, you have to hit the Spacebar to expand the abbreviation, and then go back and type in the punctuation).	Shareware programs enable you to set up AutoCorrect-like abbreviations that convert automatically into expanded text passages. Check out ShortKeys.
Create a keyboard shortcut or toolbar button for each	Keyboard shortcuts are as fast symbol you use frequently. as AutoCorrect. Toolbar buttons (on an open toolbar) give you immediate visual access to the symbol.	Setting up a keyboard shortcut or toolbar button for a symbol character requires a macro or VBA programming, except in Word. Keyboard shortcuts may be harder to remember than AutoCorrect abbreviations.	
Type in the keycode for the character (see Comments/Tips).	Fast and reliable, if you know the codes (for some people, memorizing a numeric sequence is no worse than memorizing an AutoCorrect abbreviation).	Typing numeric codes may put you off or make you feel like a computer nerd. No visual guidance.	Here's the technique: Hold down Alt while typing the four-digit ANSI code on the numeric keypad (NumLock must be on). When you release Alt, the corresponding character appears in your document in the font currently active at the insertion point. If necessary, select the character and change its font.

Inserting special characters

It sometimes seems as if a glass wall stands between you and all those special characters—you can look, but you can't use. Actually, the problem is one of inconvenience. Nonkeyboard symbols often don't get used because the common techniques for accessing them are too much bother.

To tell the truth, there is no perfect solution. But Table 8-3 lays out a variety of ways to access special characters, and their advantages and drawbacks.

Font aesthetics

Once you've mastered the mechanics of fonts, you still have to know how to use your fonts artistically. Here are a few suggestions.

Keeping the family together

Fonts come in families. In addition to the mama font (the standard version of the font, which may be called regular, roman, or book), there's a papa font (the bold version), two babies (italic and bold italic versions), and sometimes various aunts, uncles, and cousins (light, heavy, condensed, and expanded versions are common). The characters belonging to each of these family members were designed separately for best appearance. Although Windows can thicken any TrueType font to make it bold or slant it for *faux* italics, the results look second-rate. You need a separate font file—regular, bold, italic, and bold italic—for every member of a font family.

Using expert font sets

To lend a professionally typeset look to your documents, invest in a font set that includes an *expert set*. The fonts in an expert set are variations on the regular versions of the same family with special characters. Adobe is the main purveyor of expert sets, but several other font design companies also sell them.

Among the various types of characters included in expert sets, the following are the most important:

- ✦ **Ligatures:** Certain letter combinations beginning with lowercase *f* are set by typesetters as special single ligature characters, not a series of separate letters. Ligatures prevent unsightly clashes between the *f* (its curved top and the bar through its middle) and the character that follows.

- ✦ **Small caps:** When setting a word in all capitals, a typesetter avoids overwhelming the surrounding text by using small uppercase letters specially designed for this role. Word can convert ordinary capital letters into small caps via a checkbox in the Format ⇨ Font dialog box, but the results look wrongly proportioned to the practiced eye. Expert sets include honest-to-goodness small uppercase letters designed to harmonize with mixed-case text of the same font size.

- ✦ **"Old-style" numerals:** In most Windows fonts, the numerals are designed so that they'll line up properly in tables and spreadsheets. But they're harder to read than mixed-case letters.

Unlike the proportionally spaced characters of the alphabet, standard numerals are monospaced—each numeral occupies the same amount of space horizontally, along the line of text. And like uppercase letters, they're monotonously tall and lack *descenders*, the portions of letters as in *g* or *q* that fall below the baseline on which most letters sit. The old-style numerals in expert sets are analogous to lowercase letters: Their heights and widths vary from character to character, making them easier to distinguish and giving your work a distinguished look.

The Top Ten Font and Layout Rules

Consider the following formatting and font suggestions as you create your documents:

1. Use a maximum of three fonts per document, not counting italic and bold variations—and try to get by with two. Settle on one font for the body text, one font for the headings and fine print, and optionally, a third for the main title or banner headline.

2. Select simple fonts with clean lines for the body text and headings. Reserve those fancy font designs (*display fonts*) for judicious use in the title or headline, selecting the one that best evokes the right mood in your reader.

3. Match the type size to the importance of your message, but above all, size the text so that it's easy to read. It should be big enough so that the reader doesn't have to squint, but not so large as to look crowded. Make the headings noticeably larger than the body text. You can set your two main fonts in a few different sizes in distinct areas of the document, but again, go easy on the variety.

4. In body text, *use ordinary italics for emphasis*—avoid underlining or using ALL CAPITALS. Use bold cautiously in body text, because it can draw too much attention. But headings often look best in bold.

5. Except in the most formal of publications, left-align body text rather than fully justifying it. This goes double for layouts that use columns or narrow text boxes.

6. Be generous with white (empty) space on the page. If space is limited, cut the text to preserve breathing room; otherwise, you'll lose potential readers.

7. Except in fiction, use lots of subheadings to break up the visual monotony.

8. Be sure that each subhead is visually linked with the text that follows. Leave more space above the subhead than below. Ruling lines are best placed *above* a subhead, setting the new section off from the text above.

9. Strive for consistent spacing and alignment between the page elements. Spacing variations and misalignments irritate the reader.

10. Use restraint with visual elements such as ruling lines and borders, rotated text, and 3D effects. A little goes a very long way.

11. Try breaking these rules.

Sources for fonts

If you're in the market for top-quality and distinctive fonts, you'll want to browse the catalogs of the major digital type foundries, including Adobe, Bitstream, and Monotype. But don't overlook the offerings of smaller type-design outfits, where you can find some of the most elegant, original, and offbeat fonts. Try the following sources:

✦ **Emigre, Inc.:** www.emigre.com

✦ **Will Harris Fontomat:** www.will-harris.com/store.htm

✦ **Letter Perfect:** www.letterspace.com

✦ **U-Design Type Foundry:** www.gs1.com/UTF/UTF.html

✦ **Vitatype:** www.primenet.com/~jeffib/index.htm

Additionally, at www.microsoft.com/typography/links/ the Microsoft Web page has links to tons of font designers.

Cross-Reference   Font size is measured in points. See Chapter 9 for a discussion of measurement units in Office.

Using Advanced Formatting

In addition to using fonts wisely in your efforts to polish your text, you should make full use of the other formatting options available to you. Most of the commonly used text formatting commands — the commands to make text bold or italic, for instance — are, as you would expect, available from the Formatting toolbar in all Office applications.

Some of the more complex formatting commands, however, must be accessed through dialog boxes — and as you would also expect, the most complete set of such commands is available through Office's word processing application, Word.

First, take a look at Word's Font dialog box, accessed by choosing Format ⇨ Font (see Figure 8-9). (PowerPoint offers a Font dialog box, too, but it doesn't have as many options as Word's.)

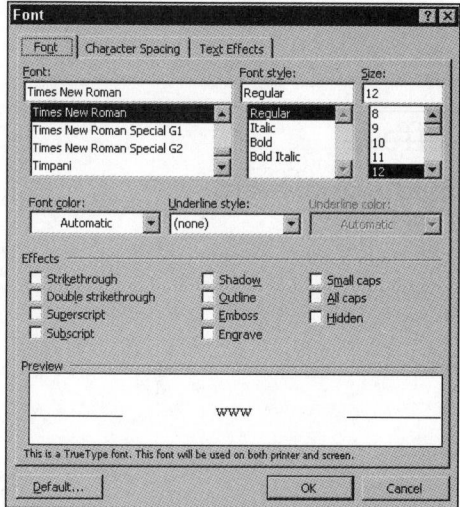

Figure 8-9: The Font dialog box lets you take advantage of all of Word's character formatting options.

The Font dialog box has three tabs, each of which controls a different aspect of character formatting.

Font tab

Under the Font tab, you can access most of the character formatting options available on the Formatting toolbar, sometimes with enhancements. For example, not only can you choose to underline selected text, but you can also choose what type of underlining you want to use (including Single, Words Only, Double, or Dotted). You can also choose to use a different color for underlining than you do for text.

You also have fancier formatting options, called Effects, which include Strikethrough, Double strikethrough, Superscript, Subscript, Shadow, Outline, Emboss, Engrave, Small caps, All caps, and Hidden. These effects are illustrated in Figure 8-10; you can also see them as you apply them in the Preview window at the bottom of the Font dialog box.

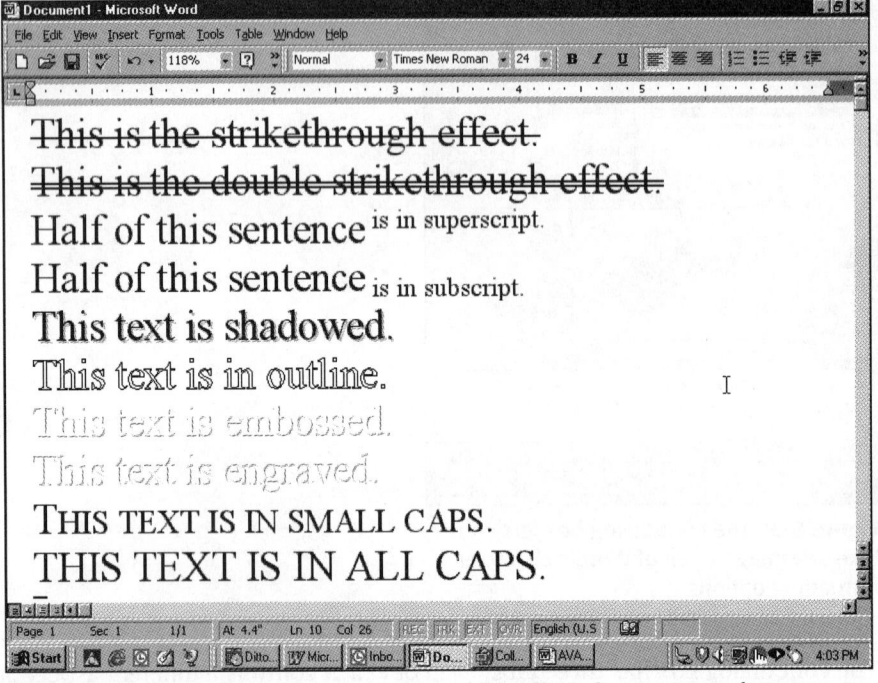

Figure 8-10: Word offers numerous eye-catching effects for you to apply to your text.

Character Spacing tab

The Character Spacing tab offers a new set of controls (see Figure 8-11):

✦ **Scale** adjusts the width of the selected text without affecting its point size. If you adjust this upward, the letters look fat and squat; if you adjust it downward, the letters look tall and skinny. The Preview window at the bottom of the dialog box shows you what your text will look like.

✦ **Spacing** adjusts the amount of space between letters. You select whether you want the text spacing Normal, Expanded, or Condensed; and then you specify the amount of space (in points) you want to add or subtract from between letters. Again, use the Preview window to get just the effect you want.

✦ **Position** adjusts the location of the selected text relative to the normal baseline for text. As with spacing, you select whether you want the text Normal, Raised, or Lowered; and then you specify how many points you want to raise or lower the text above or below the baseline.

✦ **Kerning** adjusts the spacing between certain letters to make text as legible and attractive as possible. If you select the Kerning checkbox, Word will automatically adjust kerning in TrueType or other scalable fonts whenever they're equal to or larger than the size you specify.

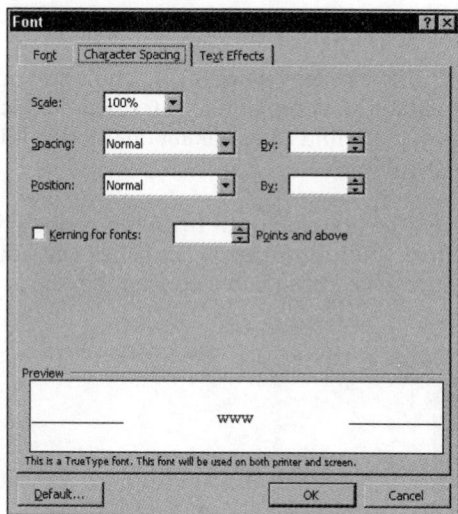

Figure 8-11: Fine-tune your characters with these controls.

Figure 8-12 demonstrates some of these formatting options.

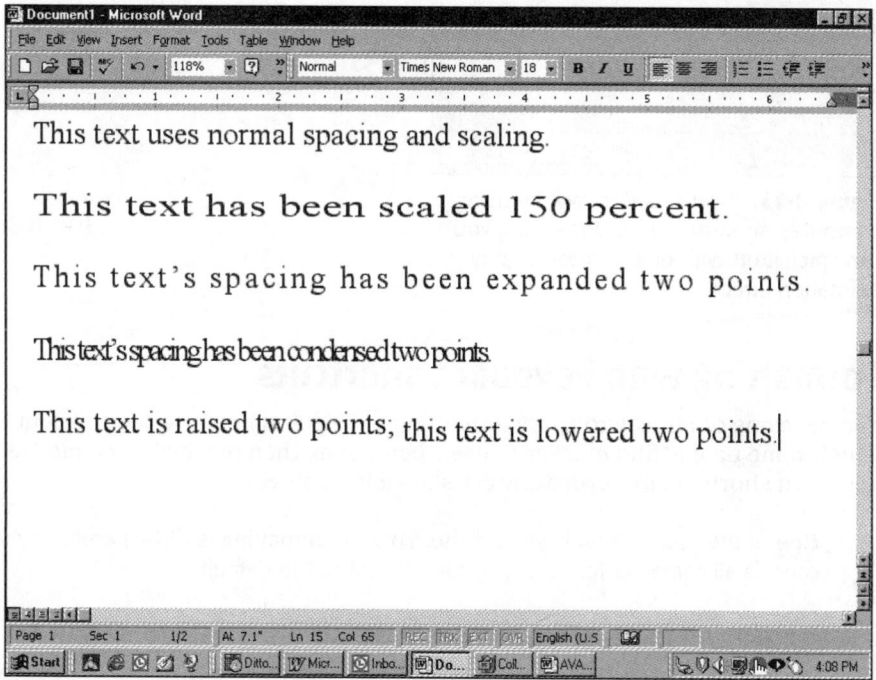

Figure 8-12: Character spacing can be used to achieve a number of interesting effects.

Text Effects tab

The third tab in the Font dialog box, Text Effects (see Figure 8-13), won't do you much good if you're preparing a document for printing, but if your document is going to be read on other computers, you might find that making characters blink, shimmer, or sparkle really makes them stand out.

To apply any of the text effects, just select the text you want to animate, open the Font dialog box, and then choose the effect you want to apply and click OK. You can preview each effect in the Preview window to be sure you've chosen the one you want.

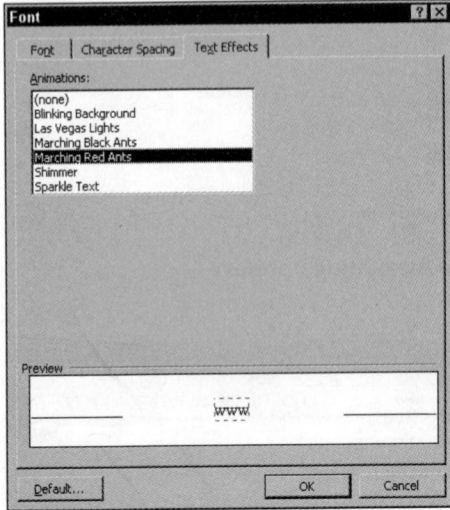

Figure 8-13: If your readers will be using computers to peruse your document, you can spice it up with one of these snazzy animation effects.

Formatting with keyboard shortcuts

You have one other way to apply formatting to selected text: use the shortcut keys, which some people find quicker to use when typing than reaching for a mouse. The keyboard shortcuts for formatting are shown in Table 8-4.

Tip

One of the most useful keyboard shortcuts for formatting is Ctrl+spacebar, which cancels all character formatting, returning text to the default.

Table 8-4
Keyboard Shortcuts for Character Formatting

Format	Shortcut
Bold	Ctrl+B
Italic	Ctrl+I
Underline	Ctrl+U
Word underline	Ctrl+Shift+W
Double underline	Ctrl+Shift+D
Subscript	Ctrl+equal sign
Superscript	Ctrl+Shift+plus sign
Small caps	Ctrl+Shift+K
All caps	Ctrl+Shift+A
Change case	Shift+F3
Hide text	Ctrl+Shift+H
Remove formats	Ctrl+spacebar
Font	Ctrl+Shift+F
Symbol font	Ctrl+Shift+Q
Point size	Ctrl+Shift+P
Next larger size	Ctrl+Shift+>
Next smaller size	Ctrl+Shift+<
Up one point	Ctrl+]
Down one point	Ctrl+[

Formatting paragraphs

In addition to formatting characters, Word provides tools to let you apply formatting to whole paragraphs at a time. Word considers a paragraph to be any section of text that falls between two paragraph marks, which are inserted whenever you press Enter. (The only exception to that rule is the first paragraph of a document, which Word recognizes as being the text from the top of the document to the first paragraph mark.)

Tip   To see where the paragraph marks are in your document, click the Show/Hide ¶ button in the standard toolbar. This makes all the paragraph marks visible.

Paragraph formatting affects the spacing and alignment of all the lines in a paragraph. As with character formatting, you have more than one way to format a paragraph, but all of them begin with your placing your cursor somewhere inside the paragraph you want to format (it doesn't matter where, as long as it's between the two paragraph marks that define the paragraph).

Again, the most commonly used paragraph formatting options, as with character formatting, are available on the Formatting toolbar. To access the more advanced paragraph formatting, you have to open the Paragraph dialog box by selecting Format ➪ Paragraph, or by right-clicking on a paragraph and choosing Paragraph from the shortcut menu (see Figure 8-14).

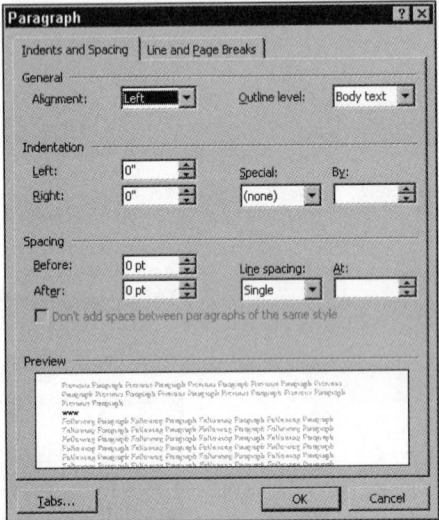

Figure 8-14: The Paragraph dialog box lets you precisely control the alignment and spacing of your paragraphs.

The Paragraph dialog box has two tabs, which are covered in the following sections.

Indents and Spacing tab

The controls on the Indents and Spacing tab not only let you apply formatting to a paragraph, but they also provide valuable information about the current formatting of the paragraph. From here, you can change the paragraph's alignment, adjust the indentation with much greater precision than the Indent buttons on the Formatting toolbar allow, and adjust the amount of space that appears both above and below the current paragraph. As usual, there's a Preview window that shows you the effects of your formatting choices. The darker text in the middle of the Preview window is the currently selected paragraph.

 **Cross-Reference** You can also assign an outline level to a paragraph from the Indents and Spacing tab. For detailed information on creating and using outlines in Word, see Chapter 19.

The Paragraph dialog box also gives you control over line spacing—the amount of space between lines. You have six options:

✦ **Single:** This leaves a minimum amount of space between lines, just enough that their characters don't overlap.

✦ **1.5:** This leaves one and a half times as much space between lines as Single does.

✦ **Double:** This leaves the equivalent of a blank line between lines.

✦ **At Least:** When you choose this, Word will automatically adjust line spacing in the paragraph to allow for smaller or larger font sizes or graphics, but it will never leave less space between lines than the point size you specify.

✦ **Exactly:** When you choose this and enter a value in points, Word will use that line spacing regardless of font size or graphics.

✦ **Multiple:** This lets you enter line spacing as a multiple of single spacing: 1.6, for example, or 2.4.

First Line and Hanging Indents

One of the indentation controls on the Indents and Spacing tab gives you the option to apply first line or hanging indents. Both align the first line of a paragraph differently from the following lines.

A *first line indent,* like the one that starts this paragraph, begins the paragraph's first line to the right of the rest of the lines. This is the kind of indent usually used to set off the first line of a paragraph in many books, magazines, and newspapers.

A *hanging indent,* like the one that starts this paragraph, begins the paragraph's first line to the left of the rest of the lines. It's often used to start off a list of items.

Line and Page Breaks tab

The Line and Page Breaks tab (see Figure 8-15) lets you control the flow of text within a paragraph. It offers several options:

✦ **Widow/Orphan control:** This prevents widows (the first line of a paragraph that appears all by itself at the bottom of a page) and orphans (the last line of a paragraph that appears all by itself at the top of a page).

✦ **Keep lines together:** This prevents any page break at all in the middle of a paragraph, even if it doesn't result in a widow or orphan.

✦ **Keep with next:** This prevents a page break from occurring between the selected paragraph and the one that follows.

✦ **Page break before:** This inserts a page break before the selected paragraph.

✦ **Suppress line numbers:** If you've got line numbering turned on within a document, this option keeps those line numbers from being displayed for the currently selected paragraph.

✦ **Don't hyphenate:** This prevents the selected paragraph from being automatically hyphenated if Hyphenation is enabled.

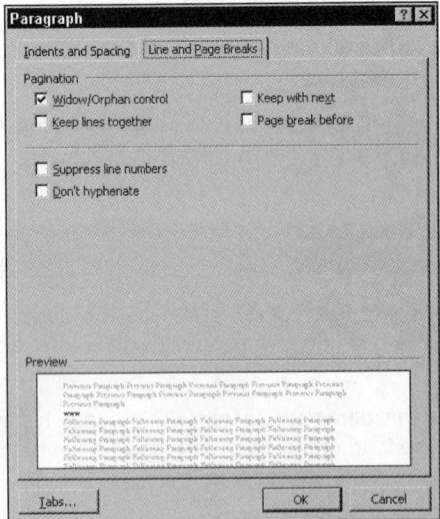

Figure 8-15: Controlling the flow of text with these controls can make your document look cleaner and more professional.

Tabs

In addition to the preceding tabs, the Paragraph dialog box includes a button, Tabs, that brings up the Tabs dialog box shown in Figure 8-16. (You can also access this dialog box by choosing Format ➪ Tabs.)

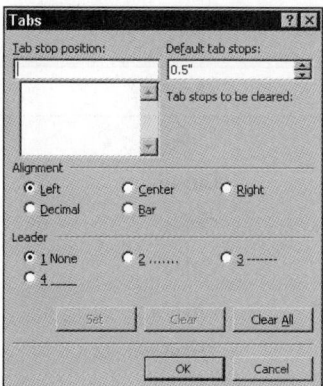

Figure 8-16: Set tabs and their leaders using the Tabs dialog box.

Enter the tabs you want in the box at the left and then set their alignment at the right. You have several options:

✦ **Left:** If you press Tab, the cursor will go to this spot, and any subsequent text you type will appear to the right of the Tab stop.

✦ **Right:** Press Tab and, again, the cursor will go to this spot, but any subsequent text will appear to the left of the Tab stop.

✦ **Center:** Press Tab to send the cursor to this spot, and any subsequent text will be centered on the Tab stop.

✦ **Decimal:** This is most commonly used when you're creating a column of monetary figures. Set the Tab stop where you want the decimal to appear. Press Tab and then type in the number. The numerals to the left of the decimal will appear to the left of the Tab stop, but once you enter a decimal, subsequent numerals appear to the right of the Tab stop.

✦ **Bar:** This draws a vertical bar at the spot where you insert the Tab stop. It has no effect when you press the Tab key.

In addition to setting Tab stop alignments, you can assign each Tab stop a leader — characters that will be inserted in the tabbed line before the stop. You can use dots, dashes, or underline marks.

Keyboard shortcuts

Shortcut keys are also provided for paragraph formatting. They're shown in Table 8-5.

<table>
<tr><td colspan="2" align="center">Table 8-5
Keyboard Shortcuts for Paragraph Formatting</td></tr>
<tr><td>*Format*</td><td>*Shortcut*</td></tr>
<tr><td>Left-align text</td><td>Ctrl+L</td></tr>
<tr><td>Center text</td><td>Ctrl+E</td></tr>
<tr><td>Right-align text</td><td>Ctrl+R</td></tr>
<tr><td>Justify text</td><td>Ctrl+J</td></tr>
<tr><td>Indent from left</td><td>Ctrl+M</td></tr>
<tr><td>Remove indent from left</td><td>Ctrl+Shift+M</td></tr>
<tr><td>Increase hanging indent</td><td>Ctrl+T</td></tr>
<tr><td>Decrease hanging indent</td><td>Ctrl+Shift+T</td></tr>
<tr><td>Single-space lines</td><td>Ctrl+1</td></tr>
<tr><td>Use 1.5-line spacing</td><td>Ctrl+5</td></tr>
<tr><td>Double-space lines</td><td>Ctrl+2</td></tr>
<tr><td>Add or remove 12 points of space before a paragraph</td><td>Ctrl+0 (zero)</td></tr>
<tr><td>Remove paragraph formats not applied by a style</td><td>Ctrl+Q</td></tr>
<tr><td>Restore default formatting (reapply the Normal style)</td><td>Ctrl+Shift+N</td></tr>
<tr><td>Display or hide formatting marks and nonprinting characters</td><td>Ctrl+*</td></tr>
</table>

Using the ruler

In Word, you can also set indents and tabs using the ruler that normally appears across the top of the document space in Normal, Print Layout and Web Layout views. (If for some reason the ruler isn't visible, you can turn it back on by choosing View ➪ Ruler.) The ruler is a useful tool that reminds you of how wide your document, and various items in it, will be when printed, and where they are located on the page. To set indents, use the following directions:

✦ **Left indent:** Go to the left end of the ruler and click and drag the little square below the two diamond-shaped arrows pointing at each other. Place the arrows however far from the left margin you want the indent to be set and release the square.

✦ **First line indent:** Drag the top diamond to the right of the bottom arrow by the amount you want the first-line indent to be.

✦ **Hanging indent:** First set a left indent as above, and then drag the top arrow to the left of the bottom arrow by the amount you want the hanging indent to be.

✦ **Right indent:** To change the right margin of a paragraph, drag the arrow at the right end of the ruler to the left.

To set tabs, follow these steps:

1. Click the button at the far left of the ruler to cycle through the various types of Tab stops. Pick the one you want.

2. Click on the ruler at the point you want the Tab stop to be set.

3. Adjust the Tab stop as necessary by dragging it left or right along the ruler.

4. If you make a mistake, delete the Tab stop by dragging it off the ruler.

✦　　✦　　✦

Getting Graphical

Text may be your communication vehicle, but if your message lacks rakish fins, a bold grille, and a shiny hood ornament, no one will be watching when it arrives. Polished documents need graphical elements to illustrate their points, to summarize key information in immediately understandable form, and simply to break up the monotony.

Office lets you beautify your documents with pictures of all sorts, from the simplest lines and boxes to complex illustrations, from charts and graphs to scanned photographs. The new drawing tools built into Office approach the power of those in professional graphics software. And if they don't do the trick, you can add artwork from essentially any paint, photo-editing, or line art application. Office's features for manipulating imported and embedded graphics have been improved as well. And for that matter, you can add other kinds of embellishments to your documents, such as video and sound clips.

Line Art Graphics from Scratch

In four of the Office applications — Word, Excel, PowerPoint, and Publisher — you can embellish your documents with graphics of your own design with Office's drawing tools. Now we're not talking about just a few simple shapes and lines, maybe with some basic patterns. Office's drawing tools give it much of the power of the major-league drawing programs for creating line (vector) art. Professional graphic artists are still going to want standalone applications such as Corel Draw or FreeHand, but you can often accomplish comparable results with Office alone.

In addition to the traditional set of simple lines, rectangles, and ovals, Office comes with a whole palette of prefab AutoShapes that you can add to your document with a couple of quick clicks. You can choose from polygons, hearts, arrows, flowcharting symbols, scrolls, and even those word balloons you see in cartoons (see Figure 9-1 for a few examples). Office also offers a full set of features for drawing complex freehand shapes. After laying down a shape with one of three freehand tools, you can edit the points that define its perimeter one by one, which is the kind of control needed for serious line-art work.

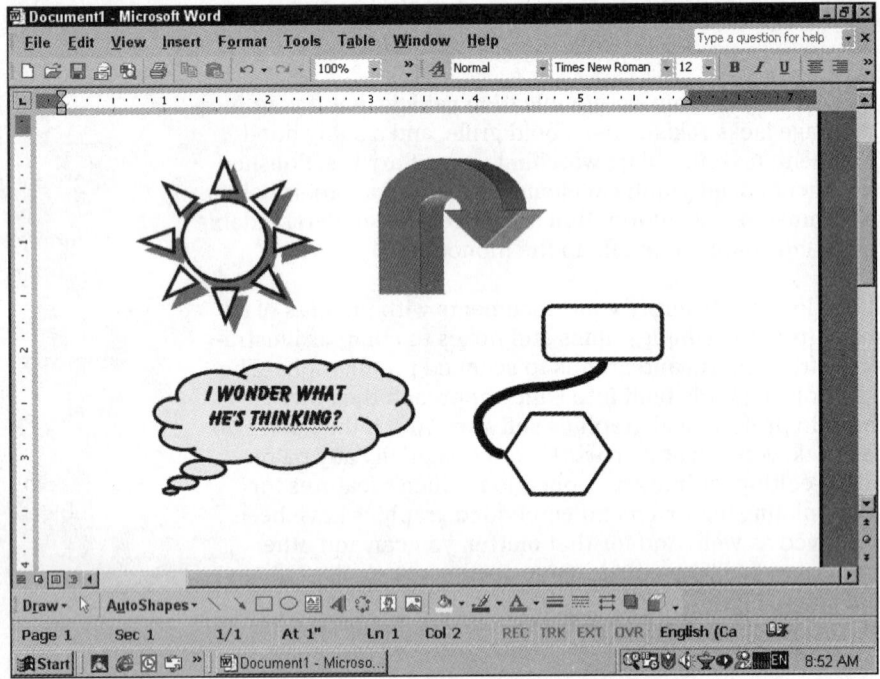

Figure 9-1: A few of the AutoShapes available in Office, some after special effects have been applied

When you've created a shape, Office lets you enhance it with special effects. The 3-D effect is especially powerful: You can apply the illusion of three-dimensional depth, perspective, and lighting to almost any shape, rotating the shape freely in imaginary 3-D space. Simpler shadow effects are also available. You can freely rotate any shape. And you can use text as visual spice, adding text to any AutoShape, and making sophisticated graphical effects with WordArt.

Using the Drawing toolbar

All of the Office drawing tools are accessible from the Drawing toolbar, one of the standard toolbars. Shown in Figure 9-2, the Drawing toolbar looks exactly the same in all the applications in which it is available. If it's not already visible, you can display it by clicking the Drawing button. This button toggles the Drawing toolbar on and off. You can also show the Drawing toolbar by right-clicking any toolbar and selecting Drawing from the shortcut menu.

Figure 9-2: Use the Drawing toolbar to add your own graphics and edit imported clip art.

Starting from the left, the first section of the toolbar has the tools for selecting and editing existing shapes. Next comes a section devoted to laying down new shapes and text elements. The buttons in the third section let you select colors, patterns, and line width, and turn on the shadow and 3-D effects.

Adding drawing shapes to a document

To insert drawing shapes into a document, start by clicking the button for the shape. The buttons for the basic shapes (line, arrow, rectangle, and oval) appear on the Drawing toolbar. Access the buttons for the other prefab shapes on the AutoShapes menu, described in the next section.

When you choose a drawing shape, the mouse pointer changes to a simple cross. Click in the document to produce the shape at a predetermined size. Drag the pointer in to size it to your own requirements, releasing the mouse button when the shape takes on the right size and proportions.

To create an object within a perfectly square boundary, hold down Shift while you draw it. Use this technique to add impeccable squares and circles, isosceles triangles, and perfectly proportioned hearts, stars, and whatnot. Holding down Shift while you draw a line or arrow constrains a line to preset angles — this is especially useful for drawing true horizontal or vertical lines.

To have the new object expand out symmetrically in the opposite direction (like a mirror image of what you draw), hold down Ctrl while you draw. To center an object on a particular spot, begin drawing from that location using this Ctrl+drag technique.

Tip Ordinarily, the mouse pointer reverts to normal as soon as you've drawn a shape, enabling you to select shapes or return to editing your document. To draw multiple shapes of the same type without having to reactivate the tool each time, double-click the button for the shape. To bail out of this repeat-draw mode, click it once more, right-click anywhere, or press Esc.

Inserting AutoShapes

To insert an AutoShape, choose AutoShapes on the Drawing toolbar and select from one of the submenus (see Figure 9-3). You can also insert AutoShapes from a toolbar by that name, or from toolbars for each of the AutoShapes submenus. To display these toolbars, tear them off from the AutoShapes menu by dragging the colored bar at the top of each menu or submenu. You can also choose Insert ➪ Picture ➪ AutoShapes to display the AutoShapes toolbar.

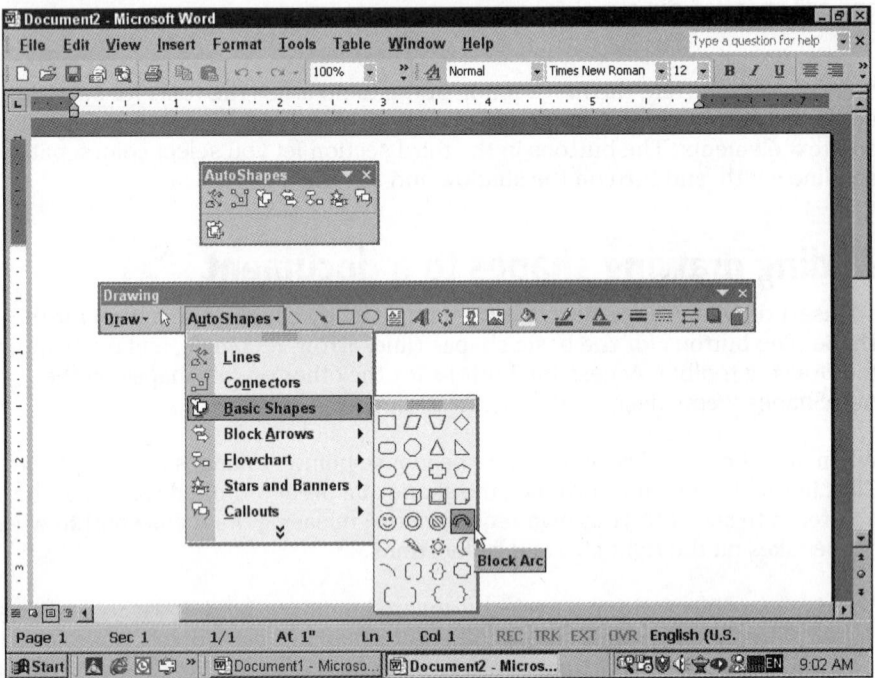

Figure 9-3: Place AutoShapes in your documents by selecting them from the menu system on the Drawing toolbar, shown at bottom, or the AutoShapes toolbar, shown at top.

You can't double-click the buttons on the AutoShapes submenus. If you want to draw any of these shapes repeatedly, you must first tear off its submenu to make it a floating toolbar. You can then double-click the shape's button.

More AutoShapes? Not really

The shapes accessible via the More AutoShapes item on the AutoShapes menu or toolbar aren't really AutoShapes. Instead, the More AutoShapes command displays the Clip Organizer, discussed in "Managing clip art and other content with the Clip Organizer" later in this chapter. Items in the Clip Organizer are ordinary pictures, not AutoShapes. You can't size them as you're inserting them (as you do with other toolbar shapes), you can't add text to them, and you can't reshape them as you can with most AutoShapes.

Special AutoShapes — connectors and action buttons

Among the available AutoShapes is a collection of *connectors*. Connectors have built-in smarts: you use them to connect two objects. Once two objects are connected, you can move them and they stay connected. (There's a curved connector in Figure 9-1.)

When you choose a connector from the collection and point at an object you've already drawn, four blue dots appear around the edges of the object. Point at the object you want to start the connector from (some connectors have arrows on them, so it can matter which object you choose first) and then click and drag to the object you want the connector to lead to. Once you reach it, four blue dots will appear on it, too. Drag the connector to the side of the object you want it to connect to, and release the mouse button. The connector will appear. You can adjust the shape of the connector by clicking and dragging the yellow diamond that appears midway along its length.

In PowerPoint alone, you also have access to an AutoShapes menu of *action buttons*. An action button does something, such as display another slide, when you click it in a PowerPoint presentation. Action buttons are resizable rectangles, shadowed to look three-dimensional, that contain an icon representing what they're for — an arrow pointing right to indicated "next slide" or one pointing left to indicate "previous slide." You can rotate action buttons just like you would any other shape; a yellow diamond control lets you vary the "depth" of the 3-D effect.

Tip   You can add action buttons, minus their intelligence, to a document created in another Office application. Put the shape into a PowerPoint document and then move it to its destination via the Office Clipboard.

Copying Pictures from Office to Non-Office Applications

You can usually paste pictures into Office from non-Office applications, such as an outside graphics program, by copying the picture from the non-Office application to the Windows Clipboard and then pasting it into the Office document.

However, it doesn't work the other way. Office uses the Office Clipboard, which is separate from the Windows clipboard. You can only paste pictures from the Office Clipboard into other Office applications.

So how can you move a picture you've edited or created in Office to a non-Office application?

You have to save it as a separate graphics file on your computer, then open or import it into the non-Office application. In PowerPoint, you can do this simply by right-clicking on the picture and choose Save Picture As. In Word and Excel, it's more roundabout; you can either copy the picture to the Office Clipboard, paste it into a PowerPoint document, then save it, or you can save the document as a Web page. When you do save a document as a Web page, Office saves any images in the document into a special folder with the title (Name of document)_files. You can then retrieve the images from that folder and use them in your non-Office application.

Selecting drawing objects

As is the norm with drawing software, you must select a shape before you can change it. You can tell when a shape has been selected by the little white squares (the sizing handles) arranged in a rectangle around the shape. When a shape containing text is selected, the bounding rectangle appears shaded.

Immediately after you draw a shape, Office selects it automatically. Thereafter, you can select it by clicking anywhere over it. Alternatively, you can activate the Select Objects tool first (the Drawing toolbar button with the arrow pointer on it). This approach is useful in the following situations:

✦ **To select objects that are behind text or other objects.** If other elements in the document make it hard to see what you're doing, you can still select the object they're hiding. See "Organizing and aligning graphics" later in the chapter.

✦ **To select groups of objects by dragging to enclose them in a selection rectangle.** You can also select two or more objects by Shift+clicking them one at a time.

✦ **To work only with drawing objects and pictures.** The Select Objects button is a toggle, and as long as it's pressed in, the selection pointer is active. You can then be sure that you're only selecting graphics objects.

Moving, resizing, rotating, and duplicating graphics objects

As usual, you have multiple options for altering the size or position of a graphics object. Table 9-1 summarizes the available techniques.

To move an object, just drag it where you want it to go. You don't need to select it first, but if text or objects are in the way you may need to use the Select Objects tool to do the dragging.

You know you're in position to drag-move an object when the mouse pointer becomes a four-headed arrow. For most objects, including WordArt objects, you must drag over the enclosed parts of the shape or its outlines, not the bounding rectangle marked by the selection handles. For an object that contains editable text, drag by the object's outline, or by the shaded rectangle surrounding the object.

Table 9-1
Keyboard and Mouse Actions with Graphics Objects

To Do This	Use This Mouse Action	Or This Keyboard Action
Select an object.	Click the object with the standard mouse pointer or with the Select Object pointer.	After first selecting an object with the mouse, press Tab or Shift+Tab to select the next or previous object.
Select multiple objects.	Shift+click each object in turn, or drag a selection rectangle around all the objects using the Select Object pointer.	
Move an object.	Drag over the shape (or its outline), or drag with the right button to the new location, selecting Move Here after releasing the button.	Select the object and then press the arrow keys (Ctrl+arrow to move in smaller increments).
Move an object in horizontal or vertical directions only.	Hold down Shift while dragging the object.	
Duplicate an object, moving the new copy	Hold down Ctrl while dragging the object, or drag with the right button to the new location, selecting Copy Here after releasing the button.	Select the object; press Ctrl+C and then Ctrl+V; now move the duplicate object.
Resize an object.	Drag a sizing handle.	

Continued

Table 9-1 (continued)

To Do This	Use This Mouse Action	Or This Keyboard Action
Resize an object, preserving its proportions.	Hold down Shift while dragging a corner sizing handle.	
Resize an object from the center outward.	Hold down Ctrl while dragging a sizing handle.	
Resize an object from the center outward, preserving its proportions.	Hold down Ctrl+Shift while dragging a corner sizing handle.	
Resize an object without the settings for the grid and guides.	Hold down Alt while dragging a sizing handle.	
Specify a new location or size by precise numeric measurements.	Double-click the object.	Select the object. Then choose Format, followed by the type of object (at the bottom of the Format menu); or display the shortcut menu and choose Format at the bottom.
Rotate an object.	Select the object and then drag over any of the circular green rotation handles.	Select the object; then choose Draw ➪ Rotate or Flip. Choose a flipping option from the menu.

You can also use the keyboard to move an object once it's selected. Each press of an arrow key nudges the object in the arrow's direction. Hold down Ctrl while you press an arrow key to move the object in smaller increments. And you can position objects at precise locations using the Format dialog box, described in the section "Formatting Objects: The Master Control Center" later in this chapter.

Resize a selected object by dragging the sizing handles (the white boxes along the edges of the selection rectangle enclosing the shape). You can also enter new measurements in the Format dialog box.

Reshaping AutoShapes

Experiment with dragging those yellow diamonds you see when you select many AutoShape objects. Depending on the object, you can use this technique to affect parts of the object—changing its width, contour, or rotation—without affecting its overall size (see Figure 9-4).

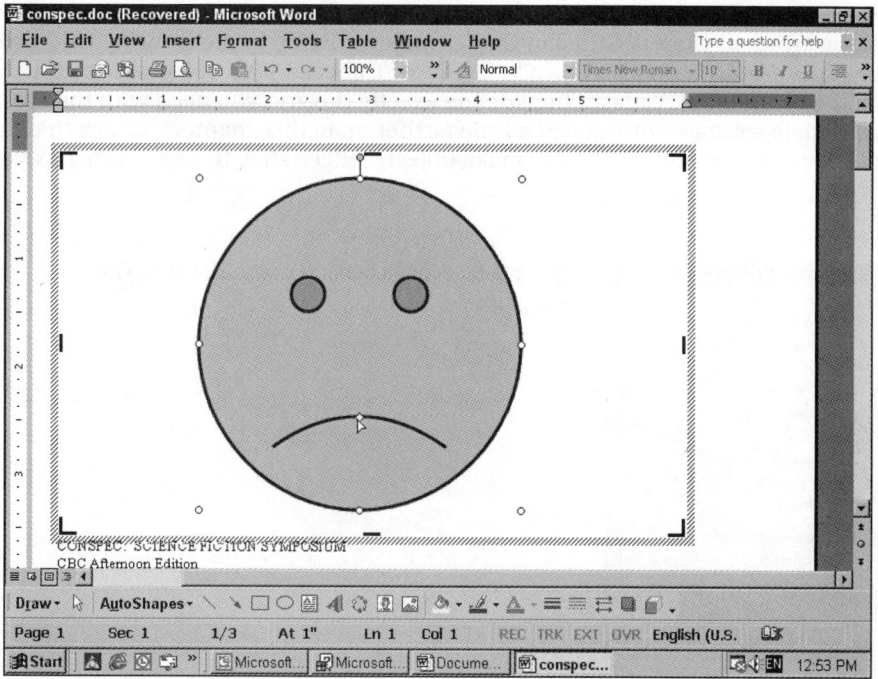

Figure 9-4: The face of anxiety, produced by dragging a happy face's diamond handle

Tip

You can transform just about any enclosed AutoShape into any other. After selecting the object, open the Draw menu on the Drawing toolbar, choose Change AutoShape, and pick out the new shape you want from the submenus. This technique works for text boxes and other shapes containing text. It doesn't work if the original shape was drawn freehand using the tools on the AutoShapes ⇨ Lines menu. (Text boxes and freehand drawing are covered later in this chapter.)

Precision work with the grid and guidelines

In Word and PowerPoint, you can turn on an imaginary grid of evenly spaced horizontal and vertical lines, to which your objects stick when you draw, move, or resize them. With the grid on, you can't position an object in between two adjacent gridlines — it's as if a magnet pulls the object edges so they always line up on the grid. (Excel comes with its own grid, formed by the cells of the spreadsheet, to which you can also snap objects.)

You can also rig things so objects automatically align with one another. With this option turned on, the rectangular boundary of an object you're moving or resizing seems to cling to the boundary of any object it passes over.

To control these autoalignment settings, choose Draw ⇨ Grid on the Drawing toolbar in Word, or Draw ⇨ Grid and Guides in PowerPoint. In the Drawing Grid dialog box (the Word version is shown in Figure 9-5), check "Snap objects to grid" to turn on the overall grid. You can then define exactly the grid you need with the spacing and origin settings (introduced a little farther on in this chapter). Check the "Snap objects to other objects" box to make objects' edges stick to one another as you draw.

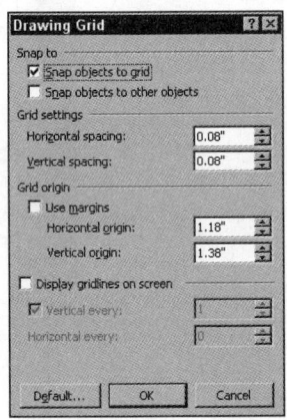

Figure 9-5: Word's version of the Drawing Grid dialog box

Tip

Holding down Alt while you work disables the snap-to features.

Working with text boxes and callouts

Text boxes are just what the name implies — on-screen rectangles ready to receive text. You can place a text box anywhere you want on a document, overriding the basic layout.

The Drawing toolbar has a separate button for creating text boxes. After you click the button, you can insert the text box by clicking or dragging in your document, just as with other drawing toolbar shapes.

However, almost any enclosed AutoShape can contain text. To add text to, say, an AutoShape heart, activate the Text Box tool and then click the shape. Alternatively, select the shape, display its shortcut menu, and choose Add Text. As soon as you do, a rectangle (representing an attached text box) encloses the shape on the screen.

Note You can't add text to plain lines or freehand shapes. Note also that text added to an AutoShape is constrained by the attached rectangular text box—you can't type within the entire shape.

Using callouts

A *callout* is just a text box with a line (called a *leader*) connecting it to another location in your document. Use a callout to add text that comments on another item, as shown in Figure 9-6. Via the AutoShapes menu, callouts come in a multitude of shapes and line configurations.

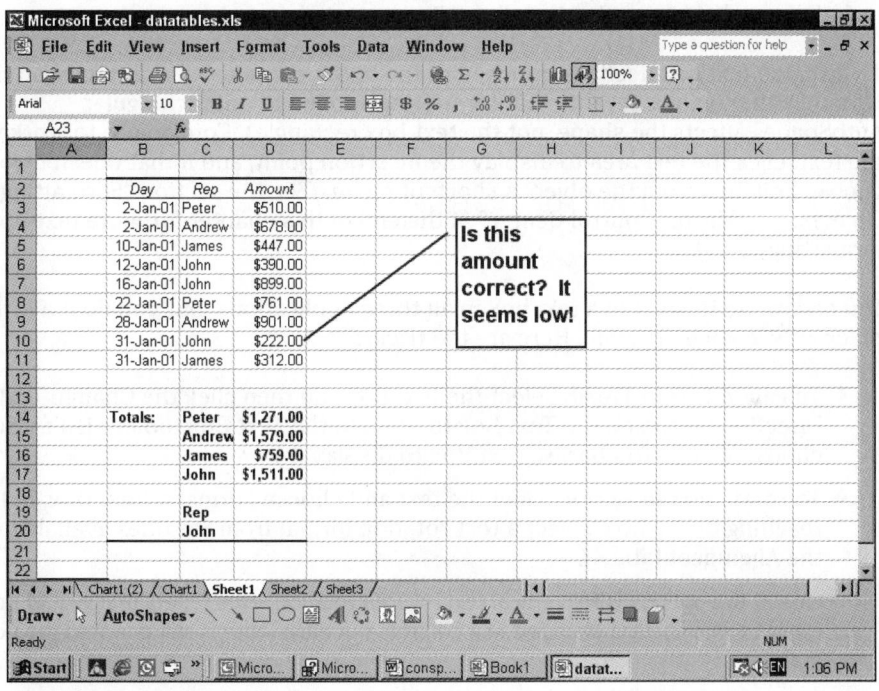

Figure 9-6: A callout in action

When you've inserted a callout, you can modify the leader by dragging on the yellow handles that define the leader's endpoint and the points where it bends, if any. To see these handles, you must select the callout itself by clicking the rectangle, not the space inside, where text goes.

Tip For all but the first row of shapes on the AutoShapes ➪ Callouts menu, you can also change the leader's configuration, the gap between the leader and the callout shape, the side where the leader attaches to the callout, and so on. Right-click the callout and choose Format AutoShape.

Formatting text boxes and the text inside them

You can do anything to text in a text box, callout, or AutoShape that you can do to text elsewhere in your documents. In Excel and PowerPoint, you can apply character formatting. In Word, however, you can also set paragraph alignment, control the spacing between lines and between paragraphs, add bullets or numbers, and apply paragraph styles, just as with text in the body of the document. Word text boxes can also be linked together, letting text added to one box flow through a series of boxes.

Because text boxes are drawing objects, however, you can also apply to them most of the Drawing toolbar's formatting options. Detailed later in this chapter, these include fancy backgrounds, as well as alignment and grouping commands.

To format a text box itself, as opposed to the text it contains, click directly on the rectangle that defines it (note that formatting applied to nonrectangular AutoShapes affects the shape, not the text box rectangle). Conversely, to work with the text, click the text area to display the insertion point, and if that doesn't work, choose Edit Text from the object's shortcut menu. (See the section "Formatting Objects: The Master Control Center" at the end of this chapter for more text-box formatting secrets.)

You can rotate the text in a text box in all three applications, but you do it a little differently in each program. Here are the tricks:

✦ **To rotate text in Word:** Select the text box and then click the Change Text Direction button on the Text Box toolbar. (If the Text Box toolbar isn't visible, choose View ➪ Toolbars ➪ Text Box to display it.)

✦ **To rotate text in Excel:** Select the text and choose Format ➪ Text Box. In the resulting dialog box, select a text rotation format from the ones available on the Alignment tab.

Note   One of the options is for vertical text *without* rotation—the letters that would normally be in a line are arranged in a column, but each letter is still oriented the normal way.

✦ **To rotate text in PowerPoint:** You use the same process as in Excel, except you can rotate the text only 90 degrees. Check the relevant box in the Format ➪ Text Box dialog box under the Text Box tab.

Drawing and editing freehand shapes

Modeled on the features of high-end drawing applications like CorelDRAW!, Office's trio of freehand drawing tools—curve, freeform, and scribble—are quite powerful. Don't get the wrong idea—you wouldn't want to rely on Office for a major design project. But you can use the drawing tools to do acceptable freehand sketches (see Figure 9-7).

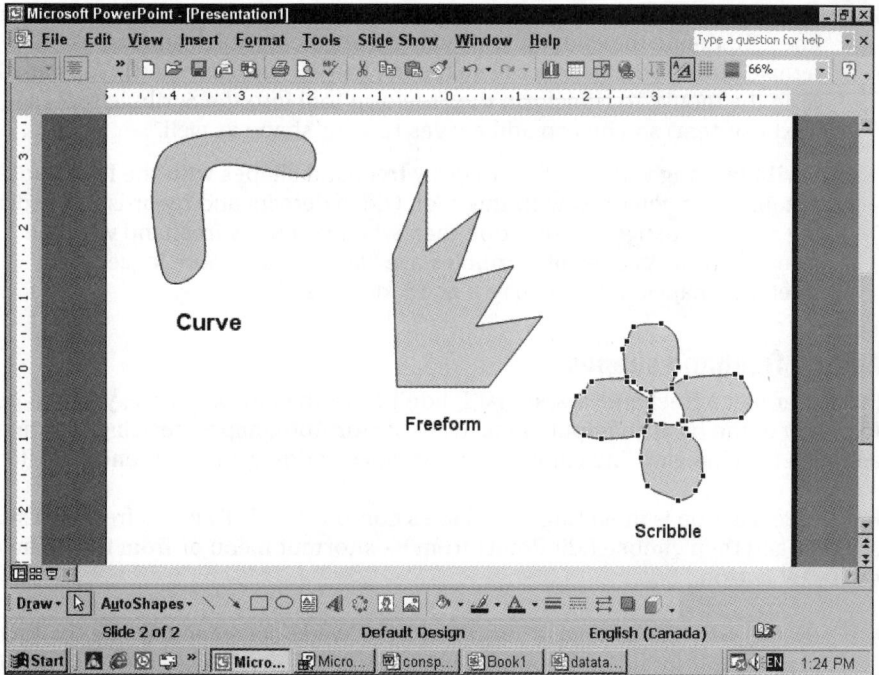

Figure 9-7: Sample freehand shapes drawn with the curve, freeform, and scribble tools

The Office drawing tools provide a critical capability: You can edit what you draw. Drawing with a mouse is hard (to put it mildly); you can't expect to lay down lines where you want them. But as long as you can go back and push them into place, you can gradually sculpt the curve you had in mind. In Figure 9-7, the scribble shape on the right has been selected for editing the points that define the line.

Before starting work on a freehand drawing object, magnify your work by at least a 200-percent zoom factor. Then, to draw the object, choose AutoShapes ⇨ Lines to display a graphical menu of six line-drawing tools. The top row contains ordinary straight lines, but clicking one of the tools on the bottom row starts a new freehand drawing. Here's how they work:

✦ **Curve.** Imagine you're playing with a really long rubber band that you can pin down anywhere you like on the drawing surface—that's sort of how this tool works. Click and release the mouse button to pin down the starting point. Moving the mouse pointer now extends the line straight out from that point. When the free end reaches a place where the curve should bend, click again to pin down the rubber band there. When you stretch the line out from that spot in any new direction, the line curves accordingly—and smoothly. You can remove previous direction-change points—in reverse order—by pressing Backspace. Finish the curve by double-clicking the final anchor point.

✦ **Freeform.** Use this tool to draw shapes that include both straight and curving lines. To define the endpoints of straight segments, click and release the mouse button (that's how the shape in Figure 9-7 was created). You can also drag the mouse to transform the Freeform tool into the Scribble tool (see the next list item) so you can add curves to your shape as well.

✦ **Scribble.** Drag with this tool to draw freehand shapes with the finest possible detail. When you draw with this tool, Office detects and records in the drawing smaller changes of direction than when you draw freehand with the freeform tool. As a result, scribbles are likely to look more jagged than freeform shapes unless you're a good mouse artist.

Editing freehand shapes

I've never met a freehand shape that I didn't have to edit. Of course, you can perform any of the basic manipulations available for AutoShapes: resizing, rotating, adding a fill, changing line color or size, and even adding shadows and 3-D effects.

But the real action is in editing the shape's contour itself. To edit a freehand shape, select it and then choose Edit Points from its shortcut menu or from the menu of the Draw button.

Tip   By the way, the technique described here works for imported line, or vector, graphics too, including clip art — but to apply it, you need to see the tip in the section "Editing line art" later in this chapter.

When Edit Points is turned on, you see black squares along the shape's outline, one for each point where the line changes direction. Microsoft refers to such a direction-change point as a vertex. It's really critical that you zoom in on the object to work with the points comfortably. It also helps to distinguish the points from the line by setting the line width to 0 points. With the shape selected, click the Line Style button on the Drawing toolbar, choose More Lines, and then enter **0** for the Weight setting. You can change back to the correct line style after you finish the edits.

When you've taken care of these preliminaries, you can manipulate lines and points in various ways:

✦ Move a point by dragging it.

✦ Delete a point to smooth out an overly wiggly stretch by holding down Ctrl while you click the point.

✦ Add a new point by clicking at any point-less location along the curve.

✦ Change the degree and direction of deflection for the segment passing through a point. Click the point to select it, and then drag its tangent handles. This is an extremely powerful technique for shaping and smoothing freehand lines, so be sure to familiarize yourself with how it works — see the next section.

Working with tangent handles and tangent lines

As shown in Figure 9-8, the *tangent handles* are those white boxes you see when you select a point. (Microsoft calls them tangent *points*, but if you use that name you'll mix them up with the direction-change points on the freehand line.)

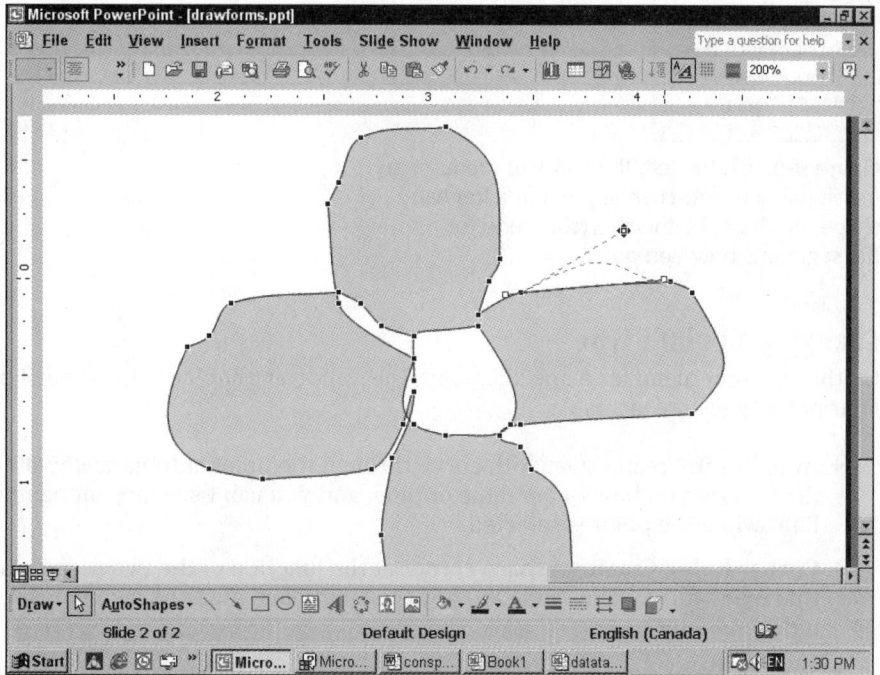

Figure 9-8: Reshaping a freehand line by dragging a point's tangent handle

Dragging the tangent handles gives you control of the pair of blue *tangent lines* to which the handles are attached. The angle of one tangent line to the other determines the direction of stretch it places on the curve. The tangent line's length determines how far that part of the curve gets stretched. If you see only one handle, it means that the segment on the other side of the point is a straight line and can't be bent (but see "Changing a segment's type" later).

Of course, the line that takes shape as you work with the tangent handles also depends on the location and types of the points (vertices) on either side of the one you're working with. Practice — you'll see what I mean.

Changing point and segment types

With Edit Points turned on, to further refine the contour at a specific point, right-click along the outline to display a shortcut menu. The choices listed in the second menu group of the shortcut that appears vary, depending on whether you right-clicked directly over a point or elsewhere along the outline (see Figure 9-9).

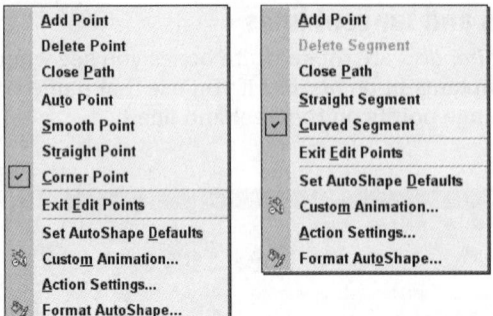

Figure 9-9: On the left, the shortcut menu of an individual direction-change point in a freehand shape; on the right, the shortcut menu for the segments between points

Changing a point's type

On the shortcut menu for a specific point, the important choice is the type of point. Four point types are available:

✦ **Auto Point.** Creates a smooth curve through the point automatically. Office decides for you how to bend the outline, and you can't see tangent handles or lines when the point is selected.

✦ **Corner Point.** Creates a sharp corner at the junction of the two segments that meet at the point. You can vary the length and angle of each tangent line independently.

✦ **Smooth Point.** Select this type of point to have the outline curve smoothly through the point, but with customizable deflection. You can bend the outline at will by dragging either tangent handle, but the two tangent lines always extend equally in opposite directions (you can't vary the angle between them).

✦ **Straight Point.** Use this point type when you want the segment on one side of the point to be "flatter" than the segment on the other, but you don't want a sharp corner. You can stretch the two tangent lines by different amounts, though they always extend in opposite directions.

Note   You don't need a straight point to create a straight line passing through the point — a smooth point will work just as well, so long as you stretch the tangent lines far enough.

More weird facts about editing curve points

You can convert a straight point or smooth point to a corner point by holding down Shift while you drag a tangent handle. Likewise, hold down Ctrl to change a corner point or straight point into a smooth point. If you hold down both Shift and Ctrl, Ctrl wins.

You can pop up the points shortcut menu by right-clicking a tangent handle. Selecting a new point type from the menu changes the handle's point accordingly. But if you choose Add Point, you get a new point at the current location of the handle.

 **Tip** When you first draw a shape with the Curve tool, all the points are AutoPoints. Scribbles and freeform shapes, however, have corner points instead.

Changing a segment's type

With a freeform shape's points showing, you can change the shape by right-clicking over a portion of the outline between two points (that is, a *segment*); the shortcut menu that appears offers you two options:

✦ **Straight Segment.** This type of segment connects two points with a straight line that can't be bent, no matter what type of point lies at either end. If you turn on point editing and select one of the points, you'll notice that it lacks tangent handles on the side toward the straight segment.

✦ **Curved Segment.** Although this type of segment sometimes *looks* perfectly straight (depending on how the shape was drawn and edited), you can deform it by pulling on the tangent handles of the points at either end of the segment.

Not only can you see in the menu which type of segment you're dealing with, you can also convert one type of segment into the other type by selecting it on the menu.

Closing and opening freehand shapes

One more option is available on the shortcut menu when you're editing the points of a freehand outline: If the shape is closed (with a continuous outline), choose Open Path to break it apart at the direction-change point nearest where you right-clicked the outline. If the shape is an open line with a beginning and an end, choose Close Path to have Office connect the two endpoints.

WordArt for designer text

If you like graphically powerful text effects, WordArt is for you. This feature takes any text of your choosing and warps it to one of many shapes, adding 3-D effects in the process. Sample results are shown in Figure 9-10.

WordArt is incorporated into the Drawing toolbar. To add a WordArt object, click the corresponding button to display the WordArt Gallery dialog box. If the Drawing toolbar is hidden, you can choose Insert ➪ Picture ➪ WordArt instead. From there, picking out a style (or entering and editing the text you want displayed) is a breeze.

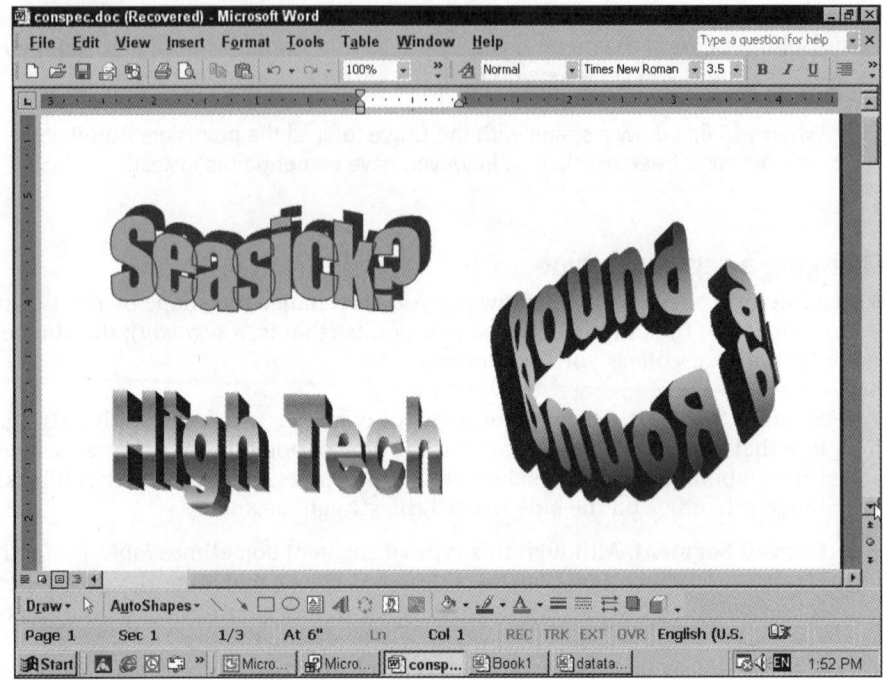

Figure 9-10: Samples of WordArt

Don't overlook those yellow diamond handles that appear when a WordArt object is selected. As usual, they let you change the shape of a curve, but this time you're working with an *invisible* curve along which the WordArt text is stretched and bent. Dragging the yellow diamond either distorts the characters more or straightens them out.

Note When you select a WordArt object, a special toolbar appears automatically. You can use the buttons here to alter the basic WordArt settings for the object, including the shape it's based on, the text it displays, and whether the text appears horizontally or vertically. You can also adjust such fine points as letter height, character spacing, and paragraph alignment. You can add 3-D and shadow effects with the Drawing toolbar.

Adding a diagram

Next to WordArt on the Drawing toolbar is a new button: Insert Diagram or Organization Chart. This opens a dialog box offering you six different types of diagrams, as shown in Figure 9-11: an organization chart (used to show hierarchical relationships), a cycle diagram, a radial diagram, a pyramid diagram, a Venn Diagram (overlapping circles that depict the overlap among various elements) and a target diagram.

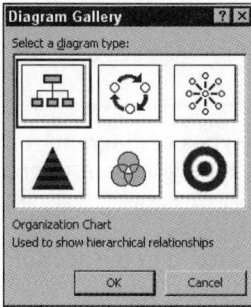

Figure 9-11: Insert an organization chart or diagram from this dialog box.

The organization chart

Although inserted by the same button, the organization chart and various diagrams open different subsidiary toolbars. The Organization Chart toolbar offers four buttons:

✦ **Insert Shape.** This button is for adding boxes to the chart — such as subordinate, coworker, or assistant, each inserted in relation to the box your insertion point is currently in.

✦ **Layout.** This button lets you choose from various types of organization charts — Standard, Both Hanging, Left Hanging, Right Hanging

✦ **Select.** This button lets you select all the boxes on the same level, all the boxes in a particular branch, all the assistants or all the connecting lines, which you can then format using the Drawing tools just as you would format any other Drawing object.

✦ **Autoformat.** This final button opens the Organization Chart Style Gallery, which provides preformatted organization charts and a preview of each.

Diagrams

Inserting any of the diagrams creates a default diagram of the type chosen, which you can then modify using the Diagram toolbar. On this toolbar, the buttons serve the following functions:

✦ **Insert Shape.** This button inserts a duplicate of the basic shape of the diagram (another circle in the Venn Diagram, for instance, or another layer in a pyramid diagram).

✦ **Move Shape Forward.** Use this option to move the shape you just inserted to the foreground of the diagram.

✦ **Move Shape Backward.** Use this button to move an inserted shape into the background of the on-screen image.

✦ **Reverse Diagram.** This button (you guessed it!) flips the entire diagram.

✦ **Diagram Style Gallery.** This button calls up a set of preformatted styles for your diagram.

Finally, you can change your diagram to one of the other types of diagrams — anything except an organization chart — by choosing the type you want to convert it to from the Change to menu.

Edit the text in your diagram or organization chart as described in the section on working with text boxes, earlier in this chapter.

Working with color, line, and texture

You can control the width and color of the line defining any drawing object, and you can fill most objects with a color, simple pattern, textured background, or clip-art image or other picture.

Most of the objects you can draw are closed, meaning that they have a continuous outline around an enclosed area. When Office refers to the line of a closed shape, it means this outline. Of course, you can also draw ordinary open lines, the kind with two free ends. Either way, a line can be straight, jagged, or smoothly curving.

Tip   In addition to the techniques covered in this section, you can also control fill and line options from the Format dialog box, described in the section "Formatting Objects: The Master Control Center" later in this chapter.

Filling objects

To fill an object, select it (of course) and then click the Fill Color button on the Drawing toolbar. Click the main portion of the button to fill the object with the currently selected color. If you want to change colors or apply a pattern or texture, click the vertical bar at the right of the button to display a pop-up menu of colors. You can choose from these, but if you want an even fancier fill, select More Fill Colors or Fill Effects.

Tip   The dialog box displayed when you choose More Fill Colors is the secret residence of the Transparency slider. Use this slider (it displays transparency in percentages, with 100 percent being completely transparent and zero percent being completely opaque) to allow text or other documents behind the object to peep through a bit. This slider is also available on the Format dialog box, described in the section "Formatting Objects: The Master Control Center" later in this chapter.

The Fill Effects choice brings up the Fill Effects dialog box, shown in Figure 9-12.

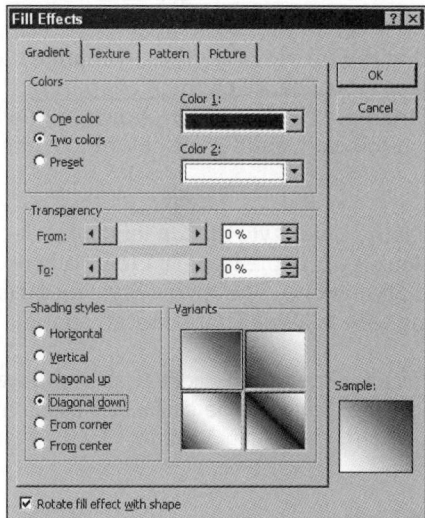

Figure 9-12: The Fill Effects dialog box

Here, select among four types of complex fills by switching to the corresponding tab, as follows:

✦ **Gradient.** Creates a fill with a gradual transition between two or more colors. The One Color option blends the chosen color into black or white, depending on the setting of the Dark/Light slider. You can select the colors involved and control the geometric pattern of the transition. You can also set the transparency of the start point and the end point of the gradient fill, so different parts of the filled object will let different amounts of whatever's under the object peek through.

✦ **Texture.** Fills the shape with a pattern designed to imitate a textured surface. You can select a texture from the available presets, or choose Other Texture to pick an image in a disk file. The chosen image has to be small so it can be displayed at full size within shapes. Office tiles copies of the image so the shape is completely filled.

✦ **Pattern.** Fills the shape with one of 48 simple preset patterns. You can select foreground and background colors for the pattern.

✦ **Picture.** Fills the shape with an imported picture. The picture is scaled larger or smaller as necessary to completely fit the shape.

Note You can "fill" lines that don't completely enclose an area. Office adds the fill on one side of the line.

Controlling line options

Use techniques similar to those described in the previous section to change the color, width, or pattern of the selected shape's outline. Click the main part of the Line Color button on the Drawing toolbar to apply the line color shown on the button. Click the vertical bar beside the button to select a different color or to choose a patterned outline from a dialog box.

The pop-up menu displayed when you click the Line Style button lets you select the line width and whether you see a single, double, or triple line. To create a broken line, select one of the choices on the Dash Style menu. The Arrow Style menu is only available if the "shape" you're working with is a line (not a closed shape).

Tip The Line Style pop-up menu lacks a choice for lines of no width at all. If you want a selected object to have a fill but no outline, bring up the Line Color menu and choose the No Line option.

Adding shadow and 3-D effects

Office art can be deep, really deep — if you use shadow or 3-D effects. To get started, you just select the object and then click the appropriate button, Shadow or 3-D, on the Drawing toolbar. This pops up a menu of preset effects shown as little graphical examples. Click one of these, and your shape takes on the settings of the chosen preset.

But who wants to be stuck with presets? The illusion of depth is enchanting, and no one can resist playing with shadow and 3-D effects. The keys to controlling them yourself are the Shadow Settings and 3-D Settings toolbars. Display them by clicking the corresponding choice at the bottom of the pop-up menu displayed by the Shadow and 3-D buttons.

Tip By the way, you can add shadows to just about any object, including placeholders for multimedia clips. But you *can't* add the Drawing toolbar's 3-D and shadow effects to selected text. When you add 3-D to a text box, the text itself remains flat, and it just sits there as you tilt the 3-D object. To place 3-D text in a 3-D shape, slap a WordArt object on top of the graphical one.

Both the 3-D and Shadow toolbars have On/Off buttons at the left that toggle the relevant effect. The object remembers its most recent settings for both effects, so you can turn an effect on or off or switch back and forth between 3-D and shadow effects without losing your previous work.

Tip You don't need the On/Off buttons to switch between 3-D and shadow. Clicking any button of the other effect's toolbar immediately restores that effect with its previous settings.

The Shadow effect includes presets that make the selected object look embossed or engraved. Choose the leftmost style on the bottom row to apply the embossed effect, the one to its right for an engraved effect. Both effects remove any existing border.

Customizing shadow and 3-D effects

The Shadow Settings toolbar has buttons for moving the shadow relative to the object itself, as well as one for changing the shadow's color. These tools are adequate, but the 3-D Settings toolbar is a lot more fun. The Shadow Settings tools include the following:

✦ **Tilt.** These four buttons rotate the faux 3-D object about its horizontal and vertical axes — but only through 180 degrees at most. For example, you can stand an object on its face so the backside of the 3-D effect becomes the top, but you can't turn the new top surface closer toward you.

✦ **Depth.** This button is for determining how far, in points, the 3-D effect extends out from the original drawing. Remember, there are 72 points to an inch. So if you're entering a custom depth and you think in inches, multiply the depth you want by 72. The 0 pt. setting doesn't actually produce a flat object, just one with very little depth. Use it to display the object as a planar surface (changing the 3-D color can make the edges more obvious). When available, the Infinity setting extends the 3-D effect off toward the horizon, although the shape may stop before it reaches the edge of the page.

✦ **Direction.** Use this button to determine which way (left, right, up, or down) the 3-D effect extends from its object. In addition, you can control the manner in which the effect extends. Select Perspective to give it an artist's perspective, with all the lines converging toward a single point in the distance. Choose Parallel to have the lines extend parallel to one another — this option doesn't give the illusion of reality, but it's the usual technique in technical drawings.

✦ **Lighting.** This button is for selecting the brightness and direction of the imaginary lighting source. As you pass the mouse over a direction button on the pop-up menu, the cube in the center gives you an idea of how that choice would look. Click the center cube to light the object directly from the front.

✦ **Surface.** This button lets you select from four options controlling how reflective the surface of your 3-D shape will appear. Matte gives it a dull look, whereas Metal supposedly makes it look like polished metal, with Plastic somewhere in between. Wire frame removes the surface entirely.

✦ **3-D Color.** This button is for choosing the color of the 3-D effect. Select Automatic to have Office choose the color for you based on that of the original object (use the standard Fill Color and Line Color buttons on the Drawing toolbar to change the object's color even when a 3-D effect is in place).

Organizing and aligning graphics

Be sure you're aware of the many options Office provides for working with groups of objects. These fall into three basic categories of commands: alignment, grouping, and ordering.

Aligning objects

It's bad enough trying to get a picture to hang straight, but the human nervous system is sorely inadequate to the task of lining up two or more graphics objects on a screen using a mouse. One alternative, typing in numeric coordinates, takes too long. The solution can be found on the menu you get by choosing Draw ➪ Align or Distribute (Figure 9-13).

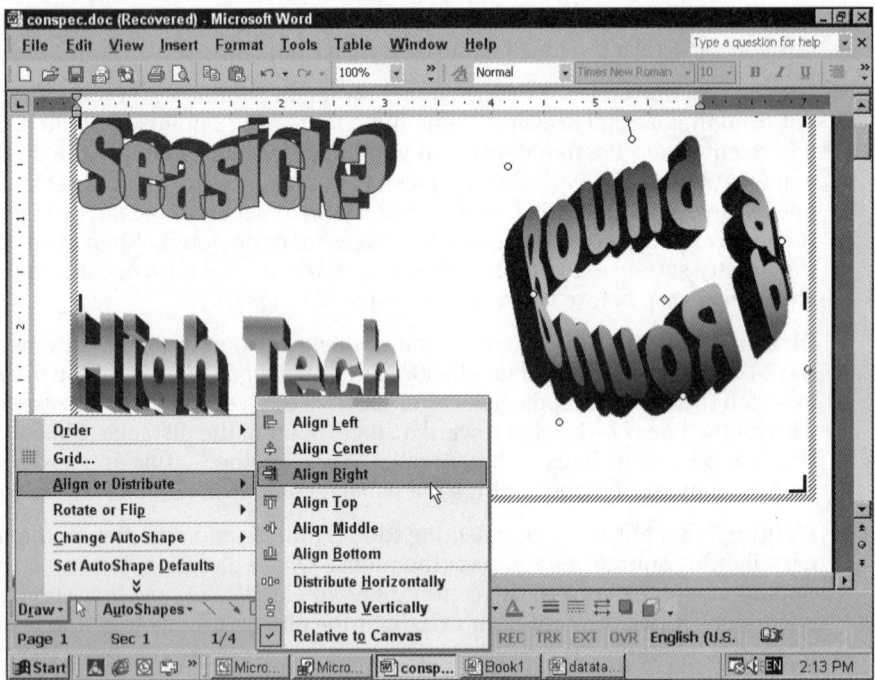

Figure 9-13: The Align or Distribute menu

Before you open this menu, select the objects that you want to bring into relationship with one another, or with the page they're on. It doesn't matter which order you select them in. Then display the menu of alignment tools. In Word or PowerPoint, if you want to align or distribute the objects relative to the whole page rather than to one another, turn on the Relative To option at the bottom of the menu (to Drawing Canvas in Word, to Slide in PowerPoint).

The basic functions of the alignment options should be self-explanatory. What may not be so obvious is that objects are moved so they line up with the one that's already located farthest in the selected alignment direction. For example, if you select three objects and choose Align Left, the object that is farthest left remains in place, while Office moves the other two objects so their left sides line up with it. Also, remember that Office aligns the objects based on the imaginary rectangles that surround them.

The distribution choices arrange three or more selected objects at equal distances from one another. The two objects at the top and bottom of the page remain in place, while the ones in between divide the intervening space evenly. If the Relative to Page option is on, distributing two or more objects moves them all so they're evenly spaced on the page.

Grouping objects

You can and should group objects together to preserve their relative positions and sizes, during moving and resizing operations, or if you know you'll always be applying the same effects to all the objects. All you have to do is select all the objects and choose Draw ➪ Group. The selection handles are removed from the individual objects but appear around the entire group, which you can now move, size, or color as a unit.

To work with the objects individually again, select the conglomerate object and choose Draw ➪ Ungroup. This is the only way to edit the points of a grouped freehand object, for example. After making any changes you like, you can reconstitute the last group you ungrouped by choosing Draw ➪ Regroup. This works even if you have moved the objects onto different pages — Office will bring all the chickens home to roost on the same page when you use the Regroup command. The trio of grouping commands is also available from the Grouping menu on an object's shortcut menu.

You can group smaller groups of objects into larger groups for as many levels of organization as you like. The Ungroup command only breaks apart the top-level group. If a drawing is composed of groups of grouped groups, you have to use the Ungroup command repeatedly to get to the individual shapes so you can edit their points.

Tip   In Word, the DrawDisassemblePicture command — available from the Tools ➪ Customize dialog box (click on the Commands tab and choose All Commands under the Categories list, then scroll through the list of Commands in the Commands box) — can ungroup all the groups in one fell swoop.

Ordering objects

I'm talking order as in sequence of placement, not as in, "I'll have two objects to go, hold the tacky fill patterns." Anyway, as in all drawing programs, Office graphics objects are ordered in an imaginary stack, one on top of the next. You only notice this when two objects overlap, or when you place an object on top of text. The object on top covers up the one below it, although if the top object has no fill color, you can still see the object below.

Use the Draw ➪ Order menu to change a selected object's position in the stack (the menu, shown in Figure 9-14, is also available from an object's shortcut menu). You can do this to change the look of the object landscape, but also just to retrieve an object that's buried underneath others.

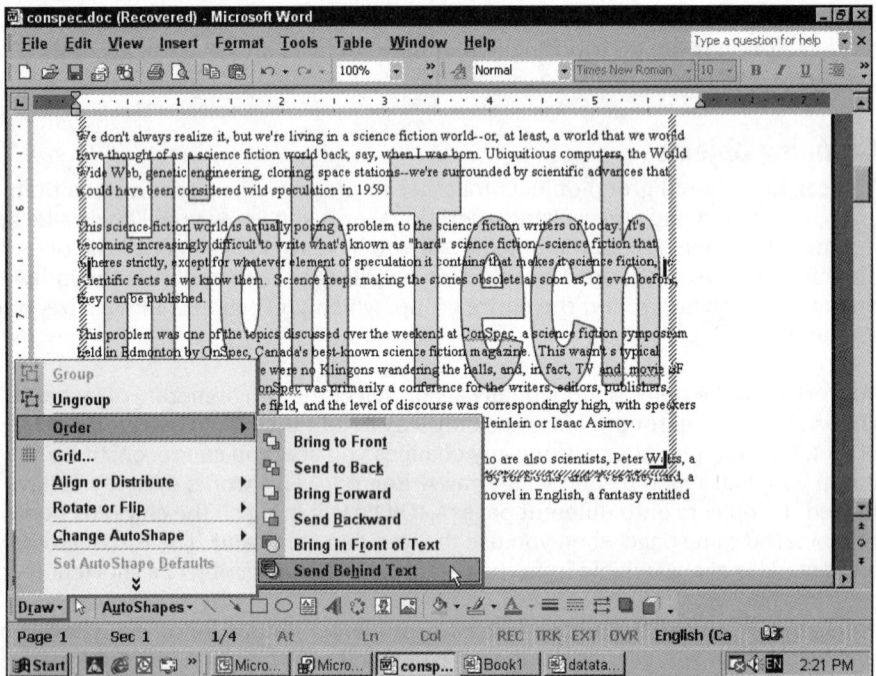

Figure 9-14: Use the commands on this menu to bury an object beneath something else or pull it out again.

On the menu, the Bring to Front and Send to Back commands move the selected object to the very top or bottom of the pile, whereas the Bring Forward and Send Backward choices just promote or demote it by one level. In Word, the menu also lists commands to move the object in front of or behind the document text, which is initially at the bottom of the stack of objects.

Toolbar modifications for efficient drawing

You have room on the standard Drawing toolbar for a few more buttons. Don't hesitate to fill up that space with any tools you find useful (see Chapter 5 for information on customizing toolbars).

Aside from obvious choices such as the Alignment and Grouping commands, some suggestions include:

✦ The EditPoints command. If you do any work with freehand shapes, for example, by all means add this button. Turning on point-editing via the shortcut menu is cumbersome, and it's too easy to mistakenly turn it off. (For that matter, a keyboard shortcut for this command might come in handy too.)

✦ The Select Multiple Objects command. Clicking this button displays a dialog box with a list of the shapes in your document by type. Click the shapes you want and OK the box to select them.

✦ In Word, the DrawMarquee command. This lets you select multiple graphics just as you can with the pointer tool. However, it shuts off as soon as you release the mouse button. You can't use it to select objects by clicking.

✦ The command to turn outlines on or off. See the section "Controlling line options" earlier in this chapter.

If you work extensively with special effects, customize your toolbar setup so the buttons of the Shadow Settings and 3-D Settings toolbars are automatically available whenever you draw. That way, you won't have to manually display them each time you start working on a shape. The easiest way to do this is to create a custom toolbar and fill it with the buttons found on both of the Settings toolbars — just Ctrl+drag the buttons from the existing toolbars to your new one. If you regularly use any particular depth, direction, lighting, or surface settings, you can drag out their buttons onto the custom toolbar for one-click access. Then dock the new toolbar so it's always at the ready. If you do keep the 3-D Settings and Shadow Settings toolbars (or their buttons) at the ready, you can dispense with the 3-D and Shadow buttons on the main Drawing toolbar and use their slots for other buttons. With an object selected, clicking any of the 3-D Settings buttons turns on the 3-D effect, which you can then tweak to taste.

Setting defaults for fill, line, and special effect

To set up defaults for all future shapes you draw, format an object in your document with all the options you want as your defaults for fill color, line color and style, and 3-D or shadow effects, if any. Select this object of your affections and choose Set AutoShape Defaults from the Draw button's menu or the selected object's shortcut menu. From here on in, every shape you draw will take on those same characteristics.

New in Word: The Drawing Canvas

The new version of Word has a new way of dealing with inserted graphics that doesn't exist in the other Office applications. Called the Drawing Canvas, it's essentially a graphic (a rectangle) into which you can insert other graphics. Previously, each graphic inserted into Word was in its own separate box. Using the drawing canvas makes it easier to create a graphic made up of several different drawings.

The Drawing Canvas opens immediately whenever you insert a picture of any kind. You can't miss it; as you can see in Figure 9-15, it tells you in no uncertain terms to "Create your drawing here."

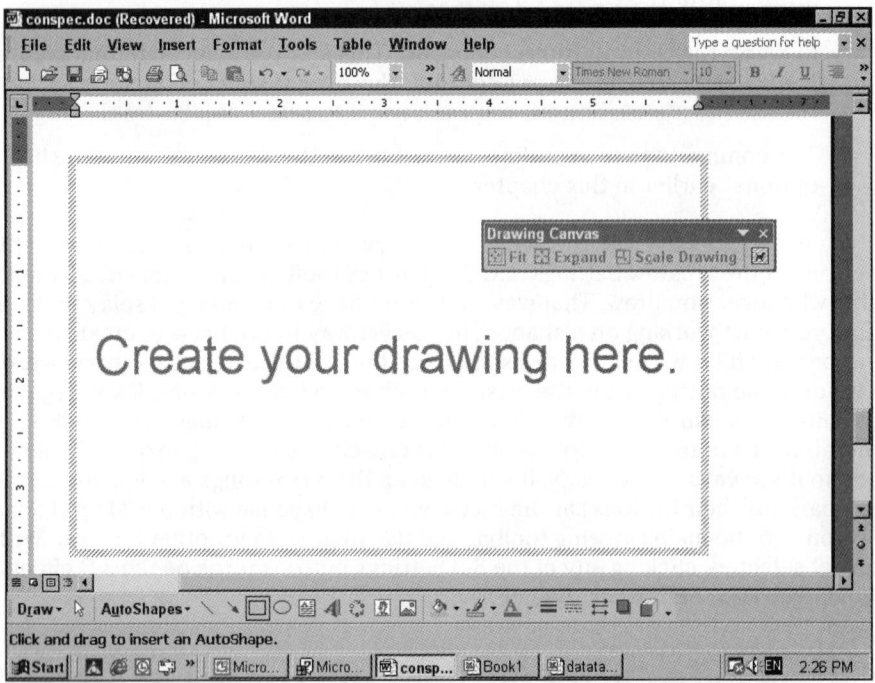

Figure 9-15: Word's new Drawing Canvas makes it easier to insert graphics into Word documents.

Do as it says. You'll also see a new toolbar, the Drawing Canvas toolbar (also visible in Figure 9-15), with a handful of new tools. (If you don't, right-click the Drawing Canvas and choose Show Drawing Canvas Toolbar from the shortcut menu.) The buttons allow you to shrink the Drawing Canvas to fit the drawing, or to expand it to make room for more drawings. (You can expand drawings within the Drawing Canvas as usual without affecting the size of the canvas.) If you click and drag the handles on the sides of the canvas, you can adjust the size of the canvas without affecting the drawings it contains. If you click the Scale Picture button, however, the handles change, and you can then adjust the size of the canvas and the drawings on it at the same time. Finally, the Text Wrapping button allows you to control how text interacts with objects inside the drawing canvas (more on text wrapping later in this chapter).

Tip   Although by default the Drawing Canvas has no fill or border, you can add both. Adding a fill turns it into an attractive background for the drawings you create inside it; adding a border turns it into a kind of frame for those drawings. Both can be a useful effect. To access the formatting commands for the Drawing Canvas, choose Format ➪ Drawing Canvas or right-click the Drawing Canvas and choose Format Drawing Canvas from the shortcut menu.

Inserting and Editing Pictures

When the built-in drawing tools won't suffice, adorn your document with graphics from other sources. Office uses the term picture to mean any type of graphical image you acquire from a source other than the built-in drawing tools. This encompasses both paint-type bitmaps and draw-type (vector art) metafiles in any format Office recognizes.

Pictures are, of course, *objects* (the general term for anything from an external source placed, in its original form, into an Office document). This chapter surveys specific types of objects you're likely to use to make your documents presentable, as well as the commands used to format objects once they reach an Office document.

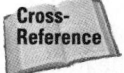

Cross-Reference   Chapter 11 covers the basics on how objects behave and how you can manipulate them in Office.

Inserting pictures

The standard way to add pictures created in other software is the Insert ➪ Picture command. Use the two choices at the top of the submenu, Clip Art and From File. (The other items, some of which vary depending on the application you're using, don't insert pictures in the sense that Office usually uses that term. They are covered elsewhere in this chapter.)

The Insert ➪ Picture ➪ From File choice brings up a fairly standard Office file dialog box. As shown in Figure 9-16, however, the Insert Picture dialog box lets you preview images rather than documents before you select them.

Choosing Insert ➪ Picture ➪ Clip Art opens the Insert Clip Art task pane, through which you access the Clip Organizer, described in the next section. But keep in mind that the only real difference between clip art and other pictures in Office is where you find the graphics. Once in your document, clip-art pictures function just like ones you insert from a file or by scanning them in.

Cross-Reference   You can create a button that always inserts a specific picture into the current document. See Chapter 5 for more information.

Figure 9-16: The Insert Picture dialog box gives you a preview of the images you might want to place into your document.

Managing clip art and other content with the Clip Organizer

In Office XP, what used to be called the Clip Gallery is now called the Clip Organizer — and it's been given a major makeover that takes advantage of the new task panes. Figure 9-17 shows the new Insert Clip Art task pane displaying the results of a search for sports pictures.

The Insert Clip Art task pane has two main sections: Search For and Other Search Options.

Use Search For to search the Clip Organizer for images that match the keywords you enter — sports, in Figure 9-17.

The Other Search Options section lets you fine-tune your research. Search in lets you choose where to search for Clip Art collections (pictures have to be in a collection before Clip Organizer recognizes them — see "Organizing your clips" later in this chapter to learn how to put other pictures on your computer into collections that Clip Organizer can recognize). The Results list box lets you choose what kind of objects you want to search for: clip art, photographs, movies or sounds.

Using content items in Clip Organizer

When you've conducted a search, Clip Organizer displays thumbnail images of the items it has found. Inserting a clip-art image or other content item from Clip Organizer couldn't be easier: just double-click the thumbnail.

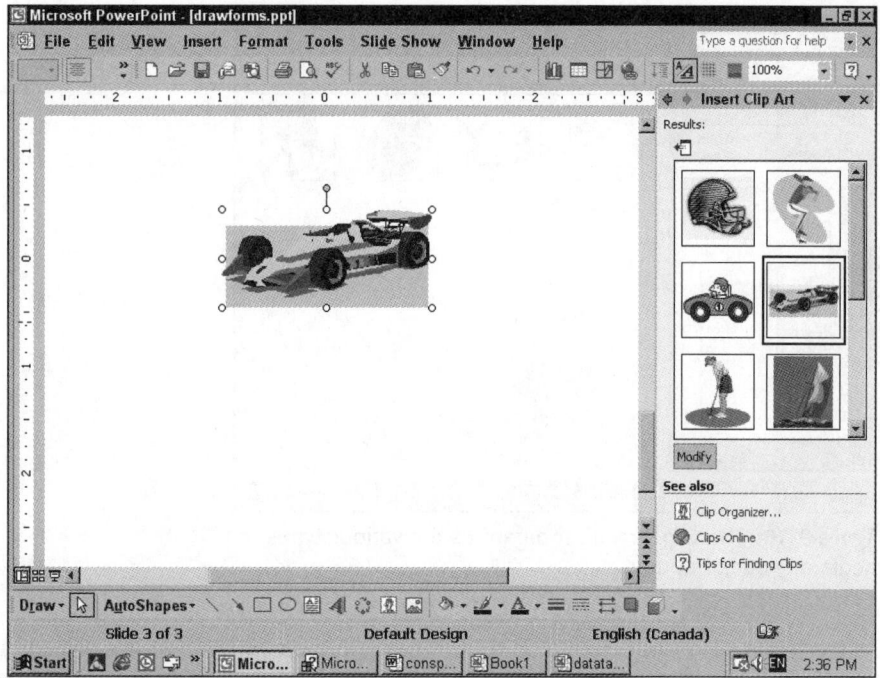

Figure 9-17: Microsoft Clip Organizer (formerly Clip Gallery) now resides in one of the new Office task panes.

Clicking the down-pointing arrow to the right of the object opens up a shortcut menu with several other options. Not only can you Insert the item, you can also copy it to the Office Clipboard, delete it from the Clip Organizer, open it in another program, copy it to a different collection, find other items of a similar style, and preview it and check out its properties (size, graphic format, and so on).

Organizing your clips

A collection of clip art, sounds, and video clips can quickly become overwhelmingly large. Clip Organizer helps you keep track of all the content and arrange it so you can find it in the Insert Clip Art task pane.

To organize your clips, click the Clip Organizer link at the bottom of the Insert Clip Art task pane. A message appears asking you if you want to organize your clips now or later. If you choose Now, Organizer immediately starts searching your hard drive and organizing your clips into collections based on the folders they're found in.

If you'd prefer to specify exactly how Clip Organizer goes about organizing your content, click later. The Clip Organizer itself opens (see Figure 9-18).

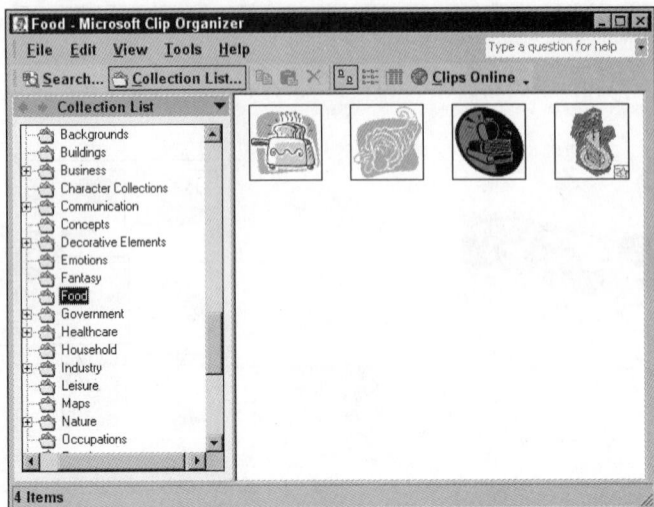

Figure 9-18: The Clip Organizer organizes the various types of media on your computer.

On the left is your Collection List; this shows you the content that has already been organized into collections. Clicking a collection brings up thumbnail previews of all the images in that collection at right. Each image has the same attached menu you've already seen in the Insert Clip Art task pane.

To add content already on your computer to the Clip Organizer, choose File ➪ Add Clips to Organizer. You can choose to do so automatically — in which case Clip Organizer searches your hard drive for all the media types it recognizes and collects them all — to input images from a scanner or camera, or to choose which specific images you want to add to the organizer. If you choose that option, you'll see a pretty standard Office browsing window; choose the clip or clips you want to add to a collection and click Add To to choose a collection to add the clip to. In the resulting Import to Collection dialog box, you can also start a new collection by clicking New.

The thumbnail images in Clip Organizer work exactly the same as the thumbnail images in the Insert Clip Art task pane. The menu attached to them is the same, too. If you choose one and then choose Edit Keywords from the attached menu, you'll see the dialog box in Figure 9-19.

Type in a caption for the item that will jog your memory. Your description appears in Clip Organizer when you hover the mouse over the item for a second or so. You may want to include technical information, such as the number of colors the image contains or the file format "flavor" (subtype). The caption you see automatically includes the main file type (GIF, WMF, BMP, or what have you) and the file's size.

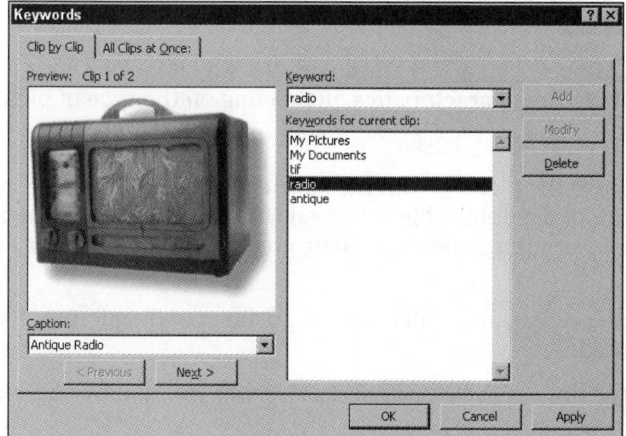

Figure 9-19: Use the Keywords dialog box to add a caption and keywords to content items.

Type in keywords that Clip Organizer matches when you type in a search. To apply the same keyword to several different clips in a collection, select them by choosing Edit ➪ Select All in Clip Organizer. Open the menu attached to any of the selected clips and choose Edit Keywords; then choose the All Clips at Once tab. This looks just like the Clip by Clip tab open in Figure 9-19, but any captions and keywords you add will be attached to all of the open clips.

Working with Photo Editor

Bundled with Office is Photo Editor, a reasonably capable program for scanning images and modifying the resulting bitmap pictures by using a variety of special effects. Comparable in function to Adobe Photoshop, Photo Editor doesn't claim to have as many bells and whistles, but it does a decent job within its limits. Photo Editor isn't installed by default, so if you want to try it out you should rerun Office Setup and select an appropriate installation setting for it.

If you install Photo Editor, it automatically opens when the image has been scanned. You can posterize the image, emboss it, or otherwise add special effects, as well as perform more mundane adjustments to brightness, contrast, and color. When the picture looks right, choose File ➪ Exit and Return To (your document).

Note   Although you can create "new" pictures in Photo Editor, this isn't a paint program — it offers no tools at all for adding new dots to a bitmap image.

Modifying pictures

When you've inserted a picture, you aren't stuck with the way it looks. Office lets you fuss with all sorts of picture characteristics, depending on the type of picture you're working with:

✦ You can resize or move the picture. With the mouse, you use the same techniques as you would for a graphic object created with the built-in drawing tools (see "Moving, resizing, rotating, and duplicating graphics objects" earlier in this chapter.)

✦ You can add a border, a line, and a fill color for portions of the picture that aren't already colored.

✦ You can crop the picture—covering up parts of it that you don't want to show in the document.

✦ You can adjust the picture's brightness and contrast.

✦ If the picture is a line-art (vector) image, you can convert it into individual shapes that you can then edit with Office's built-in drawing tools.

✦ If the picture is a paint (bitmap) image, you can remove one of its colors. You ask why? See the next two sections.

✦ If need be, you can go back to the application in which the picture was created and edit it there. Assuming the other software is installed on your system, this process is as simple as double-clicking the picture—provided you have linked or embedded it instead of simply importing it wholesale.

Using the Picture toolbar

When you select a picture, the Picture toolbar (Figure 9-20) pops up automatically. You can display it at other times too, as you would any other toolbar. The Picture toolbar has most of the controls you need for modifying your digital art.

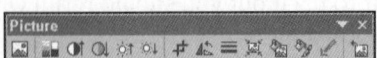

Figure 9-20: The Picture toolbar lets you manipulate art.

From left to right, the buttons on the Picture toolbar work as follows:

✦ **Insert Picture.** This button duplicates the Insert ➪ Picture ➪ From File menu selection.

✦ **Color.** This button offers four presets for settings affecting the picture's appearance. Choose Grayscale to convert the picture's colors to corresponding shades of gray. The Black & White option converts all colors to either black or white. Washout makes the image bright and low-contrast so it can be placed behind the rest of the document, simulating a watermark (use the Draw ⇨ Send to Back command). Select Automatic to let Office decide the settings.

✦ **More Contrast and Less Contrast.** This button raises or lowers the color saturation (intensity), decreasing or increasing the gray content.

✦ **More Brightness and Less Brightness.** This button adds white or black, making all the colors lighter or darker.

✦ **Crop.** This button hides the edges of the picture as though clipping them away. To crop the picture, click the Crop button and then drag a sizing handle.

✦ **Rotate Left.** This button rotates the image 90 degrees left.

✦ **Line Style.** This button is the same as the Line Style button on the Drawing toolbar. It applies a border around the picture itself (or in Word, around the picture boundary).

✦ **Compress Picture.** This tool is new with Office XP. It ensures that the size of the image file is as small as possible. Clicking it opens a dialog box that allows you to change the resolution of the picture to Web/Screen (96 dots per inch, or dpi), Print (200 dpi) or No Change (its original resolution). You can also choose to delete cropped areas (when you crop a picture, all of the picture is still there; part of it is just hidden). You can compress only the selected picture, or all pictures in the document.

✦ **Text Wrapping.** This button controls the flow of text in the underlying document around the picture. (Available only in Word.)

✦ **Recolor Picture.** This button is available only if the selected picture is a draw-type image, not a bitmap. Click it to change the picture's existing colors.

✦ **Format Picture.** This button displays the Format Picture dialog box. See the section "Formatting Objects: The Master Control Center" later.

✦ **Set Transparent Color.** Available only for bitmaps, this tool makes one color in the image transparent, letting the document behind it show through. Click the button, and then click the color you want to strip away. The color becomes transparent throughout the image, not just where you clicked. It's a neat effect, but see the sidebar "Transparent Pitfalls" for some further information.

✦ **Reset Picture.** This button removes cropping from the selected picture; restores it to its original size; and returns the color, brightness, and contrast controls to their original settings.

Editing line art

You can edit the underlying shapes in imported draw-type pictures just as if you had drawn them with Office's built-in graphics tools. The only trick is, you have to break up the picture into its component shapes and edit each one individually. For example, you can rearrange parts of the image, change fill and line colors, and even edit the points of the individual shape outlines. This technique also lets you combine parts of two or more images.

Transparent pitfalls

The Set Transparent Color tool on the Paint toolbar is handy for removing a one-color background from a bitmap picture so the foreground artwork stands out. Images with transparent areas are commonly used in Web pages to make the graphics look embedded directly in the background. However, you should be aware of some caveats pertaining to the Set Transparent Color tool.

For one thing, some bitmaps already include transparent areas, and if these are present, you can't use the tool. For another, the really cool bitmaps you probably want to use have palettes of 256 colors or more. With that many colors available, you'll rarely find large areas of all one color. Because you can make only one color transparent, you'll end up with a field of pinholes rather than a transparent background. And finally, it's common to find the background color in the foreground design — in which case, you get holes in the foreground as well.

The basic technique is simple: You just select the picture and choose Ungroup from the shortcut menu or the Draw button's menu (see "Grouping objects" earlier). What you're likely to discover, though, is that the picture consists of groups of grouped objects. In other words, you'll have to Ungroup a succession of objects until you finally expose the individual shapes for editing.

Tip   When you're done making changes, you can put the whole image back together by using the Group command on the individual elements. Regroup won't work, because it only reassembles the last set of ungrouped items.

All pictures are objects — but are they art?

In Office, all pictures are objects — items that function semiautonomously within a document. Depending on how you insert a picture, it may or may not enter your document as an OLE object. OLE objects retain their connection to another application, while an ordinary picture object is a loner image that takes up residence, for a time at least, in an Office document.

When you bring in a picture with the Insert ➪ Picture ➪ Clip Art command, the picture arrives as a Clip Art OLE object. That's why double-clicking it takes you back to Clip Organizer. By contrast, pictures inserted via the Insert ➪ Picture ➪ From File command normally aren't OLE objects — if double-clicking them does anything, that something happens within Office.

You can insert a picture with a link to the file it came from, the simple type of OLE connection, by checking Link to File in the Insert Picture dialog box. If the information in the linked file later changes, Office will then update your document to show the revised image. Of course, it's also possible to insert a picture as an embedded OLE object. You must use the Insert ➪ Object command, choosing a suitable Object type from the list.

Besides pictures, you can use lots of different types of objects to gussy up a homely document. See Chapter 11 for the scoop on the Insert ➪ Object command.

Office places no limits on the types of objects you can insert in your documents. All the loud fuss over multimedia has long since blown over, but there are definitely times when it makes sense to illustrate a document with a video clip or some recorded speech or music.

The Clip Organizer can house such objects for your ready retrieval according to category or keyword. You can also insert these items directly from disk via the appropriate commands on the Insert menu.

Formatting Objects: The Master Control Center

Whether you're working with a drawing object you created with the Office drawing tools, a picture, or any other type of object, the Format dialog box consolidates a comprehensive assemblage of settings with which you can control the object's appearance in your document.

The settings you see when you select an object and choose Format ➪ Object vary, depending on the type of object and the Office application you're working in. You can also get to the dialog box from the object's shortcut menu. Figure 9-21 shows a representative sample.

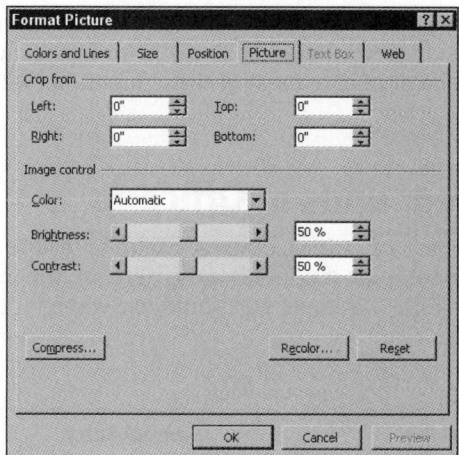

Figure 9-21: The Format Picture dialog box

Secrets of the Format dialog box

Get to know the Format dialog box. The Size, Position, and Picture tabs enable you to control the object spatially with much more precision (though more slowly) than you can with the mouse. Tabs on this key dialog box include:

✦ **Colors and Lines.** You don't need this tab if you use the Drawing toolbar — it duplicates the Fill Color, Line, and Arrow Style buttons there.

✦ **Size.** This tab lets you specify the object's size in absolute units (with the Size and Rotate settings), or as a percentage of the object's current size (using the Scale settings). For picture objects, you can check Relative to Original Picture Size to scale the picture based on its original size rather than its current size (in PowerPoint, you should also specify your slide show monitor's resolution). Whether you use the Size or Scale settings, check Lock Aspect Ratio to maintain the object's original proportions as you change either height or width.

✦ **Position.** In PowerPoint, use this tab to specify the object's position on a slide. Use the From settings to indicate the starting point for the measurements you enter. Word doesn't have the Position tab. Instead, you must switch to the Layout tab and then click the Advanced button to bring up the Advanced Layout dialog box and there, switch to the Picture Position tab.

✦ **Properties.** In Excel, you can select one of three options governing how the object changes as its underlying cells move or change size (handy for sorting tables containing pictures).

✦ **Layout.** In Word, this tab specifies how text wraps around the object.

✦ **Picture.** This tab lets you crop a picture object and set brightness and contrast with numerical precision.

✦ **Text Box.** In Word, this tab lets you set the margins between the boundaries of a text box and the text it contains. PowerPoint adds controls for fine-tuning the look of your text boxes. You can duplicate most of these functions with Word's sophisticated formatting options.

Working with measurement units in Office

Any time you change size, spacing, or position, Office expects you to enter the information using one of the measurement units it understands. Here are the measurement units and the corresponding abbreviations you should use when typing them into a dialog box.

Unit	Abbreviation	Sample Entry
Inches	in	.25 in
Inches	"	.25"
Centimeters	cm	.1 cm

Unit	Abbreviation	Sample Entry
Points	pt	18 pt
Picas	pi	1.5 pi
Lines	li	2 li

Points and picas are typographic units. A point is approximately 1/72-inch and a pica contains 12 points — so an inch contains about 6 picas.

You can't use every measurement unit with every formatting choice. When you're setting font size, for instance, Word accepts an entry only in points, not inches or lines. However, in many Word dialog boxes, you can type in new values in your choice of several units. If you're not using the default units, you just have to include the abbreviation for the units you've settled on. In Word, you can change the default units on the General tab of the Tools ➪ Options dialog box.

✦   ✦   ✦

Using Active Documents

Although people still tend to think of a document as a
stack of paper, many Office documents are never
printed at all. A document that spends its entire existence in
electronic format, displayed only on a screen, is less portable
than a paper counterpart—but it has advantages of its own.
You can build interactive Office documents by filling them
with controls—push buttons, checkboxes, scroll bars, and
the like—that alter the document's appearance or content
depending on the user's action. (And, by the way, you *can*
print a document containing controls—the controls and any
information they contain appear on the page, although, obviously, they don't work there.)

This is a short chapter because many of the techniques that
make the controls in your documents actually do things are
covered elsewhere—specifically, in Chapter 56. In this chapter, after an introduction to the concept of active documents,
you learn how to add controls to the documents you create
with Office and how to control their appearance and behavior
without programming.

When to Use Active Documents

By now, Web pages have introduced everyone to the concept
of active documents. But you don't need to have a Web site to
take advantage of them with Office. You might create an exclusively electronic document for your personal use, storing it on
your own PC in a file that you open whenever you need to see
the document. You might send copies of the document on
disk or via e-mail to other people, who can then display it on
their own computers even faster than they could access it on
the Web.

One typical use for an active document is as an on-screen form. Controls make it easy to create a document with fill-in-the-blank entry fields and boxes for checking off options. While you can accomplish the same end using custom-crafted dialog boxes (the VBA forms described in Chapter 56), why go that route when you can embed controls directly in a document? Figure 10-1 shows an example.

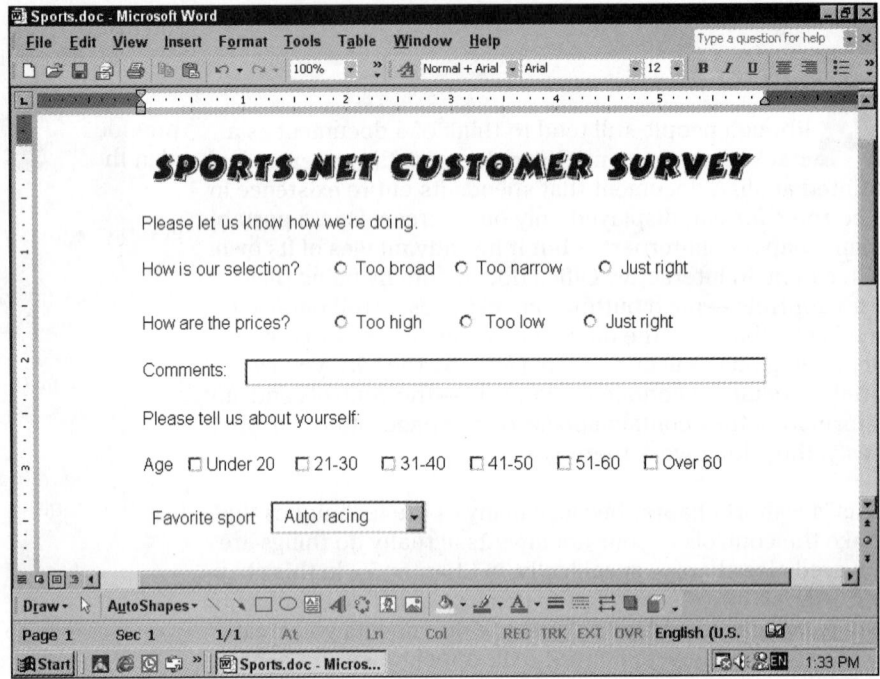

Figure 10-1: This Word document looks and functions like a paper form.

But you don't need to build an entire document around controls. Just a few simple checkboxes can enhance many on-screen documents.

About Controls in Office Documents

You can think of a control as any element in an on-screen document that reacts to a user action such as a mouse click. Controls supply checkboxes and entry blanks where the user can enter responses to questions or fill in information. The controls at your disposal fall into a number of overlapping groups:

✦ **Hyperlinks:** Hyperlinks are hotspots that when clicked take you to another location in the current document, to a different document, or to a Web page. You can use hyperlinks to make any Office document interactive. Simple text hyperlinks — the kind that typically appear on a Web page in blue type with an underline — are the most common. You can also assign a hyperlink to any picture (graphic) you insert in a document. Hyperlinks work just as well in ordinary Office documents as in Web pages.

Cross-Reference

For detailed information on working with hyperlinks in Office, see Chapter 45.

✦ **HTML controls:** In Word only, the Web Tools toolbar lets you insert standard HTML forms controls directly into documents destined to be Web pages. These controls work only on Web pages.

✦ **"Forms" controls:** The Forms toolbars in Excel and Word provide various controls unique to these two applications. These are discussed in the next section, "About Forms in Word and Excel."

✦ **AutoShapes:** AutoShapes were discussed in Chapter 9 as graphical elements, but you can turn them into active push buttons via simple menu commands. In Word, PowerPoint, and Excel documents they can serve as hyperlink buttons. In Excel, you can assign macros to AutoShapes. PowerPoint AutoShapes have special talents — when clicked, they can perform actions such as navigating to another slide or playing a sound. See the section "Working with Active AutoShapes" later in this chapter.

✦ **ActiveX controls:** ActiveX controls are standard software components that can be used in applications developed with programming tools such as VBA, Visual Basic, or C++. Office lets you place these same controls directly into your Word, Excel, and PowerPoint documents and then add VBA code "behind" them to get them to do tricks.

About Forms in Word and Excel

In Office, the term "form" means different things in different contexts. Generically, of course, a form is any document that has blanks, checkboxes, or other areas with which users of the document are expected to interact. However, other uses for the term are more specific. The custom dialog boxes and other windows you can build with VBA are technically called *forms*; Web pages can contain HTML forms, which you can readily create with Word — and both Word and Excel have their own special sorts of forms.

Long before VBA and HTML became universal Office tools, the forms tools in Word and Excel were making it possible to build active documents. You can still access these tools by displaying the Forms toolbar in either application. These toolbars provide various controls you can insert into your document, along with related buttons that help in forms design.

Word's Forms toolbar: Avoid it

In Word, the "old-style" controls on the Forms toolbar are few in number, limited in functionality, and really quite obsolete — everything you can do with them, you can do with ActiveX controls. They're provided only so you can display and edit documents created in older versions of Word.

Excel's Forms toolbar: Try it

In Excel, the controls on the Forms toolbar (see Figure 10-2) provide an easier way to create interactive on-screen worksheets, compared to the ActiveX controls described later in this chapter. That's because no VBA programming is required to make them work.

To activate the Forms toolbar, choose View ➪ Toolbars and select it from the list provided.

Figure 10-2: Excel's Forms toolbar is the easiest way to add controls to worksheets.

After you add a control to a worksheet, you can then build a formula that produces results based on the current value of the control. This requires that you link the control to a worksheet cell and then refer to the linked cell in your formula. To specify the linked cell, right-click the control and choose Format Control on the shortcut menu. In the resulting dialog box, switch to the Control tab. Then, in the Cell Link box, specify the cell that will display the current entry in the control as follows:

- ✦ For a checkbox, the linked cell displays either TRUE or FALSE.

- ✦ For a list or combo box, the linked cell displays the number of the item selected in the list.

- ✦ For spinner and scroll bar controls, the linked cell displays the numeric value selected by the control.

- ✦ In the case of a set of option buttons, the linked cell shows the number of the selected button.

To specify the items that are to appear in a list or combo box, type them into a worksheet column and then open the Format Control dialog box, switch to the Control tab, and enter the column in the Input Range field.

Tip   Although Excel controls aren't ActiveX controls, you can write VBA code for events, such as mouse clicks, that occur to the control. To add code, select the control by right-clicking it and then click the Edit Code button on the Forms toolbar. VBA event procedures for Excel controls appear in standard VBA code modules, whereas code for ActiveX controls embedded in a worksheet goes in the special code module for that worksheet. See Chapter 56 for details on writing event code for controls.

Working with Active AutoShapes

The basic technique for creating an active AutoShape — one that does something when you click it — has two steps: First you add the AutoShape to your document; then you select it and assign an action to it.

Cross-Reference   To learn how to add AutoShapes to documents, see Chapter 9.

To make an AutoShape into a hyperlink, select the AutoShape and choose Insert ⇨ Hyperlink. Alternatively, right-click the AutoShape and choose Hyperlink from its shortcut menu.

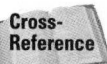

Cross-Reference   For details on working with hyperlinks, see Chapter 45.

To assign a macro to an AutoShape in Excel, right-click the shape and choose Assign Macro. The resulting Assign Macro dialog box lets you choose an existing macro for the shape or record a new one.

PowerPoint's AutoShapes have more capabilities than those in Word or Excel, probably because PowerPoint documents are usually presented rather than printed. In addition to triggering hyperlinks, PowerPoint AutoShapes can navigate to other slides, play sounds or video clips, run macros or other applications, or perform any actions permitted by OLE objects inserted on the slide. None of this requires any programming.

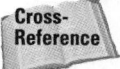

Cross-Reference   For details on working with AutoShapes in PowerPoint, see Chapter 37.

Adding ActiveX Controls

AutoShapes are great for graphical hyperlinks and triggering simple functions, but they can't display information. ActiveX controls are far more flexible and powerful. The controls that come with Office represent most of the standard types you see in Windows programs, and you can choose from a cornucopia of other ActiveX controls from Microsoft and third-party developers.

In Word, PowerPoint, and Excel you can use ActiveX controls directly in documents and on the custom VBA forms discussed in Chapter 56. By contrast, in Access and Outlook you can place controls only onto custom forms. However, Access and Outlook forms aren't standard VBA forms, and Access and Outlook forms are distinct from one another to boot. These variations can seem very confusing at first, but don't worry — you use the same basic methods to work with ActiveX controls in all applications.

Types of ActiveX controls

Table 10-1 lists the standard ActiveX controls included with Office, along with their uses.

Table 10-1 Office ActiveX Controls	
Control Name	*Use*
Checkbox	Indicates one of two possible values, such as *yes* or *no*, or *on* or *off*.
Text Box	Provides a place to type in text or information.
Command Button	Lets the user click the button to activate a hyperlink or VBA procedure.
Option Button	Used in groups; lets the user select one of several choices (also known as radio button).
List Box	Lets the user select one of several preset choices.
Combo Box	Lets the user select one of several preset choices or type in a new entry from scratch.
Toggle Button	Switches back and forth between two settings.
Spin Button	Contains two buttons that raise or lower a setting's value each time it's clicked.

Control Name	Use
Scroll Bar	Like a spin button. but with a bar between the buttons that displays the relative value of the setting graphically (also known as a slider).
Label	Displays text specified by the creator of the document.
Image	Displays a graphic that can be clicked.

Inserting ActiveX controls

To place an ActiveX control in a Word document, Excel worksheet, or PowerPoint slide, begin by activating the Control Toolbox, a special toolbar shown in Figure 10-3. The button for the Toolbox is located on the Visual Basic toolbar, but you can also display the Toolbox directly by choosing it from the View ➪ Toolbars menu.

Figure 10-3: Use the Control Toolbox to insert ActiveX controls into Office documents.

With the Toolbox on your screen, you can get down to the business of inserting the control. In Word, start by placing the insertion point where you want the control to appear. The location must be in the main part of your document — you can't place controls inside tables or text boxes. (You don't need to select a location first in PowerPoint or Excel.)

Now click the Toolbox button for the type of control you want. Word automatically places the control near the insertion point, but in the other two programs you must then click in the document where you want the control to go.

To insert an ActiveX control that's installed on your system but not visible on the Toolbox, click the More Controls button. A scrollable list of the available controls appears; select the control you want. Again, Chapter 56 goes through the technique for installing new ActiveX controls.

Using design mode

As soon as you insert an ActiveX control, Office switches to design mode — you can tell because the Design Mode button looks pressed in. When design mode is off, clicking a control triggers some response from the control. But when design mode is on, clicking a control selects it so that you can change its look or behavior. Use the handles (the little black squares) bordering a selected control to resize it, just as you would a graphical object. Drag anywhere else over the control to move it to a new location. To turn design mode on or off manually, just click the Design Mode button.

Tip   Word inserts each new ActiveX control into the document "in line" with the text at the insertion point—that is, as if the control is itself a text character. Although you can move the control around in the text, you can't position it freely anywhere on the page. To gain this freedom, right-click the control and choose Format Control from the shortcut menu. In the Format Control dialog box, switch to the Layout tab and click a Wrapping style other than In Line with Text—Tight or Square is usually the best choice. You can then move the control around in the document with abandon.

Controlling controls with properties

To change the look or behavior of a selected control, use the Properties dialog box. This box appears when you click the Properties button on the Control Toolbox. Although the properties available depend on the type of control you're working with, common ones include the foreground (text and arrow) and background colors, the font for text that appears on the control, and properties determining the control's size and location.

Cross-Reference   Control properties are discussed in much more depth in Chapter 56.

Tip   Normally, all the option buttons you insert in a document are part of one group—if you click one option button to turn it on, all the other option buttons get turned off. However, you can set up more than one group of option buttons in the same document using the `GroupName` property. To assign option buttons to a particular group, just type the identical text in each button's GroupName field. The buttons in each group then function independently so that each group has its own active button.

Working with controls—with and without programming

As soon as you add any control to a document and leave design mode, the control is ready to react to mouse clicks. But these reactions aren't usually useful by themselves. For example, clicking a checkbox makes the box looked checked but doesn't do anything else unless you write VBA code that responds to the click event. Likewise, you can drag the thumb in a scroll bar control to a new position, but to make that change do something useful in a document you must write code that carries out some action in response.

To get started writing a VBA procedure that dictates a control's behavior, select the control and click the View Code button on the Control Toolbox. You're whisked to the control's Code window in the Visual Basic Editor, where you can type in the code. Chapter 56 covers the details on writing VBA code for controls.

However, some of Office's ActiveX controls respond in useful ways without any programming, especially because their current settings are saved with the document. These include the checkbox, option button, and text box controls.

When you click a checkbox control, for example, you see a check mark alternately appear and disappear in the box. You might insert a checkbox to enable an editor to indicate whether he or she has finished reviewing the document. Similarly, clicking an option button activates it and deactivates the previously active option button. And when you click a text box, a blinking insertion point appears in the box and you can start typing text. Because Office saves the current control settings and text, you can use these controls to give users a way both to highlight current information in a graphically interesting way and to store it directly in the document. To store control values in a database, however, requires the programming techniques discussed in Chapters 49 and 50.

✦　　✦　　✦

Sharing Information

Opening up the dams of divergent file formats to let the information within flow freely can be a challenge. Office places at your disposal three main methods for transferring information among documents:

♦ Through the Clipboard, cut- or copy and paste, or drag and drop

♦ By exporting and importing the information to and from disk files

♦ By using Object Linking and Embedding (OLE), which enables you to edit the information in the destination document using the commands native to the application from which the information came

Note   This list omits one of the most powerful information-sharing techniques: automated data passing using VBA techniques. To get a taste of what that method can accomplish, consult Part XI.

Power Clipboard Techniques and Utilities

The standard Cut and Copy commands send information from a source document to the Clipboard, a temporary holding area available to all Windows applications. Any type of data — text, graphics, sound files, anything — can be sent to the Clipboard. From the Clipboard, you can then paste the information into any application that understands that data type.

When you use the Edit ➪ Paste command to place the Clipboard contents into a destination document, the information merges with the document without retaining any connection to its source document or to the source application. The pasted data can be edited only with whatever tools the destination application provides.

Of course, as a Windows user you already know all about these Clipboard basics. But Office XP applications introduce some wrinkles, including a new Clipboard task pane that gives a boost to cut- or copy-and-paste operations. In addition, special Paste commands and a new Paste Options button enables you to control the way the receiving application inserts the data.

When to use the Clipboard

Transferring information into a document using the conventional Cut- or Copy-and-Paste commands via the Clipboard makes sense when:

✦ Speed is important.

✦ You're sure you won't need to update the data in the future.

✦ You plan to share the document with someone who doesn't have access to the application that created the information you're transferring (in which case an OLE connection wouldn't work).

✦ Your computer is too slow or has too little memory to use OLE efficiently.

Using the Clipboard taskbar

Office's Clipboard taskbar gives a major boost to information transfers via the Cut, Copy, and Paste commands. Office now stores cut or copied items in 24 separate slots in its own Office Clipboard for later retrieval when you need them. What's more, the Office Clipboard can receive these items from any Windows program. Figure 11-1 shows the Clipboard task pane.

Tip   To display the Office Clipboard task pane at any time, choose Edit ⇨ Office Clipboard, or press Ctrl+C twice.

In the task pane, the items you have copied to the Office Clipboard are listed one above the other in a menu that scrolls as necessary to accommodate up to 24 items. You'll also see a snatch of text or a thumbnail image to remind you of what each item is, while the icon of the program it originated in is displayed along the left edge of the task pane.

If you hold the mouse pointer over an item in the task pane, a downward-pointing arrow will appear. Click that to bring up a small menu that lets you either paste the item into the application you're currently working in or delete it from the Clipboard. However, you don't need that menu to paste an item; simply clicking on it has the same effect.

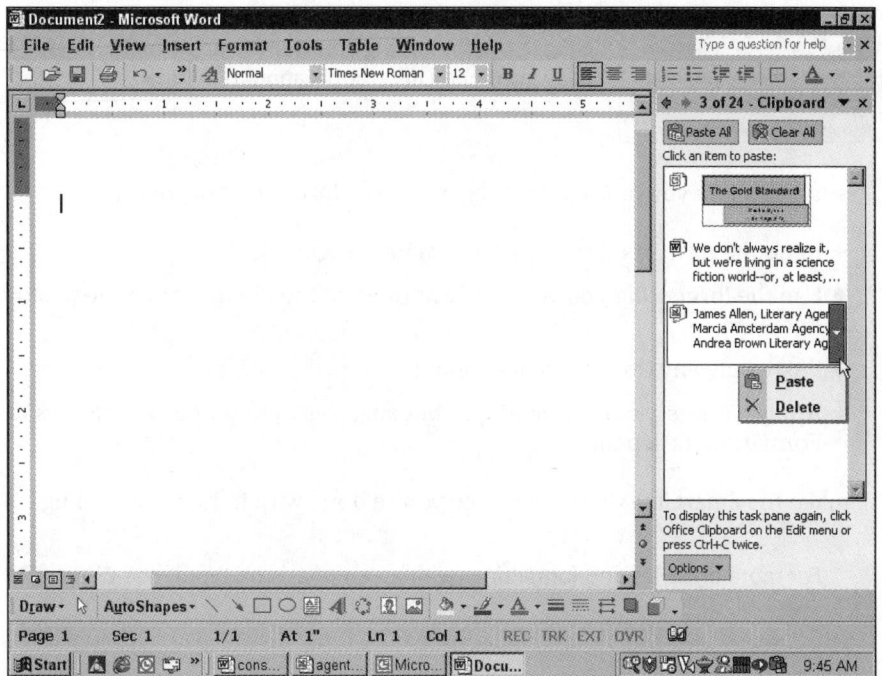

Figure 11-1: The Clipboard task pane shows chunks of data from PowerPoint, Word, and Excel, all ready to be pasted whenever and wherever you need them.

At the top of the task pane are two buttons. One enables you to paste everything in the Clipboard into your current application at once (starting with the bottom item in the Clipboard task pane—which was the first one you copied into the Clipboard—and working up to the top item in the task pane, the most recently copied). The other button clears the entire Clipboard.

Note   When you paste an item from the Clipboard toolbar into a document, that item is passed to the Windows Clipboard. In other words, you can paste the same item again and again using the standard Windows Edit ➪ Paste command or its Ctrl+V shortcut.

Using paste options

As soon as you paste an item, Office pops up a Smart Tag—in this case, a small image of a Clipboard. If you point at this tag a downward-pointing arrow will appear; clicking it opens the new Paste Options menu (see Figure 11-2).

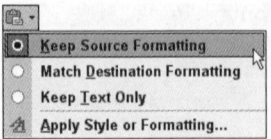

Figure 11-2: The new Paste Options Smart Tag lets you choose the formatting you want to apply to items you copy from one Office application to another.

This menu offers you four choices regarding the formatting of your item:

✦ Keep the formatting the pasted item had originally.

✦ Use the formatting you've already applied to the document you're pasting the item into.

✦ Paste only any text the item contains.

✦ Apply a new style or formatting. Choosing this option opens the Styles and Formatting task pane.

To make the Smart Tag disappear once you're done with it, just start typing.

For more on styles and formatting (with an emphasis on Word) see Chapter 18.

When you paste a drawing or picture, the Paste Options Smart Tag doesn't appear.

Placing items in the Office Clipboard

Pasting items from the Clipboard task pane into a document is easy enough, but how do you get those items onto the Office Clipboard in the first place? No special techniques are required—anything you cut or copy in any Windows application automatically enters the Office Clipboard as long as the item is stored in a format recognized by Office.

Alternatives to the standard Paste command

Office provides two variations on the plain old Paste command for placing Clipboard data into an application: the Edit ➪ Paste Special and Edit ➪ Paste as Hyperlink commands.

Specialty pasting

When an application places information on the Clipboard, it often does so in more than one form. That way, the receiving application (or the person using it) can decide which form should go into the document.

In all five Office applications, the Edit ➪ Paste Special command lets you control how Clipboard information reaches the destination document.

Figure 11-3 shows the Paste Special dialog box as you see it when information from another application is on the Clipboard (in Excel, the Paste Special dialog box looks completely different when you're pasting information placed onto the Clipboard from within Excel itself). The options within the dialog box will vary depending on what kind of information you're pasting. In this case, the options are to past the copied material as HTML coding, Unicode text, or ordinary text.

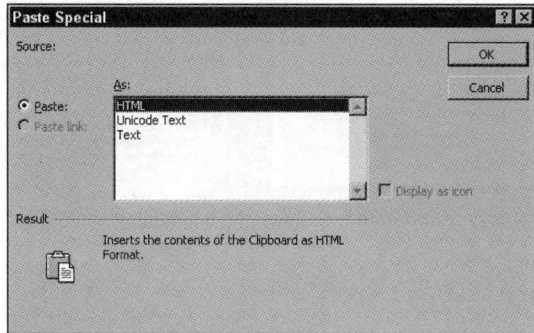

Figure 11-3: Pasting Word text into Excel with the Edit ➪ Paste Special command

Cross-Reference

The Paste Special dialog box is also one route to placing OLE objects into your document. See "Specialty pasting, part II: Pasting objects" in the section on OLE later in this chapter.

Pasting data as a hyperlink

In all the Office applications except Outlook, you can create a hyperlink to another document by pasting data from the source document. Once the hyperlink is in place, one click on it jumps you to the original document. There, the Web toolbar automatically appears, so you can return to the document containing the hyperlink by clicking the Back button.

To insert a hyperlink this way, place text or numeric information on the Clipboard and switch to the destination application. There, use the Edit ➪ Paste as Hyperlink command instead of doing a regular paste. This isn't an OLE link—the pasted data are treated as if pasted the regular way (Excel cells become a table in Word, for example), but they appear with the telltale underlined characters of a hyperlink (see Figure 11-4).

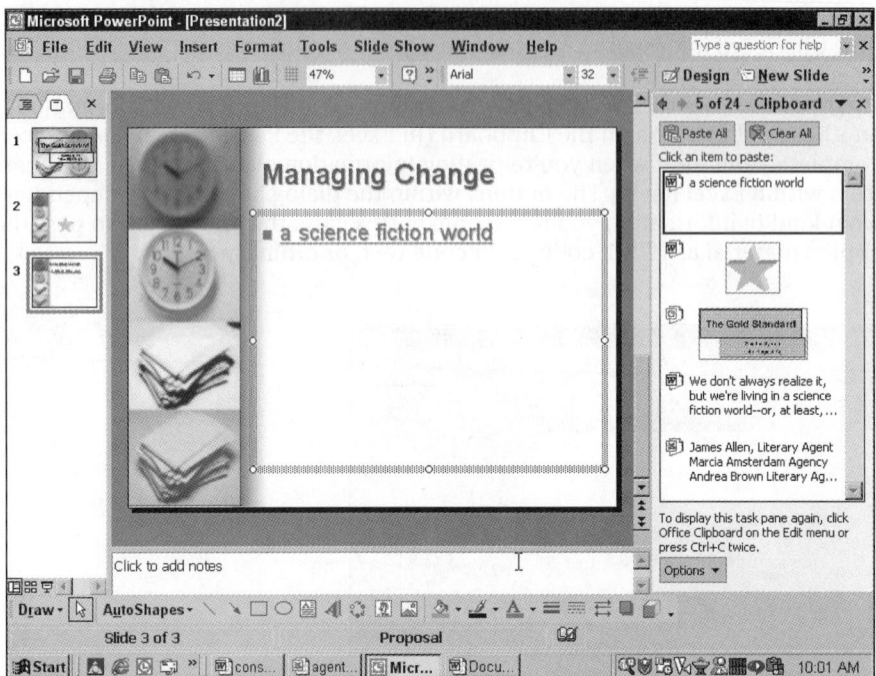

Figure 11-4: I've just pasted a line of text from a Word document into a PowerPoint slide as a hyperlink. Someone viewing the PowerPoint presentation online can now click on that hyperlink and read the full text of the article it refers to.

> **Note** One important first step: The source document must have been saved first, or Paste as Hyperlink won't be available because the receiving document won't know where to find it.

Using the Clipboard with specific types of data

Office applications often differ in their treatment of information transferred through the Clipboard, either on the sending or receiving ends of the transfer. The next few sections describe some of these variations on the cut-copy-paste theme.

Transferring Word text to other Office applications

PowerPoint, Excel, and Outlook all recognize character formatting in pasted text originating in Word. But all formatting is lost when you paste text from Word into Access, which converts pasted text into its default font.

Transferring tabular data into Word

When inserted via the ordinary Paste command, information from an Excel worksheet or Access database ends up in Word as a table. Again, you have the option, via the Paste Options Smart Tag, to keep the source formatting, match the destination table style, or paste the table as text only. In Figure 11-5, the table originated in Excel, and its original color coding was kept when it was pasted into Word, as you can see on the Smart Tag menu.

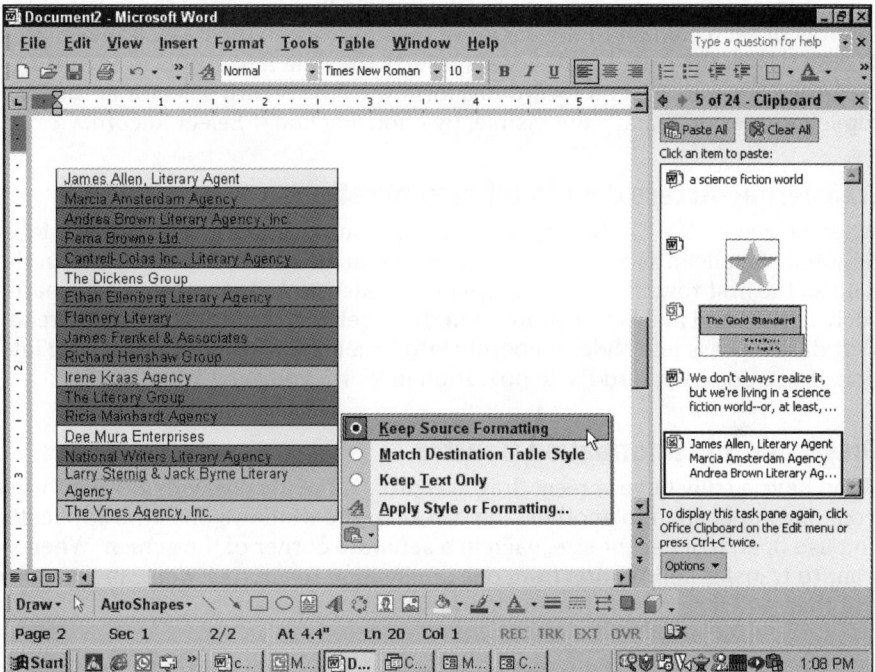

Figure 11-5: Word created this colored table from information pasted from an Excel worksheet.

Inserting information into Access via the Clipboard

To bring information into Access from another application via cut- or copy-and-paste, the data must be organized in tabular format. Sources that Access accepts include Excel worksheets, Word tables, and text manually formatted in tabular form with a tab between each column.

To paste the information into an Access datasheet (a table, a query, or a form displayed as a datasheet), select enough rows or columns to hold all the incoming data. Of course, the order of the columns in the source information should match that of the destination datasheet. You can choose whether to replace current records or add the pasted data in new records. To replace existing records in the datasheet, select their rows and choose Paste. To add the data as new records at the bottom of the table, choose Edit ⇨ Paste Append.

Pasting into a form that displays a single record at a time is a little trickier. In this case, Access checks the data you're transferring in, comparing the entries in the top row of each column to the names of the controls on the form. If they match, Access pastes the data. If not, Access inserts the data into the form according to its tab order. You can select a record in a form with the record selector at the form's top-left corner or, if that's not visible, by choosing Edit ⇨ Select Record.

Transferring Access data to other applications

When placed on the Clipboard, information from Access is formatted with tabs between each field, as you'd expect. The field names are always included in the data as the first row. Rich Text information is also included, so simple formatting such as bold and italics will show up in the receiving application, if it can read Rich Text data. Access info slides smoothly into Excel complete with formatting information. If you do a standard Paste operation in Word, you get a Word table.

Drag-and-drop information transfer

If you have a truly huge screen, drag and drop is the ideal way to move information from one application to another. You can keep the windows of all the applications you use open to a decent size, each in a separate corner of the screen. When you want to transfer information from one application to another, you can just select it and then pull it across with a quick drag-and-drop operation.

Office permits just such supereasy information transfers. Anything you can place on the Clipboard, you can drag to another application where you can drop it into place. That goes for graphics as well as text or worksheet cells. Take a look at Figure 11-6.

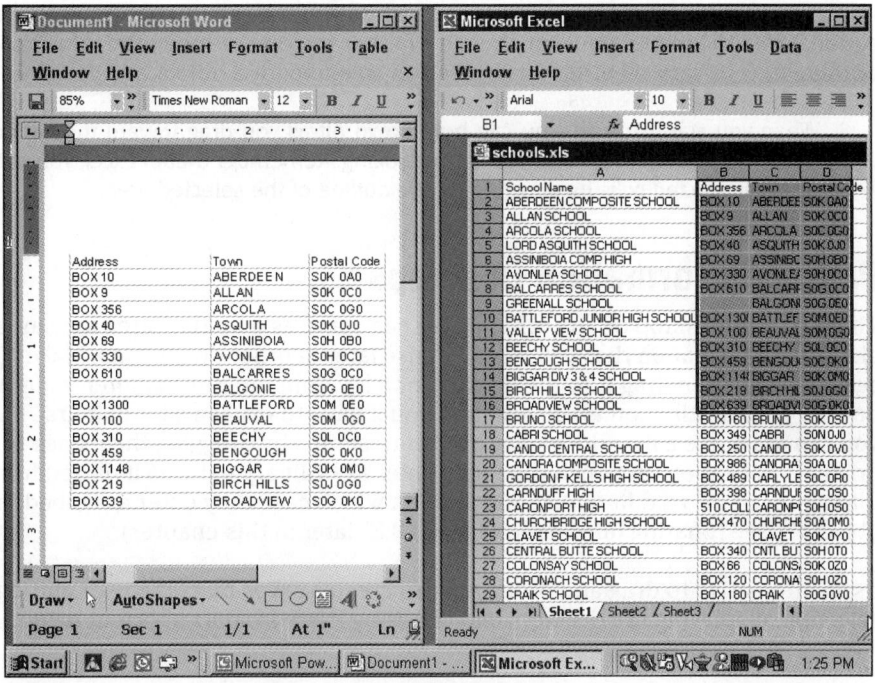

Figure 11-6: I've just dragged the highlighted portion of the Excel spreadsheet at right into the Word document at left.

Left- and right-button dragging

Left-dragging moves the selected item from the source document to the destination. Hold down Ctrl while you left-drag to copy the item instead. Note that depending on which two applications are involved and where you start, the information may be transferred as ordinary Clipboard data or as an embedded object (see the "Sharing Information Using OLE" section later).

Tip

In real life, few screens are big enough to permit multiple windows of any useful size. Most people work with only one application at a time, keeping its window maximized to fill the whole screen. If that's your practice, you can still take advantage of drag and drop. The key is the Windows taskbar. Select the information you want to move or copy, and drag it to the icon on the taskbar for the destination application. Keep the mouse button held down there, until the second application appears on the screen. You can now deposit the information in its new home.

If you right-drag, you get a shortcut menu when you release the button at the destination. From the menu, you can choose whether to copy or move the information, or to paste it in various other forms such as an embedded object or hyperlink.

Tip When you start in Excel, you can hold down Alt as you drag toward the window border to prevent the worksheet from scrolling. Remember that in Excel, you move or copy selected cells by dragging on the outline of the selected area.

Parking information in scraps

The Windows desktop or any other folder can serve as a holding area for random chunks of information that you intend to use later in other documents. Make a selection and then drag it to the desktop or a My Computer or Explorer folder window. (If your destination is the desktop, you'll have to expose a bit of it first.) Later, you can assemble a new document from your scraps by dragging them back to the original application (in which case they enter as ordinary data, as if pasted from the Clipboard) or into a different application (in which case they enter as embedded objects — see "Sharing Information Using OLE" later in this chapter).

As an alternative to drag and drop, you can create scraps by copying or cutting a selection, displaying the desktop, and choosing Paste from its shortcut menu.

Importing and Exporting

When you need to add large amounts of data created in another application to a document, the best approach is often to import information stored in a disk file. In Office, importing information stored in a foreign file format is as simple as opening the file, via the File ➪ Open, Insert ➪ Picture, or (in Word) Insert ➪ File commands. The only catch is that you must have installed a converter for the file format you're trying to import. Also known as filters or translators, converters are software plug-ins that perform the translations between foreign data formats and that of the Office application you're using.

Office comes with converters for a large number of common file formats of various types: word processor documents, database and spreadsheet files, graphic images, and files of personal information managers (Word even has an import converter for Excel worksheets). Some of these converters are automatically installed, but you can select among many optional converters when you run Office Setup.

To see whether a converter for the import file's format is installed, look at the list at Files of Type in the Open or Insert dialog box. File types are listed either by the name of the source application (as in WordPerfect 5.*x*) or by description (for some graphics file formats, and generic formats for tabular data).

Importing: Techniques and troubleshooting

The easiest way to import any file is simply to try to open it, without specifying what format it's in. Select All Files at Files of Type, locate the file, and choose Open or Insert. Office can usually figure out what format the data is stored in without any help from you.

If you like, you can select the correct format — assuming its converter is installed — at Files of Type. When you do, Office modifies the file list to show only files with the extensions typically associated with files of that type. The main value of this step is just to help you pick out the file you want to import in a sea of other files.

Sometimes, however, Office needs your help in determining how to convert the file. Access and Outlook have special commands for importing data. In Access, choose File ➪ Get External Data ➪ Import. Outlook comes with an Import and Export Wizard for converting to and from the formats of other personal information manager (PIM) software. Use File ➪ Import and Export to start it.

The import process goes smoothly most of the time. But what if the import file's format isn't listed at Files of Type? What if you can't see the import file in the file list? And worst of all, what if Office bungles the import process and the incoming data appears in your document as gibberish?

Installing additional file format converters

If you don't see the import file's format in the list at Files of Type, don't get too excited until you've checked to see whether you just forgot to install the necessary converter. To see what's available, run Setup and select Add or Remove Features. In the resulting dialog box, open up Office Shared Features and then Converters and Filters. You'll find both Text Converters and Graphic Filters to choose from (see Figure 11-7). The Setup items for Word, PowerPoint, and Excel each offer one or more miscellaneous converters as well.

Tip   Additional converters are available through Microsoft. Visit the Microsoft Office Web site at `www.microsoft.com/office`.

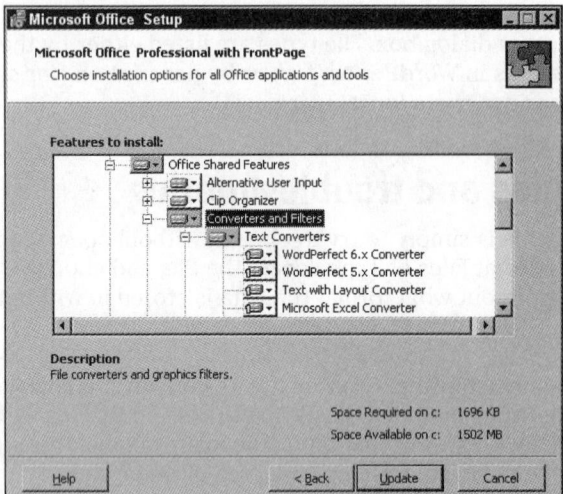

Figure 11-7: Use this item in Setup to install your choice of the many file converters provided with Office.

If you don't see your files when trying to import them

When you select a specific file format in the Open or Insert dialog box, Office displays only files having the extension it thinks files of that type ought to have. If your import file has a different extension, it won't appear in the file list. You can deal with this in two ways:

✦ Rename the import file, giving it the extension Office prefers. You can do this directly from the Open or Insert dialog box by selecting All Files (*.*) at Files of Type, locating the file, and choosing Rename on its shortcut menu.

✦ After selecting the proper format at Files of Type, enter the import file's extension into the File Name box, as in *.art or *.cog, pressing F5 or Enter to refresh the display. A caveat: If the import file has a filename extension that Office recognizes as belonging to a different format, Office may get confused about which converter to use. If necessary, rename the file to match Office's expectations.

If the import converter is missing or doesn't work

Despite the wealth of converters that come with Office, at times you will want to import a type of file that your Office application can't convert properly. This may be because the import file was created in VisiCalc, MacWrite, or some other long-forgotten or extremely alien program, and a converter for that file format just doesn't exist. In some cases, however, it's because the Office converter isn't as accurate as it ought to be. Recent versions of Word, for example, are well known for making goofs when importing files created in Word for DOS.

Whatever the cause, this problem can be remedied — if you're lucky — in one of two ways:

✦ By using the source application to export the information into a format that the destination application does understand. Even the most obscure software usually provides an Export command that will generate a file Office can read, even if it's just straight text. Of course, this works only if you have access to the source application.

✦ By using third-party utilities to convert the file from its current format to one that the destination application can read. See "Mass conversions" later in this chapter.

Importing database and spreadsheet data

Using the File ➪ Open command, you can quickly import a database object (usually a table) into Word or Excel. The problem is that all the information in the object enters your document or worksheet, leaving you to delete columns or rows that aren't germane to your purposes at the moment. Also, this works only with database objects that are stored in their own separate files — you can't open a single table residing in an Access database, for example.

You need other tools to reach inside complete databases and extract specific information from one or more of its objects. Office comes with data source drivers for many different database formats, including dBase, Paradox, 1-2-3, and — through ODBC — many others, including high-end, networked databases such as Oracle.

To import via these drivers in Word, click the Insert Database button on the Database toolbar and choose Get Data. (You can display the Database toolbar by choosing View ➪ Toolbars and selecting it from the list displayed.)

In the Select Data Source dialog box, pick the type of database file you're importing at Files of Type, browse to and select the file itself, and choose Open.

You can also click New Source to start the Data Connection Wizard, which will lead you through the process of connecting to a specific data source (see Figure 11-8).

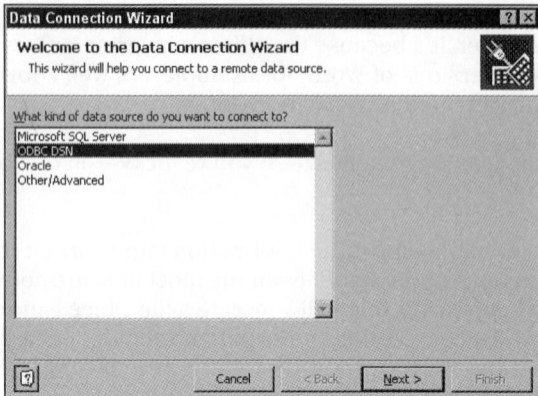

Figure 11-8: The Data Connection Wizard makes the process of connecting to a specific database much easier.

Although Excel can import a variety of database files by opening them with the File ➪ Open command, to focus on records meeting your criteria or to import data relationally, use the command Data ➪ Import External Data ➪ New Database Query. This opens the Choose Data Source dialog box. Check the "Use the Query Wizard to create/edit queries" box to have Office lead you through the process step by step.

Exporting data

You can look at the data transfer problem from either the source or the destination. When your data are bound for another program, you can be sure they'll get there by exporting them to a file format that you know the other program can read.

Even within Office, exporting is sometimes useful for data transfers between applications. More often, though, you'll be exporting to share your information with others who don't use Office XP. Exporting your data to a file format their programs recognize will help them out.

Here are some tips on exporting from Office:

✦ In most Office applications, you export using the File ➪ Save As command. In the Save As dialog box, select the format for the export file from the list at Save as Type. As with importing, you may need to install additional converters to export the data in the desired format (see "Installing additional file format converters" earlier in this chapter).

✦ If you routinely share files with users of another program, you can set Excel, Word, and PowerPoint to save automatically in any supported format you choose. In the Tools ➪ Options dialog box, go to the Save tab (for Excel, the Transition tab). Make your selection from the Save As drop-down list.

✦ In Access, you can use Access's File ➪ Export command to export an Access object. Your choices for the format of the exported information are numerous. You can create an Excel worksheet (Excel can open that, of course), a Rich Text Format file (which Word and other word processors can import with preservation of the tabular database layout), or a plain text file. You can also export the object in a database or Web format.

✦ In Outlook, you export to other personal information managers via the File ➪ Import and Export command.

✦ Because Office files are so sophisticated these days, what with all the formatting information, versions, comments, and so on, it's a near certainty that some elements in your document will be left behind when you export the information. *C'est la vie*; but if you want to be sure that at least all the text in a document gets to its destination, you may have to manually copy items to the Clipboard and then into Word for export.

Generic import/export file formats

When more sophisticated converters are unavailable or don't work properly, you can usually transfer textual data from one application to another in one of several generic, lowest common denominator formats:

✦ At the very lowest level, it's usually possible to extract the raw text from a document without too much trouble. Most applications store text in a linear fashion, so you can import the document into Word as a text file and then use Find and Replace supplemented by manual editing to remove extraneous garbage. Better yet, open the file in Word by first selecting Recover Text from Any File at Files of Type in the Open dialog box. This choice tells Word to comb the chosen file for data that's recognizable as text and import only that information.

✦ Nearly every spreadsheet and database program can read and write (import and export) comma- or tab-delimited files. Word and many word processors can handle these files too. They're stored in plain text format, but the data are organized in a structured way. Each row of the table occupies a single line of the file, and the columns within a row are separated by commas or tab characters. These files contain no formatting, but they work well for transferring the essential information from one application to another.

✦ Most up-to-date word processors understand the Rich Text Format. RTF files contain very sophisticated formatting information, but they are stored as ordinary text, with special bracketed codes representing the font and layout instructions — similar to the way HTML does it (see Figure 11-9). RTF files have a two-sided appeal. If the destination application understands them fully, the document should translate with formatting preserved. If not, because these are stored as standard text files, it's relatively easy to extract their text.

✦ All Office applications enable you to import and export files in HTML format, readable by a Web browser.

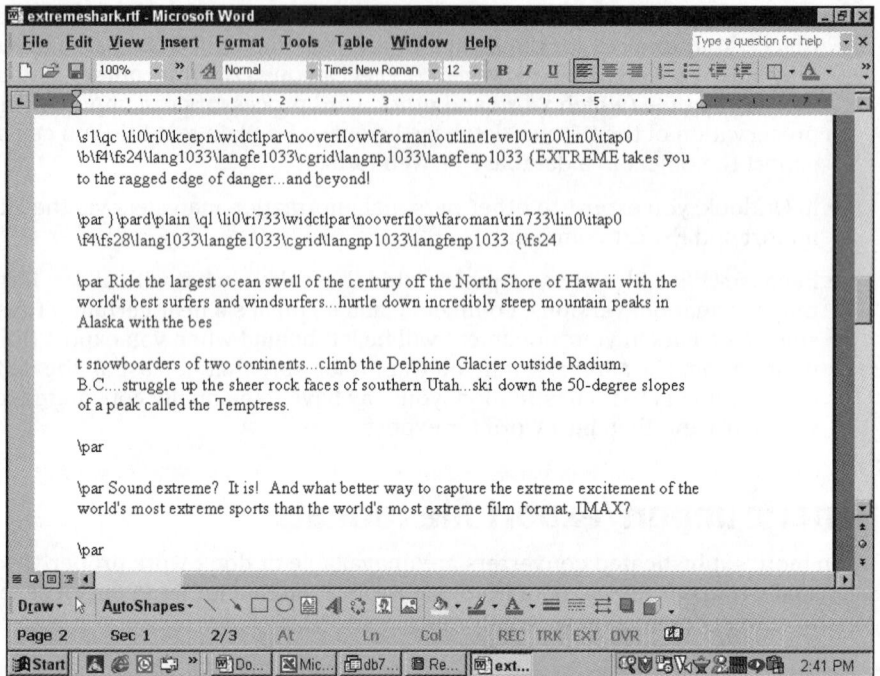

Figure 11-9: A Rich Text file opened in Word using the Recover Text from Any File option. Those unintelligible codes are formatting instructions.

Cross-Reference   See Chapter 45 for more on saving Office files in HTML format.

Mass conversions

When Office mangles data you're trying to import, or if it lacks an export converter for a desired file format, investing in a utility to handle the translation may make sense. Here are products to look into:

✦ **General:** To convert from or to almost every common format, check out Conversions Plus (DataViz, www.dataviz.com). It contains converters for most PC and Macintosh word processors. Graphics, spreadsheet, and database formats are well represented as well. In addition to the converters, Conversions Plus includes a viewer that lets you peek into any file of a supported file type from My Computer or Explorer, and MacOpener, a tool that lets you open Mac-formatted disks (including SCSI hard disks, Zip and SyQuest cartridges, and CD-ROMs).

✦ **Graphics:** While Conversions Plus converts a number of graphics file formats, Paint Shop Pro (JASC, `www.jasc.com`) handles many more and is a great choice for this specific need. In my tests, Paint Shop Pro has been flawless at converting one image format into another.

✦ **Database:** Data Junction (Data Junction, `www.datajunction.com`) is a powerhouse conversion tool for tabular data from just about any source, from structured text files on up to mainframe database tables. It handles complex data structures that can gag the importing routines in Office, and it supports far more file formats. The same publisher markets Content Extractor (formerly known as Cambio), a remarkable tool for extracting information stored in unstructured text files and organizing it into tabular format.

Tip   You can download free trial versions of Paint Shop Pro, Data Junction and Content Extractor from the Web sites mentioned above. Although you'll have to pay for the software if you want to keep using it, downloading a free trial version is a great way to find out if the software does what you want it to do — and to get a feel for how conversion tools work.

Sharing Information Using OLE

Object Linking and Embedding isn't mentioned much any more in the Office documentation or help files — maybe because OLE just isn't a very sexy acronym. But OLE technology is still very much alive in Windows and in Office XP.

OLE permits a document to serve as a kind of container for distinct hunks of information created in other applications. In the obvious Office example, a Word document can contain — interspersed with text created in Word itself — an Excel worksheet, a PowerPoint slide, and, via DDE (a predecessor of OLE), the results of a query of an Access database.

Instead of being merged into the destination document, each of these information hunks remains an independent object, rather like an apple bobbing in a bucket of water, and retains its connection with the source application. As a result, the information within an object can't be edited with the tools of the destination application (Word's, in this example).

OLE, however, lets you open the object for editing. When you do, the source application's menus and toolbars appear, and all of its functionality is at your disposal. But as Figure 11-10 shows, you haven't left the container document: you can still see the rest of the document, and the title bar still bears the destination application's name.

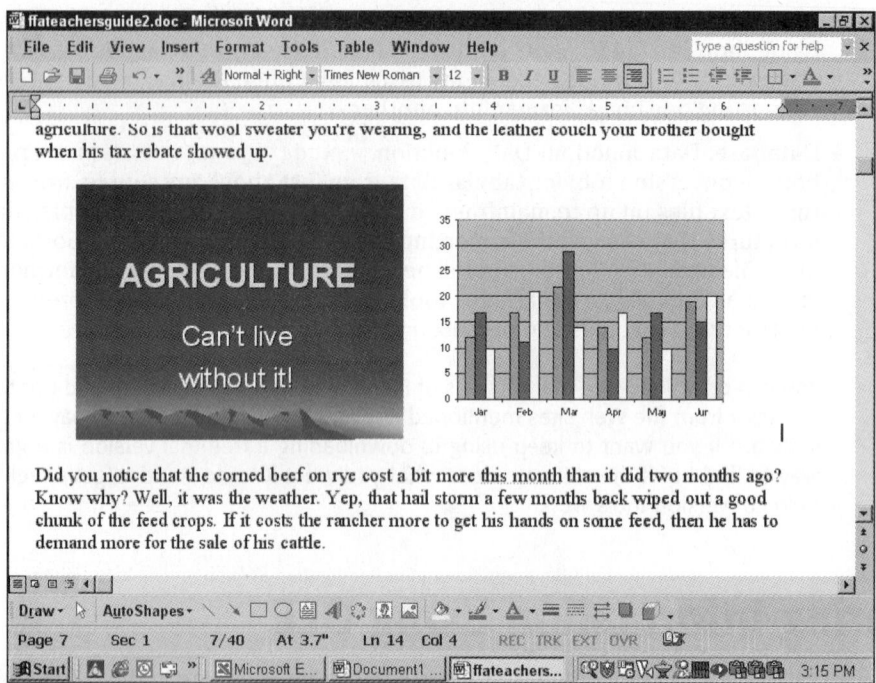

Figure 11-10: Here are a PowerPoint slide (at left) and an Excel chart (at right) embedded in a Word document.

The difference between linking and embedding

Office may no longer talk about OLE, but it does talk about linking and embedding a fair amount. Although both of these OLE techniques place objects created in one application into documents created in another, there's a key difference.

An embedded object exists only in association with the destination document and can be opened only there. Think of embedding as a connection to the source application. Embedding is the default type for most OLE connections in Office.

A linked object represents a gateway to all or part of a source document, stored independently in its own disk file. You can open a linked object from within the destination document, yes, but you can also open the file it represents with the object's source application. If you make changes to the document in the source application, those changes appear in the destination document — after all, the linked object in essence is the source document, or at least part of it.

So insert a linked object if you want to be able to edit it separately with the source application, even when the destination document isn't open.

The pros and cons of OLE

OLE offers huge benefits, but they don't come free. The cost/benefit analysis appears in Table 11-1.

Table 11-1 Counting the Blessings and the Cost of OLE	
Advantages	*Disadvantages*
Allows mixing and matching of information from different applications.	Must have continuous access to the source application.
Places information from another application into the document without any loss of formatting.	If the object is linked, the source document must remain accessible and must not be moved or renamed.
Allows later editing of the object with the full functionality of the source application.	Slows down the system and requires lots of memory.

Placing objects in your documents

If you decide OLE is for you, you can take any of several routes to your destination, as usual:

✦ The Edit ➪ Paste Special command.

✦ The Insert menu. Relevant commands include Insert ➪ Object, Insert ➪ Picture, and Insert ➪ Chart, among others.

✦ Application-specific commands (for example, you can send a PowerPoint slide as an object to a Word document using a menu command, File ➪ Send To ➪ Microsoft Word).

Specialty pasting, part II: Pasting objects

Probably the simplest way to embed or link an object is with the Edit ➪ Paste Special command. If the information on the Clipboard is packaged as an object, one of the choices on the Paste Special dialog box will let you insert it in that form.

For example, when you copy Excel cells to the Clipboard, Excel bundles them up as an object. In Word, the standard Paste command ignores the object packaging, inserting the cell data as a Word table. But on the Paste Special dialog box, you have the choice of pasting the same information as a Microsoft Excel Worksheet Object, as shown in Figure 11-11.

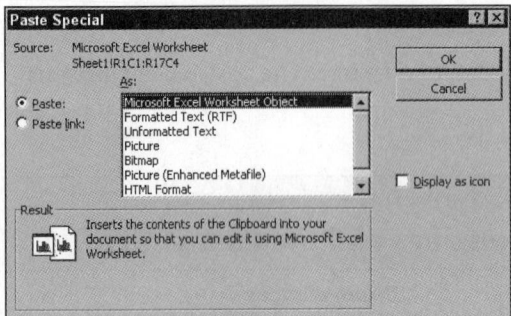

Figure 11-11: The Paste Special dialog box in Word, as it appears when Excel data is on the Clipboard

Note Whether information on the Clipboard winds up in the destination document as an embedded object, a linked object, or ordinary merged information depends on your choice of settings in the Paste Special dialog box, and also on the information itself.

To embed an object, choose the Paste radio button. This button's behavior is a little tricky. With ordinary Clipboard information — that isn't packaged as an object — choosing the Paste radio button inserts the information without any connection to the source application. When an object is on the Clipboard, the same Paste button embeds the object. How can you tell which type of information you're dealing with? The item name listed at "As" should give you a clue, but look at the help text listed at "Result" — if the explanation listed there ends with something like "... so you can edit it with (*source application*)," the item will be embedded.

To link the object, choose Paste Link, which is available only if the Clipboard contains an object. The wrinkle here is that you can often paste the object as a link in any of the formats listed in the Paste Special dialog box, when embedding is possible only with the standard object type. For example, Word lets you paste an Excel object as a link in plain text format. You can then edit and format this text within Word. Because the text you're working with is actually a Link field, however, updating the field (F9) removes your edits and displays the current values from the source file. You can also select the field and choose Edit ➪ Linked Object to edit the object using the source application.

Some objects can be displayed in your document as an icon, which the viewer then clicks on to open the object itself. This option is discussed further later in this chapter.

Inserting objects

If you don't already have the source application running, creating an object by inserting it is often the way to go. The relevant commands on the Insert menu in Word, Excel, and PowerPoint include Picture and Object. (To insert objects in Access, you must use the Insert ⇨ Object command, the Unbound Object Frame tool, or an image control, depending on issues too complex to discuss here.)

Inserting items named on the Insert menu

When is an inserted item not an object? When you choose Insert ⇨ Picture ⇨ From File or in Word, Insert ⇨ File. The inserted information enters your document as if you had used the standard Paste command, not as an embedded or linked object that you can edit with the source application. However, if you choose Insert as Link (by clicking on the downward-pointing arrow on the right end of the Insert button), a link is established between the inserted object and the source file — that is, any changes you make to the file in the source file object will show up in the object inserted in your document.

Other items listed on the Insert menu and on the Insert ⇨ Picture submenu are always inserted as objects, almost always as embedded objects. These items vary from application to application. Excel has an Insert ⇨ Diagram command, whereas PowerPoint offers Insert ⇨ Chart and Insert ⇨ Movies and Sounds. In Word, the Picture submenu lets you insert a chart or a scanned image. In Excel and PowerPoint, you can insert organization charts from the same submenu.

Note That these items are objects isn't obvious, in that the source applications are often hidden applets included with Office. Clip art, charts, WordArt text effects, maps, equations, organization charts, and all drawing objects created in Office work this way. Because you can't run the applets as standalone applications, you can only embed their objects. You can't store the objects in separate files, so linking is impossible.

Inserting objects of any type

The Insert ⇨ Object command is a fallback technique for placing any type of object into your document. The resulting dialog box (see Figure 11-12) has two radio buttons: one for creating a new object from scratch, the other for inserting an existing file as an object.

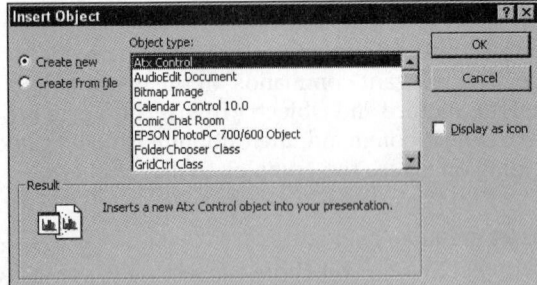

Figure 11-12: The Insert Object dialog box gives you many options.

The "Create new" button inserts embedded objects only. It lists all the object types registered on your system. When you select an object type, the corresponding application starts up with a new item at the ready. Add and edit information to taste, and then select File ➪ Exit. You'll be back in your own document where the newly embedded object should be visible.

You can embed or link objects with the "Create from file" button. Just locate the file with the Browse button and then specify whether the inserted object should be embedded or linked by clearing or checking the Link box.

Note

You can insert any file as an object of sorts, but you can only edit the object within your document if its file type supports OLE, as registered with your system. A non-OLE file appears in your document as an icon (see Figure 11-13). If the file type is associated with an application (non-OLE), you can open the file in its source application in a separate window by choosing Edit ➪ Package Object ➪ Activate Contents. You aren't automatically returned to your document when you close the file.

Other ways to place objects in documents

Depending on the Office applications you're working with, you may be able to tap special commands for transferring objects from one application to another. The list includes these possibilities:

✦ In PowerPoint, the File ➪ Send To ➪ Microsoft Word command creates a new Word document containing the current PowerPoint slide or presentation. You're given a choice of page layouts and the option to simply paste the slide or paste it as a linked object.

✦ In Access, you can create an Excel PivotTable object to analyze information in your Access database. Select Forms in the Database window, click the New button, and in the New Form dialog box choose PivotTable Wizard.

✦ In Word, you can insert an updateable database using the Database toolbar. After displaying the toolbar, click the Insert Database button, click New Source, and then choose Other/Advanced in the first window of the wizard. This will provide a long list of OLE database providers. Choose the type of database you want, then continue with the wizard.

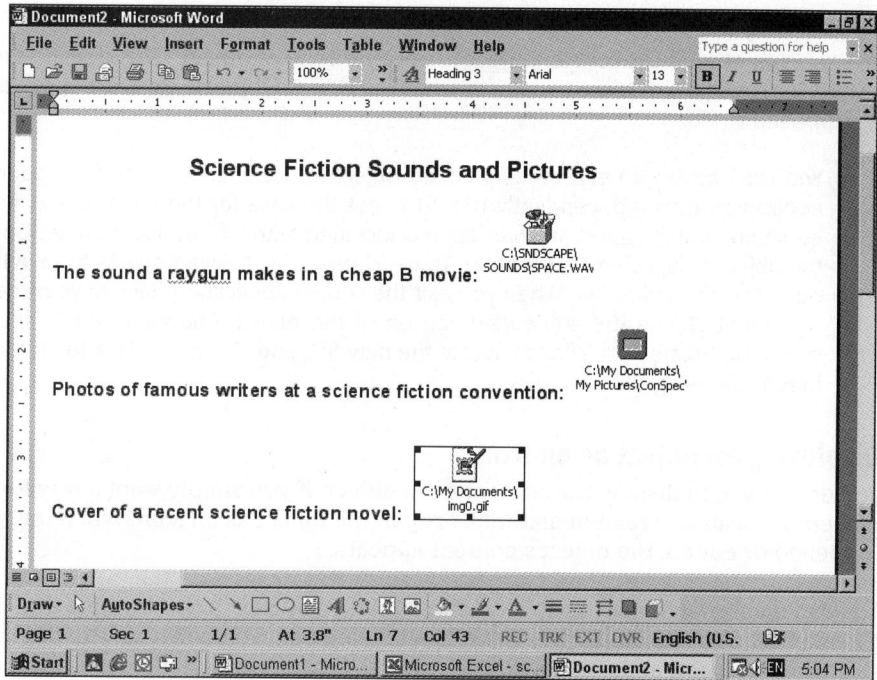

Figure 11-13: The icons represent files created in a non-OLE application packaged as an object.

Working with objects in documents

Once you've placed an OLE object into a document, editing its contents is as simple as double-clicking the object. You can also choose Edit ➪ Object ➪ Edit or Object ➪ Edit from the object's shortcut menu—the method you must use with multimedia objects, which play when you double-click them. When you edit an embedded object, the title bar doesn't change, but the menus and toolbars become those of the source application. Return to the main document by clicking somewhere outside the object.

If you prefer, you can edit the object in the source application's own window. Choose Edit ➪ Object ➪ Open, or from the object's shortcut menu, Object ➪ Open. When you're through making changes, choose File ➪ Close or File ➪ Exit.

Note   Linked objects can be edited only in the source application. The Edit Link and Open Link options on the Object submenu are equivalent.

Converting an object to another type

You can sometimes convert an object to another type of object. This doesn't work very often, but now at least you know what the Edit ➪ Object ➪ Convert command is supposed to do.

Tip   You can convert an existing embedded object into a linked object if the source application runs independently (which is not the case for the chart, draw, map, equation, and organization chart applets included with Office). Here's how: Open the object in its source application. There, choose File ➪ Save Copy As to save the object in a separate file. When you exit the source application back to your main document, delete the embedded version of the object. Choose Insert ➪ Object, select the Create from File tab, locate the new file, and check the "Link to file" box before choosing OK.

Displaying an object as an icon

You don't have to display the content of an object. If you simply want a way for readers to easily see related material, drop in the object as an icon. When the icon is opened or edited, the object's content appears.

You can display an object as an icon at the time you insert it by checking the "Display as icon" box in the Insert ➪ Object dialog box. To display an existing object as an icon, select it and choose Edit ➪ Object ➪ Convert and on the resulting dialog box, check "Display as icon."

Managing links

If a document contains any linked objects, you can use the Edit ➪ Links dialog box to view and modify those links (see Figure 11-14).

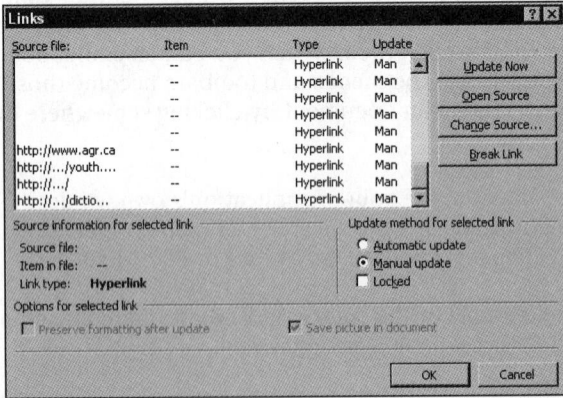

Figure 11-14: Manage linked objects in the Links dialog box shown here.

The box lists the current links and provides various options for controlling them, which include the following:

✦ **Update Now:** Updates the selected link using the current contents of the source file. Useful if the object is set to manual updating (see last bullet).

✦ **Open Source:** Opens the object in the source application.

✦ **Change Source:** Lets you replace the current link with a different file name, which is most useful for reconnecting the link after the source file has been moved (this command isn't the same as Edit ⇨ Object ⇨ Convert — think of it as "change source file," not "change source application").

✦ **Break Link:** Removes the link between the object and the source file. What you end up with is just a picture of the original data as it appeared at the time you broke the link.

 Tip

In Word, you can perform the same conversion on a linked or embedded object right in the document with the Unlink Fields command — the shortcut is Ctrl+Shift+F9.

✦ **Update:** Choose Automatic to keep the data in your document always current with the source file, or choose Manual if you want it updated only on command. Checking the box labeled Locked prevents updates of either type.

✦ ✦ ✦

Advanced Document Management

I n Office, as in Windows, the *document* reigns supreme— not the software you use to create it, and not the operating system that permits that software to run. This makes perfect sense, because it's the way we work in the noncomputer world, too. When you paint a picture, you concentrate on the scene before you. You pick up brushes and paints as you need them, but your concentration remains on the artwork emerging before you. This chapter looks at techniques for working with documents as complete units, and for integrating component documents into larger ones.

Power Techniques for Document Management

If you're going to be making documents, you need to know how to create them, store them, name them, organize them, and find them when you need them. Building on your knowledge of basic Windows skills, this section leads you through a more advanced discussion of document management in Office.

Starting and opening documents

Windows and Office combine to give you a profusion of ways to start new documents and open existing ones. But which one is best? That you must decide for yourself, based on your work habits and aesthetic preferences, and shoe size.

To create a new document, you have these choices:

✦ From the Start menu, choose New Office Document, and then select and open a template for the type of document you want to create.

✦ Click the New Office Document button, located on the Office toolbar of the Shortcut Bar.

✦ In almost any My Computer or Explorer folder, or on the desktop, display the shortcut menu (right-click or press Shift+F10) and choose New. Then select the type of document you want to create from the submenu. The only time this won't work is if you're viewing My Computer itself or a special folder such as Printers or Control Panel.

✦ In a My Computer or Explorer folder, open an Office template directly (double-click the template icon, or highlight it and press Enter).

✦ From any running Office application, choose File ➪ New or click the New button on the Standard Toolbar. Then make your choices from the New Document task pane.

To open an existing Office document, you have these choices:

✦ From the Start menu, choose Open Office Document. This brings up the Open Office Document dialog box — the mother of all Open dialog boxes, set to list all the standard types of Office document files (the next two sections in this chapter have lots of tips on using the Open dialog box).

✦ From the Start menu, choose Documents to list your most recently used documents. Choose the one you want to reopen.

✦ Display the Shortcut Bar and click the Open Office Document button on the Office toolbar.

✦ In a My Computer or Explorer folder, locate and double-click the document, or highlight it and press Enter.

✦ In any running Office application, choose File ➪ Open or click the Open button on the Standard Toolbar and then select and open one or more documents.

✦ In any running Office application, choose from the list of recently used documents at the bottom of the File menu.

Secrets of the Open and Save As dialog boxes

When you're working in an Office application, you open existing documents and save new ones via a pair of similar dialog boxes labeled Open and Save As (of all things). Nearly all Windows applications use versions of these dialog boxes, but in Office they're souped up with special features.

When you choose File ➪ Open to access existing documents, the Open dialog box appears as shown in Figure 12-1. Similar or identical dialog boxes appear when you use any command that accesses existing files, such as Insert ➪ File or Insert ➪ Object in most Office applications, or Format ➪ Apply Design in PowerPoint. The Save As dialog box looks much the same, just a little less complicated.

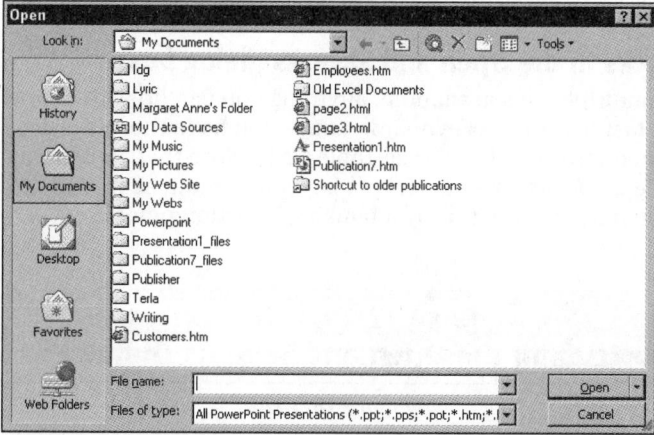

Figure 12-1: The File ➪ Open dialog box. You see essentially identical dialog boxes with different names when using various file-related commands in Office.

The *File list*, where the file and folders are displayed, consumes the bulk of each dialog box. Of course you're familiar with the basic operations of these dialog boxes, but you may not appreciate all you can do with them. The section "Locating files" covers the finer points of finding and displaying groups of files that meet specific criteria in these dialog boxes. This current section gives you the inside story on their other powerful hidden features.

Selecting multiple files in the Open dialog box

As in My Computer and Explorer, you can select two or more files at once in the Open dialog box and then choose Open to open them at the same time. You can make two kinds of multiple-file selections:

✦ **Select two or more files in a continuous range:** With the mouse, click the first file, hold down Shift, and click the last file. Using the keyboard, highlight the first file in the sequence, hold down Shift, and extend the selection by pressing any standard cursor-movement key (the arrows, PgUp, PgDn, Home, or End).

✦ **Select files randomly:** With the mouse, click the first file, hold down Ctrl, and click the remaining files one at a time. If you mistakenly select a file, be sure you're still holding down Ctrl and then just click the file again.

Note   Because you can only save one file at a time, the Save As dialog box doesn't permit multiple selections. To perform Windows file-management chores from within Office, use the Open dialog box, not Save As.

More keyboard tricks in the Open and Save As dialog boxes

Aside from selecting multiple files at random, anything you can do with the mouse, you can probably do faster with the keyboard — once you have the necessary keyboard shortcuts burned into your brain (see Table 12-1). Note that an item in a dialog box is said to *have the focus* when it accepts keyboard input, as is made evident by a faint dashed rectangle around it or by a blinking insertion point.

Table 12-1
Keyboard Shortcuts in the Open and Save As Dialog Boxes

Task	Keyboard Shortcut
Select a file	Space (to select the file marked by a dotted rectangle); cursor keys (to move the selection highlight to another file)
Rename a file	F2 (The file has to be selected first. Learn this one — it's definitely easier than using the mouse.)
Press (activate) any of the dialog box toolbar buttons	Alt+1 through Alt+9 (see the "Buttons in the Open and Save As dialog boxes" section)
Open the Look In list (when File list has the focus)	F4 (also drops down any list that has the focus)
Refresh the list of files (in the Open dialog box, search for files using the current search criteria — same as Find Now)	F5
Go up one level in the disk/folder hierarchy	Backspace (when the file list has the focus)
Display a shortcut menu for selected file (same as right-click)	Shift+F10
Display a shortcut menu for the current *folder* (not a specific file), in order to see the folder's Properties, or to use the Paste command	Shift+F10 with no file selected (to deselect all files, press Alt+N to activate the File Name list, in which you type *; then press Tab to switch back to the list)
Display properties for a selected file or folder	Alt+Enter

Task	Keyboard Shortcut
Display properties for the current folder	Alt+Enter with no file or folder selected
Move selected file(s) to the Recycle Bin	Delete
Delete selected file(s)	Shift+Delete

Buttons in the Open and Save As dialog boxes

The Open and Save As dialog boxes are both equipped with one-click buttons for common functions. These include the big folder management buttons in the vertical bar along the left side of the dialog box, along with the toolbar buttons across the top. Although some of these buttons duplicate functions available through other keyboard shortcuts or the shortcut menu, others supply unique capabilities that you should take advantage of (see Table 12-2 for details).

Tip Clicking a button works fine, but you can also activate any of the buttons along the top of the Open or Save As dialog boxes by pressing Alt plus the number key corresponding to the button's position on the toolbar, starting with 1 for the Back button. Use the typewriter number keys along the top row of your keyboard, not those on the numeric pad.

Table 12-2
Buttons in the Open and Save As Dialog Boxes

Button	Button Name	Function
Navigation buttons		
	History	Displays the Recent folder, into which Office automatically places shortcuts for the documents you've opened and the folders from which you obtained them. (Note: Folder shortcuts are listed in the currently active sort order, rather than at the top of the list.)
	My Documents	Takes you immediately to the My Documents folder, or another "home base" folder you've specified for documents in the Windows Registry (see the sidebar "Changing the My Documents and Favorites Folders" later in this chapter).
	Desktop	Takes you directly to the Windows Desktop.

Continued

Table 12-2 *(continued)*

Button	Button Name	Function
	Favorites	Switches to the Favorites folder. See the "Using the Favorites folder to access frequently used items" section later in the chapter.
	Web Folders	Switches to the Web folders.
	Back	Moves to the folder or disk you were last using.
	Up One Level	Moves to the parent folder or disk.

File-management buttons

Button	Button Name	Function
	Search the Web	Opens your browser's default search page.
	Delete	Deletes the currently selected file or files. Hold down Shift when you click this button to delete the file permanently rather than send it to the Recycle Bin.
	Create New Folder	Creates a new subfolder in the current folder.

Views button and menu

Button	Button Name	Function
	Views	A split button. Clicking the main part of the button cycles between the List, Details, Properties, and Preview views described next. To switch directly to a specific view, click the thin bar on the right part of the button and choose from the drop-down menu.
	List view	Displays filenames.
	Details view	Displays the name, size, type, and date of each file. See the "Tips on Details view" section later in the chapter.
	Properties view	Displays the properties of the selected file in the right pane.

Button	Button Name	Function
	Preview view	Shows you a preview of the selected file in the right pane. This works on just about any type of file you can open in Office, including documents from the other Office applications, text files, files from various word processors and spreadsheets, and even pictures. One drawback to using this button is that displaying documents takes a lot longer than simply listing a bunch of filenames. When this view is active, use the mouse to move from file to file, because scrolling via the keyboard takes too much time. Another problem: You can't delete a file you're previewing, because it is technically open in Windows, and Windows protects open files from deletion.

Tools menu

	See Figure 12-4	Displays a menu of relevant choices (see the section "The Tools menu" later in the chapter).

Tips on Preview view

Among the modes accessible through the Views button listed in Table 12-2, the Preview and Details views deserve further comment. Preview view, entered by pressing the Preview button described previously, is actually fairly complicated:

✦ In Office applications except Word, you can only preview graphics files and Office documents — but you can only preview those Office documents saved with the Save Preview Picture box checked in the File ⇨ Properties dialog box (Summary tab). Checking this box stores in the document file a little graphic image of the first page. This *preview picture* graphic is what you'll see when you preview the file.

✦ In Word, you can preview many files without the preview picture. This works for most file types that Word can import, such as text, HTML, or Excel files. Note that you can't preview PowerPoint files saved without a preview picture.

Cross-Reference Chapter 11 discusses the text and graphics converters necessary for importing files.

✦ If you save a *Word* document with a preview picture, you see only that tiny, barely recognizable picture when you preview it, even in Word — not the entire document in a small scrollable window, as you otherwise would. Therefore, it may make sense to save preview pictures only when you want to preview your Word documents in other Office applications (but see the "Tips on using and setting properties" section later in this chapter). Although you can decide whether to save the preview picture for each document independently, this setting is stored in Word's templates.

Cross-Reference   Templates are discussed in Chapter 18.

Tips on Details view

Details view in the Open and Save As dialog boxes — the view you see if you click the Details button described in Table 12-2 — works just like its counterpart in My Computer. Each file appears on a separate line, with columns for the file's name, size, type, and date modified. As in My Computer or Explorer, you can change the width of these columns by dragging the separators between them.

To make more room for important information — namely, long filenames — change the way Office documents are listed in the dialog boxes. In the Type column, Office documents are always preceded by the Microsoft moniker, as in "Microsoft Excel Worksheet," "Microsoft PowerPoint Presentation," and even "Microsoft HTML Document." This naming style eats up way too much room, leaving less for the filenames.

To remove those superfluous *Microsoft*s, open My Computer or Explorer (it doesn't matter which folder you display) and choose View ➪ Folder Options. In the Folder Options dialog box select the File Types tab so the dialog box appears, as shown in Figure 12-2.

Here, scroll the list of Registered File Types until you get to the long section of those that start with *Microsoft*. Select one of the common types, such as Microsoft Word Document, and click Edit to bring up the dialog box shown in Figure 12-3. In the box at "Description of type," delete the word *Microsoft*. If you like, shorten the entry further, so long as you can understand it (Word Doc would probably do). Click OK to return to the Options dialog box, where you can repeat the procedure for as many types of files as your patience permits.

The changes take effect in Details view the next time you use each Office application. Removing the *Microsoft* from Office document descriptions has another benefit: It's easier to pick out the different types in the Details list when they don't all start with the same word.

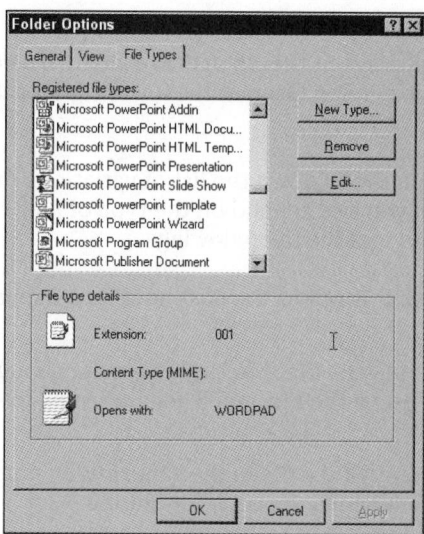

Figure 12-2: The File Types tab of the Folder Options dialog box in My Computer

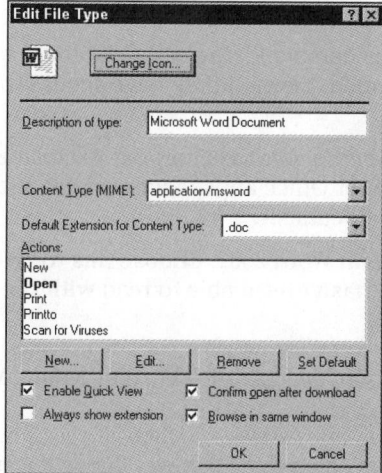

Figure 12-3: Edit file type descriptions in this dialog box.

Sorting the File list

To sort the File list, click the arrow on the Views split button. Then choose Arrange Icons, followed by the sort type you want (by Name, Type, Size, or Date).

Protecting a document's contents with special file-opening options

You can open a disk file in several different ways in the Open dialog box. To select one of the alternatives, use the split button labeled Open at the lower right of the dialog box.

Clicking the arrow at the right of the button drops down the list of variations on the standard Open command. The commands you see depend on the type of file selected and the Office application, but can include the following:

✦ **Open:** The standard opening method, this opens the file under its current name and lets you edit it.

✦ **Open Read-Only:** Although you can edit the file, you can't save the changes using the original name (if you try to save the file, you'll get a warning followed by the Save As dialog box).

✦ **Open as Copy:** Office first makes a copy of the file in the same folder, naming it "Copy of *original filename,*" and then opens the copy for editing.

✦ **Open in Browser:** For HTML and other Web page files, you can choose to open the file in your browser rather than the Office application you started from.

✦ **Open in *application*:** Opens the file in the specified Office application, no matter which application created it.

✦ **Open Exclusive:** In Access, choosing this command opens the database for your exclusive use — other users can't open it even if they have access to it on the network.

✦ **Open Exclusive Read-Only:** Opens an Access database for your exclusive use and as a read-only version. Unlike the other Office apps, Access won't allow you to make any changes to a read-only document.

✦ **Open and Repair:** This is a new function in Word 2002. Choose this to attempt to repair a corrupt document that Word hasn't been able to read with the normal Open command.

You can access these same commands more quickly from the shortcut menu for one or more files.

Note   A document opened as read-only in Office is only treated that way during the current use. After you have closed it, you can open it again the regular way later (although you get a reminder that you last opened it as read-only). The file's operating system read-only attribute is *not* set, so other programs can modify it as well.

Use these alternative file-opening methods when you want to be sure that the original file won't change. Open the file as read only if you simply want to review it, or if you want to copy information from it to another document. If you plan to edit the document contents and save the changes without disturbing the original document, open it as a copy.

Tip To protect a file from modification by Office or by any other program, turn on the read-only attribute using My Computer or Explorer: Select the file, display its properties (Alt+Enter), and check the Read-Only box on the General tab. (You can also do this from within an Office file-related dialog box such as Open or Save.)

The Tools menu

When you open the Tools menu, you get a little list of special commands and options. Figure 12-4 shows the version of this menu you get in the Open dialog box.

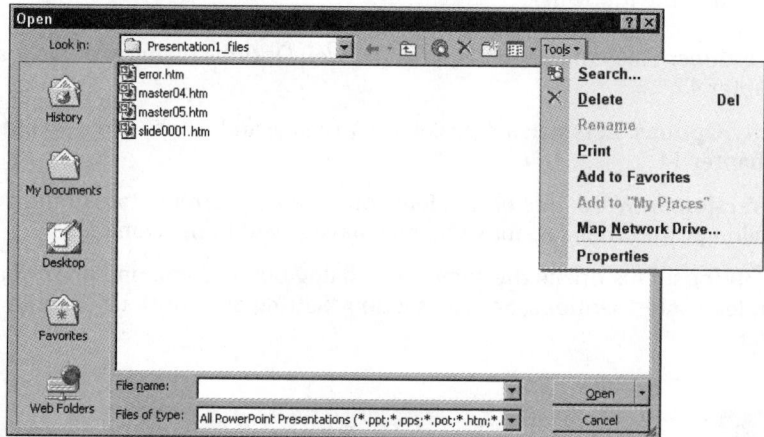

Figure 12-4: The Tools menu of the Open dialog box

Choices on the Tools menu in the Open dialog box

The items on the Tools menu are as follows:

✦ **Search:** Displays the Search dialog box. Here you can specify criteria for documents that Office should find and display in the main dialog box. (See the section "Locating files" later in this chapter.)

✦ **Delete:** Erases the selected file or files, of course. The Delete button on the main dialog box toolbar is faster.

✦ **Rename:** Performs the obvious function.

✦ **Print:** Prints the selected document without opening it. See Chapter 13.

✦ **Add to Favorites:** Adds a shortcut to the selected item (file or folder) to your Favorites folder.

✦ **Map Network Drive:** Lets you connect to a drive on your network. See Chapter 7.

✦ **Add to My Places:** Adds a shortcut to the selected item to a network place, a folder on a network file server, Web server or Exchange 2000 server. Before you can add a shortcut to a network place, you have to create it by opening the New File task pane in any Office application and clicking Add Web Folder.

✦ **Properties:** Displays the selected file's Properties dialog box. If you select more than one file, you see only the first file's properties. The keyboard shortcut to display the Properties dialog box is Alt+Enter.

Tools menu choices for the Save As dialog box

In the Save As dialog box, the Tools menu omits the Find and Print commands but adds a set of save-related choices. Depending on the application you're running, these may include the following:

✦ **Web Options:** This command displays the Web Options dialog box, discussed in Chapter 45.

✦ **Security Options:** Lets you set password, privacy, and macro security options. See Chapter 14.

✦ **Save Version:** In Word, this option lets you save the current state of the document along with other versions you may have saved in the same file.

✦ **Save Options:** This opens the same Save dialog box you can find on the Save tab under Tools ➪ Options. See the section "Setting Save options" later in this chapter.

Changing the My Documents and Favorites Folders

Suppose you think that My Documents is a pretty dorky name and you want to keep your main document stash in a folder called Strange, Rare, and Peculiar. Well, you're free to do so — but you'll run into trouble in Office's Open and Save As dialog boxes. They don't provide a way to redirect the navigation button to your chosen folder. However, you can specify a folder of your own. The surest way to do so is by tinkering with the Windows Registry. If and only if you know how to recover from a Registry meltdown, run the Registry Editor — using File ➪ Export to make a copy of the Registry, please, before you change anything. Then search for the following Registry branch:

```
[HKEY_CURRENT_USER\Software\
Microsoft\Windows\
CurrentVersion\Explorer\
User Shell Folders]
```

Within the User Shell Folders branch, identify the Personal key and replace the existing value with the correct path for your new documents folder. Close the Registry Editor and test the changes by opening an Office Open or Save As dialog box. You should see a button labeled Strange, Rare, and Peculiar (or whatever folder you selected) in place of the original My Documents button. Use the same basic technique to specify a different Favorites folder by changing the Favorites key in the same Registry branch. In this case, the name of the button doesn't change in the Open and Save As dialog boxes.

Using the Favorites folder to access frequently used items

Favorites is a subfolder created automatically in your main Windows folder (on single-user PCs) or in your user profile folder (on systems that support multiple users). The Favorites folder enables you to navigate instantly to any location available to your system.

The idea is to fill up the Favorites folder with shortcuts to the drives, folders, and individual documents that you access most often. When the shortcuts are in place, a click on the Favorites button gets you to its folder; click the shortcut again and you're there.

Because Favorites is just a folder like any other, you can put shortcuts into it in the usual Windows ways using My Computer or Explorer. But by far the fastest way to place a shortcut in the Favorites folder is with the Open dialog box in any Office application. Navigate to the item, then choose Tools ➪ Add to Favorites. The deed is done—a shortcut to the item is now listed every time you display the Favorites folder. And the best way to do that, of course, is by clicking the big Favorites button.

Playing many favorites: Fast access to specific folders

If you store documents regularly in several different folders, you can save lots of time and dialog-box fiddling by writing little macros that display the Open or Save As dialog box open to a specific folder. The following example is for the Open dialog box in Word:

```
Public Sub FolderOpenPuppyTales()
With Dialogs(wdDialogFileOpen)
    .Name = "E:\Puppy Tales\"
    .Show
End With
End Sub
```

In your version, substitute the full path of the target folder within the quotation marks on the line beginning with .Name. Be sure to include the final backslash. For a Save As macro, replace the term in parentheses with wdDialogFileSaveAs.

Here's the comparable macro in Excel. (No, VBA is not yet as consistent across the Office applications as Microsoft promised to make it.)

```
Public Sub FolderOpenBudgieBudgets()
Application.Dialogs(xlDialogOpen).Show ("D:\Budgie Budgets\")
End Sub
```

Use xlDialogSaveAs in the parentheses for the Save As dialog box.

Disk housekeeping with the Open and Save As dialog boxes

If you dislike leaving the safe haven of the Office environment, the Open and Save As dialog boxes give you a serviceable alternative to My Computer or Explorer for tidying up your disks and all their folders and files. In either dialog box you can do the following:

✦ **Move or copy files:** Select the files and on the shortcut menu, choose Cut (for a move) or Copy. Then open the destination folder, display the shortcut menu (with no file selected), and choose Paste. Alternatively, if the destination folder's icon is visible in the File list, select it and choose Paste from its shortcut menu.

✦ **Rename files:** Select a file and press F2, or wait a second and then click again (don't double-click), or choose Rename from the shortcut menu.

✦ **Delete files:** Select the files and then press Del or choose Delete from the shortcut menu to move them to the Recycle Bin, or press Shift+Del to rid yourself of them more permanently.

When Open is open, you can perform move, copy, and delete operations on more than one file at a time. That's not allowed in Save As.

If you like the idea of managing your files from within Office, check out Outlook's special features for this purpose, described in Chapter 31.

Saving documents

After you've saved an Office document for the first time in the Save As dialog box, saving again requires only a quick Ctrl+S. Practice that key combination until it becomes an automatic finger-twitch, and you'll never have to wail, "I just lost an hour's work!"

Office XP works harder than any version of Office before it to keep you from losing an hour's work, even if you don't use Ctrl+S at every opportunity. See Chapter 14 for more information.

Saving documents in other formats

Whether you're working with a brand-new document or one that's been around the block a few too many times, you have the option of saving it in a format other than the standard, or *native*, one used by preference by its Office application. To change the format, choose File ➪ Save As (of course, Save works if your document is new and previously unsaved). Then use the drop-down list at Files of Type to select an alternative format for the document.

More information about file formats and conversions can be found in Chapter 11.

Tip To save a document with a different extension from the default Office supplies for the chosen format, enclose the whole name in quotation marks. For example, to save a Word document called My Summer.Fun, you would type **"My Summer.Fun"** in the File name field. If you just type the name without the quotes, Office appends the default extension to the name. In this example, you would end up with a file called My Summer.Fun.doc.

Setting Save options

Excel, Word, and PowerPoint offer various options for fine-tuning the way they save your documents. You can display these settings by choosing Options from the Save As dialog box, or in Word and PowerPoint, by displaying Tools ⇨ Options and selecting the Save tab. Some available options include the following:

✦ **Allow Fast Saves:** Available in PowerPoint and Word, this setting speeds up the saving process — often dramatically — but makes your files bigger. When it's on, the application records at the end of the file the changes made to the document since the last save, without removing previously saved information. Eventually a limit is reached and the current contents of the document get saved in their entirety. Although it's generally best to leave this setting active, turn it off if you want to ensure the file is as compact as possible, perhaps to send it over a modem. Turning this option off also enables the file to be read by text editors and viewers that can't translate the Office file formats.

✦ **Allow Background Saves:** Another speed-up option, but available only in Word, this setting sends information to the disk in bits and pieces while you work instead of forcing you to wait until the entire file is saved. It's a little risky, because if the computer happens to crash while the background save is in progress, you may lose your work.

Crash protection

Several Save options specifically relate to protecting your work against human error or computer crashes. These are as follows:

✦ **Always Create Backup:** Available in Word and Excel, this option renames the existing file first (using the .wbk extension in Word, .xlk in Excel) and then saves a new copy of the file. In Word, this setting applies to all documents and is found on the Tools ⇨ Options dialog box; you can't do fast saves if this option is active, which makes sense if you think about it. In Excel, you can turn it on or off for each document independently in the Save As dialog box. Go to the General Options choice on the Tools menu. An alternative backup strategy is to use a macro to force your application to make two copies of your file each time you save it. The results are different — you can't recover a previously saved version, but your current version is more secure.

✦ **Save AutoRecover Info:** This setting causes the application to automatically save the document's current contents at the interval you specify, placing them into a folder designated in the File Locations tab of the Tools ⇨ Options dialog box (at least in the case of Word). If the computer quits on you unexpectedly, which it's bound to do from time to time, your application should automatically load the AutoRecover version of the document.

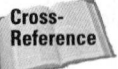

Cross-Reference

See Chapter 14 for more information on recovering from AutoRecover and other tips on handling crashes.

✦ **Read-Only Recommended:** If this box is checked, the file can't be saved under its current name. This is a weak form of security, but it's adequate when you and your coworkers know what you're doing. See also the discussion in "Protecting a document's contents with special file-opening options" earlier in this chapter.

Locating files

Often, Windows' long filenames tell you enough about your documents' contents that you can pick out the files you want to work with in the Open dialog box. But plenty of times arise when you need more help finding the right files. The document you want to open may have been stored in any one of a zillion different folders, and the question is, "Which one?" This problem is compounded if you have more than one hard disk, and it gets really serious if you're accessing files on a network or over the Internet.

Besides, even if you know which folder to look in, you may have trouble picking out the correct files by name alone. You may remember that you once reported on last year's failed investment in an eggshell recycling project, burying the details somewhere below a minor sub-subheading in a document. When suddenly eggshells become a vital constituent in a premium clean-burning gasoline, searching for your write-up in a sea of documents with names such as "Quarterly report 3, Fall 1996" gets old in a hurry. Instead, tell Office to look for files containing the word *eggshell* and the right document appears in moments. (Unless, of course, you've written dozens of reports on other egg-related topics in the interim, in which case, choose a more specific word or words.)

In the Open dialog box, the four boxes at the bottom covered in the next section are usually all you need to track down the files you need and show them in the File list. More complicated winnowing requires an advanced search, covered in "Constructing searches," a bit later in this chapter.

Specifying files in the Open and Save As dialog boxes

When you first use the Open or Save As dialog boxes, they are set to show you all documents in the current folder that belong to the Office application you're using. But with only a little effort you can filter the File list to display a more limited group of files.

Using the File name box

In both the Open and Save As dialog boxes, the File name box does double duty, depending on what you type into it:

✦ If you enter a complete filename at File name, pressing Enter opens that file (in the Open dialog box) or saves the current document using that name (in Save As).

✦ If you type in a filename containing wildcards, or a disk path and then press Enter, the File list displays files matching your entry, opening the requested folder if you specified a new path. This can save a lot of time when you're trying to display files of a certain type or navigate to a particular folder.

Displaying groups of files using wildcards

The Open and Save As dialog boxes come with the obligatory drop-down lists for specifying file types (these lists are labeled Files of Type in the Open dialog box and Save as Type in the Save As dialog box). Although you can use these lists to filter the File list so it shows only a particular kind of file, wildcards give you more flexibility. Besides, you can type them just as fast as you can pick an item from the list. Note that entries in the File name box override the selection at Files of Type or Save as Type.

Wildcards in the File name box work much as they do in DOS, only better. The * character represents any number of characters, whereas a ? represents any single character. For example, to display files that include the word Access at the beginning of the name, type **Access*** at File name. To display all files of a given type, say, .prn files from an old copy of Lotus 1-2-3, type ***.prn**. You don't have to type the * to show filenames that contain a given bit of text. If you want to find files with *Office* anywhere in the name, just type **Office** (actually, **office** will do).

You can even combine two or more requests on the same line by separating them with a semicolon. To see .PRN and .NRP files only, type ***.prn;*.nrp**. To see all files whose names contain either the word *monitor* or the word *printer*, type **monitor; printer**.

Unfortunately, this technique can fail if you combine filename extensions listed in the Files of Type drop-down with unlisted extensions. In this situation, only the files with the listed extensions appear in the dialog box. Combining two or more unlisted file types works, as does combining two or more listed types.

Tip

Here's a little-known amazing fact: You can display files from two or more folders on completely separate paths. Type in each path, separating the entries with a semicolon. You might, for example, type **c:\consultations;e:\references**. Only the first folder named appears in the Look In field, but all the files from all the folders are there.

Navigating with the File name box

If you're a decent typist, and if you know DOS conventions and your hard disk hierarchy, typing entries in the File name box zooms you directly to your destination at another folder or drive. Just type the destination path, as in **C:\My Documents**. You don't have to enclose the path in quotation marks.

What's really cool about File name in the Office file dialog boxes is that it completes your entry for you. Start to type a file or folder name, and it fills in the first matching item it finds. It manages this trick even if you begin by specifying a different disk, for example, by typing **D:**.

With this improvement, keyboard navigation to a buried subfolder becomes truly practical, even if all the folders have long names. After you type the first character or three of the top-level folder, Office should find the right match. Press the right arrow to move beyond the entry it supplies and start typing the subfolder at the next level down. Again, Office finds the match. Keep going in the same way, remembering to press the right arrow after every match so you don't erase the entry Office has supplied.

You can also use DOS-type special path characters and conventions to shorten your typing. Try the following:

To Move	Type
To the root folder of the current drive	Backslash
To the parent folder of the current folder	.. (two periods)
Up the folder hierarchy a specific number of levels	Two periods plus another period for each level you want to move (to move up to the third level above, type five periods)
To a subfolder in the current folder	The subfolder's name, followed by a backslash

You should definitely use this technique to switch to another drive. Instead of hunting for the drive in the Look In list, just type its letter name and a colon at File name. When you press Enter, the active folder on the new drive opens in the dialog box (by active folder, I mean the one that Windows registered as the last one used). If you don't want to type any more, you can now use the File list or the Look In list to navigate to the right folder.

Using this technique, you can toggle back and forth between folders on different drives in one step — without having to navigate to the destination folder each time as you would using the Look In list.

Constructing searches

If you can't locate the files you need using the controls of the main Open dialog box, choose Tools ➪ Search to display the Search dialog box, shown in Figure 12-5. For the uninitiated, this dialog box can be a bit daunting, but you can master it if you take it slowly.

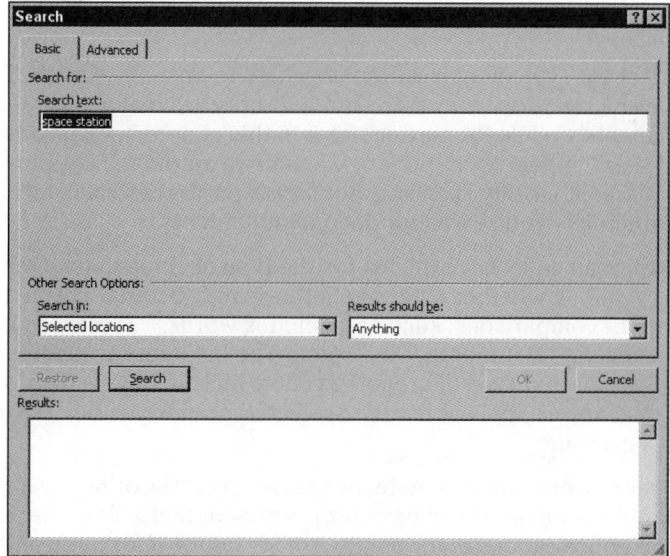

Figure 12-5: The Search dialog box, available from any Office Open dialog box

This dialog box contains two tabs, Basic and Advanced. Look at the Basic tab first.

Conducting a Basic Search

Basic searches are fairly straightforward. Enter the text you'd like to search for in the Search text box. Office looks for the text you enter in files, filenames, and file properties.

Next, set your Other Search Options. Clicking on the down arrow to the right of the box containing the text "Selected locations" lets you specify exactly where on your hard drive you want the search conducted. You can be as detailed as you want, selecting only half a dozen subfolders, for instance, in as many folders, anywhere on your hard drive. Or you can be inclusive and simply check Everywhere.

Click on the down arrow to the right of the "Results should be" box, and you can be equally as specific about what kind of files you want to search for, although you are limited to Office-related files; this is Office Search, after all.

When you've established your search criteria, click Search. The names of files that match your criteria appear in the Results box. You can double-click on any of the listed results to open that file in the appropriate Office application.

Conducting an advanced search

The Advanced Search tab includes the Other Search Options tools just like the Basic Search tab did, but it also includes less intuitive options labeled Property, Condition, and Value.

1. At Property, select the type of information on which to base the search. The list here includes all the properties listed in the Properties dialog box (see "Tracking Documents via File Properties" later in this chapter), with various properties that don't appear there but are maintained automatically, plus other items that aren't, strictly speaking, document properties, such as "Text or Property" (which lets you search for document contents).

2. At Condition, select an entry from the list for the type of comparison Office performs when deciding whether a file meets the search criteria. This list includes all sorts of comparisons, such as "includes words," "is (exactly)," "any number between," "last month," and so on. The list items available change depending on what type of property you've picked, but even so, some of the choices may not be applicable to the selected property — be careful to select one that's germane.

3. At Value, type in the word, number, date, or logical term (*yes* or *no*) against which Office should compare the chosen property's contents. To enter times or dates, use the abbreviations *m* for minutes, *h* for hours, *d* for days, and *w* for weeks. Specify months by typing the month's number (you can't specify years without entering the complete date). If the Condition specifies a range "anytime between" or "any number between," type the word *and* between the two items that define the range.

4. With the search criterion definition complete, select one of the radio buttons And or Or. Choose And if you want to display only files that meet this criterion *and* the last one you entered, or choose Or if you want to see files that meet either this criterion or the previous one.

You can add as many criteria to your search as you like.

Note   These Search dialog boxes are just variations on the Search task pane you'll see if you choose File ⇨ Search in any Office application, as described in Chapter 1.

Fast searching

When you want to find information in a big book, you turn to the index and look up the page number where the topic is covered. The alternative — scanning through the pages one by one — is much too slow.

That's the concept behind fast searching, a document-indexing ability built into Office (it used to be called Find Fast and ran as a more or less separate program, but now it's much better integrated and more transparent). True, computers are uncomplaining, tireless, and much faster readers than people. But if you ask your PC to look for the word *needle* in a haystack of files, a word-by-word search can still take quite a while. If (instead) the computer can look up the term in an index, the search time is shorter.

Fast searching is installed automatically with the rest of Office, and it runs automatically. Every so often it sneaks around on your hard disk looking for new or changed files. When it finds one, it adds the new information to the index.

All this work pays off for you when you search for files in the Open dialog box of any Office application. Rather than rummaging through every file in the folder to see if it matches your search criteria, Office consults the fast searching index, looking up the criteria there.

Maintaining Find Fast indexes

Because the indexing process is automatic, there's usually no need for you to deal with fast searching at all. But there are several situations where you need to manage the indexes yourself:

✦ To change the folders included in the index

✦ To update an index prior to an important search

✦ To free up disk space by deleting the index

To access the fast searching options, choose File ➪ Search in any application. When the Basic Search task pane opens, click on Search options. When the Indexing Service Settings dialog box opens, click Advanced. This opens the dialog box shown in Figure 12-6.

Choosing which folders to index

By default, all folders are indexed. To remove some folders from those indexed, click Modify. Locate the folder you don't want indexed and remove the check mark from the box in front of it.

Updating the index

Although fast searching reindexes your documents every two hours automatically by default, you can order an early update by clicking Update Now. Do this if you want to be sure that the index is completely current before you conduct a critical search. Select the drive or folder you want updated at "Index in and below," and make sure you uncheck the "Do not update while the computer is in use" option. However, be prepared for some serious disk activity; updating the index is not a minor task.

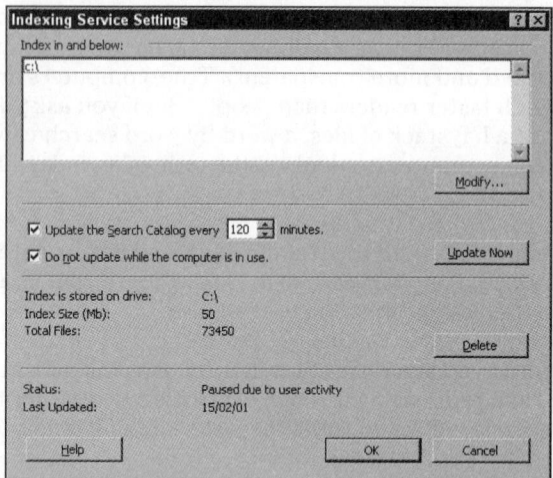

Figure 12-6: The Indexing Service Settings dialog box gives you control over fast searching.

Deleting the index

If you're desperately short of disk space, you can free up several megabytes by deleting the fast searching index. To do so, click Delete.

Changing the automatic update interval for indexes

You can adjust how often fast searching does its updates by changing the interval from 120 minutes to something else.

Tip   If an up-to-date index is your highest priority, set the update interval to 0 and uncheck the "Do not update while the computer is in use" box. Fast searching updates the index as soon as it detects any changes. This is likely to slow down your computer, however.

Tip   Another way to find a particular Office document is with Windows' own Find utility (Start ➪ Find ➪ Files or Folders).

Tracking Documents via File Properties

Part and parcel of every Office document is an attached set of *properties* — named items that hold identifying information about the document. In any Office application, to display or edit the *active* document's properties, choose File ➪ Properties. To work with *any* document's properties sheet, select the document in the Open or Save As dialog box and choose Properties from its shortcut menu.

Either way, you'll get the dialog box shown in Figure 12-7. You can also see this dialog box by displaying the file's properties in My Computer or Explorer, but you can't edit the Office-specific properties there.

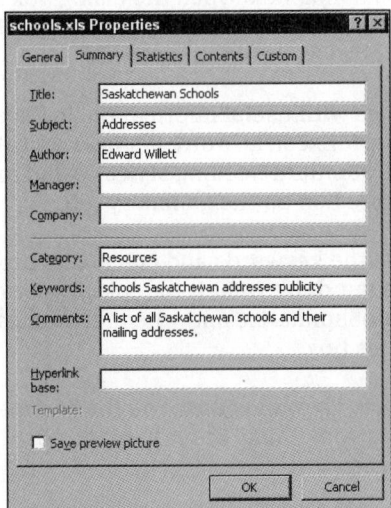

Figure 12-7: The Properties dialog box provides you with details about a particular document.

Office maintains a set of *automatically updated* properties containing current data on such items as the number of words and characters the file contains, and the dates it was created, last used, and last printed. You can inspect these in the Statistics tab of the Properties dialog box. The filename and path also fall into the automatic category, of course, and are displayed on the General tab.

Other properties can be edited to hold whatever information you think is appropriate. Of this type, Office implements more than a few *preset* properties. It records default information into some of these automatically, such as the title and author's name, while in other cases it leaves the properties blank until you fill them in. An example is the Keywords property, which lets you specify a series of words related to the document's contents or function. You can also create any number of *custom* properties, filling them with information directly or linking them to an item in a document — for example, via a Word bookmark.

After you've entered the relevant information, you can search for documents based on their properties. That topic is covered in the "Locating files" section earlier in the chapter.

Tips on using and setting properties

To improve the odds that you'll actually fill in the Properties dialog box, you can have Office applications display it automatically when you first save each document. This is a setting on the Tools ➪ Options dialog box. Open the dialog box and switch to the Save tab (in Word or PowerPoint) or the General tab (in Excel). Check the box labeled Prompt for document (or workbook, or file) properties.

The Contents tab is filled in for you, sometimes with useful information. In Excel, it displays the names of macro sheets in Microsoft Excel. In Word, it shows you all the headings in the document (if you've used the standard heading styles) — but only if you have also checked the Save Preview Picture box on the Summary tab.

In Word, the AutoSummarize command fills in the keywords and comments properties automatically. If you use AutoSummarize but don't want it to replace your own keywords and comments, choose Tools ➪ AutoSummarize and when the process is complete, clear the Update document statistics box.

Unlike the other properties, the preset property Hyperlink base (on the Summary tab of the Properties dialog box) actually does something. Enter here the base address for relative hyperlinks in the document.

Cross-Reference   See Chapter 45 for information on relative versus fixed hyperlinks.

Creating custom properties

If the preset properties supplied by Office aren't enough to satisfy your need to pigeonhole things, just create some more properties of your own. In the Properties dialog box, select the Custom tab shown in Figure 12-8.

Microsoft has already thought of many of the custom properties you might want to use, and these semicustom properties are available in the list at Name. If you don't find a suitable name in the list, type in your own. Then select a Type for the new property (text, date, number, or yes or no). After entering the information you want assigned to the property at Value, choose Add to store the custom property with the information.

To link a custom property to content in an Office document, start by defining the content in the document itself. In Word, bookmark the text that should be inserted into the property. In Excel, name a cell or cell range. In PowerPoint, just select whatever text you want assigned to the property.

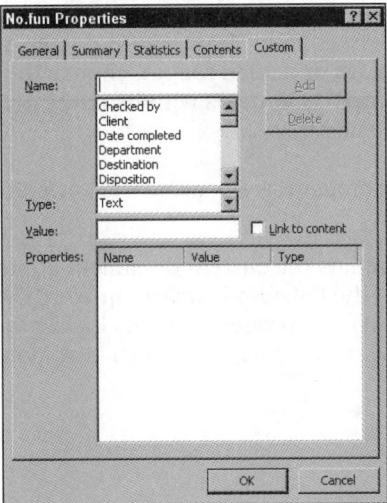

Figure 12-8: The Custom tab of the Properties dialog box lets you create your own properties.

What Happened to Binder?

Previous versions of Office included an application called Binder, which enabled you to create compound documents containing, for example, a Word document, an Excel spreadsheet, and a PowerPoint presentation. Office XP does not include Binder; it would be a bit redundant since you can already build such compound documents by using one application, usually Word, for the main document and by placing links in it to documents from the other applications.

However, you can still pull information out of a Binder file created in a previous version of Office if you need it for an Office XP document and then save it in whatever format you like.

To do so, use My Computer or Windows Explorer to locate the Binder file (Binder files use the extensions .obd or .obt, if you want to conduct a search for them) and then double-click on it. The Unbind program starts, removing the individual files from the Binder. In the resulting dialog box, select a folder to save the unbound files in and click OK.

You can now work with the files from the old Binder file individually in Office XP.

With the content ready, create a custom property as described previously. Instead of typing in a Value, however, check the "Link to content" box. If your document contains more than one linkable item (bookmark or named range), choose the correct name from the list at Source. The new property appears with its current value in the list that follows with a little link icon beside it.

Tip   See Chapter 37 for a tip on using a custom property as a bookmark in PowerPoint.

From now on, the property automatically contains the current document content referred to by the link. However, if you delete the linked bookmark (in Word), named range (in Excel), or text (in PowerPoint), the property retains its last value, and this can't be changed. The Properties list shows it with a Broken Link icon.

✦   ✦   ✦

Printing: From Screen to Paper

Producing printed documents is an everyday task and, fortunately, one that usually isn't very complicated. That's why this chapter is short. But you'll still find some useful suggestions here to help you feel less put out by your output chores.

Matching Print Orientation to Document Layout

Most likely your monitor is wider than it is tall. People designing worksheets in Excel and forms and reports in Access or Outlook tend to do the natural thing, laying them out to fit the available screen real estate. But when you print such a document, you're likely to end up with the contents running off the right side of the page or squashed to illegibility at the top.

To avoid such embarrassments, you should train yourself to set each individual document's orientation when you first create it, choosing portrait (tall) or landscape (wide) as appropriate. But if you work primarily with worksheets and forms, consider setting the default print orientation to landscape using the printer's Properties dialog box (available in Office from the Print dialog box, or in Windows proper, via Start ➪ Settings ➪ Printers).

Previewing Before You Print

All Office applications let you see what your document will look like on paper before you actually print it, using the File ➪ Print Preview command or the corresponding button. Print Preview saves time and resources, not to mention wear and tear on your printer.

Tip   Don't wait until you're actually ready to print to use Print Preview. Call it up from time to time as you work to make sure your document is laid out the way you want it to be. It may save you grief at the end of the process, when you may be in more of a rush.

What you see in Preview

Each Office application has a different Print Preview screen—Excel's being the most rudimentary style-wise, lacking cool graphical buttons (see Figures 13-1 and 13-2). But they all work in essentially the same way.

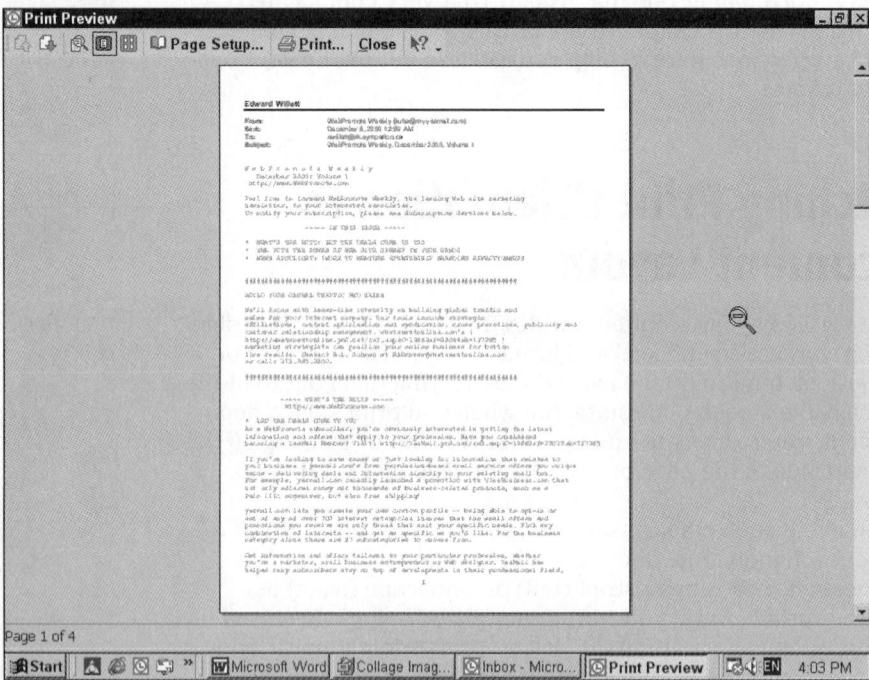

Figure 13-1: Outlook's Print Preview, with lots of cool buttons

Print Preview shows you exactly what your Office application intends to print, except that resolution is lower on the screen than it is in print. Document elements that in other views you can't see (or can't see well), such as headers and footers, appear in their proper locations and in the proper color.

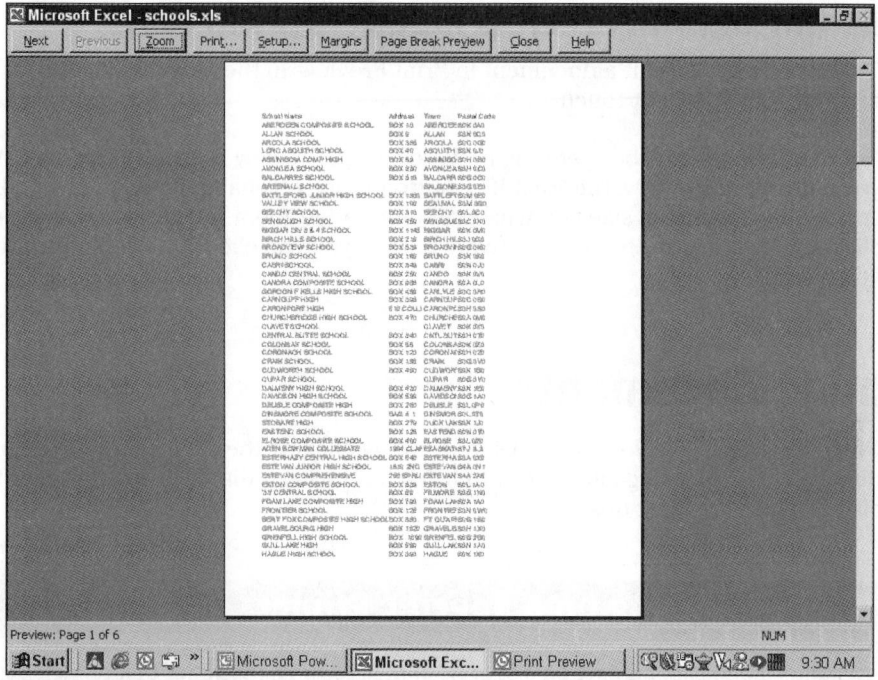

Figure 13-2: Excel's more pedestrian Print Preview window

Each program provides one or more buttons to toggle between a full-size view of the document and at least one zoomed-out view that shows the whole page at once. (Word, Access, and PowerPoint provide Zoom drop-down lists that let you choose what percentage of full-size you want the page displayed at.) In Word and Access, the Multiple Pages button on the Print Preview toolbar lets you display a variable number of pages. If you've ever used the Insert Table button in Word, you should find the workings of the Multiple Pages button familiar. You click the button and then use the mouse to sweep an area in the displayed grid to select the number of pages to be previewed and their arrangement, in rows and columns.

There's a limit to how many pages you can display with this technique, although it varies with the document and the resolution of your monitor. Of course, the more pages you display, the less detail you see. Displaying multiple pages is useful mainly for getting a crude overview of your pages. It can also help you find one specific page of interest quickly.

Editing in Print Preview mode — only in Word

Only Word lets you edit a document in Print Preview. In the other applications, you can look, but you can't touch.

Not that how you go about editing in Word's Print Preview is exactly obvious. When you enter Print Preview, the Magnifier button is active, enabling you to switch back and forth between full size and whatever alternative zoom setting is active. To edit, click the Magnifier button to deactivate it. Now you can click your document and edit away.

Printing Documents

Office programs give you two ways to print: by clicking the Print button to print directly or by choosing File ➪ Print to bring up the Print dialog box (pressing Ctrl+P also displays the Print box).

One-Click Printing on a Specific Printer

For guaranteed one-click printing on a specific printer, record a macro for that printer. Using the method discussed in Chapter 5, start recording the macro, naming it something like PrintToNetworkLaserPrinter and assigning it to a button. Next, open the Print dialog box and select the desired printer. The other options in the dialog box will also be recorded, so change them to whatever settings you want in your macro. After you choose OK to start the print job, stop the macro recorder (you can cancel the print job too unless you actually want to print the current document).

If you want a button that opens the Print dialog box with a specific printer already selected, you need to write the macro in VBA as shown here. Substitute the name of the printer as shown in the Name box in the Print dialog box for `"printer name"` (don't forget the quote marks).

```
Sub PrintUsingPrinterName () ' Word version
    ActivePrinter = "printer name"
    Dialogs(wdDialogFilePrint).Show
End Sub
```

In Excel, you must explicitly state the Application object (it's understood in Word), and you must also include the port on which the printer is connected as in this sample:

```
Sub PrintUsingPrinterName() ' Excel version
Application.ActivePrinter = "HP LaserJet 4 on LPT1:"
Application.Dialogs(xlDialogPrint).Show
End Sub
```

The Print button bypasses the Print dialog box, sending the document immediately to the printer you last selected with the settings you last chose. If you're not sure which printer is currently selected, hover the pointer over the Print button for a moment, and you see the printer name on the ScreenTip that appears.

Tip

For one-click access to the Print dialog box, place the File ➪ Print menu command on a toolbar. See Chapter 5 for the techniques required to place menu items on toolbars (a quick hint: You must open the Tools ➪ Customize dialog box). I suggest placing a *copy* of the Print menu command on the toolbar, rather than moving the command off the menu (so hold down Ctrl when you drag the command). You'll find that the button image for the Print dialog box looks exactly like the one for the standard Print button, so a paint job (editing one of the twin button images) is in order. (Chapter 5 covers the technique.)

Shortcut and drag-and-drop printing

A tip that works for many Windows applications: If all you want to do is print a document, you don't have to bother opening it in its application and then choosing the Print command. Instead, locate the document in My Computer or Explorer and right-click it, choosing Print from the shortcut menu. The document appears on-screen within its application, but only long enough to prepare the print job. With that complete, the application exits.

Tip

You can also use the preceding trick from within Office's file-related dialog boxes, such as Open and Save As. You never see the document or its application on your screen, except that you may be asked to specify what to print. If you want to work your mouse a little harder, and if you have more than one printer available on your system, drag and drop can save you some time. Drag the document's icon from a My Computer or Explorer window, dropping it onto the icon of the printer you want to use or into the printer's window (the one displayed when you double-click the Printer icon). Unless you keep the Printers folder open, you must first create a shortcut to the target printer by dragging the Printer icon from the Printers folder to the Desktop.

Working with the Print dialog box

If you've seen one Print dialog box in any of the Office applications, you've seen them all, more or less. Figure 13-3 shows one example.

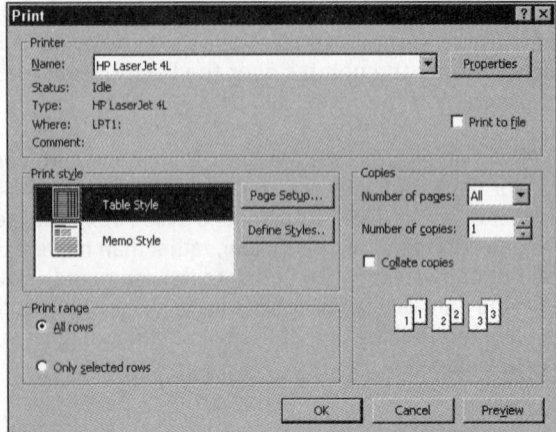

Figure 13-3: Outlook's Print dialog box. Note that Outlook lets you select from various print styles, a choice not available in other Office apps.

Note

One basic fact to remember regarding the Print dialog box is that the settings you select remain in effect *during the current session* until you change them again. The next time you run the program, the settings revert to their defaults.

Controls in common

The Print dialog boxes of all the Office applications have a set of controls in common. Click the Properties button to change setup options for the printer currently displayed in the Name field. If you have more than one printer installed on your system, you can select the one you want to print to by dropping down the Name list. The printer initially selected is the one set as the Windows default in the Printers folder of the Control Panel. Other controls common throughout Office include Print to File, Number of Copies, and Collate. These controls are covered later in the chapter.

The typical Office Print dialog box also has some way to specify a print range — which pages, worksheets, binder sections, and so on to print.

If you select something before calling up the Print dialog box, you often get a chance to print only the selection. In Word, you can include noncontiguous pages in the print range by separating the pages with a comma. To print pages 3, 4, 5, 7, 8, and 9, enter **3–5, 7–9**. You can also specify pages within a specific section, an entire section, or noncontiguous sections, as shown in Table 13-1.

Table 13-1	
Printing Specific Sections and Pages	
What You Want to Print	*Example Entry in Print Dialog Box*
A complete section	s2
Noncontiguous sections	s3,s6
Specific pages in a section	p30s2–p40s2
Specific pages spanning two or more sections	p30s2–p65s5

Collating

If you check the Collate box, Office prints the entire document all the way through for as many times as you've specified by the entry at Number of Copies. That way, each copy emerges from the printer in proper page order, and you have nothing to do but clip or staple.

This is dandy, so Collate is checked by default. But you should turn off collation if:

✦ The file you're printing contains complex graphics that take a long time to translate into a page image.

✦ You're printing multiple copies of a one-page file.

✦ You're printing to a file.

Need some explanation? One downside of having Office do the collating can be slower printing. This applies to page printers such as lasers. It takes time for the print information for a page to be transferred from your PC to the printer, and still more time for the printer to convert those bytes into an image of the page. Once the page image has been formed, however, the printer can make any number of copies at top speed. When you turn on collation in the Print dialog box, the data transfer-translation process must be repeated for every single page. This makes no sense whatsoever for a one-page file, and it's also very time-consuming if the pages contain complicated graphics or many fonts.

Printing to a file can also be affected. Generally, when you print to a file you want to generate the smallest file you can. If collation is on, the file contains as many copies of all the page information as you requested. See "Printing to a File" later in this chapter.

Application-Specific Printing Tips

Each Office application has a few wrinkles of its own when it comes to printing.

Word

In the Word Print dialog box, the Options button brings up the same print-related settings you get when you select the Print tab from the Tools ⇨ Options dialog box. You can also print items other than the current document, such as document properties and field codes, by choosing them from the "Include with document" area.

Knowing what you're printing in Word

It's time to print — do you know where your insertion point is?

Selecting the Current Page option from Word's Print dialog box prints the current page, of course. But wait — which is the current page? It's not (necessarily) the page you see displayed behind the dialog box. For printing purposes, the current page is the one that contains the insertion point. But when you scroll with the mouse, the insertion point stays behind until you click the document. For this reason, the current page may be at one end of the document, while the page you see on your screen is at the other.

So if you plan to print only the page on the screen, make sure the insertion point is blinking somewhere on that page before you call up the Print dialog box. If you forget to check the location of the insertion point before you get to the dialog box, you can look down at the status bar to see which page is current.

Tip   Word has a great feature for converting regular documents into compact booklets or drafts. In the Zoom section of the File ⇨ Print dialog box, change the setting at "Pages per sheet" from 1 to any of the available values up to 16. When you print, Word shrinks each page appropriately. With a typical document, a setting of 2 gives you reasonably legible text and uses only half the paper. Higher settings are usually best for previewing the document's overall layout.

Shrinking a Word document to fit on the page

If you originally laid out your document for a specific page size and now plan to print it on smaller sheets, you may not have to reformat the whole thing. Instead, adjust the Scale to Paper Size setting in the File ⇨ Print dialog box (Zoom section). (You can condense a document intended for legal paper so much that it fits onto an envelope, but don't blame me if no one can read it!)

Word's Shrink to Fit command works differently. Use it when a document is just a bit too long for a single page, with a little bit of leftover text flowing over onto the next page. Shrink to Fit automatically reformats the document so that it fits on one page less than its current length, changing type size and line spacing. Don't expect miracles or typographic elegance from the Shrink to Fit command, but it does shorten your document. The Undo command restores the document to its previous condition if the results are just too ugly.

The only trick about using this command is knowing where to find it: By default, it's available only via a button on the Print Preview toolbar. If you don't routinely use Print Preview, you can place the ToolsShrinkToFit command on another menu or toolbar or assign it to a keyboard shortcut with the customizing techniques presented in Chapter 5.

Other things you can print in Word

Open up the "Print what" list box in Word's Print dialog box if you want to print something other than the document. You can choose to print the document properties, the document showing any markup you've added, a list and descriptions of the styles you used, and even the current key assignments (a great way to get a printed list to refer to if you have trouble remembering key assignments on your own).

PowerPoint

PowerPoint too has a Print tab in the Tools ➪ Options dialog box. Among other choices, it lets you fix some print settings for the current document, overriding the current settings in the Print dialog box when you print by clicking the Print toolbar button.

In PowerPoint's File ➪ Print dialog box, use the Print What list to specify whether you want to print slides, paper handouts, speakers notes, or an outline and whether you want to print in grayscale, color, or pure black and white. PowerPoint also lets you scale slides to fit paper and even automatically add a thin frame around the border of printed material.

Excel

Excel locates additional print-related settings on the Sheet tab of the File ➪ Page Setup dialog box. Here, you can control the sequence in which different sections of a worksheet print, and thus the order in which those sections are numbered.

You can find additional Excel printing tips in Chapter 23.

Outlook

Outlook's Print dialog box lets you select a print style for the item you're printing. The options depend on the type of item you're printing. For instance, if you're printing a calendar, you can pick from styles such as daily, weekly, monthly, and so on. The Page Setup button duplicates the File ➪ Page Setup command. It displays a dialog box chock-full of controls for specifying the size and format of printed items (see Figure 13-4) based on settings dictated by the styles. You can define new styles at your whim.

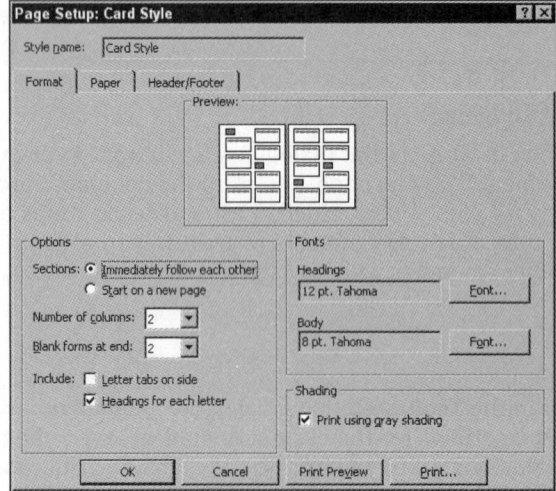

Figure 13-4: Outlook's Page Setup dialog box is used to define the format of printed items.

Access

In Access, you must print each object, such as a data table, form, or report, separately. It follows that each object has its own print settings. To define margins and columnar layouts, you can either choose File ➪ Page Setup or click Setup in the Print dialog box. However, only the File ➪ Page Setup dialog box lets you designate a specific printer for a given form or report. If you use a fast laser printer to print out your financial reports but rely on a dot matrix printer to produce invoices or receipts, use this feature to ensure that each item always comes out of the correct printer.

Access forms and reports have two print-related properties (accessed by choosing View ➪ Properties or pressing F4): When Layout for Print is set to Yes, the text Access displays on your screen conforms to the spacing it will have when printed, even if your screen fonts don't match your printer fonts. The text may look distorted on the screen, but at least you know it's in the right place. Setting the Fast Laser Printing property to Yes causes Access to substitute underscore and vertical bar text characters for real lines, which makes printing quicker — but only on laser printers.

Printing to a File

If you check the Print to File box, your Office application saves on disk the entire stream of instructions and information that it would normally send to the printer. If all goes well, you can then copy the resulting print file directly to a printer at any time without opening the original application (see "Printing a print file" later in this chapter). Because every printer speaks a different language, you must specify the type of printer you plan eventually to use when you create the print file.

Why go to the trouble of preparing a print file? For either of the following two reasons:

✦ You want to be able to reprint the document frequently without running the application that spawned it. Copying a print file to the printer is considerably faster than running the application, opening the document, and then printing.

✦ You want to output it on a device that isn't available to your system. One possibility is that you're preparing documents for output on high-end equipment on slides or film, the kind used by professional printing shops. You can print to a file and then send that file to the service bureau that produces the final product. (Note, however, that most service bureaus want a copy of the document itself in case something goes wrong.) In another scenario, a friend or someone in your company might give you physical access to a fancy color printer, but you can't connect to the machine from your PC, directly or via a network link. A simple solution is to print to a file, take that file on a floppy disk to the computer connected to the printer, and copy it from that computer to the printer.

To print to a file bound for a printer that isn't already installed on your system, you must first install the necessary printer driver. Use the Add Printer icon in the Printers folder (Start ➪ Settings ➪ Printers). Realize that you can install a driver for any printer any time — the printer doesn't have to be connected.

Tip Printing to a file also gives you an alternative way to export information crudely. By installing (in Windows) the Generic/Text Only printer driver, you can produce text files by "printing" them to a file.

Creating the print file

In the Print dialog box, select the driver for the destination printer. Again, Windows doesn't care if the printer isn't accessible to your system. Then check the Print to File box. You can choose other options as usual, but see the comment on the Collate box in the "Collating" section earlier in this chapter.

When you print, you get a dialog box asking you to enter a name for the print file. The extension .prn is customary for most print files, while .ps is usually used for PostScript files (remember that you must type quotation marks around a filename to save it with a nondefault extension). However, if you create print files intended for two or more different printers or other output devices, choose different extensions for each printer.

If the print file is destined for a printer unavailable on your system, you can copy it to a floppy disk or other removable medium as soon as it hits the hard disk. Then either send the floppy to the service bureau or use it to copy the file to a computer connected to the printer. Alternatively, send the file via the Internet or by direct modem transmission to its destination.

Tip

The Print to File checkbox in Office applications is always available, but you have to remember to use it. If you use a particular printer driver only for creating print files, set up the driver to print to a file automatically. In Windows, just select FILE as the port for that printer when you first install it, or later, on the Details tab of the printer's Properties dialog box.

Printing a print file

Once you've gone to the trouble to create a print file, your next challenge is sending it to the intended printer. Follow these steps:

1. Choose Start ➪ Programs ➪ MS-DOS Prompt (Windows 95 or Windows 98) or Start ➪ Programs ➪ Command Prompt (Windows NT or Windows 2000).

2. To send a PostScript file to the printer, enter this command:

   `copy file path\filename.ps port`

   where *port* is your printer port (typically LPT1). For example, if you want to print `Myfile.ps`, stored in the `c:\Windows\Programs` folder, you would enter `copy c:\Windows\Programs\Myfile.ps LPT1`.

3. To send a non-PostScript printer file to the printer, enter this command:

   `copy /b path\filename.prn port`

   An example of this is `copy /b c:\Windows\Programs\Myfile.prn LPT1`.

Most printers can print plain text files using this technique. If you need a quick printout of a Read.me file or some such file, use these commands to put the file on paper.

"But wouldn't it be easier," I hear you asking," if you could just drag the printer file icon onto the printer icon and it would print?" Indeed it would be, but ordinarily Windows simply plays dead if you try this. Fortunately, you can teach it to do better tricks. Try the following techniques.

Printing files by drag and drop

For printing print files by drag and drop:

1. Use a text editor to write and save a batch file called PRNTFILE.BAT; make sure it contains the following line:

```
copy /b %1 lpt1:
```

(If necessary, replace lpt1 with the printer port to which your printer is connected.)

2. On the Windows Desktop (or in any convenient folder), create a new shortcut for the batch file. Name it something like *Send File to LaserJet*.

3. After the new icon appears, right-click it and then select Properties.

4. On the Program tab of the Properties dialog box, select Minimized in the Run field, and check the Close on Exit checkbox (leave it unchecked if you want to see a DOS box on your screen while printing is in progress, and then close the box when you're done).

When the shortcut is ready, you can send any file to the printer by dragging it and dropping it onto the shortcut's icon. Alternatively, you can select the file, choose Copy from its shortcut menu, and then choose Paste from the shortcut menu of the new shortcut icon.

Printing files via the file's shortcut menu

For printing print files via the file's shortcut menu, follow these steps:

1. Create the PRNTFILE batch file and its shortcut as in steps 1-3 in the preceding section.

2. Make a copy of the shortcut in the Send To folder (in the main Windows folder).

Now, when you right-click any file, you can choose Send To ⇨ Send File to Printer (or whatever you named the shortcut in the Send To folder).

Faxing Your Documents

Two truths: In Office, printing documents is one way to fax them. Conversely, faxing documents is one way to print them.

If you have a fax modem—and assuming you've installed the fax services that come with Windows or comparable faxing software—you can fax any document by printing it. Just choose the name of your fax software driver in the Print dialog box. This works in any Windows application.

In Excel, Word, and PowerPoint, you can also fax documents using the File ⇨ Send To ⇨ Fax Recipient, which is probably a bit simpler. In Outlook, you can send messages by fax instead of e-mail by selecting the appropriate version of the recipient's name from the address book, as in *Sue Smith (Business Fax)* or *Jane Jones (Home Fax)*.

Tip   If you travel with a notebook PC but without a printer, remember that you can always produce a paper copy of any document by faxing it to the nearest fax machine using either of the preceding methods.

✦   ✦   ✦

Document Integrity and Security

You put a lot of work into your documents. You don't want something happening to them. You don't want to lose them when the computer crashes, and you really don't want to lose them because somebody's let a virus into your system.

This chapter talks about how Office works to keep your documents safe from crashing computers, corrupting influences, and prying eyes — and additional steps you can take to help Office protect your work.

Office's "Robustness Features"

Microsoft's term *robustness features* is another way of saying they're trying really hard to make software that doesn't crash. It's an admirable goal, but it's a simple fact of computing life that the more complex the software, the more likely it is to occasionally stop working — and Office is very complex software indeed.

Document Recovery feature

Fortunately, Microsoft isn't sticking its head in the sand and simply pretending Office will never crash, thus leaving you and your documents out to dry when it does. Instead, it has added a new feature to Office called Document Recovery (although I prefer the name that appeared in some earlier versions of the documentation — "Save on Crash.") When PowerPoint, Word, Excel, or Access encounters a problem that stops them in their tracks, they don't just shut down;

instead, you see a message offering you the opportunity to save your current document before the application shuts down. You can even connect to the Internet and report the problem to Microsoft by clicking on a hyperlink, providing Microsoft with valuable information about what conditions caused the crash, so they can attempt to address the problem with future patches or in the next version of Office.

Once you've either reported the problem or chosen not to, the Office application closes down and automatically restarts. When it comes back up, it opens a task pane on the left side of the screen, showing you the documents saved at the time the application stopped working — or, if you chose not to save the document, the last version of the document saved by AutoRecover (see the next section). It also offers you the original version of the document. You can choose which of those documents you wish to open or you can choose to discard them.

In every crash I have experienced, the Document Recovery feature worked perfectly — making it a life- (or at least document-) saving tool that Office users everywhere can greatly appreciate.

Note   If you don't retrieve the saved documents from the task pane before closing the program, Office warns you that the recovered documents will be lost, giving you one more chance to be sure that you've saved everything you needed to after your unfortunate crash. If you prefer, you can save the recovered documents and view them later.

AutoRecover

Before the new Document Recovery feature came along, AutoRecover provided (and continues to provide) another level of security against document loss. For the first time, it's been added to Excel and Publisher, as well as Word and PowerPoint.

AutoRecover saves the document's current contents at an interval you specify on the Save tab of the Tools ⇨ Options dialog box (see Figure 14-1), placing them into a folder designated in that same dialog box.

The AutoRecover feature can bail you out when your computer crashes — particularly if, for some reason, you don't have the opportunity to use the new Document Recovery feature to save your document at the time of the crash (for instance, because of a power outage, for which see the nearby Tip) — but it doesn't always work as you might hope. If you've trained yourself to save your documents frequently anyway, the AutoRecovered version of a document may actually be older than the one stored in the original file.

Caution   Don't replace the original file with the AutoRecover document until you've inspected both files to see which is really more current.

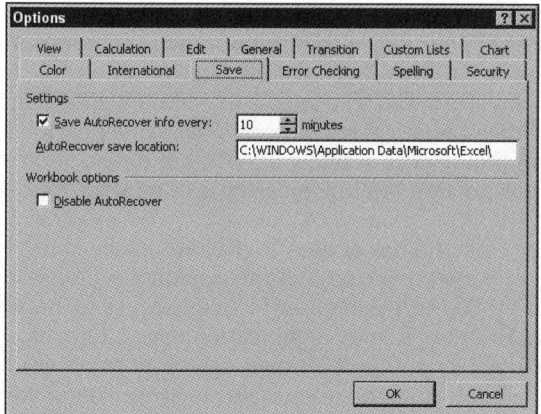

Figure 14-1: The Excel version of AutoRecover options set in the Save tab of the Tools ➪ Options dialog box

Fortunately, using the Save command on an AutoRecovered document doesn't automatically wipe out the original file. Instead, choosing File ➪ Save brings up the Save As dialog box. If you want to replace the original file, you must enter its name yourself at File Name; you must then confirm the replacement in a warning dialog box.

Tip

When you restart your application after a crash, it may fail to load one or more of the AutoRecovered documents, especially in the event of a power outage, which kills the program before it has a chance to undertake any shutdown procedures (which is one good reason to investigate adding an emergency battery backup power system to your computer). If you're pretty sure that the AutoRecovered documents should be there, you can just open them yourself using the File ➪ Open dialog box. You find them in the folder designated in the Tools ➪ Options dialog box, Save tab. (PowerPoint AutoRecover files are stored in the Temp folder, or whatever other folder is designated on your system for temporary files.)

Caution

You only get one chance to manually recover these AutoRecover files — they are deleted when you quit the application.

Office Security

Now that everybody has a portable computer, is on a network, or both, "personal computing" no longer means "private computing." If your laptop gets lost or stolen, or if your network's security system is less than impenetrable, your sensitive personal or business data may fall into the wrong hands.

Additionally, if your computer is hooked up to a local network of some type, chances are good you have a choice of saving your files either to your own computer or to a location somewhere on the network. This arrangement also makes it possible for others who are working on the same (or related) projects to access your files and borrow from them, comment on them, or suggest changes. That's fine provided that only the people you want to have that access actually have it, but not so good if access is also available to people who shouldn't be messing around with your files.

Fortunately, in Office you can control who has access to files you place in network folders. It has simple features that keep novice users from opening or modifying your files without your permission. You can also allow or deny access by network users to your own computer's hard drive. If your organization uses Microsoft Exchange Server for e-mail, Outlook lets you protect messages sent to others in the group. But to keep out thieves and determined snoops, and to secure all of your e-mail, you need stronger security measures in the form of special software designed for that purpose.

The Security tab

Word, Excel, and PowerPoint all provide the same basic password protection for their files, which you access in each application the same way, by opening Tools ⇨ Options and then clicking on the Security tab.

Type your password(s) into the "Password to open" and/or "Password to modify" boxes. Passwords can be up to 15 characters long; can contain letters, numbers, spaces, and symbols; and are case-sensitive. As you type them in, only asterisks are displayed.

Click OK when you're done; another dialog box will open asking you to re-enter the password to confirm it. Do so and click OK again. The next time you open the document, you'll be prompted to enter the correct password; if you've set a password to modify the document, you'll be given the choice of either entering the password to modify or to open the document as read-only.

To change or remove a password, open the document using the current password, then return to the Security tab, and either type a new password over top of the old one or remove the old password altogether.

Caution   Don't forget the password you've chosen! Once its been entered and you've closed the document, you won't be able to open it and/or modify your document without the correct password, any more than anyone else can.

There are slight differences among the options displayed on this tab. Word, for instance, whose Security tab is displayed in Figure 14-2, has a couple of checkboxes the others don't.

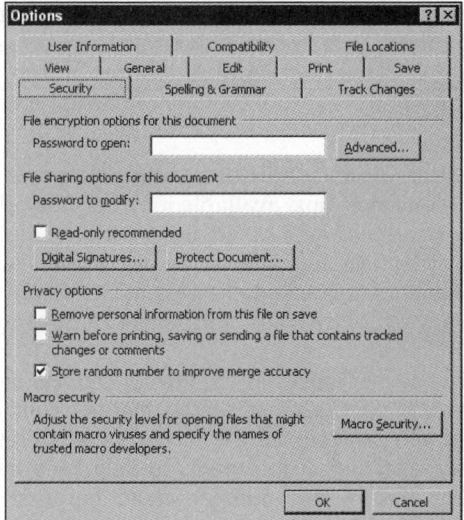

Figure 14-2: Word's version of the Security tab under Tools ⇨ Options, your central headquarters for setting security features

Note

> Protect Document (a button available only on the Word version of the Security tab) allows you to enable the Track Changes command so other users can change the document but all changes they make are tracked so you can review them later. The idea is to prevent other users from changing the document but allow them to insert comments, or to prevent any changes to the document except in form fields. You can reinforce document protection by entering yet another password, if you choose. (Information on protecting Excel and Access files is included later in this chapter.)

All three applications have the same four general areas on this tab, however:

✦ **File encryption options for this document.** Here you can assign a password to the document that must be entered before it can be opened. Assigning password protection also ensures that the document is encrypted, which makes it even more secure. You can set the type of encryption used by clicking the Advanced button; the encryption available depends on what you have installed on your system. By default, Office XP uses its own encryption system, which is also compatible with Office 97 and Office 2000.

✦ **File sharing options for this document.** Here you can apply varying levels of security. If you check "Read-only recommended," users who open this file get a message suggesting they open it as a read-only file. If they do, they won't be able to change the original document; instead, any changes they make must be saved as a new document, under a different name. If you enter a password in the "Password to modify" field, anyone can open the file, but only someone who knows the password can modify it. Users who don't know the password can open the file only as read-only. Clicking the Digital Signatures button allows you to add a digital signature to a file, proof to someone who receives it that it really came from you.

✦ **Privacy options.** This is a new feature in Office XP. Checking the "Remove personal information from this file on save" box, available in Excel, PowerPoint and Word, limits the personal information that is saved along with the file. This means you won't unintentionally distribute the name of the document's author or the names associated with comments or tracked changes, which could otherwise be found on the Summary tab of the File ➪ Properties dialog box.

Word, again, has a couple of additional checkboxes in the Privacy Options area; you can ask it to warn you before you print, save or send a file that contains tracked changes or comments, and you can turn off the function that stores a random number when you compare and merge documents to help keep track of related documents. Conceivably, this hidden number could be used to demonstrate that two documents are related.

Unchecking the "Store random number to improve merge accuracy" box in Word's security tab degrades the effectiveness of the Compare and Merge process.

✦ **Macro security.** Macros are very useful, but they can also hide viruses that can do nasty things to your system and compromise your documents' security. Click the Macro Security button to choose from three levels of security:

   • **High:** Allows only signed macros from trusted sources to run (click the Trusted Sources tab to see who your trusted sources are).

   • **Medium:** Allows you to choose whether to run potentially unsafe macros.

   • **Low:** Lets all macros run.

You should only set Macro Security to Low if you have trustworthy virus-scanning software installed, or if you are absolutely sure all the documents you open are safe (which, if you're connected to a network, you can never be sure of).

Security in Excel

Excel gives you precise password control over which elements in worksheets or workbooks other people can view or modify. Use the options on the Tools ➪ Protection submenu for this purpose:

✦ **Protect Sheet.** For a single worksheet, you can choose, in great detail, exactly what users of the worksheet can do (see Figure 14-3). Choose from the list of options. You can also set a password that must be entered to unprotect the sheet.

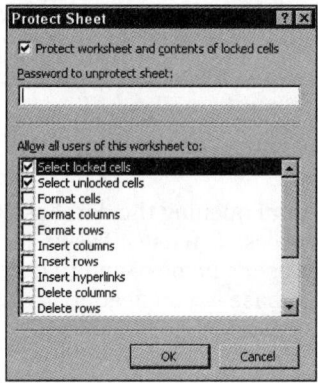

Figure 14-3: Excel lets you fine-tune the protection of a worksheet in great detail.

✦ **Allow Users to Edit Ranges.** You can set certain ranges to be unlocked by a password even when the sheet is protected — and, of course, you can then specify that password. This is useful if you want other people to be able to edit some ranges, but not the entire sheet. There's also an option to summarize the ranges and permissions specified with this command and paste them into a new worksheet for handy reference.

✦ **Protect Workbook.** This option offers two choices. You can protect the structure of the workbook (so sheets can't be deleted, moved, hidden, unhidden, or renamed, and new sheets can't be inserted) and/or you can protect the workbook's windows (so they can't be moved, resized, hidden, unhidden, or closed). Again, you can assign a password that unprotects the workbook.

✦ **Protect and Share Workbook.** This command prevents changes to the sharing settings of a shared workbook. In particular, this ensures that the change history can't be turned off, so you can always see what changes were made to the workbook and by whom. Check the box at the top of the dialog box that appears; then assign a password so nobody else can alter this setting without your permission.

Password-protecting Access databases

If you're used to tweaking the security settings in Excel, PowerPoint, and Word, then you know about choosing Tools ➪ Options and then choosing the Security tab. In Access, however, the Security tab doesn't exist; instead, you choose Tools ➪ Security. When you've found your way there, Access provides two kinds of passwords: One restricts the opening of a database; the other prevents access by unauthorized users (even when the database is already open).

Setting up a database password

To require a password each time a database is opened, set up a *database password*. Start with the closed database file (all users must close it). In the File ➪ Open Database dialog box, click the part of the Open button on the right with the arrow to drop down a short menu. Here, choose the Open Exclusive box (which prevents anyone else from opening it while you're using it). Then click the main part of the Open button to retrieve the database. When the database is open, choose Tools ➪ Security ➪ Set Database Password and type your password.

Setting up user passwords

A database password prevents unauthorized users from opening the database in the first place; once it's open, anyone with network access can use it freely. To prevent someone else from logging in under another user's name — and to define exactly what each user can and can't do with the database — you need to set up *user passwords* (security account passwords for each user).

To set up security account passwords, begin by defining a password for the default user account, called Admin. (Until you define this password, Access doesn't require a login procedure, and anyone can open and modify the database.) Then go on to define additional passwords for other authorized users.

In brief, here's how you define a security account password:

1. Start Access from the workgroup containing the user account for which you're creating the password, logging in with the correct user name.

2. Open the database and then choose Tools ➪ Security ➪ User and Group Accounts.

3. Enter the new password on the Change Logon Password tab.

You can go on to define the user's privileges in the Tools ➪ Security ➪ User and Group Permissions dialog box (see Figure 14-4).

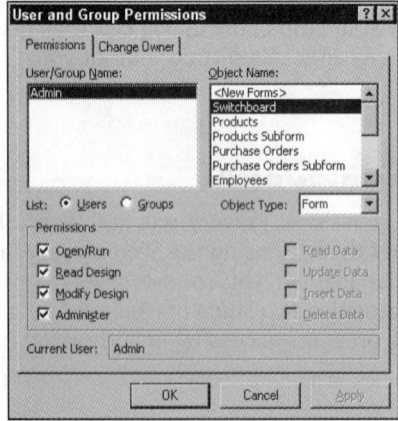

Figure 14-4: In addition to requiring an individual password, you can control a user's access to database features and objects with this dialog box.

Encrypting a database

Encrypting a database is the only way to ensure that a knowledgeable hacker can't extract the information in the file (which can happen even if you've password-protected the database). After a database has been encrypted, Access can still work with it normally, without any special steps on your part — it decrypts the information on the fly, as needed.

To encrypt an Access database, start with the database closed (all users must close it). Then choose Tools ➪ Security ➪ Encrypt/Decrypt Database. You'll see a version of the usual Save As dialog box. Enter a name and path for the encrypted copy and then click Save. You can replace the existing file with the encrypted copy by entering the name of the current file, but if you do so, only an encrypted version of the database will exist.

Encryption only protects the contents of the file when you're not using Access to examine them. Password protections remain in effect, however.

Security in Outlook

Outlook's security features pertain to messages you send to or receive from other users, not your own Outlook items. The relevant settings are on the Security tab of the Tools ➪ Options dialog box. They fall into three categories, as follows:

✦ **Secure e-mail.** Provides security for the messages you send over the Internet based on digital IDs. A digital ID is used to verify that messages actually came from the person who claims to have sent them and that they have arrived unaltered. You can encrypt (scramble) messages sent with a digital ID to prevent their contents from being read until they get to the intended recipient.

✦ **Secure content.** Enables or disables active content in the e-mail messages and Web pages you receive, content that could monkey with your disks and files, such as ActiveX controls, scripts, and Java applets. You select a named security zone for your messages corresponding to the degree of confidence you place in your sources. You can change the security settings of the zone you select, but note that the changes apply in any program that uses the zone — Internet Explorer being the main example.

✦ **Digital IDs (Certificates).** Enables you to obtain a new digital certificate via the Web and to move existing digital certificates to or from other computers.

Firewalls

A *firewall* offers better security from prying eyes than anything built into Office. A firewall is software or hardware that prevents unauthorized people from gaining access to your computer through its network connections.

If your computer is part of a network in a large corporation, the network itself is probably protected already by a firewall designed to keep out hackers; ask your IT staff. If, however, you use your computer at home, you might want to look at installing a personal firewall.

One excellent choice is ZoneAlarm, from Zone Labs, Inc. (`www.zonelabs.com`). **This down-loadable firewall is free for personal use, as are more elaborate versions for business use.**

Macro Viruses

After giving birth to a fledgling document and spending untold hours of hard work nourishing it to robust maturity, no one wants to see the child of their labors get sick or die. As we all know, the real world is a dangerous place. Danger is one of many ways in which the online world reflects the real world—but you can take measures to rescue your documents from infections and major trauma.

The macro virus—what a concept

Unleashed on an innocent world in 1995, the Concept virus was the first known example of a macro virus, a computer infection carried through macros rather than executable programs. Wouldn't you know it—the Concept virus infects Word documents. It displays a cryptic message box containing only the numeral 1.

Before Concept came along, people generally thought only their *programs* were vulnerable to attack by viruses—documents were considered safe. But because macros are very much executable programs—and because Office applications can be made to execute macros automatically when documents are opened or closed—a document containing macros makes a perfect virus vehicle. Since Concept, many more macro viruses have shown up, with names such as DMV, Nuclear, Colors, Hot, Wazzu, and Laroux.

Because documents are so often copied from user to user, even organizations that don't allow individual users to install new programs are vulnerable to infection. Although the Concept virus wasn't much more than a nuisance, causing no serious damage to the systems it infected, it could easily have been programmed to modify or wipe out files. Depending on the programming involved, Office macro viruses can act like those swine-flu germs that infect both people and pigs—they are potentially infectious across platforms (that is, on the Mac OS and any version of Windows).

What Are Viruses, Worms, and Trojan Horses?

The real world often provides useful metaphors that describe (and name) things in the online world. For example, consider viruses (tiny bits of genetic material that infect living cells, turning them into virus factories that create many copies of the original virus) and worms (primitive cylindrical life forms that live by insinuating themselves into a variety of environments, including the insides of some animals). Mythology is also a source of terms; consider the Trojan Horse, a giant wooden horse left as a "gift" for the enemy city of Troy — which the Trojans took in, unaware that it was full of invading Greek soldiers. In the computer world, the terms *virus, worm,* and *Trojan horse* have something in common: They're bad news for your computer.

Technically, a *computer virus* is any program designed to copy itself, usually without the user's knowledge, by attaching itself to a program or file on your PC. When you run the infected program or open the file, you also unwittingly activate the virus. The virus may lurk in your computer's memory, infecting every program you run and every disk you access. The virus may destroy files, take up disk space, make your computer display strange characters, or seemingly do nothing at all. More viruses probably fall into the "annoying" category than the "destructive" category, but that's all the more reason to take precautions. The most common type of virus, the *macro virus,* is the only type that infects Office documents (which is why I discuss them in detail in this section of the chapter) — but it's not the only type of virus.

Worms can be just as destructive as viruses (just as a tapeworm can cause as much grief as a flu virus) but in a different way. Worms, like viruses, can replicate themselves, but instead of spreading from file to file (as viruses do), they spread from computer to computer. Typically, they mail copies of themselves, usually attached to a "harmless" message, to every address they can find in your Outlook address book. When someone opens the attachment to the e-mail, the worm runs itself just once and then starts looking for more connections to other machines it can exploit.

Trojan horses are well named. When such a program arrives at your computer looking like something highly desirable, it is really hiding a nasty surprise in its belly. The part of the program you can see may seem to be doing exactly what you expect it to — but a hidden part of the program could be destroying files or stealing your passwords and e-mailing them to someone else. Although a Trojan horse isn't a virus or worm, it can be a vehicle for delivering viruses and worms.

To avoid viruses, worms, and Trojan horses, never open attachments sent to you by people you don't know (or even people you *do* know who didn't warn you that the attachment was coming) without double-checking with the person who sent it to make sure it's harmless. In addition, scan all incoming files with good third-party antivirus software; several examples are mentioned later in this chapter.

Preventing infection

As a preventive measure, good computer hygiene is virtuous but not really practical—so many files come and go that you can't hope to evaluate the health of each one. But you can cut your risk of viral infections, and Office gives you some tools to help you do it.

Because macro viruses depend on the capability of Office applications to execute macros automatically, the basic prevention technique is to shut off automatic macro execution. In Word, to disable the auto-execution of macros for all documents, all the time, create a macro of your own named Autoexec, with the following code:

```
    Sub DeepSixAutoMacros()
WordBasic.DisableAutoMacros
MsgBox "AutoMacros have been shut down", 64, "Office XP Bible
Message"
End Sub
```

If you have created your own automatic macros, however, this technique disables them, too. In this situation, you can manually disable automatic macros in documents with suspect pedigrees by holding down Shift while you open or close a document.

Another step you can take is to set the default templates (`Normal.dot` in Word, `Book.xlt` and `Sheet.xlt` in Excel) to read-only status. Because macro viruses typically attack these templates, this setting stops them in their tracks. The drawback here is that your programs then can't automatically update the template by saving the changes you make on purpose.

As noted earlier, via the Security tab in the Tools ➪ Options dialog box, Word, Excel, and PowerPoint offer you three different ways to deal with macros. Choose the medium level of security to get Office applications to display a warning message every time you open a document or template containing macros, and therefore possibly a macro virus.

Disinfecting your documents

If a macro virus takes hold of your system, often you can remove it from your documents manually by deleting the macros from each infected document individually. After opening the document, choose Tools ➪ Templates and Add-Ins ➪ Organizer. After switching to the Macro Project Items tab, delete the document's macros (which should be listed in the left pane of the Organizer dialog box).

A better solution is third-party antivirus software such as McAfee VirusScan (McAfee Software, www.mcafee.com) or Norton AntiVirus (Symantec Corporation, www.symantec.com). These programs act as "disinfectants" to purge existing viruses; they can also scan your computer at regular intervals for new infections (whether macro or other kinds of viruses) and can be regularly updated via the Internet so they're always ready for the latest virus infections.

✦   ✦   ✦

Creating Effective Documents with Word

◆ ◆ ◆ ◆

◆ ◆ ◆ ◆

Word is the most used—and arguably the most powerful—application in the Office suite. This part looks at Word in detail, pointing out tools and possibilities you might not otherwise use right away. These chapters show how to customize Word to suit your style of working and get more out of your text. They also look at the Word templates and styles and explore how to create reference tables of various types. Working with others on a Word document is covered in detail; the last two chapters offer suggestions on how to take Word to the next step by exploring fields and VBA programming.

Power Customizing Word

✦   ✦   ✦   ✦

In This Chapter

Customizing your view in Word

Customizing keyboard shortcuts

Redefining Word's built-in commands

Working with Word templates

✦   ✦   ✦   ✦

Word is easily the most customizable of the Office applications. While all Office programs let you tweak the toolbars and menus to taste, Word has many more special options governing the look and function of the program. And you have far more control over keyboard layout and shortcuts than you do in the other Office applications.

Selecting Word Options

Choosing Tools ⇨ Options brings up a dialog box of more than 100 options that control all facets of Word's operations. Figure 15-1 shows the View tab of the Options dialog box in Word. As you can see, and as in the other Office applications, the Options dialog box groups its options on separate tabs — and Word has no less than 11 of them.

I'm not going to cover the available options exhaustively, because many of them are self-explanatory and many others are useful to very few people. In general, I'll mention specific options at the places in the text where they're relevant to the task at hand. For now, I simply recommend that you set aside a few minutes sometime to acquaint yourself with what the Options dialog box has to offer. Page through all the tabs, using the Help tool to explain any choices whose functions aren't clear.

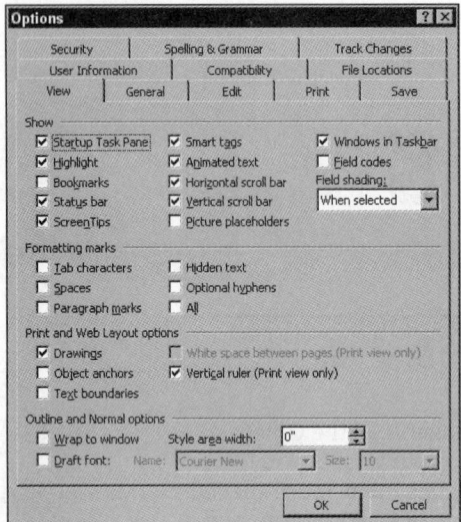

Figure 15-1: Word's Options dialog box, with the View tab (one of eleven) selected

Customizing the Screen

Most Word users quickly get comfortable with the main views: Normal, Print Layout, and Web Layout. Two additional views — Outline and Master Document — are covered in Chapters 19 and 20, respectively. At any rate, the quickest way to "customize" your screen is to switch between these views as your needs dictate. The following is a quick review of the main views with their chief characteristics:

✦ **Normal view:** Shows text with character and (most) paragraph formatting. You can also see imported graphics, but not where they will appear in print or on a Web page. AutoShapes you draw within Word and columns aren't displayed. Page and section breaks appear as lines.

✦ **Print Layout view:** Shows the document as it will appear when printed. All graphics, columns, and tables look just as they do on the printed page, allowing for the reduced resolution of the screen. If you zoom out, Word displays the document on convincing looking "pages."

✦ **Web Layout view:** Shows the document as it would look in a browser, more or less. All page breaks are removed from the screen (although they're preserved in the document). Some formatting elements available in Print Layout view are limited or missing altogether in Web Layout view.

Using the entire screen for a document: Full Screen view

There's another "view" you may not even know exists. It works in conjunction with the three usual views described above, but expands the space you have to work in by hiding everything except for the document.

Even if you know that Word's Full Screen view exists, I bet you haven't trained yourself to use it. If on-screen space is at a premium, I suggest you make the effort now. Choose View ⇨ Full Screen to switch to Full Screen view. This works in Print Preview mode as well, but there, the Print Preview toolbar includes a Full Screen toggle button by default. (You can add this button to other toolbars, of course, using the standard customization methods covered in Chapter 5.)

Sure, with today's larger monitors and higher resolutions, more of us can have our cake (scads of toolbars) and eat it too (with plenty of room on the screen left for documents). But lots of folks are still making do with 14- or 15-inch screens, and notebook users have even less screen real estate to work with.

Full Screen view hides the menu, the toolbars, the status bar, the scroll bars, and even the title bar at the top of Word's window. The only extraneous item left is a tiny floating Full Screen toolbar. It contains a single Escape button that takes you back to the regular window layout. If you prefer, you can dock the Full Screen toolbar along any of the four sides of the Word window, a configuration that keeps it out of the way of your text. But then the toolbar takes up too much space, so I recommend against it.

Once the initial anxiety passes (No toolbars! How can I cope?), you'll find that you still have access to all of Word's power. Of course, all your keyboard shortcuts still work. But so does the top menu bar. All you have to do is open it via a keyboard shortcut (Alt+F for the File menu, for instance). Pressing Alt alone while in Full Screen view displays the menu bar itself.

You can also make the menu bar appear by moving the mouse pointer to the top of the screen. It doesn't matter if you've stationed the Office Shortcut Bar or the Windows taskbar up there, even on Auto Hide — when you move the mouse pointer to the top of the screen, it's the Word menu that appears.

Adding back window elements to Full Screen view

OK, so that covers the menu bar. But what if you can't be happy unless you can see the ruler, one of the toolbars, or maybe the horizontal scroll bar? No problem — just turn on whatever components you need individually. To display the ruler, choose View ⇨ Ruler. If your security blankets are the scroll bars or the status bar, display them by choosing Tools ⇨ Options and checking the appropriate boxes on the View tab.

To turn on that certain toolbar, choose View ➪ Toolbars and pick it from a list, or for more choices, pick Customize and check off the toolbar you want displayed. Full Screen view remembers which toolbars you unhide in this view and displays them again the next time you switch to this view.

If all you need are 10 or 20 crucial buttons, you can add them to the Full Screen toolbar. Just be aware that you can only customize this toolbar while you're in Full Screen view. To do so, choose Tools ➪ Customize and start adding buttons with the techniques detailed in Chapter 5.

Dumping the Full Screen toolbar

For a perfectly pristine, fully full screen, you can use a VBA macro to remove the Full Screen toolbar when you toggle Full Screen view on and off. You can still return to an ordinary view by pressing Esc. The code you need is listed in the section "Redefining Word's Built-In Commands" later in this chapter.

Customizing tips for special screen situations

The tips here all rely on selections in the View tab of the Options dialog box. Choose Tools ➪ Options, and then click the View tab to display the relevant set of choices, as shown back in Figure 15-1.

Toggling the zoom factor

Chapter 4 includes a VBA macro that enables you to flip back and forth between two different magnifications of your document with a single button click. This macro is much more efficient than manually adjusting the zoom setting over and over again.

Maximizing performance

When your main concern is efficient text editing, fine-tuning Word's screen-related options can boost the program's performance. Try the following settings on the View tab:

✦ **Picture placeholders:** Check this box to have Word display plain rectangles in place of the pictures in your document. This can be a major timesaver while you're working on the text — it takes a lot of computer horsepower to display complex drawings or large bitmaps, particularly if they contain many different colors. When it's time to proof the document as a whole, just uncheck the box again and the pictures will reappear. Obviously, this setting doesn't help if your document has no pictures.

✦ **Draft font:** Checking this box displays all text in a single plain-looking font in Normal and Outline views. That saves time, because Word no longer spends time figuring out how to display all those different typefaces, sizes, and colors. In draft mode, Word displays all text at the same size, ignores most paragraph formatting, and indicates character attributes like bold, italics, and highlighting by underlining the affected text. But you'll only notice a significant speedup if you're trying to run Word on an old, underpowered PC—fancy screen fonts just aren't a strain for a Pentium.

Minimizing on-screen distractions

Many people find that they write better if they concentrate on document content first, and then go back and format the text so that it looks nice. Here are some options to consider if you're one of those people:

✦ **Draft font:** See the last point in the preceding section. Even if it doesn't appreciably speed up your screen, the Draft font option can still be helpful if you prefer to focus on content alone when you're writing. When you want to work on the document's format, just turn off the Draft font.

✦ **Animated text:** Text animation may have a place in Web page design and custom applications—although I'm not convinced—but it's definitely annoying when you're writing. Uncheck this box to turn off the special effects without removing the animation.

✦ **Highlight:** If someone has marked up the document with colored highlights, you may find it difficult to focus on the nonhighlighted text when you have to edit it. Uncheck this box to display everything in plain black and white.

Maximizing screen space, when you don't want to use Full Screen view

The following options in the View tab can give you more room for your work:

✦ **Status bar:** Uncheck this box to hide the status bar, opening up another third of an inch or so (depending on your monitor) for your document.

✦ **Horizontal scroll bar and Vertical scroll bar:** If you're good with the keyboard, the scroll bars just get in the way. Turn them off. Note that the horizontal scroll bar contains the buttons for the various views (Normal, Page Layout, Outline, and Web Layout), but you can change views quickly enough with the View menu or the corresponding keyboard shortcuts (Alt+Ctrl with N, P, O—Word doesn't have a default shortcut for the Web Layout view).

✦ **Style area:** The little-known style area is a vertical region along the left edge of the window where Word displays paragraph style names. It's handy for scanning visually through a document to see how styles look in use, or to hunt for paragraphs with incorrect styles. On the other hand, it cuts into your usable screen area significantly. The easiest way to remove it is by dragging the vertical line separating it from the document all the way over to the left side of the window. You can also set its size in inches via the View tab of the Options dialog box—a 0 setting in the Style area width box in the Outline and Normal options area shuts it off. (The style area is visible only in Normal and Outline views.)

One Step to a Smaller Window

Switching to Word's Web Layout view turns on the "Wrap to window" function automatically. However, Web Layout view has other effects you may not want, such as removing page breaks, and it doesn't resize the window. What you really need is a VBA procedure to switch to a smaller window and change the word wrapping setting in a single step, and then return to the standard wrapping setting when you maximize the window again. Ideally, the macro would take effect when you use the standard Windows buttons for restoring and maximizing an application, but that won't work. Instead, the following macro toggles between the two window configurations. Place it on a toolbar button or give it a keyboard shortcut:

```
Sub ToggleWindowSizeAndWrapToWindow ()
Dim WrapStateAs Boolean
WrapState = True ' Set variable default
If Application.WindowState = wdWindowStateNormal Then
    Application.WindowState = wdWindowStateMaximize
    WrapState = False
Else
    Application.WindowState = wdWindowStateNormal
End If
ActiveWindow.View.WrapToWindow = WrapState
End Sub
```

Using Word effectively in a small window

Word processing is best done in the largest possible editing space. If you need to work with other applications, however, you may need to shrink Word's window so that you can see all your programs at once.

In this situation, you are still able to see your text if you check the "Wrap to window" checkbox on the Tools ⇨ Options dialog box (View tab). Now, instead of truncating each line at the right edge of the window, Word temporarily reformats each paragraph so that text that would normally fall past the edge wraps to the next line. The document still prints with the original formatting and returns to its normal appearance on the screen when you uncheck the box.

Activating the Word calculator

Word has always had a command for performing calculations on numbers visible on the screen, in your documents. Unfortunately, Word buries this handy command where you're not likely to come across it — in the Customize dialog box. To find and activate the command, choose Tools ⇨ Customize and switch to the Commands tab. Select All Commands in the Categories list, and then scroll way down in the Commands list until you see the ToolsCalculate command. Haul it out and put it on the Tools menu or on a toolbar.

Once the Calculate command is accessible, performing a calculation is as simple as selecting the numbers in your document and clicking the button or menu item. It doesn't matter how numbers are arranged—in a row, in a column, or even within or across paragraphs, separated by any amount of text. The result appears in the status bar and is placed on the clipboard, so doing a quick Ctrl+V (Paste) deposits it at the insertion point. By default, Word adds the selected numbers, but it will dutifully perform subtraction, multiplication, or division if the appropriate symbol precedes a number in the selected text.

Customizations, Templates, and Documents

Please note that Word can store customizations, including macros, customized toolbars and menus, and keyboard shortcuts, in templates or in documents. Only templates can contain AutoText entries, however. By default, all of these items are placed in the Normal.dot template, making them available in all documents. But if two or more people share the same copy of Word, each can have a different custom setup by maintaining a unique template where these customizations are stored. And if a particular customization is only useful with a specific document, you can store it in that document rather than in a template.

As you might expect, you decide where a new toolbar, macro, keyboard shortcut, or AutoText entry is to be stored when you create it. In Word, the dialog boxes for creating each of these items contain drop-down lists from which you can select a destination: Normal.dot, any other templates currently active or attached to the current document, or the document itself.

Cross-Reference

See the section "Using Word templates" later in this chapter for details on how templates work; they're also discussed in Chapter 18. Chapter 5 covers customizing toolbars, menus, and shortcut menus. Just remember, Office blurs the distinction between toolbars and menus—you can place buttons on the top menu bar and put menus into the toolbars.

Tip

Place the Cut, Copy, and Paste commands on the Grammar and Spelling shortcut menus. That way, you won't have to stall when you want to edit text that Word thinks is misspelled or grammatically weak.

Customizing the Word keyboard

Keyboard efficiency matters more in Word than in any other Office application. You need both hands on the keyboard for full-tilt typing and editing, and you must break your stride every time you reach for the mouse.

That's why Word, of all the Office applications, gives you the most freedom to customize the keyboard. Do yourself a favor and take advantage of that power. Create a keyboard shortcut for every item you use regularly, whether it's a command, macro, style, font, or AutoText entry, or a character that isn't already available on the keyboard. For that matter, you should change any of the stock shortcuts that you find hard to remember or inconvenient to reach.

Creating and changing keyboard shortcuts

The Customize Keyboard dialog box described later works for every kind of item to which shortcuts can be assigned, from Word commands to individual special characters. However, you can also assign shortcuts to styles via the Style dialog box and to any single character via the Symbol dialog box. In fact, I recommend you use the latter dialog box (display it by choosing Insert ➪ Symbol) to create shortcuts for individual characters, because it can display all available characters at once and in any font.

To create or redefine a keyboard shortcut, start by choosing Tools ➪ Customize. Click the Keyboard button to bring up the Customize Keyboard dialog box, shown in Figure 15-2.

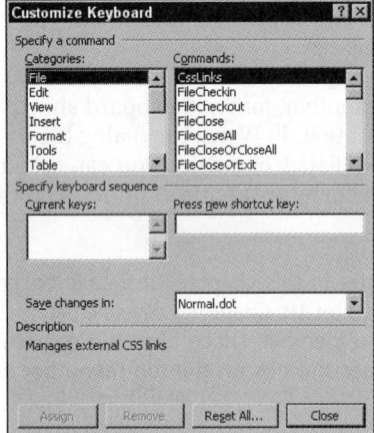

Figure 15-2: Use the Customize Keyboard dialog box to customize your keyboard.

To assign a keyboard shortcut to a Word command or other function, start by finding the item in the Commands list on the right.

Cross-Reference Chapter 5 reviews how to navigate the Categories and Commands lists when customizing Office applications.

When you've selected the item, its existing keyboard shortcuts appear in the Current Keys list at the lower left (who knows — maybe you don't need to create a new shortcut after all). You can have as many keyboard shortcuts as you like for each command, so there's no "pressing" need to delete any of the existing shortcuts, but if you do wish to remove one, highlight it and click the Remove button. To create a new shortcut, click in the "Press new shortcut key" field and then press the key or keys you've chosen for the shortcut. The shortcut appears in written form.

Before you choose Assign to create the new shortcut, check to make sure that the keys you've chosen aren't already assigned to some other command. If they are, the message Currently Assigned To: appears just below your entry. You're free to replace the existing assignment, but you probably shouldn't unless it's one you're definitely not using already.

By default, the changes are saved in the Normal.dot template, but you can choose to save them in any other template you have open, or only in one of the documents you have open. All the available options are displayed in the Save changes in drop-down list.

If you've really confused yourself or made a mess of things, you can always return to the original key assignments for the template or document selected in the Save changes in box by clicking the Reset All button.

Note When you choose Assign, the new shortcut is added to the Current Keys list. The list can hold only eight shortcuts, but shortcuts nine and above will work even though you can't see them on the list.

Choosing keys for shortcuts

When you're cooking up shortcuts, make an effort to be organized — try to assign similar shortcuts to similar commands. You might use the Alt+Ctrl combinations for file- and document-related commands, Alt+Shift combinations for formatting commands, and so on.

However, there's a problem with this advice: It conflicts with another good idea — that you should stick to Word's default shortcuts whenever possible — because few of the defaults follow any sort of recognizable pattern! That means imposing consistency means sacrificing defaults.

In any case, don't neglect any key as a possible shortcut. Except for nonstandard keys — like those Fn keys on most notebook PCs — most keys can be used as shortcuts, alone or in combination with Alt, Ctrl, or Shift. On my computer, Alt+Scroll Lock and Ctrl+Break are valid combinations (you may have different results with these system keys depending on who made the computer and keyboard).

Note The Scroll Lock key deserves special mention. Here's a perfectly good key that almost all programs treat as a taboo. In Word, you can use Scroll Lock — all by itself — as a shortcut key, though it takes a little doing. See "Using off-limits keys in custom keyboard shortcuts" later.

Maximum control with two-step shortcuts

If you're really hungry for more keyboard shortcuts, you'll get all you can eat with Word's two-step shortcuts. In a two-step shortcut, the first key or combination you press initiates the sequence; you press another key combo to complete it. Let's say you set aside F10 as the first key for all your two-step shortcuts. You can now create shortcuts such as F10, 5 (you press F10, then the 5 key), or for that matter F10, F10.

Note   You can't use the Ctrl or Alt keys in the second step of a two-step shortcut.

Yes, two steps take longer than one, but many people find they're still faster than using the menus or the mouse. Besides, they're often easier (to remember and to press) than some complex combination involving Alt, Ctrl, and Shift (and think of the possibilities they open!).

Two-step shortcuts are great for groups of similar commands. Sticking with the F10 example, you could assign F10, F1 through F10, F10 to your most commonly used paragraph styles. You might activate your favorite fonts via F10, 1 through F10, 0 (using the typewriter number keys), while F10, a through F10, z might be given over to special dingbat characters. Of course, that still leaves you with F10, Shift+a through F10, Shift+z and tons of other combinations with the punctuation keys. By the way, this is the system Word uses for entering accented characters—for example, Ctrl+' followed by e inserts an é into your document.

Using off-limits keys in custom keyboard shortcuts

The Customize Keyboard dialog box refuses to recognize many keys on your keyboard—it just beeps when you type them as part of a new keyboard shortcut. These off-limits keys include all the alphanumeric characters, the punctuation keys, and all of the numeric keypad keys, plus system keys such as Scroll Lock. (Mind you, the Customize dialog box does allow these keys when used in combination with Alt or Ctrl, but not alone.)

Word is trying to protect the novice user from making a mess of the keyboard. I appreciate the thought, but I'm a grown-up now and willing to live with a little risk. I *never* type a reverse apostrophe, hardly ever \ or |, and only occasionally [or] (the square bracket characters located just to the right of the P key). Therefore, these keys are much more useful to me as ultrafast one-key shortcuts to Word commands.

On my keyboard, for example, I use the ` key to swap the last two characters I typed, when I typed them in reverse order—which is pretty darn often. The \ key changes the case of the next letter, and the [and] keys cut the word to the left or right of the insertion point, respectively.

Putting the off-limits keys to work just takes a little VBA. Behind the scenes, Word keeps track of each key by a code number. For example, the F1 key is 112, the X key is 88, and the Delete key is 46. You use these key codes in VBA procedures to specify the keys you want to redefine.

Word also supplies named constants for the key codes. Table 15-1 lists the named constants and key codes of some of the keys you can't access in the Customize Keyboard dialog box. As you can see, the table lists only plain and shifted keys. The reason? You don't need VBA if you're using Alt or Ctrl in your shortcut, because the Customize Keyboard dialog box reads any combination that includes either of those keys. (For special projects, you can also redefine the standard alphanumeric and punctuation keys; to learn their key codes and named constants, search for wdKey in the Object Browser.)

| Table 15-1 | | | |
| **Selected Key Codes for Customizing** | | | |
Key	Key Code Constant	Key Code (Key Alone)	Key Code (with Shift)
5 on the numeric keypad (with Num Lock off)	wdKeyNumeric5Special	12	268
Scroll Lock	wdKeyScrollLock	145	401
`	wdKeyBackSingleQuote	192	—
~	*	—	448
[	wdKeyOpenSquareBrace	219	—
{	*	—	475
\	wdKeyBackSlash	220	—
|	*	—	476
]	wdKeyCloseSquareBrace	221	—
}	*	—	477
Spacebar	wdKeySpacebar	32	288
0 on the numeric keypad	wdKeyNumeric0	96	352
1 on the numeric keypad	wdKeyNumeric1	97	353
2 on the numeric keypad	wdKeyNumeric2	98	354
3 on the numeric keypad	wdKeyNumeric3	99	355
4 on the numeric keypad	wdKeyNumeric4	100	356

Continued

<table>
<tr><th colspan="4">Table 15-1 *(continued)*</th></tr>
<tr><th>Key</th><th>Key Code
Constant</th><th>Key Code
(Key Alone)</th><th>Key Code
(with Shift)</th></tr>
<tr><td>5 on the
numeric keypad</td><td>wdKeyNumeric5</td><td>101</td><td>357</td></tr>
<tr><td>6 on the
numeric keypad</td><td>wdKeyNumeric6</td><td>102</td><td>358</td></tr>
<tr><td>7 on the
numeric keypad</td><td>wdKeyNumeric7</td><td>103</td><td>359</td></tr>
<tr><td>8 on the
numeric keypad</td><td>wdKeyNumeric8</td><td>104</td><td>360</td></tr>
<tr><td>9 on the
numeric keypad</td><td>wdKeyNumeric9</td><td>105</td><td>361</td></tr>
<tr><td>* on the
numeric keypad</td><td>wdKeyNumericMultiply</td><td>106</td><td>362</td></tr>
<tr><td>+ on the
numeric keypad</td><td>wdKeyNumericAdd</td><td>107</td><td>363</td></tr>
<tr><td>- on the
numeric keypad</td><td>wdKeyNumericSubtract</td><td>109</td><td>365</td></tr>
<tr><td>. on the
numeric keypad</td><td>wdKeyNumericDecimal</td><td>110</td><td>366</td></tr>
<tr><td>/ on the
numeric keypad</td><td>wdKeyNumericDivide</td><td>111</td><td>367</td></tr>
</table>

Note: To specify the keys marked with *, you need the `BuildKeyCode` method of the `KeyCode` argument of the `KeyBindinds.Add` method. Use `wdKeyShift` as Arg1 and the constant for the key immediately above it in the table as Arg2 (see Word VBA Help on `BuildKeyCode`).

The following sample macro shows how to assign the Scroll Lock key to a command, in this case the Word Count command. The `Add` method of the `KeyBindings` object takes a `KeyCategory` argument for the type of item you're working with (command, macro, style, or what have you). Then come the `Command` and `KeyCode` arguments for the command name and key code, respectively. The example uses the named constant for the Scroll Lock key, but the equivalent numeric key code, 145, would work just as well.

```
Sub AssignWordCountToScrollLock()
    KeyBindings.Add KeyCategory:=, _
        Command:="ToolsWordCount", KeyCode:=wdKeyScrollLock
End Sub
```

If you don't want to type a new macro every time you redefine a key, use the macro listed below. When you run it, it asks you whether the keyboard shortcut you're creating is for a macro or one of Word's built-in commands. Next, you type in the name of the macro or command. You must enter the exact spelling. To find a command's official name, locate it in the Customize Keyboard dialog box, just as if you were going to assign a keyboard shortcut to the command. Finally, type in the code number for the chosen shortcut key—you have to use the number, not the corresponding named constant.

```
Sub AssignHiddenKeys()

On Error GoTo BYE

strMacroQuery = "Are you defining a keyboard shortcut " & _
    "for a macro? " + Chr(13) + "If so, click Yes. " & _
    "For built-in commands, click No."
Style = vbYesNo + vbQuestion + vbDefaultButton2
strTitle = "Office XP Key Assigner"
strMessage1 = "Type the name of the command or macro " & _
    "you want to assign to a shortcut."
strMessage2 = "Type the code number of the keyboard " & _
    "shortcut key or keys you want to assign."
MacroOrCommand = MsgBox(strMacroQuery, Style, Title)

If MacroOrCommand = vbYes Then
    KeyCategoryName = wdKeyCategoryMacro
Else
    KeyCategoryName = wdKeyCategoryCommand
End If

CommandName = InputBox(strMessage1, strTitle)
KeyValue = InputBox(strMessage2, strTitle)
CodeNumber = Val(KeyValue)

If CodeNumber < 8 Or num > 1919 Then
    MsgBox _
        "Shortcut key code must be between 8 and 1919"
Else
    CustomizationContext = NormalTemplate
    KeyBindings.Add KeyCategory:=KeyCategoryName, _
        Command:=CommandName, KeyCode:=CodeNumber
End If

BYE:
End Sub
```

Shortcuts for standard keyboard characters

Suppose you take my advice and assign the | key to a shortcut. What happens if one day, ten years from now, you finally need to type a |? No problem—just use the Insert ➪ Symbol command to place the character you need from the Symbol dialog box into your document.

For me, the bracket and backslash keys fall into a different category. They're great as shortcut keys, but I do need those brackets in my documents at least three or four times in a blue moon.

The solution is to create a shortcut combining Alt or Ctrl with the key in question. The shortcut inserts the original symbol in one step, and is easy to remember because it's based on the symbol's real key. The best way to set up such a shortcut is again the Insert ➪ Symbol command. Choose Insert ➪ Symbol. In the Symbol dialog box, start by selecting (normal text) in the Font list. Then select the character to which you're assigning the new shortcut and click Shortcut Key. Type the key combination for the new shortcut so that it appears at "Press new shortcut key". Combinations with the Alt key usually don't conflict with Word's default shortcuts, which use Ctrl for the most part. To create a shortcut for], for example, enter Alt+] at "Press new shortcut key".

Keeping track of keyboard shortcuts

Whether or not you change the default keyboard shortcuts, you should be aware of ways to learn the current shortcuts (default and customized) as you work, and to find out what the current shortcuts are.

Word automatically displays keyboard shortcuts for menu commands on the menus themselves. If you like, you can also see them in the ScreenTips that pop up when the mouse pointer rests over a button for a second or two. To turn this feature on, choose Tools ➪ Customize, select the Options tab, and check the Show Shortcut Keys in ScreenTips box.

Other tricks for acquainting yourself with keyboard shortcuts include the following:

✦ To learn the current keyboard shortcuts for any command, macro, or other item, open the Customize Keyboard dialog box and highlight the item in the Commands list. All shortcuts assigned to the item appear in the "Current keys" box.

✦ To print a list of all current custom keyboard shortcuts, choose File ➪ Print and select "Key assignments" in the Print What field. Only custom shortcuts, not Word's defaults, appear in the printout.

✦ To create a document containing a table of Word commands with their keyboard shortcuts and menu locations, use the ListCommands command. Select All Commands in the Categories list on the Commands tab of the Tools ➪ Customize dialog box, locate the item for ListCommands, and drag it onto a toolbar or menu.

Redefining Word's built-in commands

Uniquely among the Office applications, Word enables you — invites you, really — to modify the way its own commands work. The trick is simple: You create a VBA macro (a Sub procedure) with the same name as the built-in command you want to alter or replace.

Often, figuring out the name of the command you want to modify is the hardest part of this trick. The sample macro listed here, for example, replaces the built-in View ⇨ Full Screen command, which toggles Full Screen view off and on (for a diatribe on Full Screen view, see "Using the entire screen for your document in Full Screen view" earlier in this chapter). Unfortunately, Word's official name for this command is `ToggleFull`, not necessarily your first guess. Equally unfortunately, I know of no reference list of menu commands with their corresponding official names. You may have to scroll through the list of commands in the Customize dialog box, placing likely candidates on a toolbar and trying them until you hit on the right one.

After you have found the correct command name, it's on to writing the macro. Typically, you use this technique when you want a built-in command to work just a little differently, not because you want to completely replace the command. For this reason, a macro of this type almost always includes the built-in command as part of its code. For example, the macro shown here toggles Full Screen view on and off sure enough, but also hides the Full Screen toolbar when switching to a Full Screen view.

Now to explain the sample macro: The first executable line (the one beginning with `ActiveWindow`) is the VBA code corresponding to Word's `ToggleFull` command. After that command has done its work, the remaining code steps in to ensure the Full Screen toolbar doesn't appear.

```
Sub ToggleFull()
ActiveWindow.View.FullScreen = Not ActiveWindow.View.FullScreen
    If ActiveWindow.View.FullScreen = True Then
        For Each cb In CommandBars
            If cb.Name = "Full Screen" Then
                cb.Visible = False
            End If
        Next
    End If
End Sub
```

In this type of macro, the macro's name must exactly match that of the command it modifies. In addition, if you're including the original command in your macro, you need the correct VBA syntax for the command. To be sure you get the spelling and code right, have Word start the macro for you, and then add your custom code. Follow these steps:

1. Open the Tools ⇨ Macro ⇨ Macros dialog box.

2. Select the choice "Word commands" from the Macros In drop-down list.

3. Select the command you want to modify in the long scrolling list in the main part of the dialog box.

4. Returning to the Macros In list, choose the template or document in which you want to store the macro for your modified command. Selecting All Active Templates and Documents stores it in the Normal template.

5. Choose Create. This takes you to the Visual Basic Editor, where the macro has been started for you and already contains the VBA code corresponding to the command you're modifying.

6. Once you've added your custom code, return to Word. Now, every time you use the menu item, toolbar button, or keyboard shortcut for that command, your macro runs instead.

Using Word templates

Throughout Office, you use templates to endow new documents with preset layout, formatting, and content that you can then add to or modify. With the template responsible for elements that remain constant from document to document, you can devote your energies to defining the items that make each document unique, and you can be sure that documents based on the same template share consistent common elements.

In Word, however, templates do more. Word templates contain customizations to the program itself, such as custom toolbars and shortcut keys, macros, and AutoText entries. All these customizations are available automatically in documents you base on a template they reside in. What's more — and this is where Word really parts company with its suitemates — Word lets you use multiple templates simultaneously with the same document. Using a hierarchy of templates, you can retain personal customizations to the program while sharing layout and boilerplate content with others in your organization.

Word also enables you to change the templates on which the document is based. This means that in midstream, you can radically alter a document's format, the available customizations, or both. However, content in the new template does not appear in the document.

Word template basics

Among the many details a Word template can store are the following:

✦ The settings of the File ➪ Page Setup dialog box

✦ Paragraph and character styles

✦ Macros

✦ Custom toolbars, menus, and shortcut keys

✦ AutoText entries

✦ Layout and content of headers and footers

✦ Text, graphics, and other content items

Formatted AutoCorrect entries are stored only in the Normal template, the subject of the next section.

By default, Word templates are stored in the Templates folder, a subfolder of your main Office folder. The General tab of the File ➪ New dialog box lists all the templates — and shortcuts to templates — stored directly in the Templates subfolder. It provides additional tabs for any subfolders and folder shortcuts within the Templates folder, so long as these other folders contain Word templates. You can change the default main, or user, templates folder and specify an additional workgroup templates folder in the Tools ➪ Options dialog box, or via the Office Shortcut bar.

Parallel with other Office applications, a Word template is essentially just a standard document stored with the special .dot extension. True, Word templates can contain a few types of information not included in ordinary documents, such as AutoText entries. However, you can use any Word document as a template for the layout, formatting, and content of new documents simply by storing it in one of the templates folders. But documents based on such ersatz templates don't acquire the toolbars, macros, and other customizations of the "template."

Creating and modifying templates

To create a new template, start by setting up a document with the layout, formatting, and content you want in the template. Add new macros, toolbars, and keyboard shortcuts as discussed in the "Customizations, Templates, and Documents" section earlier in this chapter. Then choose File ➪ Save As. When you select Document Template at Save as Type, Word automatically takes you to your main templates folder. Navigate to one of its subfolders if you wish, name the new template, and save the file. Once a document is saved as a template, you can add AutoCorrect entries as well. To modify an existing template, open it by selecting Document Templates at Files of Type in the File ➪ Open dialog box. Make any changes you wish and save the file again.

Using the Normal template

In Word, one master template has an all-important role: This is the Normal template, stored in the `Normal.dot` file. The Normal template governs the layout and content of each new document that appears when you start Word without any startup switches or click the New toolbar button. You can change the layout and content for these default documents by modifying the Normal template with the technique described in the previous paragraph. In addition, customizations stored in the Normal template are always available no matter what document you're working with and what other template it's based on.

If Word doesn't find the Normal template in any of your templates folders or in the main Office subfolder, it automatically makes a new Normal template containing the default formatting, layout, and program settings. This gives you a quick way to restore the defaults if your experiments produce an unusable ab-Normal template — just rename the current version of `Normal.dot` or copy it to another folder, and then restart Word.

Scaling the template hierarchy

Because you can use more than one template with a given document, and because the settings stored in these templates may well conflict, Word has to decide which template's settings take priority. The Word template hierarchy has three levels, which work as follows:

1. The **attached template** — the one on which the current document is based — rules supreme. Other settings defined here supersede those in other active templates. Again, you can change the template attached to the document, as the next section discusses in detail.

2. The **Normal template** occupies the second rank of the template hierarchy.

3. At the bottom of the barrel are any other **global templates**. Any settings they contain that don't conflict with those in the attached or Normal templates are available. If you load two or more global templates, Word prioritizes them alphabetically.

Tip   As an individual user, storing all of your routinely used custom macros, toolbars, and keyboard shortcuts in the Normal template works fine. However, you might consider placing them instead in a separate global template. That way, to revert to Word's default settings you simply unload this template by unchecking its box in the Tools ➪ Templates and Add-Ins dialog box.

If you use Word in a group, you can individualize it for different users without sacrificing document consistency. Store layout, formatting, and boilerplate text in the Normal template and other templates reserved for this purpose. Whether the group is networked or uses Word on the same computer, these templates should be placed in the workgroup templates folder. There, they will be available to all users for new documents, or to be attached to existing ones. Each user stores personal customizations in a separate template placed in the user templates folder defined for that person. This personalized template can then be loaded as a global template.

Attaching a different template

The template you select when you create a new document is, in Word's jargon, attached to the document. You can attach a different template to change the document's paragraph and character styles, and to make the new template's customizations available when you work with the document.

To change the attached template, choose Tools ➪ Templates and Add-Ins. In the resulting dialog box (see Figure 15-3), choose Attach to bring up a dialog box displaying the templates in your main templates folder. Select the template you want to attach and choose Open.

When you attach a different template, its paragraph and character styles are copied into the document, replacing any existing styles with duplicate names. The template's customizations and AutoText entries become available to the document but aren't copied there. However, text, graphics, and page setup settings in the template do not become part of the document. (If you need content items from the template, you can open the template itself in Word and copy the elements to your document.)

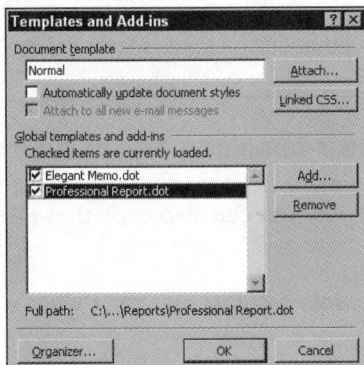

Figure 15-3: Change the document's template in the Templates and Add-ins dialog box.

In the Tools ➪ Templates and Add-Ins dialog box, the setting labeled Automatically Update Document Styles is worth noting. When this box is checked, Word updates the document's paragraph and styles with those currently in the attached template each time you open the document. This is a great way to keep documents automatically consistent with changes you make in your personal or corporate typographic identity by way of template modifications.

To copy individual styles in the reverse direction, from your document to the attached template, choose Format ➪ Styles and Formatting, then select Custom from the Show drop-down list at the bottom of the task pane. This box is used primarily to determine which available styles will be displayed in the Styles and Formatting task pane, but it also includes the option to Save settings in template. Select that, and when you save the document, the styles you have created for it will be saved in the template you're using for it.

Loading global templates

Global templates are those whose AutoText entries, macros, and customizations are available in any Word document. The Normal template is a global template, but as described earlier in this section, it is always loaded and takes precedence over other global templates. You can use any template as a global template with either of the following techniques:

✦ Load the template manually. Choose Tools ➪ Templates and Add-Ins, and then choose Add. Select the template and click OK. It should then appear in the large box in the middle of the Templates and Add-ins dialog box.

✦ Load the template automatically each time Word starts. Copy the template file to the Office startup folder. By default, this is the Windows\Application Data\ Microsoft\Word\Startup folder. You can select a Startup folder of your own on the File Locations tab of the Tools ➪ Options dialog box.

Add-ins — special-purpose software plug-ins that you can obtain from third-party suppliers or that you can write yourself — are managed the same way as global templates.

Managing styles and customizations across templates and documents

Word's Organizer (see Figure 15-4) lets you rename or delete individual styles, VBA modules and forms, toolbars, and AutoText entries. You can also copy these items from one template or document to another.

> **Note**   Only templates can store AutoText entries. Note too that you can't work with keyboard shortcuts in the Organizer.

You activate the Organizer button from either of two dialog boxes: Tools ➪ Templates and Add-Ins, or Format ➪ Style. The Organizer has separate tabs for each of the items you can work with.

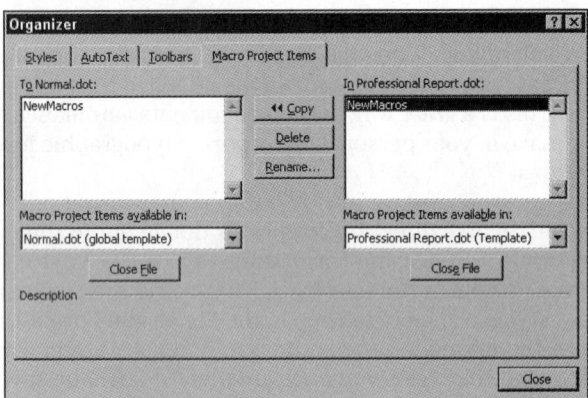

Figure 15-4: The Organizer lets you modify items stored in templates and documents.

Use the two pairs of "available in" drop-down lists and Close/Open File buttons on either side of the Organizer to activate the document or template you wish to work with. (Before you can open a new file, you must first close the one currently displayed.) You can then select the items you want to rename, delete, or copy. The standard Windows Shift+click and Ctrl+click tricks work for selecting more than one item at a time.

If you're copying toolbars, don't forget to copy any macros their buttons depend on as well.

> **Note**   You can also use the Visual Basic Editor to copy macros from one document or template to another (see Part XI).

A Better Way to Save Your Template Customization

If you customize your templates frequently, you need a macro that saves your changes without all those steps. Word includes a SaveTemplate command that you can drag from the Tools ➪ Customize dialog box (look under All Commands in the Categories list) onto a toolbar or menu. However, this command doesn't save changes to the Normal template.

The following code saves the current document's attached template — even if the template is `Normal.dot` — and displays a confirmatory message:

```
Sub SaveTemplate()
On Error GoTo SaveTemplate_Err

With ActiveDocument.AttachedTemplate
   .Save
   MsgBox "Saved " & .Name
End With
Exit Sub

SaveTemplate_Err:
   MsgBox Err.Description
   Exit Sub
End Sub
```

Put this macro into `Normal.dot` or another global document and hook it up to a toolbar button for one-shot access.

Saving template customizations right now

When you add or change the macros, toolbars, or keyboard shortcuts that reside in a template, Word doesn't save the changes until you exit the program. This means that lots of work can be at risk for quite some time. Although the AutoRecovery and Save on Crash features usually protect you, I recommend saving your templates manually whenever you make important changes.

To accomplish this, you must open the Visual Basic Editor by choosing Tools ➪ Macro ➪ Visual Basic Editor, or pressing Alt+F11. There, choose File ➪ Save or click the Save button. This method is labor intensive, but at least it does the job.

✦   ✦   ✦

Making Text Work for You

Word is more than just a glorified typewriter. You can also use it to add special formatting touches such as bulleted lists, columns, and borders to your text, as well as reference tools such as footnotes, endnotes, cross-references, and more. In this chapter, you explore some of the ways you can use Word to make your documents more visually effective and practically useful in this chapter.

Creating Bulleted and Numbered Lists

Word provides three different methods for creating numbered and bulleted paragraphs. For the first two, you place the insertion point in the target paragraph, or select a group of paragraphs, and then do either of the following

◆ Click the appropriate button, Numbering or Bullets.

◆ Choose Format ➪ Bullets and Numbering and select the bullet or number format you want from the resulting dialog box (see Figure 16-1). This is the option to use when you want direct, certain control over the format of your numbering scheme (as in 1., 2., 3. . . . ; I., II., III. . . . ; or even (A), (B), (C) . . .) or bullets.

To use the third method, just place the insertion point on a blank line and let Word format your list automatically as you type it — details on this option follow later in this chapter.

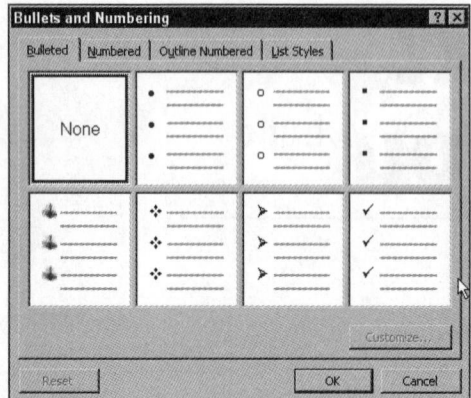

Figure 16-1: The Bullets and Numbering dialog box. Select a format for bulleted lists from the Bulleted tab, one of four tabs.

Using the Bullets and Numbering buttons

When you apply bullets to a paragraph during editing by placing your insertion point inside the paragraph and then clicking the Bullets toolbar button, the bullet character applied to the paragraph is the last one you used. Likewise, when you click the Numbering button, the paragraph receives the numbering scheme you last applied.

Note

The numbers and bullets that Word adds are part of the paragraph format. When you apply either to a paragraph, Word doesn't insert a numeral or bullet character into the text. Instead, the program adds the numbering or bullet information — including the specific numbering scheme or bullet character you choose — to the paragraph format.

Among other things, this means that you can't click alongside or select a paragraph number or bullet. When you cursor through a numbered list, you'll see that the insertion point skips over the numbers as though they are protected by a force field. It also means that when you copy the paragraph mark of a numbered paragraph and paste it elsewhere, Word numbers the destination paragraph automatically.

Removing numbering and bullets

Two quick ways to turn off paragraph numbering or bullets are

✦ Select the paragraphs (for a single paragraph, just place the insertion point in it) and click off the appropriate button (either the Bullet or Numbering button).

✦ Click just to the left of the first character in the paragraph (not counting the number or bullet) and press Backspace.

Using automatic numbered and bulleted lists

To activate the automated, as-you-type method for adding simple numbered and bulleted lists, check the "Automatic numbered lists" and "Automatic bulleted lists" boxes in the AutoFormat As You Type tab of the Tools ⇨ AutoCorrect Options dialog box.

I recommend this method because it's so easy. Not only are you spared the extra steps of selecting the paragraphs, but also you don't need to call up and fiddle with a dialog box to choose the format for your numbering system or bullets.

Instead, here's all you need do:

1. On a blank line, type the "number" for your first point, as in (1), I., or A) — you must either include punctuation after the number or press Tab in step 2. Or, type a bullet character (see "Characters to type for automatic bullets," later in this chapter).

2. Press Space or Tab.

3. Type the paragraph text.

4. Hit Enter.

Word starts the next point in the sequence with the appropriate, correctly formatted number or bullet. From then on, you can add more numbered or bulleted paragraphs by simply pressing Enter after typing some text in the current paragraph. Word also applies this formatting to the original paragraph, converting the numbers or bullet character you typed there into the automatic kind.

Tip   Office XP inserts a Smart Tag to the left of the first entry in your list after you hit Enter when automatic numbering or automatic bulleted lists are turned on. Clicking on the down arrow to the right of the tag opens a shortcut menu which enables you to undo the automatic numbering Word just inserted, stop automatically creating numbered lists, or go to the Tools ⇨ AutoCorrect Options dialog box.

To finish the list, hit Enter a second time after the last point to start a new ordinary paragraph. Alternatively, you can press Backspace to "delete" the number or bullet character. What this actually does, as I noted a few paragraphs ago, is turn off the numbering or bulleting setting in the paragraph format.

Remember, the number or bullet character Word displays is actually part of the paragraph formatting, not the document proper. Therefore, it can't be directly edited. The automatically formatted paragraphs use an indent setting to imitate any spaces or tabs you typed in front of the number or bullet. In addition, Word copies any character formatting, such as bold or italics, that you applied to the number or bullet characters you originally typed.

Even if you've turned automatic bulleted lists off, Word automatically adds bullets to each new paragraph you insert after a bulleted paragraph. Automatic bulleting really refers to the way Word recognizes certain ordinary characters typed at the beginning of a paragraph and adds a bullet to the paragraph automatically.

Multiple-level automatic numbering and bullets

Many numbered and bulleted lists are organized hierarchically. The classic multiple-level list is the standard outline format you learned in grade school:

I. Main point

II. Second main point

    a. Subsidiary point 1

        i. Sub-subsidiary point 1

        ii. Sub-subsidiary point 2

    b. Subsidiary point 2

III. Third main point

Word's automatic numbering and bulleting can create such lists with a minimum of effort on your part.

Start an automatic multiple-level list with the technique outlined in the previous section: Type a number or bullet character, press Space or Tab, type the text for the first item, and then hit Enter. At the start of the new paragraph, Word places the appropriate number or bullet for the same level of the hierarchy.

If the new paragraph is supposed to be at the same level as the previous paragraph, all you have to do is type the text. If you want to change the level, press Tab to demote the paragraph to a lower level in the outline, or Shift+Tab to promote it. Finish the list the same way you would a single-level list — by pressing Enter twice.

When not to use automatic numbering and bullets

When shouldn't you use on-the-fly numbering and bullets? Only when you're creating unusually fancy numbered or bulleted lists. Word's attempt to manage lists automatically will almost certainly screw up any complicated format you design, so turn off the autonumber and bullets feature.

Using automatic lead-in emphasis

In numbered and bulleted lists, the first phrase or sentence of each point often gets special formatting to make it stand out. Here's an example:

✦ **New features.** This year, Tony's Toy Turtles are made of wood, not plastic, and they now have moveable, jointed feet.

✦ **New price.** We've rolled back the suggested retail price to $25.99.

✦ **New possibilities.** Tony's Toy Turtles go where your imagination goes!

When automatic numbering and bulleting is on, Word detects such "lead-in emphasis" in the first point and automatically turns on the same formatting at the beginning of each subsequent numbered or bulleted point. When you conclude the lead-in text by typing a punctuation mark — dashes, colons, and semicolons work as well as periods, question marks, and exclamation points — Word reverts back to the standard formatting for the paragraph's style.

Creating empty numbered or bulleted lists semiautomatically

Automatic numbering or bulleting only works if you type something — anything other than spaces or tab characters — in the paragraphs. In other words, you can't create an empty list of numbered or bulleted points and then go back and fill in the list.

The closest you can get is to place a single character in each paragraph, perhaps an *x*. If you're using as-you-type automatic numbering, you type the initial number or bullet character, press Space or Tab, and then type **x**, finally pressing Enter to finish the line. On the next line, because Word has entered the number or bullet already, all you have to do is type another *x*. If you'll be applying the numbers or bullets using the toolbar buttons or the dialog box, begin by entering a series of paragraphs, each containing an *x*. Select the group of paragraphs and then apply the numbers or bullets. With either method, once the numbers or bullets are in place, you're free to erase those *x*'s, if you really must have an empty list.

Characters to type for automatic bullets

For bullets, you don't actually type the bullet symbols at the beginning of the first bulleted point. Instead, you type one or two ordinary keyboard characters and Word converts it (or them) into a corresponding bullet. Table 16-1 shows the characters to type to get different types of automatic bullets.

Table 16-1 Word Creates Automatic Bulleted Lists		
For Bullets Like These	**Type As the First Characters on the Line**	**Followed By**
•	o (the letter)	Tab
•	*	Space
(	>	Space or Tab
-	- (hyphen)	Space or Tab
–	– (en dash)	Space or Tab
■	-- (two hyphens)	Space or Tab
—	— (em dash, not entered with AutoFormat as you type)	Space or Tab
⇨	=> (equal sign followed by right triangle bracket)	Space or Tab
→	->	Space or Tab

Maintaining a consistent format: List styles for automatic numbering and bullets

Because lists are used so often in documents, Office XP has made them part of the style feature. That means you can create a specific list, then save its formatting information as a style that can be easily applied to future lists.

Cross-Reference   For detailed information on working with styles, see Chapter 18.

You can create a list in the style you like and then save that style; or you can create a style from scratch, using the New Style dialog box (see Figure 16-2).

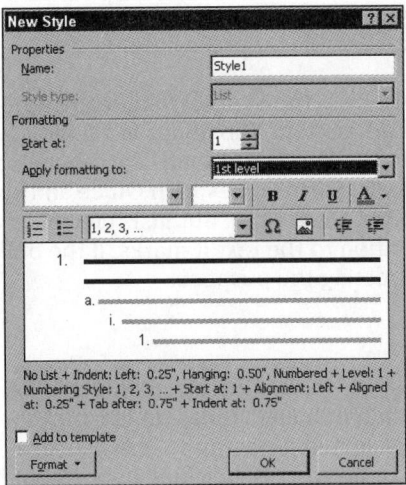

Figure 16-2: The New Style dialog box enables you to create a list style that perfectly suits your needs.

You can get to it by clicking New Style on the Styles and Formatting pane (which is opened by the Styles and Formatting button on the Standard toolbar or by choosing Format ⇨ Styles and Formatting) and choosing List in the "Style type" box; or you can choose Tools ⇨ Bullets and Numbering, click the List Styles tab to see the current styles available, and then click Add to open the New Style dialog box.

Once there, you'll find a complete set of formatting tools that enable you to create as fancy a bulleted or numbered list as you like.

Bullet-specific secrets

Although bulleted and numbered items share much in common, you should know a few details that are specific to bulleted lists.

Any character can be a bullet

One reason to apply bullets via the Bullets and Numbering dialog box rather than automatically is to access alternative bullet symbols. You're limited to the choices shown in Table 16-1 when you use as-you-type automatic bullets. With the dialog box, you can select any character from any active font as the bullet.

From the main dialog box, select an existing bullet format and click Customize and then Character. (Don't bother with the Font button unless you want to change the bullet's size or style — you can select a bullet character from any installed font using the character chart that appears when you click Character.) Once you've custom "bulletized" the first paragraph in your list, Word automatically adds the same custom bullet to subsequent paragraphs until you press Enter twice.

While most of the standard bullets are drawn from the Symbol font, many other fonts also contain suitable symbols. The Windows font Wingdings is a good place to start looking. Monotype Sorts (equivalent to the PostScript font Zapf Dingbats) has a wide selection of more conservative symbols; Sorts comes with Office and should already be installed on your system. Wacky bullets are fun, but just remember that the whole point of the bullet is to draw attention to the text it marks. If the bullet itself attracts too much attention, you're defeating the purpose.

Using graphical bullets

To use graphical bullets in your list, click Picture in the Customize Bulleted list instead of Character. Word presents a selection of bullets it has on file; pick the one you want and then click OK to add it to the selected paragraphs. You can also import a graphics file from your hard drive or network by clicking Import, but be aware that large graphic images will generate an error message; Word only lets you use very small images as bullets.

Word formats the paragraphs just as it does for ordinary bulleted paragraphs. Subsequent new paragraphs pick up the picture bullet, too, until you press Enter twice.

Note   The bitmap bullets look great within Word and when displayed in your browser, but because they are bitmaps they don't print quite as sharply as ordinary bullets.

Using Columns

Arranging text in columns is a good way to break up an otherwise gray mass of print with a little white space. You can set columns before you begin entering text into a document, or you can apply columns to a document that's already underway. To set columns, follow these steps:

1. Choose Format ➪ Columns. This opens the Columns dialog box (see Figure 16-3).

2. Decide how many columns you want. Word offers you five preset column designs: One, Two, Three, Left, or Right. The latter two create pages with two columns of unequal width: If you choose Left, the left column is narrower than the right; if you choose Right, it's the other way around. If you want more columns, enter the number you want in the Number of Columns box.

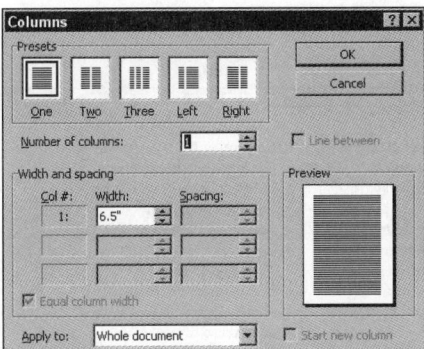

Figure 16-3: Setting your text in columns, using these controls, can make it more visually appealing.

3. By default, the checkbox marked Equal Column Width is checked. To specify different widths for different columns, uncheck it; then enter the width of each column in the Width boxes above it, followed by the amount of space you want between that column and the next one to the right in the Spacing boxes. The Preview box will show you roughly what your document will look like with those settings.

4. If you would like to draw a dividing line between columns, check the Line Between box.

5. Finally, use the Apply To drop-down list to choose whether to put the whole document into columns, or just use columns from the current location of your insertion point onward. If you choose the latter, you also have the option to have the columns start immediately, even if they're in the middle of a page, or check the Start New Column box to jump to a new page to start the columns. If you're already using columns, checking this box forces your current column to end, and any text after the insertion point will go into the next column on the same page.

Note

You can also choose to set a selected portion of text into columns. Just highlight the text you want in columns before beginning the procedures above; when you get to Step 5, the Apply To drop-down list will include the option of applying columns just to the selected text. If your document has more than one section, the Apply To drop-down list will include the option of applying columns just to the current section, the whole document, or just from your insertion point onward.

6. When you're satisfied with your selections, click OK (see Figure 16-4).

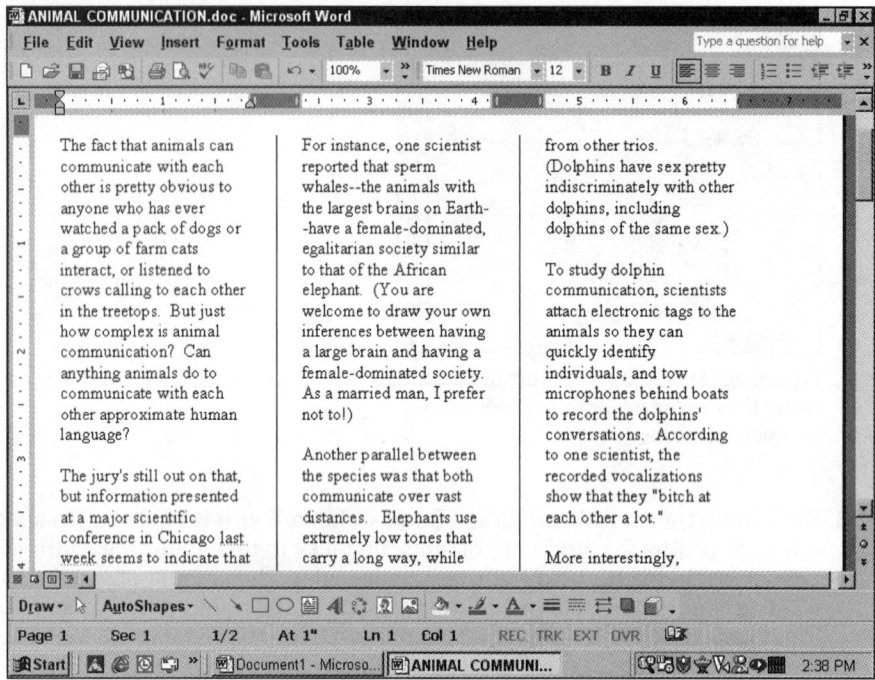

Figure 16-4: Text set in columns can be easier to read, and more pleasant to look at, than text that runs across the page. Note that you can only see what the columns will look like by using Print Layout view; Normal view shows only a single column.

Headers and Footers

A *header* is text or a graphic that appears at the top of every page in a document; a *footer* is text or a graphic that appears at the bottom of every page.

To create a header or footer, select View ➪ Header and Footer. Word automatically switches to Print Layout view. The main text in the document is grayed out; at the top and bottom of the page, you'll find boxes into which you can enter text or graphics for your headers and footers. You'll also see the Header and Footer toolbar, shown in Figure 16-5.

Figure 16-5: The Header and Footer toolbar lets you control the placement and content of your headers and footers.

Type text into the header and footer boxes just the way you would into the main document. All of the formatting options available for regular text are also available for headers and footers.

In addition, you can use the Header and Footer toolbar to automatically add certain features to your headers and footers, including the following:

✦ **AutoText:** Click Insert AutoText to pull down a menu of AutoText items you might want to add to your headers or footers, including the date it was last printed, the date on which it was created, who created it and the filename, and so on. Just select the AutoText item you want to use and Word automatically adds it to the header or footer you're currently creating.

✦ **Insert Page Number, Insert Number of Pages, and Format Page Number:** We'll look at all three of these in more detail in the next section.

✦ **Insert Date:** Click this button to insert the current date into your header or footer. The date is inserted as a field, so it will always display the current date when you view the document.

✦ **Insert Time:** Click this button to insert the current time as a field.

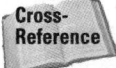 **Cross-Reference** For detailed information on using fields in Word, see Chapter 21.

The Header and Footer toolbar also includes several other useful buttons:

✦ **Page Setup:** This opens the standard File ➪ Page Setup dialog box. Under the Layout tab, you can choose to have different headers and footers on odd and even pages, and a unique header and footer for the first page. If you choose those options, place your insertion point on an even page before opening the Header and Footer toolbar in order to create the header and footer for even pages, and then do the same for odd pages and/or the first page. In the Page Setup dialog box, you can also choose how close to the top or bottom edge of the page you want your headers and footers positioned.

✦ **Show/Hide Document Text:** Clicking this button hides even the grayed-out version of the document's main text, so you can work on your header or footer without distraction.

✦ **Same as Previous:** This button is only active if you have more than one section in your document. If you do, it makes your header or footer for the current section the same as the header or footer for the previous section.

✦ **Switch Between Header and Footer:** You can get from the header box to the footer box (or vice versa) by scrolling down (or up) the page — or you can simply click this button to instantly switch back and forth between them.

✦ **Show Previous, Show Next:** If your headers and footers are different on odd and even pages, or on the first page, or across sections, you can move from one to the other using these buttons.

Page Numbering

One of the most common uses of headers and footers is to add page numbers. All you have to do to add a page number to either a header or footer is click the Insert Page Number button on the Header and Footer toolbar. There are also several AutoText options that include the page number.

If you want to automatically include the total number of pages in the document, click the Insert Number of Pages button on the Header and Footer toolbar.

Of course, you have more than one way to indicate page numbers. For instance, sometimes you want Roman numerals, sometimes you want Arabic. That's where the Format Page Number button on the Header and Footer toolbar comes in. Click it to bring up the Page Number Format dialog box.

Here you can choose a format for your page numbers: regular numerals, Roman numerals (both uppercase and lowercase) or letters (again, both uppercase and lowercase). If you like, you can ask Word to add a chapter number in front of the page number, and specify the character that will separate the two numbers (for example, 1-2 or 2:A). You can also specify how Word will recognize the beginning of a chapter, by telling it which style of text is used to start one. Finally, you can have page numbering be continuous from section to section, or start anew at the beginning of each new section — and specify which number page numbers in a new section should start with.

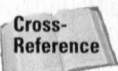
Cross-Reference   For more on styles, see Chapter 18.

If all you want in your header or footer is the page number, you don't have to use the Header and Footer toolbar at all. Simply choose Insert ⇨ Page Numbers. This opens the Page Numbers dialog box, which lets you choose a position for your page numbers (top or bottom of the page — as a header or footer, in other words) and an alignment (right, left, center, inside, or outside — the latter two apply only if you're creating a document that will be bound and have mirrored margins). You can also choose whether or not to show a page number on the first page.

Inserting Captions

The Insert ⇨ Reference ⇨ Caption command sounds promising when you first come across it. It's a real challenge to come up with pithy, informative descriptions for figures and tables, and I would love to delegate the task to my computer. Figure 16-6 shows the Caption dialog box.

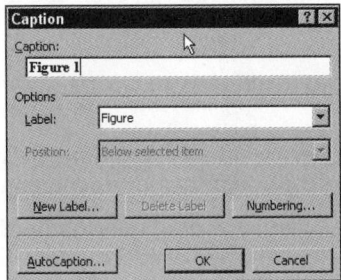

Figure 16-6: The Caption dialog box

Alas, the Caption command doesn't write your captions for you. Instead, it simply gets you started, placing a caption label at the insertion point and applying the Caption paragraph style to your text.

But what makes Word's captions so useful is that the numbers in that caption label are fields. You can add captions anywhere in the document in any order; as soon as you update the fields, Word numbers all your captions in proper sequence. Another nice touch is that you can tell Word where the caption should go — above or below the selected item.

Even better is the AutoCaption feature. When you turn on AutoCaption for a particular item type, Word starts a new paragraph with a caption label formatted to your specifications every time you insert an item of that type. Items you can AutoCaption include pictures, tables, and any object type you can link or embed in the document via OLE. If the item is a picture or a linked or embedded object, Word places the caption in a text box sized to match the object.

Problems with the Caption command

Unfortunately, the Insert Caption command has its dark side:

✦ Although you can include the chapter number in a caption label (as in "Figure 23-2"), this only works if you use one of the built-in heading styles for your chapter title and number that style via the Format ⇨ Bullets and Numbering command. If you use a style called Chapter Title instead of Heading 1 to announce new chapters, you're sunk.

✦ For some reason, Word won't add a period or colon for you at the end of an automatic caption. Many caption labels have the form "Figure 23-3:" or "Figure 23-4.", but Word forces you to type the extra punctuation every time.

Better captions

If you're willing to give up automatic captions, an AutoText or AutoCorrect entry overcomes the limitations of the Insert Caption command. You can even use the command to get you started:

1. Place the insertion point into a blank paragraph and choose Insert ➪ Reference ➪ Caption.

2. Choose the label you want and select a numbering scheme, but don't activate chapter numbering. Choose OK to insert the caption into your document.

3. Place the insertion point in the caption label, just in front of the Number field. Here, insert a field for the chapter number. Here are two of several possible solutions:

   If you use a single document to hold all the chapters in your book, you can number the chapter title paragraphs using an autonumbered paragraph style. In this case, you would use a STYLEREF field to enter the chapter number in your caption via a reference to that style of the chapter title paragraphs. The field you need looks like this: { STYLEREF "Chapter Title" \s }. (Put the name of the paragraph style inside the quotes.)

   If your chapter titles are numbered "by hand" (you just typed the number where it belongs in your document), use a Ref field such as { REF ChapterNumber }. You must also assign a corresponding bookmark—in this case named ChapterNumber—to the chapter number where you typed it into your text.

4. Type a hyphen (-) after the field you entered at step 3, and then go to the end of the label inserted by Word at step 2. Type a colon or a period if you want.

5. At this point, you may want to change the Caption paragraph style to a custom style specific for this type of caption, such as Table Caption, Equation Caption, and so on.

6. Select the entire caption label, including the paragraph mark. Assign it to an AutoCorrect entry (such as fg) or to a named AutoText entry (go with AutoText if you want to assign it to a button).

From then on you can insert a complete caption into any document by typing the AutoCorrect abbreviation or inserting the AutoText entry. If you later add, delete, or reorder your chapters, you have only to update the fields in the document to correct all your captions. (If you type in the chapter numbers yourself as discussed in step 3, you must first locate and change the bookmarked chapter numbers.)

Forging cross-references

Word's Cross-Referencing feature will save you truckloads of time in big documents, once you learn how to use it.

Creating a cross-reference

In outline, the mechanics of setting up a cross-reference are easy. Choose Insert ➪ Reference ➪ Cross-reference, make a few selections from the dialog box shown in Figure 16-7, and click OK. Voilà, instant cross-reference.

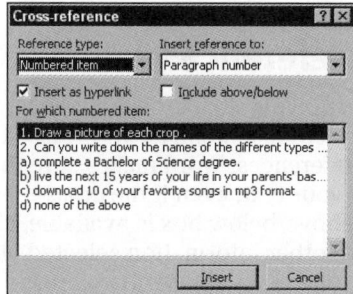

Figure 16-7: The Cross-reference dialog box

Ah, but the devil is in the details. All those choices in the dialog box can be confusing. The following explanations may help:

✦ **Reference type:** Select the type of item you want the cross-reference to refer to — a figure, a table, or what have you — not the type of reference, whatever that would mean. But even this clarification is a bit misleading: In many cases, what you're really selecting is the type of caption to refer to, not the underlying item type. For example, when you select Figure, you're telling Word you want to cross-reference a figure caption, not the graphic it describes. You'll see why this matters in a moment.

✦ **Insert reference to:** Choose the information you want to place at the insertion point. The function of this field would have been clearer if Microsoft had labeled it "Insert the Following information" or just "Insert."

✦ **Insert as hyperlink:** If this box is checked, as it is by default, you can click the cross-reference to move directly to the item it references. This makes the cross-reference command the easy way to build hypertext documents.

✦ **Include above/below:** See "Creating "above" and "below" references" next.

✦ **For which (item type):** This area contains a list of all the items of the selected Reference type, from which you can pick the one item you want to cross-reference. Just be aware that when you have selected a type of caption, what you see is a list of captions, not a list of the actual pictures, tables, or equations they describe. If you haven't inserted a caption, you can't cross-reference the corresponding item. And if you choose, say, Table as the Reference type, but you haven't captioned any tables, the box will be empty no matter how many tables your document contains.

By the way, the Cross-Reference feature works fine with captions inserted using the alternative method described in "Better captions" earlier.

Creating "above" and "below" references

You can have Word automatically add "above" or "below" to a cross-reference, depending on the relative location of the cross-referenced item, as in "Please see Figure 23-2 above." When you update the cross-references, Word makes sure that the correct term (above or below) is inserted in your text, even if the cross-referenced item has been moved. If the Include above/below box is available, checking it adds an above/below cross-reference to the other information selected via the Insert reference to field. If the box is grayed out, you need to insert two cross-references to build an entry like the example at the beginning of this paragraph: first, one for the main cross-reference information, and then another to the same caption or other object with above/below selected in the Insert reference to field.

More cross-reference arcana

If your document contains numbered paragraphs, you can insert a cross-reference consisting of the number of any numbered paragraph. In legal documents, for example, cross-references such as " . . . exceptions noted in paragraph I.A.2.e . . . " are common.

Set up paragraph number cross-references by selecting Numbered item or Heading in the Reference type field of the Cross-reference dialog box. Among the items that then appear in the Insert reference to field, three create these paragraph number cross-references (see Table 16-2). The actual appearance of the cross-reference in your document depends on which item you choose. It may also depend on the relative locations of the current paragraph and the paragraph you're cross-referencing.

Say you're working in paragraph c of section 3 and you want to cross-reference paragraph b in the same section. If you select the Paragraph number item, the cross-reference appears as b in the document. If you cross-reference paragraph e in section 2 instead, you would get 2e as the cross-reference. On the other hand, if you select Paragraph number (full context), the two cross-references would read 3b and 2e, respectively.

Table 16-2
Options for Paragraph Number Cross-References

Choice in Insert reference to	Cross-reference Inserted in Document	Example			
			Number of referenced paragraph	Number of paragraph where cross-reference appears	How cross-reference appears in document
Paragraph or Heading number	The paragraph's own number, along with enough of the complete number sequence specifying its location in the outlined numbered list to identify it		I.A.2.b. I.A.2.b. I.A.2.b.	I.A.2.d. I.A.5.g. III.C.3.b	b 2.b I.A.2.b
Paragraph or Heading number (no context)	Only that paragraph's number, no matter what its location in the outline numbered list		I.A.2.b.	III.C.3.b	b
Paragraph or Heading number (full context)	The full number sequence that specifies the paragraph's location in the outline numbered list		I.A.2.b.	I.A.2.d.	I.A.2.b

Adding Footnotes and Endnotes

Adding a footnote or endnote to a document couldn't be easier: Choose Insert ⇨ Reference ⇨ Footnote and complete the dialog box shown in Figure 16-8. When you choose OK, Word inserts a reference mark (the number or symbol in the body text that signifies an associated note) and places the insertion point into a special area at the bottom of the window where you can type in the note text.

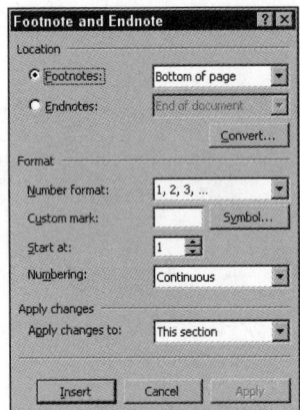

Figure 16-8: The Footnote and Endnote dialog box

If you're working in Normal, Outline, or Web Layout view, this area is a separate pane, with its own scroll bars. In Print Layout view, you work with the notes directly on the document, but Word keeps them where they belong (at the bottom of the page or at the end of the document). When you insert a footnote, you can choose whether to restart the note numbering scheme on every page or with every section, or to number the footnotes continuously throughout the document. Indicate which of those options you want using the Numbering drop-down list on the Footnote and Endnote dialog box.

Tip   You can insert a note directly, bypassing the Footnote dialog box, with a keyboard shortcut. By default, Alt+Ctrl+F inserts a footnote, and Alt+Ctrl+E an endnote.

Resting the mouse pointer over a footnote or endnote reference mark displays a ScreenTip containing the note text, right there in the document. The only reason to reopen the footnote or endnote pane is to edit or format the note text.

Note

When you save a Word document containing footnotes or endnotes as a Web page, Word converts the reference marks into bona fide HTML hyperlinks. Each reference mark, of course, is linked to its note text at the bottom of the page — which in turn is linked back to the reference mark. Regardless of whether the notes are officially footnotes or endnotes, they all wind up at the end of the Web document, because Word converts the entire document, no matter how long it is, into a single Web page.

Using symbols instead of numbers for reference marks

Select the number format for footnotes and endnotes and their reference marks in the Footnote and Endnote dialog box. If your document includes both footnotes and endnotes, they should have different number formats or your readers won't know which is which.

In documents that have both types of notes, symbols (such as *, †, ‡, and §) are often used for the footnotes and numbers for the endnotes. You find these symbols as the last option in the Number Format list in the Footnote and Endnote dialog box. If you select symbols, choose Restart Each Page from the Numbering list unless you're sure the document or section will have no more than eight to ten footnotes or endnotes. Alternatively, you can assign each note individually to any character or symbol you like. Type the character at Custom Mark or choose Symbol and select any character from any active font.

Locating a footnote fast

Use the Browse Object command to locate the next or previous note in a hurry. To jump to a specific footnote by number, choose Edit ⇨ GoTo, select Footnote at Go to What, and type in the footnote number you want to track down.

The footnote or endnote pane contains all notes of the relevant type. Use the cursor keys or vertical scroll bar to scroll through the notes. As you move from note to note, Word keeps the text in the main document window synchronized — you can always see the line containing the current note's reference mark.

Editing and formatting footnotes and endnotes

You can use all of Word's editing and formatting commands on footnote or endnote text — you just have to get to the text in the first place. In Print Layout view, you can just scroll to the note in question and edit away. In Normal and Outline views, you must open the note pane to edit footnotes or endnotes. Do so by double-clicking the reference mark or by choosing View ➪ Footnotes. Know these things about the note pane:

✦ If a document has both footnotes and endnotes, switch between them by choosing the desired item in the drop-down list at the top of the note pane.

✦ You can set the note pane to a different zoom factor than the main document pane.

✦ You can change the height of the note pane (and in the opposite direction, that of the main document pane) by dragging the thin horizontal separator between them.

Tip

A reference mark is more than just a superscripted number or symbol — it contains the note's text. So when you want to move, copy, or delete an entire note, work with the reference mark. Select the mark, and then choose Cut or Copy to move it and its text to the clipboard, or hit Delete or Backspace to remove the note. You can also move a footnote or endnote simply by dragging the reference mark to a new location, or delete a footnote or endnote simply by selecting the reference number and then pressing delete. In either case, all the reference marks are renumbered automatically as necessary.

More about formatting footnotes and endnotes

Word automatically applies the Footnote Text or Endnote Text paragraph style to the note text. It applies a character style — Footnote Reference or Endnote Reference — to the reference mark. So if you want to reformat note text or reference marks, just change the relevant style or styles.

Cross-Reference

See Chapter 18 for details on working with styles.

You can control the position of your footnotes via the Footnote and Endnote Options dialog box. Your choices for footnotes are bottom of page or below text (which isn't necessarily the bottom of the page, if the text ends part way down), while your choices for endnotes are the end of the section or the end of the document.

You can also modify several elements that Word displays and prints in conjunction with footnotes and endnotes. These include the separator, by default a short line above the first note; the continuation separator, a longer line that appears on the second page when a note is split over two pages; and the continuation notice, a message Word adds to the second page of a two-page note.

To choose the element you want to modify, select it from the drop-down list at the top of the note pane (you must be in Normal or Outline view to see this list). You can add text or other characters or delete the special line characters used to form the separators.

Cross-Reference The other item under the Insert ➪ Reference menu command, Index and Tables, is described in detail in Chapter 19.

Using – or Not Using – AutoSummarize

AutoSummarize, activated by choosing Tools ➪ AutoSummarize, analyzes your document to determine the key sentences, and then automatically creates a summary. You can choose how long you want the summary to be (anywhere from 10 sentences to 75 percent of the length of the original), and choose how to present it from the dialog box shown in Figure 16-9: as highlighted sentences in the original document, as a separate document, as an executive summary or abstract at the top of the original document, or by hiding everything except the summary (in that case, a toolbar pops up that lets you show or hide more of the original document as you see fit).

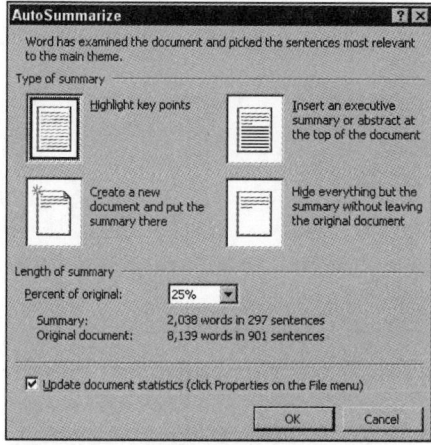

Figure 16-9: AutoSummarize analyzes your document and does its best (which, alas, isn't very good) to boil it down to a few key sentences.

It's a grand idea, and someday, maybe, we'll have computers that think like people and can really summarize a document effectively, but whenever I've tried to use AutoSummarize, all I've ended up with are meaningless snippets of headings and body text, basically useless to anyone.

To be fair, Microsoft warns that you may have to "fine-tune" the summary, and if they mean by that "throw the whole thing out and do it yourself," well, true enough. My advice: If you need to create a document summary, make a copy of the document and use Outline view to pare away the details.

✦   ✦   ✦

Expert Editing

Word is great at making your documents look as fancy as you want, but its core function is helping you create the content of those documents. That's where the advanced techniques for locating, entering, and changing text included in this chapter shine!

Setting Editing Options

The Options dialog box (Tools ⇨ Options) devotes a whole tab to choices related to text editing, as shown in Figure 17-1.

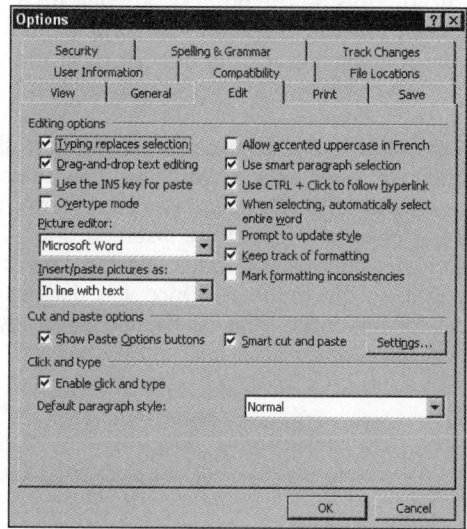

Figure 17-1: The Options dialog box with the Edit tab selected

For many of these text-editing items, the default settings are fine for almost everyone—you can just forget these options exist. Here are the options I recommend you focus on:

✦ **When selecting, automatically select entire word:** This box refers to selecting with the mouse, not with the keyboard. It's checked by default, meaning that when you drag over any part of a word, the entire word gets selected. This is great if you have lousy aim with the mouse pointer. The problem is, you can never make a selection that begins or ends in the middle of a word. I would rather have precise control, so I clear (uncheck) this box.

If you prefer to leave this box checked, you can override its function whenever you like, selecting only the desired portion of a word by holding down the Alt key while you drag.

✦ **Use the INS key for paste:** Checking this box turns the Insert key into a shortcut for the Paste command, just like Ctrl+V or Edit ⇨ Paste. Most Word works discourage this use of Insert. They argue that because Ctrl+V works the same in all Windows applications, you might as well stick with it in Word.

The point is well taken, but here's my counterpoint: Having a one-key shortcut for Paste is great, considering that it's a command you use all the time. And because Insert is just under the cursor keys on the numeric keypad on a standard keyboard, it's the perfect key for this purpose—as soon as you reach the destination using the cursor keys, a quick tap of your right thumb finishes the paste.

Tip

What really makes the Insert key sing in this role is to give it a partner: Turn the Delete key into a one-shot Cut command for selected text. Word gives you no such option, but the VBA macro here does the trick. Here's how it works: If there's no selection, the macro deletes the character to the right of the insertion point—in other words, it functions just like Delete does normally. If text is selected, however, the macro cuts the selection, placing it on the clipboard. Once you define the Delete key as the keyboard shortcut for this macro, the cursor pad becomes a cut-and-paste hot rod:

```
      Sub DeleteKey()
  If Selection.Type = wdNoSelection Then GoTo DeleteKey
      If Selection.Type = wdSelectionIP Then GoTo
DeleteKey
          Selection.Cut
          GoTo LeaveOff
      DeleteKey:
          Selection.Delete Unit:=wdCharacter, Count:=1
      LeaveOff:
      End Sub
```

✦ **Overtype mode:** By default — that is, unless the "Use the INS key for paste" box is checked — the Insert key toggles between ordinary insert-mode text editing and the overtype mode, where what you type replaces what's already at the insertion point. If you do use Insert as a Paste key, you can activate overtype editing by checking the "Overtype mode" box. But you can also turn on Overtype mode by double-clicking OVR in the status bar.

Working with Files and Windows

Before you can edit a document, you need to display it on the screen. That's my justification for this brief section on opening and saving document files and working with their windows.

Cross-Reference For general information on opening and saving files in all Office applications, including Word, see Chapter 12.

Opening previously used files

The File menu displays up to nine of the last files you opened. To reopen one of these, choose File and pick it from the list or press the corresponding number key.

What if you want to be able to quickly load a specific file, whether you happen to have recently opened it or not? Word has a deeply hidden, completely undocumented Work menu that enables you to specify files that you always want fast access to. To use the Work menu, you must first add it to a toolbar or another menu. Open the Customize dialog box and switch to the Commands tab. In the Categories list, scroll down to and click Built-in Menus. You can then find the Work menu at the very bottom of the Commands list. Drag it to the File menu (or any other menu or toolbar of your choice). Once the Work menu is installed, you can add any file to it by opening the file and then choosing Work ⇨ Add to Work Menu. From then on, you can open that document at any time by choosing it from the list on the Work menu.

Deleting entries on the Work menu list requires a secret keyboard shortcut. Before you open the menu, press Ctrl+Alt+- (that's the hyphen key near Backspace, along the row of number keys at the top of the main part of your keyboard). The mouse pointer becomes a heavy black horizontal bar. Now open the Work menu and choose the file you want to delete from its list. The Ctrl+Alt+- technique deletes commands from any of the built-in Word menus.

Closing and saving documents: Quick tips

This section covers useful but otherwise unrelated hints on the common operations of closing and saving your documents.

Closing all documents

It's always a good idea to close the documents you aren't using, because they take up memory and thereby slow down your system, and because extra open documents make it harder to switch quickly to the document you want to work with.

To close all open documents at once, hold down Shift while you open the File menu. The Close All command appears on the menu in place of the ordinary Close command. The Close All command is also available in the Customize dialog box, from which you can add it to a toolbar or menu.

Minimizing file size, maximizing file integrity

The Allow Fast Saves box on the Save tab of the Tools ➪ Options dialog box directs Word to add changes to the end of the disk file each time you save your document. If you clear this box, Word saves the entire file each time. Turning off fast saves is slower, of course, but it has two significant advantages:

✦ It keeps the file to the minimum size possible. Disallow fast saves if you're running short on disk space.

✦ It ensures that your text appears in the disk file in the same order as it does in the actual document. If something goes wrong with the file so that Word can't open it, you may still be able to retrieve the latest text using the "Recover text from any file" import filter in Word, or via a text editor.

Copying a block of text to a new file

Word lets you insert other documents (in any word processing format it can read) into the current document. Use the Insert ➪ File command for this purpose. For some reason, though, it doesn't provide a command for the reverse procedure. In other words, you can't save a portion of the current document as a separate file, at least not without a lot of manual labor. Here's a macro that streamlines the process:

```
Sub CopyBlockToFile ()
On Error GoTo StopNow
If Selection.Type = wdSelectionIP Then
 ActiveDocument.Content.Select
End If
Selection.Range.Copy
Documents.Add
Selection.Range.Paste
Dialogs(wdDialogFileSaveAs).Show
ActiveDocument.Close
StopNow:
End Sub
```

Highlight a portion of your current document and run this macro; it automatically and quickly pastes the highlighted text into a brand-new document, ready for saving under any name you choose.

Working with document windows

Switching from one open document or document window to another via the Window menu is fine if you rarely move back and forth between them. If you're a fairly frequent flyer, however, that procedure gets old fast.

Quick cycling through open documents and windows

Word 2002 shortens your travel time from one document to the next by placing a separate item for each open document window on the taskbar. To access a different document window, click its taskbar icon. To switch even faster, use the keyboard: Alt+Tab and Alt+Shift+Tab cycle you in opposite order through all open applications, including each Word window. Another option is to press Alt+W; this opens the Window menu, which lists all open documents and assigns numbers to them. Just press the number that corresponds to the document you want to switch to.

If you're good with keyboard shortcuts, however, you should also learn and use the Next Window and Previous Window commands—these commands are more direct than Alt+Tab because you don't have to deal with other applications. Ctrl+F6 or Alt+F6 takes you to the next window in this cycle, while Ctrl+Shift+F6 or Alt+Shift+F6 moves you back. You can place these commands on toolbar buttons, too, using the standard techniques for customizing covered in Chapter 5.

Note There's only one problem with the Next Window and Previous Window commands: they often work in reverse of the way you'd expect. After you move from one window to another you have to use the Next Window command to get back to the first document again.

Quick access to all open windows

Using the Window menu to switch gets even older if you open more than nine documents. If the document you need isn't one of the selected nine still on the Window menu, you have to choose the More Windows command at the bottom of the menu and then pick your document from a dialog box. To get around the nine-document limit on the Window menu, assign the WindowList command to a toolbar button. It displays the dialog box showing all your open documents so you don't have to open the Window menu first. Find the WindowList command in the list of All Commands in the Customize dialog box (Commands tab).

Multiple views of the same document

You can view the same document in a split window, or even in two or more windows at the same time. This makes it easier to move or copy items within a long document—you can use drag and drop if you like.

To split a document window into two parts, or panes, position the mouse pointer over the split box, a squat gray button located above the top arrow button on the vertical scroll bar. Wait a moment until the pointer changes to a double-headed arrow. Then drag the split bar—the horizontal separator between the two panes—downward until the two panes are sized the way you want them. If you've turned off the vertical scroll bar, you can always choose Window ➪ Split instead to turn on the split bar.

You can adjust the pane size at any time by dragging the split bar up or down. To reunite the windows, double-click the split bar, or drag it up to the toolbar area.

Tip   You can move back and forth between the two panes with the mouse, but the quick way is to press F6.

To open a new, completely separate window for the document, choose Window ➪ New Window. When the same document appears in two or more windows, the windows are numbered in the title bar and on the Window menu, as in TopSecret:1, TopSecret:2, and so on.

Advanced Navigation

Before you can make changes in the text, you have to get to where the changes need to be made. That's why editing expertise begins with mastery of all the ways you can get around in a document. While you're probably familiar with basic cursor-movement keys and mouse-navigation techniques, don't neglect the features covered here, including advanced mouse and keyboard skills, the Document Map, browsing by object, and the Go Back and Go To commands.

Mousing around

Here are some quick tips on navigating with the mouse in Office:

- ✦ If ScreenTips are turned on in the Customize dialog box, you see the page number and the first heading of the current page as you scroll through a document by dragging the vertical scroll bar's scroll box.

- ✦ Clicking in the vertical scroll bar above or below the scroll box scrolls up or down by one screen, just as if you had pressed PageUp or PageDown.

- ✦ In Normal view, to scroll left past the left margin, hold down Shift while you click the arrow at the left end of the horizontal scroll bar.

- ✦ With any three-button mouse, clicking the middle button places Word into a special AutoScroll mode—dragging up or down moves you smoothly through the document until you click the middle button again.

Navigating with Document Map

Choose View ➪ Document Map or click the corresponding button to display Document Map along the left side of your document.

As shown in Figure 17-2, Document Map gives you a quick outline-type overview of the document's organization, showing the headings arranged hierarchically in a narrow, scrollable pane. You can expand or collapse any branch of the outline containing subheadings by clicking the little box beside it. You can control the overall level of detail by right-clicking Document Map and selecting a heading level from the shortcut menu.

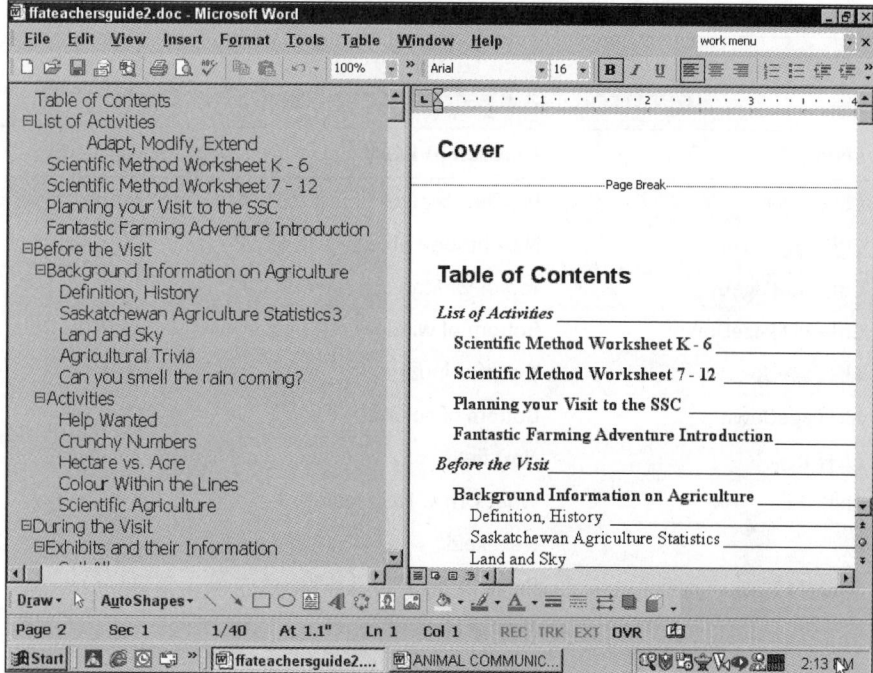

Figure 17-2: Displaying a document with Document Map

But Document Map's real value is as a navigation aid. Click a heading and Word takes you there instantly. As you move about in the document by any method, Document Map highlights the heading for the section containing the insertion point. To access the Document Map pane via the keyboard, press Shift+F6. You can then navigate with the cursor movement keys. To move in the main document to the heading selected in Document Map, hit Enter.

A paragraph appears in the Document Map only if it has been assigned to a numbered outline level (rather than body text) in the Paragraph dialog box.

Cross-
Reference   For more information on using the Word Outline features, see Chapter 19.

Navigation keyboard shortcuts

While everyone knows the common navigation keys, it's easy to forget the ones you don't use regularly. If you prefer keyboard navigation to using the mouse (many people find it more efficient), I suggest you keep a cheat sheet handy for those situations when advanced movement commands are called for. If you haven't made up your list yet, feel free to consult Table 17-1.

Table 17-1 Advanced Navigation Keyboard Shortcuts	
Shortcut	*Function in Word*
Ctrl+PageUp	Previous browse object (see "Browsing by objects" later)
Ctrl+PageDown	Next browse object
Ctrl+Alt+PageUp	Top of window
Ctrl+Alt+PageDown	Bottom of window
Alt+PageUp	Top of column
Alt+PageDown	Bottom of column
Alt+F1	Next field
Shift+F1	What's This? Help feature
F11	Next field
Shift+F11	Previous field
Ctrl+F6	Next document window
Ctrl+Shift+F6	Previous document window
Alt+Up	In Page Layout view only, previous document object (text column, table cell, footnote, text box, or frame)
Alt+Down	In Page Layout view only, next document object

Browsing by objects

Word lets you browse your document by jumping from one item to the next (or previous) item of the same type with a mouse click. The controls you need are the Previous Object and Next Object buttons, those arrow buttons at the bottom of the vertical scroll bar. (By default, Ctrl+PgUp and Ctrl+PgDn are the keyboard shortcuts for the Previous Object and Next Object browse buttons.)

When you first use Word, the two buttons function to take you to the next and previous pages. Between the buttons, however, the Select Browse Object button lets you choose which type of item to jump to as you browse. Click the button to see a little fly-out graphical menu. If you then select, say, the Browse by Field icon on the menu, clicking an arrow button now moves you directly to the next or previous Word field in your document. For most of the menu choices, the text at the bottom of the menu indicates clearly what happens. A few of the choices need some extra comments, as follows:

✦ **Go To:** Pops up the Find and Replace dialog box with the Go To tab selected. After you pick an item type in the Go to What box, that item becomes the object for browsing with the Next and Previous object buttons. This lets you browse by objects that aren't on the menu, including bookmarks, equations, and objects (meaning those linked to or embedded in your document, as discussed in Chapter 11).

✦ **Find:** Displays the Find and Replace dialog box. The text you enter becomes the target for the browse-by buttons.

✦ **Browse by Edits:** Cycles through the current location of the insertion point and the last three locations where you edited text. This is just like the Go Back command discussed in the next section, except that you can go forward once you've gone back. It does not jump to the next revision (tracked change). The Next Change and Previous Change buttons hop to revisions, but they're on the Reviewing toolbar.

Go Back tips

The Go Back command in Word can be incredibly handy. Go Back cycles through the last three locations of the insertion point at which you edited text (sensibly, it doesn't return to locations you just visited with the cursor keys without changing anything). Press Shift+F5 to go back.

Go Back is great, though I sure wish Microsoft would give it a longer memory, say for the last five insertion-point locations. Better yet would be an adjustable number — jumpy writers like me would probably set it to ten or more. But you can partially compensate for this deficiency with the instant-bookmark macros I describe later in this chapter.

Tip

Immediately after opening a document, you can pick up where you left off in your last editing session by pressing Shift+F5 (Go Back). Word saves with the document only the one editing location last used — the rest of the Go Back information is tossed out. If this trick doesn't work, it means either the file in question has never been edited or it's stored in a non-Word format such as RTF.

Optimizing the Go To command

Choosing Edit ➪ Go To or pressing F5 brings up the Go To controls as a tab in the Find and Replace dialog box, which serves as a master navigation control panel. You can still display the Go To controls quickly by double-clicking the left side of the status bar, in the area where the page and section numbers are displayed. Figure 17-3 illustrates the dialog box with the Go To tab active.

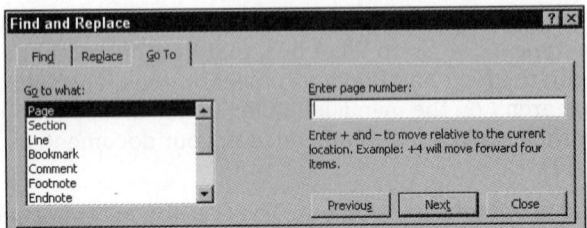

Figure 17-3: The Go To controls are a tab of the Find and Replace dialog box.

You can use the Go To controls to seek out just about any identifiable landmark in the document. You can, for example, go to the next or previous heading of a particular level (Heading 1, Heading 2, and so on). Just type the level number—to locate the next Heading 3, you would type **3**—and click Next or Previous.

The dialog box stays on the screen after you reach your destination; to get rid of it, you have to close it manually.

Bookmarks

Bookmarks are wonderfully helpful when you're editing a long document. Drop a bookmark at any location you expect to revisit later, giving it an appropriately descriptive name.

To create a bookmark, open the Insert ➪ Bookmark dialog box (Ctrl+Shift+F5 is the default shortcut). When you want to return, open the dialog box again, select the bookmark by name from the list, and click Go To—you're there in a flash.

Tip   You can go to any bookmark using the Go To dialog box, described in the previous section. It's easier to press F5, the keyboard shortcut you use in the Go To dialog box, than Ctrl+Shift+F5, the keyboard shortcut to open the Bookmark dialog box. Also, the Go To dialog box remembers the last type of item you located. So if you use it for bookmarks repeatedly, they will already be selected in the Go To What list. Then again, if you know the bookmark name, you never need to select Bookmark at Go To What—just type the bookmark name in the Enter field and click OK.

For ordinary users, bookmarks are simply great navigation aids. But once you start using fields and VBA, you'll find bookmarks are a key element in many automated procedures for manipulating specified text passages and displaying them elsewhere in a document. I cover some of these uses for bookmarks when I detail various advanced techniques later in this chapter..

Bookmark secrets

One complexity of bookmarks is that a given bookmark can identify a location only (this is an empty bookmark) or enclose a text selection within it. For navigation purposes, there's no reason to select text before you drop a bookmark. However, bookmarking a text selection lets you manipulate the bookmarked text on automatic pilot with fields and VBA macros.

Tip

Bookmarks are normally invisible, but you can see them by checking the Bookmarks box in the Tools ➪ Options dialog box's View tab. If you do, they appear as heavy square brackets enclosing whatever text they identify. Empty bookmarks look like a thick I-beam because the pair of brackets sit on top of one another. Figure 17-4 shows how both types of bookmarks look on the screen.

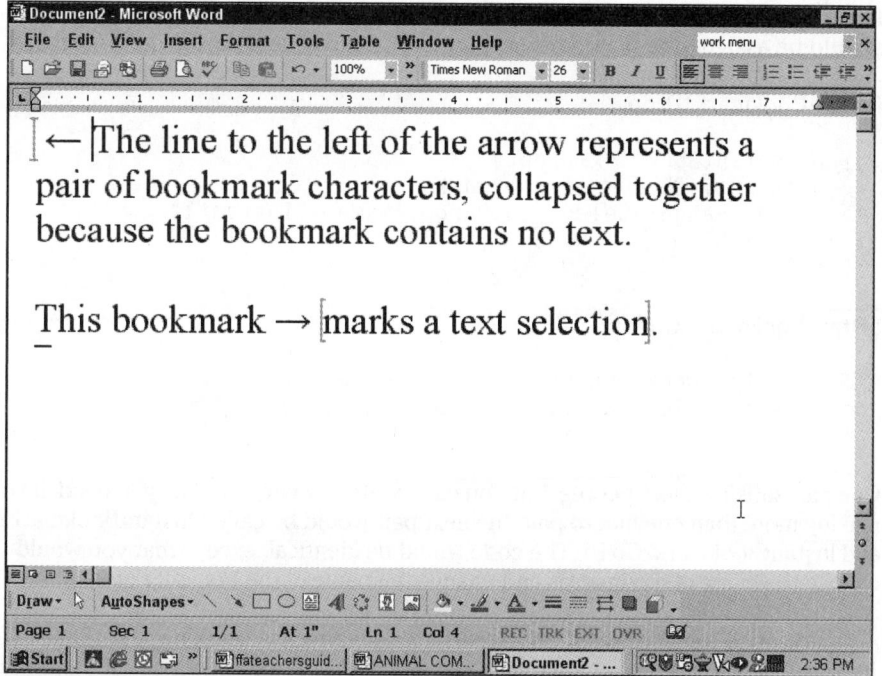

Figure 17-4: Word indicates a bookmark on-screen with a pair of bracket-like symbols. On the left is an empty bookmark, with both brackets in the same location. The bookmark on the right marks a text selection with brackets at either end.

When you work with text containing a bookmark, the bookmark behaves as you probably want it to. If you copy text to another location, the bookmark stays in its original spot. If you move the text, however, the bookmark goes along for the ride. Cutting or clearing the text removes the bookmark, but you can't delete it with the Backspace or Delete key. If you copy text to another document, both the original selection and the copy contain the bookmark (each document has its own set of bookmarks). You're free to edit the text within the bookmark, whether or not you've displayed the brackets on the screen.

Using instant bookmarks

Word's named bookmarks are perfect for finding your way back to key spots when you work with a document over a period of days or weeks. But they're too much trouble for on-the-fly navigation during the course of a single editing session. For this purpose, you want to be able to drop a temporary bookmark with a single keystroke and return to it just as easily. That way, if you suddenly realize how to handle a writing problem in another part of the document, you're free to follow the muse. Just drop the bookmark, go make the changes, and come right back when you're done.

If you like this idea, what you need is one or more pairs of instant-bookmark macros. In each pair, the first macro sets a bookmark, the second takes you to it. The macros should be assigned to keyboard shortcuts or toolbar buttons for quick access.

InstantBookmark1Drop:

```
Sub InstantBookmark1Drop()
  With ActiveDocument.Bookmarks
    .Add Range:=Selection.Range, Name:="Instant1"
  End With
End Sub
```

InstantBookmark1GoTo:

```
Sub InstantBookmark1GoTo()
  Selection.GoTo What:=wdGoToBookmark, Name:="Instant1"
End Sub
```

One pair satisfies most people, but you can create as many pairs as you need. If you're making more than one macro pair, the next pair would be called InstantBookmark2Drop and InstantBookmark2GoTo. The code would be identical, except that you would change the name of the macros and change the name of the bookmark to Instant2.

Actually, of course, it doesn't matter what you name the bookmark in these macros. Just choose something meaningless, a name that you would never use for a real bookmark. Use a unique bookmark name for each pair of macros, entering the same name in both macros in the pair.

Bookmark tricks with AutoText

Try this: Select text containing a bookmark and then create an AutoText or AutoCorrect entry. The bookmark becomes part of the AutoText or AutoCorrect entry (you must save the AutoCorrect entry as Formatted text). Thereafter, each time you insert the entry in your document, Word inserts the bookmark too — any previous bookmark by the same name vanishes.

What's this trick good for? Well, instead of having to think up and type in new bookmark names for each document, you might want to create a battery of generic bookmarks and store them as AutoText entries. For example, you could create a Today's Focus bookmark as an AutoText entry that identifies the location in the document where you're currently working.

The only problem is that you can't save a bookmark all by itself as an AutoText or AutoCorrect entry — you must include with it at least one character of text.

What are hidden bookmarks?

The Insert ➪ Bookmark dialog box offers a checkbox labeled Hidden Bookmarks. Hidden bookmarks are those that Word adds automatically for its own purposes when you insert cross-references, tables of contents, and other such items. If you check this box, you see the automatically generated names for these bookmarks in the list. Figure 17-5 shows the Bookmark dialog box with several hidden bookmarks on display.

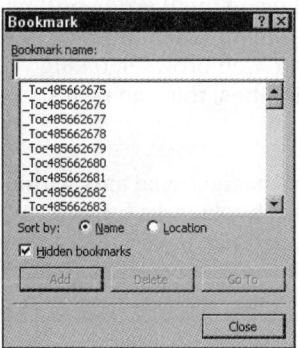

Figure 17-5: The bookmarks in the list shown here were all created by Word, which explains why they look like gibberish.

As you can see, the names Word concocts for hidden bookmarks look pretty meaningless to humans. Although you can tell from the first few characters what type of item the bookmark marks, you won't know which specific item it stands for. For example, a "ref" hidden bookmark may represent any one of many captions, footnotes, or other items.

So what can you use hidden bookmarks for? Not much. But you can go to a hidden bookmark, and this gives you one way to hunt down a cross-reference or other such item that you might otherwise miss if you had to page through a long document.

Note Hidden bookmarks are always invisible in the document itself. Even if you make bookmarks visible by checking the relevant box in the View tab of the Options dialog box, you won't see the telltale brackets around the item marked by a hidden bookmark.

Predefined bookmarks — for macros only

The predefined Word bookmarks are even more hidden than the hidden bookmarks just described. Predefined bookmarks mark many locations that you might want to go to in macros, which is where they come in handy. They never appear in the Bookmark or Go To dialog boxes, but you can go to any predefined bookmark by typing its full name (including the backslash) in either dialog box. For example, the \Sel predefined bookmark takes you to the current selection or the insertion point.

To see a list of these bookmarks, look up the topic "Predefined bookmarks" in Microsoft Visual Basic Help — you can find it in the Contents tab under Concepts, P.

Using hyperlinks as cross-document bookmarks

When you work with multiple related documents at the same time, it would be nice to flip directly to text passages of interest in one step. Ideally, you wouldn't have to know which document contains the text you want to display. Bookmarks don't give you that ability. Each bookmark is stored with a specific document and is only accessible when that document is already active. There's no one-step way to go directly from one document to a specific bookmark in another document.

However, you can accomplish roughly the same goal using the Word hyperlinks. Available throughout Office, hyperlinks are discussed in full in Chapter 45. In brief, hyperlinks work in your documents as they do in your Web browser, taking you immediately to another location. Among other possibilities, this can be a specific spot in a document — any document.

While you can use this technique to give your readers navigational aids within the current document, it's not ideal as a substitute for real bookmarks for your own use while editing. Compared to real Word bookmarks, hyperlinks have the disadvantage that you can only jump to the location they point to from the hyperlink itself. You can jump to a bookmark from anywhere.

The easiest way to create a hyperlink between two Word documents (or within a document) is simply to copy text from the second document. Returning to the location where you want to place the hyperlink, insert the copied text using the Edit ⇨ Paste as Hyperlink command (in Word, hyperlinks are actually fields, and this command inserts the necessary field).

Clicking the hyperlink takes you to the location from which the text was copied.

Note To change the hyperlink's destination, and the text it displays, click anywhere inside it and then press Ctrl+K to open the Edit Hyperlink dialog box.

Find and Replace Secrets

I'm sure you know how to hunt down text and to carry out basic find-and-replace operations with the Find and Replace commands. Just remember that these functions are part of the master Find and Replace dialog box that includes Go To, as well (see Figure 17-6). When you press F5 to bring up Go To, the Find tab is just one click away.

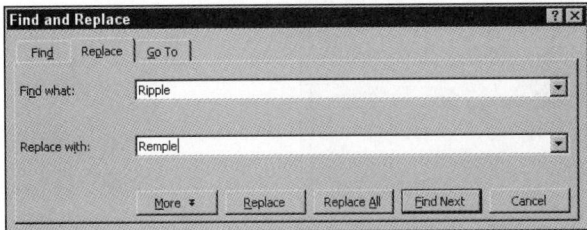

Figure 17-6: The Replace tab on the Find and Replace dialog box. In the default version shown here, you can enter only Find and Replace text — the controls governing advanced features are hidden.

Find and Replace: More options

The advanced features of Find and Replace are hidden when you first open the dialog box — you won't see checkboxes for controlling Find and Replace options, nor are the No Formatting, Format, and Special buttons visible. The idea is to protect beginners from too many confusing options.

Figure 17-6 shows the Replace tab as it first appears, while Figure 17-7 shows it with the extra buttons. To display the checkboxes and buttons if they're not already visible, choose More. (If you then want to hide these extremely useful, can't-live-without-them controls, well, that's your business — choose Less.)

Note
The Find and Replace dialog box always appears without the advanced options the first time you display it during a given session with Word — there's no setting to make the box automatically appear with the advanced options visible. Once you click More, however, those options remain visible until the next time you start the program.

Find and Replace tips

Here are two quick suggestions for making Find and Replace operations more efficient:

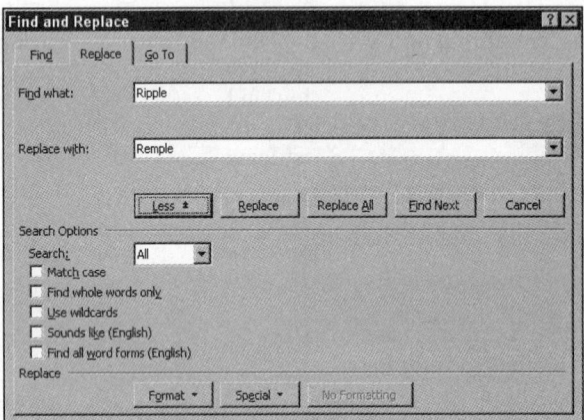

Figure 17-7: The Replace tab of the Find and Replace dialog box shown with its boxes and buttons for advanced features

> ✦ **Stop using Find — use Replace instead.** All the functionality of the Find dialog box is included on the Replace tab, so you just don't need Find. If you have limited screen space for toolbar buttons, dump the Find button but keep the Replace button.
>
> ✦ **Assign the Find Next command a one-key keyboard shortcut.** Once you've entered text in the Find dialog box, you can close the box and use the shortcut to find the next hit without a dialog box blocking your view.
>
> The default shortcut for the Find Next command (called Repeat Find in the Commands list) is Shift+F4, hardly the most convenient choice for such a commonly used command. I make mine F3, as do most text editing programs. If you're already stuck on using F3 for AutoText (the default command for the F3 key) consider F8 or F10 as your shortcut for Find Next. After all, most people don't much use the commands Extend Selection and Activate Menu Mode that these keys normally trigger. Another good choice would be the Insert key, if you're not using it for the Paste command (see the "Setting Editing Options" section at the beginning of this chapter).

Advanced Find and Replace 1: Remember these features

Many competent Word users don't fully appreciate the power lurking under the hood of the Find and Replace commands. Remember that these commands can do the following:

✦ **Search for and replace variant forms of the word you enter in the "Find what" field.** If you ask Word to find "be" and check the "Find all word forms" checkbox, it scoops up "is", "are", "was", "were", and "been". If you're replacing a verb, you're usually offered the correct conjugation for the found word. If Word has suggested a conjugation that isn't correct, you can choose the right one from a drop-down list.

✦ **Search for and replace formatting you specify.** If you want to find that one place in the document where you typed "big dog" in bold italics, use the Format button to refine your search criteria. Remember, too, that you can search for formatting independent of text — just leave "Find what" blank.

Advanced Find and Replace 2: Using special characters

Find can track down essentially anything in a document. In addition to text and formatting, your potential targets include paragraph marks, tabs, annotations, and line, page, and section breaks. In long documents, getting Word to find these items is much easier and more accurate than visually scanning for them yourself. And with Replace, Word can insert these items or substitute them for others.

Codes for special characters in the Find and Replace dialog box

Table 17-2 lists the codes you must enter in the "Find what" and "Replace with" boxes to represent special characters. You can have Word enter these codes for you by picking the special characters by name from a menu. If the More button is visible, choose it. Then choose Special and make your selection from the menu.

Table 17-2
Special Character Codes for Find and Replace

Item	Code to Enter	Availability (Find and/or Replace)
Paragraph mark	^p	Both
Tab character	^t	Both
Annotation mark	^a	Find only
ANSI or ASCII characters where *nnn* is the ANSI or ASCII character code	^0*nnn*,	Both
Any character	^?	Find only
Any digit	^#	Find only
Any letter	^$	Find only

Continued

Table 17-2 *(continued)*

Item	Code to Enter	Availability (Find and/or Replace)
Caret character	^^	Both
Clipboard contents	^c	Replace only
Contents of the "Find what" field	^&	Replace only
Endnote mark	^e	Find only
Field	^d	Find only
Footnote mark	^f	Find only
Graphic	^g	Find only
Breaks		
Column break	^n	Both
Line break	^l	Both
Manual page break	^m	Both
Section break	^b	Both
Hyphens and spaces		
Em dash	^+	Both
En dash	^=	Both
Nonbreaking space	^s	Both
Nonbreaking hyphen	^~	Both
Optional hyphen	^-	Both
White space (any combination of consecutive spaces, tab characters, and paragraph marks)	^w	Find only

What good are special characters?

Here are a few practical tasks that you can accomplish by finding and replacing special characters.

Reviewing or removing optional hyphens

Optional hyphens can cause unexpected errors in a document, so you should review their placement in each word if you want to be absolutely certain your opus will print flawlessly. Instead of laboriously scanning the document, use Find to locate them for you (don't forget, optional hyphens are invisible unless you turn them on in the Options dialog box's View tab). Or blow 'em away with Replace.

To find all optional hyphens, place their code (^-) as your only entry at Find What. To eliminate optional hyphens from the document, enter ^- at Find What, make no entry at Replace With, and then choose Replace All.

If you want to search for specific words containing an optional hyphen, your best strategy is not to use the optional hyphen code in the "Find what" box. If you leave out the optional hyphen code, Find locates all occurrences of the word—including those containing an optional hyphen anywhere in the word. If you do include the optional hyphen code, Word finds the word only when it has the optional hyphen in the same location as you entered it in Find What.

Getting rid of manual paragraph indents

Word novices often indent the old typewriter way, pressing Tab or Space when they start a new paragraph. If you have to work on such documents, a replace operation with special characters fixes it up in no time. In the replace dialog box, enter **^p^w^** at Find What and **^p** at Replace With. Choose Replace All and you're done. You can now go back and format the document the proper way.

Finding, adding, or removing page or column breaks

Word lets you insert page and column breaks any place in a document you see fit. When you don't want to split up a paragraph over two pages or across two columns, or if you want to reserve space for an illustration that you'll physically paste into the printed document, adding a break is the solution.

However, those manual breaks lead to formatting *faux pas* if, later, you insert text toward the beginning of the document, or change margins, paragraph indents, fonts, or just about any other formatting setting. Word repaginates the document as it should, but this renders your manual page and column breaks obsolete. More than likely, you'll end up with pages or columns containing little or no text.

If you know or suspect that a document contains manual breaks, you should inspect them before you print to avoid nasty surprises. Enter the code for each break (**^m** for page breaks, **^n** for column breaks) in turn in the "Find what" box. Alternatively, you can zap the breaks and start fresh using Replace. After entering the appropriate special character code at "Find what", clear the "Replace with" box and choose Replace All.

You might also have a document that needs manual page or column breaks inserted at predictable locations. Normally, you would want forced page breaks to occur before a new heading, and you can set this up by modifying the heading style by checking the "Page break before" box in the Paragraph Format dialog box.

Occasionally, however, the page break locations are marked by a word or phrase rather than a paragraph style. In this case, you can have Replace insert the breaks for you. Type the text at "Find what". At "Replace with", type **^&^m**. That ^& code reinserts whatever you type at "Find what"—without this code, your Replace operation would substitute a page break for the specified text.

Because there's no formatting option to force a column break before a given paragraph, you can't set up styles to automate the task. The method just mentioned works—if you enter ^&^n at "Replace with"—but only if there's some repeating unit of text to search for.

Cleaning up plain DOS text files

Word can import ordinary, unformatted text files just fine, but they don't always show up on your screen the way you want them to. The biggest problems are with DOS text files, which contain a paragraph mark (technically, a carriage return and line feed pair) at the end of every line. Real paragraphs are separated by blank lines, so the file contains two paragraph marks in a row between paragraphs.

If you import a DOS text file by selecting Text Files at Files of Type in Word's Open dialog box, each line becomes a separate paragraph. Things will look okay at first, maybe (if space above and space below are both set to 0 in your Normal paragraph style). But when you start editing, you'll know something is wrong.

Look at the sample in Figure 17-8. Text doesn't flow from line to line because Word assumes you're working with a series of separate paragraphs. Of course, this assumption becomes obvious if you turn on the Paragraph Marks.

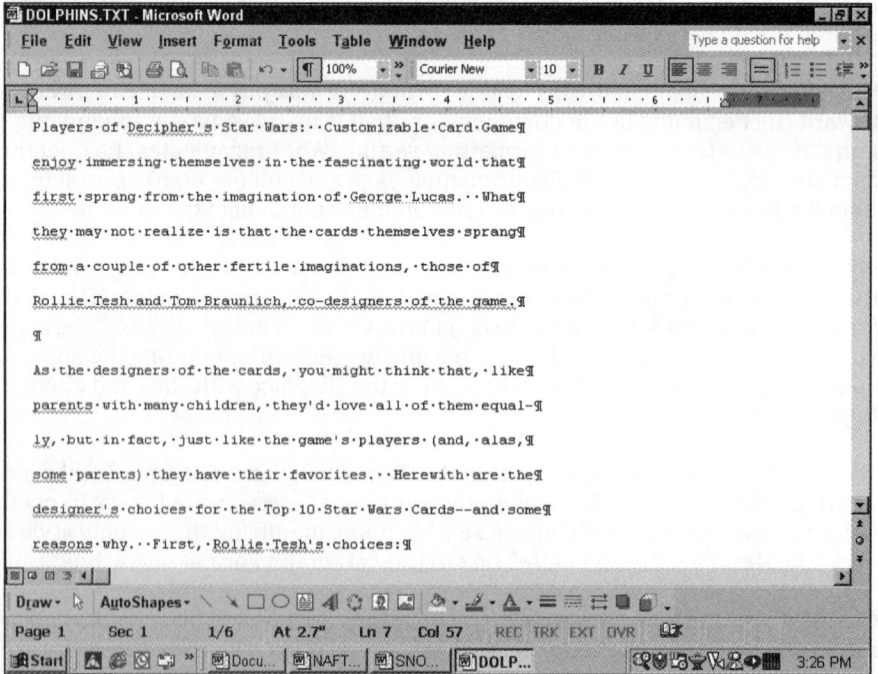

Figure 17-8: A text file opened in Word. Each line ends with a paragraph mark.

You may have somewhat better luck if you import the file using the "Text with layout" choice—but don't count on it. I find that Word's efforts to autoformat text files usually make the file harder to clean up, stuffing it with unwanted section breaks and assigning multiple paragraph styles.

So, sticking with a text file imported without layout, you need a three-step procedure to find and replace using special characters to clean up the file.

To be safe, start by moving the insertion point to the top of your document, then call up the Replace dialog box. For each of the three steps listed here, make the indicated entries and then choose Replace All.

1. First, locate and mark the breaks between real paragraphs:

   Find what: **^p^p** (for two consecutive paragraph marks)

   Replace with: **xxx** (the replace entry can be any sequence of characters as long as you're sure they don't already occur in the document)

2. Next, get rid of all those extra paragraph marks falling at the end of lines:

   Find what: **^p**

   Replace with: (make no entry, not even a space)

3. Finally, revive the real paragraph breaks:

   Find what: **xxx**

   Replace with: **^p**

Tip   If you plan to import a lot of text files, record a macro following these steps and assign it a keyboard shortcut or to a toolbar or menu. Then, just run the macro as you need it.

Advanced Find and Replace 3: Using wildcards

Rare indeed is the hardy soul who takes advantage of Word's capability to find and replace text that matches an abstract pattern rather than an exact sequence of characters. But this capability can be a huge timesaver for some complex text modifications.

The "wildcards" name is an analogy to a card game where a deuce or joker, for example, can stand in for a range of other cards. In Word, wildcards are special characters you can enter in Find and Replace operations that represent one or more characters (from a defined range) in the document.

You can only enter the wildcards in the "Find what" box, not in "Replace with". If you think about it, this makes sense—Word can't read your mind and choose from a range of possible characters to insert in the document. However, you can include the text located by the wildcard Find in the Replace entry. That means you can use Replace to revise variable text, which gives this feature its real power.

Of course, you won't be using the wildcards by themselves—they're valuable only when mixed with ordinary characters in a complete expression. As a simple but far-fetched example, say your computer products company has decided to abandon the Macintosh market and climb on the Windows bandwagon. All your new products work just like the old ones did, but you do have to change the names in all your press releases and product information sheets. MacMathWhiz has become PCMathWhiz, MacScanWhiz will now be called PCScanWhiz, and so on.

Wildcards let you make all the changes in one step for each document. In outline, you would simply enter **Mac*Whiz** at "Find what" and a corresponding expression at "Replace with". The actual process involves a few wrinkles, so stick around for the details that follow.

Performing a wildcard Find and Replace

The mechanics of finding and replacing with wildcards are simple. Once you have the Find and Replace dialog box open, your first step is to make sure its advanced options are visible. If you don't see a set of checkboxes and buttons at the bottom of the dialog box, choose More to display them.

All you have to do now is check "Use wildcards". Once the box is checked, Word interprets wildcard characters entered at "Find what" as such, rather than as ordinary characters. If you don't want to type in the wildcards yourself, choose Special and select them from the pop-up menu.

Replace operations using wildcards

In almost every case, you use a wildcard-based Replace operation to modify the existing text, not to replace it entirely with something new. Your goal is to change text that may vary with different text that likewise varies, based on what was originally there. That means you need a way to insert portions of the variable text located by Find into the new text inserted by Replace.

In Word, here's how you handle the problem: First, use parentheses to separate the "Find what" entry into sections based on which portions you want to use in the replacement text. Using the Macintosh-to-PC example introduced earlier, you would make the following entry at "Find what": **(Mac)(*Whiz)**

In this example, because everything after the "Mac" should be retained in the new product names, you only need to divide the Find text into two sections.

Second, enter your replacement text, referring to the section(s) you want to retain by number. You must enter the backslash character (\) in front of the section numbers. The sample entry would look like this: PC\2

Tip

Because the sections of a wildcard Find entry can include both wildcards and ordinary characters, you can use this procedure to change the order of portions of the find text — even if you use no wildcards at all. Suppose you write a report referring frequently to a Mr. John George. When it turns out that you got his first and last names backward, set things right by entering **(John)( )(George)** at "Find what" — that middle section encloses the space between the two names — and **\3\2\1** at "Replace with".

Wildcard reference

This section collects a miscellany of important tips related to wildcard Find and Replace operations. Table 17-3 lists all the wildcard characters (operators) along with a few other special characters used in conjunction with wildcards. Table 17-4 lists additional characters to use in wildcard Find and Replace operations.

Table 17-3
Wildcards and Other Special Characters Used in Wildcard Find and Replace Operations

To Find	Enter This Wildcard or Character	Sample
Any of the actual characters used as wildcards including ?, *, ( ), [ ], { }, <, @, \	\ followed by the wildcard character	"\?" finds "?"; "*" finds "*"; "\\" finds "\"
Any one character	?	"d?g" finds "dig", "dug", and "dog" but not "drug"
A sequence of characters of any length	*	"d*g" finds "dig", "drug", and "digressing"
Any one character from a specified group	[character list]	"d[iu]g" finds "dig" and "dug" but not "dog"
Any one character in an ascending alphabetical or numeric sequence	[beginning character-ending character]	"do[a-p]e" finds "dole" and "dome" but not "dote" or "dose"
Any one character except those specified	[!character list]	"di[!e]" finds "dig", "din", and "dip" but not "die"
Any one character except those in a specified sequence	[!beginning character-ending character]	"du[!a-f]" finds "dug" and "dun" but not "dub" or "dud"
An exact number of repetitions of the previous character or expression	{n}	"20{2}24" matches two and only two additional 0s — it finds "20024" and "20025", but not "2024" or "200024"

Continued

Table 17-3 *(continued)*

To Find	Enter This Wildcard or Character	Sample
At least a specified number of repetitions of the previous character or expression	{n,}	"20{2,}24" matches two or more additional 0s—it finds "20024" and "2000024" but not "2024"
Repetitions of the previous character or expression within a specified range	{n,m}	"20{1,3}24" matches 1 to 3 repetitions of 0—it finds "2024", "20024", and "200024" but not "2000024"
One or more repetitions of the previous character or expression	@	"dro@l" finds "drol" and "drool"
The beginning of a word	<	"<(de)" finds "demure" and "deranged" but not "sulphide"
The end of a word	>	"(ed)>" finds "red" and "detangled" but not "educational"

Table 17-4
Other Characters to Use in Wildcard Find and Replace Operations

To Perform This Function	Enter These Characters	Sample
Identify sections of a wildcard in a "Find what" entry	() (parentheses)	The following entry has been divided into three separate sections: (Part No.) (A-)([0-9]{1,})
Include a section of the current wildcard Find entry in the Replace text (you must first have enclosed all the sections of the Find entry in parentheses)	\ followed by section number	The following Replace entry is based on the preceding sample: \1BX-\3. It would convert the text "Part No. A-43254" into "Part No. BX-43254"

Caution While it may not be obvious, wildcard Finds are always case sensitive. Word looks only for the exact characters you enter in the "Find what" box, whether you type in real, individual characters or use a wildcard to refer to a range of characters.

Tip Oddly, Word doesn't include distinct wildcards for numerals, letters, lowercase or capital letters, or punctuation marks. However, you can create stand-ins for the missing wildcards using the available tools. For example, to hunt down any numeral, you would enter **[0-9]**; to find one or more numerals in succession, enter **[0-9]{1,}**. As detailed in Table 17-3, square brackets are used to match any character in a consecutive sequence, whereas braces (curly brackets) indicate the number of times the previous character must occur for a match to be found.

Watch out for the repeater wildcard, the @ symbol. According to Microsoft, this is supposed to locate any number of occurrences of the preceding character or wildcard expression. If the repeater worked as promised, you could type **[0-9]@** to locate any number from 1 to 999 (even up to 9999999 if there are no commas). But it doesn't, at least not when used alone: You must enter it between other characters, or it finds only one matching character at a time. Use {1,} instead, which works as the repeater should.

One last point: You can use most of the codes for special characters such as tabs, page breaks, and so on in wildcard finds. However, the codes for certain items, including paragraph marks, don't work. Fortunately, Word gives you substitute numeric codes for most of these items for use in wildcard Find and Replace operations — see Table 17-5 for a listing. Note, though, that you can't search for fields if you're using wildcards.

Table 17-5	
Substitute Codes to Use in Wildcard Find and Replace	
To Find or Replace This Item	*Enter This Code*
Footnote or endnote mark	^2
Paragraph mark	^13
Section or manual page break	^12
White space	*space*{1,}

Speeding Text Entry

Word comes with lots of features that accelerate text entry. The most important of these to master is AutoCorrect, covered in full in Chapter 8. However, Word suffers from an embarrassment of riches in this category. Keeping track of which feature performs which function can sometimes be tough. Table 17-6 summarizes some of the most useful text entry features.

Table 17-6 Word Text Entry Features	
Feature	**Explanation**
AutoCorrect	Corrects various common typing errors and converts abbreviations into complete words or phrases
AutoFormat as you Type	Converts hyphens into dashes and straight apostrophes and quote marks into paired, typographically correct curly marks.
AutoText	Inserts stock text passages from a list or via a toolbar button
Repeat	When used immediately after typing text, inserts the same text
Insert Date and Time	Inserts the date, the time, or both in one of many available formats

AutoText secrets

Over time, the Word AutoText feature has really been beefed up. You can select individual AutoText entries from a toolbar button or from the Insert menu without having to open the AutoText dialog box. Also appreciated is the capability to group your AutoText entries by category. Word comes with a rich set of prefabricated AutoText entries for stock phrases such as salutations and closings in letters.

Even better, AutoText is almost as automatic as AutoCorrect. Once you've typed the first four letters of an AutoText entry, the AutoComplete feature pops up a little ScreenTip offering the entire item. If that's what you're trying to type, just press Enter to have Word insert the whole word or phrase. If not, just keep typing — Word leaves you in peace.

When to use AutoText

Although I prefer AutoCorrect for most automated text entry chores, AutoText definitely has its place. For one thing, AutoText entries are specific to a template. If the text you reuse varies with the type of document, you can store the appropriate AutoText entries in separate templates (AutoText entries stored with the Normal template are available in all documents, of course). Another AutoText advantage is that you can recall its named entries from menus and toolbar buttons. That means that your shorthand is always readily available, even if you forget a code name.

Including formatting in an AutoText entry

To create a formatted AutoText entry, apply the formatting to text in your document first, select the text, and then choose Insert ➪ AutoText ➪ New or press Alt+F3. A small dialog box will open telling you Word will create a new AutoText entry from the current selection and inviting you to name it.

You can also include bookmarks in AutoText entries to mark document locations quickly. See "Bookmark tricks with AutoText" in the section on bookmarks.

Using the AutoText menu — watch out for disappearing entries

The AutoText menu (and the AutoText toolbar button, if you choose to display it) lets you access AutoText entries in categories of your choice. Figure 17-9 shows the AutoText menu with several submenus, each offering a collection of related entries.

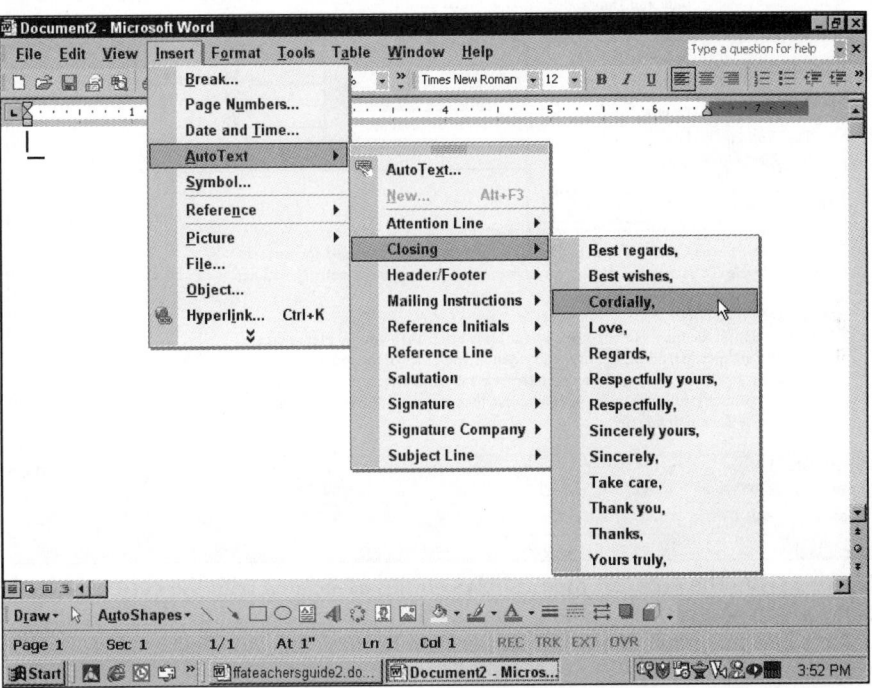

Figure 17-9: When the insertion point is in a Normal paragraph, the AutoText menu shows all your AutoText entries organized into categories as a series of submenus.

Note   Those submenus are actually the names of paragraph styles, present or past: A Word AutoText entry is associated with the paragraph style in which it was created (Chapter 18 covers paragraph styles in detail). The relationship between specific paragraph styles and AutoText entries can be confusing and problematic, so I try to explain it here. But you can use this relationship to customize the AutoText menu, as described in the next section.

Suppose you happen to be in a Heading 1 paragraph when you create an AutoText entry. From now on, as shown in Figure 17-10, the bottom of the AutoText menu displays that entry, and all others created from Heading 1 paragraphs, whenever you're working in any Heading 1 paragraph.

Notice, however, that you can no longer access the other AutoText submenus shown in Figure 17-9, nor the entries they contain—they've all disappeared. It turns out that you can only see the submenus when you're working in a Normal paragraph (all AutoText entries are available in paragraphs assigned to the Normal style) or if the paragraph style you're working in has no AutoText entries of its own.

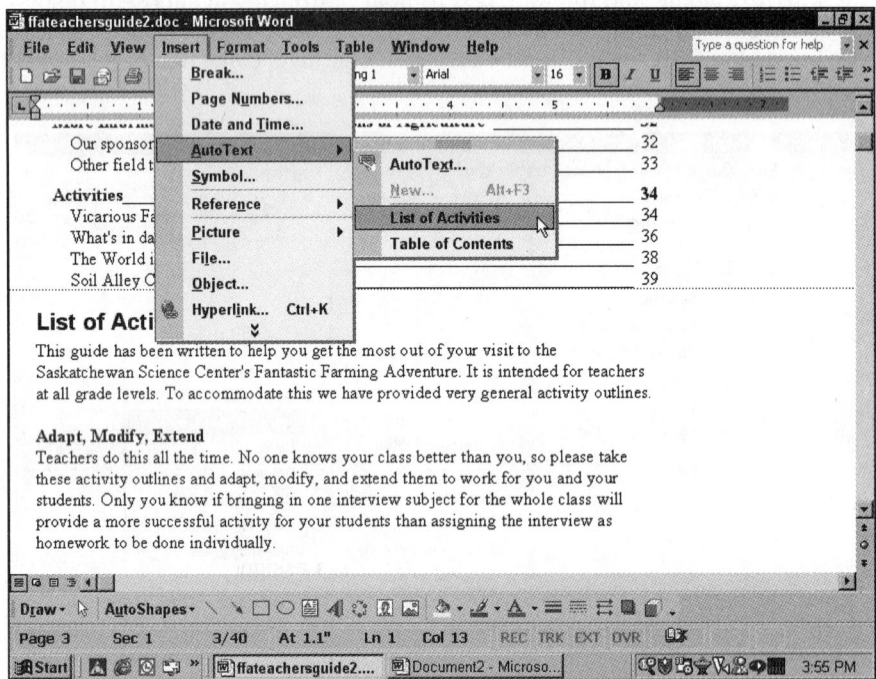

Figure 17-10: The AutoText menu shows entries associated with the current style so that you can access them without opening the AutoText dialog box. If the insertion point is in a paragraph of any style other than Normal, only AutoText entries associated with that style appear on the menu.

With this system, the Word designers have made what I believe is an erroneous assumption. They think that when you're working in a given paragraph, you only need access to AutoText entries associated with that one style. As a result, at times the bulk of your AutoText list is inaccessible via the menu. Instead, to access it you have to open the AutoText dialog box by choosing Insert ➪ AutoText ➪ AutoText and selecting the entry there.

 **Caution** Be careful when you create an AutoText entry. Check the style of the current paragraph and be sure that you really want to associate the entry with the style.

 Tip If you want all your AutoText entries to be available on the menu at all times, always create them from Normal paragraphs. There are trade-offs: You give up the ability to organize the list, and to include paragraph formatting with the text.

Organizing your AutoText entries using virtual paragraph styles

You can organize the entries on the AutoText menu into submenus with descriptive titles. Here's the technique:

1. For each submenu you want, create a new paragraph style, naming it what you want the AutoText submenu title to be.

2. In a document, assign a paragraph to the new style.

3. Create all your AutoText entries for this category.

4. Now delete the style in the Styles and Formatting task pane. Word retains the association between the style's name and the associated AutoText entry, and a submenu with the deleted style's name appears on the AutoText menu. I call the style name a "virtual style," because the AutoText feature thinks it exists but it really doesn't function as a paragraph style.

Deleting the style isn't technically necessary—the associated AutoText entry is still available when you're in a paragraph assigned to the Normal style (or to the new style). It's just that if you don't delete it, you'll be cluttering your template with a style you don't need. To add new entries to the submenu later, you must again re-create the style with the same name, define the new AutoText, and then delete the style once more. Consistent with the previous discussion, you can see the submenus only when you're working in paragraphs assigned to the Normal style, or to a style with no associated AutoText entries.

Creating one-shot AutoText entries

For fastest possible insertion of a specific AutoText entry, assign it a keyboard shortcut or toolbar button. Choose Tools ⇨ Customize to make the assignment— AutoText is one of the items in the Categories list on the Commands tab.

Editing AutoText entries

You can delete AutoText entries in the AutoText dialog box, but you can't edit them there. To revise or replace an existing entry, retaining its current name, follow these steps:

1. Insert the entry in a document and make the revisions there. If the new text is radically different than the existing entry, just type the new text into your document.

2. Still in the document, select the revised or new text you now want to use as the AutoText entry.

3. Choose Insert ➪ AutoText and then click New. The Create AutoText dialog box appears.

4. Here's the key step: Type the exact original name of the AutoText entry you're revising or replacing. When you click OK in the dialog box, the revision becomes final.

Using AutoText fields to keep documents automatically up-to-date

It's common to use a repeating passage of text that changes over time. Say you've developed several different documents that quote the company dress code. Your first thought might be to place the dress code in an AutoText entry that you could then insert in any document as many times as necessary. The problem is, fashions change. When the bigwigs revise the dress code, you're going to be stuck with wading through each document to make the updates. But if you insert a field that refers to the dress code AutoText entry, all you would have to do is make the changes once, replace the existing AutoText entry with them, and then auto-update your documents.

To enter an AutoText field, put the insertion point where you want the entry and choose Insert ➪ Field to display the Field dialog box (see Figure 17-11). Select Links and References in the Categories list and then AutoText in the list of Field Names. Next, select the specific AutoText entry the field should refer to. Click Field Codes, then click Options, pick the AutoText name from the list, and choose Add to Field.

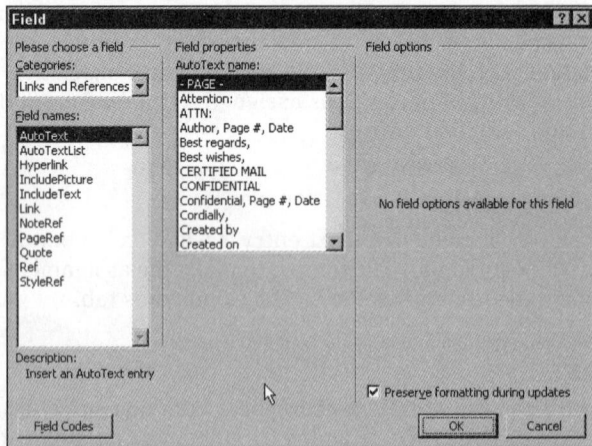

Figure 17-11: Inserting an AutoText field in the Field dialog box.

As soon as you OK the dialog boxes, the AutoText field appears in your document. If field codes are visible (the setting is in the View tab of the Tools ⇨ Options dialog box), you'll see a bracketed expression such as { AUTOTEXT dresscode * MERGEFORMAT }. If you've turned off field codes, the text of the AutoText entry appears instead. You can toggle back and forth between the two views of the entry by placing the insertion point anywhere in it and choosing the ToggleFieldDisplay command (the default shortcut is Shift+F9).

When the dress code policy changes, you must first revise the AutoText entry (see the previous section, "Editing AutoText entries," for instructions). After that, updating all the documents that contain it will be a breeze. Open each document in turn, press Ctrl+A to select the entire document, and then choose the Update Fields command (F9 by default).

Using the Spike

The Spike, a special AutoText item in Word, is a neat idea but it's not implemented well. The enhanced Clipboard toolbar (discussed in Chapter 11) can do the same tasks.

The Spike is a clipboard-like holding station for text and graphics. Each time you cut a selected item to the Spike, it just adds itself to the bottom of the Spike clipboard without erasing the existing contents. Once you have all the material you want in the Spike, you can place it en masse at any location.

Problems with the Spike

So what's wrong with the Spike? One glaring problem is that you can only cut — not copy — information to it. If you want to assemble a document that summarizes information from several others, leaving the source documents intact, you have to fall back on a repeated sequence of ordinary copy-and-paste operations.

As well, all the information you place in the Spike becomes one continuous chunk — you can't reorder it. That means you have to plan carefully the sequence of cuts you make to the Spike, or do a lot of reorganizing once you place the contents in the destination document.

Spike tips

If you do insist on using the Spike, the following points are here to get you started:

✦ The default keyboard shortcuts for getting your text into and out of the Spike are as follows: Ctrl+F3 cuts selected text to the Spike, while Ctrl+Shift+F3 pastes the Spike contents into your document.

✦ If you want to set up toolbar buttons for these operations, the commands you need in the Customize dialog box are Spike and InsertSpike. Word doesn't include button bitmaps for either command, so you have to design your own or use them as text buttons.

✦ Because the Spike is a special AutoText entry, you can also paste its contents via the Insert ➪ AutoText command.

✦ AutoComplete works with the Spike, too. Just type **spik** and you get a ScreenTip showing you the first two lines of text stored in the Spike. Pressing Enter at this point inserts the Spike contents into your document.

Using Repeat to clone text you just typed

The Repeat feature (F4 is the default keyboard shortcut) is great for repeating Word commands, but did you realize it will repeat what you've just typed? If you need to make several copies of a word, phrase, or sentence, use Repeat to speed the task as follows:

1. Start by moving the insertion point to clear any previously typed text. If the insertion point is already where it should be, just press the left arrow and then the right arrow.

2. Type the text, including a space or paragraph mark at the end to leave room for the next copy. You can use the Backspace key to make corrections. But don't press the cursor keys—if you do, you'll clear the text that Repeat is storing for you.

3. Press F4 to place into your document as many copies as you like of the text you typed.

Inserting the current date or time in one step

When you choose Insert ➪ Date and Time, the dialog box lets you tell Word to insert the current date, time, or both into your document in one of a host of available formats.

If you leave the Update Automatically box cleared, Word inserts the date and time information as ordinary text—the date you insert stays the same unless you edit it. If you check the box, however, Word actually inserts a Date field, which it updates every time you open or print the document (and whenever you update the field manually). Given that the dialog box doesn't say anything about Date fields, this might not be obvious.

The Insert Date and Time command is flexible, but you probably only use one or two date formats most of the time. Wouldn't it be nice to be able to insert a date in a single step, without having to deal with the dialog box? Something you could access via a toolbar button or keyboard shortcut? Word does offer a one-shot Date command and a corresponding toolbar button on the Header and Footer toolbar. You can add this button to other toolbars via the Customize dialog box. But be aware that this Date command has two potential problems.

First, it inserts the date or time using the current default format set in the Date and Time dialog box—this is usually okay, but if you want a button to insert a nondefault format, it won't do the trick.

Second, the Date command can only insert the date or time as a field, not as plaintext. If you don't want the information to be updated every time you open the document, you're out of luck.

The only real solution is a simple macro, in which you specify which format you want and whether to insert the date or time as a field or as ordinary text. After you've entered the macro, assign it a custom toolbar button, keyboard shortcut, or both. Here's the macro to try:

```
Sub DateAsText()
Selection.InsertDateTime _
  DateTimeFormat:="MMMM d, yyyy", InsertAsField: = False
End Sub
```

This example inserts a date, in the very standard format "October 12, 2001," as ordinary text. Type **True** instead of **False** if you want your own macro to insert a Date field rather than ordinary text. To use a different format, enter the "picture" of the format, just as you would for a Date field, in the quote marks. To see a list of these format pictures, choose Insert ⇨ Field, select Date in the Field Names list, and look in the Field properties area.

 **Cross-Reference**   Chapter 21 covers the whys and wherefores of formatting pictures.

Quick Text Changes

All professional writers will tell you that good writing is rewriting. Whether you're editing for clarity, to make a more powerful argument, or simply to correct minor errors, affording the means to make these changes painlessly is the word processor's greatest strength. Of course, the Word editing functions are so fundamental that you probably have a good grasp on most of them already. But look through the pointers that follow—you may find some new ideas for faster text editing.

Mouse text-selection shortcuts

The mouse makes it easy to select any quantity of text for editing operations such as cutting, pasting, or moving via drag and drop. The standard way to select with the mouse is to drag over the text, and you can extend selections by holding down the Shift key while you click. But just in case you've forgotten them, Table 17-7 shows Word's mouse shortcuts for text selection.

Table 17-7 Mouse Text-Selection Shortcuts	
This Mouse Action	*Selects This Text*
Double-click	Entire word
Triple-click	Entire paragraph
Click the selection area (to the left of the text)	Entire line
Click anywhere in a sentence while holding down Ctrl	Entire sentence
Double-click the selection area	Entire paragraph
Triple-click the selection area	Entire document

Tip   You can select columnar blocks of text by holding down Alt as you drag. This is sometimes extremely useful, especially when working with tabular material imported from plaintext files. Switch to a monospaced font such as Courier for best results before making columnar selections. (With the keyboard, select a columnar block of text by pressing Ctrl+Shift+F8 and then use the arrow keys to define the block. Press Esc to cancel this mode.)

Take advantage of the shortcut menus

Once you've selected a block of text with the mouse, the fastest way to cut or copy it to the clipboard is via the shortcut (right-click) menu. On this point, I recommend adding the Cut, Copy, and Paste commands to the shortcut menu that appears when you right-click a misspelled word. Otherwise, Word forces you to stop and deal with the spelling error before you can cut or copy the word.

Cross-Reference   Chapter 5 explains how to modify shortcut menus.

Using the selection bar

The selection bar is the invisible column between the left edge of the document window and the left margin of the page. To select text with it, point in this area and click once to select a line, twice to select a whole paragraph, or thrice for the entire document. Dragging selects entire lines as you cross over them.

Mouse moves — an alternative to drag and drop

No book on Office would be complete without mention of this slick mouse-keyboard maneuver for moving or copying text. To move a chunk of the document, first select the text and then point at the destination and hold down Ctrl while you right-click. To copy, Ctrl+Shift+right-click instead.

A great secret keyboard move technique

Hold down Alt+Shift while you press the up or down arrow to move the paragraph containing the insertion point up or down in the document as a unit. You don't need to select the paragraph first. However, if you do select two or more paragraphs, the whole set of paragraphs moves. This is a really cool way to rearrange paragraphs and an alternative to Outline view for shuffling entire sections.

Keyboard shortcuts for cutting words, lines, sentences, or paragraphs

Selecting text with the mouse is easy, yes, but it slows you down: You have to take your hands off the keyboard. And even with the shortcut menu, cutting a selection is still a two-step procedure. That's why many writers favor keyboard shortcuts that cut units of text in a single step.

These shortcuts should cut text (rather than copy or delete it) because cutting is the most versatile of the three procedures. If you need the text again at the same or another location, pasting brings it back. Creating a copy of what you cut is as simple as cutting, pasting at the same place, and then pasting again at the new location.

At the very least you should make up a pair of word-cutting shortcuts. The simple macros listed here cut the word (or word fragment) to the left or right of the insertion point, respectively (I mention the lines emphasized by bold type in a moment — when you type them, they appear in the regular VBA font):

```
Sub CutWordLeft()
  Selection.MoveLeft Unit:=wdWord, Extend:=wdExtend
  Selection.Cut
End Sub
and
Sub CutWordRight()
  Selection.MoveRight Unit:=wdWord, Extend:=wdExtend
  Selection.Cut
End Sub
```

Now, where to park these macros on the keyboard? My modest proposal is the two square bracket keys, [and]. You must use the technique described in "Using off-limits keys in custom keyboard shortcuts" in Chapter 15 to assign the bracket keys to the word-cutting macros, because you can't type the brackets in the Customize Keyboard dialog box. But once the shortcuts are in place, you can speed through your text, chopping out words or phrases effortlessly. Most people use brackets only rarely. Still, if you assign the shortcuts Alt+[and Alt+] to the original bracket characters, you can type the brackets immediately when you do need them.

You can create similar macros to cut text in larger chunks moving left or right from the insertion point whole. In each of the preceding macros, the first line (in bold) creates the selection unique to that macro. In your new macros, substitute the lines in Table 17-8 for those printed in bold in the version shown earlier.

Table 17-8
Sample Cutting-Text Macros

Unit of Text	Macro's Specific Job	First Line of Macro
Sentence	Cut to beginning of current sentence	`Selection.MoveLeft Unit:=wdSentence, Extend:=wdExtend`
	Cut to end of current sentence	`Selection.MoveRight Unit:=wdSentence, Extend:=wdExtend`
Line	Cut to beginning of current line	`Selection.HomeKey Unit:=wdLine, Extend:=wdExtend`
	Cut to end of current line	`Selection.EndKey Unit:=wdLine, Extend:=wdExtend`
Paragraph	Cut to beginning of current paragraph	`Selection.MoveUp Unit:=wdParagraph, Extend:=wdExtend`
	Cut to end of current paragraph	`Selection.MoveDown Unit:=wdParagraph, Extend:=wdExtend`

Improving on Word's case-changing functions

As befits a sophisticated text editor, Word includes a panoply of functions for changing the case of your text (we're talking about going from BIG LETTERS to baby letters or vice versa). Unfortunately, your access to these functions is restricted.

Swapping Characters

Word still is missing a useful command that was common among many of the old DOS word processors: a function to swap the position of two adjacent characters. It's so easy to mess up and type "teh" when you meant to type "the."

AutoCorrect fixes many common errors of this kind, detecting and setting straight "agian," "esle," and "bakc," as well as "teh." But AutoCorrect only works on the specific sequences of characters in its list, and you can't possibly anticipate all the mistakes you're going to make.

Solve the missing feature problem with a quick little macro called SwapCharacters. It works on the two characters to the left of the insertion point, picking up the closest one and tucking it one position back in the stream of text. If you like this macro, I suggest putting it on a very accessible key.

```
Sub SwapCharacters()
If Selection.Type <> wdSelectionIP Then GoTo NoSwap
   Selection.MoveLeft Unit:=wdCharacter, Count:=1
   Selection.MoveLeft Unit:=wdCharacter, Count:=1,
Extend:=wdExtend
   Selection.Cut
   Selection.MoveRight Unit:=wdCharacter, Count:=1
   Selection.Paste
NoSwap:
End Sub
```

The standard keyboard layout places a keyboard shortcut for the Change Case command on Shift+F3. Like a good-looking person with bad teeth, this command has a lot of initial appeal but tends to put people off after they take a second glance, for the reasons reviewed in the next section.

How the Change Case command works

As you press Shift+F3 repeatedly, Change Case cycles the affected text through three different case states. But the exact effect varies, depending on whether and how much text is selected first. Now, it's asking a lot to memorize such variations, and this is one of the command's problems. (There are others, as you'll soon see.) Anyway, just so you can look it up for easy reference, Table 17-9 shows how Change Case works.

Table 17-9 Effects of Word's Change Case	
Condition	**Effect of Change Case (Shift+F3 by Default)**
No text is selected.	1. Converts the entire word to UPPERCASE.
	2. Converts the entire word to lowercase.
	3. Capitalizes the word containing the insertion point.
Less than a full sentence is selected.	1. Converts the entire selection to UPPERCASE.
	2. Converts the entire selection to lowercase.
	3. Capitalizes every word in the selection, changing all other letters to lowercase.
A full sentence or more is selected.	1. Converts the entire selection to UPPERCASE.
	2. Converts the entire selection to lowercase.
	3. Capitalizes the first word in every sentence in the selection, changing all other letters to lowercase.

So what else is wrong with the Change Case command? I can list three problems:

✦ At any one time, Change Case performs only three of Word's five useful case-changing functions (there is a sixth, mentioned later). You can get to some of the other options via a dialog box (choose Format ⇨ Change Case), but that route usually takes more time than just retyping the text.

✦ The Change Case dialog box also leaves out the Word command for capitalizing the first word in the selection, regardless of its sentence location.

✦ When text isn't selected, Change Case always works on the whole word containing the insertion point. You can't use Change Case to make "Powerpoint" into "PowerPoint" (unless you select just the second "p" before pressing Shift+F3).

Note

Word also offers the interesting but nearly useless "toggle case." Use it on the selection PowerPoint, and you would end up with pOWERpOINT. Once in a blue moon you may find a use for this conversion, and if you do, activate it via Format ⇨ Change Case.

Keyboard shortcuts for changing case

Editing often moves a word from somewhere in the middle of a sentence to the lead-off position, and vice versa. Because changing case is such a frequent chore, keep the necessary keyboard shortcut close at hand. I put my case-changing macro on the \

(backslash) key, where it's immediately accessible. As a backup, I assign the | key (Shift+\) as the shortcut for Word's standard Change Case command—that way, I can still capitalize a whole word without selecting it first.

Cross-Reference   See Chapter 15 for a discussion of how to create keyboard shortcuts.

✦   ✦   ✦

Saving Time with Styles and Templates

Styles and templates are one of the greatest timesavers Word has to offer — and one of the best ways to ensure that all your documents look their best and (just as importantly) have a look consistent with other, related documents.

Best of all, they're easy to use — as you'll see in this chapter.

What Are Styles?

A style is a set of preset formats for text — size, font, indent, etc. — that is given a name. You can apply a style to a paragraph of text, or to a few words, and all the formatting is done at once. For example, as I'm writing this book I'm using a set of styles provided by the publisher. There's one style for the chapter title, another for major headings within the chapter, another for figure captions, and another for Tips and Notes. Using the styles provided saves both my editors and me a lot of manual formatting.

Note   Styles are also used to format automatic tables of contents and outlines. See Chapter 19 for more information.

One of the major advantages of using styles is that when you make a change to a style (for example, you decide to change the font of your headings) all the paragraphs using that style also change, throughout your document. This saves you searching through your document and changing each paragraph individually.

Types of styles

There are four types of styles: paragraph, character, table and list:

✦ **Paragraph styles:** These styles, as the name implies, format a whole paragraph. Paragraph styles can include not just font type and size, but any formatting that can be applied to paragraphs, including alignment, indents, and justification. The style called "Normal" is the default paragraph style. This means that if you do not choose another style, all text is formatted with the Normal style.

Be aware that there is both a Normal style and a Normal template (covered later in this chapter) — it's easy to confuse the two. You can recognize a paragraph style when its listed in the Styles and Formatting task pane (see Figure 18-1 in the next section) by the paragraph symbol (¶) that appears beside it.

✦ **Character styles:** These styles are used to format words and phrases instead of whole paragraphs. Unlike paragraph styles, they do not include alignment, indents, spacing, and so forth. You could use a character style if you regularly need to highlight words in your document by making them bold, underlined, or italic. The character style called Default Paragraph Font contains the same character formatting information as the Normal paragraph style. (You can use a paragraph style as a character style — it just ignores all the alignment and indent information.) Character styles can only include the formatting options that are available when you choose Format ⇨ Font, Format ⇨ Borders and Shading, or Tools ⇨ Language.

One of the advantages of using a character style is that you can use it to change the look of text without changing the size. For example, you may want to use blue, bold Arial text whenever you refer to one of your company's products. You can select the product name and apply the character style; the text size, whatever it is, remains the same. Character styles are identified in the Styles and Formatting task pane by an underlined a (again, see Figure 18-1 in the next section).

✦ **Table styles:** Want all your tables to look the same throughout your document? A table style can include everything from text formatting to borders and shading to vertical and horizontal alignment within cells. You can create table styles that apply to the entire table or just to portions of it — just the header row, for instance, or the first column. Table styles are identified in the Styles and Formatting task pane by a grid icon.

✦ **List styles:** Once you've perfected the look of a list, make it a style and use it over and over. List styles let you choose whether to start the list with a bullet, number, or symbol, and set indenting and other formatting. As with tables, you can apply different styles to different parts of the list: level 1, level 2, level 3, and so on. List styles are identified in the Styles and Formatting task pane with a small icon of a list.

Saving style information

When you save any document, the styles used within it are also automatically saved, so they're automatically available the next time you edit that document. However, if you want to use those styles in another document, you'll have to copy them from the first document to the second. If you find you need to use the same styles over and over again in a multitude of documents, it's time to create a template.

What Are Templates?

A template is a special Word document with the filename extension .DOT that is used to maintain a consistent look from document to document. Word comes with templates for many common types of documents, including letters and faxes, memos, reports, newsletters, and Web pages.

In a template, all the unchanging items — the company logo and company name and address, for example, in the case of a letterhead — are inserted automatically. As a result, when you create a document using a template, all the fixed text and pictures are already in place, and you only need to enter your additional text.

Templates also contain styles, as well as macros and any changes that have been made to Word's default menus, keyboard shortcuts, and toolbar settings. Using the styles included with the template ensures that all documents created using that template will use the same fonts, sizes, alignment, and so forth. For example, in the Contemporary Report template (see Figure 18-1) styles are provided for document, chapter and part titles and subtitles, body text, and more.

 Note   Actually, all documents are based on templates — even the blank document Word opens automatically when you start the program. The default template is called `Normal.dot`; if you haven't chosen another template, that's the one you're working with.

In addition to the many templates you can use as is or modify, Word provides several wizards — miniprograms that can help you automatically create faxes, letters, and other documents.

The Template That Wrote This Book

Templates are very useful for long documents. This book is a good example: It was written using a special template created by Hungry Minds, Inc., for all the books in its *Bible* series.

The page formats and the styles for the headings, bullets, lists, and so on, which all stay the same from book to book, are all stored in the template. This ensures that all the *Bible* books have the same "look," and also makes the formatting of each book a (relatively) quick and simple task.

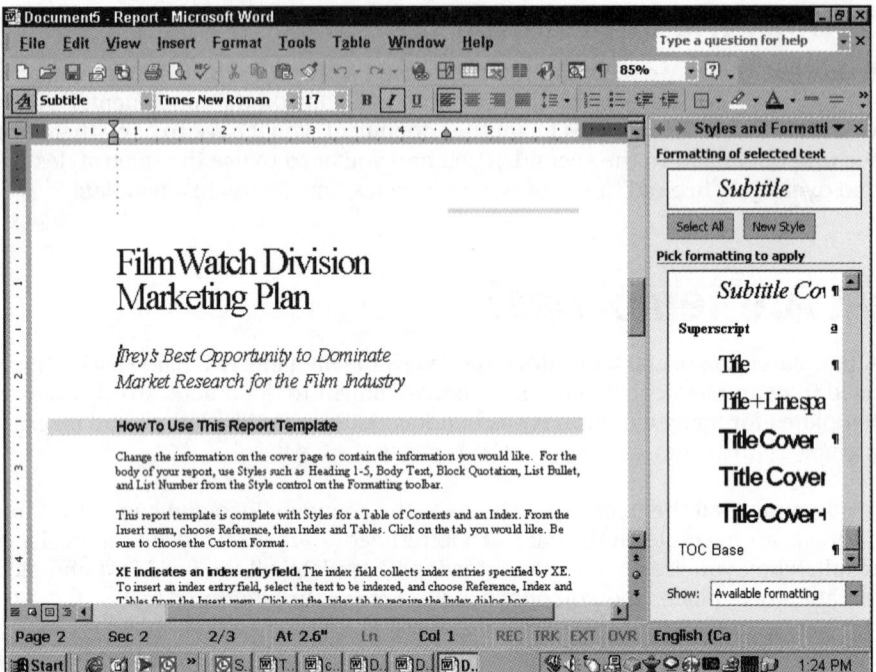

Figure 18-1: This is the Contemporary Report template that comes with Word. Different styles (shown in the task pane down the right side) are used to format the various sections of the report.

Applying Word's Built-in Styles

The Normal template includes several built-in styles. You can use them as they are or change them to suit yourself. Later in this chapter you'll learn how to create your own styles and modify them, but in this section you'll simply apply them.

Applying a style with the task pane

The easiest way to apply a style is to open the Styles and Formatting task pane. To do so, click the Styles and Formatting button at the far-left edge of the Formatting toolbar.

By default, the task pane shows you the formatting of the selected text in the top box, and a menu of all available formatting. "Available formatting" includes any direct formatting you have applied, any styles you have created, and three built-in heading styles. In a long, complex document, this can be an extensive list.

To see only the styles that have been used in your document, choose Available Styles from the Show drop-down list at the bottom of the task pane. To see all the styles that are available in the template you're using, choose All Styles from the drop-down list.

To apply a style, simply select the text you want to apply the style to, then click on the name of the style you want to use in the list in the task pane.

Select the text to be formatted as follows:

✦ If you want to apply a style to a whole paragraph, place the insertion point anywhere in the paragraph.

✦ If you want to apply a style to several consecutive paragraphs, highlight the paragraphs to be changed.

✦ If you want to apply a style to selected text only, highlight the text to be changed.

To change all the text of one style within a document to another style, follow these steps:

1. Select a small sample of the text whose style you wish to change. Its current formatting will be displayed in the top box in the task pane.

2. Click the Select All button to select all examples of text using that formatting throughout the document.

3. Click the style you wish to apply to the text from the list of styles.

Note   Refer to Figure 18-1 earlier in the chapter and note that all of the styles except Superscript have a paragraph symbol in the gray box at the right end. The paragraph symbol means that that's a Paragraph style. The underlined "a" next to the Superscript style tells you it's a character style. List styles are designated by a stack of three dots and three lines, just like the ones on the Bullets button on the Formatting toolbar, and Table styles by a box bisected horizontally and vertically by lines.

Tip   The alternative to using the task pane is to highlight the text you want to apply a style to and choose the style you want from the Style list box on the Formatting toolbar (see Figure 18-2). This method has an advantage: If the list of styles is too long for you to see all of them, you can find a style quickly by clicking on the Style list box's drop-down arrow and typing the first letter of the style you are looking for. For example, press H if you are looking for Heading 1. The first style starting with H moves into view at the top of the list, where you can select it with a click.

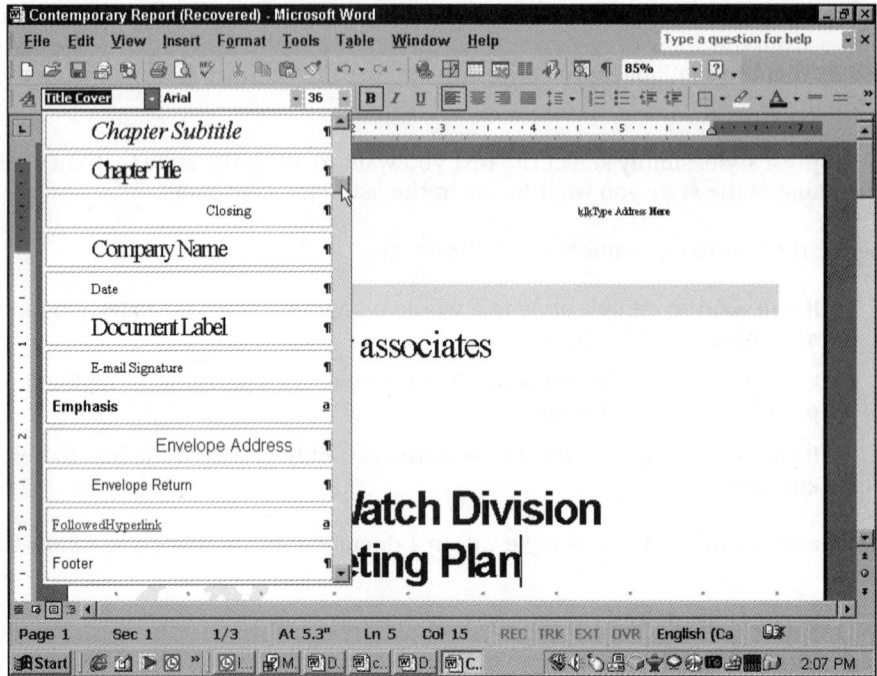

Figure 18-2: You can apply a style using the Style list box on the Formatting toolbar.

Applying a style with a keyboard shortcut

You can also apply styles with keyboard shortcuts; just select the paragraph(s) or text you want to apply the style to as outlined above and then press the appropriate key combination. Table 18-1 lists the keyboard shortcuts assigned by default to the Normal template.

Table 18-1 Built-In Styles		
Style Name	**Main Features**	**Shortcut Key**
Heading 1	Arial, 16 pt, bold	Ctrl+Alt+1
Heading 2	Arial, 14 pt, bold, italic	Ctrl+Alt+2
Heading 3	Arial, 13 pt, bold	Ctrl+Alt+3
Normal	Times New Roman, 10 pt	Ctrl+Shift+N

Alternative ways to apply styles

There are a couple of other ways to apply styles. You can apply one style repeatedly to different paragraphs using the Repeat Style command; you can also copy a style from one section of text onto another section by using the Format Painter tool.

Using Repeat

To apply the same style to a series of paragraphs, use the Repeat Style command, by following these steps:

1. Apply the style to the first paragraph you want to format.

2. Move your insertion point to the next paragraph you want to format.

3. Choose Edit ⇨ Repeat Style, or press Ctrl+Y.

4. Move to the next paragraph you want to format and repeat Step 3.

5. Continue until you've applied the style to all the paragraphs you want.

Using the Format Painter

To copy a style from one section of text to another, use the Format Painter. Follow these steps:

1. Highlight text that uses the style you want to apply to additional text.

2. Click the Format Painter tool on the Standard toolbar to switch it on.

3. Use the Format Painter tool to highlight the text to which you want to apply the same style as the first text.

Removing a style from text

If you apply a style to a paragraph by mistake, you can reapply the default Normal style by selecting the paragraph and pressing Ctrl+Shift+N.

Similarly, if you have applied a character style and want to remove it, select the text and change it back to Default Paragraph Font by pressing Ctrl+Spacebar.

Seeing which styles have been applied

You can see which style has been applied to a paragraph by clicking on it and looking at the Style box on the Formatting toolbar or in the "Formatting of selected text" box at the top of the Styles and Formatting task pane.

Tip   If you switch on the Show/Hide Paragraph tool on the Formatting toolbar, you'll also see a small black spot to the left of each paragraph that has had a style other than Normal applied to it.

If you're in Outline or Normal view, you can also have Word display style names down the left side of the screen (see Figure 18-3). If you use styles a lot, this can be very helpful.

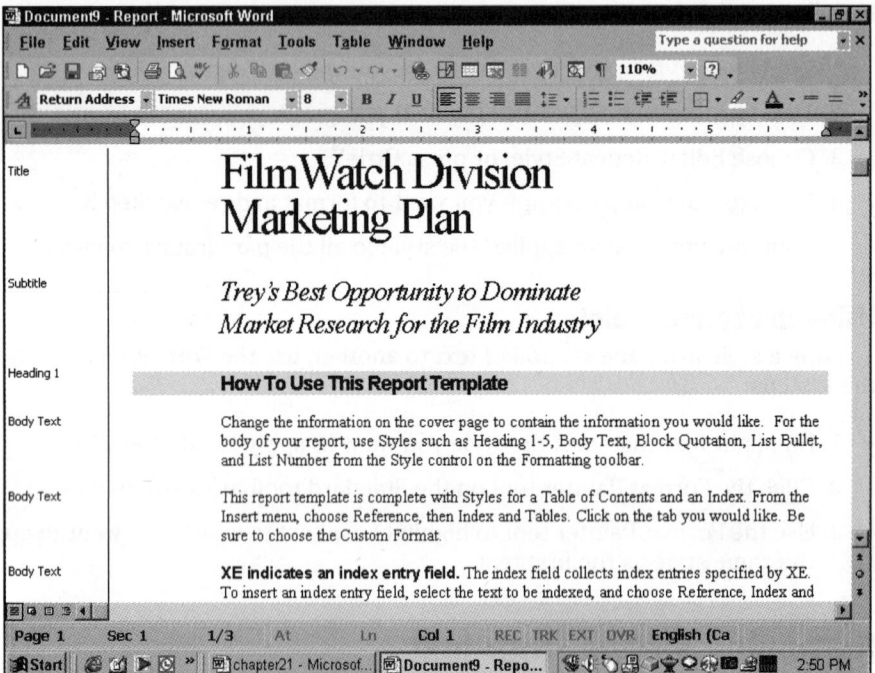

Figure 18-3: You can make Word display style names alongside the document text.

Displaying style names

To make Word display style names, follow these steps:

1. Make sure you are in Normal or Outline view.

2. Choose Tools ⇨ Options, and go to the View tab.

3. In the "Style area width" box in the Outline and Normal Options section at the bottom of the View tab, enter how wide you would like the area used to display style names to be (one inch is a convenient width).

4. Click OK. The style names are now displayed down the left side of the document. You can adjust the width of the style names display area by dragging the on-screen divider left or right.

Using Reveal Formatting

Another way to get information about how text has been formatted is to place your insertion point within the text you want information about, then open the Reveal Formatting task pane by choosing Format ➪ Reveal Formatting (see Figure 18-4). If you check the "Distinguish style source" box at the bottom of the task pane, the style used for the text will be revealed. As long as this task pane is open, you can view details of any other formatting by clicking elsewhere in the document.

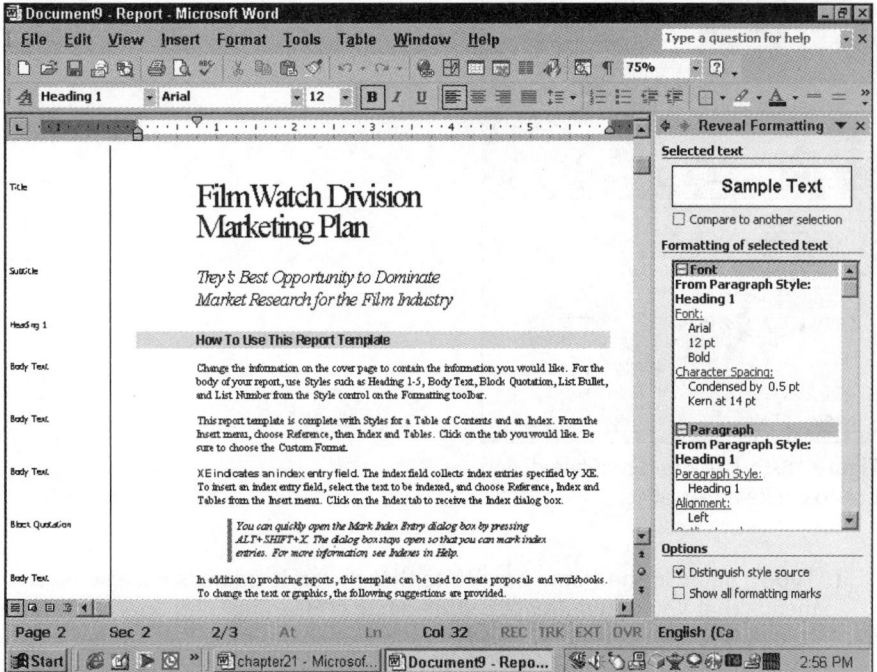

Figure 18-4: The Reveal Formatting task pane can show you details about the formatting within your document — including applied styles.

Creating Styles

You have two ways to create a style:

✦ Name a style and use dialog boxes to select the formatting features you require. This is the most complete method, as it gives you access to some features that are not easy to see (such as rules for page endings and special line spacing).

✦ Create the style using some existing text, which you have already formatted the way you want. In effect, you are giving Word an example of what the style should look like.

Creating a style using dialog boxes

To begin, click the Styles and Formatting button on the Formatting toolbar to open the Styles and Formatting task pane. Then click New Style within the task pane. This opens the New Style dialog box (see Figure 18-5). To continue, follow these steps:

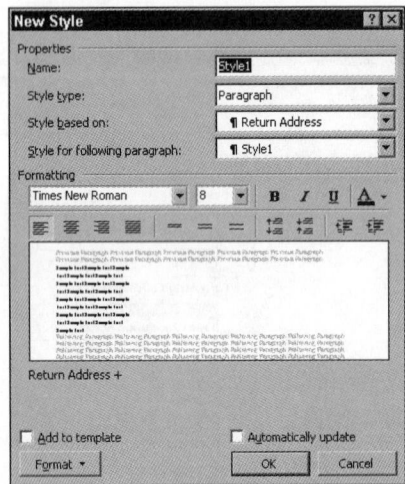

Figure 18-5: Use the New Style dialog box to create a new style.

1. Type a name in the Name box. Note that the style name is case sensitive. This means that you could create a style named "Heading" and another one called "heading." The style name can be up to 253 characters. You cannot use the backslash(\), curly braces ({ }), or the semicolon (;), but you can use spaces.

2. Names appear in alphabetical order, so it's a good idea to name related styles in a similar way—for example: Head 1, Head 2, Head 3, rather than Major Head, Subhead and Sub-Subhead. This makes styles easier to find because they end up grouped together.

3. Click the Format button to gain access to all of the formatting dialog boxes, which are normally accessed by choosing Format from the menu bar. Many of the basic formatting tools have been made readily available in the New Style dialog box itself. The Preview box shows a thumbnail view of what your paragraph looks like, and beneath it is a description of the various elements of the style. Other options in this dialog box include the following:

   • **Style type:** You can choose character, paragraph, list, or table. The basic formatting tools visible in the New Style dialog box will change depending on which type of style you're creating.

• **Style based on:** If you base your new style on an existing style, all the formatting of the existing style is used and you need only make changes in format where the two styles differ. For example, if your base style is Arial 12-point normal, your new style will also be Arial 12-point normal. If you want your new style to be bold and italicized, you only need to add those two formatting instructions.

 **Tip**

If the base style changes—say, the font is changed to Times New Roman instead of Arial—all the styles based on it change, too. Suppose you want all headings in a document to use the same font. Create the major heading and use it as the base style, and then base the rest of the headings on this style.

• **Style for following paragraph:** This feature sets which style will be used in the paragraph following any paragraph that uses the style you're currently defining. For example, suppose you're defining your Heading 1 style. If you know that every time you use the Heading 1 style, the next paragraph in the document should be in Normal style, then choose Normal here. When you press Return after typing Heading 1, the next text you type in will automatically be set to Normal style.

• **Add to template:** New and modified styles are automatically saved with the document, but not the current template. To alter the current template to permanently include the new style, check this option.

• **Automatically update:** This has no effect when using the Normal template. If you are using any other template and change the format of a paragraph, the style gets redefined and all the paragraphs using the same style are automatically changed. This can surprise you if you are not expecting it! We'll look at how to modify styles in the next section of this chapter.

Creating a style by using an example

To create a style by using an example, follow these steps:

1. Format a paragraph, section of text, list, or table with all the elements you want in your style. Use any of the Word formatting tools, such as font, borders, indents, and so on.

2. Click anywhere in the paragraph, section of text, list, or table.

3. Click the Styles and Formatting button on the Formatting toolbar to open the Styles and Formatting task pane.

4. Click the New Style button inside the task pane.

5. Type the name you want to give the new style in the Name box in the Properties area.

6. Select any other properties you wish to add to the style just as you did with a style created from scratch. The preview area will show you what your new style will look like.

7. Click OK.

Modifying Styles

Just as there are two ways to create new styles, so there are two ways to modify existing ones. You can use dialog boxes or use an example.

Modifying a style using dialog boxes

To modify a style using dialog boxes, follow these steps:

1. Click the Styles and Formatting button on the Formatting toolbar to open the Styles and Formatting task pane.

2. Select the style you wish to modify from the list and right-click on it.

3. From the pop-up menu that appears (see Figure 18-6), choose Modify.

4. The Modify Style dialog box appears; except for its title and the fact that you cannot change the Style type, it looks and works exactly like the New Style dialog box. Make any changes you wish, then click OK.

5. When you have finished, you'll find that all text within the document that uses the style has changed to reflect the modification.

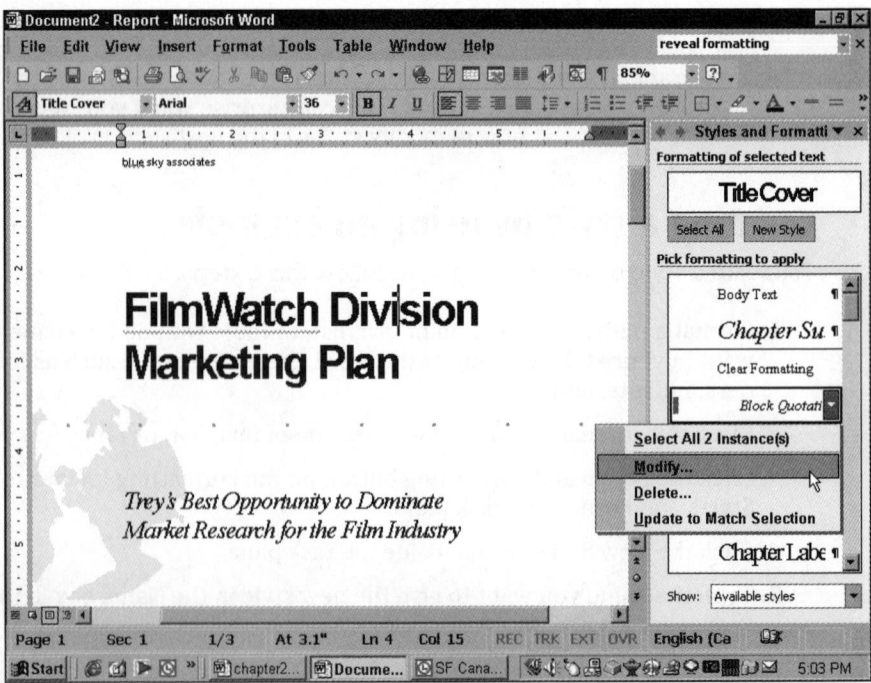

Figure 18-6: Right-clicking on the name of a style enables you to quickly modify or delete it.

Modifying a style by using an example

This is a quick and easy way to modify a style:

1. Click the Styles and Formatting button on the Formatting toolbar to open the Styles and Formatting task pane.

2. Select any paragraph, table, text, or list that uses the style you wish to modify by highlighting it or clicking somewhere within it.

3. Make whatever formatting changes you want.

4. Right-click on the name of the paragraph's original style in the "Pick formatting to apply" list in the task pane and choose Update to Match Selection.

5. You should find that all paragraphs using the same style have changed.

Copying, deleting, and renaming a style

You can copy a style from one document or template to another using the Organizer (see Figure 18-7). To access the Organizer, choose Tools ➪ Templates and Add-Ins to open the Templates and Add-Ins dialog box, then click the Organizer button within that box. When the Organizer dialog box opens, make sure the Style tab is selected.

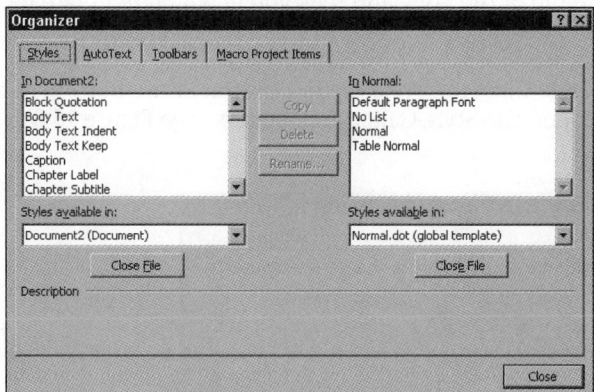

Figure 18-7: The Organizer dialog box lets you copy styles from one document or template to another.

This dialog box has two sides, listing the styles in two different files. If you open this dialog box while you have a document open, you'll see the style in use in your open document on one side and the styles in the normal template on the other. However, you can open the file of your choice on either side. If one of them shows the incorrect document or template, click Close File under the incorrect one first, and then click Open File to bring up the Open dialog box. Make sure you have the correct setting in the "Files of type" box. To open a document, choose Word Documents; and to open a template, choose Document Templates:

✦ To copy a style using the Organizer, make sure the source file is on one side and the destination file is on the other. Highlight the style you want to copy by clicking on it and then click Copy. You should see the selected style appear in the destination file's Style list.

✦ To delete a style, click on the style name and then click Delete.

✦ To rename a style, click on the style name on either side of the dialog box and then click Rename. Type a new name for the style, click OK, and then click Close.

Note   You cannot delete the two built-in styles from the Normal template.

Using the Style Gallery

The Style Gallery is a tool to help you find styles, no matter which template they are in. It shows you an example of the style and tells you in which template it is saved. To use the Style Gallery, follow these steps:

1. Choose Format ➪ Theme. Click the Style Gallery button at the bottom of the Theme dialog box to open the Style Gallery dialog box (see Figure 18-8).

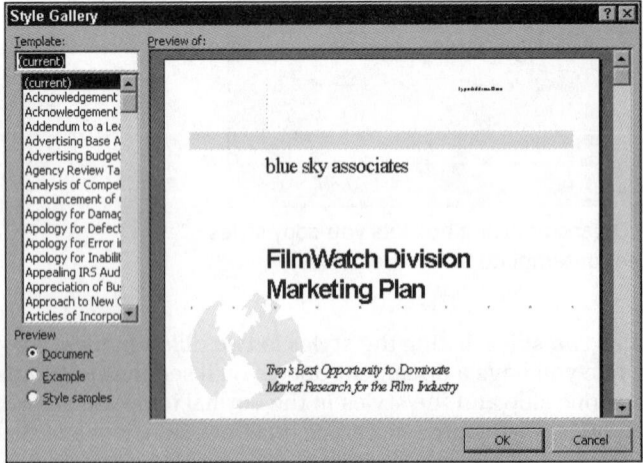

Figure 18-8: The Style Gallery dialog box can help you find the style you want from all those Word has to offer.

2. Select the template you want to look at from the list at left.

3. Click the Document radio button to see what your document would look like formatted with the styles in the selected template.

4. Click Example to see a sample document formatted with the template.

5. Click Style samples to see a document showing a sample of each style in the template.

Once you have found a style you wish to use, you can copy it into your template using the Organizer.

Applying a Template

As noted earlier, when you create a new document by clicking the New button on the Standard toolbar, you are creating a document based on the Normal (default) template.

However, if you create a new document using the menu instead of the toolbar, you can choose from a variety of other templates. Choose File ➪ New to open the New Document task pane, then choose the General Templates option from the New from template area. This opens the Templates dialog box (see Figure 18-9). The templates available are grouped by type under various tabs. Word has several built-in templates, and you can add your own later. You can also use the wizards supplied with Word to create your own documents.

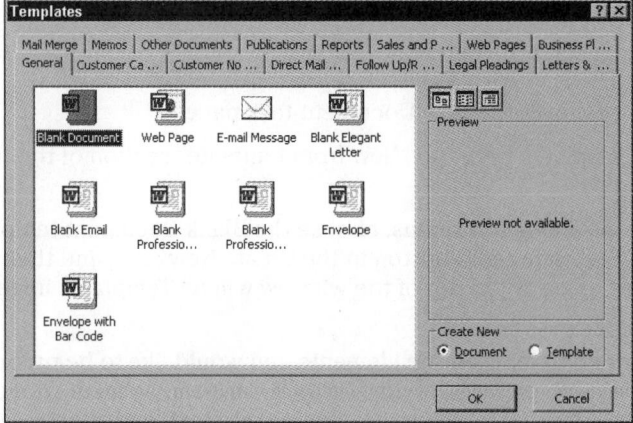

Figure 18-9: The Templates dialog box offers a multitude of templates for you to choose from.

Creating a new document with a template

To use a template, select the tab you require and then the template. When you create a document using a template other than Normal, it has no filename; you can treat it just as you would a document created using the Normal template and name it whatever you wish.

Applying a template to an existing document

To apply a template to a document you have already created, choose Tools ➪ Templates and Add-Ins. The dialog box shows the current template in use. Click Attach to select another template to use with the document. The styles from the attached template are added to the current document.

You can choose whether to automatically update the document with the styles in the saved template each time you open the document.

Creating and Modifying Templates

You can create a new template in two ways:

✦ From scratch

✦ From an existing document

Creating a template from scratch

To create a template from scratch, follow these steps:

1. Choose File ➪ New to open the New Document task pane.

2. Choose General Templates from the "New from template" section of the task pane.

3. When the Templates dialog box opens, choose the Blank Document template, then click on the Template radio button in the Create New area, and then click OK. The document name at the top of the window will be Template1 instead of Document1.

4. Create a document containing all the elements you would like to be part of your new template: text, pictures, styles, fields, forms, and so forth. You can also include macros, special toolbars, or menus, AutoText, and shortcut key entries.

5. Save the document as usual. It will be automatically saved with the filename extension .dot in the Templates folder.

To add a new tab to those on the Templates dialog box, add a new folder under the Templates folder and add one or more templates to that folder. A new tab by that name, containing the templates you've stored in that folder, will automatically appear the next time you open the Templates dialog box. Note that the tab will not appear if your new folder doesn't contain any templates.

Creating a template from an existing document

If you have an existing document that you would like to use as a template — maybe you've created a document you've been using as your letterhead but you've only just learned about the Template feature — follow these instructions:

1. Open the document you want to use as a template.

2. Choose File ➪ Save As. The Save As dialog box appears.

3. Type a name for your template and then select Document Template in the "Save as type" box. Word automatically switches you to your Templates folder.

4. Click Save.

Modifying templates

You can modify a template in much the same way you modify any other document. Follow the same procedures you use to create a template from scratch, but instead of opening a Blank Document as a template, open the template you want to modify. Make your changes, then save it as usual.

You cannot save changes to a template when it is in use. If you created your current document by choosing a template, you cannot save it as a template using the same name. You have to give it a different name.

Modifying the Normal Template

For certain features, you need not use the method described in the previous section to modify the Normal template. If you wish to change the default font, choose Format ➪ Font, select the font type, size, and style you wish to use, and click the Default button. You are prompted to verify that you really want to change the Normal template.

The same Default button appears in the Page Setup and Language dialog boxes. Choose File ➪ Page Setup to set the default paper size, printer bin, margins, and many other options. Choose Tools ➪ Language ➪ Set Language to select the default language for spell checking, the thesaurus, and grammar checking. (Some language dictionaries have to be purchased separately.)

To change any of the styles other than the Normal style in the Normal template, you need to open the template as instructed in the previous section.

Note   You may have difficulty locating the file `Normal.dot`. (On my system it is in c:\Windows\Application Data\Microsoft Office\Templates.) You may need to do a search to find it on your system. Click Tools on the toolbar of the Open dialog box to search for document templates on your disk.

✦   ✦   ✦

Organizing Information with Outlines, Tables of Contents, and Indexes

Good organization is crucial to the success of any document. If the information presented isn't in some sort of logical order, it's much harder for the reader to understand it. That not only undermines communication (the primary purpose of creating a document in the first place), it undermines your credibility.

Fortunately, Word provides several organizational tools that can help you present your thoughts in crystal-clear fashion, and make it easier for your audience to find the information they're looking for within your documents.

What Is an Outline?

An outline is a hierarchical listing of the headings within a document. This book, like most nonfiction books, began life as an outline, and that outline can still be traced in the various levels of headings that appear in each chapter. Major headings, like "What Is an Outline?" above use the largest type; each subsequent level of heading uses slightly smaller type.

Sub-subheadings all relate in some way to the subheadings they're grouped under, which in turn relate in some way to the major heading under which they are grouped.

Word includes, as part of its normal template, several levels of heading styles. By using these styles for your headings (Heading 1 for main headings, Heading 2 for subheadings, Heading 3 for sub-subheadings, and so forth) as you build your outline, you can create an organizational structure that's easy to modify and easy to move around in within Word.

Using Outline View

Word offers a special view, Outline view, to help you work with outlines. A typical outline in Outline view looks something like the one shown in Figure 19-1, which is part of the outline for this book. You can turn on Outline view by choosing View ➪ Outline.

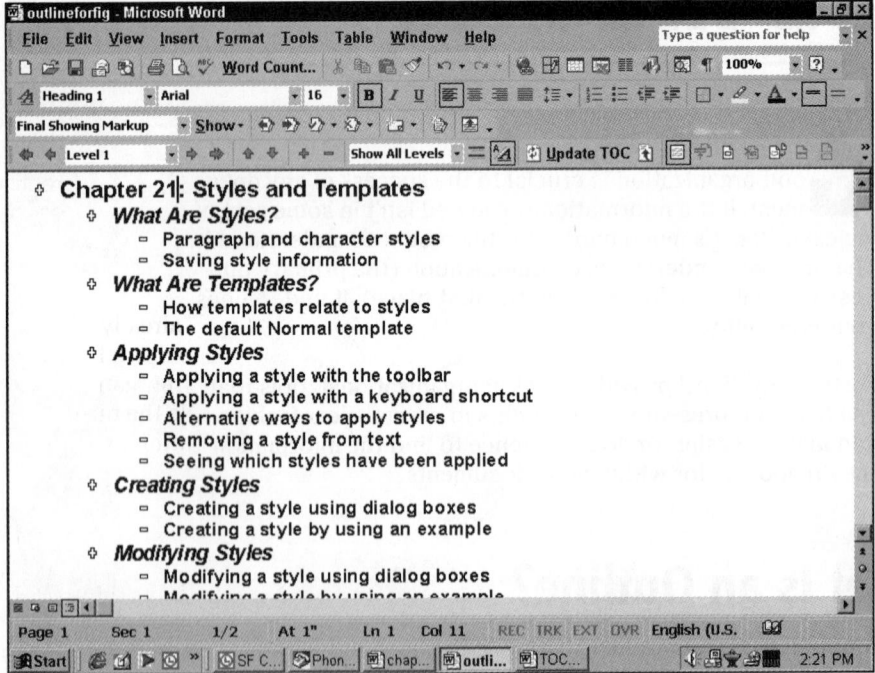

Figure 19-1: Outline view shows you the various levels of headings within your document.

In Outline view, Word automatically indents headings to show their relative importance to one another. In addition, it enables you to view only the level of headings that you want by using the Show Level drop-down list on the Outlining toolbar, which you can see in Figure 19-1 just above the document window. Clicking on this list enables you to view only those levels of the outline you want to, from Level 1 all the way down to Level 9. Choosing Show Level 1 shows you only your Level 1 headings; choosing Show Level 2 shows you only your Level 1 and Level 2 headings, and so on. You can also choose Show All Levels to see the entire outline, including paragraphs that don't use a heading style.

To the right of the Show Level drop-down list is the Show First Line Only button. Click this to see only the first line of all the paragraphs in your document (of all the styles you're viewing).

To the right of the Show First Line Only button is the Show/Hide Formatting button; click this to toggle formatting on and off. In general, though, it varies from template to template — every heading style has its own character formatting, which can be distracting when all you want to do is organize your document.

We'll look at the other buttons on the Outlining toolbar in the next section.

Creating and Modifying Outlines

All you have to do to create an outline is assign each level of the outline the appropriate heading style: Heading 1 for top-level heads, Heading 2 for subheads, and so on. You can write your outline first, and then assign heading styles as appropriate, or you can assign heading styles as you go along. It doesn't matter.

Rearranging your outline

Rearranging the order of your outline is also easy. If you're not already in Outline view, choose View ➪ Outline to get there. The buttons and drop-down list on the left end of the Outlining toolbar are controls for quickly and easily reorganizing your outline — and your thoughts. Place your cursor anywhere inside the outline element you want to rearrange, and then press the appropriate button or choose the level you want to assign that element from the drop-down list.

From left to right, these outlining controls are as follows:

✦ **Promote to Heading 1:** This makes the element a top-level heading.

✦ **Promote:** This moves the selected item one notch higher in the hierarchy by assigning it the next-highest outline level.

✦ **Outline level:** You can choose any of the nine available outline levels, or body text, from this drop-down list.

✦ **Demote:** This moves the selected item one notch lower in the hierarchy, assigning it the next-lowest outline level.

✦ **Demote to Body Text:** This assigns the Normal style to the selected item.

✦ **Move Up:** This moves the selected item above the item above it. The outline level doesn't change.

✦ **Move Down:** This moves the selected item below the item below it. Again, the outline level doesn't change.

Using outline paragraph levels

Although the Heading 1, 2, 3, and so forth styles are assigned outline levels 1, 2, 3, and so on and can't be changed, you can apply the same outline levels to other paragraph styles. You could choose to make Normal style correspond to outline level 1 just like Heading 1 style, if you wished. This gives you enormous flexibility in designing your outline.

There are nine outline levels in all. You can't change the outline levels assigned to various paragraph styles directly from Outline View, oddly enough; instead, you have to return to Normal or Print Layout view. Once you've done that, click on the paragraph you want to apply an outline level to and then either choose Format ➪ Paragraph or right-click and choose Paragraph from the pop-up menu. Either method will open the Paragraph dialog box shown in Figure 19-2.

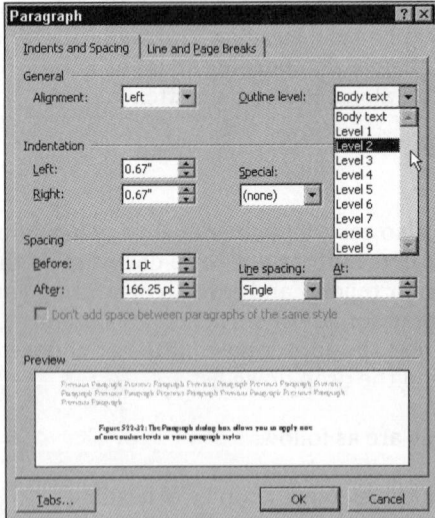

Figure 19-2: The Paragraph dialog box enables you to apply one of nine outline levels to your paragraph styles.

Choose an outline level from the Outline Level drop-down list. To remove an existing outline level, choose Body Text.

Tip

Because these effects can't be seen in Normal or Print view, using outline paragraph levels enables you to "invisibly" outline a document. You could, for example, use levels simply to remind yourself which paragraphs are most important — in the event you have to later shorten the document — without someone reading a printed copy ever being able to tell.

To view the results of your outline paragraph levels, switch to Outline view (see Figure 19-3). Level 1 paragraphs are flush with the left margin, Level 2 paragraphs are indented, and Level 3 paragraphs are indented still further. Body text paragraphs are always indented one level further than the heading level they are within. Note that the paragraph outline levels are independent of the heading levels.

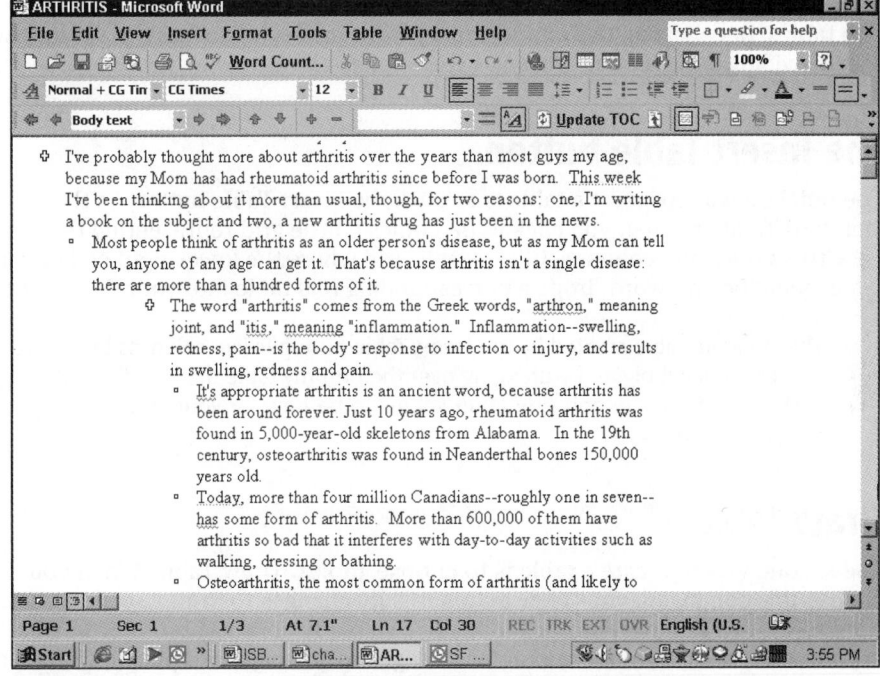

Figure 19-3: In Outline view, the outline levels applied to the paragraphs become clear.

Tip

An outline not only keeps you organized, it also makes it easier to move around in a lengthy document. By going to Outline view and collapsing a lengthy document to first-level heads alone, you can effectively shrink the document to a size much easier to work with — it might fit on one page instead of a hundred. Then you can simply click on the heading of the section you want to work on and expand it, make your changes, and then collapse that section again. This can save you a lot of scrolling.

Printing an outline

You can print an outline just like you would any other document. Go to Outline view, collapse or expand sections as you see fit, and then choose File ⇨ Print or click the Print button on the Standard toolbar.

Creating Tables

Tables are another useful way of organizing information to the benefit of both the creator of a document and the reader. Readers benefit from a clearer understanding of the relationships among the various items inserted into the table. Creators benefit from Word's ability to sort, sum, and otherwise manipulate information entered into tables. Recognizing their importance, Word makes tables easy to set up and use, providing two different ways to create them.

The Insert Table button

The quickest way to insert a table is to click the Insert Table button on the Standard Toolbar. When you click it, up comes a little grid representing the table-to-be with its rows and columns. Click in this grid where the lower-right cell of your table would be and Word drops a corresponding real table into your document.

Tip   The standard table created by the Insert Table button is five columns by four rows. You can make it bigger by dragging over the dummy table that pops up when you click the button. The only limitation seems to be how far your screen will let you drag the mouse.

Draw Table

The second way to create a table is to choose Table ⇨ Draw Table. When you choose this command, your view automatically changes to Print Layout if you are in Normal view (it remains unchanged if you're already in Print Layout or in Web Layout view) and your mouse pointer changes to an image of a pencil, which you can use to draw the rows and columns of your table just as you might draw a table on a piece of paper with a regular pencil and a ruler. (Don't worry; Word keeps all of your lines straight automatically, creating your table on an invisible grid that everything snaps to.) You can make the table as large as you want, and add as many vertical and horizontal lines as you want (see Figure 19-4).

Draw Table is a very powerful command for creating nonstandard tables — tables that have different numbers of columns in different rows, for instance; or tables in which columns and rows are of varying widths and heights. Notice that when you choose Draw Table, you also automatically open the Tables and Borders toolbar. This toolbar provides handy access to tools for applying borders and shading.

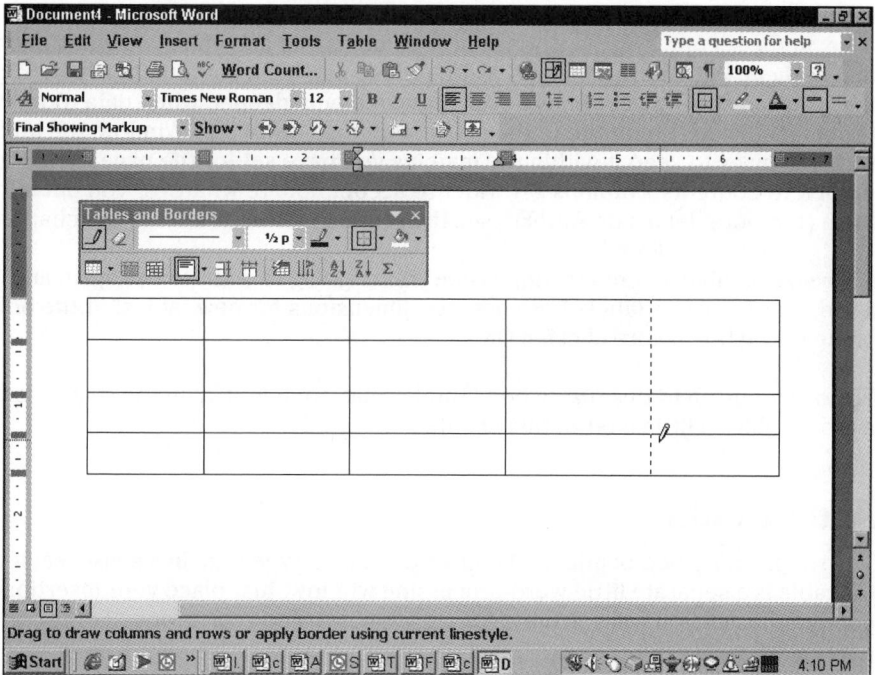

Figure 19-4: Here I've drawn a table with four rows and five columns.

Insert Table

The other way to create a table is to choose Table ⇨ Insert ⇨ Table. This opens the Insert Table dialog box shown in Figure 19-5.

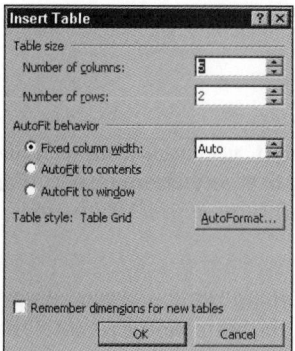

Figure 19-5: Specify the size of the table you want to create in this dialog box.

In the top section, enter the number of rows and columns you want your table to have. In the second section, choose how columns will act when you enter information in them. With a fixed column width (which can be set automatically by Word or that you can specify), columns never get wider, only deeper, when data too wide for the current width is entered in them. If you choose AutoFit to Window, the table's width changes to keep it within the margins you have set for the page. If you choose AutoFit to Contents, columns get wider to accommodate whatever you put into them (for more details on AutoFit, see the section "AutoFit" later in the chapter).

If the size of table you're creating is one you're going to want to use again and again, check the box labeled "Remember dimensions for new tables" at the bottom of the dialog box before clicking OK.

The other button in this dialog box, AutoFormat, we'll look at in the section on formatting tables a little later in this chapter.

Adding data

The simplest method of adding data to a table is to type it in. In a sense, each cell of the table is a separate little word-processing window; just place your insertion point in the cell you want to enter information into and type away.

You can also add data by copying it from elsewhere into the clipboard and then pasting it into your table cells. If you have a lot of data already in tabular form in another Office application, such as Excel or PowerPoint, you don't have to rely on cut and paste or retype it. You can import that table directly into Word as a linked or embedded object.

Cross-Reference For more information on linked and embedded objects and sharing data among Office's various components, see Chapter 11.

Editing and Formatting Tables

Once you have created your table and entered data in it, you may want to make changes. Editing text in a table is the same as editing text anywhere else in Word. You can copy text from place to place, highlight it and type over it or delete it, and so forth.

You can also format text the same way you do in the main body of a document, with one major difference: You can set individual margins, indents, and even tab stops for each cell in a table.

Whenever you click inside a cell, you'll see the same controls that appear in the main document area ruler appear inside a smaller ruler that corresponds to the size of the cell. You can use these controls just as you do in your main document, moving the upper triangular slider at the left to set an indent, clicking on the ruler to create a tab stop, and moving the left-bottom and far-right triangular sliders to set margins (see Figure 19-6).

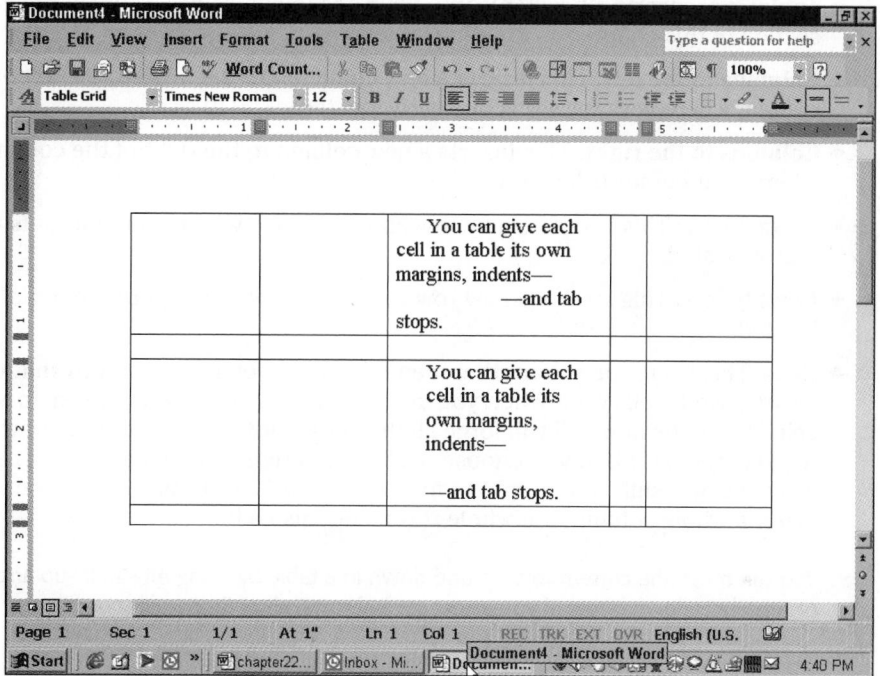

Figure 19-6: You can set the margins, indents, and tab stops individually for each cell in a Word table.

Note   To use a tab stop within a table cell, press Ctrl+Tab instead of just pressing Tab. The latter will move you to the next table cell instead of to the tab stop.

Similarly, you can change fonts and their sizes and styles within each cell just as you do anywhere else in your Word document, using the usual text formatting commands.

In addition to formatting the text within a table, however, you'll probably want to format the table as a whole to give it a unified look or simply to make the information you've entered into it more easily accessible to your audience.

The Table menu

Choose Table and you'll find many commands to help you make your table look just the way you want to. The first three commands, covered in the following sections, let you add or delete cells, rows, columns, or whole tables.

Insert

Choose Table ⇨ Insert and you're presented with a new menu featuring several options:

✦ **Table:** This inserts a new table into your document, as described in the earlier section of this chapter on creating tables.

✦ **Columns to the left:** This inserts a new column into the table to the left of the column where your cursor is currently located.

✦ **Columns to the right:** This inserts a new column to the right of the column where your cursor is located.

✦ **Rows above:** This inserts a new row above the row where your cursor is currently located.

✦ **Rows below:** This inserts a new row below the row where your cursor is located.

✦ **Cells:** This brings up yet another menu that asks you if you want to shift cells down or shift cells right when you insert your new cell. If you choose to shift cells down, the new cell will force all the cells below it in its column down one to make room for it. If you choose to shift cells right, all the cells in the new cell's row will shift to the right to make room for it. You can also choose to insert a whole column or a whole row using this menu.

Tip

You can move the current row up and down in a table by using Alt+Shift+up arrow or Alt+Shift+down arrow. If you select several rows, all of them will move.

Delete

Choose Table ⇨ Delete and you're presented with commands that are essentially the opposite of the Insert commands. You can delete the entire table, or just the row or column where your cursor is currently located. If you choose Table ⇨ Delete ⇨ Cells, you'll see a Delete Cells dialog box just like the Insert Cells dialog box, except instead of being asked if you want to shift the other cells in the column or row down or right, you're asked if you want to shift them up or left.

Note

Insert Cells and Delete Cells work a little differently if you use them with multiple cells selected (see the next section of this chapter). If you choose to shift cells to the right in the Insert Cells dialog box, Word inserts the same number of cells as you've selected and shifts the rows in which they appear to the right. If you choose to shift cells down, however, Word doesn't just insert the number of cells you've selected; it inserts a number of rows equal to the number of rows of cells in your selection. In the Delete Cells dialog box, you can choose only to shift cells left; if you choose to shift cells up, Delete Cells has no effect at all.

Tip

If you select several rows or columns and simply press Delete, the contents of those rows or columns will disappear, but the rows and columns themselves stay put. To delete them without using the menu commands, select them and press the Backspace key or use the Cut command (Ctrl+X).

Select

Table ⇨ Select offers you the same options as Table ⇨ Delete. Click Table to highlight the whole Table for formatting, Column to select the entire column where your cursor is located, Row to select the entire row, or Cell to select the cell where you've placed your cursor.

Tip

You can also select parts of a table with your mouse. To select a cell, triple-click anywhere inside it. To select an entire row, move your mouse pointer to the left edge of the table. Just outside the table boundaries, the pointer will turn into a white arrow pointing back at the row. Click once to select the row. Similarly, to select a column, move your pointer to just outside the table's top edge. Your pointer will turn into a black arrow pointing down at the column. Click once to select the column. The quickest way to select an entire table is to place your insertion point inside it, then press Alt+5.

You can also select a specific range of cells by clicking and dragging from one cell to another. The next section of the Table menu lets you merge and split cells, or even split the entire table.

Merge Cells

Suppose you want to create a single headline that runs across the top of your table, or subheads that cover two or three columns further down inside your table. To do that, you need to combine two or more cells into one larger cell that spans one or more columns or rows.

To combine cells, simply highlight the cells you want to combine into one, and then choose Table ⇨ Merge Cells (see Figure 19-7).

Split Cells

Sometimes, of course, you want to do just the opposite: you want to subdivide an existing cell into two or more smaller cells. To do that, select the cells you want to subdivide and then choose Table ⇨ Split Cells. Choose how many rows and how many columns you want to subdivide the selected cell or cells into. You can choose to split each cell you've selected individually into that many rows or columns, or, by checking Merge cells before split, combine all the selected cells into one large cell that is then subdivided into the number of rows and columns you've specified.

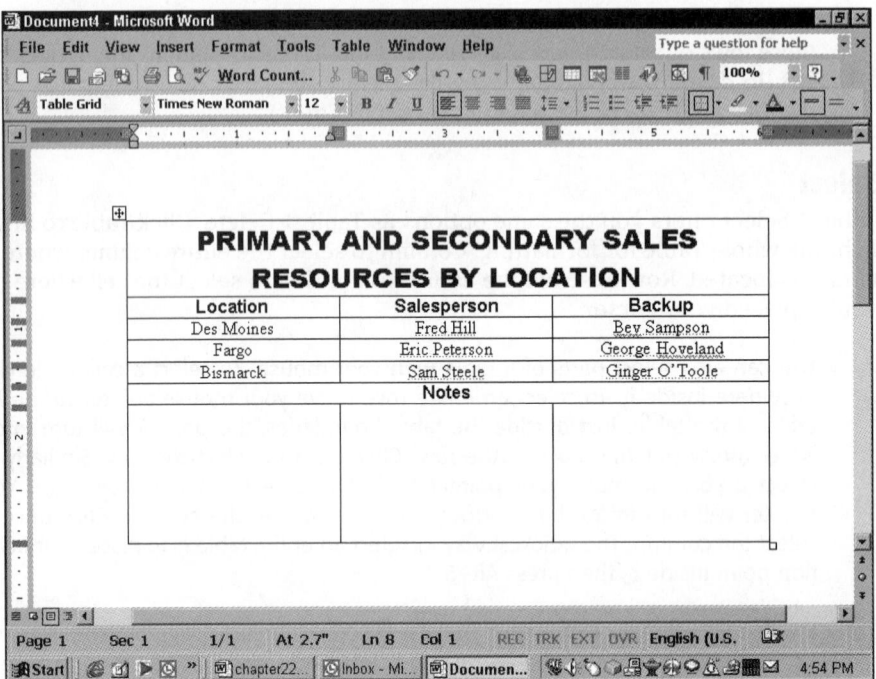

Figure 19-7: Using the Merge Cells command, you can create larger cells within your table's regular grid.

Tip   You can use the Split Cells command to quickly change the number of rows and columns in your whole table. Choose Table ➪ Select ➪ Table to highlight every cell in your table, and then choose Table ➪ Split Cells. Enter the new number of rows and columns you want in your table, making sure Merge cells before split is checked, and then click OK. Your table will instantly change from whatever it was before to the number of rows and columns you've specified.

Tip   Another way to merge or split cells is to use the Draw Table and Eraser tools. To break one cell into two, draw a line across the cell with the Draw Table tool. To merge two cells into one, drag the Eraser tool along the boundary between the two cells.

Split Table

You can turn a single table into two separate tables with the Split Table command. Just place your cursor in the row that you want to be the first row of the bottom table and choose Table ➪ Split Table. The table will split apart above the row you've selected (see Figure 19-8).

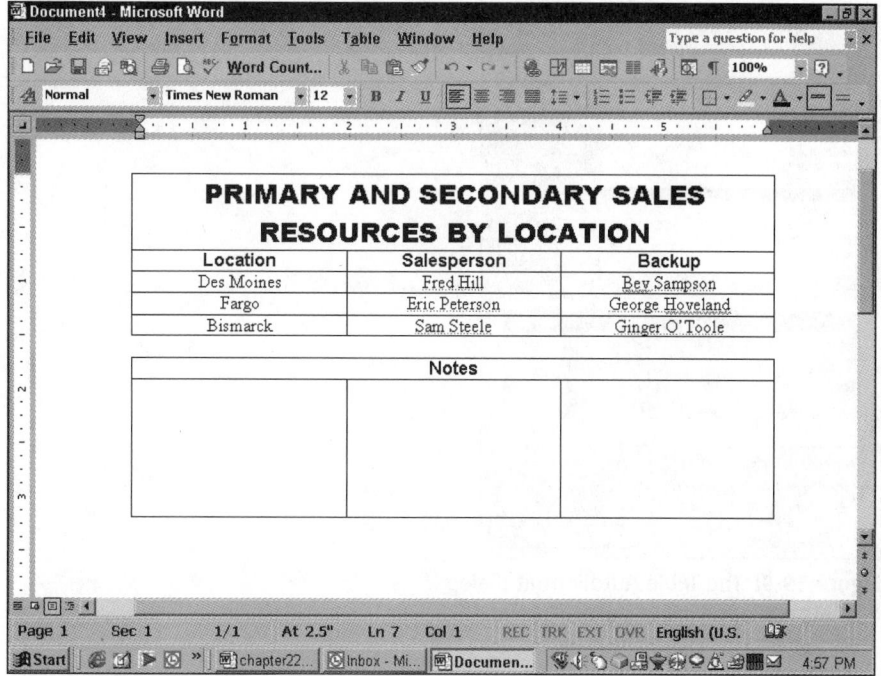

Figure 19-8: Only have one table when you really need two? Use the Split Table command to remedy the situation.

Tip   The cursor, after the Split Table command, is between the two tables. This enables you to enter text between the tables. If you've created a table as the first thing in a new document and decide you want text to appear above it, place your cursor in the top row of the table and use the Split Table command to make room for the text.

Using automatic formatting with tables

Also within the Table menu are several options to apply automatic formatting to Tables. Automatic formatting can save you time and effort and ensure a consistent, professional look.

AutoFormat

AutoFormat automatically applies shading, borders, colors, and other interesting formatting elements to your table. You can apply AutoFormat to a table either when you first create it (by clicking AutoFormat on the Insert Table dialog box) or at any time by placing your cursor anywhere within the table and choosing Table ⇨ Table AutoFormat (see Figure 19-9).

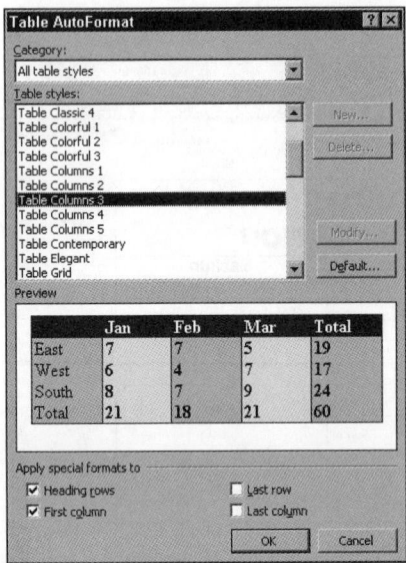

Figure 19-9: The Table AutoFormat dialog box lets you apply all or parts of several predesigned formats to your table.

Choose the format you want from the Table Styles list; the Preview box will show you exactly what it will look like. You can choose whether or not to accept any special formatting that might be included in the design for the heading (top) row, first column, last column, or last row by checking the boxes in the area labeled "Apply special formats to".

Applying an AutoFormat won't change the size of your table unless you check AutoFit; if you do, your table's columns and rows may change to fit snugly around the text they contain.

Cross-Reference   See the next section of this chapter for more details on how AutoFit works.

Once you're happy with your choices, click OK to see your new table.

AutoFit

AutoFit, under Table AutoFormat on the Table menu, determines how rows and columns change to accommodate the text you enter into cells. AutoFit offers five options:

✦ **AutoFit to Contents:** If you choose this option, your table will automatically adjust itself to wrap snugly around the text entered in cells.

✦ **AutoFit to Window:** If you choose this option, your table will adjust its width to fit within the margins you have set for the page.

✦ **Fixed Column Widths:** If you choose this option, your column widths will remain the same and text will automatically wrap when it comes to the end of the column, instead of making the column expand.

✦ **Distribute Rows Evenly:** This makes all rows in your table the same height — the same height as the tallest row in your table — which means your table may suddenly get much taller.

✦ **Distribute Columns Evenly:** This makes all columns the same width by subdividing the width of the column evenly. In other words, while Distribute Rows Evenly makes your table higher, Distribute Columns Evenly keeps the column the same width and makes some rows wider and some narrower.

Heading Rows Repeat

This command is useful if your table is going to span more than a single page. To use it, select the top row or rows of your table and then choose Table ➪ Heading Rows Repeat. If your table jumps to another page, the top rows you selected will be displayed again as heading rows.

Other Table menu commands

The remaining commands on the Table Menu are Convert, Sort, Formula, Hide Gridlines, and Table Properties. We'll look at Table Properties, Sort, and Formula in detail in a moment.

Convert

Convert allows you to turn a table into text, or text into a table.

Table to text

To convert a table to text, follow these steps:

1. Select the portion of the table that you want to convert to text.

2. Choose Table ➪ Convert ➪ Table to Text.

3. From the dialog box, choose what you want to use to separate the items from the table once it's converted into text: paragraph marks, tabs, commas, or any other character you specify.

4. If any of the cells in the table you're converting contains a nested table, check Convert Nested Tables; if you'd like to keep the nested table as a table, don't check it.

5. Click OK.

Text to table

Convert also allows you to turn text into a table. To do so, follow these steps:

1. Highlight the text you want to convert.

2. Choose Table ⇨ Convert ⇨ Text to Table.

3. A dialog box almost identical to the usual Insert Table dialog box appears (see Figure 19-10), with one difference: At the bottom, you have to tell Word what character it should look for to figure out how to break the text into table entries. Also, note that while you can choose the number of columns, you can't choose the number of rows — it's set automatically. That's because the total number of cells created has to match the number of entries that Word will form from the converted text.

4. Click OK.

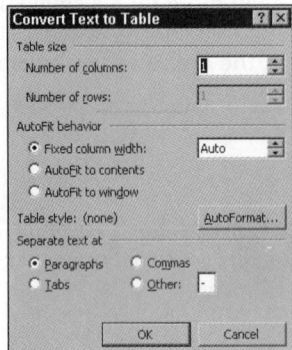

Figure 19-10: You can instantly place text into a table by using the Convert Text to Table dialog box.

Hide Gridlines

Choose this command to hide the gridlines that Word otherwise provides to outline your table's cells. Click Show Gridlines to bring the gridlines back.

Note   These gridlines are not the same as the borders you can apply to tables (outline borders are used by default on new tables — unless you change these borders, this command will appear to have no effect). Also note that this command applies to all tables in the document.

Table Properties

Table Properties, at the bottom of the Table menu, is one of the most powerful commands the menu has to offer. It opens a dialog box that lets you handily specify most of your table's characteristics. The Table Properties dialog box has four tabs, as described here.

Table

Here you can specify three major properties of your table as a whole (see Figure 19-11):

✦ **Size:** Set the preferred width of your table, in inches or a percent of the page width. Note that this width may change later as you add or edit entries to the table, depending on your AutoFit choices.

✦ **Alignment:** Set your table against the left margin, centered on the page, or against the right margin, or enter a specific amount for it to be indented. (Note that the Indent from Left command is available only if you choose left alignment.)

✦ **Text wrapping:** Choose None if you want text to appear only above or below your table; choose Around if you'd like text to wrap around the table on the page. Around can sometimes improve the look of your page, particularly if your table is small. If you choose Around, click Positioning to detail exactly how you want text to relate to your table; options including horizontal and vertical positioning relative to margins, columns, paragraphs, or the page as a whole, and how much white space you want to add around the table. You can also choose whether to let the table move with the text or allow text to overlap it.

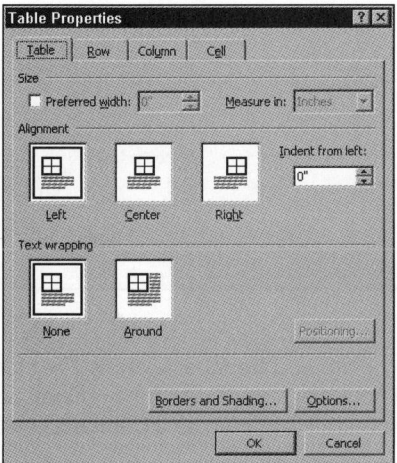

Figure 19-11: The Table tab of the Table Properties dialog box lets you position your table just where you want it on the page.

Row

Use the Row tab (see Figure 19-12) to specify the height of a range of rows (if you've highlighted several of them) or individual rows (if you haven't). Here's how the options work:

✦ **Size:** Word tells you which row or range of rows you're working with. Specify the height you want the row or rows to be and whether you want the row(s) to be exactly that height, or if that's a minimum measurement.

✦ **Options:** You can choose to allow or disallow the row to break across pages. If you're working with the first row, you can choose to make it a header row that will repeat on each page the table takes up.

✦ **Previous Row or Next Row:** Click here to adjust the next row above or below the currently selected row or rows.

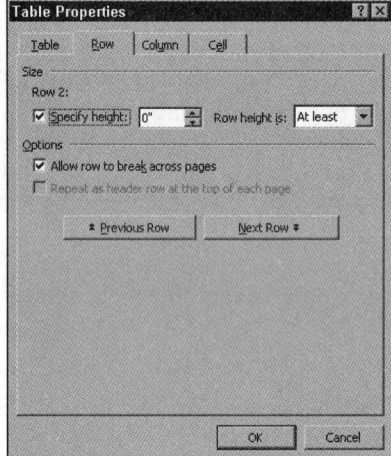

Figure 19-12: Specify row height, and other options, from the Row tab of the Table Properties dialog box.

Column

The Column tab looks very much like the Row tab and behaves exactly the same way, except you specify width, not height. There are no options for breaking across pages, and you can specify width not only in inches but also as a percentage of the total table width.

Cell

The Cell tab (see Figure 19-13) lets you specify the preferred width for a selected cell or cells. Again, you can specify width in inches or as a percentage of the total table width. Below that, you can choose how to align text within the cell: flush against the top, centered vertically, or flush against the bottom.

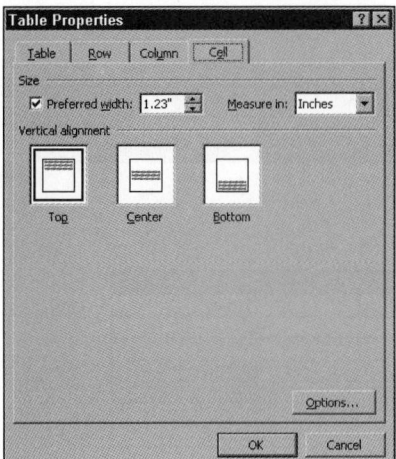

Figure 19-13: Control the size of your table's cells, and how text fits within them, with these controls.

Finally, clicking Options brings up a small dialog box in which you can set the cell's margins (or choose to leave them the same as for the rest of the table) and set whether to wrap text when it gets too long or to squeeze or widen it to make it fit the width of the cell.

Using Sort

If you're planning to sort, sum, or otherwise manipulate a lot of data, you're better off doing it in Excel than in Word. But if all you need are some simple calculations or you want to create an alphabetically sorted list of names, Word's tables can probably do it for you.

To use Sort, make sure your cursor is inside the table you want to sort and then choose Table ⇨ Sort. Word automatically selects the entire table. (The table in Figure 19-14 is unsorted.) After choosing Table ⇨ Sort, the Sort dialog box appears, looking like the one shown in Figure 19-15.

Word lets you sort your table in three ways: by text, by number, or by date (depending on what type of data is entered). In the "Sort by" area, you choose which column you primarily want to sort, whether to sort by text, number, or date, and whether to sort in ascending order or descending order. In the two "Then by" areas, you enter the criteria you want to apply to settle any ties, where the initial criteria are identical for two or more entries. You should choose to use the data in one of your remaining columns to decide which of the tied entries comes first. Then choose whether to sort the tied entries in ascending or descending order.

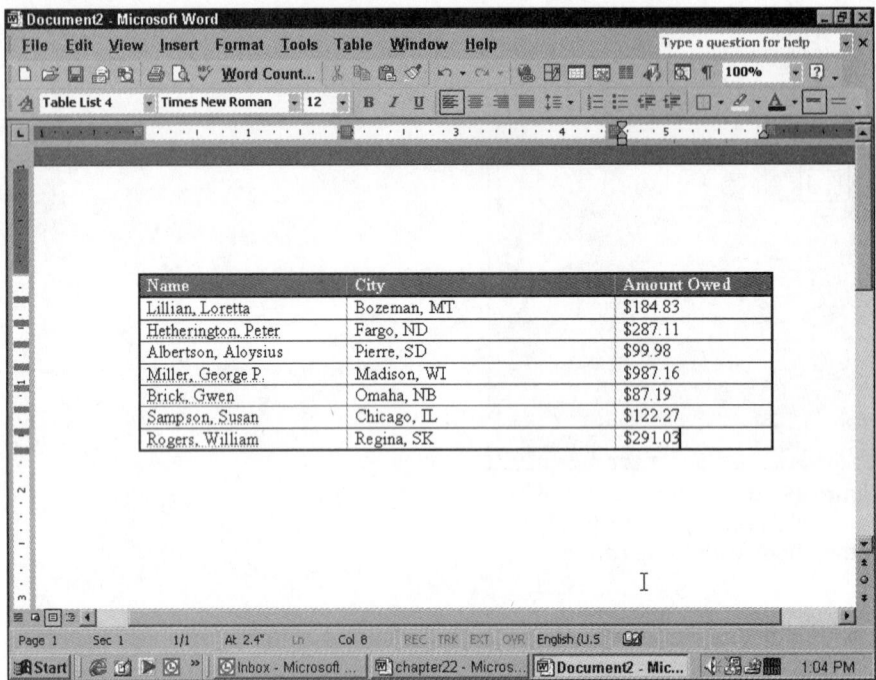

Figure 19-14: Here's a table in dire need of sorting.

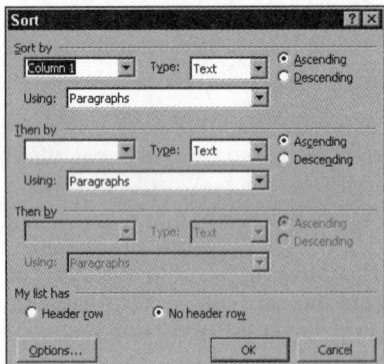

Figure 19-15: Here are the options Word provides for sorting tables.

At the bottom, indicate if your table has a header row or not. If you indicate that it does, the entries in the top row will not be sorted with the others. Also, columns will be indicated by the entries associated with them in the header row, instead of just being listed as Column 1, Column 2, and so forth as they otherwise are.

When you've made the selections you want, click OK. The table from Figure 19-14, sorted in ascending order by amount owed, is shown in Figure 19-16.

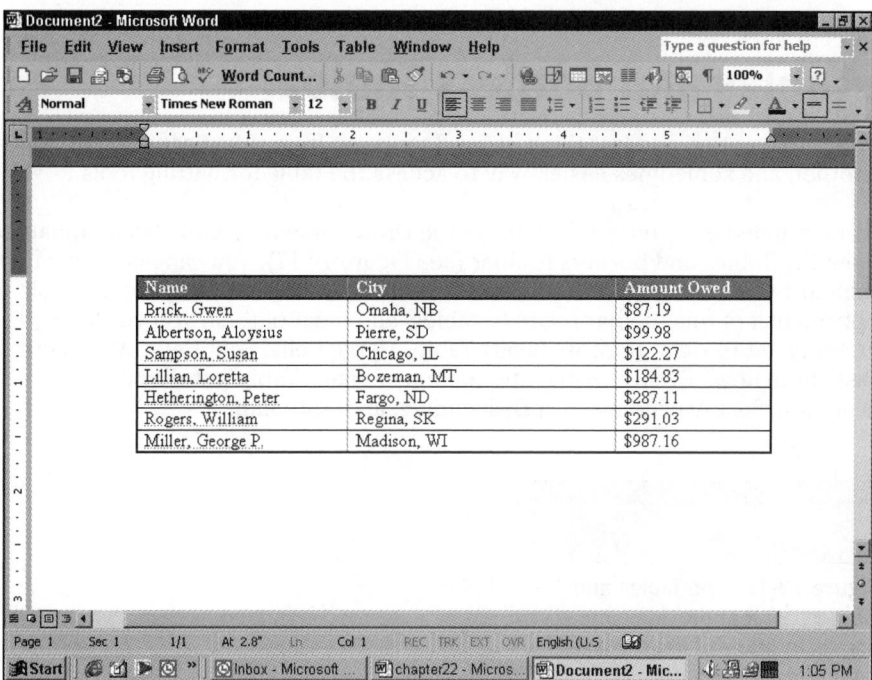

Figure 19-16: The Sort command can quickly make sense of a complicated and convoluted list.

Click Options to fine-tune the sorting command. For example, you can specify what language Word should use to sort with and whether the sorting order should be case sensitive.

Sorting Tips and Tricks

To sort a single column without affecting the columns on either side of it, first highlight the column and then choose Table ⇨ Sort and click Options. Check the box marked "Sort column only", and then return to the main Sort dialog box and choose your criteria as usual. Click OK. Only the selected column will be sorted.

You can also sort a text list that isn't in a table with the Table ⇨ Sort command, provided each item in the list ends with a paragraph mark. Highlight the list and then choose Table ⇨ Sort. A dialog box will open; choose ascending or descending order and whether you're sorting text, numbers, or dates, and then click OK.

Note   Word also enables you to perform calculations on the entries in your table's cells using formulas; however, Microsoft itself, in its Help files, suggests that if you're going to be performing calculations, you're much better off doing it in Excel.

The Tables and Borders Toolbar

I want to mention one last thing before I move on from this discussion of tables: another, and sometimes easier, way to access the table formatting tools.

As mentioned early on, when you use the Draw Table tool, you also automatically open the Tables and Borders toolbar (see Figure 19-17). You can also bring up this toolbar by choosing View ⇨ Toolbars ⇨ Tables and Borders. Most of the tools on the bottom half of this toolbar relate to tables, and most of them you've already looked at. From left to right, they are Insert Table, Merge Cells, Split Cells, Alignment, Distribute Rows Evenly, Distribute Columns Evenly, Table AutoFormat, Text Direction, Sort Ascending, Sort Descending, and AutoSum.

Figure 19-17: The Tables and Borders toolbar provides one-click access to many of the most useful table-formatting tools.

The Text Direction command

One of the commands I haven't yet looked at is the Text Direction command, which is also available by right-clicking on a table. Text Direction lets you run text vertically on the page instead of horizontally. To use it, highlight the text you want to apply it to, or simply place your cursor inside the cell where you want it to apply and click the Text Direction button. The text will move from horizontal to vertical, with what was at the left margin now at the top. Click the button again and the text will remain vertical, but what was at the left margin when the text was horizontal is now at the bottom. Click the button a third time and the text returns to its original horizontal position.

If you choose this command from the right-click pop-up menu instead, you'll get a dialog box that shows you the three positions and illustrates what each looks like to help you make your choice.

Using AutoSum

Another useful command on this toolbar is AutoSum. This calculates and displays the sum of the values in the cells above or to the left of the cell containing the insertion point.

Building a Table of Contents

Another organizational tool Word offers is an automated method of creating a table of contents. A table of contents (TOC) is very similar to an outline in that it displays the information contained within a document in the form of a series of headings, usually arranged in a hierarchical format. In Word, however, the big difference between an outline and a table of contents is that the table of contents also lists the page in the document on which the information can be found.

Creating and formatting a TOC

You could create a table of contents by printing an outline, printing the whole document, and then figuring out which page the various headings fall on. Fortunately, you don't have to. Word will automatically build a table of contents for you, and let you format it as you see fit. Here are the steps to create a table of contents:

1. Apply a consistent series of paragraph styles to your document. The simplest ones to use are the same ones you use to create an outline: Heading 1, Heading 2, Heading 3, and so on. If you haven't used heading styles, however, you can still build a TOC as long as you use a different style in your document for each level you want to show in the TOC: chapter heads, section heads, and so forth.

2. Place your insertion point where you want the TOC to be inserted into your document, then choose Insert ➪ Reference ➪ Index and Tables and click on the Table of Contents tab (see Figure 19-18).

 **Tip**
The Table of Contents takes up space in your document — which means it affects the page numbers of everything else in your document. In other words, with a two-page TOC at the front of your document, something that was originally on Page 3 is now on Page 5. To avoid that, insert the TOC at the end of your document.

3. The window at the left shows you what your TOC will look like in a printed document; the window at the right shows you what your TOC will look like in an HTML document. In Print Preview, by default, page numbers are displayed and right-aligned, and a tab leader is already assigned. You can remove the page numbers and the right alignment, and remove or change the tab leader, as you see fit. (In the HTML version, your TOC entries are direct links to the appropriate pages.)

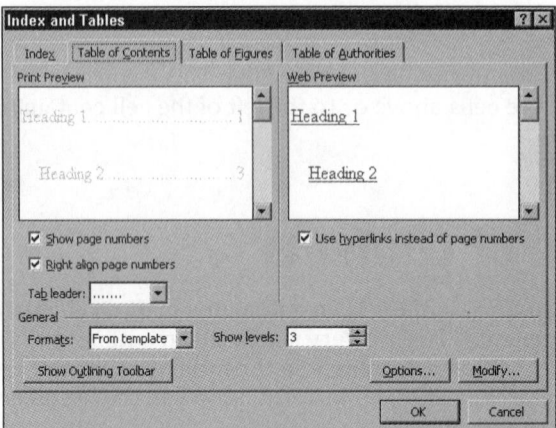

Figure 19-18: The Index and Tables dialog box includes controls for designing and formatting a table of contents for your document.

4. By default, your TOC is formatted in the way your current template calls for, which is pretty basic if you're using the Normal template. Word offers you a list of other formats to choose from in the Formats drop-down list. Select each to see it previewed, and then choose the one you want. Also, choose how many levels you want in your TOC. If you're using the From template option in the Formats drop-down list, you can click the Modify button to see all the available TOC styles in the current template, and choose the one you want to use.

5. Click Options to open the Table of Contents Options dialog box, which lists all the currently available styles and shows you which ones Word is currently looking for to include in the TOC. By default, TOC level 1 is assigned to paragraphs with Header 1 style, TOC level 2 to those with Header 2, and so on. If you outlined your document in the usual way, these default options should work well for your table of contents. If you didn't, however, you can scroll through the list of styles to find the ones that you did apply to your headings and indicate which level of the TOC you'd like items bearing those styles to appear as. Type the TOC level you'd like to assign to it in the space next to each style's name.

6. Click OK to return to the Index and Tables dialog box.

7. Click OK to insert the TOC into your document (see Figure 19-19).

Keeping your TOC current

The entries in the table of contents are built using field codes. This is helpful because as headings and page numbers change due to editing of the document, you can keep the TOC current simply by updating the field codes. To do so, right-click on any entry in the TOC and choose Update Field. In the little dialog box that appears, choose whether you want to update the page numbers alone or the page numbers and the TOC entries' names, and then click OK.

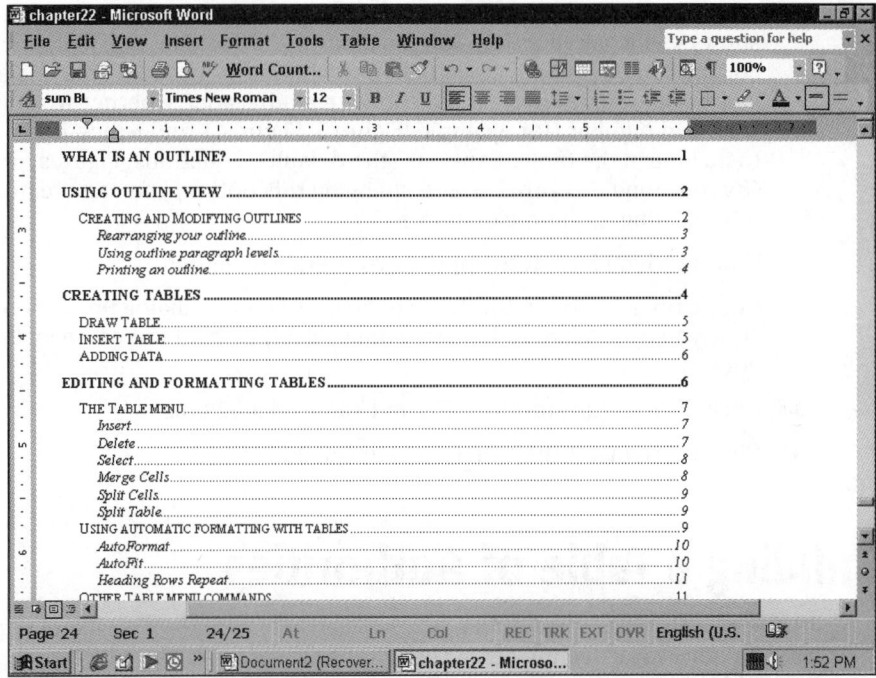

Figure 19-19: A newly inserted table of contents looks something like this. This example uses the Formal template.

Cross-Reference For more information on editing, formatting, and updating field codes, see Chapter 21.

Building a Table of Figures

A table of figures is a list of all the figures, equations, or illustrations in a document. Building one is very similar to building a table of contents: Word looks for a set of elements that all have the same style (the Bullet style, for instance; another common choice is the style applied to captions, as each figure is probably accompanied by one) and places them in a table linked to the pages they appear on. To create a table of figures (TOF), follow these steps:

1. Consistently apply styles to your figures or their captions.

2. Place your insertion point where you want the TOF to appear and choose Insert ➪ Reference ➪ Index and Tables, and then click on the Table of Figures tab.

3. In the resulting dialog box, essentially identical to the TOC dialog box, Word shows you what your TOF will look like in print and in an HTML document. For the print version, you can choose whether or not to display page numbers and if you want them right-aligned with a tab leader, whether to include a label and number (for example, Figure 3, Figure 4), and which items you want to include in the table: Captions (the default), Equations, Figures, or Tables. (By repeating this process and changing this option, you can create separate tables listing each type of item.)

4. Choose which format to apply to your table of figures.

5. Click Options to open the Table of Figures Options dialog box. Choose the style you want Word to look for when selecting the items to be included in your TOF.

6. Click OK to return to the Index and Tables dialog box.

7. Click OK to insert the TOF into your document.

Building a Table of Authorities

A table of authorities is used primarily in legal documents — it's a list of references made to other legal documents. Although the process is essentially the same as building a table of contents or a table of figures, marking the citations you want to add to the table is a little more complicated than simply assigning each the same style.

Marking citations

To mark citations, follow these steps:

1. Select the first full citation.

2. Choose Insert ➪ Reference ➪ Index and Tables, then select the Table of Authorities tab.

3. Click Mark Citation. This opens the Mark Citation dialog box shown in Figure 19-20.

4. In the Selected Text box, edit the long citation until it looks the way you want it to appear in the table of authorities. (You can also format it using keyboard shortcuts such as Ctrl+B to bold it, Ctrl+I to italicize it, and so on.)

5. Select the category that applies to the citation from the Category drop-down list.

6. In the Short Citation box, enter any short versions of the citation that appear in the document, so Word can search for them.

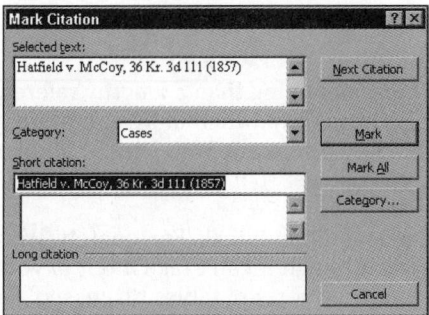

Figure 19-20: Mark your citations using this dialog box before creating your table of authorities.

7. To mark a single citation, click Mark; to mark all the citations that match both the long and short versions you've just entered, click Mark All.

8. To move on to the next marked citation in the document, click Next Citation. To mark another citation, return to the document, highlight it, and then repeat the steps above.

9. Once you've marked all your citations, click Close.

Inserting your TOA

You can insert a table of authorities (TOA) just as you would a table of contents or a table of figures. Place your insertion point where you want the TOA to appear; then, as before, open the Index and Tables dialog box. From the Table of Authorities tab, perform the following steps:

1. Click the category of citation you want to include in your TOA, or click All to include them all.

2. Choose the format you want to use from the Formats list box.

3. If you want to replace any instance of five or more page references to the same citation with the text "passim," make sure the "Use passim" checkbox is checked.

4. If you want to keep long citations' original formatting in the TOA, make sure "Keep original formatting" is checked.

5. Click OK.

Creating an Index

Personally, I can think of few things more annoying than a lengthy reference article or book without an index—especially these days, when more and more people are accustomed to the search function built into so many Web sites. A good index isn't as handy as that, but it's as close as you can get to it in a print document.

Creating an index by hand is a tedious and difficult task. Fortunately, Word can simplify the procedure for you somewhat (although it can't take it out of your hands altogether). Just as with building the various sorts of tables discussed earlier, Word does require you to first mark the words or phrases that are to be included in the index. You can either do this one word or phrase at a time, or you can use a concordance file to semiautomate the process.

By marking words and phrases

Here are the steps to create an index by marking individual words and phrases:

1. Start at the very beginning (a very good place to start). Locate the first word or phrase you want to include in the index.

2. Highlight it, and then choose Insert ➪ Reference ➪ Index and Tables.

3. Click the Index tab and choose Mark Entry. This opens the Mark Index Entry dialog box (see Figure 19-21). The word or phrase you highlighted appears in the Main Entry box. (You can also get to the Mark Index Entry dialog box faster by pressing Alt+Shift+X.)

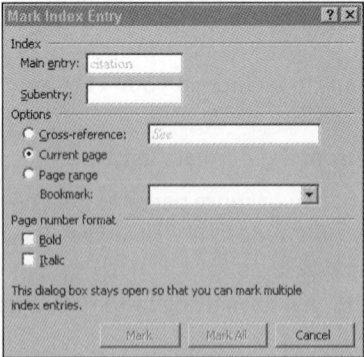

Figure 19-21: Build an index word by word using the Mark Index Entry dialog box.

4. If you want to add another word or phrase as a subentry under the main entry, type it into the Subentry box.

5. Sometimes, instead of giving a page number, you want to point readers to a different entry in the index. If that's the case, click the Cross-reference radio button and enter the appropriate text in the "Cross-reference" box.

6. By default, Word inserts the page number of the highlighted word or phrase into the index. This is what the "Current page" option does.

7. If you'd prefer to have Word insert a range of pages instead of a single page number, click "Page range". (You can only do this if you've already bookmarked the range; you select the range by choosing the correct bookmark from the Bookmark drop-down list.)

8. If you'd like page numbers to be in bold or italic, click the appropriate "Page number format" checkboxes.

9. Once you're satisfied with your choices, click Mark to mark the current selection as you've indicated, or click Mark All to mark every instance of the highlighted text within the document.

10. Repeat this procedure with every word or phrase you want to add to the index.

Using a concordance file

The other method of creating an index, with the use of a concordance file, is particularly useful if many of the documents you create contain the same keywords or phrases. If you're already looking for a tool on any of the Word toolbars to help you create a concordance file, you can stop looking: It doesn't exist. A concordance file is simply a separate Word file set up as a two-column table.

Creating a concordance file

To create a concordance file, follow these steps:

1. Create a two-column table.

2. In the left column, enter the text you want Word to search for and mark as an index entry.

3. In the right column, enter what you want to appear in the index for that entry. You can create a subentry by typing the main entry followed by a colon, and then the text for the subentry.

4. Do the same for every other word or phrase you want Word to search for and create an index entry for.

5. When you're done, save the concordance file. (You can use any name you want.)

Marking index entries

Once you have a concordance file, you can use it to quickly mark index entries in any document. To do so, do the following:

1. Open the document you want to index.

2. Choose Insert ⇨ Reference ⇨ Index and Tables; click the Index tab.

3. Choose AutoMark.

4. Word shows you the standard Open File dialog box; find the concordance file and then click Open. Word searches for the words and phrases you entered in the left-hand column and marks them as you indicated in the right-hand column.

Building your index

Once you've marked all the entries for your index, either one at a time or by using a concordance file, you're ready to create your index:

1. Place your insertion point wherever you want the index to appear (typically at the end of the document, but it doesn't have to be).

2. Choose Insert ⇨ Reference ⇨ Index and Tables.

3. In the resulting dialog box, select a format for your index from the Format drop-down list. You can see what each format looks like in the Print Preview box.

4. Fine-tune the formatting with the other controls: you can right-align the page numbers and add a tab leader, change the number of columns used to display the index, and choose to indent subentries or simply run them straight on after the main entry.

5. Once you're satisfied with your formatting choices, click OK. Your index will be automatically inserted into your document in a new section of its own.

Updating your index

As with the three types of tables (table of contents, table of figures, and table of authorities), what you really end up with is a series of field codes, which you can update at any time to reflect the changing page numbers of the words and phrases you've marked as index entries. Just place the insertion point anywhere in the index and press F9, or right-click and choose Update Field from the pop-up menu.

✦   ✦   ✦

Working with Others on Word Documents

As do the other Office applications (though to a greater extent), Word has bunches of features designed to facilitate document creation, review, and revision by teams of writers, editors, and know-it-all bosses. Many of these features are equally useful for individuals who want to keep track of the changes made to a document over time. With Office XP, these features are easier than ever to use.

Collaborating with Many Users on a Single Document

There are two main components to collaborating with other users on a document in Word: comments and the track changes feature. But first, I want to say a few words about the Reviewing Toolbar, which you'll use to work with both tools.

The Reviewing toolbar

The Reviewing toolbar (see Figure 20-1) collects buttons pertaining to document review and group document development. Word displays the Reviewing toolbar automatically when you edit a comment, but you can choose View ➪ Toolbars to activate it at any time. Buttons on the toolbar give fast-track access to commands for viewing comments and changes, adding comments, tracking changes, and accepting or rejecting those changes.

Figure 20-1: Activate the Reviewing toolbar for quick access to commands used in collaborating on documents.

Inserting comments

When you hand a paper document to someone for a critique, you expect to get the pages back all covered with questions, corrections, suggestions, and personal reactions. There's nowhere to attach a paper clip or sticky note to a Word document, but Word's Comments feature serves the same purpose, without all the smudges and wrinkles.

To insert a comment, select the text you want to comment on and then choose Insert ⇨ Comment or press Alt+Ctrl+M (if you don't select text first, Word applies the comment to the word containing the insertion point).

What happens next depends on which view you're using. If you're in Normal view, you can type the comment in the pane Word opens for that purpose at the bottom of the window (see Figure 20-2).

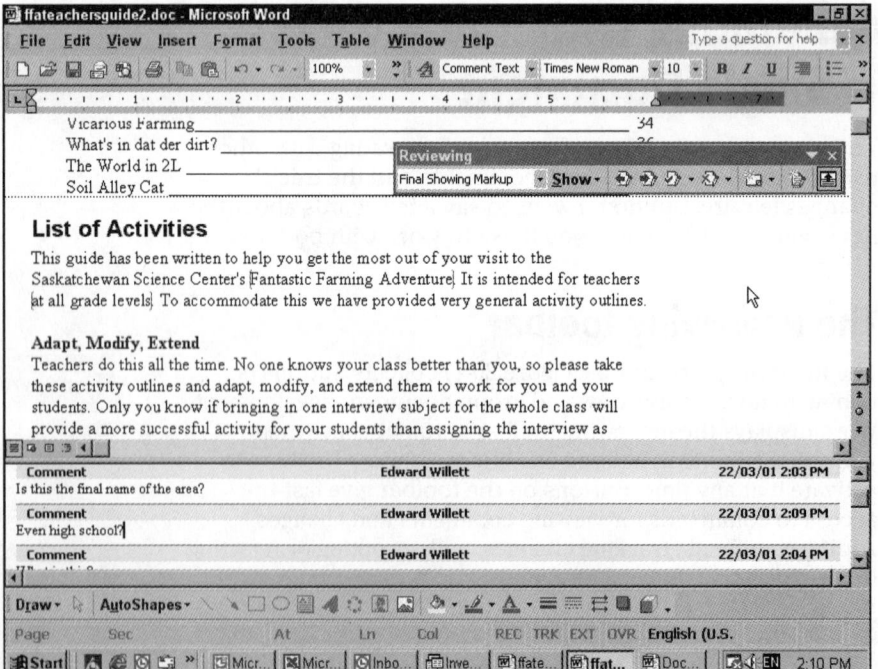

Figure 20-2: Type your comment into the window Word opens for you at the bottom of the screen.

Word indicates the comment with brackets around the text to which the comment is attached. To read the comment itself, just hold the mouse pointer over the text to which the comment is attached, and comment itself appears in a ScreenTip box. The ScreenTip also lists the reviewer's name for reference. Figure 20-3 shows an example.

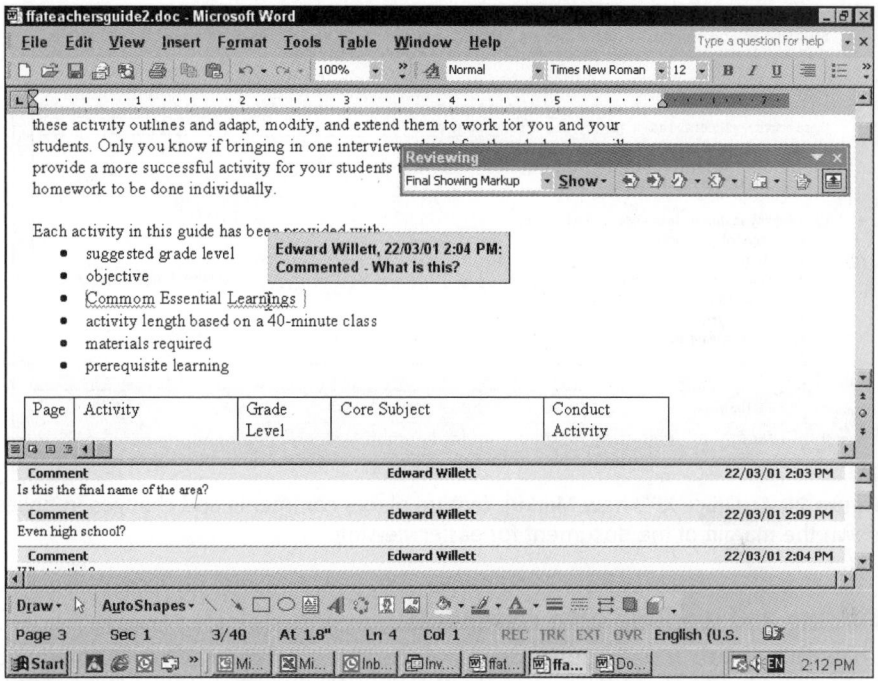

Figure 20-3: Here's a sample comment displayed as a ScreenTip over the text it refers to.

Note You can record spoken comments if your computer has a sound card with a microphone, and you can write them by hand if you're set up for pen input. See Chapter 4 for info on using voice and handwriting recognition with Office.

New Feature If you're in Print Layout or Web Layout View, comments are displayed in boxes, like the speech balloons of cartoons, down the right margin of the document (see Figure 20-4). A line is drawn from the comment box to the text it refers to. When you insert a new comment, you type it directly into one of these boxes.

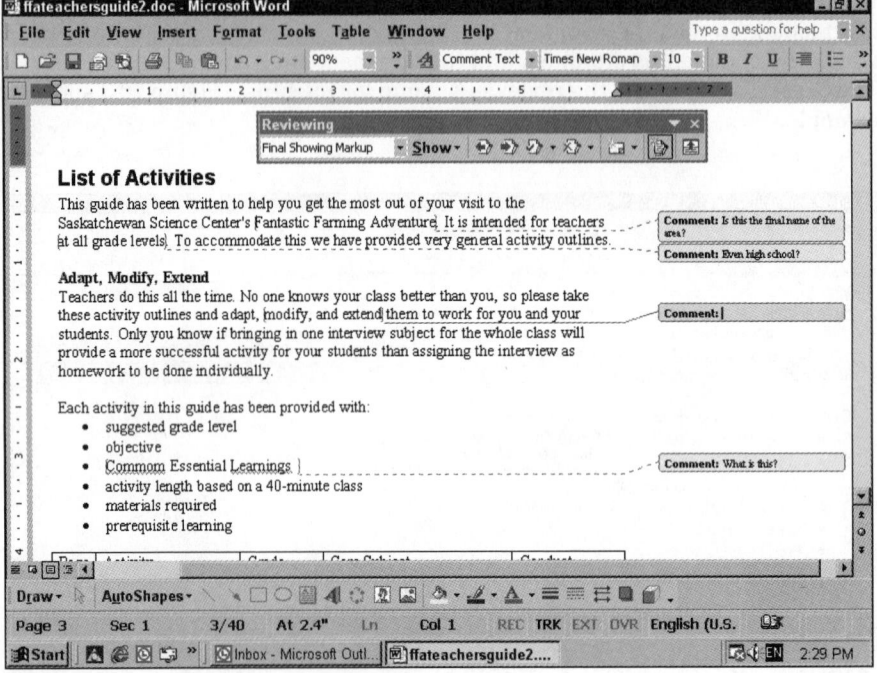

Figure 20-4: Office XP's new Markup feature places comments and changes in boxes down the margin of the document for easier viewing.

Finding and working with comments

To jump instantly from comment to comment, use the Browse Object command (described in Chapter 17), or click the Previous Comment and Next Comment buttons on the Reviewing toolbar.

Alternatively, you can open the comment by right-clicking the comment mark and choosing Edit Comment from the shortcut menu or clicking the Reviewing Pane button on the Reviewing toolbar. After the pane is open, you can scroll through all the comments in the document.

Note   You can view comments in the Markup style you see in Print Layout and in the Reviewing Pane at the same time; opening the Reviewing Pane doesn't effect the view in the main window.

To display only the comments of a particular comment maker, choose that person from the Show ➪ Reviewers list on the Reviewing toolbar.

You can edit a comment in the comment pane or in one of the Markup boxes, of course, but you can also change character or paragraph formatting, directly — perhaps to add highlighting — or by applying styles. By default, Word applies the Comment Text paragraph style to comments. (By the way, comment marks receive the Comment Reference character style.) To delete a comment, right-click in the text it pertains to or in its Markup box and select Delete Comment from the short-cut menu, or left-click it and choose Reject Change/Delete Comment button on the Reviewing toolbar.

Printing comments

Comments normally don't print, but you can get them onto paper by choosing "Document showing markup" from the "Print what:" drop-down list on the main Print dialog box. Word prints the comment marks (and all other hidden text) where they belong in the document, and it prints the comments themselves at the end of the document, beginning on a separate page.

Changing identifying information for comments

Word displays comments with the name and initials of the person who made them. This information comes from the User Information tab of the Tools ➪ Options dialog box. If someone else uses the same computer to comment on the document, that person should change the User Information so Word can keep track of who made which comments. Better yet, each person using the PC should have his or her own Windows user profile. That way, each person's user information is automatically activated at logon while activating Windows and starting Word.

Reviewing documents

When you work with somebody else on the same document, each of you needs to know when changes have been made, and by whom. Word's Track Changes command (select Tools ➪ Track Changes or click the Track Changes button on the Reviewing Toolbar) fits the bill.

You can have Word identify changes made to a document in two main ways: by turning on the Track Changes command, so changes are recorded while the document is being edited, or by comparing the current document to another version. With either approach, changes are marked in the document the same way.

Tip When you print a document containing tracked changes, the changes can appear in the printout if you choose Document showing markup from the Print what list in the Print dialog box.

Tracking changes during editing

With Track Changes turned on, Word displays changes made to the text in several ways. In the text itself, added text appears underlined and in a different color. If you're in Normal view, deleted text appears struck-through; if you're in Print or Web Layout view, deleted text is indicated by Markup boxes along the right margin (see Figure 20-5). If you turn on the Reviewing Pane, you also see all the changes listed there.

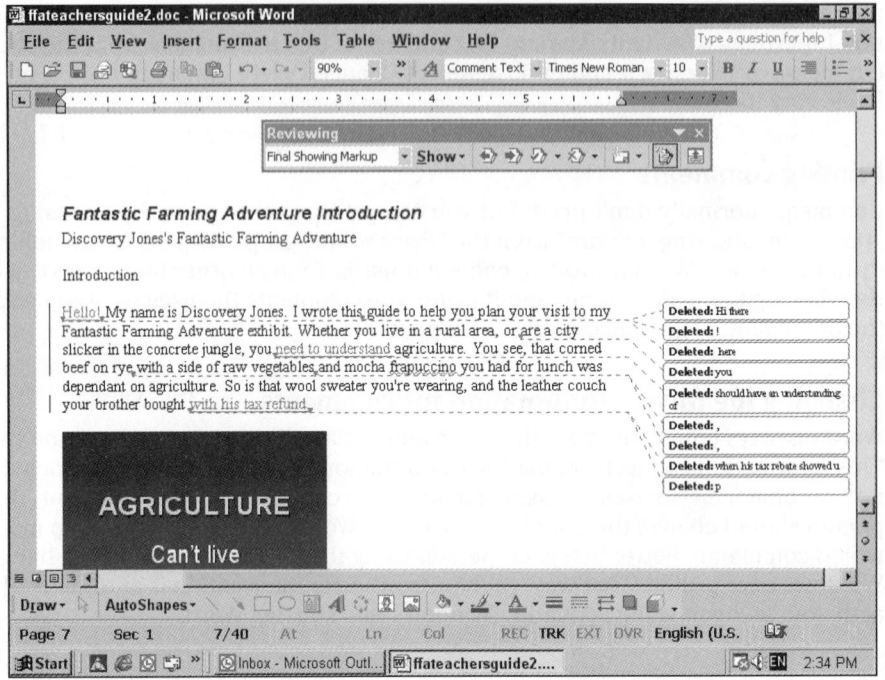

Figure 20-5: Changes to text are marked both in the text and (in Print Layout or Web Layout view) in Markup boxes down the right side of the document.

Note   Word displays a little box showing who made a change when you point at the change with the mouse.

Changing the way changes are displayed

If you care to, you can change the defaults governing tracked changes on the Track Changes tab on the Tools ➪ Options dialog box. Good reasons to change these settings include the following:

✦ **To minimize distracting colors:** Letting Word pick the color ensures that each reviewer's changes get a unique color. If the riot of color blows your mind, select a specific color to use for all changes. You can still see who made the changes by holding the mouse pointer over a section until a ScreenTip appears (the author of each change is also listed in the Reviewing Pane).

✦ **To track formatting changes:** By default, formatting changes are "marked" in ordinary text. Select a different color, mark, or both to see them.

✦ **To change the location of that vertical line indicating changed lines:**
Alternatives to the default (Left Border) include None, Right Border, and
Outside Border. The last choice places the line in the left margin of even-
numbered pages and in the right margin of odd-numbered pages, but only if
you have set up different odd and even pages in the Page Setup dialog box. In
Normal view, the line always appears on the left.

Hiding and displaying changes

Sometimes you need to work with a document containing many tracked changes
without being distracted by Word's on-screen marking of additions and deletions.
You can turn off the display of tracked changes while Word continues to track new
changes you make. Open the Show menu on the Reviewing Toolbar and uncheck
the items you don't want displayed—Comments, Insertions and Deletions, and/or
Formatting.

To hide all changes at once, choose View ➪ Markup. To show changes again, choose
View ➪ Markup again.

Note   You can still see any changes and comments in the Reviewing Pane if you turn it
on, even if they're not visible in the text.

Accepting and rejecting changes

It's all well and good to keep track of the changes made to a document, but eventually the moment of truth arrives: Which changes are you going to keep?

I'll leave the tough decisions to you, but the mechanics are simple: Using the
Reviewing toolbar, click the Next or Previous button to locate a change. Inspect
the changed text and then click the Accept Change button to confirm the change
or the Reject Change button to rescind it.

Note   When you accept a deletion, the text marked as deleted disappears from your
document. The same is true when you reject an insertion.

For more options, click the downward-pointing arrows to the right of the Accept
and Reject buttons. Now you have the option to Accept or Reject All Changes in
Document. You can also Delete All Comments in Document from the Reject button
menu.

To reject or accept all comments or changes from a single reviewer, choose the
reviewer from the Show ➪ Reviewers list on the Reviewing Toolbar and deselect any
other reviewers on the list to show only the changes or comments that reviewer
has made. Then you can select Accept or Reject All Changes Shown or Delete All
Comments Shown from the menus attached to the Accept and Reject buttons.

Comparing and merging two copies of a document

When you want to incorporate changes made by another person in a separate copy of the document, use the Tools ➪ Compare and Merge command. This command imports marked changes from the other copy, including any comments it contains.

To perform the merge, choose Tools ➪ Compare and Merge Documents to display an Open dialog box. Find the document you wish to merge with your copy, and click Merge to display the results of the comparison in the original document; you can then open the original document and view the results. If you'd prefer to Merge the new document into a document you currently have open, choose Merge into current document from the menu you can open by clicking the downward-pointing arrow to the right of the Merge button. If you'd prefer to merge the new document and the original document into a brand-new document, choose Merge into new document.

You can now go on to review the changes made as described in the previous section.

Using versions

You can store multiple versions of a given document in one big file. The Versions feature helps you keep track of who was responsible for each saved revision, when it was saved, and what it contains. Retaining intermediate versions of a document isn't just a boon for obsessive administrators. If you suddenly realize that after all, you *really need* that big section you deleted three revisions ago, you don't have to panic — just pull the version that has that section out of storage.

Of course, you can maintain multiple versions of a document using Save As, storing each version in a separate file. But this is cumbersome and it litters your hard disk with large numbers of files whose purpose is quickly forgotten. In addition, this method wastes disk space, because there is bound to be a lot of redundant information in all those copies of the document. By contrast, when you save multiple versions in the same file, Word stores only the differences between the versions, not a complete copy of each version (nevertheless, a file containing versions is still significantly larger than a standard file).

 **Tip**   You can insert into your document a field that shows the date and time that the document was last saved as a quick way to identify the version of a printed document. After opening the Insert ➪ Field dialog box, select SaveDate in the Field Names list. Typically you'll place the field in a header or footer.

Saving versions

You can save the current state of the document as a separate version at any time. Choose File ➪ Versions to display the dialog box shown in Figure 20-6. To save a new version, choose Save Now and type in identifying comments in the secondary dialog box for that purpose.

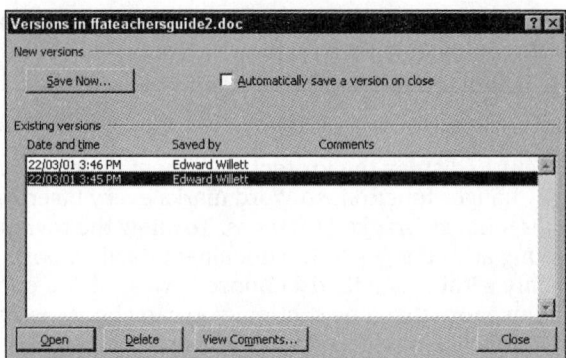

Figure 20-6: Use the Versions dialog box to view and manage versions stored together in a single file.

You can also have Word save a new version each time the document is closed. This is a good way to handle revisions made by multiple authors, especially when an audit trail is required. Just check the *Automatically save a version on close* box in the Versions dialog box. You can't add your own comments to versions saved automatically.

Working with earlier versions

When you have saved one or more versions of a document, the Versions dialog box displays information about each version, including who saved it, the time it was saved, and any comments that were entered (you can see the entire comments text by choosing View Comments). To work with an earlier version, double-click it in the dialog box. Word displays the current document and the selected version in separate, horizontally tiled windows. You can open only one previous version at a time. You can edit the earlier version, but you can't save the changes in the current document — instead, you must use Save As to save it in a new file.

Note

It's a good idea to save a version in its own file if you plan to send a document to a reviewer, so the reviewer only gets to see the one version that's fit for semi-public consumption. You must also convert a version as a separate file when you want to compare the current version to an earlier one. If you start the comparison from the earlier version instead, you don't have to create a new file first.

To delete a version you no longer need, select it in the Versions dialog box and choose Delete.

Setting up a document to be reviewed

Before you distribute a document to others for review, make some basic preparations to ensure that you send out only the information you want to send out, and so you can easily incorporate changes made by the reviewers.

After opening the document, choose File ⇨ Versions to see if the file contains multiple versions, and if so, save separately only the version you want to send out. Then comes the important step: controlling the kinds of changes your reviewers can make.

Choose Tools ⇨ Protect Document to display the Protect Document dialog box. To enforce activation of the Track Changes function, so Word marks every insertion and deletion the reviewer makes, choose Tracked Changes. To allow the reviewer only to add comments, preventing any changes to the document itself, choose Comments. To allow changes only within form fields, choose Forms. (If you choose Forms and the document contains more than one section, you can choose which sections to protect or unprotect by clicking the Sections button.) Then enter a password so the reviewer can't change these settings — and write down the password now, so you won't be locked out when you get the file back.

Ensuring document security with digital signatures

A digital signature is an electronic, encryption-based, secure stamp of authenticity. Office XP allows you to digitally sign documents by attaching a digital certificate, a special file that is issued by certificate authorities (such as VeriSign, Inc., at www.versign.com), or from your company's own internal security administrator or information technology department. Essentially, whoever issues you your digital certificate vouches to whomever is interested that you are who you say you are.

If you're sending a document to a series of reviewers sequentially, you might find it useful to ask each one to sign off on the document with a digital signature. When the file arrives at the next reviewer on the list with the digital signature intact, it verifies that the previous person to review the file was who it was supposed to be, and also that the file has not been altered since that person signed it. (Once the file is altered, the digital signature disappears.)

To digitally sign an Office file, first obtain a digital certificate. Then choose Tools ⇨ Options, and click on the Security tab.

Click the Digital Signatures button, then, in the Digital Signature dialog box, click Add; this opens the Select Certificate dialog box, which lists all the digital certificates currently installed on your computer. Choose the one you want to use to sign the file, then click OK to close the Select Certificate dialog box, and OK again to attach the certificate to the file.

To check and see who last digitally signed a file, just choose Tools ⇨ Options, click on the Security tab, and click the Digital Signatures button.

Cross-Reference   For more on protecting documents, see Chapter 14.

Using Master Documents

A master document is a document that contains a set of related documents. For example, if you were writing a book, you could create a master document (the book as a whole) made up of, say, 25 subdocuments (the chapters of the book).

In a network environment, master documents can be even more useful. A corporate annual report could be stored as a master document while the subdocuments that made it up—reports from various departments, and so on—get worked on by different individuals. That way the master document itself would always be as up-to-date as possible and all the people working on its various components could refer to it.

Creating master- and subdocuments

To create a master document and subdocuments, follow these steps:

1. Create an outline of your master document. (For each section you want to turn into a subdocument, be sure to use the same heading style.)

2. Select the part of the document you want to break into subdocuments. (Make sure it begins with the heading style you've selected.)

3. On the Outline toolbar, click the Create Subdocument button. Word creates a new subdocument everywhere in the selection where the heading style that begins the selection appears. For example, if the selected area begins with Heading 2, a new subdocument will be inserted everywhere you used the Heading 2 style.

4. Save the outline. The outline becomes the master document; each subdocument is saved with a name based on the text you used in its heading.

Tip You can also convert an existing document to a master document and then divide it into subdocuments simply by going to Outline View and following the same procedure.

Converting documents to subdocuments

You can also turn an existing document into a subdocument of a master document. To do so, open the master document, place the insertion point where you want to insert the new subdocument, click the Insert Subdocument button on the Outlining toolbar, and locate and select the file you want to insert.

Rearranging and editing subdocuments

You can quickly change the structure of a master document by adding, removing, combining, splitting, renaming, or rearranging its subdocuments. By default, the subdocuments are hidden when you open a master document, but you can use the

Expand and Collapse Subdocuments buttons on the Outlining toolbar to see them in detail. When they're collapsed, each subdocument's name appears as a hyperlink; to open any subdocument, click its link (see Figure 20-7).

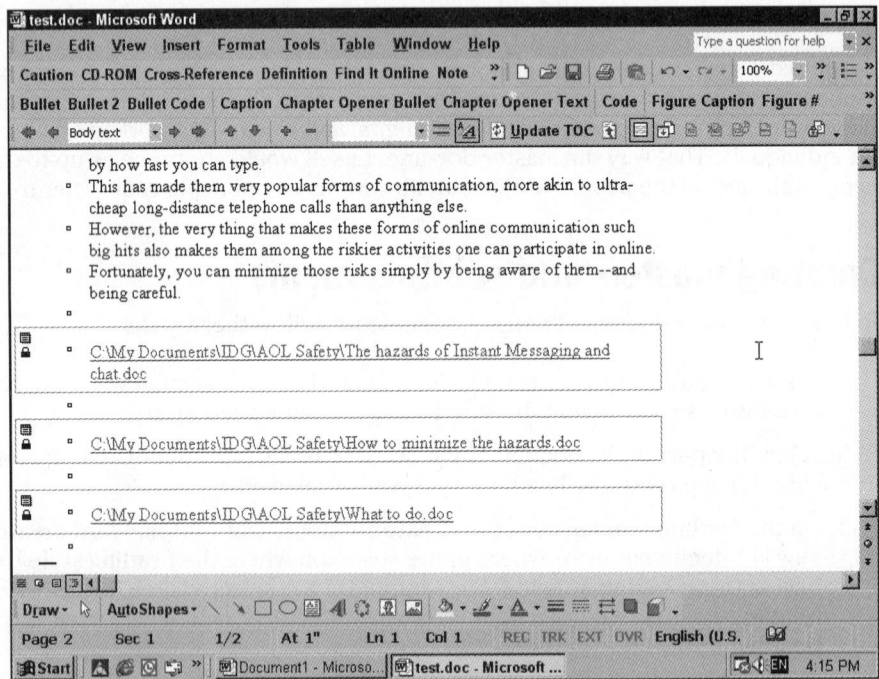

Figure 20-7: When collapsed, subdocuments show up in the master document as hyperlinks.

The easiest way to manage rearranging, combining and splitting subdocuments is to use the standard outlining procedures to drag a heading and its subsidiary text where you want it to go:

- ✦ **To move an entire subdocument to a new position in the outline:** Drag its square icon at the far left of the window.

- ✦ **To combine any part of a subdocument into another subdocument:** Select and drag the relevant heading markers, dropping them inside the destination subdocument.

- ✦ **To remove a subdocument, placing its contents back in the master document:** Drag the main subdocument heading marker, dropping it at its destination between subdocuments.

- ✦ **To divide a subdocument into two:** Drag the portion you want to place in a new subdocument into the main master document, between existing subdocuments. With the heading or headings still selected, click the Create Subdocument button.

You can edit each subdocument just as you would a regular Word document. The master document's template applies to all the subdocuments, which ensures a consistent design, and you can print all of the subdocuments at once simply by printing the master document.

Master- and subdocument security

Within a workgroup, if someone is working on a subdocument, that document is "locked" to everyone else. Users can view it, but they can't modify it until the subdocument is closed. Also, master documents and subdocuments can both be assigned passwords to limit access.

 **Cross-Reference**   See Chapter 14 for more on protecting files with passwords in Office.

✦   ✦   ✦

A Dream of Fields

*F*ields are codes inserted in your document that instruct
Word to carry out some special function. The typical field
functions as a kind of text-making machine—Word translates
the field's instructions into text that appears in your document.

One important benefit of this feature is that the resulting text
isn't static—it reflects prevailing conditions at the time Word
performs the translation. Take a simple date field, for example. On each different day that Word processes the field, it displays that day's date in the document.

This type of field can perform far more complex tasks, such as
gathering all the headings in your document into a formatted
table of contents. But some fields perform other kinds of wiz-
ardry without directly inserting text into the document.

Fields are most commonly used in headers and footers. The
Header and Footer toolbar has buttons for inserting common
fields. In addition, the same toolbar's AutoText menu offers
prefab selections that insert useful combinations of text and
fields into your headers and footers.

VBA can probably accomplish everything that fields can, and
VBA is certainly the tool to use if the document tasks you're
automating are of any complexity. But fields often give you a
shorter route to the destination, they're less demanding in
terms of memory and system resources, and they don't take
you out of the document to a separate software universe. But
it's not an either-or proposition—you can manipulate fields
with VBA to capitalize on the strengths of each.

A thorough discussion of fields would fill up the entire Word
section in this book. If you need more information than is provided here, consult the Help files.

Working with Fields

Behind the scenes, Word relies on fields to perform many of the functions you use regularly. But Word lets you work directly with fields if you so choose, editing the fields it has inserted or creating new fields from scratch.

Keyboard shortcuts for field commands

Word's default menus and toolbars offer little help for field explorers, but all the field-related commands are available via default keyboard shortcuts. Most of these involve the F9 key, though F11 plays a role too. If you forget any of the items listed in Table 21-1, just keep pressing various combinations of Ctrl, Alt, and Shift with F9 until you get the desired results, relying on Undo to reverse accidental unlinking.

Table 21-1
Keyboard Shortcuts for Fields

Shortcut	Name	Function
F9	Update Field	Causes Word to reevaluate the field(s) in the current selection, bringing the results up to date.
Ctrl+F9	Insert Field	Inserts a new empty field, signified by heavy curly braces.
Shift+F9	Toggle Field Code	Toggles the display of field codes versus field results for the field(s) in the current selection.
Alt+F9	View Field Codes	Toggles the display of all fields in the document.
Ctrl+Shift+F9	Unlink Fields	Converts the current results of the selected fields to ordinary text. No further updating of the original fields will then be possible.
Alt+Shift+F9	Do Field Click	Activates button fields such as MACROBUTTON or GOTOBUTTON as if you had clicked them with the mouse.
F11	Next Field	Jumps to the next field in the document.
Shift+F11	Previous Field	Goes back to the last field.
Ctrl+F11	Lock Field	Locks the field so it can't be updated.
Ctrl+Shift+F11	Unlock Field	Unlocks a locked field so it can again be updated.

Using field commands on toolbars and menus

Although keyboard shortcuts are the fastest way to access field-related commands, they work only if you memorize them. Until then, you can use the shortcut menu that appears when you right-click a field to get to two important field-related commands: Update Field and Toggle Field Codes.

Tip   Consider adding the remaining field commands to one or more shortcut menus or to a regular menu or toolbar.

Drag the field-related commands from the Tools ⇨ Customize dialog box (Commands tab) to the destination toolbar or menu using the techniques laid out in Chapter 5. With a few exceptions, the items you select in the dialog box are the same as the command names, as listed in Table 21-1 (but without any spaces). The exceptions are listed in Table 21-2.

Table 21-2	
Field-Related Commands That Have Different Names in the Customize Dialog Box	
For This Command	*Select This Item in the Customize Dialog Box*
Toggle Field Codes	`ToggleFieldDisplay`
Insert Field	`InsertFieldChars` (Note: The command called `InsertField` in the dialog box brings up the Insert Field dialog box, rather than immediately placing a new blank field in the document.)
Previous Field	`PrevField`

How fields work

Each field can appear in your document in one of two forms: as a *field code* (the instructions used to specify the field and its options) or as *field results* (the information that Word derives according to the field code's instructions). It's an either-or kind of thing: Either you see the field code or you see the field results, not both at the same time. Here's an example of a field code:

```
{ DATE \@ "dddd, MMMM dd, yyyy"}
```

And here's how the same field looks when its results are displayed instead:

```
Saturday, March 10, 2001
```

A field's results are expected to change over time. To display the correct current results, you must update the field (see "Updating fields," later in this chapter).

Field codes — anatomy

A field code consists of three main elements, as shown in this example:

```
{ REF CurrentTopic \* Caps }
```

✦ **Field characters:** the pair of bold, curly braces that enclose the rest of the field code.

✦ **Field type:** The name of the field. This name gives at least a hint of its function. In the example, the field type is REF, which stands for reference (to a bookmark).

✦ **Instructions:** Various items that follow the field type and further define what the field should do and how the results should look in your document. The example field has two instructions, CurrentTopic and * Caps. CurrentTopic is the name of the bookmark the field refers to. The * Caps instruction capitalizes the first letter of each word in the bookmarked text. Instructions that begin with a backslash are called *switches* because they switch on optional functions or formatting.

Fields can often be *nested*, meaning that you can include one field as part of the instructions within another field. This enables you to build fields that carry out very sophisticated procedures to finally produce the results you want.

Inserting fields

You have three main ways to insert fields into your documents:

✦ **You can have Word insert the field for you behind the scenes:** You tell Word how to do it by making selections in various dialog boxes.

✦ **You can build the field code with Word's help:** Use the Insert ➪ Field dialog box. (See the paragraphs following this list.)

✦ **You can insert the field manually:** Press Ctrl+F9 to place an empty field — with the requisite pair of heavy curly braces — into your document. You then type in the entire field code yourself. Note that you can't create a field by simply typing in the braces — even if you format them in bold, Word still treats them as ordinary text.

Choosing Insert ➪ Field brings up the dialog box shown in Figure 21-1. Here Word guides you in putting together a field code that produces the results you're after, but don't expect wizard-like pampering: You still have to know when and how to use field code components, and you're not protected from errors that give the wrong results (or none at all).

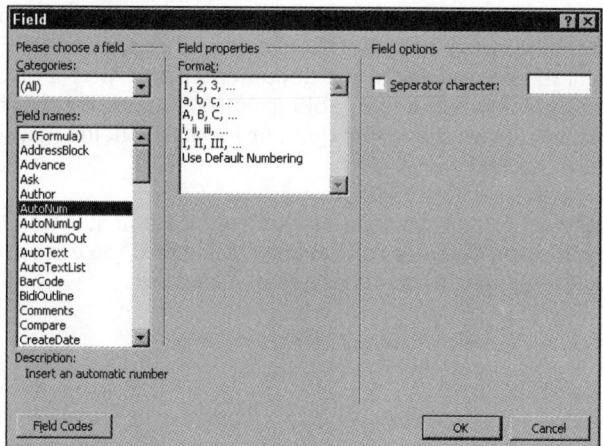

Figure 21-1: The Insert ⇨ Field dialog box

To assemble a field in the dialog box, your first step is to select the right field type by name in the Field Names list. If you know which category your field belongs to, selecting that first in the Categories list reduces the names you have to look through. Otherwise, just leave "(All)" selected at Categories.

As you move through the list of field names, Word automatically displays a description of what the field does underneath the Field names box, and changes the dialog box to reflect the additional choices you need to make to use the field. Make additional choices from the Field properties and Field options areas as appropriate.

Clicking the Field Codes button shows you the name of the code in a text box and allows you to manually add instructions and switches. In some cases, the Field codes button summons an additional Options button that offers (in a separate dialog box) the same field properties and options that appear in the Field dialog box when the Field Codes button is not yet clicked.

Note   Whether you generate a field in the Field dialog box or type it yourself, the order of the instructions makes a difference, so follow the correct syntax. You should leave at least one space between each instruction except the switches (Word identifies them by the backslash character). Instructions containing spaces should be enclosed in quotation marks, but you can usually omit the quotation marks otherwise.

Toggling between field codes and field results

Because information is what you're after, the finished document normally displays and prints the field results. Before the document is finished, however, you can switch back to the field codes to ensure that the field is set up to produce the right information.

Switching back and forth between codes and results is also a good way to learn how fields work. You have several ways to switch between field codes and field results. If you want to see all the field codes in the document, press Alt+F9, or check Field Codes under Show on the View tab of the Tools ➪ Options dialog box. To toggle between field codes and results for a specific field, or for all the fields in a selection, press Shift+F9 instead.

Tip   If for some reason you want to print field codes with your document, check the Field Codes box on the Print tab of the Tools ➪ Options dialog box. You can access these same choices via the Options button on the Print dialog box.

Selecting a field

You don't have to fully select a field to work with it (for example, to update it or to toggle the display of field codes). It's enough to position the insertion point anywhere within the field or just to the left of the first character. On the other hand, the field remains unselected if the insertion point is immediately to the right.

Updating fields

Keep in mind that Word doesn't automatically update fields, except when you open a document or (optionally) when you print it. Before you can believe the results of a field in your document, you have to update the field yourself. Unfortunately, the UpdateField command isn't on any of Word's regular menus; the corresponding button is found only on the Database toolbar, which isn't normally visible. But Word does give you two quick ways to access the UpdateField command: via the shortcut menu you get by right-clicking on a field, or the default keyboard shortcut, F9.

Tip   To ensure that all fields contain updated values in the printed version of a document, check the Update Fields box on the Print tab of the Tools ➪ Options dialog box.

Locking a field to prevent updating

Sometimes you don't want a field to be updated. As a simple example, you might delete some text from the field results. If the field gets updated, your edits would be nullified. You can lock the field to prevent updates by pressing Ctrl+F11. To unlock it, press Ctrl+Shift+F11.

Converting fields into plain text

If you're sure that you'll never again want to update the results of a field, unlink the field. This command converts the current field results into ordinary text. Aside from Undo, there's no going back. The keyboard shortcut is Ctrl+Shift+F9.

Working with field results

When you display a field's results, the results look and behave almost like ordinary text. I say "almost" for two reasons:

✦ The field results may be shaded in gray, depending on the Field Shading setting in the View tab of the Tools ➪ Options dialog box. I prefer the default "When selected" choice for this setting; it's good to know when the insertion point is within a field rather than ordinary text, but shading fields all the time is distracting.

✦ Although you can edit the text of the field results, you'll find the editing process quirky. Specifically, with the insertion point just to the right of the field, pressing Backspace once simply selects the field, and pressing it again deletes the entire field. Be aware that any changes you make in the text will be wiped out if you update the field, or if Word does so at print time.

Formatting field results and field codes

You can format a field's results or any portion thereof just as you would ordinary text. If you select the entire field before making a formatting change, the new format survives after the field is updated. On the other hand, an update nullifies formatting applied to selected text within the field results.

When the field code is visible, you can format selections within it. These changes do endure following an update. In combination with the * switch (described later) for the charformat command, this is one way to control the appearance of the entire results. You can control other types of formatting with switches in the field itself. Read on.

Controlling the display of field results with switches

Switches, as I noted earlier, are instructions that switch on optional functions or formatting. All switches begin with a backslash.

Although many switches are specific to individual field types, you can use four in many different fields:

✦ In fields that give text results, the Format switch (*) controls capitalization of text. In fields that give numeric results, it controls the way Word displays the numbers (as Roman numerals, written out as text, and so on). The Format switch can also be used to preserve or apply character formatting to the field results.

✦ The Numeric Picture switch (\#) controls other aspects of the appearance of numeric field results.

✦ The Date-Time Picture switch (\@) controls the way Word displays date and time information in field results. The Date-Time Picture switch and the Numeric Picture switch are called Picture switches because their formats are represented using symbols.

✦ The Lock Result switch (\!) keeps Word from updating a field when it is included in another field of one of the following types: BOOKMARK, INCLUDETEXT, or REF. These fields are used to reference information in other locations, and if you include this switch, the information they report will always match the results of the included field as displayed in the original location.

Except for Lock Result, these switches must be followed by an additional instruction that tells Word which of the available options you want to activate.

Using the Format switch

Tables 21-3, 21-4, and 21-5 show instructions for the Format switch to control capitalization, number schemes, and character formatting, respectively.

Table 21-3
Format Switch Instructions Controlling Capitalization

Instruction	Results Displayed
* caps	Capitalizes the first letter of each word.
* firstcap	Capitalizes only the first letter of the field results.
* lower	Displays the field results in all lowercase.
* upper	Displays the field results in uppercase.

Table 21-4
Format Switch Instructions Controlling Number Schemes

Instruction	Results Displayed
* alphabetic	Displays each numeral as a corresponding letter of the alphabet.
* arabic	Displays ordinary numbers. This is the default.
* cardtext	Writes out the numbers in words.
* dollartext	Writes out the amount as you would on a check.
* hex	Displays the amount in hexadecimal notation (base 16).
* ordinal	Displays the number in ordinal form (1st, 2nd, 3rd, ... 999th).

Instruction	Results Displayed
* ordtext	Displays the number in text form (twenty-second, thirty-first, etc.).
* roman	Displays the number in Roman numerals.

Table 21-5
Format Switch Instructions Controlling Character Formatting

Instruction	Results Displayed
* mergeformat	Preserves any character formatting you have applied to the field result during field updates. If you don't include this switch, character formatting is removed when Word updates the field.
* charformat	Applies the formatting of the first letter of the field type to the entire field result.

Using the Numeric Picture switch

The Numeric Picture switch (\\#) lets you control how Word displays numeric results, in terms of the number of decimal points, whether or not commas are included in large numbers, whether a dollar sign is added, and how negative numbers are listed. Following the \\# switch itself, combine the instructions in Table 21-6 to taste:

Table 21-6
Numeric Picture Switch Instructions and Results

Instruction	Results Displayed
,	Adds commas between groups of three digits (as in 12,345). When added to a field by Word, this instruction contains additional # characters, but they aren't necessary.
0	Rounds the value to the nearest integer, with no decimal places.
0.00	Rounds the value to the number of decimal places specified (in this example, two). When you select a decimal format, the field results always display all the specified decimal positions, even those whose value is 0.
% or $	You can include these symbols (or any text for that matter) by typing them into the field code where you want them to appear in the results.

To tell Word to use different formatting for negative numbers, type a semicolon after the numeric picture for positive numbers and then enter the picture for the negative ones. Table 21-7 includes some examples that should clarify how to use these instructions.

Table 21-7 Numeric Picture Switch Examples	
Numeric Picture	**Example Results**
\# $,0.00;($,0.00)	$112.52 (positive number) ($45.68)
\# $0	$65
\# ,0.000%	6,324.445%

Using the Date-Time Picture switch

Normally, fields that display date or time information do so using the format set as the default in the Insert ➪ Date and Time dialog box. And if no default is set there, you get the format set in the Windows Control Panel on the Date tab in the Regional Settings Properties dialog box.

The Date-Time Picture switch (\@) lets you take complete control. The field results can list, in any order, the named day of the week, the numeric day of the month, the month, the year, the minute, and the hour. You can include punctuation or even extra text, to produce automatic results such as, "It was in the year 2001. The day was Thursday, February 15. The time was 5:00 AM." Examples of date-time pictures are shown in Table 21-8. Table 21-9 lists the elements you use in date-time pictures to specify various date- and time-related results in fields.

Table 21-8 Examples of Date-Time Pictures	
Switch	**Sample Result**
\@ "yyyy"	1999
\@ "dddd, MMMM d"	Monday, September 22
\@ "h in the AM/PM"	6 in the PM

Unfortunately, I don't know of a way to include apostrophes within a date-time picture. That's why the last example doesn't read "6 o'clock PM."

Table 21-9
Components Available for Use in Date-Time Pictures

Entry in the Date-Time Picture	Field Results Displayed
Month (uppercase M)	
M	Number of the month without a leading 0 (zero) if it's a single-digit month
MM	Number of the month with a leading 0 (zero) if it's a single-digit month
MMM	The three-letter abbreviation of the month
MMMM	The month's full name
Day (lowercase d)	
d	Day of the month without a leading 0 (zero) if it's a single-digit day
dd	Day of the month with a leading 0 (zero) if it's a single-digit day
ddd	The three-letter abbreviation of the day of the week (Mon, Tue, and so on)
dddd	The day of the week spelled out in full
Year (lowercase y)	
yy	The last two digits of the year (works for dates in both the twentieth and twenty-first centuries). The result includes a leading 0 (zero) for the years 01 through 09.
yyyy	The full year as a four-digit number
Hours (H or h): Use lowercase h for 12-hour time, uppercase H for 24-hour time (military time)	
h or H	The hour without a leading 0 (zero) if it's a single-digit hour
hh or HH	The hour with a leading 0 (zero) if it's a single-digit hour
Minutes (lowercase m)	
m	The minute without a leading 0 (zero) if it's a single-digit minute
mm	The minute with a leading 0 (zero) if it's a single-digit minute
AM/PM	
AM/PM	A.M. or P.M. in uppercase (that is, 3 AM, 6 PM)
am/pm	A.M. or P.M. in lowercase (that is, 3 am, 6 pm)
A/P	A.M. or P.M. in abbreviated uppercase (that is, 3 A, 6 P)
a/p	A.M or P.M. in abbreviated lowercase (that is, 3 a, 6 p)

Using VBA with Fields

Word's VBA library includes plenty of support for fields, which means you can create macros that take full advantage of Word fields to accomplish specific tasks more efficiently and quickly.

Field-related objects, properties, and methods

This section offers a quick but deep look at the most important VBA objects, methods, and properties related to fields.

✦ You access the individual fields in a document, range, or selection object using the `Fields` collection of the object in question. An individual field is represented by a `Field` object, of course. Return a particular `Field` object from a `Fields` collection using the field's index number. Check out these examples:

```
Set FirstField = ActiveDocument.Fields(1)
' Fields(1) refers to the first field in the document,
' FirstField now refers to that field object.
Set SomeField = Selection.Fields(3)
' Fields(3) refers to the third field in the selection.
```

✦ Use the `Count` property of a `Fields` collection when you want to know how many fields the collection contains, as in the following:

```
intHowManyFields = SomeRange.Fields.Count
```

✦ You can determine what sort of field you're working with using the `Field` object's `Type` property. Word supplies a named constant for each field type (for instance, `wdFieldAutoText`, `wdFieldRef`, and so on). See the next line of code for an example.

✦ A `Field` object's `DoClick` method activates the field, as if it had been clicked. The following line of code executes the `DoClick` method if the field is a Hyperlink:

```
If AField.Type = wdFieldHyperlink Then AField.DoClick
```

✦ The `Next` and `Previous` properties for a `Field` object return the next and previous fields in the `Fields` collection. After this example executes, the variable `FieldDay` refers to the next field (you don't have to search through the collection for the next field, because a `Field` object itself knows where the next field is):

```
Set FieldDay = FieldDay.Next
```

✦ To examine or use a field's *result*, use its `Result` property. This property returns a `Range` object, not text, so you must use the range's `Text` property to place those results in a string variable:

```
strResultory = LeftField.Result.Text
```

✦ Other `Field` properties include `ShowCodes`, which you can use to switch between the field's results and code in your document, and `Locked`, with which you can lock or unlock the field. Both can be either `True` or `False`.

✦ Use the `Add` method on a `Fields` collection to insert a new field into the document. The method takes arguments specifying the location for the field—via a `Range` object—and the type of field (see the previous discussion on the `Type` property). The first line of this example ensures that the new field doesn't replace any existing text:

```
Selection.Collapse Direction:=wdCollapseStart
ActiveDocument.Fields.Add _
    Range:=Selection.Range, Type:=wdFieldDate
```

✦ To delete a field, use the `Delete` method directly on the `Field` object in question, as in these examples:

```
OutField.Delete ' OutField refers to a Field object
ActiveDocument.Fields(5).Delete
' Deletes the fifth field in the Fields collection
```

Table 21-10 includes some other useful field-related methods.

Table 21-10
Some Useful Field-Related VBA Methods

Method(s)	Use	Applies to (Field Object or Fields Collection)
`Select`	Selects the field.	`Field` object
`Cut, Copy`	What you'd expect.	`Field` object
`Update`	Updates the results of the field.	Both
`Unlink`	Converts field results to ordinary text.	Both
`ToggleShowCodes`	Toggles field code display for all fields.	`Fields` collection

A procedure for finding fields

Word's Find command and Browse By feature can both locate fields in your document, but they do so indiscriminately—they locate the next field of any type. To hunt down fields of a specific type, use the following VBA procedure. In the `Do...Loop` statement near the end of the procedure, replace `wdFieldRef` with the `Type` property constant appropriate for the type of field you want to search for.

Table 21-11
Word's Document Information Fields

Field Name	Description	Syntax	Details	Comments, Samples
Author	Inserts the document author's name as listed on the Summary tab of the Properties dialog box.	{ AUTHOR ["Author's name"] }	If no one has typed in another name, the author's name is on the User Information tab of the Tools⇨Options dialog box. *Author's name.* To change the author's name, enter the new name in quotation marks here. The entry replaces the existing one in the Properties dialog box.	{ AUTHOR" { FILLIN "Please enter the author's name: " } " } } This field asks the user to type in the name, which is printed in the document and added to the Properties dialog box (File menu).
Comments	Inserts the text in the Comments box on the Summary tab.	{ COMMENTS ["New Comments"] }	*New Comments.* To change the current comments, place the new ones in quotation marks here.	
CreateDate	Inserts the date and time the document was first saved under the current name (from the Created box on the Statistics tab).	{ CREATEDATE [\@ "Date-Time Picture"] }	See "Using the Date-Time Picture switch."	This deposition taken {CREATEDATE \@ "MMMM d, yyyy" }.
DocProperty	Inserts specified document information from the Properties dialog box.	{ DOCPROPERTY "Property"}	*Property.* Enter the name of any property listed in the Properties dialog box (including custom properties). You can list only one property per field.	Contact: { DOCPROPERTY Project }

Field Name	Description	Syntax	Details	Comments, Samples
EditTime	Inserts the time in minutes that the document has been open for editing since it was first created, or since it was saved under a new name (Statistics tab).	{ EDITTIME }		
FileName	Inserts the document's filename (General tab).	{ FILENAME [\p] }	\p. Includes the full path with the filename.	
FileSize	Inserts the document's size in bytes (Statistics tab).	{ FILESIZE [\k] [\m] }	\k displays the file size in kilobytes (KB). \m displays the file size in megabytes (MB).	
Info	Inserts specified information from the Properties dialog box.	{ [INFO] Property ["NewValue"] }	Info Type. The property type. NewValue. You can change the entry for any of the following properties — AUTHOR, COMMENTS, KEYWORDS, SUBJECT, and TITLE — by placing the new value in the field.	Similar to DocProperty, but enables you to change some properties
Keywords	Inserts contents of the Keywords box from the Summary tab.	{ KEYWORDS ["NewKey-words"] }	NewKeywords. To change the current keywords, place the new ones in quotation marks here.	
LastSavedBy	Inserts the name of the person who last saved the file, as listed on the Statistics tab.	{ LASTSAVEDBY }	Despite the name, this field reports the current entry at Author on the Statistics tab, whether or not the document has been saved since the author's name was changed.	

Continued

Table 21-11 *(continued)*

Field Name	Description	Syntax	Details	Comments, Samples
NumChars	Inserts the number of characters in the document (Statistics tab).	{ NUMCHARS }		Use the following field to calculate the average word length: { = { NUMCHARS } / { NUMWORDS } }
NumPages	Inserts the total number of pages in the document (Statistics tab).	{ NUMPAGES }	Use this field with the PAGE field to create entries such as Page 3 of 300. If the document begins on a page number other than 1, calculate the total page count with this field: { = (StartingNumber – 1) + { NUMPAGES } }	
NumWords	Inserts the total number of words in the document (Statistics tab).	{ NUMWORDS }		
PrintDate	Inserts the date and time when the document was last printed (Statistics tab).	{ PRINTDATE \@"Date-Time Picture" }	See "Using the Date-Time Picture switch."	
RevNum	Inserts the number of times the document has been saved (Statistics tab).	{ REVNUM }	This field is worthless! You're supposed to save your documents frequently, not just when you consider a "revision" complete. If you follow this advice, this field actually reports "number of times I felt that it was prudent to save the document."	
SaveDate	Inserts the date and time a document was last saved ("Modified" on the Statistics tab).	{ SAVEDATE [\@"Date-Time Picture"] }	See "Using the Date-Time Picture switch."	

Field Name	Description	Syntax	Details	Comments, Samples
Subject	Inserts contents of the Subject box (Summary tab).	{ SUBJECT ["NewSub-ject"] }	NewSubject. To change the subject as listed in the Properties dialog box, add the new subject here in quotation marks (up to 255 characters).	You can use a FILLIN field to ask the person working on the document to enter a new subject: { SUBJECT" { FILLIN "Enter the document subject" } " }
Template	Inserts the filename of the document's template (Summary tab).	{ TEMPLATE [\p] }	\p includes the full path with the template's filename.	
Title	Inserts the document title, as listed in the Summary tab.	{ TITLE ["NewTide"] }	NewTitle. To change the title as listed in the Properties dialog box, add the new subject here in quotation marks.	
UserAddress	Inserts the address from the Mailing Address box on the User Information tab in the Tools⇨ Options dialog box.	{USERADDRESS ["New Address"]	NewAddress. To place an address (or any text) you specify in the document, enter it here in quotation marks. The entry can include line and paragraph breaks. It does not affect the information in the User Information tab.	
UserInitials	Inserts the user's initials from the Initials box on the User Information tab (in the Tools⇨ Options dialog box).	{ USERINITIALS ["New Initials"] }	NewInitials. To place initials (or any text) you specify in the document, enter them here. The entry does not affect the information in the User Information tab.	
UserName	Inserts the user's name from the Name box on the User Information tab (in the Tools⇨ Options dialog box).	{ USERNAME ["NewName"] }	NewName. To place a name (or any text) of your choice in the document, enter it here. The entry does not affect the information in the User Information tab.	

```
        Sub Field_FindNextOfOneType ()
Dim FoundFieldFlag As Boolean
Set thisDoc = ActiveDocument
Set FieldRange = thisDoc.Range(Start:=Selection.Start,
End:=thisDoc.Content.End)
If FieldRange.Fields.Count >= 1 Then
    Set SearchFields = FieldRange.Fields
    Set CurrentField = SearchFields(1)

' Check to make sure that the insertion point isn't
' already at a field
    Selection.Collapse
    Selection.NextField
If Selection.Start = FieldRange.Start Then
    If FieldRange.Fields.Count >= 2 Then
        Set CurrentField = SearchFields(2)
    Else
        Exit Sub
    End If
End If
    Do Until (CurrentField Is Nothing)
        If CurrentField.Type = wdFieldRef Then
            CurrentField.Select
            FoundFieldFlag = True
            Exit Do
        End If
    Set CurrentField = CurrentField.Next
    Loop
End If
If Not FoundFieldFlag Then
    MsgBox "Your field type not found."
End If
End Sub
```

If you're a little more ambitious, you could wrap up this procedure in a little dialog box (UserForm) using a list box to enable the user to choose the type of field to search for.

A Field Guide to Fields

This section provides brief but critical reference information on some of the most useful Word fields. The section begins with a big table (see Table 21-11) of the fields available for working with information in the current document. The remainder of the chapter covers many other important fields individually, in alphabetical order.

The discussion of each field begins with a schematic of the field's syntax. *Instructions enclosed in brackets are optional.* As a rule of thumb, you can omit the quotes surrounding an item in an instruction if the item contains no spaces. After the syntax comes an introduction explaining the field's purpose and use. In most cases, the functions of each of the individual instructions are detailed in a table after the field's purpose and use are explained.

Document information fields

Table 21-11 lists the many fields you can use to extract information from the document itself. References to the dialog box tabs (as in "the Statistics tab") refer to those on the File ⇨ Properties dialog box.

= (Formula or Calculation) field

Field syntax: { = *Formula* [\# *Numeric Picture*] }

Use an = field in the body of a document or in a table to calculate a mathematical expression.

A *formula* is any mathematical expression Word can interpret, which can be quite complex. The expression can contain numbers as such, of course. But it can also include other fields that give numeric results (not the least of which are nested = fields), bookmarks that refer to numbers in the document, and (when you use it in a table) references to cells that contain values. And while Word doesn't have Excel's mathematical prowess, it does offer an impressive list of mathematical operators and functions you can use to manipulate these numeric values (see Tables 21-12 and 21-13).

Cross-Reference

See "Using the Numeric Picture switch," earlier in this chapter, for the number format choices you can use with the \# Numeric Picture switch to display the field's results.

Table 21-12 Operators Available in = Fields	
Operator	**Description**
+	Addition
–	Subtraction
*	Multiplication
/	Division
%	Percentage
^	Powers and roots
=	Equals, equal to
<	Less than
<=	Less than or equal to
>	Greater than
>=	Greater than or equal to
<>	Not equal to

Table 21-13
Functions Available in = Fields

Function	Result
ABS(x)	Absolute value of x
AND(x,y)	True (1) if both x and y are True, otherwise False (0)
AVERAGE(x,y,z . . .)	Arithmetic mean of x + y + z + ...
COUNT(x,y,z, . . .)	Number of items listed
DEFINED(x)	True (1) if x is a valid expression, False if Word can't calculate the value of x
False	False (0)
IF(x,y,z)	y, if x is True; otherwise z
INT(x)	The integer portion of x
MAX(x,y,z . . .)	The largest item listed
MIN(x,y,z . . .)	The smallest item listed
MOD(x,y)	The remainder of x divided by y
NOT(x)	False (0) if x is True, otherwise True (1)
OR(x,y)	True (1) if either x or y is True, False if both x and y are False
PRODUCT(x,y,z . . .)	Product of x times y times z ...
ROUND(x,y)	x rounded to y decimal places
SIGN(x)	1 if x is positive, 0 if zero, −1 if negative
SUM(x,y,z . . .)	Sum of x + y + z ...
True	True (1)

Tip   It's easier to insert an Excel worksheet (or a portion thereof) into your document than to create a Word table using = fields for your calculations. Creating formulas of any complexity without Excel's help is bound to waste time and lead to errors. Use the = field only if Excel isn't installed on your system for some reason or if you're sending the document to someone who doesn't have Excel.

Any portion of the expression calculated by an = field can be a bookmark that refers to a value somewhere else in the document. The bookmarked text can be a single number, a field that produces a numeric result, or even a complete expression. Examples include the following: { = 4*Bookmark }, { = Max(33, Bookmark, 78)+Bookmark2 }, and even { = Bookmark }.

To place a mathematical expression in your document for bookmarking purposes, just type it in as it would appear inside the = field. If you bookmark a sequence of numbers or numeric expressions separated only by commas or spaces, Word adds them together to calculate the value of the bookmark.

Ask

Field syntax: { ASK *Bookmark* "*Prompt*" [\d "*Default*"] [\o] }

Each time an ASK field gets updated, it displays a little dialog box asking the reader of the document to type in a response. When the reader clicks OK, Word stores the typed text in a bookmark. If you want to display the newly bookmarked text, you must insert another field (a REF field) to do so. Alternatively, you can use the book-marked information in other fields. For example, you can ask the reader to type in a number and use the entry in a calculation performed by an = field. Table 21-14 has further information about the ASK field.

<table>
<tr><th colspan="2">Table 21-14
Ask Field Instructions</th></tr>
<tr><th>Instruction</th><th>Function</th></tr>
<tr><td>Bookmark</td><td>This is the bookmark name that will be assigned to the entry typed by the reader in the dialog box.</td></tr>
<tr><td>"Prompt"</td><td>This is text to be displayed as instructions to the reader in the dialog box, such as "How many were going to St. Ives? Please enter a number from 1–100."</td></tr>
<tr><td>\d "Default"</td><td>Use this switch to provide Word with a default response that it can use if no entry is made in the dialog box. If you don't include this switch, Word suggests the previous entry, if any. If an undefined entry would cause trouble in other fields referring to the bookmark, you can specify a blank entry as the default by entering only a pair of quotation marks after the \d.</td></tr>
<tr><td>\o</td><td>When an ASK field resides in a mail merge main document, its dialog box normally appears every time a new data record is merged. If you include the \o switch, however, Word displays the dialog only once and uses that response in every document created during the mail merge.</td></tr>
</table>

AutoNum, AutoNumLgl, AutoNumOut

These fields are holdovers to ensure compatibility with earlier Word versions. Use ListNum instead.

AutoText

Field syntax: { AUTOTEXT *AutoTextEntry* }

This field inserts the text or graphics stored in *AutoTextEntry* into your document. Use it when you expect a component of the document to change over time. When the item does change, just redefine the AutoText entry and update the fields for an instant revision.

AutoTextList

Field syntax: { AUTOTEXTLIST "*LiteralText*" [\s "*StyleName*"] [\t "*TipText*"] }

This field builds and displays a drop-down list of AutoText entries drawn from the current template. You can limit the list to AutoText entries associated with a particular character or paragraph style. Table 21-15 has further information about this field.

| | Table 21-15 |
| | **AutoTextList Field Instructions** |
Instruction	*Function*
LiteralText	This is text that displays in the document before the user displays the drop-down list. If the text contains spaces, enclose it in quotation marks.
\s "*StyleName*"	To limit the AutoText entries displayed in the list to those associated with a particular style, enter the style's name here. If no entries are associated with the style, Word displays all AutoText entries.
\t "*TipText*"	Lets you specify ScreenTip text for the field.

Barcode

Field syntax: { BARCODE \u "*LiteralText*" or Bookmark \b [\f "*char*"] }

This field inserts a postal barcode based on an address ("LiteralText") that you type in or that is marked by a bookmark (in which case, LiteralText is the bookmark name and must be followed by the [\b] switch). The \f switch inserts the Facing Identification Mark based on the letter in quotation marks.

Compare

Field syntax: { COMPARE *Expression1 Operator Expression2* }

This field compares two numeric expressions or character strings with a single-minded purpose: to determine whether or not they are equivalent. The field result is 1 if the comparison is true, zero if it is false. The COMPARE field is almost always nested within an IF field, so some action can be taken based on the result of the comparison. Table 21-16 has further information about this field.

Table 21-16 Compare Field Instructions	
Instruction	**Function**
Expression1 and *Expression2*	These are the expressions or character strings to compare. See the section on the = field for a discussion of the forms numeric expressions can take. If you're comparing strings of characters with the = or <> operators, you can use wildcard characters in Expression2: ? stands for any character, * for any string. In this case (or if an expression contains spaces), you must enclose it in quotation marks.
Operator	May be any of the comparison operators in Table 21-12 (equal to, less than, less than or equal to, greater than, greater than or equal to, or not equal to).

Date

Field syntax: { DATE [\@ "*Date-Time Picture*"] [\l] }

The DATE field inserts the current date, time, or both. See the discussion in "Using the Date-Time Picture switch," earlier in this chapter. Table 21-17 also has further information about this field.

Table 21-17 Date Field Instructions	
Instruction	**Function**
\@ "*Date-Time Picture*"	Use this switch to specify a custom date and time format.
\l	Inserts the date and time information in the same format last selected in the Insert ⇨ Date and Time dialog box.

Eq

Field syntax: { EQ [*Switches*] }

The EQ field places a formatted mathematical equation into your document. I mention it only to warn you off; please don't use this field. The Equation Editor that comes with Office is a much more capable tool.

Fill-in

Field syntax: { FILLIN ["*Prompt*"] [\d "*Default*"][\o] }

This field works much like the ASK field. The difference is that instead of creating a bookmark that you can reference in other fields, a FILLIN field simply displays the reader's entry.

GoToButton

Field syntax: { GOTOBUTTON *Destination DisplayText* }

Now that Word has hyperlinks for instant point-to-point navigation, GoToButton fields are less valuable. To add a graphical button that the reader can push to another location, you can now insert a hyperlink onto an AutoShape or a control from the Control toolbox. Unlike hyperlinks, however, GoToButton fields can jump by number to a specific page, line, section, footnote, or comment — you don't need to bookmark these locations first.

You can use a GoToButton field to jump to any item that has been cross-referenced by a page number, or to any footnote. Instead of entering a literal page number or footnote number, insert into the field a cross-reference (itself a field) after the appropriate code letter, as in these examples:

```
{GOTOBUTTON "p{ PAGEREF _Ref375226869 }" "Jump to Table 12.12"}
```

and

```
{GOTOBUTTON "f { NOTEREF _Ref375225952 }" "Push here to jump to
relevant footnote" }.
```

Table 21-18 has further information about this field.

Table 21-18
GoToButton Field Instructions

Instruction	Function
Destination	This is either a bookmark name or a code indicating by number a line, page, section, footnote, or comment. For example, you would enter p4 to jump to page 4. Use l (the letter "el") to jump to a specified line number, s for a section, f for a footnote, and a for a comment.
DisplayText	Type the text that should serve as the jump button, or insert an INCLUDEPICTURE field to display a graphic button. The text or graphic must appear on one line in the field result; otherwise, an error occurs. You can also enter a field that gives text.

Hyperlink

Field syntax: { HYPERLINK "*Filename*" [\h] [\l] [\m] [\n] [\o "*Screen Tip*"] [\t] }

"*Filename*" is the name of the file or URL you want to jump to. Single backslashes in a path name should be entered as double backslashes here. Enclose the destination in quotation marks if it contains spaces. Table 21-19 has further information about this field.

Table 21-19
Hyperlink Field Instructions

Instruction	Function
\l	Sets the specific target location in the destination file, typically a bookmark.
\m	Adds server-side image map coordinates.
\n	Opens the destination in a new window.
\o "*Screen Tip*"	Specifies the screen tip text for the hyperlink.
\t	Another switch you shouldn't add manually. t is for the target when Word redirects a link.

If

Field syntax: { IF *Expression1 Operator Expression2* "*TrueText*" "*FalseText*" }

An IF field gives one of two possible results depending on the outcome of a test you set up within the field. Typically, at least one of the expressions compared in an IF field is based on another field or fields. That way, the outcome of the IF comparison varies depending on the current values of the nested fields. As a simple example, you would use the following field to insert in your document either long or short (depending on whether the current document is longer than 30 pages):

    { IF {NUMPAGES}> 30 long short }

Expression1 and *Expression2* can also include numbers, mathematical formulae, bookmark names, and text (character strings), as well as nested fields that return a value. If you're comparing strings of characters with the = or <> operators, *Expression2* can contain wildcard characters: ? stands for any character, * for any string. If you use a wildcard, or if a text expression contains spaces, you must enclose it in quotation marks. Text comparisons are case sensitive. If either expression is based on a field, include a format switch (*) in that nested field to ensure that the field results are capitalized like the other expression (see "Using the Format switch," earlier in this chapter).

Operator can be any of the comparison operators. Insert a space before and after the operator. *TrueText* and *FalseText* are the results you want the field to display, depending on whether the comparison is logically true or false. The final result of an IF field can be based on multiple comparisons if you include nested COMPARE or IF fields. Another trick is to test two COMPARE fields simultaneously using nested = fields based on the AND or OR functions.

IncludePicture

Field syntax: { INCLUDEPICTURE "*FileName*" [\c *Converter*] [\d] }

Use this field to insert a graphic file. The best use for INCLUDEPICTURE is as a nested field in GOTOBUTTON and MACROBUTTON fields, where it serves to insert a graphical button for the reader to press. Table 21-20 has further information about this field.

Table 21-20
IncludePicture Field Instructions

Instruction	Function
FileName	Enter the name of the graphics file with the full path, replacing single backslashes with double backslashes. Enclose the whole thing in quotation marks if it contains spaces.
\c Converter	Specifies the graphics filter Word should use to display the image, omitting the .flt extension. This switch is rarely necessary.
\d	If you include this switch, the graphic is not stored in the document.

Index

Field syntax:

```
{ INDEX [\b Bookmark] [\c Cols] [\d "Separator"] [\e
"Separator"] [\f "GroupID"] [\g "Separator"] [\h "Heading"] [\k
"Separator"] [\l "Separator"] [\p "Range"] [\r] [\s Sequence]
[\y] [\z]}
```

This is one powerful little field. Each time you update it, it combs through the document collecting index entries (XE fields) and assembling them into a complete index, which it then displays. Table 21-21 has further information about this field.

Table 21-21
Index Field Instructions

Instruction	Function
\b Bookmark	Limits the index to just the bookmarked text.
\c Cols	Cols is a number between 1 and 4 specifying the number of columns for the index.
\f "GroupID"	Limits the index to XE fields containing an \f switch with the same GroupID. The \f switch lets you create separate, special-purpose indexes (for example, Index of Authors, Index of Song Titles).

Continued

Table 21-21 *(continued)*

Instruction	Function
\h "*Heading*"	Inserts *Heading* text between alphabetical sections in the index, formatted with the Index *Heading* style. If *Heading* contains any single letter (with or without surrounding punctuation), the letter is replaced by the correct letter for each section. Insert a blank line between sections with the switch.
\p "*Range*"	Limits the index to the letters specified by *Range*. For example { INDEX \p x-z } creates an index listing only entries that start with *x*, *y*, or *z*. Use an exclamation point for entries beginning with symbols.
\r	Places subentries on the same line as the main entry, with a colon between main entries and subentries and semicolons between subentries.

The remaining switches specify separators between numbers or, in the case of \y and \z, related to the language used.

ListNum

Field syntax: { LISTNUM "*Name*" [\l] [\s] }

By default, each LISTNUM field in the same paragraph inserts the formatted number (or other list item) at the next lower level. To see how this works, select and copy the field and paste it repeatedly at the insertion point. If necessary, turn off field codes display. You should see something like this next example, depending on which numbering scheme you started with:

    Section 2.01 (a) (i) 1) a) i) a. i.

If you insert LISTNUM in consecutive paragraphs that aren't already numbered, you get the next number in the sequence at the current level. Table 21-22 has further information about this field.

Table 21-22
ListNum Field Instructions

Instruction	Function
\l	Specifies the level in the named list for the current field, overriding the automatic sequence Word would otherwise use.
\s	Specifies the starting value.

MacroButton

Field syntax: { MACROBUTTON *Macro DisplayText* }

This field places the macro named *Macro* directly into the document where the reader can run it by double-clicking the field results or by pressing Alt+Shift+F9. *DisplayText* is what appears in the document as the button. You can type in text or enter a field that gives text or graphics as its result (see the "IncludePicture" section earlier in the chapter). The text or graphic must appear on a single line in the results.

Print

Field syntax: { PRINT "*PrinterInstructions*" [\p *Rectangle* "*PS*"] }

This field sends control codes to the printer when you print the document. If you're a PostScript or PCL wizard, here's your magic wand. Use the \p switch to send PostScript code: Specify the drawing rectangle at *Rectangle*, and then list the PostScript instructions in quotation marks at *PS*. To print PostScript "on top" of the rest of the document, check the Print PostScript Over Text box in the Print tab of the Tools ➭ Options dialog box.

Quote

Field syntax: { QUOTE "*LiteralText*" [\@ "*Date-Time Picture*"] }

This field inserts *text* into the document. You can type text directly into a document, of course. The real value of this field lies in its ability to reformat dates calculated numerically by other fields nested inside it. (See "Using the Date-Time Picture switch" for details on how to specify date formats.)

In the following example, the IF nested field calculates next month's number (1 if next month will be January, 5 if it will be May). The QUOTE field converts those results to text, displaying the next month's name. Pretty slick!

```
{ QUOTE { IF { DATE \@ M } = 12 1 {= { DATE \@ M } +1 } }/1/99
\@ MMMM }
```

REF

Field syntax: { [REF] *Bookmark* [\f] [\h] [\n] [\p] [\r] [\t] [\w] }

This field inserts the text or graphics marked by the specified bookmark. REF fields are so often useful that Word doesn't even make you include the REF within the field brackets — just type the bookmark name inside a pair of field brackets. (Such fields without an explicit REF are also called BOOKMARK fields.) The only time you must include "REF" in the field is when the bookmark name is the same as another field type (such as Page or Time). You can only reference bookmarks in the active document—use INCLUDEPICTURE or INCLUDETEXT to insert bookmarked information from another document. Table 21-23 has further information about this field.

	Table 21-23 **REF Field Instructions**
Instruction	**Function**
\f	If the bookmark marks a footnote, endnote, or comment number, the REF field inserts a copy of the note or comment, and the correctly numbered reference mark.
\h	Makes the field a hyperlink to the bookmarked information.
\n	If the bookmark is a numbered paragraph, includes only the paragraph number of the bookmarked paragraph as it appears in the document.
\p	Displays above or below based on the location of the field relative to the bookmarked information. When used with the \n, \r, or \w switches, above or below appears at the end of the field result.
\r	If the bookmark is a numbered paragraph, includes the paragraph number of the bookmarked paragraph in its relative context in the numbering scheme.
\t	Removes alphabetic text from the paragraph number produced with the \n, \r, or \w switches (a reference to a paragraph numbered "Subsection 2.23" becomes 2.23).
\w	If the bookmark is a numbered paragraph, includes the complete paragraph number of the bookmarked paragraph, in its full context in the numbering scheme.

SECTION

Field syntax: { SECTION }

This field inserts the number of the current section of the document.

SECTIONPAGES

Field syntax: { SECTIONPAGES }

The SECTIONPAGES field inserts the total number of pages in a section. When using this field, you should restart page numbering from 1 in each section after the first section.

SEQ

Field syntax: { SEQ *Identifier* [*Bookmark*] [*Switches*] }

Use SEQ fields to set up a sequential numbering scheme for any items you want to count. Use LISTNUM fields instead to number paragraphs in complex lists. The Insert ⇨ Caption command inserts SEQ fields, but it makes other changes in your document. So when you need SEQ fields for more complicated jobs, you should insert them yourself. SEQ fields in headers, footers, comments, and footnotes are numbered separately from those in the body of the document. Table 21-24 has further information about this field.

Table 21-24
SEQ Field Instructions and Switches

Instruction	Function
Identifier	A name you choose for a given set of numbered items. It must start with a letter.
Bookmark	Includes a bookmark name to refer to an item elsewhere in the document. For example, to cross-reference an illustration, mark the SEQ field numbering for that illustration with the bookmark Pic2, and then insert a cross-reference to it using { SEQ illust Pic2 }.
Switches	
\c	Repeats the last number in the sequence — good for listing numbered items in headers or footers.
\h	Hides the field result. This is useful when you want to refer to the SEQ field by number in a cross-reference but don't want the number given by the SEQ field itself to appear. For an example of this switch in action, see Chapter 26.
\n	Default setting. Inserts the next number in the sequence.
\r *n*	Restarts numbering at *n*.

SET

Field syntax: { SET *Bookmark* "*Text*" }

Use a SET field to set up an invisible bookmark that you can then use in other fields, or in VBA procedures. SET fields produce no visible results, so if you want to display or print the bookmarked information, you'll need a REF field. Table 21-25 has further information about this field.

Table 21-25
SET Field Instructions

Instruction	Function
Bookmark	This is the name for your new bookmark.
Text	This is the information to be bookmarked in the form of text or a nested field. Use quotation marks if the information contains spaces.

STYLEREF

Field syntax: { STYLEREF *StyleIdentifier* [\l] [\n] [\p] [\r] [\t] [\w] }

A STYLEREF field displays text formatted with the specified style, which should be listed in quotation marks if it contains spaces. This field is often useful in headers and footers, where it searches the current page, displaying the text passage to which *Style* is applied. That lets you include the current main heading in a header or footer. With the \l switch you can also set up dictionary-style headers or footers listing the first and last entries on the page.

The placement of the STYLEREF field in your document is important. When placed in document text, or within footnotes, endnotes, or comments, it first searches backward in the document (not the note or comment text) for the nearest preceding occurrence of *Style* text. If none is found in that direction, it then searches forward from the field.

In headers and footers, the field's behavior varies depending on whether you're printing the document or just displaying it on screen. During printing, it starts by searching the current page from top to bottom. If it finds no *Style* text there, it starts from the top of the current page and works backward to the beginning of the document, and then searches from the bottom of the current page to the end of the document. For ordinary display, the search starts at the beginning of the current section rather than the current page and continues to the end of the document. Table 21-26 has further information about this field.

Table 21-26
STYLEREF Field Instructions

Instruction	Function
\l	Inserts the last passage of *Style* text on the current page, instead of the first *Style* text.
	The remaining switches work the same way as their counterparts in REF fields.

SYMBOL

Field syntax: { SYMBOL *CharNum* [\a] [\f "*Font*"] [\h] [\j] [\s *Points*] [\u] }

This field inserts a character or text specified by its number in the ANSI, Shift-JIS, or Unicode character sets. You can insert special characters much more easily with the Insert ➪ Symbol command or via keyboard shortcuts, but there's one excellent reason to use this field: It lets you place the symbol into a line without changing line spacing. While you accomplish a similar end by setting the paragraph line spacing to an exact value, doing so prevents Word from adjusting the spacing when you change font size. Table 21-27 has further information about this field.

Table 21-27
SYMBOL Field Instructions

Instruction	Function
CharNum	The code for the symbol you want to insert.
\a	Tells Word to regard the specified code as an ANSI character.
\f "*Font*"	Tells Word which font to use to display the character. If you omit this switch, Word uses the current font.
\h	Inserts the symbol without changing the paragraph's line spacing. This can chop off the top of tall characters, but used with care it prevents unsightly variations.
\j	Tells Word to regard the specified code as a Shift-JIS character.
\s *Points*	Specifies the font size — in points, of course.
\u	Tells Word to regard the specified code as a Unicode character.

TC

Field syntax: { TC "*EntryText*" [\f *GroupID*] [\l *Level*] [\n] }

This is one of two Word fields related to tables of contents (see TOC for the other). A TC field marks a table of contents entry if you don't want to use the standard, automated method for creating a table of contents (from headings). Place the TC field just before each heading or other passage you want to include in the contents. TC fields are hidden text, appearing in the document only if you display their codes. Table 21-28 has further information about this field.

Table 21-28
TC Field Instructions

Instruction	Function
EntryText	Specifies the entry's text as it will appear in the table of contents.
\f GroupID	Marks the entry as belonging to the Type group. You can then use the \f switch in the TOC field to build a reference table consisting only of entries belonging to the Type group.
\l Level	Specifies the level for this entry. For example, the field { TC "Entering Data" \l 4 } marks a level-4 entry, and Word applies the built-in style TOC 4 to that entry in the table of contents. If no level is specified, Word assumes you mean level 1.
\n	Omits the page number for the entry.

TOC

Field syntax:

```
{ TOC [\a ID] [\b Bookmark] [\c ID] [\d "Separator"] [\f
GroupID] [\h] [\l Levels] [\n Levels] [\o "Headings"][\p
"Separator"] [\s ID] [\t "Style,Level, Style,Level, . . ."]
[\u] [\w] [\x] [\z] }
```

A TOC field inserts a finished table of contents or other reference table in your document based on headings or other styles, or on TC fields. Although you can insert a TOC field via the Insert ➪ Reference ➪ Index and Tables dialog box, you often need to add or edit switches to customize the results. Table 21-29 has further information about this field.

Table 21-29
TOC Field Instructions

Instruction	Function
\a ID	CrZeates the table of contents from paragraphs in which SEQ fields of type ID reside. Only the text you typed in the document is listed in the table of contents — not the sequence number itself, or any other text inserted by the SEQ field. Typically used to create tables of figures, equations, and so on, as described in Chapter 19.
\b Bookmark	Limits the table of contents to entries taken only from the bookmarked part of the document.

Instruction	Function
\c *ID*	Like \a, except that the sequence number and text inserted by the SEQ field are included in the table of contents, along with the paragraph text in which the SEQ field resides.
\d *"Separator"*	Used with the \s switch to specify up to five characters that separate the sequence numbers from the page numbers. Word inserts a hyphen by default.
\f *GroupID*	Bases the reference table on TC fields. If you include a GroupID, the table is limited to TC fields with the corresponding letter.
\h	Hyperlinks the entries and page numbers within the table of contents.
\l *Levels*	Builds a table of contents from TC fields that assign entries to one of the specified levels. For example, { TOC \l 1-4 } builds a table of contents from TC fields that assign entries to levels 1 through 4 in the table of contents. TC fields that assign entries to lower levels are skipped.
\n *Levels*	Omits page numbers from the specified range of level numbers (as in \n 4-5), or from the entire table of contents if you don't specify a Level.
\o *"Headings"*	Bases the table of contents on paragraphs formatted with built-in heading styles (Heading 1, Heading 2, and so on). Headings is optional, specifying a numeric range (as in \o "1-4"). If you leave out the range, the table of contents includes all heading levels listed.
\p *"Separator"*	Specifies up to five characters separating each entry and its page number. The default is a tab with a leader of periods.
\s *ID*	Displays the number of the last SEQ field of type ID, placing it before the page number. You can use this switch to create Chapter Number or Page Number references in the table of contents, as long as the chapter numbers in the document are actually SEQ field results.
\t *"Style, Level, Style, Level, . . ."*	Creates the table of contents based on paragraphs formatted with specific named styles. The number after each Style item specifies the level for text of that style. You can combine the \o and \t switches in the same TOC field.
\u	Builds a table of contents by using the applied paragraph outline level.
\w	Preserves tabs within reference table entries.
\x	Preserves line breaks within reference table entries.
\z	Hides page numbers within the table of contents in Web Layout View.

XE

Field syntax: { XE "*Entry*" [\b] [\f *GroupID*] [\i] [\r *Bookmark*] [\t "*Text*"] [\y "*Text*"]}

An XE field marks a location that is to be referenced in an index. Don't create these fields from scratch—you should get Word to make them for you, via the Mark Index Entry dialog box. But you have to edit them in at least two situations: if you want to create two or more specialized indexes in the same document, or if you want an index with more than two levels, main entries and subentries. XE fields are hidden text, invisible unless field codes are displayed. Table 21-30 has further information about this field.

Table 21-30 XE Field Instructions	
Instruction	**Function**
Entry	This is the text that actually appears in the index. To specify subentries, place a colon between the subentry and the main entry, or the previous subentry, like this: "Washington, George:Fables about:Cherry tree, chopping down." The Mark Index Entry dialog box has room for main entries and subentries only, but you can add up to nine levels this way. In the resulting index, each level receives the corresponding built-in paragraph style (Index 1, Index 2, and so on).
\b	Displays the entry's page number in bold.
\f *GroupID*	Specifies that the entry is part of the GroupID group. See the earlier section on the INDEX field.
\i	Displays the entry's page number in italics.
\r *Bookmark*	Lists in the index the range of pages marked by the Bookmark instead of a single page number.
\t "*Text*"	Displays *Text* in the index instead of a page number.

✦   ✦   ✦

Word Power Programming

The VBA concepts and techniques covered at length in Part XI apply in all Office applications. Still, each app has its own object model, through which you access the specific features of that program. In the Office suite, Word's object model offers the richest array of programming treasures. Understanding Word objects such as `Range` and `Find` can be a challenge, but getting the hang of them is crucial if you want to construct VBA routines of any power in Word. That's where this chapter comes in.

Word's object model encompasses so many objects and collections that you'd need a sizeable wall poster to portray the object hierarchy in graphical form. Obviously, I can cover only a fraction of the objects, properties, and methods you can tap for your own programs. This chapter turns the spotlight on the most important Word VBA techniques. Once you grasp these fundamentals, turn to the Help files in Word for details.

Exploring the Word Object Model

The Word Object Model defines the objects and collections available to you as a Word/VBA developer — the objects and collections you can use to extend the functionality of your Word application. Most objects in the Word Object Model belong to associated collections; the name of a particular `Collection` object is usually the plural form of its associated object. The `Documents` collection, for example, holds `Document` objects; the `AutoCaptions` collection holds `AutoCaption` objects.

As shown in Figure 22-1, the Application object resides at the top of the Word hierarchy of objects; it represents the functionality of the entire Word program. Below the Application object are all other Word objects.

The figure shows the Object Model in generalized form to illustrate relationships among objects. For example, some objects have a specific *parent object* besides the Application object; Object A is the parent of Object A1. Some other objects (such as Object B) are part of a collection. Finally, objects like Object C are *children* of the Application object — but they are neither parents of other objects in the hierarchy nor part of a collection.

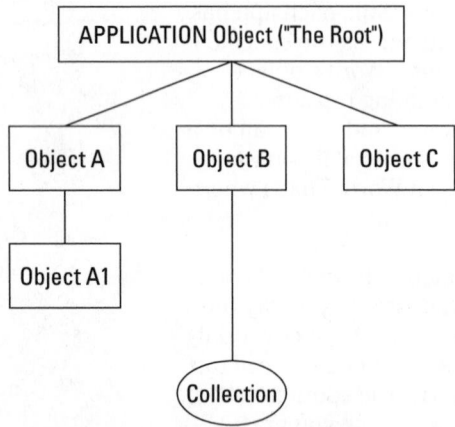

Generic Word Object Model

Figure 22-1: Exploring the generic Word Object Model

Table 22-1 lists the different Word objects, their associated collections, and parent object(s) (wherever applicable). Remember: Not all Word objects are part of a collection.

Table 22-1
Word Objects and Collections

Object	Collection	Description	Parent
AddIn	AddIns	Each `AddIn` object represents a Word add-in library.	`Application`
Adjustments		Holds a collection of numbers used for moving the adjustment "handles" of the parent `Shape` object.	`Shape`
Application		Root object of the model. Only this object can provide access to all other objects.	
AutoCaption	AutoCaptions	Each `AutoCaption` object represents one item that can have a caption automatically added.	`Application`
AutoCorrect		Represents all functionality of Word's AutoCorrect features.	`Application`
AutoCorrectEntry	AutoCorrectEntries	The `AutoCorrectEntries` collection holds a list of words and their AutoCorrect entries.	`AutoCorrect`
AutoTextEntry	AutoTextEntries	Provides functionality for implementing AutoText feature of Word.	`Template`
Bookmark	Bookmarks	Provides functionality for implementing the Bookmark feature of Word.	`Range`, `Find`, `Document`

Continued

Table 22-1 *(continued)*

Object	Collection	Description	Parent
Border to a side or some sides of a border around a parent object.	Borders Paragraph, Table	Each border object corresponds	Range, Find,
Browser		Provides navigation functionality in Word.	Application
CalloutFormat		Represents modifications that may be made to line callouts.	Shape
CaptionLabel	CaptionLabels	A *caption label* is identifying text added (sometimes automatically) to figures, tables, equations, and so on.	Application
Cell	Cells	Each Cell object represents a cell in a table.	Range, Find
Characters	Characters	Allows access to individual characters in a string of text.	Range
Checkbox		Represents a checkbox form field.	FormField
ColorFormat		Describes a specific single color used in a gradient or a patterned fill.	
Column	Columns	Each Column object represents a column in a table.	Find
COMAddIn	COMAddIns	A COMAddIn object refers to a COM component available in Word.	Application
Comment	Comments	Each Comment object represents a single cell (in a document, selection, or range) that contains a comment.	Range, Find, Document
CustomLabel	CustomLabels	Each CustomLabel object represents a custom mailing label.	MailingLabel

Object	Collection	Description	Parent
`DefaultWebOptions`		Allows programmatic changes to items associated with the default settings of the Web Options dialog.	`Application`
`Dialog`	`Dialogs`	A `Dialog` object represents a single built-in dialog box in Word.	`Application`
`Dictionary`	`Dictionaries`	Each `Dictionary` object represents a single custom dictionary active in Word.	`Application`
`Document`	`Documents`	Each open Word document is equivalent to a `Document` object.	`Application`, `Find`, `Template`, `Window`
`DropCap`		Use this object to create a dropped capital letter of the first letter in a paragraph.	`Paragraph`
`DropDown`		Each `DropDown` object represents a dropdown form field object.	`FormField`
`Email`		Each `Email` object represents an e-mail message.	`Document`
`EmailAuthor`		Each `EmailAuthor` object `Email` represents the author of the e-mail message.	
`EmailOptions`		Each `EmailOptions` object holds application-level attributes that Word uses when you create and edit e-mail messages.	`Application`
`EmailSignature`		Each `EmailSignature` object holds information about the signatures used by Word in e-mail messages.	`Email`

Continued

Table 22-1 *(continued)*

Object	Collection	Description	Parent
EndNote an endnote in a document, selection, or range.	EndNotes Document	Each EndNote object represents	Range, Find,
Envelope		Each Envelope object represents a single envelope available for a Document object.	
Field	Fields	Each Field object represents a single field in the parent collection.	Range, Find, Document
FileConverter	FileConverters	Each FileConverter object represents a file converter in Word (such as WordPerfect file converter).	Application
FillFormat		The FillFormat object represents the fill effects available for shapes.	Shape
Find		This object represents the Find and Replace dialog box in Word.	
FirstLetterException	FirstLetterExceptions	Each FirstLetterException object represents an abbreviation that is not included in the AutoCorrect object capitalization rule.	AutoCorrect
Font		This object contains formatting attributes related to fonts of the parent including font type, size, and color.	Range, Find
FontNames		This object represents a list of fonts available in Word.	Application
Footnote	Footnotes	Each Footnote object represents a single footnote in a Word document, selection, or range.	Range, Find, Document

Object	Collection	Description	Parent
FormField **a single form field in a Word document, selection, or range.**	FormFields Document	Each FormField object represents	Range, Find,
Frame	Frames	Each Frame object represents a single form field in a Word document, selection, or range.	Range, Find, Document
Frameset		Each Frameset object represents a frames page or a single frame on a frames page.	
FreeformBuilder		The FreeformBuilder object is used by the Shape object to create new 'free hand' shapes	
	GroupShapes	The GroupShapes collection holds all of shape objects that make up a grouped shape.	Shape
HangulAndAlphabetException	HangulAndAlphabetExceptions	These objects are used in Korean version of Word. Each HangulAndAlphabetException represents a single hangul.	AutoCorrect
	HangulHanjaConversionDictionaries	This collection represents a list of custom dictionaries.	Application
HeaderFooter	HeaderFooters	This collection represents a list of headers and footers in a particular section of a document.	Find
HeadingStyle	HeadingStyles	Use this object to create a table of contents or table of figures.	
HorizontalLineFormat		Use this object to format a horizontal line.	InlineShape
Hyperlink	Hyperlinks	Each Hyperlink object represents a single hyperlink in a document, range, or selection	Range, Find, Document, Shape

Continued

Table 22-1 *(continued)*

Object	Collection	Description	Parent
Index	Indexes	Each Index object represents a single index in a document.	Document
InlineShape	InlineShapes	Each InlineShape object represents a single inline shape in a document, selection, range, or field.	Range, Selection, Document
KeyBinding	KeyBindings	Each KeyBinding object represents a single custom key assignment.	Application
Language	Languages	A Language object includes formatting and proofing abilities for a specific language.	Application
LetterContent		This object represents the different parts of a letter that Word's Letter Wizard uses to create letters.	Document
LineFormat		The LineFormat object represents the formatting associated with the line of the parent Shape object.	
LineNumbering		Use this object to view line numbers for each page or column.	PageSetup
LinkFormat		The LinkFormat object represents the linking attributes associated with an OLE object or picture.	
ListEntry	ListEntries	A ListEntry object represents a specific list item in a drop-down type form field.	DropDown
ListFormat		This object represents the list formatting options that can be applied to the paragraphs in the parent Range object.	Range

Object	Collection	Description	Parent
ListGallery	ListGalleries	Each ListGallery object represents one of the three tabs in the Bullets and Numbering dialog box.	Application
ListLevel	ListLevels	Each ListLevel object represents a single list level of a particular list template.	ListGallery
	ListParagraphs	This collection represents the list of paragraphs in a document, list, or range that are formatted with list formatting. represents formatting options for a particular list.	Range, Document, Lists
ListTemplate	List object	Lists Each Document	List
ListTemplate	ListTemplates	A ListTemplate object represents a particular list format.	ListGallery, Template, Document
Mailer		The Mailer object, which is available only on Macintosh, represents the PowerTalk mailer for a document.	
MailingLabel		This object represents a mailing label in Word.	Application
MailMerge		This object allows access to the mail-merge abilities of Word.	Document, MailMerge
MailMergeDataField	MailMergeDataFields	A MailMergeDataField object represents one mail-merge data field of a mail-merge data source.	MailMerge
MailMergeDataSource		This object represents the properties of the mail-merge data source.	MailMerge
MailMergeField	MailMergeFields	This collection represents the list of mail-merge fields in a particular document.	MailMerge

Continued

Table 22-1 (continued)

Object	Collection	Description	Parent
MailMergeFieldName	MailMergeFieldNames	Each MailMergeFieldName object represents a single field name a mail-merge data source field.of	MailMergeDataSource
MailMessage		This object represents the properties of an e-mail message composed by using Word as the e-mail editor.	Application
OLEFormat		The OLEFormat object represents all of attributes associated with an OLE object, ActiveX object, or a field, except for linking.	
Options		This object allows access to all options available in Word's Options dialog box.	Application
OtherCorrectionsException	OtherCorrectionsExceptions	This object represents a single word that AutoCorrect will not correct.	AutoCorrect
PageNumber	PageNumbers	This object represents a single page number in an associated header or footer.	HeaderFooter
PageSetup		This object allows you to manipulate the page properties for a document, range, selection, or section.	Range, Selection, Document, Section
Pane	Panes	This object represents a single pane for a window.	Window
Paragraph	Paragraphs	Each Paragraph object represents a single paragraph in a document, range, or selection.	Document
ParagraphFormat		This object provides formatting options for a specified paragraph.	Range, Selection, Paragraph

Object	Collection	Description	Parent
PictureFormat		Use this object to manipulate the picture properties of the parent Shape object.	Range, Document
	ProofreadingErrors	This collection includes the list of spelling and grammatical errors for a document or range.	
Range		This object represents a specific area in a document.	Selection, FormField, Document, List, Paragraph
ReadibilityStatistic	ReadibilityStatistics	Each ReadibilityStatistic object represents a single statistic for the current document or range.	Range, Document
RecentFile	RecentFiles	Each RecentFile object represents one of the recently opened files in Word.	Application
Replacement		This object represents the Replace part of the Find and Replace dialog box.	Find
Revision	Revisions	Each Revision object represents a single revision made to a document or range.	Range, Selection, Document
RoutingSlip		This object represents the routing slip of a document.	Document
Row	Rows	Each Row object represents a single row in a selection, range, or table.	Range, Selection
Section	Sections	Each Section object represents a single section in a selection, range, or document.	Range, Selection, Document
Selection		This object represents the selected part of a document.	Application, Window Sentence

Continued

Table 22-1 (continued)

Object	Collection	Description	Parent
Sentences		This object returns a collection of Range objects.	Range, Selection, Document
Shading		This object represents the shading properties associated with the parent object.	Range, Paragraph
ShadowFormat		The ShadowFormat object allows manipulation of the shadow formatting properties of a parent Shape object.	Shape
Shape	Shapes	The Shape object represents a single shape such as an AutoShape, a freeform shape, an OLE object (like an image), an ActiveX control, or a picture.	Hyperlink, ShapeRange, Selection, Document, FreeformBuilder
ShapeNode	ShapeNodes	The ShapeNode object specifies a single node or curved segment that makes up a freeform shape.	Shape
	ShapeRange	This collection holds a collection of Shape objects for a certain range or selection in a document.	
SpellingSuggestion	SpellingSuggestions	This object represents a spelling suggestion for an incorrectly spelled word.	Application
	StoryRanges	This collection represents a collection of all stories in a document.	
Style	Styles	A Style object represents a built-in or user-defined style in a document.	Document

Object	Collection	Description	Parent
Subdocument	Subdocuments	This object represents a single subdocument in a master document or range.	Range, Document
SynonymInfo		This object returns the synonyms, antonyms, and related words found for a word or phrase.	Range, Application
System		This object contains information about the computer system of the user.	Application
Table	Tables	Each Table object represents a single table in a selection, range, or document.	Range, Selection, Document
TableOfAuthorities	TablesOfAuthorities	This object represents a single table of authorities in a document.	Document
TableOfAuthoritiesCategory	TablesOfAuthorities Categories	This object represents a single category table of authorities.	Document
TableOfContents	TablesOfContents	This object represents a single table of contents in a document.	Document
TableOfFigures	TablesOfFigures	This object represents a single table of figures in a document.	Document
TabStop	TabStops	This object represents a single tab setting for a particular paragraph or collection of paragraphs.	Paragraph
Task	Tasks	Each Task object represents one of the running tasks on the system.	Application
Template	Templates	Each Template object represents the currently loaded template in the Word session.	Application, Document

Continued

Table 22-1 *(continued)*

Object	Collection	Description	Parent
TextColumn	TextColumns	Each TextColumn object represents a column of text in a section or document.	PageSetup
TextEffectFormat		This object contains all properties and methods associated with WordArt objects.	Shape
TextFrame		This object contains the properties and methods that can manipulate text frame shapes.	
TextInput		This object contains the properties and methods associated with a single text form field.	FormField
TextRetrievalMode		This object contains the properties and methods associated with how text is accessed from a Range object.	Range
ThreeDFormat		This object contains all three-dimensional formatting properties of the parent Shape object.	
TwoInitialCapsException	TwoInitialCapsExceptions	This object represents an abbreviation that is not included in the AutoCorrect object two caps rule.	AutoCorrect
Variable	Variables	A Variable object represents a single variable stored in a template or document.	Document
Version	Versions	Each Version object represents one version of a document.	Document

Object	Collection	Description	Parent
View		This object represents all view properties and methods associated with a window or a pane.	Window
WebOptions		Use this object to change the items associated with the Web Options dialog box of a document.	
Window	Windows	Each Window object represents a single window associated with a document or the Word session.	Application, Document
	Words	This collection contains a list of words in a range, selection, or	Selection Document document.
WrapFormat		This object includes properties and methods associated with how text wraps in a shape or shape range.	
Zoom	Zooms	Each Zoom object represents the magnification options for a pane or window.	View, Window

Understanding the Application Object

As in the other Office applications, the root object in Word's object model is `Application`. In other words, all other Word objects are contained by the `Application` object. The `Application` object is so central to VBA programming in Word that often you need not even mention it explicitly when you work with many important Word objects. Even so, you shouldn't forget its role; you need it to work with properties and methods of the application itself, as well as to include in some object references. For example, the following statement triggers the `ListCommands` method of the `Application` object:

```
Application.ListCommands ListAllCommands:=True
```

By the way, the `ListCommands` method creates a new document and places in it a table containing the keyboard shortcuts and menu locations of all Word commands. When you supply `True` as the value of the `ListAllCommands` argument, the new document contains both the custom keyboard and your menu assignments. Switch the value to `False` if you want to see only custom assignments in the table.

Accessing Word Documents in VBA

If the VBA procedure you're writing acts directly on a document, you must specify that document as an object in your code. Often, you can do so implicitly by using the `Selection` object, covered later in this chapter. In other situations, however, you must identify the target document explicitly.

Working with the active document

The typical VBA procedure in Word performs its magic on the document that's currently being edited. Use the `ActiveDocument` object to specify this active document. The statement `ActiveDocument.Close` closes the active document, of course. The point is, you don't have to write any code to figure out which document is the one being edited at the time the procedure runs — just use the `ActiveDocument` object.

Specifying a particular document

If you want to work with a particular document that isn't necessarily active, you must specify it as a member of the `Documents` collection. This collection contains all the documents currently open in Word. As with the generic VBA collection, you can refer to an individual document in the collection by its title, which in this case is its file name (use the file name only, not the complete path). Here's an example:

```
Documents("Toy Store Newsletter.doc")
```

Because you may not know the file name of the target document in advance (and because a user can change the document's file name), you may want to create a variable to hold the name. You can then use the variable to specify the document object your code, as in `Documents(strDocName)`.

You can also refer to a document by index number. The object reference `Documents(3)` specifies the third object (document) in the `Documents` collection. As simple as this technique may be, it's of limited value — typically, you don't know the index number of the document you want to work with. One use for it, however, is to learn the name of an open document. The following statement places the second open document's file name in a variable:

```
strDocName = Documents(2).Name
```

Creating, opening, and activating documents

To create a brand-new document, use the `Add` method of the `Documents` collection. Used without arguments, the `Add` method starts a document based on the Normal template. To specify another template, add its full path as the argument, as in this example:

```
Documents.Add template:= _
"C:\Windows\Application data\Microsoft Office\Hidden templates"
```

To open an existing document, you need the `Open` method (again, a method belonging to the `Documents` collection). Of course, you have to include the complete path of the document file, as in the following:

```
Documents.Open FileName:="C:\Toys\Toys for infants.doc"
```

When you open an existing document, by default, that document becomes the active document. You may activate a document that's already open, but not currently active, with the `Activate` method. Suppose you want your VBA program to activate a specific document that may (or may not) be open already when the program runs. Use code similar to the following to activate the document if it's already open, or to open it if it isn't:

```
Sub DocActivateOrOpen()
    Dim docFileName As String, docPath as String
    docFileName = "Pull toys.doc"
    docPath = "C:\Toys\"

    For Each targetDoc In Documents
```

```
        If targetDoc.Name = docFileName Then targetDocIsOpen =
True
    Next targetDoc

    If targetDocIsOpen = True Then
        Documents(docFileName).Activate
    Else
        Documents.Open FileName:=docPath & docFileName
    End If
End Sub
```

Closing and saving documents

To close an existing document, window, task, or pane, you need the `Close` method. You can use any of three different command syntaxes for using the `Close` method.

Syntax 1

The syntax is for closing specified *document(s)*:

```
expression.Close(SaveChanges, OriginalFormat, RouteDocument)
```

where

- ✦ *expression* is an expression that returns a Document or Documents object

- ✦ `SaveChanges` is an optional variant that specifies the save action for the document and can be one of the following `wdSaveOptions` constants: `wdDoNotSaveChanges`, `wdPromptToSaveChanges`, or `wdSaveChanges`.

- ✦ `OriginalFormat` is an optional variant that specifies the save format for the document and can be one of the following `wdOriginalFormat` constants: `wdOriginalDocumentFormat`, `wdPromptUser`, or `wdWordDocument`.

- ✦ `RouteDocument` is also an optional variant. True to route the document to the next recipient. If the document does not have a routing slip attached, this argument is ignored.

The following example saves the document displayed in the window; then it closes the active window:

```
ActiveWindow.Close SaveChanges:=wdSaveChanges
```

Syntax 2

The syntax for closing the specified *window* is as follows:

```
expression.Close(SaveChanges, OriginalFormat)
```

where *expression* is an expression that returns the specified window. For instance, the following example prompts the user to save before closing the active document.

```
ActiveDocument.Close SaveChanges:=wdPromptToSaveChanges,
OriginalFormat:=wdPromptUser
```

Syntax 3

The syntax for closing the specified *pane* or *task* is as follows:

```
expression.Close
```

where *expression* is an expression that returns the specified pane or task. For instance, the following example closes the active pane if the active window is split:

```
If ActiveWindow.Panes.Count >= 2
Then ActiveWindow.ActivePane.Close
```

Working with document sections

Because each Word document has one or more sections, you would expect Word VBA to provide a Sections collection and individual Section objects to work with these elements. One important use of Section objects is to access their headers and footers (via the HeaderFooter object). You can add new sections to a document using the Add method of the Sections collection or the InsertBreak methods of a range or selection.

Opening Windows with VBA

Each open document has at least one window, but a Word user can open as many windows as desired for any given document. Remember, each of these windows is an object in its own right. In the Word object model, the Application object has a Windows collection containing all the windows of all open documents. In addition, each Document object has its own separate Windows collection that contains only the windows for that document.

You have two main reasons to work with Window objects in Word: to control the appearance of the window and to manipulate document content via the Selection object. The Selection object is discussed later in the chapter; here I focus on the technique for specifying a particular window—and on introducing the properties you can use to alter a window's appearance.

Specifying windows in code

The easiest window to work with in code is the one that's currently being edited when the procedure runs. Use the `ActiveWindow` object to specify this window.

To designate a specific window in code, identify it as a member of one of the `Windows` collections. You don't have to name the `Application` object when you work with the global `Windows` collection, but when you access a specific document's `Windows` collection, a reference to that document is required. You can identify the window by its name or index number in the collection. A window's name is the same as the name of the document it displays — except you have to add a colon and the window number after the document name if more than one window is open for the same document.

Table 22-2 displays typical document references for `Windows` object.

Table 22-2 Document References for Windows Object	
Reference	*Comments*
`Windows("Document4")`	Valid if Document4 has only one open window
`Windows("Kites, tops, and skip ropes.doc:3")`	Specifies the third window of the named document
`Documents("Window display.doc").Windows(2)`	Specifies the second window of the named document's `Windows` collection

Working with window panes

A Word window has at least one pane, but it can have more than one. When you split a window vertically using the Window ➪ Split command, the top and bottom portions of the window are separate panes. The areas where Word displays headers, footers, footnotes, endnotes, and comments are also panes.

If you have to access the appearance settings or the selection in an individual pane, you must first identify the target `Pane` object in your code. Refer to that object by index number in its window's `Panes` collection.

Tip   When you simply want to work with the main part of the window (or the top pane if the window is split), that's the default pane; you can omit pane references.

Changing window appearance

Window objects offer a host of properties representing the state of all the elements you see on the screen that are pertinent to an individual window. A number of these properties act as toggles — their values can be either True or False. For example, to turn on the Document Map for the active window, enter this statement into your code:

```
ActiveWindow.DocumentMap = True
```

Use similar statements to turn on or turn off properties such as DisplayScreenTips or DisplayVerticalScrollBar.

Tip   Remember that the keyword Not reverses the current value of a Boolean variable or property. Using that keyword is the easiest way to toggle such properties, as shown here:

```
ActiveWindow.DisplayRulers = Not
ActiveWindow.DisplayRulers
```

The Left, Top, Height, and Width properties let you set the size and location of a nonmaximized window.

Using the View object

Several aspects of the appearance of a window or pane are governed by a subsidiary object, View. Table 22-3 lists a few of the View object's many properties.

Table 22-3
View Object's Properties

Property	What It Does
Type	Corresponds to the selection at the top of the View menu (Normal, Outline, Print Layout, and so on). To change the view type, use one the following predefined constants: wdMasterView, wdNormalView, wdOutlineView, wdPrintView, wdWebView, or wdPrintPreview. For example, the statement ActiveWindow.View.Type = wdPrintPreview switches the ActiveWindow to the Print Preview view.
FullScreen	Controls whether the window is displayed in standard or full-screen view (see Chapter 15 for information on full-screen view).
TableGridlines	Determines whether table gridlines are visible.
ShowAll, Show . . .	ShowAll determines whether all nonprinting characters are visible; it corresponds to the setting of the All checkbox on the View tab of the Tools ⇨ Options dialog box. You can display or hide any type of nonprinting character, as well as other items (such as text highlighting and boundaries), by using various properties that start with Show—for example, ShowBookmarks and ShowHighlight.

Zooming in and out — in code

To control a window's magnification, you have to drill down still deeper into the object hierarchy to the Zoom object and then modify its Percentage property. Here's an example:

```
ActiveWindow.View.Zoom.Percentage = 135
```

If you want to preset the zoom factor for a view type that isn't currently displayed, include the constant for its type as an argument to the View property, as in

```
ActiveWindow.View.Zoom.Percentage = 75
```

The next time the user switches to that view, the document appears at the specified zoom percentage.

Alternatively, you can use the `PageFit` property of the `Zoom` object to duplicate the Page Width and Full Page choices in Word's Zoom toolbar button. With either of these settings active, Word rezooms the document whenever the window size changes, ensuring that the correct fit is maintained. This statement is equivalent to selecting Page Width in the Zoom button:

```
ActiveWindow.View.Zoom.PageFit = wdPageFitBestFit
```

The Full Page choice is available only in Print Layout view, but you can duplicate it with the following code:

```
Windows("Document1").View.Zoom.PageFit = wdPageFitFullPage
```

To shut off automatic rezoom, set the `PageFit` property to `wdPageFitNone`.

Working with the Selection Object

In Word VBA, the `Selection` object refers to whatever is currently selected in a window pane. That's right, the `Selection` object belongs to a window pane, not to a document; a document can have more than one open window, each window can have more than one pane, and each of these contains a selection. (Although a `Selection` object technically belongs to a window pane, it's okay to think of it as belonging to a window instead, unless you specifically want to work with the selection in a special pane such as a header or footer.)

Although you can manipulate selections in your code through the `Selection` object, it's often better to use a `Range` object instead. For a discussion of when to use each of these objects, see the section "Working with Text in Word VBA" later in this chapter.

The content of a selection can be a block of text, a table, a text box, a graphic, or anything else you can select with the mouse or keyboard. Key point: If nothing is selected, the `Selection` object represents the current location of the insertion point.

Every window pane contains a selection; if the selection you want isn't in the main pane of the active window, you need only refer explicitly to the target window. To work with the selection in the main pane (of whichever window is active when the procedure runs), just use the `Selection` object by itself. For example, you can use the following statement to replace the active window's selection with the text in quotes:

```
Selection.Text = "My dog has fleas."
```

If you want to refer to a selection in one of the windows that isn't active, you must specify the window in full. Here's an example:

```
Documents("Sea chanties.doc").Windows(2).Selection.Text = _
    "My bonnie lies over the ocean."
```

Because the Selection object can refer to many different types of content, it's always best to check to see what type of content is selected before you perform some action on it. Otherwise, you risk unexpected results or errors. Use the Selection object's Type property to provide this information. For example, the following code tests the selection to be sure it's a regular text selection of one or more consecutive characters before cutting the selection to the Clipboard:

```
With Selection
If .Type = wdSelectionNormal Then
    .Cut
End If
```

You can use the selection constants listed in Table 22-4 in such tests.

Table 22-4
Selection Constants

Selection.Type Constant	What Is Selected
wdNoSelection	No selection at all
wdSelectionBlock	A vertical block of text
wdSelectionColumn	A table column
wdSelectionFrame	A frame
wdSelectionInlineShape	A graphic residing in text
wdSelectionIP	Just an insertion point — nothing is actually selected
wdSelectionNormal	A standard selection consisting of consecutive text characters
wdSelectionRow	A table row
wdSelectionShape	A floating graphic, not in line with text

Understanding Range Objects

When you're editing a document yourself, you must position the insertion point or make a selection before adding, deleting, or formatting the text. In VBA, however, Word's Range objects free you from that necessity. A Range object simply specifies a continuous block of text of one or more characters anywhere in a document. Range objects are completely independent of the insertion point or highlighted selection the user sees in the document window. Once you've created a Range object, you can then manipulate the text it encompasses with VBA equivalents for all of Word's powerful editing commands, just as you can with Selection objects.

You can specify Range objects in your code in two ways:

✦ By accessing predefined ranges via the Range property

✦ By defining ranges yourself using a Document object's Range method

Using the Range property

An open Word document already contains Range objects corresponding to many document elements. Each paragraph defines a range, as does every table, individual table cell, comment, and footnote, to name just a few examples. You can think of these ranges as existing only in a sort of virtual reality until you access them using the Range property of the object in question. For example, to specify the Range object represented by the first paragraph in the active document, you would use the following object reference:

```
ActiveDocument.Paragraphs(1).Range
```

Because these predefined ranges already exist in Word's mind, you can use object references to them directly, without assigning them to object variables. This is the way to go if you want to use a given range for a single operation. The following statement copies the document's second table to the Clipboard using the Range object's Copy method:

```
ActiveDocument.Tables(2).Range.Copy
```

When multiple consecutive statements use the same range, you can use a With... block to speed up code entry and the program. Here, this technique is used with a range representing the document's third section to sort the paragraphs in the range and then make the first sentence bold:

```
With ActiveDocument.Section(3).Range
    .Sort SortOrder:=wdSortOrderAscending
    .Sentences(1).Range.Bold = True
End With
```

The preceding example illustrates how a Range object typically contains other objects which themselves encompass ranges. The statement on the third line accesses the range corresponding to the first sentence in the original range and then makes that sentence bold. Note too that you can't apply formatting directly to objects such as words, sentences, or paragraphs — you must use their Range properties.

> **Tip** If you plan to use a range in multiple statements that aren't consecutive, assign the range to an object variable. Doing so makes your code easier to type and your procedure a bit faster.

Selection objects also have the Range property. That fact makes it easy to use the properties and methods belonging to Range objects on existing selections. This example assigns the selection's range to a variable, moves the selection, and then converts the text of the original range to all-lowercase characters:

```
Set deRange = Selection.Range
Selection.Move Unit:=wdParagraph, Count:=3
deRange.Case = wdLowerCase
```

Defining your own ranges using the Range method

When existing objects don't contain the text you want to work with, create your own Range object. You can define as many Range objects as you want in any open document(s). The technique relies on the document's Range method, which requires you to specify the new range's starting and ending points in terms of character position in the document. Check out this example:

```
ActiveDocument.Range (Start:=10, End:=20)
```

The preceding expression is an object reference to a range beginning with the eleventh character in the document and ending with the twentieth character. The "character position" values actually refer to the place just to the left of a given character where the insertion point would go. A value of 0 corresponds to the location immediately to the left of the first character in the document, and a value of 10 to the spot just past the tenth character and just left of the eleventh character. Word counts all characters in the document, including hidden and nonprinting characters, whether or not they're currently visible.

> **Tip** To create a range that is just a location and contains no text, set the Start and End values to the same number. To include the entire document in the Range object, use the document's Range method with no arguments, or use the document's Content property.

It's easy enough to create a Range object — as long as you know the values for the starting and ending characters you want to include in it. The trouble is you rarely want to work with an arbitrary number of characters at an arbitrary location in your document. Normally you're interested in text at meaningful places in the document. You might want to begin a range at an existing bookmark (for example), or at the start of the current selection (or an existing range), or at a particular word or phrase that you know is somewhere in the document.

To define a range based on some such item, use the Start or End properties of a Selection, Range, or Bookmark object to learn the character-position value you need. If you want to create a 10-character range starting at a bookmark named ForgetMeNot, these statements do the trick:

```
With ActiveDocument
    Set myBkMark = .Bookmarks("ForgetMeNot")
    Set homeOnTheRange =.Range (Start:= myBkMark, End:=
myBkMark + 10)
End With
```

Here's another example, showing how you can use the Range property to locate a paragraph, focus on a particular word it contains, and then use the beginning of that word as the start of a new range. Here, the End argument is omitted, so the range extends from its starting point to the end of the document:

```
With ActiveDocument
    Set firstWord = .Paragraphs(160).Range.Words(3)
    Set RangeTop =.Range (Start:= firstWord.Start)
End With
```

As discussed in the section later in this chapter, using Find with a range or selection redefines the object to encompass only the text it finds. So after Find locates a phrase in a range or selection, the Start or End properties for the same range or selection now identify the start and end positions of the found text.

Working with Text in Word VBA

Range and Selection objects are the starting points for almost everything you can do to text in Word VBA. Some text manipulations can be applied to documents as a whole, but in general, you must specify a range or a selection before you can make changes.

Range and Selection objects have a great deal in common, but they also have important differences. Both objects represent continuous sequences of characters (upon which you can perform all kinds of editing magic); they also share the majority of their properties and methods. However, some properties and methods are unique to selections and some to ranges. The big differences, of course, are that a Selection object corresponds to a window pane's one visible selection—which can be text, graphics, or other items — but Range objects exist independently of the selection, always consist of text, and can be accessed in any quantity.

Use the Selection object when your procedure depends on the user to identify the text to be manipulated, or when you want to show the user just which text is being changed. Range objects are better otherwise. They make your program faster and less distracting to the user. One reason is that Word leaves the screen alone when modifying a range — but updates the screen every time a selection changes. In addition, range modifications politely leave the user's selection undisturbed.

Selecting ranges and creating ranges from selections

Despite their differences, Selection and Range objects can be created easily from one another. This capability is crucial. Many important editing functions work only with ranges. Contrariwise, the only way to display the contents of a range to the user is by selecting the range. Use these simple techniques:

✦ To select a range, use the range's Select method. For a range object called RangeR, the code would be RangeR.Select.

✦ To access a range representing the same contents as a selection, use the selection's Range property, as in Selection.Range.

Remember, if a text-related method calls for a range but you want to use it on the selection, just type Selection.Range.MethodName into your code.

Redefining ranges and selections

Word VBA offers scads of methods for moving and resizing ranges and selections. I cover some of the most important of these in this section, but you can find more with careful study of the Help files.

Expanding a range or selection

The Expand method makes an existing range or selection bigger by tacking on at its end a unit of text. The unit can be a character, word, or paragraph, or any of a number of other predefined chunks. You can only add one of the specified units at a time, however, and you can't add units to the beginning of the range or selection. To add to the selection the word that immediately follows it, use the following statement:

```
Selection.Expand(wdWord)
```

You can use any of the following constants to expand the object: wdCharacter, wdWord, wdSentence, wdParagraph, wdSection, wdStory, wdCell, wdColumn, wdRow, wdTable, and (for Selection objects only) wdLine. The default is wdWord.

Perhaps confusingly, `Selection` objects (but not ranges) also have an `Extend` method. This method turns on Word's extend mode, which extends the selection when the user moves the insertion point. Each time your program calls the `Extend` method, the selection grows by a larger unit of text to encompass in sequence the current word, sentence, paragraph, section, and document. If you specify a character argument, as in `Selection.Extend("C")`, the selection extends to the next occurrence of that character instead.

Moving a range or selection

Word VBA permits you to redefine the beginning and end of a range or selection at will. Just be aware that the methods that include `"Move"` in the name change the location of the range or selection — they don't actually move the text contained in the object.

The `Move` method alters the range or selection by first collapsing it so that it marks a location only and no longer contains any text. This location is the starting position of the original object. The method then moves this collapsed object according to your instructions. After the move is complete, you can use the `Expand` or `MoveEnd` methods to make the object encompass text.

The following example moves the named range backward in the document by two paragraphs. Note that you use a named constant for the `Unit` argument (see the earlier section "Expanding a range or selection" for a list of these constants). The `Count` argument is a positive integer if you want to move forward in the document (toward the end) and negative to move backward. If the range or selection isn't already collapsed, or if it falls inside a unit, the beginning or end of the current unit is counted as the first one of the move. In this example, no parentheses appear around the arguments because the method's return value — how many units were actually moved — isn't used here.

```
onTheRange.Move Unit:=wdParagraph, Count:= -2
```

The `MoveStart` and `MoveEnd` methods work like `Move`, except that they only change the starting or ending position of the range or selection. The statement

```
Selection.MoveStart Unit:=wdWord, Count:=3
```

moves the beginning of the selection three words closer to the end of the document. Note that if you move the object's starting point past the end, Word collapses the range or selection and moves it as specified. The result is vice versa when moving the object's end to a point before the start.

Yet another pair of methods, `StartOf` and `EndOf`, move or extend the start or end position of a range or selection. `StartOf` moves the start of the object backward to the start of the current unit; `EndOf` moves the end of the object forward to the end of the current unit. With either method you can use the `Extend` argument to control whether Word moves both the start and end positions simultaneously, collapsing the object or only the side being moved. If the side of the object being moved is already at the side to which you're moving, nothing happens. Here's an example:

```
Selection.StartOf Unit:=wdSentence, Extend:=wdMove
```

Use the `wdMove` constant to collapse the object or `wdExtend` to move only the specified side.

Collapsing a range or selection

Often you must collapse a range or selection to a single position that doesn't enclose any text. In technical terms, a collapsed range or selection is one in which the start and end are the same. One situation where collapsing these objects is critical is when you want to insert a field, table, or other item before or after a selection or range without replacing the object's text. (You can insert plain text, new paragraphs, and some other items at a noncollapsed range or selection.)

Use the `Collapse` (what else?) method to collapse a range or selection. You can collapse the object to the original starting or ending position, as you prefer, using the optional `Direction` argument. The first of the following examples collapses the selection to its start, while the second collapses a range object to its end:

```
xSelection.Collapse
Selection.Collapse(Direction:=wdCollapseEnd)
```

If you collapse a range that ends with a paragraph mark to its end (using `wdCollapseEnd`), Word places the collapsed range after the paragraph mark (that is, the collapsed range is located at the start of the next paragraph). If you want to insert something in front of the original range's paragraph mark, you must first move the range backward with the `MoveEnd` method via a statement such as this:

```
someRange.MoveEnd Unit:=wdCharacter, Count:=-1
```

Deleting, copying, and pasting text

Erasing all the text in a range or selection is easy — just use the object's `Delete` method. You can use the `Cut` method instead if you want to remove the text and place it on the Windows Clipboard. Of course, the `Copy` method puts the text on the Clipboard without affecting the text in the range or selection.

You can insert text placed on the Clipboard into any range or selection with that object's `Paste` method. If the destination object isn't already collapsed, the pasted text replaces the text in the object — just the way the `Paste` command works in Word.

Although using the Clipboard to transfer text from one location to another is a familiar method, it's not the most efficient one. A better approach is to use the Text or FormattedText properties of the destination range or selection. Set these properties equal to the range or selection containing the text you want to transfer, and you're in business. The destination object should be collapsed unless you want the transferred text to replace the object's existing text.

The following example transfers the text from the selection to a collapsed range based on a bookmark (the fourth line actually performs the transfer). Only the text itself, without any formatting, gets copied to the new location.

```
With ActiveDocument.Bookmarks("TheBookmark")
    Set RangeY = ActiveDocument.Range(Start:=.Start, End:=.Start)
End With
RangeY.Text = Selection.Text
```

To transfer all the formatting along with the text, just substitute the FormattedText property for the Text property on both sides of the equal sign.

Inserting new text

The easiest text-adding technique to remember is to set the Text property of a range or selection to the text you want to insert. The following statement illustrates this:

```
Range2.Text = "Hey, ho, nobody home"
```

Tip

Just remember that setting the Text property replaces the existing text, if any, in the range or selection. Collapse the object beforehand unless your intention is, in fact, to replace the existing text.

Use the InsertBefore or InsertAfter methods of a range or selection object to insert text at a specific location in a document without destroying the object's existing text. These methods place the new text immediately before the start or after the end of the object in question, respectively. Word includes the inserted text in the selection or range.

With either method, the only argument is the text you want to insert. The following example inserts a new paragraph containing the text "Diary entry" at the beginning of the selection (note the use of the VBA constant vbCr to insert a paragraph mark). It then adds a paragraph stating today's date at the end. If you select an entire paragraph before running this code, the date paragraph appears after the paragraph mark in the selection:

```
Dim strInsertText As String
Selection.InsertBefore "Diary entry" & vbCr
```

```
strInsertText = "Today" & Chr(146) & "s date is "
strInsertText = strInsertText & Format(Now, "Long date") & ". "
Selection.InsertAfter strInsertText & vbCr
```

The example shows how inserted text can include string variables and VBA functions that return strings, as well as literal text and VBA constants. See Chapter 53 for information on working with strings in VBA.

The easiest way to add a new, empty paragraph to a document is to insert a paragraph mark (represented by the constant vbCr) with the Text property or InsertBefore/InsertAfter methods. The Add method used on a Paragraphs collection also works, but it's more cumbersome. Use it only if you want to place the new paragraph within a range or selection rather than at the beginning or end.

Formatting text

Several key properties of a range or selection are your gateways to changing the appearance of the text. These properties correspond to the items in Word's Format menu, and they function as indicated in Table 22-5.

Table 22-5 Text Formatting Properties	
This Property	**Gives Access To**
Font	Subsidiary properties for each aspect of character formatting, such as Name, Size, and Bold. For some reason, you can directly access the most common character formatting properties on Range objects, without going through the Font property, but not on selections.
ParagraphFormat	Subsidiary properties for each aspect of paragraph formatting, such as LeftIndent and LineSpacing.
Style	The name of the character or paragraph style applied to the range or selection.
Borders	The borders around the text.
TabStops	Types and locations of tab stops. You can access this property only through Paragraph objects, not directly via ranges or selections.

Finding and Replacing in Word VBA

Although it sounds like an imperative, `Find` is an object in Word VBA. `Find` objects belong to ranges and selections. Locating text or formatting with a `Find` object requires the following steps:

1. Access the `Find` object for a particular range or selection. If you want to search the entire document, use the `Document` object's `Content` property to access the corresponding range, as in

   `ActiveDocument.Content.Find`

2. Set the `Find` object's properties corresponding to what you're looking for and how you want to look for it.

3. Trigger the `Find` object's `Execute` method.

Here's an example of the technique:

```
With OpenRange.Find
    .ClearFormatting
    .Text = "pogo sticks"
    .Execute
End With
```

For properties you don't explicitly set, the `Find` object takes on the options that were last used or that are currently set in Word's Find and Replace dialog box. That's why you should always include the `.ClearFormatting` method when you're starting a new search — it removes any formatting that may have been previously specified from the search request.

Working with found text

The `Execute` method's job is to locate the first occurrence of the search text or formatting in the specified range or selection. Once the `Execute` method runs, your first programming concern is to see whether it found the text you were looking for. Use the `Find` object's `Found` property with an `If...Then` statement to perform this test, as in this sample code skeleton:

```
If .Found = True Then
    (take action on the found text)
Else
    (display an appropriate message)
End If
```

If the `Execute` method does find the search text, the original range or selection is redefined so that it encompasses the found text. This is a key point; it means you can work directly with that text through the original object's properties and methods. In the following code, an expansion of the first example in this section, the statement .Parent.Italic = True refers to the parent of the Find object, that is, the range called OpenRange. If that statement runs, OpenRange now encompasses only the found text — so only that text is formatted in italic.

```
With OpenRange.Find
    .ClearFormatting
    .Text = "pogo sticks"
    .Execute
    If .Found = True Then
        .Parent.Italic = True
    Else
        MsgBox "No pogo sticks found."
    End If
End With
```

Replacing text or formatting

The Replacement object belongs to (that is, is a property of) the Find object. To code a search and replace operation, you set properties and trigger methods of the Replacement object.

The following example replaces all occurrences of the words *pogo sticks* with *skateboards*. The selection changes when the find criterion is found because the Find object is accessed from the Selection object:

```
With ActiveDocument.Content.Find
    .ClearFormatting
    .Text = "pogo sticks"
    With .Replacement
        .ClearFormatting
        .Replacement.Text = "skateboards"
    End With
    .Execute Replace:=wdReplaceAll
End With
```

Note that the Execute method can take a Replace argument, used to control whether all occurrences of the found text, or only the first, get replaced.

Finding and replacing formatting

To search for text that's formatted a certain way, use the Find object's format-related properties. These are identical to the properties you use to work with formatting of a range or selection, as discussed in "Formatting text" earlier in this chapter. You use these same properties on the Replacement object if you want to specify formatting for the replacement text.

To search for any text with particular formatting, set the relevant `Find` properties and then set the `Text` property to an empty string using a pair of adjacent quotation marks. To change the formatting of found text without altering the text itself, use an empty string for the `Text` property of the `Replacement` object. The following code searches for paragraphs currently assigned to the `Drab` style and applies the `Frilly` style to them instead:

```
With Selection.Find
    .ClearFormatting
    .Style = "Drab"
    .Text = ""
    With .Replacement
        .ClearFormatting
        .Style = "Frilly"
        .Text = ""
    End With
    .Execute Replace:=wdReplaceAll
    .ClearFormatting
    .Replacement.ClearFormatting
End With
```

Including the two format-clearing statements in your procedures after the `Execute` method is a good idea. Otherwise, the next time the user opens the Find and Replace dialog box, he or she has to clear formatting options manually.

Using Document Variables

Unique among the Office applications, Word enables you to define in your code special document variables that it records with an individual document for later use. Document variables make it possible to store values used by a procedure between editing sessions.

Create and access document variables as members of the document's `Variables` collection. Like ordinary variables, document variables have names. The following statement places the value of a document variable called `Henry` into an ordinary variable called `FriendOfAnais`:

```
FriendOfAnais = ActiveDocument.Variables("Henry").Value
```

To create a new document variable, use the `Variables` collection's `Add` method as shown here:

```
Documents("Document1").Variables.Add _
    Name:="TimesThisMacroHasRun", Value:=0
```

Because you get an error if you try to add a document variable that already exists, the safe way to create variables is by checking to see if the variable name already exists. If so, you can retrieve the value; if not, you can create the variable and assign it an initial value. The following code illustrates this technique:

```
For Each DocVar In ActiveDocument.Variables
    If DocVar.Name = "LastCaption" Then DocIndex = aVar.Index
Next DocVar
If DocIndex = 0 Then
    ActiveDocument.Variables.Add Name:="LastCaption", Value:=1
    CaptionCounter = 1
Else
    CaptionCounter = ActiveDocument.Variables(DocIndex).Value
End If
```

Even though the object models of the other Office applications don't explicitly provide document variables, you can commandeer custom document properties for the same purpose. See Chapter 57 for more information.

✦   ✦   ✦

Crunching Numbers Efficiently with Excel

Excel becomes more powerful with every new version of Office, and Office XP is no exception. This part looks at Excel in detail — at how to customize it and how to navigate around in it. Editing and formatting are covered, as are the all-important use of formulas and functions. Charts (which can be used in all Office applications) get an in-depth look, as do the data-analysis capabilities of Excel. Finally, this part addresses the processes for finding and eliminating mistakes in Excel worksheets — and the ways VBA programming can make Excel even better.

Power Customizing Excel

Excel may offer fewer customization options than Word, but you still have extensive control over the way the program operates, how it looks on the screen, and perhaps most important, what information, formatting, and special features it adds automatically for you in new workbooks.

Startup Options

If you routinely use one or more workbooks, you can have Excel open them for you when you start the program. Just put shortcuts to the workbooks (or the workbooks themselves) into the XL Start folder (use Start ➪ Find ➪ Files or Folders to track it down).

If another folder suits you better, or if you want to automatically open worksheets stored elsewhere on your network, specify the location by typing its full path in the "At startup, open all files in:" box. This setting is on the General tab of Excel's Tools ➪ Options dialog box. Each time it starts, Excel opens the documents in *both* the folder you specify here and the XL Start folder. The alternate folder is a good place to put shared workbooks so each user doesn't require a separate copy.

You can place workspace files in either startup folder to have a group of workbooks open simultaneously just as you last used them (workspace files are covered in Chapter 24). Just be sure to place only the workspace file in the startup folder, and not shortcuts to the workbooks within it.

Excel templates stored in either startup folder appear in the General tab of the File ➪ New dialog box, right along with templates in the Templates folder.

Caution   Excel attempts to open *every* file it finds in the startup folders, be it word processing documents, sound recordings, or whatever—so place only workbooks,
workspaces, and their shortcuts in these folders.

Setting Excel Options

As in Word, Excel's Tools ⇨ Options dialog box is the central control panel for configuring the program. As shown in Figure 23-1, the settings in the Options dialog box
are organized as 13 tabs. I cover many of these options later, and others are pretty
much identical to their counterparts in Word, but a few bear mention here.

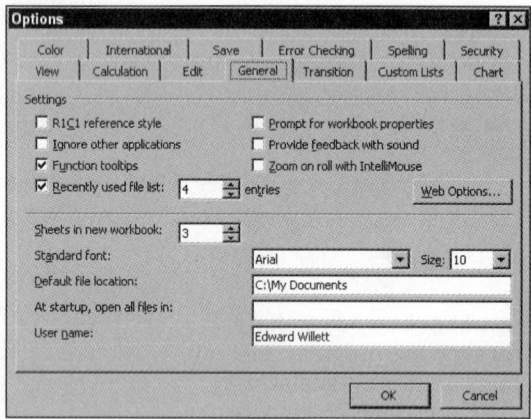

Figure 23-1: Excel's Tools ⇨ Options dialog box.
This illustration shows the General tab.

The General tab offers miscellaneous settings affecting overall program operation:

✦ I recommend maxing out the "Recently used file list" setting to 9. Being able to
   reopen files with a quick menu choice instead of going to the Open dialog box
   is a real boon.

✦ Note that you can change the number of blank worksheets Excel places into
   each new workbook you create, to a maximum of 255. Consider changing this
   setting to 1 — for many uses, a single sheet is plenty; it saves memory and
   disk space, and you can always add extra sheets as you need them.

✦ The "User name" you specify here applies to your other Office applications as
   well.

The settings on the Transition tab are mainly designed to ease the process of
switching from Lotus 1-2-3 to Excel. Because Excel has long since won the

spreadsheet wars, few people now need these options. But the "Save Excel files as" setting can be useful if you share files with others who use an earlier version of Excel or a different program.

Customizing the Screen

The View tab of the Tools ⇨ Options dialog box contains most of the controls you need to customize the way Excel looks. Most settings are self-explanatory. A few comments should suffice:

✦ To control which elements of the Excel user interface appear on the screen, use the settings at Show and Window options. The four Show choices apply throughout Excel, no matter which window you have open. The Window options settings, however, apply only to the current worksheet or chart sheet, or to the current workbook.

✦ Check "Page breaks" to display dotted lines indicating the current page breaks for printing, whether or not you've changed the ones Excel sets automatically. This doesn't affect the display of page breaks in Page Break Preview mode (see Chapter 25).

✦ If the "Zero values" box is checked, you see a 0 in each cell containing a zero value. Otherwise, Excel displays the cell as empty, even if you explicitly entered the numeral 0.

✦ To change the color of the *worksheet* (not workbook) gridlines, choose from the drop-down menu at Gridlines Color.

✦ The Objects section governs the visibility of charts, graphics you create with the Drawing toolbar, clip art and other pictures, text boxes, and buttons. Select the Show Placeholders button to display charts and imported pictures (only) as gray rectangles to speed up scrolling. Other objects remain visible. The Hide All button, on the other hand, hides all types of objects both on your screen and in printed worksheets.

Working with the color palette

Excel limits you to a selection of 56 distinct colors that you can apply to just about anything that appears in a worksheet. However, you're welcome to customize this color palette, replacing any of the individual colors with any available on your system.

Use the Color tab of the Tools ⇨ Options dialog box to modify the color palette. To specify a new color, select one of the colors and choose Modify to bring up the requisite dialog box. The colors selected at "Chart fills" and "Chart lines" define the first 8 colors Excel automatically applies to these chart elements. The remaining 40 colors are available for general use. The Reset button restores all 56 colors to their default hues.

Excel stores the current color palette with the workbook. You can copy the palette from any open workbook using the drop-down list at "Copy colors from". To change the default palette used in new workbooks, change the color palette in your default or custom workbook template.

When you apply a color to a worksheet element, you're actually assigning one of the palette's numbered slots — not a color per se — to the element. Change a palette color, and all elements to which that palette slot have been assigned change color accordingly. When you copy elements between workbooks with different palettes, their colors change as well.

Tip

You can apply the 16 "Chart fills" and "Chart lines" colors to nonchart worksheet elements. The catch is, these colors aren't displayed on the drop-down color menus of the Fill Color and Font Color buttons (Formatting toolbar). To apply the chart-related colors, you must make a worksheet selection, choose Format ➪ Cells, and choose a color from the Font, Border, or Pattern tabs (use the latter tab to select a cell shading color).

Using Full Screen view

If you want more room to see the numbers, choose View ➪ Full Screen to hide the title bar, the toolbars, and the status bar. Full Screen view works differently in Excel from the way it does in Word. For one thing, it doesn't remove the menu bar. On the other hand, Excel doesn't require a macro to hide the Full Screen toolbar, which is small but potentially annoying. Just click the Close box in the toolbar's upper-right corner to put it to sleep. Also, pressing Esc doesn't return you to Normal view. Instead, you have to choose Close Full Screen on the Full Screen toolbar, or again choose View ➪ Full Screen.

Storing a view of the current workbook

Save a *view* to record a worksheet's current look so you can return it to those settings by opening the view later. In addition to the settings on the View tab of the Tools ➪ Options dialog box, a view can store hidden rows, columns, and sheets; filter settings; and print settings.

After setting up the worksheet the way you want it to look for future use, choose View ➪ Custom Views. When you then choose Add to create a new view, the dialog box shown in Figure 23-2 appears. Enter a name for the view and check or clear the boxes for optional components of the view. If you do include print settings, the view records the print area, or, if none is defined, the entire sheet.

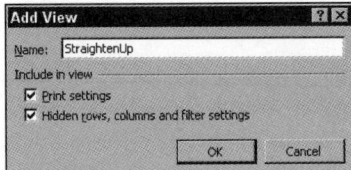

Figure 23-2: Define a new view in this dialog box.

Custom views define settings for an individual worksheet. When you open a view from any worksheet in the same workbook, Excel activates the worksheet for which you defined the view.

Recording and Using Macros

Macros are great for automating repetitive tasks and extending Excel's functionality. Chapter 5 explains how to record macros in Office, so I confine myself to Excel-specific issues here.

Defining a keyboard shortcut for the macro

You can assign a keyboard shortcut for a new macro directly from the Record Macro dialog box (see Figure 23-3). Excel limits you to keyboard shortcuts that combine Ctrl with a lowercase or uppercase letter (Ctrl+Shift+the letter). In other words, macro shortcuts are case sensitive. You can't use numbers, punctuation marks, or other symbols in a macro keyboard shortcut. Alt and the function keys are off-limits, too.

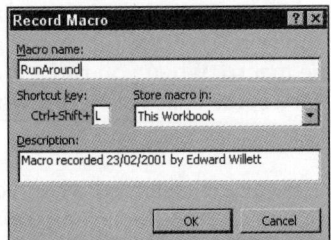

Figure 23-3: When you're about to record a new macro, you use this box to name the macro, assign a keyboard shortcut, and pick a storage location.

To change the keyboard shortcut assigned to a macro, open the Tools ⇨ Macro ⇨ Macros dialog box and choose Options.

Storing a macro

Use the drop-down list at "Store macro in" in the Record Macro dialog box to select the destination for a new macro. If you want the macro to be available always, no matter which workbooks are open, pick Personal Macro Workbook. When Excel exits, the macro is saved in the personal.xls workbook file in your XL Start folder. Excel opens personal.xls automatically each time it starts up, but as a hidden workbook.

Alternatively, you can select This Workbook in the "Store macro in" field to record the macro in the current workbook, or New Workbook to have Excel create a work-book from scratch and place the macro there. If you make the latter choice, just be aware that Excel doesn't announce the new workbook's arrival and doesn't identify it as a special macro workbook. The new workbook is simply listed on the Window menu as Book1.

Storing macros in a separate new workbook makes sense for special-purpose macros that you plan to use with more than one workbook but don't want available in all workbooks.

Tip   Excel doesn't automatically save workbooks in which you place macros. To protect your work against unforeseen system crashes, get in the habit of saving the work-book containing a new macro immediately after you record it. If you stored the macro in the Personal Macro Workbook, you must unhide the workbook (Window ⇨ Unhide) before you can save it.

Recording absolute versus relative cell references

Before recording a macro, decide whether you want it to record absolute or relative cell references. By default, Excel keeps track of absolute references, the actual row and column locations you select while recording the macro. When you run a macro recorded with absolute cell references, it selects these same cells no matter which cell is selected when you start the macro.

To record relative cell references instead — relative to the cell selected when you run the macro — click the Relative Reference button on the Stop Recording toolbar. Clicking it again turns absolute cell references back on. Excel graciously enables you to record a combination of absolute and relative cell references. All you have to do is toggle the Relative Reference button at the appropriate steps as you record the macro. Just remember, when the button is activated, the macro is recording rel-ative references.

Running macros

When you run a macro, it acts on the current worksheet, even if the macro is stored in another workbook.

Use the Run button in the Tools ➪ Macro ➪ Macros dialog box to start any macro stored in the Personal Macro Workbook or any of the open workbooks. Use the "Macros in" drop-down list to control which workbooks' macros appear in the dialog box.

You can assign a macro to a button, to another control, or to any graphic object, so the macro runs when you click the item (use the Forms toolbar to add controls to your worksheet). Excel asks you to specify or record a macro when you add a button. To assign macros to other controls or graphics, choose Assign Macro from the item's shortcut menu. You can then assign an existing macro or record a new one.

Macros can also be assigned to menus and toolbar buttons. The basic procedure for customizing toolbars applies (see Chapter 5), with this wrinkle: When you select Macros in the Commands tab of the Customize dialog box, the available macros themselves don't appear in the Commands list.

Instead, you're offered two items, Custom Menu Item and Custom Button. Drag either of these items to a desired location on a toolbar or menu. Then right-click the new item and select Assign Macro at the bottom of the shortcut menu.

Tip   To make any macro faster, turn off screen updating while the macro runs. To do this, you need to edit the macro's VBA code as discussed in Chapter 30.

Saving Custom Toolbar Layouts

Use the techniques laid out in Chapter 2 to customize toolbars in Excel. Then, to store a custom toolbar for future use, use the techniques described here.

Creating global custom toolbars

Excel automatically saves the customizations you make to your toolbars and menus in a configuration file named `Excel.xlb`. By default, the toolbar file is stored in your `\Application Data\Microsoft\Excel` folder.

If you want to be able to switch between two or more alternate toolbar setups no matter which workbook is open, follow these steps:

1. After setting up the toolbars to suit your preferences, exit Excel. This is the only way to save the setup.

2. Using My Computer or Explorer, rename the `Excel.xlb` toolbar file (if you want to start a new toolbar setup from scratch) or make a copy under a new name (if you want to base a new setup on this one). You can use any descriptive name you like, but keep the file's `.xlb` extension.

3. Restart Excel, which opens with the default toolbars and menus. You can now create an alternative set of customizations. When you next exit the program, Excel again saves these in `Excel.xlb`.

To activate a customized toolbar setup, just use the File ➪ Open command to open it. Excel reverts to the toolbar configuration in the standard toolbar file each time you start the program unless you make further changes. If you want Excel to start up with one of your alternate toolbar configurations, copy that file to `Excel.xlb`.

Attaching custom toolbars to a workbook

You can attach custom toolbars to a particular workbook so these toolbars are always available when the workbook is open. Open the Tools ➪ Customize dialog box and choose Attach on the Toolbars tab. The resulting dialog box lets you copy currently active custom toolbars to the active workbook. Custom toolbar setups can also be stored in templates, by saving a workbook to which they've been attached as a template (read on).

Using Excel Templates to Store Customizations

Excel templates can contain the following:

✦ The number of sheets in a workbook, and their names and types

✦ Formatting for individual cells and entire sheets, cell styles, page formats, and custom print areas

✦ Repeating text or values, including page headers and row and column labels

✦ Protected and hidden sheets, rows, columns, or cells

✦ Settings from the Tools ➪ Options dialog box

✦ Custom toolbars, macros, hyperlinks, and ActiveX controls

Creating and saving workbook templates

To create a new template, all you do is save a workbook in one of the folders Excel recognizes. Obviously, you should set up the workbook with all the formatting, content, and customizations you want in your template before saving it as such. To create a work*sheet* template, you just create a one-sheet workbook.

Note   Worksheet templates are simply workbooks containing only one sheet — there are no other differences between the two types. You can use worksheet templates for workbooks and workbook templates for worksheets.

You can recognize an Excel template by its .xlt extension, and the File ➪ Save As dialog box lists a Template choice in the "Files of type" box. However, you don't need to select this before saving the new template. All that really matters is where you save a workbook destined for template-hood:

✦ To create a new *default workbook* template, save the workbook in the XL Start folder or the alternate startup folder using the name book.xlt. Excel uses this template as the basis for new workbooks it opens when you start the program or when you click the New button.

✦ To create a new *default worksheet* template, save a one-sheet workbook in one of the startup folders using the name sheet.xlt. Excel uses this template for new worksheets inserted into the current workbook using the Insert ➪ Worksheet command.

✦ To create any other template, save the workbook (or a shortcut to it) in the Templates folder (located in the main Office folder) or any of its subfolders. Templates stored in the Templates folder appear on the General tab of the File ➪ New dialog box. Those stored in subfolders appear on separate tabs.

Inserting a new worksheet based on a custom template

The worksheet added by the Insert ➪ Worksheet command is always based on the default worksheet template. To insert a sheet based on a different template, right-click the worksheet tab where you want the new sheet to be inserted. Choose Insert from its shortcut menu to display the available templates. It's okay to choose a workbook template here, but doing so inserts however many sheets the template contains.

✦   ✦   ✦

Advanced Navigation and Selection

◆ ◆ ◆ ◆

In This Chapter

Using keyboard
shortcuts to move
around in Excel

Naming ranges

Selecting multiple
and nonadjacent
ranges

Using AutoFill

◆ ◆ ◆ ◆

Moving around in worksheets, selecting cells of interest, and filling them—these are the basics of working
in Excel, right? So what's the big deal?

In a word: efficiency. Navigating your worksheet and selecting
cells is probably the single most important thing you'll ever
do in Excel. Because these are the tasks you'll be performing
almost constantly, you need to learn tricks to get them done
as quickly and painlessly as possible.

On the Move

Face it: With 16,777,216 cells to play in, worksheets can get
pretty large. And that's only counting one sheet in your workbook! There's got to be an easy and fast way to get around.

Knowing your place

It doesn't take a rocket scientist, or a whole village, to figure
out which is the active cell—the one in which you can type or
edit data. The active cell has a thick black border, and Excel
puts its address up to the left of the Formula Bar in the Name
box. But there's another way to know where you are: Excel
gives a subtle highlight to row and column headings of the
selected area, so a quick glance tells you the current range.

Keyboard navigation

As soon as your worksheet fills more than a single window, you feel a hunger for quick ways to travel to the cell with which you want to work. Table 24-1 should give you something to chew on.

<table>
<tr><td colspan="3" align="center">Table 24-1
Keyboard Shortcuts for Navigation</td></tr>
<tr><td>*To Go Here*</td><td>*Press This*
Key Combination</td><td>*Notes*
(If Applicable)</td></tr>
<tr><td>Active cell</td><td>Ctrl+Backspace</td><td>Use this shortcut if the active cell has scrolled off the screen.</td></tr>
<tr><td>Next unlocked cell</td><td>Tab</td><td></td></tr>
<tr><td>Beginning of current row</td><td>Home</td><td></td></tr>
<tr><td>Last column containing any filled cells in the current row</td><td>End, then Enter</td><td></td></tr>
<tr><td>Beginning of the worksheet</td><td>Ctrl+Home</td><td></td></tr>
<tr><td>Last worksheet cell</td><td>Ctrl+End; or End, then Home</td><td>Cell at intersection of last row and column used.</td></tr>
<tr><td>Last filled cell in current block</td><td>Ctrl+arrow key; or End, then arrow key</td><td>Repeat to jump over the blank cells to the next filled cell in the same row or column. See the section "Making a run for the border," in this chapter.</td></tr>
<tr><td>Up or down one screen</td><td>Page Up or Page Down</td><td></td></tr>
<tr><td>Left or right one screen</td><td>Alt+Page Up or Alt+Page Down</td><td></td></tr>
<tr><td>Upper-left corner of the window</td><td>With Scroll Lock on, Home</td><td></td></tr>
<tr><td>Lower-right corner of the window</td><td>With Scroll Lock on, End</td><td></td></tr>
<tr><td>Next or previous worksheet</td><td>Ctrl+Page Up or Ctrl+ Page Down</td><td></td></tr>
<tr><td>Next or previous workbook or window</td><td>Ctrl+Tab or Ctrl+ Shift+Tab</td><td></td></tr>
<tr><td>Next or previous pane</td><td>F6 or Shift+F6</td><td></td></tr>
</table>

Making a run for the border

Spreadsheets are made up of filled-in cells and empty cells. And usually, filled-in cells come clumped together. Empty or full, there are many times when you want to reach the edge of one of these areas. From either the mouse or the keyboard, some easy tricks are at hand.

With your hand on the mouse, you'd be surprised how much agility you have in moving the active cell. Let's say you're in the heart of a large worksheet, and you want to find the next empty cell in the current column. By merely double-clicking the bottom border of the active cell, you immediately jump to the bottom of the current block of filled-in cells. The selected cell lies now just above that empty cell you were looking for. If you had double-clicked the right border of the active cell, you would have jumped to the right border between filled and empty cells in the current row, and so on.

The same holds true when you're in the middle of a blank area. Double-click the active cell's edge to jump in that direction to the place where blank cells meet filled-in cells. (You have to point directly over the cell outline so that the mouse pointer becomes two crossed arrows.)

You can use this trick in several ways. From inside a block of filled-in cells, double-click a cell's top edge to see the heading for that column. Double-click its right edge to see the totals for that row. Or if you're out in the middle of a field of blank cells, double-click in the direction of your data to find its closest border.

If you have any previous spreadsheet experience, you're no doubt aware of the keyboard equivalent for this trick: Press Ctrl+arrow to quickly accomplish the same task. If you're in the middle of a table of data and you press Ctrl+down arrow, you immediately jump down to the last row. (Caveat: If "Transition navigation keys" are activated on the Transition tab in Tools ➪ Options, these keys work slightly differently.)

Border crossings have never been so easy. (No passports or visas required!)

Jumping to a defined name

Any cell or range of cells can be given a name that you can jump to instantaneously. Using range names, you never again have to scroll around thinking, "Now where did I put that table?" Excel treats names exactly as it does all other cell addresses.

To add a name, position yourself in a cell, select a significant range of data, or make a nonadjacent selection (see "Making multiple selections" later in this chapter). Now click the Name box on the left side of the Formula Bar (it should currently show the address of the active cell). Type a name that's easy to remember — naming do's and don'ts are covered in the "Naming conventions" section — and press Enter. From now on, you can refer to the cells in the range by name rather than address.

Named ranges are valuable enough for clarifying the purpose of important regions of your worksheets. But learn to put them into action for superfast navigation. From wherever you are in the workbook (even on a different sheet), click the Down Arrow button next to the Name box to drop down the list of named ranges defined for the workbook. Figure 24-1 shows the list in action. Now click your destination range, and Excel transports you there faster than Scotty could beam you. (If the Formula Bar is hidden for some reason, you can also press F5 to bring up the Go To dialog box and double-click the destination range name.)

Named ranges have other uses besides navigation. You can refer to them in formulas, which are discussed in Chapter 26. You can also print a named range by selecting it via the Name box, then opening the File ⇨ Print dialog box and choosing Selection in the "Print what" area.

Note   When the worksheet is zoomed out to 39 percent or less, Excel indicates explicitly defined ranges with a border and the name in blue. The border and the name do not print, and they are not displayed when the zoom is above 39 percent.

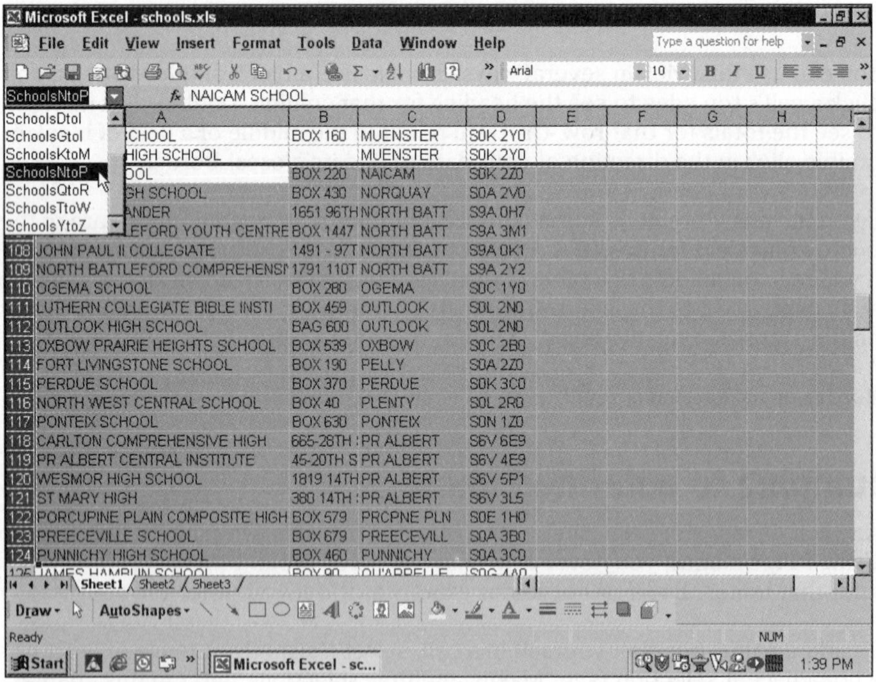

Figure 24-1: Selecting a named range from the Name box transports you to the range instantly.

Naming conventions

Though you can use up to 255 characters, I suggest something that's easily visible in the Name box. The first character of a name must be a letter or an underscore, and spaces and most other punctuation are not allowed (you can use underscores or periods as word separators). Of course, Excel won't accept names that are identical to cell addresses. Case is significant, and I recommend using an initial cap.

Managing named ranges

Manage named ranges using the Insert ➪ Name ➪ Define dialog box (see Figure 24-2). To assign an existing name to a different range, make the change in the "Refers to" box—you can type in the new cell reference or use the Collapse Dialog button as discussed in "Selecting from within a dialog box" later in this chapter.

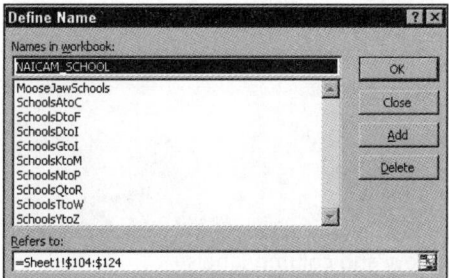

Figure 24-2: The Define Name dialog box enables you to add and delete named ranges.

You can't directly rename a range. Instead, you must highlight the range name in the "Names in workbook" list so that it appears in the box above that list, click the name there, change it as you see fit, click Add—and then delete the original range name.

Naming cells automatically based on row and column labels

Why go to the trouble of creating range names for the rows and columns in your worksheet when you've already labeled them on the worksheet itself? Excel can create the names for you from existing row and column labels. Select a range that includes both data and the row and column labels, and choose Insert ➪ Name ➪ Create to display the dialog box shown in Figure 24-3.

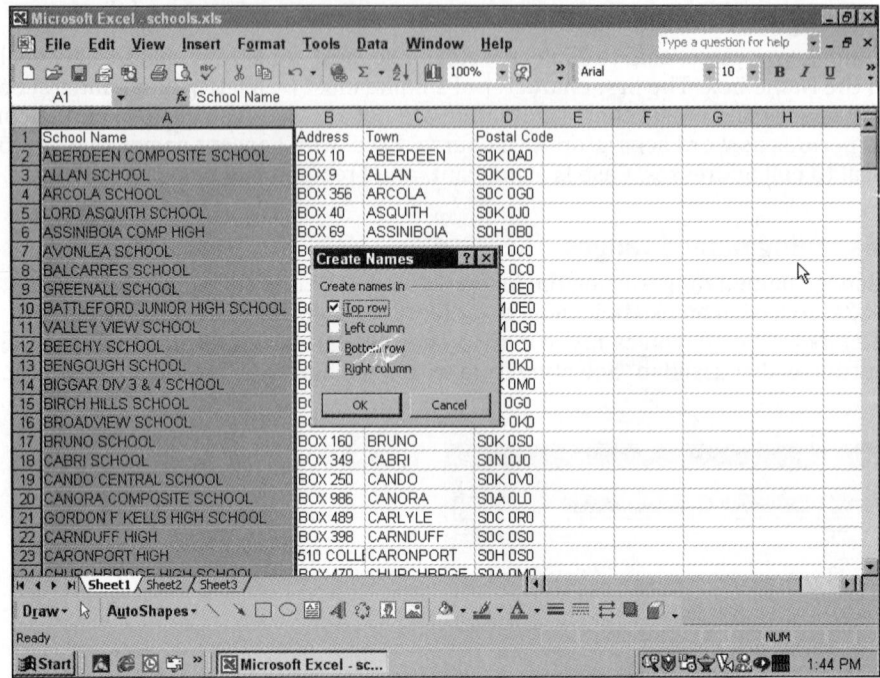

Figure 24-3: Creating names using existing row and column labels

In the Create Names dialog box, Excel makes an educated guess as to where the ranges you want to define are located on the worksheet. Confirm that it has chosen the rows or columns you intended and click OK. Excel creates new names based on the headings of the chosen rows or columns, substituting any impermissible characters with underscores. Note that the resulting named ranges encompass only the cells containing data, not the cells with the labels themselves.

You can also create a name that represents the same cell or range of cells on more than one sheet in the workbook

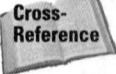
Cross-Reference See Chapter 26 for more information on 3D references.

Going out for a scroll

Though defined names make it simple to navigate a large spreadsheet, at times you may need to take a scroll and look around. Knowing a few simple tips makes it easy.

Using the mouse to scroll through your worksheet is as simple as using a scroll bar. When you drag the scroll box to move a larger distance, a ScreenTip appears showing you how far you've gone. (In a very large worksheet, hold down Shift while dragging to scroll faster—much faster—through the sheet.) The size of the scroll box shows proportionally what percentage of the entire worksheet you see on the screen. The position of a scroll box indicates the relative location of the top line of the screen within the worksheet.

Dragging the vertical scroll box displays which row number would be at the top of the screen if you stopped at this moment. And likewise, dragging the horizontal scroll box displays the letter of the column that would be at the left of the window. Long distances are now a cinch to navigate.

When you use keys on your keyboard to scroll around, the active cell moves as you're scrolling. As long as the Scroll Lock key is turned off (which it is by default), keys such as Page Up, Page Down, and the arrow keys move the active cell. However, if you want to scroll through the spreadsheet and *preserve* your selection, make sure that Scroll Lock is turned *on*. When it's on, you can use these keys as much as you like without affecting the current selection. When you're ready to return, press Ctrl+Backspace to bring the current selection back into view.

The Scroll Lock key also enables a few selection shortcuts, as listed in Table 24-1. (If you're not sure of Scroll Lock's status by looking at the keyboard, look in the status bar at the bottom of the Excel screen. When you see the letters "SCRL," you know Scroll Lock is on.)

Tip   So which way does the cell selection travel when you type an entry and hit Enter? It's totally up to you. Go to Tools ➪ Options and look at the Edit tab. If you check "Move selection after Enter", you can decide if the selection should move down, right, up, or left. Or, clear the box to turn off this feature completely — if you do, you stay in the current cell when you press Enter.

Navigating by IntelliMouse

Smarter than the average mouse, the Microsoft IntelliMouse has a repertoire of Quick Scroll and Zoom functions that are sweet music if your worksheets are large. Table 24-2 summarizes these talents.

Table 24-2 IntelliMouse Functions to Navigate Faster	
What to Do	**How to Do It**
Scroll up or down	Turn the wheel up or down.
Pan the worksheet	While holding down the wheel button, drag toward a window edge. The farther you drag, the faster the worksheet pans.
Pan automatically	Click the wheel button and then move towards a window edge. To return to normal operations, click any mouse button. This works with any three-button mouse.
Zoom in or out	Hold down Ctrl while turning the wheel up or down.
Show or hide detail in outlines	Point to a cell containing an outline, hold down Shift, and then turn the wheel up or down.

Tip   The Quick Zoom feature may be worth the investment in an IntelliMouse. To jump to a different location on a worksheet, roll the wheel back until you see the destination, click there, and then roll the wheel forward for a comfortable magnification. If you use the IntelliMouse mostly for zooming, set it up so you don't need to hold down Ctrl to zoom. Go to the General tab on the Tools ⇨ Options dialog box and check the box labeled "Zoom on roll with IntelliMouse".

Navigating to other worksheets

Excel lets you keep multiple worksheets in the same workbook. To move from one worksheet to the next, click the named tab for the destination sheet (the tab controls are at the lower left of the window). If all the tabs aren't visible, you can use the scrolling buttons to the left of the tabs to bring the one you want into view. Ctrl+Page Up and Ctrl+Page Down are the keyboard shortcuts for moving from one worksheet to the next.

Tip   For even faster worksheet hopping in workbooks with lots of worksheets, right-click over the scrolling buttons to the left of the worksheet tabs and choose the destination sheet from the shortcut menu. This doesn't work when you right-click the tabs themselves — in that case, you move to the sheet whose name you clicked on and also bring up a menu that lets you insert, delete, copy, move, and rename sheets.

The Contents tab of a workbook's Properties dialog box lists the included sheets by name. Because you can access the Properties dialog box from the shortcut menu for a worksheet file in Explorer or My Computer, this can help you get more information on workbooks when you're nosing around your hard disk outside of Excel.

Using workspace files

Use a workspace file to open a group of workbooks (not just multiple sheets in the same workbook) all at once. The workspace file records the window size and location of each workbook in the group. However, it doesn't contain the workbooks themselves, which you continue to edit and save individually once you open them via the workspace file.

To create a workspace file, open the workbooks you want it to include and arrange them on the screen to taste. Choose File ⇨ Save Workspace. Excel saves the file with the .xlw extension. Use the standard File ⇨ Open command to open workspace files, which are displayed by default in the Open dialog box's File list. As with individual workbooks, you can have Excel open a workspace file automatically whenever you start the program by placing the file in the XL Start folder described in Chapter 23 (only the workspace file needs to be there, not the component workbooks).

The Art of Natural Selection

Selecting cells is critical in anything you do in Excel. You need to select data before moving it, copying it, bolding it, shading it, or adding a polka dot background.

The typical user selects ranges with a simple drag of the mouse, and you may be thinking, "What could be easier?" But the truth is, the larger the range, the more that dragging becomes a drag.

Shift magic

There's much more magic to the Shift key than merely allowing you to create capitals or bleeping unmentionables (#@$%^&*!). If you hold down Shift whenever you move the cursor, you also extend the highlight.

Say you're using the arrow keys to move to a cell nearby. Hold down Shift while you're arrowing, and *voilà*! The highlight goes along for the ride. All the cells you've passed have been selected.

You can also add Shift to a simple mouse click. How often do you need to select an area that's larger than the screen, so you drag down past the last visible row, only to find you're suddenly scrolling way past the speed limit and now have to drag upward and — oops, too far in the other direction — and back down, and #@$%^&*!...?

Next time, use the Shift-click trick: Click without the Shift key in the top corner of the desired range. Now, using the scroll bar only, scroll down until the bottom of the range comes into view. Press Shift while you click the opposite corner. If the range isn't exactly the right size, keep Shift down while you reclick. It's as easy as that.

You'd be surprised how often you can add the Shift key while moving around on the keyboard. Here are just a few more examples:

✦ **With the Go To box:** While sitting in a cell, bring up the Go To box (choose Edit ➪ Go To, or press Ctrl+G or F5). Enter a cell address in the Reference box, and hold down Shift as you press Enter or click OK. The selected range now spans from the original cell to the new address you typed.

✦ **With the Name box:** While sitting in a cell, click the Name box on the left side of the Formula Bar. Type the address of a new cell and hold down Shift as you press Enter. The entire range is selected.

✦ **While double-clicking a cell border:** As mentioned under "Making a run for the border," you can double-click a cell's border to jump to the edge of the current region. While you're doing so, merely hold down Shift to carry the highlight along with you. It's a quick way to select a large area.

Experiment on your own and you'll find some other handy examples. With one named range selected, try holding down Shift while you specify another in either the Go To box or the Name box. Even multiple selections become easy.

Making multiple selections

Don't forget that Excel lets you make multiple, or nonadjacent, selections; that is, you can select cells or ranges that are not adjacent to each other (see Figure 24-4). Once you've selected the first cell or range you want in the normal fashion, hold down Ctrl and select some more. This is a great way to add formatting to cells that aren't sitting together.

Back to square one

When you're done with the selected area, you can collapse the selection to just the top-left cell in the selection by pressing Shift+Backspace. If you're working with a multiple selection, the active cell is the top-left cell of the block that was last added to the selection. Ctrl+Backspace, by contrast, brings the current selection back into view no matter where you've scrolled.

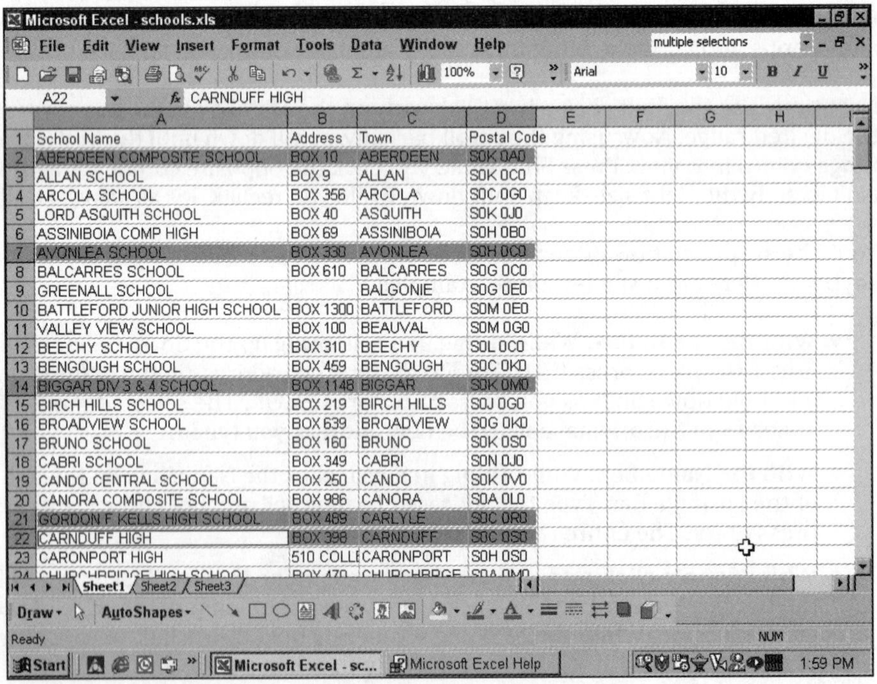

Figure 24-4: Using the Ctrl key, I made a multiple selection of only the schools I was interested in. Now I can make them bold to make them stand out.

Selecting from within a dialog box

There are many occasions when you need to specify a specific cell reference in a dialog box. It could be a single cell or a range of cells. And, of course, the easiest way to do this is to click inside the dialog box's field and click or drag the worksheet. But as dialog boxes offer more increased functionality, they also become bigger and cover more screen area. Arranging the box on your window so you can see it, without it obscuring the area to select, can get pretty tricky.

Dialog box fields that accept range references are called range selection boxes. You can type a range into a range selection box or enter the range by dragging on the worksheet with the dialog box as is. But learn to take advantage of the Collapse Dialog button on the right side of each range selection box. Clicking the button hides all of the dialog box except its title bar and the range selection box you're working with, as shown in Figure 24-5. You have complete freedom (and space!) to select the area you choose. As you do, your selection is echoed in the range selection box. When you're done, you can restore the entire dialog box by clicking the corresponding Expand Dialog button.

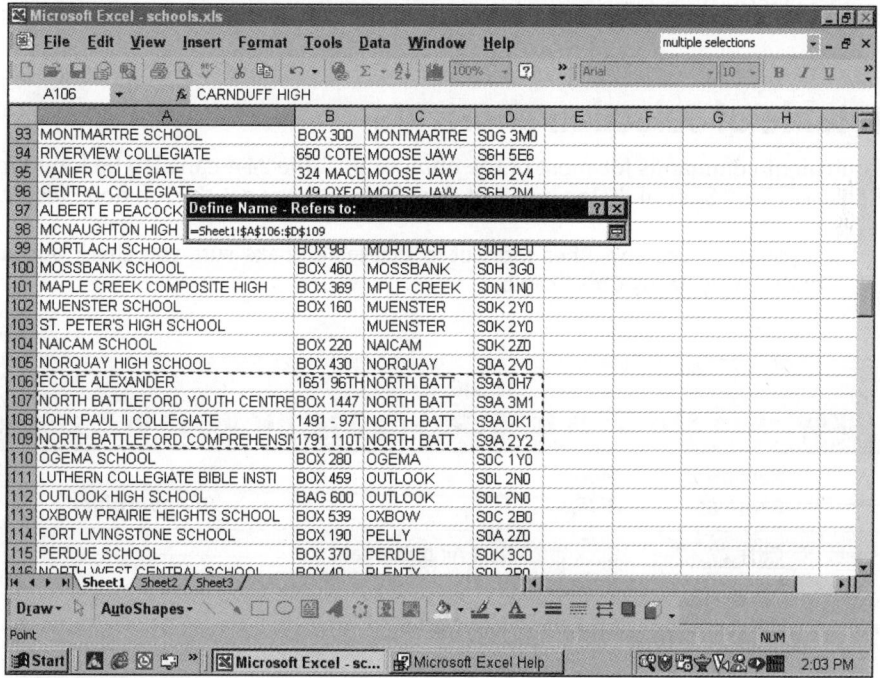

Figure 24-5: Selecting a range while working in a dialog box. Most of the box has been hidden to make it easier to see the worksheet while selecting.

Navigating inside a selection

Once you've gone to all the trouble to select some data, you'll often want to move around inside without disturbing the selection. Don't use arrows, Home, End, or click—the selection disappears. Instead, try the keys suggested by Table 24-3.

Table 24-3 Moving within Selected Data	
Keys	**Function**
Enter	Moves cell by cell in the direction set on the Edit tab of the Tools ➪ Options dialog box.
Shift+Enter	Moves cell by cell in the opposite direction as Enter.
Tab	Moves right.
Shift+Tab	Moves left.
Ctrl+Period	Jumps to each corner.

A table of selection shortcuts

Equivalent commands for most of the choices in Table 24-4 can also be found in the Edit ➪ Go To ➪ Special dialog box, but the shortcut keys get the job done faster.

Tip   If you don't use any other shortcut in this table, make sure you check out how enormously handy Ctrl+* can be.

Table 24-4 Keyboard Shortcuts for Selecting Specific Items in Excel			
Range to Select	**Keyboard Shortcut**	**Mouse Action**	**Notes (If Applicable)**
Entire worksheet	Ctrl+A	Click the Select All button at the upper-left corner of the worksheet.	
Whole column	Ctrl+Space	Click the column letter.	
Whole row	Shift+Space	Click the row number.	

Range to Select	Keyboard Shortcut	Mouse Action	Notes (If Applicable)
Create or extend selection	Shift+cursor movement keys in Table 24-1	Shift+click.	
Current region	Ctrl+* (hold down Shift if you use the	Click the Select Current Region button	Selects the rectangular area of filled cells that includes the active cell, asterisk on the 8 key) bordered by blank rows or columns. To place the Select Current Region button on a toolbar, drag it from the Commands tab of the Customize dialog box (select Edit in the Categories box).
Filled cells in current column up or down	Ctrl+Shift+up or down arrow	Shift+double-click on the top or bottom of active cell.	Selects from the current cell to the next empty cell in the current column.
Filled cells in current row left or right	Ctrl+Shift+left or right arrow	Shift+double-click on the left or right side of active cell.	Selects to next empty cell in the current row.
Last filled cell in the active cell's column or row	End, then Shift+ arrow key		
Last cell in the current row	End, then Shift+ Enter (same as End, then Shift+right arrow)		Doesn't work if Transition Navigation Keys is checked on the Transition tab of the Tools ⇨ Options dialog . box.
Upper-left corner of the window	With Scroll Lock on, Shift+Home		In the subsequent entry for Last filled cell, note different response toShift+Home after pressing End.
Lower-right corner of the window	With Scroll Lock on, Shift+End		
Last filled cell (lower-right corner of the worksheet)	End, then Shift+Home		
Visible cells	Alt+Semicolon		Selects nonhidden cells in the existing selection.

Continued

Table 24-4 *(continued)*

Range to Select	Keyboard Shortcut	Mouse Action	Notes (If Applicable)
Current array	Ctrl+/		Selects array containing active cell.
Row differences	Ctrl+\		Selects cells in current row whose contents are different from active cell. If multiple rows are selected first, the comparison cell for each row is in the column of the active cell.
Column differences	Ctrl+|		Selects cells in current column whose contents are different from active cell. If multiple columns are selected first, the comparison cell for each column is in the row of the active cell.
Cells with comments	Ctrl+Shift+O (letter O)		
Direct formula precedents	Ctrl+[	Click the Trace Precedents button on the Auditing toolbar	Select cells referred to by formula in active cell. Display the Auditing toolbar by checking its box in the Tools ⇨ Customize dialog box.
Direct and indirect precedents	Ctrl+Shift+{		As in the preceding entry, but also selects cells referred to by the direct precedents.
Direct formula dependents	Ctrl+]	Click the Trace Dependents button	Selects cells with formulas that refer to active cell.
Direct and indirect dependents	Ctrl+Shift+}		As in the preceding entry, but also selects cells that refer to the direct dependents.
All sheet objects	Ctrl+Shift+Space		You must select at least one object first.

Automatic Calculations on Selected Cells

Whenever you select two or more cells containing numbers, the status bar at the bottom of the screen shows the sum of the values in the selection (text is ignored). Even multiple, nonadjacent selections are allowed (see "Making multiple selections" earlier in this chapter). Right-click the status bar to change the type of calculation Excel displays. The shortcut menu for the status bar lets you select the type of calculation Excel displays there when two or more cells containing numeric values are selected.

Details of Data Entry

If you filled every cell on an entire worksheet with the maximum number of characters, you'd have typed 536,870,912,000 characters from your keyboard (more, if you made any mistakes). Multiply that by the number of sheets in your workbook and you'd end up with a worksheet whose calculations run at a glacial pace—not to mention carpal tunnel syndrome.

While you're not likely to do this, your worksheets undoubtedly have large amounts of significant data. The more efficiently you lay them out, the more efficiently they reflect the correct results. You need data entered to your exact specifications. (And more than likely, you need it by yesterday.) With some shortcuts in hand, it can be done.

Single cell entries

You probably enter most of your data by typing it one chunk at a time. The tips in this section should make this basic chore much easier.

Getting it right the first time

Back in the olden days, after entering a number into a worksheet cell, you needed to then go somewhere else to apply the appropriate format. Nowadays, spreadsheets can sense what you want the moment you type in the data. Dates and times are recognized automatically. Enter one and it's formatted for you. Same with numbers containing commas, dollar signs, or percent signs. For the most part, Excel knows just what you mean. (Excel depends upon the Regional Settings you've set in the Windows Control Panel when it chooses default formats for your numbers, dates, and times. From the Control Panel folder, open Regional Settings and confirm that everything is set correctly.)

Occasionally, you may be intending one thing while Excel is assuming another. If Excel is confused, generally it accepts whatever you've typed as straight text, but generates a Smart Tag in the form of a yellow diamond with an exclamation mark inside it. Click on the down arrow beside that tag to see a shortcut menu (see Figure 24-6) giving you a number of options to deal with the error.

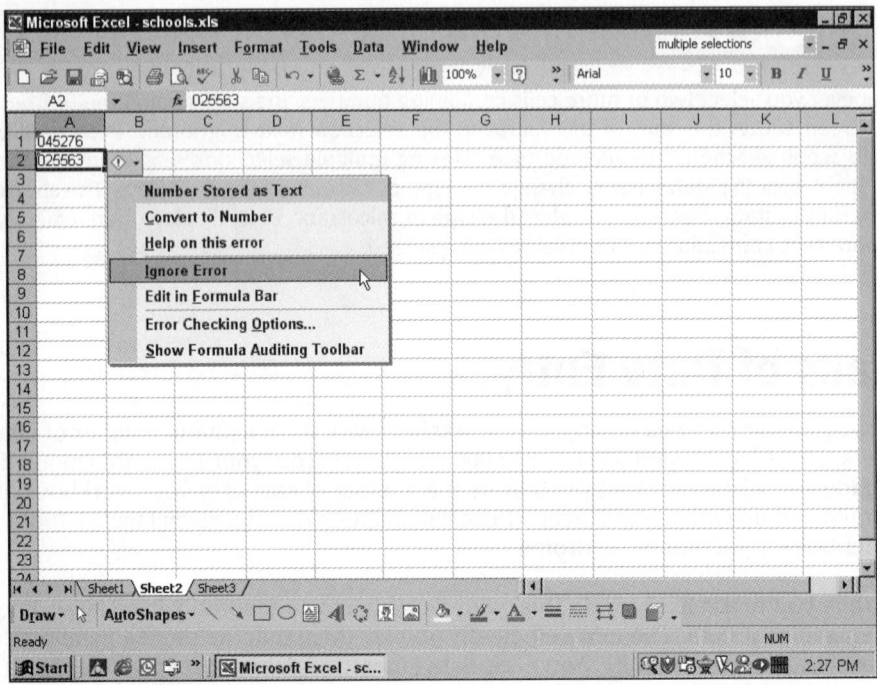

Figure 24-6: When Excel is confused by the information you entered, it creates a Smart Tag to help you.

In Figure 24-6, it's an Eastern ZIP code, a number beginning with zero, that has Excel confused. It stored the number as text, then flagged the "error." It gives you several options: You can convert the entry to a number (which removes the zero — not a good idea!), edit the entry in the Formula Bar, ignore the error (the best choice in this case), get help, or display the Formula Auditing toolbar.

To avoid this Smart Tag, you could precede the number with an apostrophe (for example, '05454). Then Excel would recognize it as text right off the bat and not consider it an error.

Caution   Excel treats text composed of numerals differently than real numbers for calculations and sorts. If you want to be able to sort a ZIP code list correctly, you must precede all the entries with an apostrophe, not just the ones that start with 0.

Tip   To enter a hard carriage return in a cell, press Alt+Enter where you want the line to break. This automatically turns on the Wrap Text format (otherwise found on the Alignment tab of the Format ➪ Cells dialog box) and adjusts the row height so that the text can fit.

Copying data from neighboring cells

Copying from neighboring cells can come in handy more often than you'd think. When you need to do it, here are the tricks to use:

✦ Press Ctrl+D to copy the contents and formatting of the cell directly above (you're copying in a downward direction).

✦ Use Ctrl+R to copy from the cell directly to the left (you're copying toward the right). This also copies both contents and formatting.

✦ Ctrl+' copies only the formula from the cell directly above. No formatting comes across.

✦ Ctrl+" copies only the resulting value from the cell above. Again, no formatting.

Confining data entry to a range

If you know that your data belongs only within a specific range of cells, select the whole range before you start entering the data. As you fill each cell and press Enter, Excel respects the range boundaries. By default, pressing Enter moves the active cell down one row in the same column, until you're at the bottom of the range. When you then press Enter, the active cell pops up to the top of the next row. And when the active cell gets to the bottom right of the selected range, pressing Enter takes you back to the top left.

You can also move around inside a selection without using the other keyboard shortcuts described in "Navigating inside a selection" earlier in this chapter. And by the way, you can change the direction in which Excel moves the active cell within the range on the Edit tab of the Tools ➪ Options dialog box.

Taking advantage of AutoComplete

Excel uses AutoComplete to guess what you're typing in a cell. If the first few characters match an existing entry in that column, Excel completes the entry for you. To accept, merely press Enter. To reject, continue typing. It's that easy.

Actually, it's even easier. If you're really lazy, you can press Alt+down arrow to display a small list of existing entries in that column. Click the one you want and you're done. You can also right-click a cell in the column (even if it's completely empty) and choose Pick From List on the shortcut menu. Figure 24-7 illustrates how all this works.

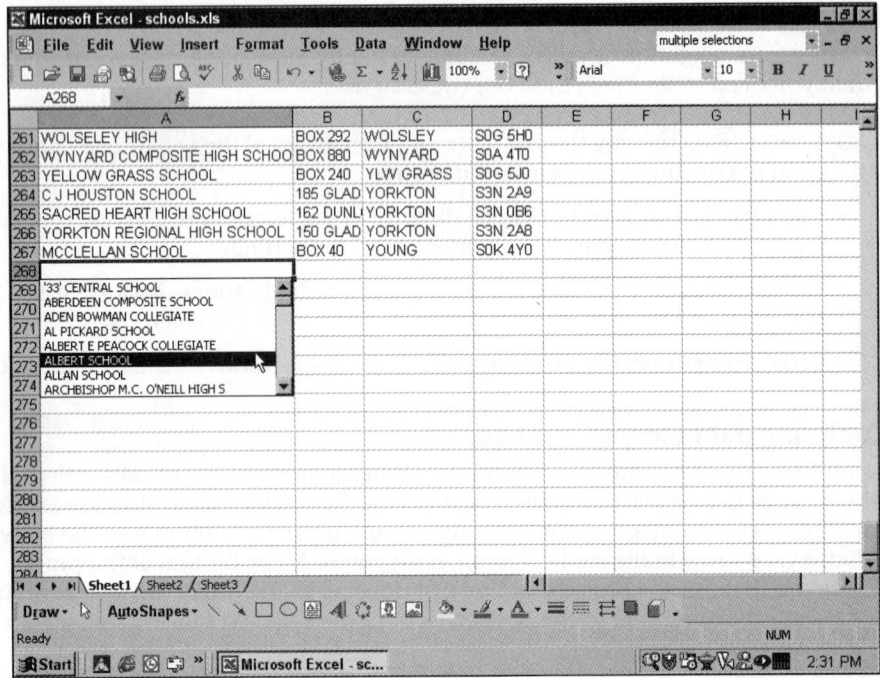

Figure 24-7: Either choose Pick From List on the right-click menu or press Alt+down arrow to choose from a list of existing entries in the current column.

Note   AutoComplete works only with entries that contain text or a combination of text and numbers. Numbers, dates, and times are not completed.

You can turn AutoComplete off (though who'd want to?) as follows: Go to Tools ➪ Options, and on the Edit tab, clear Enable AutoComplete for Cell Values.

Entering nondynamic dates and times

Although the =NOW function displays the date and time dynamically (that is, it's constantly updating), you may have occasion to enter the date and time as static text. You can do this easily with two shortcuts. Press Ctrl+; to enter the current date as text, and Ctrl+: to enter the current time. When you do so, the Formula Bar remains active, in case you'd like to add anything to the cell. (Remember that these entries are static, and they don't update when you calculate the worksheet.)

Home on the range

As worksheets grow and become more complex, patterns begin to emerge. You might have found a formula that works on an entire series of values (calculating a row or column in a database). Or maybe your data calls for some sort of logical progression of values, perhaps a progression that you've designed. Either way, the bases are covered.

Filling a range with a single entry

Let's say that an entire row or column of your database has the same calculation — a sum, perhaps. As long as the formula doesn't change, you should only have to type it one time.

The important thing to remember here is to select the entire range first. Before typing a single character, select all the cells you want to fill. (For some great tips on selecting, see the previous section.) Now begin typing the formula or value into the active cell (residing anywhere within the selection). As you know, if you merely press Enter, the data goes into the active cell and the cursor moves down. Instead, press Ctrl+Enter. The data is filled immediately into the entire selection.

AutoFilling a list of entries

Few things get as many oohs and aahs in Excel as the AutoFill feature. It is without a doubt the most powerful way to fill a range of cells with a single drag. With each fill, not only do you have several built-in lists to choose from, but you can even customize your own.

At the bottom-right corner of the selection, be it a single cell or a range, you see a small black square. This is called the fill handle. When you position the mouse pointer on top of the fill handle, it changes to a black cross. You are now ready to autofill. By merely dragging the fill handle in any direction, you begin to fill the adjacent cells with a logical progression. The way in which they're filled depends upon the cells initially selected and the kind of progression you've chosen.

Note   If you don't see the fill handle even on a selection of a single cell, go to Tools ⇨ Options. On the Edit tab, make sure the "Allow cell drag and drop" box is checked. (Note that you cannot autofill from a multiple selection.)

Sample AutoFill progressions

If the initial selection is a single cell that Excel recognizes (such as a date or time), the neighboring cells are filled in a very logical fashion (see Table 24-5). If Excel doesn't recognize the string, it does a simple copy.

Table 24-5
AutoFill and Consecutive Cells

Initial Selection	Filled Cells
January	February, March, April
Jan	Feb, Mar, Apr
Monday	Tuesday, Wednesday, Thursday
Mon	Tue, Wed, Thu
Week 1	Week 2, Week 3, Week 4
Quarter 1	Quarter 2, Quarter 3, Quarter 4, Quarter 1
Qtr 1	Qtr 2, Qtr 3, Qtr 4, Qtr 1
9:00	10:00, 11:00, 12:00
2001	2001, 2001, 2001
Potato	Potato, Potato, Potato

If the initial selection is more than one cell, you've specified a trend. Excel calculates the trend and extends it for you (see Table 24-6).

Table 24-6
AutoFill and Cells in a Trend

Initial Selection	Filled Cells
3, 6	9, 12, 15
2/23/97, 2/24/97	2/25/97, 2/26/97, 2/27/97*
Jan, Apr	Jul, Oct, Jan
2000, 2001	2002, 2003, 2004
Jan-96, Apr-96	Jul-96, Oct-96, Jan-97*

* Excel's not quite as smart as you might think. Once these sequences hit the year 2000, the "year" starts showing as 100, 101, 102 instead of 00, 01, 02 as you might hope. To avoid this problem when dealing with a sequence of dates starting in the twentieth century and extending into the twenty-first, always use the full four-digit date—something the whole Y2K mess should have taught all of us is a good idea! (Excel flags this "two-digit-date" error with a Smart Tag, by the way.)

Other AutoFill options with the shortcut menu

Other date and time progressions are also possible. Attached to the lower-right corner after you've done an AutoFill is a Smart Tag. Click on it to see the AutoFill shortcut menu (see Figure 24-8). Depending upon the initial selection, a variety of these choices is available.

Notice that autofilling can be used to copy formatting only.

With some progressions, you can choose between a linear trend and a growth trend. A *linear trend* extends the selection arithmetically 3, 6 to 3, 6, 9, 12, 15. *A growth (geometric) trend* would appear as follows: 3, 6, 12, 24, 48."

Tip If a simple autofill doesn't give you what you intended (for example, it copies when you wanted a progression, or vice versa), hold down Ctrl while you drag the fill handle. You'll get the opposite of the default action.

Creating custom AutoFill lists

AutoFill's magic capabilities can be extended to include lists of your own design. These can include anything from names of people within your group, to product part numbers, sales regions, or all seven Disney dwarves. (Quick! How many can you name?)

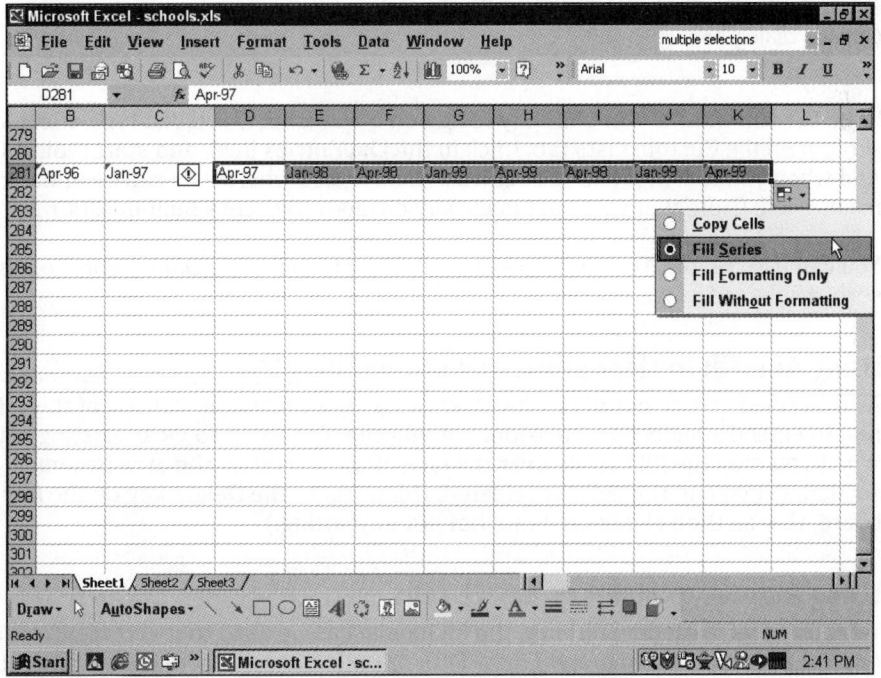

Figure 24-8: The AutoFill shortcut menu

Custom lists can be defined in one of two easy ways. If the list you want to define already exists somewhere on your spreadsheet, select it and go to the Custom Lists tab of the Tools ➪ Options dialog box, shown in Figure 24-9. The "Import list from cells" field at the bottom shows the reference to your list. If it's not correct, or if you haven't yet selected the proper range, you can make changes or reselect on your worksheet now. Once the reference is correct, click the Import button. You'll see your new list appear to the left under Custom lists.

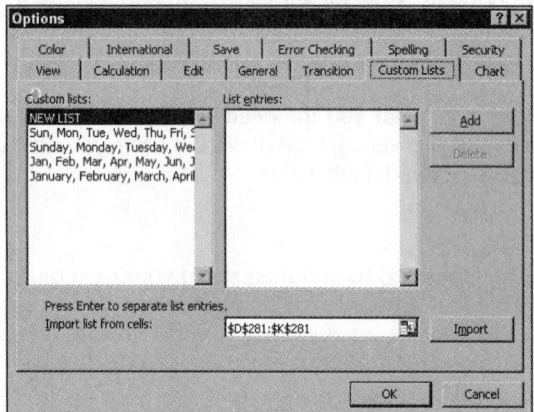

Figure 24-9: The Custom Lists tab of the Tools ➪ Options dialog box

If the list you want doesn't already reside on a worksheet, you can type one in from scratch on the Custom Lists tab. Click in the List Entries field, and start typing. Click Add when you're done. The "List entries" field is also where lists can be updated and maintained. (Note that you can't make any changes to Excel's built-in lists.)

You can use custom lists to define the order in which Excel's Data ➪ Sort command sorts a selected range.

Using AutoFill to clear entries ("Auto-unfilling"?)

As described earlier, autofilling involves dragging a fill handle outside of the selection to extend a logical progression. But you can also use it to clear existing entries. When you drag the fill handle over the face of the selection, the area becomes shaded. Let go and the cells are cleared. (Identical to the Delete key on the keyboard, this method clears contents but not formatting.)

Using AutoFill to insert or delete cells

When coupled with the Shift key, the fill handle can be used to insert blank cells into the spreadsheet (same as Edit ➪ Fill), or to delete cells from the worksheet (same as Edit ➪ Delete). Depending upon the initial selection, you can use this method to insert or delete a single cell, a range of cells, or entire rows and columns.

Beginning with a single cell or a range, you can shift-drag to insert new cells in neighboring rows or columns (cells are shifted in the same direction as your drag). The number of cells inserted matches the dimension of the initial selection. If you begin with a selection of whole rows or columns, you can shift-drag the fill handle to insert more of the same.

Deleting cells is done in a similar fashion. However, as in the clearing process described previously, you shift-drag over the face of selected cells. Excel deletes the shaded cells and shifts cells in the same direction as you drag to fill the space.

Entering data in groups of worksheets

When workbooks contain worksheets with similar designs (for example, each shows the same accounting data for a different region), any changes made to formatting or layout must be made to all sheets in the same way. When worksheets are grouped together, changes made to one worksheet affect the entire group.

Worksheets are grouped using the worksheet tabs at the bottom of the screen. You can select tabs exactly the way you would select cells on the sheet itself:

✦ To select sheets that are all in a row, click the first tab, and shift-click the last one.

✦ To select sheets that aren't adjacent, click the first tab, and Ctrl-click each other one.

✦ To select all the sheets in the workbook, merely right-click anywhere on the tabs, and choose Select All Sheets from the shortcut menu.

When sheets are grouped, each selected sheet tab becomes white. Once you've created a group, any edits made to the active sheet are reflected on all the sheets in the group in exactly the same location.

When sheets are grouped, you can also take existing values or formats from the active sheet, and fill the rest of the sheets in the group. Select the values or formats you want to fill, and choose Edit ⇨ Fill ⇨ Across Worksheets. You can then choose whether you want to fill Contents, Formats, or both.

Want to print a particular set of sheets in the workbook? Group just those, go to File ⇨ Print, and select the Active Sheets button at the bottom.

Finally, to ungroup a group of worksheets, click the tab for any worksheet that isn't in the group. If you can't see the tabs for any ungrouped worksheets, right-click the tab for any sheet in the group and choose Ungroup Sheets.

Data validation

If you're working on a spreadsheet that compiles data from many sources, chances are you're not the only person who contributes to it. Of course you know what kind of data goes where and how to enter it, but how can you guarantee that the others are entering data properly?

When you want to make sure that correct data is entered on a worksheet, you can specify specific constraints for cells or cell ranges. You can restrict the data to a particular type (such as whole numbers, decimal numbers, or text) and set limits on the valid entries. These limits can depend upon data being entered, or a calculation in another cell. You can specify certain messages to pop up on the screen to aid users. After data has been entered and calculated, you can audit the worksheet to find and correct data that isn't valid.

Setting the constraints

Select the cell or cells that need validation, and choose Data ➪ Validation. On the Settings tab, shown in Figure 24-10, choose the type of data to be entered under Allow. You can constrain the entry to be a whole number, decimal, date, or time, or to have a specific length. Once you've done so, you can use the Data field to further limit the data to those that fall within a particular range.

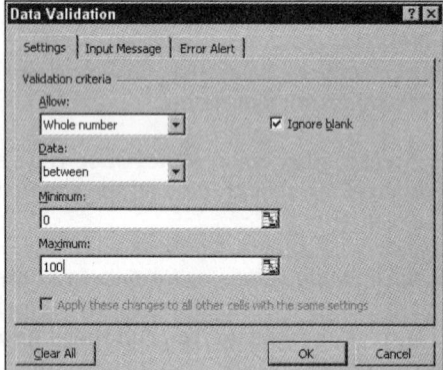

Figure 24-10: The Settings tab of the Data Validation dialog box

You can restrict the valid entries for a cell to come from a list of your own design. From short lists ("low, medium, high") to long lists (every NASCAR race Richard Petty ever won), you tailor it to your exact specifications. Choose List, and type in the entries or select a range on the spreadsheet. Then, at any time, a user can drop down the valid choices and select one. Or, the entry may depend upon a calculation that doesn't reside on the worksheet. Merely select "Custom" in the Allow list and specify the formula in the Formula field.

Displaying an input message

An input message can be displayed whenever a user selects or clicks the cell. You can use this message to explain the cell's constraints and offer help on entering data. To set up a message, choose the Input Message tab in the Data ⇨ Validation dialog box. Enter a message of up to 255 characters, and a title that appears in bold. Even if you leave the "Input message" field blank, a default message still appears when a user selects a restricted cell. To turn off all Input messages, clear the "Show input message when cell is selected" box.

An input message can also be displayed on a nonrestricted cell. Under the Settings tab, select "Any value" at Allow. Enter a message on the Input Message tab. The message is displayed until the user moves to another cell.

Displaying an error message

An error message can be displayed whenever a user enters invalid data in the cell. To set up a message, choose the Error Alert tab in the Data ⇨ Validation dialog box. As with the input message, you can enter a message of up to 255 characters, and a bolded title. A default error message alerts the user even if you've left this field blank, but you can turn off all error messages by clearing the "Show error alert after invalid data is entered" box at the top. Invalid entries may still find their way onto your worksheet. See Chapter 29 for more information on dealing with these entries.

Can't remember which cells are restricted?

You can easily find all the cells with the same restrictions as the active cell, or all the cells that have restrictions of any kind.

Bring up the Edit ⇨ Go To box (shortcut: F5) and choose Special. Turn on "Data validation" down at the bottom. Choose All to find all cells on the worksheet that have data validation applied. Choose Same to find cells with the same validation as the active cell.

Tip   Data validation attributes can be copied and pasted just like other cell formatting. After copying a cell with the restrictions you want, right-click the destination, click Paste Special, and choose Validation.

AutoCorrecting as you go

The beauty of AutoCorrecting is twofold: Common spelling errors are corrected as you type them, and long entries can be linked to shortcuts that immediately expand. The downside is that you must define these words in advance. But the convenience definitely makes it worthwhile.

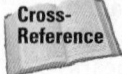

Cross-Reference   Chapter 8 has detailed information on AutoCorrect.

✦   ✦   ✦

Essentials of Editing and Formatting

How many times have you entered data and had it look perfect the very first time? (Okay, now uncross your fingers and answer the question again.) All cells need some basic editing and formatting to give them *savoir faire*. It takes very little effort to create a professional-looking spreadsheet. And if you change your mind, you can undo or redo up to 16 previous actions.

Rearranging Information

Excel is chock-full of power tools for moving data around in and among your worksheets.

Life's a drag

When you position the mouse pointer on top of a selection's border (multiple selections not included), and the pointer turns into crossed arrows, you're ready for a move or copy. Simply drag the border to move, or press Ctrl and drag to copy. As you do so, you'll see an outline of the selected area and a ScreenTip showing the address of the destination. Read on — your powers are just beginning.

Right on the button

Dragging a selected area with the right mouse button gives you a shortcut menu with a powerful array of options, as shown in Figure 25-1.

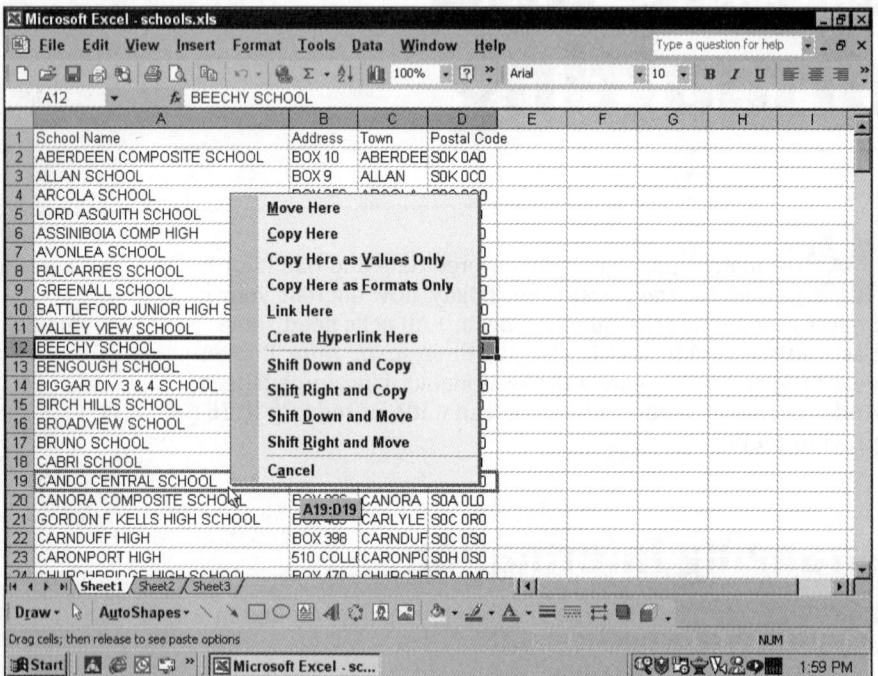

Figure 25-1: Drag with the right mouse button to get this list of choices.

✦ **Move/copy:** The first two choices are identical to the classic drags described previously. Move Here is the same as a simple left-button drag, and Copy Here is the same as a Ctrl+drag.

✦ **Selected attributes:** You can choose to copy only specific attributes of a selection, such as the resulting value of a formula (Values Only), or the formatting (Formats Only). (To copy other attributes, see "Pasting particular cell attributes," later in this chapter.)

✦ **Links:** Link Here creates in each target cell a simple formula referring to the value of the corresponding cell in the original selection (for example, =B7). As a result, Excel updates the value displayed in the target cell when the source changes. Create Hyperlink Here inserts a hot spot where the user can click to be immediately transported to the site of the original selection.

✦ **Inserting by shifting cells:** While moving or copying a selection, you can insert it between existing cells to avoid pasting over data. The four choices on the menu let you determine the direction in which existing cells are shifted to make room for new cells. (The next section tells how to do the same thing without the menu.)

Inserting within an existing range

When doing a move or copy, you can shift existing cells to the right or down to make room for the new range. All you need do is hold down Shift while you move a cell or selected range by dragging its border. When you drop the selection at its destination, Excel inserts it between existing cells. A gray line tells you whether you're inserting into a column (existing cells are shifted down) or into a row (existing cells are shifted to the right). As a bonus, a ScreenTip shows you the new address. If you're doing a copy, hold down Ctrl as usual, and add Shift to it to insert the copied cells.

Going to another sheet in the workbook

Just because your destination is a different worksheet doesn't mean you have to give up dragging and dropping. You still have tricks to use. Hold down Alt and drag the selection onto the destination's sheet tab at the bottom of the screen. When the sheet tab lights up, that sheet is active. Drag back up to your destination; drop your selection into place.

Resizing rows and columns

You can change the height of any row or the width of any column by typing in a new measurement. Use the Format ➪ Row ➪ Height and Format ➪ Column ➪ Width commands. If you select multiple rows or columns first, the new size applies to all the selected items.

Resizing rows or columns with the mouse is easy. Here's the technique when you're working with rows: Place the mouse pointer in the row heading and point to the boundary between the target row and the next one down. When the pointer becomes a thick horizontal line with arrows extending up and down, hold down the mouse button to see the row's current height in a ScreenTip, and drag to change the height.

The method is essentially the same for columns, but you hold the pointer over the boundary between the target column and the one to the right, and the pointer is oriented vertically. If you select more than one row or column before you resize, you can drag over any heading border within the selection. All the selected rows or columns take on the new size.

Note   Excel displays a bunch of number signs (as in #####) in a cell if the cell is too narrow to display its contents using the current formatting choices. If you see number signs in some of your cells, just widen the columns until they disappear.

Hiding rows and columns

To hide one or more adjacent rows or columns, select them in the appropriate heading. Then right-click anywhere over the selection and choose Hide. The hidden rows or columns disappear from view, but their contents remain intact and can be used in formulas. Use this trick to prevent underlying data from distracting you as you view calculation results.

Finding and unhiding a hidden column

You're a pretty bright person. When you see "ABCEFG", you know something is missing, even if it has been a few years since you went to elementary school. In your spreadsheet, it can only mean one thing: a hidden column. And you'd like to unhide it, but you just can't seem to get the pointer in there to touch it.

There are two quick tricks for unhiding hidden rows or columns with the mouse. Using the previous example of a hidden column D, the first technique requires you to select columns C:E by dragging over their column headings. Now right-click anywhere within the selection and select Unhide. Column D immediately appears.

The second trick is even fancier, a variation on the technique you probably already use for resizing columns (and rows) with the mouse.

Suppose that your row headings show "1:2:3:7:8:9", and you just want to see row 6. As far as you're concerned, rows 4:5 can remain hidden. In this case, the first trick just won't cut it. Instead, try this: Position the mouse pointer in the row heading over but a little below the boundary between the two rows that adjoin the hidden rows (in this case, the boundary between 3 and 7). When you get the pointer in just the right place, it changes to two horizontal lines attached with arrows pointing up and down. Hold down the mouse button right in that spot and you see a ScreenTip showing the height of the lowest of the hidden rows (in this case, 6). Initially, of course, this height is 0.00, but as you drag downward to unhide row 7, the height readout changes accordingly. Figure 25-2 shows this tip in action on a hidden column.

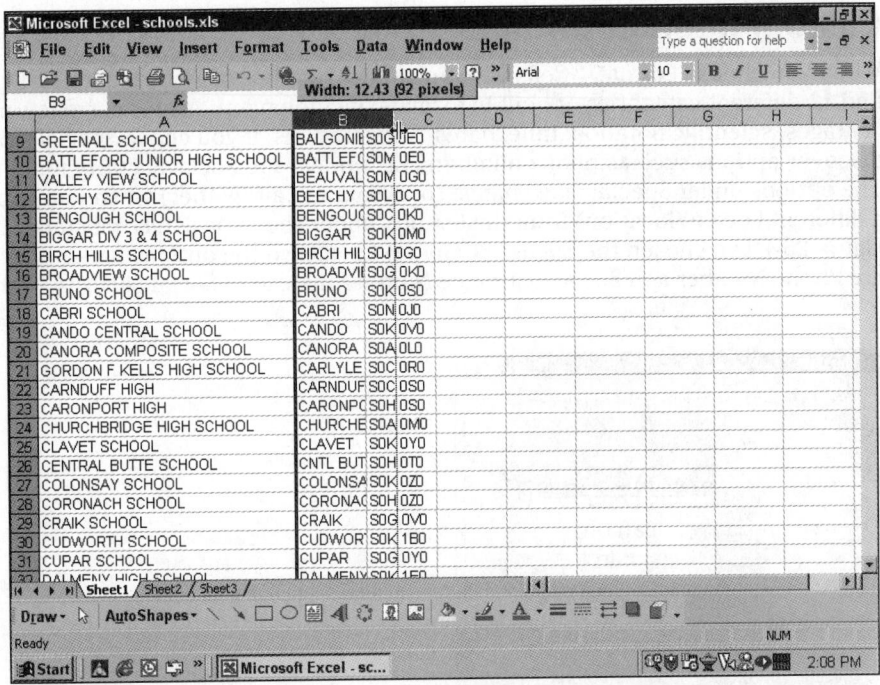

Figure 25-2: The mouse pointer changes to show you've found a hidden column.

Formatting

Over the years, Excel has gained sophisticated graphical and layout features so that now you rarely need a separate desktop publishing or drawing program to dress up your spreadsheets. Most of the formatting commands can be found on the Formatting toolbar, shown in Figure 25-3.

Figure 25-3: Use the Formatting toolbar for your most common format changes.

Here you can choose a typeface and point size; bold, italicize, and underline; left align, center, right align, or center across columns; apply a number format of currency, percent, or comma; increase or decrease decimal places; increase or decrease indents; add a border; and add a background fill or font color. These formats were put on the toolbar because they're the ones used most often—there are many more to choose from. And if that's not enough, you also have freedom to create your own customized formats.

Custom number formats

When you choose Format ⇨ Cells and look at the Number tab (see Figure 25-4), you find 12 different categories of built-in formats, including options for currency, percentages, scientific notation, time, dates, and fractions. If you chose Special, you'll discover options such as phone numbers, ZIP codes, and Social Security numbers. The options under Special may change (or disappear altogether) when you choose a different Locale (location) from the list box under the Type list. For instance, in Figure 25-4, I've chosen the English (Canada) Locale, so the options under Special are Phone Number and Social Insurance Number instead of Social Security Number.

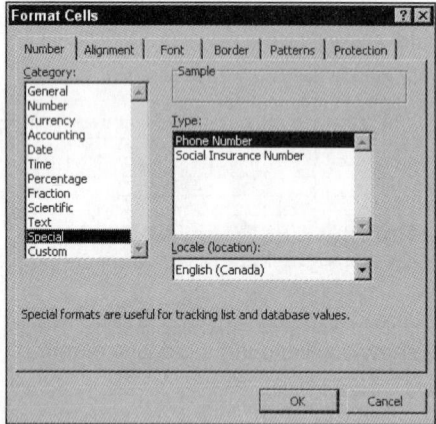

Figure 25-4: Use the Format ⇨ Cells dialog box to apply existing formats, or to customize your own.

Whereas these formats will meet your need in a great majority of cases, you still may need to create your own formats from time to time. That's when some fancy footwork comes in.

Note   The number format you apply does not affect the actual value that Excel uses for calculations. The actual value displayed in the Formula Bar is the one Excel computes with.

Rounding

Although Excel's formats give you *carte blanche* when it comes to choosing decimal places, commas, and so forth, no built-in formats will round numbers to the nearest specified whole number (larger than 1). The ROUND function does the trick, but you can accomplish a similar effect with a custom number format.

On the Number tab of the Format ⇨ Cells dialog box, choose the last category in the list, Custom, to enter a number format code for your custom format (see Figure 25-5). At Type, enter the codes in Table 25-1 for the specified rounded results.

Table 25-1		
Number Format Codes for Rounding		
Number Format Code	**Result**	**Example**
#,	Rounds to the nearest thousand, excluding insignificant zeroes.	54,223 becomes 54
#,",000"	Rounds to the nearest thousand, including insignificant zeros.	54,223 becomes 54,000
0.0,,	Rounds to the nearest million, including one decimal place.	54,789,223 becomes 54.8

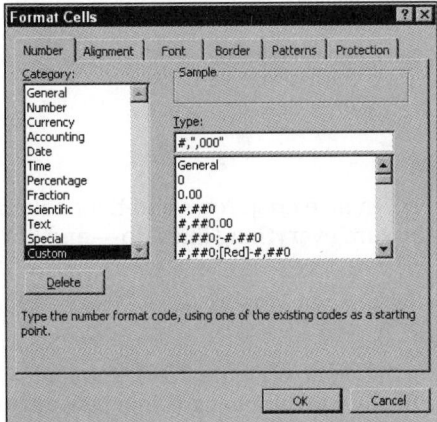

Figure 25-5: Creating a custom number format

 **Tip** See the Help topic "Number format codes" for a list of custom codes and their meanings. You can find this topic by searching for "number formats" in the Ask a Question field on the menu bar.

Using special currency symbols

To specify a currency symbol in a custom number format, you can enter a code using your numeric keypad. First make sure that your Num Lock key is turned on (Excel shows the word NUM in the status bar). Then hold down Alt and type the code using the keypad. When you lift up, the symbol appears.

The symbols in Table 25-2 can be inserted into the Type field when creating a custom format, or directly onto your spreadsheet.

Table 25-2 Codes for Special Currency Symbols	
For this Symbol	*Enter this Number Code*
¢ (cents)	0162
£ (British pounds)	0163
¥ (Japanese yen)	0165

Cross-Reference For more about inserting special characters, see Chapter 8.

Aligning data

You want your numbers to fall in line just so, in nice crisp rows and tight columns, right? Excel has the tools you need to make sure everything lines up—and fits in the available space.

Alignment options

On the Alignment tab in the Format ⇨ Cells dialog box (Figure 25-6), you find options to align cell data horizontally, vertically, and at an angle. In a new feature, you can also choose to run text left-to-right, right-to-left, or allow Excel to choose which way text should run based on the context—that is, what's in the surrounding cells.

If you choose Left (Indent) in the Horizontal list box, you'll also be able to specify an indent. You can also set the data at an angle from 0–90° (but not if you specify an indent or choose the "Fill" or "Center across Selection" options in the Horizontal field). The Orientation box shows you what angle your text will be at; in fact, if you prefer, you can set the orientation by clicking and dragging the Text line inside the Orientation box with your mouse. If the cell has borders, they're rotated to the same degree as the rotated text.

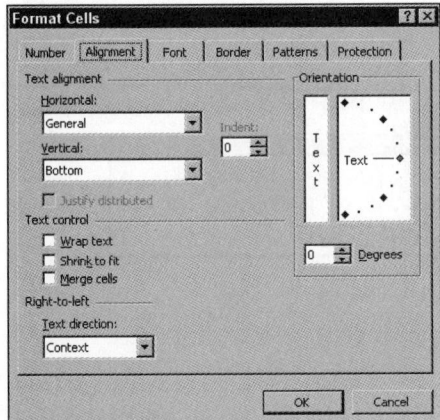

Figure 25-6: Use this tab on the Format ➪ Cells dialog box to control alignment within a cell.

If the cell fits . . .

When not all the contents are visible in a cell, you may choose to have the font size adjusted instead of resizing the column width. Turn on Shrink to Fit in the Alignment box, and Excel will adjust the font size automatically. If you later change the column width, Excel readjusts the font.

Merging cells

Cells can be merged both horizontally and vertically. With the data in the upper-left-most cell, select as many cells across and/or down as you want to merge, and click the Merge and Center button on the Formatting toolbar. Figure 25-7 shows the results of one such merger.

Excel places the contents from the upper-left corner into a single resulting merged cell. The cell address of the merged cell is that of the upper-left cell in the original selection.

If for some reason you decide you don't like the results of your cell-merging, click the Merge and Center button again. It's now a toggle switch, which means it will return the merged cells to their pre-merge multiplicity if you click it a second time.

Tip   Merged cells retain their original alignment, which could result in a small amount of text sitting in the corner of a very large cell. It's usually a good idea to center the text both horizontally and vertically after merging. Go to the alignment tab of the Format ➪ Cells dialog box (see Figure 25-6).

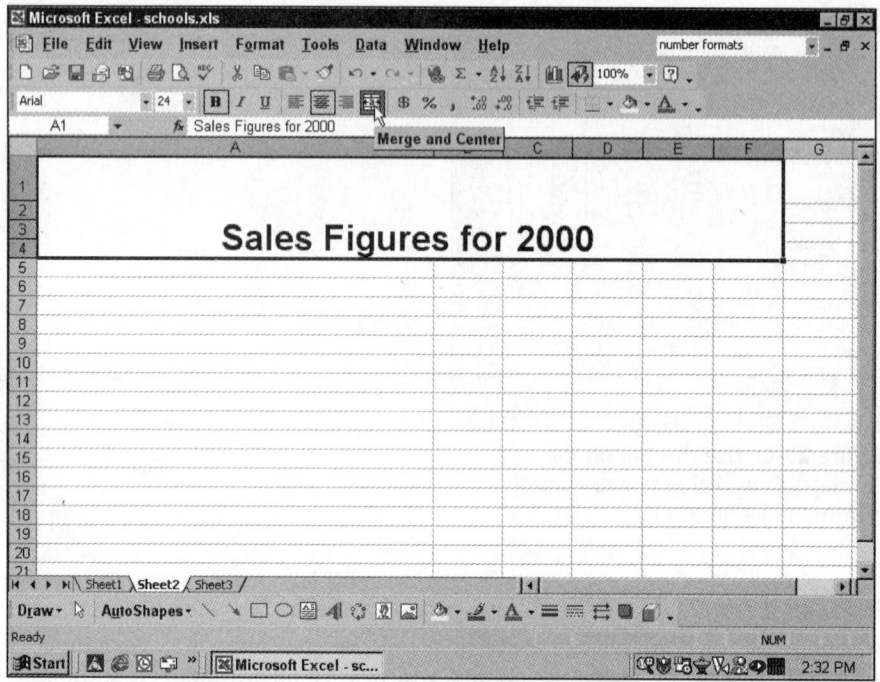

Figure 25-7: With data in cell A1, I selected A1:F4 to create this mega-merger.

Caution Only the data in the upper-left cell of the selection survives after a merge. You get a warning message if Excel finds data elsewhere in the selection. To include all data in the range in the merged cell, move it into the upper-leftmost cell.

AutoFormatting

Not very artistic? Have Excel do the formatting for you. You can apply one of 16 built-in table designs, called AutoFormats. These designs use distinctive formats for the various elements of the table, such as column and row labels, summary totals, and detail data. Click anywhere in the table, and take a look at the options in the Format ⇨ AutoFormat dialog box (Figure 25-8). You can browse through the 16 different designs, and choose one to decorate your data. Excel is aware of row and column totals and will format those differently from the detail data.

The Options button lets you choose only a portion of the formatting; let's say you like the fonts but not the background colors. Clear the Patterns checkbox and away go all the shades. To remove the AutoFormatting, go back into the AutoFormat dialog box and choose None, the final choice at the bottom.

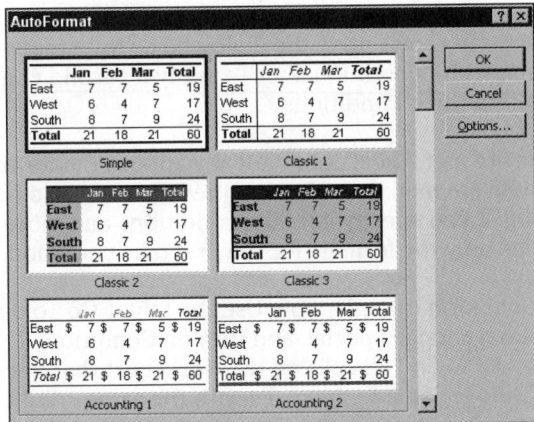

Figure 25-8: Use this dialog box to select among 16 built-in table designs.

Conditional formatting

You can monitor the values of particular cells by applying conditional formats. As the results change, the formats automatically change too. You can set certain formats to appear when values fall outside of a set range, or when a particular formula meets certain conditions.

Select the cells you want to monitor, and go to Format ⇨ Conditional Formatting (the dialog box is shown in Figure 25-9). To use cell values as the formatting criteria, choose "Cell Value Is" in the box labeled Condition 1. Then select a comparison phrase and type a value in the appropriate box. You can compare the values to either a constant or a formula, but you must include an equal sign (=) before any formula.

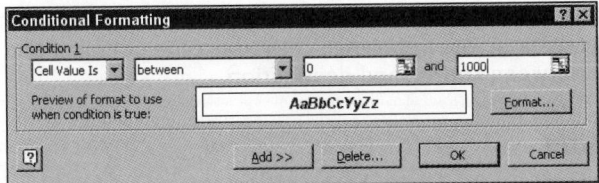

Figure 25-9: You can conditionally format cells based upon their values.

You can also evaluate data using a formula as the criteria. Choose "Formula Is" in the Condition 1 box, and enter the formula in the box on the right. The formula must evaluate to a logical value of True or False.

After you've specified a condition, choose Format to define the formatting Excel will apply if the condition is met. A sample shows up in the dialog box. (Note that you can't change row height or column width conditionally.) To apply a second condition, click Add. You can specify up to three conditions.

When the appropriate conditions are met, Excel automatically applies the formats you've set. If none of the conditions are met, the cell takes the formats it had before you added Conditional Formatting. If you specify multiple conditions and more than one condition is met, Excel applies only the formats for the first true condition.

Excel can find cells with conditional formatting for you. Use the Edit ➪ Go To dialog box (shortcut: F5). In the dialog box, choose Special, and turn on Conditional Formats near the bottom. Choose All to find all cells on the worksheet that have conditional formatting applied. Choose Same to find cells with the same conditional formatting as the active cell.

Tip   There's a special trick to copying just the conditional formatting of a cell. Select the cells to receive the formatting, plus one cell that already has the conditions you want to copy. Go to Format ➪ Conditional Formatting and click OK.

Pasting particular cell attributes

Instead of copying the exact contents of cells, you can copy specific attributes only, such as the resulting value of a formula, formatting, comments, data validation restrictions, and so on.

The Paste Special command

After copying the cells with the desired attributes, go to the destination and bring up the Paste Special dialog box. You can either choose Edit ➪ Paste Special or right-click the destination's upper-left corner and choose Paste Special from the shortcut menu. As shown in Figure 25-10, Excel's Paste Special dialog box lets you choose from a variety of cell attributes to apply, including: formulas with or without formatting; resulting values; formatting only; comments; or validation restrictions. You can also, among other things, transpose the new range (rows become columns and vice versa), or create a hot link between source and destination.

The Format Painter button

When formatting is all you're concerned with, Format Painter is a quick and easy way to transfer the font, borders, alignment, and so on from a cell to another location. Excel's Format Painter works much like the one in Word. Select a cell with the attributes you'd like to copy and click the Format Painter button on the toolbar. The mouse pointer shows a small paintbrush attached to it. With a click (for one cell) or a drag (for several cells), "paint" over the range to be formatted. It adopts the original cell's format instantly.

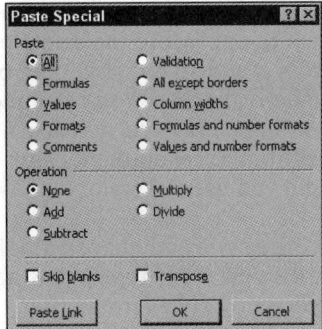

Figure 25-10: Have it your way
using the Paste Special dialog box.

Format Painter can also be used for multiple pastes. Double-click the button to
paint as many different cells and ranges as you like. When you're done, press Esc to
get out of paint mode.

Autofilling values or formats

Using the fill handle is another way to copy specific cell attributes. As the section
on AutoFill in Chapter 24 points out, selecting a cell and dragging the fill handle
with the right mouse button displays a shortcut menu asking which attributes
you'd like to copy to the neighboring cells. Note the Fill Formats choice, which
copies formatting only.

The List AutoFill feature

List AutoFill automatically copies the existing format from a list or table when you
add new rows or columns. Let's say you build a table with a standard background
shade, font, and other formatting in each column. When you add a new row to the
table, Excel automatically duplicates the column formatting in the new row.

Tip

If all this "help" bugs you, clear the box labeled "Extend list formats and formulas"
in the Edit tab of the Tools ⇨ Options dialog box.

Applying multiple formatting options quickly with styles

Much like Word, Excel lets you apply a group of predetermined formatting choices
all at once to a cell or range by specifying a named style. Excel styles can govern
any combination of the following formatting attributes: number formatting, alignment, font choice, borders, pattern or shading, and cell protection (this last one
isn't a format as such, but it's one of the characteristics you can control with a
style).

To apply a style to a range, or to create or modify styles, choose Format ➪ Style. In the resulting dialog box, select a style and choose OK to apply it to the selection. Note that the types of formatting options (font, borders, and so on) governed by a style depend on which of the boxes in the dialog box are checked. You can check or clear these boxes at will to control which of the style's presets Excel actually applies to the selection. You should realize, however, that Excel automatically remembers the changes, retaining them the next time you use the style.

To modify the formatting choices themselves, select the style and choose Modify. You get the standard Format Cells dialog box. To add a new style, type a new name first, and then choose Add. The Merge button lets you copy styles from other worksheets.

Tip   Why Excel omits the Style drop-down list button from the default Formatting toolbar is beyond me. But you can put it there, or on any other toolbar that's convenient. In the Customize dialog box, select Format on the Commands tab, and then drag the Style list button to its new home. You can then apply styles without having to call up the dialog box.

Formatting shortcut keys

Table 25-3 lists some keyboard shortcuts to format your worksheets in Excel.

Table 25-3 Formatting Shortcut Keys	
To Do This	**Press This**
Display the Format ➪ Style dialog box	Alt+' (apostrophe)
Display the Format ➪ Cells dialog box	Ctrl+1
Apply the General number format	Ctrl+Shift+~ (tilde)
Apply the Currency format with two decimal places (negative numbers appear in parentheses)	Ctrl+Shift+$
Apply the Percentage format with no decimal places	Ctrl+Shift+%
Apply the Exponential number format with two decimal places	Ctrl+Shift+^
Apply the Date format with the day, month, and year	Ctrl+Shift+#
Apply the Time format with the hour and minute, and indicate A.M. or P.M.	Ctrl+Shift+@
Apply the Number format with two decimal places, 1000 Separator, and – (minus sign) for negative values	Ctrl+Shift+!

To Do This	Press This
Apply an outline border	Ctrl+Shift+&
Remove all borders	Ctrl+Shift+_ (underscore)
Toggle bold formatting	Ctrl+B
Toggle italic formatting	Ctrl+I
Toggle underlining	Ctrl+U
Toggle strikethrough	Ctrl+5
Hide rows	Ctrl+9
Unhide rows	Ctrl+Shift+(
Hide columns	Ctrl+0 (zero)
Unhide columns	Ctrl+Shift+)

Adding Comments

Some entries on your spreadsheet need extra explanation: where the data came from, how a certain value was calculated, tips for entering data into this cell, or why this month there's less money allocated to home care and more money allocated to M&Ms. If you want to say this about that, attach a comment.

Attaching a comment to a cell

Right-click the cell and choose Insert Comment. As shown in Figure 25-11, a little "sticky note" appears with your name. Speak your mind, and when you're done, click outside the comment box.

A small red triangle (a comment indicator) appears in the cell's upper-right corner to indicate an attached comment. To see the comment box, merely rest the mouse pointer over the cell.

Tip

If you tend to be long-winded, you'll probably need to adjust the size of the comment box. Only the first four lines show up by default. Right-click the cell again, and choose Edit Comment. Small white handles appear around the comment box. Drag the handles to resize.

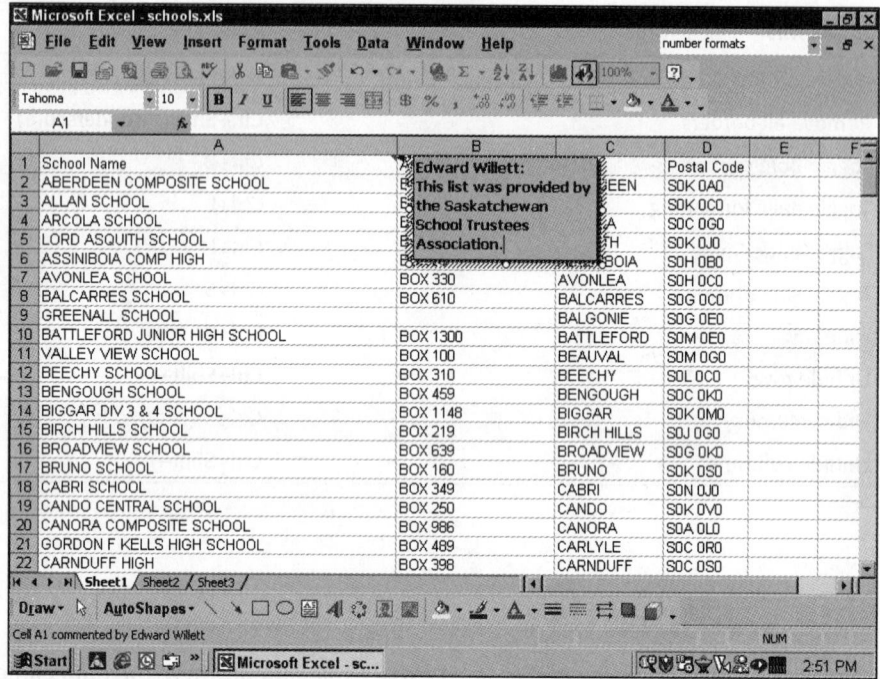

Figure 25-11: A comment tells others where information in a database came from.

Viewing comments

By default, comment indicators appear in cells, and comments show up when you rest the mouse on top. If you'd like to change this default, you can under the View tab of Tools ⇨ Options. Here's where you decide if you want to see neither indicators nor comments, indicators only, or both.

The easiest way to control the display of some but not others is to use the View ⇨ Comments command. When you do, every comment on the spreadsheet is revealed, and the Reviewing toolbar appears. From here you can cycle through each comment one by one; edit, hide, or delete; and choose ones to send via e-mail.

Tip   You can also hide a particular comment by right-clicking the cell and choosing Hide Comment. If you've hidden certain comments and now decide to display them all, choose View ⇨ Comments twice.

Editing comments

To change a comment, right-click the cell it's attached to and choose Edit Comment. If you're a keyboard user, press Shift+F2.

Finding comments

You can quickly select all cells with comments by pressing F5 (shortcut for Edit ⇨ Go To) and choosing Special, then Comments. All cells with attached comments are selected. To find a comment with a particular word or words, specify Comments in the "Look in" field of Edit ⇨ Find.

No comment at this time

To delete a comment from a cell, right-click the cell and choose Delete Comment. (The same option also appears on the Reviewing toolbar, and under Edit ⇨ Clear.) To remove all the comments from the entire worksheet, select them using F5 (as described previously), go to Edit ⇨ Clear, and choose Comments.

Note If you click a cell and press the Delete key, Excel removes the cell contents, but not comments or other formatting.

Quick Printing Tips

Learn to use the Page Break Preview option. Located on the View menu, it lets you clearly see and easily modify the boundary between one printed page and the next. Just drag those heavy blue lines to change the page break locations.

Remember, too, that you can print only a selected region of the worksheet. Open the File ⇨ Print dialog box and choose Selection in the "Print what" area before you OK the box. To print a named range, first select it via the Name box, and then print the selection. To print a particular set of sheets in the workbook, group them first (see "Entering data in groups of worksheets" in Chapter 24). Then go to File ⇨ Print and select the Active Sheets button at the bottom.

You can control whether Excel prints individual worksheet objects — such as graphics, buttons, text boxes, pictures, and OLE objects — using the Format Object dialog box. The Properties tab has a Print Object checkbox. Excel won't print any objects if you hide them all via the View tab of the Tools ⇨ Options dialog box.

✦   ✦   ✦

Formulas and Functions

Formulas are the basis for all of your work in Excel. After all, the reason you bought the program in the first place is because your pocket calculator — or worse, your slide rule — just won't cut it anymore. The more you know about formulas, the more powerful your spreadsheets become.

Formulas often contain functions, which are the source of their power. Functions perform predefined calculations using specific values. Excel has more than 200 built-in functions available for you to use. If you require a particularly complex calculation and the existing functions don't meet your needs, you can even create your own.

The Secret Formula

As time goes on and Excel becomes more sophisticated, formula creation just becomes easier. The key to success with formulas is to understand the essentials behind how Excel calculates, and to know when to ask for help (and where to get it).

Automatic versus manual calculation

Anytime you change or edit your spreadsheet, Excel recalculates your formulas to keep them up-to-date. Whenever possible, Excel recalculates only those cells dependent on values that have changed. This type of calculation helps to save time by avoiding unnecessary number crunching. But unless you specify otherwise, Excel always completely recalculates when a workbook is opened or saved.

The Calculation tab on the Tools ➪ Options dialog box (see Figure 26-1) enables you to control whether Excel performs its calculations automatically or manually. When set to manual calculation, you can get around in complex worksheets more quickly, but you have to remember that the values you see may not be current. Another option, "Automatic except tables", is useful when a worksheet contains data tables of any size, which typically demand lots of Excel's attention during recalculations (data tables are discussed in "Creating dynamic data tables," later in this chapter).

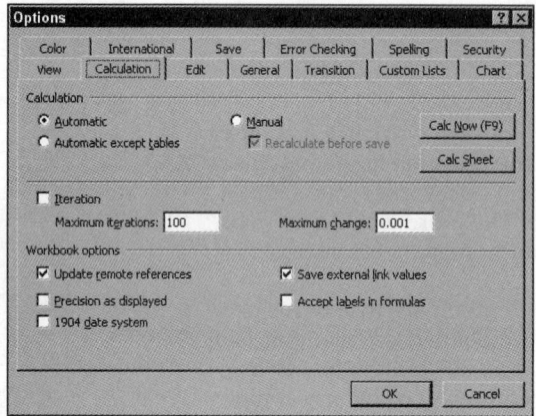

Figure 26-1: The Calculation tab of the Tools ➪ Options dialog box tells Excel how to go about calculating formulas in the current workbook.

With manual calculation on, press F9 to calculate all open worksheets, or Shift+F9 to calculate the active worksheet only. If you do choose manual calculation, you'll most likely want to check the box labeled "Recalculate before save" to guarantee your data will be updated when you save.

Note that all open workbooks use the same calculation mode (automatic or manual). The calculation mode is not saved with workbooks or with templates.

Tip   To see the contents of all the formulas on your worksheet, press Ctrl+backquote (the backquote character [` ] is located on the same key as the tilde [~] character). Every column on your worksheet widens, and every formula cell displays its contents. This shortcut is a toggle; each time you press it, the screen toggles between formula display and result display. Ctrl+` is the shortcut for selecting Tools ➪ Options, going to the View tab, and turning on Formulas.

How does Excel calculate formulas?

Regardless of how a cell has been formatted, Excel normally uses the underlying stored values for all calculations. No matter how many decimal places you've hidden or shown, or how many other cosmetic changes you've made, Excel relies upon the stored values.

To force Excel to calculate using the values displayed in your worksheet rather than the underlying stored values, go to the Tools ➪ Options dialog box and check the "Precision as displayed" box on the Calculation tab. You can set this option independently for each workbook.

Smooth operators for your formulas

The most important thing to remember when creating a formula is that it must begin with an equal sign. You can type an equal sign as the first character in a cell to start a new formula, or type it into the Formula Bar.

A formula can consist of nothing more than an equal sign followed by a value as in =2 or =TRUE or, using a function, =DATE(). But garden-variety formulas consist of at least two numbers or cell references strung together by operators. Excel calculates the result of the formula by performing the operations specified by these operators on the values they connect.

In a formula containing more than one operator, Excel follows a predetermined scheme to decide the order in which to make its calculations. Even if you commit this operator precedence scheme to memory — and I've never been able to — you can and should use parentheses to group values with their operators in your formulas. Instead of =2*3+5, for example, type =(2*3)+5 or =2*(3+5), whichever is correct. That way, you can see at a glance which operations should be done first, and you can be sure Excel follows your intentions.

Excel and VBA share many of their operators (see Chapter 53). However, each has a different set. VBA has the Mod operator and a whole set of logical operators not found in Excel (Excel's Mod function performs the same calculation as the Mod operator, but it isn't an operator). On the other hand, VBA lacks Excel's operators that work on cell references, of course, as well as its percent and exponentiation operators.

Of course, the characters +, –, *, and / are the operators for addition, subtraction, multiplication, and division, respectively. Other operators available in your Excel formulas include those in Table 26-1 and Table 26-2.

Table 26-1
Arithmetic Operators

This Operator	Performs This Function	Example
%	Percent	A5% (result is 1/100th the value of cell A5)
^	Exponentiation	4^3 (4 raised to the 3rd power — result is 64)

Table 26-2
Comparison Operators (Same as in VBA)

Text Operator	Performs This Function	Example
&	Concatenates two values into a single text string.	"Foot" & "ball" (result is "Football")

Referring to cells and ranges in your formulas

To refer to a cell in a formula, just type its address. If you put the formula =A1 into cell B2, cell B2 shows the current value of cell A1 whenever Excel recalculates the worksheet.

Another basic point: You don't need to type in the address of a referenced cell yourself. Whenever you're editing a formula, clicking or dragging on a worksheet places the addresses of the cells or ranges of cells you touched into the formula automatically.

The referenced cell or range is outlined in color. Each additional cell or range of cells you reference is highlighted in a new color, which matches the color of its reference number in the Formula Bar. This makes it easy to adjust your formula; just drag the colored boxes around the spreadsheet to change the references in the formula.

Referring to ranges of cells

Excel provides special operators to refer to multiple cells in your formulas. The most common is the range operator, : (colon). The reference B4:U8 is not only a cute way to refer to your appetite before dinner, but also defines a rectangle of cells spanning B4 at the top left and U8 at the bottom right. Table 26-3 displays the available cell reference operators.

Table 26-3
Reference Operators (Combine Ranges of Cells for Calculations)

Operator	Type of Cell Reference	Example
:	Range — creates a reference to all cells between and including two other references.	A3:C19
,	Union — creates a reference to all cells included in two other references (either single cell or range references).	A3:C19,D34:D39
(a single space)	Intersection — creates a reference to any cells common to two other references.	X10:X20 W5:X11

The union and intersection operators are probably most useful when used with named ranges, because then it's easier to understand the range you're trying to target. More on this in the next section.

Referring to named cells and ranges

Chapter 24 introduced the concept of (and the techniques for) naming cells, whether individually or as ranges. Although named ranges are great for navigation, they're maybe even better when used in your formulas. Instead of typing an obscure, arbitrary code, you just enter the name as in:

```
= (Height + Weight)/ShoeSize
```

You don't have to remember where the target cells reside in your workbook, and the formula remains understandable when you return to it 10 minutes (or 10 days, or even 10 weeks) later.

Although they can make formulas look unduly complex when used with ordinary cell or range references, the union and intersection range operators come into their own when teamed with named ranges.

Consider the little worksheet table shown in Figure 26-2. I've named each column (using the length of business trips I've made) and each row (using the names of the months). Suppose I want to know how many short business trips I took in May. Using the intersection operator — which is just a space — I can write the following formula to read the table for me, without looking up any cell coordinates:

```
=short may
```

Excel outlines the referenced ranges, each in its own color, and assigns those same colors to the names of the ranges in the formula bar. This makes it easy to see exactly what it is doing: finding the intersection of the ranges Short and May.

The union operator is probably less often useful. Still, if for some reason I had to know the total number of long trips I took in the first half of the year *and* the total number of trips of all lengths I took in the month of April, my formula would be as follows:

```
=SUM(Long,April) -Long April
```

The second term keeps Excel from counting the long trips in April twice.

Relative versus absolute references

By default, cell references are relative. If the address of the cell to which you referred changes, Excel automatically changes the formula to preserve the reference. If, say, you've given cell B2 the formula =A1, then you cut cell A1 and paste it into cell C5, the formula in B2's cell automatically becomes =C5.

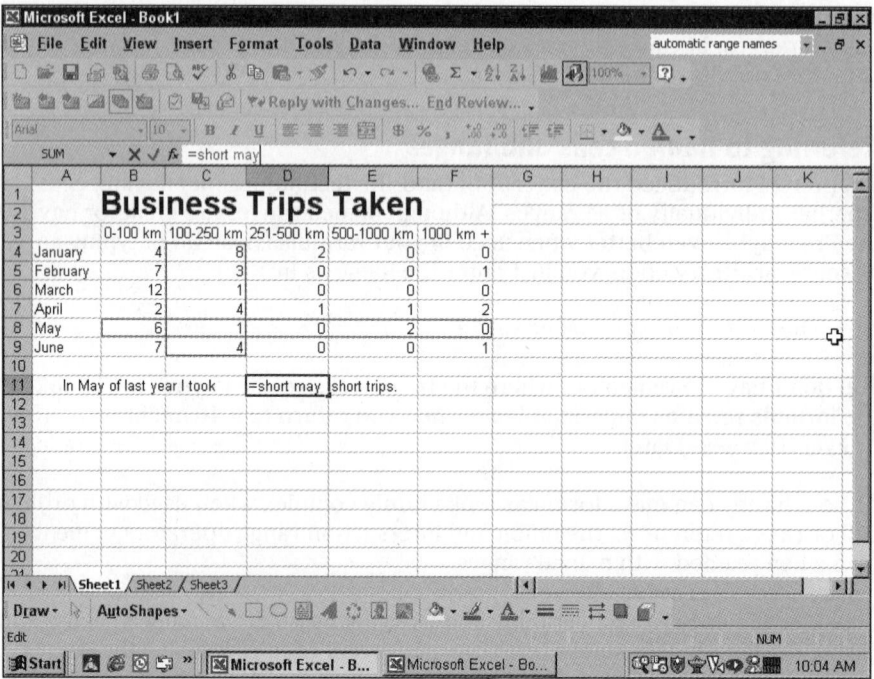

Figure 26-2: Naming ranges lets you write formulas without knowing exact cell references.

In similar fashion, sort of, if you then copy cell B2 to cell B3, B3's formula becomes =D5. Note that in this case, the cell you're referring to hasn't changed at all. But Excel assumes you want to create a table, and because you copied the formula to the next column, Excel thinks you would want the formula in the new cell to refer to the cell one column over from the original cell.

Relative references are great, most of the time — they enable you to reorganize your worksheets on the fly without having to retype every formula. However, sometimes your formula should always point to the same cell, even if the formula's cell changes. To create an absolute cell reference, add a $ character before the row and column coordinates, as in =$A$1. Then, if you copy the formula to another column, the formula will still be =$A$1. You can add the dollar sign to only one of the coordinates, as in $A1 or A$1, if you want the reference to remain absolute in only one dimension.

Even with absolute references, Excel still updates your formulas if the referenced cell changes its address. You can prevent this — but you would rarely want to — with the Indirect function, which allows you to refer to a cell using a text string; for instance, =INDIRECT ("A10") would return the value of A10, even if you've taken out a couple of rows and what is now A10 used to be A12.

Cell references outside the current worksheet

When you're editing a formula, Excel lets you create cell and range references using point and click, even when the referenced cells lie in other sheets or other workbooks. Still, it's good to know how such out-of-sheet references look.

To refer to a cell or range in another worksheet in the same workbook, precede the cell address(es) with the sheet's name followed by an exclamation mark (!). If the name contains spaces, enclose it in single quote marks, as in: =SUM('Spring sales'!C2:D5).

To enter a reference to another open workbook, list the workbook in square brackets, followed by the sheet name, the exclamation point, and then the cell reference. This time, single quote marks should go before the opening bracket and before the exclamation point if the names include any spaces. Here's an example: =SUM('[Toy sales 1999]Spring sales'!R20:T35). When you close the alien workbook, Excel adds its complete path to the reference.

Tools for Fixing Formulas

Excel 2002 has several new tools for finding and correcting problems with formulas, which you can access most easily through the new Formula Auditing toolbar. To turn it on, choose View ➪ Toolbars ➪ Formula Auditing (see Figure 26-3).

Figure 26-3: The Formula Auditing toolbar includes a number of useful tools for understanding, monitoring, and correcting formulas.

Error checking

The Error Checking tool on the Formula Auditing toolbar will search through the worksheet for formulas that don't look right to Excel. If it finds one, it will pop up a dialog box giving you options on dealing with the error. If you don't think the formula is an error, you can simply choose to ignore it; Error Checking won't mention it again.

Here are the rules Error Checking looks for (you can turn these rules on or off by going to the Error Checking tab of the Tools ⇨ Options dialog box):

✦ **Evaluates to error value:** That means the formula doesn't include the expected syntax, arguments, or data types. It might include division by zero, for instance, or a reference to a nonexistent cell. Note that you can choose to deliberately enter an error value directly into a cell, in which case, Error Checking doesn't mark it.

✦ **Text date with two-digit years:** Better late than never; this warns you that the cell contains a text date that could be interpreted to be in the wrong century—that is, 1/1/21 could be January 1, 1921 or January 1, 2021 (or January 1, 1821, for that matter).

✦ **Number stored as text:** Just what it sounds like. This often happens when you import data from other sources. Since Excel can't properly sort such data, it's best to convert these text numbers to number numbers.

✦ **Inconsistent formula in region:** This compares the formula to the others around it, and if it's radically different, Error Checking flags it.

✦ **Formula omits cells in region:** If the formula refers to a range of cells, but other cells that seem like they might belong in that range also contain data that's not referenced, Error Checking flags the cell. This could pop up if, for example, you created a formula in cell A8 that summed cells A2:A4, then added more data in cells A5:A7 but forgot to update your formula.

✦ **Unlocked cells containing formulas:** It's usually a good idea to lock a cell containing a formula so it can't be changed without being unlocked—that prevents accidental changes. If Error Checking finds a cell containing a formula that isn't locked, it flags it just to be sure it wasn't unlocked by accident.

✦ **Formulas referring to empty cells:** A reference to an empty cell can cause unintended results.

Trace precedents, dependents, and errors

No, precedents are not what we elect every fourth November, nor even what you receive on your birthday. They're the cells referred to by a formula. Precedent cells contain data that the formula uses for calculation.

Similarly, dependents, in Excel-speak, are not people you get a tax break for looking after. They're the cells containing a formula-generated result that references the current cell.

The Trace Precedents and Trace Dependents tools on the Formula Auditing toolbar make it easy to locate a formula's precedents, or a cell's dependents, and to control the relationships among them: They draw blue lines showing you exactly where those cells are located (see Figure 26-4).

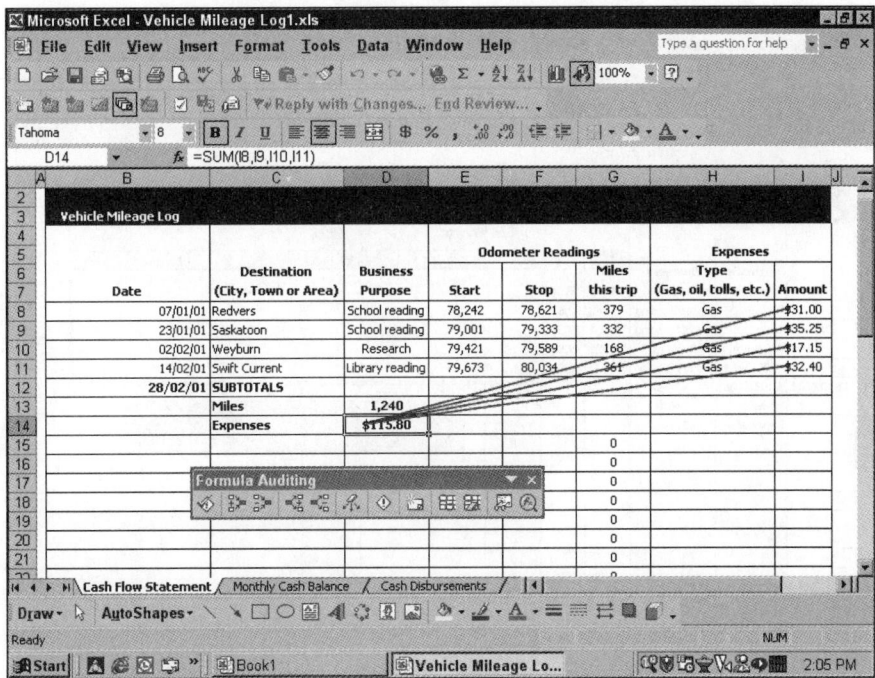

Figure 26-4: Trace Precedents uses blue lines to draw your attention to the cells a formula references.

The Trace Error tool works in much the same way, except it points to a cell that the selected cell references that contains an error, such as division by 0. Trace Error lines are red.

You can clear the lines by clicking Remove Precedent Arrows, Remove Dependents Arrows, or Remove All Arrows.

The Watch Window

Excel 2002 provides a new tool for keeping an eye on troublesome formulas. The Watch Window, activated from the Formula Auditing toolbar, lets you keep track of the values of specific cells as you add data and additional formulas to a spreadsheet.

Just click Add Watch, then either type in the reference to the cell whose value you want to watch, or click on it within the spreadsheet. The Watch Window tells you what book the cell is in, what sheet, and its reference and name (if any), and shows you the formula and the current value resulting from that formula (see Figure 26-5).

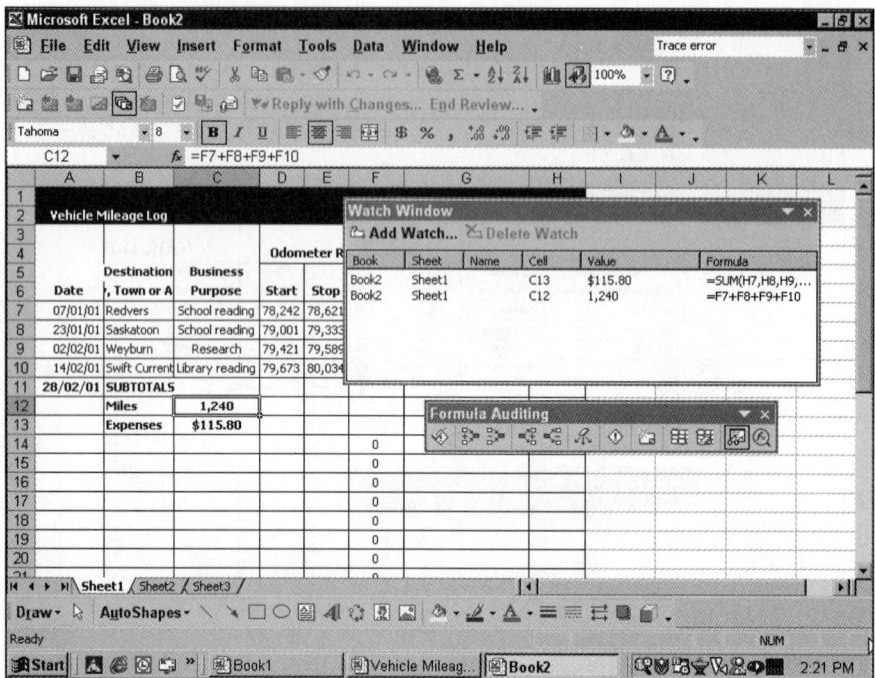

Figure 26-5: The Watch Window is a handy tool for keeping an eye on the values of certain cells as you go about your business.

Evaluate Formula

If you've got a complex formula that contains several other formulas nested inside it, the Evaluate Formula tool on the Formula Auditing toolbar can help you debug it. The Evaluate Formula dialog box will show you the current value of the formula you're evaluating, and it also enables you to step into a nested formula to evaluate the formulas that comprise it.

Working with 3D references

Workbooks are designed to hold several worksheets for a reason: The worksheets have some relationship to each other. So it follows that you may need to analyze data in the same cell or range of cells on adjacent sheets within the workbook. To do so, you can use a 3D reference. These 3D references come in two varieties: formulas or defined names. They're just as easy to create as the 1D or 2D kind, and they can be great timesavers.

Using 3D formulas

A 3D formula comprises first a range of sheet names from the current workbook, then an "!" as a delimiter, and finally a cell or range reference. When calculating the formula, Excel includes the cell reference from each and every worksheet within the range.

Suppose you have a workbook with the four sheets whose tabs and names are shown in Figure 26-6. Each worksheet has exactly the same layout, but different data. A 3D formula like this:

```
=SUM(North:South!J54)
```

returns the sum of cell J54 on the first three worksheets.

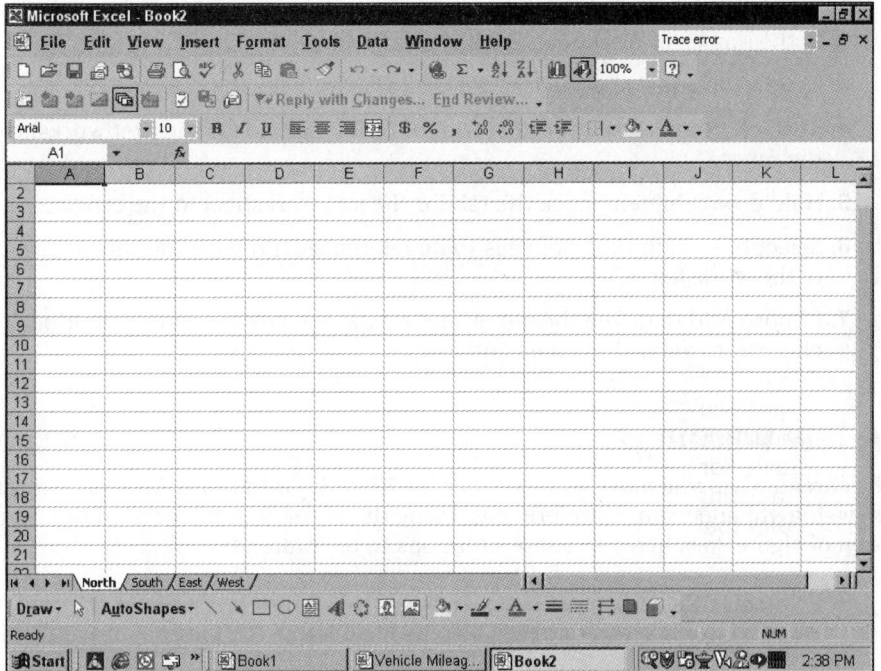

Figure 26-6: A typical use of different worksheets: sales data for each of four regions

An easy way to create a 3D formula is to use point-and-click. Position yourself in the cell where you want the formula, and try this:

1. Type = (an equal sign), the name of the function, and an opening parenthesis.

2. Click the tab for the first worksheet in the range.

3. Hold down Shift and click the tab for the last worksheet in the range.

4. Select the cell or range to be calculated.

Excel drops the corresponding 3D reference into your formula. You can now complete the formula.

Defining 3D range names

Just as a regular range name represents a single cell or group of cells on a single worksheet, a 3D range name represents a group of cells whose members reside on more than one worksheet. One name may refer to cells residing on several sheets in a workbook. The only restriction is that the named cell or range must be the same for each sheet:

1. Go to Insert ⇨ Name ⇨ Define.

2. In the Names in Workbook field, type any name you like.

3. Type = (an equal sign) in the "Refers to" field.

4. At the bottom left of the Excel window, click the tab for the first worksheet in the range.

5. Hold down Shift and click the tab for the last worksheet in the range.

6. Select the cell or range of cells to be referenced. (You can do this on any one of the worksheets.)

7. Choose Add to define the name, and stay in the box for more definitions or click OK to define the name and exit.

A few warnings

Be careful when you move or copy sheets within the workbook. Always be aware of how it might affect any 3D references. Using the scenario referenced in the discussion of Figure 26-6, here are some situations to be aware of:

✦ If you insert a worksheet between North and South (via a move or copy), the inserted worksheet's data will also be included in the formula or name.

✦ If you move West to a location somewhere outside the range, Excel removes the values from the formula or name.

✦ If you move either North or South to another location in the same workbook (such as after East), Excel adjusts the formula or name to accommodate the new range of sheets between them.

Keep in mind that Excel considers the first and last worksheets in the range (in this case, North and South) as the "anchors."

Performing Complex Calculations: VBA versus Formulas

In a real sense, adding formulas to a worksheet is a form of programming. After all, you're creating a customized piece of computer software – your worksheet automatically changes the results it calculates according to the current values of other cells.

As long as your formulas are fairly simple, you can ignore VBA and enter your calculating "programs" – formulas – directly into worksheet cells. As your skills and ambitions grow, however, you require formulas of greater complexity. At some point, it may make sense to design your computations as VBA modules instead of Excel formulas.

VBA lets you do anything you can do with Excel, and more (all of Excel's built-in functions are accessible in your VBA procedures). Here's an analysis of the trade-offs:

Excel formulas have the following advantages:

✦ **Immediacy.** Just type the formula into a worksheet cell.

✦ **Worksheet-specific debugging tools.** Features like the Range Finder and the Formula Auditing toolbar help you understand your formulas and home in immediately on potential problems with cell references.

VBA, on the other hand, has advantages with the following:

✦ **Room.** Whereas an Excel formula is limited to 255 characters, VBA routines can be as long as you want to make them.

✦ **Clarity.** Because you have plenty of room, you can separate the steps of a complex calculation on individual lines of your VBA procedure and add line-by-line comments. Confined to your worksheet, you either have to build highly complex formulas that are very difficult to understand or break them up into separate cells, making the flow of computation hard to follow.

✦ **Powerful, full-featured debugging tools.** Your ability to set break points, monitor watch values, and trace through the computation step by step makes a VBA procedure much easier to debug than a comparable Excel formula.

✦ **Strong error-handling features.** A VBA program can respond much more flexibly if the routine encounters an error such as a reference to an empty cell.

Using Functions in Your Formulas

An Excel function calculates a value for you. You use functions in your formulas sometimes to perform complex calculations that would take much more work if you constructed them from scratch, and sometimes to obtain values you just couldn't get otherwise.

Given Excel's vast wealth of functions, and the way you can combine them into highly complex formulas, I could never introduce them all to you, let alone cover the ways in which they solve real-life problems. What I can do is give you a decent introduction to the techniques required to use them effectively, and list the types of functions Excel provides with some representative examples in each category.

Tip

If you plan to build dynamic worksheets that adapt their behavior to changing conditions, plan to master the IF function. I discuss it in "Using the IF function" later in this chapter.

Function anatomy

A function consists of the function name followed by paired parentheses, which contain the function's arguments, if it has any. A function may have any number of arguments (multiple arguments must be separated by commas), and some have none. Table 26-4 shows some examples.

Table 26-4
Function Examples

Function	Value It Returns
NOW()	The current date and time.
COLUMNS(range)	The number of columns in range.
MEDIAN(number1, number2 ...)	The median of the numeric values specified in the argument list.
PMT(rate,nper,pv)	The payment amount for a loan expressed as a negative number. The arguments specify the interest rate, the number of payments, and the loan amount.

Entering functions

The easiest way to insert a function is to click the Insert Function button to the left of the Formula Bar and select a function from the Insert Function dialog box (see Figure 26-7). If you're not sure what function you want, try typing a brief description of what you want the function to do in the "Search for a function" box and click Go. The Function Arguments dialog box will then appear that enables you to enter the arguments for the function, and then shows you their current values.

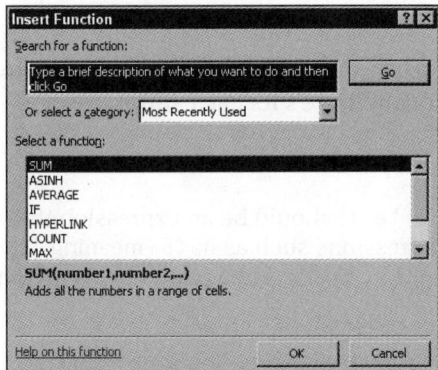

Figure 26-7: You can choose functions to insert into your formulas via the Insert Function dialog box.

If you do know which function you want, you can type the function name directly into your formula. If you know how to use its arguments, just go ahead and type an opening parenthesis, the list of arguments, and the closing parenthesis. If you're hazy on the arguments, press Ctrl+A to display the Function Arguments dialog box after typing the function's name (don't type parentheses).

Nesting functions

A formula can consist solely of a single function, as in =NOW() or =PMT(7%/12, 60, 20000). Often, however, you include one or more functions mixed with cell references and values you type in. Functions can even be nested inside other functions — in other words, you can use the result of one function as an argument in another function. Here's a simple example:

    =ABS(SUM(C2:C20))

Here, the SUM function sums the values in cells C2 through C20. That value becomes the argument for the ABS function, which returns the absolute value of the sum. You can nest functions up to seven levels deep.

Cross-Reference

With VBA, you can create custom functions to use in formulas (and call from within other VBA procedures) just as you do the built-in ones. Custom functions are a great way to condense and simplify complex formulas that you use repeatedly. Basic techniques for building and using custom functions are covered in Chapter 30.

Using the IF function

If you forego VBA, the IF function is an absolute necessity for creating worksheets that adapt to current conditions automatically. Here's its basic form:

```
IF(logical_test, truevalue, falsevalue)
```

The IF function's first argument, logical_test, should be an expression that can be evaluated as either TRUE or FALSE. Expressions such as B9<6 (meaning, "the value of cell B9 is less than 6") and Q10<>R15 ("Q10 is not equal to R15") are typical examples of such expressions.

The next two arguments determine what value the IF function returns. If the logical_ test expression is TRUE, the function returns truevalue; if logical_ test is FALSE, the function returns falsevalue. The return values can be numbers or text.

Now for an example:

```
=IF(TodaysSales > 1000, "Celebrate", "Ordinary day")
```

This formula places the text "Celebrate" in its cell if the value in another cell named TodaysSales is greater than 1000. If not, the cell containing the formula reads "Ordinary day."

Though simple in concept, IF becomes a very powerful tool when applied to changing data and coupled with other functions. In particular, it's often very useful to nest IF functions. See if you can follow the logic here:

```
=IF(Jackpot>3000000,IF(WEEKDAY(TODAY())=7,"Wednesday special
bonus!","Big jackpot"),"Meager winnings")
```

In this example, the outer IF function tests to see whether Jackpot is greater than $3 million. If not, the formula produces the discouraging message, "Meager winnings." However, if the threshold for big jackpots was passed, the inner IF takes over — because it is the truevalue argument for the outer IF, its value becomes the final result of the formula. The inner IF checks to see whether today is a Wednesday, and if so, posts a special Wednesday message. Otherwise, it gives a run-of-the-mill message touting the large payout.

A survey of Excel functions

Although Excel has far too many functions for me to cover in detail, you deserve at least a quick tour of the calculating power that's yours for the asking — if you know where to look. You owe it to yourself to become familiar with the array of chores these functions can perform — you don't want to spend valuable time creating a formula of your own when a built-in function could give you the same results.

Excel's functions are grouped into categories. This section lists the categories and describes a few representative functions in each one — but remember, Excel has many more functions than I show here. (By the way, many functions are identical or very similar to comparable functions in VBA.)

Information functions (see Table 26-5) give you information about the kind of data stored in cells. The `IS...` functions return TRUE if the cell contains the specified type of data, and FALSE if not.

Table 26-5
Information Functions

Function	Value It Returns
CELL	Information you specify about a given cell (such as its value, formatting, data type, or color)
COUNTBLANK	The number of blank cells in the specified range
INFO	Specified information about your computer (the current path, how much memory is available, and many other info items are available)
ISBLANK	TRUE if the specified cell is blank
ISEVEN	TRUE if the specified cell contains an even number
ISTEXT	TRUE if the specified cell contains text
TYPE	A number representing the type of data the specified cell contains

The most important function in the logical functions (see Table 26-6) group is the all-important `IF`, which returns one of two values depending on whether its first argument is TRUE or FALSE. The remaining logical functions return TRUE or FALSE, depending on the values of the arguments. These arguments are themselves logical values. For example, an argument might be a statement such as 2+2=4, which has the value of TRUE.

Table 26-6
Logical Functions

Function	Value It Returns
AND	TRUE if all the arguments are TRUE; otherwise, FALSE
IF	The first of two values you specify if the test argument is TRUE; otherwise, the second value
NOT	TRUE if the input argument is FALSE, FALSE if the input is TRUE
OR	TRUE if any of the arguments are TRUE, FALSE if none are TRUE

Date and time functions (see Table 26-7) let you write formulas that update themselves based on the current date and time and let you make calculations with dates. Like VBA, Excel uses a special serial number (the date value) to store and manipulate dates. You can use the DATE function to convert a "human" date into a date value. Functions such as DAY, YEAR, and MONTH convert date values into human dates.

Table 26-7
Date and Time Functions

Function	Value It Returns
DATE	The date value for a date specified as a year, month, and day.
DAY	An integer corresponding to the day of the month specified by the input date value (similar functions are YEAR, MONTH, HOUR, MINUTE, and SECOND).
NOW	The date value for the current date and time according to your PC. Use TODAY to return only the date, and TIME for only the time.
WEEKDAY	The day of the week for a specified date value.
WORKDAY	The date value for the next workday after a specified start date.
YEARFRAC	The decimal fraction of the year represented by the interval between two dates. Good for prorating employee benefits.

Lookup and reference functions (see Table 26-8) locate cells in a worksheet range or identify values in an array. The functions in the database category are somewhat complementary and may be easier to use if you set up your worksheet properly.

Table 26-8
Lookup and Reference Functions

Function	Value It Returns
CHOOSE	The value at a specified position in a list.
COLUMNS	The number of columns in a range. ROWS gives the number of rows, of course.
INDEX	The value of a specified cell within a range, or the cell address.
INDIRECT	The value of another cell whose address is given by the cell you specify in the arguments. Use this when you want your formula always to refer to the same cell address, even if the original contents move to another address because the cell is moved or if you insert or delete rows or columns.
MATCH	The relative position of an item you're searching for in a range (not the item's value).
OFFSET	A cell or range reference that is a specified number of rows and columns from another cell or range.

Math and trigonometry functions (see Table 26-9) perform a wide variety of mathematical computations.

	Table 26-9 **Math and Trigonometry Functions**	
Function	*Value It Returns*	
ABS	The absolute value of the input value.	
COS	The cosine of the input value. Excel includes a complete set of basic trigonometric functions.	
FACT	The factorial of the input number.	
LOG	The logarithm of the input number in the specified base (use LN to return the natural log).	
PI	The value of pi.	
PRODUCT	The product of all the input values (you can input a range of cells, just as with the SUM function).	
ROMAN	The Roman numeral equivalent of the input number.	
ROUND	The input number rounded off to a specified number of digits.	
SIGN	1 if the input number is positive, 0 if the number is zero, or –1 if the number is negative.	
SQRT	The square root of the input value.	
SUMPRODUCT	Multiplies together corresponding elements in two or more arrays and then sums all of the products.	
TRUNC	The integer portion of the input value, truncating any decimal portion.	

Text functions (see Table 26-10) alter text strings in all sorts of useful ways, or they create text from numbers.

	Table 26-10 **Text Functions**	
Function	*Value It Returns*	
CLEAN	The input text stripped of all nonprinting characters.	
DOLLAR	Converts a numeric value to text formatted as currency with the decimals rounded to two places.	

Continued

Table 26-10 *(continued)*

Function	Value It Returns
LEFT	A specified number of characters starting at the left side of the input string. (MID and RIGHT extract characters from the middle and right side of the input string.)
LEN	The number of characters in the input text string
LOWER	The text converted to lowercase. UPPER performs the opposite conversion.
TEXT	Converts a number into corresponding text, formatted according to a pattern you specify (similar to VBA's FORMAT function).
TRIM	The text with all extra spaces removed (single spaces between words are preserved).

As befits the essential business software tool, Excel has hordes of functions for calculating loans, investments, and the like (see Table 26-11).

Table 26-11
Financial Functions

Function	Value It Returns
ACCRINT	The accrued interest for an interest-paying security (requires Analysis ToolPak).
DB	The depreciation of an asset using the fixed-declining balance method.
DISC	The discount rate for a security (requires Analysis ToolPak).
FV	The future value of an investment, assuming a constant interest rate.
INTRATE	The interest rate for a security. Use RATE for an annuity.
IPMT	The interest payment for an investment or loan.
IRR	The internal rate of return.
PMT	The payment for an investment or loan including interest and principal.
PV	The present value of an investment.
YIELD	The yield on an interest-paying security.

Not for the mathematically challenged, Excel's 80-or-so statistical functions (see Table 26-12) can handle all manner of complex statistical analyses. I've listed a few of them here that even math boneheads may find useful, plus a smattering of the more arcane.

Table 26-12
Statistical Functions

Function	Value It Returns
AVERAGE	The arithmetic mean of the arguments.
CHITEST	The test for independence based on the chi-squared (^{2}) distribution.
CONFIDENCE	The confidence interval for a population mean.
COUNT	The number of cells containing numeric values within the input range.
FISHER	The Fisher transformation.
FREQUENCY	An array containing the frequencies within which values occur in specified ranges of values.
LARGE	The value in a series that occupies a specified rank (to identify, say, the third-best selling CD during the third quarter). SMALL gives the inverse result.
MAX	The largest value in a series. MIN gives the smallest value.
MEDIAN	The median of the argument values.
MODE	The value in a series that occurs most often.
NORMDIST	The normal distribution.
STDEV	An estimate of the standard deviation.

Many people use Excel as a flat-file (nonrelational) database manager, storing database records in worksheet rows and fields in the columns (the column labels function as field names). The dozen or so functions in the database and list management functions category (see Table 26-13) help you analyze such data. Typically, you specify the range containing your database, the field you want to work with, and selection criteria.

Table 26-13		
Database and List Management Functions		
Function	**Value It Returns**	
DCOUNT	The number of records (cells) matching your criteria	
DMAX	The maximum value of those records matching your criteria	
DSUM	The sum of the values in a field for all records matching your criteria	

Formula Tips and Tricks

The rest of this chapter is devoted to some extremely useful tips for working with formulas in general.

Cross-Reference

To learn how cell formatting can be set to change based upon the results of a particular formula, see Chapter 25.

Defining named constants

The standard method for defining a constant is to place its value into a cell and then refer to that cell when you need to use the variable in your formulas. That way, if the "constant" changes, you can type a new value in the cell to recalculate all the dependent results automatically. If the value is truly a constant, however, you can define it as a name that exists only in Excel's working memory, not in a worksheet cell.

Choose Insert ➪ Name ➪ Define. In the Define Name dialog box, type in the name for the constant and then type its numeric value in the field labeled "Refers to", erasing the existing contents (don't precede the value with an equal sign). From then on you can use the named constant in any formula.

Out-of-range date arguments

Some Excel date functions permit arguments outside the expected range. This allows for some fancy footwork to create handy results. You can find the dates before and after the current month by using numbers outside of the range 1–31. The "zeroth" date of one month (the day before the first, of course) gives you the last date of the previous month. You can also do the same with months and years. Here are some examples:

```
=DATE(2001,3,0)     February 28, 2001
=DATE(2000,0,3)     December 3, 2000
=DATE(2002,2,30)    March 1, 2002
```

```
=DATE(2000,13,32)   February 1, 2001
=DATE(2001,-2,-3)   September 27, 2000
```

Programmers, especially, may find this handy when designing loops.

Creating dynamic data tables

A dynamic data table is one of the most powerful devices in Excel. It combines two wonderful features (data tables and the DSUM function), and it has a million and one uses.

Analyzing variable inputs with data tables: Feature 1

A data table shows the results found when a range of different values is substituted into a formula. It provides a shortcut for calculating multiple variations, and it's a good way to compare the results you can expect under different conditions.

Data tables can have either one or two variables (called input cells). A simple example of a one-variable data table is shown in Figure 26-8.

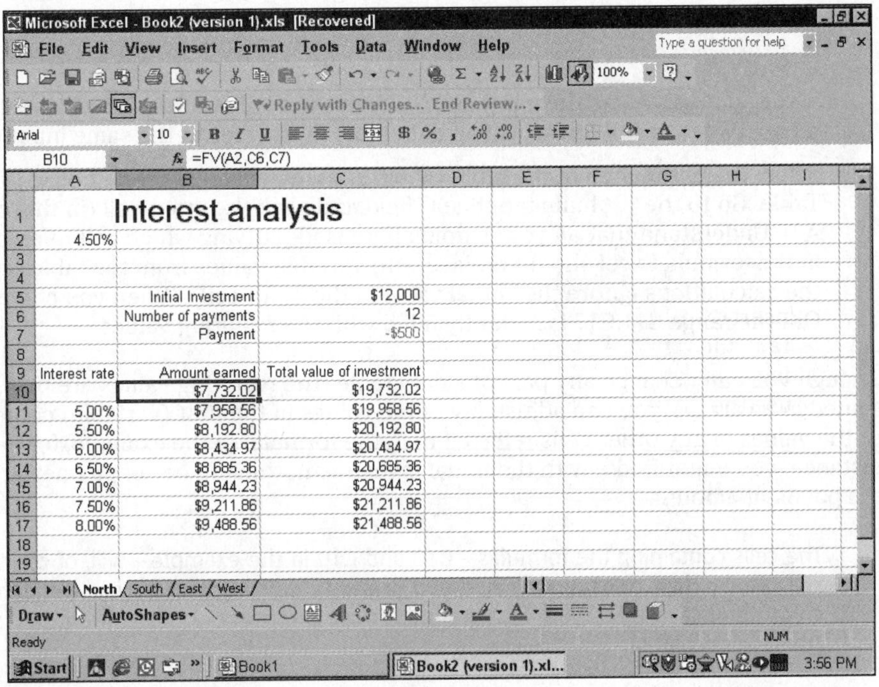

Figure 26-8: A data table comparing the total annual return on a monthly investment of $500 at various interest rates

Using the FV function, the data table in the example takes a variety of interest rates and calculates how much money a $500 per month investment will earn over one year at each of them. That result is then used to compute the total value of the investment at the end of the year. Though your data table may be completely different, the setup will be similar:

1. List the values to be substituted into the formula in a column. In the example, the interest rates are in A11:A17.

2. The formula itself goes into the cell one column to the right and one row higher than the first variable value. The values will be returned below this formula. Enter the formula as you normally would, but at the place in the formula where the variable belongs, type a cell reference as a placeholder (this is called the input cell). Actually, it doesn't matter which cell reference you use here, as long as the cell isn't in the table itself—the value it contains is used as an input to the formula only in this cell and doesn't affect the results displayed in the table itself. In the example, the formula =FV(A2,C6,C7) was placed in B10. *A2* is the input cell (placeholder), while C6 and C7 contain actual values to be used in the formula, the number of payments and the payment amount.

    You can place additional formulas to the right of the first one. In the example, the second formula in C10 calculates the ending balance:

    ```
    = FV(A2,C6,C7)+C5
    ```

    and again uses *A2* as the input cell (C5 holds the value of the initial investment). Note that all formulas in a data table must refer to the same input cell.

3. Select the entire area of the table (A10:C17 in the example) and choose Data ⇨ Table. Go to the "Column input cell" field and click the input cell (in this case, A2). Understand that all you're doing here is identifying which cell reference in the formula Excel should replace with variable values from the table (again, the calculations ignore the actual value in the input cell). When you choose OK, the range B11:C17 is instantly filled with the resulting values.

Though you can't change any part of a data table (the resulting values are presented in an array), you can adjust any of the values in the first (variable) column or the values of any other cells referred to in the formula. In the example, for instance, you might fiddle with the initial investment, the number of payments, or the payment amount.

Tip   The cells containing the formulas—B10 and C10 in the example—will, of course, still display their original results. If you prefer to hide such cells, you can either color the text to match the background, or use a custom number format of ";;;" (three semicolons).

Tip   Workbook calculation may take more time when you're using data tables. If it's a problem, go to the Calculation tab of the Tools ⇨ Options dialog box and turn on "Automatic except tables". Afterward, press F9 or Shift+F9 to manually update any tables.

Two-variable data tables

For really powerful analysis, construct a two-variable data table. The example shown in Figure 26-9 illustrates the concept by extending the earlier example to show the effects on effective yield of changing the payment amount, as well as the interest rate.

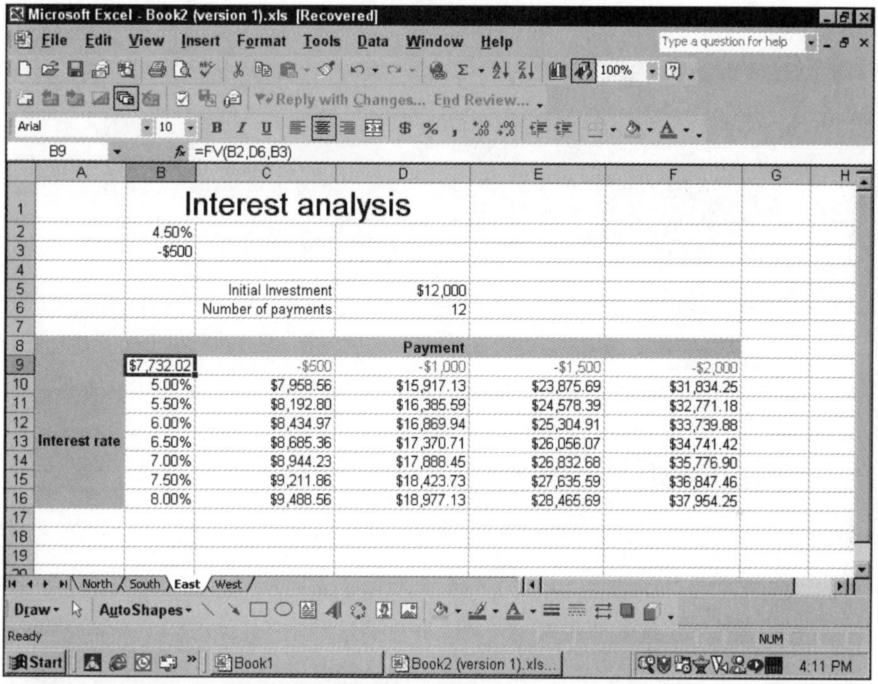

Row	A	B	C	D	E	F
2		4.50%				
3		-$500				
5			Initial Investment	$12,000		
6			Number of payments	12		
8				Payment		
9		$7,732.02	-$500	-$1,000	-$1,500	-$2,000
10		5.00%	$7,958.56	$15,917.13	$23,875.69	$31,834.25
11		5.50%	$8,192.80	$16,385.59	$24,578.39	$32,771.18
12		6.00%	$8,434.97	$16,869.94	$25,304.91	$33,739.88
13	Interest rate	6.50%	$8,685.36	$17,370.71	$26,056.07	$34,741.42
14		7.00%	$8,944.23	$17,888.45	$26,832.68	$35,776.90
15		7.50%	$9,211.86	$18,423.73	$27,635.59	$36,847.46
16		8.00%	$9,488.56	$18,977.13	$28,465.69	$37,954.25

Figure 26-9: A two-variable data table

To construct a two-variable data table, place one series of variable values down the leftmost column of those you plan to use in the table, and the other across the top row. Enter the formula in the top-left corner cell of the table. The formula should contain two input cells (placeholders): one for the variables listed in the left column, the other for the values in the top row. Once again, the cell references you use for the input cells don't matter (except that they should be different).

A look at the formula used in the example should help clarify things. The formula used is `=FV(B2,D6,B3)`, where B2 is the input cell for the variable column values and B3 is the input cell for the row variables.

Once the variables and formula are in place, select the whole table, choose Data ➪ Table, and enter the correct references in the "Row input cell" and "Column input cell" fields (A3 and A2, respectively).

Using DSUM for selective sums: Feature 2

The DSUM function sums the values in a specified column of a table, according to criteria you've defined. Unlike data tables, it returns only a single value, but it's just as useful. The simple DSUM shown in Figure 26-10 adds up all of John's sales during the month of January. His total of $1,511 (D14) was calculated using this formula:

```
=DSUM(B2:D11, "Amount", C13:C14)
```

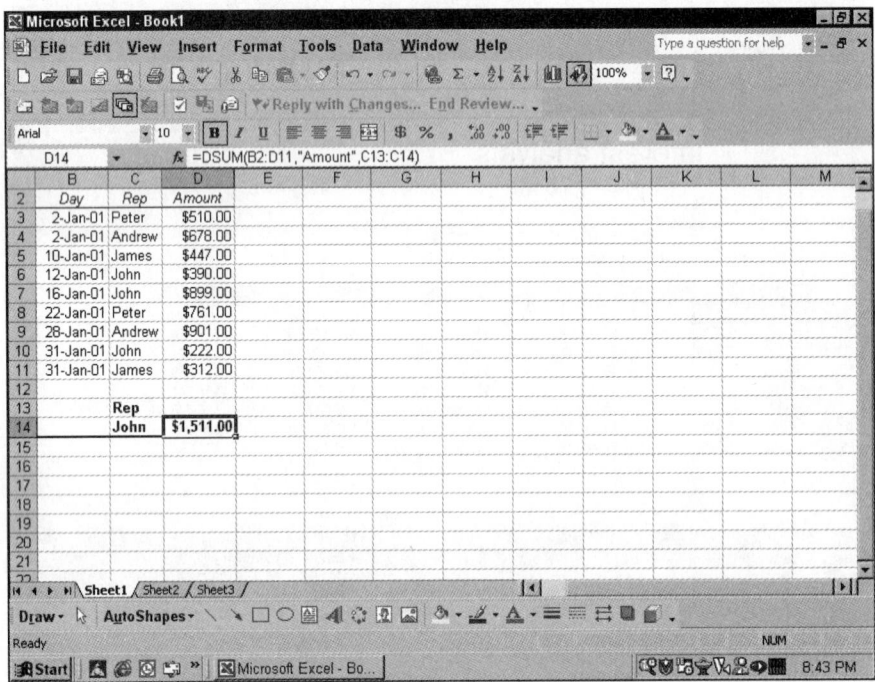

Figure 26-10: Using the criteria in cells C13:C14, the DSUM in D14 sums the sales for one particular rep.

Excel searches the specified range (B2:D11), and sums the values from a particular column ("Amount") that meet the criteria (C13:C14). You could click C14 and type a different rep's name to immediately get results for that rep in D14.

Putting data tables and DSUMs together

Let's say you had 25 rep names in the preceding example. You could be inefficient and sloppy, and tediously enter 25 DSUM formulas to keep track of all their totals. Or you could be a totally cool Excel whiz and create a data table, using the DSUM function as the pivotal formula to calculate the sales total for each rep. To combine these two features, build a one-variable data table that includes the reps' names in the first column. While I used the FV function last time, this time I'll use a DSUM. I use a data table to put it all in motion and sum all the reps at once.

Using this example, I'll build a table that adds the sales of Peter, Andrew, James and John. In Figure 26-11, you can see the new data table directly below the data. The reps' names for the table reside in C14:C17 with the table Excel has built right alongside in D14:D17. Note also that the two cells containing the DSUM criteria argument are still there but they've moved from C13:C14 in Figure 26-10 to C19:C20.

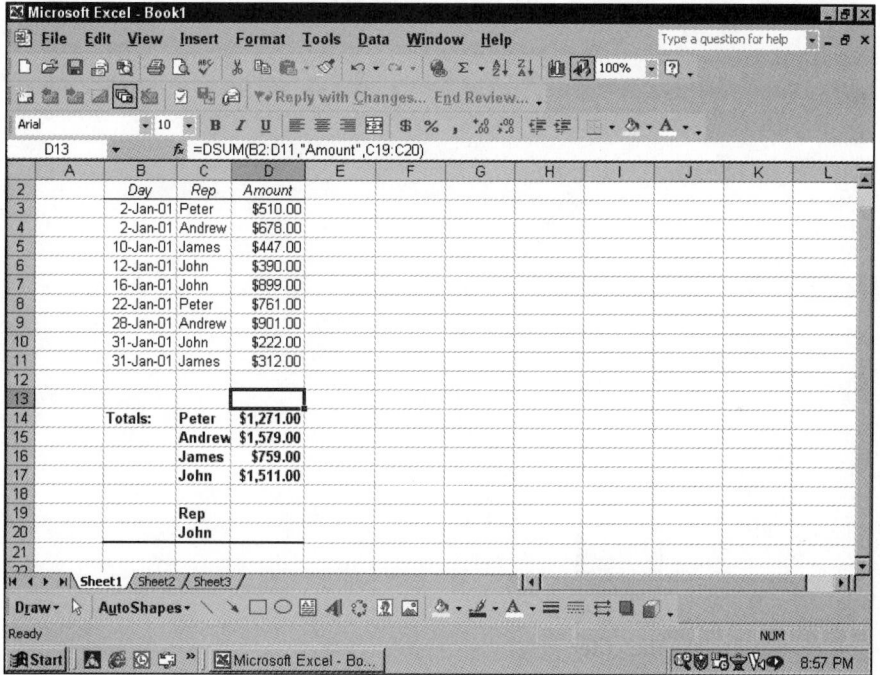

Figure 26-11: Using a dynamic data table to total the sales of several reps at once

Because the data table covers C14:D17, the formula for the table belongs in cell D13 — look back to the beginning of the "Creating dynamic data tables" section if you've forgotten how that works. In the illustration printed here, the formula is =DSUM(B2:D11,"Amount",C19:C20). Just as in Figure 26-10, this DSUM is looking at the table in B2:D11 and adding the values in the column "Amount" that match the Rep = Bloe criteria, although this time the criteria appear in cells C19:C20. By the way, the formula is there in D13, all right. It's just that you can't see it in the picture — I've colored it white to keep my spreadsheet clean. However, D13 is selected so that if you look in the Formula bar you can see the formula there.

Now, let's get fancy. Of course I want the DSUM to use the criteria of "John," but I also want to use the criteria of "Peter," "Andrew," and even "James" (who hasn't been doing very well!). That's where the data table comes in. With my DSUM formula sitting in D13, I select C13:D17. (The label in B14 is outside the data table.) Then I go to Data ⇨ Table, click in the "Column input cell" field, and click in C20. Cell C20 is the one I want to vary: First I want to use the criterion "Peter," followed by "Andrew," and so on. I click OK, and *voilà*! My results instantly appear.

Although the example table is small, the technique applies to real-life databases you maintain in Excel — a table with many more rep names would be just as easy to create. Once you catch on to the way they work, you should be able to think of loads of useful applications for dynamic data tables.

✦   ✦   ✦

Charting New Territory

Charts are indispensable for their ability to illustrate your data in a graphical fashion. While you can investigate details by scrutinizing the individual values in your worksheet, a chart shows you the big picture, clarifying the way the numbers change from month to month, region to region, or person to person.

Charts are pretty and lively, too. That's reason enough to use them liberally in the otherwise drab and orderly universe of the Excel worksheet.

Remember, you can place Excel charts in any of your Office documents. In fact, I recommend that you use Excel charts for all your charting needs and ignore the Microsoft Graph application that also comes with Office.

Chart Speak

Before we start, let's agree on some lingo: A chart is the graphical representation of your data. It has a hot link to your data, meaning that as the data changes, Excel immediately updates the chart. You may also hear people call a chart a graph—the two terms mean exactly the same thing.

Each single value on the chart is called a data point. Data points can come in many different varieties, such as columns, bars, lines, pie slices, and even ice cream cones! (Yes, you can import clip art and use it to represent data points.) A group of related data points is called a data series. All data points within a single data series are formatted with the same colors and patterns. Data series' names and colors are shown in a key called the legend. (Pie charts are examples of charts with only one data series.)

The category axis, running horizontally along the bottom of the chart, is also called the x-axis. It separates data into groups based on such things as months or regions. The value axis, running vertically along the left, is called the y-axis in a 2D chart, and the z-axis in a 3D chart. It defines the values shown by data points. The area bounded by the axes is called the plot area. A 3D chart also has a series axis (in 3D charts, the y-axis is synonymous with the series axis). The series axis runs from the front to the back of the plot area. (Pie and doughnut charts, because of their circular shapes, do not have axes.)

An embedded chart is in the form of an object that resides on the worksheet. You can manipulate it like a picture and embed it on any sheet in the workbook. A chart sheet is a separate sheet in the workbook containing only the chart. Both maintain a hot link to your data.

Choosing a Chart Type

Excel offers 14 basic built-in chart types from which to choose, each one with several of its own variations. Can't decide? Click the Chart Type tool on the Chart toolbar to instantly change from one to another:

✦ A **column chart** shows data changes over a period of time. It helps compare individual values and percentages to the whole in a vertical format. Variations include clustered columns and stacked columns.

✦ A **bar chart** also shows data changes over a period of time. It helps compare individual values and percentages to the whole in a horizontal format. Variations include clustered bars and stacked bars.

✦ A **line chart** shows trends in data over time. Lines are displayed in a horizontal format. Variations include stacked lines and lines with markers.

✦ A **pie chart** shows the ratio of each point within a single data series to the total. Variations include bar of pie and exploded pie (clean-up service not included).

✦ A **doughnut chart** is similar to a pie chart, but it can contain more than one data series. Variations include exploded doughnut. (Note: Using a pie chart and a doughnut chart at the same time is not recommended for those on calorie-reduced diets.)

✦ An **area chart** emphasizes the degree of change over time and the relationship of data points to the whole. Variations include stacked area.

✦ A **surface chart** shows trends and finds optimum combinations between different sets of data. Variations include wireframe and contour.

✦ An **XY** or **scatter chart** plots data points against each other to portray differences in trends. It is often used to illustrate uneven intervals or clusters. Variations include connecting lines (with or without data point markers).

✦ A **bubble chart** is a type of XY (scatter) chart that compares sets of at least three values. Each data point has at least two values, and the size of the bubble represents the value of a third.

✦ A **radar chart** compares the changes in values relative to a center point. Variations include filled radar and radar with markers.

✦ A **stock,** or **high-low-close, chart** illustrates stock prices and scientific data. Variations include open high-low-close and volume high-low-close.

✦ **Cone, cylinder,** and **pyramid charts** are column charts with special shapes.

Most of these chart types offer 3D variations. And as if these choices weren't enough, Excel complicates your life further with a host of options for custom chart formats — fancier variations on the standard 14 chart types. You can save your own custom-formatted charts for reuse.

A fifteenth chart type, the Pivot Chart report, is a hybrid Pivot Table-and-Chart, and you need special techniques to create it. Chapter 28 covers Pivot Tables and Pivot Charts.

Worksheets à la Chart

A chart can be either embedded on a worksheet or stored on a separate chart sheet by itself. Both methods offer a simple creation process and umpteen formatting options.

Using the Chart Wizard

The simplest way to create a chart is with the Chart Wizard. Once you've entered your data, click the Chart Wizard button on the Standard toolbar and sit back as Excel asks you everything it needs to know. The four-step process guides you through selecting a chart type (see Figure 27-1), specifying the source data, adding special options, and choosing a location for the chart (embedded site or new chart sheet).

Note
An embedded chart must be created from adjacent selections within the source data. If you need to pull data from multiple areas, you can add it afterward by copying and pasting.

If you've chosen an embedded chart, a chart object appears on the worksheet you chose in step 4 of the wizard. You can move it or resize it (using the black handles around the edges) to your heart's content. If a chart sheet is more your style, a new sheet is inserted in your workbook with your new chart filling the window.

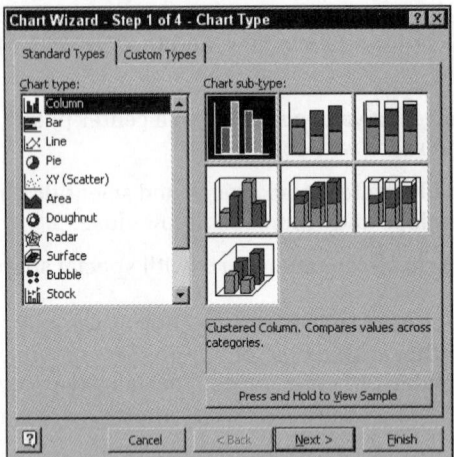

Figure 27-1: Step 1 of the Chart Wizard lets you choose a chart type and then select from among the built-in subtypes. Or you can create your own customized chart type.

Tip   You can create a chart sheet without the Chart Wizard by selecting the source data and pressing F11. There's no default keyboard shortcut to create an embedded chart.

Viewing chart items

Rest the mouse pointer over any chart item to see its name appear in a ScreenTip. If you rest it over a data point, you'll see its series number, point number and value.

Tip   If you don't see the ScreenTips, go to Tools ⇨ Options and look at Chart Tips on the Chart tab. The "Show names" and "Show values" boxes must be checked.

The name box on the Formula Bar shows the currently selected chart element. Click any chart element to select it. You can also select chart elements using the arrow keys. If you're working with an embedded chart and the worksheet data is in view, you also see the corresponding values highlighted when you select a data series. And it's all color-coded!

Changing the chart type

If you don't see the chart toolbar on the screen, right-click any existing toolbar and choose Chart. Clicking the Chart Type button drops down a graphical menu of 18 different chart types as shown in Figure 27-2. Click one, and your chart instantly changes.

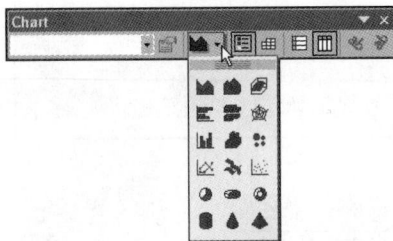

Figure 27-2: The menu displayed by
the Chart Type button

If you'd like to view more options, right-click the chart and choose Chart Type, or
use the Chart ➪ Chart Type command. You see a dialog box similar to step 1 of the
Chart Wizard. Here you can peruse the various chart types. For a preview, use the
button labeled Press and Hold to view a sample.

Adjusting Data

Although you can, you don't need to return to the source data to make changes.
Changes can be made right on the chart itself, so you can watch how other values
are affected. Imagine you worked for the federal government and had to chart those
inflation indexes that come out every month. Given that Washington economists
are always releasing revised figures, you would need a way to modify your charts as
the "facts" change. With Excel, all it takes is a simple drag to remedy the situation.

Dragging points on the chart

Data marker is the term for any chart element that depicts an individual data point
or value, such as a bar, pie slice, or bubble. Some line charts have visible rectangles
marking each data point, but if not, each location that represents a value in the
source data is a data marker.

At any rate, the quickest way to change the value of a marker in a 2D column, bar,
pie, doughnut, line, XY (scatter), or bubble chart is to drag the data marker.
Figures 27-3 and 27-4 show this technique in action on a sample chart. When Excel
detects such changes to a chart, Excel instantly updates the underlying values on
the worksheet.

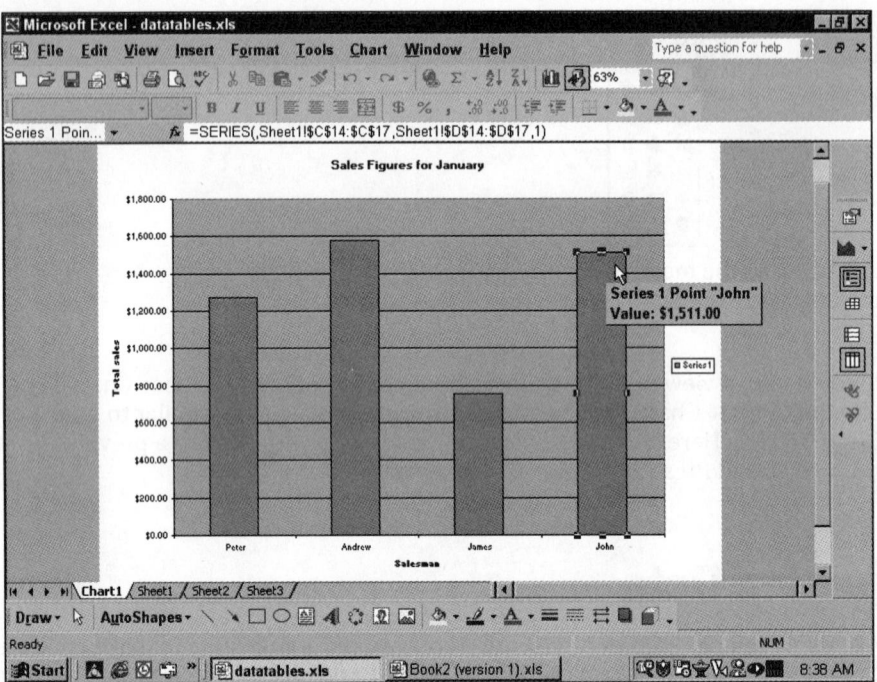

Figure 27-3: A sample chart before a data marker is resized with the mouse. The data marker in question has been selected, though this isn't necessary.

To change a chart item, click the data series containing the data point you want to manipulate, and then click again until the specific data point is selected. You can tell it's selected by the presence of handles around its outline. Then drag the largest handle to change the data point's value. On columns and bars, the handle you want is at the top center. On pies and doughnuts, it's on the outer edge. You'll know when you've found it because the mouse pointer becomes the familiar double-edged arrow.

As you drag the marker, a ScreenTip displays the changing value so you know exactly when you've reached your destination. If the data marker was based on a cell containing a fixed value, the cell's value changes accordingly. If the cell contains a formula, however, you have a bit more work to do, as discussed in the next section.

Goal-seeking using charts

Adjustable data points are not limited to those represented by constant values. Formula values can be changed, too. But formulas are often dependent on other cells in the spreadsheet (their precedent cells). When this is the case, you turn to goal-seeking, the process whereby Excel varies the value in a precedent cell until the dependent formula returns the result you want.

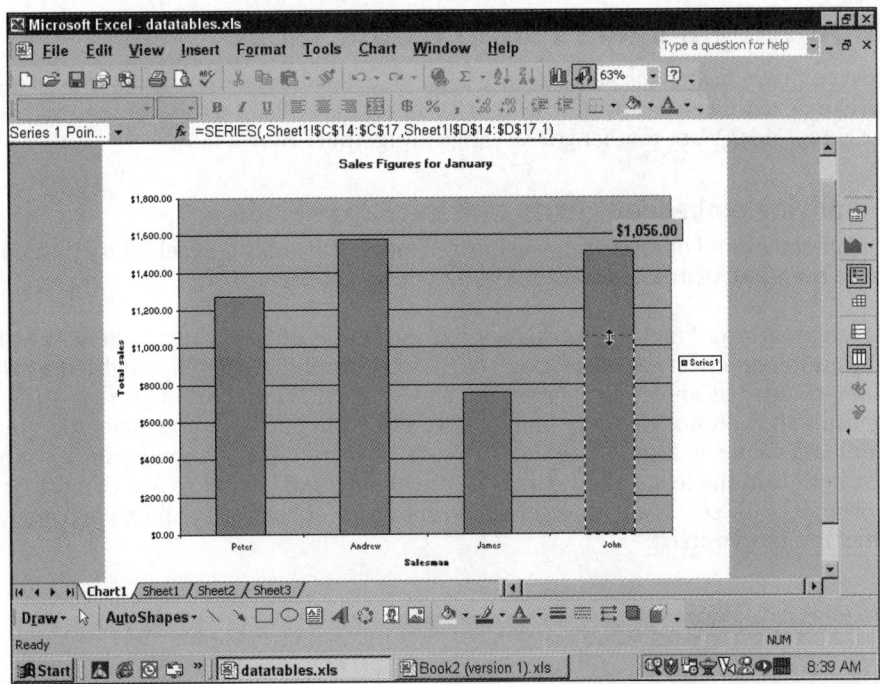

Figure 27-4: Dragging the data marker to a new position to change a value in the chart

On the chart

Select the data point you want to change (as described previously). Drag the largest handle to the approximate value you'd like it to be, and let go (a little tip displays the changing value). When you do, the Goal Seek dialog box immediately appears.

The cell that contains the formula appears in the "Set cell" field, and the value you want the formula to reflect appears in the "To value" field. Adjust either of these, as necessary, and in the "By changing cell" field, tell Excel which precedent cell you'd like to change. (Though the formula may have more than one precedent cell, you can adjust the value of only one.)

Excel then lets you watch as it cycles through numbers, looking for the right fit for the precedent cell, to match the requested formula value. When it finds a solution, it shows you the results, and you have the option to OK or Cancel the change.

On the worksheet

To change values generated from worksheet formulas in 3D, surface, radar, and area charts, you can use the Goal Seek feature right on the worksheet. To do so, select the formula to be changed, and choose Tools ➪ Goal Seek. Follow the same procedure that you did for goal-seeking on the chart.

Modifying a chart's source data range

Just to prove nothing is set in stone, you can even change the source data of an already existing chart. Want to add or subtract data? Want to add or subtract labels or categories? Want to change the range altogether? Here's how.

Modifying embedded charts with the Range Finder

On an embedded chart sheet, use Range Finder, the built-in Excel utility that out-lines ranges of cells in various colors as you select them.

Arrange the chart and the worksheet data so that both are easily in view. As you click different chart elements, you see the corresponding data highlighted by the Range Finder, as shown in Figures 27-5 and 27-6. The monochrome screen shot doesn't show it, but category names are outlined in purple, series names in green, and data values in blue. To add or subtract adjacent cells to a range, simply drag the handle in the lower-right corner of the highlighted border to select more or fewer cells. To select a completely different range of cells altogether, you can even drag the border itself.

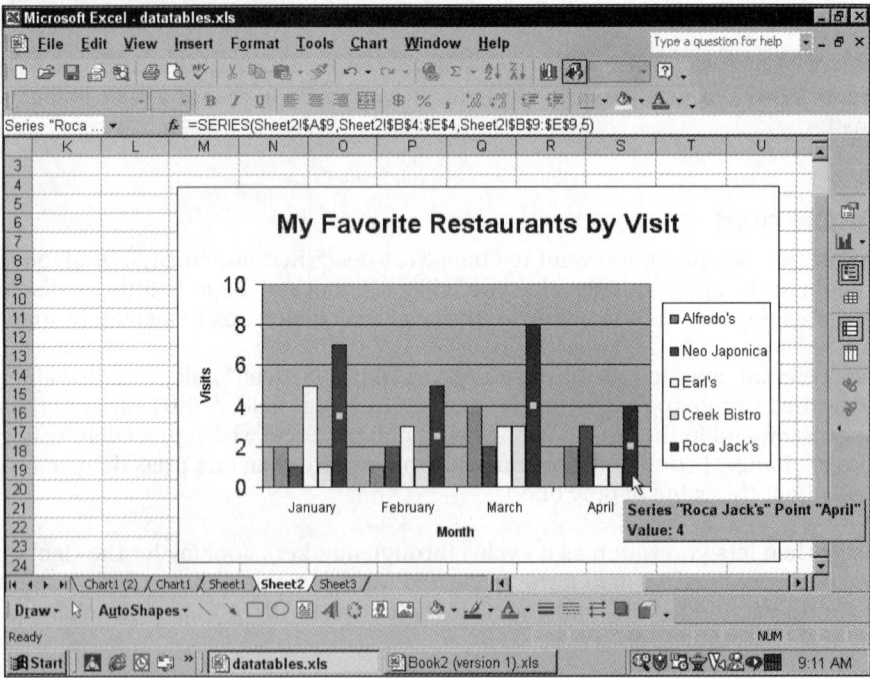

Figure 27-5: In this sample chart, the Roca Jack's series has been selected. Excel highlights the corresponding worksheet data, shown in Figure 27-6.

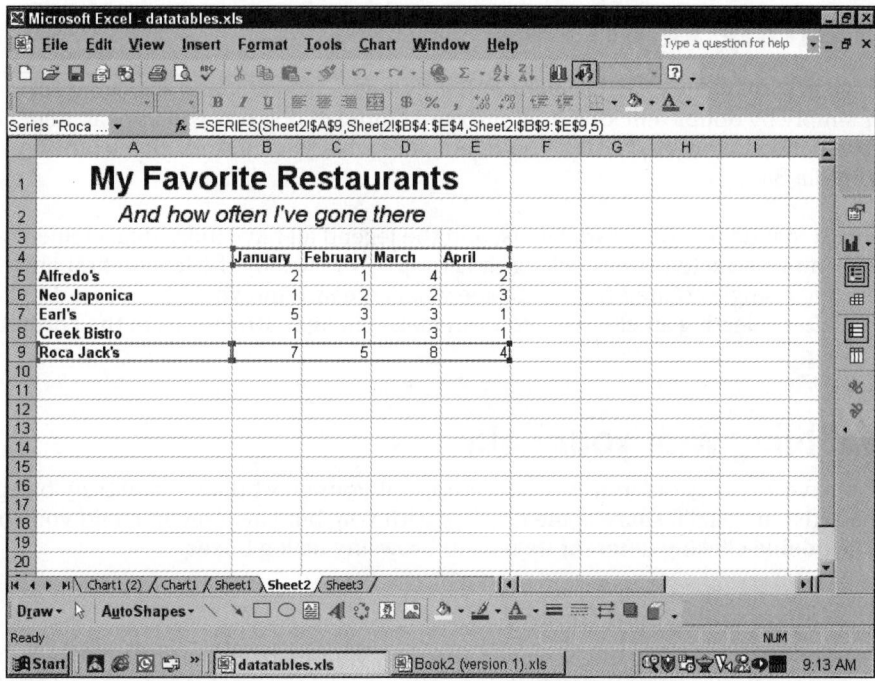

Figure 27-6: The chart in Figure 27-5 is based on this worksheet. As shown here, Excel's Range Finder highlights data corresponding to selected chart elements.

Note The Range Finder works on embedded charts only. To adjust the data on a chart sheet, right-click the chart and choose Source Data, or use the Chart ➪ Source Data command.

Including multiple selections in a chart

Yes, it's true. A chart can be made from nonadjacent areas of data. If you're starting from scratch (for example, the chart doesn't exist yet), make your multiple selections as you normally would and start the Chart Wizard. To add a nonadjacent area to an existing chart, copy it to the clipboard, activate the chart, and paste it in. Excel can usually sense where the data should be added, but if you need to make some adjustments, right-click the chart and choose Source Data, or use the Chart ➪ Source Data command.

Changing a chart's orientation

By default, Excel uses the leftmost column of your worksheet data for category names and the topmost row for series names. Each column of data is considered to belong to one data series. To change the way data series are plotted, click the By Row or By Column tool on the Chart toolbar. (You can also right-click the chart and go to Source Data.)

Formatting Charts

You can format any chart element either by right-clicking it and choosing Format, or simply by double-clicking it. A custom-tailored dialog box will appear, depending on which item you clicked. (If you're not sure what you clicked, check out the Formula Bar.)

Notice that data series, data labels, and the legend all have individual elements that can be selected after clicking the group. (Try clicking the legend first and then clicking a single colored marker to see what I mean.) And you'll be pleased to know that after selecting an element, you can make changes straight from the Formatting toolbar.

Dabbling with your data

You have so many different ways to represent your chart data, it will truly bring out the artist in you. I'll share some goodies with you, but I also recommend you spend time double-clicking different items and browsing dialog boxes.

Displaying worksheet figures

The first thing that you might want to do with your chart data is display the numbers at the bottom of the chart, showing the part of the worksheet from which it's derived. Figure 27-7 illustrates how a chart with an attached data table looks. Right-click the chart outside the plot area and choose Chart Options (you can also use the Chart ➪ Chart Options command). Go to the Data Table tab and turn on "Show data table". The data used to create the chart is placed directly below it; you can format the data table just like any other chart element.

Tip   When you hide or filter worksheet data, the corresponding chart doesn't show it either. By default, charts show only visible rows and columns. If you'd like your chart to display all the data, go to Tools ➪ Options. On the Chart tab, turn off "Plot visible cells only".

Controlling the way empty cells are plotted

If the values in a complex chart contain zeros or blank cells, you can specify how these values are plotted. Click anywhere on the chart and select Tools ➪ Options. Make sure the Chart tab is selected. Under "Plot empty cells as", specify whether you want to leave gaps (creating a segmented line), treat the blanks as zeros (causing the line to drop), or interpolate (filling the gaps with connecting lines).

Choosing colors and patterns for chart elements

Who said chart elements have to be one solid color? A few clicks can create an eye-catching display. And if your heart so desires, every data point in the chart can have a different design. The Format Data Series dialog box offers a dazzling array of choices on its Patterns tab (see Figure 27-8).

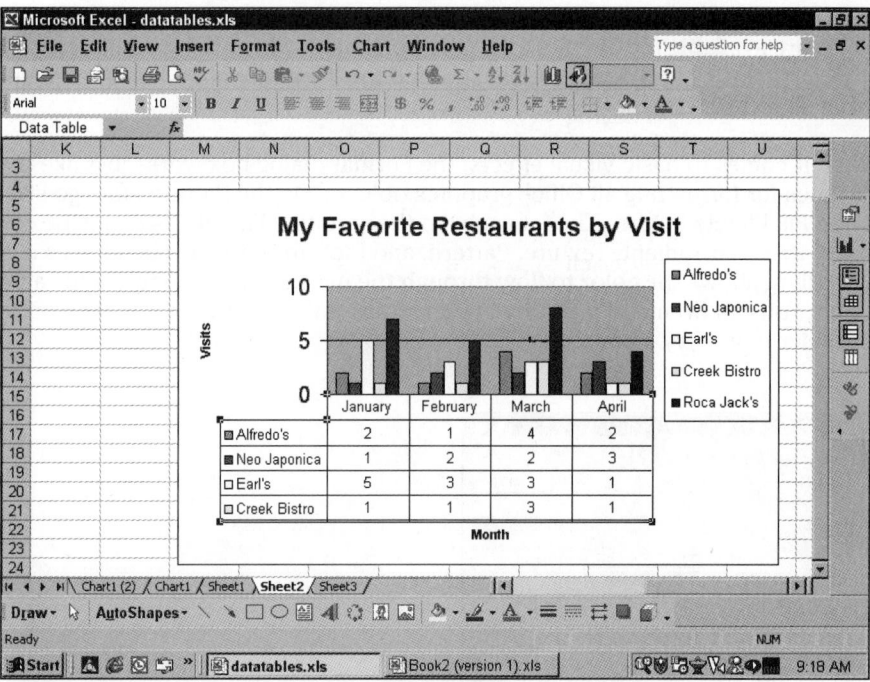

Figure 27-7: A chart with an attached data table

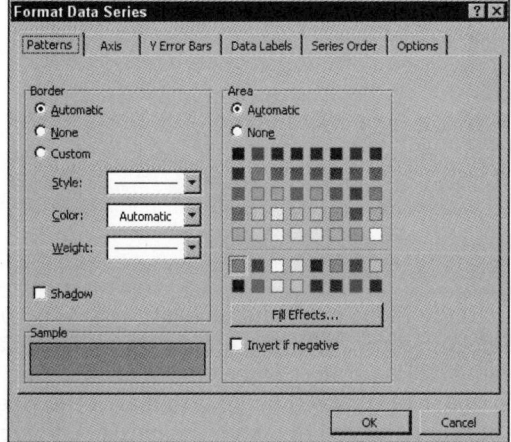

Figure 27-8: The Patterns tab of the Format
Data Series dialog box

To change an entire data series, double-click any marker in the series. To change a
single data point, first click the series and then either double-click the point or
right-click the point and choose Format Data Point from the shortcut menu. In this

case, the dialog box you see is titled Format Data Point, of course. Similar dialog boxes are available for the plot area (the portion on which the data markers appear) and the chart area (the background for the entire chart) by double-clicking these elements.

When it comes to basic visual effects, the Format dialog box works just like the similar ones for formatting all Office graphics objects. On the Patterns tab, go straight to the Fill Effects button. The four tabs in the resulting Fill Effects dialog box (see Figure 27-9) — Gradient, Texture, Pattern, and Picture — are as much fun as a game. A gradient allows the color to flow through the marker, and a texture adds a fancy touch. You can even add a gradient to a texture (talk about cool!). When you're in a splashier mood, try a pattern.

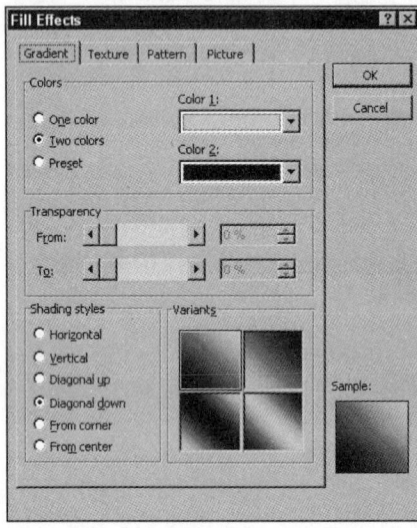

Figure 27-9: Use the Fill Effects dialog box to add splashy visual effects to your chart.

For a completely different effect, go to the Picture tab and navigate your way to that clip art you've been saving. Click Select Picture and find a simple object (a dollar bill is a classic example, especially in a 3D line chart). Once you've chosen one, you can Stretch it (for example, a single dollar bill is stretched out to match the size of a marker) or Stack it (several dollar bills are stacked to match the marker). If you're working in a 3D chart, you can even specify which sides of the markers should be formatted.

Tip Adding pictures this way works for column, bar, area, bubble, 3D line, and filled radar charts. To use a picture as a data marker in 2D line, XY (scatter), and unfilled radar charts, copy the picture onto the clipboard, click the data series, and paste it in.

Tip   You can also add a picture or textured background to the chart area, the plot area, or the legend, and in 3D charts, to the walls and floor. Right-click the element you want to work on, select Format from the shortcut menu, and off you go.

Timelines on the x-axis

X-axes often show timelines. And on occasion, the time units are not equidistant from each other (for example, Feb, May, Oct, Nov). When Excel sees times on the category axis, it automatically uses a type of axis called a time-scale axis. A time-scale axis places categories at equal intervals, which in the preceding example would cause blank gaps.

If you prefer to place the categories spaced next to each other, you can change from a time-scale axis to a standard category axis. Right-click the chart outside the plot area and choose Chart Options (or go to Chart ⇨ Chart Options). On the Axes tab, you'll see an option to change from Time-Scale to Category.

Adding trendlines

A trendline is the graphical representation of the direction or course of the data in a data series. Trendlines can be used for regression analysis, by extending the data forward or backward to indicate trends. They can also show a moving average, which smoothes out fluctuations to show a clear pattern. (Trendlines can be added to all data series but those in 3D, stacked, pie, doughnut, or radar charts.)

Right-click a data series and choose Add Trendline (or go to Chart ⇨ Add Trendline). On the Type tab, select the type of line you want. You can also customize a Polynomial's Order (the highest power for the independent variable) and a Moving Average's Period (the number of periods used during calculation). You can find the equations for calculating trendlines in Help.

Note   A moving average on an XY (scatter) chart is based on the order of the x-axis values. To get the result you want, you might need to sort the values before adding the moving average.

Displaying ranges of error

Data series can display error bars, a graphical representation of potential error or uncertainty relative to each data point within the series. You can add error bars to y-axis values on column, bar, line, and area charts. For XY (scatter) and bubble charts, you can add error bars to y-axis values, x-axis values, or both. (A caveat: Except on bubble charts, Excel doesn't allow error bars on 3D charts.)

Double-click a data series. If you're using one of the preceding chart types, you'll see the appropriate Error Bars tab on the Format Data Series dialog box. Here's where you determine the type of display and the method used to determine the range of error. You can even define your own custom error settings. In the Plus and Minus fields, either specify a worksheet range to use as error amounts or enter the values you want to use, separated by commas. To delete error bars for a data series, click one and press Delete. When you delete one error bar, all error bars for the entire series are deleted.

Toying with your text

What good is a chart without some helpful explanation? Empty columns and lines mean nothing without clarification. It's up to you to make your chart user friendly. You can do that in several ways. Just remember to keep it simple: No more than two or three fonts per chart should do the trick.

The two flavors of text

Chart text comes in two flavors: text that comes from the source data on the worksheet, and embellishments you add later. Both are easy to manipulate, but it's important to know how they differ.

Text that comes from the worksheet

Upon chart creation, Excel captures certain text items from the worksheet source data. These items include things like row and column headings (which become category and series names), and the heading directly above the data (which becomes the chart title). Though you can format as much as you like right on the chart, if you want to change the wording of this text, you should probably go back to the worksheet to do it in order to maintain the link.

Text that you add later

Added embellishments can include things such as axis titles, chart titles, data point labels, and text boxes. The first three are labels that are affixed to a particular chart element (axis, chart area, and data series or point, respectively). You can add them simply by formatting that element. A text box is a free-floating piece of text that can be positioned anywhere on the chart. It's often used in conjunction with an arrow to point out a noteworthy characteristic, such as the month you actually sold more widgets than thingamabobs.

The easiest way to create a text box is to just select the chart (unnecessary on a chart sheet) and start typing, pressing Enter when you're finished. As you type, the text appears in the Formula bar, but when you press Enter, Excel deposits it in a box in the middle of the chart. You can reposition and format the new text box as you please. Alternatively, you can use the Drawing toolbar to add text boxes (see Chapter 12).

Rotating chart text

Most chart text can be rotated or angled to some degree. This not only adds some interest, but it could be of great help when you're trying to fit everything into a limited space. The chart title, axis titles, and data point labels can all be angled at any increment from 90 degrees to –90 degrees. They can also be vertically aligned so that they're read from top to bottom. Double-click any text item and go to the Alignment tab to see your choices. If you're looking for a quick fix, click either of the Angle Text buttons on the Chart toolbar to quickly rotate the selected text up or down by 45 degrees.

Note You can rotate text boxes using the Alignment tab of the Format box, but the toolbar buttons are unavailable. You cannot rotate legend text.

Tip Normally, fonts in a chart scale proportionally when you resize either an embedded chart or the chart area of a chart sheet. To keep the font sizes constant, right-click the chart area (outside the plot area and near the border) and choose Format Chart Area. On the Font tab, clear the Auto Scale checkbox.

Perspective and rotation

Sometimes a chart needs more pizzazz even after you've chosen the perfect colors and fiddled with the fonts. Excel's 3D and rotation options may be what you need to make the chart stand out.

Wanting a new perspective?

Three-dimensional charts can be manipulated in many different ways to suit your taste. The most common way to give one a new look is to rotate it. All 3D charts are easily rotated in the Chart ➪ 3D View box. But you can also rotate one by dragging it.

Click the edge of the plot area to select the corners of the chart (make sure it says "Corners" in the Formula Bar). Drag a corner handle to adjust the elevation and rotation of the 3D view. You might want to drag slowly until you get the hang of it.

If you get into trouble, go back into the 3D View box and click the Default button. Then slowly try again. To view an outline of the data markers as you rotate the chart, hold down the Ctrl key.

Rotation is not the only option available. For a new look, you can also do the following:

✦ **Change the height and perspective:** The 3D View box lets you try out a host of different angles from which to view the chart. (The Perspective option is not available for 3D bar charts.)

✦ **Change the chart depth, gap depth, and gap width:** Double-click a data series and go to the Options tab. Here's where you have complete control over the spacing between markers and categories. (You can change the chart depth in 3D charts with axes, the gap depth in 3D perspective charts, and the gap width in 3D bar or column charts.)

2D pie and doughnut rotations

The order in which Excel plots data series in pie and doughnut charts is determined by the order of the data on the worksheet. If you'd like to change the rotation, you've got 360 angles from which to choose.

Double-click the data series you'd like to change and go to the Options tab. In the "Angle of first slice" box, specify any value from 0 degrees to 360 degrees for the angle of the first slice. A sample box shows you a preview.

Mixing Different Data Types in the Same Chart

Just as people come in all shapes and sizes, so, too, does data. And Excel gives you the flexibility to mix data to create more complex charts (see Figure 27-10 for an example). Combination charts and charts with secondary axes are often used to emphasize certain information.

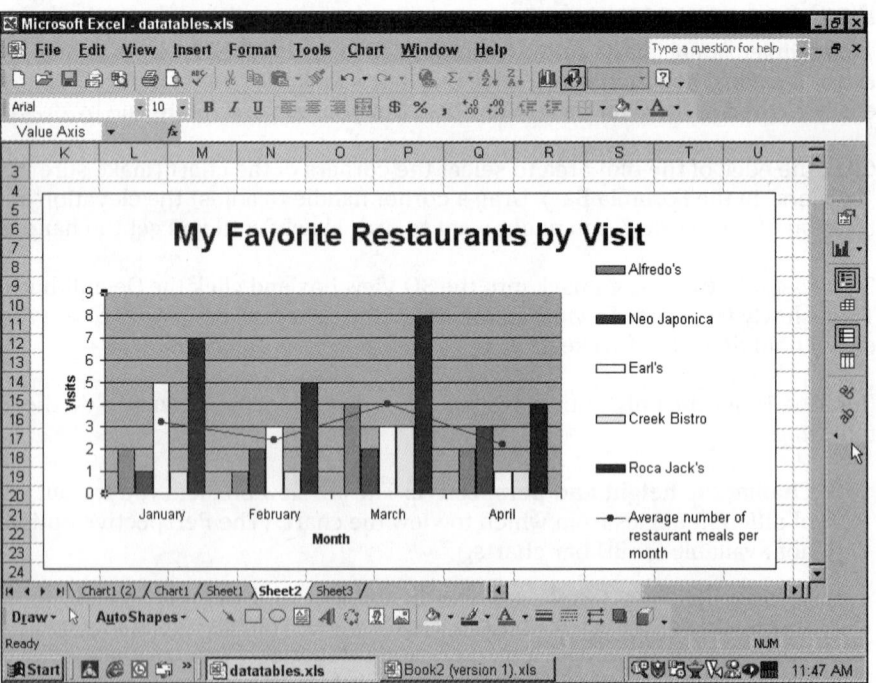

Figure 27-10: A sample combination chart

Using combination charts

A combination chart has at least one data series with a different chart type (you may have also heard this called an overlay). A common use for this is to plot actual values in columns, and as a contrast, add a line series showing the average values, which is what I've done in Figure 27-10. To change the type of a data series, right-click the series and go to Chart Type. You can also select a series and use the drop-down list on the Chart toolbar.

Charts with secondary axes

When you have different kinds of data to show in the same 2D chart (such as cost and quantity), you can plot one or more on a secondary value (y) axis. Double-click the data series you want to plot along a secondary value axis, and go to the Axis tab. Click Secondary Axis to plot this series separately from the others. The secondary axis appears on the opposite side of the chart and can be formatted completely independently from the primary value axis. Data markers associated with the secondary axis are positioned in front of other markers.

Saving Chart Options to Use Again

Once you've gone to all the trouble of creating the chart of your dreams, you'll probably want to use it again next time. You have a couple of different ways to save your work.

With the chart selected, go to Chart ➪ Chart Type. On the Custom Types tab, click the Set as Default Chart button. You'll then be asked to supply a name and a description for this type of chart. Once the default is set, all new charts will appear in this style. You can also save this chart formatting without making it the default, which enables you to select it only when you're ready to use it. On the Custom Types tab, go to the "Select from" box, and click "User-defined". Click the Add button to define your new type. At any time, you can choose this chart type from the custom list.

✦　　✦　　✦

Analyzing Data

Entering data onto the spreadsheet and arranging it is merely part of the preparation process. Now we get down to the heart of the matter. It's time to analyze, scrutinize, poke at, peek into, and otherwise examine your data in many different ways. Excel has many ways to do this; I'll show you a few of the more efficient ones.

Filtering Data

Any list or table can be used as a database (no special definitions are needed). When you perform database tasks, such as finding, sorting, or filtering data, Excel automatically treats the information as a database and assumes that the columns are the fields and the rows are the records. Filtering data in lists is one of the most common uses of Excel. With just a few simple clicks, you can easily display the records that match any criteria.

AutoFilter

The AutoFilter feature is a quick way to find a subset of the data in a list. To prepare to AutoFilter a list or table, click anywhere inside it and choose Data ➪ Filter ➪ AutoFilter. Excel treats the cells of the first row in the list or table as column labels (field names) and places small arrow buttons next to each one.

Click any arrow to drop down a list of conditions for that column (see the example in Figure 28-1). The available choices work as follows:

- ◆ To display only the records (rows) that equal a particular value, click that value in the list.

- ◆ Choose Blanks at the bottom of the drop-down list to see only the blank cells in the list. Once you've found any blank records, it's a cinch to delete them. A NonBlanks choice is also available.

✦ To display a certain number of top or bottom values in a list of numbers, click Top 10. You can then specify how many top or bottom values you want to see.

✦ If these choices aren't enough, you can create fully customized filter conditions by choosing Custom in the drop-down list, as detailed in the next section.

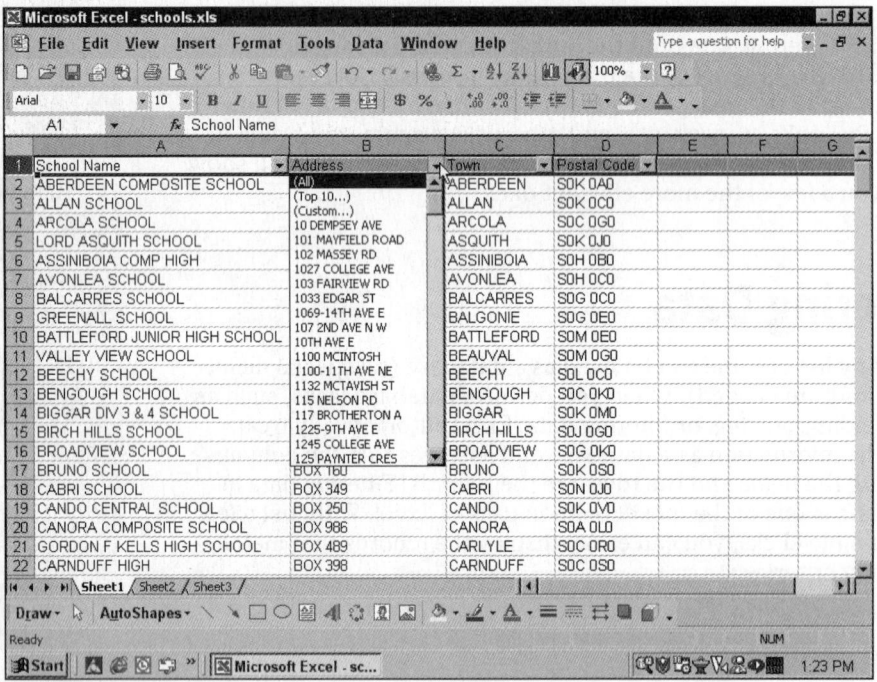

Figure 28-1: When AutoFilter is turned on, column names provide drop-down lists of built-in filtering options.

Further, some miscellaneous AutoFilter facts are as follows:

✦ Once you've filtered a list, Excel displays filtered row numbers in blue, and the drop-down arrows on columns that are in use also turn blue.

✦ You can filter values in more than one column at the same time. After filtering the list in one column, click the arrow in another column to restrict the filter even further.

✦ When a list or table has been filtered, the AutoSum command totals only the visible rows.

✦ To remove a filter from a column, click the arrow again and choose All (it's at the top of the drop-down list and you may have to scroll up to see it). Turn off AutoFiltering altogether by again choosing Data ➪ AutoFilter.

Note You can apply filters to only one list on a worksheet at a time. To begin filtering a different list on a worksheet, turn off the existing filter and then turn on the new filter.

Creating custom filters

Custom filters let you set two criteria in the same column or apply a comparison operator other than "equals." Click the arrow in the column you want to filter, and click Custom. The first field is a drop-down list of 12 different comparison operators, ranging from "is greater than" to "begins with" to "does not end with" and everything in between (see Figure 28-2). In the second field, you enter the value that completes the condition.

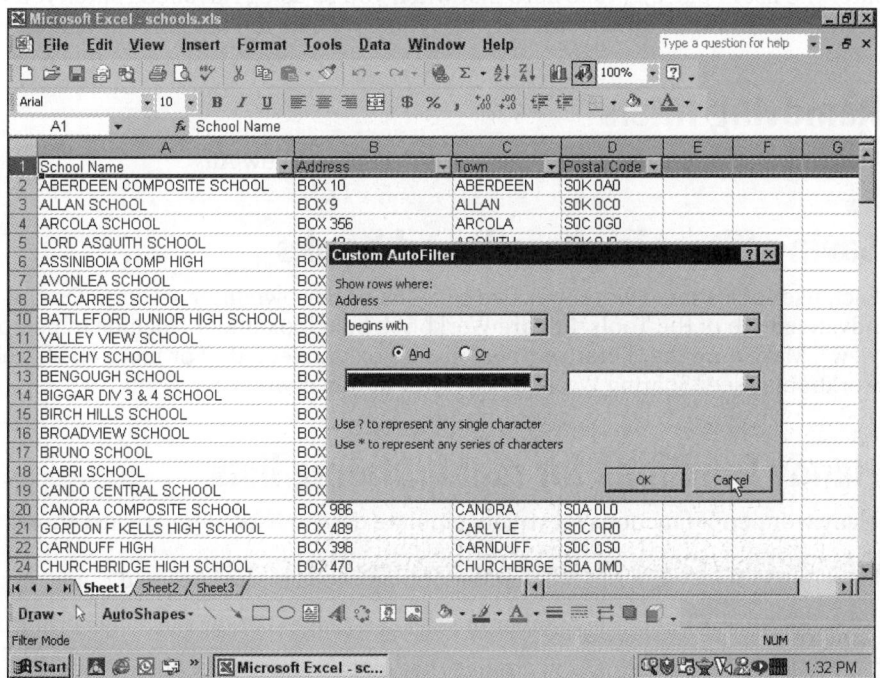

Figure 28-2: In the Custom AutoFilter dialog box, you can filter a list using one or two specifications.

To further restrict the filter, you can also enter a second criterion. Choose either And or Or, and enter another condition. AutoFilter displays all records that match both conditions (And), or all records that match at least one condition (Or).

Tip   To find blank or nonblank fields with the Custom Filter box, use "equals" as the criterion to find blanks, and "does not equal" to find nonblanks. Leave the field to the right blank.

Using advanced filters

If you need to apply more than two conditions to a column, use calculated values as your criteria, or if you need to copy records to another location, you can use advanced filters. Using the Data ⇨ Filter ⇨ Advanced Filter dialog box, you can extract data the old-fashioned way. Enter a criteria range directly on your spreadsheet. You can use as many conditions as you need, and you can apply complex criteria or calculated values (see Help for some examples). In the Advanced Filter box, specify the list range, the criteria range, and an optional extract range (you can also filter the list in place). (Take note that when you're using Advanced Filter you won't see the arrows with drop-down lists like you do when you're using AutoFilter.)

Removing filters

To remove all filters of any kind, use Data ⇨ Filter ⇨ Show All.

Saving filters in shared workbooks

Each user of a shared workbook can save his or her own filter settings. On the Advanced tab of the Tools ⇨ Share Workbook box, look under "Include in personal view". Make sure the "Filter settings" checkbox is selected. (For more on shared workbooks, see "Sharing Workbooks," later in this chapter.)

Handy functions for manipulating lists

Many wonderful functions let you manipulate data in lists. Here are just three:

✦ COUNTBLANK: Counts the number of blank cells in the specified range.

✦ COUNTIF: Counts the number of cells in a range that meet a single criterion.

✦ SUMIF: Totals the cells in a range that meet a single criterion.

Cross-Reference   For more information on using functions in Excel, see Chapter 26.

Pivot Tables and Pivot Charts

A pivot table is an interactive table that quickly summarizes large amounts of data. You can rotate the rows and columns to see different summary views, filter the data by displaying different pages, or display details for any data field. You can also have Excel produce a complementary chart from a pivot table automatically.

Other neat pivot table features include the following:

✦ One-click updating of table data and headings when the source data changes

✦ Formatting that stays in place even when you refresh a table or change its layout

✦ Data that sorts automatically and maintains its sort order (including dates)

✦ The capability to specify precedence for multiple calculations

✦ Dynamic sorting or hiding of items based on items in the table

You construct a pivot table based on an existing database. The data can come from Excel, stored in a worksheet database-style with rows as the records and labeled columns as the fields. Alternatively, you can draw on an external database, such as an Access table.

It's much easier to see how pivot tables work by experimenting with one than by reading about them. If you're trying to see whether a pivot table would help you understand your own real-life database, I strongly encourage you to make a copy of your workbook and use the copy to try out these techniques now.

Tip   Prior to Excel 97, pivot tables were called cross-tab tables. You can easily convert a cross-tab table to a pivot table. After selecting a cell on the sheet where the cross-tab table resides, start the PivotTable Wizard. The wizard tells you what to do to complete the conversion.

Note   You can't create pivot tables or change the layout of existing pivot tables in shared workbooks.

When to use pivot tables

In general, it's appropriate to use a pivot table when you use your database to summarize and consolidate information from detailed records so you can see larger trends. A pivot table can summarize data using functions such as Sum, Average, or Count. You can also automatically include subtotals, grand totals, and calculated fields of your own.

The worksheet shown in Figure 28-3 offers an example of a database that's prime for pivot table making. As in the sample, such a database normally includes fields of both of the following types:

✦ **Numeric information:** Fields for quantity, cost or price, weight, size, or some other measured amount. These are the details you want to summarize.

✦ **Categorical information:** Fields defining the categories into which you summarize the numeric information on a category-by-category basis.

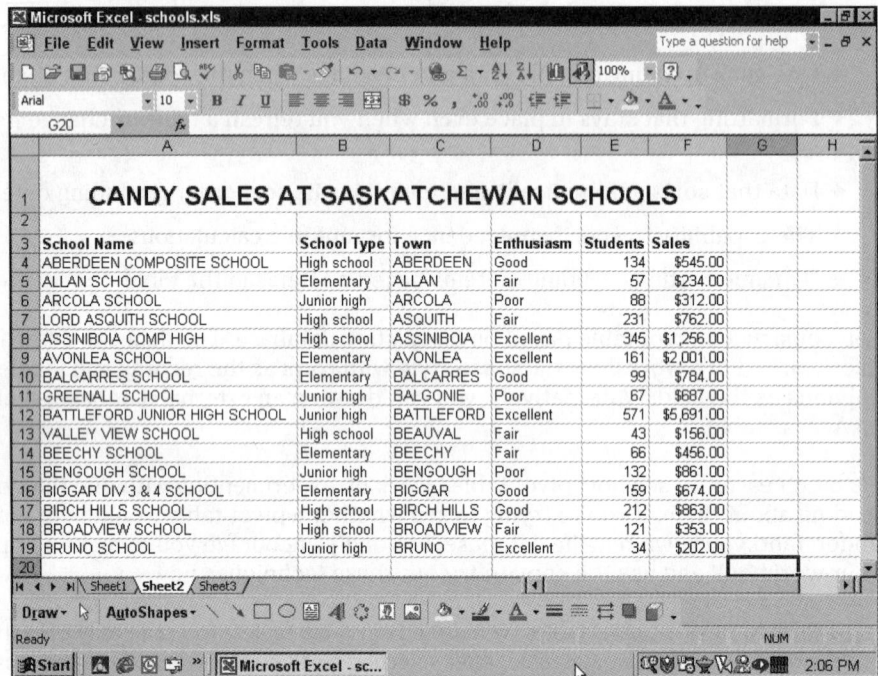

Figure 28-3: The worksheet shown here contains a database suitable for summarizing with a pivot table.

Of course, categorical information is often expressed numerically, especially when the categories represent rankings on a scale. For example, ratings such as "Good," "Fair," "Poor," and "Excellent" could just as well be represented by numbers 3, 2, 1, and 4. Such fields can be used in pivot tables as either kind of information. Another wrinkle: You can always use a pivot table to summarize categorical information by simply counting the number of records in each category.

Creating a pivot table

If the target database is in a worksheet, activate the sheet and click anywhere in the database. Choose Data ⇨ PivotTable and PivotChart Report to start the PivotTable Wizard. It walks you through the creation process:

1. Begin by specifying the type of source data and type of report. You can create a pivot table from information on a single worksheet, on several worksheets, on another pivot table, or on an external database. If you want a pivot chart as well as a pivot table, click the appropriate button and see the section "Creating pivot charts" later in this chapter.

2. Depending upon your answer in step 1, the wizard helps you specify the data's exact location. In the case of worksheet data, if the active worksheet contains a suitable database, Excel selects it for you—but you can adjust the range or choose another one as necessary.

3. All you need to do in step 3 is decide whether the table should appear in its own new worksheet or in an existing sheet. (However, you can use the Layout and Options buttons to control the organization and look of the table as discussed later in "Using the PivotTable Wizard.") Click Finish to complete the wizard.

These first three steps produce only the skeleton of the pivot table, which appears in your workbook as shown in Figure 28-4. The real fun starts when you actually lay out the information the way you want to see it in the table.

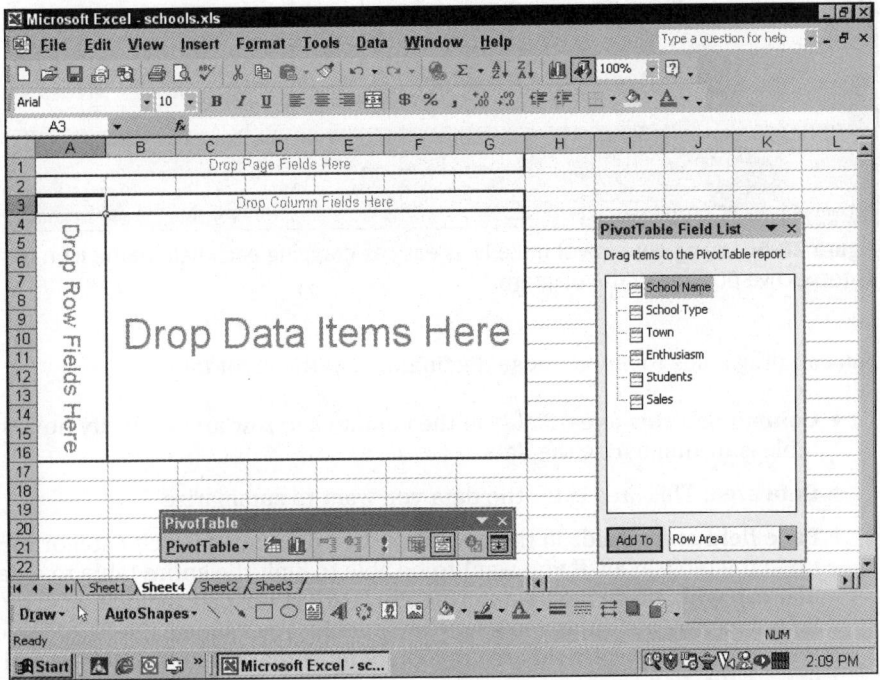

Figure 28-4: The outline of a new pivot table appears like this in your worksheet, ready for you to lay out its fields.

Laying out fields

Note the PivotTable Field list, a task pane visible in Figure 28-4. The Field list includes a labeled icon for each field (column) in the original database. As shown in Figure 28-5, all you have to do is drag these icons to the desired locations on the pivot table outline.

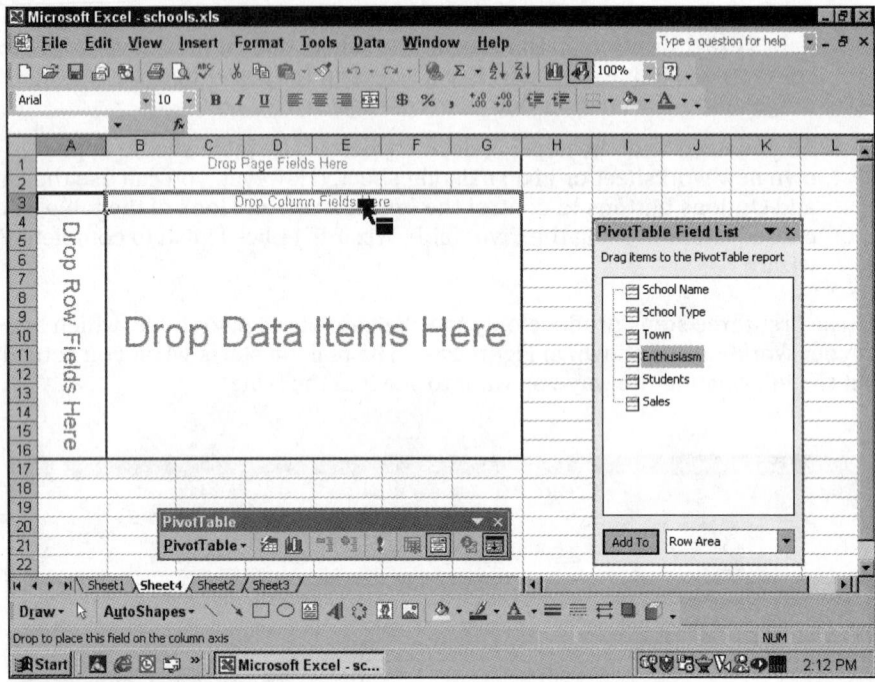

Figure 28-5: Laying out a pivot table is as easy as dragging each field name icon to its respective position in the diagram.

You can drag fields to any of these destinations in the pivot table:

✦ **Column and row axes:** Fields in the column and row areas specify how the table is to summarize the data.

✦ **Data area:** This area is for the data you want to summarize.

✦ **Page field area:** Fields in the page field area determine which categories show up in the table at all. If you want to be able to limit the entire table to a particular category, place the field for this category in the page field area. (The page field area may not appear in a new pivot table. You can use the PivotTable Wizard to add a page field area to a pivot table that doesn't have one and place fields in it — see "Using the PivotTable Wizard," later in this chapter.)

So which fields go where? Until you become pivot-table adept, you can use this simple rule for making effective tables: Fields containing numeric values go in the data area, while fields that define categories belong in the rows and columns and the page area. Text fields that contain unique entries rather than category information can be placed usefully in the data area if you want to count the number of records in the categories defined by other fields. At a minimum, you must place at least one field in the data area, and one in either the row axis or the column axis.

Don't be concerned in the slightest about getting the layout perfect the first time. You can reorganize the table just as easily as you laid it out initially, as detailed in the section "Pivoting the data," later in this chapter.

Pivot table anatomy and physiology

Figure 28-6 shows a completed pivot table after fields from the sample database have been laid out. The final column (the one labeled "Grand Total") contains the overall summary calculations for the fields in the data area.

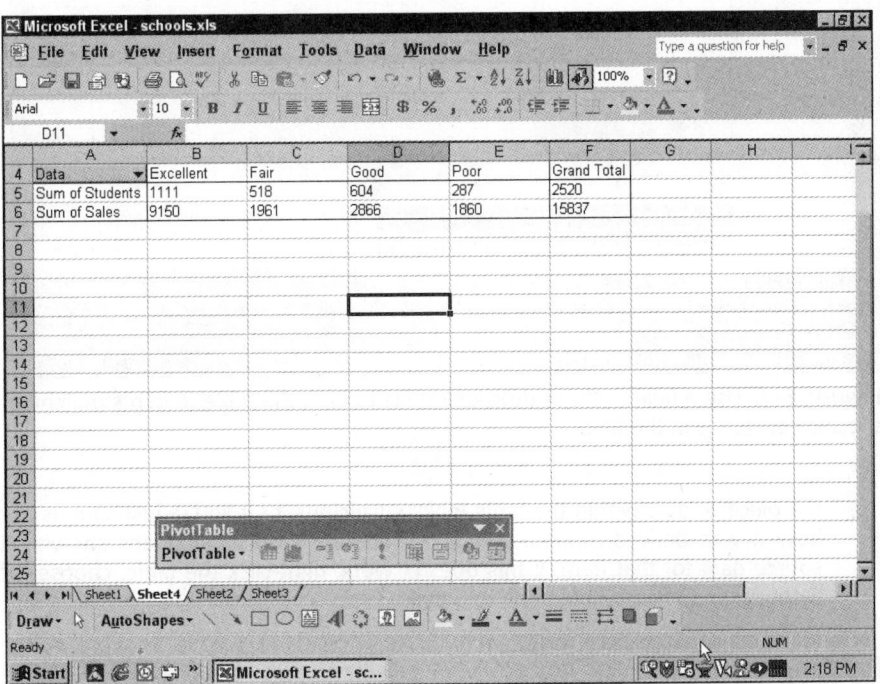

Figure 28-6: A completed pivot table, before additional formatting has been applied

By default, the calculations shown in a pivot table are simple sums of the values for numeric data, and simple counts of the number of items for text. You can change the calculations performed for each data field using the technique covered in "Controlling summary calculations," later in this chapter.

A pivot table has a button for each field in the table, except that you get only one button for the data area no matter how many fields it contains. Each button is titled with the field name. Clicking the arrow on the button opens a drop-down list that lets you select the elements that are to appear in the table (see Figure 28-7). This is a great way to focus in on a specific category of information.

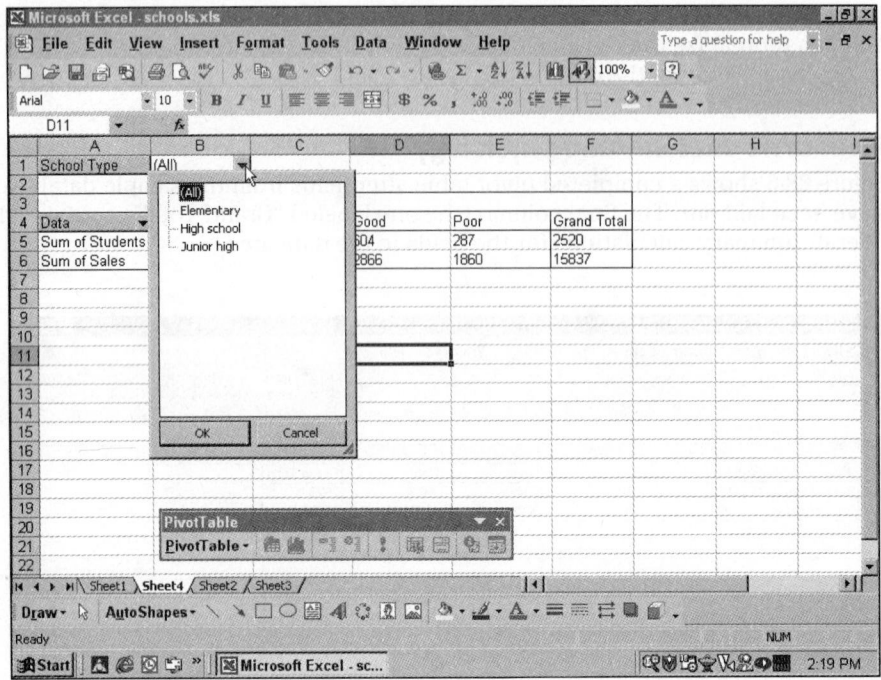

Figure 28-7: Use a field button's drop-down list to limit the table to items matching specific categories in the field.

Tip   If a piece of data within the table looks suspicious, or if you're just curious about how it was derived, double-click it. A separate worksheet opens showing the source data for that item. If this doesn't work, right-click the table, choose Table Options, and check Enable drill to details.

Pivoting the data

They don't call it a "pivot" table for nothing. By dragging fields to different parts of the table, you can view your data from different perspectives. Excel automatically reformats the table according to the field locations, relabeling column and row headings according to the current fields in those areas.

To remove a field altogether from the page, row, or column areas, just drag its button out of the pivot table and back to the Field List task pane. (If you've closed the Field list, you can reopen it by clicking the Show Field List button on the far-right end of the PivotTable toolbar). If you remove all the fields in either the row or column area, the table's data disappears—you see the empty skeleton again. As soon as you add back one or more fields into the empty area, the table comes to life again.

If you've placed only a single field in the data area, its name appears in the top-left corner of the table, and you can drag it off the table from there. However, you can't drag individual fields out of the data area when it contains two or more fields. Instead, remove them from the table by clicking the Data drop-down button (it will be labeled with the field name if the data area contains only one field). In the pop-up list of fields, clear the checkbox for the field you want to remove. Alternatively, you can remove all data fields by dragging the Data item off of the table, and then you can add fields back individually.

Using the PivotTable toolbar and shortcut menu

Once you create a pivot table, the PivotTable toolbar remains on the screen until you dismiss it. However, while you can always use it to activate the PivotTable Wizard, the toolbar is otherwise active only when you select some portion of an existing pivot table. Then the toolbar's buttons become available.

Note   You don't really need the toolbar; you can access all of its functions, plus some additional ones, by right-clicking the pivot table to open the shortcut menu.

Fine-tuning pivot tables

Once you've decided on your table's basic layout, you have a host of options for controlling how it summarizes the data, for displaying additional calculations, and for making the table pretty.

Working with field options

To fine-tune the way your pivot table handles an individual field, right-click the field heading in the table and choose Field Settings in the resulting shortcut menu. (Alternatively, you can just double-click row, column, and page fields.) The PivotTable Field dialog box appears, as shown in Figure 28-8.

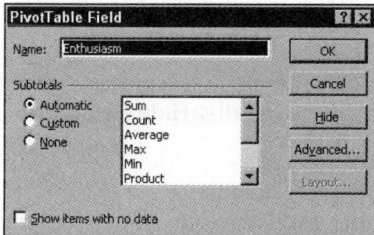

Figure 28-8: Fields in a pivot table can be customized using the PivotTable Field dialog box. Numeric fields include a Number button for formatting numbers.

If the field contains numeric data, you'll see a Number button that lets you control the formatting. On fields in the row, column, and page areas, the Advanced button gives you further display and sort options.

Controlling summary calculations

Use the list in the middle of the PivotTable Field dialog box to control which calculations appear in your pivot table. For data fields, you're choosing the calculation displayed in the cells in the body of the table. You can pick only one calculation for data fields. For row, column, and page fields, you're determining the calculation displayed in special "subtotal" rows or columns. These subtotals only appear when you place two or more fields in one area (row, column, or page). You can select as many subtotal calculations as you like for fields in the row, column, and page areas.

Comparing fields

Another option lets you compare the values of the current field with those in a different field. Bring up the PivotTable Field dialog box for an item in the data area and click the Options button. Now select the type of comparison you want under Show data as. In the "Base field" and "Base item" boxes, choose which field and individual item you want to base the comparison on.

Refining pivot table layout

Suppose you just want to reorder a pivot table's rows or columns, perhaps because the headings represent rankings that should appear in rank order rather than alphabetically. To move a row or column heading, activate the cell and then drag its border to the new location.

To merge two or more row or column headings into a group, follow these steps:

1. Select the headings you want to include. You can hold down Ctrl while you click to select nonadjacent headings.

2. Right-click a selected cell and choose Group and Show Detail ⇨ Group from the shortcut menu. Excel adds a new heading labeled Group1 or the like to your table.

3. To consolidate the entries from the rows or columns in the group, right-click the group heading and choose Group and Show Detail ⇨ Hide Detail.

Using the PivotTable Wizard

Although you can lay out fields on the pivot table itself, you can also do so in the PivotTable Wizard when you're creating the table in the first place, or later, to modify the layout of an existing table.

To use the wizard for layout, click the Layout button on the wizard's third panel. (You're taken immediately to this panel when you activate the wizard for an existing pivot table — to do so, right-click anywhere in the table and choose Wizard from the shortcut menu.)

The Layout dialog box displays a diagram of the pivot table structure, with page, row, column, and data areas, along with a series of buttons representing the fields. Drag the fields of interest to the diagram, just as you would on the actual table. Because the diagram doesn't display data, you may find it easier to make layout modifications here, especially when the table includes many fields. And you may need the Layout dialog box to use the page area — the page area is always visible here, even if it isn't displayed on the pivot table itself.

Using the PivotTable Options dialog box

Clicking Table Options on a pivot table's shortcut menu brings up a big dialog box (see Figure 28-9) stuffed full of formatting options. The box also includes options dealing with the table's underlying data. You can also get to this dialog box from the third panel of the PivotTable Wizard.

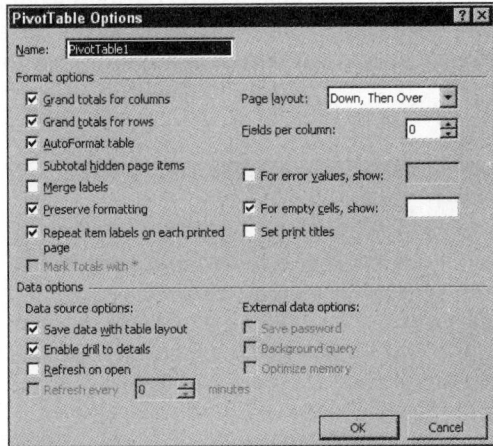

Figure 28-9: From the PivotTable Options dialog box, you can define how error values and empty cells are displayed (among other things).

Handling empty cells and error values

Use the PivotTable Options dialog box to control what Excel does with empty cells and error messages. To change how errors are displayed, select the "For error values, show" box, and enter the value you want to display instead of errors. To change how empty cells are displayed, select the "For empty cells, show" box, and enter the value — zero, or a specific word, for instance — you want to display in empty cells. (By default, empty cells are left blank.) The changes you make affect the entire pivot table. If you don't check the "For error values, show" box, Excel displays a default message.

Formatting pivot tables

The easiest way to give your table a classy format is with one of the AutoFormat choices available via the Format Report button, found on the PivotTable toolbar or shortcut menu. You can apply any of 21 different formats in report or table styles. Use the None option at the bottom of the Format list to remove automatic formatting.

Creating pivot charts

You can chart your pivot table summaries instantly, either by selecting PivotChart during step 1 of the PivotTable Wizard, or from an existing pivot table (choose PivotChart from the table's shortcut menu or click the Chart Wizard button on the Standard or PivotTable toolbar).

Pivot charts work almost exactly like pivot tables, only graphically. Once you have one in your workbook, you can play around with its layout and control the data it displays just as you can a pivot table. Looking at Figure 28-10, you can see the sample chart has the field buttons just like those in pivot tables, in addition to a conventional legend.

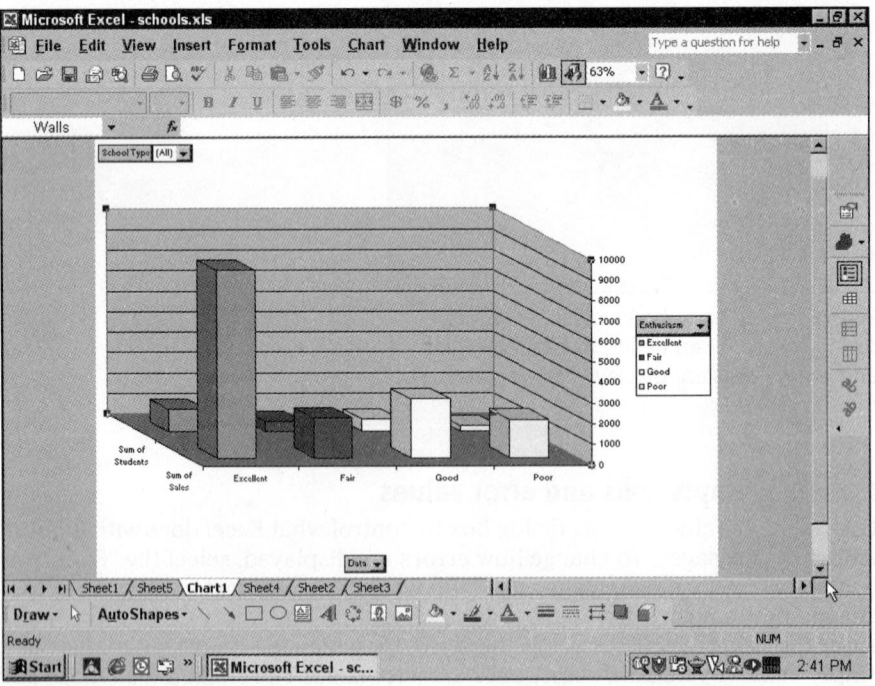

Figure 28-10: A pivot chart based on the pivot table shown in Figure 28-6

Some of the modifications you can make to pivot charts include the following:

✦ Dragging fields on or off the chart or to different locations inside it

✦ Selecting items from the field button drop-down lists to control which data the chart displays

✦ Altering field options via the PivotTable Field dialog box (display it by double-clicking a field button)

The chart remains connected to the table from which you created it, so these changes appear on the table as well. Of course, you can format the chart visually just as you would an ordinary chart — see Chapter 27 for details.

Using Goal Seek

Goal Seek is an Excel tool that automatically adjusts the value of one cell to get a specific result in another cell. Suppose you were working on a budget for a project, and needed to show break even. The only variable you can adjust is the wage to be offered to the six people needed to complete the project. On your first crack at it, you put too much money into wages and the budget shows you losing money. You can use Goal Seek to find out how much the pay rate needs to be cut in order to bring it in on budget.

To use Goal Seek, follow these steps:

1. Click on the cell whose value you want to change.

2. Select Tools ⇨ Goal Seek from the menu.

3. In the Goal Seek dialog box (see Figure 28-11), the "Set cell" value is already filled in because you selected it before invoking Goal Seek. If you had not done so, or if you had clicked on the wrong cell, you would need to click on the desired cell at this point.

4. In the "To value" box, type the result you want — zero in this case, because you just want to break even.

5. In the "By changing cell" box, enter the reference for the cell (you can also set it by clicking on the cell) that holds the value you want Goal Seek to adjust to achieve the value you specified — in this case, the cell that contains the hourly pay rate you want to adjust to the point where the project doesn't operate at a loss.

6. Click OK.

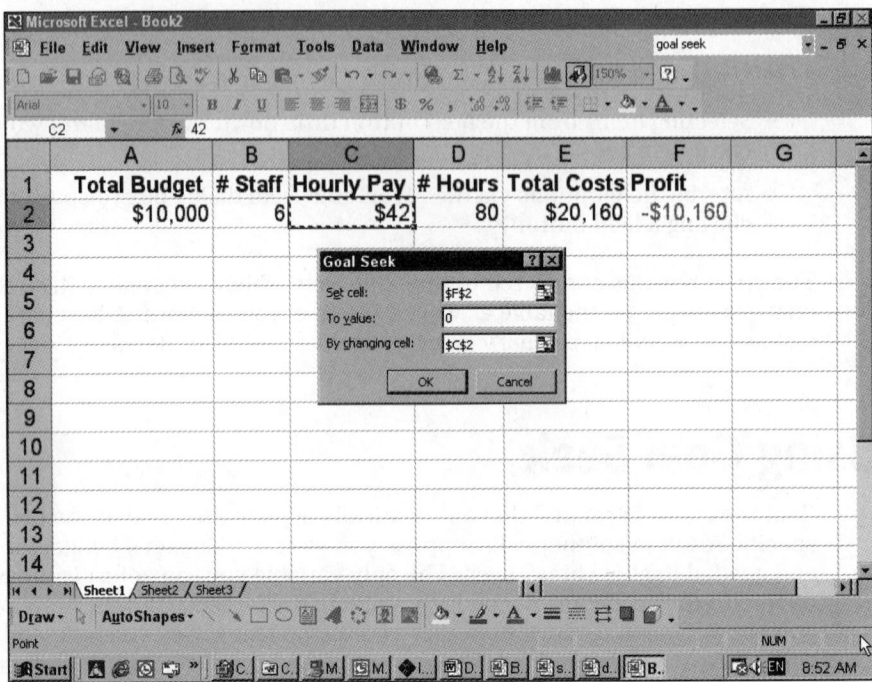

Figure 28-11: Use Goal Seek to figure out how the value in one cell needs to be changed to produce a specific value in another cell.

7. Goal Seek will now run through a series of calculations, trying out various possibilities, and rapidly find an answer, which it displays in the Goal Seek Status dialog box. In this case, the answer is $21. Goal Seek automatically inserts that amount in the cell you wanted to change.

8. To accept the new values, click the OK button. To reject them and return the values to the original ones that were there before you ran Goal Seek, click the Cancel button.

The Step and Pause buttons in the Goal Seek Status dialog box aren't of much use unless you're calculating a very large value using a very slow computer or are very fast with a mouse. Goal Seek is so fast that it'll usually find the final value before you can react. If you are quick enough, you can click the Pause button to freeze the calculation and then use the Step button to walk through the calculation as it tries different values. When you click Pause, it becomes a Continue button, which you can click on to resume the normal mode of calculation.

Working with Add-ins

Add-in programs are optional components that add functionality to Excel. Although some add-ins are installed automatically when you install Excel, others must be installed separately by you.

After installing an add-in onto your hard drive, use the Tools ➪ Add-Ins command to load the add-in into Excel. This makes the feature available and adds any associated commands to the menus. The Tools ➪ Add-Ins dialog box (see Figure 28-12) is very easy to use: If the add-in is listed in the box, you know it's been installed onto your hard drive. If it has a check next to it, you know it's been loaded into Excel.

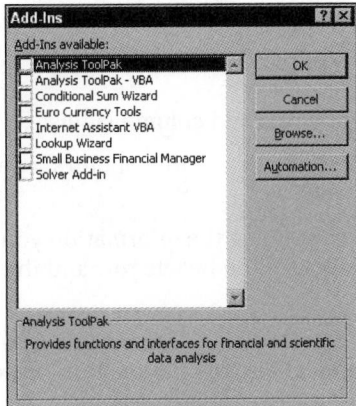

Figure 28-12: These add-Ins have been installed, but not yet loaded into Excel.

Some add-ins may delay the time it takes to launch Excel. To conserve memory, you might want to unload add-ins that you don't use often. (Unloading an add-in removes its features from Excel, but the program remains on your PC so that you can easily reload it.)

The sections that follow offer quick looks at some add-ins that are especially helpful in analyzing data. If you can't find one of the commands or features mentioned, go to Tools ➪ Add-Ins to install the appropriate add-in program.

Lookup Wizard add-in

Use the Lookup Wizard add-in when you need to determine the current value of an item in a list. Suppose you keep track of your pet store's canine menagerie in a simple Excel list. Each row of the list (which is basically a table) shows a dog breed in the first column and how many of them you have on hand in the second column, which is labeled In Stock.

What you want is a way to find the current number of beagles on hand. The list is long, and it's too much trouble to comb through it yourself. Besides, another worksheet needs to know how many beagles are in stock so that it can calculate how many beagle puppies to buy each month. Whenever you update this second worksheet, it must have access to current information, even if the beagle row has changed places in the list.

To count your hounds reliably, use the Lookup Wizard. Follow these steps:

1. Start by selecting the entire list, including the row and column labels.

2. Choose Tools ➪ Wizard ➪ Lookup. In the first of four wizard windows, confirm the list range.

3. Specify the labels for the row and column containing the information you seek. In the example, you would pick the label for the beagle row and the label for the In Stock column.

4. Tell the wizard how you want to enter the results — as a formula in a single cell, or as the formula along with the column labels (the parameters) used to do the lookup.

5. The last step is really easy: Just designate the cell or cells where Excel should enter the lookup formula (and the parameters if you chose to include them in step 4). You can switch to a different worksheet to deposit the cell(s) there. The formula cell displays the results of the lookup, of course, so you simply see the same value as in the list. If you choose to include parameters, their cells simply contain the selected row and column labels.

Whenever Excel recalculates the formula, the current value from the inventory list is transferred to the target cell. Because the formula sniffs out the desired information in the list based on row and column labels, not on predefined cell coordinates, you always get the correct answer — even if beagles have moved up one row in the list after your store stopped carrying basset hounds.

If you chose not to include parameters, the formula used for the lookup includes the literal characters of the row and column labels you selected. If you opted to include cells for the parameters, however, the formula refers to the current contents of those cells. That means you can type a different breed name in the row label parameter cell and instantly see how many afghans, poodles, or spaniels are in stock.

Analysis ToolPak add-in

The Analysis ToolPak is a set of 19 data-analysis tools that assist in complex statistical and engineering analyses. You provide the data and parameters for each analysis; the tool calculates the results and displays an output table. Some tools generate charts in addition to tables.

To use the Analysis ToolPak, you must first install it by checking its box in the Add-ins dialog box (refer back to Figure 28-12). Then choose Tools ➪ Data Analysis to display the Data Analysis dialog box. Select an analysis tool from this dialog box. When you then choose OK, a dialog box with options relevant for that tool appears.

Solver

The Solver is another add-in for those who need advanced data analysis. It calculates solutions to "what-if" scenarios based on variable cells. Unlike Goal Seek, which finds a single value, Solver can find multiple values and enables you to define constraints. (When you use Solver, the cells involved must be related through formulas on the worksheet.)

When using Solver, you specify the target cell whose formula result you want to optimize. You then designate the cells to be changed (up to 200) — those that are related, either directly or indirectly, to the target cell. You can apply constraints to restrict the values in the cells or their relationships. Solver changes the values in the input cells to produce the desired result in the target formula cell.

To use Solver, choose Tools ➪ Solver and fill in the dialog box shown in Figure 28-13. For a bit of general information about the algorithm used by Solver, choose Help in the Solver Parameters dialog box.

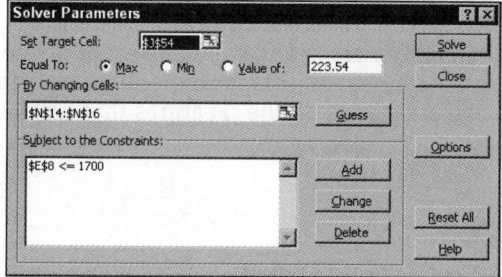

Figure 28-13: Cells N14:N16 contain values that drive the formula in cell J54. Use Solver to vary them until J54 equals the target value of 223.54.

For nonlinear problems, it can be helpful to experiment with different starting values for the input cells, especially if Solver has found a solution that is significantly different from what you expected.

Tip   Use Goal Seek when you know the desired result of a formula, but not the input value from a single cell that the formula needs. Use Solver when you need to change the values in several cells and have multiple constraints for those values.

Sharing Workbooks

"Share and share alike," your mother used to say. Well, I'm not sure if she was referring to Excel spreadsheets, but I'm sure she'd be pleased that everyone in your group can edit workbooks at the same time, by creating a shared workbook.

You can allow others to review and edit a workbook simultaneously. During the process, their changes are highlighted (in different colors, of course), change histories are tracked, and comments are stored. And if you decide to, you can put limits on access.

To open a workbook for sharing, open the workbook and go to Tools ➪ Share Workbook. On the Editing tab, select "Allow changes by more than one user at the same time". The list on the Editing tab shows the current users for this workbook. If you've just enabled sharing right now, the only user shown is you. You can return to this box at any time to see who is currently working on this shared workbook.

When you filter data in a shared workbook and set print options, your settings are saved independently of those made by other users. Whenever you open the shared workbook, your personal settings appear. (See the section "Filtering Data," earlier in this chapter.)

Many Excel features are off-limits in shared workbooks. You can't delete worksheets, merge cells, or define conditional formats. Nor can you insert or delete blocks of cells; insert or modify charts, pictures, objects, or hyperlinks; or create or modify macros. For a list of such commands, look up the "Features that are unavailable in shared workbooks" Help topic.

Keeping track of changes

Excel keeps track of all changes made to a shared workbook and which user made the changes. Whenever a change is made, Excel identifies it using the name in the Tools ➪ Options box (look in the "User name" field on the General tab). You can later view a complete history of every change, including information about those that conflict.

You can keep a history in two ways: by highlighting changes directly on the worksheet, or by maintaining a separate History worksheet.

If you protect a workbook for sharing, others cannot remove it from shared use or turn off the change history. In this way, you guarantee that all changes are tracked. Use the Tools ➪ Protection ➪ Protect and Share Workbook command.

Highlighting changes on the sheet

Individuals can highlight their changes right on the sheet, making them easily visible. To highlight changes to the current workbook, open the Tools ➪ Track Changes ➪ Highlight Changes dialog box, shown in Figure 28-14. Turn on "Track changes while editing". This also turns on sharing and the change history, if they're not already on.

Check the "Highlight changes on screen" field to mark changes as you make them. "List changes on a new sheet" saves the changes to the change history (discussed in the next section).

The When, Who, and Where fields let you fine-tune the Track Changes command. Under When, you can choose to limit tracking to changes made since you last saved or since a specific date, or to those changes that have not yet been reviewed; under Who, you can choose to track changes made by everyone, or everyone but yourself; and under Where, you can choose to track changes made only to a specific range of cells.

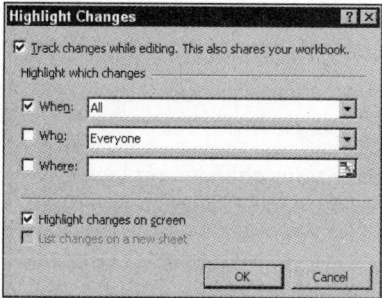

Figure 28-14: You can track changes while editing to keep a record of all your edits.

When a change is made to a cell, the cell is outlined in color, and a small indicator is placed in the upper-left corner. Changes are color-coded according to the user. Rest the pointer over a highlighted cell to see a small note with the user's name, the date, the time, and the change that was made.

 **Note**   When highlighting changes, Excel does not track certain things, such as formatting.

Keeping a change history

You can view a complete list of changes to the workbook by maintaining a History worksheet. The History sheet (called the Conflicts sheet prior to Excel 97) includes information on who made the change, when and where it was made, what data was changed, and how conflicts were resolved. The column labels have filter arrows that you can use to find specific information.

To keep a change history, you must first save the workbook in shared, protected form with the command previously described. Then, go to Tools ➪ Track Changes ➪ Highlight Changes. Turn on "List changes on a new sheet". A sheet named History is added to the workbook.

When viewing the History sheet, you can filter the information in several ways. Each column heading has a filter arrow, with a drop-down list. Any column can be filtered to show changes made by particular users on particular dates. You can review changes in the order that they were made, or view changes to particular areas of the worksheet.

Information about how conflicts are resolved is also available on the History sheet. You can find information about any changes that are replaced by other changes, and print the change information.

The History worksheet shows only the changes that have been saved. To include all changes from your current session, save the workbook before viewing the History sheet.

Merging changes

When you save a shared workbook, you can have your changes replace any conflicting changes made by others, or you can review each change and decide whether to accept it.

Updating settings

If you plan to merge copies of a shared workbook, you must prepare some settings ahead of time. Select Tools ➪ Share Workbook. On the Advanced tab, you determine how long changes are tracked, when they're updated, and how conflicting changes are resolved.

In order to merge changes, each copy of the shared workbook must track changes from the day when the copies were created, through the day when they're merged. If the number of days specified is exceeded, you can no longer merge the copies. (If you aren't sure how long the review will take, enter an unusually large number of days.)

On the verge of a merge

Open the shared workbook into which you want to merge changes. Choose Tools ➪ Compare and Merge Workbooks. If prompted, save the current version. In the dialog box that appears, select the copies that have changes to be merged and click OK.

Excel incorporates changes from all shared copies selected and resolves conflicts according to the settings on the Advanced tab of Tools ➪ Share Workbook. Even cell comments from different users are identified by individual user names and merged into a single comment box.

The entire process is recorded on the History sheet for viewing any time. Revisions by different users are color-coded. When it's done, you can have the final word by going to Tools ➪ Track Changes ➪ Accept or Reject Changes. Excel steps through every change, displays it for you, and allows you to give your yay or nay. (On the History worksheet, rejected changes display "Undo" or "Result of rejected action" in the Action Type column.)

✦   ✦   ✦

CHAPTER 29

Debugging Your Worksheets

◆ ◆ ◆ ◆

In This Chapter

Understanding cell interdependence

Tracing with the Formula Auditing toolbar

Tracking down cell errors

◆ ◆ ◆ ◆

Want more control over what's going on behind the scenes? I have a few tricks here that are guaranteed to make you feel like a power user, including more information about the Formula Auditing toolbar, which is also discussed in Chapter 26.

Using the Formula Auditing Toolbar

To display the Formula Auditing toolbar, choose View ➪ Toolbars ➪ Formula Auditing (see Figure 29-1).

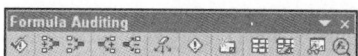

Figure 29-1: The Formula Auditing toolbar is a handy little gadget.

Who's dependent on whom?

In a complex spreadsheet, the values in many cells depend on the values in other cells — and other cells depend on the values in them. Who's dependent on whom? Excel gives you several quick and easy ways to find out.

Cell *precedents* are the cells that provide data to the formula in the active cell. These precedents contain the input values that the formula needs. Cell *dependents* are those cells that depend on the value in the active cell. The active cell provides data to them. The diagram in Figure 29-2 shows a very simple example. To help debug problems on your worksheet, Excel provides tools for tracing precedents and dependents.

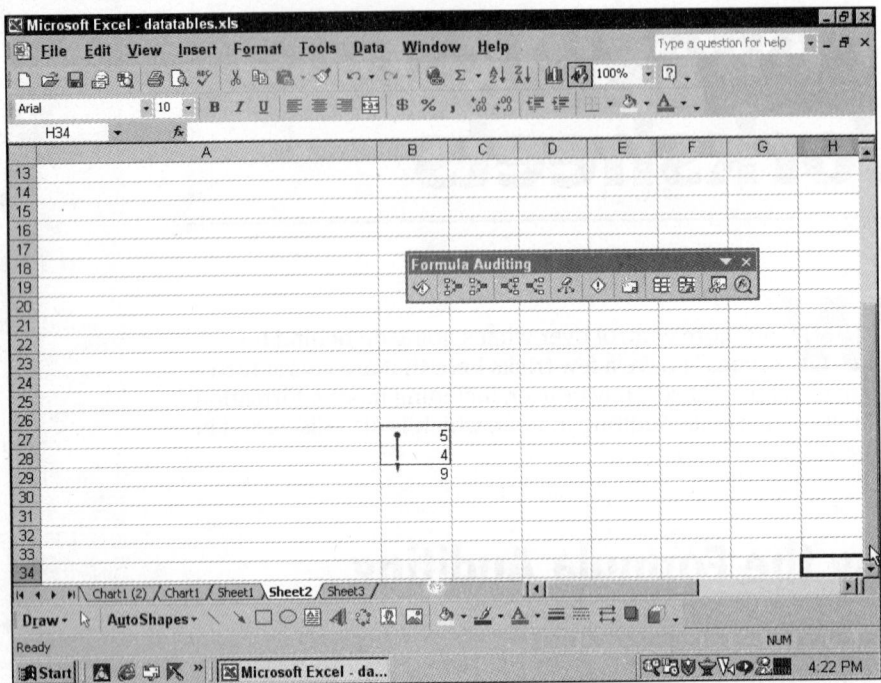

Figure 29-2: The sum of "9" depends upon the two values above it—"9" is the dependent cell, and "5" and "4" are the precedent cells.

Tracing with the Formula Auditing toolbar

On the Auditing toolbar, four buttons give you the ability to show and hide tracer arrows on your worksheet. When you click the Trace Precedents button, blue tracer arrows indicate cells that are precedents of the selected cell. Cells off the current worksheet are indicated by arrows with a small worksheet icon. When you click the Trace Dependents button, blue tracer arrows indicate cells that are dependent on the selected cell.

In each case, the arrow shows the direction of the reference (see Figure 29-3).

Each time you click a button, one level of precedents or dependents is shown. The first time you click the Trace Precedents button, for example, Excel locates and displays the immediate precedents (the *parents* of the active cell). With each additional click, successive levels of indirect links—grandparents, great-grandparents, and so on—are shown by additional arrows.

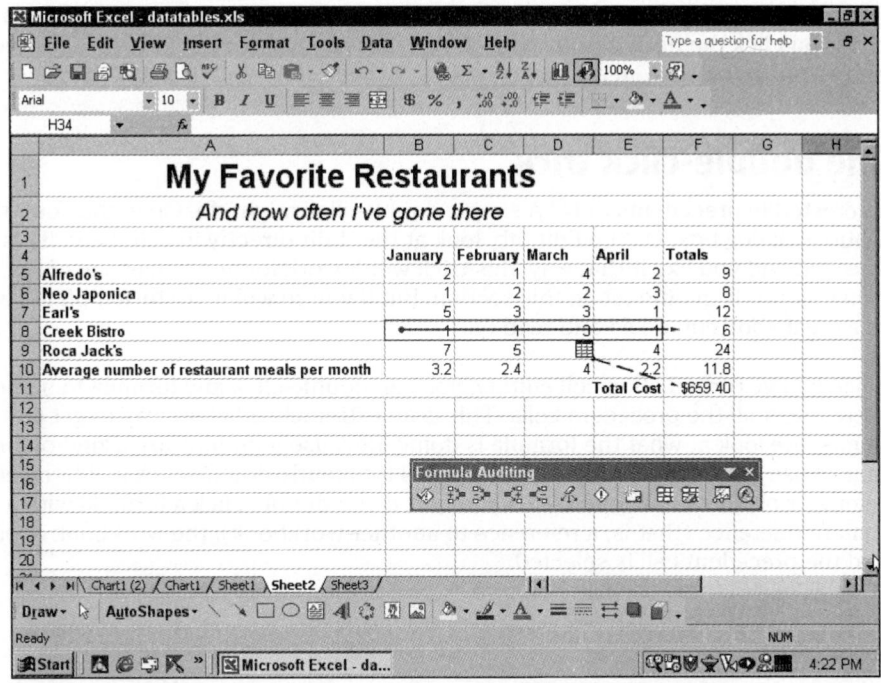

Figure 29-3: With a single click, you can trace several dependencies (as in `Creek Bistro`). The `Total Cost` value came from another worksheet.

If you want to find the cell at the other end of a tracer arrow, you can simply double-click anywhere along the arrow. This also works for cells on other worksheets or in other workbooks. Double-click the arrow, and in the Go To box that appears double-click your destination.

Note You can't trace the following referenced items with the auditing tools: text boxes, embedded charts, pictures, pivot tables, named constants, and dependent cells residing in a closed workbook. Also, because tracer arrows are graphical objects, you won't see them if objects are hidden on the worksheet. If they aren't visible, check the View tab in the Tools ⇨ Options dialog box. Under Objects, make sure that Show All is selected.

Select a formula cell and click the Remove Precedent Arrows button to remove the arrows that point from its precedent cells. Select a precedent cell and click the Remove Dependent Arrows button to remove the arrows that point to its dependent cells.

If several levels of links are shown, they are removed one level at a time. The first time you click the button, the arrow indicating the most indirect link is removed, and so on. To remove all tracer arrows, click the Remove All Arrows button.

The double-click trick

Interested in precedents only? A simple double-click might do. Open the Tools ➪ Options dialog box. On the Edit tab, look at the "Edit directly in cell" field. If it's checked and you like it that way, this trick won't work for you — use one of the other methods mentioned in this section. But if you're willing to turn it off in favor of a great shortcut, do so and read on.

Once you've turned off in-cell editing, you can double-click any formula to immediately select all the precedent cells. This is an extremely efficient way to get an immediate look at what the formula is doing. Because functions are a kind of formula, I use it liberally on my SUM formulas. I frequently double-click a SUM to get a reminder of what I'm summing. As a bonus, if you double-click a formula with a remote reference (that is, a reference to another workbook), the workbook opens and the precedent cell is selected.

For keyboard users

There are keyboard shortcuts that reveal precedents and dependents, too, and Table 29-1 lists them.

Table 29-1
Keyboard Shortcuts for Precedents and Dependents

Press This	To Do This
Ctrl+[	Select direct precedents of the active cell.
Ctrl+Shift+[	Select direct and indirect precedents of the active cell.
Ctrl+]	Select direct dependents of the active cell.
Ctrl+Shift+]	Select direct and indirect dependents of the active cell.

Cell Errors

Cell errors are usually traceable. If you understand what the error means, it's an easy fix.

Understanding cell error messages

Error messages in cells can be awfully cryptic. Table 29-2 reviews a few of the meanings.

	Table 29-2 Cell Error Messages	
Error	**Meaning**
#DIV/0!	The formula is dividing by zero.
#N/A	A value is not available to the function or formula.
#NAME?	Text in the formula is not recognized. (For more on the #NAME? error, see "Error checking on-the-fly" later.)
#NULL!	The formula refers to an intersection of two areas that do not intersect.
#NUM!	A problem occurs with a number in the formula or function.
#REF!	A cell reference is not valid.
#VALUE!	The wrong type of argument or operand is used.
#####	The formatted number is too wide to display within the column. (This is the only error that is not traced with the Auditing toolbar. Simply widen the column to fix it.)

Tracing errors

Sometimes the source of cell errors is immediately obvious. If it's not, select the cell that has the error and click the Trace Error button on the Formula Auditing toolbar. Red arrows point to formulas that cause error values, and blue arrows point to cells containing values that create errors.

To select and display the cell at the other end of an arrow, double-click the arrow. If more than one error path exists, Excel stops tracing at the branch point when you use Trace Error. To continue tracing, click Trace Error again.

Auditing Data Validation errors

If you've used Data Validation to constrain entries in a cell, chances are you defined error messages to pop up for incorrect entries. But invalid entries can still find their way onto your worksheet.

Input and error messages only appear when a user is typing directly into the cell. Copying, autofilling, formulas, and macros can also alter worksheet information, and these incorrect entries don't produce error messages. But rest assured, they can easily be tracked down. (This is the one time you'll be pleased to have an audit!)

When you audit a worksheet for incorrect entries, Excel identifies all cells containing values outside the limits you've set using Data Validation. To trace these errors, you need merely turn to a button on the Auditing toolbar. On the toolbar, click the Circle Invalid Data button. Excel immediately checks the worksheet and places red circles around the first 255 cells containing data that do not meet the criteria you set with Data Validation. Once the errors have been found and corrected, click the Clear Validation Circles button to erase the red circles.

 Note The auditing buttons are not available on a protected worksheet.

Identifying circular references

A circular reference is a formula that directly or indirectly refers back to itself. Excel cannot automatically calculate all open workbooks when one of them contains a circular reference. While many of them happen by accident, some scientific and engineering formulas require circular references to perform their calculations.

When a circular reference occurs, Excel alerts you with a message and the Circular Reference toolbar. If you didn't mean to create one, you can use the toolbar to track it down and correct it. If you intended to create one for a specific process, you can control how the reference is calculated.

Accidental circular references

When a circular reference occurs, Excel automatically displays an alert, opens the Circular Reference toolbar, and places blue auditing arrows in the cells involved (see Figure 29-4).

If you're familiar with the Auditing toolbar, you'll recognize the Trace Dependents, Trace Precedents, and Remove All Arrows buttons on the Circular Reference toolbar. Use these buttons to display tracer arrows. You can move between cells in a circular reference by double-clicking the arrows or by choosing them from the toolbar's drop-down list. As you move to each cell in turn, you can redesign the logic to break the circular reference.

Another visual cue can be found in the status bar. You'll see the word "Circular" followed by a reference to one of the guilty cells. If the status bar message appears without a cell reference, it means the error is found on a different sheet in the workbook.

You can display the Circular Reference toolbar manually. Choose View ➪ Toolbars ➪ Circular Reference.

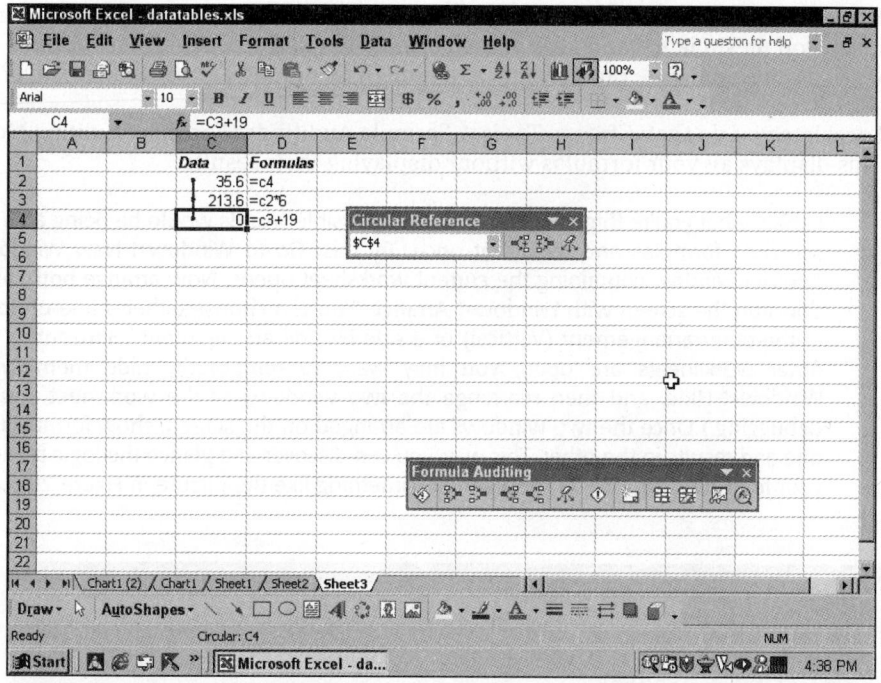

Figure 29-4: The Circular Reference toolbar and blue auditing arrows alert you to the location of circular references.

Intentional circular references

If you're using a scientific or engineering formula that requires a circular reference, it might be helpful to know how Excel treats them, and how to control the process by which Excel calculates results that depend on circular references.

To have Excel calculate circular references, you must go to the Calculation tab of the Tools ⇨ Options dialog box. There, check the Iteration box. When you turn iteration on, Excel iterates (that is, repeatedly calculates the worksheet) the number of times specified at "Maximum iterations", or until all values in the circular reference change by less than the value at "Maximum change", whichever comes first.

Finding errors in logic

While tracer arrows and validation circles are a fast, efficient way of finding errors, what they can't find is errors in your logic. But if some values on your worksheet seem fishy, you can take a closer look at your formulas to see whether they're really doing what you intended them to do.

By default, your worksheet displays formula results; to see the contents of a formula, you must click it and look in the Formula Bar. But debugging is laborious
when you can only see one formula at a time. Why not look at them all at once?

Excel lets you do that: Choose Tools ➪ Formula Auditing ➪ Formula Auditing Mode.
This displays all your formulas without displaying their results.

Tip

I know what you're thinking. The best of all possible worlds would be being able to
see *both* formulas and results at once. Try this: Go to Window ➪ New Window.
Another window containing the current worksheet opens. Now arrange both windows on the screen with Window ➪ Arrange. You can choose either a one-on-top-
of-the-other arrangement (Vertical) or a side-by-side arrangement (Horizontal). (If
other worksheets are open, you may want to temporarily hide them with
Window ➪ Hide, and then rearrange the two windows of the worksheet you're
debugging.) Once the two windows are arranged on the screen, show formulas in
one and results in the other. This way, you can discover at a glance the logic behind
your formulas. The results should look something like the picture in Figure 29-5.

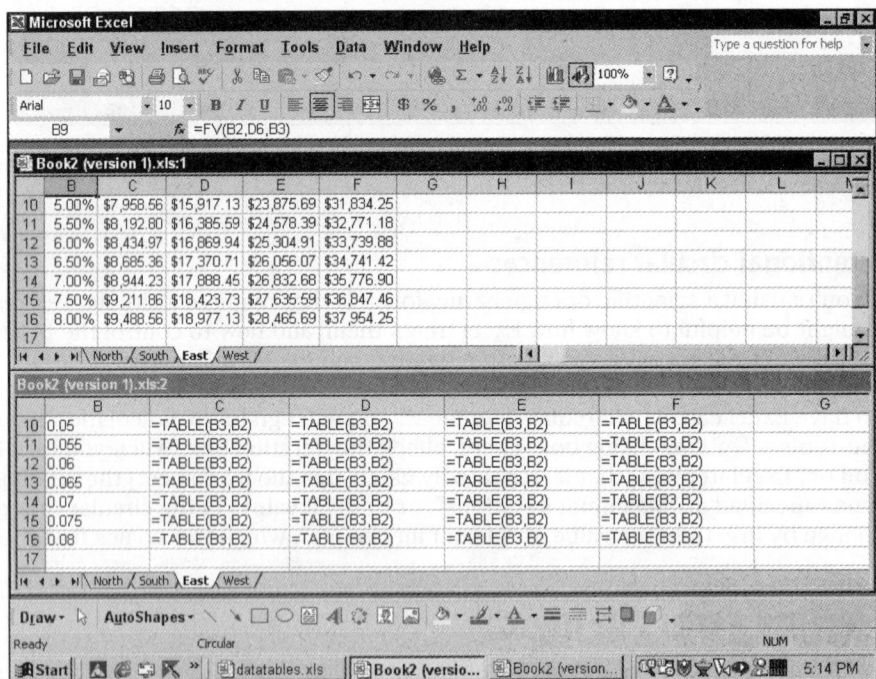

Figure 29-5: While both windows display the same worksheet, the top window
shows results, and the bottom window shows formulas.

Error checking on-the-fly

If in the best of all possible worlds you can find your errors at a glance, in the best of all possible universes your mistakes would be fixed for you as you made them. As detailed in Chapter 8, the AutoCorrect feature corrects errors in spelling and punctuation in text you enter on your worksheets. Excel's Formula AutoCorrect feature automatically catches the most common mistakes when creating a formula. And the following few extra tips show that sometimes just knowing how Excel thinks can give you the edge.

Formula AutoCorrect

So you know your way around Excel pretty well, and you've typed a gazillion formulas before, so you tend to do it pretty fast. Well, even the most experienced make mistakes sometimes. Thanks to Formula AutoCorrect, now you can continue to make them. Excel catches many of the most common formula errors, bringing them to your attention (see the list in Table 29-3). You can then accept or reject the suggested correction, which appears in an alert message (see Figure 29-6). For example, if you end a function with an extra parenthesis, Excel finds the extra parenthesis and proposes the correction. In some cases, such as when a parenthesis is missing in a simple formula, Excel corrects the problem without bothering you with a message.

Table 29-3
Errors Formula AutoCorrect Catches

Common Error	*How Excel AutoCorrects the Problem*
Missing parenthesis	Creates a matching pair.
Missing quote mark	Creates a matching pair.
Cell reference as `row-col` instead of `col-row`	Changes the reference to `col-row`.
Semicolon instead of colon	Replaces the semicolon with a colon.
Colon in the wrong place	Moves the colon to between two cell references.
Extra space in cell reference or number	Removes the space.
Two decimal points together	Removes the second decimal point.
Two operators together	Removes the second operator.
Extra operator at the beginning or end	Removes the operator.
=> or =< or ><	Reverses the operator symbols.
Commas in values over 999	Removes the commas.
Letter X instead of *	Replaces the X with *.
Implied multiplication, as in: `=2(a+b)`	Inserts *, as in `=2*(a+b)`.

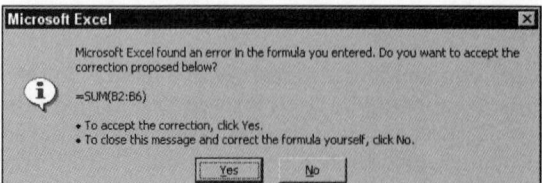

Figure 29-6: Excel displays an alert message if you make one of the errors listed in Table 29-3.

Playing the parentheses match game

Ever been haunted by the infamously cryptic message `Parentheses don't match`? Parentheses are the bane of most users who type formulas, and when they don't match, it's always been up to us to figure out which one is missing.

Not anymore. Excel displays parentheses in color as they are entered. While the outermost pair is in black, the inner pairs are displayed in a series of up to seven different colors. Not only that, but as you type a closing parenthesis, the pair is momentarily highlighted. If the parentheses are already entered, move the cursor across one to highlight the pair. It couldn't be simpler to see how they match up.

As mentioned in the preceding section, Formula AutoCorrect catches several common parentheses errors. It's actually difficult now to create an error that Excel can't help you with (I tried). But these tips will help you if and when you do.

Using lowercase is a capital idea

Another common error message, #NAME?, can actually be pretty obscure. If you've just entered a complex formula full of functions and defined names, which one is causing the problem? To avoid puzzling over the source of the message, take advantage of Excel's built-in error checking. You can do this by regularly entering all formulas in lowercase, and giving all defined names an initial cap.

When you enter a formula, Excel goes through an error-checking routine. At this time, it does two things:

  ✦ It bumps all recognized function names to uppercase.

  ✦ It converts all recognized defined names to the case in which they were defined.

If you've defined names with an initial cap but regularly type in lowercase, #NAME? errors are a cinch to track down. When you see one, simply check the formula for a name still in lowercase—that's the one Excel couldn't recognize (see Figure 29-7).

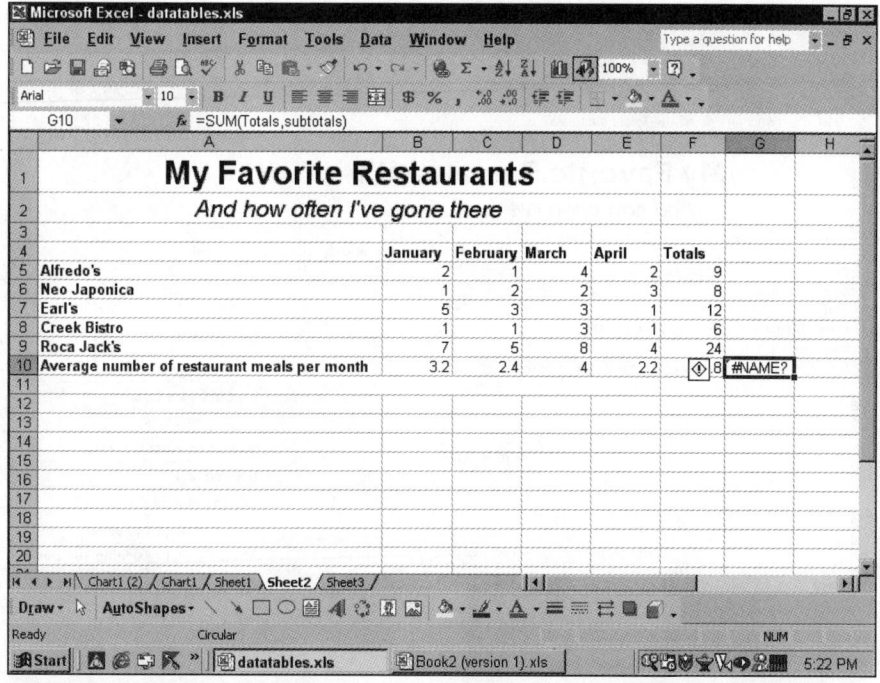

Figure 29-7: Excel capitalized the known function SUM, and gave an initial cap to the known range name Totals. Because subtotals remains in lowercase, I know that's the unrecognized name.

Tip   Complex formulas can pass Excel's error checkpoints but still deliver wrong or suspect results. One way to investigate potential problems is to calculate formulas one portion at a time. In the Formula Bar, select one piece of the formula. (Make sure it can stand on its own—parentheses should still be paired.) Press F9. Only that portion is calculated, and the result appears in the Formula Bar. You can do this to other parts of the formula if more detective work is required. By seeing how Excel interprets each piece, you can more easily track down where the error lies. After calculating the desired portion, press Esc to restore the original formula.

Smart Tags stand on guard for thee

Refer back to Figure 29-7. See that square with the little diamond containing an exclamation mark next to the #NAME? error message? That's one of Office XP's new Smart Tags, and they'll catch most formula errors before you're even aware of them—and help you solve them.

Whenever you see a Smart Tag, clicking on it brings up a shortcut menu like the one in Figure 29-8. Here you'll see what kind of error has been detected, and you can get help on the error, check the calculation step by step, choose to ignore it, or edit it in the Formula Bar.

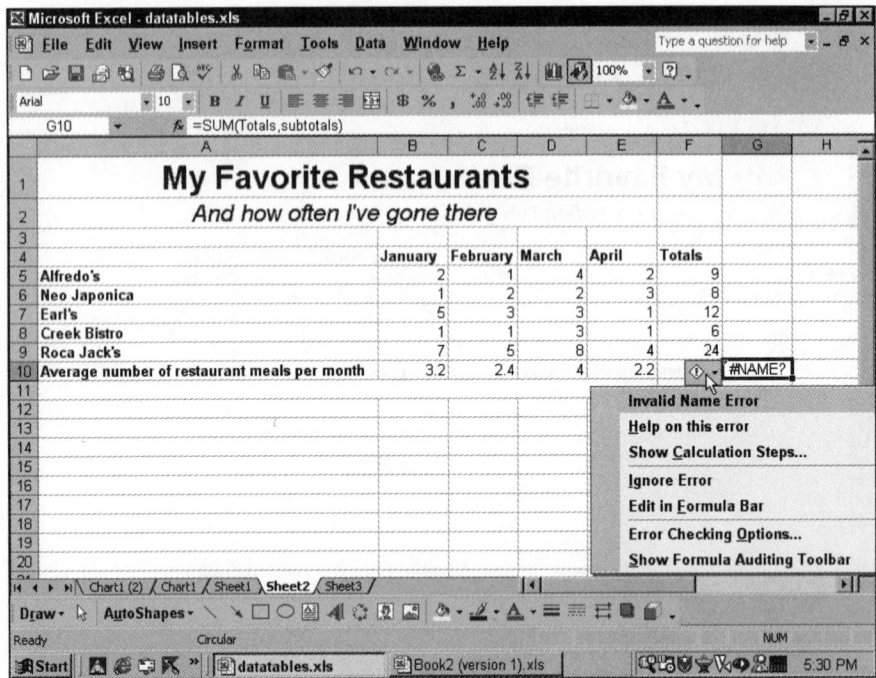

Figure 29-8: Smart Tags flag errors as you make them and help you correct them.

Smart Tags are one of the most user-friendly additions to come to Office in several generations, and they'll help keep your spreadsheets error free.

✦   ✦   ✦

Excel Power Programming

I f you've ever written a worksheet formula, you're already a
programmer of sorts, so don't think VBA is beyond you.
When you get used to working in the Visual Basic Editor
instead of directly on your worksheets, you're likely to find
that writing VBA code is actually easier than writing
formulas — you can spread out in an editing window and add
explanatory comments to your code. But VBA also offers the
power to create customized, spreadsheet-based applications
that perform feats of calculation and automatic formatting
that almost no one could achieve without it. Just be sure to
ground yourself in the VBA fundamentals (covered in Part XI)
before you get too ambitious with the monster Excel-coding
techniques presented here.

Navigating the Excel Object Model

Before you start writing VBA code for Excel, you may find that
reviewing a few essential concepts can save you some work:

✦ **The Object Model of programming:** The Excel Object
Model defines the available objects and collections that
you (as an Excel/VBA developer) can use to extend the
functionality of your Excel application. Most objects in
the Excel Object Model include objects with associated
collections. The name of a `Collection` object is usually
the plural form of the object associated with it. (For
example, the `Dialogs` Collection is an object that holds
a collection of `Dialog` objects; and the `Shapes`
Collection holds `Shape` objects.)

✦ **The Excel hierarchy of objects:** All Excel objects are subordinate to the Application object, and also to each other in specific instances; a collection may, for example, "own" collections of other objects (as the Windows collection "owns" — that is, holds — a collection of Window objects).

As shown in Figure 30-1, the Application object resides at the top of the hierarchy; it represents the functionality of the entire Excel program. Below the Application object are all Excel objects. Note that the figure shows the Object Model in a generalized form: Some objects have a parent object, as when Object A is the parent of Object A1. Other objects — such as Object B — are part of a collection. The remaining objects are children of the Application object — but they are not parents of other objects, nor are they part of a collection. For example, Object C is a child of the Application object, but it is not part of a collection, nor is it a parent of another object.

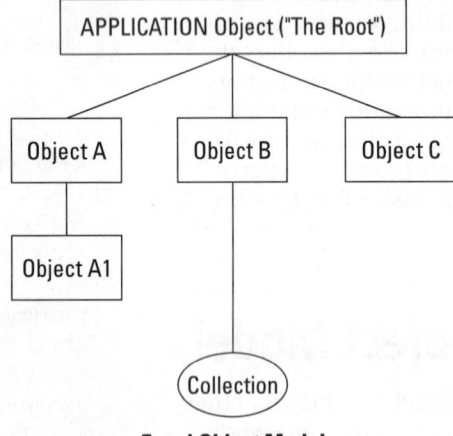

Excel Object Model

Figure 30-1: Exploring the generic Excel Object Model

Table 30-1 lists the different Excel objects, their associated collections, and their parent object(s) wherever applicable. Remember: Not all Excel objects belong to collections.

Table 30-1
Excel Objects and Collections

Object	Collection	Description	Parent
AddIn	AddIns	AddIn object represents an Add-in shown in the Excel Add-Ins dialog box.	
	Areas	Holds a collection of Range objects.	Range
Adjustments		Holds a collection of numbers used to move the adjustment handles of the parent Shape object.	Shape
Application		Root object of the model. All other objects may be accessed only through this object.	
AutoCorrect		Represents the entire functionality of Excel's AutoCorrect features.	
AutoFilter		Provides the functionality equivalent to the AutoFilter feature in Excel.	Worksheet
Axis	Axes	Each Axis object is equivalent to an axis in an Excel chart.	Chart
AxisTitle		Contains formatting and words associated with a chart axis title.	Axis
Border	Borders	Each Border object corresponds to a side or some sides of a border around a parent object.	Range, Style
CalloutFormat		Corresponds to the line callouts on shapes.	Shape
Characters		Allows access to individual characters in a string of text.	AxisTitle, ChartTitle, DataLabel, Range
Chart	Charts	Allows access to all attributes of a specific chart in Excel.	Workbook

Continued

Table 30-1 *(continued)*

Object	Collection	Description	Parent
ChartArea		Contains formatting options associated with a chart area.	Chart
ChartColorFormat		Describes a color of the parent ChartFillFormat object.	ChartFillFormat
ChartFillFormat		Represents the fill formatting associated with its parent object.	Chart
ChartGroup	ChartGroups	ChartGroup object includes all plotted points associated with a particular chart type.	
ChartObject	ChartObjects	ChartObject acts as a wrapper for embedded chart.	
ChartTitle		Contains all text and formatting associated with a chart's title.	Chart
ColorFormat		Describes a single color used by the parent object.	FillFormat, LineFormat, ShadowFormat, ThreeDFormat
Comment	Comments	Each Comment object represents a single cell comment.	Range
ConnectorFormat		Represents the connector line used between shapes.	Shape
ControlFormat		Contains properties and methods used to manipulate Excel controls such as text boxes and list boxes.	Shape
Corners		Represents the corners of a 3D chart.	Chart
CubeField	CubeFields	Each CubeField object represents a measure of hierarchy field from the OLAP cube.	PivotTable

Object	Collection	Description	Parent
CustomView	CustomViews	Each CustomView object holds the attributes associated with a workbook custom view.	Workbook
DataLabel	DataLabels	Each DataLabel object represents a single data label for a trendline or a point.	Series
DataTable		The DataTable object contains formatting options associated with a chart's data table.	Chart
DefaultWebOptions		Allows programmatic changes to items associated with the default settings of the Web Options dialog box.	
Dialog	Dialogs	Each Dialog object represents a single, built-in Excel dialog box.	
DisplayUnitLabel		The DisplayUnitLabel object contains all text and formatting associated with the label used for units on axes in charts.	Axis
DownBars		The DownBars object contains formatting options for down bars in a chart.	ChartGroup
DropLines		The DropLines object contains formatting options for drop lines in chart.	ChartGroup
ErrorBars		The ErrorBars object contains formatting options for error bars in a chart.	SeriesCollection
FillFormat		The FillFormat object represents the fill effects available for shapes.	Shape
Filter	Filters	Each Filter object defines a single filter for a single column in an AutoFiltered range.	AutoFilter
Floor		The Floor object contains formatting options for the floor area of a 3D chart.	Chart

Continued

Table 30-1 *(continued)*

Object	Collection	Description	Parent
Font		The Font object contains all formatting attributes related to fonts of the parent including font type, size, and color.	AxisTitle, Characters, ChartArea, ChartTitle, DataLabel, Legend, LegendEntry, Range, Style, TickLabels
FormatCondition	FormatConditions	Each FormatCondition object represents some formatting that will be applied if the condition is met.	Range
FreeformBuilder		The FreeformBuilder object is used by the parent Shape object to create new freehand shapes.	Shape
GridLines		The GridLines object contains formatting properties associated with the major and minor gridlines on a chart's axes.	Axis
	GroupShapes	The GroupShapes collection holds all shapes that make up a grouped shape.	Shape
	HiLoLines	The HiLoLines object contains formatting attributes for a chart's high-low lines.	ChartGroup
HPageBreak	HPageBreaks	Each HPageBreak object represents a single horizontal page break for the printable area of the parent object.	Worksheet, Chart
Hyperlink	Hyperlinks	Each Hyperlink object represents a single hyperlink in a worksheet or range.	

Object	Collection	Description	Parent
Interior		The Interior object contains the formatting options associated with the inside area of the parent object.	AxisTitle, ChartArea, ChartObject, ChartTitle, DataLabel, DownBars, Floor, FormatCondition, Legend, LegendKey, OLEObject, PlotArea, Point, Range, Series, Style, Upbars, Walls, ChartObjects, DataLabels, OLEObjects
LeaderLines		The LeaderLines object contains the formatting attributes associated with a chart's *leader lines* (which connect data labels to actual points).	Series
Legend		The Legend object contains the formatting options and legend entries for a particular chart.	Chart
LegendEntry	LegendEntries	Each LegendEntry object represents a single entry in a legend.	Legend
LegendKey		The LegendKey object contains properties and methods to manipulate the formatting of legend key entries.	Legend
LineFormat		The LineFormat object represents the formatting associated with the line of the parent Shape object.	Shape
LinkFormat		The LinkFormat object represents the linking attributes associated with an OLE object or picture.	
Mailer		The Mailer object is used on the Macintosh to mail Excel files by using the PowerTalk mailer.	

Continued

Table 30-1 (continued)

Object	Collection	Description	Parent
Name	Names	Each Name object describes a range of cells in a workbook that may be accessed by a specified name.	Workbook, Application, Worksheet
ODBCError	ODBCErrors	Each ODBCError object contains information describing an error that occurred on the most recent query using an ODBC connection.	
OLEDBError	OLEDBErrors	Each OLEDBError object contains information describing an error that occurred on the most recent query using an OLE DB provider.	
OLEFormat		The OLEFormat object represents all attributes associated with an OLE object or ActiveX object for linking.	Shape
OLEObject	OLEObjects	An OLEObject represents an ActiveX control, a linked OLE object, or an embedded OLE object on a worksheet or chart.	
Outline		The Outline object represents the outline feature in Excel.	Worksheet
PageSetup		The PageSetup object contains the functionality of the Page Setup dialog box.	Chart, Worksheet
Pane	Panes	A Pane object is equivalent to single pane of a window.	Window
Parameter	Parameters	Each Parameter object represents a single parameter for a query table.	QueryTable
Phonetic	Phonetics	The Phonetic object represents a single phonetic text string.	Range

Object	Collection	Description	Parent
PictureFormat		The PictureFormat object allows manipulation of the picture properties belonging to the parent Shape object.	Shape
PivotCache	PivotCaches	Each PivotCache object represents a single memory cache for a PivotTable report.	Workbook
PivotField	PivotFields	Each PivotField object represents single field in a single PivotTable report.	PivotTable
	CalculatedFields	The CalculatedFields collection holds the collection of calculated fields associated with the parent PivotTable report.	PivotTable
PivotFormula	PivotFormulas	Each PivotFormula object represents a formula being used in a PivotTable report.	PivotTable
	PivotItems	The PivotItems collection holds all the individual data entries in a field.	PivotField
	CalculatedItems	The CalculatedItems collection holds all individual calculated entries in a field.	PivotField
PivotLayout		The PivotLayout object describes how the fields of a PivotChart are placed in the parent chart.	Chart, ChartGroup
PivotTable	PivotTables	Each PivotTable object in the collection allows manipulation and creation of Excel PivotTables.	Worksheet
PlotArea		The PlotArea object contains the formatting options associated with the plot area of the parent chart.	Chart
Point	Points	A Point object describes the particular point of a series on a chart.	Series

Continued

Table 30-1 *(continued)*

Object	Collection	Description	Parent
PublishObject	PublishObjects	Each PublishObject object contains items from a workbook that have been saved to a Web page; their values may need occasional refreshing on the Web page side.	Workbook
QueryTable	QueryTables	Each QueryTable object represents a single table in a worksheet filled with data from an external data source.	Worksheet
Range		Because it corresponds to a range of cells, the Range object is one of the most versatile objects in Excel.	Worksheet
RecentFile	RecentFiles	Each RecentFile object represents one of the recently modified files.	
RoutingSlip		The RoutingSlip object represents the properties and methods of the routing slip of an Excel document.	Workbook
Scenario	Scenarios	Each Scenario object represents a single scenario in a worksheet.	Worksheet
Series	SeriesCollection	Each Series object contains a collection of points associated with a chart group in a chart.	ChartGroup
SeriesLines		The SeriesLines object provides access to the series lines that connect data values from each series.	ChartGroup
ShadowFormat		The ShadowFormat object allows manipulation of the shadow-formatting properties of a parent Shape object.	Shape

Object	Collection	Description	Parent
Shape	Shapes	The Shape object represents an individual shape, such as an AutoShape, freeform shape, OLE object (for example, an image), ActiveX control, or other picture.	Worksheet, Chart
ShapeNode	ShapeNodes	The ShapeNode object specifies a single node or curved segment that makes up a freeform shape.	
	ShapeRange	The ShapeRange collection holds a specified group of Shape objects for a certain range or selection in a document.	Range, Selection
	Sheets	The Sheets collection contains all sheets in the parent workbook.	Workbook
Style	Styles	The Style object represents formatting attributes associated with the parent object.	Range, Workbook
TextEffectFormat		The TextEffectFormat object contains all properties and methods associated with WordArt objects.	Shape
TextFrame		The TextFrame object contains the properties and methods that can manipulate text frame shapes.	Shape, ShapeRange
ThreeDFormat		The ThreeDFormat object contains all three-dimensional formatting properties of the parent Shape object.	Shape
TickLabels		The TickLabels object contains the formatting options associated with the tick-mark labels for the tick marks on a chart axis.	Axis

Continued

Table 30-1 *(continued)*

Object	Collection	Description	Parent
TreeviewControl		The TreeviewControl object allows manipulation of the hierarchical member selection of a cube field.	CubeField
Trendline	Trendlines	The Trendline object describes a trendline in a chart of a particular series.	Series
UpBars		The UpBars object contains formatting options for up bars on a chart.	ChartGroup
Validation		The Validation object contains the properties and methods that represent validation for a range in a worksheet.	Range
VPageBreak	VPageBreaks	The VPageBreak object represents a single vertical page break for the printable area of the parent object.	Worksheet, Chart
Walls		The Walls object contains formatting options for all the walls of a 3D chart.	Chart
WebOptions		The WebOptions object contains attributes associated with opening or saving Web pages.	Workbook
Window	Windows	Each Window object represents a single Excel window; it also contains scrollbars and gridlines for the window.	Application, Workbook
Workbook	Workbooks	A Workbook object represents a single workbook.	Application
Worksheet	Worksheets	The Worksheet object allows access to all attributes of a specific worksheet in Excel.	Workbook
WorksheetFunction		The WorksheetFunction object contains all Excel worksheet functions.	Application

Using the Application object's properties

At the top of the hierarchy sits the `Application` object, representing the functionality of the whole Excel program. This object occupies a privileged position, and with good reason: The `Application` object can affect how any object under its dominion works — and you can use that power to advantage in your VBA programming.

Take, for example, speed. Many Excel VBA programs run faster if you turn off screen updating (the default setting displays every change made to your workbook as your VBA code runs). Though useful for tracking down errors, screen updating can be a drag on performance while your program is actually doing the work you created it to do. Use the `Application` object's `ScreenUpdating` property to shut off this behavior with the following statement:

```
Application.ScreenUpdating = False
```

It's considered good form to set the `ScreenUpdating` property back to `True` at the end of the procedure.

> **Tip**
>
> Restoring the properties of Excel objects to their default values is always a good programming practice. This practice helps avoid unexpected behavior of Excel; by following it, you don't risk disturbing the functionality of Excel.

When you set the `ScreenUpdating` property, you must name the `Application` object explicitly in your code. Generally, however, you can use the `Application` object's properties directly, without having to name the object they come from. For example, the `ActiveSheet` property of the `Application` object refers to the worksheet or chart sheet that's currently active (in the currently active workbook, of course). To refer to this sheet in your code, you can simply use `ActiveSheet` rather than `Application.ActiveSheet`.

The `Workbooks` collection of the `Application` object contains all the workbooks currently open. Use a workbook's name in parentheses to identify a specific workbook you want to refer to. The following example activates a workbook called `Consolidated toy statistics.xls`:

```
Workbooks("Consolidated toy statistics.xls").Activate
```

Individual worksheets are also objects in their own right, of course. They belong to the `Worksheets` collection and must be specified as such. The expression `Worksheets("Sheet3")` refers to the sheet named `Sheet3`. Similarly, a chart housed in its own separate sheet has an individual `Chart` object that is a member of the `Charts` collection. Refer to that object via an expression such as `Charts("Parts Chart")`. (Coding to embed charts in worksheets is another matter, and beyond the scope of this book.)

Using individual Window objects

`Window` objects offer access to the screen appearance of your workbooks (and sometimes to their contents). When you see a window on-screen, it also serves as a `Window` object (a member of the `Windows` collection, which belongs to the `Application` object). You can refer to a window (that is, a `Window` object) by referring to the file name of the workbook it contains — simply specify that file name as an index into the `Windows` collection, as shown here:

```
Windows("Toy Sales Trends.xls")
```

 Note   The Windows collection refers only to Window objects of Excel.

If more than one window is open for the workbook, type a colon and the window's number after the workbook name, as in `Windows("Toy Sales Trends.xls:2")`.

Working with Cells in Code Using Range Objects

Surprising fact: Excel doesn't have a Cell object (the `Cells` property, mentioned later in this section, is not an object). So remember this basic coding principle: To refer to one or more cells in your VBA code, use the `Range` object. In Excel, a `Range` object can encompass one or more cells — and can even include more than one noncontiguous area of the sheet.

As a source of capabilities for a VBA program, Excel's `Range` object has similarities to Word's object of the same name. As in Word, for example, a VBA program can refer to as many `Range` objects as needed. You're not confined to working with the user's visible selection, and you don't have to select an area before you can act on it in code. At this point, however, the Excel version of the `Range` object starts to show significant differences that are tailored to the needs of a spreadsheet.

Specifying a Range object

When you want your code to act on one or more cells, Excel provides eight different methods you can use to identify those cells as a range:

✦ **Standard cell references.** So-called *A1-style cell references* are probably the easiest way to get started with `Range` objects. To specify a range, enclose the reference in quotation marks and parentheses; then put it immediately after the `Range` keyword, as in these examples:

```
ActiveSheet.Range("B3")
Worksheets("Sheet2").Range("M5:S20")
```

✦ **Named ranges.** If your worksheet contains named ranges, you can base VBA Range objects on them, as shown here:

```
Worksheets("Budget Summary").Range("Interest payments")
```

To name a range in your code, set the range's Name property with a statement such as:

```
Range("A3:B4").Name = "SalePrices"
```

✦ **Shortcut notation.** Range objects are used frequently enough that Excel lets you omit the Range keyword when you specify a Range object (whether with A1 notation or by name). To use this trick, place the cell reference or range name in square brackets, as in these examples:

```
ActiveSheet["A1:Z26"]
["Quarterly subtotals"]
```

✦ **The Cells property of a Worksheet object.** This technique is important to master because it's the best way to define a range by variables rather than by fixed cell addresses. The basic idea is to list the row and column coordinates of the range numerically. (See "Using the Cells property to define a range" later in this chapter.)

✦ **The Selection property.** Use the Selection property when your code needs to work with the range that corresponds to the user's selection. (See "Working with selections," later in this chapter.)

✦ **The ActiveCell property.** Use the ActiveCell property to access the range that represents the active cell of a given window. If you use ActiveCell as a property of the Application object (or without any object qualifier), the ActiveCell property refers to the active window. The following code snippet illustrates such use:

```
ValueStorageBin = ActiveCell.Value
```

✦ **The Rows or Columns property of a Worksheet object.** You can access a range that encompasses an entire row or column via the Rows or Columns property of the worksheet (that is, of its Worksheet object). Simply use the index number of the target row or column (you can't address columns by their letter designation). The following example defines a range covering column E, the fifth column:

```
Workbooks("IOU.xls").Worksheets("Sheet Shootout").Columns(5)
```

✦ **Object references you define.** Because a range is an object, you can set a named object reference to it and then access the range by using the reference's name. This technique is faster and easier than repeatedly specifying the original range. After setting an object reference to a name such as RanGer (as shown in the following example), you can then use its properties in expressions such as RanGer.Value. Here's the code fragment:

```
Dim RanGer As Range
Set RanGer = Worksheets("Sheet1").Range("B12:H13")
```

Using the Cells property to define a range

Used without coordinates, the `Cells` property of a `Worksheet` object refers to a range that encompasses all the cells of that worksheet. Similarly, the `Cells` property of the `Application` object (`Application.Cells`) refers to all the cells of whatever worksheet is currently active.

If you want to hone in on a more localized range, the `Cells` property requires that you specify row and column coordinates numerically, rather than using a letter name for the column. The following example refers to a range encompassing cell E3:

```
Worksheets("Old news").Cells(3,5)
```

Looks a little weird, doesn't it? The second value in the cell reference refers to the column number (5, because E is the fifth column); what's really confusing is that the row coordinate (3) comes first — it's just the opposite of A1 notation. Because this system is counterintuitive, you should probably avoid it unless you need its special virtue. Yes, it has one: Because both coordinates are numeric, they're easy to specify with variables. Variable coordinates allow your program to decide — as it runs — where the target range is, basing its decision on typed user input, calculations, or the like. The following example selects a row according to a familiar variable, the current month of the year:

```
CurrentMonth = Month(Now())
aGoal = Worksheets("Monthly Projections").Cells(CurrentMonth, 8)
```

The syntax required to refer to a range that covers more than one cell is shown in this example:

```
Worksheets("Sheet1").Range(Cells(3, 5), Cells(3, 6))
```

Acting on cells en masse

You can change a characteristic of an entire range in a single step by using the properties of the range. The following line of code, for example, changes the font size for all the cells in a range:

```
Worksheets("Sheet1").Range("B12:H13").Font.Size = 14
```

Of course, you can (and should) use `With` structures when you want to work with several properties or methods that apply to the entire range, as shown here:

```
With someRange  ' a previously defined object reference
    .Value = 20 ' sets the value of all the cells to 20
    .Font.Name = "Garamond"
    .Font.Italic = True
    .Locked = True
    someRangeName = .Name ' store the range name
End With
```

Acting on individual cells in a range

Although you can use one statement to assign a single value to all cells in a range (as in the preceding example), Excel provides no one-step method for modifying existing values in a multicell range. A statement such as *someRange.Value = someRange.Value + 10* won't work. Instead, you must cycle through all the cells in the range individually, using a For Each...Next loop. With this technique, you don't need to know how many cells the range contains. The following code does the work:

```
For Each aCell In Selection
    aCell.Value = aCell.Value + 10
Next
```

Often you need to examine the individual cells in a range before deciding whether or how to act upon them. Based on the current value of the cell, your code may decide to change the cell format, change the value itself, or use the value in some other computation. Again, use a For Each...Next loop. Here's an example:

```
For Each aCell In Worksheets("Sheet2").Range("A5:B10")
    If IsNumeric(aCell) Then
        Select Case aCell
            Case 5 To 10
                aCell.Font.Underline = xlUnderlineStyleSingle
            Case 10 To 20
                aCell.Font.Italic = True
            Case Is > 20
                aCell.Font.Bold = True
        End Select
    End If
Next
```

Working with selections

Before editing or formatting worksheet cells in Excel, a user must select one or more of those cells. In VBA, however, selecting cells isn't necessary; you can use Range objects to identify the cells you want to work with. Even so, VBA does provide selection-related tools for two reasons: so your code can tell which cells the user has selected, and so your code can show the user where something important is happening on the worksheet.

Identifying the current selection

Often custom code must act like most of Excel's built-in commands when it affects cells the user has selected. To access the range corresponding to the user's selection, use the Selection property of the Application object or a Window object. The Application object's Selection property returns the range that represents whatever the user has selected on the active worksheet. The following two statements, for example, are equivalent:

```
Application.Selection.Value = 20
Selection.Value = 20
```

> **Note**   Generally, however, you may use the `Application` object's properties directly, without having to name the object they come from. For example, the `ActiveSheet` property of the `Application` object refers to the worksheet or chart sheet that's currently active (in the currently active workbook, of course). To refer to this sheet in your code, you may simply use `ActiveSheet` rather than `Application.ActiveSheet`.

Use a window's `Selection` property to ensure that you always refer to the object selected on that particular window, regardless of which window is currently active. The following example demonstrates this technique; it also shows how you can set an object reference to the range representing the current selection (so you can reuse the same range later):

```
Dim SelRange As Range
Set SelRange = Windows("Toy Inventory.xls").Selection
With SelRange
    .CheckSpelling
    .AutoFit
    .Copy
End With
```

Selecting a range

When your VBA program makes a change to the worksheet that you want the user to notice, use the `Select` method to move the selection to that range, chart, or what have you. The `Select` method applies to just about any worksheet object available in Excel — it's available for `Chart` objects and all their components (each part of a chart is also a separate VBA object); for `Shape` (drawing) objects; and, of course, for `Range` objects.

To select a range, you must first activate its worksheet; then use the `Select` method for the `Range` object, as shown in this example:

```
With Worksheets("Love Statistics")
    .Activate
    .Range("BrokenHearts").Select
End With
```

By the way, the `Select` method for `Worksheet` objects apparently does nothing more than activate the specified worksheet and doesn't change the existing selection there. In other words, it's equivalent to the worksheet's `Activate` method. Similarly, you can use the `Activate` or `Select` methods to activate a chart sheet, but neither method actually selects the chart. Here's an example:

```
Charts("Customer Demographics").Select
```

To select chart components or embedded charts, use the `Select` method on the object in question.

Activating a specific cell

To set the active cell for user input, use the `Activate` method of the `Range` object corresponding to that cell. If the activated cell is in the current selection, the entire range remains selected. The following example works that way:

```
Worksheets("DoNothingTillYouHearFromMe").Activate
Range("A1:E7").Select
Range("C4").Activate
```

If the activated cell is outside of the selection, the selection moves to the new active cell.

Determining the selection type

Code designed to work on selected cells is likely to fail if you try to apply it to a chart instead. That's why before doing anything with a selected object you should check to make sure the current selection contains exactly the type of object that the code expects. Use VBA's `TypeName` function to return a string containing the object type of the selection. You can use this string in `If...Then` or `Case Select` structures to decide what (if anything) to do with the selected object, as in the following example:

```
With Selection
Select Case TypeName(Selection)
    Case "Range"
        .Value = 2001
    Case "ChartArea"
        .Interior.ColorIndex = 3 ' 3 = bright red
    Case "Nothing"
        MsgBox "Nothing is selected"
    Case Else
        MsgBox "I refuse to recognize this selection type!"
End Select
End With
```

Programming Custom Worksheet Functions

You should consider working in VBA even if Excel's built-in data-analysis tools seem to meet all your needs. The reason: With VBA, you can create custom worksheet functions that have big advantages over formulas you type directly into cells.

Custom functions enable you to carry out calculations (and other operations) that extend beyond the capabilities of formulas based on built-in Excel functions. Even if you did write a formula to get the same results, a custom function has major benefits: It's easier to write, easier to test, and easier to understand later on. Instead of struggling in the cramped confines of the formula bar, you have the entire code window to work with; you can break up complex logical operations into separate lines of code. Equally important, you can (and should) put explanatory comments right next to the code they pertain to.

Writing custom worksheet functions

Custom Excel functions are simply ordinary VBA function procedures. All the details on function procedures and their syntax laid out in Chapter 53 apply. In brief, a function procedure begins with a declaration of its name and ends with an End Function statement. Somewhere in-between, you need a statement that assigns a value to the function's name; that is the value that the function returns. A trivial example can show these rudiments:

```
Function MemoryAvailable()
    MemoryAvailable = Application.MemoryFree
End Function
```

This function simply returns the current amount of memory (in bytes) that's available to Excel. Note that the function takes no arguments; it merely retrieves the quantity of available memory from your system. Here's another (slightly more complex) Excel function that does take arguments:

```
Function CheckForValue(aRange, Value)
    For Each objCell In aRange
        CheckForValue = False ' default return value is False
        If objCell.Value = Value Then
            CheckForValue = True
            Exit For
        End If
    Next objCell
End Function
```

This function checks a range of cells for a specific value. If the value is present anywhere in the range, the function returns True; if not, it comes back False. When you trigger this function, you must supply two arguments: the range of cells and the value you want to look for.

Running custom functions

One way to run custom functions, of course, is the regular VBA way: by calling them from in a Sub procedure. That technique is covered in Chapter 53.

To insert the return value from a custom function into a worksheet, use your function just as you would one of the built-in Excel functions: Type the function's name in a cell after an equal sign. After the name, type a pair of parentheses, adding

inside them any arguments you want to use with the function. You need the parentheses even if there are no arguments, as in this example:

```
=MemoryAvailable()
```

As with built-in Excel functions, a custom function can be part of a more complex
cell formula, as in these simple examples:

```
=MemoryAvailable() & " bytes are now available"
=If(CheckForValue(B8:B18,C8)),"Value found","Value not found")
```

Using the Formula palette with custom functions

What's really cool is that the Formula palette recognizes custom functions. If you
don't remember what arguments your function requires (or whether it takes any
arguments), no matter — the Formula palette shows you exactly what's required
(see Figure 30-2).

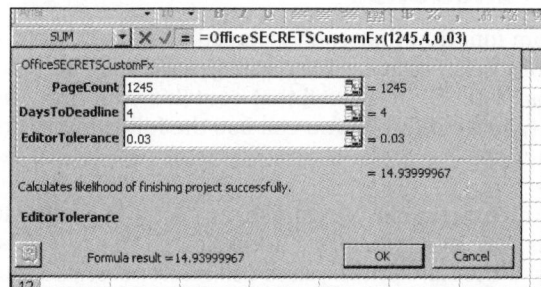

Figure 30-2: Using the Formula palette to enter
the arguments for a custom function

Tip   To edit functions within formulas, use the Formula Palette. To display this Palette,
choose a cell that contains a formula and click Edit Formula. The palette displays
the first function in the formula, along with each of its arguments. You may edit
the first function (or edit another function in the same formula) by clicking in the
formula bar anywhere within the function.

If you don't remember the name of your custom function, choose More Functions
from the drop-down Functions list. In the resulting Paste Function dialog box,
choose User Defined at the bottom of the Function category list. You can then
select from among the available custom functions.

You can add a description of your custom function that appears in the Paste
Function dialog box when the function is selected. To create the description,
choose Tools ➪ Macros and type the function name in the Macro Name box (functions don't appear in the macro list). Now click Options and enter a description of
the function in the appropriate field.

Accessing custom functions in other workbooks

If the custom function you want to use is stored in the current workbook, you only need to type its name in your cell formulas. To use a function stored in a different open workbook, precede the function name with the workbook's name and an exclamation point, as in this example:

```
=SECRETfunctions.xls!TopSecretFunction(C4:D6,M9)
```

To access functions stored in a workbook that isn't open (or that might not be open the next time you need what's in it), set up a VBA reference to the workbook. Choose Tools ➪ References. If the workbook isn't already listed in the resulting dialog box, click Browse to locate it; then add it to the list. If the box beside the workbook isn't already checked, check it to activate the reference. You can then use the functions it contains by name only, without having to specify the workbook they come from.

Testing your custom functions

When an error occurs in a custom function that you've placed in a worksheet formula, you don't get the benefit of VBA's normal error messages. Instead, all you see is a vague error message such as #VALUE! in the cell that contains your function. When you're building a custom function in VBA, you can use the following tricks to help you test and debug the function:

✦ **Pretest.** Before you place the function into a worksheet, test it by calling it from a Sub procedure. This way, you gain direct access to VBA's error messages and debugging tools. If the function requires cell references, you must use the Range object when you call the function, as in this example:

```
Sub FxTester()
    ReturnVal = CheckForValue(Range("B8:B13"), Range("C8"))
    MsgBox ReturnVal
End Sub
```

✦ **Set a breakpoint.** With the function in a worksheet formula, set a breakpoint in the function's code in the Visual Basic Editor. Then your function runs whenever Excel recalculates the worksheet. As soon as VBA reaches the line of code that has the breakpoint, you're taken into the Editor, ready to debug.

Fancier functions

Don't hesitate to write functions that give you exactly the output you want — why leave anything to a formula when you can do all the work in the function itself? For example, the following modification of the CheckForValue function (presented earlier in "Writing custom worksheet functions") returns an explanatory text string rather than merely True or False:

```
Function CheckForValue2(aRange, Value)
For Each objCell In aRange
```

```
      CheckForValue2 = "Search value " & Value & " not found"
      If objCell.Value = Value Then
         CheckForValue2 = "Search value " & Value & _
            " found in Cell " & objCell.Address
            Exit For
      End If
   Next objCell
   End Function
```

If the modified function finds the target value anywhere in the range, it returns a string such as Search value 3.57 found in Cell $F$83; if not, it comes back saying Search value 3.57 not found.

Using Built-in Functions in Your Code

Whether you're writing a custom function or a Sub procedure, don't be bashful about calling on the wealth of calculating and data analysis power offered by Excel's built-in functions. Using them in your own code is simple: You just call them as methods of the WorksheetFunction object. For example, suppose you're writing a procedure that makes a calculation based on an average of the values in a worksheet range. To obtain the average, you would use code similar to the following:

```
OnAverage = WorksheetFunction.Average(Range("B8:B13"))
```

Some of Excel's built-in functions are off limits to VBA. These are the functions that duplicate VBA's own built-in functions (which are introduced in Chapter 53).

Programming for Excel Events

Writing code for events often assumes a more important role in Excel than it does in the other Office applications. That's because a spreadsheet's whole mission involves responding to changes made by the user. Changing the value of a single cell can produce ripple effects throughout an entire workbook as Excel recalculates dependent formulas and charts. As a VBA programmer, you can intercept the events (such as the changing of the value of a single cell) that drive this process to enhance and supplement Excel's built-in responses.

Choosing the right object

Before you start writing event code, one of your first considerations is to decide which object should respond to the event. Four Excel objects recognize events: charts, individual worksheets, workbooks, and the entire Excel application. If you want to write code that responds to events that affect a specific chart, your code belongs in that Chart object's event procedures. For events that occur in response to worksheet changes, however, you have choices to make.

Although some Excel events are recognized only by a particular object, many are passed up the object hierarchy from the Worksheet object to the Workbook and Application objects. For example, a change occurring on a worksheet triggers the Worksheet object's Change event, which in turn triggers the SheetChange event for both the Workbook object and the Application object. With this arrangement in mind, you must decide whether your code belongs in the event procedure for the worksheet, the workbook, or the application. The choice shouldn't be too difficult:

✦ If you want the code to run only in response to changes occurring on a single worksheet, it belongs in that worksheet's event procedure.

✦ If you want your procedure to run when a change happens to any worksheet in a particular workbook, put the code in the workbook's event procedure.

✦ If your code should be active throughout all open workbooks, it belongs in the application's event procedure.

Starting an event procedure

The fundamental technique for writing an event procedure for one of Excel's objects is no different from writing event code for a VBA form or control. Chapter 56 has the details, but the basic steps are the following:

1. Display the code window for the object.

2. Select the object by name from the Object drop-down list at the top left of the code window.

3. Select the event for which you want to write code from the Procedure drop-down list at the top right of the code window. When you do, the skeleton for your chosen event procedure appears in the window.

Aside from writing the code itself, the only tricky part can be to bring up the object's code window in the first place (Step 1). For Worksheet and Workbook objects (and for Chart objects that occupy separate sheets), you face no special challenges: Just select the object in the Project Explorer and click the View Code button. Objects appear by their names, which you can change in the Properties window.

The situation is more challenging when it comes to charts that are embedded in worksheets (or in the Excel Application object). You must write special class modules to make these objects available in the Project Explorer. Details on how to do this are beyond the scope of this book, but you can find them in the Help system.

Reacting to worksheet changes

If your goal is to make things happen as the user interacts with the worksheet moment by moment, the tools you need are the Change, Calculate, and SelectionChange events (for Worksheet objects) and the corresponding

SheetChange, SheetCalculate, and SheetSelectionChange events (for Workbook and Application objects). To fire custom procedures when worksheets themselves or charts are activated or deactivated, use the Activate and Deactivate events.

The Change and SheetChange events

The Change and SheetChange events are triggered every time the value of any cell or cells change via a user action or the updating of a link. Changes in calculated values don't trigger the event, however. The corresponding event procedures let you zero in on the specific cells whose value has changed. The following example checks the changed values — which are contained in the range called Target — to see whether they fall within a specified range. If they do, they receive highlighting — a large, bold, green font:

```
Private Sub Worksheet_Change(ByVal Target As Range)
    For Each oCell In Target
        If oCell > 4 And oCell < 11 Then
            With oCell.Font
                .Bold = True
                .Size = 16
                .Color = RGB(0, 255, 0) ' green
            End With
        End If
    Next oCell
End Sub
```

Note that Target can include more than one cell — it's a range, after all — because operations such as filling, clearing, and pasting can be performed on more than one cell at a time. For this reason, your Change event procedure should include a For Each...Next structure whenever you want it to act on the contents of an individual cell or cells, as shown in the preceding example.

Actually, the Change and SheetChange events may fire even if a value doesn't change. These events are bound to occur when the user starts editing a cell (by clicking in the formula bar or pressing F2), even if the user stops the edit without making any changes (by pressing Enter, clicking the Enter check button, or clicking the worksheet). The events don't fire if the user abandons the edit by pressing Esc or clicking the Cancel button.

The Calculate and SheetCalculate events

The Calculate event, recognized by both Worksheet and Chart objects, happens whenever Excel updates a worksheet or chart. The SheetCalculate event for the Workbook and Application objects occurs in response. If automatic calculation is on, these events fire immediately when any cell value changes — meaning that they occur in tandem with the Change event. When you switch to manual calculation, the Calculate events occur only when the user presses F9 to initiate the recalculation.

Use event procedures for the `Calculate` and `SheetCalculate` events to modify the worksheet according to the results of a calculation. For example, if you know that recalculation may change the items in a sorted list, you might want the `Worksheet_Calculate` event procedure to resort the list following the calculation. These event procedures don't tell you which cells changed after a calculation; you must specify, as part of your code, the addresses of the cells you want to change.

The SelectionChange and SheetSelectionChange events

Excel registers a `SelectionChange` event for the worksheet every time the active cell moves or a selection expands or contracts. Parallel `SheetSelectionChange` events also occur for the `Workbook` and `Application` objects. You can use the event procedures for these events to provide feedback about the current selection. In the following simple example, the `SelectionChange` event is used to display the address of the active cell in the current worksheet's top-left cell, and to show the worksheet's name (along with the selection's address) in the status bar. Note how the `Sh` argument enables you to identify and work with the current worksheet:

```
Private Sub Workbook_SheetSelectionChange(ByVal Sh As Object, _
    ByVal Target As Excel.Range)
        Sh.Range("A1") = ActiveCell.Address
        Application.StatusBar = Sh.Name & ":" & Target.Address
End Sub
```

Getting a little fancier, you might instead have a selection change trigger some response (say, displaying a custom dialog box) only if the new selection encompasses a specified cell or range. The following example shows what the code would look like:

```
Private Sub Worksheet_SelectionChange(ByVal Target As
Excel.Range)
    If Target.Address = "$B$2" Then
        MsgBox "You found the SECRETS cell!"
    End If
End Sub
```

Programming dynamic charts

Because Excel's `Chart` objects recognize a multitude of events, many of them mouse-related, you can think of them as big ActiveX controls parked in your workbooks. Charts recognize the `Activate`, `Deactivate`, and `Calculate` events. Other chart events you can write code for include the following:

✦ `DragOver` and `DragPlot`. These occur when cells are (respectively) dragged over a chart embedded in a worksheet, and when they are dropped onto the chart.

✦ MouseDown, MouseUp, and MouseMove. These occur in response to mouse actions.

✦ Select. This occurs when any part of the chart is selected. Your code can determine the type of element and the specific element that was selected, and respond accordingly.

✦ SeriesChange. This occurs when the user changes a value on the chart by manipulating the chart itself (rather than by changing the underlying value in the worksheet).

✦   ✦   ✦

Communicating and Organizing with Outlook

O utlook is used primarily to create, send, receive, and manage e-mail, but it's also a powerful productivity tool. This part gives the message-management side of Outlook full coverage, but also examines how it keeps track of contacts (and makes them available for use in other programs) and how it helps you manage your appointments, meetings, and events.

Outlook Overview

Outlook is a productivity enhancement and information-management tool for both personal and workgroup use. Outlook gives you features aplenty for keeping track of your own e-mail messages, appointments, meetings, tasks, and contacts. It enables you to store and recall random facts, too, and can even substitute for Explorer as a disk- and file-management utility.

Because most people work in groups, Outlook is designed from the ground up to facilitate information exchange and group collaboration throughout an organization. Outlook lets managers assign tasks and schedule meetings and appointments for members of the workgroup and then monitor meeting attendance and task completion.

As the *client* (individual user) portion of Microsoft's groupware solution, Outlook is at its most powerful when used in conjunction with Exchange Server. But if your organization doesn't run Exchange, don't let that stop you from using Outlook—some of the more arcane networking features will be unavailable, but you can still tap a wealth of information-management power.

Though Outlook delivers plenty of power right out of the box, you're not locked into the stock forms supplied with the product. With its extensive customization features, you can build a productivity command center tailored to your information management needs. If the options on the toolbars aren't enough, Outlook's Visual Basic interface lets you put its resources to work in custom applications using the techniques covered in Part XI.

> **Note** Even before you install Office, you may be familiar with Outlook Express. Outlook Express is the basic message management software that comes with Windows. While it shares similarities with Outlook, particularly in the way it handles e-mail, it doesn't have all the other productivity tools that make Outlook such a powerful program.

Getting Started with Outlook

Outlook's e-mail and groupware features rely on the messaging capabilities built into Windows. If you go with Outlook's Internet Only configuration, or if you don't use Outlook for e-mail at all, setting up the program is straightforward. If you're working on a network with the Corporate or Workgroup configuration, you must choose or set up a user profile, a collection of settings that defines the way Windows messaging applications function. For one thing, the user profile specifies where (that is, using which information services) the program stores and retrieves data.

If you have previously set up a user profile for Exchange or a previous version of Outlook, Outlook 2002 uses it automatically. If not, a wizard leads you through the process of creating a new profile. To use Outlook successfully, you must configure your user profile properly. Because understanding and configuring user profiles and information services is challenging, I discuss the necessary steps in detail in Chapter 32. If you're anxious to get started with Outlook, it's okay to accept the default profile configuration choices that the wizard suggests for now.

Customizing Outlook

In common with the other Office applications, Outlook places most of its customizing settings on the Tools ➪ Options dialog box and enables you to customize its menus and toolbars.

Using the Tools ➪ Options dialog box

As shown in Figure 31-1, the Outlook 2002 version of this dialog box has plenty of controls to help you set up Outlook just the way you want it.

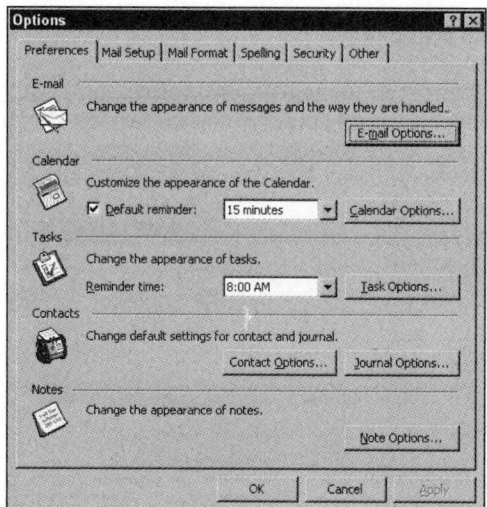

Figure 31-1: The Preferences tab in Outlook's
Tools ⇨ Options dialog box

Your choices in the Options dialog box occupy six separate tabs, as follows:

✦ **Preferences:** This tab offers basic settings controlling the look of Outlook
items and includes options governing contact and journal items.

✦ **Mail Setup and Mail Format:** The settings on these tabs pertain mostly to
e-mail and are covered in Chapter 32.

✦ **Spelling:** Options governing Outlook's spell checker reside on this tab. See
"Spell Checking in Outlook," later in this chapter, for details.

✦ **Security:** This tab has controls that can help protect you and your organization from unauthorized access to mail and sensitive data.

✦ **Other:** Though burdened with an uninspired name, this tab houses some key
Outlook settings. Take special note of the Advanced Options button — many
of the settings in the dialog box it produces are useful.

Customizing Outlook toolbars

Outlook lets you add and remove toolbars at will using the same techniques you
use in the other Office applications. The simplest way is to right-click any toolbar to
display a shortcut menu. You can select any other toolbar you want to display or
hide. To customize the toolbars themselves, use the methods common throughout
Office (see Chapter 5).

Working with Outlook Folders

Right out of the starting gate, Outlook is set to manage your information with its collection of built-in folders. Access the contents of individual folders by clicking their icons in the Outlook bar on the left of the screen, shown in Figure 31-2.

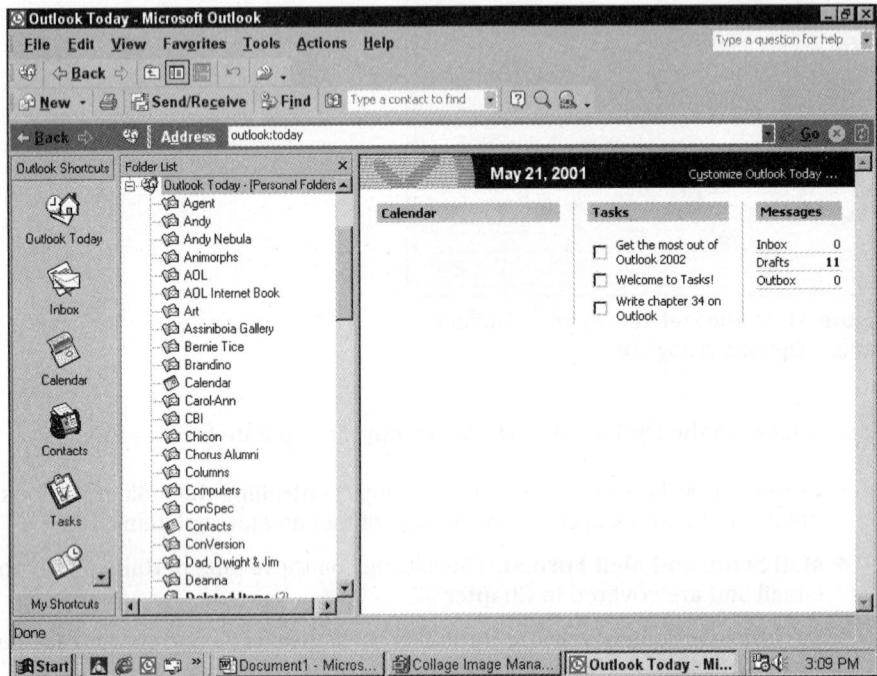

Figure 31-2: The Outlook window, showing the Outlook bar on the left with large icons and the Outlook Today folder

Although you can add folders of your own at any time, Outlook's default folders include the following:

✦ **Outlook Today:** Strictly speaking, the top Outlook folder isn't a folder at all, but a panel that collects important information from multiple folders.

✦ **Inbox, Outbox, and Sent Items:** These folders list e-mail messages you've received, written, and already sent, respectively. Only the Inbox folder appears by default in the Outlook Shortcuts group, the primary group on the Outlook bar (see "Working with Outlook bar groups," later in this chapter).

✦ **Calendar:** As initially configured, this folder displays events scheduled for the day, a small monthly calendar for access to other days, and a To Do list.

✦ **Contacts:** This is your little black book. This folder collects names, addresses, and other critical information about the important people in your world. You can have Outlook dial any number or send mail to any e-mail address listed in a contact.

✦ **Tasks:** This folder displays tasks you have defined for yourself or that have been assigned by the powers that be. You can change the priority of any task on the list or double-click it to obtain or modify details.

✦ **Journal:** This folder records activities of all types. You can use it to track interactions with your contacts or to keep a record of which Office documents you open and when, all automatically.

✦ **Notes:** This folder stores random notes. From here, you can post individual notes on your screen in their own windows as electronic sticky notes.

✦ **Deleted Items:** Outlook moves items deleted from all other folders here, where you can retrieve them until you empty this folder. See "Outlook Housekeeping Secrets," later in this chapter, for details on using the Deleted Items folder.

If you have been using Exchange for e-mail, the corresponding Inbox and Outbox folders in Outlook contain messages you've previously composed, sent, and received. Otherwise, these folders are empty when you first start Outlook, except for a message or two from Microsoft.

Note   The Outlook folders do *not* correspond to folders on your hard disk, and their contents are not individual files. Instead, Outlook stores all of your information in one gigantic mailbox file specified in the properties for your Personal Folders information service.

Selecting a folder

The quickest way to get around the Outlook folders is to simply click an icon in the Outlook bar, and—boom!—up pops the corresponding folder. Depending on factors such as your screen resolution and the Outlook window size, the default folder icons may not all fit in the Outlook bar. Use the arrow buttons at the top and bottom to scroll the bar. To squeeze in more icons, right-click in the bar and choose Small Icons from the shortcut menu. To widen or (more likely) narrow the Outlook bar, drag the divider separating the Outlook bar and the main part of the screen.

To turn the Outlook bar off, choose Hide Outlook Bar from its shortcut menu. With the Outlook bar hidden, you can use one of two other options to select and display folders:

✦ Choose View ➪ Go To, and click on the folder you want.

✦ Click the Folder List button on the Advanced toolbar button (or choose View ➪ Folder List) to display the Folder list.

Once you've switched to at least one other folder, you can use the Back and Forward arrow buttons on the Advanced toolbar to retrace your steps in either direction, just as you would move among Web pages you've visited in your browser.

 **Tip**

If you right-click a folder in the Outlook bar or the Folder list, you can choose Open in New Window on the shortcut menu to display the folder in a separate Outlook window. Unlike the Outlook bar, where you can control which folders are displayed and how they're grouped, the Folder lists and the View menu both display all the Outlook folders.

If you'd like to always start in a particular folder, you can arrange that, too. Choose Tools ➪ Options and select the Other tab; then click Advanced Options. Choose the folder in which you'd like Outlook to start from the Startup in this folder list box.

Creating new folders

To create a new Outlook folder, choose File ➪ New ➪ Folder. In the Create New Folder dialog box, select the level in the folder hierarchy where the new folder should go using the folder list at the bottom of the dialog box. Use the "Folder contains" drop-down list to specify the type of Outlook folder you want — contacts, calendar, mail items, and so on.

Using Outlook Today

The Outlook Today "page" is a simple but effective summary view of your daily activities. It lists the appointments and tasks you've scheduled, displays an inventory of your mail folders, and lets you look up names in your Contacts folder quickly. Figure 31-3 shows Outlook Today in action.

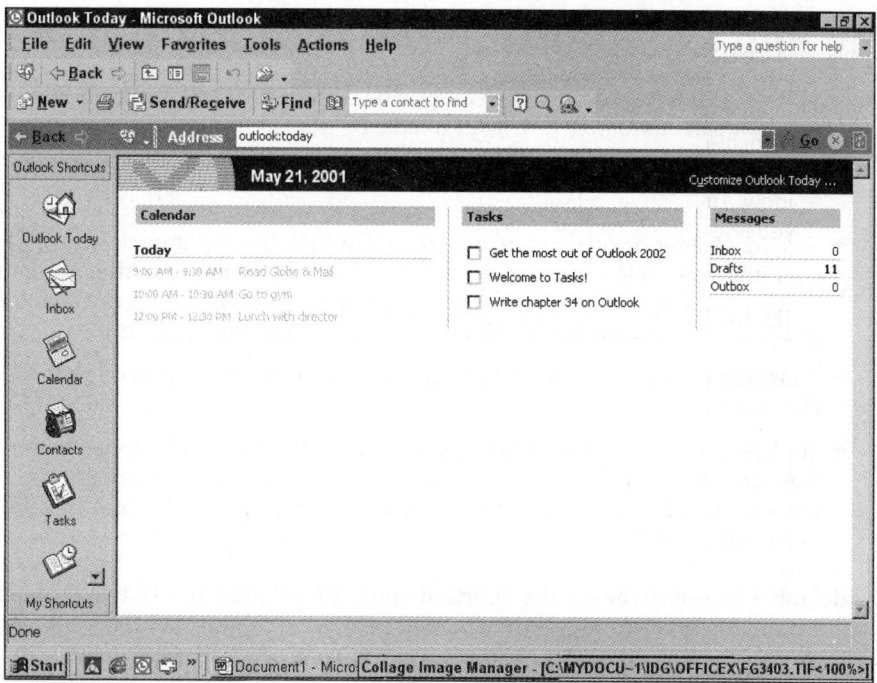

Figure 31-3: Outlook Today lets you see the challenges that face you today at a glance.

Because Outlook Today is designed for ease and simplicity, I don't need to say much about it. Keep in mind these few points:

✦ Outlook Today works like a browser. To view an item listed on the page, just click it once. Clicking a calendar or task item displays the item details in a separate window. Clicking a heading such as Calendar or Tasks displays the corresponding folder.

✦ Contacts aren't listed in Outlook Today, but you can still look them up: Type a portion of the person's name in the Find a Contact box that appears in the Standard toolbar. When you press Enter, Outlook displays the matching contact in a separate window. If more than one contact matches your request, you see instead a box listing all the matches — from which you can choose the correct one.

✦ You control Outlook Today's behavior by clicking Customize Outlook Today. The resulting page has a box you can check to ensure that Outlook Today is the first thing you see whenever you start the program. Other options govern what you see in each of the three main headings (Messages, Calendar, and Tasks) and Outlook Today's style — that is, its overall look.

Using and Customizing the Outlook Bar

Once you've gotten the hang of the Outlook bar—which should take about a minute—you can customize it to your needs. By adding, moving, or removing shortcuts for folders and other items, you can create an environment that fits your personal information management needs:

✦ To add a folder or other shortcut to the Outlook bar, right-click over the bar (but not over an icon) and choose Outlook Bar Shortcut. Use the "Look in" list in the resulting dialog box to display Outlook's special folders or the folders available on your system (including network-accessible folders).

✦ Reorganize shortcut icons by dragging them to new positions on the Outlook bar.

✦ To delete any unwanted shortcuts, right-click the icon and choose Remove from Outlook Bar. You're deleting the icon from the Outlook bar, not the underlying folder or other item, and you can restore the shortcut by adding it again any time.

By default, Outlook arranges the shortcuts on the Outlook bar into two groups: Outlook and My Shortcuts. As you would expect, though, you can reorganize the filing system, creating, renaming, or deleting groups as need or whimsy dictates.

The Outlook bar includes a button for each group at the top or bottom of the bar. To view the shortcuts of a different group, just click the corresponding button. Note that by default, the only mail-related shortcut in the Outlook group is Inbox. Switch to the My Shortcuts group by clicking its button to display all the folders associated with your e-mail messages, including Inbox (again), Outbox, and Sent Items.

To add a new group, right-click the Outlook bar and choose Add New Group. Outlook adds a button for the group below the existing ones. After naming the new group, click its button to display the empty group (Outlook slides all the other group buttons to the top or bottom of the Outlook bar). You can now add Outlook bar shortcuts to the new group.

To remove a group from the Outlook bar, right-click a group button and choose Remove Group. Or, with the doomed group active, right-click an empty area of the Outlook bar, again choosing Remove Group. You can rename a group by choosing Rename Group from its shortcut menu.

Working with Views

When you open an Outlook folder, the program presents the information it contains in one of many possible views available for the folder. A view defines the way

Outlook displays the information in a folder. You can change the view at any time, modify existing views, or create new ones of your own.

The Outlook Calendar's standard view is the Day/Week/Month view. When you switch to the Calendar folder, notice that separate sections of the window display appointments, a monthly calendar (the Date Navigator, which in the maximized Outlook window actually shows two months), and a list of tasks (the TaskPad, located in the lower-right corner). The Day/Week/Month view has several viewing options of its own. To see a week's or month's worth of appointments at once, choose Week or Month from the View menu, or click the corresponding toolbar buttons. Figure 31-4 shows the Calendar folder in the Week view.

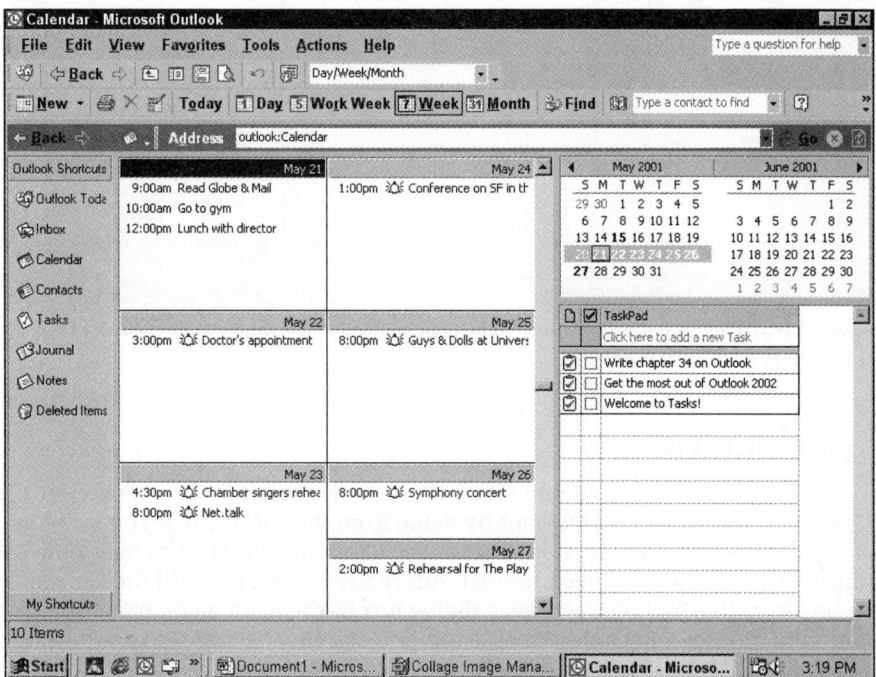

Figure 31-4: The Calendar folder's Week view, one of the options for a Day/Week/ Month view

This view provides a pretty fair time-management tool. You can see details of your schedule and To Do list, while the two-month calendar alerts you to all days with scheduled events and appointments by displaying them in bold type. However, my main point is that this is only one way to look at your date-related information. Figure 31-5 shows the same information in the Month view, which displays a larger calendar.

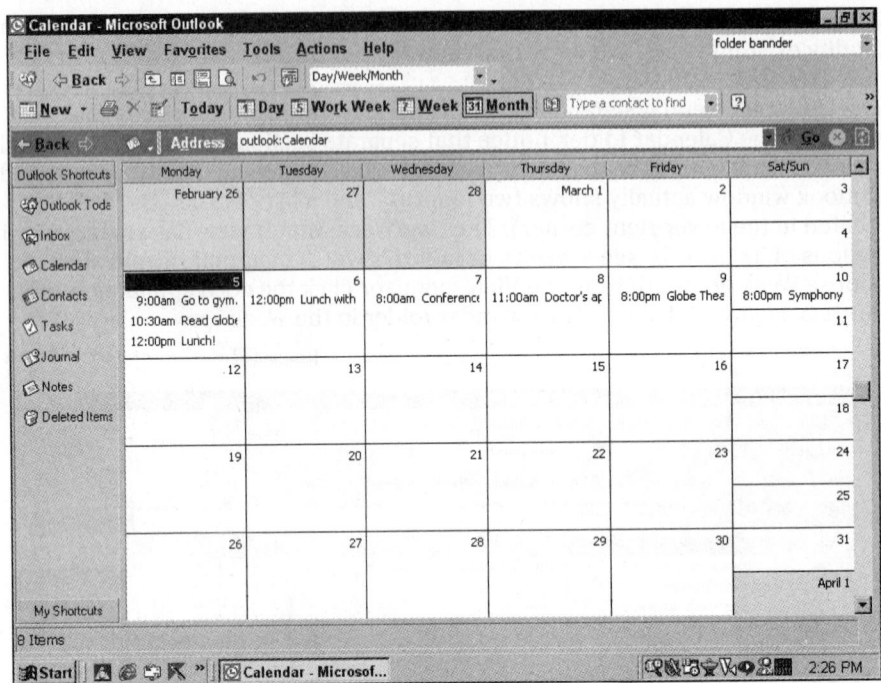

Figure 31-5: Here's the same information displayed in Week view in Figure 31-4, shown here in Month view.

Switching views

To switch between the available views for the current folder, choose View ➪ Current View and select the view you want by name from the submenu. If you frequently alternate between different views, get in the habit of using the Current View list button — it's on the Advanced toolbar. Alternatively, you can add the Current View list box from the Tools ➪ Customize dialog box to the main menu bar. You can add or modify the views in each available folder using the techniques laid down in "Customizing Views," later in this chapter.

Figure 31-6 shows one more view; this time I selected the Active Appointments view for the Calendar folder. The window now displays details about future appointments in tabular form. This view can help you locate an appointment quickly, without bothering to search in your monthly, weekly, or daily calendar.

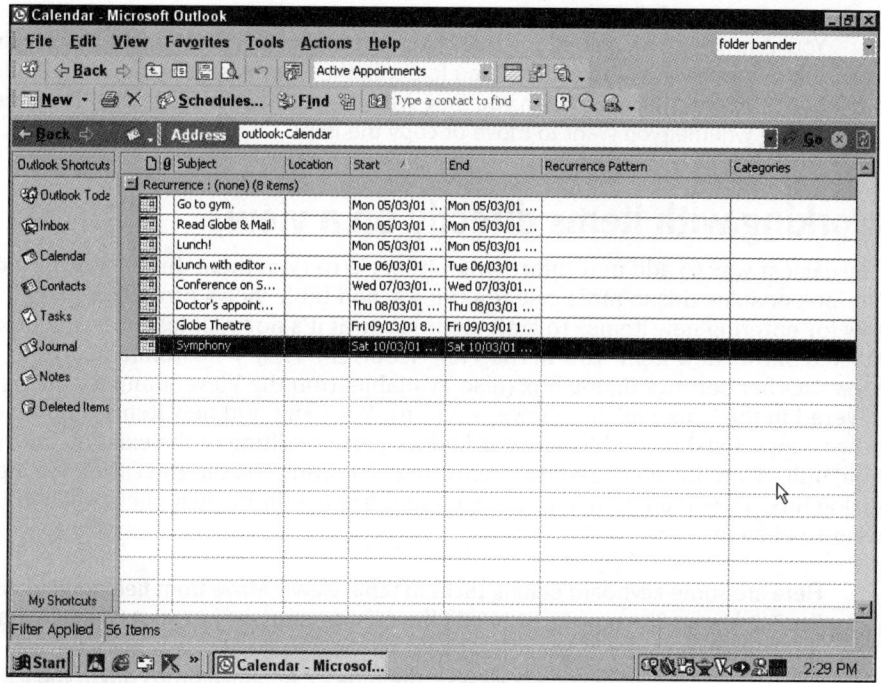

Figure 31-6: The Calendar, now showing Active Appointments view

Types of Outlook views

Probably the most commonly used Outlook views are table views. They display information in tabular form, organized with items in the rows and specific fields of information in the columns.

But Outlook offers four other view types. You've already crossed paths with Day/Week/Month views, which show items by date and time on a calendar. Timeline views also present chronological information, but along a horizontally scrolling bar. Card views show information about each item in a rectangular block rather than a row. Icon views are the simplest type; they only show an icon for each item in the view. A view's name usually doesn't tell you which type of view it is — you have to display the view to see. You can change the view type for any view, as detailed in "Customizing Views," later in this chapter.

Adding and Editing Information Items

Outlook lets you enter or edit individual items of information — mail messages, contacts, tasks, and so on — either by typing directly into a view or by opening a separate form for that specific item.

Tip   You can move or copy information items between Outlook folders by dragging them from a view to the destination folder in the Folder list. Dragging with the left button moves the item. When you drag with the right button, you get a little menu asking whether you want to move or copy the item.

Working with items directly on a view

The easiest way to add new information items is to type them directly into a view. Outlook enables this in most calendar views, and table views provide a special top row for entering new items. To activate this row if it's not visible, check the box labeled Show "new item" row in the View ⇨ Current View ⇨ Customize Current View ⇨ Other Settings dialog box (also available from the View Summary dialog box covered in the "Customizing Views" section). You can't add new items directly on other views. Calendar, table, and card views permit editing of the existing informa- tion, unless you have cleared the "Allow in-cell editing" box in the Other Settings dialog box. To edit an item in any view that permits editing, just click the field you want to change.

Tip   Here are some keyboard editing tricks in table views: Move from field to field with the Tab key and then press F2 to edit the existing entry, or just start typing to erase the current contents. If you're in a field offering several preset choices—such as the Flag Status field in contact views—pressing F2 or Space drops down the list of choices. You can then use the Up and Down arrow keys to make your selection. Use Space to check or clear checkboxes.

Some fields can't be edited at all. However, if you can't type in *any* field, go to the Other Settings dialog box (View ⇨ Current View ⇨ Customize Current View ⇨ Other Settings). There, check the "Allow in-cell editing" box. However, you can't directly edit Notes in any view, even if you turn on in-cell editing.

Deleting items from a view

To delete an item by moving it to the Deleted Items folder, highlight it and click the Delete button (the one with the artistic X), press Ctrl+D, or drag the item to the Deleted Items folder. Depending on the view you're working in, the Del key alone may or may not perform the same chore. You can delete any item listed in a view permanently, without moving it to the Deleted Items folder, by highlighting it and pressing Shift+Del.

Entering and editing items on forms

Although entering new items in the main Outlook window is convenient, Outlook doesn't permit it in all views. Besides, space is cramped and you have access only to a subset of the available fields. To add a new information item no matter what view you're using, enter it on a form designed for that purpose. You have many choices for starting new items, but the fastest way is to press Ctrl+N, which opens the default item form for the current folder. (Some folders let you add variations on the standard item type. In the Calendar folder, for example, you add appointments, or events, and meeting requests on different — if very similar — forms.) Other methods for adding new items via forms include these:

✦ Click the New button at the far left of the toolbar. Clicking the main part of this button opens a new default item form. To add an item to another folder, click the right portion of the button, the thin bar with the arrow — this drops down a menu of all item types.

✦ Choose New from a view's shortcut menu or from the menu specific to the open folder (such as Journal, Calendar, or what have you) to open a new default item form. If the folder permits more than one item type, the menu lists those alternatives, too.

✦ Choose File ➪ New and select any item type from the submenu.

To edit an existing item on a form, double-click it, or select it and press Ctrl+O or Enter.

Working with forms

The supplied forms for entering and editing information items are clearly organized, and I'm sure you can figure out how to fill them in without my help. Just be aware that most forms have two or more tabbed pages, and you may find just the right basket for a particular detail on one of the pages that isn't showing when you first open the form. Of course, Outlook's form designers couldn't think of everything. If you need to add special fields for the information you require, you can customize the existing forms or create your own from scratch (see "Customizing Forms," later in this chapter).

Assigning categories to items

Categories are keywords that can help you organize information you store in Outlook. You can use them to help you find, sort, filter, or group items in any folder.

Categories can help you get over your anxiety about keeping similar yet distinct groups of items in the same folder. For example, instead of creating separate folders for personal and business contacts, you can place both in your main Contacts folder and then create two distinct views filtered by category to display them separately.

To assign a category to an item visible in a view, right-click the item and choose Categories from its shortcut menu. You can add and delete Outlook categories using the Master Category list, accessible from the Categories dialog box.

Customizing Views

Outlook doesn't just give you plenty of alternative prefab views; it lets you customize the existing views or develop your own views from scratch. The multitude of options may make your head swim, so ready your cranial flotation device.

Creating new and modified views

The rest of this section describes the specific techniques you can use to customize views. First, though, you should know that Outlook 2002 automatically saves any changes you make to a view. This leads me to a simple point: If you want to preserve the current view for later use, start with a new view before you begin your customizations.

Assuming you want to base your changes on the view you're currently using, the technique for creating a copy of the current view is as follows:

1. Choose View ➪ Current View ➪ Define Views to display the Define View dialog box, shown in Figure 31-7.

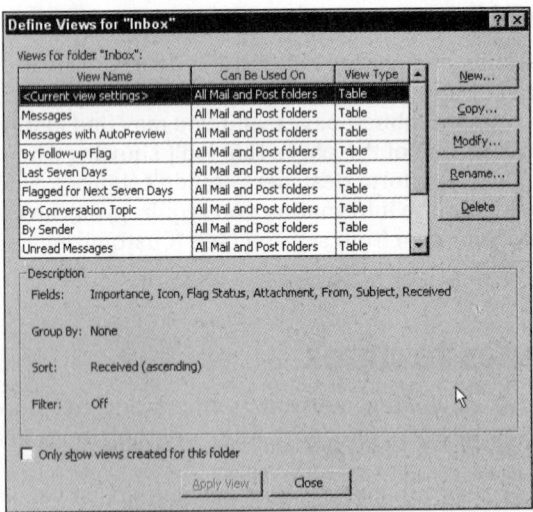

Figure 31-7: Use Outlook's Define Views dialog box to create, copy, and modify views.

2. Leave selected the top choice in the Views list, "Current view settings," and click Copy.

3. Outlook presents a little Copy View box asking you to name the copied view and designate where it will be available. Make your selections and click OK.

4. Outlook presents the View Summary dialog box for accessing all the controls pertaining to view layout and content. As discussed in the next section, this box gives you access to all of Outlook's view customizing commands. But if you want to use the copied view immediately, just click OK at this point to return to the Define Views box, and there click Apply View to activate the view.

After you've added a new view, it appears by name on the View ➪ Current View submenu.

If you want to start work on a custom view from scratch, open the Define Views dialog box and click New. In this case, you must select the type of view you want to build (see "Types of Outlook views," earlier in this chapter) in addition to choosing a name and specifying the view's availability.

Note   Once you've created a view, you can't change its type or where it can be used.

Defining views comprehensively

The View Summary dialog box, shown in Figure 31-8, is a master control panel for customizing views. You can display it:

✦ From the Define Views dialog box (refer back to Figure 31-7), by selecting a view and clicking Modify. This technique lets you customize any view.

✦ By choosing Views ➪ Current View ➪ Customize Current View.

The View Summary dialog box contains buttons that in turn display the dialog boxes for specific customizing functions, such as Group By, Sort, and Filter. However, you can perform many of these same functions more quickly with other techniques described in the relevant sections that follow.

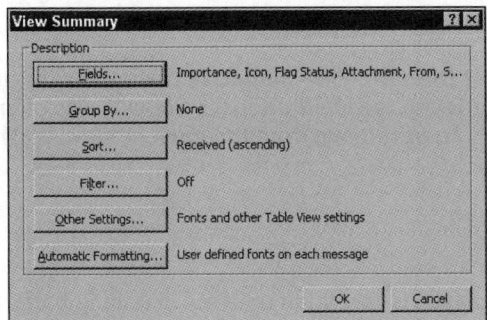

Figure 31-8: The View Summary dialog box is an access point for all functions governing views.

Adding and reorganizing fields in a view

Customizing the existing fields works much like customizing toolbars in the other Office applications. To move a field, drag it horizontally to a new location. To remove a field, drag it vertically until you see a big black X and then release the mouse button. To add a field, however, you need the Field Chooser, shown in Figure 31-9. Display it by choosing Field Chooser from the shortcut menu you get by right-clicking a column header, or by clicking the Field Chooser button on the Advanced toolbar.

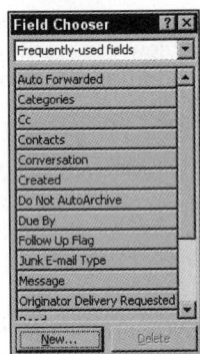

Figure 31-9: The Field Chooser dialog box

The Field Chooser provides a collection of buttons based on the existing fields in your Outlook folders. To add a field to the view, just drag its button from the Field Chooser to the desired location along the column heading area. You can use the drop-down list at the top of the dialog box to select the type of fields displayed.

The Field Chooser also gives you a fast way to add new fields to the folder represented in the view. Choose New, enter a name for the field, and specify its type and format. When you return to the Field Chooser, the new field shows up under the heading "User-defined fields in this folder." You can then add it to the view. In doing so, you make it part of the folder, available for use in other views and in custom forms.

The Show Fields dialog box (available from the View Summary dialog box discussed in the previous section) is an alternative to the Field Chooser. Show Fields offers a simple list of fields that you can copy to or remove from the current view. It also lets you reorder the view's fields.

Filtering a view

Filtering a view lets you limit the displayed information to items matching particular criteria. Click Filter in the View Summary dialog box to bring up the dialog box shown in Figure 31-10. The choices in the Filter dialog box depend partly on the folder that you're working with. In general, you can filter a view based on text present in one or more fields, or by people associated with the item (for example, those who have been invited to a meeting).

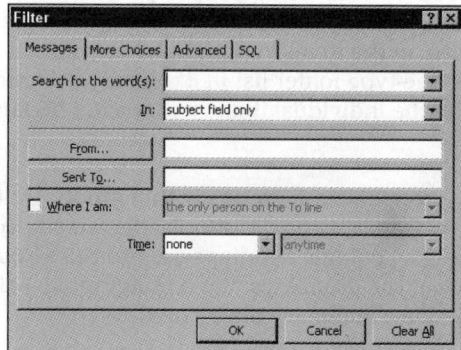

Figure 31-10: Use the Filter dialog box to focus in on items of particular interest in an Outlook view.

You can use additional filtering options based on the categories you can associate with items in Outlook (see "Assigning categories to items" earlier in this chapter). Switch to the More Choices tab and choose Categories to select from those available. This tab has miscellaneous filtering options that are often useful.

If you're still hungry for more filtering choices after that big meal, you're bound to reach satiety with the dessert offered on the Advanced tab. Here, you can build complex sets of filtering criteria using conditions for the contents of every field in Outlook individually.

To add a criterion for filtering, select the field from the submenus in Field and then choose appropriate conditions and values from the subsequent boxes. Appropriate conditions (and often values) for each field have been predefined, so you won't have to worry about writing these from scratch. Many of Outlook's stock views are based on advanced filters, and it may pay to start a custom filter by modifying what's already been done for you.

Sorting a view

To sort a view on any field, right-click the column heading for that field and choose Sort Ascending or Sort Descending. Quicker still, click the column heading for the field to sort it in ascending order, and click it again to reverse directions. Fancier sorts can be had using the Sort dialog box. Click Sort in the View Summary dialog box to display it. Here, you can select up to four separate fields for four separate sorting levels.

Grouping related items

To group related items together visually, group them by a field. When you right-click a column heading and choose Group by This Field, Outlook puts together an outline-like representation of the information. Each unique value from the chosen field is displayed as a main heading, with all the items containing that value grouped together beneath it. As with a tree-type folder list in Explorer (or Outlook, for that matter), you can display or hide the individual items under each heading by clicking its little +/– icon to the left.

For more complex groupings (showing groups within groups within groups), click in the column heading area and choose the Group By box. Outlook adds an empty area just above the items. You can now drag column headings up into this Group By box, arranging them in the order you want the groupings. For a nongraphical alternative, click the Group By button in the View Summary dialog box.

Formatting choices

Outlook's formatting tools for views are "satisfactory," I guess you might say. Although you can pick fonts and specify field alignment and field size options, don't expect to create fancy custom formats within a view.

The formatting options are grouped in various menu choices and dialog boxes. To control column size and alignment, right-click over the column headings and make your selections from the Best Fit and Alignment choices, or choose Format Columns to open a dialog box. To select fonts for the column headings and item details, click Other Settings in the View Summary dialog box.

Limitations on customizing views

View types vary regarding how many customization options they offer, but you always have some choices. In Day/Week/Month views, for example, you can switch between the daily, weekly, and monthly calendars, filter the items displayed, and specify the intervals for dividing your daily schedule.

Outlook Housekeeping Secrets

Although Outlook excels at organizing large amounts of information, the sheer volume of material you have to deal with can become overwhelming. You have to be able to find the particular information you need, when you need it. And one of your main tasks is to throw out the stuff you don't need on a regular basis, so that you can find the stuff you do need — and so that your hard disk doesn't become clogged with old e-mail you no longer need.

Using the Mailbox Cleanup command

One useful new feature in Outlook 2002 is the Mailbox Cleanup command. To access it, choose Tools ➪ Mailbox Cleanup. This opens the dialog box in Figure 31-11.

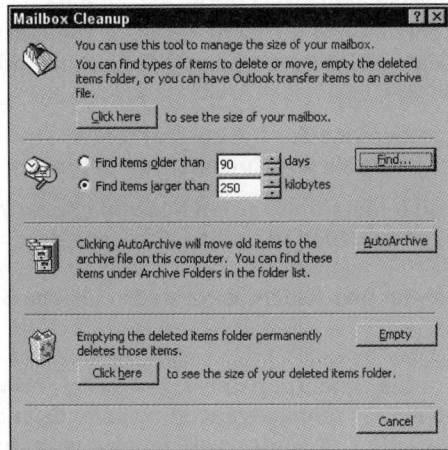

Figure 31-11: Mailbox Cleanup helps you keep your mailbox organized.

Mailbox Cleanup provides several useful tools. The button at the top of the dialog box lets you find out just how big your mailbox is getting — you may be shocked to see how much disk space it's taking up. If it's bigger than you expected, then you have added incentive to clean it up.

The Find button lets you track down items that are older than a certain number of days, or larger than a certain size. It can help you target old and overstuffed items for removal or archiving.

AutoArchive activates AutoArchiving (described later in this chapter), while the final section of the Mailbox Cleanup dialog box lets you see how big the collection of deleted items in your deleted items folder is getting, and empty it permanently if you wish.

Using the Organize command

Outlook's Organize command helps you locate information via visual cues and place related information in appropriate folders. Choose Tools ➪ Organize or click the Organize button to display a special pane above the items in the current folder. Here, you can click the various options listed on the left to display commands that make your information easier to work with. The options available depend on the type of folder you're working with. They include

- ✦ **Using Folders:** Enables you to move a selected item to another folder, presumably one where it better belongs.

- ✦ **Using Categories:** Enables you to assign categories to the selected items, and to create new categories. You can accomplish the same tasks via the Edit ➪ Categories command, or with the Categories item when you're editing individual information items.

- ✦ **Using Views:** Lets you switch to another view for the current folder. The Change Your View list is equivalent to the View ➪ Current View submenu.

- ✦ **Using Colors:** Available only for mail folders, this option lets you choose colors for mail items according to the people they're sent to or received from.

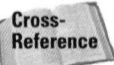

The Junk E-mail option, also exclusively for mail folders, is covered in Chapter 32.

Pay attention to the upper-right corner of the Organize pane as you switch between the options. It offers buttons that let you access more advanced commands and settings related to the option you're working with (the buttons are labeled with text only, not icons). To close the Organize pane, click the big X in the far upper-right corner of the pane or click the Organize button again.

Finding information

Outlook can search for information you want to locate in two main ways: the easy way, and the powerful way. For the easy way, click Tools ➪ Find or click the Find button on the Standard toolbar. A special pane appears at the top of the folder window offering a "Look for" box in which you type your search request and a "Search in" box offering you options for places to look. Click Find Now to begin your search.

When Outlook completes the Find operation, matching items appear in the folder window, though the view changes automatically as appropriate. When you're finished working with the search results, click Clear to return to the original view.

When you want more control over your search operations, click the Options button at the right end of the Find pane and choose Advanced Find, or if the Find pane isn't open, choose Tools ➪ Advanced Find. You can add the Advanced Find button to a toolbar from the Tools ➪ Customize dialog box, but if you want it to display an icon rather than text, you have to create your own picture for it (see Chapter 5).

The Advanced Find dialog box, shown in Figure 31-12, is a compact but sophisticated search tool. Type or select search criteria in the controls of any of the three tabs and then click Find Now to begin the search. The dialog box expands downward with a list of the items found by the search. You can double-click an item to open it in its own window.

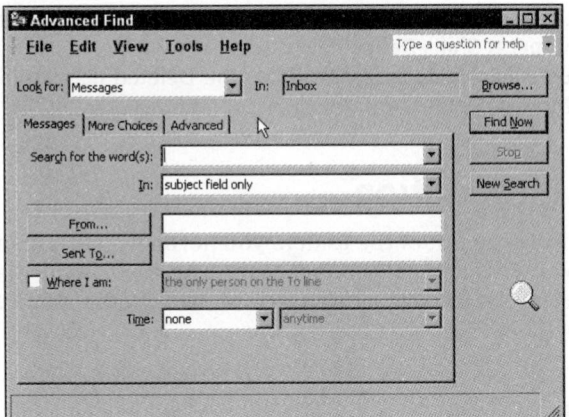

Figure 31-12: Use the Advanced Find dialog box to create complex Outlook searches.

I don't have space to detail how to use each of the myriad Advanced Find options individually, but you can figure them out with a few trial searches. The first tab provides the search choices most commonly used for the type of item you're working with. When you change the item type in the "Look for" box—"Any type of Outlook item" is one of the available types—the tab's title and fields change accordingly. The controls on the More Choices tab are a bit more stable, but not entirely—they change if you select Files in the "Look for" box. The Advanced tab lets you create search criteria based on any field associated with the items you're searching.

Tip

Outlook's Advanced Find dialog box offers an alternative to the search tools available in Windows and Office for locating files on disk or your network—and you don't have to run Outlook to use it. To search for files according to any combination of hordes of different characteristics, select Files in the "Look for" box. To activate Advanced Find when Outlook isn't open, click the Windows Start button and then choose Find ⇨ Using Microsoft Outlook.

Deleting items permanently

Remember that deleting an item moves it to the Deleted Items folder but doesn't actually erase the item altogether. To empty the Deleted Items folder manually, you have to choose Tools ⇨ Empty "Deleted Items" folder (or use the button in the Mailbox Cleanup dialog box described earlier).

To set Outlook so that it empties the folder automatically when you exit the program, check the appropriate box on the Other tab of the Tools ⇨ Options dialog box.

Tip   To delete an Outlook item permanently without moving it to the Deleted Items folder, select the item and press Shift+Del or hold down Shift while you click the Delete toolbar button. To retrieve a deleted item from the Deleted items folder, right-click it and choose Move to Folder from the shortcut menu.

Archiving Outlook information

Archiving means moving information out of the folders you normally use and into a special folder for storage. To archive manually, choose File ⇨ Archive. In the dialog box shown in Figure 31-13, select the folder you want to archive, choose a cutoff date, and select a destination file.

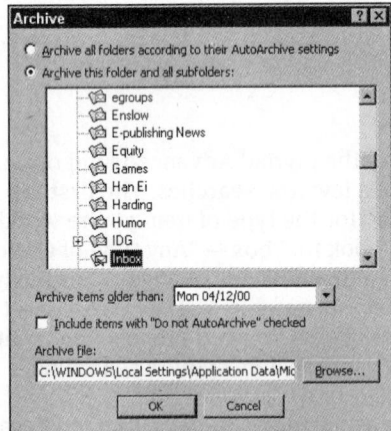

Figure 31-13: Archive outdated information using this dialog box.

It's often handy to let Outlook automatically do your archiving. To turn on AutoArchive, open the Tools ⇨ Options dialog box, switch to the Other tab, and click AutoArchive. Use the settings on the resulting AutoArchive dialog box to switch on the process, specify how often it takes place, and select a default archive file. You must then activate AutoArchive on a folder-by-folder basis. Open each folder in turn, using the AutoArchive tab on the File ⇨ Folder ⇨ Properties dialog box to tell Outlook how old items should be to be automatically archived.

Tip   As you delete unwanted items from your personal folders file, Outlook doesn't necessarily free up disk space accordingly. To reclaim at least some of this real estate, you must compact the file. To do so, choose View ⇨ Folder List so that the Folder list is visible. Right-click the very first item, Outlook Today, and choose

Properties for "Outlook Today" from the resulting shortcut menu. In the Personal Folders Properties dialog box, click Advanced, and in the subsidiary dialog box click Compact Now.

Spell Checking in Outlook

Outlook can check the spelling in any of your individual information items, including e-mail messages, appointments, contact entries, and tasks. However, only text in the body of the item, not in the individual fields, is checked.

Outlook uses the Office spell-checking engine, so the details spelled out in Chapter 8 apply as much here as in Excel or Access. Just be aware that you can only check spelling of a single Outlook item at a time, and only when that item is open in its own window. To check the spelling of an item, locate the item in its Outlook folder, double-click the item to open it, and then choose Tools ➪ Spelling from the item's own menu to start the check.

Customizing Forms

As you know, Outlook opens a distinct window, or form, for each information item you work with individually, be it an e-mail message, contact, meeting or appointment, task, or journal entry. If the forms supplied with Outlook don't meet your needs, customize them.

Opening a form for customizing

Use the following steps to ready a form for customization:

1. Open the existing form on which you want to base your custom version, just as if you were creating a new information item of that type.

2. On the form's menu, choose Tools ➪ Forms ➪ Design a Form. As shown in Figure 31-14, the form window now includes new menu items, toolbars, and tabs, as well as the Field Chooser window. You use all of these to shape your custom form.

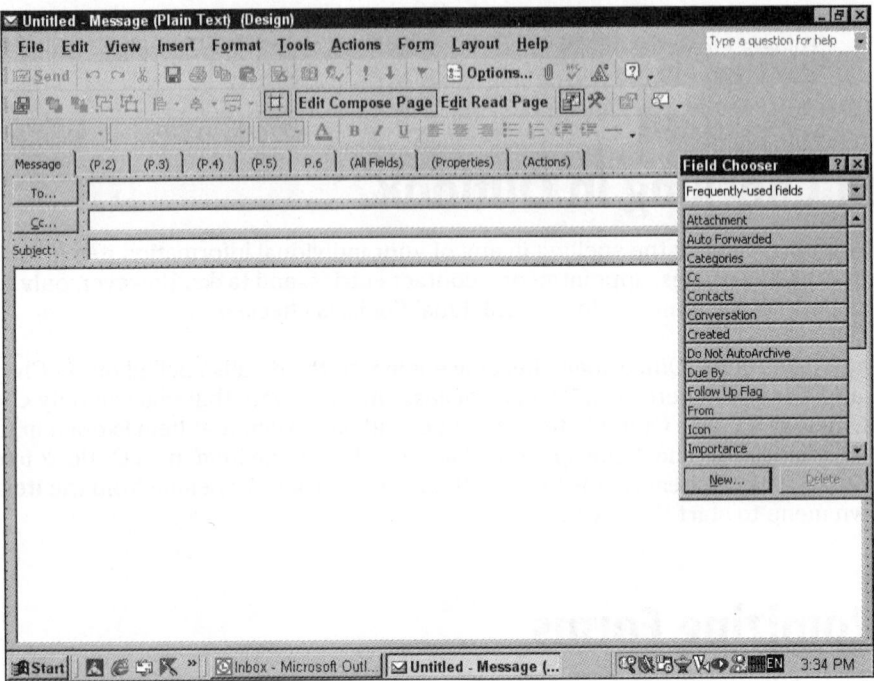

Figure 31-14: The standard New Message form is displayed ready to be customized in design mode.

Working with form pages in design mode

In addition to its standard, prefab pages, an Outlook form has five customizable pages (six for a message form). When you first open a form in design mode, the customizable pages are labeled P.2, P.3, and so on. These labels are in parentheses, indicating that the pages are hidden when you display the form for normal use in editing information. To add or modify the contents of a customizable page, start by displaying it (click the page's tab). Outlook displays the page as a blank grid on which you place new fields and buttons, and it shows the Field Chooser window from which you can drag the fields you want to display on the page.

Tip   You can't modify a form's prefab pages. However, you can create a custom form with a customizable page that duplicates the fields on the prefab tab, and then hide the prefab one.

One prefab page, All Fields, is common to all form types. This page gives an unobstructed view of all the available fields via a big table. For efficiency's sake, some users may prefer to enter information in the table instead of on the other, more elegantly designed pages. Note, though, that the All Fields page is hidden in most of the standard Outlook forms (you can tell because its name is in parentheses in design mode). If you want this page to appear in a form, you must display the page as described in "Displaying, hiding, and renaming pages" (coming up shortly), and then publish the custom form.

Working with special design mode pages

To the right of the tabs for the pages that actually appear on your form when it's in use are two additional pages exclusively for the design process. These are

✦ **Properties:** Use this page to define the custom form's properties. If you're creating lots of different forms, you can use the Category and Sub-Category fields to organize them hierarchically. The Contact field lets you add the name of the form's designer or anyone else that users of the form should contact if they have questions.

✦ **Actions:** This page enables you to add to the form a command that automatically opens another form, usually to reply or respond to the arrival of the form from another user. Use the New, Properties, and Delete buttons at the bottom of the page to add new, modify, and remove actions, respectively.

Displaying, hiding, and renaming pages

To hide or display a page in the normal view of the form (not while designing it), toggle the Form ➪ Display This Page command. When a page is hidden, its name appears in parentheses. To rename a page, choose Form ➪ Rename Page and type in the new name.

Adding fields and controls to a custom page

To add content to a custom page, drag fields from the Field Chooser onto the page. You can select from fields associated with items in the current folder, and from fields from other folders as well.

To add controls (radio buttons, checkboxes, combo boxes, and so on), display the Control Toolbox by choosing Form ➪ Control Toolbox or clicking the corresponding button, the one with the wrench and hammer. Chapter 56 explains how to write code to make controls do useful work, but in Outlook you must use VBScript rather than VBA for this purpose. To get started, select the control and choose Form ➪ View Code.

Just as in the Visual Basic Editor, you can use the toolbar buttons or Layout menu commands to align, group, and order the fields and controls you add. To modify characteristics of an individual field or control, right-click it and select Properties from the shortcut menu. Also on the shortcut menu, the Advanced Properties choice displays a list of properties in tabular form. You can leave the latter dialog box open while you select different items on the page.

Adding default information to a custom form

Information you type into the fields on a custom form will be saved with the form. If you want to supply yourself (or other Outlook users) with default content, just add it before saving the form.

Saving forms

Once you've customized a form, you're faced with a decision about how to save the new version. You have three choices:

✦ You can save it as an individual item in the corresponding Outlook folder.

✦ You can save it as a separate template or message file.

✦ You can save it in an Outlook forms library, which makes it easy to access from anywhere in Outlook.

These choices aren't mutually exclusive — you can save a custom form with all three methods if you feel the urge.

Saving a form as an information item

Whether or not you're working in design mode, a form's File ⇨ Save command saves the custom form as a single item in the Outlook folder associated with that form type. If you ever plan to use the custom form again, save it as a template or in a forms library, too.

Tip   Because plans change, there may come a time when you want to use a "one-time" custom form for a second item. The quickest way is to make a copy of the original item on a view. Use the Edit menu Copy and Paste commands or their keyboard equivalents, Ctrl+C and Ctrl+V. As detailed in the next section, you can't save a second copy of the same item using the File ⇨ Save As command.

Saving a form as a separate file

Use the Form's Save As command to save a form and any accompanying information in a separate file — not in one of the special Outlook folders — in one of four formats. As usual, you use the "Save as type" box to select the format you want in the Save As dialog box.

The first two of the available formats are plaintext and Rich Text, both of which are useful if you want to transfer the information in the form to someone who doesn't own Outlook or Exchange. To save the form itself as well as its contents in a separate file, save it as an Outlook template (.oft) or message (.msg) file. Outlook templates are covered briefly in "Using Outlook forms" later in the chapter. The message format is used by both Outlook and Exchange for storing information in separate files. Either are good formats in which to send someone else a copy of the form on a floppy disk when the recipient isn't on your network.

Saving a form in a forms library

Outlook provides two separate but equally effective ways to store custom forms for reuse: as templates — as just described — and in a forms library. These libraries house stockpiles of custom forms for your own use (in the personal library) or for use throughout an organization (in the organization library).

To store a custom form in a forms library, click the Publish Form button on the Forms toolbar. In the dialog box shown in Figure 31-15, Outlook asks you to supply a name for the new form (this is the name that will appear on its title bar, unless you've changed the Form caption on the form's Properties page).

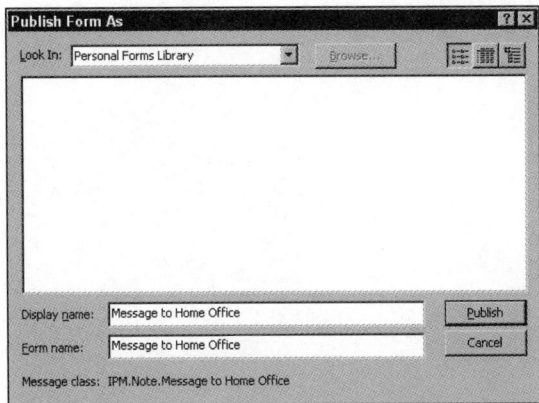

Figure 31-15: Store custom forms using the Publish Form As dialog box.

In addition, you must decide where the form should be stored by choosing "Look in":

✦ **Personal Forms library:** A choice in the Forms Library drop-down list, the Personal Forms library stores forms for your use only.

✦ **Organization Forms library:** This library resides on a network server and stores forms accessible throughout the organization. It's available in the "Look in" list only if your PC is on a network.

✦ **Outlook folders:** Select a specific Outlook folder in which to store the form. If you don't see the folder you want in the list, click Browse and locate it in the tree-type list that appears.

Note   The name you assign to a custom form appears in the form's title bar only after you save a new item based on the form. When you first create the item, Outlook displays only the name of the generic item type on which the custom form is based (note, message, contact, or what have you).

Using Outlook forms

To create a new Outlook item based on a custom form or template, choose File ⇨ New ⇨ Choose Form (or the equivalent command, Tools ⇨ Forms ⇨ Choose Form). When Outlook displays the Choose Form dialog box, use the "Look in" drop-down list to select from the available form libraries, Outlook folders, and template locations.

Forms stored as such are kept together in libraries, while templates are form designs stored in separate files with the .oft extension. Take a few minutes to see what, if any, prefab templates may be included with your software. Outlook supplies its templates in two forms: as Outlook (.oft) templates and as standard Word (.dot) templates.

✦   ✦   ✦

Managing Messages Efficiently

Although Outlook is many things, most people will come to know and love this powerhouse information-management software as an e-mail organizer. (Okay, so maybe you don't love software. Outlook will earn your respect, at least!)

Setting Up Outlook for E-Mail

Setting up Outlook for e-mail is straightforward, especially now that Outlook no longer has separate modes for Internet and Microsoft Exchange.

Your main task is to create and specify settings for at least one mail *account*. Each Outlook account corresponds to a particular e-mail address on a particular Internet server to which you connect via a particular method. If you have multiple e-mail addresses, or if you connect to your mail server over a LAN at some times but by modem at others, you can create as many Outlook accounts as you need.

Choose Tools ➪ E-mail Accounts to get to the E-mail Accounts dialog box, shown in Figure 32-1. As an alternative route to the same box, click the Accounts button on the Mail Delivery tab of the Tools ➪ Options dialog box.

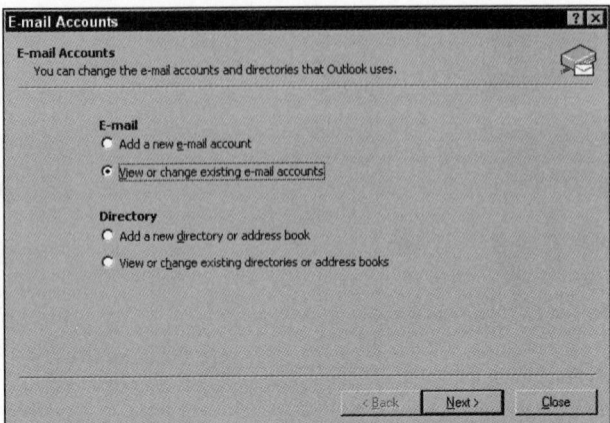

Figure 32-1: Create and modify Internet e-mail accounts in this dialog box.

Creating and modifying e-mail accounts

Before you start a new Outlook e-mail account, you should gather a few pieces of vital information. You need the e-mail address for the account, the server names and types, and your logon name and password. With these facts handy, start the account by clicking the "Add a new e-mail account" radio button in the E-mail Accounts dialog box; then click Next.

Your first choice is to select what type of e-mail account you want to add. The options include Microsoft Exchange Server, POP3, IMAP, HTTP (this covers Web-based e-mail services such as Microsoft's Hotmail, which — big surprise — Outlook is now designed to work with very well indeed). Additional Server Types covers all the other options.

From this point, all you have to do is fill in the blanks in the series of simple dialog boxes you see.

To make changes to an existing Outlook account, select "View or change existing e-mail accounts" in the initial E-mail Accounts dialog box, then click Next. Select the account in the list provided (see Figure 32-2) and click Change. You see the same dialog box you saw while creating a new account, with the current settings already filled in. Make any changes you need to make here.

You can test your account settings to make sure they work by clicking Test Account Settings.

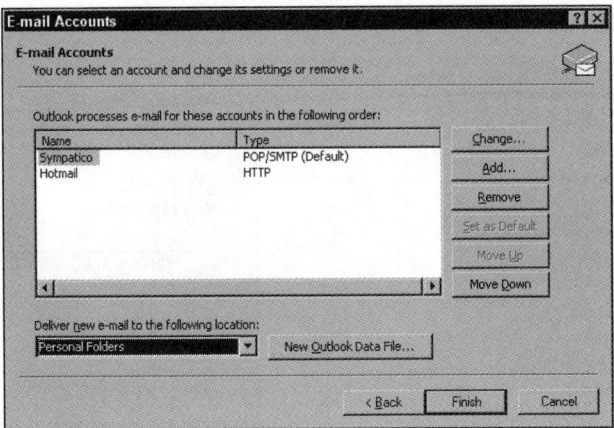

Figure 32-2: As you create e-mail accounts, Outlook adds them to this list.

Don't neglect the More Settings button as you're providing information about your new account. If you click it, a tabbed dialog box presents an array of pertinent settings, including those you worked through when creating the account. The General tab lets you give the account a name you see in Outlook, different from the user name that recipients see when they get messages from you. You can also specify a return address for an account other than the one used to send messages.

The Advanced tab (which may or may not be visible, depending on which type of account you're setting up) mostly contains technical settings that probably won't require your intervention. However, if you want automatic backups of your messages, or if you want to pick them up from more than one computer, you can check the box "Leave a copy of messages on the server."

Managing your accounts

If you create more than one mail account, you have some choices to make about how to use them together. A mandatory task is to set a default account—the one from which messages are sent unless you specify otherwise. Use the Set as Default button in the E-mail Accounts dialog box shown in Figure 32-2.

The typical Outlook user relies on one or two accounts on a daily basis, using other accounts only under special circumstances. Outlook now makes it easy to choose which account you want to access or use to send an e-mail. When you retrieve or send messages by choosing Tools ➪ Send/Receive, the menu includes all your active accounts, plus the option to run Send/Receive on All Accounts (a task you can also accomplish by pressing F9). Just choose the account you want to use (see Figure 32-3).

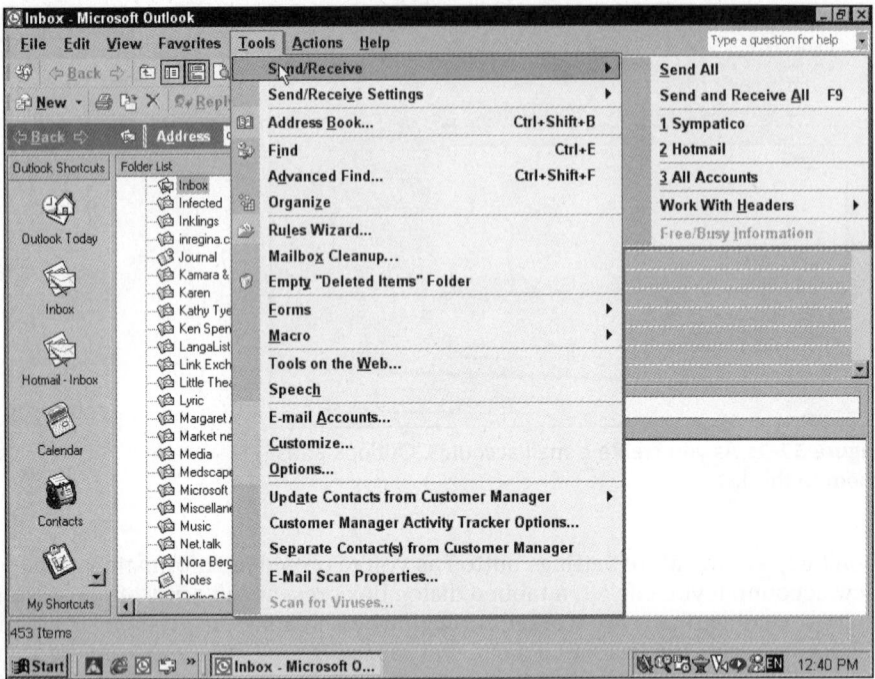

Figure 32-3: Choose which accounts you want to send or retrieve messages from using the Send/Receive menu.

Working with Messages in Your Mail Folders

Like your typical e-mail software, Outlook organizes your messages into Inbox, Outbox, Sent Items, and Deleted Items folders. You can display messages in any of these folders in a multiplicity of views depending on your needs at the moment. Remember that by default, only the Inbox and Deleted Items folders appear in the Outlook Shortcuts group.

You open a message by double-clicking it or selecting it and pressing Enter. By default, Outlook uses Word as its e-mail editor, so the message appears in a modified version of the same word processor you use for your most complex documents (see "Using Word as your e-mail editor," later in this chapter).

Tip

In past versions of Outlook, Word was very slow to load as the e-mail editor, so many people chose not to use it. In Outlook XP Word loads quickly, so there's no good reason not to use it as your e-mail editor; however, if you'd really prefer to use Outlook's less powerful built-in e-mail editor, you can turn off Word in Tools ➪ Options. Under the Mail Format tab, uncheck "Use Microsoft Word to edit e-mail messages."

Using AutoPreview to peek inside your messages

Outlook's AutoPreview feature lets you read a bit of your mail before you open it, so you don't waste time with messages that are of absolutely no interest. With AutoPreview, you can quickly scan your messages for meaningful content and choose whether to read them right away, read them later, or simply discard them. Figure 32-4 illustrates AutoPreview in action on my Inbox.

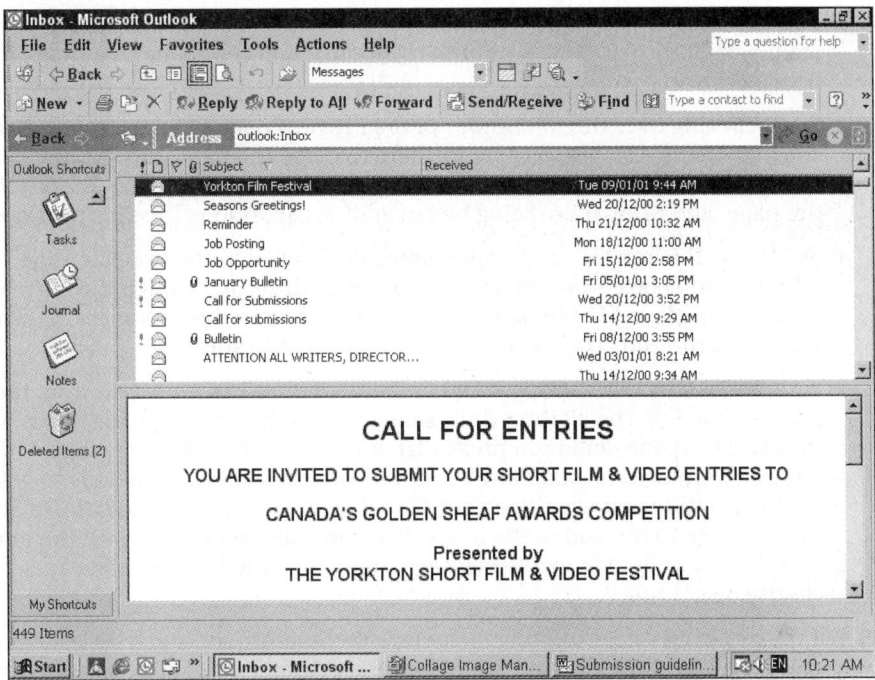

Figure 32-4: Inbox messages, displayed with AutoPreview and the Preview pane turned on

To toggle AutoPreview on or off, click the AutoPreview toolbar button on the Advanced toolbar (the button with the magnifying glass). To control AutoPreview settings, choose View ⇨ Current View ⇨ Customize Current View and click the Other Settings button. The resulting dialog box has a section in which you can decide which messages Outlook previews (all, or only those that are unread), and what font it should use for the AutoPreview text.

Viewing mail with the Preview pane

Even better than AutoPreview for making your mail easier to read is the Preview pane. With the Preview pane activated, Outlook displays the text of a selected e-mail message in a separate area at the bottom of the window. This is a much faster way to read your mail than opening each message in an individual separate window. Though the Preview pane takes up space you could use for displaying more messages, it's worth it. Figure 32-4 shows the Preview pane in operation.

If the Preview pane isn't already visible, display it by choosing View ➪ Preview Pane or clicking the Preview Pane button on the Advanced toolbar.

Other facts you need to know about the Preview pane include the following:

✦ You can resize the pane by dragging up or down the bottom border of the main part of the window. Wait until the mouse pointer becomes a double-headed arrow.

✦ Right-clicking over the top border of the Preview pane itself brings up a short shortcut menu. Use the commands here to close the pane, hide or display header information for the current message and select a font for the text in the pane, and bring up a dialog box of additional options (see the next tip).

✦ As long as the box for single key reading is checked in the Preview Pane options dialog box, you can use the Spacebar to scroll through the current message displayed in the pane, and then move on to the next message when you get to the end. Train yourself to use this handy shortcut.

✦ You can use the Edit ➪ Copy command or Ctrl+C to place the text from the Preview pane on the clipboard. To select text in the Preview pane, press Tab to select the pane, and then press Ctrl+A to select the entire message. Alternatively, use the standard Windows text navigation commands to get to the information you want to select. To select a block of text, hold down Shift as you move to the end of the block. You can make selections with the mouse as well — to select the whole message, right-click the Preview pane and choose Select All.

✦ If the message you're viewing includes attachments, you see a series of icons along the top of the Preview pane indicating what kind of attachments they are and their names. Click one of those icons to open the attached document immediately — if the document type is acceptable — or to see a box asking whether you want to open the attachment or save it on disk.

✦ You can follow a hyperlink, respond to meeting requests, and display properties of an e-mail address in the Preview pane without having to open the message.

Tip   To ensure that you're always asked whether to open or save the attachment, use the File Types tab in the View ➪ Options dialog box in Explorer or My Computer. There, pick the file type you want, click Edit, and then check "Confirm open after download."

Selecting a view

Outlook provides many alternative views for the mail-related folders via the View ⇨ Current View menu. Here are a couple to try:

✦ **By Follow Up Flag:** Displays messages flagged for some follow-up action at the top of the folder, with the accompanying message and due date visible in each item. See "Flagging messages," later in this chapter.

✦ **Message Timeline:** Shows graphically when your messages came in or went out.

Flagging messages

Outlook lets you mark messages that require some kind of further attention with a little Red Flag icon. You see this icon for all flagged items in any view that includes the corresponding column in the heading. The standard flag type is Follow Up, but you can select from several others.

To flag an e-mail message, choose Follow Up from the Actions menu or the message's shortcut menu. The dialog box that pops up lets you choose the type of flag you want to apply and a date when you want to be reminded about the pending concern. To mark a message flag as completed, check the Completed box in the same dialog box.

Managing your mail with the Rules Wizard

The Rules Wizard lets you set up automatic handling procedures for e-mail messages. For example, when a message arrives from a certain person, you can have Outlook shunt it into a special folder, play a distinctive sound, or display an appropriate message — or do all of these things. To set up custom rules, choose Tools ⇨ Rules Wizard or, if the Organize pane is active and you're working with the Using Folders options, click the Rules Wizard button at the top right.

Note   Mail sent and received using HTTP mail accounts can't be filtered using the Rules Wizard.

The main Rules Wizard dialog box displays existing rules and lets you create, delete, and modify individual rules and rearrange their order — the order in which Outlook applies the rules can be important if a message meets the criteria for two different rules. Clicking Create or Modify starts the Rules Wizard proper (see Figure 32-5), which walks you through the steps of specifying the rule.

Tip   Use the Run Now button in the Rules Wizard dialog box to test your new rules immediately, so you're sure that they work properly.

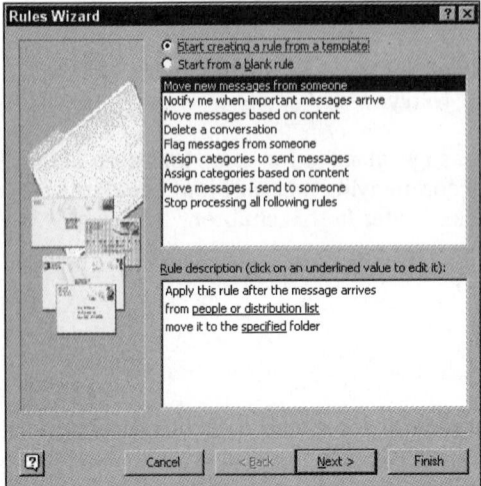

Figure 32-5: Use this box to start defining a new mail-handling rule.

Managing your junk mail

Outlook now includes unobtrusive (and ineffective, unfortunately) junk mail filters. Although I keep the junk mail filters turned on, I can't tell you why — in my experience they often incorrectly identify spam messages as desirable and vice versa.

The junk mail filters work by identifying visually messages that are from a known spam purveyor or an unknown source, or that contain suspect content. The filter attempts to differentiate between generic spam and X-rated ads separately, assigning each type of detritus its own color. If you want to take chances on missing important mail, you can even set up an automatic rule to route the presumed trash to a special folder, or delete it altogether.

To turn on the junk and adult e-mail filters, and set the options for how they deal with e-mail, click the Organize button on the Standard toolbar and choose the Junk E-mail link.

If junk mail sneaks through — and it will — you can at least ensure you don't get a message from that same address again by selecting the message, then choosing Actions ➪ Junk E-mail ➪ Add to Junk Senders list or Add to Adult Content Senders list.

Writing Messages

To start a new e-mail message from within Outlook, use any of the methods to create new items described in Chapter 31. If you already have one of the mail-related folders open (Inbox, Outbox, Sent Items, or Deleted Items), the fastest way is to press Ctrl+N or click the New Message button.

 **Note** Outlook's drag-and-drop capabilities shine when you're viewing a folder containing contact items and want to send a message to someone in the database. Just drag the person's contact item over to any of the mail-related folders — Inbox will do — and Outlook starts a new message with that contact's address already filled in. When you're in another folder, you can choose Tools ⇨ Address Book to start the Address Book, pick a name from the list there, and click the Send Mail button to open a new message to the person. Chapter 34 has more info on the Address Book.

Outlook supplies an assortment of *stationery* options (which produce fancy, pre-formatted e-mail) for use with HTML-formatted messages. See "Understanding message formats," later in this chapter.

Using special commands for messages

A message appears in its own window, of course (see Figure 32-6), complete with its own menu items and toolbar buttons — they're blended with Word's (see "Using Word as your e-mail editor," later in this chapter).

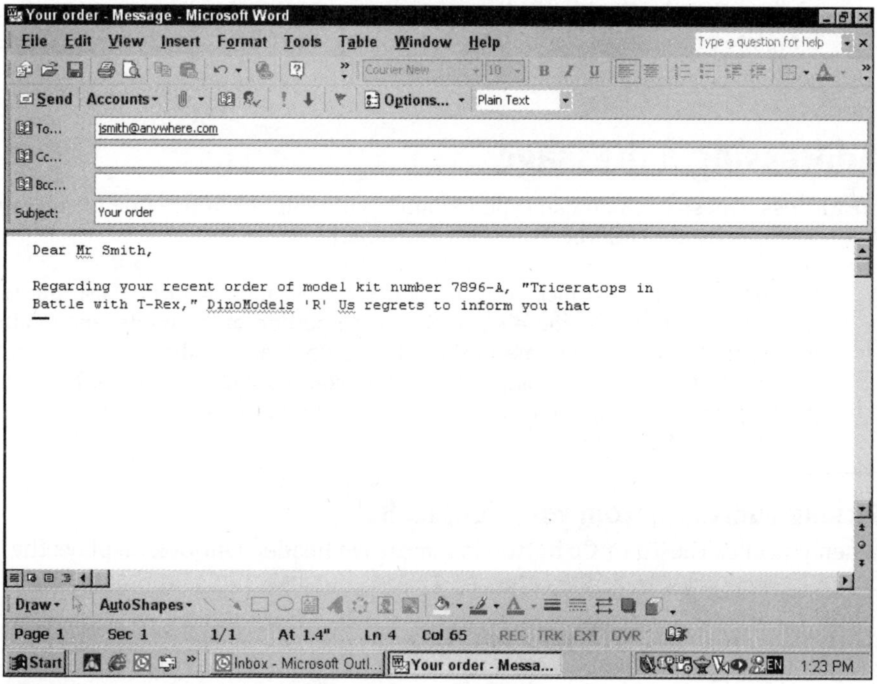

Figure 32-6: Writing an e-mail message using Word

Special elements of note include the following:

✦ Click the Send toolbar button to save your message and close it, storing it in the Outbox until it's actually sent.

Tip   To send e-mail immediately whenever you're connected to the Internet, go to the Mail Setup tab in the Tools ⇨ Options dialog box and check "Send immediately when connected" in the Send/Receive section.

✦ Click Accounts to choose which account to use to send the message.

✦ The Save button (and menu command) saves the message but doesn't close it. When you're working in Word, the Save button saves the document in Word format, not as a message. If you're working in Outlook's e-mail editor, the message is saved in the Outbox folder but is marked as unsent. Even if you close the message manually, it won't be sent until you reopen it and click Send.

✦ The File ⇨ Save As command lets you save the message in a separate file. The file formats you can choose depend somewhat on whether you're using Word as your editor, and on what message format you're working with — plaintext, Rich Text, or HTML. With Word, you can save it in any available format. If you're using the Outlook editor, you can save a message as text, as an Outlook template or message, or in Rich Text Format or HTML, whichever of these formats is in effect at the time.

Addressing a message

To address a message, you can type in names yourself or choose one from your Address Book by clicking the To and Cc buttons.

Tip   It may seem easier to pick your recipient's e-mail address from a list, but with Outlook, typing may be more efficient. Enter a portion of the name, and Outlook tries to find a matching name in the Address Book and in the addresses you've previously sent e-mail to, filling in the e-mail address if it's successful. To address the message to multiple recipients, separate their addresses with a semicolon in the To and Cc fields.

Picking addresses from your Contact list

When you click the To or Cc button in a message header, Outlook displays the Select Names dialog box (see Figure 32-7). This box lists the names and e-mail addresses from your Outlook folders that contain contact information. If you have more than one such folder, you must select the one you want to draw from in the drop-down list just above the main list of names. (Note that folders containing contact items appear in the Select Names dialog box only if the box for "Show this folder as an e-mail address book" is checked in the Properties dialog box (Outlook Address Book tab) for the folder.) To address a message to more than one recipient, you can Shift+click or Ctrl+click to select multiple names and then click To, Cc, or Bcc to identify them all as recipients.

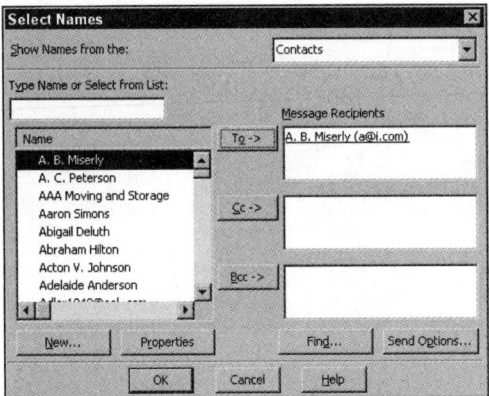

Figure 32-7: The Select Names dialog box displays names from your contact folders for quick selection of e-mail addresses.

Hiding names of other recipients

Addressing a message using the Bcc (blind carbon copy) field prevents recipients from seeing the addresses of the other recipients. This is a courtesy to the person reading the mail (because it keeps the message header free of clutter) and the other recipients (whose privacy is protected a bit, although a savvy recipient can still recover their addresses).

Mailing to the masses with Outlook

You can mail a message to a whole slew of recipients in one step, more or less, once you've created a *distribution list*. With the list in place, sending any message to the distribution list sends a copy to everyone on the list.

To create a personal distribution list, follow these steps:

1. Choose File ➪ New ➪ Distribution List. An Outlook item for the distribution list opens, as shown in Figure 32-8.

2. Type a name for the distribution list.

3. Click Select Members to add recipients from your Contacts folders, or Add New to include a recipient who isn't listed in Outlook (you can add the new recipient to your Contacts folder, but you don't have to).

4. Click Save and Close to store the list. Outlook places it in your Contacts folder, where its name is listed in bold type in the Full Name field.

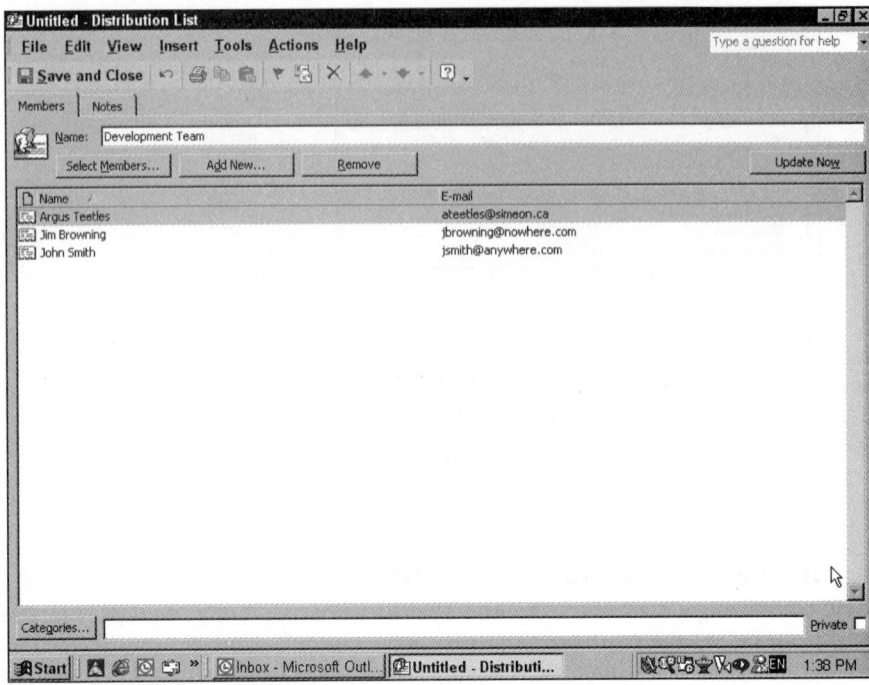

Figure 32-8: Create a group for mass mailing in this dialog box.

You can address a message to a distribution list using Outlook's standard addressing techniques. With the Contacts folder open, right-click the list item and choose New Message to Contact to start a new message to the list. Working within a message item, you can type the distribution list's name in the To or Cc fields, or click the associated button and choose the list from the Select Names dialog box—distribution lists appear in bold type.

You can also create distribution lists in the Address Book, although they're called *groups* there. In the Address Book window, click the New Entry button; from the New Entry dialog box, choose New Distribution List. This takes you to the same dialog box shown in Figure 32-8.

Tip   To send a message to an ad hoc group, start in your Contacts folder and select multiple addresses for the mailing by Shift+clicking (to select a range of consecutive items) or Ctrl+clicking (to select contacts one by one). If all the contacts are members of a single category, you don't need to select them—just display the Contact list in the By Category view. Now, starting from any of the selected contacts or from the category heading, drag onto a mail folder icon on the Outlook bar. After you approve a warning, Outlook displays a new message with the To field filled with the e-mail addresses of all those contacts.

Using message options

Don't neglect the Options button for individual messages. Click Options to open a shortcut menu, from which you choose Message Options to open the dialog box in Figure 32-9.

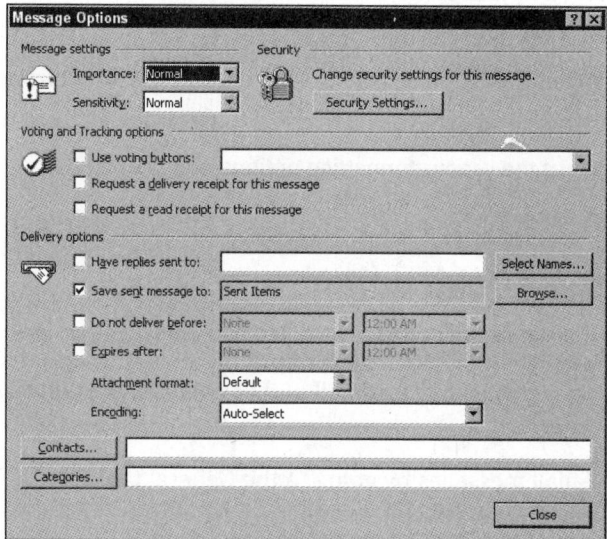

Figure 32-9: The Message Options dialog box lets you control settings for individual messages.

Use the Message Options dialog box to do the following:

✦ Assign importance and sensitivity ratings.

✦ Specify a folder in which your copy of the message should be saved after it's sent.

✦ Indicate who should receive replies to your mail.

✦ Postpone delivery of the message until a specified time (useful when you need to record an idea but want to control when it arrives).

✦ Assign Outlook categories to the message.

✦ Set security options for the message.

Understanding message formats

The lowest common denominator for e-mail messages is *plaintext* (also known as *ASCII text,* because it uses only the limited ASCII character set). If you store e-mail messages in the Rich Text Format, Outlook can send and display them as HTML (the formatting language of the Web, which can store complex formatting), or as Word documents, Access Data Pages, or Excel Worksheets. Rich Text Format preserves the full formatting of your text, including fonts, paragraph indents, bullet points, and so on.

To select a default format for new messages, go to the Mail Format tab on the Tools ⇨ Options dialog box and select a format in the Message Format area near the top. To create a new message in a specific format, choose Actions ⇨ New Mail Message Using and select the format from the resulting submenu. If you're already composing a message, you can switch to another format by choosing the one you want from the Format menu.

Cross-Reference For a more detailed look at the various formatting options, see Chapter 33.

Using Word as your e-mail editor

As noted earlier, by default Word is the editor for the e-mail messages you write, and for viewing incoming messages. Obviously, Word has far more editing and formatting power than ordinary e-mail editors, and all of that power is at your disposal when you edit e-mail with Word.

Specify settings for Word e-mail messages by going to the General tab of the Tools ⇨ Options dialog box (in Word) and clicking the E-mail Options button. As shown in Figure 32-10, the resulting dialog box has three tabs.

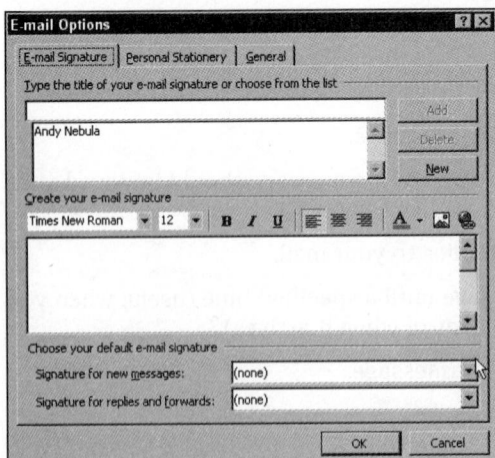

Figure 32-10: Set e-mail options for Word messages in this dialog box, available from the General tab of Word's Tools ⇨ Options dialog box.

The three tabs work as follows:

✦ Use the E-mail Signature tab in the E-mail Options dialog box to create signatures for e-mail messages and designate default signatures that appear automatically when you start a new message.

✦ The Personal Stationery tab lets you select formatting options for new e-mail messages.

Cross-Reference

Both of these options are discussed in detail in Chapter 33.

✦ The General tab offers three self-explanatory options for how HTML messages will be sent.

Word also includes the following features specifically useful for e-mail editing:

✦ By default, Word displays messages with the text wrapped to the window no matter how long the lines are formatted to print.

✦ Word's on-the-fly spell checker works when you compose e-mail messages just as it does in other Word documents — you see those wavy red lines under misspelled words.

✦ If the message you're reading is a response to someone else's message (and in turn, that message responded to an earlier one), the View ➪ Document Map command displays names of all the authors of the messages in the chain. You can click a name to jump directly to the corresponding message, if it's available to your system.

✦ Right-click a name in the body of a message and choose Who Is from the shortcut menu to display that person's listing in the Address Book.

Sending and Receiving Messages

The standard way to manually send the messages in your Outbox and check for new incoming mail is by clicking the Send/Receive button on the Standard toolbar. The keyboard shortcut for this command is F5. You get the dialog box shown in Figure 32-11, as Outlook connects to your network or dial-up service provider and transfers messages.

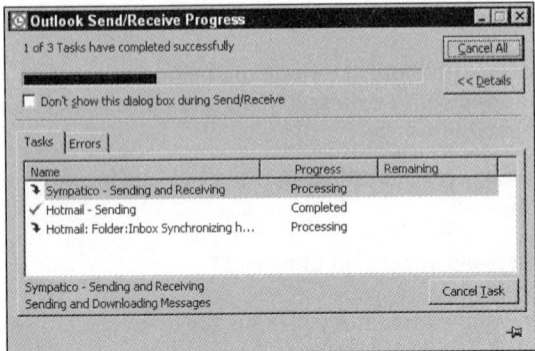

Figure 32-11: Outlook displays the progress of a
mail session in this dialog box.

Working with the mail dialog box

Figure 32-11 shows the mail dialog box (I call it that, anyway) in its expanded version. Click the Details button to display or remove the lower portion of the box. Other items on this dialog box work as follows:

+ The top part of the dialog box is for messages from Outlook. When an account is connected and Outlook is actively sending or receiving messages, this area tells you how many messages need to be processed and displays progress graphically along the horizontal bar.

+ The tabbed box below shows pending mail tasks. It lists a separate task for each send or receive operation on each account included in the current mail operation. You see a send task only for those accounts for which you have unsent outgoing mail. As each task is completed, Outlook displays a message and icon indicating whether the task is executing, was completed successfully, was canceled, or experienced an error. If you do get errors, you can see details on them in the Errors tab.

+ If you're mailing via a dial-up connection—that is, using a modem—the "Hang up when finished" box lets you decide whether to disconnect automatically after completing the mailing or to stay online so that you can surf the Web or do another mailing.

+ If you never want to be bothered with the mail dialog box, click the box "Don't show this dialog box during Send/Receive."

Sending an individual message

Suppose you want to send a key message you just wrote, but your Outbox is full of other messages that are in progress and not quite ready to send. To send a message individually, select it in your Outbox (or another appropriate mail folder) and choose Tools ⇨ Send.

Mail-handling options for networked computers

Outlook can automatically send and receive your mail on a schedule. To control if, and how often, automatic mail handling kicks in, open the Tools ➪ Options dialog box. Go to the Mail Setup tab and click Send/Receive.

In the Send/Receive Groups dialog box you can specify how many minutes should elapse between automatic send/receives both when Outlook is online and when it is offline (in which case, if you're using a dial-up connection, it automatically dials to check for messages and sends any messages in your Outbox). In the When Outlook is Online area, you can also choose to perform an automatic send/receive whenever you exit Outlook.

Customizing Outlook's E-Mail Settings

Choose Tools ➪ Options to examine and change your e-mail settings in Outlook. Every tab has some options related to e-mail; many are covered elsewhere in this chapter (or in the next), but here are some additional pointers:

✦ On the Preferences tab, click E-mail Options to check out the options for including the text of an original message when you reply to or forward it (see Figure 32-12). Try the "Include and indent original message text" and "Attach original message" choices. The latter is the most courteous and probably the best: It lets recipients read the original if they want to; they can trash it without reading it if they prefer.

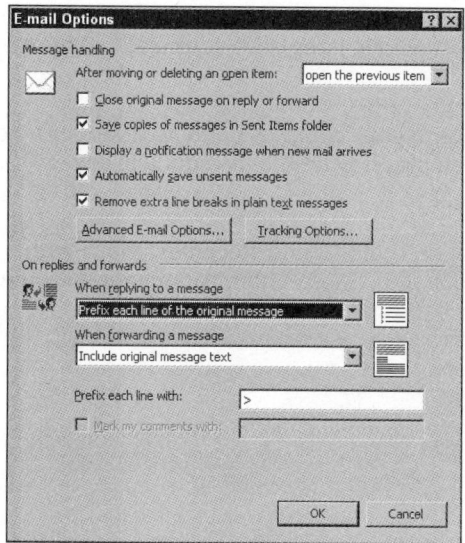

Figure 32-12: This dialog box offers many, but by no means all, of Outlook's e-mail-related settings.

✦ On the same E-mail Options dialog box shown in Figure 32-12, click Tracking Options to see some powerful settings for working with receipts so that you and your correspondents can know who got what mail, when.

✦ The choices on the Spelling tab are straightforward. Your big decision is whether or not you want every message spell checked before it goes out.

Using Remote Mail

Remote mail lets you spend less time connected to the Internet and operate offline most of the time, by enabling you to pick up only the headers of your e-mail and then decide offline which ones you want to download entirely.

To use remote mail, first set up your computer to connect to your e-mail server, as described in the earlier section on setting up e-mail accounts.

Now, to download headers, choose Tools ➪ Send/Receive ➪ Work With Headers ➪ Download Headers From and then choose the account you want to download headers from, or choose All Accounts.

Once the headers are downloaded, you can mark the ones you want to work with by right-clicking them. You have two choices:

✦ **Mark to Download Message(s):** This option downloads the message to your current computer and removes the original message from the server.

✦ **Mark to Download Message Copy:** This downloads a copy of the message to your computer, but leaves the original on the server. This is the best choice if you want to be able to access the message later from your main computer back in your office or home.

You can also delete the message from both your computer and your server by clicking the item you want to delete and then pressing Delete. A red X will appear in the header column.

Once you've made your decisions, choose Tools ➪ Send/Receive ➪ Work With Headers ➪ Process Market Headers From and choose either All Accounts or the specific account the headers came from.

✦ ✦ ✦

More Than Text: Advanced Messaging

There's more to sending e-mail then just sending plaintext, or at least there can be. Outlook also enables you to send fancily formatted messages that look like Web pages instead of typewritten script, attach files to those messages, and add a personalized "signature" — as you'll see in this chapter.

Attaching Files to Messages

Attaching files to messages is a great way to send word processing documents, pictures, music and video clips, and even programs to other people. In fact, you can attach just about any file on your computer to an e-mail message and send it to someone else — although they'll have to have the right program to open it for it to do them any good.

Attaching a file is easy. With a message open, click the Insert File button (it looks like a paper clip) or choose Insert ➪ File. Alternatively, drag and drop the attachment file from a file-management window (My Computer, Explorer, or a file-management view in Outlook) into the body of the message.

Tip　　Don't forget that you can also send most Office documents as an e-mail message attachment from within the applications you use to create them. Choose File ➪ Send To ➪ Mail Recipient (as Attachment).

To send an Outlook item of any type (such as a contact or task item) to a person who also uses Outlook, right-click the item and choose Forward from the shortcut menu, or press Ctrl+F. This starts a new e-mail message with the item attached. If you started the message already, choose Insert ➪ Item instead, or drag the item onto the body of the message. The recipient just drags the item from the message onto the icon for the Outlook folder where it belongs.

Tip   Using cut and paste or drag and drop, you can attach documents or other files of any type to *any* Outlook item, not just to messages. For that matter, you can add them directly to mail-related folders.

Originally designed to handle sequences of ordinary text, e-mail systems must take special measures to send files. Files attached to or inserted in an e-mail message must be encoded in ordinary text characters for the trip and then decoded and converted back into files on the recipient's computer. Outlook and other e-mail programs handle the encoding and decoding process automatically. Your only worry is to ensure that the mail programs at the sending and receiving ends use the same encoding formats.

Two encoding formats are in widespread use: UUENCODE and MIME. They enable you to send e-mail messages containing embedded objects and files inserted at specific points in the message, not just attached at the end.

MIME, Outlook's default, is generally preferable and is the only choice if you're sending HTML messages. However, if your recipient's software understands only the UUENCODE format, you must set up Outlook accordingly.

To use UUENCODE format, open the Tools ➪ Options dialog box and click on the Mail Format tab, then the Internet Format button. This opens the dialog box shown in Figure 33-1. Check the box labeled "Encode attachments in UUENCODE format when sending a plaintext message." Outlook will still send attachments with HTML messages in MIME format — the only choice that works — but will send any attachments to plaintext messages in UUENCODE.

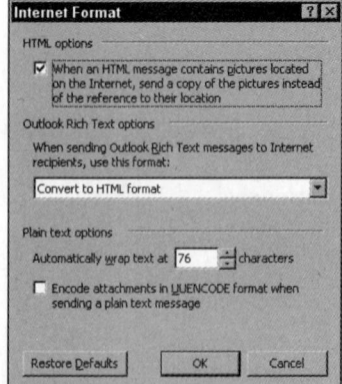

Figure 33-1: Use this dialog box to change the format Outlook uses to send attachments to plaintext messages.

Even when both the sending and receiving programs are using the same encoding format, attached or inserted files still won't get through unless both sides use the same character sets for the encoding/decoding process. This is most likely going to be a problem when you are communicating internationally. Clicking the International Options button next to the Internet Format button on the Message Format tab opens a dialog box that enables you to change the character sets for default and individual messages.

Rich Text and HTML Formatting

As noted in the last chapter, Outlook can send and display messages in several formats. Those formats include a variety of Office-only formats, such as Word documents or Excel spreadsheets, but the three formats available for straightforward messages are plaintext, Rich Text Format, and HTML.

Plaintext is just what it sounds like, and it's by far the safest choice when you don't know what your recipient's computer is capable of deciphering.

Rich Text Format stores sophisticated formatting information as ordinary text, with special bracketed codes representing the font and layout instructions. RTF permits much fancier formatting than plaintext, though not as much as HTML — it can preserve fonts, paragraph indents, bullets, and so on. As well, RTF can be read by most modern word processors, so there's a good chance your recipient will be able to view the message the way it was intended.

Finally, HTML is the language used to create Web pages, and permits all of the fancy formatting we've come to expect on the World Wide Web, from photos to background colors to text of all sizes and shapes.

Setting the default format

To select a default format for new messages, go to the Mail Format tab on the Tools ⇨ Options dialog box and select a format in the Message Format area near the top. To create a new message in a specific format, choose Actions ⇨ New Mail Message Using and select the format from the resulting submenu. If you're already composing a message, you can switch to another format by choosing the one you want from the "Message format" list box just to the right of the Options button.

Creating RTF and HTML messages

The biggest difference between a plaintext message and RTF and HTML messages is that a large chunk of the Word Formatting bar that's grayed out when you're writing a plaintext message is active when you're working in RTF or HTML. Use these tools — font, font size, tables, lists, drawing, styles, and so forth — just as you would working on a Word document. If it's not active, you can't use it in that format — it's as simple as that.

The Perils of RTF and HTML

The ability to use Rich Text Format and HTML sounds great, but it takes two to format—your recipient must also be using Outlook or another e-mail program that supports the format you've chosen.

If Outlook sends a Rich Text or HTML message to a recipient whose software can't understand the format, one of two things may happen. If you're lucky, the message will show up as ordinary text—the formatting will be missing, but at least the information will be readable. More likely, however, the receiving software will let the formatting codes through. Your recipient will see a more or less unreadable message and may end up angry instead of impressed. (If the recipient is savvy and wants to read your message anyway, it can be exported to a separate file, which can then be opened in a word processor, such as WordPad, that can import Rich Text Format files or a browser—but the recipient has to really want to read your message to go to all that trouble!)

If the Rich Text, HTML, or Word format works for most of your recipients but not for everyone, you can force Outlook to send messages to certain people in plaintext format.

Open the contact item for the person. There, double-click on the e-mail address. From the Internet Format list at the bottom, choose "Send Plain Text only".

If you want to see that Outlook always sends messages to a certain recipient in Rich Text format, regardless of the default message format setting, choose "Send using Outlook Rich Text format".

If you don't choose either, Outlook will decide the best sending format, based on other messages sent to and received from that recipient.

One of the most powerful features is the ability to use the Styles and Formatting task pane just as you use it in regular Word documents. Choose Format ➪ Styles and Formatting to open the Styles and Formatting task pane (see Figure 33-2). If you choose Available Formatting or Available Styles from the Show list at the bottom of the task pane, you'll see a list of all the formatting options supported by RTF or HTML, depending on which advanced format you're using. This list includes the Hyperlink and Followed Hyperlink styles, several heading styles, and the Plain Text style, which uses a fixed-width font as opposed to the Normal style, which uses a proportional font.

Using E-Mail Stationery

One of the interesting options opened up by HTML is the use of e-mail "stationery." Like the paper stationery you probably already use, this provides a special background for your messages, which can contain images (a business logo, for instance), colors, textures or text.

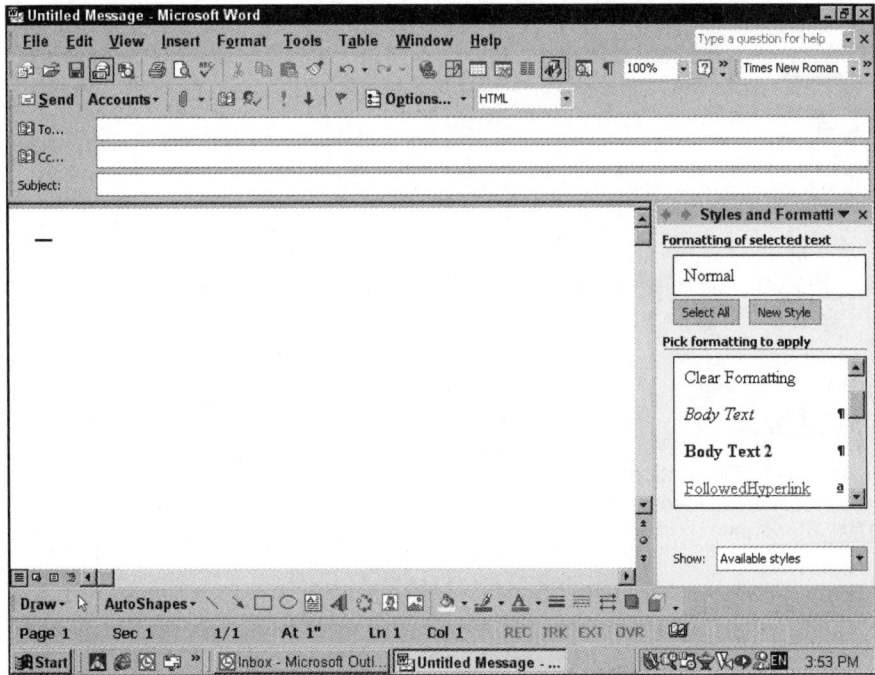

Figure 33-2: HTML and RTF have a variety of formatting styles available for use in your messages.

You can create a new message using HTML and stationery at any time by choosing Actions ➪ New Mail Message Using ➪ (stationery name) or More Stationery, even if your default mail format is not HTML.

If you want to use Outlook's built-in stationery as your default, you have to have HTML as your default e-mail format. Furthermore, you have to have a default stationery selected, even if you want to choose from the selection of stationery instead of having one default type.

You can set both by selecting Tools ➪ Options from the menu and clicking the Mail Format tab in the Options dialog box. From the drop-down list under "Send in this message format", select HTML. To set your default stationery, click the Stationery Picker button in the Stationery and Fonts section. This opens the dialog box shown in Figure 33-3.

Click on the various listings under Stationery and look at their appearances under Preview. When you find one you like, click the OK button and that one will be set as your default stationery.

Note   Clicking the Get More Stationery sends you to Microsoft's Office Update Web site, so be prepared to go online if you make that choice.

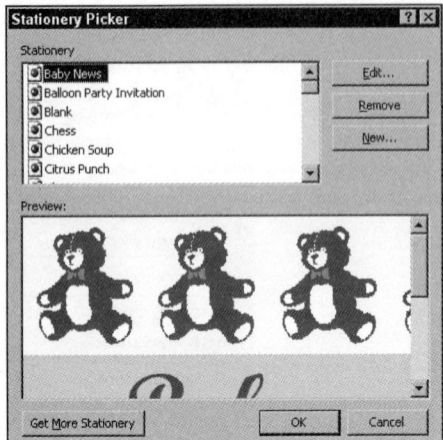

Figure 33-3: The Stationery Picker lets you choose a background for your HTML messages.

You will be returned to the Options dialog box, where you'll need to click one more OK button to finish.

From now on, when you start a new e-mail message, the default stationery will be there without any effort on your part. If you want to change it for a message, select Actions ⇨ New Mail Message Using ⇨ More Stationery from the menu. This will bring up the Select a Stationery dialog box, which is functionally identical to the Stationery Picker.

Editing your stationery

You're not limited to the stationery that comes with Outlook. To begin with, you can fiddle around with the ones provided until they suit you better. To do so, go to the Stationery Picker, click on the stationery you want to use as the basis for your new stationery, then click Edit. This opens the Edit Stationery dialog box shown in Figure 33-4.

Here you can choose the font you want to use with your stationery, change the background picture by browsing for a new one, or replace the background with a solid color. (You can even choose not to include a background with the stationery, although if you're going to make that choice, what the heck do you want stationery for in the first place?)

When you're happy with the changes you've made to the stationery, click OK.

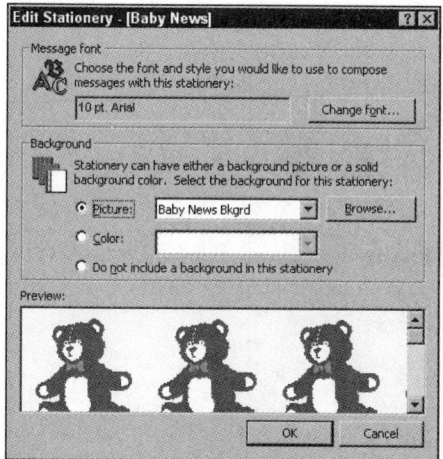

Figure 33-4: Edit stationery to suit yourself in this dialog box.

Creating a new stationery

You can also create a stationery from scratch. To do so, click the New button in the Stationery Picker. This starts up a wizard that leads you step by step through the process of creating your own stationery.

First you're asked to name the stationery, then to either start from scratch, use an existing stationery as a template, or use some other file as a template. Then you're kicked over to the Edit Stationery dialog box shown in Figure 33-4, where you make the same choices as before.

Using themes as stationery

When you're using Word as your e-mail editor, as Outlook does by default, you can use any of Word's built-in themes as the basis for your e-mails.

To do so, open a Word message form in HTML or RTF format and click the arrow to the right of the Options button. From the resulting menu, choose Stationery. This opens the E-mail Options dialog box with the Personal Stationery tab selected. This initial dialog box lets you set fonts for new mail messages and replying and forwarding messages, as well as the font you'll see when you're composing and reading plaintext messages.

However, it also lets you access Word's themes. Click the Theme button to open the Theme or Stationery dialog box shown in Figure 33-5. Choose the theme you want, then click OK. You can modify the font used with it in the Personal Stationery tab.

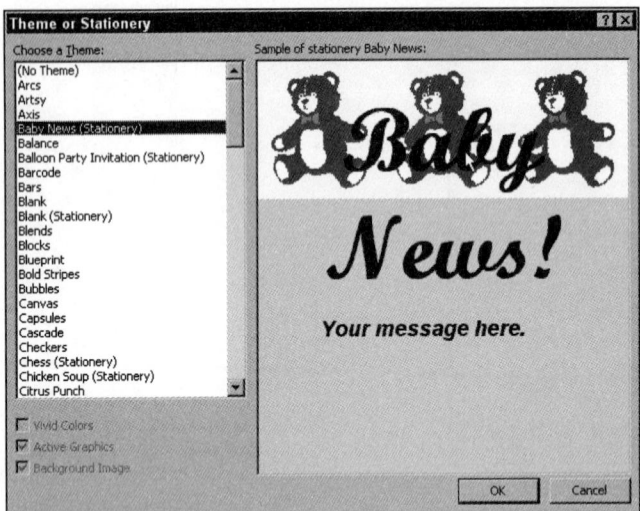

Figure 33-5: Word lets you use its themes as stationery for e-mail messages.

Sending Business Cards

Digital business cards, or *vCards,* are the modern equivalent of the cardboard that clutters up Rolodexes all over the world. These files are imported into address books like Outlook's Contacts listings.

To send a vCard via e-mail, you must have a listing in your Contacts folder. Select it, and then choose Actions ➪ Forward as vCard from the menu. This will create a new e-mail message with the vCard (.VCF file) attached to it, as shown in Figure 33-6.

All you need to do is address the message and click the Send button.

Tip

You can also save a contact as a vCard. This is useful in case you want to include it with a signature on your e-mail (see the following section). To do so, double-click on a contact to open it and select Export to vCard File from the File menu. Outlook will let you select a folder and a name for the file. The default folder is Signatures, and the default filename is the name of the contact. Click the Save button to finish.

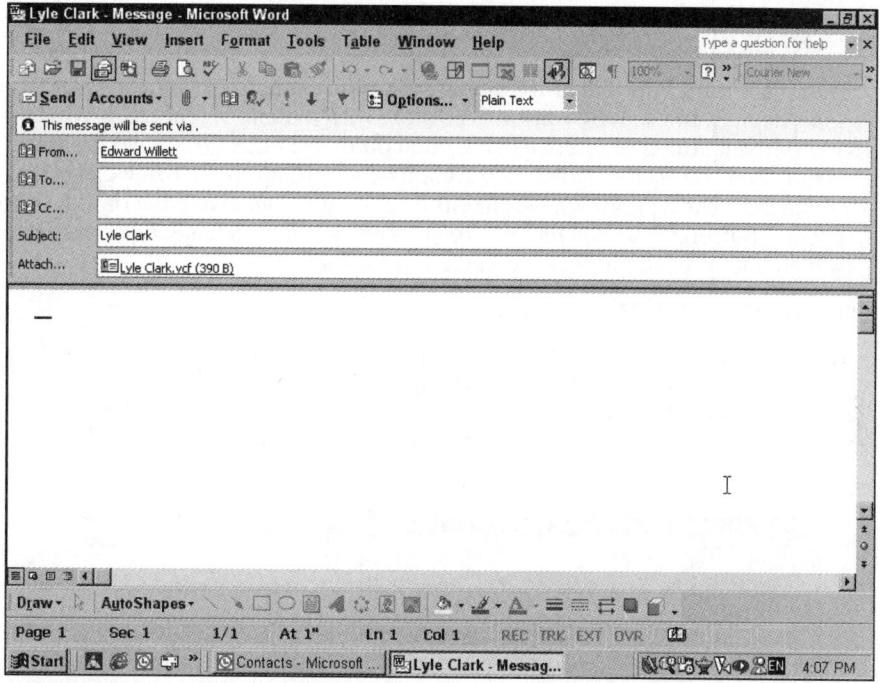

Figure 33-6: Sending a vCard

Using Signatures and Receipts

A signature is not necessarily just your name. It's a bit of text that's added automatically at the end of e-mail messages you send out. Of course, there's nothing to prevent you from using your name as the signature on your messages, but most people use quotations, statements of company policy, addresses of Web pages, and so on instead.

Creating a message signature

To make a signature for your messages, follow these steps:

1. Select Tools ⇨ Options from the menu.

2. In the Options dialog box, click the Mail Format tab. If you already had some signatures created, you could select which one you wanted to use as your default signature from the drop-down list at the bottom of the tab.

3. Click the Signatures button.

4. The Create Signature dialog box is blank at first, as there are no signatures yet. Click the New button.

5. In the Create New Signature dialog box, type a name for your new signature. By default, the second option is to start with a blank signature. If you had other signatures to choose from, you could also click on the second radio button, which is "Use this existing signature as a template:". You would then pick one from the drop-down list. In either case, you can also click on the third radio button, "Use this file as a template:" — in which case, type the template filename or click the Browse button to locate it.

6. Click the Next button.

7. Type your signature text into the text area of the Edit Signature dialog box (see Figure 33-7). The Font and Paragraph buttons, which let you choose fonts and alignment, are not available for plaintext. The Clear button erases the text area, and the Advanced Edit button lets you edit the signature in Notepad.

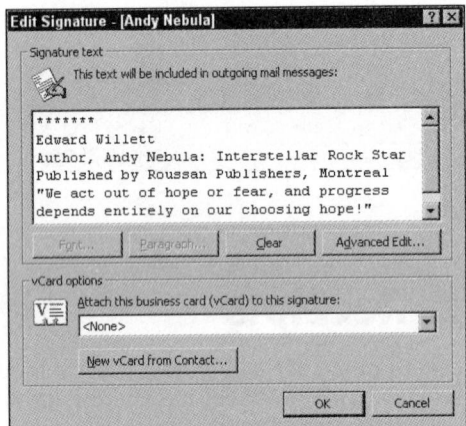

Figure 33-7: The Edit Signature dialog box, where you can create a new signature

8. If you want to attach an existing vCard file as part of the signature (see the preceding section), select it from the drop-down list. It's probably not the best idea to do this, as you wouldn't give someone a physical business card every time you saw him or her. Nobody needs 200 copies of your vCard, either.

9. Click the Finish button to complete the signature creation.

10. Back in the Create Signature dialog box, the signature is now listed and the Edit and Remove buttons are active. Repeat steps 4–9 to create more signatures.

11. Click the OK button to return to the Options dialog box.

12. In the Options dialog box, click the OK button to finish the process.

When you send a message, if you have selected a default signature in the Mail Format tab, it will automatically be included. Otherwise, or if you want to add another signature in addition to the default, you'll have to pick one by clicking the Signature button in the message form's Standard toolbar before you send the message.

Creating a signature in Word

For a more powerful signature editor, you can turn to Word. With a Word message form open, choose Options ⇨ E-mail Signature. This opens the E-mail Options dialog box shown in Figure 33-8, with the Signature tab selected.

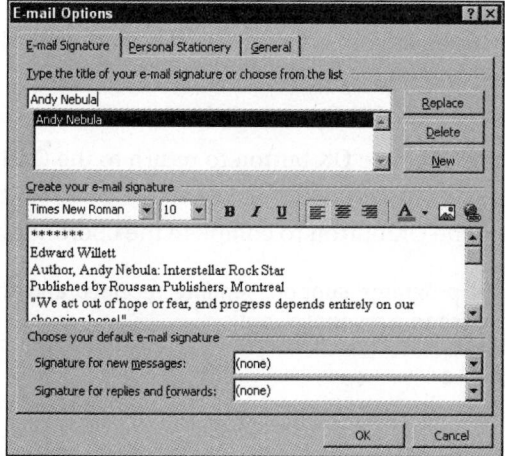

Figure 33-8: When you use Word as your e-mail editor, you have access to a more powerful signature editor.

This dialog box looks in the Signature folder just like the Outlook Signature Editor does, so the signature I created in the last section appears in the list of those available. But now I can edit it more easily using a miniformatting toolbar that includes font, font size, font style, alignment, font color, an Insert Picture button, and an Insert Hyperlink button.

When I've finished editing the signature, I can click Replace to replace the original version of the signature with the new version.

At the bottom of this dialog box are options to choose two different default signatures for different purposes — one for new messages, and one for replies and forwards.

Setting up message receipts

Making sure your e-mail has arrived is much like sending snail mail with a return receipt requested form. To set things up so you get confirmation, follow these steps:

1. Select Tools ➪ Options from the menu.

2. If it is not already selected, click the Preferences tab.

3. Click the E-mail Options button.

4. In the E-Mail Options dialog box, click the Tracking Options button.

5. In the Tracking Options dialog box, click the two checkboxes labeled "Read receipt" and "Delivery receipt".

6. If you don't want other people to be able to get such receipts from you, click the radio button labeled "Never send a response".

7. Click the OK button to return to the E-Mail Options dialog box.

8. In the E-Mail Options dialog box, click the OK button to return to the Options dialog box.

9. In the Options dialog box, click the OK button to complete the operation.

Note   Bear in mind that not all e-mail programs support sending receipts, and that someone else may use the "Never send a response" option.

✦   ✦   ✦

Keeping Track of Contacts

If Outlook is best known for its e-mail management tools, as
I said in the last chapter, then it should come as no surprise that it also excels at managing lists of contacts. After all,
what's the point of being able to make and manage messages
if you have no one to send them to?

This chapter covers using Outlook's contact database, beginning with using the built-in forms to enter contact data. You
can also use the All Fields tab to enter more detailed data not
covered in the General and Details tabs of the contact form.

As I've already pointed out, Outlook has several built-in views
(and the capability of creating custom views) for everything,
and contacts are no exception. Contact data can be edited
either in the views or via the data entry forms.

Contact listings can be grouped the same way as messages
can, and contacts can be associated with other contacts, as
well as items in other Outlook folders.

Adding a Contact

There are several ways to get into the Contacts folder (see
Figure 34-1), but the easiest is to click the Contacts shortcut
on the Outlook bar.

Cross-Reference For more information on the Outlook bar, see Chapter 31.

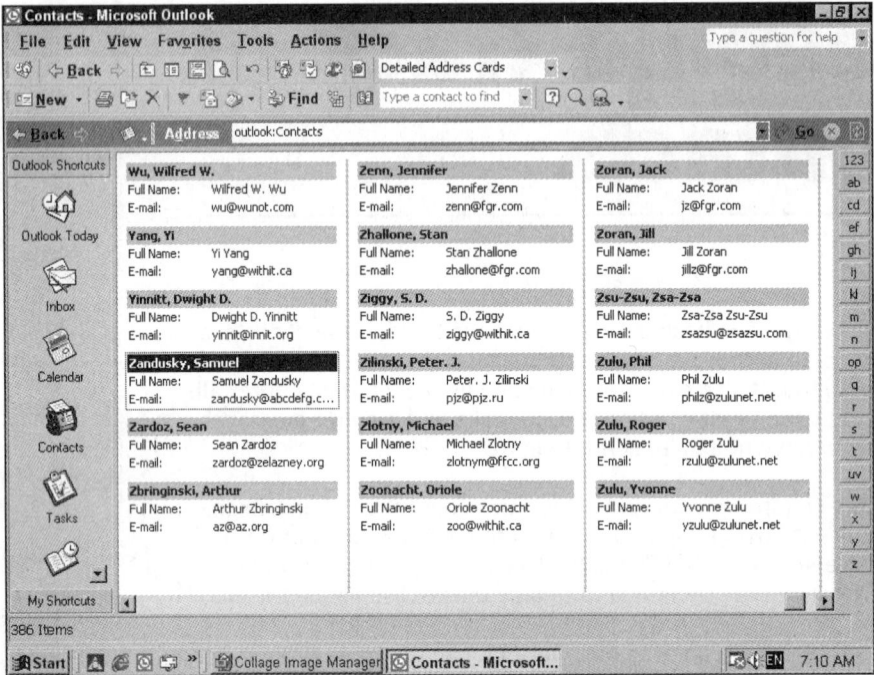

Figure 34-1: The Contacts folder

Adding a contact listing is even easier. Just click the New Contact button on the toolbar while you're in the Contact folder, or choose File ➪ New ➪ Contact at any time.

Where things can get complex is if you gather all the information that Outlook can hold. Of course, there's no requirement that you fill in all the blanks — it's just that Outlook can cover anything you come up with. If all you've got is basic data such as name, phone number, and e-mail address, just use that. On the other hand, if you want a place to keep track of things like nicknames, birthdays, and anniversaries, and even to store digital certificates, you've got it.

To add a contact listing, follow these steps:

1. Click the New button or choose File ➪ New ➪ Contact.

2. In the new contact form's General tab (see Figure 34-2), enter the contact's full name in normal format, like "John Smith." The name will automatically be entered in the format "Smith, John" under File As when you tab out of the Full Name box.

Tip

If you would prefer to have the name filed as "John Smith" instead of "Smith, John," choose that option from the File As drop-down menu.

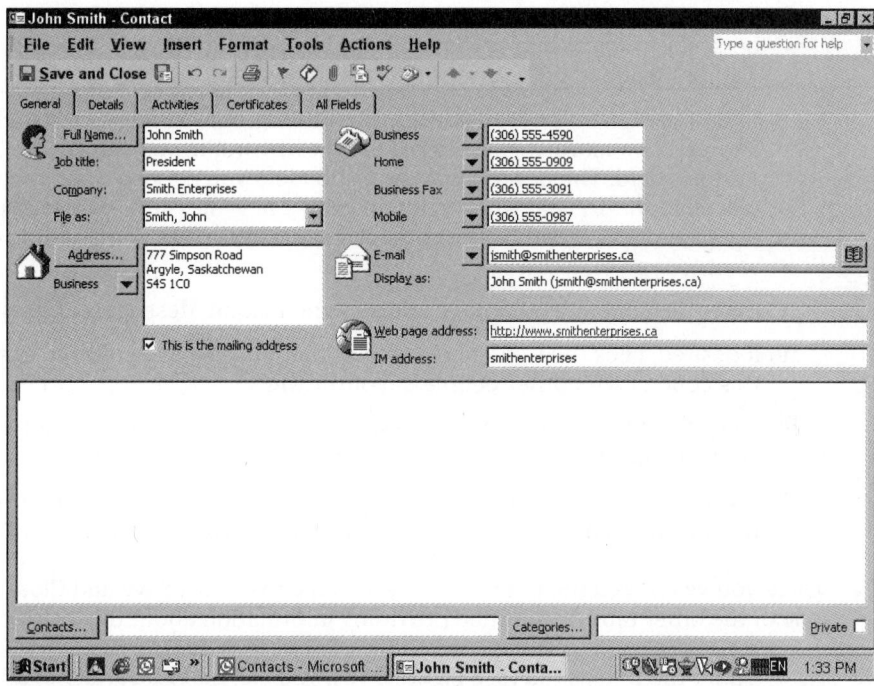

Figure 34-2: The General tab of the Contact form

3. If you wish to enter more detailed name information, click the Full Name button. This will bring up a dialog box with such options as title, suffix (Jr., Sr., and so on), and middle name. Enter the data and click the OK button to return to the new contact form. Although this information does not appear in separate fields on the main form, it is included in separate field entries in the database.

4. Fill out the Job title and Company fields. When you enter a company name, three more options appear in the drop-down list under File As: to file by company name, to file by "Smith, John" with the company name in parentheses after it, or to file by company name with "Smith, John" in parentheses after it.

5. The Address field is set by default to the business address, but three different addresses can actually be entered — business, home, and other. Select which one you want to enter by clicking the downward-pointing arrow. You can enter all three if you wish. Clicking the Address button brings up an address listing where Outlook has already parsed the information you entered into its component parts, such as street address and ZIP code. You can also specify the Country/Region, which you can select from a drop-down list (Outlook does a very good job of determining the country from most addresses). After doing so, click the OK button.

6. If you have entered multiple addresses, display the one you want snail mail to go to and click the checkbox labeled "This is the mailing address."

7. Enter the contact's telephone numbers. Although the form lists only four numbers, several more are accessible via the arrow buttons, just as with the Address field.

8. Enter the contact's e-mail addresses. Although the form lists only one e-mail address, two more are accessible via the arrow button, just as with the Address field. The new Display As option lets you choose what you want displayed in the To field when you compose a new message — instead of the e-mail address, it can be the contact's name, nickname, or anything else you want to type in.

9. Enter the contact's Web page address and Instant Messaging address.

10. If desired, click the Contacts button at the bottom of the form to associate this contact with other people in your listings.

11. If you want to assign a category (such as "competition" or "personal") to this contact, click the Categories button at the bottom of the form.

12. If you don't want other people with access to your Contacts folder to be able to view this contact's information, check the Private checkbox.

Once you've entered the information, you can either click Save and Close, or click one of the other tabs to continue providing information about this contact:

✦ Under the Details tab (see Figure 34-3), you can enter a variety of additional data, such as the contact's nickname, spouse's name, the directory server and e-mail alias the contact uses for Online NetMeetings, and so forth. The Birthday and Anniversary fields have a calendar available by clicking the downward-pointing arrow. By default, the current date is shown, but other months are available by using the left- and right-pointing arrows to scroll through the year. Once you're in the right month, click the date.

Tip   If you want to enter the year, too, as I did in Figure 34-3, you can type it in directly. Outlook's perpetual calendar will even tell you what day of the week that was — which makes it a pretty good way to find out on what day of the week you were born (or anyone else, for that matter).

✦ The Activities tab doesn't take any entries from you. It simply lists all Outlook items with which the contact is associated, such as other contacts, e-mail messages, and so forth.

✦ If you have a digital certificate for this person and wish to use it in secure e-mail messages, click the Certificates tab, then click the Import button, find the certificate, and open it to add it to the list. (A *digital certificate* is a piece of security software that acts as an identification card to computers that can read it; it vouches for the identity of the person who possesses the certificate.)

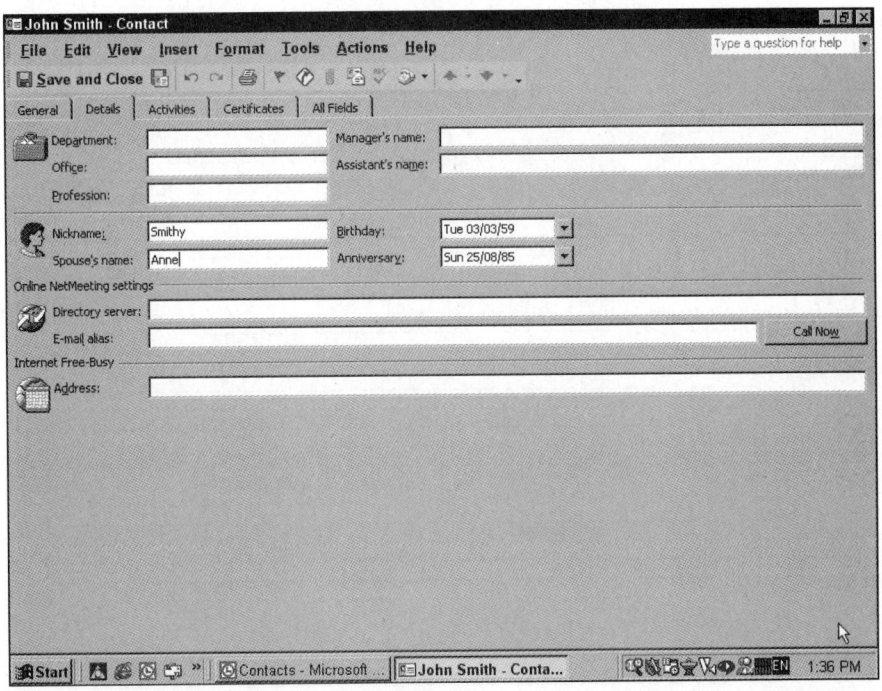

Figure 34-3: Enter additional information about a contact using the Details tab.

✦ To view or change specific fields, click the All Fields tab (see Figure 34-4). The drop-down list under "Select from" lets you choose various types of fields to display, such as phone number, address, and so on. (The most all-inclusive of these options is "All Contact fields.") Enter data under the Value column next to the field name. Press Enter or click anywhere else on the form and the information is accepted in the field (the contact must still be saved to keep the change, though). In addition to entering new information here, you can also edit existing data. All changes you make here are instantly reflected in the appropriate fields on the other tabs.

Outlook even lets you add new fields so you can provide additional information about a contact: for instance, Pet Name or Shoe Size. To add a new field:

1. With the All Fields tab selected, click the New button.

2. In the New Field dialog box, type a name for the field.

3. Select a Type for the data (text, number, date/time, and so forth) from the drop-down list.

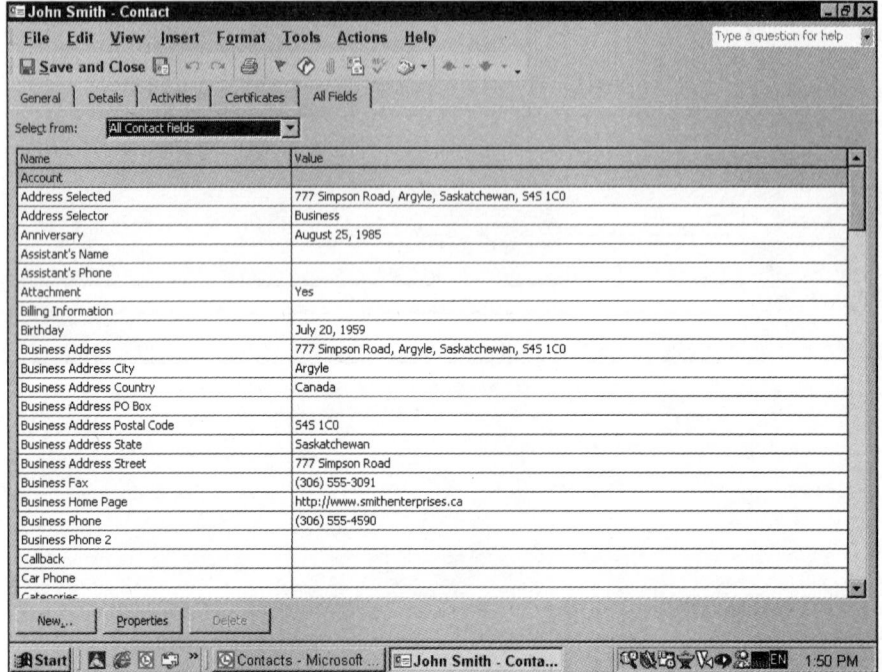

Figure 34-4: The All Fields tab is an alternative place to enter data for your contacts.

4. Select a format (this varies depending on the data type) from the second drop-down list.

5. Click the OK button to complete creation of the new field.

6. Enter the data for the new field under the Value column. Unless you enter data, this field is only visible by selecting "User-defined fields in this folder" under "Select from." If there is an entry under this field, it can also be viewed by selecting "User-defined fields in this item."

To complete the entry of contact information using any of the tabs, click the Save and Close button on the toolbar or use the Ctrl+S key combination.

Note   You can also add a contact in any of the Contact folder views except the address card views by clicking in the first row under the column headers and then entering the data for the new contact. However, this is a comparatively awkward approach because you must scroll or tab to fill in the fields for the new contact.

Tip   If you're entering information for a lot of contacts one after the other, choose File ➪ Save and New whenever you finish entering information for a contact. This saves the information for that contact and automatically opens a blank Contact form for your next entry.

Importing Addresses

Sometimes you may want to import addresses into your contact folder that are stored in some other format: as a vCard file, for instance, Netscape Mail, or even an Excel spreadsheet or other database.

To do so, choose File ⇨ Import/Export. This opens the Import and Export Wizard (see Figure 34-5).

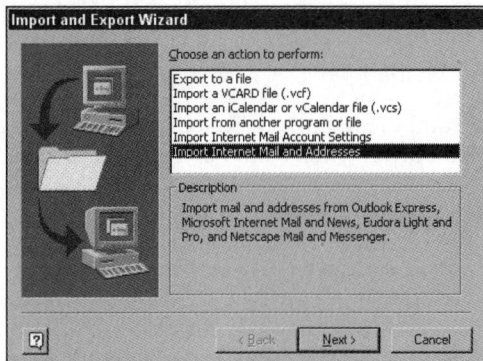

Figure 34-5: Use this wizard to import addresses stored in another format.

First you're asked to choose which of several actions to perform. To import a database file, for instance, you'd choose "Import from another program or file." When you click Next, you're asked to choose the specific type of file you want to import, then to locate the specific file. You're given the option of replacing any duplicates that turn up in the imported data with the imported data; allowing duplicates to be created; or to not import duplicate items. Finally, you're asked to select a destination folder.

In my experience, importing and exporting can be kind of hit-and-miss, with the resulting data sometimes requiring a lot of cleaning up; still, it's generally faster than typing all that information in yourself, contact by contact.

Note   For contacts stored in another file to have a hope of being successfully imported, the data must be labeled in a way that matches up with fields in Outlook. If they don't, you're likely to get an error message and importing will abort. It's a good idea to go to the original program that created the file you want to import and relabel the data to match what Outlook is looking for.

Opening and Editing a Contact

You can edit contact fields directly in the Address Cards, Detailed Address Cards, or Phone List views (see the following section on viewing Contact lists). However, not all fields are visible in these situations, and the easiest way to edit contact data is by using the same form you used to add the contact to begin with. To do so, follow these steps:

1. Double-click the contact's listing.

2. Select the tab containing the data you want to edit. If neither the General nor Details tab lists the fields you want to edit, select the All Fields tab.

3. Edit the data.

4. To save the listing, click the Save and Close button. To exit without saving, press the Esc key and click the No button when asked if you want to save changes.

Viewing Contact Lists

The Current View drop-down list on the toolbar offers you seven different ways to look at your contact information. Table 34-1 shows these seven views and their contents. The By Category, By Company, By Location, and By Follow-Up Flag views are grouped by those parameters (see the following section on grouping contacts).

Table 34-1 Contacts Views	
View	**Contents**
Address Cards	Name, follow-up flag, address, phone numbers, e-mail addresses
Detailed Address Cards	The full listing from the General tab
Phone List	Flag status, icon, attachment, name, company, file as, phone numbers, journal, categories
By Category	Flag status, icon, attachment, name, company, file as, categories, phone numbers
By Company	Flag status, icon, attachment, name, job title, company, file as, department, phone numbers, categories
By Location	Flag status, icon, attachment, name, company, file as, state, country/region, phone numbers, categories
By Follow-Up Flag	Flag status, icon, attachment, name, company, file as, phone numbers, categories

Cross-
Reference

Remember, you can also create your own views if you don't like any of the available ones. For detailed information on customizing and creating views, see Chapter 31.

Creating Groups

Although there is no Group By Box command for contacts in the Address Card views, you will find that you can use it in every other view. In fact, the By Category, By Company, By Location, and By Follow-Up Flag views are grouped by those parameters (see the preceding section on viewing contact lists).

In this method of grouping, the Group By Box button on the toolbar is pressed, opening the Group By box above the listings. Field headers are dragged into the Group By box, and the listings automatically group themselves accordingly. Up to four fields can be stacked in this manner, with each group being subordinate to the one before it. The order of the fields, and therefore the stacking of subgroups, can be changed by dragging the field headers into new positions in the Group By box.

The second method of grouping is to right-click the blank record at the top of the window (the one containing the field labeled "Click here to add a new contact") and select Group By from the pop-up menu. In the Group By dialog box, shown in Figure 34-6, fields are chosen from drop-down lists.

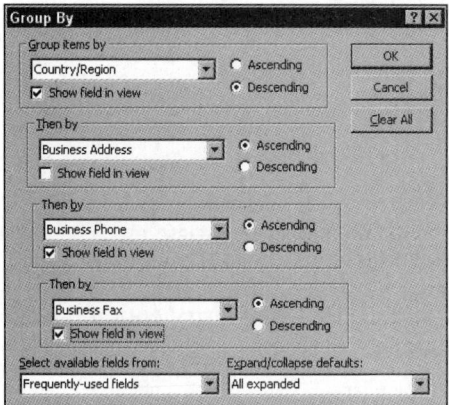

Figure 34-6: The Group By dialog box

Once again, up to four fields can be stacked. When you're finished choosing the fields, click the OK button to implement the grouping. Figure 34-7 shows contacts grouped by last name.

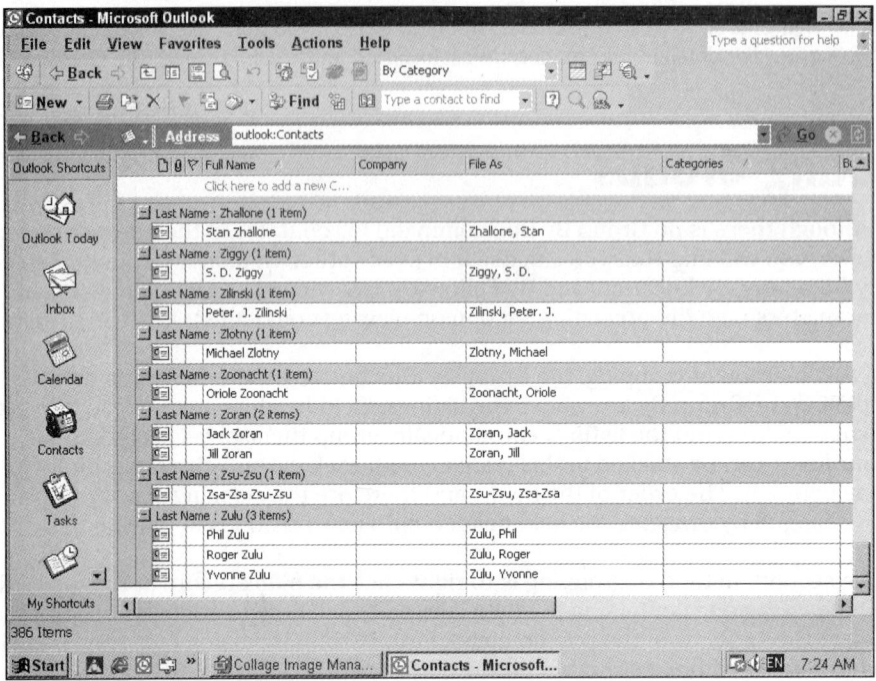

Figure 34-7: When you display contacts by group, they look like this (these contacts are grouped by last name).

Associating Contacts with Other Outlook Items

It's often useful to know not only who's who, but also who's associated with whom or responsible for what. Outlook takes this need into account and provides a simple method for associating contacts with different items in the various folders. You can associate a contact with other contacts, with tasks, with journal entries, and so forth. To link a contact with an item, follow these steps:

1. Select the contact you want to associate with an item.

2. Select Actions ⇨ Link ⇨ Items.

3. In the Link Items to Contact dialog box (see Figure 34-8), select the folder in the top panel that contains the item you want to associate.

4. In the bottom panel, select the item or items you wish to associate with the contact. To select a contiguous range of items, click the first item in the range, hold down the Shift key, and click the last item in the range. To select a non-contiguous group of items, hold down the Ctrl key while clicking each item.

5. Click the OK button.

The associated items appear on the Activities tab in the form for the contact.

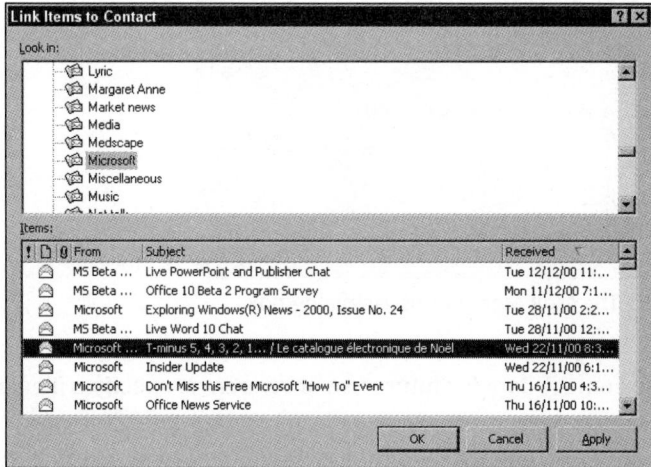

Figure 34-8: The Link Items to Contact dialog box

Mail Merging Outlook Contacts with Word

From time to time, you may want to use your Outlook Contacts listings with Word in a mail-merged document. Thanks to the integration of Office applications, you can do so easily. To use your contacts in a Word mail merge, follow these steps:

1. Open the Contacts folder.

2. Select those contacts you wish to use in the mail merge. To select noncontiguous contacts, hold down the Ctrl key while clicking their listings.

3. Select Tools ⇨ Mail Merge from the menu.

4. The Mail Merge Contacts dialog box will appear (see Figure 34-9). Choose which contacts you want included in the mail merge by clicking the appropriate radio button under Contacts.

5. Choose which fields you want included in the mail merge by clicking the appropriate radio button under "Fields to merge."

6. Choose whether to create a new document or to use an existing document by clicking the appropriate radio button. If you decide to use an existing document, you can click Browse to open a standard file Open dialog box from which you can navigate to the mail merge document you want to use. When you find it, select it and click the OK button to return to the Mail Merge Contacts dialog box.

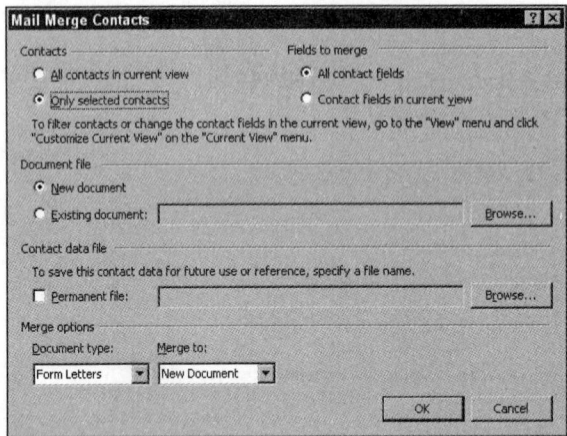

Figure 34-9: The Mail Merge Contacts dialog box

7. To save the contact data for future use or reference, specify a filename where indicated.

8. Choose the appropriate Merge options: "Document type" (form letters, mailing labels, envelopes, or catalog) and "Merge to" (new document, printer, or e-mail).

9. Click the OK button to proceed.

10. Next, either the existing document will be opened or the new one will be created. Click the Insert Merge Fields button to open a list of available fields and insert them into your Word document as desired (see Figure 34-10).

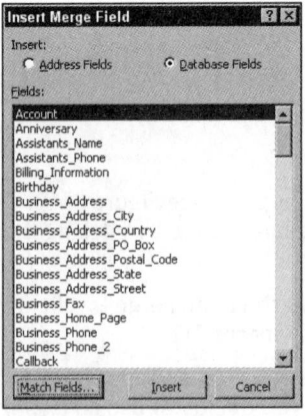

Figure 34-10: The Insert Merge Field dialog box in Word

✦　　✦　　✦

Managing Your Time with Calendar

Beyond the message-and-contact-related capabilities of
Outlook is another thing the application is really good
at: helping you manage your time (and, if you're in a position
to do so, other people's time, too!). This chapter helps you get
a grip on Outlook's Calendar feature, beginning with the
Outlook Today view, which gives you a quick handle on your
day by showing you the appointments and tasks you need to
deal with and monitoring your current e-mail situation all in
one place.

This chapter also explores how you can assign tasks to yourself or to other people (alas, other people can assign you
tasks as well!); how Calendar is used to schedule appointments, keep track of events, and invite other people to meetings; and how you can import scheduling data into Calendar
from other scheduling programs and send information from
Calendar to others.

The Outlook Today View

Outlook Today, as I mentioned back in Chapter 31, is designed
to give you a quick handle on what's facing you right now (see
Figure 35-1). It lists calendar events for the next several days,
shows you your current e-mail message situation, and provides a list of pending tasks. The checkboxes next to the tasks
are there so you can signify that you've finished them. When
you check one, the task is crossed off. You can go to the
Calendar, Messages, or Tasks folders by clicking on their
names.

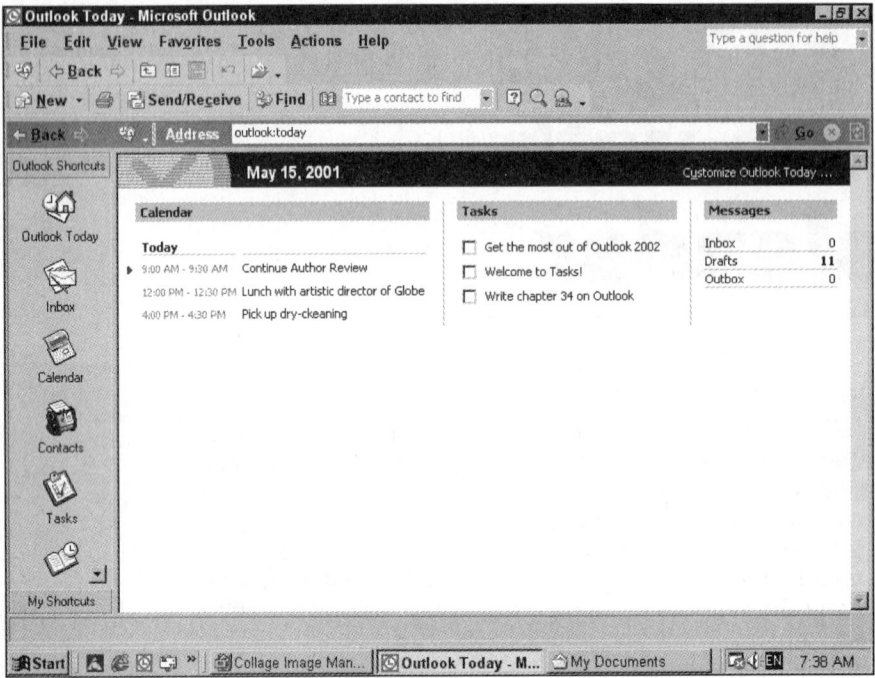

Figure 35-1: The Outlook Today view

Outlook Today's settings aren't graven in stone. As you've probably come to expect in Office in general and Outlook in particular, you can customize it to suit yourself. You can set it up so it's the default opening screen in Outlook, can add other e-mail folders, change the number of days shown in the calendar, and can control how the Tasks list is presented.

To customize Outlook Today, follow these steps:

1. In Outlook Today, click the Customize Outlook Today link. This brings up the Outlook Today options page (see Figure 35-2).

2. To make Outlook Today your default start-up screen in Outlook, click the checkbox labeled "When starting, go directly to Outlook Today."

3. To add or remove folders from the e-mail message listing, click the Select Folder button. In the resulting dialog box, check a folder to include it in the e-mail messages listing or uncheck it to remove it from the listing. By default, Outlook already has the three most likely candidates included—Drafts, Inbox, and Outbox. Depending on your personal needs, however, you may want to remove one or more of these or even add the Sent Items folder or the Deleted Items folder. If you don't want any folders in your e-mail message listing, click the Clear All button. Click OK to return to the options page.

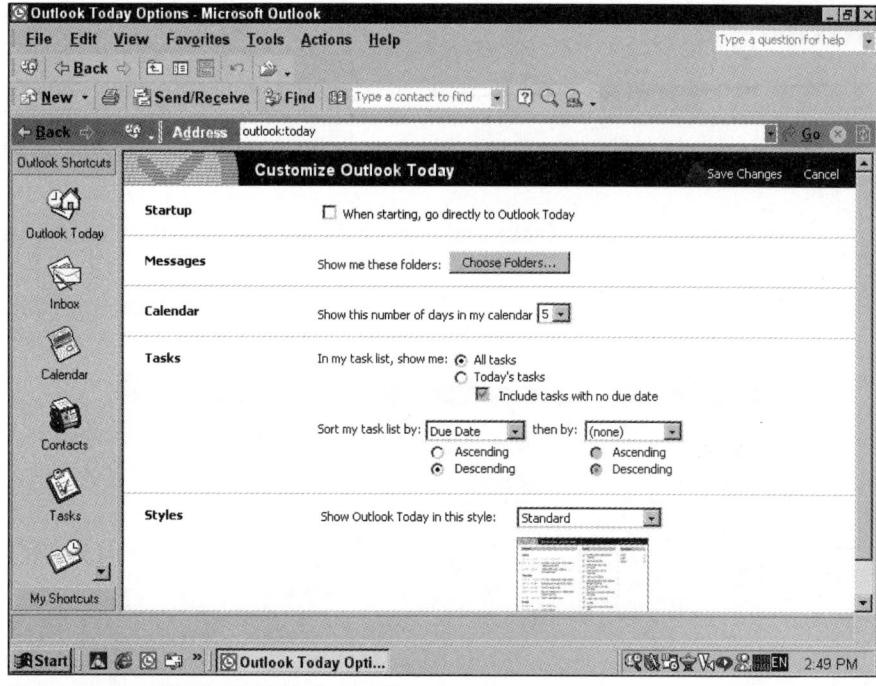

Figure 35-2: The Outlook Today options screen

4. To set how many days of calendar events are shown, choose a number from 1 to 7 from the list box labeled "Show this number of days in my calendar."

5. The Tasks list has the most options. Under the "In my task list, show me" category, the default is "All tasks." If you want to see only one day's tasks, click the "Today's tasks" radio button instead. Check the "Include tasks with no due date" checkbox if you don't want some of your tasks to slip by unnoticed.

6. Next, you can choose how the Tasks list is sorted. The default is by due date. However, you can also choose to sort by importance, creation time, or start date. You can add a second layer of sorting by specifying another field under "then by." The possible fields are the same for both. The default sort order is descending. If you'd prefer to change this, select the Ascending radio buttons.

7. From the Show Outlook Today in this style list box, select the layout you want for Outlook Today. A small preview area below the list box will help you choose.

8. Click the Save Changes button.

Adding and Editing Tasks

You can either assign a task to yourself or send a request to someone else to take on a task (of course, they can send you such a request as well). (In theory, the person you send a task request to can refuse it, but in most companies the chain of command makes this moot!) To create a task, follow these steps:

1. While viewing the Tasks folder, click the New Task button, or choose New ➪ Task at any time.

2. In the task form (see Figure 35-3), type a name for the task under Subject.

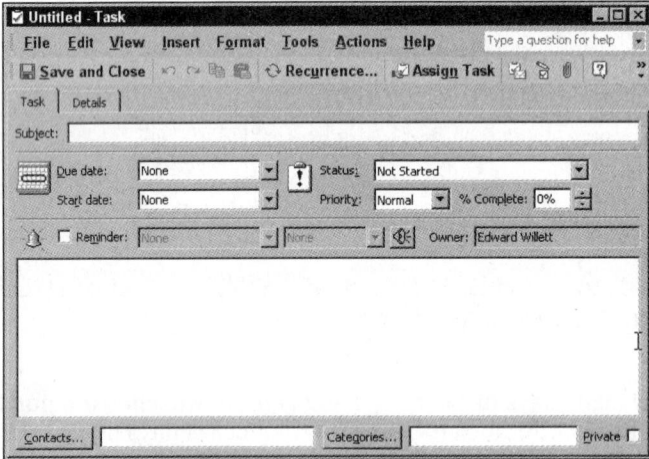

Figure 35-3: The task form

3. Select a Due Date and Start Date. This is done by clicking on the downward-pointing arrows next to those boxes and selecting dates from the pop-up calendars.

4. Select a status for the task from the drop-down list. The options are Not Started, In Progress, Completed, Waiting on Someone Else, and Deferred.

5. Select a priority for the task from the drop-down list. The options are Low, Normal, and High.

6. Select a % Complete from the drop-down list. The options are 0%, 25%, 50%, 75%, and 100%. You can also type any number into the % Complete box.

7. If desired, check the Reminder checkbox and select a date and time. The date is selected from a pop-up calendar. The time is selected from a list of half-hour increments for the day.

8. If desired, click the Speaker icon next to the time box to select a sound that will be played at the reminder time. This brings up a dialog box in which you can click on a Browse button to select a sound file.

9. You can use the buttons on the bottom of the task form to associate contacts or categories with this task.

Note   Associating a contact is *not* the same as assigning a task.

10. Click the Private checkbox if you don't want other people with access to this folder to be able to view this task.

11. Click the Save and Close button on the toolbar.

To edit an existing task, click on it in Outlook Today view or in any other view that displays tasks. This opens the task form, which you can then alter as you desire. Once you've made your changes, click Save and Close to save them.

Assigning a Task to Someone Else

If you followed the procedure above, you've created a task that you own. This may be exactly what you want, if you're planning your own time, but if you're in the fortunate position of being able to plan someone else's time, too, then you'll want to assign the task to someone else.

To do that, create a new task as I've just described and then click the Assign Task button on the toolbar. This causes some changes to the task form, as shown in Figure 35-4.

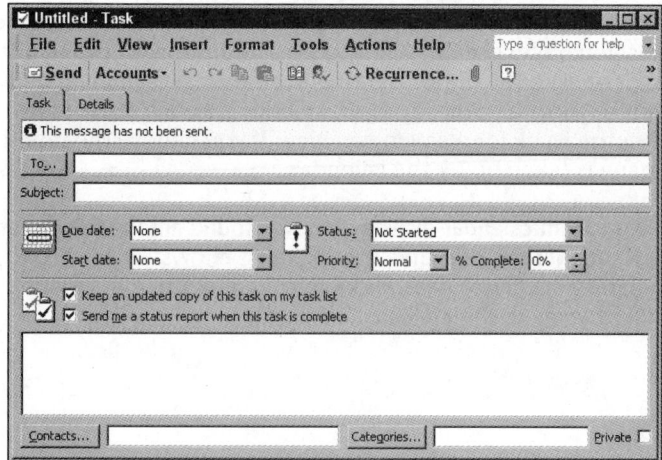

Figure 35-4: The task assignment form

The Assign Task tool has vanished, and the task blank now has a To field just like an e-mail message and, as the notation at the top says, it is currently an unsent e-mail message. Click the To button to select a recipient and then click the Send button.

Note   The Details tab is used for recording such information as the amount of time spent on completing the task, the mileage run up in the process, and so forth.

Using Calendar

If you've ever said to someone, "Yeah, Tuesday at 4:30 will be fine," only to realize later that you already have something scheduled for that time slot, you're going to love Calendar. Calendar lets you manage your time more efficiently, scheduling appointments and events with ease.

First, you should understand some definitions. In Outlook parlance:

✦ An *appointment* is time blocked off on your calendar for a specific purpose over a limited period of time.

✦ A *meeting* is an appointment to which you invite other people. During that time, you normally can't be doing anything else, and your calendar will show that you are busy and unavailable (unless you specify otherwise).

✦ An *event* is something that takes place over a period of at least 24 hours, and it doesn't necessarily mean that you're unavailable during it. For example, a three-day-long seminar is an event, but you may have free periods during those days when you would be available for appointments.

Figure 35-5 shows the basic Calendar screen. Although this is a one-day view, you can also select weekly or monthly calendar views. There are actually two categories of the weekly view — you can choose either a five-day week or a seven-day week. The five-day week, of course, is for Monday through Friday, the typical workweek. Each of these views is selected by clicking the appropriate button on the toolbar. The two-month calendar view in the upper right-hand side of the screen shows a highlight on the current day for the one-day view, Monday through Friday for the five-day view, and the entire week for a seven-day view. If you choose the monthly view, the entire view pane is taken up by the calendar.

Tip   You can use the two-month calendar display to move around among the months, scrolling back and forth via the left- and right-pointing arrows. To bring up the appointment listing for a particular date, click on it. To return to the current day, click the Go to Today button on the toolbar.

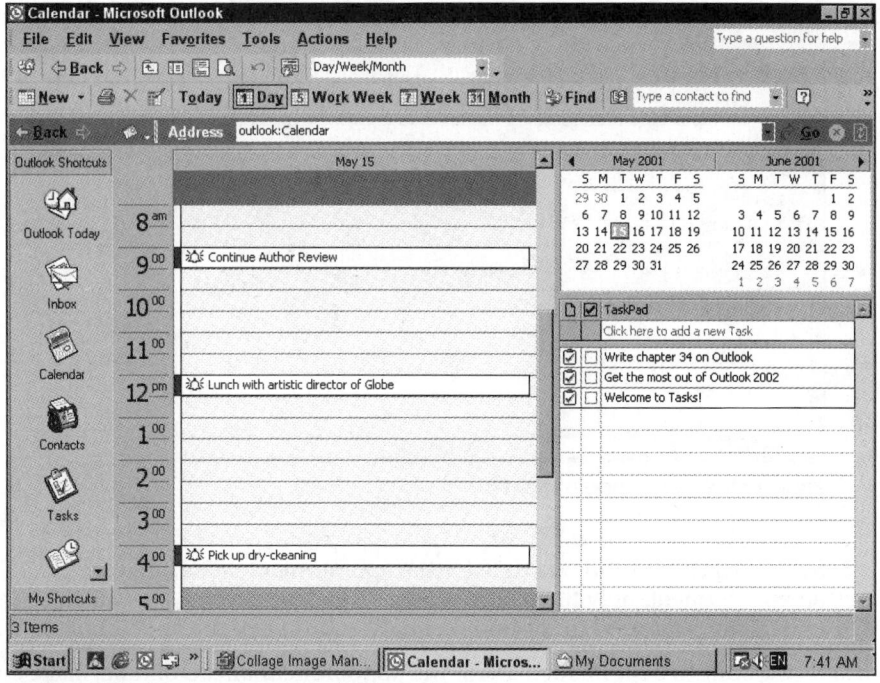

Figure 35-5: The Outlook Calendar

Creating and Managing Appointments and Events

You can add a new appointment to a particular date and time by double-clicking on the time slot in the appointment book while viewing that day. Alternately, you can just click the New button while you're in Calendar view. The only difference between the two approaches is that the first one brings up the appointment form with the correct date and time already inserted. Once you're in the appointment form, follow these steps:

1. Type a subject for the appointment into the first field in the Appointment tab (see Figure 35-6).

2. Enter the location of the meeting in the second field.

3. If this is to be an online meeting, click on the checkbox to the right of the location and select the online program to be used from the drop-down list to the right.

4. If this is an event, check the "All day event" checkbox.

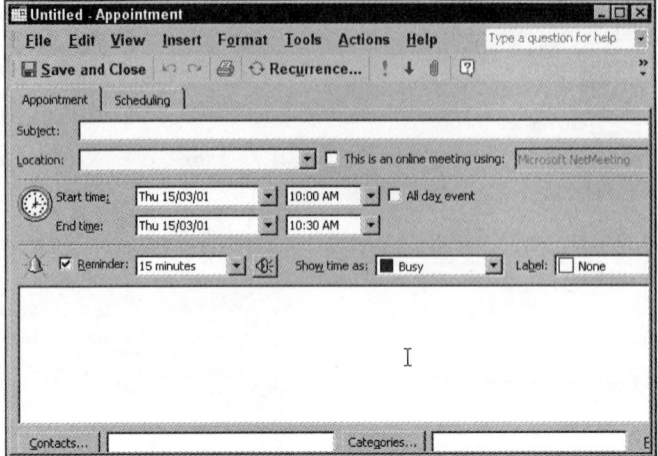

Figure 35-6: The Appointment tab

5. Set the start time and end time for the appointment. If it's an event instead of an appointment, only the starting day and ending day will be available. Otherwise, you need to set both the date and time of the appointment.

6. If you want to be reminded about the appointment ahead of time, make sure the Reminder checkbox is checked and select an amount of time before an appointment when you will be reminded. Click the Speaker icon to select a sound file to be played at that time.

7. Under "Show time as," choose Free, Tentative, Busy, or Out of Office.

8. Add any comments in the text area.

9. If desired, specify which contacts are associated with this appointment by clicking the Contacts button at the bottom of the screen and selecting them from your Contacts listings.

10. If desired, assign categories to the appointment by clicking the Categories button.

11. If you want the appointment to be private, enable the Private checkbox.

12. Click the Save and Close button on the toolbar.

If you are dealing with other people also using Outlook on your network, you can invite others to the meeting, appointment, or event by clicking the Scheduling tab (see Figure 35-7).

Now, to invite others to the meeting, appointment or event, follow these steps:

1. Click the Add Others button.

2. Choose where to add others to the appointment from—your address book or a public folder (if available). In the Select Attendees and Resources dialog box

(see Figure 35-8), select a contact and click the Required button if their presence is necessary (notice that you're already listed as required, since it's your appointment!). Click the Optional button if their presence is desired, but not necessary. Click the Resources button if they're someone providing necessary information for the meeting.

3. Click the OK button to return to the Scheduling tab.

4. Click AutoPick Next to automatically find the next time when the people you've listed are available. Use the << button to find the previous time slot when all the people are available. The box to the right of the list of attendees gives you a graphical representation of people's availability.

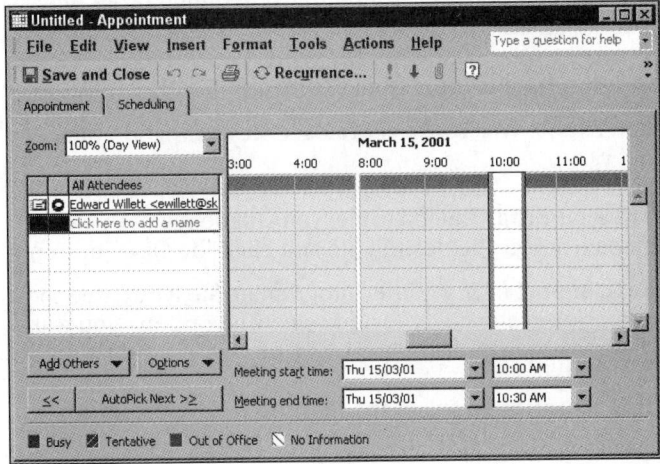

Figure 35-7: The Scheduling tab

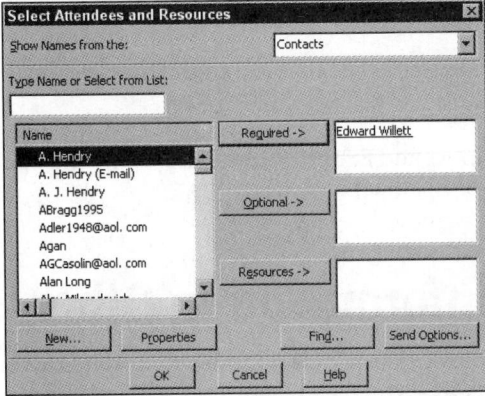

Figure 35-8: The Select Attendees and Resources dialog box

5. Click the Appointment tab.

6. Because others from your Contacts listings are being invited, the appointment blank now has a To field with their names filled in. Click the Send button to issue the appointment notification.

Importing Appointments and Events

If you have scheduling data such as appointments in another program, Outlook can convert it to its own format. You can import calendar data either in the vCalendar format (a format designed for the exchange of calendar data among people using different scheduling applications) or from other scheduling programs, such as Lotus Organizer or Schedule+. To do so, follow these steps:

1. Select File ⇨ Import and Export from the menu.

2. In Import and Export Wizard, select the action you wish to take.

3. Click the Next button.

4. If you chose to import a vCalendar file, you will be taken to a standard file Open dialog box. Select the desired file and click the Open button.

5. If you chose to import from another program or file, you'll see the Import a File dialog box. Select the file type and select the options you want.

6. Click the Next button.

7. Click the Browse button to select the file. You will be taken to a standard file Open dialog box. Select the desired file and click the Open button.

8. Select the duplicate handling option you desire. Your options are to allow duplicate items to overwrite current ones, to allow duplicates to coexist, or to not import duplicates.

9. Click the Next button.

10. Make sure that Calendar is selected as the destination folder.

11. Click the Next button.

12. The final screen of the Import and Export Wizard shows the file you're importing; click Finish to (what else?) finish.

Sending Calendar Information to Other Users

Although other users on your network can view your calendar data (at least the data you haven't marked as private), you may want to send information to others who are not on your network. In that case, you can simply e-mail them the appointment. If they're using Outlook, you can just attach the appointment, but if they're not, you'll need to convert it to iCalendar format. (iCalendar, like vCalendar mentioned earlier, is a calendar format designed to enable people using different scheduling programs, and even different types of computers — iCalendar works with Macintosh systems, too — to exchange calendar information successfully.) Fortunately, Outlook takes care of that little detail for you, and it's simply a matter of making an alternate menu selection. To send calendar data to others, follow these steps:

1. If you are looking at the appointment listing on the main Calendar screen, click on the appointment you want to send. If you're looking at the appointment form itself, the appointment is already selected and you don't need to do anything special.

2. Select Actions ⇨ Forward (to send to another Outlook user) or Actions ⇨ Forward as iCalendar.

3. An e-mail message will be created (see Figure 35-9) with the calendar data included as a file attachment, which shows in the Attach... field. If it's in Outlook format, it'll just list the name of the appointment. If it's in iCalendar format, the file extension .ics will be appended to the name.

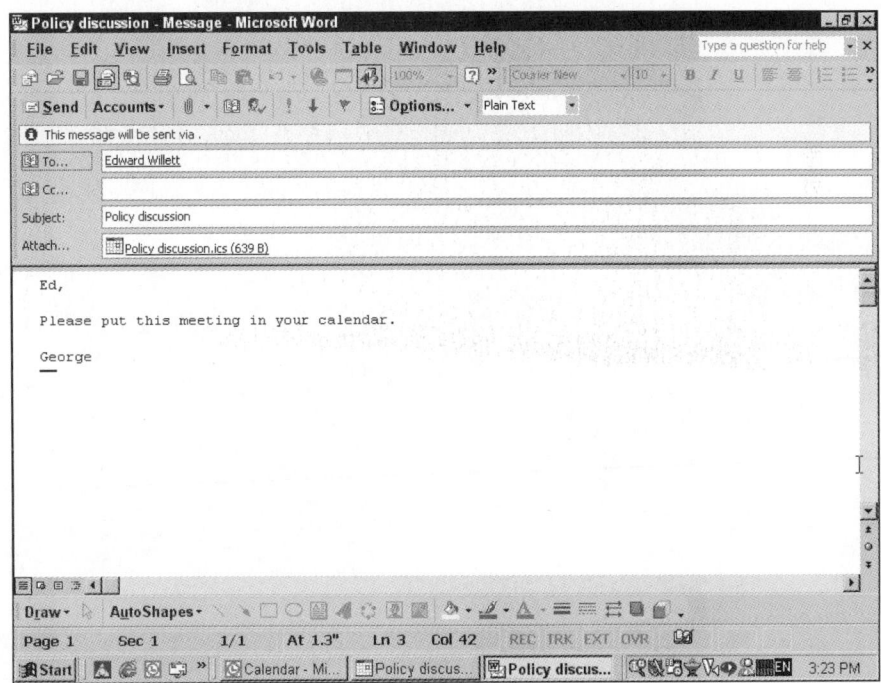

Figure 35-9: Forwarding calendar data in iCalendar format

4. Click the To button to select the recipient(s) from your Contacts listings or type in an e-mail address if they're not among your contacts. If desired, do the same with the Cc field.

5. Type a message in the text area.

6. Click the Send button.

✦   ✦   ✦

Using Journals and Notes

With Outlook's Journal, you can track all your actions in Microsoft Office, showing them as a timeline that you can set for daily, weekly, or monthly views. You can also add items manually to the Journal timeline, and the Journal entries are subject to alteration through direct editing.

Outlook's Notes, meanwhile, are the digital equivalent of Post-it pads. Although they're created within Outlook, Notes are separate applications, which can remain open even when Outlook isn't open.

This chapter on Outlook takes a look at these sometimes underappreciated features.

Viewing Your Journal

The Outlook Journal, which you access buy clicking on the Journal icon in the Outlook bar, keeps track of your actions in Office.

The first time you click on the Journal icon, you'll receive a message asking if you want to activate the journal. If you do, you'll see the Journal Options dialog box shown in Figure 36-1. Here you can choose which items to record in your journal (e-mail messages, meeting cancellations, meeting requests, meeting responses, task requests, and task responses are the options) for which contacts (all the names in your Contacts folder are listed). You're also given the option of recording files from Access, Excel, PowerPoint and Word—checking those options is how you use Journal to keep track of your day-to-day Office activities.

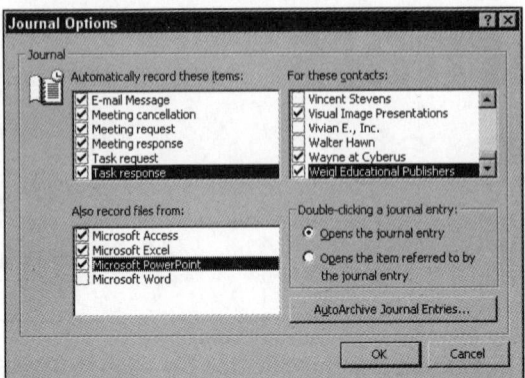

Figure 36-1: Choose what you want your journal to record using the Journal Options dialog box, which opens automatically the first time you activate your journal.

Finally, you can choose to have double-clicking a journal entry either open the journal entry or open the item referred to by the journal entry. Choosing the latter can make it easier to find files you were working with on a particular day of the week in the course of a particular project.

Clicking OK opens the journal.

Tip   Whether you set up your Journal so double-clicking an entry opens the journal entry or opens the item, you can always access the other choice; just right-click the Journal entry and choose either Open Journal Entry or Open Item Referred To on the shortcut menu.

Note   You can return to the Journal Options dialog box and change the way the journal operates at any time by choosing Tools ➪ Options, then clicking on Journal Options in the Contacts section of the Preferences tab.

By default, it shows a weeklong timeline on-screen (see Figure 36-2), although you can change this to a one-day or one-month view. Unlike with Calendar, there is no five-day-week option; a week in the journal is seven days.

The different timelines give different levels of detail. The daily listing, for example, shows what hours a particular file was in use, while the monthly listing doesn't even give the file's name unless you specify that it should (see the following section on configuring your Journal).

You can view by type, contact, category, entry list, last seven days, and phone calls. Just select the desired view from the View ➪ Current View drop-down list. Type is the default view, grouping together all Word documents, Excel worksheets, and so on.

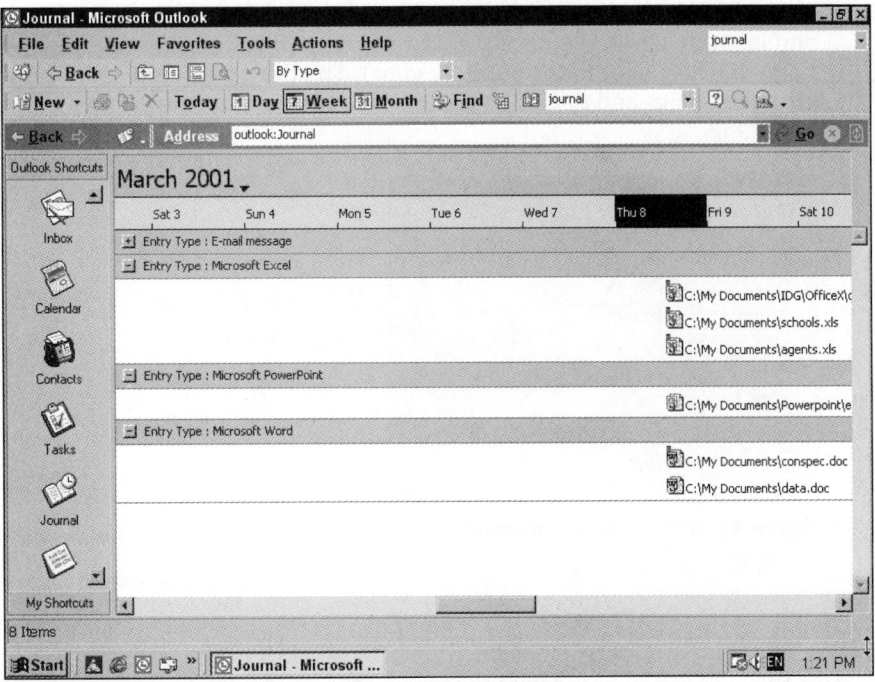

Figure 36-2: The journal, with items viewed by type

Configuring Your Journal

In addition to deciding which timeline view you're going to use, you can also set the journal to use specific fonts for different parts of the timeline, to show week numbers (Week 1 ends on the first Saturday of the year), and to specify the size of Item labels and choose whether or not they should be displayed during the month-long timeline view. To set these options, follow these steps:

1. Right-click anywhere in an open space — not on a journal item — and select Other Settings from the pop-up menu. If your screen is filled with journal items, use the scroll bar at the bottom of the screen to get to a view in which you've got some blank space, or switch to another timeline (daily, weekly, or monthly) in which you can find some blank space to right-click in.

2. In the Format Timeline View dialog box (see Figure 36-3), the top panel contains three buttons for font selection. The first one, Upper Scale Font, is for the top line in the Journal. In the daily view, this line shows the day, month, and year; in the weekly and monthly views, it shows the month and year only (if you're showing week numbers, they'll appear in the daily and weekly views). The second font button, Lower Scale Font, is for the second line in the

Journal. In the daily view, this line shows the hours of the day; in the weekly and monthly views, it shows the day and date (if you're showing week numbers, they'll appear in the monthly view). The third one, Item Font, is for the group headings and the individual journal items within the groups.

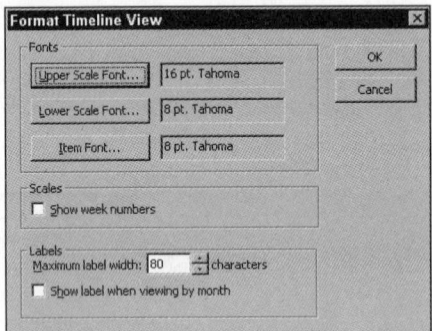

Figure 36-3: The Format Timeline View dialog box

3. Click any font button to bring up the Font dialog box.

4. In the Font dialog box, select the font face from the list under Font, the style (bold, italic, and so on) from the list under Font style, and the font size from the list under Size. You can also choose a different script (that is, Hebrew or Chinese) if you have one installed.

5. Click the OK button to return to the Format Timeline View dialog box.

6. If you want to show the number of the week, check the Show Week Numbers checkbox.

7. The bottom panel is for label-handling options. By default, the maximum length of the label on any item is 80 characters. This number can be set anywhere from 0 to 132 characters. Either type in the desired number or use the arrows to increase or decrease the number.

8. If you want the item labels to be visible in the monthly view, as they are in the daily and weekly views, check the box labeled "Show label when viewing by month".

9. Click the OK button to save your changes.

Adding and Editing Journal Entries

Because not everything is tracked automatically by the journal, you may want to manually add some entries. Or you may want to make changes to the journal entries that already exist.

The easiest way to add a journal entry for an item that is not available for automatic entry is to drag the item onto the Journal icon on the Outlook bar. This brings up a Journal Entry form (see Figure 36-4), in which you can fill out any pertinent data relating to the item.

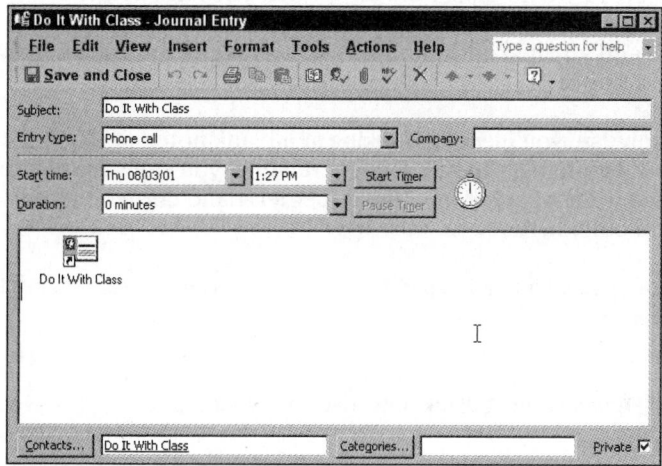

Figure 36-4: The Journal Entry form, set up to track a phone call

In this example, we've decided to make a phone call to a contact, so we dragged the Contact listing onto the Journal icon in the Outlook bar. The Journal Entry form shows the name of the contact, along with other information such as the date and time. To start tracking the call, click the Start Timer button. When the call is finished, click the Pause Timer button. (If you're interrupted during the call, click the Pause Timer button, and then click the Start Timer button once you're able to resume the call. If you want to reset the timer to zero, choose 0 minutes from the Duration list box.) To finish the Journal entry, click the Save and Close button. If there wasn't already a phone call group in the Journal, it's created now and the journal entry for the phone call is placed in the timeline.

To edit an existing journal entry, right-click on it and select Open Journal Entry from the pop-up menu. This brings up the same Journal Entry form, and you can change any of the data in it, including the time, date, and duration of the item. Clicking the Save and Close button puts the new information into the journal, and the journal entry is moved along the timeline to reflect the new data.

Creating and Editing Notes

Notes in Outlook are just like sticky notes in the real world. They're little bits of digital paper that you scribble hasty notes on and pin up where you can find them later.

There are several different ways to create notes. If you're in the Notes folder, just click the New Note button or right-click in an empty space and select New Note from the pop-up menu.

Often, though, you're not there when you want to jot down a note, so it's convenient that Outlook lets you create them from any folder. Click the downward-pointing arrow to the right of the New button. This brings up a listing of all the new items you can create, and you just click on Note. Alternatively, you can choose File ➪ New ➪ Note from the menu.

Whichever method you use, you'll end up looking at a blank note (see Figure 36-5). All you have to do is start typing. Then, when you're done, you can save the note by either double-clicking on the paper icon in the upper left-hand corner of the note or just clicking anywhere outside the note.

 **Tip**   If you need more space, you can expand the note by clicking and dragging the lower-right corner.

   **Figure 36-5:** A blank note, ready for your input

To delete a note, select it by clicking on it, and then press the Del key or click the Delete button on the toolbar.

Viewing Notes

Notes show up as icons in the Notes folder in Outlook. The first couple of words in the notes are shown beneath each icon so you can tell which is which. To view a note, open the Notes folder and double-click on the note's icon.

Although notes are created within Outlook, they're actually totally independent windows, and an open note will show up on your taskbar along with other open applications. You can even close Outlook and the open note will still remain.

If you want to get to notes that aren't open, though, you'll have to go into Outlook and find them in the Notes folder. Figure 36-6 shows the Notes folder with a few notes in it.

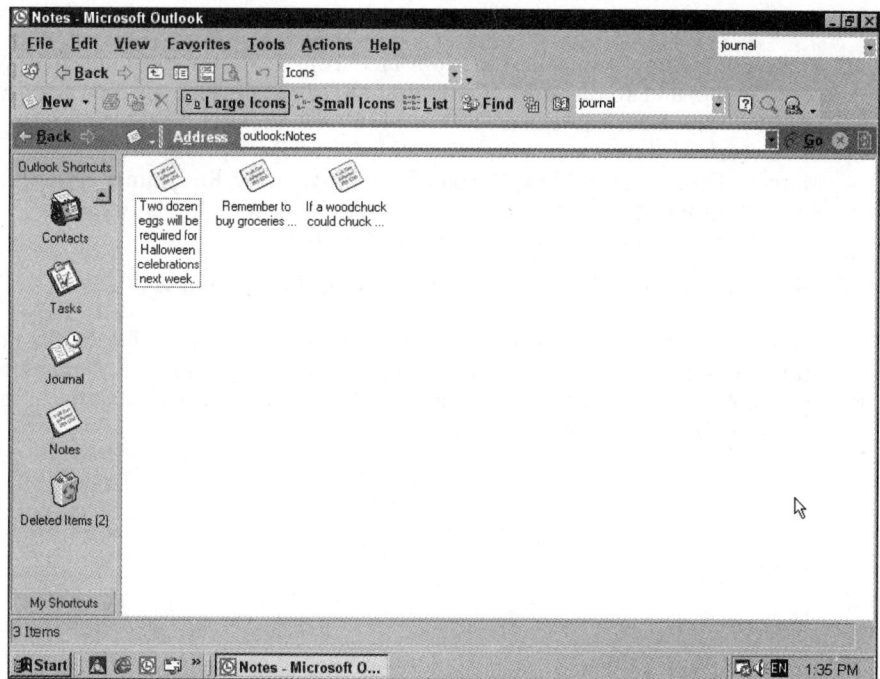

Figure 36-6: The Notes folder displays notes with an icon and a few words.

Configuring Notes

You have very few options for configuring the appearance of your notes.
Essentially, you can set the color and size of the sticky pad, and you can also set
the font, style, size, and color of the text you type within it. To modify these values,
follow these steps:

1. Select Tools ➪ Options from the menu.

2. In the Options dialog box, if it is not already selected, click the
   Preferences tab.

3. Click the Note Options button.

4. In the Notes Options dialog box, you can select the note's color and size from
   the lists. Color options are Blue, Green, Pink, Yellow, or White. Size options are
   Small, Medium, or Large. The default options are Yellow and Medium. (You
   can also change the note's color by clicking its icon on the top left corner,
   choosing Color, and then choosing the color you want from a drop-down list
   of choices.)

5. Click the Font button to bring up the Font dialog box.

6. In the Font dialog box, select the font face from the list under Font, the style (bold, italic, and so on) from the list under Font style, and the font size from the list under Size. You can also choose to have the text be struck out or underlined, and pick a color for the text. Font color options are Black, Maroon, Green, Olive, Navy, Purple, Teal, Gray, Silver, Red, Lime, Yellow, Blue, Fuchsia, Aqua, and White. You can also set the script (that is, Western, Hebrew, or something else you have installed).

7. Click the OK button to return to the Notes Options dialog box.

Tip

You can forward a note to someone else as an e-mail; just right-click on the note and choose Forward. A blank e-mail form opens; type in the address of the person you want to send the note to and click Send. The note is sent as an attachment, not as text in the body of the e-mail.

✦   ✦   ✦

Presenting Your Thoughts Powerfully with PowerPoint

PowerPoint can help you make your point with greater conviction and emphasis — if you know how to use it effectively. This part discusses the basics of powerful presentations and how to use PowerPoint's templates, wizards, graphics, and special effects to achieve that level of power.

Powerful Presentations

Arguably today's premier presentation software, PowerPoint turns out attractive, professional-looking slide shows and electronic presentations with a minimum of hassle. Over and above its rock-solid, basic slide layout and editing features, it can endow your presentations with a raft of special animations and multimedia effects. But don't be put off by the glitzy stuff — PowerPoint ably handles mundane-but-essential chores, such as printing your speaker's notes and audience handouts.

By the way, a quick word on PowerPoint terminology is in order at the outset. A PowerPoint document is referred to as a *presentation*, even if it isn't currently being presented to anyone. A PowerPoint *slide show* displays a presentation's slides one by one, without the distractions of the screen tools used to design the presentation.

Planning Great Presentations

Spending time planning before leaping in with both feet is critical for a successful presentation. Important factors to consider during the planning process include the following:

✦ **Your message.** Start by identifying the core ideas that you want to communicate and organizing the facts you will use to support them. You can think intelligently about the text, images, sounds, or other items you actually need in order to convey the information most clearly.

✦ **Your audience.** The most important consideration in planning a presentation is knowing who you're presenting it to. Is this a technical-minded crowd responsive to factual details presented in a serious tone? Or will the audience be partying during your presentation and looking to you for more good times?

✦ **Your medium.** Obviously, if you plan to present your work on conventional photographic slides or overhead projector transparencies, you won't be incorporating animation and multimedia special effects. An 8-by-10-foot projection screen effectively conveys much more information than a cramped laptop display, so you can include more detail on each slide. Performance considerations become critical if you're going to offer your presentation over the Web, so minimizing the complexity of your slides becomes an especially high priority.

✦ **Room size and lighting.** All things being equal, the larger the room, the larger the type and images you should use (and the less information you should squeeze onto each slide). If the lights will be dimmed during your talk, consider going with light-color slide backgrounds to help lighten the room and enable your audience to see you (and, ideally, pay more attention to what you're saying).

The virtues of simplicity

Keep your slides simple. You can commit no greater sin in the presentation world than bombarding your audience with so much information that the slides look like an eye chart — and leave your audience needing an eye doctor.

You certainly face that danger with PowerPoint. You can sculpt slides with richly detailed backgrounds, captivating graphics, and lists of multiple bullets, each branching into further subcategories — and then add sound, animation, and video. Unfortunately, piling these elements on can be as attractive as a resumé with 30 different fonts, à la the dreaded ransom note style.

Tip   Content is king. When designing a presentation, focus on driving the key points into the minds of your audience as your priority.

Ensuring consistent presentations

Variety is the spice of life, but too much spice causes indigestion. Typically, a presentation audience appreciates a surprise when it occurs within a stable framework of design elements that repeat from slide to slide. Consistency from one presentation to the next makes sense, too, helping you create a professional identity, a sort of visual trademark. Three PowerPoint features help give your slides thematic consistency: masters, color schemes, and templates.

Cross-Reference   Templates and masters are discussed in detail in Chapter 38. Color schemes are accessed through the Slide Design task pane, which is also discussed in Chapter 38.

Starting New Presentations

Whenever you open PowerPoint, it creates a blank title slide and opens the New Presentation task pane, which gives you lots of options as to how you want to go about starting your presentation (see Figure 37-1).

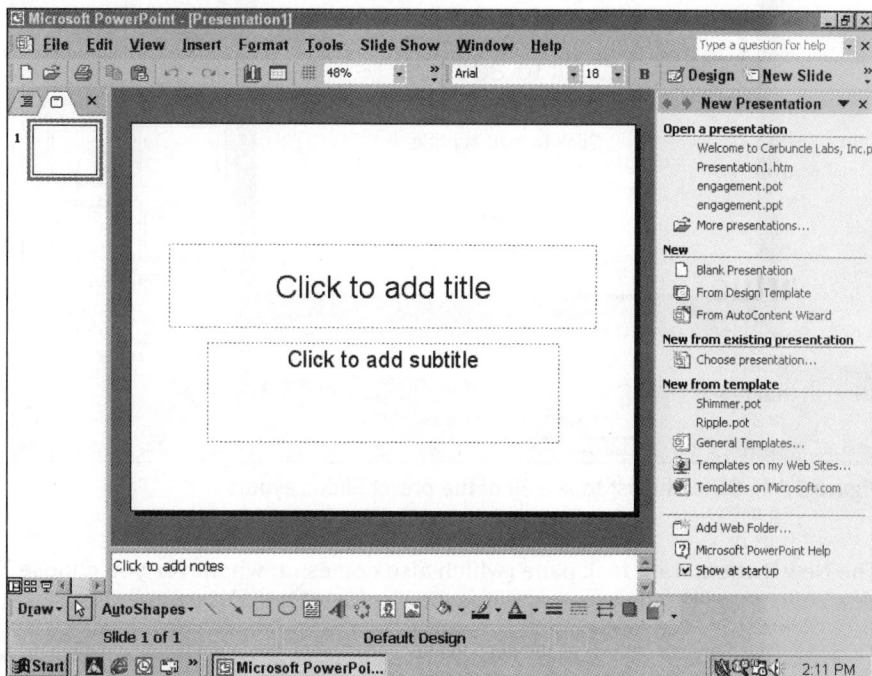

Figure 37-1: The New Presentation task pane presents you with all the different ways you can start a new presentation.

If you select a new blank or design template presentation, PowerPoint asks you to create the first slide, choosing from one of 24 *Slide Layouts*. Figure 37-2 shows the Slide Layout task pane. A Slide Layout choice dictates the number of layout elements or *placeholders*, the type of information each placeholder will contain (text, charts, tables, and so forth), and their arrangement relative to one another.

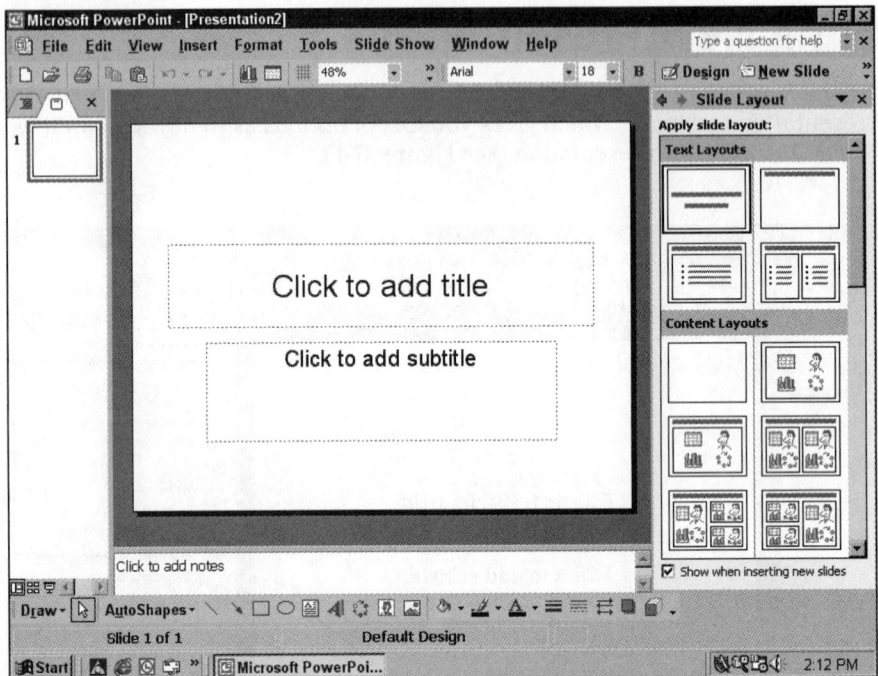

Figure 37-2: Scroll the list to see all of the preset Slide Layouts.

The New Presentation task pane (which also comes up whenever you choose File ⇨ New) offers you three ways to create a new presentation. You can

✦ **Activate the AutoContent Wizard.** Based on your responses, it builds a wide range of boilerplate presentations with skeletal, fill-in-the-blanks content.

✦ **Select a template on which to base the new document.**

✦ **Start a blank presentation devoid of background color or graphics.**

Cross-Reference

The AutoContent Wizard is described in detail in Chapter 38.

Creating Great Slides and Presentations

Once you have your design ideas in mind, you can turn to this section for loads of little tips and background facts that make it easier to bring the slides you imagine into electronic reality.

Working with the PowerPoint user interface

For starters, a quick run-through of a few general user interface topics is in order.

Working with views

PowerPoint's View menu offers three ways to see your presentation while you edit it, plus a Slide Show view to display the slides alone:

✦ **Normal.** Divided into three resizable panes, Normal view is your main presentation-editing tool. The upper-right pane displays a single slide and enables you to edit the slide's contents. The pane on the left shows you either a scrolling list of all your slides and their text in outline form, or thumbnail images of your slides in order, top to bottom, depending on which tab is selected: Outline or Slides. (You can edit as well as browse slide text in the outline pane — see "Reviewing and editing slide text in the outline pane" for details.) The pane at the bottom lets you type in your speaker's notes using a simple word processor.

✦ **Slide Sorter.** Displays thumbnail miniatures of all the slides in the presentation. You can assign special animation effects with the Slide Sorter toolbar (as described in Chapter 39) — if you do, corresponding icons and notations appear below slides with the effects.

✦ **Notes Page.** Displays an editable print preview of your speaker's notes. PowerPoint creates a separate page of notes for each slide with a copy of the slide as well as the note text. You can move the slide and text box around on the page, and you can add more text boxes and graphics, but you can't change the slide content in this view.

✦ **Slide Show.** The Slide Show view is crucial for testing and giving presentations, but you can't edit slides while you're showing them. See Chapter 40 for more information.

Take note of the three little buttons at the bottom left of the PowerPoint window (shown in Figure 37-1, just to the left of the horizontal scrollbar). Clicking these buttons gives you an alternative way to switch between different views, although you don't get a button for the Notes Page.

Tip　To display the Slide master, which determines basic design choices such as the fonts and color scheme used in all slides, Shift+click the Slide View button. Shift+click the Slide Sorter View button to see the Handout master, where you can lay out the printed copies of your slides for distribution to your audience (masters are covered in Chapter 38). Shift+clicking the Slide Show button — the rightmost of the three — displays the Set Up Show dialog box.

Zooming in PowerPoint

Don't forget that PowerPoint lets you change the magnification at which you view your slides. Even when the entire slide fits into the window at a reasonable enlargement, it can pay to zoom in still farther (with the Zoom toolbar button) for detail work. The default zoom setting, Fit, lets PowerPoint adjust magnification automatically so the entire slide always fits as you resize its pane.

> **Note**   If you zoom in so close to a slide that you lose track of what it looks like, just make sure the Slides tab of the left viewing pane is selected. You can keep an eye on the miniature version of the slide in that pane while you work on details in the main pane.

Previewing in black and white

If you plan to print handouts and notes on a black-and-white printer, you can view your slides in Grayscale or in Pure Black and White by clicking the Color/Grayscale button on the Standard toolbar or by choosing View ➪ Color/Grayscale.

Arranging slides in a presentation

Use Slide Sorter view or the outline pane to shuffle the slides in your presentation. In Slide Sorter view, just drag and drop slides where you want them to fall in the presentation sequence. In the outline pane, drag the icon for the entire slide to the destination (for a discussion of the icon, see the section "Reviewing and editing slide text in the outline pane," later in this chapter). You can cut, copy, and paste selected slides in either view. Select a slide in the outline pane by clicking its icon. In Slide Sorter view, you can select nonadjacent slides by pressing Ctrl and clicking.

Modifying the layout of individual slides

You can resize, move, or delete with reckless abandon any placeholder whose content you can change (on non-masters, that means you can't alter the date, slide number, or footer placeholders). If you need a place for additional text, add it via a text box.

Aligning objects with guidelines

Like any self-respecting graphics program, PowerPoint includes optional guides that help you align objects visually or automatically. When guides are visible, dragging an object in a guide's vicinity makes its corner or center (whichever is closer) line up with the guide.

> **New Feature**   PowerPoint 2002 also includes, for the first time, a visible grid that can help you align objects more precisely.

To turn on the grid, simply click the Show/Hide Grid button on the Standard toolbar. A grid made up of dotted lines appears on your slide (see Figure 37-3).

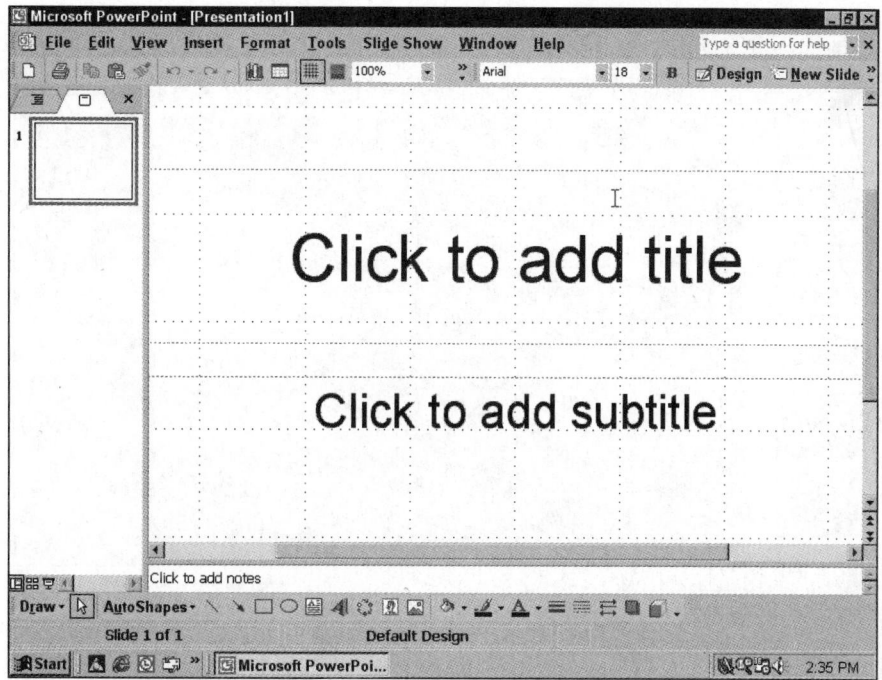

Figure 37-3: PowerPoint now includes a visible grid to help you align objects.

To turn on the guides, choose View ➪ Grid and Guides. The resulting dialog box not only lets you turn on the guides (by checking the appropriate box at the bottom), it also lets you snap objects to grid (as though they had a mysterious magnetic power), snap objects to other objects, and adjust the spacing of the grid. You can make the settings you put into this dialog box the default settings for presentations by clicking the Set as Default button.

The guides are simply horizontal and vertical dotted lines. When you first turn them on, they neatly bisect the slide both vertically and horizontally, dividing it into four quarters. You can drag a guide to wherever it will do you the most good, or drag it off the slide altogether if you want to delete it. To create an additional guide, hold down Ctrl while you drag one of the existing ones. To turn off the Guides, go back to the View ➪ Grid and Guides dialog box and uncheck their checkbox.

Using the pasteboard

If you're making extensive edits to a slide's graphics, use the *pasteboard,* a blank area surrounding the slide as a temporary parking place for objects you might want to reuse. Figure 37-4 shows this technique in action. To place an object on this pasteboard, just drag it off the slide and drop it there. As always, pressing Ctrl while dragging makes a copy of the object, whether you're dragging it to or from the pasteboard.

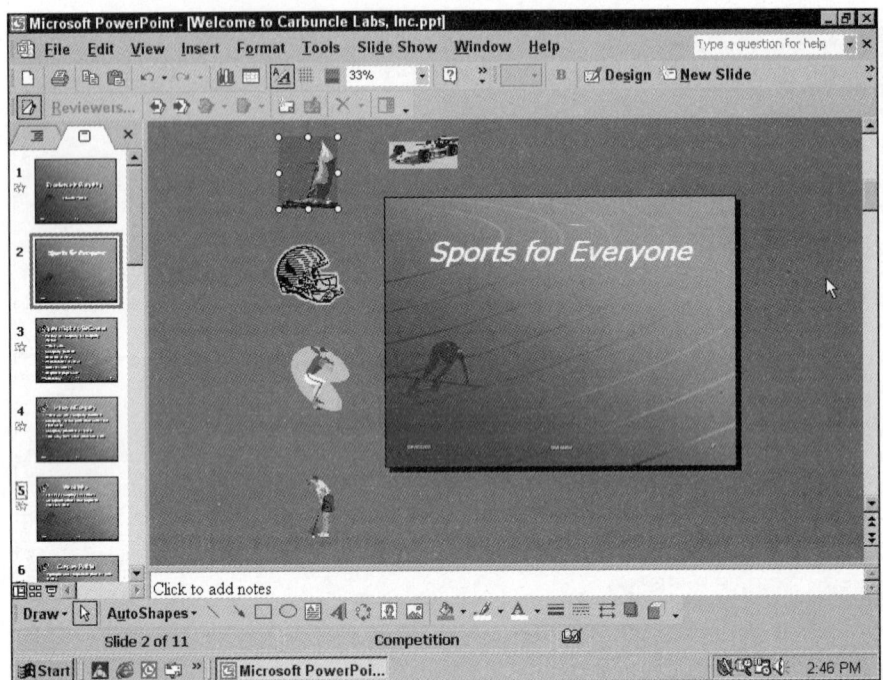

Figure 37-4: Design elements have been parked temporarily on the pasteboard for easy access as slides take shape.

Caution   Unfortunately, the pasteboard moves with the slides when you scroll — when you move to a new slide, you can't access an item you parked alongside another one.

Adding and formatting text

In PowerPoint, text must have a receptacle. You can type text only into placeholders, text boxes, or AutoShapes, not directly onto the slide background.

Editing and navigating text on slides

PowerPoint inserts dummy text into each empty placeholder on a new slide. The dummy text disappears as soon as you add any text of your own. When you're working inside a text placeholder, you can use the arrow keys to move around and the standard Windows Shift+arrow keys to select text. Cut, Copy, and Paste work as expected, of course.

However, cursor movement keys often function differently in PowerPoint than they do in Word or other word processors. Table 37-1 lists the important keyboard navigation commands.

Table 37-1	
Text Navigation Keys on Slides	
To Do This	*Press These Keys*
At All Times	
Move to the next or previous slide	Page Down or Page Up
Move to the next text placeholder and select the text within it; if at the last placeholder in the slide, insert a new slide	Ctrl+Enter
When Text Editing Isn't Active inside a Text Placeholder	
Move to the first or last slide	Shift+Home or Shift+End
Select the next or previous text placeholder on the current slide	Tab or Shift+Tab
When a Text Placeholder Is Selected, but Text Editing Isn't Active inside It	
Select the placeholder's text	Enter (you can then use the arrow keys to move to a specific location in the text)
Unselect the placeholder	Esc
When Text Editing Is Active inside a Text Placeholder	
Move up or down a line	Up or Down arrow. Home and End also work, when pressed with the insertion point at the beginning or end of a line.
When Text Editing Is Active inside a Text Placeholder	
Remove the insertion point and select the placeholder	Esc
Demote or promote the current bulleted point to the next lower or higher level in the outline	Alt+Shift+Right arrow or Alt+Shift+Left arrow. Tab or Shift+Tab also works when pressed at the beginning of the paragraph.

Note   If you have an IntelliMouse, you can use the wheel to scroll through the slides in Normal, Outline, or Slide view.

Reviewing and editing slide text in the outline pane

You can edit your presentation's text in the outline pane rather than on the slide itself. Editing in the outline pane lets you develop content for the entire presentation in one editing window, and it enables you to focus on organization and ideas without distracting layout concerns.

Figure 37-5 shows the outline pane at work. Icons and an outline layout make the presentation's organization easy to understand. Each slide has a number and a slide icon. The text in bold alongside these symbols is the slide's title and appears in the title placeholder. Additional text on the slide appears below that, in point form.

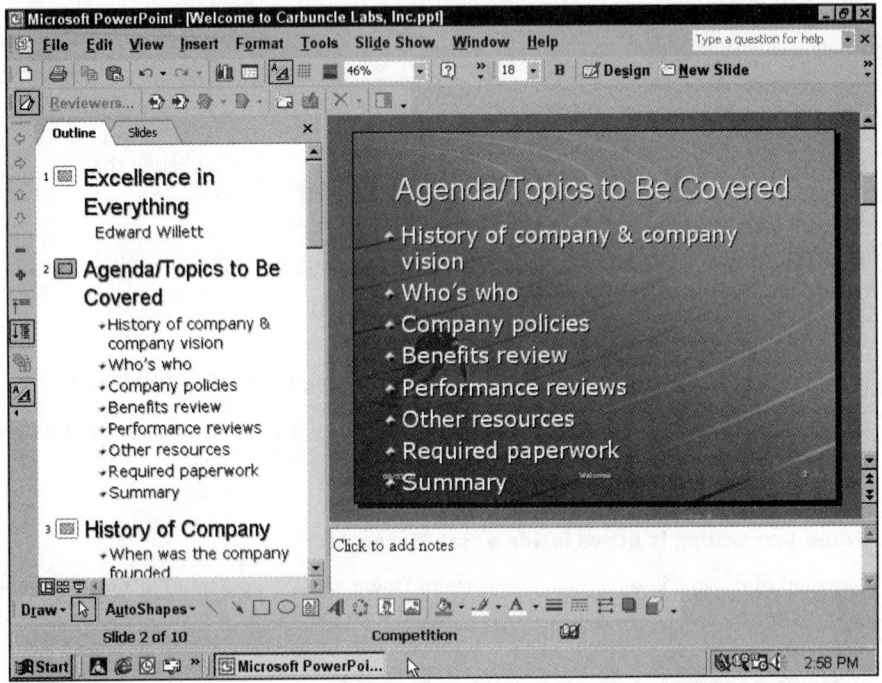

Figure 37-5: PowerPoint's outline pane lets you work with multiple slides in text format. I've activated the Outlining toolbar, which is docked along the left side of the screen.

The outline pane works much like Word's Outline view (see Chapter 19). To take full advantage of it, you need to turn on the Outlining toolbar by choosing View ➪ Toolbars ➪ Outlining. Once you've done that, you can

> ✦ **Collapse or expand any selected slides of the outline.** Doing so enables you to show only the slide titles or all of the subsidiary points. Select the slides you want to work with — you have to Shift+click each slide individually — and then click the Collapse or Expand button on the Outlining toolbar.

> ✦ **Demote or promote bulleted items in the outline.** Drag them to the right or left or use the Demote and Promote buttons (the ones with the big green arrows) on the toolbar.

> ✦ **Reorder bulleted points or entire slides.** Just drag them up or down or use the Move Up or Move Down buttons.

✦ **Demote or Promote items within the outline.** For example, you can turn title text into just another bulleted point, or vice versa, with the Demote and Promote buttons.

✦ **Create a Summary Slide.** Use this slide to present the titles of the selected slides as bulleted points; create it by using the Summary Slide button.

✦ **Show or hide formatting.** Just click the Show Formatting button. In Figure 37-5, Show Formatting is turned on.

In general, editing keys work in the outline pane like they do when you're working directly with your slides (see Table 37-1). One exception: Page Up and Page Down move you up and down through the outline a page at a time, rather than to the previous or next slide.

When the text placeholders specified by a slide layout aren't enough, you can add as many text boxes as you need via the Drawing toolbar or the Insert ➪ Text Box command. But text boxes aren't quite like text PowerPoint placeholders. For one thing, they and their content don't appear in the outline pane. For another, although they do take on the slide's default font, they don't pick up the custom bullets specified by the slide's template.

Bookmarking text in PowerPoint

You can use a custom document property to jump to a specific text location in a PowerPoint presentation. This trick is sort of like a one-legged version of the bookmark feature in Word.

First create the custom property, linking it to the content you want to be able to jump to. To do that, select the text you want to bookmark—you can't bookmark an unselected insertion point—and choose File ➪ Properties. On the Custom tab, type in or select a property name and check the Link to Content box.

Thereafter, you can move immediately to the bookmarked text. Choose Edit ➪ Go to Property, select the name of the custom link, and then choose Go To.

Splitting and merging slides

To divide up an overly long text passage over two slides, use Outline view. Place the insertion point where you want the break and press Enter. Now, without moving the insertion point, click the Outline Promote button until you see a new slide icon. You can then give it a title.

Similarly, you can combine two slides into one, incorporating the text of the second slide into the body text of the first. In the outline pane, begin by moving the slides to be merged so they're in consecutive order in the presentation, with the one that will receive the merged text first. Select the title of the second slide and click the Demote button or press Alt+Shift+Right arrow. After you OK a warning message, PowerPoint merges the slides.

Importing text from an outline

You can also import text formatted as an outline from just about any kind of file and have PowerPoint convert the outline into slides automatically. Choose Insert ➪ Slides from Outline to create new outline-based slides in an existing presentation. Alternatively, if you're starting a new presentation, you can base it on an outline by choosing File ➪ Open and selecting All Outlines in the "Files of type" box. Each top-level heading becomes the title for a new slide, with the points beneath it entering the slides as body text, indented according to their outline level in the original file.

As you would hope, this technique works especially well with outlines created in Word. Paragraphs assigned to the Heading 1 style in a Word document become titles of PowerPoint slides; Heading-2 paragraphs get converted to the top level in bulleted lists, and so forth. If you're currently working with the document in Word, you can jump-start the presentation by choosing — in Word — File ➪ Send To ➪ Microsoft PowerPoint.

Formatting text

Text formatting works in PowerPoint as it does elsewhere in Office, with a few wrinkles:

✦ The Formatting toolbar has a button for Shadow Format Text.

✦ For fast modifications of font size, use a pair of buttons on the Formatting toolbar: Increase and Decrease Font Size. You can make similar quick adjustments of line spacing for paragraphs with the Increase and Decrease Paragraph Spacing buttons, but you have to add them to a toolbar first. For more precise work, use the Font and Line Spacing commands on the Format menu.

✦ You can add or remove the bullet from any paragraph with the Bullets button. To change the bullet character or its size or color, right-click the paragraph and choose Bullets and Numbering from the shortcut menu. You can select any character from any available font as a bullet or choose a graphic from the Clip Organizer. To create an automatically numbered list, pick one of the number formats from the Numbered tab of the Bullets and Numbering dialog box.

✦ In an ordinary text placeholder containing outline-formatted text, use the Promote and Demote buttons to change the outline level of the current paragraph. Alternatively, you can use two pairs of keyboard equivalents: Tab and Shift+Tab, or Alt+Shift with the left and right arrow. If the text is bulleted, its bullet character changes accordingly. (By the way, Alt+Shift+up arrow or down arrow moves the current paragraph up or down as a unit, as in Word.)

Setting paragraph indents

PowerPoint has a ruler much like Word's, and you need it to indent paragraph text. Display the ruler by choosing View ➪ Ruler. Then use the same techniques you use in Word to change the indents of the paragraph containing the insertion point.

Adding text animation

PowerPoint lets you fiddle with text animation effects in a seemingly infinite number of permutations, although I recommend that you stick with one or two relatively simple methods, except when you want to draw attention away from the speaker and to the screen.

 **Cross-Reference** Animation is covered in detail in Chapter 39.

Checking spelling

PowerPoint shares the Office spell checker with Word and its other sisters and brothers. And like Word, PowerPoint checks your spelling on the fly if you leave the "Check spelling as you type" box checked in the Tools ⇨ Options dialog box (the Spelling and Style tab). You see little wavy red lines under words that aren't in the dictionary.

Getting suggestions

In PowerPoint 2002, as in the rest of Office XP, Smart Tags stand ready to help you out whenever Office thinks you need it. Open up the tag by clicking its downward-pointing arrow, and you'll see a list of suggestions you can choose from (see Figure 37-6).

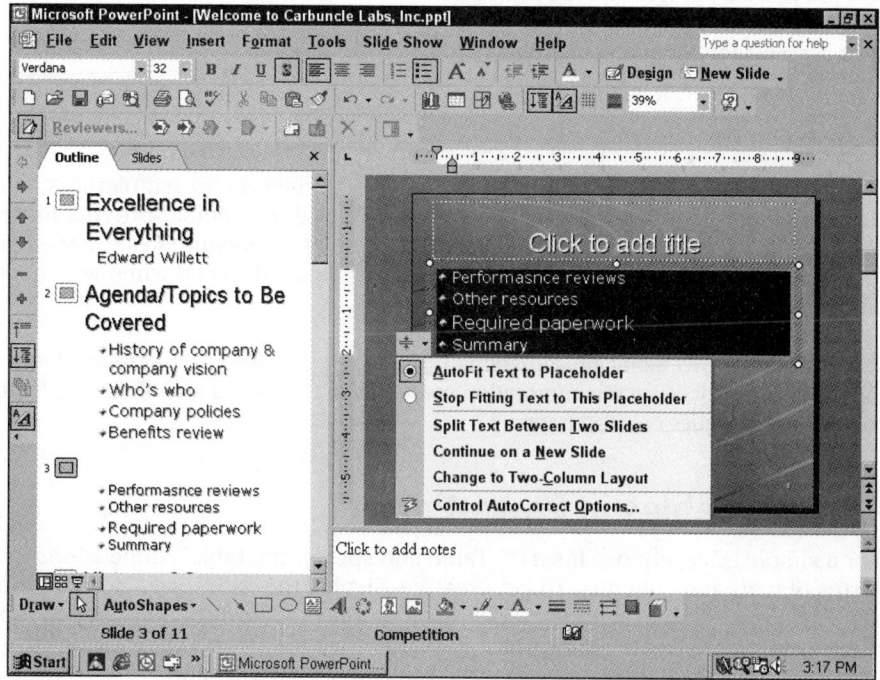

Figure 37-6: PowerPoint has determined I could use some help, and so has popped up a Smart Tag with possible solutions for my conundrum.

Use the Style Options dialog box (shown in Figure 37-7) to set the rules PowerPoint uses for analyzing style. To display this box, go to the Spelling and Style tab of the Tools ➪ Options dialog box and click the Style Options button.

The dialog box has two tabs, Case and End Punctuation and Visual Clarity. Both choices refer to text — whatever the name suggests to you, the Visual Clarity options govern text-related issues such as minimum font size and maximum number of bullets per slide.

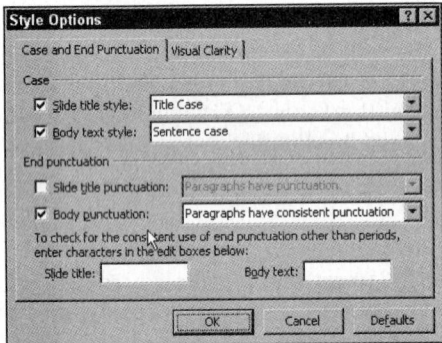

Figure 37-7: The Style Options dialog box lets you make a number of decisions about how PowerPoint should check the style of your presentation for potential problems.

Adding graphics, charts, and tables

You can draw shapes (line art), add AutoShapes, or insert clip art, pictures, maps, and charts, or any other object in your PowerPoint documents. Note that like Excel, PowerPoint's AutoShapes menu offers a Connectors submenu. These shapes are lines that connect two objects on a slide and that stay attached when you move the objects.

Tip

Because PowerPoint presentations typically rely so heavily on graphic elements, be sure to draw on the information presented in Chapters 9 and 42 to supplement the techniques covered here.

Creating tables in PowerPoint

For a simple table, choose Insert ➪ Table and specify the table's dimensions in terms of rows and columns. To get creative, display the Tables and Borders toolbar (by clicking the Tables and Borders button on the Standard toolbar), which looks and works much like its counterpart in Word. Click the Draw Table button (the one that looks like a pencil) to lay down the table divisions freehand.

Tip

Click the menu button labeled Table on the Tables and Borders toolbar to reveal a laundry list of table-related commands. If you work regularly with PowerPoint tables and don't want to keep the toolbar visible always, Alt+Ctrl+drag a copy of this menu to the main menu bar for immediate access at any time.

Inserting Word tables and Excel charts

Although you can create tables in PowerPoint, you may prefer to rely on Word's more powerful table editing and formatting features. After you perfect the table in Word, select it, copy it to the Clipboard, and then switch to PowerPoint and paste it onto a slide. The same simple technique works for Excel charts as well.

The simple Clipboard method doesn't create a hot link to the original table or chart. If you want to be able to edit the item using the originating program, or if you want changes in the source document to appear automatically in your slide, you must insert or link the item as discussed in Chapter 11.

Copying formats

When you want to duplicate a set of formatting options you've already applied to an item on a slide, use PowerPoint's Format Painter. This feature works much like the comparable command in Word. Select the text or picture with the formatting you want to copy, and then click the Format Painter button. All you have to do then is drag over the text or click the picture that you want to receive the same formatting.

Adding action buttons, interactive controls, and hyperlinks

Make your PowerPoint presentations interactive. You can insert an *action button* on any slide by choosing the desired button from the Draw toolbar's AutoShapes ➪ Action Buttons menu. For detailed information on using action buttons, see Chapter 39.

As in other Office documents, you can also add hyperlinks and dialog box–type interactive controls to any PowerPoint presentation. Hyperlinks can be placed into any area that holds text. To add controls to a slide, display the Control Toolbox by selecting it on the View ➪ Toolbars menu (see Chapter 10 for information on controls).

Multimedia madness

When does it make sense to add video and sound to a slide show? Only when they actually clarify your presentation. Using them just because you can is at best annoying and at worst a superlative means of obfuscating your point or muddying your message. Over my protests, add your multimedia objects via the Insert ⇨ Movies and Sound submenu, dealt with in more detail in Chapter 39.

✦　　✦　　✦

Saving Time with Templates and Wizards

◆ ◆ ◆ ◆

In This Chapter

Working with the
AutoContent Wizard

Understanding the
Slide Layout task
pane

Making effective use
of Masters

Using, creating, and
saving templates

◆ ◆ ◆ ◆

Not everyone has the knack, the knowledge, or (especially) the time to design a presentation entirely from scratch. Sometimes you just want to enter your information and let PowerPoint do all the work of making it look great. Well, PowerPoint is more than equal to the task, with a number of tools to get your presentation up and running as quickly as possible.

Using the AutoContent Wizard

The AutoContent Wizard gets you going quickly by providing you with both a design and suggested content for a variety of common presentation types.

Whenever you start PowerPoint or whenever you choose File ➪ New, From AutoContent Wizard is one of the options you're presented with in the New Presentation task pane (see Figure 38-1). Just click it to start it.

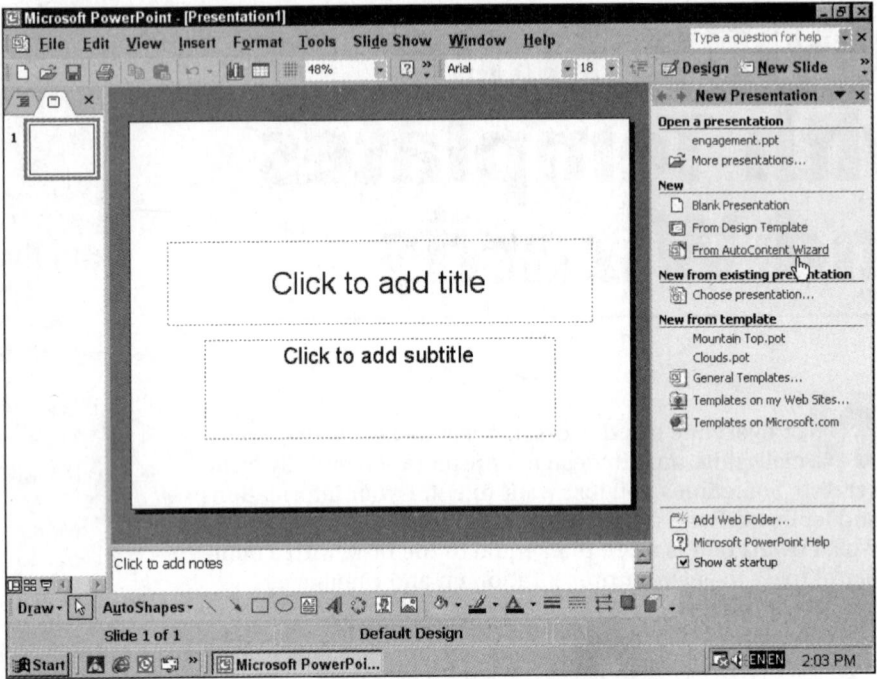

Figure 38-1: AutoContent Wizard is ready to help you every time you open PowerPoint or start a new PowerPoint presentation: just click.

From the introductory screen, click Next to open the first of three screens in which you provide AutoContent Wizard with the information it needs to help you out. The three screens are as follows:

✦ **Presentation type:** Click All (see Figure 38-2) to see all the presentation types the AutoContent Wizard can help you create (everything from "Recommending a Strategy" to a "Group Home Page" to a "Project Post-Mortem"), or click General, Corporate, Projects, Sales/Marketing or Carnegie Coach to see just the presentations in those areas. (The Carnegie Coach presentations contain content designed to help you hone your own presentation and public speaking abilities.) Choose the presentation type you want and click Next.

✦ **Presentation style:** Presentations can be designed to be displayed on a computer screen, on the Web, as black-and-white handouts, as color transparencies, or even as 35mm slides. Choose the type of final product you're aiming for, and then click Next.

✦ **Presentation options:** In the third and final screen, you enter a title for your presentation and any text you'd like to appear as a footer on each slide, and decide whether you want the date the slide was last updated and the slide number to also appear in the footer.

Once you've made all these choices, click Finish. AutoContent Wizard creates a presentation of the type you've specified with slides that are typical of that kind of presentation (see Figure 38-3). Each slide contains suggestions as to what sort of content should appear there. You can use or ignore those suggestions as you wish: At this point, the presentation is entirely yours to edit—but you're already way ahead of where you would be if you'd started from scratch!

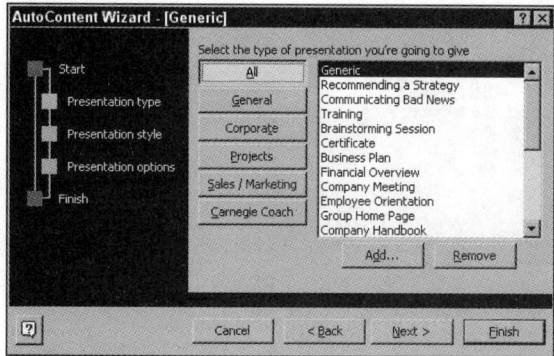

Figure 38-2: What sort of presentation would you like to create? AutoContent Wizard can help you with the most common types.

Figure 38-3: AutoContent Wizard adds suggested content to all the slides in the presentations it creates to help you with the process of adding your own content.

More about the Slide Layout Task Pane

As noted in the last chapter, whenever you start a new, blank presentation or insert a new slide, you're provided with a number of slide layouts to choose from in the Slide Layout task pane (see Figure 38-4). When you choose one, the new slide that appears has placeholders in it, into which you can insert your own content.

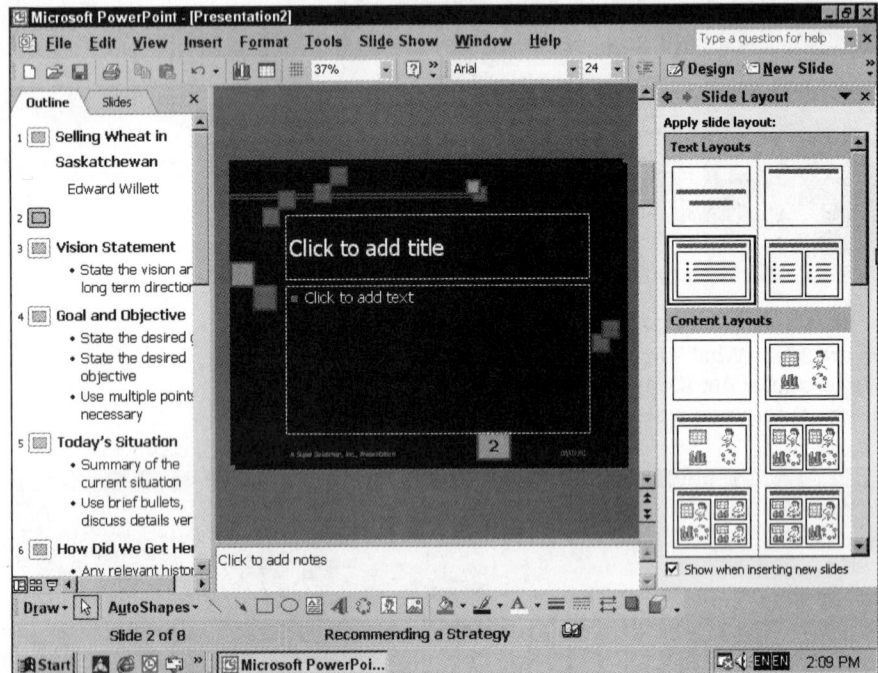

Figure 38-4: PowerPoint provides you with a wide selection of predesigned slide layouts, into which you can insert your own content.

Exploring the available layouts

The available slide layouts are divided into four categories:

✦ **Text Layouts** include only text. Options include a title slide, a blank slide with a title across the top, and slides that contain bulleted lists.

✦ **Content Layouts** include almost everything but text. As I described in more detail in the previous chapter, when you choose a content layout, you'll see one or more little boxes on the slide that contain six options: Insert Table, Insert Chart, Insert Clip Art, Insert Picture, Insert Diagram or Organization Chart, and Insert Media Clip. Just click on the button within the Content box that represents the type of content you want to insert. Content Layouts arrange this content in a variety of ways on the slide. Some slides include titles.

✦ **Text and Content Layouts** combine titles, bulleted lists, and content.

✦ **Other Layouts** are a hodgepodge of layouts that include specific types of content — for instance, a bulleted list and clip art, or a chart and a bulleted list, or a title and a chart, or a title and a diagram or organization chart.

Reconfiguring existing slides

These slide layouts are good for more than just inserting new slides; you can also use them to reconfigure existing slides. To do so, bring up the slide you want to change in Normal view, and then choose Format ➪ Slide Layout (or right-click and choose Slide Layout from the pop-up menu). This opens the Slide Layout task pane; click on the new layout you want to apply to the existing slide and it's automatically applied.

Figure 38-5 shows a slide created using the Title and Text layout from the Text Layouts section of the Slide Layout task pane, while Figure 38-6 shows the same slide with the Title, Content and Text layout from the Text and Content Layouts section of the Slide Layout task pane applied (note the Content box waiting for me to decide what kind of content I want to add).

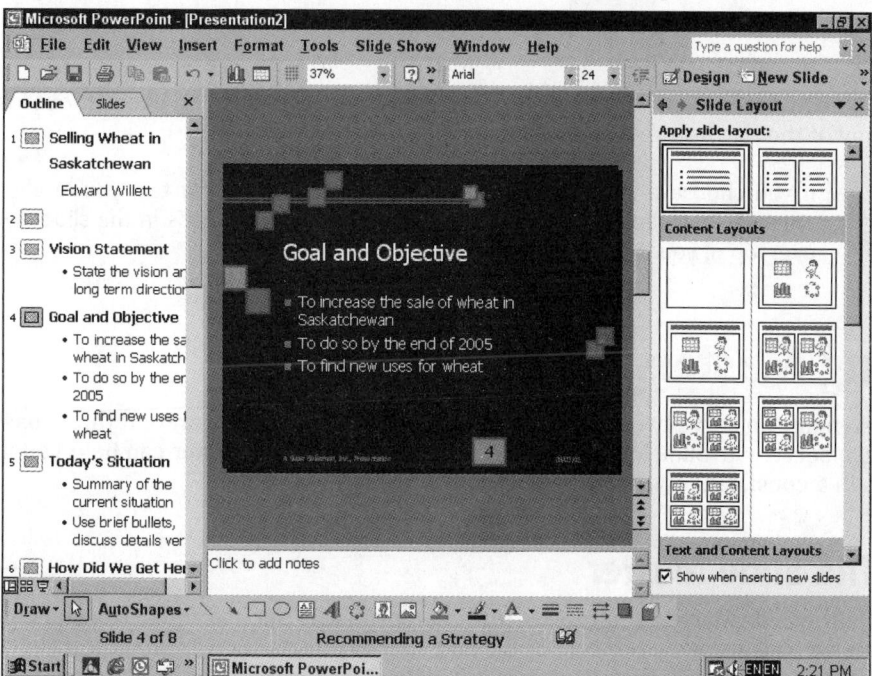

Figure 38-5: Using the Title and Text slide layout, I created this slide for my presentation.

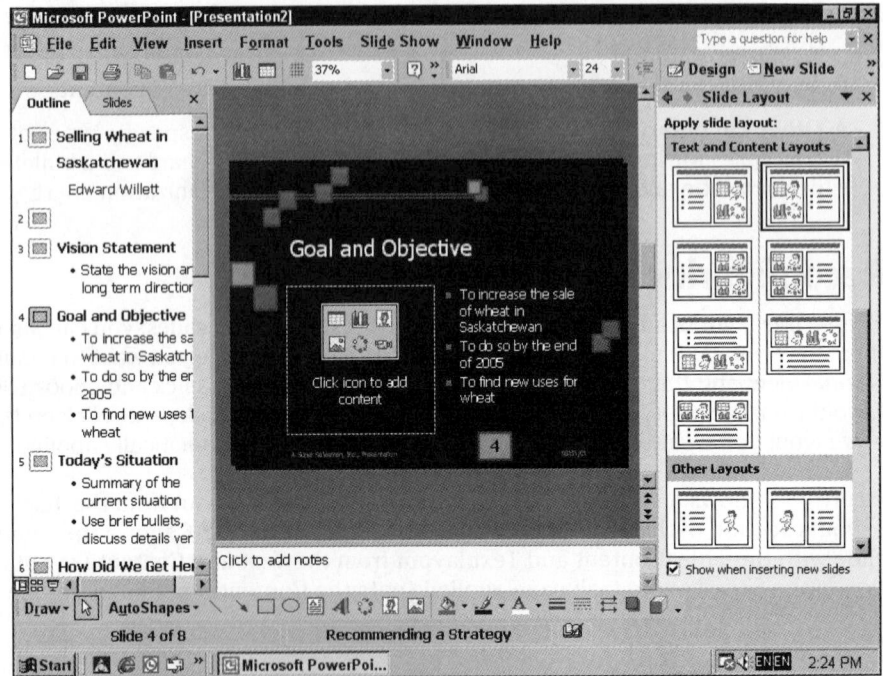

Figure 38-6: The same slide with the Title, Content and Text layout applied

You can experiment with as many different slide layouts as you like without losing any of the text you've already entered.

Caution   If you choose a slide layout that doesn't contain space for text you've already entered, PowerPoint will simply plop a box containing what's in the slide layout over top of your text (see Figure 38-7).

Using Masters

No man can serve two masters, the Bible tells us, but in PowerPoint three masters can serve you: Slide Master, Handout Master, and Notes Master can help you maintain a consistent style throughout your presentation.

The Slide Master

On the Slide Master, you can set text characteristics such as font, size, and color, plus a background color or graphic and special effects such as shadowing and bullet style, which will then be applied by default to all the slides in that presentation.

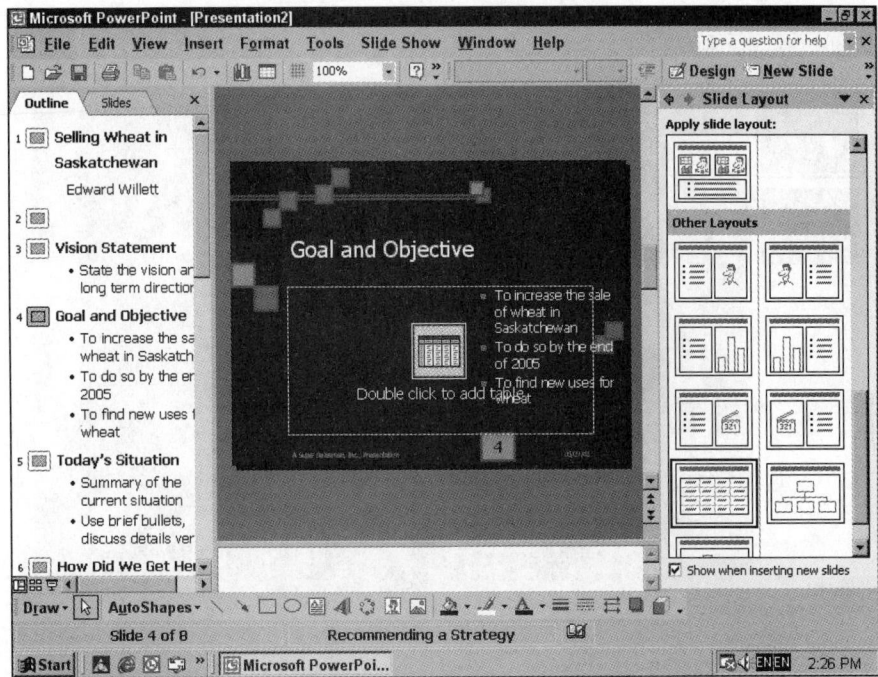

Figure 38-7: If you choose a slide layout that doesn't have a placeholder for text you've already entered, you'll end up with the content from the slide layout overlaying your text, and you'll have to do some juggling to make it all fit.

Using the Slide Master also means that if you want to make a change to the style of, say, all the slide titles in a presentation, you don't have to change each title on each slide: You can simply make the change on the Slide Master, and all the slide titles that use that Master will change appearance automatically.

You can also use the Slide Master to make anything you like appear on every slide in the presentation. A typical example would be the company logo. Rather than insert it as a separate picture on each slide, just insert it once on the Slide Master and it will appear on each slide automatically.

New in PowerPoint 2002, you can create more than one Slide Master in the same presentation, so you can base, say, your introductory slides on one Slide Master, the meat of your presentation on a second, and the conclusion on a third.

Opening the Slide Master

To open the Slide Master, choose View ➪ Master ➪ Slide Master (see Figure 38-8).

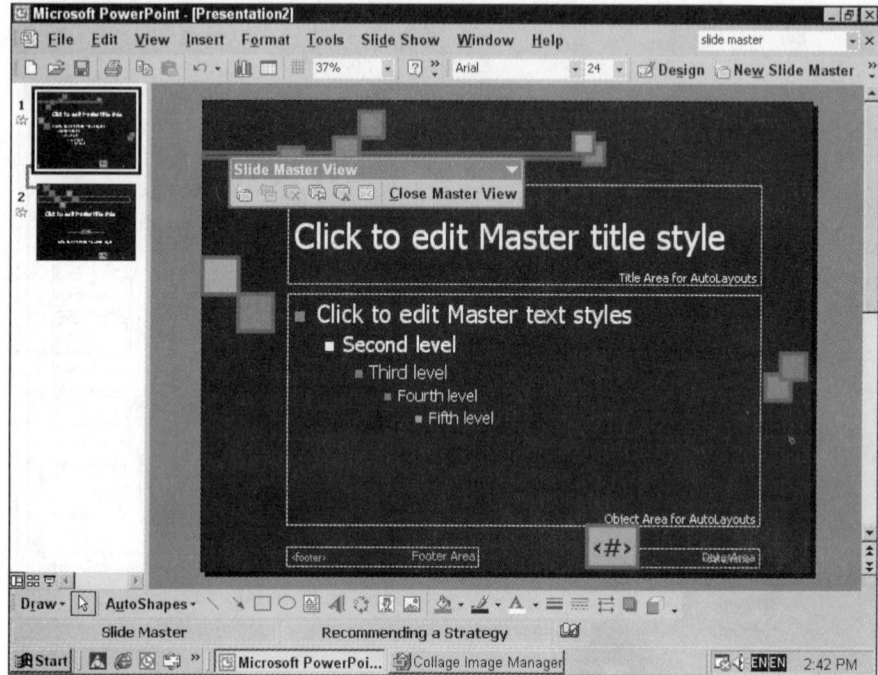

Figure 38-8: The Slide Master lets you specify the layout of elements that appear on many slides just once, a great saving of time and effort.

Formatting the Slide Master

To format the Slide Master, follow these steps:

1. Click once inside the text box containing the type of text you want to format.

2. Highlight the type of text you want to format (for example, Second level).

3. Format the text just as you would within an ordinary text box, using PowerPoint's regular formatting tools. You can change the font, style, and alignment, and add borders and a background color to the text boxes.

4. Add any content you would like to appear on every slide: for example, a picture, a diagram, a chart, a table — even a movie or a sound. You can also change the Slide Master's background, either by choosing Format ➪ Background or by right-clicking on the background and choosing Background from the shortcut menu.

5. To add text that will appear on every slide, insert a new text box by choosing Insert ➪ Text Box, and then type in the text you want to appear. (Typing into the text placeholders that appear automatically when you view Slide Master doesn't have any effect.)

6. When you're finished making changes to the Slide Master, click Close Master View on the small Slide Master View toolbar.

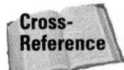

Cross-Reference For more information on working with graphics in PowerPoint, see Chapter 39.

Tip The button labeled "Preserve Master" on the Slide Master View toolbar prevents a Slide Master from being automatically deleted by PowerPoint in certain circumstances. If you want to be sure your Slide Master remains available to you next time you open the presentation you're working on, click this button.

Adding a Title Master

The Title Master is a special form of the Slide Master that applies only to the slides in your presentation that use the Title slide layout. Use it when you want your Title slides to have a different format from the other slides in your presentation.

To add a Title Master, just click the Insert New Title Master button on the Slide Master View toolbar, which opens automatically when you choose View ➪ Master ➪ Slide Master. PowerPoint creates a standard Title Master that you can then format as you like, just as you formatted the Slide Master.

Note Each Title Master is paired with the Slide Master from which it was created. These pairs are called slide-title master pairs, and they're displayed together.

Tip You can apply the various design possibilities displayed by the Slide Design task pane, discussed in detail later in this chapter, to a Slide Master as well as to individual slides.

Handout Master

The Handout Master works just like the Slide Master, except it lets you format handouts instead of slides.

Handouts can help your audience follow your presentation more easily. They can include images of slides (helpful if some of your audience members can't easily see the computer or projection screen on which you're showing your presentation, if they want to take notes, or if they want to be able to study the presentation in detail later) plus any additional information you want to supply.

To create handouts, follow these steps:

1. Call up the Handout Master by choosing View ➪ Master ➪ Handout Master (see Figure 38-9).

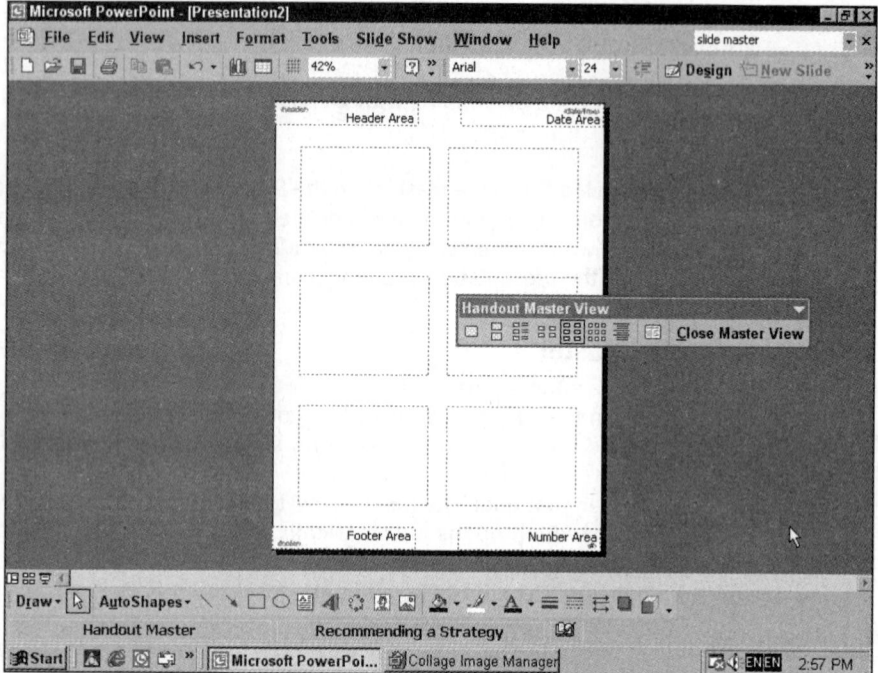

Figure 38-9: The Handout Master lets you customize handouts just as the Slide Master lets you customize slides.

2. When you print handouts, you can choose from among several different layouts in the Print dialog box. To help you design your Handout Master, PowerPoint lets you preview the various layout options using the Handout Master View toolbar. (If the toolbar isn't visible, activate it by choosing View ⇨ Toolbars ⇨ Handout Master.) The boxes in the main body of the Handout Master represent images of slides. Possible print layouts include one slide per page, two slides per page, three slides per page with room for text alongside each one, four slides per page, six slides per page, nine slides per page, or no slides per page — just the outline.

3. Make any other changes you want to the handouts — adding text that will appear on every handout, graphics, a background, and so forth.

4. When you're satisfied with the appearance of your Handout Master, click Close Master View on the Handout Master View toolbar.

5. To print Handouts, choose File ⇨ Print, and then choose Handouts from the "Print what" list box in the Print dialog box (see Figure 38-10). Choose the layout you want to use in the Handouts section of the dialog box, and whether you want slides to be arranged so they read horizontally from left to right (so that in a four-slide arrangement, slide 1 would be in the upper-left corner, slide 2 to the right of it, slide 3 under slide 1, and slide 4 to the right of slide 3); or vertically (slide 1 in the upper-left corner, slide 2 beneath it, slide 3 to the right of slide 1, slide 4 beneath slide 3). When you've made your selections, click OK to print.

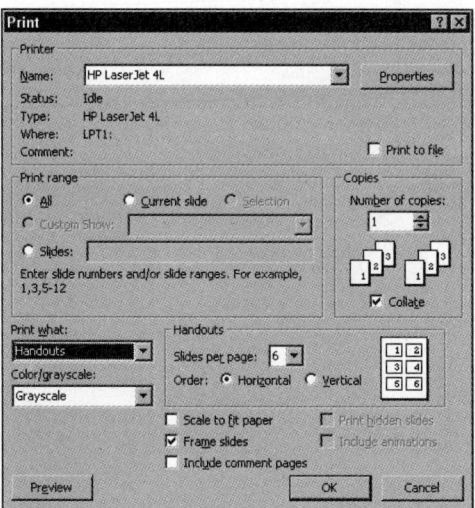

Figure 38-10: Select the layout you want to use for printing your handout in the Print dialog box.

Notes Master

Notes are even more useful than handouts. In fact, they can be used as handouts, especially if you want to provide additional information about individual slides. They're also useful for creating speaking notes for whomever will be making the presentation.

Notes pages consist of an image of an individual slide with a text area underneath. You can enter notes in Normal view in the Notes pane directly under the Slide View pane.

The Notes Master works like the other masters we've looked at: It lets you set default formats for the text you enter into notes, relocate or change the size of the slide image that appears on each notes page, and add any other graphics, fills, or backgrounds you might want.

To customize the Notes Master, follow these steps:

1. Open the Notes Master by choosing View ➪ Master ➪ Notes Master (see Figure 38-11).

2. The box at the top of the Notes Master is simply a small representation of the Slide Master. The only changes you can make to it here are to its size and position (you can change its size by clicking on it and tugging on its handles, and move it by clicking on it and then dragging it).

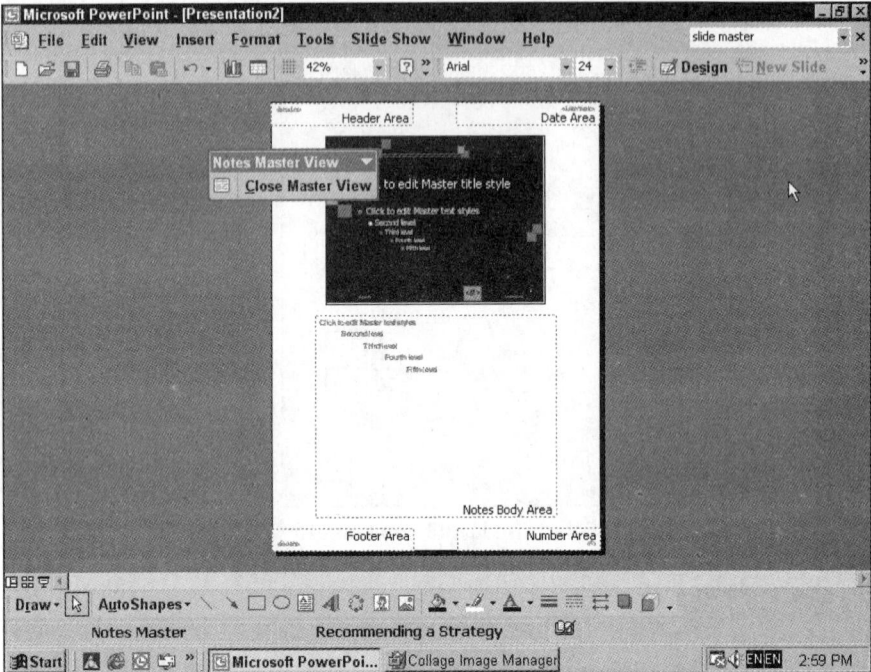

Figure 38-11: Customize your notes pages by changing the Notes Master.

3. Format the text in the Notes box the way you want text to be formatted on all your notes pages. As with the Slide Master, you can format text differently depending on which level in the hierarchy it is: that is, is it a title, a subtitle, a sub-subtitle, and so on.

4. Add any graphics you want to appear on all notes pages, along with any borders, fills, or backgrounds you want on all pages.

5. When you're satisfied, click Close Master View on the Notes Master View toolbar.

6. Print your notes pages by choosing File ⇨ Print, and then selecting Notes Pages from the "Print what" list box in the Print dialog box.

Using Design Templates

Design templates are preformatted master slides that PowerPoint provides to make it possible for anyone to create a good-looking presentation even if they don't know the first thing about design.

Accessing the design templates

Whenever you start PowerPoint or choose File ⇨ New, From Design Template is one of the options that appears in the New section of the New Presentation task pane. (Note that simply clicking New on the toolbar doesn't open the New Presentation task pane; you have to use the File ⇨ New command.)

Clicking on it opens the Slide Design task pane (see Figure 38-12), divided into three sections: Used in This Presentation (since this is a new presentation the only thing used in it is a very basic black-on-white design), Recently Used, which shows any templates you may have applied recently, and Available for Use, which shows you most of what's available — but not all; if you scroll to the bottom, you may see another "template" labeled, "Additional Design Templates". Clicking this will prompt Office to attempt to install additional templates from your Office CD, so make sure you have it handy if you choose this option.

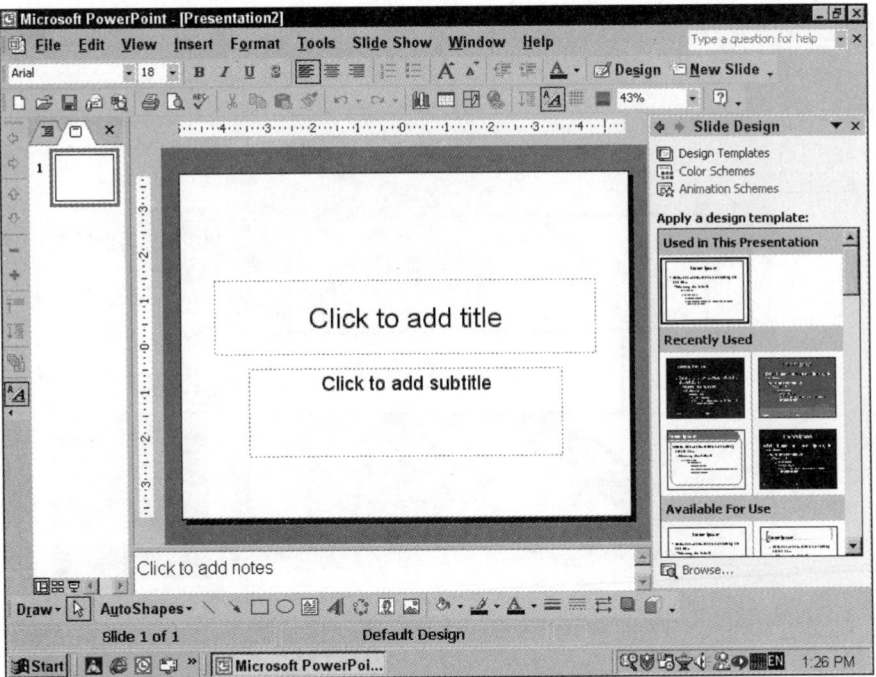

Figure 38-12: PowerPoint's design templates can help you create a good-looking presentation without having to design every aspect of it yourself.

Note   The Recently Used section of the task pane won't appear if you haven't yet applied any templates.

If you point at any of these designs, its name, indicative of its appearance (more or less), will pop up.

Tip   Having trouble really seeing what these designs look like? Point at any one of them and a downward-pointing arrow will appear. Click on that, then click on the option Show Large Previews, and you'll get a much better look at the various designs in the task pane.

Choosing a slide layout

When you've found a template you'd like to work with, double-click on it and the title slide that PowerPoint creates automatically whenever you start a new presentation will suddenly be transformed to match the design you chose (see Figure 38-13). All subsequent slides will use that same design unless you choose to change it.

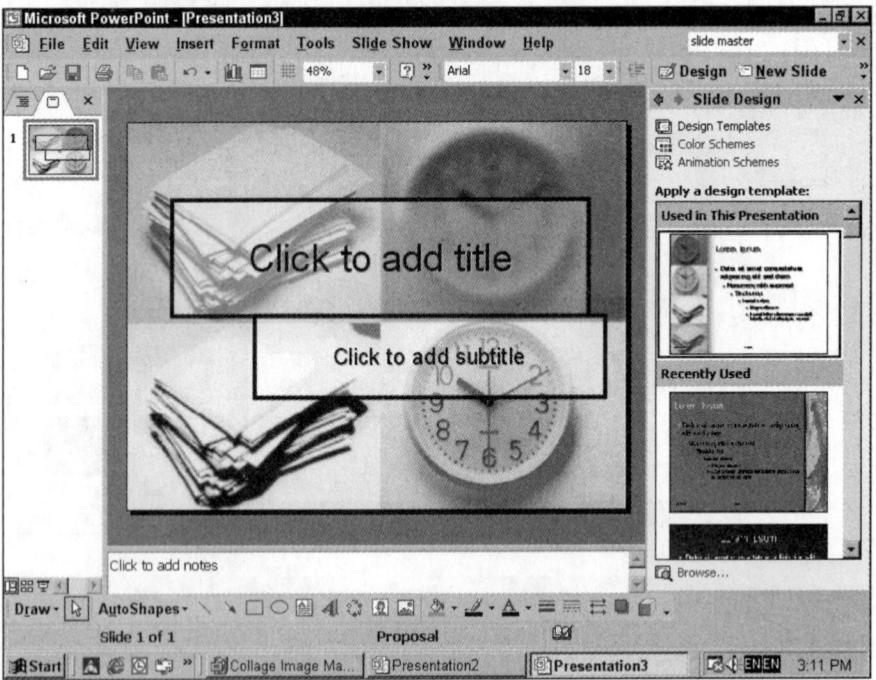

Figure 38-13: When you use a design template, all you have to do is fill in the blanks; your background and color scheme are already taken care of. (Note that I've turned on the Show Large Previews option in the task pane in this figure.)

Modifying and applying the design templates

Whenever you use a design template, what you've really done is attach a Slide Master to your presentation—which means you can modify the design template by modifying the Slide Master, as described in the previous section of this chapter.

You can apply any of the design templates in the Slide Design task pane by clicking on it. By default, the template is applied to all slides in the presentation; to apply a template to a single slide, point at the design, click on the downward-pointing arrow, and choose Apply to Selected Slides.

Creating and Saving Your Own Templates

Anytime you make changes to any of the masters, you're essentially creating your own template. If you come up with a design you really like, you'll probably want to save it so you can use it in future presentations.

To save your current presentation as a template, follow these steps:

1. Choose File ➪ Save As.
2. In the "Save as type" list box, select Design Template.
3. Type a name for your new template into the "File name" box.
4. Click Save.

The template, which includes all of the masters you've formatted plus all of the slides currently in the presentation, is automatically saved in the default file folder for templates. The next time you start a presentation using a design template, or choose Format ➪ Slide Design, you can apply the template you've saved by clicking the Browse link at the bottom of the Slide Design task pane. This will open the template folder, where you should find the template you created and saved.

✦   ✦   ✦

Sprucing Up Your Presentation with Graphics and Special Effects

Multimedia (pictures, animation, video, and sound) can bring your presentation to life. Slide transitions can be created to bring your slide on-screen with a variety of special effects. You also work with *actions,* commands that enable you to put buttons on slides that show them in a random fashion (rather than in a linear sequence), or to run other programs, macros, sounds, or video clips.

Note All computers can show transition effects. However, for good-quality sound, you need a compatible sound card, and for good video, you need a good video card. Check the Windows Control Panel to see what multimedia and sound capabilities you have.

Adding Images and Multimedia

Image is another word for picture. Most of the images you use in PowerPoint will be bitmap images. (See the sidebar "Bitmap versus Vector Graphics" for more information.) The term multimedia covers pictures, video, and sound in any combination.

Bitmap versus Vector Graphics

Be aware of the difference between a bitmap and a vector graphic image. Scanned pictures, digital camera images, and photographs are all bitmap images. All of the paint-type graphics programs also produce bitmaps.

A bitmap image is made up of dots. Bitmap images can be saved in a variety of formats, each with its own filename extension. Some common ones you may see are `.pcx`, `.gif`, `.wmf` (this is the format used by the clip art that comes with Office), `.bmp`, and `.tif`. There are many more. The thing to be aware of with bitmaps is that if you enlarge them, you may find that the straight lines develop jagged edges as each dot is enlarged. Another thing to be aware of is the size of the file. Bitmap files tend to be large.

Some graphics programs, especially CAD and graphic design programs, produce vector graphic images. The advantage of these files is that you can make the pictures any size and they always remain good quality—no jagged edges. If you use the Drawing toolbar—to draw AutoShapes, for example—you are drawing vector graphics.

PowerPoint provides many sample images for your use. You can also create your own images using PowerPoint, a scanner, a graphics program, or a digital camera. You can edit your images to a certain extent within PowerPoint, but there is usually far more editing power in a graphics program. Most scanners also provide software with which you can edit your image.

Adding images

Adding an image to a slide can enhance it significantly. You could add a picture that amuses—a cartoon character, for example—or a picture of the item being discussed. You may also want to put your company logo onto your slide or many slides. Be careful that you use images that are appropriate for the presentation: Cartoons are only suitable under certain circumstances.

You can import an image using the following methods:

✦ Choose Insert ➪ Picture ➪ Clip Art. This opens the Insert Clip Art task pane, which enables you to search by keyword for images contained in Office's Clip Art Organizer. The task pane shows you thumbnails (miniatures) of your pictures so you can easily find the right image. (The Clip Art Organizer also includes photographs, movies, and sounds.)

✦ Browse your computer's various drives to find the image you want. If you find yourself doing this often, though, you might want to move the images you're using regularly into the Clip Art Organizer. Every time you open the Insert Clip Art task pane, the Clip Art Organizer will ask you (unless you check the "Don't show this message again" box) if you would like to catalog all the media files on your computer. Be aware this may take some time, and you'll be asked to tell the Organizer where to put the files it finds, so don't undertake it unless you've got a good-sized chunk of time to deal with it.

✦ Acquire an image from a scanner or digital camera.

✦ Create your own illustrations using one of the various tools PowerPoint provides for the purpose, including AutoShapes and the Drawing toolbar.

 **Cross-Reference** Many of these options apply to all Office applications, and are dealt with in detail in Chapter 9.

Adding an image from the Clip Art Organizer

To add an image from the Clip Art Gallery to your slide, follow these steps:

1. Make sure you are in Normal view. If you want to use tools, rather than the menu, check that the Drawing toolbar is showing. If not, select it from the View ➪ Toolbars menu.

2. Click the Insert Clip Art tool on the Drawing toolbar, or choose Insert ➪ Picture ➪ Clip Art. The Insert Clip Art task pane appears (see Figure 39-1).

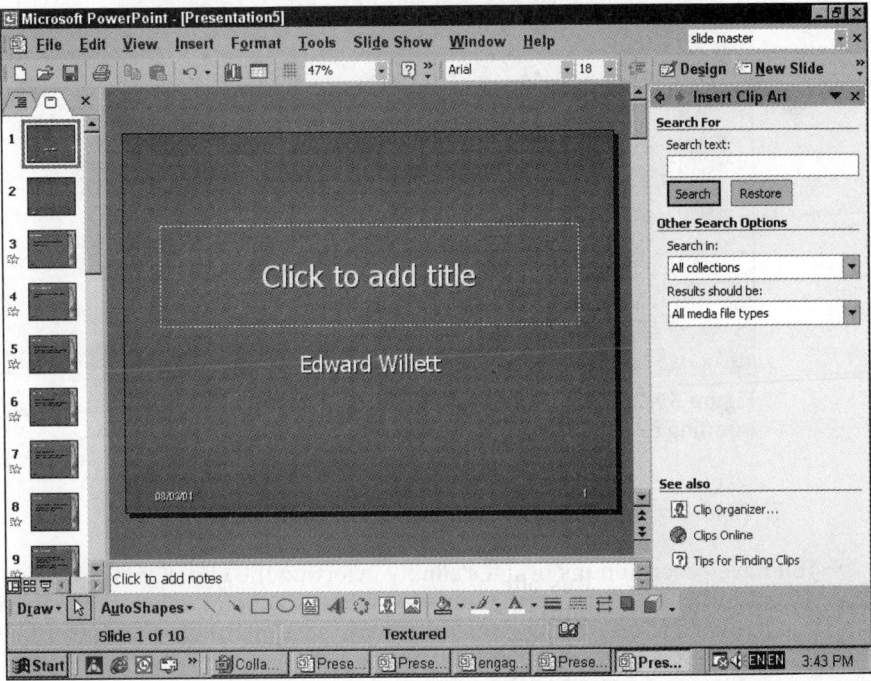

Figure 39-1: The Insert Clip Art task pane lets you search the Clip Art Organizer for pictures.

3. Enter a keyword that describes the kind of image you're looking for.

4. Clip Art is organized into collections. Choose which collections you want to search in and choose which media types you're interested in; since in this case we're inserting an image, you could limit the search by unchecking Movies and Sounds in the "Results should be" field.

5. Click Search. The Insert Clip Art task pane displays thumbnails of the images it found that matched your keyword.

6. When you place your mouse over a thumbnail of a picture, the Clip Art Organizer gives you information about its name, file type, and size, and the keywords associated with it, as shown in Figure 39-2.

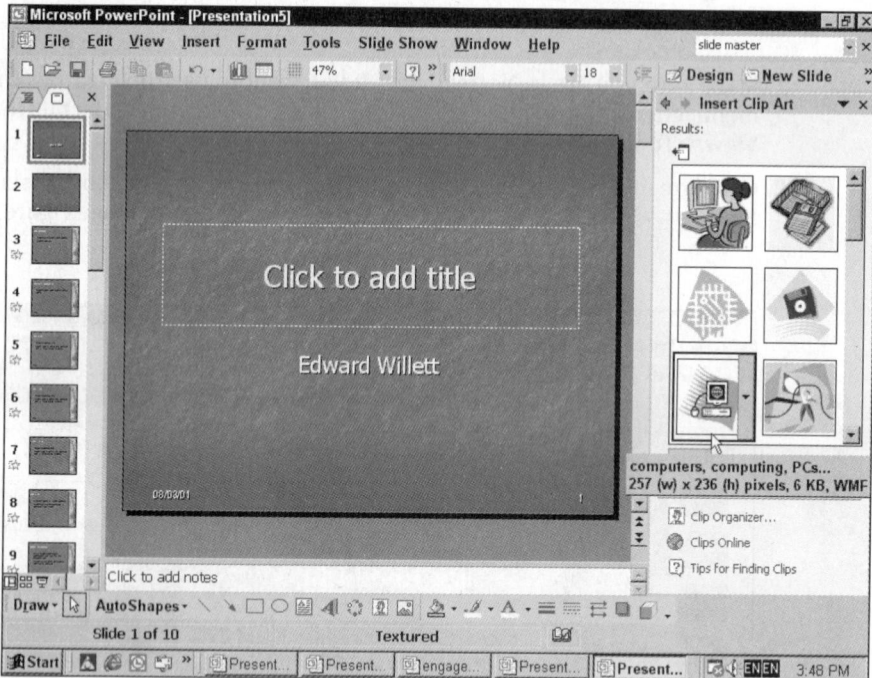

Figure 39-2: The Insert Clip Art task pane enables you to preview clip art before inserting it.

7. To insert the picture right away, double-click it.

You have other options besides simply inserting the clip. If you click on the downward-pointing arrow that appears when you point at one of the thumbnails, you'll open a shortcut menu that offers you several other choices: for instance, you can copy it to the Office Clipboard (see Chapter 11 for more details on that), delete it from the Clip Organizer, copy it to another collection, edit its keywords, or open it in your default graphics program.

You can get more detailed information about it, and get a better look at it, by choosing Preview/Properties. This opens the dialog box shown in Figure 39-3, where you can see all kinds of details and even create a caption.

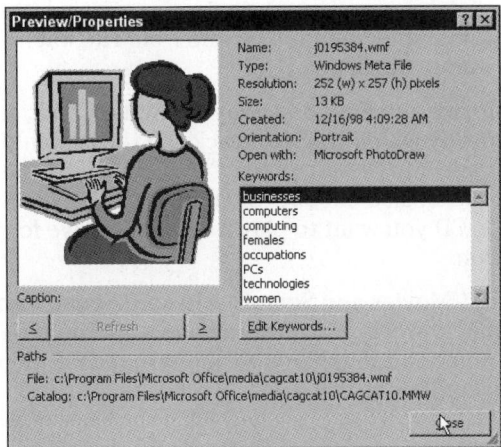

Figure 39-3: The Preview/Properties dialog box provides detailed information about any picture you may be about to insert.

Cross-Reference

When you have a picture on the slide and you select it (you can tell when a picture is selected because it has white handles around it), the Picture toolbar is automatically displayed. It contains some very useful features, described in detail in Chapter 9.

The Drawing toolbar can be used to create your own illustrations and diagrams and to edit your clip art. It, too, is described in detail in Chapter 9.

Working with sound

Adding sound to your presentation can draw the attention of the audience or add humor. I wouldn't use too many sounds, though; they'll lose their impact and may become irritating. Whether or not sound is appropriate depends on the type of presentation you are giving. Additionally, sound files — unless they're very simple ones — can take up a lot of disk space.

Inserting sounds

PowerPoint provides you with some sample sound files. You can usually find more in the Windows\Media folder and you can use any others you may have on your computer. There are also automatic links to help you download new sound files from the Internet from within PowerPoint. There are four methods for inserting sound:

✦ **From the Clip Art Organizer:** Inserting a sound from the Clip Art Organizer is exactly like inserting Clip Art: Choose Insert ⇨ Movies and Sounds ⇨ Sound from Media Gallery to open the Organizer, then enter a keyword and choose Sounds (you can be more specific about what kinds of sounds, if you wish) in the "Results should be" field.

✦ **From a file:** Choose Insert ⇨ Movies and Sounds ⇨ Sound from File, then browse for the sound file you want to insert.

✦ **From a CD:** Choose Insert ⇨ Movies and Sounds ⇨ Play CD Audio Track, and you'll be given the option to specify which track or tracks on the current CD you want to play, or even what specific section of the CD, specified by the time code, you want to play. You can also choose to loop the track indefinitely. Of course, you have to have the CD you want to play from in the drive for this to work during your presentation.

✦ **Record a sound:** Choose Insert ⇨ Movies and Sounds ⇨ Record Sound to bring up a small control panel. For this to work, you have to have a microphone hooked up to your computer. Name the sound you're about to record, then press the Record button and record away.

The Sound icon

When you insert a sound, an icon appears on your slide and you are prompted with the following: "Do you want your sound to play automatically in the slide show? If not, it will play when you click it".

✦ If you answer "Yes", the sound plays when the slide appears in the slide show.

✦ If you answer "No", the sound only plays when you place your mouse over the Sound icon and click on it.

You can move the Sound icon around and resize it as you like.

Note   You can achieve more control over the way a sound is played if you use the custom animation effects, which are covered later in this chapter.

Working with movies

Adding a video clip adds life to your presentation. You might like to use one on the first or the last slide, or insert one that runs over and over during a coffee break until you return to continue the presentation.

Tip   Some people use PowerPoint to create training modules instead of presentations, or to create continuously running demonstrations or sales presentations, which run on computers at trade shows. For such purposes, video is an excellent way of drawing attention or explaining a product. Just be aware that video files take up lots and lots of disk space.

Inserting video

PowerPoint provides you with some sample video clips in the Clip Art Organizer, which you access, as you've probably figured out, by choosing Insert ⇨ Movies and Sound ⇨ Movies from Clip Organizer. Your other option is — you guessed it! — Insert ⇨ Movies and Sound ⇨ Movie from File, which enables you to browse your computer for any movie files you may already have stored on it.

The Video Clip icon

When you insert a video clip, the first frame of the video appears on your slide and you are prompted with the following: "Do you want your movie to play automatically in the slide show? If not, it will play when you click it".

✦ If you answer "Yes", the movie plays when the slide appears in the slide show.

✦ If you answer "No", the movie only plays when you place your mouse over the picture and click on it.

You can move and resize the video frame in the same way as with any other object. If you enlarge it, you'll find the resolution drops.

Note   You can achieve more control over the way a video clip is played if you use the custom animation effects, which are covered later in this chapter.

Tip   If you find you cannot play a particular sound or video in PowerPoint, you can try playing it using the Windows Media Player. Choose Insert ⇨ Object and select Create from File. Browse to find the file. It is placed on your slide as an object and is run using the Windows Media Player.

Using Slide Transitions

Slide transitions are special effects used when moving from one slide to another in a slide show. Adding slide transitions makes a presentation more interesting. You may be tempted to use a different transition between each slide, but this can confuse the audience. Your presentation is more effective if you use the same transition between each pair of slides in a series of slides. You could use one transition for each logical section. When you change to another section, change to another transition. This is a subtle way of telling the audience that you have changed to a new subject.

Selecting the slides

The first step to applying transitions, obviously, is to select the slides you want to use for the transitions. You can do this either in Normal view or Slide Sorter view. In Normal view, click the Slides tab in the leftmost view pane to view the slide thumbnails.

✦ To apply a slide transition to an individual slide, click to select the slide (a black border appears around it).

✦ To apply a transition to a group of slides, click on the first slide and then hold down the Shift key and click on the last slide. The group of slides should now all be selected.

✦ To apply slide transitions to various slides that aren't necessarily contiguous, click on them one by one while holding down Ctrl.

Adding transitions

When you have selected the slides you want to apply a transition to, click on the Slide Transition tool or choose Slide Show ➪ Slide Transition. The Slide Transition task pane appears (see Figure 39-4). To create a transition, use the following steps:

1. Choose the transition effect you want from the "Apply to selected slides" list. When you make a selection, it's previewed for you on the slides showing in Slide Sorter view — assuming the AutoPreview checkbox at the bottom of the task pane is selected, which it is by default. (If you're in Normal view, you can see it better because the Normal view of the currently selected slide is much larger.)

2. To control the speed of the transition, choose Slow, Medium, or Fast from the Speed drop-down list in the Modify Transition area of the task pane.

3. You can choose to play a sound when the slide is shown. Choose the sound you want from the Sound drop-down list. You can also decide whether the sound is to be played once or over and over again (loop), stopping only when you play the next sound, by checking the "Loop until next sound" checkbox.

Note   If you choose to loop, and want the sound to stop when the next slide appears, you have to add the sound called Stop Previous Sound to the next slide.

4. When giving a presentation, you normally want to advance from one slide to the next by clicking the mouse. If you are creating a rolling demonstration, however, you can choose to move from one slide to the next automatically. In the Advance Slide section of the task pane, select Automatically After and enter the length of time the slide must be on the screen before moving on to the next slide.

5. Now choose Apply to Master or Apply to All Slides.

You can preview your transitions in the current view by clicking Play, or click Slide Show to view the effects as they'll appear when you run your Slide Show.

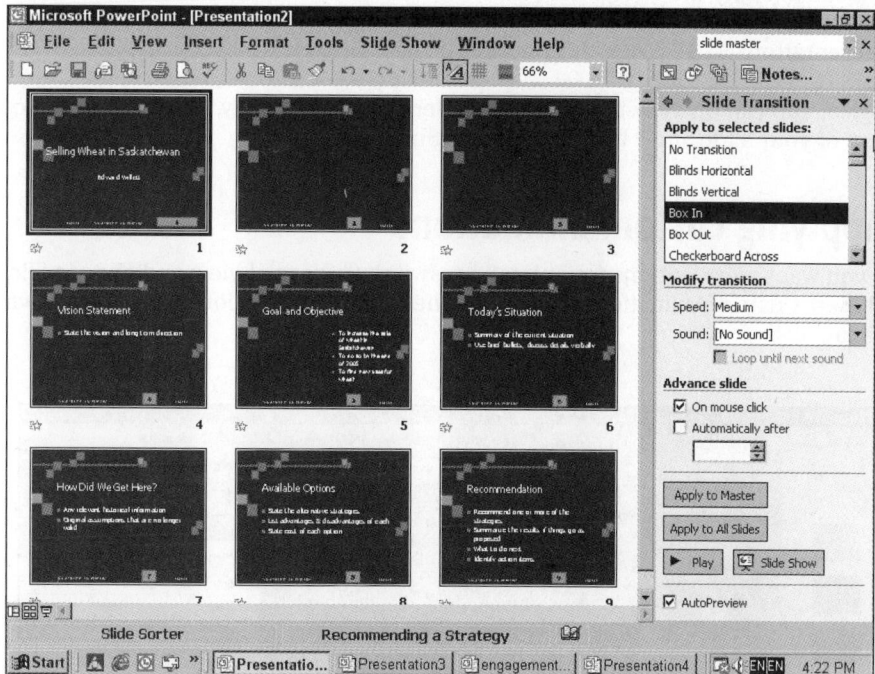

Figure 39-4: The Slide Transition task pane

Using Animation Schemes

Animation schemes take you one step beyond slide transitions, offering even more effects. You can make lines of text fade in one by one, for instance, or flash, or zoom out toward the viewer and then back into place. Animation schemes turn your slides into little bits of Hollywood, right on your desktop.

Applying an animation scheme

To apply an animation scheme, first select the slides you want to apply the scheme to, just as you did to apply a slide transition.

Choose Format ⇨ Slide Design to open the Slide Design task pane, and click the "Animation schemes" link.

The schemes are grouped as Recently Used (if there are any recently used schemes — otherwise this section won't appear), No Animation, Subtle, Moderate, and Exciting. Click the one you want to apply the selected slides. You can also choose to apply the animation scheme to the Master — in which case it will be used by all slides based on the Master — or simply apply it to all slides in the presentation.

Again, you can preview the animation effect by clicking Play, or view it in the context of your Slide Show by clicking Slide Show.

Applying custom animations

If you want more options for animation, switch to Normal view and choose Slide Show ➪ Custom Animation. This opens the Custom Animation task pane shown in Figure 39-5.

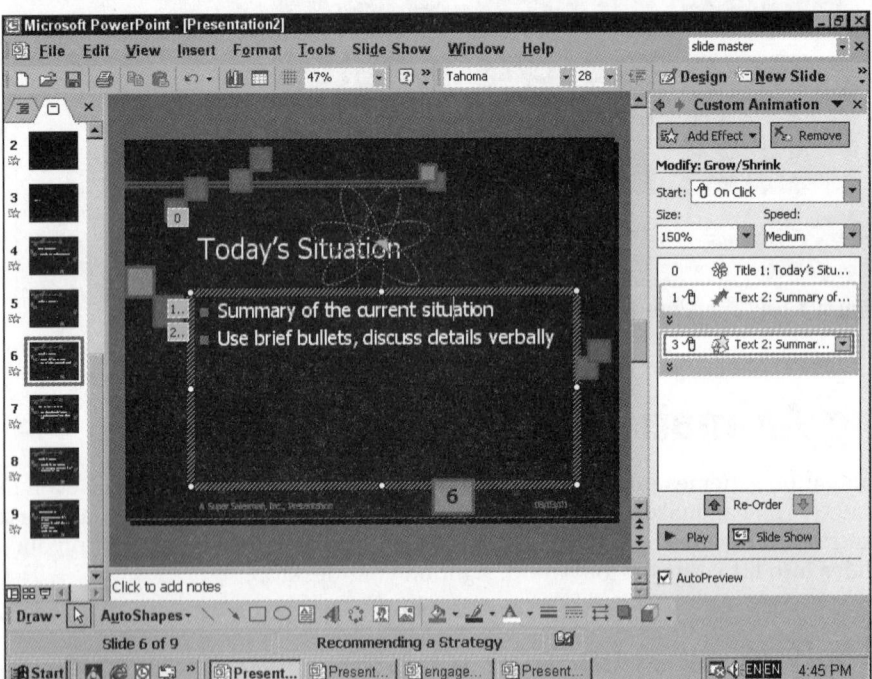

Figure 39-5: The Custom Animation task pane provides the tools that can make your slides come alive.

Here's how it works:

1. Select the element of the slide to be animated — for example, a bulleted list or an object such as a picture.

2. Click Add Effect. This opens a small shortcut menu with four categories of effects: Entrance, Emphasis, Exit, and Motion Paths. Each has dozens of options to choose from. When you choose one, it's added to the list of animations on the slide.

Tip

Have some fun with the Motion Paths choice. One of its options is Draw Custom Path. You can draw a line, curve, freeform shape, or scribble that the selected object will then follow!

3. Now modify the animation. You can choose to have it run when you click on it, at the same time as the previous animation effect you entered (if there's more than one on this slide), or after the previous animation effect. You can also modify its size and speed.

Note

You can find additional options for modifying these effects by clicking on them in the list, opening the shortcut menu by clicking on the downward-pointing arrow that appears, and choosing Effect Options. Among other options, you can attach a sound to the animation here.

4. Change the order of the effects on the slide using the Re-Order buttons.

5. If you decide you don't like an animation effect, select it in the list and click Remove.

Creating Actions

Actions are links from one item on a slide that take you to other slides or initiate other actions. The following list demonstrates some of the ways they can be used:

✦ PowerPoint provides some buttons that represent commonly used actions — to go to the next slide or the start of the slide show, for example.

✦ Actions can be started from any object on the screen, not just Action buttons. You could link an action to text, an object, a table, a graph, or an image.

✦ You can decide whether the action is to be taken when the mouse moves over the item or only when you click on it.

✦ You can use actions to link to a specific slide, another PowerPoint presentation, a Word document, an Excel spreadsheet, a macro, or a site on the Internet or intranet, or to run another program.

✦ Actions are useful if you are using PowerPoint to create a rolling demonstration or on-screen training course. You could insert action buttons that enable the person viewing the slide show to choose which section to cover next. In a training course, clicking on the right answer could take users to the next question, while clicking on the wrong answer could take users back to the beginning of the section they are covering.

Action buttons

The standard Action buttons provided with PowerPoint are Custom, Home, Help, Information, Back or Previous, Forward or Next, Beginning, End, Return, Document, Sound, and Movie.

 **Tip**   Even though each of these has a name, you can use them for any function. There are no links created in advance. You can decide what action they initiate.

To add an action button to your slide, follow these steps:

1. Make sure you are in Normal view.

2. Choose Slide Show ⇨ Action buttons or click the AutoShapes tool on the Drawing toolbar and choose Action buttons. A set of Action buttons is displayed.

3. Click the Action button of your choice.

4. Click on the slide where you would like to place the button. The Action Settings dialog box appears (see Figure 39-6).

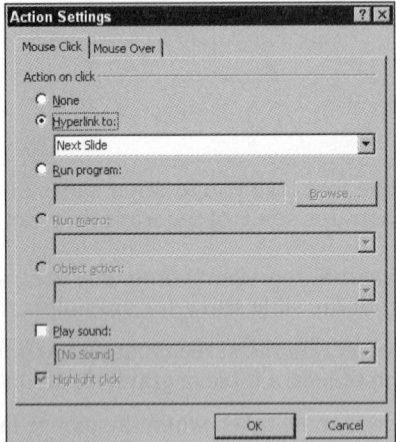

Figure 39-6: The Action Settings dialog box lets you create a variety of useful actions.

5. Decide whether you want the action to be taken when you click on the button or when the cursor moves over the button. Click on the relevant tab: Mouse Click or Mouse Over.

Tip

It is far safer to take an action by clicking, as it is easy to move your mouse over a button by mistake!

6. Select what is to happen when you click on the Action button:

   - **Hyperlink to:** This enables you to go to a specific slide in the current slide show — for example, to the first or last; to go to another slide show, run it, and return to the same place or run it and continue; to go to an Internet address; or to go to any other file.

   - **Run program:** Choose Browse to locate the program.

   - **Run macro:** This is not available from Action buttons.

   - **Object action:** This is not available from Action buttons.

7. You can also have a sound played when you click on an Action button, by selecting Play Sound. Select the sound you want to be played from the drop-down list.

8. If you select Highlight Click, then when you click on the button in the slide show, the button is highlighted for a moment to acknowledge you have clicked on it. This is only available for certain objects.

9. To test your Action button, click OK on the dialog box and run the Slide Show. Click the Action button and check what happens.

Creating a sample action

Suppose you want to place a button on a slide that restarts the slide show by going to the first slide:

1. Go to the slide on which you want to put the Action button and make sure you are in Normal view.

2. Click AutoShapes on the toolbar and select Action buttons.

3. Select an Action button and then click on your slide to place it where you would like it. The Action Settings dialog box will appear.

4. Select the "Hyperlink to:" radio button, then choose First Slide from the drop-down list.

5. Click Play Sound and select a sound from the drop-down list.

6. Click OK to close the dialog box.

7. Test the Action button by clicking the Slide Show View tool. You should see your Action button on the screen. Click it, and you should see the Action button change color, hear the sound you selected, and be taken to the first slide in your presentation.

Action settings

If you do not use one of the built-in Action buttons, you can use other objects to link to actions. You could use some text, a video clip, a sound, an AutoShape, a macro button, and so forth. The dialog box is the same as the one for Action buttons (refer to Figure 39-6), but some extra features are available, depending on which type of object you selected. Just select the object and choose Slide Show ⇨ Action Settings.

✦   ✦   ✦

Creating and Organizing a Slide Show

Now that the slides you have created are ready for a slide show, PowerPoint can take you much further than simply displaying them one slide after another. You can add special effects to the way each slide comes onto the screen and hide slides you don't want to use. You can print supporting materials to hand out to the audience and record a narration to accompany the show (as well as sound and video, as covered in the previous chapter). You can use the Pack and Go Wizard to put the whole show on disk so you can move it to another machine. In a corporate environment, you can give your presentation over a network, using the Online Collaboration feature to get everyone together to confer on the presentation. Taking this concept a step further, you can even broadcast your presentation over an intranet or the Internet.

Creating a Slide Show

The Slide Show feature is built into PowerPoint. You do not need to do anything special to create a slide show — just create the slides and save the presentation. Slide Sorter view is used to see all the slides in sequence.

Rearranging the slide show

Click the Slide Sorter View tool, which is at the bottom of your window at the left, or choose View ➪ Slide Sorter (see Figure 40-1).

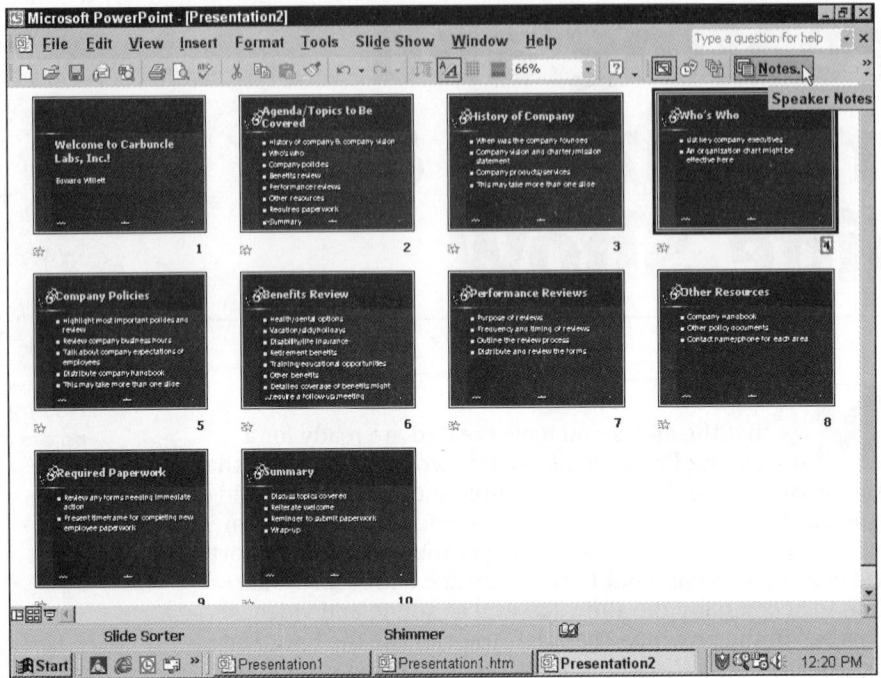

Figure 40-1: Slide Sorter view is used to change the order of your slides. Slide 4 is a hidden slide—notice the icon on the slide number.

In this view, you can drag the slides from one position to another to change the sequence in which they will appear. Use the Zoom tool on the Standard toolbar to see more or fewer slides on the screen. To delete a slide, click on it and press Delete.

Caution   There is no prompt to ask if you are sure, so be careful when deleting slides. If you make a mistake, click the Undo tool to get it back immediately.

If you want to move around the slide show in a different sequence, you can branch from one section to another, or even go to another program, by assigning actions.

Cross-Reference   For more information about branching from one slide to another, or to another program, see Chapter 39.

Hiding slides

You may change your mind and decide not to show one of the slides in your presentation. If you don't want to delete the slide, you can hide it temporarily.

Select a slide and click the Hide Slide tool on the Slide Sorter toolbar to hide it, or right-click on the slide and choose Hide Slide from the shortcut menu. This does not delete the slide, but prevents it from being shown when running the slide show. To unhide the slide, select it and click the same tool again. Figure 40-1 shows a hidden slide (slide 4).

Tip   If you are running a slide show and want to show a hidden slide, right-click and choose Go ⇨ Slide Navigator and double-click on the slide you require. Slide numbers of hidden slides are in parentheses.

Adding comments

Comments can be added to slides in Normal view. They are much like yellow sticky notes and are easy to remove. They are intended for use when reviewing the presentation. If you route the presentation to several people, they can each add their comments, and review other people's comments. Each comment starts with the author's name.

Here's how it works:

✦ You can choose to run a slide show with or without comments.

✦ To insert a comment, make sure you are in Normal view. Then, choose Insert ⇨ Comment. A window into which to type your comment appears; so does the Reviewing toolbar (see Figure 40-2). Once the Reviewing toolbar is active, you can insert a comment just by clicking on the Insert Comment button on the toolbar.

✦ Type the comment and then click outside the comment area.

✦ Comments can be formatted like any other item. You can also change the shape of the comment box by going to the Drawing toolbar and choosing Draw ⇨ Change AutoShape.

✦ You can move from comment to comment by clicking on Next Item or Previous Item on the Reviewing toolbar.

✦ Each Comment that you insert creates a little marker that appears on the slide (see Figure 40-3). You can move these markers wherever you want — even right off the slide. Pointing at a marker reveals the comment it represents. To edit a comment, click on the marker that represents it, then click Edit Comment on the toolbar.

Note   These markers only appear in Normal view; they're invisible if you run a slide show that contains slides with comments.

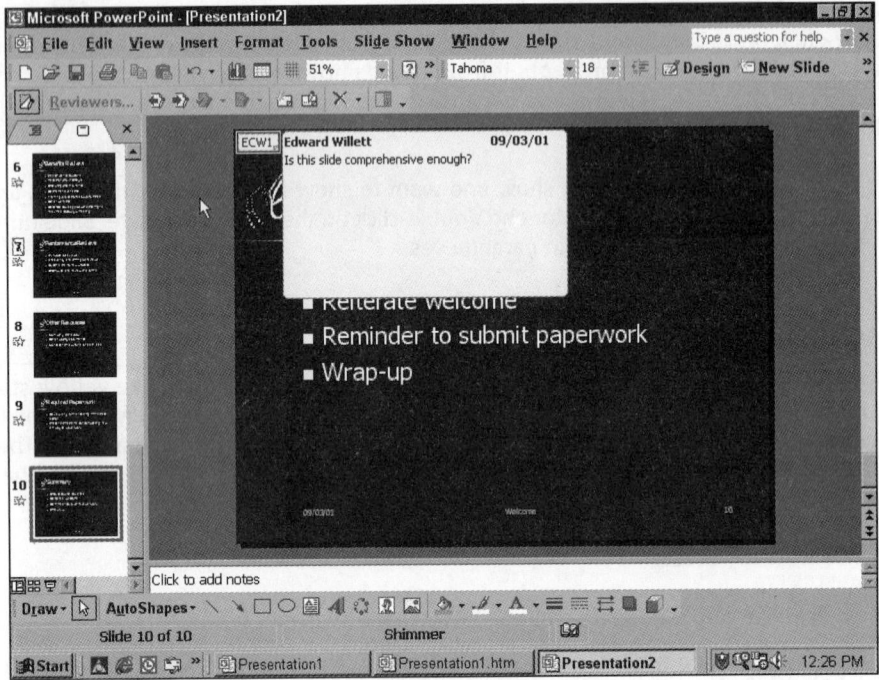

Figure 40-2: Comments are like sticky paper notes on your page. You can move them anywhere. Notice the Reviewing toolbar.

✦ Click on Insert Comment on the toolbar to add a new comment; click on Edit Comment to edit the comment.

✦ Click the Markup button on the toolbar to show or hide comments.

✦ Comments can be printed. Choose File ➪ Print, and make sure the "Include comment pages" box at the bottom of the Print dialog box is checked. (The only time it's not available is if you're printing an outline.)

Note

The Reviewing toolbar offers other options if you have several people suggesting changes to a presentation. Use the Reviewers button to view changes made by all or just certain reviewers, and use the Apply and Unapply buttons to either accept their changes (incorporating them into the presentation) or reject them. A special Revisions task pane makes this easier, offering you a view of the changes made by the reviewer in either List or Gallery form. You can send a presentation via e-mail to other people for comments by choosing File ➪ Send To ➪ Mail Recipient (for Review).

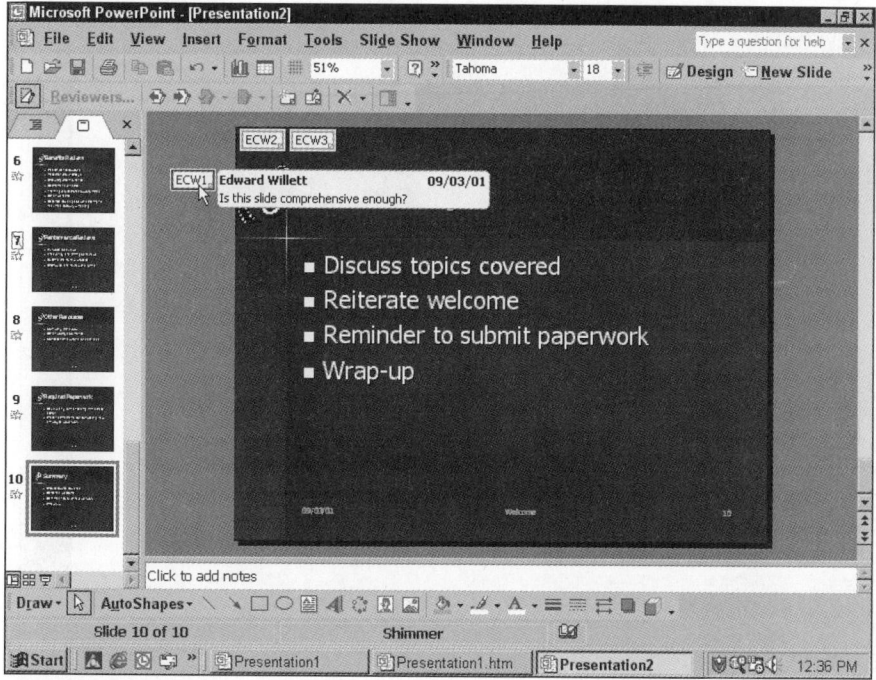

Figure 40-3: This slide has three comments on it, indicated by markers. I've moved one marker right off the slide and pointed at it to bring up its contents.

Adding speaker notes

Speaker notes are printed notes that the presenter uses as a guide while speaking. Whenever you turn around to look at your slides while giving a presentation, you run the risk of losing the attention of the audience. Speaker notes help you avoid this problem, because an image of the slide is printed on the top of the note and the points you want to make are printed at the bottom. Here are some guidelines:

✦ Speaker notes can be typed when in Normal view. Click on the words "Click to Add Notes", at the bottom of the window, and start typing.

✦ You can make this part of the screen larger by dragging the gray bar upwards. Another method is to choose View ➪ Notes Page. This shows the speaker notes as a full page.

✦ To make them readable, click the Zoom tool and select, for example, 100% (see Figure 40-4).

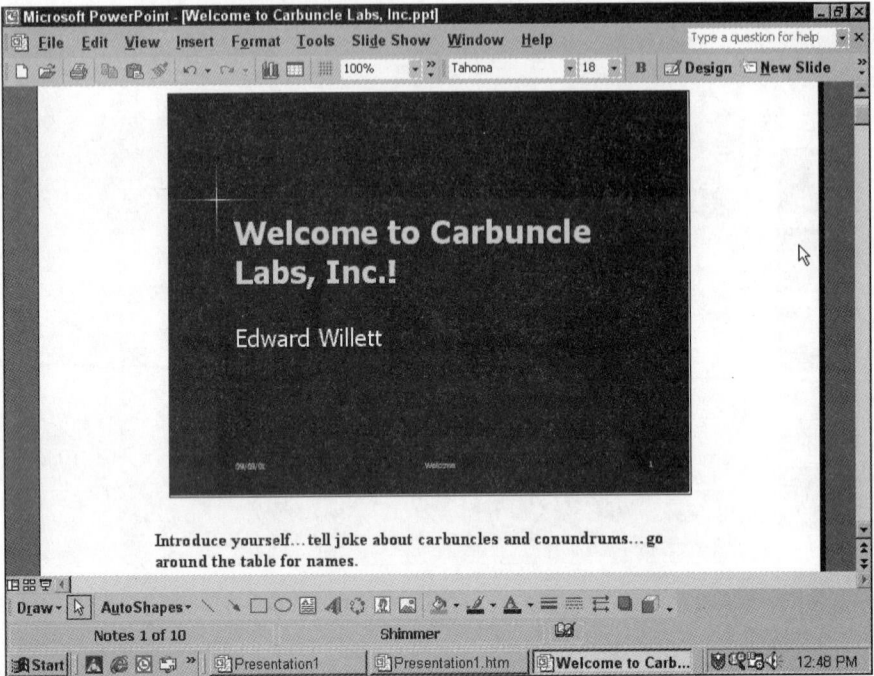

Figure 40-4: Use the Zoom tool to make the speaker notes page a readable size.

✦ You can also add speaker notes while running the slide show. Right-click to get the shortcut menu and choose Speaker Notes. Type your note and click Close.

✦ To print Speaker Notes, choose File ➪ Print. Under "Print what", select Notes Pages. The slide prints in the top half of the page and the notes are printed underneath.

Handouts

Handouts are pages with several slides printed on them. They are intended for handing out to the audience as a reminder of what was covered in the presentation. However, they are also useful for reviewing your presentation. You can fit up to nine slides on one page.

To print handouts, choose File ➪ Print. Under "Print what", select Handouts. Then decide how many slides per page you want to print and in what order. Click Preview to see how your handout will look (see Figure 40-5).

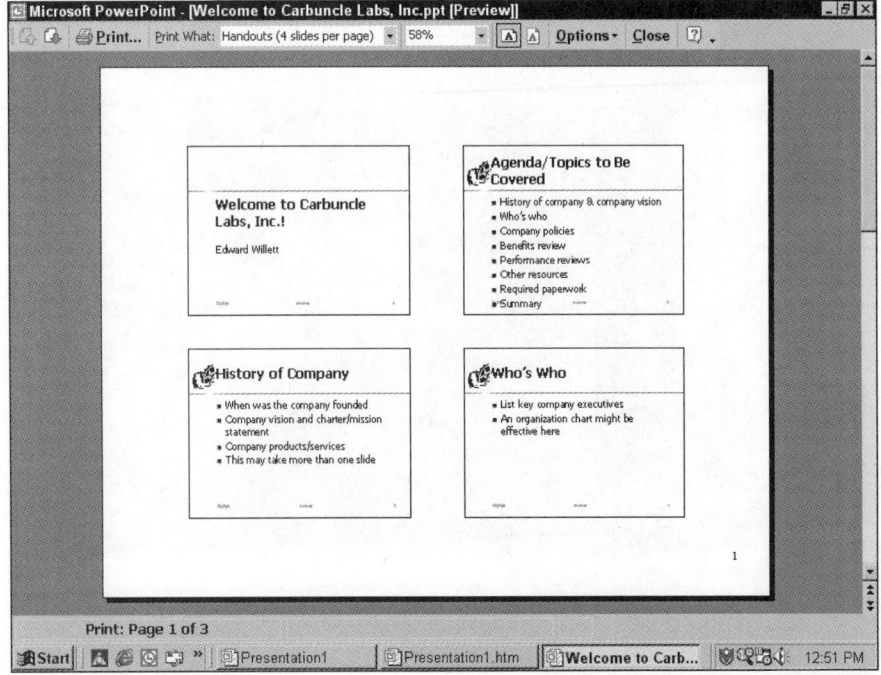

Figure 40-5: When you print handouts, you can choose how many slides per page to print. Here I've chosen to print four per page.

Summary slides

A summary slide takes the titles of selected slides and puts them on one slide. This is useful for producing an introductory slide to tell the audience what subjects you'll be covering, or a closing slide to reinforce your main points. Select the slides in Slide Sorter view by holding down the Ctrl key and clicking on each slide in turn. Click the Summary Slide tool on the Slide Sorter toolbar to insert a new slide with the title Summary Slide. The titles of each of the selected slides are listed as bullets (see Figure 40-6).

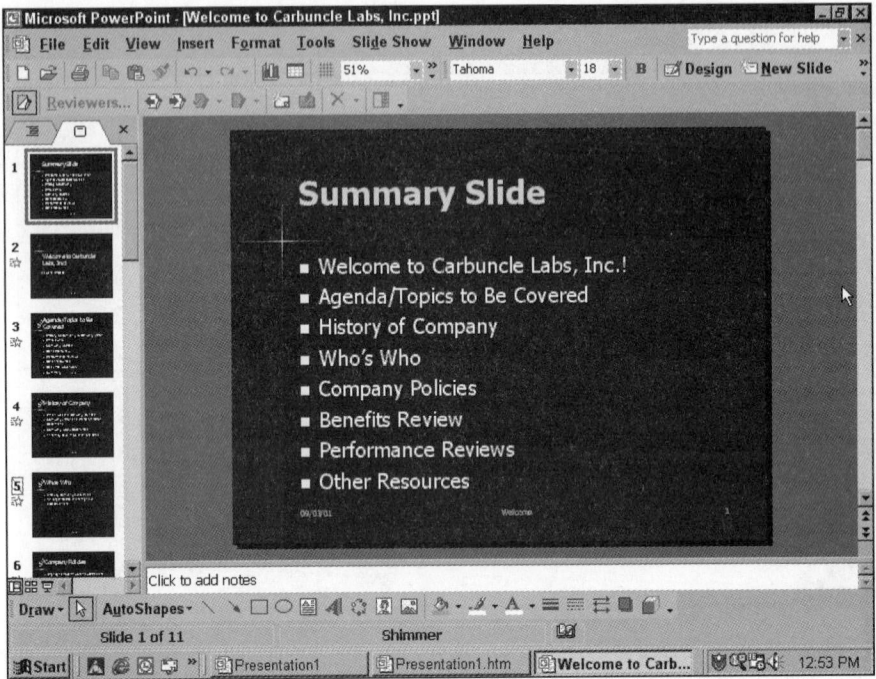

Figure 40-6: When you create a summary slide, the titles of the slides you chose in Slide Sorter view are listed as bullets.

Playing the Slide Show

To play your slide show, press F5. This will run the slide show, enabling you to move from slide to slide manually. Following are alternative methods to run the show:

✦ Choose View ⇨ Slide Show.

✦ Choose Slide Show ⇨ View Show.

✦ Click the Slide Show tool at the bottom left of your screen.

Tip   If PowerPoint is not running, you can right-click on the filename in My Computer or Explorer and choose Show to view your show.

Moving between slides

To go to the first slide, press Home. To go to the last slide, press End. To end the slide show before it is finished, press Esc. To see a list of the controls you can use in a presentation, press F1 during the slide show.

Table 40-1 shows the mouse and keyboard actions for moving between slides or points on a slide.

Table 40-1 **Moving Between Slides**	
To the Next Slide/Point	**To the Previous Slide/Point**
Enter	Backspace
Right arrow	Left arrow
Down arrow	Up arrow
N	P
PgDn	PgUp
Space	
Mouse click	

Writing on slides (annotations)

During a slide show you may want to write on the slide or circle an important item. To do this, right-click on the slide while running the slide show to call up the shortcut menu. Select Pointer Options ➪ Pen or press Ctrl+P. The cursor shape changes to a pen. Drag the mouse on the screen to draw. You can hold down the Shift key while drawing to keep your lines horizontal or vertical. You can also move the mouse around until you see a button at the bottom-left corner of the screen and click the button to view the shortcut menu. The following list covers some additional features:

✦ To choose a different pen color, right-click and choose Pointer Options ➪ Pen Color from the shortcut menu.

✦ The highlighting is temporary and disappears when you move on to the next slide. To erase it while it is on the screen, press E or right-click and choose Screen ➪ Erase Pen.

✦ To continue with the slide show, right-click and choose Pointer Options ➪ Automatic. When you choose Automatic, the pointer automatically disappears if it is not used for 15 seconds. You can also press Ctrl+A to change the pointer back into an arrow.

Black and white slides

When you are giving a presentation, it is handy to be able to display a plain black screen or a plain white screen, to ensure you have the full attention of the audience. To do this, press B for a black screen or W for a white screen. Press the same key again to continue with the slide show.

Setting up the slide show

In a presentation, the default is to move from slide to slide manually — by pressing a key, for example. But you can also create self-running presentations for use in trade shows or at kiosks. You can set the amount of time each slide must stay on the screen before automatically moving to the next slide. Choose Slide Show ⇨ Set Up Show to see the options available (see Figure 40-7).

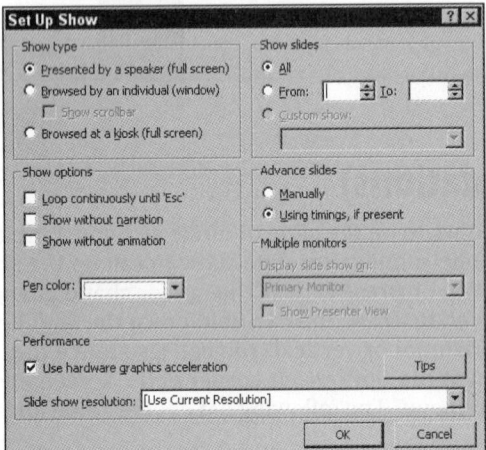

Figure 40-7: Use the Set Up Show dialog box to change the options for your slide show.

There are three show types to choose from:

✦ **Presented by a speaker (full screen):** This is the normal option for a presentation. Slides are moved manually from one to the next.

✦ **Browsed by an individual (window):** This presents the show in a special browser, a version of Internet Explorer (see Figure 40-8).

✦ **Browsed at a kiosk (full screen):** This prevents the slide show from being modified in any way by the audience. The audience can advance through slides. The slide show automatically restarts after five minutes of inactivity and repeats itself when finished.

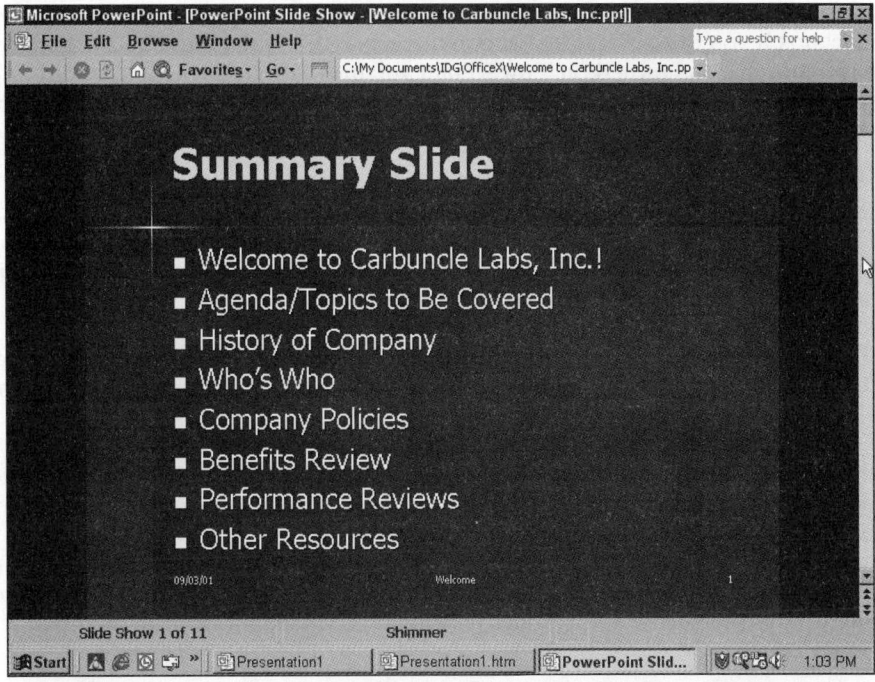

Figure 40-8: When you choose "Browsed by an individual (window)," the screen displays the slide show in a modified version of Internet Explorer. The toolbar is the same as Explorer's, but the menus are specific to slide shows.

In the Set Up Show dialog box you can also select the pen color for annotating slides. (This option is active only if "Presented by a speaker (full screen)" is selected.) You can decide to run the show without narration or without animation. The Set Up Show dialog box is also used to select the range of slides to be shown, or a custom slide show. (This is discussed later in this chapter.) You can choose to run the slide show automatically or manually. If your computer supports it, you can make use of multiple monitors: one to show the slide show, another to show the special Presenter View—new to PowerPoint 2002—which includes details on what bullet or slide is coming next, enables presenters to see their speaker notes, and lets them jump directly to any slide.

If your computer has a video accelerator card, you can make use of its capabilities to enhance your slide show (this makes animations more effective). You can also decide at what resolution you want your show to run.

Setting slide timings

To set the timings for an automatic self-running slide show, go to Slide Sorter view and select the slides you want to set a certain timing for. Click the Slide Transition tool at the left of the Slide Sorter toolbar or choose Slide Show ➪ Slide Transition. This opens the Slide Transition task pane. Enter the number of seconds the slide must be displayed in the "Automatically after" box. Uncheck the "On mouse click" checkbox if you don't want the slide to move on when the mouse is clicked. If you leave both options turned on, PowerPoint will move on to the next slide either when you click on the mouse or when the time is up, whichever comes first.

Rehearsing slide timings

Rather than set the timing for each slide in the Slide Transition task pane, you can do it on the fly, while watching your slide show, by using the Rehearse Timings command. This enables you to vary the timing by what feels right, rather than just guessing as you have to do in the Slide Transition task pane.

In Slide Sorter view, choose Slide Show ➪ Rehearse Timings or click on the Rehearse Timings tool. The slide show starts, with the Rehearsal toolbar visible in the upper-left corner of the screen.

The timer starts to run. Whenever you're ready to advance to the next slide, click the Next button on the toolbar. The timer resets. Continue this procedure until you reach the end of the slide show, at which time a dialog box informs you "The total time for the slide show was xx seconds. Do you want to record the new slide timings and use them when you view the slide show?" Choose Yes, and the next time you run the slide show automatically, each slide will display for the recorded length of time.

Note   If you want to use timings for your show, make sure the "Advance slides: Using timings, if present" radio button is selected in the Slide Show ➪ Set Up Show dialog box.

Custom slide shows

Once you have created a slide show and presented it, you'll often find you have to repeat the show to another audience, but with some changes. Perhaps you want to hide certain slides, or change the sequence. Create a custom show for this.

Choose Slide Show ➪ Custom Shows. In the resulting dialog box, click New. In the Define Custom Show dialog box (see Figure 40-9) type a name for the custom show, click on the slides you wish to use, and click Add to put them in the list. (To transfer several slides at once to the custom show, hold down the Ctrl key and click on the slides you want, then click Add.)

To change the sequence of the slides in the custom show, select a slide or slides in the Custom Show list, then use the up and down arrows.

Click OK when you're done. You can view the show by clicking the Show button in the Custom Shows dialog box.

To set up the custom show, choose Slide Show ➪ Set Up Show. In the "Show slides" area, click the Custom Show radio button and select your custom slide show.

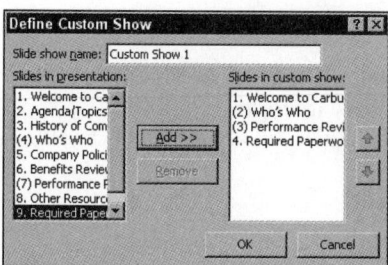

Figure 40-9: Select the slides you want to use in a custom show, and rearrange the order of them.

To switch back to the full slide show, choose Slide Show ➪ Set Up Show and change the setting under "Show slides" back to All.

Using Recorded Narration

You can record narrations to accompany a self-running slide show. Narrations are also useful to store the verbal part of your presentation so that you can put the whole presentation on the Web, to make the presentation available to someone who was not able to attend, or to simply store your presentation complete with the speech. You can also use the feature to store comments made during a presentation.

You'll need a microphone and sound card to create a narration, and anyone who wants to hear it must also have a sound card in his or her computer. The quality of the speech will vary from system to system. You can record your narration at various levels of quality; just remember, the higher the quality, the more disk space it will require.

 Tip An alternative to recording sound is to use speaker notes to type the accompanying speech. It uses far less space and avoids the potential hardware and sound quality problems.

You can record the narration before or during the presentation, and you can record the narration for the entire show or for individual slides. The narration will take precedence over all other sounds attached to a slide, so only the narration will be played. When you record a narration, a Sound icon appears on each slide (in views other than Slide Show view).

When you play the slide show, you can choose to run it with or without the narration. Choose Slide Show ➪ Set Up Show and select "Show without narration" if you don't want the narration to play.

Recording a narration

To record a narration, choose Slide Show ⇨ Record Narration. The Record Narration dialog box appears (see Figure 40-10). Here's how it works:

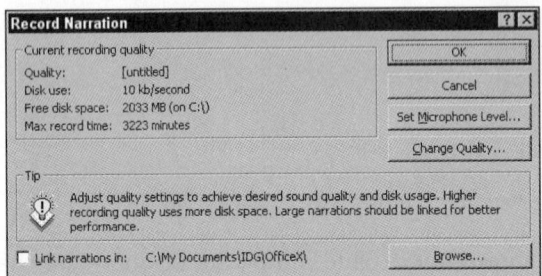

Figure 40-10: The Record Narration dialog box gives you an idea of how much space you will use on your disk. Choose Change Quality to change how much space is needed—the higher the quality, the more space you'll need.

✦ Notice the figures regarding disk use and maximum record time. You probably don't want to fill your hard disk with a sound file!

✦ Choose Set Microphone Level to ensure the volume is appropriate.

✦ Choose Change Quality, and find an appropriate combination of Format and Attributes. Choose the best quality you can use with the disk space you have available. You can save a new combination of Format and Attributes under another name.

Note   Quality levels are given in the format "11,025 Hz, 8 bit, Mono," followed by a notation such as "11 KB/s". This tells you the sampling rate, how the data is stored, whether it's monaural or stereo, and how quickly recording at this rate will eat up disk space. The higher the numbers, the higher the recording quality. The top quality offered, "48,000 Hz, 16 Bit, Stereo" will fill up your disk at the rate of 188 KB/s"—but with a good microphone, it offers near-CD-quality sound.

✦ If you are recording a large narration, choose "Link narrations in:" and select an appropriate folder. The default folder for linked narrations is the same folder as your presentation. When you link narrations, the narrations are stored in a separate file with the name: *presentation name* narration *slide number*.wav. If you don't link narrations, the audio is stored within the presentation file.

✦ Click OK and your slide show will start. Record away!

Re-recording narrations

To re-record narrations, select the slide and choose Slide Show ➪ Record Narration and click OK. Record your new narration and press Esc when you want to stop.

Caution

Be careful which slide you stop on. Go on to the slide after the one you want to stop on. For example, if you want to stop on slide 8, then go to slide 9 to stop — otherwise, the new recording will not be saved to slide 8.

Using the Pack and Go Wizard

Many people create their presentations on one computer, but want to run the slide show on another computer. The presentation computer might not even have PowerPoint loaded and the screen may be a different type and have projection equipment linked to it. The Pack and Go Wizard puts all the files you need onto a disk (or disks) and compresses them. You can take the presentation to another computer and load the slide show onto the hard disk. It is automatically decompressed at the same time. When you want to run the slide show, you can use the PowerPoint Viewer, which is covered in the next section of this chapter, or you can run the slide show from PowerPoint if it is installed.

To run the Pack and Go Wizard, follow these steps:

1. Choose File ➪ Pack and Go. The first of six dialog boxes appears. Click Next.

2. You can select the currently active presentation and you can also browse to find other presentations. Click Next.

3. Select the floppy drive (A:) unless you want to send the presentation to another destination. Click Next.

4. Select "Include linked files" and "Embed TrueType fonts" to make sure all files and fonts are included. Click Next.

5. If you are going to run your slide show on a computer that does not have PowerPoint included, you can include PowerPoint Viewer with the presentation. To do so, select Viewer for Microsoft Windows.

Note

If you don't have the PowerPoint Viewer installed, this screen will prompt you to download it. The PowerPoint Viewer must be installed on your machine before you can pack it for use on another machine.

6. The final dialog box confirms your options, states that it will compress the presentation, and will call for more than one floppy if required. Click Finish.

Here are some additional guidelines:

✦ Your slide show and the PowerPoint Viewer, if requested, will be saved on your floppy disk. If more than one disk is required, you will be prompted.

✦ To run your presentation on another computer, put the floppy in the drive and open Windows Explorer. Browse to the floppy drive and run PNGsetup. Select a folder on the computer where you would like to put the presentation. The files will be expanded and copied onto the computer.

✦ When the copying is complete, you can run the slide show either using PowerPoint or the PowerPoint Viewer.

Printing

Printing the slides themselves is becoming less important now that so many people use on-screen presentations and projection equipment attached to computers. Often you want to print the slides in black and white and not in the colors used for the presentation. You can preview how your slides and handouts will look in black-and-white by clicking one tool. You can then change the way black and white prints before you print your whole presentation. If you do want to print slides in color for proofing purposes, you will save a lot of time and resources by printing handouts instead of full-page slides.

You can print slides, outlines, speaker notes, and audience handouts. You can print them in color, grayscale, or pure black and white. Table 40-2 shows how objects print in grayscale or pure black and white.

Table 40-2 Grayscale versus Pure Black and White		
Object	*Grayscale*	*Pure Black and White*
Text	Black	Black
Text shadows	Hidden	Hidden
Embossing	Hidden	Hidden
Fills	Grayscale	White
Frame	Black	Black
Pattern fills	Grayscale	White
Lines	Black	Black
Object shadows	Grayscale	Black
Bitmaps	Grayscale	Grayscale
Slide backgrounds	White	White
Charts	Grayscale	Grayscale

Printing slides

To print your slides choose File ➪ Print. Figure 40-11 shows the Print dialog box.

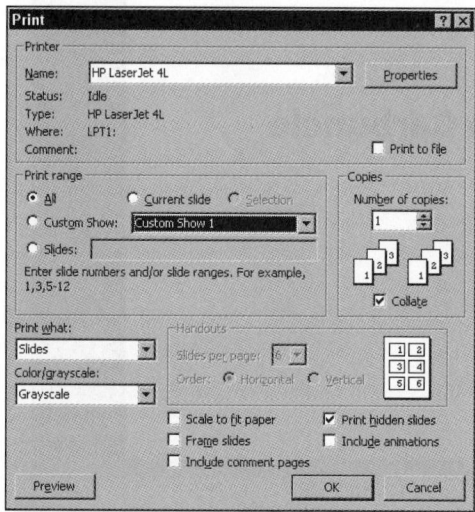

Figure 40-11: The Print dialog box has some special options for PowerPoint. The "Print what" list box is important.

You can select the range of slides to be printed. Make sure that you have chosen Slides in the "Print what" box. Choose whether you want the animated items to print, whether you want the slides to be scaled to fit paper rather than staying scaled as they are on the screen, whether you want to print a frame around the slides, whether you want to print hidden slides, and whether or not to include comment pages.

PowerPoint 2002 includes a Print Preview view that lets you see exactly what your slides will look like when printed. It will even take into account whether your printer is capable of printing color or not; if it is, and you choose to print in color, the Print Preview will be in color. If your printer can only print black and white, and you choose to print in color, the Print Preview shows you what the result will be in black and white.

Figure 40-12 shows a black-and-white version of a color slide in Print Preview. The Print Preview toolbar provides straightforward options: You can move to the next item; click Print to send the job to your printer; view slides, notes pages, or outline view; zoom in and out; change the orientation of the page (for handouts, notes pages, and Outline view only); and, using the Options button, access many of the commands you've already seen on the Print dialog box. Click Close to exit Print Preview and return to the Print dialog box.

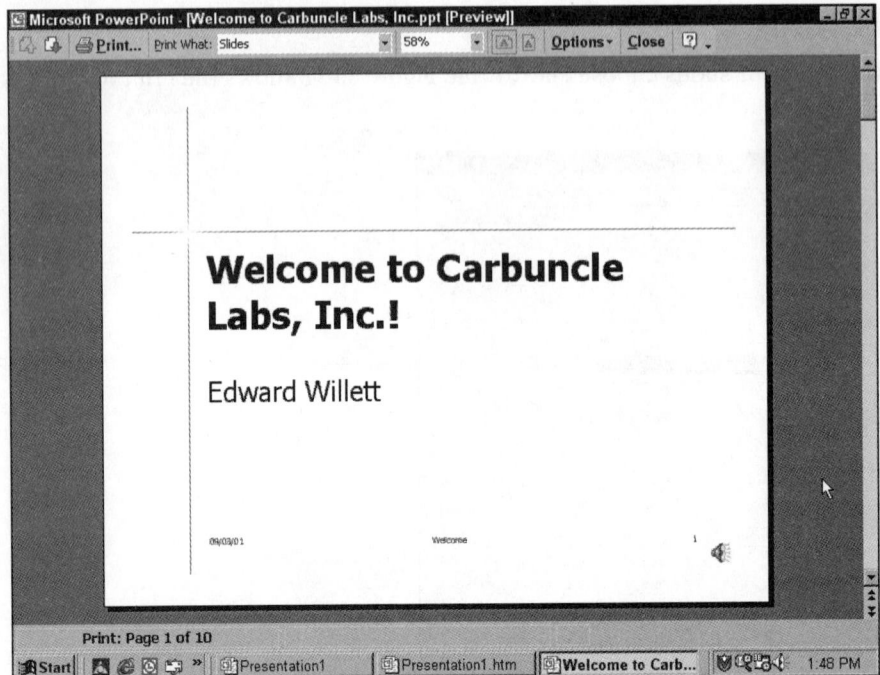

Figure 40-12: Print Preview lets you see exactly what your presentation will look like when printed.

Note You can access Print Preview any time by choosing File ➪ Print Preview.

Printing speaker notes

To print speaker notes, as noted earlier in this chapter, choose File ➪ Print and select Notes Pages under the "Print what" list box. You have the same options as for printing slides. Prior to printing, you can insert a header and footer by choosing View ➪ Header and Footer and selecting the Notes and Handouts tab.

Printing handouts

Also as noted earlier in this chapter, to print handouts, choose File ➪ Print and select Handouts under the "Print what" list box. You have the same options as for printing slides, plus you can choose how many slides to print on one page and the order in which they appear on the page—horizontal or vertical. Prior to printing, you can insert a header and footer by choosing View ➪ Header and Footer and selecting the Notes and Handouts tab.

Printing an outline

Outlines print as they are displayed in the Outline pane of Normal view. Whichever levels are showing will print — you can print all the text in your outline or just the slide titles. You can also show or hide formatting.

Printing files in Word

Choosing File ➪ Send to ➪ Microsoft Word takes you to the dialog box shown in Figure 40-13. You can send notes pages and outlines to Word and touch up the formatting there. Select Paste Link if you want to keep the copy in Word up-to-date with the information in the PowerPoint presentation.

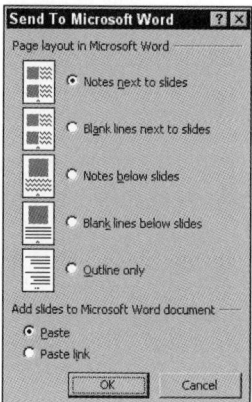

Figure 40-13: Use this dialog box to format slides, notes pages, or your outline when you send them to Microsoft Word.

When you click OK, Word is loaded and the slides and notes pages are put in a table. Outlines are created using Outline Styles.

✦   ✦   ✦

Designing Dazzling Publications with Publisher

Publisher is a powerful desktop-publishing program that is perfect for creating everything from brochures to newsletters. This part provides a quick introduction to Publisher, examining the basics of using it in the first chapter and introducing some more advanced techniques in the second.

Introducing Publisher

Once upon a time, it took designers, typesetters, and complex mechanical equipment to turn out a published document, especially if it featured pictures, fancy typefaces, and color. Today, thanks to computers, every desktop is a full-featured print shop, with designers, typesetters, and printing equipment within arm's reach—at least, it is if it has a computer with desktop publishing software installed.

You can achieve a lot of desktop publishing effects with Word and PowerPoint, but if you really want your publications to look their best, you need a dedicated desktop publishing program. If you have purchased Office XP Professional Special Edition at retail or purchased a new computer with Office XP Small Business or Office XP Professional with Publisher pre-installed on it, then you have one, because those packages include one of the most popular personal desktop publishing programs available, Microsoft Publisher.

The Publisher Workspace

Publisher shares a basic look with other Office applications, but it's still worthwhile taking a quick look at the Publisher workspace before you begin trying to use the application.

When you first start Publisher, you find yourself in something called the Publication Gallery. Here you find dozens of pre-designed Quick Publications that you can adapt to your own use. For now, though, look in the task pane at the left for the Blank Publication link under the New area. Click on it to open a default blank document in Publisher's workspace, similar to Figure 41-1 (in the figure I've added a text box—more on that later—to bring up the Formatting toolbar). The various components of the workspace are labeled in that figure.

Objects toolbar

Standard toolbar

Horizontal ruler   Page area

Scratch area   Formatting toolbar

Zoom controls

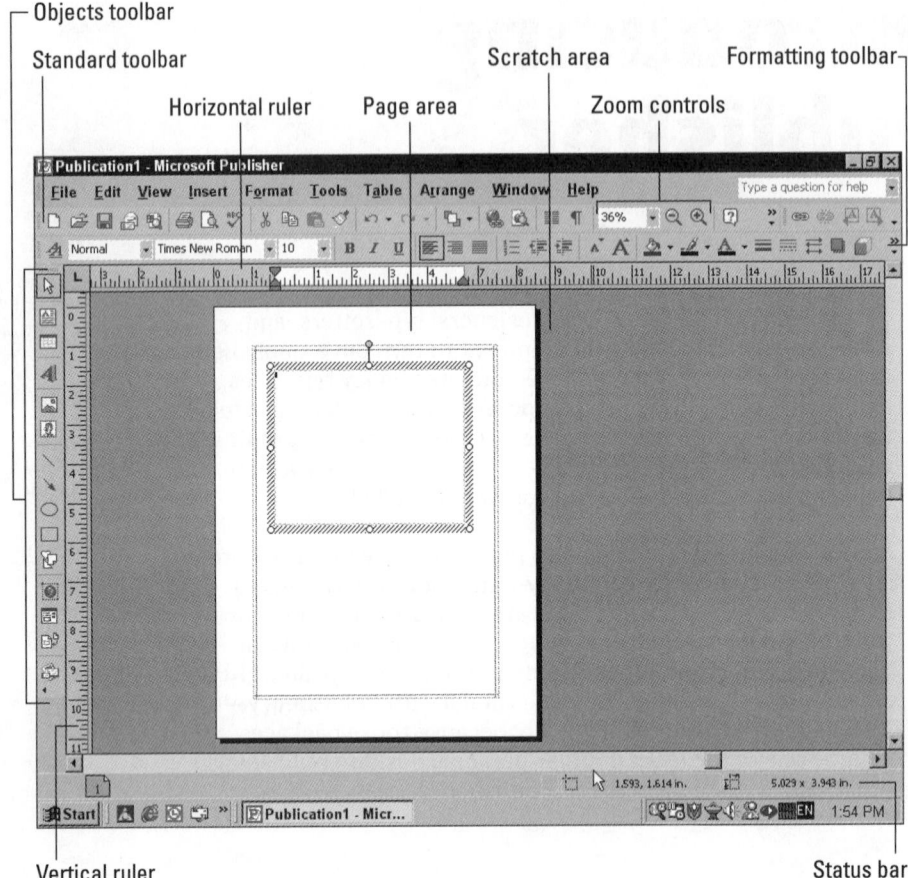

Vertical ruler

Status bar

Figure 41-1: Publisher's workspace is similar to that of other Office applications.

The main features of the workspace are the *page area* (the white rectangle) and the *scratch area*. The page area is where you place the text, graphics, and so forth that you want to appear in the final publication; the scratch area is a virtual desktop where you can drag items when you want to get them out of the way or store them for later use.

Framing the top and left sides of the workspace are the *vertical* and *horizontal rulers*, which help you position items precisely.

Like most Office applications, Publisher displays the Standard and Formatting toolbars by default. The Standard toolbar is directly under the menu bar, and the Formatting toolbar is directly under that.

Publisher also has a special toolbar called the *Objects toolbar*, which runs vertically down the left side of the workspace. These tools let you create what Publisher calls *objects,* which include text boxes, picture frames, WordArt, tables, lines, shapes, and Web-specific objects such as hotspots, form controls, and HTML code fragments.

Among the tools on the Standard toolbar are the *Zoom controls*. The Zoom list box lets you choose how large you want the display of your page to be; in addition to specific percentages of full size, it offers you the choice to view the whole page, the full width of the page, or to zoom in to a selected object. You can zoom in and out a step at a time by using the Zoom In and Zoom Out buttons, marked with a plus and minus sign, respectively.

At the bottom of the workspace is the *status bar*, which provides precise information about the location of the pointer and the dimensions of objects that are currently selected. As well, it shows a numbered icon for each page in the publication; you can jump from page to page just by clicking on its icon.

Using the Publication Gallery

As noted earlier, by default, whenever you start Publisher, you're shown the Publication Gallery. You can use the Gallery as a starting point for your publication.

Your first step is to choose how to browse through the gallery. One choice is to browse by Publication Type, first choosing a publication type, such as brochure, flyer, or Web site, from the list provided in the task pane, and sometimes then choosing a subtype.

Notice that each publication in the gallery has a name, for example, "Ascent Event Brochure" or "Floating Oval Event Brochure." The latter part of the name refers to the type of publication; the first part refers to the style in which the publication is designed.

If you prefer, you can choose to browse by Design Set instead of Publication Type. That choice shows you all the publication designs available within that particular design set (see Figure 41-2).

Note

In addition to Master Sets, which are based on common graphic elements, fonts, and so forth, Publisher offers special design sets based around common themes, for example, Special Event Sets, Holiday Sets, Fund-raiser Sets. If you're looking for something that falls within those themes, look there first.

As you've already seen, you've also got the option of starting a publication from scratch by choosing Blank Publication. Additionally, you can create a new publication based on an existing publication by choosing "From existing publication" in the New area. This opens a copy of an existing publication, which you can then modify and save without affecting the original publication it is based on. Finally, you can also open a publication from a template, or simply open an existing publication that you intend to alter.

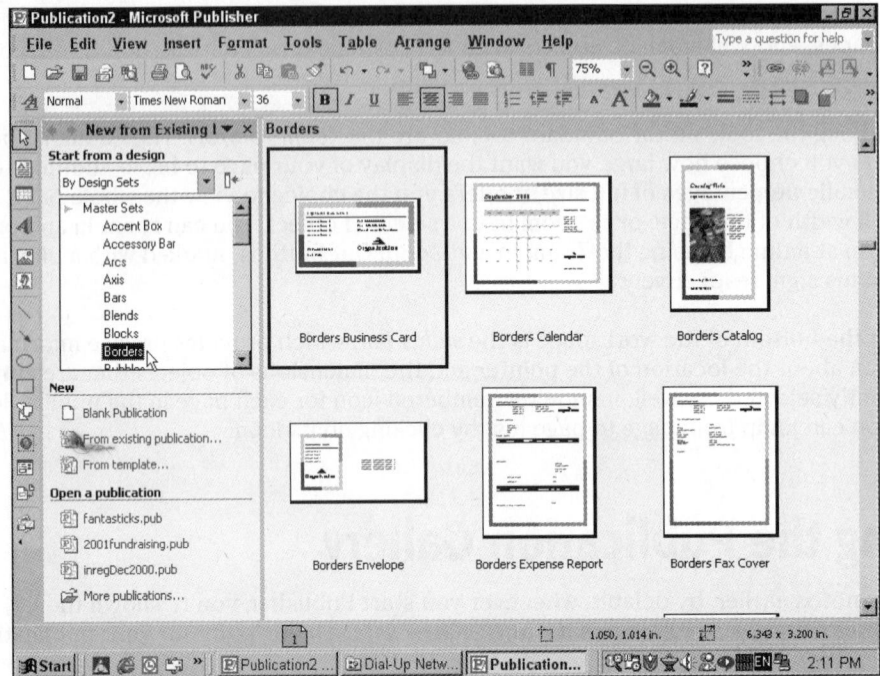

Figure 41-2: Browsing by Design Sets shows you all the publications available that use a certain basic design.

Working with Text

The primary components of any publication are text and graphics, so the rest of this chapter looks at how you insert and manipulate text and graphics in Publisher — beginning with text.

Typing in text

Once you have opened or created a Publisher publication, to type new text into it, follow these steps:

1. Click the Text Box tool at the top of the Objects toolbar.

2. Your pointer changes to a crosshairs; use this to draw a box where you want the text to appear.

3. Type your text into the frame just as if you were typing a document in Word (see Figure 41-3).

Figure 41-3: Typing text into a Publisher text box is as easy as typing in Word.

If you run out of space, you can resize your text box by clicking and dragging the handles that surround it. A text box can hold more text than is visible. If you reduce the size of the frame, some text disappears but it isn't lost; expanding the text box makes it visible again.

Inserting a text file

Sometimes you want to insert a whole text file from Word or some other application. To do so, use these steps:

1. Draw a text box as before.

2. Choose Insert ⇨ Text File from the menu bar.

3. Locate the file you want to insert and click OK.

4. Publisher inserts the file into your text box (see Figure 41-4).

Note   Notice the small box in the lower-right corner of the text box with the letter *A* followed by three dots in it. That indicates that more text is contained in the text box than is currently visible.

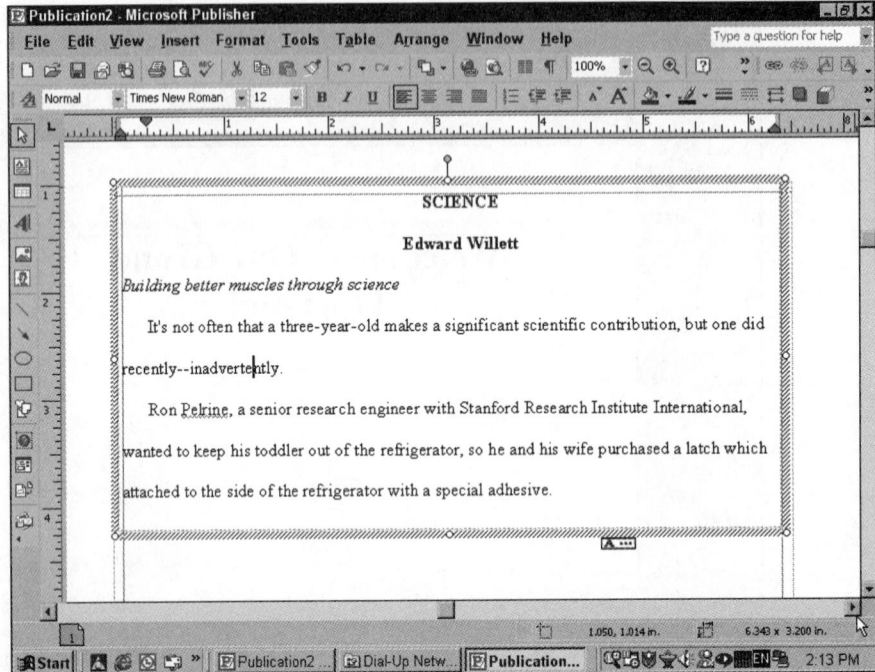

Figure 41-4: This Word file, inserted into a Publisher document, keeps all its original formatting.

Autoflow and linked frames

When you insert text into an existing text box, sometimes you get a message warning you that the inserted text won't fit. You're asked if you'd like to use autoflow. If you choose Yes, Publisher jumps to every other text box in the publication in turn, asking if you'd like to insert the remaining text into that frame. If you don't place all the text in existing frames, it eventually asks you if it should insert new pages and frames to accommodate the text.

Text inserted into multiple frames using autoflow results in a series of linked frames. When frames are linked, changing the formatting in one frame — making text larger, for instance, or reducing line spacing — results in adjustments in all of the linked frames. You can also select all the text in all of the frames simply by choosing Edit ⇨ Select All.

You can tell when frames are linked because a small image of a chain link with an arrow beside it appears in the lower-right corner of the first frame (see Figure 41-5); a similar image appears in the upper-left corners and bottom-right corners of frames further down the chain. Clicking these images takes you automatically to the next or previous frame in the chain.

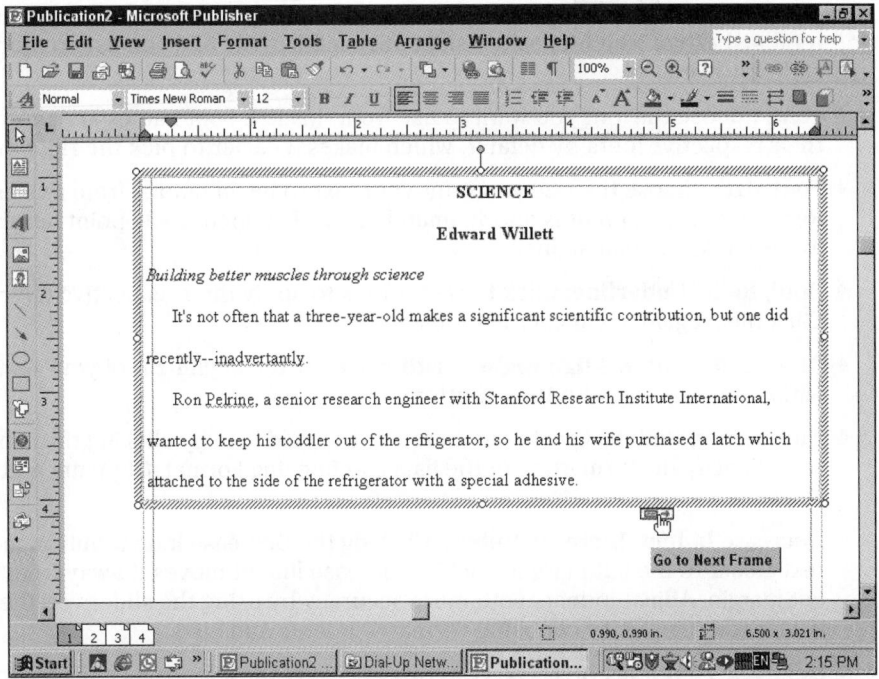

Figure 41-5: This little icon at the bottom of a text box indicates it's just one frame in a chain. Clicking on it takes you to the next frame in the chain.

You can unlink text boxes at any time by clicking the Break Forward Link button on the Connect Frames toolbar, which becomes active whenever you create linked frames. You can also link text boxes together by selecting the first frame you want to link, clicking the Create Text Box Link button, and then clicking the next frame.

Formatting text

Once you've inserted text into a text box, you can format it just as you would in Word. Many of the tools on the Formatting toolbar are, in fact, identical, so choosing font, style, size, alignment, and so forth will seem very familiar.

Note You can set the formatting for a text box before you begin typing in it, or you can apply formatting to highlighted text.

Formatting toolbar buttons

Briefly, the Formatting toolbar buttons for text are as follows:

✦ **Style:** Choose the style you want from the list box. You can create your own style or import styles from another program by choosing Format ➪ Styles and

Formatting or by clicking the Styles and Formatting button on the Formatting toolbar, both of which open a task pane much like the one you use to modify styles in Word.

✦ **Font:** Choose the font you want to use from this list. Font names are shown in their respective fonts by default, which makes it easier to pick the right one.

✦ **Font Size:** Choose the size you want your text to be, in points, from this list. Remember that a point is approximately 1/72 of an inch, so 36-point letters, for example, are half an inch high.

✦ **Bold, Italic, Underline:** Click these buttons to apply their respective effects. Click them again to cancel their effects

✦ **Align Left, Center, Align Right, Justify:** Specify the alignment of your text within the text box with these buttons.

✦ **Numbering, Bullets:** Create numbered or bulleted lists by clicking these buttons. Specify the formatting of the lists by choosing Format ➪ Indents and Lists.

✦ **Decrease Indent, Increase Indent:** Clicking the Decrease Indent button moves text closer to the left margin; clicking Increase Indent moves it away from the left margin. Adjust indents with more accuracy by using the sliders on the horizontal ruler or by choosing Format ➪ Indents and Lists.

✦ **Decrease Font Size, Increase Font Size:** Clicking these buttons changes the text size to either the next smallest size in the Font Size list or the next largest.

✦ **Fill Color, Line Color, Font Color:** Fill Color determines the color that fills the text box; you can also choose patterns as fills or create gradient fills. Line Color and Font Color determine the color of any lines used in the text box border and the color of the text itself, respectively. Each offers options for choosing colors from the color schemes mentioned earlier, or for picking your own colors from those available on your computer.

Some of these options get a more detailed treatment in Chapter 42.

✦ **Line/Border Style, Dash Style, Arrow Style:** This lets you specify the location and appearance of border lines around the text box and turn ordinary lines into arrows.

BorderArt (see Chapter 42) lets you create a variety of fancy graphical borders.

Format menu options

For more detailed formatting, choose Format from the menu bar and select the item you want to fine-tune. Options under the Format menu include the following:

✦ **Font:** Opens a dialog box that lets you choose font, font style, size, and color all in one place. In addition, it offers a variety of underlining styles and some formatting styles that aren't available by default on the Formatting toolbar, including Superscript, Subscript, Emboss, and Engrave.

✦ **Character Spacing:** Lets you set scaling, tracking, and kerning. Scaling lets you stretch or condense characters. It doesn't change their height, only their width. This can create interesting special effects or let you cram a bit more text than you'd normally be able to into a narrow text box (see Figure 41-6). Tracking adjusts the overall spacing of a block of text, while kerning adjusts the spacing between adjacent characters.

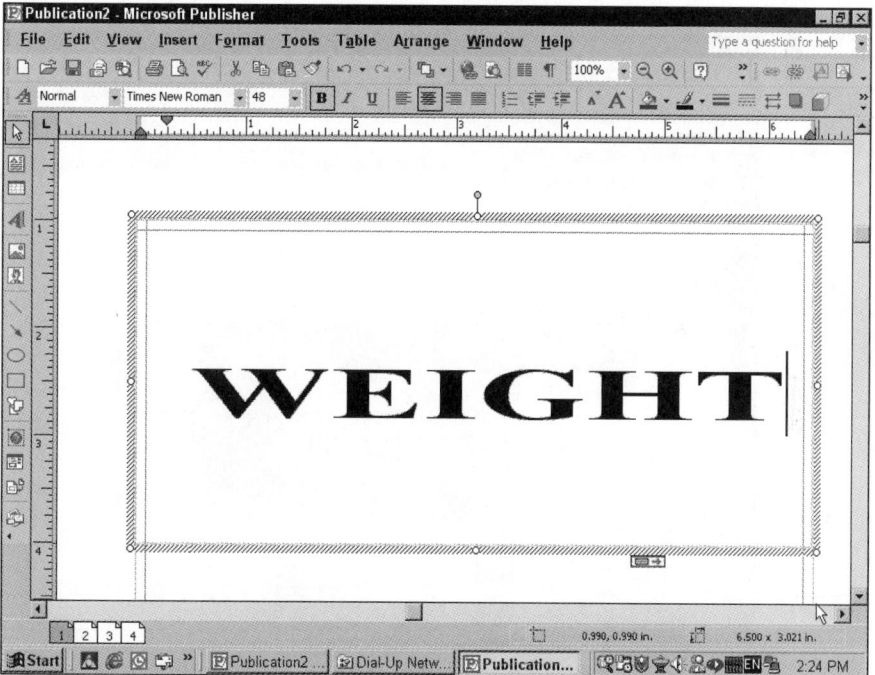

Figure 41-6: Scaling your text can create interesting effects. The word WEIGHT in this figure is scaled to 200 percent.

✦ **Line Spacing:** Lets you adjust the amount of space between lines and between paragraphs.

✦ **Align Text Vertically:** Lets you choose whether text in a particular text box should be snugged up against the top margin, against the bottom margin, or centered between the two.

✦ **Tabs:** Works the same as in Word; it lets you set tab stops and assign leaders (repeating characters, such as dots or dashes) to them.

✦ **Horizontal Rules:** Tells Publisher to automatically insert horizontal lines before or after (or both) a paragraph and lets you specify thickness, color, style, and position.

✦ **Quick Publication Options, Publication Designs, Color Schemes, Font Schemes:** All of these enable you to apply some of the professionally designed schemes included with Publisher to your current publication. Quick Publication Options (see Figure 41-7) lets you automatically add elements of a Quick Publication, Publication Designs lets you apply elements of one of the designs from the Publication Gallery, Color Schemes changes the colors of your fonts and other elements to match a set color scheme designed to look good, and Font schemes does the same with the fonts you're using.

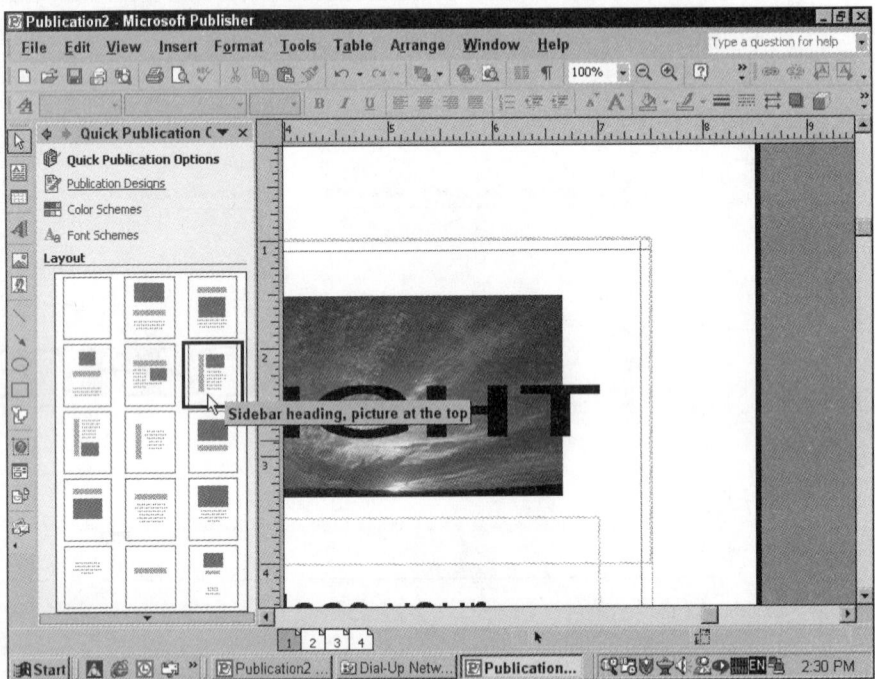

Figure 41-7: Publisher makes it easy at any time to apply one of the professionally created designs included with the program to your own publication.

✦ **Styles and Formatting:** Opens the Styles and Formatting task pane and lets you modify or apply styles.

✦ **Text Box:** Lets you format the text box itself. You can adjust its background color, the line or border that surrounds it, and its size; rotate it anyway you want; adjust the way text inside it wraps around graphics; set its internal margins; break the text inside it into columns; and even add an automatic "Continued on page . . ." or "Continued from page . . ." slug at the top or bottom of it. There are several tabs here; explore them freely.

✦ **Indents and Lists:** Lets you create normal, bulleted or numbered lists and set left, first-line, and right indents for lists and paragraphs.

✦ **Drop Cap:** Provides a selection of preformatted drop caps — extra-large capital letters at the start of paragraph, as in old-fashioned books — or lets you create your own custom drop cap, setting the font, size, and so on.

The Measurements toolbar

The Measurements toolbar lets you control many aspects of spacing and positioning of text boxes with handy control boxes.

To view the Measurements toolbar, choose View ➪ Toolbars ➪ Measurements or click View Toolbar on the dialog boxes just mentioned that have to do with spacing, such as the Line Spacing dialog box or the Character Spacing dialog box.

The Measurements toolbar is shown in Figure 41-8. Any changes you make with the Measurements toolbar controls show up immediately on the screen, which makes this a very useful mechanism for fine-tuning your publication. Here's how it works:

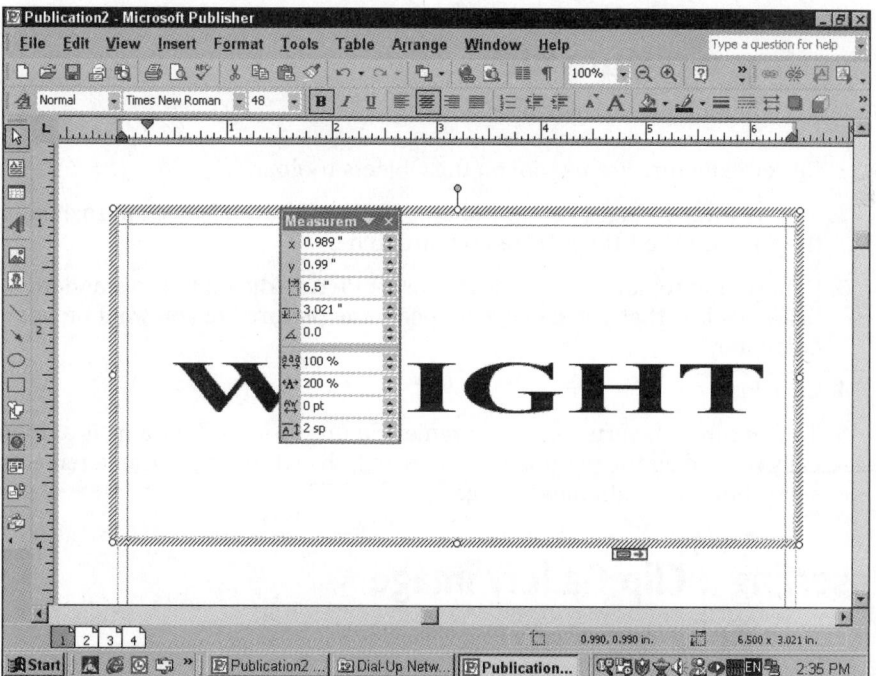

Figure 41-8: The Measurements toolbar lets you fine-tune your publication by entering precise values for a number of parameters.

✦ The two top controls, labeled x and y, control the horizontal and vertical positions of the text box, measured from the zero points of the horizontal and vertical rulers to the left and top edges of the text box. Of course, you can always drag a text box around on the page to reposition it, but if you want precise positioning, these controls can give it to you. You can either type in the coordinates you want or click the little up and down arrows beside each control.

✦ The next two controls down control width and height of the text box.

✦ The next one controls rotation.

✦ In the bottom section are spacing controls for the text itself: from top to bottom, tracking, scaling, kerning, and line spacing.

Working with Graphics

Pictures for your publication can come from several sources: the Office Clip Gallery, a file on your computer (which you may have downloaded off the Internet, for example), a scanner, or a digital camera. Once they're inserted into your publication, you can manipulate them in a variety of ways.

Inserting a picture file

To insert a picture file, follow these steps:

1. Click the Picture Frame tool on the Objects toolbar.

2. Your pointer changes to a crosshairs; use it to draw a frame approximately the size you want the inserted picture to be.

3. Publisher automatically opens the Insert Picture dialog box, a standard browsing box that you can use to locate the picture file you want on your computer.

4. Click Insert.

5. The picture is inserted into the frame you drew for it. The frame is automatically resized so the picture isn't distorted; the width of the frame remains the same, but the height may change.

Inserting a Clip Gallery image

To insert a Clip Gallery image, follow these steps:

1. Click the Clip Gallery Frame tool on the Objects toolbar.

2. Your pointer changes to a crosshairs; draw a frame approximately the size you want the inserted Clip Gallery image to be.

3. Clip Gallery opens automatically. Find the image you want and double-click on it to insert it into your publication.

4. The Clip Gallery picture is inserted into the frame. Again, the frame's size changes to prevent the picture from being distorted.

Inserting a scanner or camera image

To insert an image from a scanner or digital camera, use these steps:

1. Choose Insert ➪ Picture ➪ From Scanner or Camera ➪ Select Device to choose the camera or scanner you want to acquire the picture from.

2. Choose Insert ➪ Picture ➪ From Scanner or Camera ➪ Acquire Image to open the device's software and acquire the picture.

3. The picture is inserted into your document. You can then drag it to where you want it and work with it in a variety of ways (see the next section).

Formatting pictures

Once you've inserted a picture, you can manipulate it in a variety of ways. You can

✦ **Recolor it:** Choose Format ➪ Picture and then choose the Picture tab. In the resulting dialog box you can apply a number of color effects; the Color drop-down list includes Grayscale, Black & White, and Washout, as well as the default Automatic, which uses the picture's original colors. You can adjust the brightness and contrast here as well, or you can click the Recolor button to open the dialog box in Figure 41-9. This lets you recolor the whole picture or leave the black parts black and just recolor the colored parts. Choose the color using the Color control; you can also apply tint and shade fill effects. You can undo changes to the color of a picture by clicking Restore Original Colors.

Figure 41-9: Recolor a picture, or restore it to its original color, using these controls.

✦ **Resize it:** Choose Format ➪ Picture and choose the Size tab to open a dialog box where you can change both the height and width of the picture by entering either a specific measurement (in the "Size and rotate" area) or a percentage of its original height and width (in the Scale area). You can return a picture to its original size by clicking the Reset button. You can also rotate the picture using the rotation tools in the "Size and rotate" area.

Caution   If you scale height and weight by different percentages, your picture is distorted. To avoid this, check the "Lock aspect ratio" checkbox; this ensures that whenever you change one dimension of the picture, the other changes proportionately.

✦ **Apply a fill or a border:** Choose Format ➪ Picture ➪ Colors and Lines to apply a fill or a border to the picture frame. You can achieve the same effect by clicking the appropriate buttons on the Formatting toolbar.

✦ **Change how text wraps around the picture:** Choose Format ➪ Picture and click the Layout tab to open the dialog box in Figure 41-10, where you can set margins for the picture frame and also determine whether, if the picture is placed over a text box, text wraps around the outside of the picture frame or tucks in closely around the picture itself. This dialog box also lets you position the text frame very precisely, using the controls at the bottom.

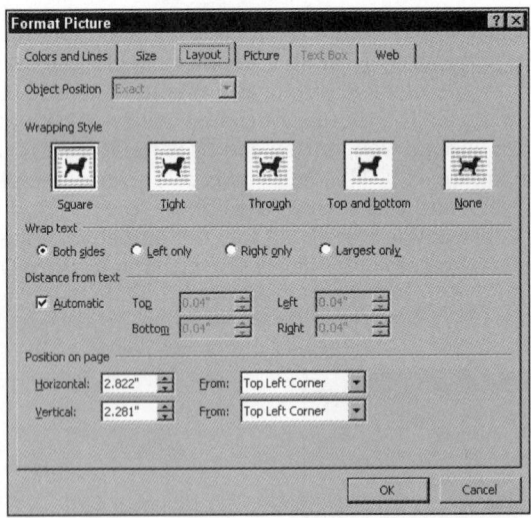

Figure 41-10: Set the text wrap properties of a picture frame using this dialog box.

✦ **Rotate the picture:** As noted, you can do this using the Picture tab of the Format ➪ Picture dialog box, but the easiest way to do it is simply to point at the green handle that sticks up from the top of the picture and rotate the picture visually, by clicking and dragging.

✦ **Crop the picture:** Choose Format ➪ Picture and click the Picture tab. Crop the picture using the controls at the top, by choosing how far from each edge to crop the picture.

Tip

A better way to crop pictures is to do so visually, using the Picture toolbar (see Figure 41-11). This comes up automatically when you first insert a picture and contains a number of useful tools, including a Crop tool, which you can use to crop the picture visually by clicking and dragging on its corners.

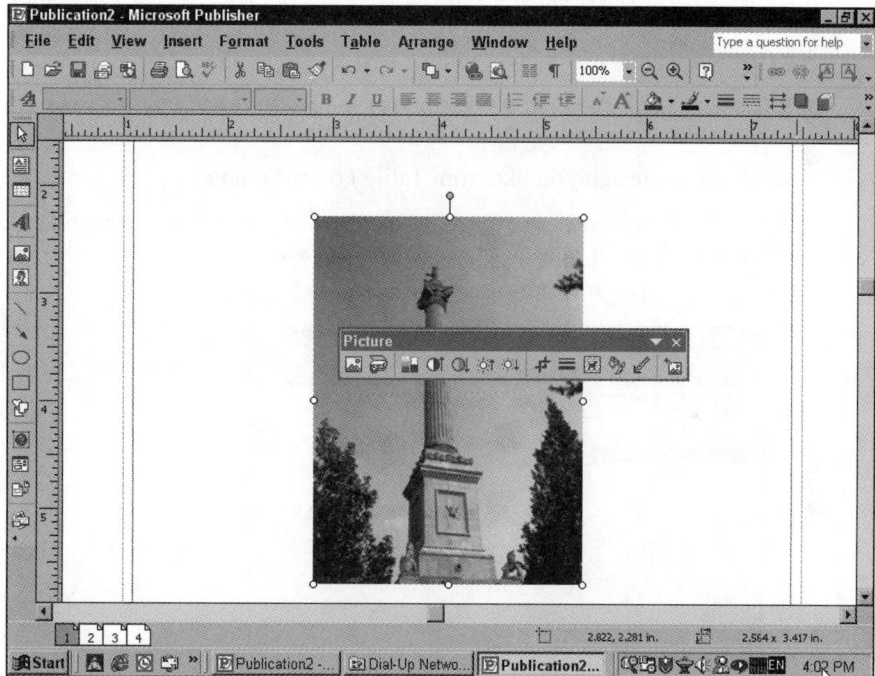

Figure 41-11: The Picture toolbar contains one-button controls for many of the options also available through the Format ➪ Picture dialog box.

Drawing lines and shapes

Publisher also lets you draw basic shapes with four simple drawing tools on the Objects toolbar: the Line tool, the Oval tool, the Rectangle tool, and the Custom Shapes tool. The Line tool also lets you draw arrows and adjust the shape of the arrowheads.

Custom Shapes provides you with a small menu of a variety of starbursts, arrows, and other useful shapes. If the shape includes a small gray diamond, its shape is adjustable; click and drag on the diamond to see what effect it has.

You can apply different line styles and fills to shapes and rotate them, as well.

Working with Tables

The third-most-common type of object you're likely to want in a Publisher publication is a table.

Inserting a table

To insert a table, follow these steps:

1. Click the Insert Table tool on the Objects toolbar.

2. Draw a frame, just as you did for text and graphics.

3. The Create Table dialog box opens (see Figure 41-12). Enter the number of rows and columns you want in your table.

4. Choose a design you like from Table Format menu.

5. Click OK. Publisher creates a table with the number of rows and columns you indicated, sized to fit in the frame you drew.

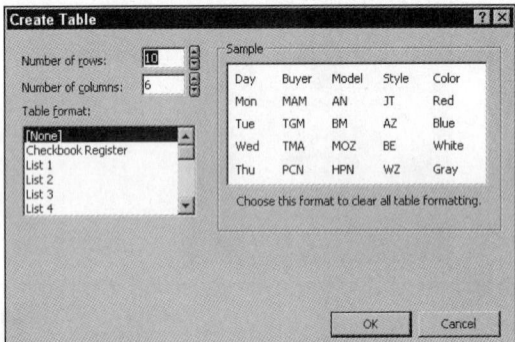

Figure 41-12: The Create Table dialog box gives you a number of table designs to choose from.

Entering data into a table

Once you've got your blank table, entering information into it is simply a matter of clicking on the cell you want to enter information into and then typing away. The same formatting tools are available to you for formatting text within a table that are available when you are working in a text box.

Editing a table

Publisher tables don't offer nearly as many options as, say, Word tables when it comes to making changes. In fact, there are only a few, all accessed by choosing Table from the menu bar:

✦ **Insert Rows or Columns:** Opens a dialog box in which you can specify whether you want to insert rows or columns, and how many, and whether the new rows or columns should appear before or after the currently selected range of cells.

✦ **Delete Rows or Columns:** Deletes the rows or columns containing the currently selected cells.

✦ **Merge Cells:** Turns any currently selected cells into one big cell, erasing the borders between them.

✦ **Cell Diagonals:** Splits currently selected cells into two divided by a diagonal line, which can slant either up or down.

✦ **Table AutoFormat:** Lets you change the format of your table.

✦ **Select:** Lets you select the entire table, the current rows or columns, or just the cell in which the cursor is currently located.

✦ **Fill Down and Fill Right:** Fill a column or row of selected cells with the contents of either the topmost or leftmost cell in the selected range.

✦ **Grow to Fit Text:** When checked, makes the table automatically increase row height to make room for whatever text you enter into it.

✦ **Merge/Split Cells:** Highlight two or more cells and choose Merge Cells to combine them into one larger cell; or highlight a merged cell and choose Split Cells to turn it back into its original individual cells.

✦   ✦   ✦

Advanced Publisher Techniques

This chapter takes a look at some advanced techniques that can add extra pizzazz to your creations and shows you how you can use Publisher to design Web pages. I'll also discuss printing: both printing to your personal printer and preparing your publication for printing by a print shop.

Adding Special Effects

Why settle for ordinary text in ordinary text frames, when you can dress up your text in a number of ways? With its border art, drop caps, and WordArt tools, Publisher can give your publication the added oomph it needs to catch and hold your reader's attention.

BorderArt

To add an ordinary border to a text box or picture frame in Publisher, click the Line/Border Style button on the Formatting toolbar, click More Lines, choose a size and color of line and which sides of the frame to apply it to in the Format dialog box (under the Colors and Lines tab), and then click OK.

Note   If you check the "Draw border inside frame" box, the entire border, no matter how wide, is drawn inside the edges of the frame. If you don't check the box, the border overlaps the edges of the frame.

But while you're in the Colors and Lines tab of the Format dialog box, you'll see a button labeled BorderArt. Click it, and the border possibilities suddenly expand exponentially (see Figure 42-1).

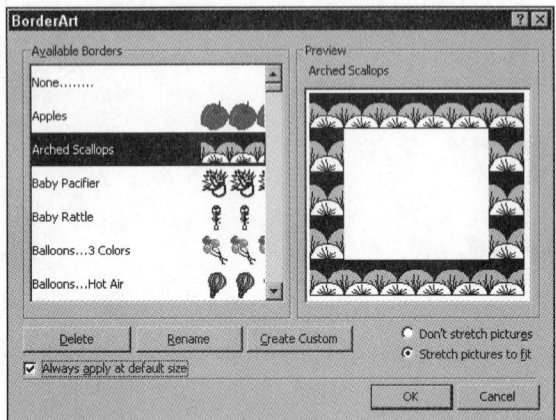

Figure 42-1: You're not limited to ordinary lines when you create borders in Publisher.

Publisher comes with a number of decorative borders, which you can peruse and choose from in the Available Borders area of this dialog box—literally everything from apples to zigzags.

Each border has a default size; if you think the border is too thick or too thin, though, you can change it by unchecking the "Always apply at default size" box and then returning to the Colors and Lines tab to set the border width as usual. You can also modify the color under the Colors and Lines tab, just like you can an ordinary line border.

The BorderArt dialog box also enables you to choose whether or not to deform the individual pictures that make up some borders (such as the apples in the figure) to make a more continuous border.

Figure 42-2 shows how the appropriate border can dress up your text.

You're not limited to the available borders; you can also create your own border using any graphic image. Click Create Custom in the BorderArt dialog box and then choose a picture file from your computer or from the Media Gallery. Publisher converts it into a border, which you can then name what you wish. That border continues to appear in your list of available borders until you choose it and click Delete.

Note   A picture has to be pretty simple to be made into a border. A digital photograph of a winter scene, for instance, would be too complex. A simple line drawing of a snow-covered tree, however, would not.

Figure 42-2: Happy Holidays looks a lot more festive with a few evergreen trees around the edges.

Drop caps

A *drop cap* is a large initial letter in a piece of text, reflecting the style of the illuminated manuscripts of the Middle Ages, when books often began with large, lavishly decorated initial letters.

To apply a drop cap to the beginning of a particular paragraph, click anywhere in that paragraph, then choose Format ➪ Drop Cap. This opens the dialog box shown in Figure 42-3.

As with borders, Publisher has several available styles of drop caps ready and waiting for you. Click the one you like and then click OK. The drop cap is added to your paragraph (see Figure 42-4).

If you don't see a drop cap you like in the Drop Cap dialog box, click the Custom Drop Cap tab and you can design your own, using the tools shown in Figure 42-5.

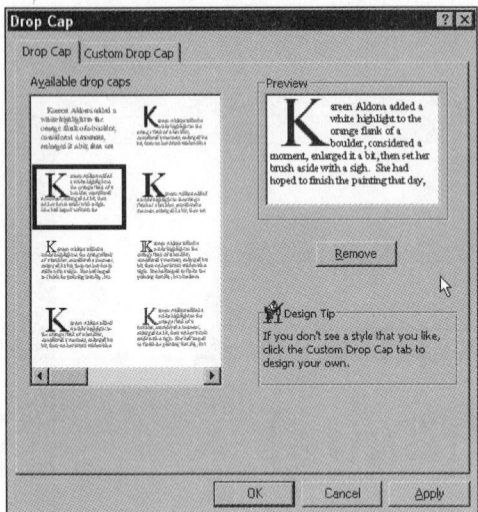

Figure 42-3: Create a fancy initial letter for a paragraph with the Drop Cap dialog box.

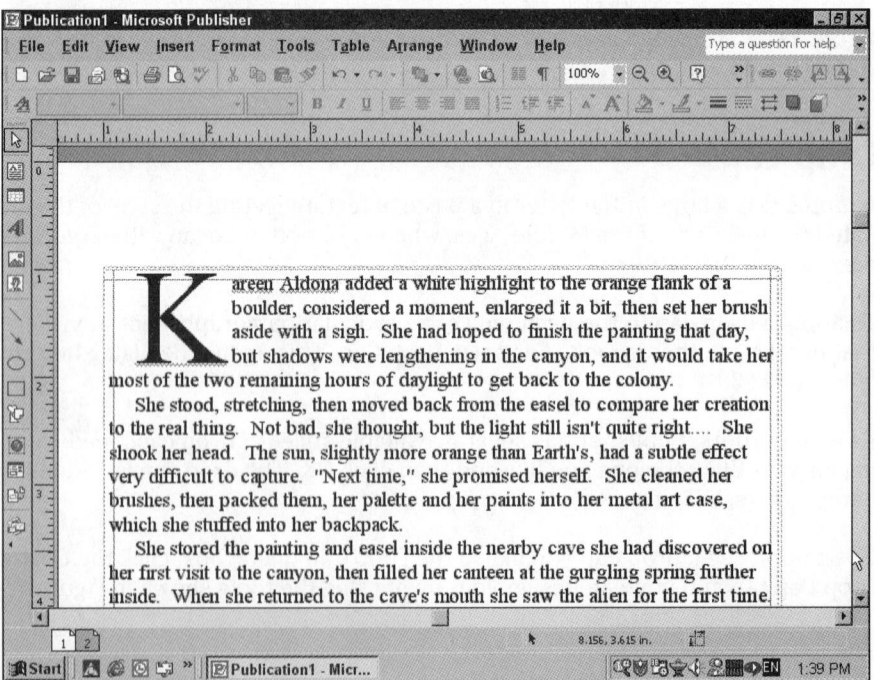

Figure 42-4: Drop caps are an ornamental touch that can bring your text alive.

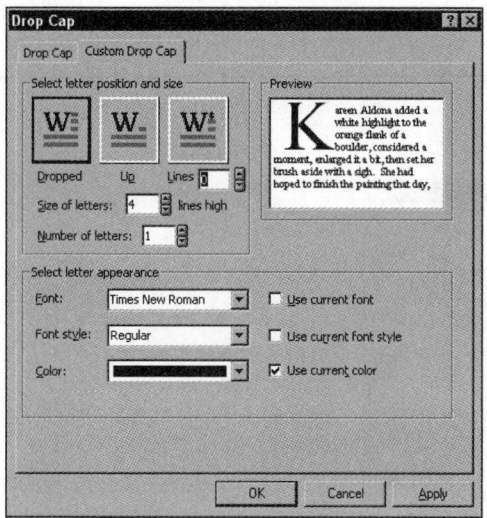

Figure 42-5: Don't like Publisher's available Drop Caps? Then design your own!

This dialog box is divided into two sections, one in which you choose the appearance of the initial letter and one in which you determine its position and size.

In the "Select letter position and size" area, you can choose to make your drop cap drop into the paragraph until its top is even with the top of the first line of text (as in Figure 42-4) or have it rise above the paragraph so that the bottom of the drop cap is level with the bottom of the first line of text. Or you can compromise, and have it rise a specified number of lines above the paragraph.

You can also set the size of the drop cap, in lines, and how many letters you want in the drop cap style—typically just one, but some of the preset drop caps include two letters, and you might want to set the entire first word in drop-cap style.)

In the "Select letter appearance" area, you choose a font for the drop cap, a style (regular, italic, bold, or bold italic), and a color. If you wish, you can automatically use the font, style, and color of the rest of the paragraph.

When you're happy with your drop cap, click OK.

WordArt

Another form of fancy text is WordArt, which applies special formatting to text—shapes, shadows, and so forth that you can't apply through the ordinary formatting tools.

To create a WordArt object, follow these steps:

1. Click the Insert WordArt button on the Object toolbar to open the WordArt Gallery shown in Figure 42-6.

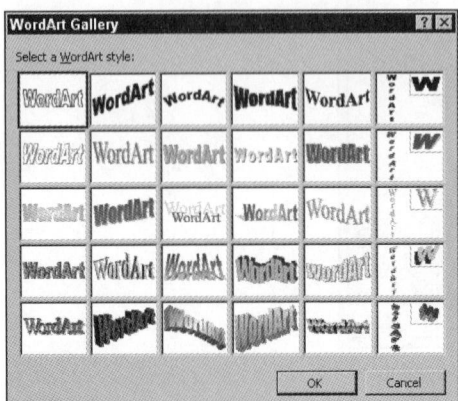

Figure 42-6: WordArt Gallery offers you a lot of fancy formatting to choose from.

2. Choose the WordArt style you'd like to use.

3. Type the text that you want to apply WordArt formatting to in the Text window in the Edit WordArt Text dialog box that now appears. Press Return to add a second line of text and any additional lines of text after that.

4. Choose a font and font size from their respective list boxes, and apply bold or italic style, if you wish.

5. Click OK. WordArt applies the style you chose to the text you entered (see Figure 42-7).

Editing WordArt is easy with the WordArt toolbar, which opens automatically whenever you create a WordArt object, and with other tools Publisher makes available. You can do all the following:

✦ **Resize it:** Use the handles as you would on any other object to adjust its height and width. Because WordArt is really a graphic, not text, the shape of the letters deforms along with the shape of the frame.

✦ **Reshape it:** Many WordArt styles, including the one in Figure 42-7, include a small yellow diamond or two somewhere inside them. Clicking and dragging this diamond adjusts the shape of the object. In Figure 42-7, clicking and dragging the diamond adjusts the amount of curve applied to the text. You can also change the shape of the WordArt object by clicking the WordArt Shape button on the WordArt toolbar and choosing the shape you want to apply from the menu provided.

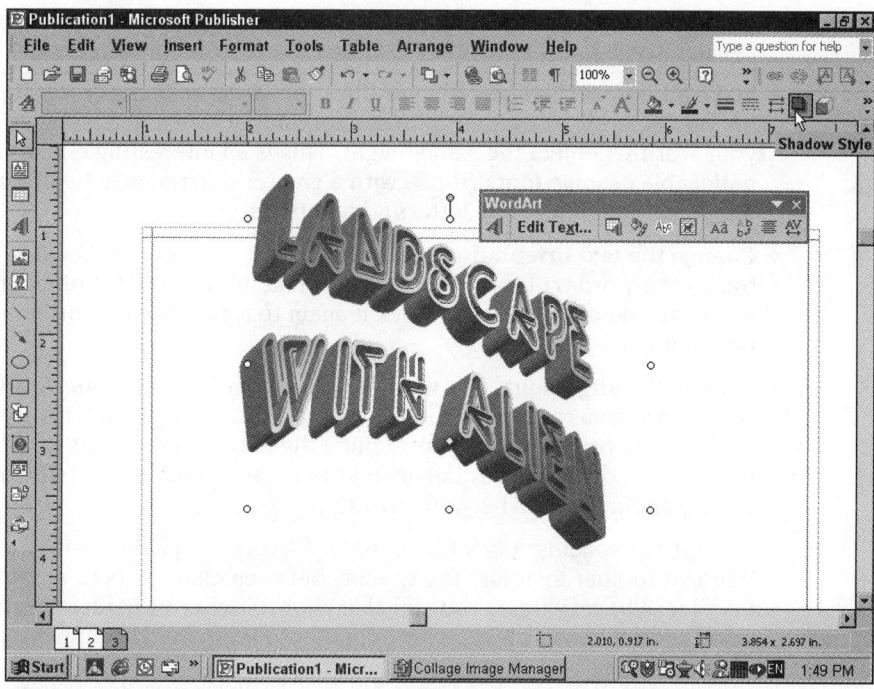

Figure 42-7: Here's the text I entered into WordArt rendered in the WordArt style I chose. Notice the WordArt toolbar that has opened automatically.

✦ **Change shadow style and 3D style:** Whenever you're working with a 3D object in Publisher, you can apply a shadow style or 3D style to it by clicking the Shadow Style and 3D Style buttons on the Formatting toolbar. Choose the style you want from those offered, and click to apply, or click Shadow Settings or 3D Settings to create your own shadow or 3D style.

✦ **Edit text:** Click the Edit Text button on the WordArt toolbar to reopen the Edit WordArt Text dialog box and change the text, or its font, style, or size.

✦ **Change the WordArt style:** Click the WordArt Gallery button on the WordArt toolbar to reopen the WordArt Gallery; click any of the styles offered to change the style of the currently selected WordArt object to the new style.

✦ **Format the WordArt object:** Click the Format WordArt button on the WordArt toolbar (or choose Format ➪ WordArt) to open the Format WordArt dialog box, which includes tabs very similar to the Format dialog boxes for text boxes and graphics. You can apply borders, change the fill of the object, and make other changes using this dialog box.

✦ **Change text wrapping:** Click the Text Wrapping button on the WordArt toolbar to change the way text in a text box wraps around the WordArt object.

✦ **Make all letters the same height:** Click the WordArt Same Letter Heights button on the WordArt toolbar to make both uppercase and lowercase letters in your WordArt object the same height. This is an interesting effect that's more noticeable in some fonts (those with a greater difference in height between uppercase and lowercase letters) than others.

✦ **Change the text orientation to vertical:** Click the WordArt Vertical Text button on the WordArt toolbar to make the text in the WordArt object run up and down instead of side to side. Click it again to return the text orientation to horizontal.

✦ **Change the alignment:** The WordArt Alignment button on the WordArt toolbar enables you to set alignment to center, left, right, stretch justify (which justifies text by horizontally stretching the letters), letter justify (which justifies text by adding spaces between letters), and word justify (which justifies text by adding spaces between words).

✦ **Change the spacing:** Click the WordArt Character Spacing button on the WordArt toolbar to adjust the spacing between characters to anything from very loose to very tight. You can also choose to Kern Character Pairs, which moves certain characters closer together to improve their appearance.

You can edit your WordArt at any time by double-clicking the frame to bring up the Edit WordArt Text dialog box and the WordArt toolbar.

Using Linked and Embedded Objects

Sometimes you may want to insert an object into a Publisher document that you can't create with Publisher's own tools. An Excel spreadsheet is a good example. Another is an image that you may have created using a specialized graphics program. You can insert these objects and continue to edit them if the program they were created in supports linking and embedding. First, a couple of definitions:

✦ A *linked* object is one that appears in your publication but isn't really part of it: it's stored somewhere else. All that's really included in your publication is the object's name and location; when you display or print the page that includes the linked object, Publisher fetches the object from wherever it is and dutifully includes it. One advantage of linking over embedding is that any changes made to the object in the original program (that is, Excel or Word) are automatically reflected in the Publisher publication to which the object is linked.

✦ An *embedded* object is created and edited with another program, but all the data for it is contained within your publication. Whereas a linked object has little effect on the amount of disk space your publication takes up, an embedded object may have a much greater effect.

Embedding a new object

To insert a new embedded object into your publication, follow these steps:

1. Choose Insert ➪ Object from the menu bar. This opens the dialog box shown in Figure 42-8.

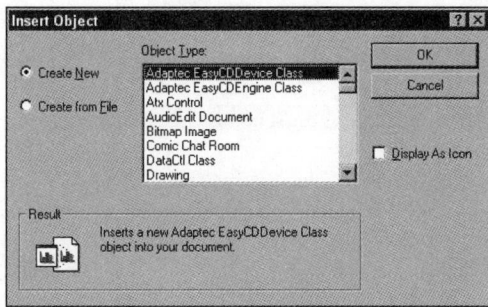

Figure 42-8: You can insert any of the objects listed here into your publication. The list that appears depends on what software is installed on your computer.

2. Choose the type of object you'd like to embed from the Object Type list. If you want to simply display an icon representing the object, check Display as Icon; otherwise, the entire object is displayed.

3. Check the Create New box.

4. Click OK. In Figure 42-9, I've chosen to embed a Microsoft Excel chart. Notice that Publisher's toolbars have vanished, replaced by the Excel toolbar — and the Excel Chart toolbar has opened, too.

When you've finished creating your embedded object, click anywhere outside the object's frame. Publisher's controls reappear, and you can continue creating your publication as normal. Whenever you want to edit the embedded object, just double-click it and its controls reappear.

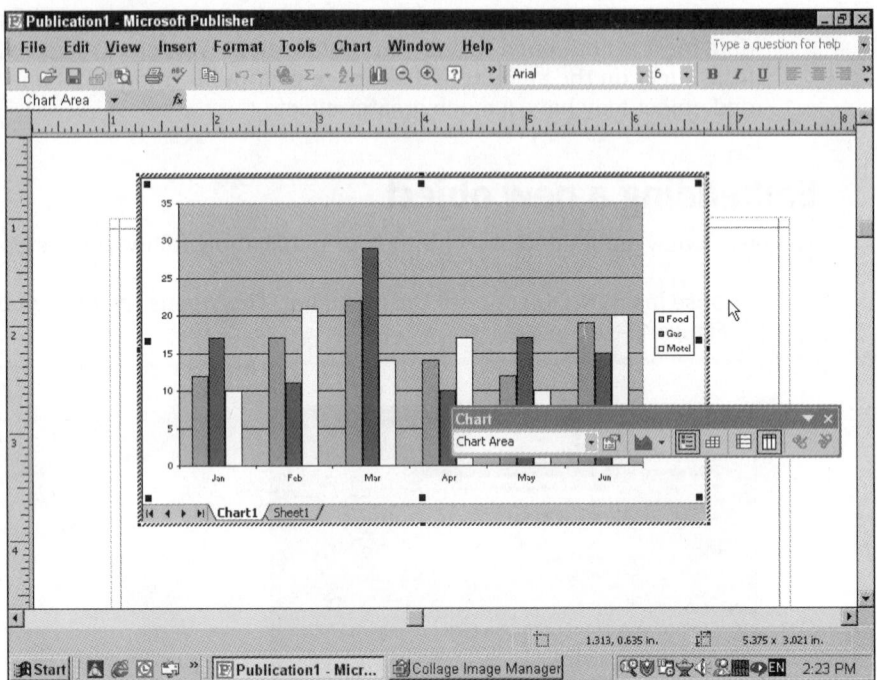

Figure 42-9: When you create a new embedded object, Publisher's controls are sometimes replaced by controls specific to that object.

Embedding an existing object

To insert an object that already exists as a file created by another program, follow these steps:

1. Choose Insert ➪ Object.
2. This time, click Create from File.
3. Enter the path to the file, or click Browse to browse for it on your computer.
4. If you want the object to be linked, check Link; otherwise the object is embedded.
5. Click OK. The file you selected is inserted into your publication (see Figure 42-10).

Figure 42-10: This PhotoDraw graphic was inserted as a linked object. Any changes to this image I make using PhotoDraw are now automatically reflected in this Publisher publication.

Mail Merging in Publisher

Another useful tool in Publisher is mail merge capability. You can create a database in Publisher specifically for that purpose, or you can use a database you created in another program. Publisher provides a helpful wizard to make the process easy.

To open the Mail Merge Wizard, choose Tools ➪ Mail Merge ➪ Mail Merge Wizard. This opens the task pane shown in Figure 42-11.

The first step is to select the recipients. You can use an existing list, create a list by selecting from among your Outlook contacts, or type in an entirely new list.

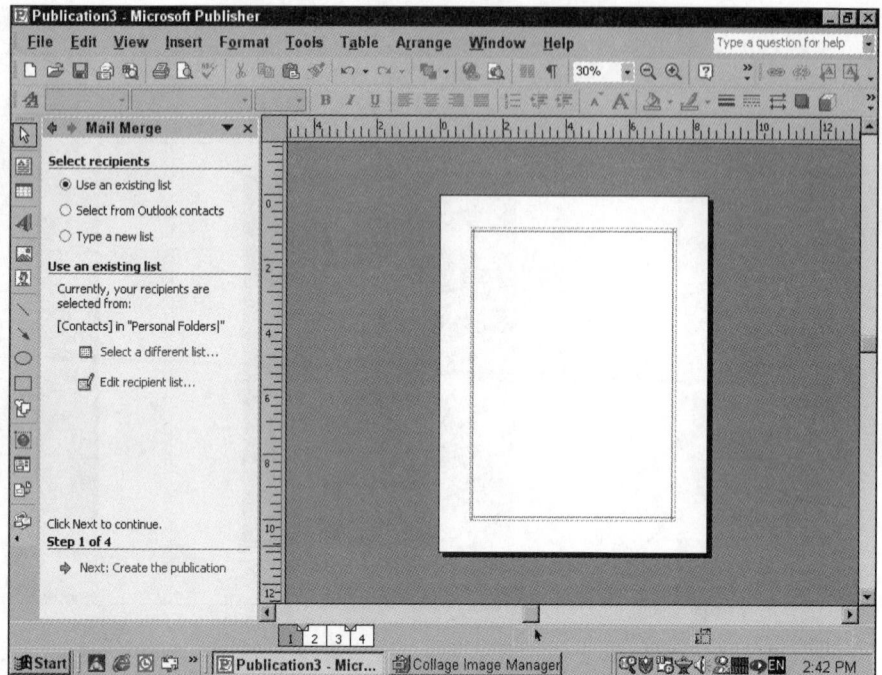

Figure 42-11: Use this wizard to set up mail merging in Publisher.

Using an existing list or Outlook contacts

If you choose to use an existing list, you'll be asked to locate the list on your computer (it must be either a database file or in table format).

When you've located it, you'll see the Mail Merge Recipients dialog box shown in Figure 42-12. This lists all the fields you have set up in the database, and lets you choose which ones to include in your mail merge, sort the list by any of the fields just by clicking the appropriate column heads, or narrow down the lists by clicking the arrow beside the column name and filtering the information. (You can choose to view only entries that have blank spaces in that column, only entries that have non-blank spaces in that column, or look for other criteria you provide by choosing the Advanced option. For instance, you could filter the database so it merges only the people whose first names are *John* or whose postal codes exceed a certain number.)

If you choose to select from Outlook contacts, you'll see them displayed in the same Mail Merge Recipients dialog box.

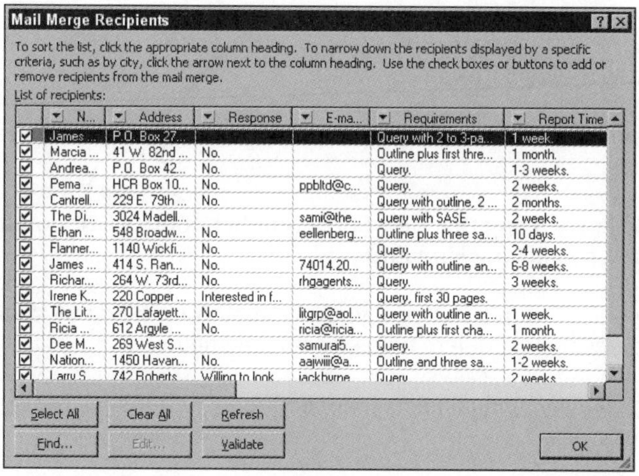

Mail Merge Recipients ? ✕

To sort the list, click the appropriate column heading. To narrow down the recipients displayed by a specific criteria, such as by city, click the arrow next to the column heading. Use the check boxes or buttons to add or remove recipients from the mail merge.

List of recipients:

▼	▼ N...	▼ Address	▼ Response	▼ E-ma...	▼ Requirements	▼ Report Time ▲
☑	James ...	P.O. Box 27...			Query with 2 to 3-pa...	1 week.
☑	Marcia ...	41 W. 82nd ...	No.		Outline plus first thre...	1 month.
☑	Andrea...	P.O. Box 42...	No.		Query.	1-3 weeks.
☑	Pema ...	HCR Box 10...	No.	ppbltd@c...	Query.	2 weeks.
☑	Cantrell...	229 E. 79th ...	No.		Query with outline, 2 ...	2 months.
☑	The Di...	3024 Madell...		sami@the...	Query with SASE.	2 weeks.
☑	Ethan ...	548 Broadw...	No.	eellenberg...	Outline plus three sa...	10 days.
☑	Flanner...	1140 Wickfi...	No.		Query.	2-4 weeks.
☑	James ...	414 S. Ran...	No.	74014.20...	Query with outline an...	6-8 weeks.
☑	Richar...	264 W. 73rd...	No.	rhgagents...	Query.	3 weeks.
☑	Irene K...	220 Copper ...	Interested in f...		Query, first 30 pages.	
☑	The Lit...	270 Lafayett...	No.	litgrp@aol...	Query with outline an...	1 week.
☑	Ricia ...	612 Argyle ...	No.	ricia@ricia...	Outline plus first cha...	1 month.
☑	Dee M...	269 West S...		samurai5...	Query.	2 weeks.
☑	Nation...	1450 Havan...	No.	aajwiii@a...	Outline and three sa...	1-2 weeks.
☑	Larru S	742 Roberts	Willing to look	jackburne	Query	2 weeks

[Select All] [Clear All] [Refresh]

[Find...] [Edit...] [Validate] [OK]

Figure 42-12: Sort and filter the entries you want included in your mail merge using this dialog box.

Creating a new list

To create a new list, choose "Type a new list" from the "Select recipients" area of the Mail Merge task pane and then click the Create link under "Type a new list." This opens the New Address List dialog box shown in Figure 42-13.

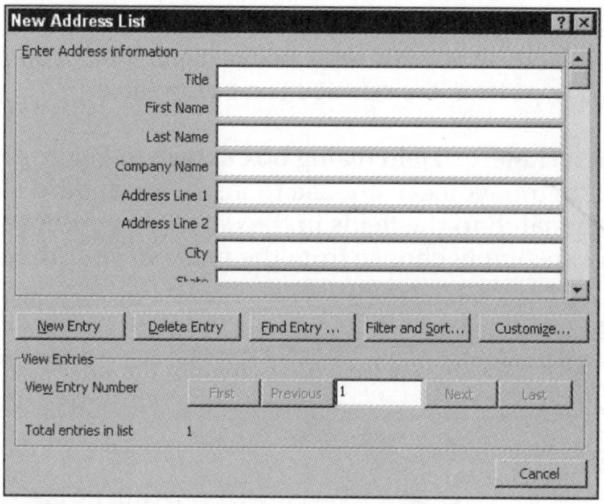

New Address List ? ✕

Enter Address information

Title [   ]
First Name [   ]
Last Name [   ]
Company Name [   ]
Address Line 1 [   ]
Address Line 2 [   ]
City [   ]
State

[New Entry] [Delete Entry] [Find Entry ...] [Filter and Sort...] [Customize...]

View Entries

View Entry Number [First] [Previous] [1] [Next] [Last]

Total entries in list   1

[Cancel]

Figure 42-13: Create a new address list for mail merging using this dialog box.

By default, the dialog box includes fields for the most common fields used in address lists. If these fields suit your purpose, just type the information into the blanks. Click New Entry to create a new entry.

When you've finished, click Close and save your database using the Save Address List dialog box that opens.

You can locate a specific entry using the View Entry Number controls, or conduct a search for a specific entry by clicking Find Entry.

If the fields included by default don't suit you, you can customize fields by clicking Customize. You can add new fields, delete fields, or rename fields.

After you've created a database, you can edit it at any time by choosing Tools ➪ Mail Merge ➪ Edit Address List.

Create the publication

The next step in the Mail Merge Wizard is to create your publication, if you haven't already done so.

To add recipient information, click where you want the information to appear and then click the items you want to add from the list provided. These include an address block (the address of the recipient, which would typically appear at the top of a business letter) and a greeting line (Dear, To, and so forth), both of which you can customize by clicking the links provided.

Note   You must have a text box or table selected in your publication before you can insert fields. The inserted field appears in the selected text box or table.

Clicking More Items opens the Insert Merge Field dialog box shown in Figure 42-14. By clicking the radio buttons at the top, you can choose to insert a standard address field, which you can then match to the fields in the database you're using by clicking Match Fields, or you can simply choose from the fields in your database.

Fields appear in your publication as the name of the field surrounded by double brackets on each side (see Figure 42-15).

Preview your publication

The next step the wizard offers is a preview of your publication. Publisher inserts the data from the database into your publication one entry at a time and lets you page through the results forward and backward to make sure that including data hasn't caused any unexpected problems within your publication, such as inserting a blank line or pushing some text out of sight in a text box.

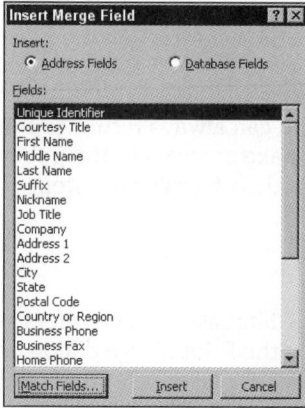

Figure 42-14: Use this dialog box to insert the information from the list you created or opened in the previous step.

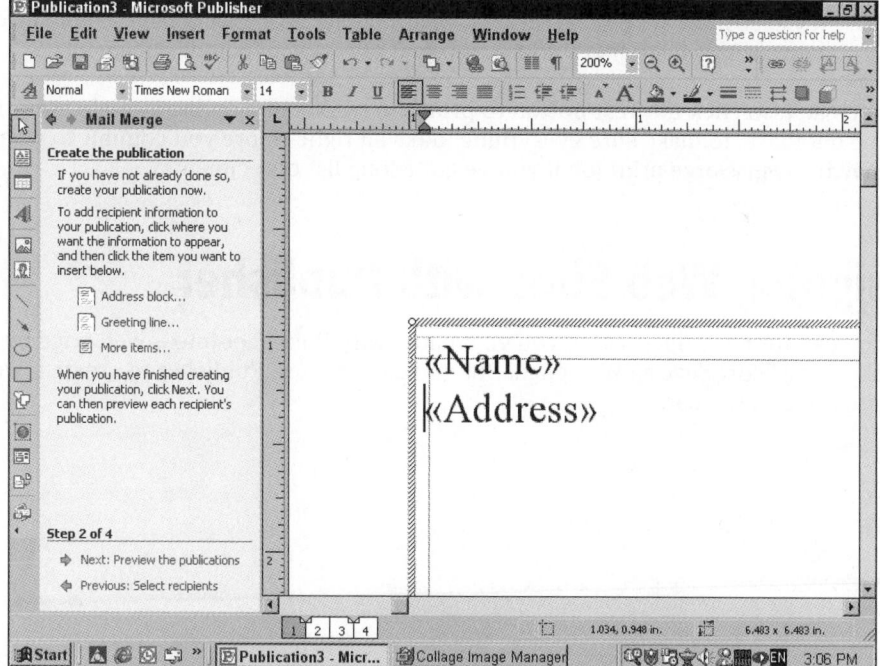

Figure 42-15: Mail merging fields look like this once inserted into your publication. They'll be replaced by data from the list once you run the mail merge.

You can click "Find a recipient" to find a particular data entry, you can edit the Recipient list further, or you can choose to exclude whichever recipient you're currently viewing.

When you're happy with the way things look (and you can always return to the previous "Create the publication" step of the wizard to make changes to the publication itself), click "Complete the merge" to move on to the wizard's final step.

Merging

Publisher replaces the field codes with data from the database file and offers you the opportunity to print. Clicking the Print link opens the Print Merge dialog box, which varies slightly from the regular Print dialog box discussed later in this chapter; it asks you which entries you want to print, if you want to skip over rows on a sheet of labels, and if you want to print lines that contain empty fields.

Tip   It's almost always a good idea to avoid printing lines that contain empty fields, because otherwise they'll create awkward gaps in your printed document.

You can also click the Test button to print the results of merging a single entry from the database, to make sure everything looks all right before you commit to what may be a very large print job if you've got a long list of recipients.

Designing Web Sites with Publisher

You can turn any publication you've created with Publisher into a Web page by choosing File ➪ Save as Web page. But you can also use Publisher to create a Web site right off the bat.

The Publication Gallery includes a number of designs for Web sites, using the same design schemes as are used for other Publication Gallery publication types (see Figure 42-16). Alternatively, you can create some other type of publication using one of the Publication Gallery designs (say, a brochure) and convert it into a Web site by clicking Convert to Web Layout on the options task pane that opens whenever you create a new publication from one of the Publication Gallery designs (see Figure 42-17).

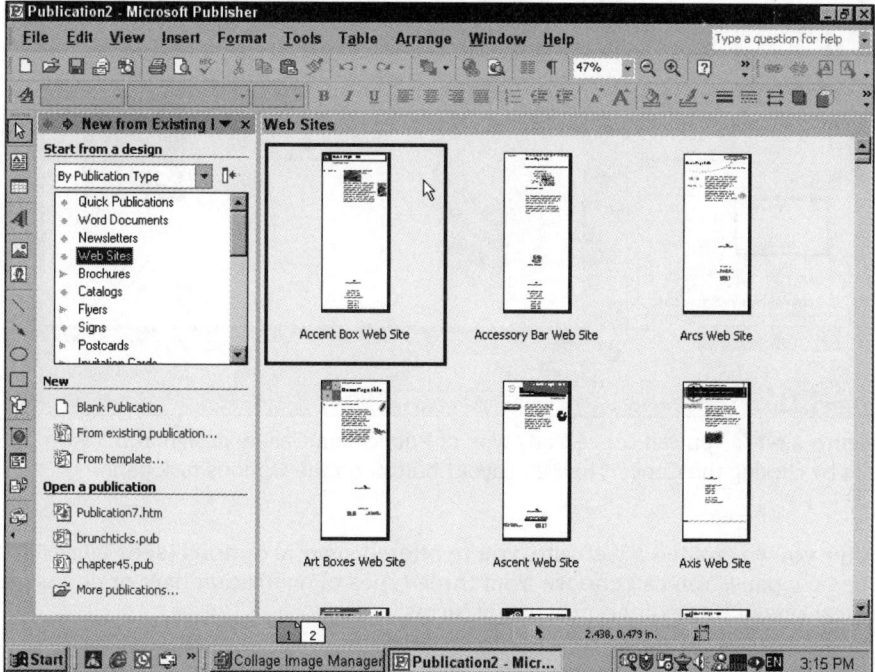

Figure 42-16: The Publication Gallery includes these designs for Web sites.

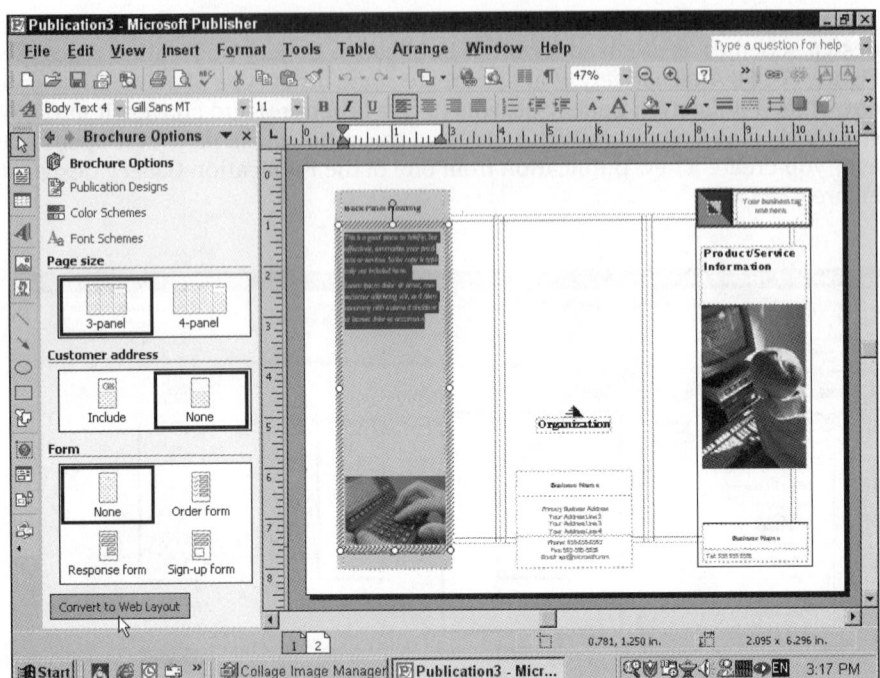

Figure 42-17: You can convert any type of Publication Gallery design into a Web site by clicking the Convert to Web Layout button on the Options task pane.

After you've created a Web site, you're offered several options (see Figure 42-18) in the task pane. You can choose from three types of navigation bars or choose to insert one of three different types of forms.

You can add to your Web site with additional pages. Click "Insert page" at the bottom of the task pane. Choose the type of page you want (from the drop-down list provided), and then click More Options to refine the page further.

If you click "Background fill and sound," you open another task pane where you can modify your page with a variety of backgrounds and fill effects — all the hundreds of options Publisher puts at your disposal to fill any object, in fact — or choose a sound file that plays whenever someone visits your site.

Tip   Clicking "Background sound" on the Background task pane opens the Web Options dialog box, which gives you many more tools for perfecting your Web site. In addition to specifying sound, you can title the page, add keywords for Web search engines to look for, add a description, specify the types of browsers that you expect to use your site, specify how to organize files within the site, choose the kind of monitor you want pictures to look best on, and more.

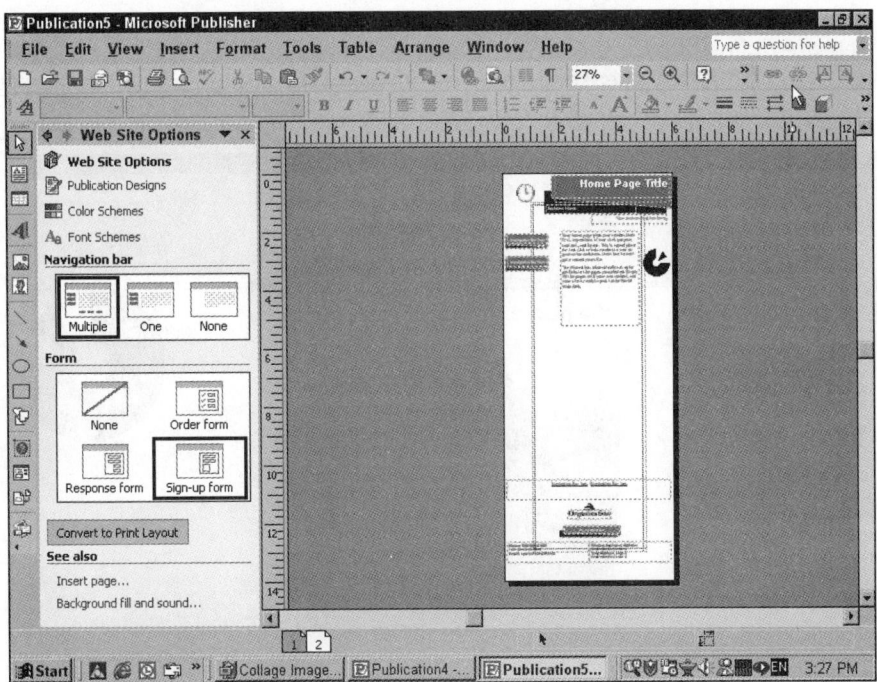

Figure 42-18: The Web Site Options task pane lets you add various elements to your Web site automatically.

Creating a hotspot

A *hotspot* is a specific area within a Web page that a viewer can click to activate a hyperlink. Hot spots are generally used in conjunction with graphics. To create a hotspot, click the Hot Spot button on the toolbar.

As soon as you do, the Insert Hyperlink dialog box pops up. It gives you four choices:

✦ **Existing File or Web page:** Enter the URL for an existing Web page in the Address blank or browse for a file or Web site you want the hotspot to link to.

✦ **Place in this Document:** You can choose from First Page, Last Page, Next Page, Previous Page, or a specific page.

✦ **Create New Document:** Provide the name and path for a new document for the hotspot to link to, and Publisher creates it for you. You can edit it now or later.

✦ **E-mail address:** Type in the address you want the hotspot to link to. You can provide a subject to be automatically appended to any e-mail sent using the link.

As soon as you close the Insert Hyperlink dialog box, you'll see a frame on your Web site. Adjust it to fit the area you want to make a hotspot. For example, in Figure 42-19 I'm turning the speaker area on the image of the antique radio into a hotspot.

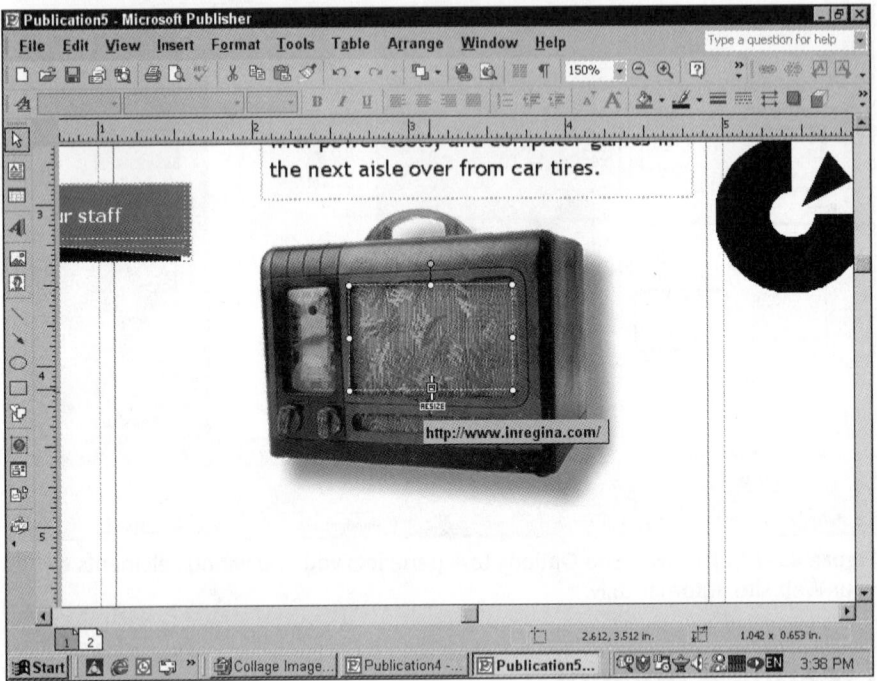

Figure 42-19: Creating a hotspot is as easy as creating any other frame in Publisher. Pointing at one of the frame's handles shows the hotspot's corresponding URL.

Inserting hyperlinks

To insert an ordinary hyperlink, simply click the object you want the hyperlink to be attached to — or highlight the specific text. Then press Ctrl+K or choose Insert ➪ Hyperlink. The Insert Hyperlink dialog box opens; make your choice, enter the necessary information, and click OK.

Tip   To remove a hyperlink, select it and press Ctrl+K or choose Insert ➪ Hyperlink — just as you did to insert it; then click the Remove Link button in the Edit Hyperlink dialog box.

Adding a form control

Form controls are objects that enable the viewer of your Web page to make choices and/or enter data that you can later retrieve (you'll have to talk to your Internet service provider or network manager about how, exactly).

To add a form control, click the Form Control tool in the Object toolbar, choose the type of form control you want to add, and draw a frame as you would for any other object. Publisher can create five form controls (illustrated in Figure 42-20): a single-line text box, a multiline text box, a checkbox, an option button, and a list box.

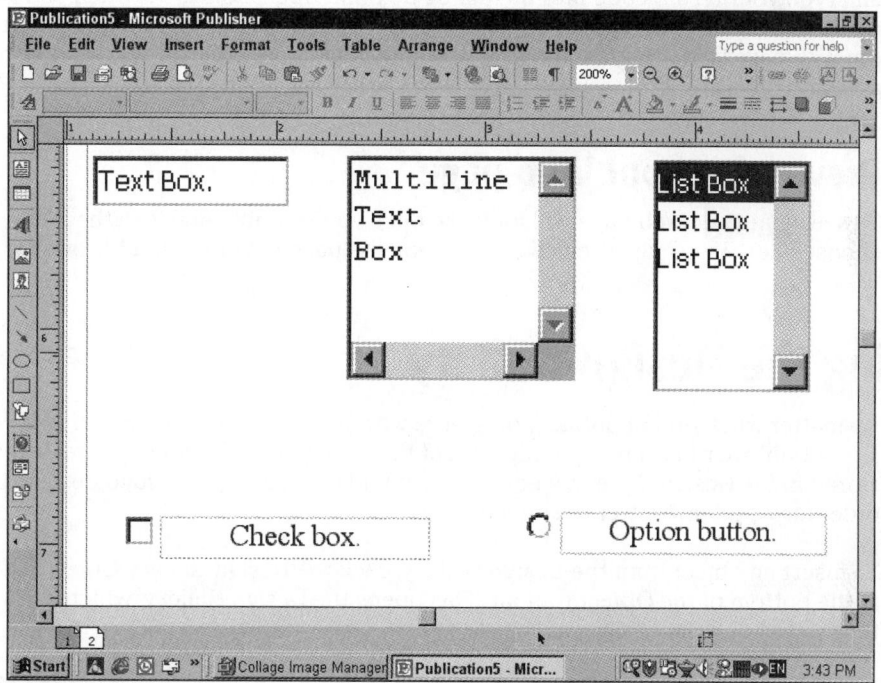

Figure 42-20: Publisher can create these five form controls for your Web page.

Each can be edited by double-clicking it. You can set a variety of options, including how the data contained in the form is labeled when it's submitted to you and the default text that appears.

The Form Control tool can also create a command button that you can define as either a Submit button (which submits the data entered in the form controls) or a Reset button (which erases everything and has the submitter start over.) When you create a command button, you're given options as to how data contained in forms is to be submitted to you: as a file on your Web server you can retrieve, as an e-mail message, or via a program that's provided by your Internet service provider.

Note   You may need to talk to your ISP or network manager to determine what settings to use with form controls.

Inserting an HTML code fragment

Sometimes you want to insert a specific piece of HTML code into your Web page. Publisher lets you do that without having to open your Web page in a text editor. Simply click the HTML Code Fragment button on the Object toolbar, draw a frame, and type your HTML code into the dialog box that opens. Click OK when you're done. The HTML code appears just as typed within the frame in Publisher; when the Web page is viewed in a browser, the specified hyperlinks, images, and so forth appear.

Previewing your Web page

To see what your Web page will look like once you've published it to the Web, choose File ➪ Web Page Preview. This opens the page in your default browser.

Using the Design Gallery

No matter what kind of publication you're working on — from a postcard to a Web site — Publisher has already done a lot of the design work for you. The results are stored in the Design Gallery, where you can find everything from logo designs to order forms to newsletter mastheads.

To insert an object from the Design Gallery, click the Design Gallery Object button at the bottom of the Object toolbar. This opens the Design Gallery, which shows three tabs:

✦ **The Objects by Category tab:** Lists all the categories of objects in the Gallery (see Figure 42-21); click the category and then choose the object you want from those displayed.

✦ **The Objects by Design tab:** Shows the same objects but organizes them differently — by related designs, rather than by category.

✦ **The Your Objects tab:** Shows objects you've created and added to the Design Gallery. To add an object, select it, then choose Insert ➪ Add Selection to Design Gallery. You'll be asked to give the object a name and assign it to a category. When you've done that, the object remains in the Design Gallery until you remove it, and you can add it to any future publications by choosing the Design Gallery Object button and clicking the Your Objects tab.

Grouping by Design

Sometimes you'll create designs that are made up of many different objects — several text boxes mixed with graphics, for example. You can make it easier to move that design or resize it by grouping all its constituent objects together.

To do that, select them, either by drawing a box around them with your mouse pointer or clicking each in turn while holding down Shift. A border appears around the outside of all the selected items, with a button at the bottom with two blue squares in it. Click that button and all the objects in the group are locked together.

Now, whenever you click one of them, the whole group is selected; you can move or resize it as you wish. (Note, however, that if you resize a group, the text in it doesn't resize like the graphics do; you'll have adjust font sizes manually to make them fit the resized group.) A border can be added only to the active object in the group selection.

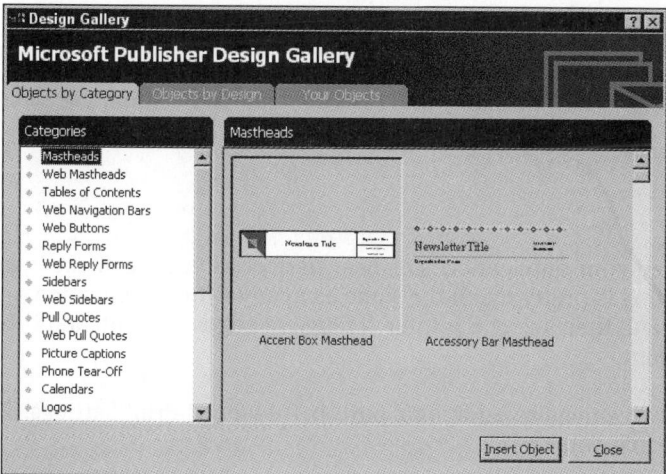

Figure 42-21: The Design Gallery contains dozens of ready-made objects you can use in your own publications.

Saving and Printing

To save a Publisher publication, choose File ➪ Save and assign the publication a name. By default, Publisher saves publications in its own file format, but you can also save them in a variety of other file formats, including word processor formats, graphics formats, PostScript, or as a Publisher template — in which case, it's accessible through the Publication Gallery and you can use it as the basis for future publications.

Caution In any format except Publisher's own, you run the risk of losing formatting, so unless you have a really good reason to do otherwise, it's probably best to leave your publications in the default format.

Using the Design Checker

Before you print your publication (or, in the case of a Web page, save it to your Web server), it's a good idea to run Publisher's Design Checker.

Choose Tools ➪ Design Checker and then choose whether to have Design Checker examine a particular selection of pages or all pages. You can also click Options to choose which problems Design Checker looks for.

Options include text in overflow areas, disproportional pictures, empty frames, covered objects, objects partially off the page, objects in nonprinting regions, blank space at the top of the page, spacing between sentences, and (for Web sites) a page unreachable by hyperlinks.

The Design Checker is particularly useful if you're new to Publisher, because it can spot errors you might not even be aware can be a problem. When you're more comfortable with Publisher, you'll probably find (as I do) that you seldom use Design Checker.

Printing

When you're satisfied your publication is as near perfect as you can make it, you're ready to print. Printing is pretty much the same as in any Office application — choose File ➪ Print and then select a printer, a range of pages to print, and the number of copies you want.

The Print dialog box contains an additional button, Advanced Print Settings. These options include the following:

✦ What resolution to print linked graphics at.

✦ Whether to allow the printer to substitute its own fonts for those used in the publication.

✦ Whether to allow bleeds (images that extend to the edge of the paper). Since most printers won't print right to the edge, you have to make your page size slightly smaller than your paper size and then trim the paper to achieve this effect.

✦ Whether to improve screen and print color matching. (As a rule, color printers can't exactly match screen colors; checking the box for color matching may help.)

Preparing for Outside Printing

Sometimes you want to be able to send your publication to a print shop for printing on a professional press rather than on your own printer. Publisher can help you prepare your files for that purpose.

Choose File ➪ Pack and Go ➪ Take to a Commercial Printing Service. (The other option here, Take to Another Computer, can split your file over multiple disks, embed necessary fonts, and include linked graphics, making it easy for you or someone else to work on your publication on another computer.) This opens a wizard that takes you step by step through the process of preparing your files for outside printing, including embedding TrueType fonts, including linked graphics, creating links for embedded graphics, compressing your publication, and adding an unpacking utility for uncompressing it when it gets to its destination.

✦   ✦   ✦

Creating and Managing a Wonderful Web Site with FrontPage

FrontPage is one of the leading programs used for creating and managing Web sites. This part takes a quick look at how to use FrontPage to design and manage Web sites; then it examines how Office's other applications can be used to create documents for Web sites — anything from ordinary static Web pages to interactive pages tied to Access databases and Excel spreadsheets.

Designing Web Pages with FrontPage

Office XP Developer includes FrontPage, the leading software tool for Windows-based Web page development and Web site management. Even with the advanced page-authoring features in Office proper, you're likely to find FrontPage a boon for some editing and formatting tasks. But FrontPage's main appeals to the Office aficionado lie in its abilities to organize a set of pages into a complete, coherent Web site, and to publish the entire site to a server.

Note Many of FrontPage's neatest features are only available on servers running the FrontPage Server Extensions. The Extensions are available as software plug-ins for operating systems other than Windows, so you may be able to access them even if your organization or ISP uses a UNIX server. Just be sure to check on this before you go hog-wild with FrontPage's special capabilities.

Using FrontPage with the Rest of Office

Functionally and cosmetically, FrontPage and Office go together like fingers of the same hand.

The availability of common themes for Web page design in the various applications demonstrates this tight coupling. Because Word, PowerPoint, and FrontPage share the same themes, you can create a given page in whichever program is most appropriate, yet maintain stylistic harmony throughout your site with no special effort.

Because you can store Office documents in HTML format, and because you can directly save and open Office documents in FrontPage webs (see the Note below for an explanation of FrontPage terminology), you face no import-export hassles. When stored in HTML in a FrontPage web, Office documents are pages of the web, automatically. Office documents serving as pages within a FrontPage web don't lose their identity, however. When you're working in FrontPage and you click a page created by another Office application, the page opens in that application for editing.

Note   At the outset, you should understand a bit of jargon: The term *web* (lowercased) is the FrontPage equivalent of a document in other Office applications — analogous to an Excel workbook or a PowerPoint presentation. Speaking practically, an individual web (that is, a FrontPage document) corresponds roughly to what most people would call a (World Wide) Web *site*. In other words, it's a collection of World-Wide-Web pages hyperlinked together to make a coherent whole, along with the graphics and multimedia content those pages contain, and any downloadable files they make accessible. Even so, a FrontPage web isn't really a Web site until you *publish* it — that is, transfer all this content to a server with access to the World Wide Web or an intranet.

From another standpoint, a web works similarly to a document in other Office applications. You use commands on the File menu to create new webs and open existing ones, just as you would work with documents in other Office applications. The (FrontPage) web is, in effect, a record of the various files and folders you have added to the (World Wide) Web site you're developing. The FrontPage web doesn't directly contain the site's content (which resides in the HTML pages and associated files that make up the site itself).

Cross-Reference   A finished Web site can contain content from more than one FrontPage web (see Chapter 44).

This web-as-document idea has a couple of holes in it, true. For one thing, FrontPage webs aren't stored in individual disk files; each web is a series of folders that contain interrelated files. For another, when you use FrontPage as a Web page editor, the page is a document in its own right. Still, if you think of a FrontPage web as a discrete unit of information that behaves much like a document, you have a useful sense of what's going on behind the scenes when you work with FrontPage.

Navigating Through FrontPage Views

When you launch FrontPage, a Views list appears on the left side of the screen, a big open space takes up the middle, and the New Page or Web task pane appears on your right. Figure 43-1 shows a typical example of what shows up on-screen.

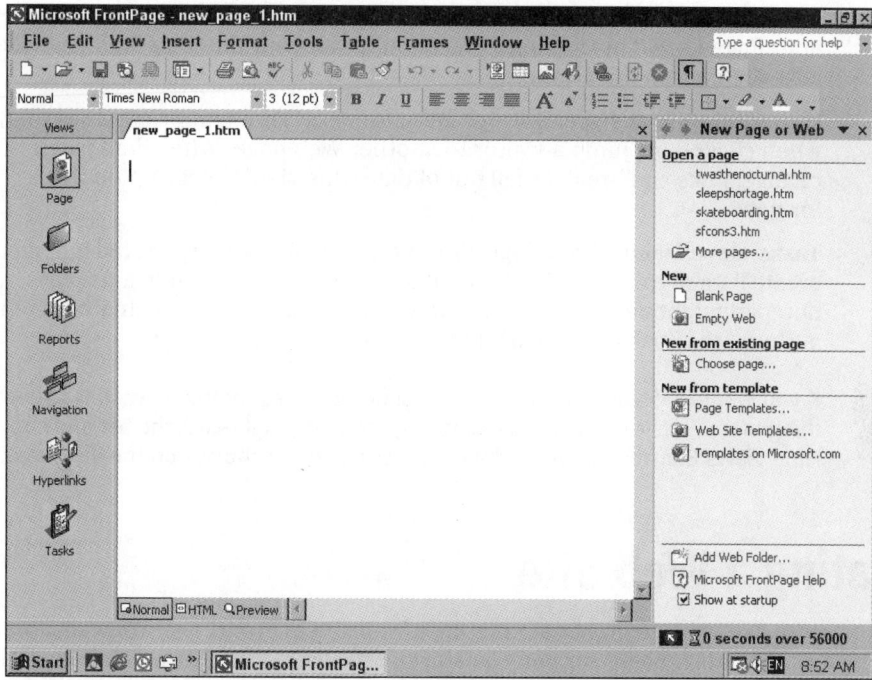

Figure 43-1: When you launch FrontPage, this is what you see.

The Views list is where you select from many different ways to look at the files you create in FrontPage. The area to the right of it is your workspace. Even before you start creating Web pages and organizing them into a Web site, you can introduce yourself to the different views in FrontPage:

✦ **Page view:** Most of us spend the vast majority of our FrontPage work time in Page view. This is where you edit individual Web pages. The workspace doesn't look that different from Word; if you've worked with Word, you'll soon feel right at home here. Figure 43-1 shows FrontPage's Page view—the New Page or Web task pane, of course, is normally closed when you're working in this view.

Tip

You can set FrontPage so the New Page or Web task pane doesn't open every time you start the program—just uncheck the Show at startup box at the bottom of the task pane.

✦ **Folders view:** Think of Folders view as a directory of the files you create in FrontPage. After you start saving Web pages, you'll see them listed here.

✦ **Reports view:** FrontPage can generate reports that provide interesting information on the state and status of your Web site. Here's where you'll find them.

✦ **Navigation view:** Navigation view is going to be your second-most-used view, after Page view. This is where you organize all your different Web page files into an integrated Web site.

✦ **Hyperlinks view:** *Hyperlinks* (or *links,* for short) are text or graphics that, when clicked on, jump a visitor to another Web page. When Web pages change, links can break or fall out of date; this view checks up on them for you.

✦ **Tasks view:** Finally, FrontPage allows the organizationally fixated among us to create lists of things to do. If you're designing a site yourself, a pocket notepad might be all you need. But if you're collaborating with other Web authors, the Tasks view helps keep you all on the same page.

Tip   If you want to devote the screen real estate occupied by the Views bar to something more practical (such as viewing page content), right-click the bar and choose Hide Views Bar. You can then change views using the choices on the View menu.

Creating a Web Site

There are two ways to go about creating a Web site in FrontPage: You can start by creating individual pages, or you can start by designing the site as a whole. Either way works; sometimes one approach works better than the other, depending on the situation. If you are creating a single Web page, for example, you need not worry about how it will connect with other pages at your Web site. If you are designing a multipage Web site, often it works best to design the whole site first, and then provide page content.

To use an architectural analogy, if you were designing an office building, you would almost always want to start by laying out the design of the building, and then worry about furnishing the individual suites and individual offices. When you design Web sites with FrontPage, you also develop site-design skills.

Creating a new FrontPage web

You have two basic options in creating a FrontPage web. You can create your web on a Web server that is accessible to the Internet or an intranet. Or, you can create your web on a local computer drive (your hard drive). Webs saved to your hard drive cannot have all the advanced features available in FrontPage, like the ability to collect data from input forms. And, of course, they can't be visited by anyone else. But you can use your local drive to design a web, and then publish it to a Web server when one becomes available.

Starting from a template

You can start a web or create a single page from scratch by choosing either Empty Web or Blank Page from the New area of the New Page or Web task pane, either when you first start FrontPage, or at any time. Simply choose File ⇨ New ⇨ Page or Web. As in other Office applications, however, you can also choose to create a page or web from a template.

If you're starting a web and not just creating a single page, choose Web Site Templates from the *New from template* area of the New Page or Web task pane. This opens the dialog box in Figure 43-2, where a number of wizards are offered to help you create various kinds of webs. These types include One Page Web, Corporate Presence Web, Personal Web, Project Web, Database Interface, Customer Support Web, and SharePoint Team Web Site. (This last type can only be created on a computer that's set up to run SharePoint — see Chapter 6 for more information on SharePoint). There's also an Import Web Wizard, which allows you to import an existing Web site into FrontPage as a new web.

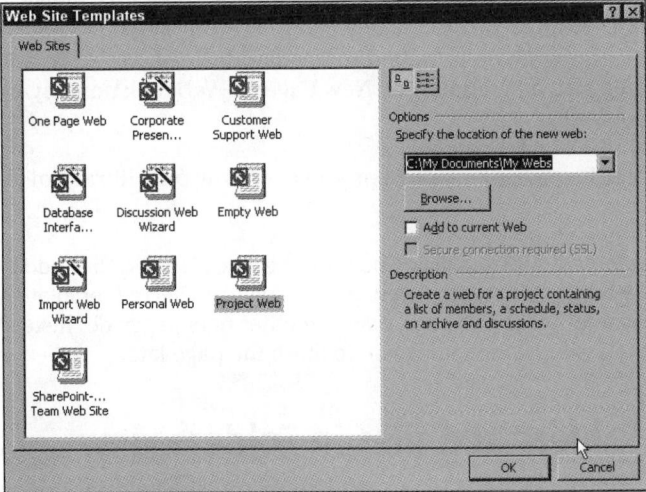

Figure 43-2: Starting a new FrontPage web from a template provides you with these choices.

You're asked to specify the location of the new web — it can be on your computer or on another server — and if you've already got a web open, you can add the pages from the template you've chosen to the current web instead of starting a new one.

Although the Web Site Templates dialog box doesn't make this clear, a FrontPage web's name is the same as the folder name or the URL you supply as the location of the new web. Be sure to choose a name that you want people to use for accessing your Web. If you're planning to publish your little web on the big World Wide Web, observe the naming limitations in force there: Use only letters, numerals, and ordinary punctuation marks, and don't include spaces in the name.

Some of the web templates are quite complex, requiring a pretty high level of expertise with FrontPage to customize. These templates — Corporate Presence Web, Customer Support Web, Database Interface Wizard, Discussion Web wizard, and Project Web — also require that you already have a Web site in place that's equipped with FrontPage Server Extensions. The Empty Web, One-page Web, and Personal Web, however, all work well without FrontPage Server Extensions on a Web server.

Starting from scratch

When you choose Empty Web to create a new Web, FrontPage sets up the Web folders and support files and leaves you with the job of creating the Web's pages. With any of the other templates and wizards, a new Web contains at least one page to get you started. Either way, though, you're bound to need additional pages. To add a brand-new page to a Web you again open the New Page or Web task pane by choosing File ➪ New ➪ Page or Web.

You can choose to either insert a blank page or you can draw on a library of page templates and wizards.

One option on the Page Templates dialog box is a checkbox labeled "Just add Web task." If you choose that, you'll create a new page using the selected template, but the page won't open for editing in page view like other new pages do; instead, a task is added to the Tasks list reminding you to finish the page later.

Working with folders and files in Folders view

FrontPage's Folders view (see Figure 43-3) works like Windows Explorer, so you shouldn't have any trouble using it to navigate the constituent files and folders of your Web. A few points bear comment, however.

You can select any arbitrary set of files in the Folders view Contents pane (the big section on the right) to carry out cut, copy, and delete operations; to find and replace text in the selected files; and to apply themes or specify shared borders. Press Shift+click to select a series of consecutive files, or Ctrl+click to select or deselect any file individually.

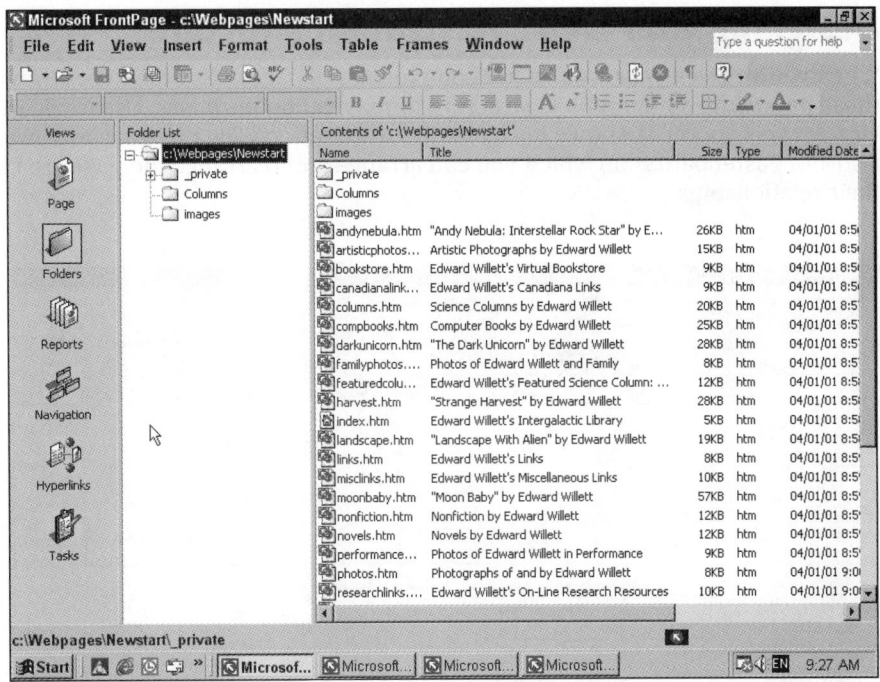

Figure 43-3: FrontPage's Folders view helps you navigate the files and folders of your Web.

As in Explorer, double-clicking a file opens it. By default, Web pages created in another Office application open in that application; those created in FrontPage or stored in generic HTML open in FrontPage's page view. Image files open in the application with which they're associated in Windows. You can change these defaults in the Configure Editors tab of the Tools ⇨ Options dialog box. All the editors you thus configure are available when you right-click a file and choose Open With.

Note that Folders view's icons for pages are informative. You can see at a glance which Office application created the page, because a mini-icon for the application is overlaid on each page's icon. Generic HTML pages, whether saved by IE, a text editor, or some other Web page editor, have icons without any identifying mini-icon. Also, when a page is open in the FrontPage editor, a little pencil gets added to its icon in Folders view.

Finally, be aware that the Folder List navigation bar, a fixture of Folders view, is optionally available in the Page, Navigation, and Hyperlinks views as well. It works a bit differently here, listing files as well as folders but enabling you to select only one file at a time. Use the View ⇨ Folder List command or the corresponding toolbar button to turn it on or off in these views.

Designing your web's navigation structure

When you've given your web its full complement of pages, it's time to organize those pages into a hierarchical structure for navigation purposes. Use Navigation view for this chore. As shown in Figure 43-4, Navigation view presents your Web on a sort of pasteboard from which you can arrange and rearrange the pages to clarify their relationships.

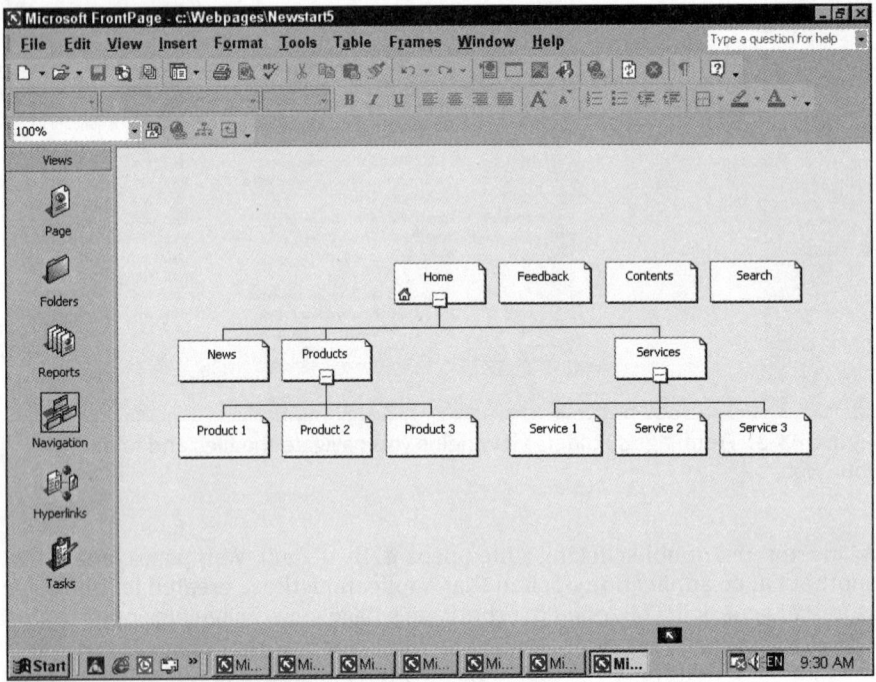

Figure 43-4: Navigation view helps you organize your Web.

You're supposed to use Navigation view in concert with navigation bars you insert in your pages. A navigation bar is a FrontPage component that automatically adds the appropriate navigation buttons to the page, based on the location of the page in the navigation structure. But even if you eschew navigation bars, Navigation view can help you turn a hazy mental picture of your site's organization into a definite road map.

Note   Placing a page in the navigation structure does *not* automatically add links to any other pages in the structure. FrontPage creates links for you only if you add navigation bars to the page.

Working with pages in the navigation structure

A Web's home page is the only one automatically included in its navigation structure. To add an additional page, open the Folder List by clicking Toggle Pane button on the Standard toolbar, then drag the pages from the Folder List to the location in the structure where you want them to reside. To position the page where you want it, watch the location of a fuzzy line that connects the icon of the page you're adding to an existing icon on the structure (see Figure 43-5). Let the fuzzy line guide you as follows:

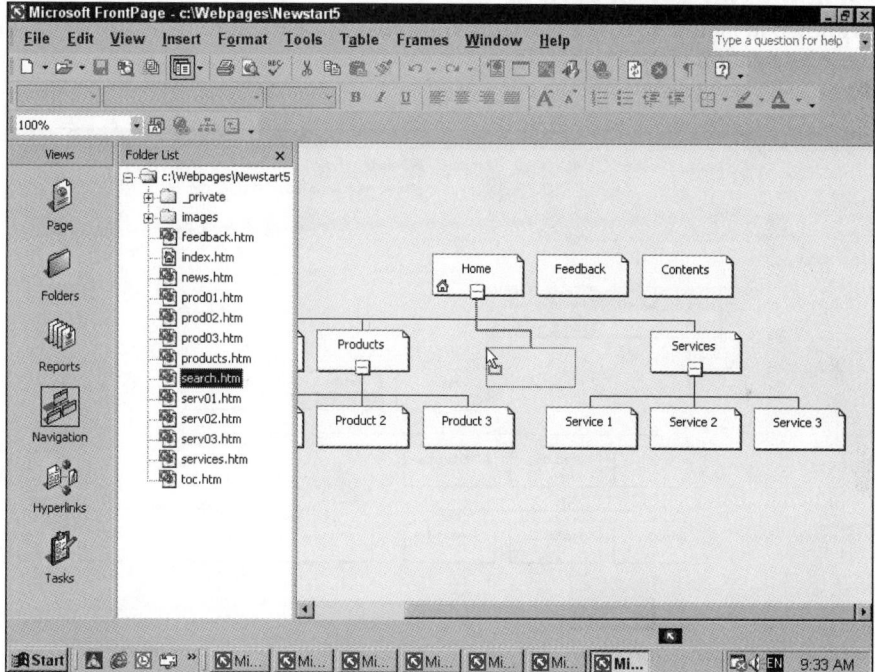

Figure 43-5: While you drag a page icon in the navigation structure, a fuzzy line shows you where the page will drop in.

✦ If you don't see the fuzzy line, the page can't be added to the structure at the current location. Drag on until the line appears.

✦ To add a page to the top level of the Web — the level of the home page — the fuzzy line should extend from the top of the home page icon (or the left side, if you're viewing the structure in the rotated portrait orientation).

✦ To add a page at a subsidiary level to an existing page, drag the icon for the new page until the fuzzy line connects it to the bottom of the existing page's icon. You can add as many subsidiary pages as you like to an existing page.

You can add a page to the structure only once.

To revise the navigation structure, just drag page icons around on the screen. The fuzzy line continues to serve as your guide to their placement. You can delete a page by clicking it to select it and pressing Del, or via its shortcut menu. In the resulting dialog box, you can tell FrontPage to delete the page from the navigation structure only, or to remove it from the web itself, erasing the page's file.

Caution If the page you're deleting has subsidiary pages in the navigation structure, deleting it removes all subsidiary pages as well.

Using the Navigation toolbar

As shown in Figure 43-6, the Navigation toolbar appears automatically when you enter Navigation view.

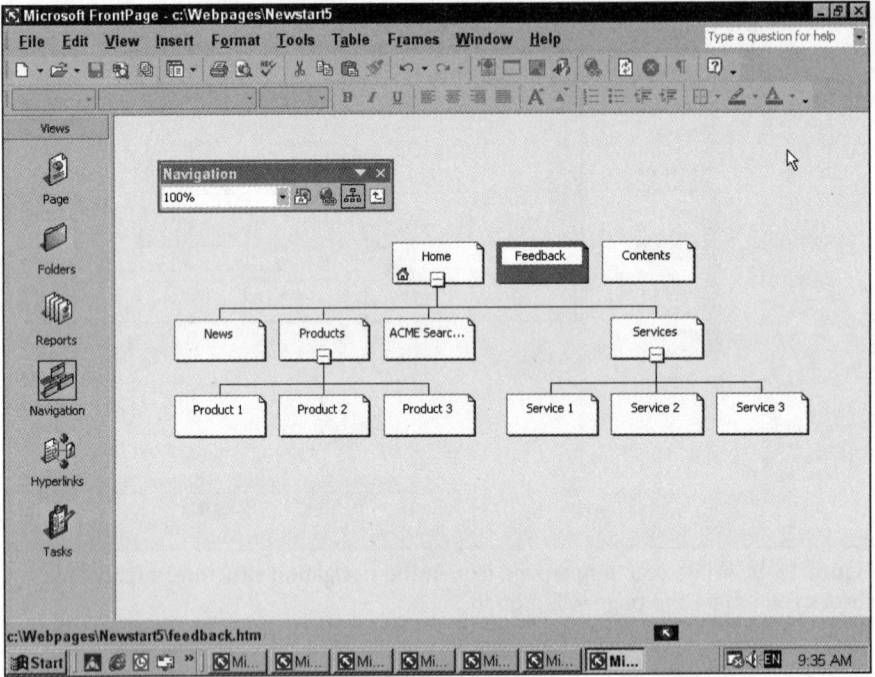

Figure 43-6: The Navigation toolbar lets you adjust the appearance of Navigation view.

From left to right, the controls on the Navigation toolbar include the following:

✦ **Zoom:** Lets you adjust the magnification by selecting one of several preset zoom factors. Size To Fit is my preferred setting. If you zoom out, a page's entire name may not fit in the icon. Hover the mouse pointer over the page icon for a second to display the name in a ScreenTip.

✦ **Portrait/Landscape:** Click here to toggle back and forth between the standard landscape (wide) view, in which the levels of the navigation structure are arranged from top down, and a portrait (tall) view, in which they're shown from left to right.

✦ **Add Existing Page:** To add to the navigation structure of a page or file located outside your Web, select the page to which you want to connect the external item and click the Add Existing Page button. In the Insert Hyperlink dialog box that then appears, navigate to a Web or intranet address or a disk file. When the existing page is part of your navigation structure, you can move it around just like any other page.

✦ **Included in Navigation Bars:** This button is selected when a page is included in navigation bars. To exclude a particular page from your navigation bars, click the page to select it and then click this button so it no longer looks selected.

✦ **View Subtree Only:** Use this button to focus in on a single branch of the navigation structure. Begin by clicking the page at the top of the branch, one that has subsidiary pages attached to it. When you then click the View Subtree Only button, you see only the chosen branch. Click the button again to see the entire navigation structure.

To hide the details of a given branch of the navigation structure, click the little white box containing a minus sign at the bottom or right side of the page at the top of the branch. All the subsidiary pages disappear. Clicking the box again (it now contains a plus sign) restores the hidden pages.

Adding and Formatting Text

Okay, so you've started your web, either using a template, or with a single blank page in Page View, or by laying out the structure in Navigation View. However you start the web, eventually you're going to want to add content to it, and probably the first content you're going to want to add is that workhorse of communication, text.

Adding text to a FrontPage Web page is not hard. The basic text editing and formatting tools you already know from Word are available here, too. Type, cut, paste, or click the Spelling button to check your spelling. Click the Bold button on the Formatting toolbar to assign boldface to selected text, and so on.

One thing you might not have expected is how easy it is to take text, graphics, and even tables from other Office applications and add them to your web. This section shows how to do that.

Getting text without typing

You can copy text from Word (or Excel, Access, and PowerPoint for that matter) right into FrontPage's Page view. Simply select the text in another Office application and click the Copy button in that application's toolbar to save the text to the Clipboard. Then, open or switch to FrontPage's Page view and paste the text at the cursor insertion point.

Much, but not necessarily all, of your formatting will be saved when you paste text. You may be using formatting in your other application that's not available in HTML pages. But FrontPage will do its best to keep your font type, size, color, and attributes when you paste in text from other applications.

Editing text

The editing tools at your disposal in Page view include the following:

✦ Edit ➪ Find and Edit ➪ Replace lets you find and/or replace text in Page view. Can you Find and Replace globally, for an entire Web site? Yes, you can — just select the All Pages radio button in the Replace dialog box.

✦ The Spelling tool in the Standard toolbar allows you to check spelling for the open page in Page view. Want to spell-check your entire document? This too can be done. Click the Spelling tool while in any view except Page view, and you get the option of selecting the Entire Web radio button. The Add a Task for Each Page with Misspellings checkbox creates a link in Tasks view to each page that needs fixing.

Formatting text

All the formatting tools in FrontPage's Page view work much the same as in other Office applications. The main difference is that when you create Web pages in FrontPage, the available options are different from those you get when you create documents to print in other applications. Following are some general guidelines:

✦ **Font sizes:** When you select font sizes from the Font Size drop-down list, you'll notice a rather limited selection. This is because Web browsers don't interpret many font sizes.

✦ **Font colors:** On the plus side, you can assign font colors with the Font Color button and every browser will interpret those colors, so long as you stick with the basic colors available on the font color palette. First select the text; then click the down arrow next to the Font Color button and choose a font color from the palette that appears.

Formatting paragraphs

The following list details the general capabilities and restrictions you encounter when formatting paragraphs with FrontPage:

✦ **Indenting:** FrontPage lets you indent selected paragraphs using the Increase Indent tool.

✦ **Alignment:** You can left-align, center, and right-align paragraphs using the toolbar buttons — but you can't justify text from margin to margin.

✦ **Numbered and bulleted lists:** Automatic numbering or bullets are assigned by selecting text and clicking either the Numbering or Bullets button. If you are adding to a numbered or bulleted list, each time you press Enter, you create a new bulleted or numbered item. Remove bullet or numbering formatting from a selected paragraph by clicking the respective button again on the Formatting toolbar.

✦ **Spacing:** There is no reliable way to control spacing between paragraphs. By default, most paragraphs have a line of spacing between them. You can create line breaks without vertical spacing by holding down the Shift key and pressing Enter to create a forced line break.

The Paragraph dialog box, shown in Figure 43-7, allows you some control over line and paragraph spacing. Although not all browsers will recognize the additional formatting features available in the Paragraph dialog box, you can apply them, and visitors using Internet Explore 4 and higher will see them. To access the Paragraph dialog box, right-click selected paragraphs, and choose Paragraph from the shortcut menu. The Preview area of the dialog box demonstrates the effect of the formatting you apply, assuming that your page is viewed by a visitor with a browser version current enough to recognize these formatting features.

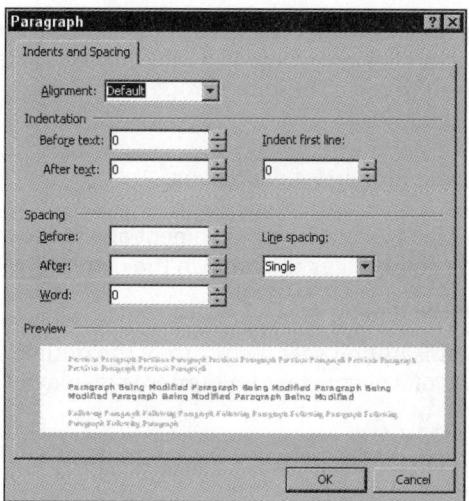

Figure 43-7: Options available in the Paragraph dialog box may or may not be viewable by your visitors' browsers.

Using Tables As Layout Tools

Tables serve two purposes in Web page layout. You can create Excel or Word-type tables to display information in rows and columns. Or, you can use tables to lay out text and graphics in newspaper style columns.

In either case, the easiest way to create a table is to click the Insert Table tool on the Standard toolbar and click and drag in the Table grid to define the number of rows and columns in your table — just like creating a Table with the Insert Table tool in other Office applications.

When you have finished creating a table, you can use it in a number of ways:

✦ **Add text:** You can add text to a table by clicking in a cell and typing.

✦ **Insert objects:** You can also insert any other object (such as a picture) into a table cell. You can apply the same editing and formatting techniques to table text as you do to text outside a table.

✦ **Select rows or columns:** You can select a row or column of a table by clicking in a cell, and then choosing Table ➪ Select ➪ Column or Table ➪ Select ➪ Row.

✦ **Delete cells, rows, or columns:** You can delete selected cells (or rows or columns) by choosing Delete Cells from the Table menu.

Defining table properties

Formatting assigned to an entire table applies to all cells in the table, and governs the overall appearance of the table. Right-click anywhere in a table, and choose Table Properties from the shortcut menu to open the Table Properties dialog box, shown in Figure 43-8.

The following options appear in the Table Properties dialog box:

✦ **Alignment:** Defines where the table is located. Left alignment aligns the table to the left; right to the right; and center aligns the table in the center.

✦ **Float:** Lets you wrap text next to the table.

✦ **Size:** Affecting the Borders area, this option sets the width of the outline placed around the table. A setting of 0 means that no border is displayed in a browser.

✦ **Cell padding:** Specifies the space, in pixels, between the contents of a cell and the border.

✦ **Cell spacing:** Defines the spacing between cells.

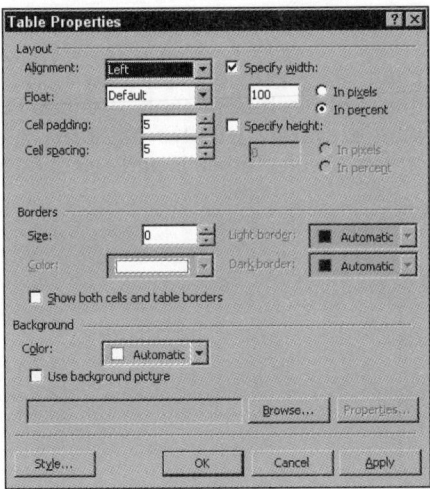

Figure 43-8: Define global table formatting in the Table Properties dialog box.

✦ **Specify width** and **Specify height:** These options set the overall height and width of a table. The height and width can be set in either pixels or as a percentage of the browser window. If the Specify Width checkbox is not checked, the table will adjust its width depending on its content. If the Specify Height checkbox is not checked, the table adopts whatever minimum height is required to display everything in your cells.

✦ **Color** and **Use background picture:** Affecting the Background area, these options define the background color (or image) for your entire table. They work much the same as assigning a background to an entire page. Click the Use Background Picture checkbox and use the Browse button to locate an image to tile as the background for the table, or choose a background color from the Color drop-down list.

✦ **The Borders area:** Lets you assign colors to the table's border. There are three settings: Color, Light Border, and Dark Border. The Color setting lets you set a single color for the entire border. The Light Border and Dark Border settings allow you to specify colors for the top-and-left and bottom-and-right edges of the border, respectively. This can help you give your table a 3-D look. Using either the Light or Dark Border setting overrides the Color setting for its respective area.

✦ **The Style button:** Opens the Modify Style dialog box. Use the Format button in the Modify Style dialog box to assign default font, paragraph, border, or numbering styles to your table.

Defining cell properties

The Cell Properties dialog box, shown in Figure 43-9, provides quick access to all the formatting options available to individual cells within the table. To open this dialog box, select the cells to which you want to apply attributes, and then select Table ➪ Properties ➪ Cell, or right-click within the selected cells and select Cell Properties from the shortcut menu.

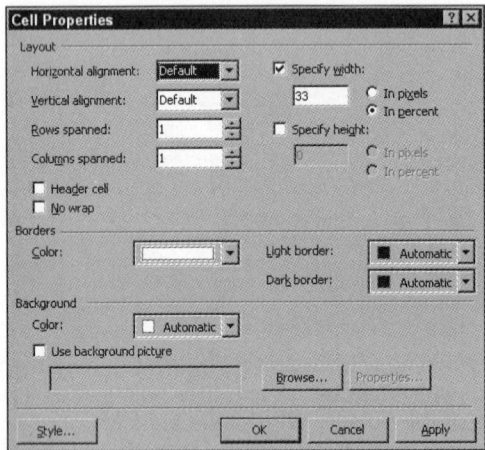

Figure 43-9: The Cell Properties dialog box

The Cell Properties dialog box offers the following capabilities:

✦ **Horizontal alignment** defines where the text or graphic is placed horizontally within the cell. The options are default, left, right, center, and justify.

✦ **Vertical alignment** determines where the text or graphic is placed vertically within the cell. The options are default, top, middle, baseline, and bottom. Baseline makes the bottom of all letters in the cell line up, no matter what the size. The default setting is middle, but you may find you usually want to select top alignment for cell text.

✦ **Header cell** formats the cell as a table header that appears in bold by default.

✦ **No wrap** forces text to remain on one line.

✦ **Specify width** and **Specify height** set the width and height for the cell. Note that the greatest width setting in a column applies to all cells in that column, and the greatest height setting in a row applies to all cells in that row. You can choose to specify width or height either in pixels or as a percentage of the overall width or height of the row or column.

✦ **Columns spanned** specifies the number of columns spanned by a cell.

✦ **Rows spanned** specifies the number of rows spanned by a cell.

✦ **Background** is an option for assigning colors or images to the background of selected cells.

✦ **Borders** is an option that affects the border area. The Color setting sets the colors for the border of an individual cell, rather than the table as a whole. Light border refers to the bottom and right edges of the cell, and Dark border refers to the top and left edges of the cell; this is the opposite of their positions for the table's outline. If the table border is set to 0 width, these settings have no effect.

Converting tables to text

You can easily convert a table into text. You won't lose any of the objects (text, graphics, and so on) in the table. Those objects become normal page objects, laid out in paragraphs. To convert a table to text, click anywhere in the table and select Table ⇨ Convert ⇨ Table to Text.

Using tables for columns

Because HTML does not support multicolumn layout for Web pages, the workaround used by most Web designers is a table. Although you don't get nice desktop-publishing features (like auto-flow between columns), you can still create two- or three-column layouts using one-row tables — provided you're willing to cut and paste your text manually and arrange it in two columns.

Adding Graphics

Perhaps you've heard a bit, or quite a bit, about Web-compatible graphics. Or perhaps you've heard nothing about Web graphics. In either case, you'll like the way FrontPage handles graphic images.

The easiest way to get graphics into your Web page is to either insert them as files, or copy them in through the Clipboard. After you copy or insert a graphic of any file format, FrontPage handles the process of saving that image as a Web-compatible GIF, PNG or JPEG (also know as JPG) file.

Inserting graphic files

As in other Office applications, you insert a picture by placing your insertion point where you want the picture to go and choosing Insert ⇨ Picture.

You have four options:

✦ **Clip Art:** This opens the Clip Organizer (discussed in detail in Chapter 9).

✦ **From File:** This opens a standard Office browsing box, which allows you to locate the graphic file you want to insert.

✦ **From Scanner or Camera:** If you have a scanner or camera connected to your computer, this allows you to scan in or download pictures from them, using whatever interface you normally use for those procedures.

✦ **New Photo Gallery:** This command is unique to FrontPage, and new to Office XP, so I've devoted the next little section to it.

Inserting a Photo Gallery

The Insert Photo Gallery command allows you to insert several photographs using one of four pre-set layouts. When you choose Insert ⇨ Picture ⇨ New Photo Gallery, the Photo Gallery Properties dialog box opens. There are two tabs, Pictures and Layout. Figure 43-10 shows the Layout tab; Figure 43-11 shows the Pictures tab.

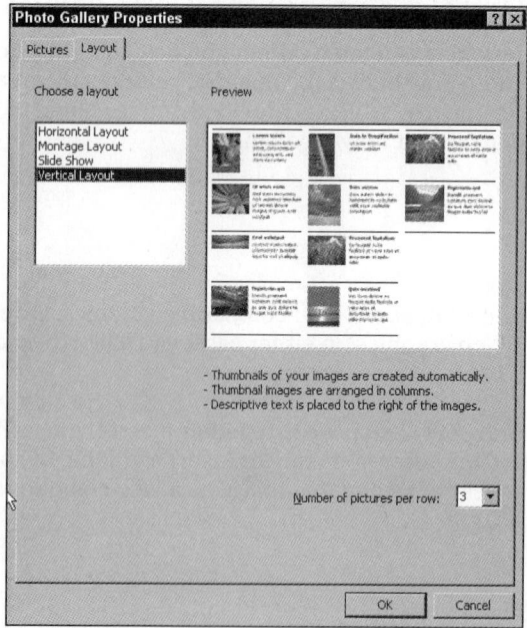

Figure 43-10: Choose a layout for your Photo Gallery from this dialog box

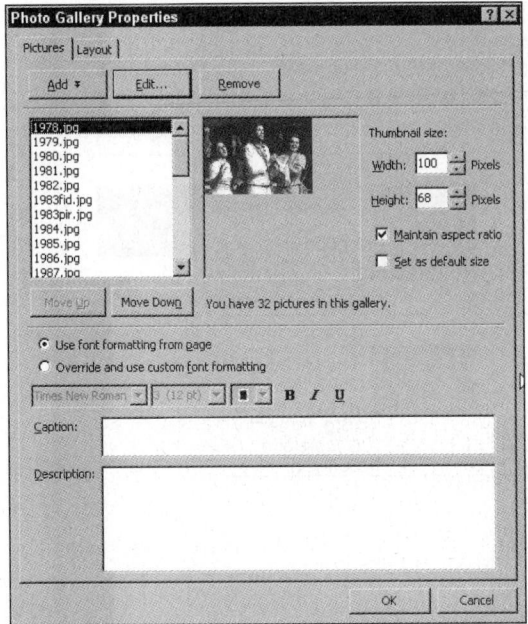

Figure 43-11: Insert pictures into your layout using this dialog box.

Choose the layout you want, based on the preview image and the description. The Horizontal and Vertical Layouts allow you to specify how many pictures you want per row.

To add pictures, click Add. (Makes sense, huh?) You can add pictures from files, or from a scanner or camera. The pictures you choose are listed in the box at upper left; you can reorganize them using the Move Up and Move Down buttons, and open another dialog box that lets you resize, rotate, and crop them by clicking Edit.

 Tip   If you've added a picture by accident to the gallery, remove it by highlighting it in the list and clicking Remove.

At the right, you can set the size of thumbnail the gallery will display. Then, at the bottom, you can type in and format a caption and a description.

When you're done, click OK. FrontPage creates the Photo Gallery in Page View (see Figure 43-12). If you Shift+Click any thumbnail, the full-size image appears.

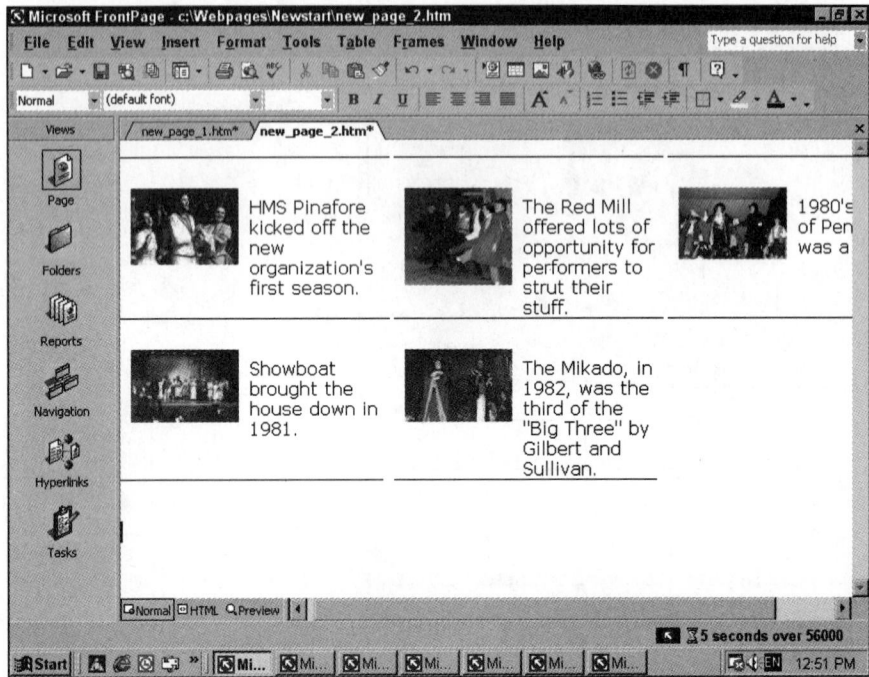

Figure 43-12: A FrontPage photo gallery looks something like this in Page View.

Note   When the Web is published and viewed through a browser, a regular click will display the full-size image; you use Shift+Click to follow any hyperlink in Page view in FrontPage because a regular click is used to select items for formatting, just as in other Office applications.

Copying a graphic

You can copy a graphic image by creating or opening it (or a file that contains it) in any application. Copy the graphic to the Clipboard, and then paste it into a Web page open in Page view.

Saving graphics

When you save your Web page, FrontPage will convert all the graphics on your page to Web-compatible formats, and prompt you to save these embedded files. The Save Embedded Files dialog box will appear, as shown in Figure 43-13. Here you can rename or relocate files; clicking Picture Options lets you set other options specific to the format in which the pictures are being saved (for example, image quality in a .JPG file, transparency in a .GIF file).

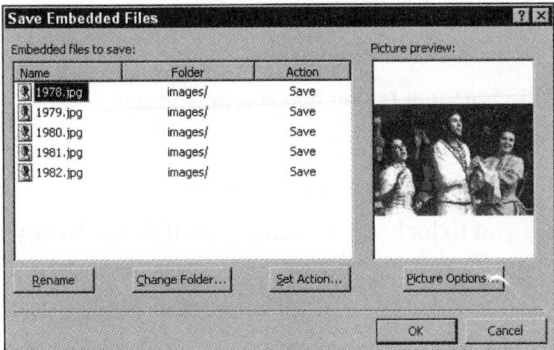

Figure 43-13: FrontPage prompts you to save all graphics on your page.

Editing pictures in FrontPage

When you select an image in Page view, the Picture toolbar appears. The tools on the Picture toolbar give you quite a bit of power to tweak the appearance of your graphic image right in FrontPage, and the ability to add hotspots — hyperlinks activated by clicking a particular part of the picture. Figure 43-14 shows the Picture toolbar.

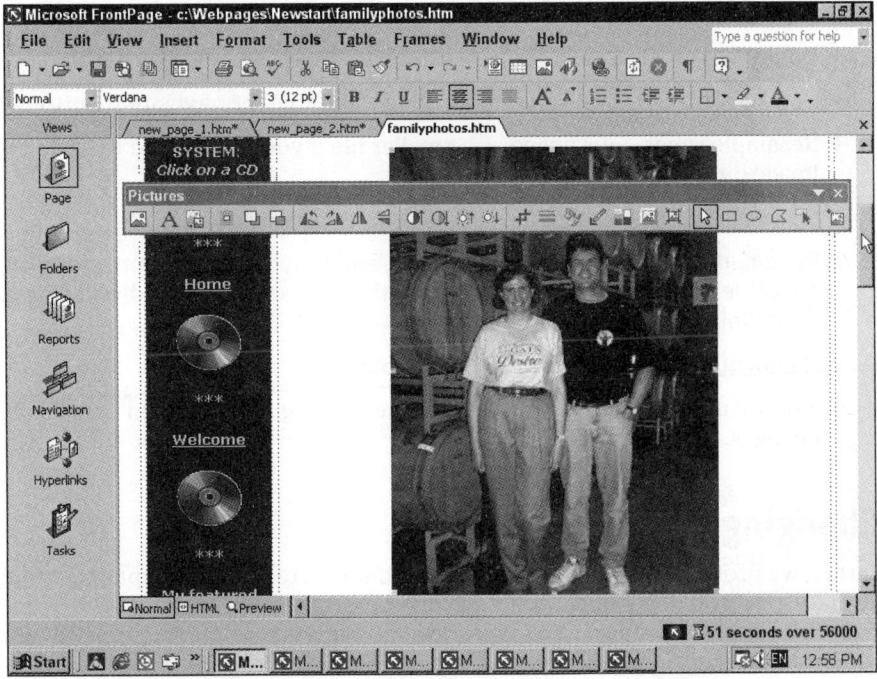

Figure 43-14: Edit pictures right in FrontPage with the Picture toolbar.

The picture tools let you add images and text to, and change the appearance of, a picture.

- ✦ The Insert Picture From File button lets you insert a new image.
- ✦ The Text button adds text to your image.
- ✦ Auto Thumbnail generates a small version of your image.
- ✦ Position Absolutely allows you to lock the position of your image to any spot on your page.
- ✦ Bring Forward and Send Backward move selected images in front of or behind other objects on the page.
- ✦ Rotate Left, Rotate Right, Flip Horizontal, and Flip Vertical rotate or flip your selected image.
- ✦ More Contrast, Less Contrast, More Brightness, and Less Brightness work like the contrast and brightness dials on your monitor or TV to change the brightness and contrast of your image.
- ✦ Crop creates a marquee around your image with movable corner and side handles. Click and drag on these handles to crop your picture, and then click the Crop button again to finalize your cut.
- ✦ Set Transparent Color displays an Eraser tool. Point and click at any one color in your image to make that color disappear, allowing the page background to show through.
- ✦ Color converts images from color to black-and-white and back again.
- ✦ Bevel adds a 3-D frame around an image, suitable for navigation buttons.
- ✦ Resample saves your image as a smaller file if you've reduced the size of your image on the page.
- ✦ Select deselects other tools and displays the arrow pointer.
- ✦ Rectangular Hotspot, Circular Hotspot, and Polygonal Hotspot create clickable links called image maps (see the next section for a discussion of hyperlinks).
- ✦ Highlight Hotspots helps identify hotspots.
- ✦ Restore undoes changes to your picture, as long as you haven't saved the changes.

Changing image properties

Earlier, we promised that if you did know about different Web-compatible graphics formats, you would like how FrontPage handles images. Up to now, we've relied on FrontPage to save images and assign a format. But you can choose from the three widely recognized Web graphics formats (.GIF, .JPEG, or .PNG). And you can assign other graphic properties to your pictures.

 **Note** Assigning attributes to Web graphics can get quite complex, but the basic picture tools and image properties you'll find in this chapter will give you the control you need to insert and format graphic images on your Web pages.

The General tab

To define image properties, right-click a picture and select Picture Properties from the context menu. The General tab of the Picture Properties dialog box includes options to set the following image options:

✦ Picture Source is the filename for the picture.

✦ The Type radio buttons (in the Type area) let you manually select a file type. Note that only the .GIF file format allows you to apply transparency to an image. The .GIF format allows for interlacing as well, which causes an image to fade in to a browser window.

✦ The Text field is the other widely used feature in the General tab, which allows you to define the text that will display either a) when a visitor has graphics turned off in his or her browser; or b) when a visitor points at a graphic.

The Appearance tab

Other formatting features are available in the Appearance tab of the Picture Properties dialog box, but you can do most of these things right in Page view. The Specify size option here is handy if you have a series of pictures that you want to be sure are all the same width or height. The Wrapping style options determine how the picture will be displayed relative to adjacent text — but for better control of that sort of thing, use tables (as described earlier in the chapter).

The Video tab

Interested in running a video on your Web page? Set that up here. Indicate the source of the video, then choose how often to loop it and whether to start it running when the page is opened or just when the mouse runs over it.

Hyperlinks and Image Maps

Hyperlinks (or *links*, for short) are text or graphic images on your Web pages that provide links to something else. The easiest way to create a link in Page view is to simply type a Web address or an e-mail address. FrontPage recognizes it as a URL or e-mail address and automatically links the text to that URL or e-mail address.

 **Note** The techniques described for assigning hyperlinks work in all Office applications, with slight variations. Master them here and you can master them anywhere.

Assigning links to text

Often, of course, you don't want the actual address to appear in your text, you just want a link from a bit of text to a Web page, an e-mail address, or maybe even somewhere further down the current page. (This latter trick requires the insertion of bookmarks; see the section on creating bookmarks a little further on in this chapter.)

To create a hyperlink, select the text you want to call up with the link and then click the Insert Hyperlink button on the Standard toolbar, or choose Insert ➪ Hyperlink, or (my favorite) press Ctrl+K (no, I don't know what the letter *K* has to do with hyperlinks). All these techniques open the Insert Hyperlink dialog box (see Figure 43-15).

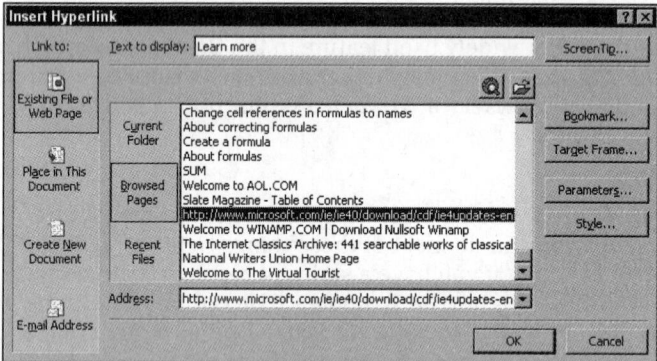

Figure 43-15: Use the Insert Hyperlink dialog box to define hyperlinks to Web sites, other Internet URLs, and documents on a local or network disk.

The box at the top of Figure 43-15 lets you enter or change the text of the hyperlink to be displayed in your document — it automatically contains any text you selected before opening the dialog box. Arranged vertically along the left side of the box, the large Link To bar contains buttons for selecting the type of hyperlink you want to create. When you click a button, the options in the main part of the box change accordingly. The Link To buttons are as follows:

✦ **Existing File or Web Page:** See the next section, "Creating hyperlinks to existing pages and documents," for details.

✦ **Place in This Document:** This button's function is better expressed as *Create a hyperlink to another location in the current document* — not *Insert a hyperlink into the current document.* See "Jumping to specific locations in documents" later in this chapter.

✦ **Create New Document:** Click here if you want to start a new document as the destination for the hyperlink you're inserting.

✦ **E-mail Address:** Click this button if you want the hyperlink to start a new e-mail message using your default e-mail program.

Creating hyperlinks to existing pages and documents

Hyperlinks can jump to and activate any document file accessible on your system, your network, or the Internet. The only requirements are that the application that opens that file type is present on your system and that the file type is associated in Windows with that application. For Web pages, of course, the requisite application is a browser.

Using the Insert Hyperlink dialog box, identify an existing Web page or document as the hyperlink's target by clicking the Existing File or Web Page button if necessary. Then use one of these three techniques:

✦ Type in a URL or a path and filename yourself.

  or

✦ Choose the target from one of the lists controlled by the three buttons just to the right of the Link To bar. Recent Files displays the files you've opened or inserted in Office. Browsed Pages displays Web pages that you've viewed in your browser recently (by title, if the title is available). (Because the HTML Help program is really just Internet Explorer with a different face, all the Help topics you've viewed show up here — this is usually a distracting nuisance.) Current Folder lists pages in the folder selected in the Look in field, which by default holds the folder containing the Web you're currently working in.

  or

✦ Click one of the Browse For buttons, to the right of the Look in field, to locate a filename or Web address. Clicking Browse for Web Page starts your browser. When you find the page you're looking for, you must manually copy its URL from the browser's address box back to the Insert Hyperlink box. Clicking Browse for File lets you find a file on your computer or local network.

The Bookmark button lets you specify a named location in the target document as the hyperlink's destination. See "Jumping to specific locations in documents" later in this chapter.

The ScreenTip button lets you write a ScreenTip that will show up when a viewer runs his or her mouse over a hyperlink. This can be a great aid to navigation around a Web site.

Editing and removing hyperlinks

To edit an existing hyperlink, right-click over the link. Choose Hyperlink ⇨ Hyperlink Properties on the shortcut menu to open the Edit Hyperlink dialog box. Its controls are identical to those of the Insert Hyperlink dialog box described earlier, except for the Remove Link button at the bottom right.

Note   Removing a hyperlink doesn't delete the text or graphics that held the link in your document; all that goes away is the hyperlink functionality.

Creating image maps

Image maps divide sections of a graphic image into different links; these sections (called *hotspots*) serve as hyperlinks. So, for example, you could post pictures of your staff and let visitors connect with anyone on the staff by clicking images of their faces.

To create an image map by assigning hotspot links to parts of a picture, follow these steps:

1. Click anywhere in the picture to which you want to add hotspot links. The Picture toolbar becomes active.

2. Click the Rectangular Hotspot, Circular Hotspot, or Polygonal Hotspot button on the Picture toolbar.

3. If you selected the Rectangular or Circular Hotspot buttons, click and drag to draw a rectangle or circle around part of your picture. Figure 43-16 shows a rectangular hotspot being drawn. You can use the Polygonal Hotspot tool to draw an outline around an irregularly shaped part of your picture. Do that by clicking to set outline points, and double-clicking to end the outline.

4. As soon as you complete your hotspot shape, the Insert Hyperlink dialog box opens. Create your hyperlink just as you did for text.

Creating bookmarks

The target of a link can be, not just a specific Web page, but a specific location on that Web page. These spots on a page are marked with bookmarks.

To create a bookmark, simply go to the spot on the page that you want visitors to be able to jump to and choose Insert ⇨ Bookmark, or press Ctrl+G. If you've selected text, that text will be the default bookmark name. If you don't, you can type a bookmark name into the Bookmark. Click OK, and the new bookmark is displayed as a small blue flag, or, if the bookmark is assigned to selected text, that text will be underlined with a dotted line. When a page includes bookmarks, you can link to them by selecting the page in your Insert Hyperlink dialog box, then clicking the bookmark button. If there are bookmarks in the currently open page, clicking the Place in this Document button in the Insert Hyperlink dialog box displays a list of the bookmarks; just choose the one you want viewers to jump to when they click the hyperlink.

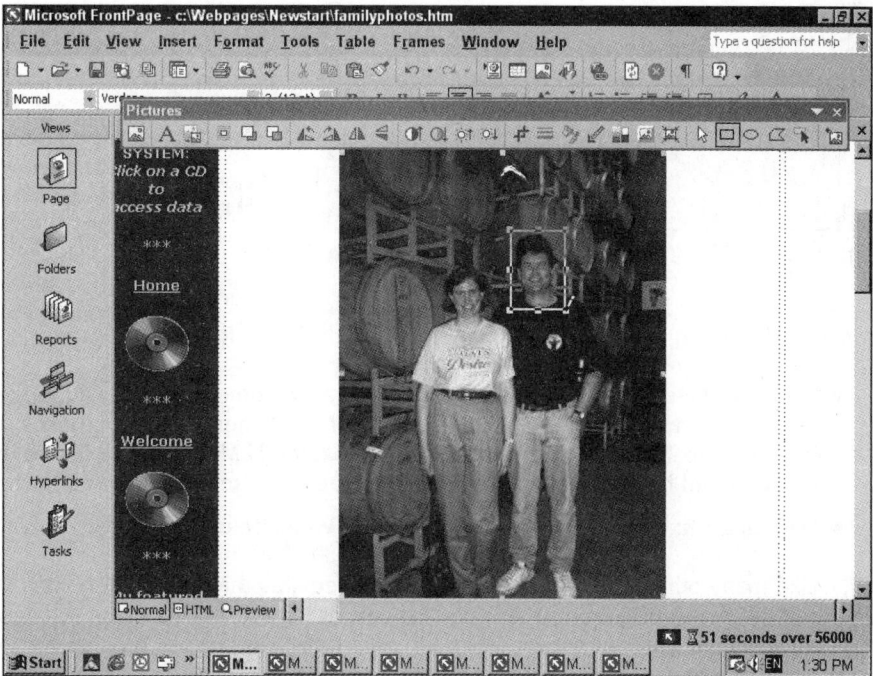

Figure 43-16: Drawing an image map hotspot

Inserting Special FrontPage Components

FrontPage offers tons of specialized prefab gadgets and gizmos that you can plug into a page to enhance its content, functionality, or looks. You can find the most-used elements by choosing either Insert ⇨ Web Component or Insert ⇨ Form.

Inserting Web components

Choosing Insert ⇨ Web Components opens the dialog box in Figure 43-17, which contains a plethora of riches to spice up your Web. Choose a component type from the box at left and then the specific component of that type that you want to insert from the "Choose a (component type)" box at right.

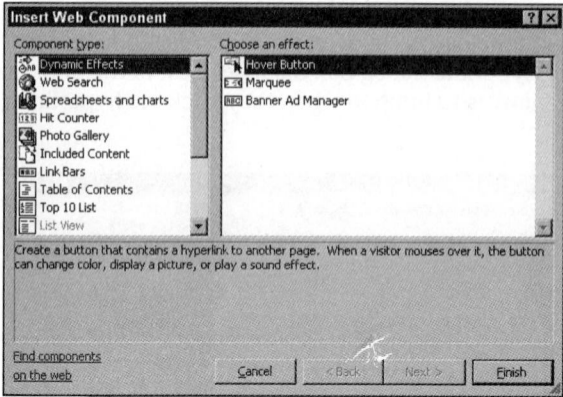

Figure 43-17: The Insert Web Component dialog box

Some especially interesting Web components include the following:

✦ **Dynamic Effects:** Want a button that changes in some way when a mouse pointer moves over it? (Or, as Microsoft puts it, "when a visitor mouses over it" — so apparently "mouse" is a verb? Who knew?) Maybe you'd like to create an animated banner ad or a scrolling marquee. Those effects are all here.

✦ **Web Search:** This lets visitors search your Web site using keywords.

Note
Like many other Web components, this one requires that you publish your Web site to a server with FrontPage Server Extensions for it to work. You can still design these FrontPage components without publishing them to a Web server with FrontPage Server Extensions, but they won't be functional. A couple of options also require a server that's running Microsoft SharePoint.

✦ **Spreadsheets and charts:** Just what they sound like. You can insert a pivot table, too.

✦ **Hit Counter:** Ever-popular, hit counters keep track of how often a particular page is visited.

✦ **Photo Gallery:** See the section on inserting a photo gallery earlier in this chapter.

✦ **Included Content:** Choose this to include author information, a description and other such data automatically.

✦ **Link Bars:** These are navigation devices, some of which include only links to other pages within your Web (based on the structure you specify in Navigation view), some of which let you add links to other sites, too.

✦ **Table of Contents:** This lists all the pages in your Web, with links to them.

✦ **Top 10 List:** No, this doesn't automatically generate jokes for David Letterman; it lists the top 10 results in a variety of categories — the 10 most visited pages on the site, for instance, or the 10 most popular browsers used to visit the site.

✦ **bCentral, Expedia, MSN & MSNBC Components:** Use these to add content to your Web that is automatically inserted from various Microsoft-related sites — giving you ever-changing content without requiring you to do the changing.

✦ **Advanced Controls:** Look here for java applets and ActiveX controls, among other things. This is also where you'll find the option to include HTML code that you've written yourself (or copied from elsewhere), with the assurance that FrontPage won't modify it (see "Experimenting with HTML," the last section in this chapter.

Inserting Forms

Forms in FrontPage are interactive components designed to elicit a response from the viewer and generate information for you. You're already familiar with them to a certain extent from being on the receiving end of them as you use Windows programs of all sorts, and you've probably run across them in Web pages you've visited.

To insert a form, choose Insert ⇨ Form, then choose the type of form you want from the list provided.

Right-click the form after you've inserted it to open the Form Properties dialog box (see Figure 43-18). This will vary depending on what kind of form you've inserted. Here you tell FrontPage how you want to deal with the information generated by the form. You can tell it to send information to a particular file or to an e-mail address or to a database, for instance. If you click Options, you'll find even more details to specify about this process.

Forms are a great way to gather information about visitors, compile an e-mail list of people interested in what you have to offer on your Web site, or just to keep people coming back. Take the time to familiarize yourself with them.

Cross-Reference For more on using forms in other Office applications, see Chapter 10.

Experimenting with HTML Code

FrontPage automatically generates HTML code when you create Web pages. That code is interpreted by Web browsers. You don't need to know HTML to create Web pages in FrontPage. That's part of its attraction! But you can enter your own HTML code, or you can examine the code FrontPage generates to teach yourself HTML.

You have a couple of ways to look at HTML code, or tags. One is to look at the
HTML tab in Page view. This view presents pure HTML, as shown in Figure 43-19.

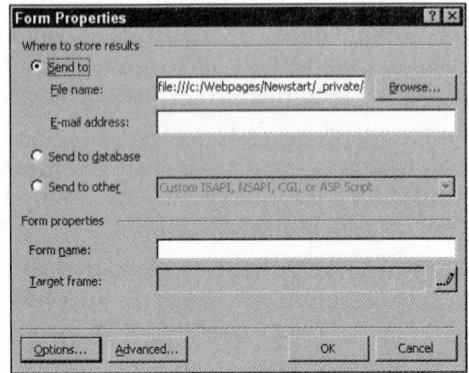

Figure 43-18: Use the Form Properties dialog
box to specify how information gathered by
forms should be dealt with.

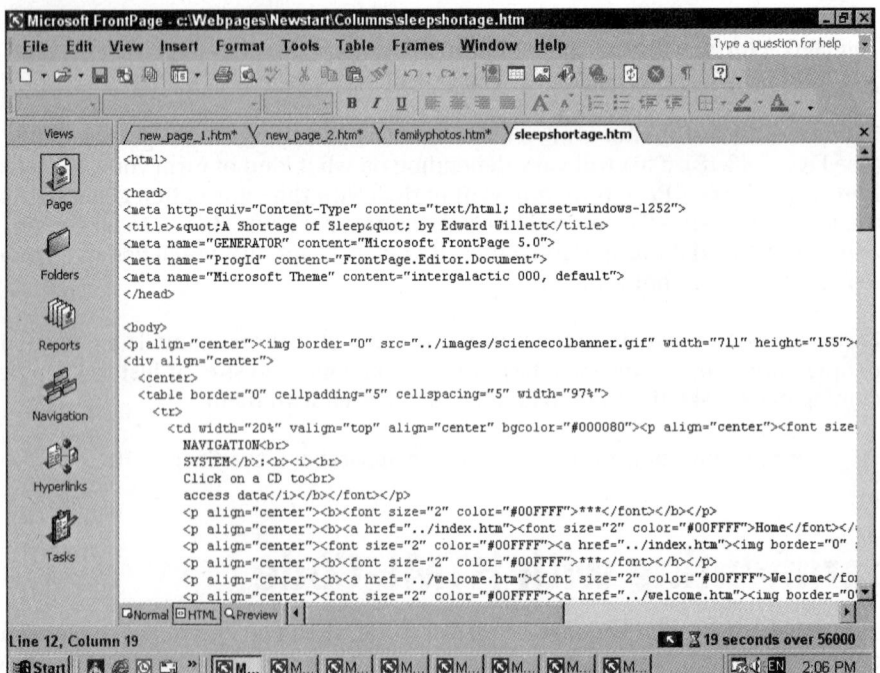

Figure 43-19: The HTML tab in Page view is a full-fledged HTML text editor.

You can examine the HTML generated by FrontPage in the HTML tab, and probably figure out what some of the tags mean. For example, `<b>text</b>` turns boldface on (`<b>`) before the word text, and then turns it off (`</b>`). You can also edit your page's HTML directly in HTML view, although, if you want to be certain FrontPage won't alter your HTML coding as it goes about its own business, use the Insert ➪ Web Components ➪ Advanced Components ➪ HTML option (described earlier in this chapter).

If you prefer, you can stay in Normal view, but make HTML tags visible. To do that, in the Normal tab of Page view, select View ➪ Reveal Tags from the menu (you could also press Ctrl+/). You'll see the WYSIWYG (What You See Is What You Get) view, but you'll see the HTML tags, too, as shown in Figure 43-20. This is another great way to learn what HTML codes mean.

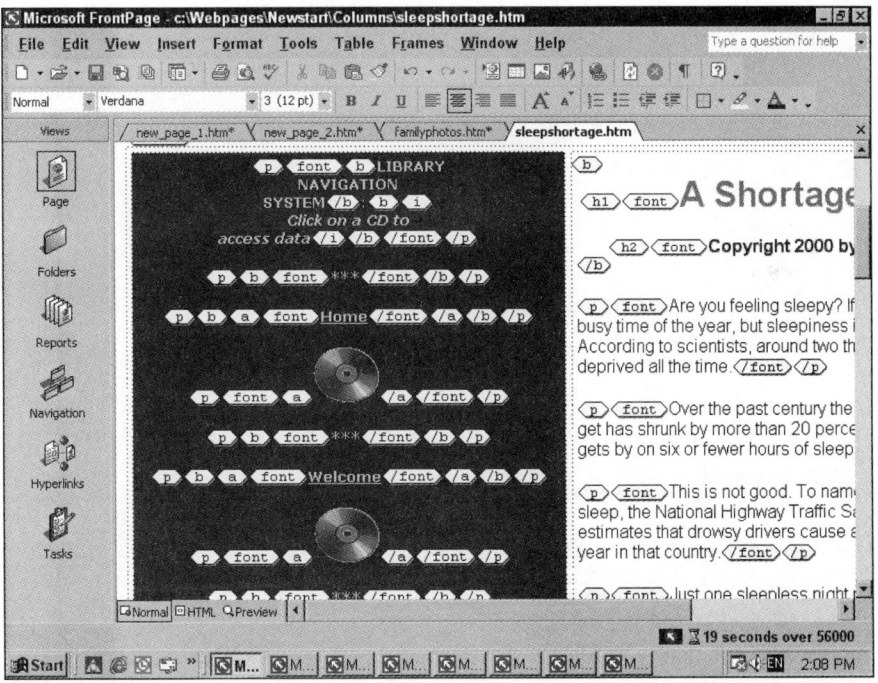

Figure 43-20: You can display HTML tags along with your formatted page on the Normal tab in Page view.

Cross-Reference

HTML is a subject for an entire book in its own right (Hungry Minds' own *HTML 4 For Dummies*, Third Edition, by Ed Tittel, Natanya Pitts, and Chelsea Valentine, is a good place to start).

No need to dip a toe any farther into that particular ocean in this chapter. In addition to other books, you can find tons of information about coding HTML online. (If there's one topic the Internet covers particularly thoroughly, it's the subject of its own inner workings!)

✦   ✦   ✦

Managing Your Web Site

In the last chapter, you learned techniques that will allow
you to create quite a nice Web site. You learned to use one
of FrontPage's templates to design a Web site, how to create
and edit Web pages, how to add text and graphics, and how to
add advanced elements, such as hit counters. You've come a
long way. In this chapter, you'll learn to use FrontPage to manage your Web site, and how to customize it to give it a unique
look and feel.

Themes, Shared Borders, and Navigation Bars

In the last chapter, you added elements to your web, page by
page. But there are also elements that can be added globally.
They include themes, which assign a universal color and
design scheme to a Web; shared borders; and navigation bars.

Selecting and assigning a site theme

Themes are collections of design elements that are assigned
to every page in a Web site. You can remove a theme from a
page, or even use different themes for different pages in a Web
site. But generally, the point is to use the same theme
throughout a site to give it a distinct and consistent look and
feel.

Themes include background colors, font size, style, and color,
and graphic elements. They are assigned in the Themes
dialog box.

Follow these steps to assign a theme:

1. With your Web open, select Format_⇨_Theme from the FrontPage menu. You can do this from any view.

2. To apply your theme to all pages in your site, click the "All pages" radio button. Alternatively, if you have selected a single page (or pages) in Folders, Page, or Navigation view, you can click the "Selected page(s)" radio button to apply the theme to only the selected page(s).

3. Click one of the themes in the list on the left side of the Themes dialog box. A preview of the theme will be displayed in the "Sample of Theme:" area on the right side of the dialog box.

   Use the checkboxes to experiment with "Vivid colors," "Active graphics," and a "Background picture," as shown in Figure 44-1.

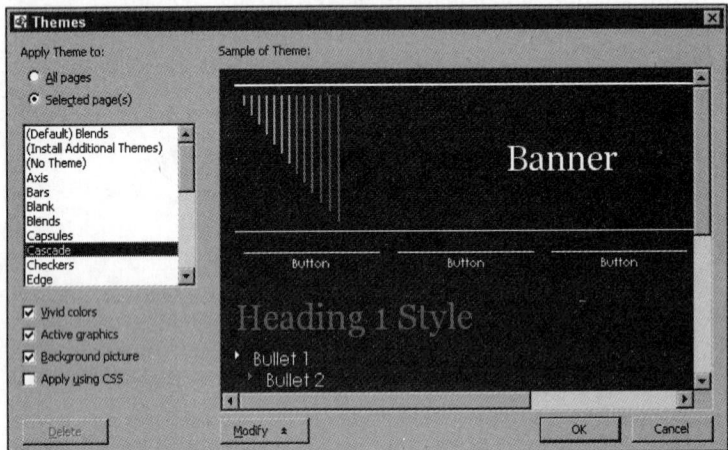

Figure 44-1: Themes provide uniform graphic elements and color schemes for your Web pages.

Note   The "Apply using CSS" checkbox allows those of you who are familiar with Cascading Style Sheets to connect one to your Web site. A full discussion of Cascading Style Sheets in FrontPage is beyond the scope of this book. You can, however, tweak and change the effects of a theme by using the Modify button in the Themes dialog box to access buttons that let you change colors, graphics, or inline styles. (More about these options later in this chapter.)

4. When you have settled on just the right theme to suit your image, click the OK button to apply the theme to your Web site (or selected pages).

You could sneak a peek at your Web pages now by double-clicking one in Navigation view to open it in Page view. However, you will appreciate the impact of themes more after you add shared borders in the next section of this chapter.

Adding shared borders

Shared borders are actually separate web pages that are attached to a border of every page in a Web site. As with themes, shared borders are most effective when applied to every page in a site. Shared borders most often hold navigation bars, but they can also contain any other object, like graphics or text.

To apply shared borders to your Web site:

1. Select Format ➪ Shared Borders from the FrontPage menu (you can be in any view).

2. Select either the "All pages" or "Selected page(s)" radio button to apply the shared borders to either selected pages, or to the entire Web.

3. "Top" and "Left" shared borders are the most widely used. Start experimenting by selecting them. Later you can elect to deselect one or both of these shared borders, and apply bottom or even right shared borders.

Note Most Web designers shy away from right-side shared borders. Visitors tend to look up, left, or possibly down for navigational links. And the right side of a Web page is sometimes out of the browser window and requires horizontal scrolling to view.

4. If you select "Top" and/or "Left" shared borders along with the "All pages" option, you can select the "Include navigation buttons" checkboxes for one or both of these shared borders. To explore the full effect of shared borders, try top and left borders with navigation buttons in each, as shown in Figure 44-2.

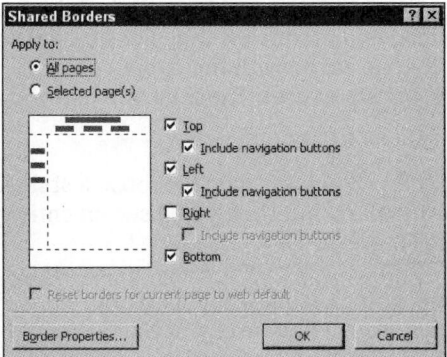

Figure 44-2: Shared borders with navigation buttons provide convenient links throughout your Web site.

5. When you have selected shared borders, click the OK button.

Tip   Shared borders can include any Web page element, including text and graphics. Shared borders act as a consistent element of each page in your Web site. To edit the content of a shared border, click in the border, and edit as you would any other Web page. When you save the Web page, the embedded shared border page is saved as well.

Inserting and editing navigation bars

You can change the logic of how navigation links get generated in navigation bars. You can define navigation bars by selecting Insert ➪ Navigation.... This opens the Insert Web Component dialog box you saw in Chapter 43, with Link Bars selected. You can choose from three types of navigation bars: "Bar with custom links," "Bar with back and next links," and "Bar based on navigation structures."

The bar with custom links displays a separate button for each hyperlink, and can point to pages both within and outside the web site. The bar with back and next links is designed to point to a sequence of pages inside the web site, and shows only "back" and "next" buttons. The bar based on navigation structure is just what it sounds like; you determine the links that appear on the bar by altering the structure of the Web site in Navigation view, as described in Chapter 43.

All three of these types of navigation bars can be edited. If you choose "Bar with custom links" or "Bar with back and next links" and click Next, you're first asked to define a style for the bar (a wide variety of styles, including one in the style of each theme, is provided), then to choose an orientation (horizontal or vertical). If you click Finish at that point, you're given the opportunity to name your new link bar, and then you'll find yourself in the Link Bar Properties dialog box (see Figure 44-3), which allows you to add a hyperlink (using the Insert Hyperlink dialog box, which you saw in Chapter 43), remove a link, and modify existing links on the bar. You can also add links to the home page (the one saved with the name index.htm) or the parent page (based on your navigation structure). The Style tab lets you change the style again, if you feel like it.

If you choose "Bar based on navigation structure," you'll choose a style and orientation just like with the other navigation bars, but then you'll see an entirely different Link Bar Properties dialog box (see Figure 44-4).

If you've ever designed a family tree, you can follow the metaphor here. Parent pages are pages one step up on the flowchart hierarchy of Navigation view. Child pages are one step below in the flowchart.

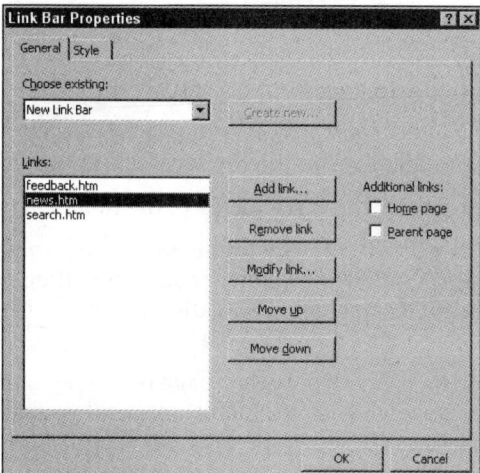

Figure 44-3: Edit your navigation bars using the Link Bar Properties dialog box.

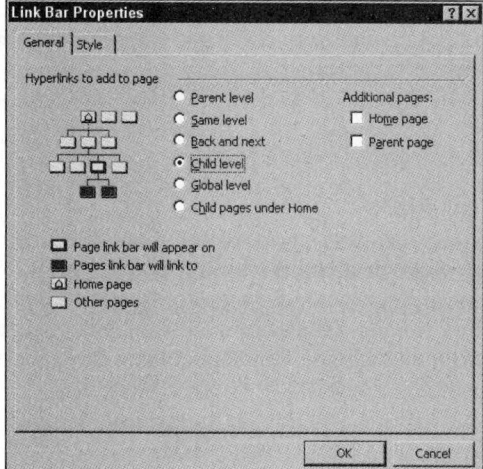

Figure 44-4: Navigation bar options use the metaphor of a family tree.

✦ "Parent level" links display only a link to the page above the page being viewed.

✦ "Same level" links display other Web pages on the same level of the Navigation view site flowchart.

✦ "Back and next" display the nearest link to the left and to the right of the current page.

✦ "Child level" links generate links only to pages directly below the current page in the Navigation view flowchart.

✦ "Global level" links display links to all pages in the top level of the flowchart.

✦ "Child pages under Home" links display the child pages of the home page.

✦ The "Home page" checkbox adds a link to the site home page on every page in the site. This is a very useful option. Allowing visitors to navigate directly to your home page is usually the most-appreciated navigational link you can provide.

✦ The "Parent page" checkbox adds a link to the parent page on each page. This is redundant if you selected the "Parent level" radio button, but if you're using other linking logic, it can be helpful.

Tip   Which type of navigational link is best? Probably the most useful navigation links for many sites are generated by selecting the "Child level" radio button, and both the "Parent page" and "Home page" checkboxes.

Tip   Why can't you assign Navigation bars to the right or bottom shared borders? Actually, you can. You just have to do it manually, by clicking in the generated border and using the Insert ➪ Navigation command.

Customizing Themes

Just because you've chosen a theme for your Web site doesn't mean you're stuck with it. You can also choose to simply use it as a starting point, then go on to modify it to suit your aesthetic sense — and practical needs — better. To do so, start by choosing Format ➪ Theme to open the Themes dialog box you saw back in Figure 44-1. This time, click Modify. This produces three new buttons under the question, "What would you like to modify?"

Modifying theme colors

Clicking the Colors button opens the Modify Theme dialog box, with three tabs, shown in Figure 44-5. These three tabs provide three different ways to change the colors in your theme.

The Color Schemes tab

The Color Schemes tab allows you to substitute the color scheme of a different theme for the selected theme. So, for example, if you like the graphics and fonts of the Citrus Punch theme, but you prefer the color scheme in the Cactus theme, you can assign the Citrus Punch theme, but select the Cactus color scheme.

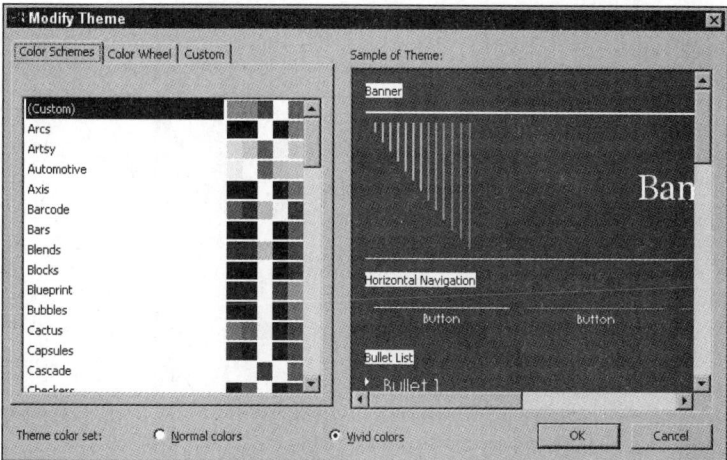

Figure 44-5: You can customize the color scheme in your theme.

The Color Wheel tab

Switching color schemes from one theme to another gives you some, but not complete, control over your theme colors. For even more options, click the Color Wheel tab in the Modify Theme dialog box. Here, you can click a location in the Color Wheel to generate a new set of colors matched in sync with the color you click in the wheel.

You can also adjust the colors in your theme color scheme by moving the "Brightness" slider. And, you can toggle between intense colors and muted colors by using the "Normal colors" or "Vivid colors" radio buttons at the bottom of the dialog box.

The Custom tab

Finally, you can modify the colors of different text elements in the Custom tab of the Modify Theme dialog box. First, pull down the "Item:" list and select the item you want to assign a color to. Then, click the "Color:" drop-down list and select a color to assign to that text element.

When you have finished modifying the color scheme of your customized theme, click the OK button in the Modify Theme dialog box.

Modifying theme graphics

Themes assign many graphics to your Web pages, e.g., a background image, a graphic to use for bullets, horizontal rules, and navigational icons. You can substitute your own graphics images for those that come with a theme, and you can customize the font of the text that gets added to these images. To do all this, click the Graphics button (after clicking Modify) in the Themes dialog box. Another Modify Theme dialog box opens, as shown in Figure 44-6.

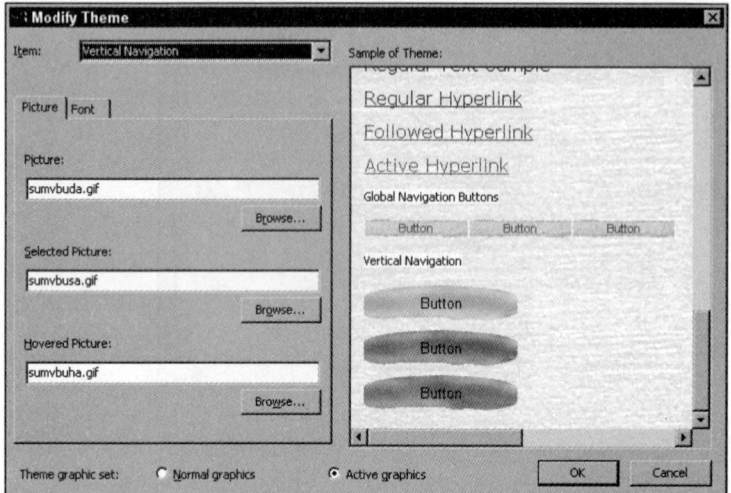

Figure 44-6: This Modify Theme dialog box allows you to substitute your own graphics for theme elements.

The Picture tab

You can assign new graphics to the various elements of the theme that use them by pulling the name of the element you want to modify from the "Item:" list at the top of the tab (that is, Vertical Navigation) and then browsing for a new picture (or, in some cases, more than one picture — Vertical Navigation, for example, requires a graphic image for the normal picture, for the picture after it's been selected, and for the picture when the mouse pointer simply hovers over it).

The Font tab

The Font tab, similarly, allows you to assign fonts, font styles, font sizes, and horizontal and vertical alignment to various items, pulled down from the "Item:" list. (Remember, you already assigned font colors in the Colors tab.)

Changing theme styles

You can assign fonts to any of the HTML styles available in the Style drop-down list in Page view. To do this, click the Text button in the Themes dialog box (after clicking Modify). Select a style from the "Item:" drop-down list, and then a font from the "Font:" list. Figure 44-7 shows a font being assigned to the Heading 1 style.

You can see additional styles by clicking the More Text Styles button. After you've assigned custom fonts to different styles, click the OK button to close this dialog box and return to the Themes dialog box.

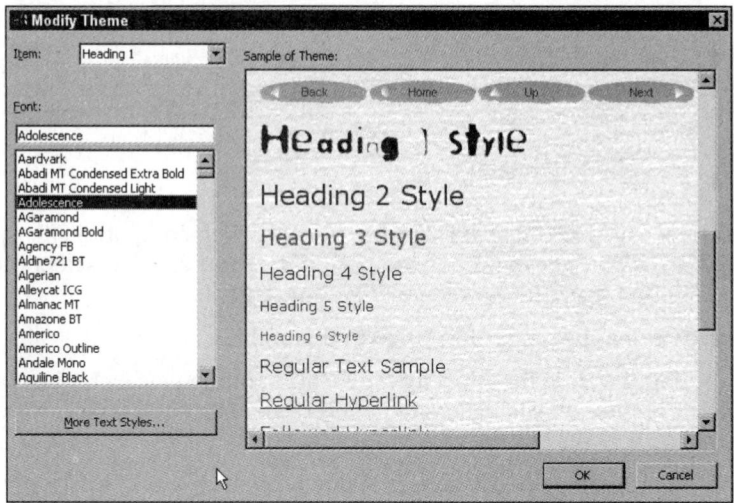

Figure 44-7: Redefining style fonts the easy way.

Saving a custom theme

By now, you've assigned custom graphics, custom color schemes, and custom text, so you've actually defined a brand-new theme of your own. To save this new theme, and add it to the list of available themes, click the Save As button in the Themes dialog box.

The tiny Save Theme dialog box appears. Enter a new descriptive theme name in the "Enter new theme title:" box, and click OK.

After you have saved a theme, it appears in your Themes list.

Organizing Office Documents into a Web Site

In other parts of this book, you learned that nearly every Office XP application easily saves files as Web pages. You may have saved a Word file as an HTML Web page. You may have saved an Excel workbook as a Web page. Perhaps you've even got a PowerPoint slideshow saved as an ActiveX object that will play like a video in a Web page.

You can incorporate all these files into a FrontPage Web site. There are different ways to do this, but one reliable approach is to break the process into three parts:

✦ Create Web-compatible files in Office applications by saving files as HTML pages, GIF or JPEG files, or other Web-compatible files.

✦ Create a FrontPage web (it can be blank), and then import the files into a FrontPage web.

✦ Organize the Web pages in Navigation view, and add other objects (such as GIF or JPEG files) in Page view.

Step by step, the process looks like this:

1. With your Office files saved as HTML files, or other Web-compatible file types, use the File ➪ New ➪ Page or Web menu option in FrontPage and select the Empty Web option from the New Page or Web task pane.

   A new empty web appears, as described in Chapter 43.

2. Name your empty web in the "Specify the location of the new web:" box, and then click OK in the New dialog box to generate an empty web with no Web pages.

3. Select File ➪ Import to open the Import dialog box.

4. Click Add File to begin to add files to your Web site. Navigate to the file you want to include in your Web site in the Add File to Import List dialog box.

5. Click Open to add the file to the list of files you will import into your Web site.

6. Add additional files to your site.

   The list of files to import appears in the Import dialog box, as shown in Figure 44-8.

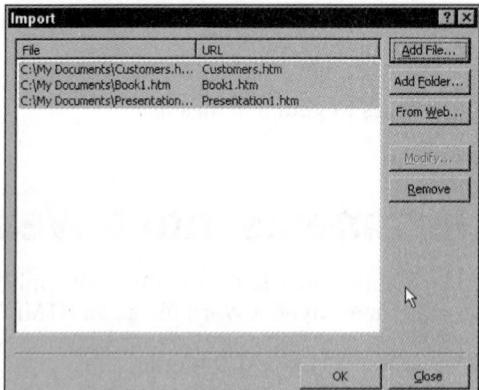

Figure 44-8: You can add all sorts of Office-generated files to your Web site. These three pages were created in Access, Excel, and PowerPoint, respectively.

 **Note**   You can add an entire folder to your Web site by clicking the Add Folder button. When you add a folder, all files in the folder are included, and the URL given to each file includes the name of the folder and any subfolders. This directory structure is also added to your web. You can also add files from an existing Web site by clicking From Web; this starts a wizard that guides you through that process.

7. When you've completed your list of files (you can always add more later), click the OK button.

   Your selected files are imported into your Web site.

8. Use Navigation view to organize the new files in your Web site. Click and drag files from the Folder list in Navigation view into the flowchart to connect them to the Web site, as shown in Figure 44-9.

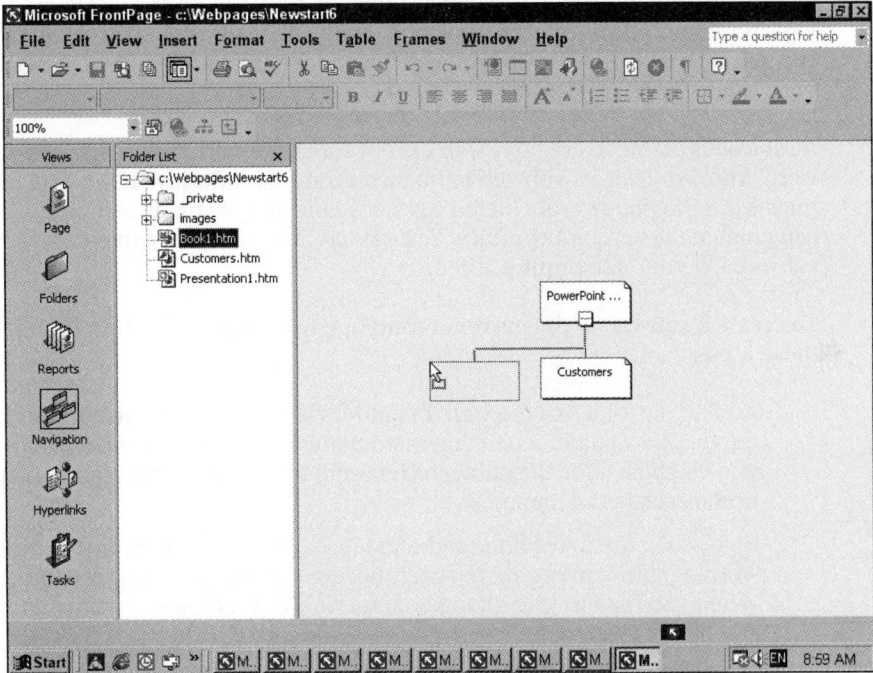

Figure 44-9: HTML files imported into your Web site can be moved into the Navigation view.

Using the _private folder

FrontPage webs always include a folder named _private. Files contained in this folder are inaccessible to visitors to your Web site. Use the folder to store form results and other information you want to keep to yourself. You can add subfolders to the _private folder to keep the material organized — everything in them remains off-limits to your visitors.

Managing complex Web site content using subwebs

If you're creating a web of significant size or complexity, you may want to break it down into sections that you develop separately. By dividing a large web into sub-webs, you may find it easier to keep track of related portions of the content. Subwebs are especially helpful when you want to house several separate Web sites at a single domain. You can also use subwebs to break up the workload by assigning a different author to each subweb. Finally, because you can assign distinct security settings to each subweb, you can use subwebs to limit access to portions of your site.

A *subweb* is just like a regular web except it resides within another web (the *parent* web). You work with a subweb in its own FrontPage window. It inherits basic settings from the parent web, including the theme and security permissions, but you can change these as appropriate. You can create subwebs within subwebs within subwebs, if your site requires them.

To create a subweb in the current FrontPage web and open it for editing, follow these steps:

1. Add a new folder to the web. In Folders view, right-click the Folder List and choose New Folder, changing the default folder name to whatever name you've chosen for the subweb (remember to avoid spaces and most punctuation marks in the name).

2. Right-click the new folder and choose Convert to Web. FrontPage displays a warning, but you can disregard it because the new folder contains no files yet. When you dismiss the dialog box, the folder's icon gains a tiny faux globe.

3. Double-click the subweb's folder to open the subweb in a separate FrontPage window.

Note   Importing a web with the Import Web Wizard mentioned in the last section doesn't convert it into a subweb. Instead, FrontPage just adds the web's files and folders to the current web. To convert an external web into a subweb, create and open the subweb first using the preceding steps and then import the external web into the subweb.

By default, subwebs aren't published when you publish the parent web. When you publish a web containing subwebs, be sure to check the Include Subwebs box in the Publish Web dialog box (you must display options for the dialog box to get to the checkbox—see the "Publishing Your Site to a Web Server" section later in this chapter).

Tip   An alternative way to create a subweb: add an existing web to one that you've already published to your intranet or the World Wide Web (or to a server-based web). All you need do is publish the web that's destined to become a subweb to the URL of the parent web.

Generating Usage and Other Reports

The Reports view provides a list of many useful statistics about your Web site. Additional reports update you on the status of navigational links, slow pages, and new files. You can select a report by choosing View ➪ Reports from the menu, and then selecting one of the available reports. Following are brief descriptions of how you can use these reports:

✦ The Site Summary report gives you an overview of your site. The rows in the Site Summary are themselves links to other views. One of the most useful things about the Site Summary view is you can get a quick idea of the size of your Web site, which is helpful when you are looking for server space for your site.

✦ The All Files report (from the Files submenu of the Reports menu) is shown in Figure 44-10. This report shows you detailed information about each file in your Web site.

✦ Recently Added Files, Recently Changed Files, Older Files, and Slow Pages (the first three are on the Files submenu of the Reports menu, the latter on the Problems submenu) are rather subjective categories. What's recent? What's old? What's slow? You define criteria for these reports by selecting Tools ➪ Options and selecting the Reports View tab

✦ The Unlinked Files report (Problems submenu) shows files in your Web site to which there are no links. These stranded Web pages are sometimes called orphan pages.

✦ The Broken Hyperlinks (Problems submenu) report shows you hyperlinks in your Web site that are either invalid or untested. You can right-click one of these untested hyperlinks and choose Verify from the context menu to test the link. If the link is to an Internet or intranet site, you must be logged on to the Internet or your intranet to test the link. After an unverified link is tested, and FrontPage determines that the link works, you'll see an OK mark in the Status column.

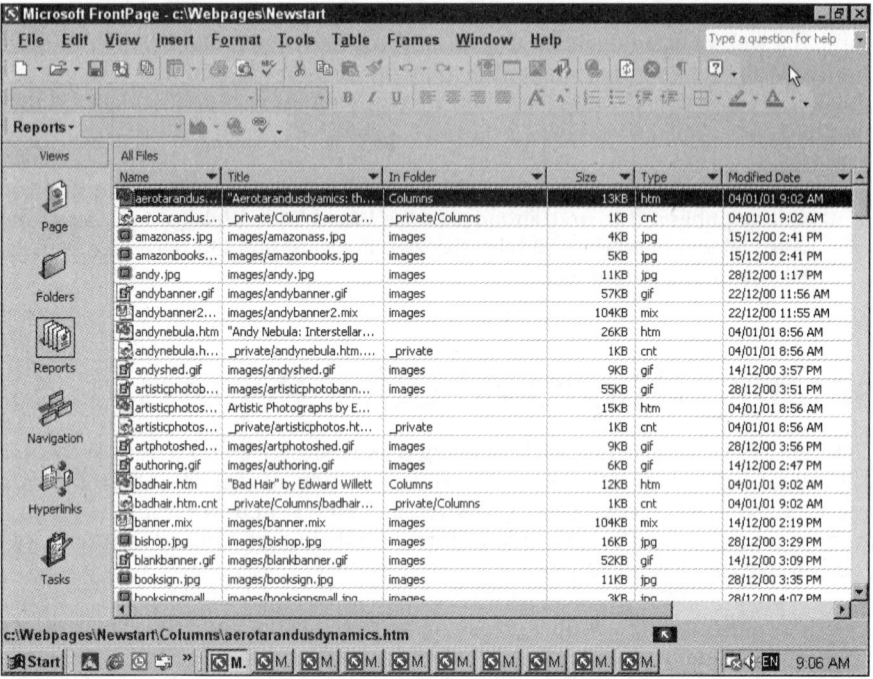

Figure 44-10: The All Files report tells you everything you need to know about files in your Web site.

✦The Component Errors report (Problems submenu) tests FrontPage Web components and forms.

✦ The Review Status and Assigned To reports (Workflow submenu) are for workgroups collaborating on a Web site. The Review Status report allows you to log pages that need to be reviewed, and track whether pages have been reviewed. The Assigned To report is similar to the Review Status report, but it tracks who is assigned to which page.

✦ The Categories report (Workflow submenu) sorts components of your Web site by category, such as Business, Competition, Expense Report, and so on.

✦ The Publish Status (Workflow submenu) report lists which pages are marked to be published to your Web server when you publish your Web.

✦ The Checkout Status report (Workflow submenu) tells you whether someone else on your network has already checked out certain files for editing. You can still open those files, but only as read-only (although you can save the file under another name and then make changes to it).

✦ The various reports under Usage are new and powerful features in FrontPage. They'll show you not just how many times your pages have been visited, but what operating systems your visitors were using, what browsers they were using, what domains they were referred from, what URLs they were referred from, even what searches were performed.

Note Usage reports are only available if your web has been published to a server that supports this kind of usage analysis.

Global Site Editing

Most of the work you do to edit the content of your Web site takes place in Page view, and is done on a page-by-page basis. But there are editing tools in FrontPage that work across an entire Web. Here, we'll look at two of them: spell-checking and search and replace.

Spell-checking your entire site

To spell-check your whole Web site, select Tools ⇨ Spelling from a view other than Page view (if you're in Page View, this command will only allow you to check the open page for spelling errors). Here's how it works:

✦ The Spelling dialog box has two radio buttons: one to check "Selected page(s)," and one to check the "Entire web." To spell-check your entire Web site, use the "Entire web" option.

✦ You can also select the "Add a task for each page with misspellings" checkbox. This handy option creates a list of pages that need their spelling corrected.

✦ After you've selected these options, click the Start button to begin the check of your spelling. After FrontPage checks all your pages for spelling problems, it produces a list in the Spelling dialog box, as shown in Figure 44-11.

✦ Double-click the page in the list to open that page and open a conventional Spelling box, as you are used to in other Office applications. Use this Spelling dialog box to correct (or ignore) questionable spellings.

Tracking tasks for your entire site

In the previous section, you learned that you can add pages that require spelling corrections to your Tasks list. To see this tasks list, click Tasks in the view bar. Figure 44-12 shows a Tasks view.

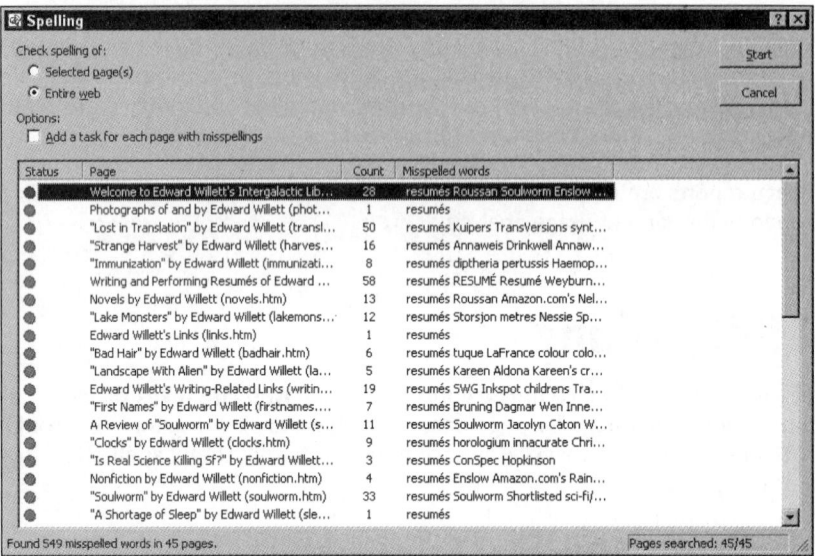

Figure 44-11: FrontPage's spell-checker creates a list of pages with potential spelling mistakes.

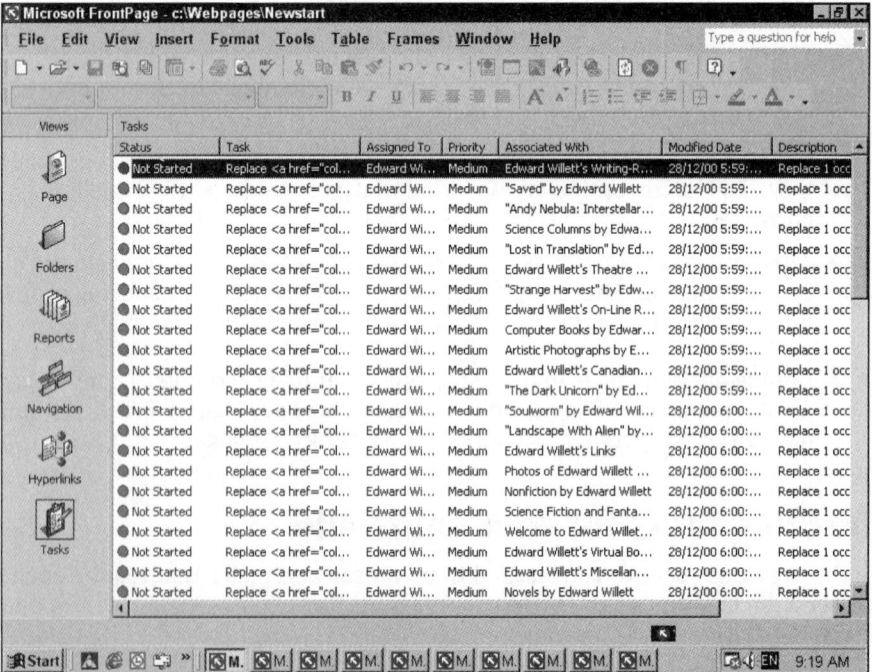

Figure 44-12: Here's a tasks view with lots of tasks—replacing bad links.

You can also add your own tasks to the Tasks view list. Select Edit ⇨ Tasks ⇨ Add Task to define a new task. The New Task dialog box appears, as shown in Figure 44-13.

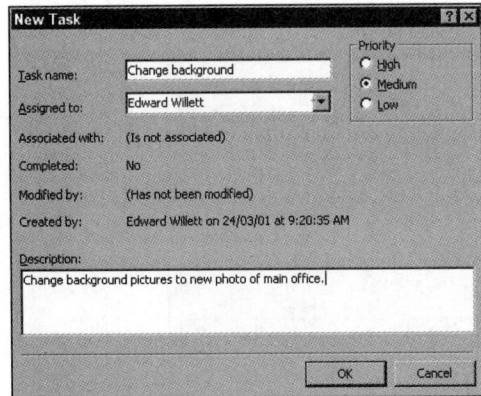

Figure 44-13: You can add your own tasks to the Tasks view list.

As you complete tasks, you can click them in the Tasks view list, and select Edit ⇨ Tasks ⇨ Mark Complete. Use the command Edit ⇨ Tasks ⇨ Show History to toggle between showing and hiding completed tasks. Tasks like correcting spelling, that were generated automatically by FrontPage, can be launched by selecting Edit ⇨ Tasks ⇨ Start Task.

Replacing throughout a site

You can use Search and Replace throughout your site. This comes in very handy when the corporate president you gushed over on every single Web page gets axed, and a new one has taken his or her place. Here's how it works:

1. To replace text throughout a site, select Edit ⇨ Replace in any view.

2. In the Find and Replace dialog box, select the Replace tab, then enter text to find in the "Find what:" box, and replacement text in the "Replace with:" box.

3. Choose the "All pages" radio button to replace the text in every page.

4. The drop-down list labeled "Direction:" lets you choose to search either up or down through a single Web page, or simply to search "All." If you've selected the "All pages" radio button, the "Direction:" option isn't available.

5. The "Find whole word only" and "Match case" checkbox options work as they do in the Find and Replace dialog box in Word and other Office applications. But the "Find in HTML" checkbox allows you to search and replace HTML code if you are so inclined.

6. After you define your replace options, if you are replacing in an entire Web, click the Find in Web button (or the Find Next button if you're only searching the current page). FrontPage will generate a list of pages at the bottom of the Replace dialog box with the text to be replaced. (see Figure 44-14).

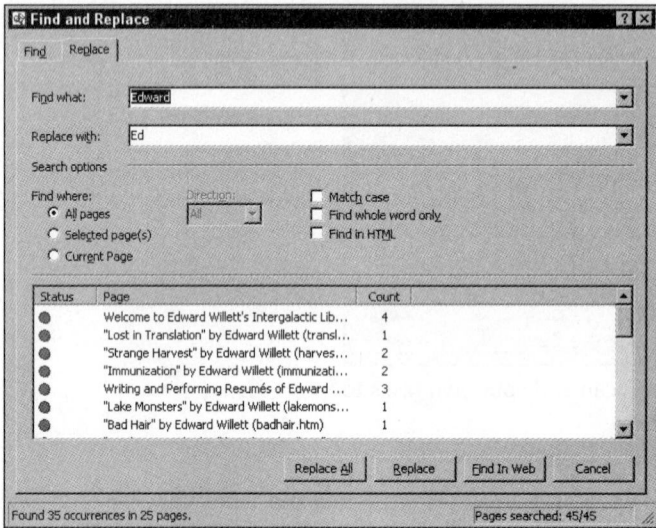

Figure 44-14: Replacing for an entire site generates a list of pages that need fixing.

7. Double-click a page to make the changes in that page. Or, select a page in the list and click the Add Task button to add a task for the selected page to your task list.

Publishing Your Site to a Web Server

Whenever you start working on Web pages in FrontPage, it's best to begin by creating a new web, rather than a single blank page, if you want to use the program's full power to manage your files.

Assuming that you've been working with a web all along, publishing your web to a web site is a breeze. Select File ➪ Publish Web to open the Publish Web dialog box. You enter a URL, get prompted for a logon name and a password, and you're in. We'll walk through that process in a bit more detail in the following sections.

Local drives versus Web servers

One of the most frequently asked questions about FrontPage is "How do I get my Web from my local computer to another computer?" The simplest way to do this is to simply enter a: in the "Enter publish destination" field in the Publish Destination dialog box, which opens when you choose File ➪ Publish Web. You'll be prompted to create a Web on your floppy disk, and then all your files will be transferred. It's a bit crude, but if all you want to do is bring the web you created at home into the office, it works.

You can also publish a Web site to other folders by specifying other folders on your hard drive or network by clicking the Browse button on the Publish Destination dialog box . Again, FrontPage will create a Web folder that can hold your FrontPage web.

If you want to share your Web site with others, however, you'll want to publish it to a Web server. To do that, enter a URL in the "Enter publish destination" field in the Publish Destination dialog box. You'll be prompted for a name and a password. If your Web server supports FrontPage, you can just enter a password and name in this dialog box, and that's it! Your entire site will be transferred to your new Web server.

Note   When you arrange for space on a Web server, either from an Internet service provider or from your local intranet administrator, you must get a logon name and a password from your administrator.

If you don't yet have a FrontPage-compatible Web site provider, read on.

Publishing to FrontPage-friendly sites

Hundreds of Web site providers are engaged in cutthroat competition to publish your Web site. If you want to shop for one of them online, click the "Click here to learn more" link in the Publish Destination dialog box.

After you contract for your site (and many providers let you do this online, instantly with a credit card or a promise to pay after a short, free trial period), you'll get a URL, a logon name and a password. With just that information, you're ready to publish your site to the Internet.

If your local intranet supports FrontPage, your intranet administrator can also give you a URL, a logon name and a password.

Other publishing options

You may find yourself in a position where you want to publish your Web site to a site provider that does not support FrontPage. These sites have not added the programs called FrontPage Server Extensions. Therefore, they do not support the Publish features in FrontPage. They also don't support other advanced elements of FrontPage Web sites; such as input forms, for example.

If you know that you will be publishing your site to a Web provider that does not have FrontPage Server Extensions, select Tools ➪ Page Options and click the Compatibility tab. Deselect the "Enabled with Microsoft FrontPage Server Extensions" checkbox, as shown in Figure 44-15.

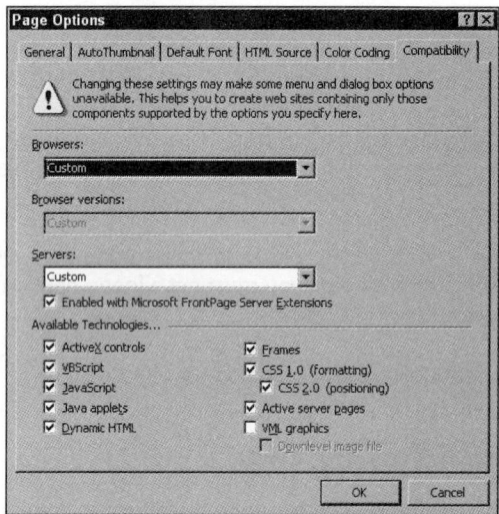

Figure 44-15: By deselecting "Enabled with FrontPage Server Extensions," you can publish a Web on a Web server without the extensions, but you can't apply some features that require the extensions.

Note   This tab also lets you turn off a host of other features that some browsers may not be compatible with, or that you just don't want to run. Use it to create Web pages that you can be confident will work well for anyone who might have access to them.

If your Web server does not have FrontPage Extension files, you can use File Transfer Protocol (FTP) to publish your Web. To do that, you will need to get an FTP server name and directory path from your server administrator. Then, in the "Enter publish destination" field in the Publish Destination dialog box, enter the location of an FTP Web server and click OK.

So, in short, you lose a couple things by going with a Web provider that doesn't have FrontPage Server Extensions: You can't use all the features you find in FrontPage. But if you still want to publish your FrontPage Web to a non-FrontPage enabled server, you will need to get instructions from your server administrator on how to transfer your files using their protocols. You can find your files using the All Files report.

Republishing a web

Whenever you make changes to a web, send these changes to the server by publishing it again. FrontPage keeps track of what has changed and what hasn't since the last time you published, so it only needs to update the changed files each time you publish. If you want to ensure that all the files on the server match those on your disk-based web—perhaps because other people have had access to them on the server—select the Publish All Pages option button in the Publish Web dialog box.

✦   ✦   ✦

Creating Web Pages in Other Office Applications

FrontPage is a wonderful tool for designing and creating Web pages, but the fact is, so are most of the rest of the applications in Office. That's because Office makes very little distinction between Web pages and other types of documents — which means that for Web page design, you have at your disposal Office's complete cornucopia of sophisticated features for text editing, graphics design, and document layout.

This chapter will tell you what you need to know to build beautiful Web pages in Word and PowerPoint and create dynamic, interactive Web pages with Excel and Access.

Authoring Web Pages in Office

Turning an Office document into a Web page is as easy as choosing File ➪ Save As Web Page and supplying a filename. Microsoft has struggled mightily to turn HTML into an alternative standard file format for Office documents. When you save a document as a Web page, all the content and formatting is preserved in the HTML file. Even if some elements don't appear correctly when the page is displayed in a browser, the document should function properly again when you reopen it in the original application.

Understanding XML

When saving a document as a Web page, Office relies on the Extensible Markup Language, or XML, to represent formatting, content, and other elements that can't be converted faithfully into conventional HTML code. XML is a simple standard format for representing structured data using ordinary text. In an Office document stored as a Web page, XML code is embedded into the body of the HTML file within HTML comments. When a browser that doesn't understand XML opens the file, it ignores these comments, but their content remains intact and can be read by Office applications.

New Feature

In Word, you now have the option of removing this XML from documents you save as Web pages, making the file size smaller. Choose File ⇨ Save as Web Page, then, in the File of Type list box, drop down and choose Web Page, Filtered.

Cross-Reference

Access and Excel now have enhanced ability to use and understand XML. See the section on creating interactive Web pages later in this chapter.

Previewing documents in your browser

In Excel, Word, and PowerPoint, you can view any open document in your browser to see how it will look as a Web page. You don't need to save the document first. Choose File ⇨ Web Page Preview to start the browser and load it with a temporary Web page version of the document.

Changing Web page titles

A Web page's title appears in the browser's title bar when you're viewing the page. The browser also stores the title on the history and favorites lists. Because the title will be publicly visible, give it some thought. If you don't assign a title of your own, Office uses the document's filename for that purpose. You can change the title in the Summary tab of the File ⇨ Properties dialog box, or by clicking the Change Title button in the Save As Web Page dialog box.

Setting options for Web pages

Each Office application provides settings that control the way its documents are converted into Web pages. For example, you can decide where to store supporting files, select a format for graphics files, and choose an encoding scheme so the correct characters are displayed in non-English Web pages. These settings are located on the Web Options dialog box. Reach it by opening the Tools ⇨ Options dialog box, switching to the General tab, and clicking the Web Options button.

Note

Some settings on the Web Options dialog box vary from application to application, but many of them are common to multiple Office programs. When this is the case, changing the settings in one application changes them throughout Office.

HTML: The Language of the Web

Hypertext Markup Language (HTML) is the language of the Web. It consists of instructions called tags, which are placed into the body of a simple ASCII text file. Files containing these tags are called HTML files, naturally enough, and are identified by the .HTM or .HTML extension. When a Web browser such as Microsoft Internet Explorer or Netscape Navigator opens an HTML file, it translates the tags and other information the file contains into a formatted document on your screen. A Web page you open with your browser corresponds to an HTML file.

Most HTML tags are paired, enclosing the information that the tag relates to. As a simple example, in the sequence `<B>great</B>` the characters in angle brackets are the paired tag for bold type. They enclose the word `great`, telling your browser to display that word in bold.

The HTML language includes scores of different tags encompassing a wide range of functionality. Some govern the appearance of elements on Web pages, making a word bold, displaying a table, or telling the browser to display a specific graphical image. Some tags control placement of text and graphics. Other tags define links to other HTML files (pages) or other sites. Form-related tags define Web page fields that can be filled out by the reader, enabling your pages to receive, store, and analyze various types of information. Still other tags activate other programs to perform functions such as returning information from a database. You can even use tags to play sound files in the background or display video clips.

Regardless of the operating system on which a browser is running, a given Web page appears basically the same. Thus, you can create and publish a single HTML document on the Web, knowing that millions of people can view it and that each of them sees what you designed, as you designed it. (There are exceptions, but this is the theory and intention of the Web's designers and of the HTML language.)

If you're interested in learning more about the HTML language, you'll find dozens of books on the subject. Of course, the Web itself is an excellent resource for this information. Go to one of the popular search sites, such as Yahoo!, and search for *html* — you'll find listings for the overseer of the HTML language, the World Wide Web Consortium (W3 Consortium), along with many other sites that offer specifications, training, tips, and other information about HTML.

Planning Your Site and Managing Your Files

Before you begin work on your Web site in earnest, take a few minutes to sketch the overall plan for your site. It won't hurt to define your goals for the site briefly but in writing, so you can be sure that your efforts are concentrated where they belong. Every page in your site should make a contribution that is consistent with this informal mission statement.

Determining the location for your finished site

You should know in advance where the finished site will be housed. The capabilities of the computer or *server* on which the site resides determine what content you add to your pages. If you have a direct connection to the Internet and are setting up the site on your own NT-based server, limitations will be few. But if you use an ISP or plan to place the site on a private intranet, you should check with the powers that be to identify content that will and won't play on the server. Ask specifically about support for forms, image maps, Active Server Pages, ActiveX controls, and the FrontPage and Office Server Extensions.

Making allowances for browser capabilities

The capabilities of the browser can also place limitations on what content the user can successfully access. It's important to plan your pages accordingly. HTML is a dynamic and rapidly evolving language. New tags are added to the language with each version, adding features that allow for increasingly sophisticated Web sites. The downside of this progress is that older browsers are unable to interpret the new commands. HTML pages produced by Office include many of the latest HTML tags, designed for viewing with up-to-date browsers. In most cases you can view pages containing the newer tags with older Web browsers, but they may look significantly different, and some of the content may not appear at all.

If you're publishing your Web site to a private intranet in a tightly standardized organization, every user should have the same browser. In this case, your work is simplified — you can plan your documents according to the features of the target browser and Office sees to it that your pages contain the correct features. (In PowerPoint and Word, you can set options that automatically adapt your documents to the demands of specific browsers.)

By contrast, browser chaos reigns on the Internet, and at many institutions, too. Although Netscape Navigator and Microsoft Internet Explorer own the vast majority of the browser market, plenty of people do use other browsers. More important, older versions of Navigator and IE are still in wide use. A lowest-common-denominator strategy is one solution. Office provides you with some help. One of the tabs in the Web Options dialog box is labeled Browsers (see Figure 45-1). On this tab you can allow or disallow a number of formatting options. You can also choose from a list of browsers, starting with Microsoft Internet Explorer 6.0 or later, all the way down to Microsoft Internet Explorer 3.0, Netscape Navigator 3.0, or later. Based on your choices, Office will allow or disallow certain features.

The problem with accommodating only the lowest common denominator is that you limit the potential appeal of your site and may alienate those who do have up-to-date browsers. In many cases your best choice is to go ahead and use all the features that you like and leave the users to worry about their browser's capabilities. After all, browsers are free and easy to get. Someone who chooses not to update his or her browser is probably not too concerned about the latest and greatest features.

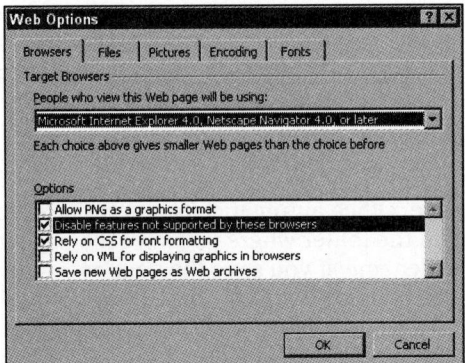

Figure 45-1: The Web Options dialog box includes a tab that lets you specify what kind of browser most viewers of your page will be using.

Tip   I do recommend that you inform your audience that you're using features that require one or more particular browsers—a small "best viewed with" message will do.

The most ambitious approach is to build code into your pages that determines which browser is running and displays the appropriate content accordingly. That option requires lots of work but is the best solution for highly visible sites. You'll have to consult books or other resources on HTML for the techniques required.

Managing files

If you're developing or working with a Web site of more than several pages, you should do some planning to avoid confusion as the site grows.

Planning your site's folders

To plan a logical hierarchy for your site, sketch it out using an organizational chart format. For example, let's say that you have a site with pages under the headings of Our Company, Personnel, Products, Employment Opportunities, and Feedback. You might set up a file structure on your hard disk consisting of a main folder called Web Pages, with subfolders named for each of these headings and perhaps another subfolder for images. As you create your pages, save them in the appropriate folders and place the images you'll be using in the Images folder.

Note   Software that specializes in Web site management can help you organize your site and make sure that every file is in its proper place. The obvious choice is FrontPage, bundled with Office XP Professional Special Edition or Office XP Developer (and the subject of Chapters 43 and 44) — but if you're reading this chapter first and ignoring those two chapters, you probably have a version of Office without FrontPage!

Caution

You may not have free rein to organize your site as you see fit—your organization, or your Internet service provider, may enforce standards as to the folders your site should contain, and which types of files belong in which folder. Be sure you're aware of any such mandates before you start work in earnest.

Dealing with Office's automatic support folders

When you save a document as a Web page, Office automatically creates a subfolder for the page's supporting files. Located in the folder where you save the page itself, the subfolder is named after the page's filename. If you save the page as HomePage.htm, the support folder will be called HomePage_files. In this subfolder go all the graphics, sound and video clips, and whatnot—all the elements that belong to the page but are housed in separate files. These files receive filenames automatically, if they don't already have them. (If you prefer to store the support files in the same folder as the page, clear the Organize Supporting Files in a Folder checkbox on the Files tab of the Web Options dialog box.)

Office keeps up with its housekeeping as your page evolves. If you delete a graphic from the page, the corresponding file is automatically removed from your disk the next time you save the page. You're on your own, though, if you move or copy the page to another location. You must also move or copy the supporting subfolder and its contents (or the files only, if you aren't using a subfolder) to the same destination.

Note

Although Office's automated file management system for Web pages prevents chaos on your hard disk, it's likely to conflict with the one you choose for your site as a whole. Typically, you're going to be using some graphics on many different pages. Instead of storing separate copies of their files in each page's subfolders, you should place the common images in a folder shared by all pages. Also, you may simply prefer to organize support files by type or content. Unfortunately, you can't specify alternative locations for support files individually. For that matter, you can't supply your own names for the support files. To take matters into your own hands, you need a dedicated page editor such as FrontPage, or you must edit the HTML code for the page yourself.

Working with Hyperlinks

You insert hyperlinks in Office applications other than FrontPage the same way you insert them in FrontPage—by selecting what you want to apply the hyperlink to and choosing Insert ➪ Hyperlink or pressing Ctrl+K. For details on using the Insert Hyperlink dialog box, see Chapter 43.

What follows here is some additional information on using hyperlinks in Office applications other than FrontPage.

Note

Hyperlinks can be inserted in ordinary Office documents not intended to be saved as Web pages, and can link not only to Web pages but to other ordinary Office documents. Although this chapter focuses on creating Web pages with Office, this seems as good a place as any to discuss these features, too.

Jumping to specific locations in documents

Although many hyperlinks just take you to the beginning of a Web page or document, your hyperlinks can jump to particular places within those same files. You can create hyperlinks to specific locations in the current document or in any other document.

You can call on three different methods to create these well-aimed hyperlinks: dragging and dropping the hyperlink content, copying and pasting it, or using the Insert Hyperlink dialog box. The first two methods are quick and easy, especially because they don't require you to first create named locations in the target document (the one the hyperlink will jump to). The Insert Hyperlink dialog box lets you work with documents that aren't currently open; it seems to be the only reliable route to hyperlinks that jump to named locations in Web pages.

 **Note**   Before you can create a hyperlink to a specific location in a document, you must save the target document first. This isn't a safety step — the method only works if the file is saved first.

Dragging Office content to create hyperlinks

The easiest way to create a hyperlink within an Office document or from one Office document to another is via drag and drop. Here are the steps required:

1. Open the target document if necessary, and be sure to save it.

2. Select the destination text or graphics in the target document.

    At this step, you're choosing the specific location that appears when the user clicks the hyperlink. (If the destination is a PowerPoint slide, you can select any text or graphic, because hyperlinks to individual items on a slide aren't allowed.)

3. Using the right mouse button, drag the selection to the document that is to contain the hyperlink.

    Unless you're creating a hyperlink within the target document, or unless both documents are visible simultaneously on the screen, you must drag the selection to the Windows taskbar, holding the mouse pointer over the icon for the target application or document until the application itself appears. Without releasing the button, continue dragging into the body of the document.

4. When you get to the location where you want the hyperlink to appear, release the mouse button.

    On the shortcut menu that appears, choose Create Hyperlink Here. (If you're creating the hyperlink within a PowerPoint presentation, release the mouse button over the destination slide in the outline pane.)

Creating a hyperlink via the Clipboard

To create a hyperlink to a specific location via the Clipboard, open the target document, or create and save it. Select the destination text or graphics in the target document and copy the selection to the Clipboard. Switch to the document that is to contain the hyperlink and choose Edit ➪ Paste as Hyperlink.

Creating location-specific hyperlinks using a dialog box

The Insert Hyperlink dialog box is the refined way to create a hyperlink to a particular spot in an Office document or Web page. The target document should already be saved in an accessible location, but it doesn't have to be open. In the document where you're placing the hyperlink, choose Insert ➪ Hyperlink to bring up the dialog box. Proceed as follows:

✦ If the hyperlink's destination is in the same document, click the Place in This Document button (in Access, the button is Object in This Database). You're presented with a list of locations in the current document.

✦ If the destination is in a different document, stick with the Existing File or Web Page button instead. After you locate the target Web page or Office document, click Bookmarks. A dialog box containing linkable locations in the document appears.

This technique works well, as long as the location you want to jump to appears in the list of bookmarks. In Word and Excel, you can create your own named bookmarks or ranges as destinations.

Bookmarks in Word documents

To create a bookmark in a Word document — or in a Web page that you're creating in Word — position the insertion point where you want the bookmark to go and then choose Insert ➪ Bookmark. The Bookmark dialog box opens, enabling you to enter a Bookmark name (see Figure 45-2).

Figure 45-2: Use Word's Bookmark dialog box to insert a bookmark that is then available as a hyperlink destination.

Cross-Reference   Chapter 17 has more on Word bookmarks.

Hyperlinks provide the next best thing to cross-document bookmarks in Word. Word lacks a command to "Go To" specific hyperlinks. But if you bookmark the hyperlink itself, you can use the Go To command to jump to the hyperlink (actually to its bookmark) and then click the hyperlink to get to your final destination in another document.

Bookmarks in Excel worksheets

Create a "bookmark" in an Excel worksheet by naming a range of one or more cells. Highlight the cell(s) you want to mark and then choose Insert ➪ Name ➪ Define. The Define Name dialog box opens, enabling you to enter a name for the selected cells, which are also specified in the Refers To: entry (see Figure 45-3). You can read more about named ranges in Excel in Chapter 24.

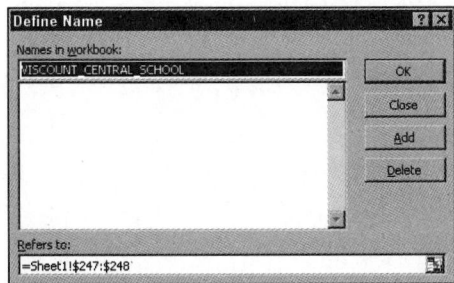

Figure 45-3: After naming a range of cells in this dialog box, you can set up a hyperlink that jumps to the named range.

Controlling the look of your hyperlinks

Office programs give you varying degrees of control over the appearance of hyperlinks. Depending on the application, you can dictate color, font, and underlining style for hyperlinks as they appear before and after they've been followed (clicked).

Formatting hyperlinks in Word and Excel

Use styles to control the look of your hyperlinks in a Word document or throughout an Excel workbook.

In Word, choose Format ➪ Styles and Formatting, or click the Styles and Formatting button on the Formatting toolbar, to open the Styles and Formatting task pane. Choose All Styles from the Show listbox at the bottom of the pane. In the list of styles, the ones you want are Hyperlink, for links that haven't been followed yet, and `FollowedHyperlink`. Choose Modify from the menu that opens when you click the downward-pointing arrow to the right of the style name. All Word text effects are available.

Note   This might be one suitable place for animated text, though text animation won't be visible if you save the document as a Web page and display it in a browser.

Cross-Reference   Themes provide a great alternative to styles for formatting Web pages that include hyperlinks. See "Working with themes," later in this chapter.

In Excel (by contrast), you must first insert a hyperlink, then choose Format ➪ Style. The Style dialog box opens (see Figure 45-4). Choose Hyperlink from the list and click Modify to make your changes to it. To change the style of a followed hyperlink, you must first follow a hyperlink; then Followed Hyperlink becomes available in the list of styles in the Format ➪ Style dialog box.

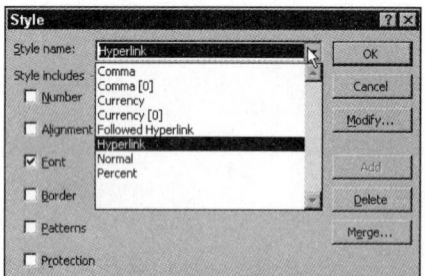

Figure 45-4: Use Excel's Style dialog box to set the formatting for hyperlinks and followed hyperlinks.

Setting hyperlink appearance in PowerPoint

In PowerPoint, the text color of your hyperlinks is determined by each slide's color scheme. To change or customize the color scheme, choose Format ➪ Slide Design to open the Slide Design task pane, then click the Color Schemes link to open the menu of available color schemes. Each scheme includes its own rules for hyperlinks and followed hyperlinks. Click the Edit Color Schemes list at the bottom of the task pane to change the preset rules; choose Accent and hyperlink or Accent and followed hyperlink from the Custom tab of the Edit Color Scheme dialog box, then choose the color you want (see Figure 45-5).

Changing hyperlink options in Access

To set the color of hyperlinks in an Access database, open the Tools ➪ Options dialog box. There, switch to the General tab and click Web Options. In Access, this dialog box is devoted entirely to the appearance of your hyperlinks. You can choose a color for regular and followed hyperlinks, and turn underlining on or off.

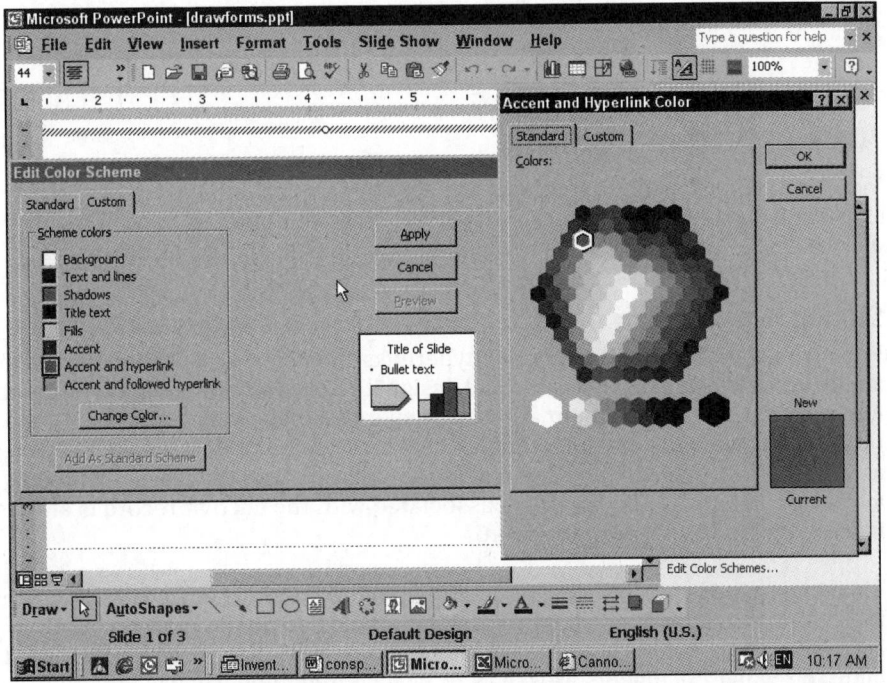

Figure 45-5: PowerPoint lets you alter the preset colors for hyperlinks and followed hyperlinks by editing color schemes.

Word and hyperlinks

This section treats a couple of hyperlink-related features that are unique to Word.

Automatic hyperlinks in Word

By default, Word automatically converts URLs and filenames into hyperlinks as you type them in your documents. This behavior can be a bit disconcerting when you're writing a book about the Web, but if you actually plan to use the hyperlinks that you type, it's very handy. To turn automatic hyperlinks on or off, open the AutoFormat as you Type tab of the Tools ⇨ AutoCorrect Options dialog box and check or clear the box labeled Internet and Network Paths with Hyperlinks. To convert an existing document's text into live hyperlinks, use the Format ⇨ AutoFormat command, choosing Options before proceeding to be sure the conversion setting is turned on.

Using HYPERLINK field switches in Word

A hyperlink inserted into a Word document is placed there in the form of a HYPER-LINK field. You can manually insert switches in the field after the linked filename or URL to control the hyperlink's behavior.

 **Cross-Reference** See Chapter 21 for details on controlling hyperlinks.

Access and hyperlinks

In Access, you can store hyperlinks as data directly in a database table using a Hyperlink data field, and you can assign hyperlinks to buttons or other controls on a form. These two methods have different functions in an Access database.

Storing hyperlinks in fields

When you want to keep track of the hyperlinks themselves as part of each record in a table, create a field in that table and assign it to the Hyperlink data type by choosing Insert ➪ Hyperlink Column. After the hyperlinks have been entered into the table, you can access any hyperlink by clicking it in the table itself. In addition, just as with any Access field, you can display a hyperlink field on a form by binding it to a text box. That way, the hyperlink associated with the current record is always visible as you flip from record to record.

This approach is appropriate if you happen to be designing a Favorite Web Sites table, but you can also use fields of the Hyperlink data type to store e-mail addresses or personal Web pages in a Contacts table. Also, because hyperlinks can jump to regular documents as well as to Web content, you can use hyperlink fields to create document archiving and retrieval databases with live links to the actual documents. The user just clicks the hyperlink to see the document and doesn't have to go hunting for it in a folder based on keywords or a description.

To add a text box that's bound to a hyperlink field to a form, start by opening the form. To be on the safe side, check the form's RecordSource property, which should be set to the table with the hyperlink field, or to a corresponding query. Now you're ready to place the field onto the form. Just click the Field List button on the Form Design toolbar. Locate the field containing the hyperlink data and drag it from the list onto the form.

Placing hyperlinks on controls

Often it makes sense to give users a stable jump gate to one Web site, document, or database object — a hyperlink that points to the same target no matter which record they're working with on the form. To set this up, use the control's HyperlinkAddress and HyperlinkSubAddress properties. After placing the control on the form in Design view, you can set these properties to point to the URL or document you want the control to jump to. When you select either HyperlinkAddress and HyperlinkSubAddress in the control's Properties dialog box, the button that appears to the right of the field (shown in Figure 45-6) pops up the Insert Hyperlink dialog box.

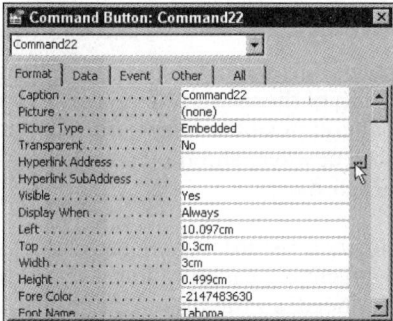

Figure 45-6: Click the little button to the right of the field for the Hyperlink Address property to display the Insert Hyperlink dialog box.

To create a hyperlink button, you must add the button to the form and then add the hyperlink to the button. You can insert a label containing a hyperlink in one step: Click the Insert Hyperlink button or choose Insert ➪ Hyperlink. After creating a hyperlink control, you can edit the text displayed on the control without affecting the underlying hyperlink. To change the text, you can click the text directly so a blinking insertion point appears, or use the control's `Caption` property.

When a hyperlink on a form is clicked, Access displays the Web toolbar, which stays on the screen even when you close the form. If this offends your sensibilities (or consumes too much space on the screen), then you must write VBA code to hide the toolbar for the form's `OnClose` event.

PowerPoint and hyperlinks

Hyperlinks in a PowerPoint presentation are active for one-click jumps only when you view the presentation as a slide show. To follow a hyperlink in a slide you're editing, right-click it and choose Open Hyperlink in the resulting shortcut menu.

Cross-Reference

As discussed in Chapter 39, PowerPoint action buttons provide an alternative way to insert hyperlinks. You assign hyperlinks to an action button using the Action Settings dialog box that appears at the time you insert it, or when you right-click the button and choose Hyperlink from the shortcut menu.

About Graphics in Office-created Web Pages

When you save an Office document as an HTML file, the application stores each graphic in the document in a separate file. The file format used to store a given graphic depends on the type of image, the number of colors it contains, and settings in the Web Options dialog box. The file format chosen has an impact on performance and image quality, so it pays to be aware of these technicalities.

Working with GIF and JPEG images

Traditionally, Web browsers have been capable of displaying two types of image files, GIF (.gif) and JPEG (.jpeg or .jpg). Both of these are bitmap (raster) formats, which represent the individual dots that compose the image. Both GIF and JPEG compress the original image, but in different ways, and they have other differences as well. Here's a summary of their characteristics:

✦ To compress files, the GIF approach finds and records where large blocks of the same color are located rather than specifying each dot in these blocks individually. Several GIF files can be interlaced, so the browser first displays every other line of dots and then fills in the missing lines. Interlacing lets the user see the entire image sooner, albeit fuzzily at first. You can also specify a transparent color in a GIF image, so the Web page underneath the image shows through everywhere that color appears. This is great for making it look like you've placed an irregularly shaped object directly onto a page, rather than on a rectangular field that blots out the page beneath. Finally, GIF files support simple animations by storing multiple images that are displayed in succession.

✦ JPEG compares the color value of adjacent pixels and records the differences between them. JPEG compression can be adjusted to ignore different degrees of color difference between pixels. The greater the difference that it ignores, the less information it records, resulting in smaller files but reduced image quality.

The bottom line: GIF is best suited for images such as logos and icons, and JPEG is best for images with many colors such as photographs, or illustrations that contain smooth gradations.

When you import an image in either format, Office preserves that format when it saves the page. If you import an image in a different format, however, Office chooses the format that best suits the image.

Saving graphics in PNG format

Portable Network Graphics (PNG) is a newer bitmap format that produces images of high quality but smaller size than JPEG or GIF. However, PNG isn't a good choice for use on the Internet at this point, because only the newest browsers can display PNG files.

Tip   If you know that all your users have Internet Explorer 5 or later (or another PNG-savvy browser), enable this format in the Options section of the Browsers tab of the Web Options dialog box. There, check the box labeled Allow PNG as a graphics format. (If you choose Microsoft Internet Explorer 6.0 or later from the list of browsers, this option is turned on automatically.) When you're done, Office stores Web page graphics in the PNG format — except for those images you import specifically as JPEG or GIF files.

Using vector graphics in Web pages

Vector (line) graphics represent images by describing them mathematically, rather than by storing information about individual dots. They are superior to bitmaps in two important ways: they're smaller, so they download faster, and they are resolution-independent, so they maintain a sharp appearance as you zoom in or out.

Office XP supports the use of vector graphics in Web pages with its Vector Markup Language (VML).

A VML graphic appears in the code for a Web page as an HTML tag. Within the tag, data describing the graphic's shape, color, and other characteristics are stored using XML coding conventions. In other words, the graphic data are part and parcel of the Web page itself, and are not stored in a separate file as they would be with a bitmap picture. Here's an example of the VML code for a simple blue oval:

```
<v:oval style='width:150 pt;height:75 pt' fillcolor="blue">
</v:oval>
```

Although you can create graphics by writing VML code, most Office Web page designers aren't that masochistic. Office automatically generates VML code for graphics you create using the standard Office drawing tools covered in Chapter 9.

Vector graphics are great, but once again, the big drawback to adopting an Office 2000 innovation is incompatibility. Only Internet Explorer 5 or above can display VML images. If all your users have that level of browser capability, you can turn on VML support in the Options area of the Browsers tab of the Web Options dialog box (choose Tools ➪ Options, then choose Web Options from the bottom of the Options dialog box). Check the box labeled Rely on VML for displaying graphics in browsers. With this box checked, Office won't generate bitmaps for images that it can represent using VML.

Note   This option is turned on automatically if you choose Microsoft Internet Explorer 5.0 or later from the list of browsers — or (naturally) Microsoft Internet Explorer 6.0 or later.

Editing HTML Code in Office

Office applications make it easy to view and edit the HTML code representing a document. After you've saved or opened an HTML-format document, the View ➪ HTML Source command becomes available. Choose this command to open the code in the Microsoft Script Editor, described later in this chapter. Opened using the HTML Source command, the Script Editor displays a simple two-window layout — the source-code pane occupies most of the screen, but the Project Explorer window is also visible. Close the Project Explorer to see more code. The Script Editor displays HTML code in various colors to designate tags, attributes, and values. You can edit the code as you would in a typical Windows text editor.

If the HTML Source command isn't listed on the View menu (and by default, it only shows up in Word), add it from the Commands tab of the Tools ➪ Customize dialog box. Select View in the Categories and then scroll the Commands list until you find the HTML Source command. Drag it up to the View menu or another suitable destination. The Script Editor is also available from the Tools ➪ Macro submenu, but its layout is busier when you activate it that way.

Cross-Reference

We'll look at the Microsoft Script Editor in a bit more detail at the end of this chapter.

Web Page Authoring with Word

Word is a natural as a Web page editor. After all, tasks such as text editing, graphics design, and layout apply equally to print and electronic documents, and Word performs all these tasks superbly. Add in a panoply of special Web page authoring features, and Word should satisfy your need for a powerful, all-purpose page development tool.

You face no special challenge when turning any document into a Web page that can be viewed in a browser. A quick trip to the File ➪ Save As Web Page dialog box is all that's required. If you haven't yet created the document, however, Word provides a set of templates to further ease the design process, and a wizard to help you construct an entire Web site in no time flat.

Basing new Web pages on templates

To create a new blank Web page, choose File ➪ New to open the New Document task pane, and then choose Blank Web Page from the New section. All you're really doing is starting a new empty document based on the Normal template, and switching to Web Layout view. However, Word also offers templates that include some content to help you get started with a new page's design. Choose the General templates option from the New from template section of the New Document task pane, and look under the Web Pages tab of the Templates dialog box. When you access a template this way, you can't see what a page based on the templates will look like until you create the new document—when you use the Web Page Wizard, you get to see a sample document ahead of time (read on).

Using Word's Web Page Wizard

Word's "Web Page Wizard," also found on the Web Pages tab of the Templates dialog box, is misnamed—it's really a Web site wizard. You can use it for single pages, but it's most useful when you're undertaking a brand new multiple-page site.

The wizard starts by asking you for the title of your new Web site and the folder where you want to store it. Simple enough. The next wizard panel, shown in

Figure 45-7, lets you choose whether to include automatic navigation frames in your pages, and if so, how they should be oriented (frames are introduced in "Working with frames in Word," later in this chapter).

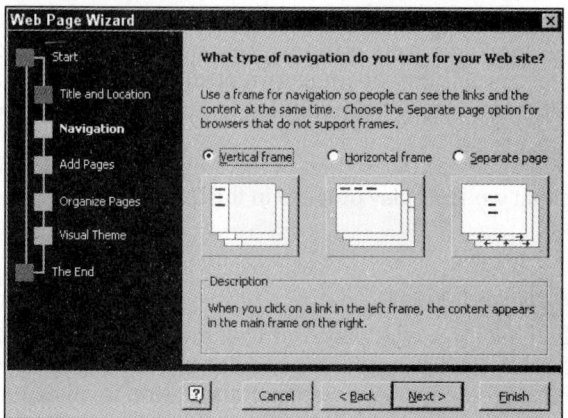

Figure 45-7: Working with Word's Web Page Wizard

In the third panel you get down to the business of adding pages to your new site. The buttons here let you create new blank pages or new pages based on Word templates, or add extant pages already available on your disk or the network. When you click the Add Template Page button, Word displays a secondary dialog box that lists the available templates. As you select the different templates in this box, Word shows you how a document based on the selected template would appear, which makes it a lot easier to choose the template that's best suited for your design goals. Because you're going to be modifying the page with your own information, don't worry if you don't find exactly what you want among the selections available.

Note The Add Existing File button works fine for Web pages created in Word or outside of Office. However, if the page you're trying to add was created in another Office application, opening it the usual way won't add it to your new Web site — instead, that other application will try to open it. You must select the page, click the arrow bar at the right of the Open button, and choose Open in Microsoft Word.

After you've assembled the pages, the next panel in the wizard lets you shuffle their order. You can't create a multiple-level hierarchy of pages, but you can specify the order in which pages appear in the navigation frame created by the wizard.

The final wizard panel lets you choose a theme for all the pages in the site. Themes are discussed in "Working with themes" later in this chapter. When you've made your selection, choose Finish. All the Web pages you've created open for editing in Word.

Editing Web pages in Word

Although you can save a Word document from any view, Word's Web Layout view is the one to use if you want to work on the document pretty much as it will look in a browser. Web Layout view disables formatting features that don't work in Web pages, and it enables Web-specific components such as frames. If you create or save your document as a Web page, Word restricts it to features that browsers can display. However, aside from the unavailability of some formatting features, you can use all of Word's standard editing and layout capabilities to author your Web pages.

Tip   If you specify a browser type in the Browsers tab of the Web Options dialog box, Word disables formatting that won't display properly in the target browser, helping you with your design tasks.

Adding tables to your Word Web page

You create and modify Word tables for a Web page in the same way as you do other documents, as detailed in Chapter 19. Although many tables in Web pages have the same function they do in print documents — to display information in an orderly fashion — they also serve a critical role in formatting. Text, graphics, and form elements placed directly on a Web page get moved around by the browser according to factors such as the size of the window and the fonts in use. By inserting those elements in a table, however, you can keep them where you want them. Tables are often used to create columnar layouts in Web pages, because true columns aren't available in HTML.

Cross-Reference   For more on using tables in Web pages, see Chapter 43.

Inserting horizontal lines

Horizontal dividing lines are a commonly used formatting element in Web pages. To add one to your Word document, place the insertion point where you want the line and choose Format ➪ Borders and Shading. Clicking the Horizontal Line button in the resulting dialog box opens a gallery of graphical lines from the Clip Organizer. You can repeatedly insert the same line by clicking the Horizontal Line button on the Tables and Borders toolbar.

Adding scrolling text

To have text scroll across your page like a marquee sign, click the Scrolling Text button on the Web Tools toolbar. Enter the text in the dialog box that appears. After you OK the box you can change the font and other formatting for the scrolling text. First click the Design Mode button on the Web Tools toolbar (if this toolbar isn't visible activate it from the View ➪ Toolbars menu). You can then select the scrolling text element and access the relevant commands on the Format menu.

Working with themes

In the Office lexicon, a *theme* represents a comprehensive design template for Web pages. A theme dictates the page's color scheme, specifies the graphics used for the background image, horizontal lines, and bullets, and determines the fonts to be used for each text style (body text, headings, bulleted points, and so on). By applying a theme to a Web page, you set the look of all these design elements in one step. And if you use the same theme for every page in your site, you automatically ensure that all the pages share a consistent look.

Themes are available in Access and FrontPage as well as Word, which gives you a no-hassle way to stick to a common design in all three programs. And although Office comes with loads of prefab themes, you can design your own using FrontPage — see Chapter 44 for details.

In Word, apply a theme to any document by choosing Format ➪ Theme. The Theme dialog box (see Figure 45-8) lists the available themes and displays a sample of the one currently selected in the list. Note that each theme has three optional variants: vivid colors, active graphics, and background image. You can turn these on or off independently using the relevant checkboxes.

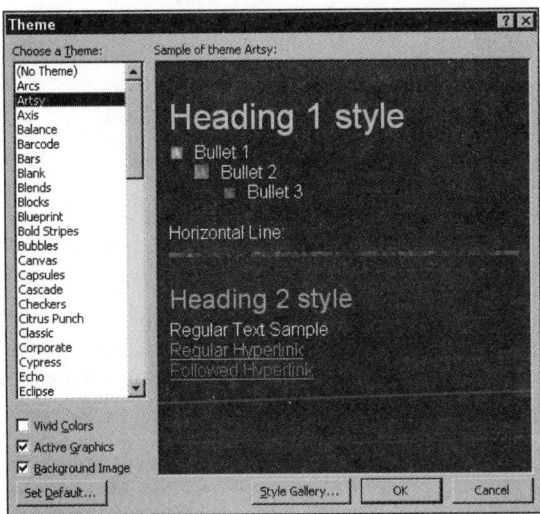

Figure 45-8: Choose themes from this dialog box

Caution Don't click the Style Gallery button. Doing so displays Word's Style Gallery, which lists and shows samples of Word templates, not themes, and you can't get back to the Themes dialog box directly.

In Access, you can assign themes only to data access pages, which are covered later in this chapter.

Working with frames in Word

Frames divide the browser window into sections that act independently of one another. In the most typical configuration, a header containing a logo and other static information appears in a frame at the top of the browser window, a menu of navigation hyperlinks is shown in a frame on the left; the page of interest is shown in a frame on the right. Technically, each frame displays a separate Web page. That's why frames are so handy for navigation — while one frame displays a constant page containing navigation links, another can show different pages according to which link has been clicked. A *frames page* is a special page that serves as a container for the various frames to be displayed. Opening the frames page displays the frames it contains and their contents.

Word knows how to build frames and frames pages; if you want to use them, you can quite easily do so. But while frames have their advantages, they have drawbacks, too. Chief among these is that some Web zealots hate them and love to let you know how strongly they feel. Don't be surprised if your gorgeous frame-based page design draws harsh words from some inspired, articulate critics (with nothing better to do).

Using the Frames toolbar and menu

Shown in Figure 45-9, the Frames toolbar gives you access to most of the commands you need to create and tweak frames in Word. It appears automatically when you work with a frames page.

Figure 45-9: Word's Frames toolbar

Creating a frames page

Word's Web Page Wizard offers an easy path to creating a simple frames page containing two frames. If you want a different or fancier design, you can create a new frames page from scratch, or modify the wizard's work.

To create a new frames page based on the document that's currently open in Word, choose Format ⇨ Frames ⇨ New Frames Page. It doesn't matter whether the document you start from is a Web page or an ordinary Word document. Word creates a new document — this is the frames page — and opens it in Web Layout view. At this point, the new frames page contains only one frame. Because that frame fills the whole window, and because the frame in turn contains the document you started with, you probably won't be able to tell that anything has changed. If you look at the title bar, however, you'll see the title of the new document, not that of the document you started with.

You use standard editing and formatting techniques to edit a document displayed in a frame. Save the frames page as you would any other Word document. When you do, Word saves the frames page itself and the documents in all of its frames.

> **Tip**
>
> To give the document contained in an individual frame a different name or store it in another location, you can save only that document: Right-click in the frame and choose Save Current Frame As. The standard Save As dialog box appears. From there, you know the drill.

Adding and deleting frames on a frames page

Add frames to a frames page by clicking one of the New Frame buttons on the Frames toolbar or by using one of the corresponding commands on the Format ⇨ Frames menu. Word creates a new document for each new frame, automatically assigning it a name when you save the frames page. To delete a frame, click inside it and then click the Delete Frame button.

Working with frame properties

Formatting options and other settings for frames are few in number and easy to learn. You control them in the Frame Properties dialog box, shown in Figure 45-10. To display it, click the target frame to select it. Then click the Frame Properties button at the right of the Frames toolbar or choose Format ⇨ Frames ⇨ Frame Properties (note that when you're working in a frames page, the commands from the Frames toolbar are also available on the Format ⇨ Frames submenu).

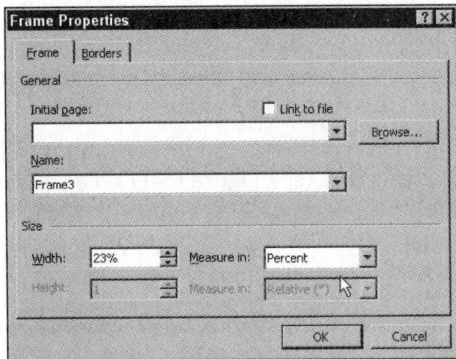

Figure 45-10: The Frame Properties dialog box lets you control the content and format of Web page frames.

Specifying a frame's name and initial Web page

Each frame has a name. You need the name to control the frame's content by hyperlinks you insert into another frame. Word assigns to each frame a name for you, but you can change the name in the Frame tab of the Frame Properties dialog box. Also on the Frame tab, the `Initial page` field lists the page or document that's currently displayed in the frame. To display a different page when the frames page is opened, enter its filename in the Initial page field.

Formatting frames

To size a pair of adjacent frames in Word, drag the frame border, if it's visible, to a new position. If the border is hidden, or if you want more precise control, you can use the Width and Height settings on the Frame tab of the Frame Properties dialog box to specify a frame's size. Settings that directly affect the borders themselves are on the Borders tab of the Frame Properties dialog box. You can choose whether or not the borders are visible, how wide they are, and their color. Clear the *Frame is resizable in browser* box if you don't want users to change frame size. Scrollbar options for the selected frame are also located here.

Inserting hyperlinks in frames

Because frames are most often used to provide Web site navigation, mastery of the techniques required to fill them with hyperlinks won't hurt. In the typical scenario, a page containing a series of hyperlinks occupies the frame on the left; clicking one of these hyperlinks displays a particular page in the frame on the right. Working in the leftmost frame, here's how to set up each of its hyperlinks:

1. Identify the location for the hyperlink. If you want to use a graphical button for your hyperlink, insert it into the left frame and select it. For a text hyperlink, just click in the frame where you want the hyperlink to reside.

2. Open the Insert Hyperlink dialog box. Use the Insert ➪ Hyperlink command, or click the corresponding toolbar button.

3. Create the hyperlink. Type in the hyperlink text and identify the page or other document that you want it to open in the right-hand frame.

4. Click Target Frame, and specify the frame where the target document will be displayed in the Set Target Frame dialog box (see Figure 45-11). The easiest way is to click inside the Current frames page box; the frame you select will turn black.. If you prefer, you can use the drop-down list to identify the frame by name.

Tip   If you forget the name of the frame, hold the mouse pointer briefly over the corresponding part of the thumbnail to see its name in a ScreenTip.

5. If you wish all hyperlinks to open in this same target pane by default, check the Set as default for all hyperlinks button.

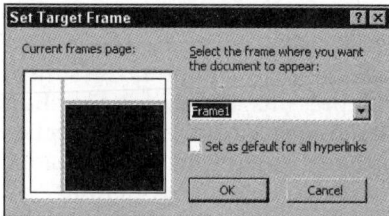

Figure 45-11: Choose which frame a hyperlink will open in using the Set Target Frame dialog box.

Building Web forms in Word

Forms are standard components of Web pages — if you've spent any time on the Web, you're bound to have come across many examples. They enable users to interact with your Web site through controls (also known as form elements) such as option buttons, checkboxes, and text boxes.

Empowering your form with scripts

Although a form control can respond visually to user interaction without any programming, it won't do much of anything useful until you endow it with a *script,* a kind of mini-program that tells it what to do. Office includes a sophisticated script editor for creating these little programs; I'll show it to you later in this chapter.

Tip

Word has the tools you need to create Web forms, all right, but to get your forms to work properly, you must know how to write scripts that power them, and how to hook those scripts up to your forms. If you have FrontPage, you're much better off creating forms with that program — FrontPage handles all those details for you, based on your entries in dialog boxes.

Creating forms

To add a form to a Web page, start by displaying the Web Tools toolbar (see Figure 45-12). It contains buttons for all the standard HTML forms controls and related functions. To insert a control, position the insertion point where you want the element to be placed, and then click the button for that element on the Web Tools toolbar. Word creates a form area in the document as soon as you insert a control from the toolbar.

Figure 45-12: The Web Tools toolbar contains what you need to add forms to Word Web pages.

As with their counterparts on VBA forms, HTML form controls have properties that you can set to govern their behavior. To set a control's properties, select it and click the Properties button. Most controls have the `Value` property. Be sure to set this — it determines the data that the control represents. In the case of a checkbox or option button, this is the value that appears in the form if the user selects the box or button. For list and drop-down boxes, the `Value` property contains the items in the list, while it specifies default text for text box and text area controls.

Adding a Submit control

Every form must have one control that the user clicks to submit his or her entries. Use the Submit control to place a standard command button on the form, or the Submit with Image control to use a graphic as your submit button. In either case, the control's `Action` property should be set to the name of the script that should run when the form is submitted. Set the `Method` property to `Post` instead of `Get` unless you want to limit the form results to 255 characters.

Using tables to format forms

A simple way to control the spacing of form elements so the page appears exactly as you want, is to create a table inside the form. The elements are then placed in cells of the table.

Here's how to be sure that the table is inside the form:

1. Place the insertion point where you want the top of the form and insert any control there by clicking the appropriate button on the Web Tools toolbar. Word creates a form area in the document and adds the control there.

2. Immediately delete the new control by selecting it and pressing Delete. The form itself remains, as indicated by lines representing its top and bottom borders.

3. Insert a table within the form. You can alter details of the table's layout as you add the controls.

Web Presentations with PowerPoint

PowerPoint presentations transfer smoothly from your computer to the Web or your company intranet. When you use the Save as Web Page command, your presentation is instantly converted into a set of Web pages, all accessible via a single master page and complete with buttons and links to navigate the site. Figure 45-13 shows a sample presentation saved in HTML format and displayed in Internet Explorer.

Note that the browser window is divided much like the Normal view in PowerPoint. The main part of the window displays the slide. A navigation bar on the left carries the titles of all the slides in the presentation — click a title to see that slide. An area below the slide is reserved for speaker notes. Running across the entire window at the bottom is a bar containing viewing controls. From left to right, these are as follows:

✦ **Outline button.** Hides or displays the outline frame.

✦ **Expand/Collapse Outline button.** Expands the outline to show subsidiary points under the slide titles, or collapses it again.

✦ **Notes button.** Hides or displays the Speaker's Notes frame.

✦ **Previous and Next buttons.** Takes you to other slides in order.

✦ **Full Screen Slide Show button.** Displays the presentation on the entire screen, as you would usually see it from within PowerPoint. The outline and speaker's notes are hidden.

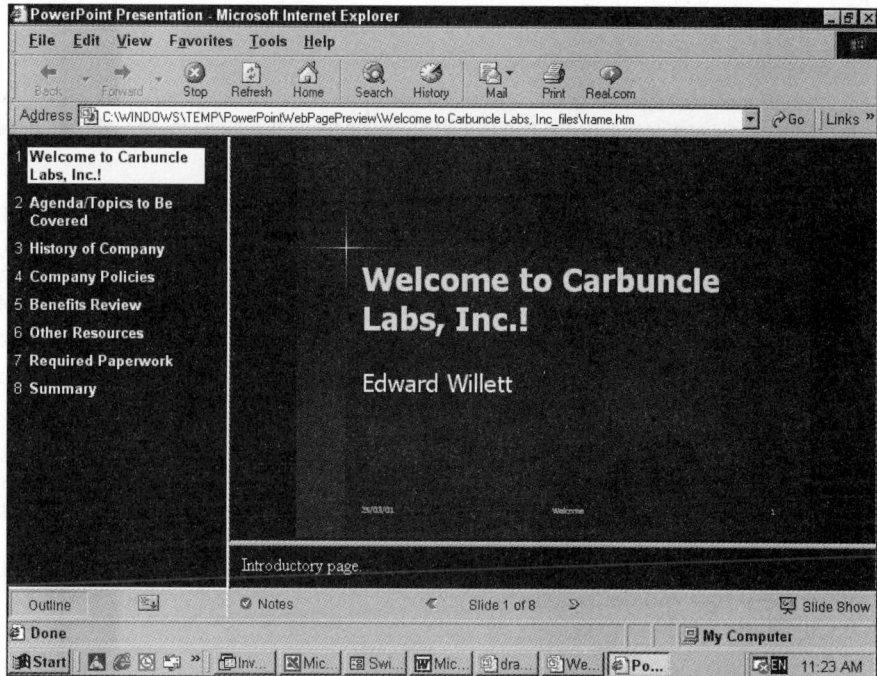

Figure 45-13: A PowerPoint presentation saved as a Web page

Saving a Web presentation

Converting an ordinary PowerPoint presentation to one for the Web is as simple as choosing the File ➪ Save as Web Page command, typing in a filename, and clicking Save. You do have options governing the way PowerPoint creates the resulting pages. To access most of them, click Publish in the Save As dialog box. The Publish As Web Page dialog box is shown in Figure 45-14.

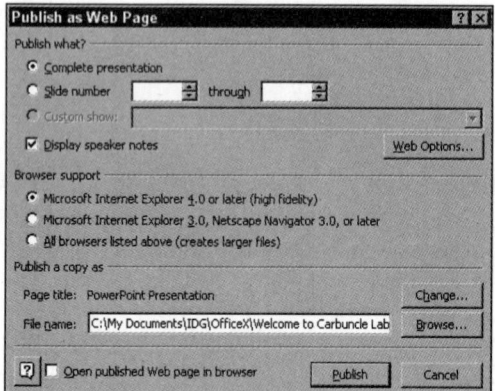

Figure 45-14: Use this dialog box to set options governing your Web presentations in PowerPoint.

Tip

Additional settings unique to PowerPoint appear in the Web Options dialog box, which you can access from the Publish box or from the General tab of the Tools ⇨ Options dialog box.

Your considerations when saving a Web-based presentation include the following:

✦ **Which slides to include.** You can include the entire presentation, select a series of slides, or choose from among the custom slide shows you've defined for the presentation, if any.

✦ **Whether to include speaker notes.** To exclude notes, clear the obvious box on the Publish dialog box.

✦ **How to handle the outline pane and control bar.** You can exclude the outline and control bar from the presentation, but don't do so casually — doing so means you can only display the first slide in the presentation. If you want to proceed, open the Web Options dialog box, and on the General tab, clear the box labeled Add Slide Navigation Controls. If you do include the outline and control bar, you get to select its color scheme using the drop-down list beneath the checkbox.

✦ **Which browser(s) to support.** You can select a target browser to tell PowerPoint how to translate presentation features into HTML code. The All Browsers choice adds code that figures out which browser is running and displays the pages appropriately.

✦ **Whether to include animation effects.** Why not, if you've taken the trouble to add animation in the first place? Maybe because you're publishing the presentation on the Internet, where animation effects won't be so impressive for users with dial-up connections. Another problem is that some animation effects don't work right or don't work at all in browsers. If all that doesn't dissuade you, go to the General tab of the Web Options dialog box and check the Slide Show Animation While Browsing box to turn on animation in the Web presentation.

Viewing a presentation in a browser

Lots of slide show features don't work properly in Web presentations, at least when you view them in a browser. These include many animation effects and action settings, as well as automatic updates of the date or time and some text formatting elements. Fewer shortcut keys for browsing the show are available. If you reopen the HTML presentation in PowerPoint, however, everything should still function.

Editing a Web presentation

You can open the Web version of a presentation in PowerPoint, edit it, and save the changes. Just remember that a Web presentation may represent a subset of the original PowerPoint document, because you can select specific slides when you first save the Web presentation. If you didn't include the entire presentation in the Web version, you're probably better off making any changes in the original PowerPoint document and then recreating the Web version from that.

Creating Interactive Pages in Office

Office Web Component controls, (introduced in Chapter 43 on the FrontPage Insert menu), include a spreadsheet control that works like a mini-Excel; a PivotTable list control, for viewing and manipulating pivot tables on a Web page; and a chart control, for working with interactive charts. Plug them into your Web pages, and people who browse your Web site gain moment-to-moment control over the information they see. Figure 45-15 shows the spreadsheet control in action in a Web page.

The only trouble is, many people won't be able to access pages that contain these components. For one thing, they work only in more recent versions of Internet Explorer. This requirement right away eliminates all the hordes of people who use other browsers. Next, a user must also have these components installed on his or her system. Otherwise, Web pages that contain them will show big empty areas where the controls belong.

The upshot of these restrictions is that until Office is as universal as the Web itself, publishing pages containing the Office Web Components will remain a dubious proposition, at least on public Web sites. If your organization standardizes on Office, however, you can put them to use on the local intranet with carefree abandon.

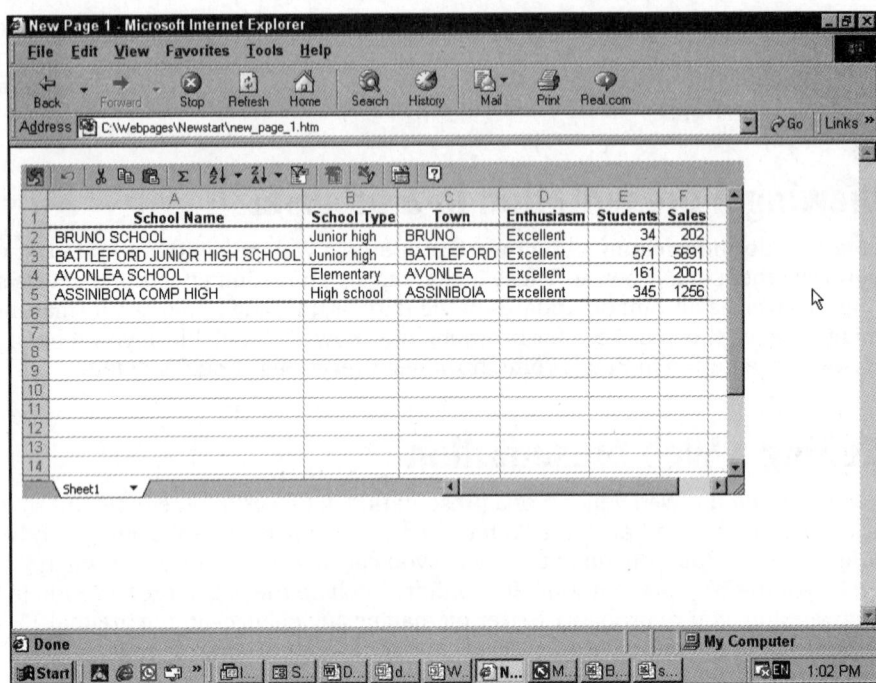

	A	B	C	D	E	F
1	**School Name**	**School Type**	**Town**	**Enthusiasm**	**Students**	**Sales**
2	BRUNO SCHOOL	Junior high	BRUNO	Excellent	34	202
3	BATTLEFORD JUNIOR HIGH SCHOOL	Junior high	BATTLEFORD	Excellent	571	5691
4	AVONLEA SCHOOL	Elementary	AVONLEA	Excellent	161	2001
5	ASSINIBOIA COMP HIGH	High school	ASSINIBOIA	Excellent	345	1256

Figure 45-15: An Office interactive spreadsheet control goes live in this Web page.

Publishing Spreadsheets on the Web

Converting any part of an Excel workbook to a Web page is as easy as saving the document in HTML format using the File ➪ Save as Web Page command. You do face a few choices, the most important being whether to convert the entire workbook or only a part of it, and whether to save the page in static or interactive form. To an extent, you can control these alternatives from the Save As dialog box itself. For a richer range of options, however, click the Publish button in the Save As box. When you do, the Publish as Web Page dialog box appears in place of Save As (see Figure 45-16). Note the checkbox at the bottom that opens the page in your browser as soon as it's saved.

Caution   Unlike Word documents and PowerPoint presentations, Excel workbooks can lose some functionality or formatting when you convert them to Web pages (although there is less risk of this in Office XP than there was in Office 2000, thanks to recent improvements). Although Excel can open the resulting HTML files again, they may not look the way they used to or contain all the original information. This limitation is especially true when you save interactive data, but some features get lost even when you save an entire workbook as a static Web page. For this reason, always save your workbooks in the standard .xls format before saving them as Web pages.

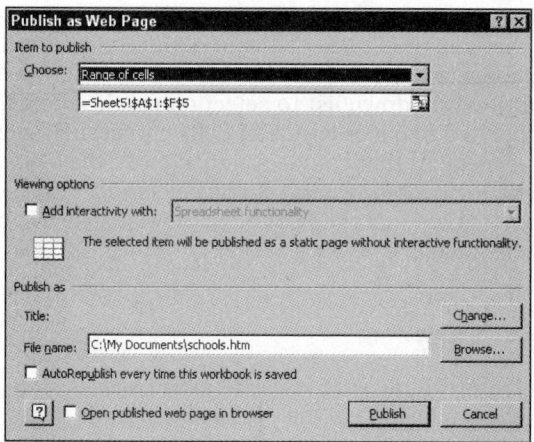

Figure 45-16: The Publish as Web Page dialog box gives you control over what part of your workbook to convert to a Web page and how to make the conversion.

You have one other option when saving a spreadsheet for Web use: You can save it in XML format (you can also open XML spreadsheets in Excel).

New Feature   Saving in XML format is a new Office XP capability that allows anyone whose browser can read XML to view the spreadsheet properly, even if they don't own Excel.

Choosing workbook elements to convert

In the Save As dialog box you can choose whether to save as your Web page the workbook as a whole, or whatever was selected before you opened the dialog box. Use the two radio buttons in the Save area to make your choice. Note that if you choose Selection rather than Entire Workbook, you can save the selection only as a Web page — the alternative file formats that would otherwise be listed at Save as Type become unavailable.

If you want fast action, then, select the part of the workbook you want in your Web page before you open the Save as Web Page dialog box. Just be sure that you select the item in its entirety, because redefining the selection requires you to leave the dialog box. To save a pivot table, for example, select it by choosing Select ➪ Entire Table from its shortcut menu. If you want to save a single worksheet, it's best to explicitly select it by clicking the Select All button at the top-left corner of the worksheet.

When you're in the Save As dialog box, if you decide that your Web page should contain a part of the workbook that you didn't select ahead of time, click Publish. You can now pick items in the Choose area to identify just about any discrete element in the workbook. First, use the drop-down list to select one of the sheets by name, or pick the Previously Published Items or Range of Cells choices. Then, if your selection has more than one element that can be saved, choose the element you want in the list box just below the drop-down list. If you selected a Range of Cells in the drop-down list, you must type in a range or click the Collapse Dialog button to select the range with the mouse.

Publishing interactive data

The distinction between interactive and static spreadsheet-based pages is simple: In an *interactive* page, users can play with the data in their browser; in *static* pages, the data just sits there. Users of interactive pages get to modify values, sort or filter the information, and enter formulas to perform calculations that give the results they want to see. In the case of pivot tables, users can reorganize the component fields and choose the level of detail to see in grouped fields. Interactive charts can be altered by changing the underlying data in the accompanying datasheet.

Caution Although interactive Web pages are a lot more fun for users, they aren't the right choice for every situation. You may want to be sure users see the correct values, and you may not want to distract them with gee-whiz interactive controls.

To save a workbook element as an interactive Web page, just click the Add Interactivity checkbox in the dialog box you use to save the data, either Save as Web Page or Publish as Web Page. The Save as Web Page dialog box automatically determines the type of interactive page you save (spreadsheet, pivot table, or chart). In the Publish as Web Page box, you get more control — you can choose to save worksheets or ranges as interactive pivot tables, or to save pivot tables as interactive spreadsheets.

Tip You can't turn an entire workbook into an interactive Web page. However, you can save each sheet individually in interactive format and then create a frames page in Word (see earlier in this chapter) to display the sheets in one frame under the control of navigation button in another frame.

Preparing to publish interactive workbook data

Some prep work may be required to realize the intended results in interactive Web pages based on Excel workbooks. Consider these points:

✦ If the worksheet or data range you're converting contains external data, saving it as a Web page "freezes" the data. If you want the Web page to retrieve current data each time it's opened, you must incorporate the data into a pivot table and then save the pivot table in interactive form.

✦ If you're saving an interactive pivot table, remove custom calculations and set the data fields to use one of the following four summary functions: Sum, Count, Min, or Max. You can save an interactive pivot table that you've already formatted, but don't bother formatting it for purposes of the Web page — all custom character and cell formatting vanishes.

✦ If you're saving an interactive chart (see Figure 45-17), confine yourself to chart types and elements that translate properly to Web pages. Surface and 3-D chart types in particular are off limits. If the chart resides on a worksheet, save it separately rather than as part of the sheet — charts are removed when you save sheets with interactivity.

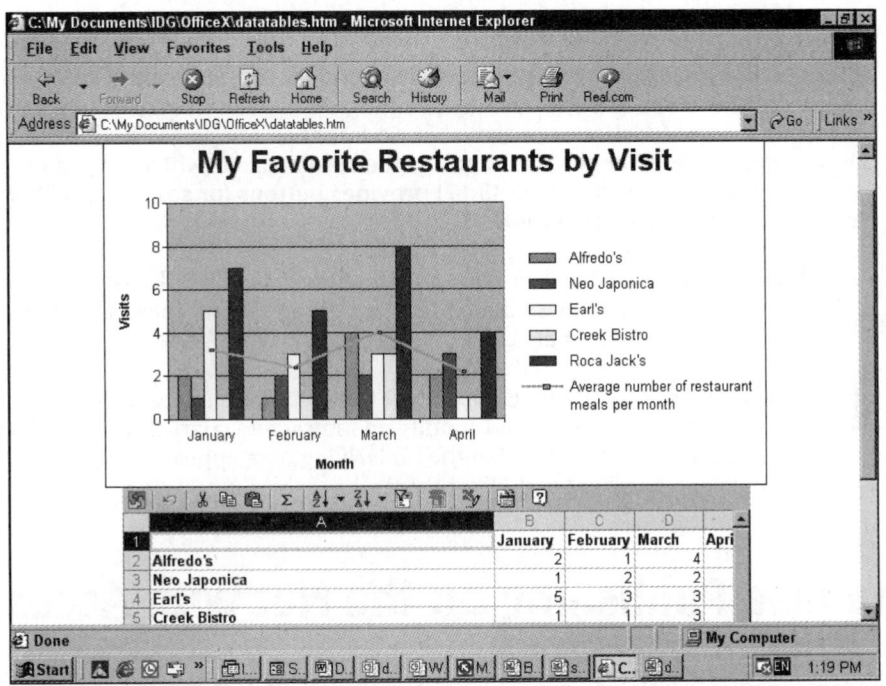

Figure 45-17: Here's an interactive chart as it appears in a browser. The chart can be altered by changing the entries in the data table at the bottom, which is saved as a spreadsheet Web component.

Note In interactive Web pages, changes in the data provided are usually only reflected in the displayed items when the Refresh button is clicked.

Formatting interactive pages

Cell and text formatting is retained in interactive spreadsheets, but not in pivot tables. If you open a page containing an interactive spreadsheet in Excel, changes you make to cell formatting are retained when you save the page and will appear in the browser when the page is opened there. However, you have to use the spreadsheet control's property toolbox to apply formatting to the cells in the control—Excel's usual formatting commands don't work.

Excel isn't a stellar performer as a page layout program. Microsoft recommends that you apply formatting to the rest of the page—the parts not occupied by the interactive control—using Word, Access, or FrontPage.

Working with interactive data in a browser

Opened in a browser, an interactive spreadsheet behaves much like a scaled-down version of Excel itself. The user can edit cell data or type in new values or formulas. Most built-in Excel functions are available, so formulas can perform sophisticated calculations. The toolbar across the top of the spreadsheet (which you can see at the top of the data table in Figure 45-17) provides buttons for sorting and filtering the information, among other tasks.

Tip Clicking the Property Toolbox button, second from the right, displays a range of other controls. Among these are a bunch for changing font, color, and other formatting characteristics of the cells.

Interactive pivot tables work much like pivot tables in Excel, except that you can't change their formatting. Users can't modify an interactive chart directly with the mouse, but a spreadsheet containing the underlying data appears below the chart and those data can be sliced and diced there.

Database Publishing on the Net with Access

Access provides several ways to distribute information over the Internet or an intranet. The easy way is to export database objects such as tables and queries as ordinary HTML documents, which you can then post to the Web or wherever. With a bit more work, however, you can make live Web pages that display current information from your database for all those who browse your site.

Tip In VBA code or macros, use the `OutputTo` method to export database information in any supported format, including HTML.

Exporting data to static Web pages

Exporting a database object as an ordinary Web page is child's play. The drawback is that the resulting file retains no link to the original data. As soon as your database changes, your Web page is out of date until you export a new version of the file. Another problem: When you export a form, only its datasheet winds up in the Web page — not the formatted form you laid out so carefully.

If you can live with the prospect of early obsolescence and minimal formatting, export the currently selected object by choosing File ➪ Export. In the Export dialog box, select HTML Documents in the Save as Type box. Check the Autostart box if you want Access to start your Web browser and open the exported document there so you can see the results.

After you choose Export, a diminutive HTML Output Options dialog box appears. If you want to merge the exported data with an HTML template to enhance the otherwise Spartan output from Access, specify the template name here. (An HTML *template* is a text file you create that specifies the location and appearance of common elements in an Access-based Web page — for details, search in Access Help for "HTML template"). Then choose OK to save the exported HTML document.

Access exports each selected datasheet and each printed page of a report as a separate HTML file, adding the page number to the end of each filename. If you save a report with multiple pages, Access supplies basic navigation controls in the form of First, Previous, Next, and Last text buttons (the HTML template you specify can include placeholders for these navigation controls). During the export, Access generates the appropriate hyperlinks for the navigation buttons on each page.

Using report snapshots on the Web

If ordinary exported datasheets look too plain, use report snapshots for fancier-looking Web pages based on static Access data. A report snapshot is a file that encapsulates an Access report as it appears when you display it in Print Preview — that is, with the current data and full formatting you see on the screen. You can distribute these snapshots to anyone, even those who don't have Access (a 32-bit version of Windows is required). A Snapshot Viewer program is required to display report snapshots. The Viewer comes with Access and is available freely from Microsoft.

Creating a report snapshot is as simple as exporting the report. In Access, select the report you want to use and choose File ➪ Export. After you select Snapshot Format in the Save as Type list and click Export, Access asks you for any parameters required by the report. When the snapshot has been saved, it appears automatically in the Snapshot Viewer, where you can proofread it before distributing the file.

One distribution method is to simply send the snapshot file on disk or via e-mail. Recipients can then run Snapshot Viewer as a standalone program and open the snapshots within it. Alternatively, however, you can include a snapshot in a Web page using either of the following techniques:

✦ **Insert a hyperlink to the snapshot file onto the page.** When the user clicks the link, the snapshot opens in the browser (with Internet Explorer 3 or above) or in a separate window.

✦ **Add the Snapshot Viewer ActiveX control to your Web page.** This control is also included with Access; set its `SnapshotPath` property to the URL of the snapshot file. When the page is viewed in a browser, the snapshot appears within the control. Obviously, this method works only with browsers that support ActiveX controls. If the Snapshot Viewer control isn't already installed on the user's computer, the browser downloads it from your Web site the first time a page containing the control is opened.

Exporting as XML

Rather than using HTML, you may get better results by choosing to publish your Access reports, forms, tables or queries as XML files, which include an associated XSL file for presentation. (XSL is the XML equivalent of Cascading Style Sheets, or CSS, for HTML. In other words, it controls formatting.)

Creating server-side dynamic database pages

If you want users to be able to interact with your database in any browser, you can export database information in either of two dynamic data formats: IDC/HTX (Internet Database Connector/HTML extension) and ASP (Active Server Pages). Both formats work by inducing your Web server software to query the database on-the-fly. The server generates an HTML file containing the requested data and sends that file to the browser. As a result, the data displayed by the browser in this dynamically generated Web page are always current. You can export tables, queries, and form datasheets, but not reports, to either format.

Server requirements for dynamic database pages

Compared to static data pages, which you must constantly update, dynamic database pages require much, much less maintenance. However, because the IDC/HTX and ASP formats rely on nonstandard enhancements to HTML, they work only when published on compatible servers. Server requirements are:

✦ **For IDC/HTX files.** Any version of Microsoft Internet Information Server (for Web servers running NT Server) or Personal Web Server (for servers running NT Workstation or Windows 95).

✦ **For ASP files.** Microsoft Internet Information Server 3.0 or greater with ActiveX Server controls, running on NT Server.

Choosing a format

Of the two formats, ASP is the most versatile. Because they support ActiveX Server controls, Active Server Pages enable users to add, modify, and delete records in the database, assuming they have permission. (By the way, the Help file for the Microsoft Script Editor contains a great deal of reference information on Active Server Pages. The Script Editor is discussed in the last major section of this chapter.)

Exporting dynamic database pages

Exporting your database objects in either IDC/HTX or ASP format requires only a smidge more work than creating static pages. Choose File ➪ Export, select the desired output format at Save as Type, and click Export. However, when you specify one of the dynamic formats in the Save As dialog box's Save as Type field, the Output Options dialog box prompts you for a number of additional entries. Figure 45-18 shows this dialog box as it appears when you save pages in the ASP format.

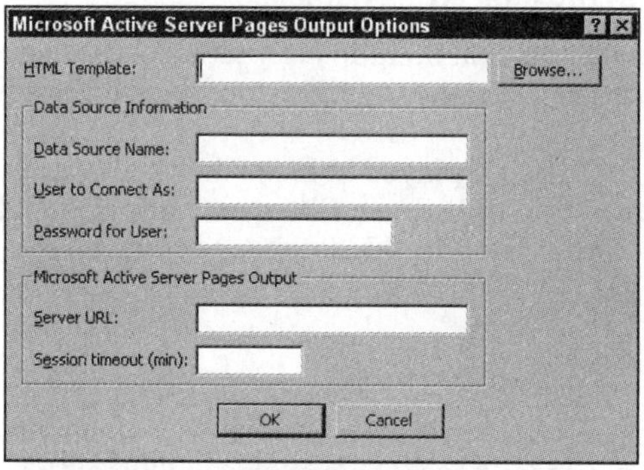

Figure 45-18: Fill out this dialog box when you export to an ActiveX Server page.

In addition to the path to an HTML template, you must specify the ODBC DSN (data source name) needed to connect to the database, along with user connection information (including a user name and password). When you're saving to the ASP format, you must give the URL for the server where the exported ASP page is to be stored during Web access. To connect to your database with either type of file, the Access Desktop driver must be installed and the correct ODBC DSN for the database must be set up. You can find information on the steps required in Access Help.

Working with data access pages

On an intranet, Access's new data access pages enable users to work with live, for-matted data in their browsers — as long as they're using Internet Explorer 5 or later.

Caution   Unfortunately, because data access pages require all users to have a late-model version of IE as well as the Office Web components, they aren't a general solution for interactive database access over the Internet.

Understanding data access pages

Unlike other objects in an Access database, data access pages are stored in individual files, separate from the database itself. In the Database window, the data access page icons represent shortcuts to these files.

You can create data access pages that function as:

✦ **Interactive reports.** Unlike a printed report, a data access page lets users determine how much detail they see and enables them to sort and filter the data.

✦ **Data entry forms.** When you add, edit, or delete a record on a data access page, the changes are entered in the underlying database.

✦ **Data analysis tools.** Data access pages can include interactive spreadsheets, pivot tables, and charts that summarize data and help you identify trends.

Each user is free to change the way data are displayed in his or her browser without affecting the data access page stored on the server. Changes made to the data themselves, however, are real — they are posted to the database on which the page is based.

Creating data access pages

The easiest way to create a data access page is to create a form or report as you normally would, then save it as a data access page. (This is new in Office XP.) Simply open the form or report you want to save as a data access page, then choose File ➪ Save As. In the small Save As dialog box, assign a name to the file, then choose Data Access Page from the As list. Click OK.

Figure 45-19 shows the form in Access, side-by-side with the Data Access Page created from it.

You can also create data access pages as you would other Access database objects. Switch to the Pages button in the Objects bar. There, your options include these:

✦ Creating a page (semi)automatically. Click the New button and choose AutoPage: Columnar in the resulting dialog box. Select a table or query on which to base the page, and click OK to open the page.

✦ Running the Page Wizard to guide you through the process of choosing, grouping, and sorting records in the page. Click Create Data Access Page by Using Wizard.

✦ Starting a new data access page from scratch in Design view. Click Create Data Access Page in Design View.

✦ Converting an existing Web page to a data access page. Double-click Edit Web page that already exists. When Access opens the page you specify, you must indicate the database you want to connect it to. You can then add interactive elements as you would to any data access page. Saving the page creates a corresponding shortcut in the Database window.

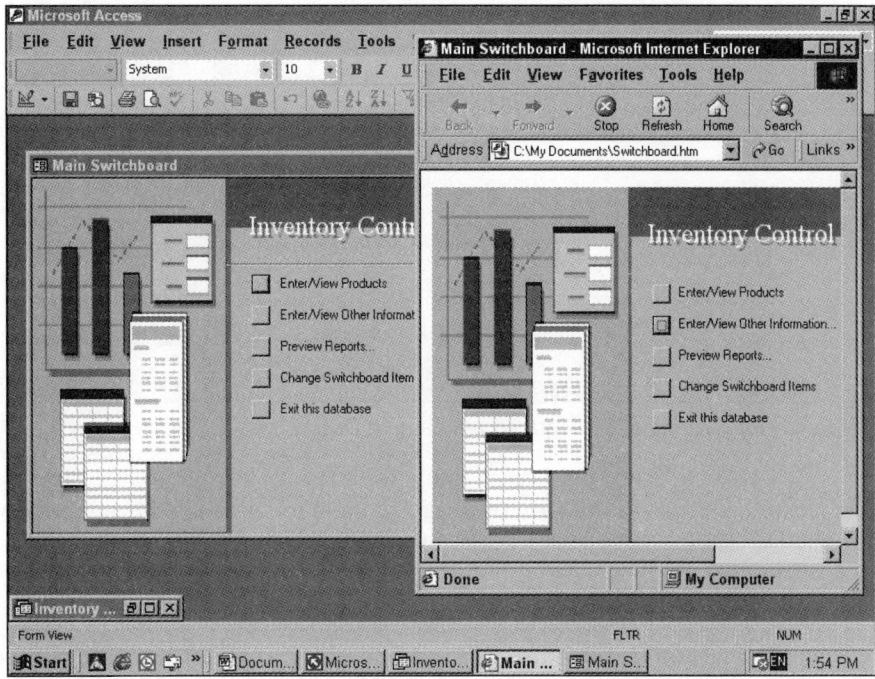

Figure 45-19: At left is a form in Access; at right is the same form saved as a data access page.

Designing data access pages

You use the same basic techniques for laying out a data access page as you would when designing an Access form or report.

Figure 45-20 shows a new data access page opened in Design view. The *body* of a data access page constitutes the page's work area, onto which you place all visible elements. When the page is viewed in IE, the body adjusts its size to fit into the browser window. The body contains a preformatted text area for typing a title. You can place controls such as labels, buttons, and checkboxes into the body, but more often they go into the *section*, a defined, gridded rectangular area intended for form-type layouts.

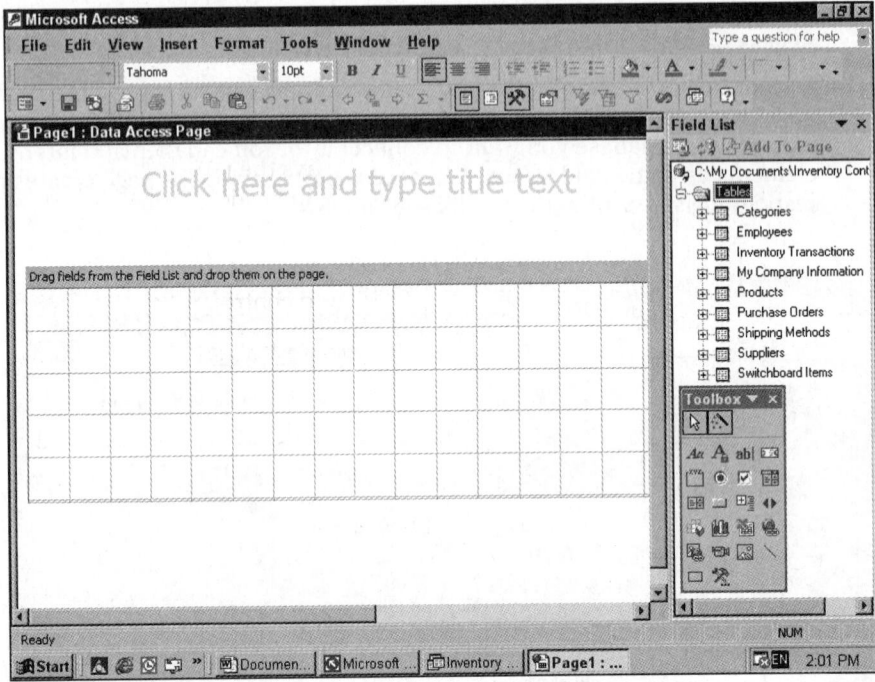

Figure 45-20: Starting a new data access page in Design view

You can add controls to the form by dragging them from the Field List, a window listing all the tables and queries in the database and their fields, or by using the Toolbox toolbar. Adding a field from the Field List produces a text box control bound (linked) to that field.

Cross-Reference   Chapter 50, on Access forms, explains how bound controls work, and the techniques described there for laying out controls work in data access pages, too.

You can add all the fields from a table or query en masse by dragging the corresponding table or query item from the Field List to the page.

Working with grouping levels and sections

A new, blank data access page like the one in Figure 45-20 opens with a single unbound section (that is, it isn't linked to any table or query in the database). After you bind a database object, sections are defined by the way you group the data. For example, if your data access page displays sales data grouped by month and then by state, you have two *group levels*, each with its own sections. Four sections are available in each group level (although you use only the sections appropriate for your needs):

✦ **Header.** Misleadingly named, this section is used to display individual records as well as for elements you might expect to see in a header.

✦ **Footer.** Displayed directly above the navigation section, the footer is used to display calculated totals for the group.

✦ **Navigation.** This section automatically displays the record navigation control for the group level and appears after the group header section. You can add unbound controls to it as well.

✦ **Caption.** Place text boxes, labels, and other unbound controls in this section, which appears above the group header. Bound controls are off-limits here, too.

Note   In data access pages used for data entry, you can have only one group level, and the Group footer section isn't available.

Setting up group levels

You can create as many nested group levels as you need. When you use the Page Wizard to create a data access page, you can set up grouping levels on the page with the wizard's help. Otherwise, you have to do it by hand.

To create the first group level in a new blank page, bind a database object to the unbound section. All you have to do is drag a field that belongs to the desired table or query from the Field List to the section. This step creates a field on the page and simultaneously binds the section to the table or query containing the field (see Figure 45-21).

The technique for adding additional group levels depends on whether you're grouping by an individual field in the same table or query, or by one of two separate tables or queries.

Here are the details on setting up each type of group:

✦ **Grouping by a field in the same table or query.** A field that contains the same data in many different records makes a useful "group-by" field. In a table of addresses, for example, you might want to group by the state fields, because the database probably contains multiple records from each state. To group by an individual field, add it to the section, make sure that it's selected, and then click the Promote button on the Page Design toolbar.

✦ **Grouping by a table or query.** You can add fields from more than one table or query to the same data access page. When two tables or queries have a one-to-many relationship, Access lets you group by the item on the "one" of the relationship. For example, if the database has a Categories table and a Products table related by a shared CategoryID field, you would group by Categories, producing a page that shows the products in each category. To set up the groups, add the fields you want to display from both tables to the section. Then select any field from the table you want to group by and click the Group by Table button on the Page Design toolbar.

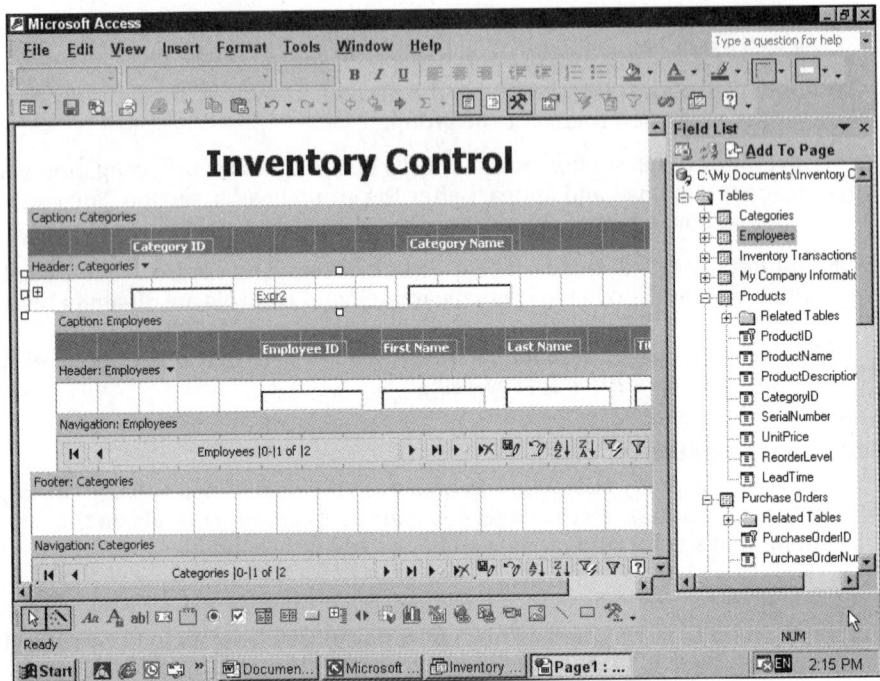

Figure 45-21: A budding data access page showing multiple group levels

After you create a new group level, Access automatically adds new sections to the page for that group. Which sections you see depends on settings in the Sorting and Grouping dialog box, described next.

Modifying group level settings

You can see and modify the settings for each group level by right clicking the title bar for that group level and choosing Group Level Properties. You can then fiddle with the group's properties.

Creating data entry data access pages

To create a data access page for entering and editing data, you must observe one essential rule: Create only one group level for the page.

Tip

You can't use group levels to work with two related tables in a single data entry data access page, but you can stitch together a workable solution using two pages. Bind each page to one of the tables. Then place a hyperlink from the page on the "one" side of the relationship to the other page. If you're feeling ambitious, you can then create a frames page in Word or FrontPage, loading the two pages into its frames. With some layout elbow grease and some luck, the result should work like a single page and enable you to see and edit data from either table simultaneously.

Using data access pages within Access

A data access page is live in the Access database where you create it — you don't have to view it in Internet Explorer. Data access pages serve essentially the same functions as forms and reports. You may want to use an existing data access page rather than go to the trouble of building a comparable form or report from scratch.

Enlivening Web Pages with Scripts

Scripts are small programs attached to a Web page that provide snippets of custom functionality. Because scripts are embedded in the page's HTML code, they are downloaded to the browser when the user opens the page. This means the script program runs on the user's computer, not the server.

Scripts make your Web pages come alive, manipulating the page to produce animations or other changes the user can see. Scripts can run when the page opens, or in response to what the user does with the mouse and keyboard, and in response to other events. As a simple example, a script might determine the number displayed on one of those counters that shows how many times a page has been opened.

Office XP features a full-blown development environment for viewing, writing, and testing Web page scripts. Shown in Figure 45-22, the Microsoft Script Editor is actually a complete HTML editing toolkit, and is available in all the Office applications except Outlook (choose Tools ➪ Macro ➪ Microsoft Script Editor to run it).

Working with scripting languages

Power has its price, and with scripts, that price is learning how to write script code. Two scripting languages are in common use on the Web: JavaScript (called JScript by Microsoft) and VBScript. Learning to program in either language is no trivial ambition, and even a worthwhile introduction to either language would eat up 50 pages or so, so I must ask you to look elsewhere for details on JavaScript and VBScript coding. (An excellent place to start is the Script Editor's Help file, which contains complete tutorials and reference information on both JavaScript and VBScript.)

I can offer brief remarks on the languages themselves.

Comparing VBScript and JavaScript

Formally known as Microsoft Visual Basic Scripting Edition, VBScript is a scaled-down version of the Visual Basic language that powers VBA. Because it's so similar to VBA, VBScript is a natural for Office developers.

Caution

The problem with VBScript is that browsers other than Internet Explorer (version 3 and later) can't execute VBScript code. Use VBScript only if all your users have IE.

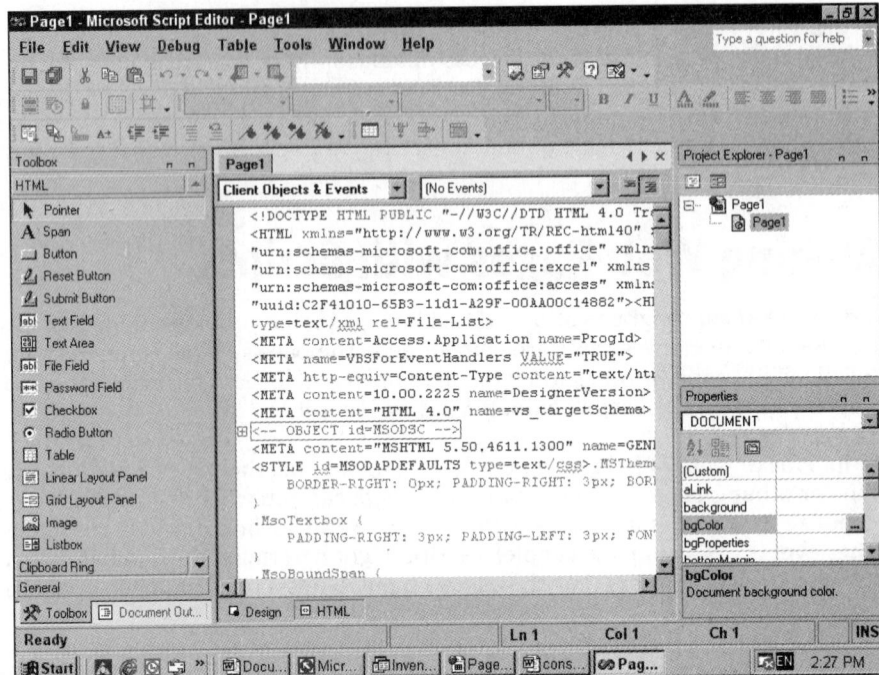

Figure 45-22: The Microsoft Script Editor is a powerful tool for editing and adding scripts on Web pages.

JavaScript enjoys much wider support among browsers than does VBScript. That makes it the scripting language to use in pages you publish on the World Wide Web, or anywhere they will be opened by users who get to choose their own browsers. (By the way, JavaScript bears no direct relationship to the Java programming language, although the two languages have some similarities.)

Selecting a default scripting language

You can choose either scripting language, VBScript or JavaScript, as the default for the Web pages you work on in the Script Editor. To change the default scripting language, locate the `defaultClientScript` property in the Properties window. Alternatively, display the View ➪ Property Pages dialog box, and on the General tab, select the preferred language in the drop-down list provided (this dialog box is just another way to access the same properties available in the Properties window when the entire page — the document object — is selected).

Adding script commands to the toolbar system

If you're at all serious about using scripts, equip yourself with some related commands that are missing from Office's default menus and toolbars. The commands are Insert Script, Show All Scripts, and Remove All Scripts. Using the customizing techniques covered in Chapter 5, place them on the menu or toolbar of your choice: Open the Tools ⇨ Customize dialog box, switch to the Commands tab, and select Tools in the Categories box. Now you can locate the three commands in the Commands box and drag them, one at a time, to the destination. You have to repeat this process for every Office application where you use scripts.

Identifying scripts in Web pages

You can tell where the scripts are embedded in a Web page by the presence of *script anchors* visible when you open the page in Office. Script anchors may not be visible, however — show or hide them using the Show All Scripts command (add it to the toolbar system as described in the previous section). Here are some script-anchor tricks:

✦ Rest the mouse pointer on a script anchor to see the first 50 characters of the script in a ScreenTip.

✦ Double-click a script anchor to edit the script in the Microsoft Script Editor.

✦ Click a script anchor to select it. You can then press Del to delete it, or cut or copy it to the Clipboard and then paste it elsewhere, even on a different document.

✦ Drag a script anchor to move the script to a new location in the document. Dragging with the right mouse button lets you make a copy of the script at the destination, preserving the original script.

Many scripts work fine no matter where they are placed in any Web page, but some are location-dependent — they won't work correctly when moved from their original location.

Editing code with the Script Editor

To open the current Office document in the Script Editor, choose Tools ⇨ Macro ⇨ Microsoft Script Editor, or press Alt+Shift+F11. If the document isn't already a Web page, it's converted into HTML code. You can scroll through the document to view the HTML and scripts, and if you know what you're doing, you can type in new scripts anywhere you like in the code. Again, to display a specific script in the Editor, double-click its script anchor in Office.

Opening a document in the Script Editor creates a separate copy that's tied only loosely to the original. The code you type in the Script Editor doesn't automatically affect the original document, and likewise, changes you make back in the original document aren't automatically reflected in the code in the Script Editor. When you modify either version of the document and switch to the other, the Refresh toolbar appears. Click Refresh to bring the two versions into synch, or click Don't Refresh to keep them distinct.

Inserting scripts

To add a script to a specific location in an Office document, you need the Insert Script command, one of the three script-related commands you should install on a menu or toolbar (see "Adding script commands to the toolbar system" earlier in this chapter). Select the target location and click the button or menu item for the Insert Script command. The document opens in the Script Editor, with the skeleton of a new script at the appropriate place in the HTML code.

Previewing pages in the Script Editor

Choose File ➪ View in browser to see how your document would look in your default browser. (To choose a different browser to view with, choose File ➪ Browse With.)

The Design View tab lets you edit a Web page graphically rather than as HTML, much like you would in Word or FrontPage. To use it, however, you must open the page directly from its disk file, rather than from an Office application.

Using ActiveX controls on your Web pages

You can adorn your Web pages with the same ActiveX controls used to power VBA forms (see Chapter 56). ActiveX controls provide extraordinary capabilities, but be aware of two potential problems. First, they tend to be relatively large chunks of software, so they can really slow down pages that contain them. However, users feel this performance drag only the first time a page is downloaded — opening the page automatically installs its controls on the user's system, and thereafter, those controls are available for immediate use with any Web page. Second, ActiveX controls work only inside Internet Explorer — users who have Netscape Navigator are out of luck without special third-party plug-ins.

If you're not dissuaded, here are the steps required to place an ActiveX control on an Office Web page:

1. Starting with your document open in its Office application, display the Toolbox, the toolbar containing ActiveX controls.

 Tip   In Word, this particular toolbar is called the Control Toolbox.

2. Click the Toolbox button for the ActiveX control you want to use, and then click in your document to insert it there.

3. Resize the control to taste.

4. Click the Properties button on the Toolbox to display the Properties window. Use it to set the initial appearance and behavior of the control.

5. Write event procedures for the control. To create an event procedure, click the Insert Script button to start a new script in the Script Editor.

Although you enter the procedure code directly into the page, you should pattern the procedure itself after the event procedure you would use in a VBA code window (see Chapter 56 for a complete discussion of event procedures). The following example shows a simple procedure for the Click event that changes the caption of a command button control:

```
<script language="VBScript">
<!-
Sub cmdBigButton_Click
    cmdBigButton.Caption = "You clicked me!"
End Sub
->
</script>
```

6. Switch to the Quick View tab to test the event procedure.

> **Caution**
>
> At Step 5, be sure you don't choose View Code from the control's shortcut menu. Doing so would take you to the Visual Basic Editor for VBA. VBA code runs on your computer, not the user's.

Publishing Your Web Pages

When you're finished creating all of your Web pages, it's time to post them to a Web server on your intranet or the Internet. If the server supports the Office Server Extensions, you can copy the files using Web Folders, described in Chapters 6 and 7. Alternatives include FrontPage (see Chapter 44), which includes a full-service Web site publishing feature, or one of the File Transfer Protocol (FTP) programs available on the Internet and elsewhere.

> **Caution**
>
> Your only real problem is to make sure that all the files involved in your Web site wind up on the server in the proper locations. Remember that most Web pages refer to a number of elements besides the HTML file, most commonly image files for photos, illustrations, charts, buttons, lines, and so on. There may also be sound and video files or other files that you're providing to your users for downloading.

All of these files must be stored on the Web server or in a location that the server has access to. They must also be in the exact location specified in the Web page (.htm file) that you've created, relative to the page being viewed. If they are not where they are supposed to be, you will have a broken link, where an image doesn't appear, another page doesn't open, or something else that was expected doesn't take place.

After you've published your Web site, be sure to test all the pages in a Web browser. Check to see that all the graphics are visible. If you see a red X where a graphic should be, it means that a supporting image file didn't make it to the server. If you have direct access to the page via Web Folders, you can open it in Office to correct the problem. Display the Web Options dialog box, and on the Files tab, check the box labeled Update Links on Save. Saving the page back to the server should fix the problem. If you aren't able to use Web Folders, try publishing the site again with whatever method you used previously, double-checking to make sure that you copy all the support files to the correct locations.

✦   ✦   ✦

Managing and Manipulating Data with Access

P A R T

✦ ✦ ✦ ✦

In This Part

Chapter 46
Getting Inside Access

Chapter 47
Fundamentals
of Access

Chapter 48
Secrets of Database
Application Design

Chapter 49
Working with Data
Using VBA

Chapter 50
Designing Access
Forms

✦ ✦ ✦ ✦

Access is designed to help you collect and work with data—and control how that data is accessed and displayed. This part introduces Access and its various parts, then delves deeply into what makes Access so powerful— the user's ability to design his or her own applications that make use of the data stored in a database. VBA comes into play again in a chapter on using that programming language to work with data. A detailed look at designing Access forms (which are different from forms in other Office applications) finishes up the part.

Getting Inside Access

In This Chapter

Customizing Access

Creating macros in Access

Choosing the database engine that works best for you

Optimizing Access performance

Everyone knows Access has something to do with databases; beyond that, the picture gets a bit fuzzy. It's not your fault you're confused — confusion is inherent in Access itself.

Access plays a variety of roles, and some of these overlap extensively with the territory of other products. This chapter sets out to clarify the mission Microsoft has set for its Office database component. It then goes on to deal with issues of setup, customization, and housekeeping that need discussion but don't pertain directly to database management — which is the focus of the remaining chapters in this section.

Getting a Grip on Access

Access has at least five major mandates. It can serve in various roles:

- ✦ **An ad hoc database manager.** Via the menus and toolbars, you can have direct, hands-on access to data drawn from a wide variety of sources on your own PC or anywhere on the network.

- ✦ **A powerful reporting tool.** Even if you rely on a non-Access application for entering and extracting data, you may want to turn to Access's reporting capabilities when it's time to analyze that data in presentable form. Access reports are easier to put together and look nicer than those available in many applications.

- ✦ **A workshop for building dynamic Web pages.** You can construct Web pages that automatically reflect changes in the underlying database.

✦ **A complete development environment for producing finished database applications.** Although other development tools can create smaller, faster, or glitzier applications, you can build complete, full-featured database applications — including true client/server applications — with Access alone. If you have Office Developer, you can distribute these applications to users who don't have their own copies of Access.

✦ **An application prototyping tool.** Even if you decide to use Visual Basic, C++, or some other tool for your finished applications, Access offers an easy-to-use test bed for building working prototypes in a hurry.

Understand that these functions are somewhat independent. You can, for example, use Access for ad hoc database management by way of the menus and toolbars and never worry about application design and VBA programming. Conversely, if you're an application developer, you may largely ignore the Access menus and toolbars in favor of the custom ones you create for the users of your application.

Power Customizing

Access enables you to reconfigure its toolbars and control what happens when the program starts, just as in the other Office applications. Scratch a little deeper, though, and you'll find a daunting array of technical settings to play with in pursuit of optimal database performance. Fortunately, Access provides some help in knowing which lever to pull, and when.

Controlling database startup behavior

To control how a specific database behaves when it is opened (as well as other aspects of its behavior), choose Tools ➪ Startup. One setting in the Startup dialog box (Figure 46-1) lets you set the startup form, the form that appears as soon as the database opens. Another lets you shut off the initial display of the standard Database window, the default Access control center. (To restore the Database window, choose Window ➪ Unhide.)

Tip   Most of these startup settings are primarily intended for customizing the look and behavior of a database application that you distribute to others. Unless you take special measures, however, they can be overridden by holding down Shift when the database is opened.

Customizing the interface and other options

The standard methods available throughout Office for customizing menus and toolbars work just fine in Access to let you create a database home of your dreams. In common with its mates, Access even lets you customize the individual shortcut menus that appear when you right-click an item.

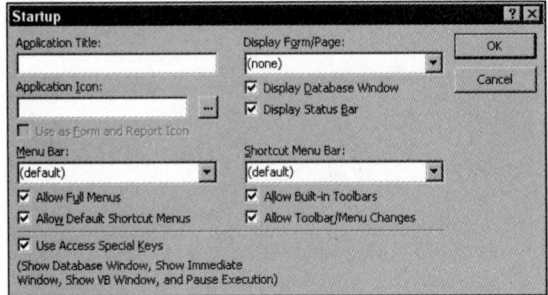

Figure 46-1: Use the Startup dialog box to set options governing how a database behaves when first opened.

Chapter 5 covers the Office customizing techniques you need.

Along with all the other Office applications, Access provides control over many program settings on the Tools ➪ Options dialog box. When you're getting started, be sure to look at the choices available on the Keyboard, View, and General tabs.

Creating macros in Access

Like the other Office applications, Access lets you perform a series of actions with a single custom command using a macro. Access is decidedly unlike the other applications, however, in the way it handles macros. The key point is that Access macros are not VBA procedures, as they are elsewhere in Office. Access also lacks a macro recorder — you have to build macros by entering commands in a special dialog box.

Among the actions that a macro can perform are RunCommand, which executes one of many available built-in Access commands; RunCode, which runs a VBA procedure; and RunMacro, which runs another macro.

To assign a set of actions to a macro, follow these steps:

1. In the Database window, click the Macros button in the Objects toolbar.

2. Click New to display the Macro window shown in Figure 46-2.

3. In the Action column, enter the series of actions you want this macro to carry out, one action per row. In each row, select an action from the drop-down list.

   If the action allows or requires additional arguments, Access displays appropriately labeled fields at the bottom of the dialog box. There, you can select them from drop-down lists or type them in.

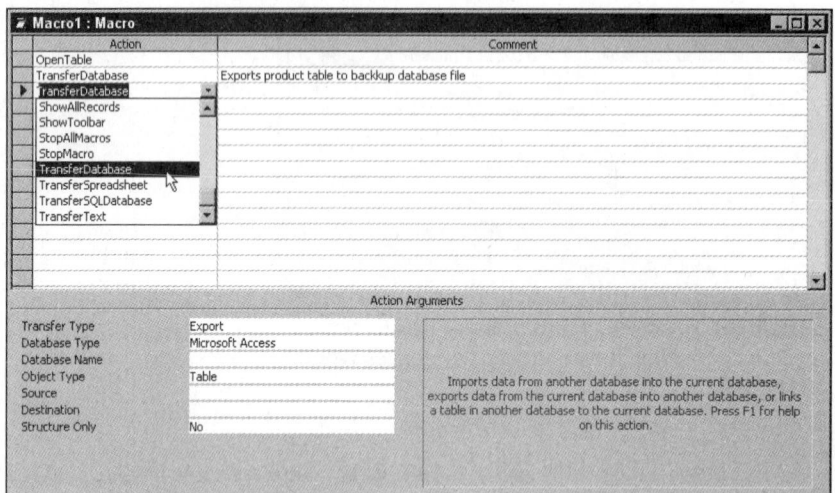

Figure 46-2: Assigning Access commands to a macro

4. To specify when the macro should be available, enter an expression in the Condition column.

Tip   If this column isn't visible, click the Conditions button on the Macro Design tool-bar. To get help creating the condition, click the Build toolbar button or right-click in the column and choose Build from the shortcut menu.

5. Save the macro by clicking the Save button, pressing Ctrl+S, or choosing File ➪ Save. Access asks you to name the macro now.

To run a macro, double-click it in the Macros tab or select it and choose Run. You can also access it from the Tools ➪ Macros ➪ Run Macro dialog box, assign it to a keyboard shortcut as detailed later, or place it on a toolbar button or menu with the techniques discussed in Chapter 5.

Tip   To run a macro automatically when you open a database, name it AutoExec.

Creating macro groups

You can define two or more separate macros in a single macro window and store them together under one name. Access refers to a macro that contains more than one individual macro as a macro group. The macros in the group still run independently. This technique enables you to organize related macros in sets rather than keeping track of many separate macro objects.

Note   A special macro group is required if you want to assign macros to keyboard shortcuts.

To create a macro group, just start a new macro as you normally would. After the Macro window appears, display the Macro Name column by clicking the Macro Names button on the toolbar.

You can now type a name for the first macro in the group in the Macro Name column. Go on to specify the actions the macro should perform in the Action column in this and subsequent rows, adding conditions in the Condition column as appropriate. (However, for this macro, leave the Macro Name column empty in the remaining rows.)

When you're finished defining the first macro in the group, start the second by typing its name in the Macro Name column on the next blank row. Continue adding macros in this fashion to complete the macro group.

Access refers to individual macros in a macro group by way of a compound name combining the macro group name and the macro name separated by a period, as in the following:

```
GeneralMacros.PrintCurrentRecord
```

Double-clicking a macro group runs only the first macro in the group. To run any of the others, choose Tools ➪ Macros ➪ Run Macro and then select the macro from the list where it appears in the format just described.

Customizing the keyboard with macros

The two "keys" to defining custom keyboard shortcuts in Access are these:

✦ Set all of them up as macros in one special macro group that you name AutoKeys (the previous section covers macro groups in detail).

✦ Type the keyboard shortcut's abbreviation as the name for each macro in the AutoKeys group. Table 46-1 lists the permissible keys and their abbreviations.

As soon as you've created and saved the macros in the AutoKeys group, Access activates the key assignment. If you assign actions to a shortcut already used by Access (for example, Ctrl+P for File ➪ Print), your shortcut replaces the default in all windows in the current database.

Tip   Another, more powerful way to control the keyboard in Access when you're working with a form is to use the KeyDown and KeyPress events for the form or any single control, assigning a custom response to the event.

	Table 46-1	
	Permissible Keyboard Shortcuts for Naming Macros in AutoKeys Group	
Key or Key Combination	**Entry in Macro Name Column**	**Example (If Applicable)**
Insert	{INSERT}	
Delete	{DEL}	
Function key	{Function key abbreviation}	{F9}
Ctrl+Insert, Delete, or any letter, number, or function key	^key	^r (Ctrl+r) ^{F3} (Ctrl+F3)
Shift+Insert, Delete, or any function key	+key	+{F6} (Shift+F6) +{DEL} (Shift+Del)

Adding and removing components

Depending on what version of Office you have, Access may come with an assortment of add-in tools that perform all kinds of useful functions. Use the Add-in Manager, available on the Tools menu, to install or remove add-ins. You can create and install your own add-ins, which are actually just specialized Access databases. Categories of Access add-ins include:

✦ **Wizards.** These tools ask you a series of questions and, based on your input, create a database object, such as a datasheet table, query, form, or report.

✦ **Builders.** These are modules that help simplify tasks by walking you through the steps of assembling, or building, complex expressions or database components.

✦ **Managers.** These help you handle housekeeping chores associated with Access components. The Add-in Manager is itself an add-in!

Choosing a Database Engine

Access itself functions mainly as a sort of customer service representative, showing you what's available in terms of commands and data, and taking your orders from the menus, the toolbars, and the keyboard. In other words, Access proper is a database front end, the part you and other users interact with. However, Access knows its limits. When it comes to the heavy labor of inserting and extracting information in the database, Access turns to a separate piece of software, a database engine — also referred to as the back end.

The Jet engine

The default database engine for Access is Microsoft Jet. Standard Access database files (with the .MDB extension) are actually Jet files and can be opened and manipulated by any development tool that can activate the Jet engine, including Visual Basic and C++. Via special drivers, Jet can also access other types of data residing on your PC, such as dBase, Excel, and Outlook files.

Alternatives to Jet

Jet is a sophisticated relational database manager; it works well for databases that serve individual users and small groups. But Jet also has its limitations.

To keep Access up to date, Access 2002 now ships with a new engine, Microsoft SQL Server 2000 Desktop Engine (also known as Microsoft Data Engine, or MSDE). Microsoft SQL Server 2000 Desktop Engine must be installed from the Office XP disks; it isn't installed by default.

In essence, Microsoft SQL Server 2000 Desktop Engine is a workstation version of SQL Server 2000, Microsoft's flagship database product intended for "enterprise-level" applications. You can use Microsoft SQL Server 2000 Desktop Engine for development work on a single PC and then switch to SQL Server 2000 itself when you're ready to deploy your database application on a larger scale.

You have still more options for the back end of your database project. Using the ODBC or OLE DB standards discussed in Chapter 47, Access can get at data in everything from dBase to high-end databases such as Oracle and Sybase (Jet is still necessary when you're working with data tables stored in formats such as dBase on your own PC or your network).

Considerations in choosing an engine

If you've decided to use Access to work with corporate data stored on a server in an Oracle database, you don't have to worry about choosing a back end — it has to be Oracle. For projects you start on your own PC, however, you face a choice between Jet and Microsoft SQL Server 2000 Desktop Engine. As you consider the strengths of each alternative, keep in mind that you can't go too far wrong — Access includes a utility that converts Jet databases into equivalent SQL Server databases (see "Upsizing a database from Jet to SQL Server," later in this chapter).

Jet advantages

Jet's main advantages are seniority and simplicity. Applications developed for Jet in previous versions of Access will run in Access 2002 without modification. Because Jet has been the standard Access database engine for a long time, many database developers know it well. Compared to Microsoft SQL Server 2000 Desktop Engine, Jet requires less memory and much less disk space, so it's definitely the way to go if your computer is limited in either of these resources. And Jet is also decidedly easier to use — it offers fewer technical settings to bedevil you. If you know for sure that the database you're building will never need to run on a large network and doesn't need to perform 24 hours a day, use Jet.

When to go with Microsoft SQL Server 2000 Desktop Engine

Starting every new Access database project using Microsoft SQL Server 2000 Desktop Engine can save you trouble down the road — assuming that your organization uses SQL Server 2000 as its organization-wide database. Because Microsoft SQL Server 2000 Desktop Engine projects transfer to SQL Server 2000 with no modifications required, you can scale up your project almost instantly to many more users and much larger datasets. As with other high-end database managers, Microsoft SQL Server 2000 Desktop Engine and SQL Server 2000 offer many sophisticated features designed to support the hard-core networked database requirements — and not available in Jet. These advantages are discussed in the next several sections.

Network performance

On a heavily trafficked network, the volume of data sent back and forth across the network is a critical factor in the performance each user experiences. Unlike Jet, Microsoft SQL Server 2000 Desktop Engine is a true client/server database manager. When the user wants to work with a particular set of data, the user's application (the client) sends a request for that data to the server. Because this query is executed by the server, which returns only the desired data, a relatively small amount of data has to be sent over the network — especially if queries are carefully designed to hone in on specific information.

By contrast, when Jet is used on a network, it functions as a file server. It sends all the raw data required to run a user's query across the network back to the user's PC, where the user's copy of Jet executes the query. If the database is of any size, network performance sags.

Data integrity and reliability

Microsoft SQL Server 2000 Desktop Engine and SQL Server log transactions as they occur — Jet does not. If the network goes down or the power goes out, Microsoft SQL Server 2000 Desktop Engine restores the data to the last known state based on its transaction log. By contrast, Jet can't recover automatically from such errors. You have to use backup files to restore a damaged database, and if you made your last backup yesterday, you're out a full day's worth of important business records.

Security

Microsoft SQL Server 2000 Desktop Engine and SQL Server rely on Windows NT security, which you should already have in place for a solid network. Because Jet's security features are independent of the operating system, they have to be administered separately, costing you time and tribulation.

Scalability

Microsoft SQL Server 2000 Desktop Engine and Jet are comparable in terms of the amount of data (2GB files) and number of users (in practical terms, only a few) they can handle. But with adequate hardware, SQL Server demolishes these limits, allowing a practically unlimited number of simultaneous users and terabytes of data.

Database administration support

Microsoft SQL Server 2000 Desktop Engine enables you to conduct administration and maintenance while the database is open and being used. Aside from the obvious convenience, this means the database can stay online 24 hours a day. With Jet, you have to shut down the database to repair, compact, or replicate it.

Database or project?

In Microsoft-speak, an *Access database* corresponds to a Jet file. The alternative choice, which is made available in the New area every time you choose File ⇨ New to open the New File task pane in Access (see Figure 46-3), is a *project*, the front end for a SQL Server database.

Project files contain Access-specific items such as forms, reports, and VBA code, but no tables or queries. Instead, the queries and tables are housed in the SQL Server database file, where they can be called on by the Access project. (I discuss database components such as tables, queries, and reports in Chapter 45.)

Tip   Multiple projects can manipulate the same SQL Server database. If the database you want to work with in your project already exists, start a new project by clicking Project (Existing Data) in the New File task pane. If you want to create a new database at the back end along with the front-end project, use Project (New Data) instead.

After you've chosen the type of database you're creating, Access database or project, Access wants you immediately to name and save a skeleton file for the item. Jet databases are stored with the .MDB extension, projects, with the .ADP extension. As soon as you save a new Jet database, the database window, Access's central control panel, appears on your screen. If you've elected to create a project, however, you see instead the Microsoft SQL Server Database Wizard dialog box (if you're starting a new database) or the Data Link Properties box (if you're creating a project for an existing SQL Server database). These dialog boxes are shown in Figures 46-4 and 46-5.

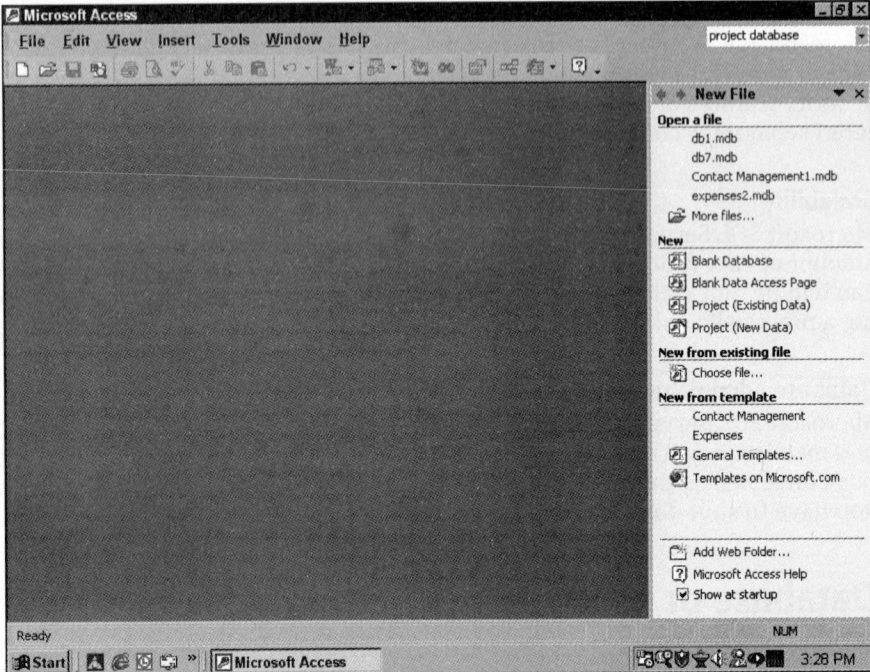

Figure 46-3: An Access database is different from a project; you choose which you want to start each time you start working in Access.

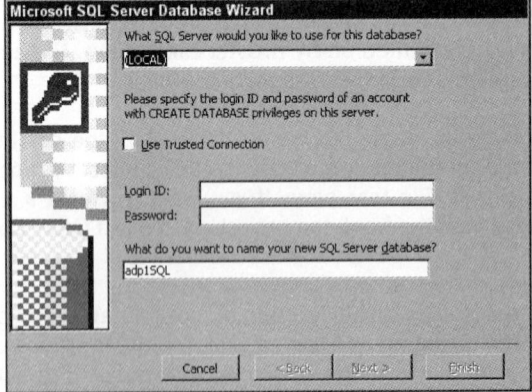

Figure 46-4: Use this wizard to start a new project and create a new SQL Server database in the process.

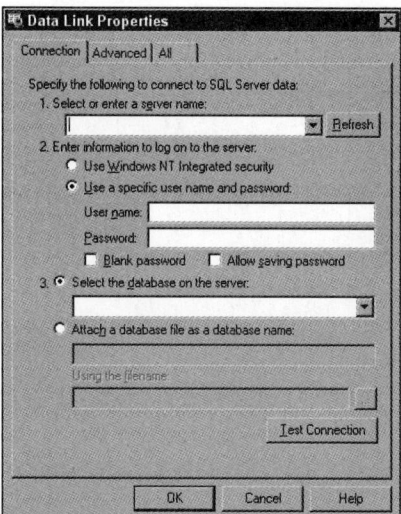

Figure 46-5: Select an existing SQL Server database for a project by specifying the server and the database name in this dialog box.

Upsizing a database from Jet to SQL Server

Suppose you decide to stick with Jet as your database engine — and later find that you need to move the data (or your entire database application) to a large network. Fortunately, you don't need to recreate the database from scratch using SQL Server. Instead, call on Access's Upsizing Wizard to convert the existing Jet database for you. If you simply want to place the data itself on the server, you're only a few mouse-clicks and some finger tapping away from the goal.

You may run into more complications if you're converting a full-fledged VBA application to an Access project — but these should be minimal if you wrote the application using ADO as your database object library.

You face somewhat more work if the code is based on DAO, but at least you don't have to redesign all the tables, queries, reports, and what not. (ADO and DAO are discussed in Chapter 49.)

To activate the Upsizing Wizard, choose Tools ⇨ Database Utilities ⇨ Upsizing Wizard (see Figure 46-6). In a series of panels, you're asked to specify options for the conversion, including which tables to include in the upsized database and how their attributes, such as default values and validation rules, are to be handled.

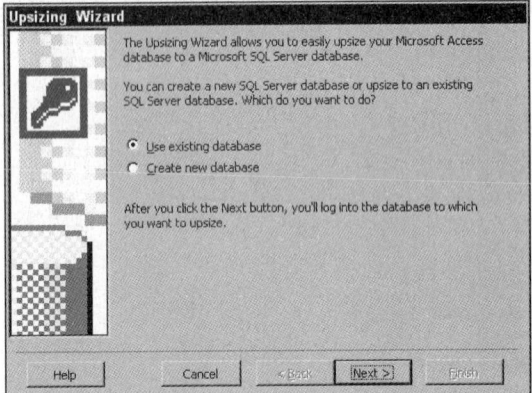

Figure 46-6: In this step of the upsizing processing, you choose the type of conversion the wizard makes.

In a key step, you can choose one of three upsizing methods:

✦ **No application changes.** This choice simply copies the data to equivalent tables in a SQL Server database. Use this choice to make your Jet data available on the network — presumably someone else is responsible for creating the front-end application for accessing the data, or perhaps you plan to use a tool other than Access to develop your own.

✦ **Link SQL Server tables to existing application.** If you select this option, the wizard creates equivalent tables in a SQL Server and then links your current Jet-based application to them. This usually isn't optimal; you gain none of SQL Server's performance, security, and scalability advantages. However, the tables are on the network where they can be readily accessed and maintained.

✦ **Create a new Access client/server application.** Choose this option to translate the existing database into a complete Access project, with the data stored in SQL Server and the .adp project file on your computer. You must specify a name for the project file.

Working in Access

Access's user interface parallels those of the other Office applications. Just be aware that Access provides an extensive set of keyboard shortcuts for navigating in database windows and editing data. I mention many of these individually in the chapters that follow, but I recommend that you refer from time to time to the comprehensive listing in the Keyboard Shortcuts Help topic.

Expanding entries for easy editing

One trick you really must master is zooming so you can much more easily edit the information in a field, text box, or property setting. Although you can edit these items directly, you often can't see the entire entry at once, and the text may be displayed in a tiny font. To edit the entry in a separate, comfortably large box, click the item or move into it with the keyboard and then press Shift+F2. In property sheets, you can right-click the setting and choose Zoom from the shortcut menu. Charitably enough, the Zoom box lets you select any font at any size for editing purposes.

Optimizing performance

Some relatively obvious ways to improve the performance of Access on your system include the following:

✦ **Equip your computer with plenty of memory.**

✦ **Keep your swap disk tuned.** Windows can usually manage its swap file (virtual memory) without your help. All you need to do is set aside plenty of free space on the hard disk containing the swap file. Regularly delete files you're not using or move them to storage disks. Defragmenting the swap file hard disk every now and then can't hurt.

✦ **Tweak virtual memory settings.** In some cases, you may want to take a more active role in managing virtual memory. Change the virtual memory settings by starting the System applet in the Windows Control Panel, selecting the Performance tab, and choosing Virtual Memory (click the Change button in NT). Increasing the minimum size for virtual memory can help, especially if your computer has barely enough RAM or you run multiple large applications simultaneously with Access. If a specific disk has more space than the one currently being used for virtual memory, tell Windows to switch to it.

✦ **Run your databases in exclusive mode.** If only one person will be using a database at any given time, opening it in exclusive mode not only locks other users out but also improves performance. To place a database in exclusive mode, check the Exclusive box in the File ➪ Open dialog box when you open the database. If you work on a single-user machine, it makes sense to set the default for all databases to exclusive mode by selecting the Exclusive radio button on the Advanced tab of the Tools ➪ Options dialog box.

✦ **Compact your databases regularly.** Compacting databases is discussed in the section "Housekeeping in Access," later in this chapter.

Using the Performance Analyzer

The Performance Analyzer is a powerful tool for improving a database's performance. It analyzes the entire database or any selected component looking for suboptimal settings and data storage techniques. After reporting its findings to you, it can carry out its recommendations at your command.

To use the Performance Analyzer, open the database to be analyzed. Then, on the Tools menu, choose Analyze ⇨ Performance. From the Performance Analyzer dialog box (see Figure 46-7), select the tab that corresponds to the type of database object you want to analyze, or switch to the All Object Types tab to see all the objects in alphabetical order. Then check off the specific objects of interest, or choose Select All to analyze every object on the current tab.

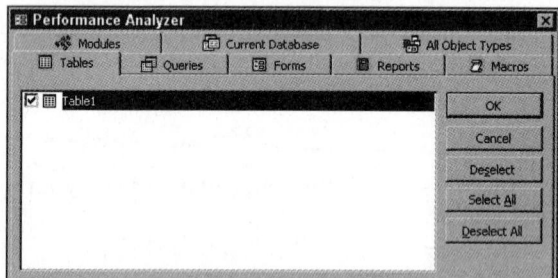

Figure 46-7: Use the Performance Analyzer to find out how to improve your database.

After the Performance Analyzer completes its work, a second dialog box displays the Analyzer's findings. These are divided into three categories of optimizations: Recommendations, Suggestions, and Ideas. When you click an item in the list, information about the proposed optimization appears at the bottom of the dialog box.

Note   As a rule of thumb, always accept optimizations in the Recommendations category. These are changes that can have no bad side effects and are virtually guaranteed to boost performance. Suggestions are optimizations that may have minor negative consequences. The Analysis Notes portion of the dialog box provides a risk/benefit analysis for the selected suggestion.

Access can make the changes advised under Recommendations and Suggestions for you. Select any combination of these optimizations and then choose Optimize. When the work is complete, the item is marked as Fixed. Optimizations listed under Ideas require manual implementation. Instructions appear in the Analysis Notes portion of the dialog box when you select the item.

Optimizing network performance

The client/server architecture of an Access - SQL Server database application is designed for efficient performance on a network. Of course, you can take steps to optimize performance for your specific application. One essential for maximum network speed is to minimize the amount of data sent and the number of trips back and forth between the server and user workstations. See to it that the server processes the data whenever possible—it should be considerably faster than any workstation. And optimize the database itself. Consider these suggestions:

✦ **Create stored procedures for any SQL statements that you expect to regularly execute.** Stored procedures are stored in the SQL Server database, where they can be activated by your application. Because they're compiled in advance, they execute faster than ordinary SQL statements.

✦ **Have the server sort records before it sends them to the requesting workstation.** You can accomplish this via stored procedures or SQL statements you place in a form or report's `RecordSource` property.

✦ **Limit the number of records users can retrieve at any one time.** Rather than allowing the user to call up an entire table, design your application so it focuses on records matching certain criteria. The smaller the number of records that have to move across the network, the faster your application seems to run—and the faster the network as a whole performs. To achieve this goal, use views, stored procedures, server filters, and WHERE clauses in SQL statements built into your code or the `RecordSource` properties of forms and reports.

✦ **Tweak the SQL server database for top performance.** Some suggestions: Turn on referential integrity to keep the relationships between tables intact as you modify the data. Define each field's data type and size so it is no larger than necessary to hold the data you expect to store in it. Create indexes for all fields used in sorts and joins, and for which criteria are set. Indexes make queries run much faster, so be sure to create them for fields used in queries you run frequently or that retrieve large sets of records.

Housekeeping in Access

As with most databases, Access files require periodic maintenance to keep them running efficiently. When you delete data from an Access database file, the file doesn't get smaller. Instead, Access just marks the data as deleted, leaving useless holes in the file. In the meantime, all new records are added at the end of the file. Note that modifying records actually causes the database file to get larger because Access deletes the old versions and adds new ones. In addition, performance is impaired because the records gradually get all jumbled up, resulting in a small-scale fragmentation problem analogous to the type that afflicts hard disks.

Access can reuse the space occupied by deleted records, but only after the file is compacted. Access can automatically compact a database at the time you close it, if it determines that doing so would recover a significant amount of disk space.

To turn on this feature, check the Compact on Close box in the General tab of the Tools ➪ Options dialog box. If you don't turn this option on, or if you keep the database open for long periods while many deletions and edits are made, you can compact the database manually by choosing Tools ⇨ Database Utilities ⇨ Compact and Repair Database.

You can compact both Access databases and projects. However, the benefits of compacting are much greater with Access databases, because compacting doesn't affect tables, views, and other objects that are actually stored in SQL Server.

Tip   The Compact and Repair Database command attempts to repair any defects found in an Access database. If your database is acting strangely, running this utility may fix the problem. Also, be sure to compact both copies of a replicated database.

✦   ✦   ✦

Fundamentals of Access

This chapter offers an intensive course in database management with Access. There is much more to learn, of course, but when you master the concepts and techniques covered here you can confidently set out to cruise the information sea.

Database Concepts: The Short Course

While the term *database* can refer to any collection of information, it's typically applied when the information in question consists of items that share common elements repeating in a regular pattern. That is, the information is structured. The standard example of a structured data collection is a set of Rolodex-style file cards. All the cards contain the same types of information (name, address, and so on), but the details vary on each card. Increasingly, however, *database* refers primarily to a digital collection of data organized and managed by database-management software such as Access.

Tables: Where the data dwells

As with all database software, Access presents each set of structured data in a *table*. The table has rows, each of which corresponds to one item (say, a person, company, product, part, or order). Each such item is called a *record*.

The table also has columns, each of which lists an individual detail about each item. If the records represent people, for example, the table might have columns for name, street address, and other details of various types. Each specific detail represented in a column occupies one of the record's *fields*.

Any given database can, and usually should, have more than one table. If you're building an order-entry database, for example, you will need one table for the customers, one for their orders, and one for the ordered items, at the very least. The alternative — mixing all kinds of information in a single table — leads to massive inefficiencies. (Imagine duplicating all the information about the ordering customer and each product ordered in every record you add to the database.) With Access, you need to store a customer's information only once — in its own separate table. When that customer places an order, you can link the customer's record to the order to show who bought what and when. This capability — linking separate tables — qualifies Access as a *relational database* in my book (after all, a link between tables is a kind of relationship), even though some experts could argue the point on purely technical grounds.

Queries: Focusing in on the data you want to see

Queries are commands you use to extract specific data from your Access tables. The most common type, the *select query,* collects records containing fields that match the criteria you specify. A query presents its findings in a table of its own, with the information arranged as you see fit. After you design a query, you can reuse it at any time to access the information in your database that currently matches those criteria. And you can base a form, report, or data access page on a query to determine which information appears on that item.

While you're designing an Access query, it appears as a special window containing tools for specifying the fields and criteria that define the query. However, Access queries are actually just graphical representations of SQL (structured query language) statements. You can convert an Access query into the equivalent SQL statement if you like, and you can even dispense with the query window and write the SQL code directly.

Forms, pages, and reports: Tools for interacting with data

On the screen, you use *forms* to work with the raw information provided by tables and queries in a more attractive, easier-to-read format. You can select specific fields you want to display, use controls such as drop-down lists and checkboxes to display them, and have the form make calculations based on the other information shown. You can add other controls such as push buttons that let the user control what information the form displays, adorn the form with formatted text and graphical touches, and customize the overall layout of all these items. The most basic kind of form simply shows the fields from one record of one table so you can focus on that item. However, a single form can combine information from more than one record and more than one table to show all the data you care about.

Data access pages are the Web equivalent of forms—they're the medium through which an Internet or network user of your database gets at the information of interest. As with forms, pages can display exactly the information you wish them to, all presented in a neatly formatted design. And compared to ordinary Web pages, data access pages are much more alive. Although you can convert an Access query into a static, unchanging Web page, a data access page lets the user interact with the information, requesting specific records at will.

When you want to print information from your database, you use *reports*. Much like a screen form, a report lets you choose criteria for the information that it extracts, and it lets you add text and graphical elements to describe and highlight the information. *Report snapshots* let you distribute Access reports in electronic form, so they can be viewed by others—even those who don't have Access.

Making things happen with macros and modules

You can analyze data well enough by viewing the database objects (the tables, forms, queries, and reports) and manipulating them with Access's menu commands. If you want Access to do more of your work for you, however, you can write *macros* and VBA *modules* to perform particular sequences of commands. The macros and modules you write are stored with your database, along with the other objects it contains.

You're free to run a macro or module whenever you like, but you can set things up so Access launches it automatically when a specific *event* occurs. Events are actions such as mouse-clicks, key presses, or changes in database content. In other words, you can program Access so it automatically responds to user actions or new information.

 **Cross-Reference** Although they can function quite similarly, macros and modules are fundamentally very different in concept. Chapter 48 discusses these differences in detail and helps you choose between the two technologies for your own applications.

Database objects

All the elements discussed so far (tables, forms, queries, reports, data access pages, macros, and modules) are, in Access jargon, *database objects*. The term is a convenient way to refer to the disparate elements of an Access database.

Planning a Database

The first step in creating a new database—one you should take even before you start Access—is to plan the database design. Start by putting into words the tasks you want to accomplish with the database.

If you run a small business, for instance, you know you want to keep track of your customers. But think in detail about what you might want to do with that information. Would you like to send mailings to select customers (such as those who haven't made purchases for more than a year, or those who have purchased a particular item or service in the past)? Be as detailed as you can be about these requirements.

With your statement of objectives in hand, get down to details by figuring out what you must do to meet your goals. List the specific items of information you'll need to store in your database; decide which database objects you must create to hold them.

Start from the finish line

This process can't be strictly linear, because the content, function, and layout of the various objects are interrelated. However, one way to proceed is to start by designing (on paper) the final output elements — on-screen forms, Web pages, and printed reports. From these, you can abstract the specific answers you need from your database — you'll need to plan queries to provide these answers. When you know all these details, you'll know what you need when it comes to the fundamental database building blocks — the tables and their fields.

As you sketch the designs of the reports and screens, write down all the individual information items each one contains on a master list. This list gives you a good starting point for determining which fields belong in the database.

 **Tip**   Keep in mind that you will probably need additional fields that don't appear on any report. Also, some items on your reports may not be fields, but calculated values.

Now rearrange the list, grouping related items together. The tables you need are likely to correspond to these groups.

Designing tables and organizing fields

Table design is probably the most difficult aspect of database planning to get right. The rule of thumb is that each field in a table should pertain to one kind of thing (or *subject,* as Microsoft puts it). A table's subject might be people, products, places, or events, but not "people and the products they bought" or "events and the people who attended."

Sometimes it's hard to know whether a particular bit of information pertains to one subject or another. Clearly, the decision on which table a field belongs in is somewhat arbitrary and depends on the particulars of the information. For example, is a phone number a characteristic of a person (like age or shoe size) or does it deserve to be considered a separate subject?

In the old days, when everybody had only two phone numbers, one for work and one for home, it would have been safe to put corresponding fields directly into the People table. Now, many people may have two home lines, a dedicated fax line, a cell phone, a pager, and sometimes more besides. Other people don't work outside the home, and have just one home number. Depending on how urgently you need to reach people, it's starting to look as if a separate Phone Number table would be a good idea.

Consider the following guidelines when deciding how to organize the information items on your master list, assigning them to fields on specific tables:

✦ If an information item can have only one entry per record, then it may be appropriate to create a field for it on the table that holds those records. A person's last name and a building's street address fit this criterion quite well. If the item represents a varying number of entries (such as orders placed by a customer), it belongs in its own table.

✦ If the information item is associated with other items that describe or qualify it, then it's a subject in its own right and probably should have its own table. A modern phone number, for instance, should be described by type (fax, pager, cell, and so on).

Of course, Access doesn't force you to place each subject in its own table. If you want to record only one phone number for each person, you could decide to place a pair of corresponding fields directly into the People table, one for the number and the other for its type (work or home).

Designing table relationships

After you have formed your own rough idea of which tables you need and the fields they should contain, your next step is to define the relationships among the tables. In Access, you must define these relationships explicitly before you can work with the data in separate tables together.

Continuing the earlier example, let's say you have a People table and a Phone Numbers table. Obviously, a table consisting only of phone numbers won't do you any good unless you like to make random phone calls. You need some way to know which phone number belongs to which person.

The classic solution to this problem is to identify or add a pair of fields, one in each table, that contain the same information. The names of the two related fields don't have to match, but the data they hold *must* match.

Because some people have identical names (did you know there's a national Jim Smith club?), you can't reliably identify the owner of a phone number only by name. In such situations — when a table contains no definitely unique field — you must create a field in both the People and Phone Number tables for a unique identifying number. Then, when you're looking at a person's record in the People table, Access can use this ID number field to locate phone number records that contain the same number in their related field.

With these ideas in mind, figure out how each pair of tables you've come up with are related, and specifically, which fields you should use to identify that relationship. As you evaluate each relationship between pairs, categorize it in one of the following types:

✦ **One-to-many.** In this type of relationship, a record in one table can have more than one matching record in the other table, but each record in the second table matches only one record in the first. For instance, a customer can place many orders, but each order is placed by only one customer. The Customers and Orders tables therefore have a one-to-many relationship.

✦ **Many-to-many.** Here, each record in one table can match to multiple records in the other. In the example of people's phone numbers, each person can have more than one phone number. But the opposite is also true — because some people live or work at the same location, a phone number can have more than one person. Thus, the People and Phone Number tables have a many-to-many relationship.

✦ **One-to-one.** In a one-to-one relationship, one, and only one, record in one table matches one, and only one, record in the other. If you find such a relationship in the tables you've designed, you should reevaluate the way you've organized them. Usually, items in a one-to-one relationship go in the same table. However, sometimes it makes sense to carve out such items as a separate table, perhaps to make a table with many fields more manageable.

Defining fields in detail

With the overall organization of your database taking shape, you can now focus on the details of each field's definition. For each field, you must do the following:

✦ **Come up with a short but memorably descriptive name.** Access allows up to 64 characters (including spaces) for a field name.

✦ **Decide on the data type for the field.** (Table 47-1 lists your options.) All items within the same field must be of the same data type.

✦ **Determine acceptable values for the field.** Access can perform data validation — that is, it can check entries to make sure they match criteria you've defined. For example, the Age field from a Grown-ups table may contain a range of permissible values "greater than 17."

✦ **Decide on how you want the field data to appear in tables and fields.** In Access, a field's format can be used to separate parts of the entry in a field making the information easier to read without changing the stored data. As a simple example, raw numbers such as 123456 might be formatted to read 123,456.

✦ **Write all these choices down for use when you create the table.**

Table 47-1
Access Field Data Types

Data Type	Type of Data Stored
Text	Letters, numerals, and punctuation to a maximum of 255 characters. Use the Text type for numbers, such as phone numbers and zip codes, that won't be used in calculations.
Memo	Letters, numerals, and punctuation to a maximum of 64,000 characters
Number	Numeric values for calculations, except monetary amounts
Date/Time	Dates and times, of course. Use the Date/Time data type rather than Number so dates and times will be sorted properly.
Currency	Dollars and cents, pounds or yen, and so on. Access doesn't round off calculated currency values. The currency symbol and other formatting shown in the field are based on the selected currency type in the Regional Settings applet of the Control Panel.
AutoNumber	A number that Access enters automatically in sequence each time you add a new record
Yes/No	1 or 0 only (interpreted as logical values Yes/No, True/False, On/Off)
OLE object	Any OLE object up to 1 gigabyte in size (Chapter 7 covers OLE)
Hyperlink	A URL or UNC path hyperlink containing up to 64,000 characters

Planning queries

Making sense of all the raw information stored in a table requires effective use of queries. During the planning stage, just write out the questions that need to be answered in ordinary English. If your database tracks dairy products and you want to know the price of eggs in Wisconsin, you'll need a query to extract that information.

Designing forms, data access pages, and reports

Although you can view, enter, and manipulate data effectively in the default table view, designing on-screen forms for these tasks improves efficiency and accuracy and makes the experience more fun. Likewise, if you're publishing database information on the Web, presenting that information as data access pages enables users of your Web site to work with just the data they need to see.

During the design phase, your job is to determine which forms and pages you need and to lay them out on paper, at least roughly. A form or page in Access has a defined area in which you can see and edit each piece of information. These areas, of course, correspond to fields in your database. A form or page can include fields from more than one table as long as you have created relationships between the tables. In addition to fields, items you can place on a form or page include text for labels and instructions; calculations based on field values; controls such as buttons, checkboxes, and drop-down lists; and graphics and OLE objects. Sketch each form, placing the fields and other items in logical order.

Access Boot Camp: Database Construction Techniques

With the plan for your database in hand, you've earned the right to let Access show you what it can do on the open road. The rest of this chapter is devoted to a whistle-stop tour of the fundamental Access objects and features you'll need to manage databases with this rich piece of software.

Using the Database window

When you run Access without specifying a database to open, the New File task pane appears, prompting you to open or create one. What you see when you eventually open an existing database or create a new one varies a great deal, depending on which database you open or which template you use as the starting point for a new database.

If you choose to create a Blank Database, you're first asked to give your database a name and choose a location for it. After you've done that, the Database window appears on your screen.

Note   In a completed database application, the Database window is often hidden from view, replaced by a switchboard form that provides buttons for activating functions specific to the application.

Shown in Figure 47-1, the Database window consists of a main panel in which you can see and work with the seven types of database objects. The Objects bar at the left of the window determines which objects appear in this main area. By clicking a button in the Objects bar, you can display all the objects of a given type together or access customized groups containing any mix of objects you want to work with together. If you click the Forms item, for example, the Database window displays any Forms objects that currently exist in the database.

Tip   Much as in My Computer or Explorer, you can change the way the window displays objects (as large or small icons, and so on) using toolbar buttons.

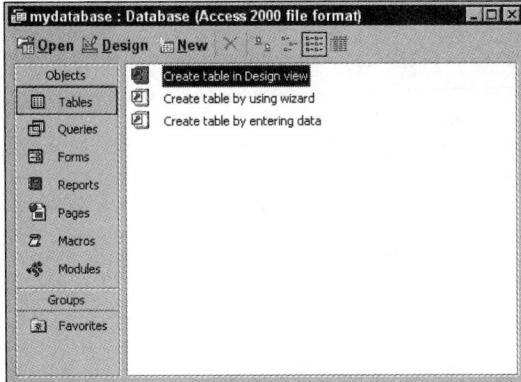

Figure 47-1: Use the Database window as your springboard to database objects in Access.

Although each type of database object serves a different purpose — and its icon is unique — you work with objects in the Database window in the same basic ways. Use the window's four main buttons as follows:

✦ **Choose New to create a new object.** Alt+N works too, but don't press Ctrl+N — that starts a new database, not a new object. The New command isn't available when you're working in a group. However, you can always create a new object of any type by choosing from the Insert menu.

✦ **Select an object and choose Design to modify it.** The corresponding keyboard shortcuts are Ctrl+Enter or Alt+D.

✦ **Select an object and choose Open, Preview, or Run to activate it.** The button label varies depending on which tab you're using. Double-clicking the object (or selecting it and then pressing Enter) accomplishes the same thing.

✦ **Right-click an object and choose Create Shortcut from the resulting menu.** Use this technique to place a shortcut to that object on the Desktop, on the Start menu, or in any folder. When you activate the shortcut in Windows, Access runs and opens the selected table, form, or other object.

Tip   You can make the Database window work like a browser (so pointing to an object selects it and single-clicking an object opens or runs it). Go to the View tab of the Tools ➪ Options dialog box and select Single-Click Open. Also, you can jump to an object in the current list by starting to type its name. As you type each character, Access selects the first object that matches your entry.

With the exception of the Run choice for macros and modules, each of these actions opens a separate window containing the object. You can open multiple objects, each in its own window, and navigate from window to window using the mouse, the Window menu, or the keyboard shortcuts shown in Table 47-2. As you open windows and switch between them, Access changes the menu and toolbars according to which type of object the active window contains.

| Table 47-2 | |
| Selected Keyboard Shortcuts for Navigating in Access | |
To Do This	*Press This Keyboard Shortcut*
Rename the selected object	F2
Select the next or the previous tab	Ctrl+Tab or Shift+Ctrl+Tab
Enter Design view for the selected database object	Ctrl+Enter or Alt+D
In Design View, go to property sheet	F4
Create a new object	Alt+N
Switch to the next window	Ctrl+F6
Switch to the previous window	Ctrl+Shift+F6
Toggle between views	Ctrl+> or Ctrl+. (period) or Ctrl+< or Ctrl+, (comma)

Tip Closing the Database window closes the entire database. If you want the Database window out of your way, *don't* click the Close button—minimize the window instead, or choose Window ➪ Hide.

Working with views

With the exception of macros and modules, you can display all Access database objects in at least two different views (three, if you count Print Preview). The views available depend on the type of object you're working with, as follows:

✦ Use **Design view** to define fields for a table, set up a query, lay out a form or report, or write a macro or module.

✦ **Datasheet view** presents information in a *datasheet*, a spreadsheet-like grid containing the data from a table, form, or query. If you view a form in Datasheet view, you see only data from the table on which the form is primarily based (the one listed as the form's RecordSource property), even though the form may include fields from other tables.

✦ **Form view**, of course, displays a form as a working unit.

✦ **SQL view** for queries displays the SQL (Structured Query Language) code that the query runs to retrieve or modify data.

✦ **PivotTable** and **PivotChart views** are new to Access 2002. With these, you can view any .MDB table or query, or .ADP table, view, stored procedure, function or form as either a PivotTable or PivotChart. This feature can help you analyze data more efficiently.

For a complete discussion of PivotTables and PivotCharts, see Chapter 28.

✦ **Print Preview** is available for all objects. The Layout Preview (available only when you're working with a report in Design view) also lets you see the report as it will print but prepares the preview faster, because it displays only a sample of your data and doesn't carry out underlying queries in full.

The quickest way to switch between available views is via the object's shortcut menu. To bring up the shortcut menu for the entire object — as opposed to the menu for a component such as a field, column, or control — right-click the title bar of the object's window. The available views are listed at the top of the menu.

You can also switch between views using the View menu or the View button, which appears at the far-left side of the default toolbar when a table, query, form, or report window is active (this is where you'll find the Datasheet view).

When you first use the View button, you may find its behavior a bit strange. It's not telling you which view you're looking at now, but rather, which one you would switch to if you clicked it. The View button is a split button. If more than one view is available for the current object and the one you want isn't showing, you can click the thin rectangle to the right of the button image to list all the available views and make your selection there.

Creating and working with tables

The first practical step in building a new database is to create its tables, defining the fields each one contains. If you have planned the database before starting work (as I previously recommended), you can focus on the mechanics at this point.

Starting from the Table item on the Database window, creating a new table is as simple as double-clicking one of the "Create table" icons. You can open the new table in either Datasheet or Design view, or you can use a wizard to build the table for you based on your input. Alternatively, you can hit the New button or press Alt+N to bring up the dialog box shown in Figure 47-2. In addition to the same datasheet, Design view, and wizard choices you get with the icons, this box also lets you add existing tables from another source to the current Access database via the Import Table or Link Table options.

Two words to the wise are in order here:

✦ **The wizard is only useful if you need one of its predefined tables.** These cover all kinds of common subjects (in the database sense of that term defined earlier), such as products, people, and personal collections and activities. They define appropriate fields for you, cutting your work to a minimum. But if the table you're creating is on a different subject, it's probably easier to start from scratch than to modify a wizard's table.

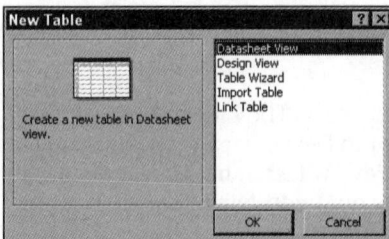

Figure 47-2: Access offers these choices when you create a new table. Note that the default choice at the top opens the new table in Datasheet view.

✦ **Use Design view for new tables if you're not using the wizard.** Note that Access selects Datasheet view as the default in the New Table dialog box. It's easy to create and reorder fields in Datasheet view, and Access figures out what type of field you've created based on the data you enter. However, you must use Design view to take control over the fields in detail. Why not start there, especially if you've gone to the trouble of planning the table in detail beforehand?

Defining fields in Design view

Figure 47-3 shows an example of a table in Design view. The top part of the window consists of a listing of the fields in the table by name, and in the order in which they appear in the table.

To create a new field, follow these steps:

1. Type in its name under Field Name.

2. Press Tab to move to the Data Type column and select the correct type from the drop-down list (as elsewhere in Windows and Office, you can drop the list down by pressing F4).

Tip
If you haven't planned the field definitions in advance, refer to Table 47-1 for a listing of data types.

3. Press Tab to add a description of the field in the appropriate column, if you like.

That was the easy part. The lower half of the Design View window, used to define field properties, is where you'll need your wits about you.

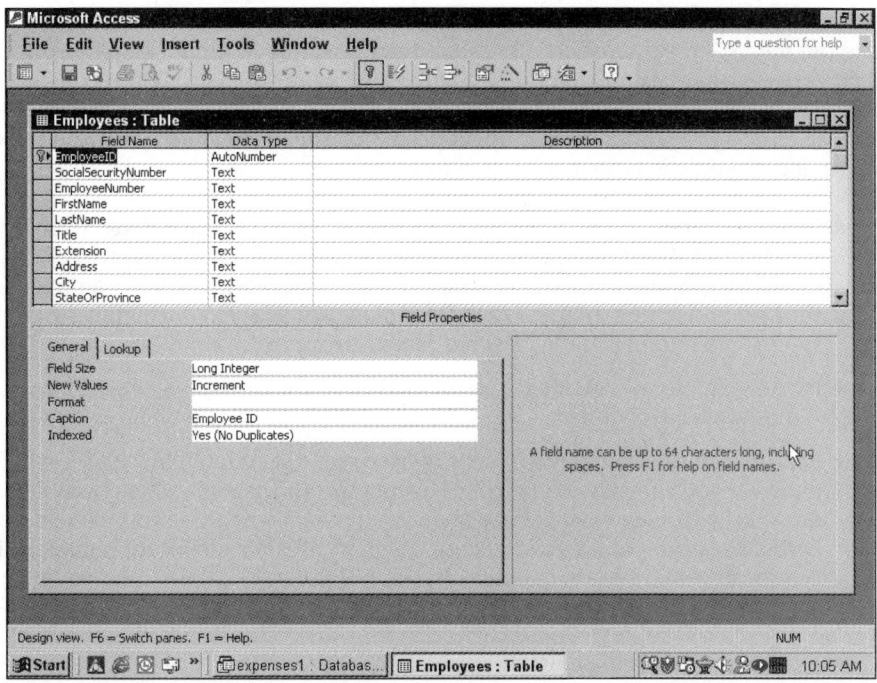

Figure 47-3: A table as it appears in Design view

Working with field properties

For each field, the General tab in the Field Properties area lists the properties you can set that are available for the field's data type. Although the available properties vary between types, most of them are common to all types of fields. As you move among the properties, the pane to the right displays a help message describing their functions. The help message should suffice for some of the items, but you'll need more background for others. I provide some critical pointers here, and you can always press F1 to get detailed information on the current property.

Although you can define a property by typing an entry, Access often helps you enter the setting. When you move to most properties, a drop-down list button, a builder button (a button which opens a dialog box that helps with the task at hand), or both appear. You can then select an entry from the drop-down list or click the builder button to get help constructing an expression.

The Lookup tab in the Field Properties area displays properties for any Lookup field that you've added. A Lookup field is one that looks in another table for the information it contains. If you haven't added a Lookup field, the Lookup tab is blank.

Formatting a field

Use the field's Format property to define the appearance of data displayed in the field — the format has no effect on the stored value of the data. When you enter data into a field, the format takes effect only when you save the data. You can choose from a predefined format appropriate for the field's data type from the drop-down list, or you can type in a custom format.

✦ In Number and Currency fields, the General format is the default, even if you don't select it — it makes no change to the way the number is entered. If you choose the Standard, Percent, Fixed, or Currency formats, you can override the default for the number of decimal places displayed — which is two — by typing in a number in the Decimal Places property.

✦ By default, Date/Time fields are displayed in the format selected in the Windows Control Panel.

✦ For Yes/No-type fields (representing Boolean data) that allow only one of two choices, you can select any of three standard formats: Yes/No, True/False, or On/Off. You can also create formats of your own for custom two-choice fields. For example, to have Access display either **In** or **Out** for a field of this type, you would type the following:

    ;"In";"Out"

✦ Text and Memo fields have no standard formats.

✦ Many fields, such as Text, Number and AutoNumber, require you to set a Field Size (the number of characters allowed in the field).

Defining an input mask

Use an *input mask* to control the way data is entered in the first place. The Input Mask property can include characters that separate portions of an entry, such as the dashes in a social security number. In addition, it controls which type of character can be typed into the field (letter or number) and which characters are required or optional. By default, these extra characters aren't stored in the table data.

Access supplies input masks for common fields such as phone numbers. Click the builder button beside the Input Mask property to display the Input Mask Wizard shown in Figure 47-4. You can select one of the prefab input masks or choose Edit List to redefine them.

Defining validation rules

The Validation Rule and Validation Text properties tell Access to check entries in the field to ensure they meet your specifications. For instance, you can require that entries fall into a certain alphabetic or numeric range.

Enter the validation rule itself into the property by the same name. You can click the builder button to run the Expression Builder, shown in Figure 47-5. The Validation Text property is for a message that Access should display when someone types data that violates the rule into the field.

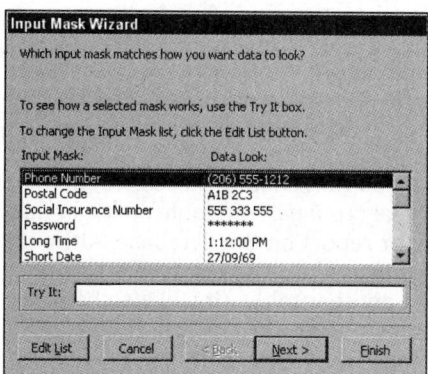

Figure 47-4: This wizard lets you select from a variety of predefined input masks.

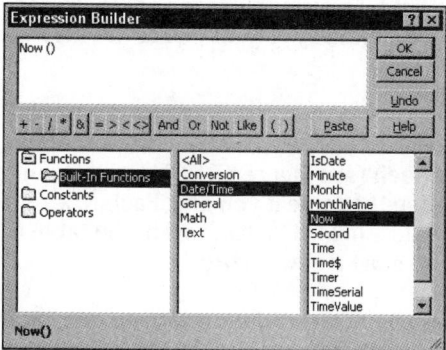

Figure 47-5: Use the Expression Builder any place in Access you need to define criteria or create a calculation.

Tip   You can also set up record validation rules that can test one field against another, for example, to confirm that the area code entered is valid for the listed city. Set up record validation rules on the Properties sheet for the table as a whole. Another tip: To see whether the data currently stored in a table meet the validation rules you've set up, choose Edit ⇨ Test Validation Rules while in table Design view. Access checks through the table and reports its findings.

Working with fields in Design view

You can perform the following actions with fields in a table's Design view:

   ✦ To move a field in the list, click and drag its row header to a new location.

   ✦ To insert or delete fields (rows), right-click over the field and choose the appropriate command from the shortcut menu.

✦ To add a new field from one of the prefab tables supplied with Access, right-click where you want the field to be inserted in the list, and then choose Build from the shortcut menu.

Specifying a primary key field

A table's *primary key* is the field or set of fields that enables Access to identify a record as unique. Access uses the primary key to *index* the table so it can find the records you want quickly when you query or report on the database. Although Access doesn't force you to specify one, you should do so because it will be required if you decide to relate the table to another table. (It will also keep Access from nagging you; if you don't define a primary key to begin with, Access will ask you if you want to do so when you close your table in Design View.)

If you know that a field in the table will have a unique value in every single record, you can use that field as the table's primary key. Otherwise, you should add a field of the AutoNumber data type as the primary key. Access automatically numbers each record you add in sequence in this field, ensuring a unique value. To set a field as the primary key, right-click it and choose Primary Key, or select the field and choose Edit ➪ Primary Key.

Working with tables in Datasheet view

Use Datasheet view to display a table as such (see Figure 47-6). Here you can enter or edit table data, but you can also redefine the table if you like. Each row represents a record, and each column represents a field. The last row in the table is marked with a star, indicating the place to start a new record.

The controls at the bottom left of the Datasheet view window let you quickly move among the records. The display there shows the number of the current record. Click this area and type in a record number to jump to that record. Starting from the left, the first four arrow buttons take you to the first, previous, next, and last records, respectively. The fifth button, the one with the star, goes beyond the last record, starting a new one.

Tip

Access datasheets based on tables let you display matching records in a subsidiary datasheet. If the table you're working with has a primary key, the first column in its datasheet consists of expand indicators, little boxes containing plus signs. Click the expand indicator of a chosen record for an instant display of records matching that primary key value from the related table.

Selecting and editing data in tables

For operations such as cut-copy-paste edits, you can select individual characters, all the contents of a single field, entire rows and columns, or a whole table:

   ✦ **To select a single record (row):** Click its record selector, the gray box at the far left of the table. An arrow or other icon appears in the record selector of the selected record.

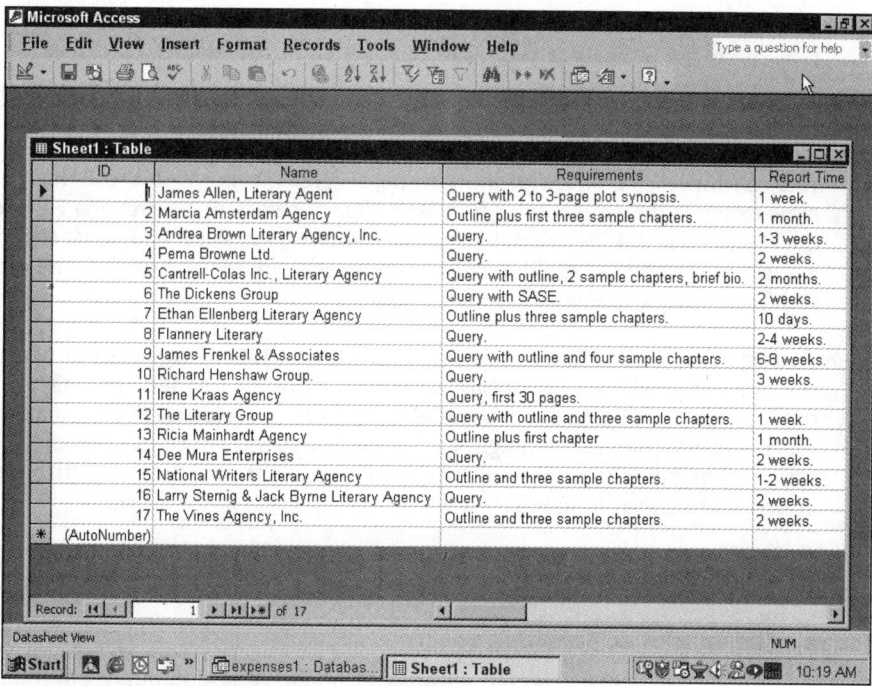

Figure 47-6: A table displayed in Datasheet view

✦ **To select a single column (field):** Click its field selector, the column heading. For many operations on single rows or columns, however, you need only click anywhere in a row or column.

✦ **To select multiple rows or columns:** Drag in the row or column header area.

✦ **To select the whole table**: Click the box at the top-left corner of the table.

✦ **To select a block of fields:** Shift+click first at one corner of the block and then at the opposite corner diagonally.

Tip

When a field contains data, moving to it with the arrow keys selects the entire field. To edit the individual characters, press F2. You can change this behavior by opening the Tools ⇨ Options dialog box, switching to the Keyboard tab, and selecting either of two buttons, Go to Start of Field or Go to End of Field. If you make this change, press F2 after entering a field to select the whole field.

Controlling table structure and appearance

Mouse acrobatics and shortcut menus provide the fastest means for manipulating a table's organization or looks in Datasheet view. Try the following techniques:

✦ **To insert a new field in the table:** Right-click in the column heading and choose Insert Column from the shortcut menu. The new column appears to the left of the one you started with. In similar fashion, insert a new record by right-clicking the row header and choosing New Record. The new record appears at the bottom of the table.

✦ **To move a column (field) with the mouse:** Click and drag the column header to its new location.

You can move columns with the keyboard. After moving to the column to be moved, select the whole entry (if it isn't already selected) by pressing F2. Press Ctrl+Space to select the column, using the arrow keys to select additional columns if desired. Then press Ctrl+Shift+F8 to turn on Move mode and execute the move with the arrow keys. Press Esc to finish up.

✦ **To resize a column:** Move the mouse pointer to the column's left boundary in the column header so the pointer becomes a double-headed arrow. Then drag the boundary. You can use a parallel technique to resize all the rows at once, but you can't change the heights of individual rows. To set the row or column size to a specific measurement, choose Row Height or Column Width from the appropriate shortcut menu.

Freeze one or more selected columns to keep them visible at the left of the window as you scroll the table horizontally. Select the columns, right-click the column heading of the selection, and choose Freeze Columns.

✦ **To hide one or more selected columns:** Choose Hide Columns from the shortcut menu. The Unhide Columns selection is on the shortcut menu for the whole table, produced by right-clicking the title bar of the table window.

✦ **To change the font for the table as a whole:** Use the Font choice on the table's shortcut menu (right-click the table's title bar) or on the main Format menu. To alter the table's appearance in other ways, choose Datasheet from either menu. The Datasheet Formatting dialog box, shown in Figure 47-7, lets you turn gridlines on or off, select table color, and activate 3-D effects.

Defining relationships among tables

Individual tables can hold a lot of information, but the key to a database's real power lies in the relationships among the tables. To set up these relationships in Access, close any open tables, and then choose Tools ➪ Relationships or click the Relationships button on the Database toolbar.

The Show Table dialog box appears automatically if no relationships have been defined for the database. Choose the tables and queries you want to work with from the lists provided and then click Add to display them in the Relationships window, the big workspace open behind the Show Table dialog box. Click Close when you've added all the tables or queries you want to work with. To re-open the Show Table dialog box again to add additional tables or queries, right-click in any blank area of the Relationships window and choose Show Table from the shortcut menu.

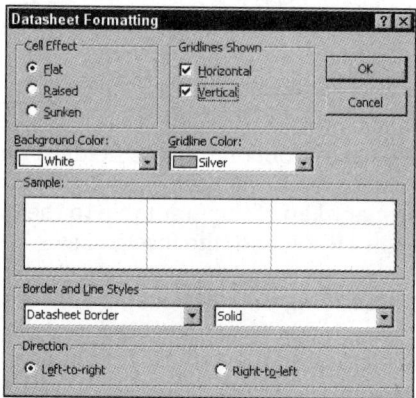

Figure 47-7: Use the Datasheet Formatting
dialog box to alter a table's overall appearance.

The Relationships window (see Figure 47-8) is where the links among your tables
can be comfortably defined, viewed, and edited in graphical fashion. Each little box
in the window is a *field list* and represents a table in the database. The primary key
field is shown in bold (tables without primary keys can't be related to other tables
or shown in the Relationships window).

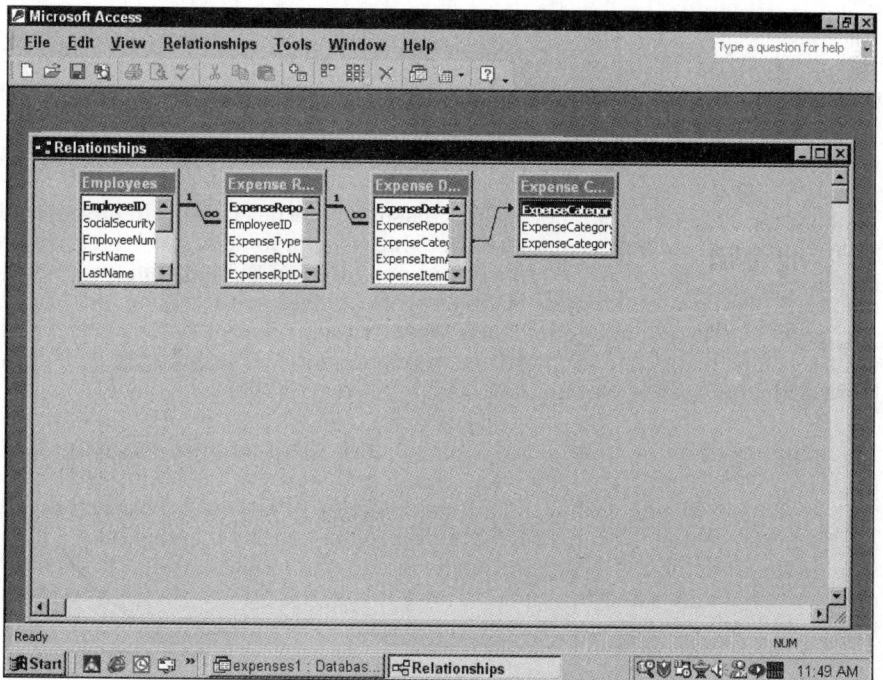

Figure 47-8: Define relationships among tables graphically in Access using this window.

Tip   Queries, which define new tables, can also be related to tables or other queries.

Setting up and editing relationships

To define a relationship, you just drag a field name from one table's field list and drop it on a field name in the other table's list. In the usual case — when defining a one-to-many relationship — you drag the primary key of the first table to the matching field that contains the same information in the second, the foreign key.

When you release the button, a dialog box describing the relationship appears. If you goofed on the fields you intended to connect, you can correct the mistake here. After you choose Create, Access draws a line between the two fields to indicate the relationship. If you can drag the field lists around on the window, this *relationship line* is redrawn accordingly.

Tip   To edit an existing relationship, double-click its relationship line.

Defining many-to-many relationships

Access doesn't provide for direct many-to-many relationships between two tables, even though they occur in many real-life situations (see "Designing table relationships" earlier in this chapter for a definition of the concept). To work around this problem, you must create a third table called a *junction table* and relate it to both of the other tables.

The *junction table* requires only two fields, defined to match those of the primary keys in each of the original tables. The junction table's primary key must be set to both of these required fields. To set a primary key to multiple fields, hold down Ctrl while you select the fields, and then choose Edit ➪ Primary Key.

The People and Phone Numbers tables discussed earlier in this chapter provide a good example of a many-to-many relationship — a person can have many different phone numbers, and a phone number can connect you to many different people. If the People table's primary key is the Person ID field, in the Phone Numbers table you might use the Phone Number field itself as the primary key. However, if you want to allow for situations where one phone number serves as both a voice and fax line, the primary key would be a Phone Number ID field.

Assuming you take the latter course, the junction table required would include two fields, Person ID and Phone Number ID. Together, these two items establish a unique entry — no person has more than one copy of a specific phone number. After you've created the junction table, you can set up the many-to-many relationship. In the Relationships window, define one-to-many relationships between each of the original tables and the junction table, using the primary keys to connect them.

Getting Answers

Unprocessed, raw information in a set of big tables is essentially useless. The whole point of database software is that it helps you dig through that data to find the specific facts you need, organized as required by your project.

Finding, sorting, and filtering data

The simplest data manipulations require very little work but produce quick, often very useful results.

Finding and replacing data

Access can perform word processing functions like find and replace operations on your data. Searching for data with this technique is much slower than using a query, but it works fine with smaller tables and is very convenient.

To look for a needle in a data stack, open a table, query, or form and press Ctrl+F or choose Edit ➪ Find. The settings you make in the Find dialog box are critical to locating the data you want. In the Match list, select Any Part of Field if you're not sure whether the items you're seeking occupy entire fields or just parts of fields.

Be sure to check the setting of the Look In box. Your selection here determines whether your search is confined to the field that was active when you opened the dialog box or covers the entire table, query, or form. As in other Office applications, Access tries to shield you from too many choices in the Find and Replace dialog box.

Tip
If you feel bold, click More to display additional options. The function of one of these choices may not be obvious: When the Search Fields as Formatted box is available, check it if you want to match the Find What entry to the field data as displayed, instead of to its stored value.

Sorting and filtering

To sort the records in a table, query, or form according to a field, right-click in the field and choose Sort Ascending or Sort Descending from the shortcut menu. These quick commands let you sort on multiple fields in a table or query, but only if they're adjacent — you have to select them as a group. To restrict the items displayed in a table, query, or form to those matching a given value or expression, right-click in the field and choose one of the following Filter options from the shortcut menu:

✦ **Filter by Selection.** This option uses the value of the current field (or block of fields, if more than one is selected) as the filter criterion. Say you have a large table of dogs and you've just clicked in the Breed column in a field containing Poodle. If you filter by selection, the table shrinks to show only the poodle records.

✦ **Filter Excluding Selection.** This option also uses the value of the current field (or block of fields, if more than one is selected) as the filter criterion. If you filter excluding selection (in the same table of dogs mentioned in the previous example) and you've just clicked the Breed column in a field containing Poodle, the table displays records for all breeds *except* poodles.

✦ **Filter For.** This option lets you type in a value or enter an expression for the filter to look for.

Other filtering techniques are available. Choose Records ➪ Filter ➪ Filter by Form to open a special window based on the original object. Here, you can type or select filter criteria into any of the fields. If you want to specify additional sets of filter criteria — to display records matching any of the criteria sets — click the Or tab at the bottom of the window and type in the new criteria. When you've completed the entries, click the Apply Filter button on the toolbar.

For more sophisticated sort and filter operations, choose Records ➪ Filter ➪ Advanced Filter/Sort.

Creating queries

Queries are your core tool for industrial-strength information-retrieval operations. Queries can also act upon your data, adding or deleting records or creating brand-new tables in response to your instructions. Filters let you display only certain records; queries not only track down specific records but manipulate them.

Note A *query* is a specification from which Access creates a temporary table each time you run the query. That means you can use queries anywhere you use tables — as the basis for forms, data access pages, reports, and even other queries.

Types of queries

There are several types of queries:

✦ **The select query.** This is the basic type of Access query. Based on criteria you specify, it extracts data from one or more tables and places the information in a datasheet. You can include calculations and totals of various types in the query, such as a count of the records with the name Fido in the Dog's Name field or an average of the values in all the Owner's Age fields. You can edit the items in the resulting datasheet, and your changes update the corresponding fields in the original tables.

✦ **The parameter query.** This type is just a select query based on criteria that you define when the query runs. The query displays a special dialog box in which you type the information for the criteria. The obvious example is a query based on a range of dates that you specify on an ad-hoc basis when you run the query.

✦ **The crosstab query.** Use a query of this type to total, average, or count the values in a field grouped by the contents of another field.

✦ **The action query.** This type alters multiple records in one step. Use one of these when you want to raise prices across the board or add a prefix to all part numbers for a certain product line.

✦ **The SQL query.** This type of query is based on an SQL (Structured Query Language) statement. (Actually, Access uses SQL statements to implement all queries, as you can see if you use View ➪ SQL View to look at any query.) In an SQL query, *you* write the SQL statement.

Designing a query

If all you want to do is look at the data in a selection of fields, the Query Table Wizard is probably the easiest way to set up your query. When it comes to finding specific information of interest, however, the wizard leaves you high and dry.

In Design view, a query window is split horizontally across the middle, as shown in Figure 47-9. The top part shows the field lists for all the tables available in the query, and the lower part contains the actual query specifications. You can add additional tables to the upper part by clicking the Show Table button on the toolbar.

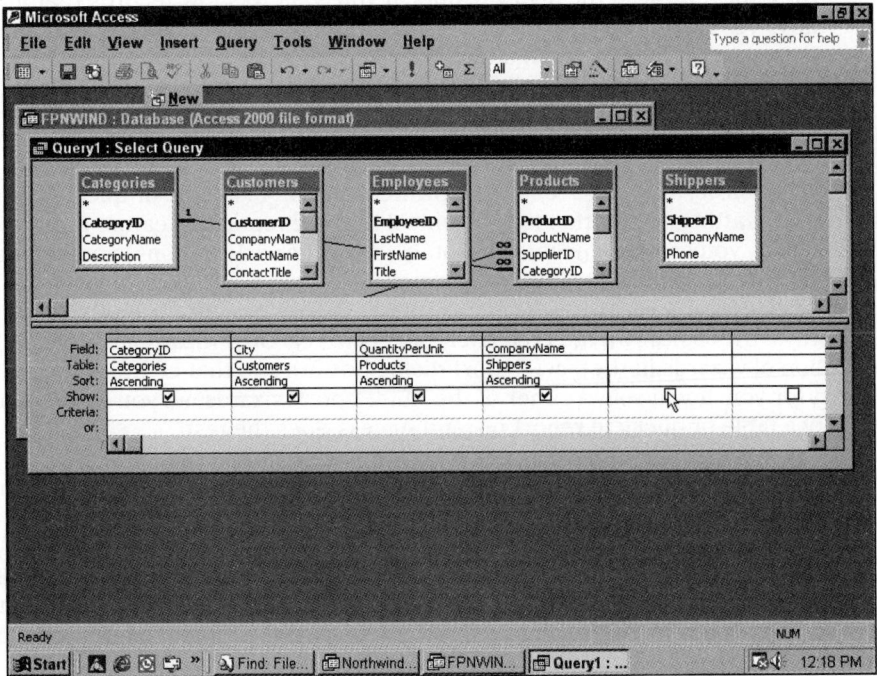

Figure 47-9: Defining a query in Design view

The *design grid* occupies the lower half of the query window. Each column represents a field used to select records for inclusion in the query. To enter a field in the query, you drag it from one of the field lists into a column.

Drag the asterisk (*) from the top of a field list to a query column to include all the fields in the query with special updating features activated. From now on, when you add or delete fields in the underlying table, these changes appear automatically in the query results datasheet. However, you can't select individual fields to show or hide, and you must add individual fields to the design grid if you want to use them to sort or filter the query results.

The remaining rows in the design grid work as follows:

✦ Use the Sort row to define fields on which the query datasheet will be sorted. If you sort on more than one field, Access performs the sorts in the order in which the fields appear in the design grid, working from left to right. You can move the column for a field by dragging it to a new location after first clicking the heading to select it.

✦ Check the box in the Show row if you want that field to appear in the query results — at times, you use a field to determine which records appear in the query, but you don't want to see that field's data.

✦ Place in the Criteria row any criteria that your records must match before they can appear in the query results. If you want to show records that match any of several different criteria sets, use additional rows labeled Or below the Criteria row to define each alternative set.

Distributing reports

At its most basic, an Access *report* is a printed version of a table or query with fancier formatting. In addition to the control that the reporting feature gives you over layout, you can also include subtotals (and other calculations) and add decorative elements to make the high points stand out.

As always, the easiest way to create a report is to rely on a wizard. Included in the selection of wizards in the New Report dialog box are two that create an entire report for you. If you select either of the AutoReport wizards, all you have to do is specify a table or query to report on, and Access does the rest.

Tip   Obviously, AutoReports lack originality. To stamp a report with your personal touch, work on it in Design view (see the next section).

If you want to distribute a report electronically instead of on paper, convert it into a report snapshot by choosing File ➪ Export and choosing Snapshot Format in the Save As Type box. You can make available a report snapshot file to interested parties on disk, via e-mail, or on the Web.

Working with reports in Design view

Design view shows the underlying structure of the report. As you can see in Figure 47-10, reports have five main sections. Items you place on the report print differently, depending on which section you put them in.(There are also two possible sections that don't appear in this figure, although I've mentioned them in the list below. That's because they're based on Groups, which haven't been set up for this report. See the section on "Grouping items in reports," later in this chapter.)

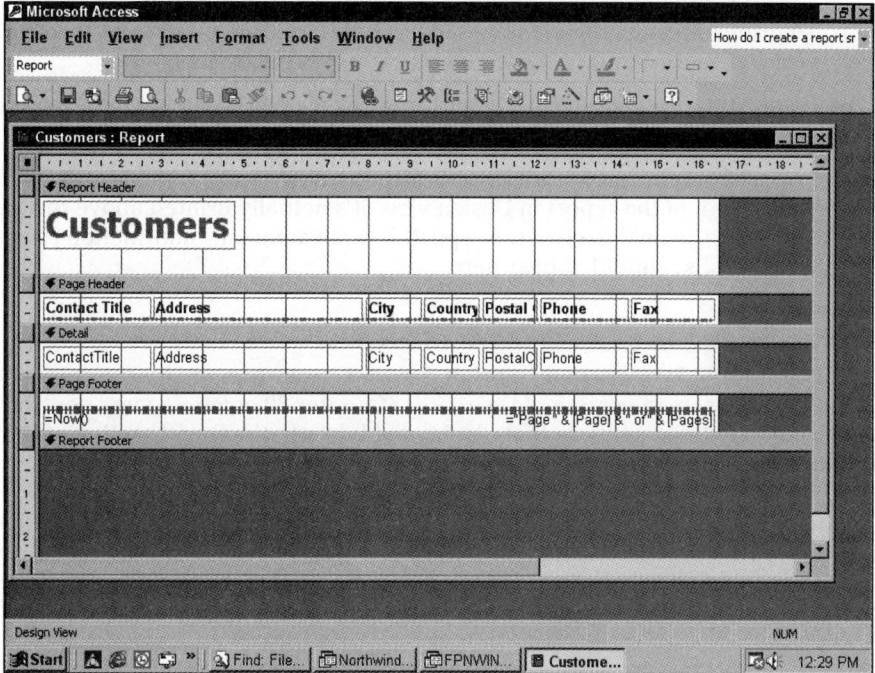

Figure 47-10: The report design takes shape in this window.

The sections work as follows:

✦ **Report Header.** This section prints at the top of the first page of the report only. Place the report title and banner ornaments here.

✦ **Page Header.** Items in the report header are printed at the top of each page. Although the header is typically used for column headings, it can also include information such as page number, date, author, and the like.

✦ **Detail.** Field data appear in this section, which is printed once for each record in the table or query on which the report is based.

✦ **Group Header.** If you plan to group together items in the report by date, salesperson, or region, for example, use the group header to label the start of each group. To set up the groups, use the instructions in "Grouping items in reports," later in this chapter.

> **Note**   In Design view, group headers and footers are labeled with the names of the fields on which the groups are based — you won't see areas labeled Group Header or Group Footer, so quit looking for them in Figure 47-10!

✦ **Group Footer.** (See the preceding description of the Group Header section.) To print summary calculations such as subtotals and counts at the end of a group of records, place them in the Group Footer section.

✦ **Page Footer.** Appearing at the bottom of every page, this is where you'd usually insert the page number, date, and author information.

✦ **Report Footer.** Here's a tricky one. Although the report footer section falls at the bottom of the report in Design view, it's actually printed above the page footer on the final page of the report. Overall summary information (such as grand totals) should appear here.

Adding fields and other items to the report

Just as in a form, every item on a printed report is represented by a corresponding control on the screen version of the report (Chapter 50 covers Access controls). Besides the text box controls that display field data in the Detail section of the report, most reports rely primarily on simple text label controls.

To add a text box bound to a field, drag it from the field list for the underlying table or query onto the report design. You can place fields in any section of the report, but they should usually go in the Detail section. Use label controls to display text that you define. These are ideal for the report title and group and column headings.

Use unbound text box controls to set up calculations in the group footer and report footer sections, and for variable items such as the page number in the page headers and footers. After adding the text box to the report, type the expression for the calculated value into the Control Source property.

For example, the expression =Now() yields the current date and time; the expression ="Page " & [Page] & " of " & [Pages] produces a "Page 2 of 4" printed result; and the expression =Sum[Daily Sales] totals the values in the Daily Sales field.

Grouping items in reports

You can group and subgroup a report based on up to ten different fields or expressions. For example, a main group might include all the orders from a region of the country. Subgroups within the main group could list the orders from a particular state, and sub-subgroups might divide those into the individual cities' orders.

Set up such groups by clicking the Sorting and Grouping toolbar button to define the grouping criteria. In the Sorting and Grouping dialog box, use the Field/Expression column to select the field you want to group, or type an expression defining the criterion (for example, as a range of values). Choose Ascending or Descending in the Sort Order column to control the order in which items print within the group.

Setting a grouping criterion isn't enough to produce a group in your report. For each criterion, you must also activate a group header or footer (or both) by setting the corresponding item or items to Yes in the Group Properties section of the Sorting and Grouping dialog box.

When you do this, the corresponding header or footer area appears in the report in Design view. You can now add controls to it, including text boxes that calculate subtotals, averages, and counts for the group — see the previous section for tips on creating such controls.

**Cross-
Reference**

Chapter 50 explains the designing of Access forms, the use of controls in forms and reports, and the differences between Access controls and standard VBA controls. Chapter 43 describes designing data access pages and using them for interactive database access in a complete Web site.

✦   ✦   ✦

Secrets of Database Application Design

When you've mastered the core database tools (discussed in Chapter 47), you're likely to find yourself hankering after better ways to harness all that power under the Access hood. After all, Access is much more than a database program — it offers a complete development environment for building custom applications.

Actually, Access offers two distinct application development environments. You can put together full-blown applications using macros alone to automate the commands available from the toolbars and menus. Alternatively, you can cut your ties to the Access user interface and turn to VBA for the ultimate in programming power. This chapter dishes out pros and cons for each of these options.

Tip   The Microsoft Web site offers loads of detailed articles on all Office development topics, including Access. Go to http://msdn.microsoft.com/office/

Understanding Access Applications

In concept, an Access *application* is a complete piece of software that performs a set of related data-management tasks, presenting its functions to the user with toolbars and forms that are custom-tailored to the job at hand. Of course, there's no need to quibble about when a database becomes an application. The point is simply that applications are more ambitious and more highly customized than the type of database in which you manage information via the standard Access user interface and its commands.

When the typical Access application starts up, a special switchboard form appears in place of Access's default Database window (see Figure 48-1 for an example). Acting as a central control panel for the application, a switchboard provides a set of buttons or other controls that activate custom commands or branch to other forms that display data for review, editing, and querying. At the same time, the application's custom toolbars and menus replace the standard ones normally available in Access. They may even display and hide themselves automatically as the user moves from form to form.

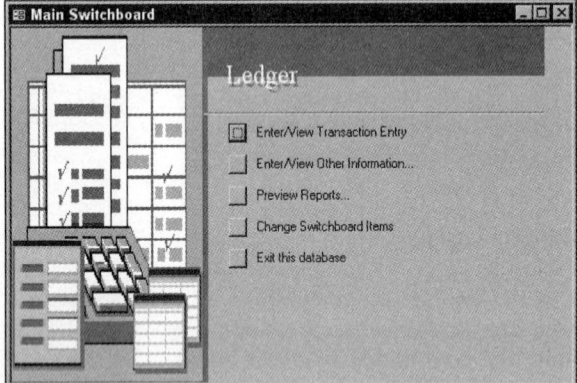

Figure 48-1: A custom application's switchboard form, the first item displayed when the application starts up.

Caution　As you create custom applications, be sure to include comments that explain exactly what each step of the macro or VBA script accomplishes. This will ensure that in the future you or someone else will be able to make necessary changes to the application to fix or update it.

Although you can build applications for your own use, they are more often intended for distribution to others. By packaging the data together with push-button controls for specific tasks, you enable users to get their work done without having to know much at all about Access itself.

Planning and implementing the application

The planning process (described in detail in Chapter 47) assumes even greater importance and requires more attention when you set out to build a complete application. The design of the underlying database's building blocks — its tables, fields, forms, queries, and reports—is crucial to the application's success. In addition, however, think carefully about what specific automated commands your users need—and how to present them on switchboards, menus, and toolbars.

As you plan, it's vital to think about the application as a series of events that may happen in any order. Clicking a button with the mouse and opening or closing a form are examples of events. In Access applications, as in VBA programs, such events trigger all custom features. If you want to let the user run a certain query, you might set up your application so the query runs when the user clicks a particular button. Your application plan must provide the macro or VBA code to activate the query when the button gets clicked.

Choose the right tool: Access macros versus VBA

To repeat a key point, Access macros are not the VBA-based macros found in Word, Excel, and PowerPoint. Because you can use either tool to create custom applications, an important step in planning a new application is to decide which tool is right for your needs.

Differences between macros and VBA

In brief, the differences between macros and VBA procedures are as follows:

✦ Access macros automate a series of actions, most of which correspond to commands you can perform in the Access user interface (via a menu or toolbar button). You can open tables, run queries, display forms, print reports, and so on.

Chapter 46 covers the basics of writing Access macros.

✦ VBA procedures in Access are like those you write in any of the other Office applications. The only thing unique about them is that they can make direct use of the programming objects that belong to Access itself. VBA isn't tied to the Access user interface, so its ways of looking at and working with databases can be very different, and more powerful, than the way the user interface works.

Despite these real differences, the division between macros and VBA isn't airtight. A macro can run VBA function procedures, and Access VBA code can use the methods of the `DoCmd` object to execute macro actions. And don't overlook Access's capability to convert macros to VBA procedures. To make the conversion, start by selecting the macro object in the Database window (but don't open the object). Alternatively, if the macro is connected to a form or report, you can open the form or report in Design view. Then choose Tools ⇨ Macro ⇨ Convert Macros to Visual Basic.

When to use macros, when VBA

How do you decide between macros and VBA? In a nutshell, macros are easier but VBA is much more powerful.

Here's my advice: Unless you're sure macros are sufficient for all your applications, skip macros. Yes, the learning curve for VBA is steeper, and it may take longer to finish your first applications. But the investment is worth it. The skills you pick up as you build simple applications apply directly to the more complicated ones you're surely going to want later. And if you find your "simple" application needs more features than you expected, coding it in VBA means you won't have to start from scratch to add them.

Note   Actually, Access doesn't force you to choose between macros and VBA—you can use both in a single application. If you're willing to learn both tool sets, you can have the best of both worlds.

Advantages of macros

Now for some details. Macros are easier to use than VBA for two main reasons. First, if you're familiar with the Access user interface, building an application using macros is a simple extension of skills you already know. Most macro actions are equivalent to commands you use regularly. In addition, Access gives you plenty of hand-holding as you construct a macro, providing fill-in-the-blank fields for the arguments needed for each action in the Macro window. And unlike VBA, with macros there isn't a lot of specialized syntax to learn.

Macros have other advantages besides ease of use. Their strengths include:

✦ You can define keyboard shortcuts for the entire application — as opposed to individual forms — only with macros, not with VBA.

Cross-Reference   Chapter 46 covers keyboard shortcuts.

✦ Macros are faster and require less memory than VBA modules. For a given form or report you realize this advantage only if no VBA code is attached to the object (see "Maximum efficiency with minimum VBA code" later in this chapter).

Advantages of VBA

VBA has many advantages over macros. Compared to macros, VBA code is

✦ **Easier to maintain.** As an application becomes more complex, VBA makes it much easier to keep track of the flow of your program because you can work with a variety of related procedures in the same module. Because the VBA code for a form, report, or data access page is part of the object, the code accompanies the object if you move it to a different database.

✦ **Easier to debug.** Access's Visual Basic Editor includes the advanced debugging tools covered in Chapter 55. Access provides no similar features for macros.

✦ **More flexible.** Although macros can test conditions and perform different actions accordingly, VBA's complete set of control structures is much more sophisticated. Combined with your ability to specify the arguments for a VBA procedure while the program runs, your programs can respond much more flexibly to current conditions than macros ever could.

✦ **Better at computations.** VBA lets you code custom functions to perform sophisticated, tailor-made calculations on numbers or text.

✦ **Better at handling errors.** Macros give you a generic error message when an error occurs. With VBA, you can decide what happens when an error occurs — your code can attempt to correct the problem, and it can display custom error messages with detailed information.

VBA offers one other big benefit: You can use the Visual Basic language to write database applications in any Office application, or in the stand-alone version of Visual Basic. When you're familiar with database objects and their methods and properties, you can work with them in any Visual Basic environment — and as discussed in the next section, a Visual Basic environment other than Access may be the right choice.

When *not* to use Access for database applications

Because Access is Office's database program, it seems only logical that you would use Access to build custom database applications. Sometimes, however, good reasons exist to consider other options.

What you have to keep in mind is that Access itself doesn't actually manage your database. That role belongs to the database engine, the software responsible for storing and retrieving data.

 The database engines available for use with Access are discussed in Chapter 46.

Access's real job is simply to provide a means for you to interact with the underlying database engine. The Access user interface is full of creature comforts, such as its graphical query designer and its customizable forms and reports, all of which make it easy to request the data you want to work with — and control how you want to see the data displayed. But as nice as those tools are, they are quite separate from the database engine that actually does the grunt-work of locating and extracting the data you're interested in. Figure 48-2 illustrates this separation of roles schematically.

Database front-end software   Back-end databases

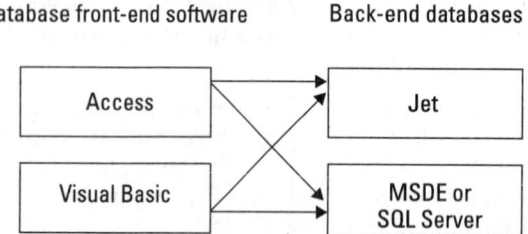

Figure 48-2: This illustration shows how you can pair different database front ends with different database engines.

The point is that because the database user interface and the database engine are distinct pieces of software, you can use tools other than Access to tell the engine what you want it to do. That's exactly what you're doing when you build a database application in VBA. Even if you code the application inside Access, your VBA code speaks to the database engine not through Access, but through a completely independent software component, such as ADO or DAO.

For a refresher on ADO, DAO, and what their acronyms mean, see Chapter 49.

Database application development options

So if Access isn't your only option for control of the database engine, what tool should you use to code your database applications? Your choices and their respective benefits include the following:

✦ **Access itself.** VBA applications built from inside Access can make direct use of Access objects, such as forms and reports. Because Access forms and reports have built-in database functionality, they can shorten the development cycle significantly over generic VBA. Also, Access is the best choice for applications that you create for personal use, when you expect to be adding new features frequently as the need arises and your time permits.

✦ **Another Office application such as Word or Excel.** In many custom applications, database access is only part of the function. If your planned application requires significant word processing or number crunching features, creating it in Word or Excel lets you take direct advantage of that program's resources. Through ADO or a similar component, your VBA code can still retrieve, display, and manipulate database data. And the application can be smaller, faster, and less complicated than it would be if you use COM to automate Access from, say, Word (or automate Word from Access). Unaided, VBA forms and reports aren't database-aware, but the code required to manually connect a form to data isn't all that daunting. Besides, you can buy Office Developer or third-party toolkits to bind controls and forms to data. And you can transfer your work directly to other VBA applications because it won't be dependent on Access-specific forms.

✦ **Visual Basic proper (not VBA).** Visual Basic (the mighty ancestor of VBA) is a great tool for database development. Your Visual Basic code can connect to databases via ADO just as in VBA, and Visual Basic forms are database-aware much as those of Access are. An application created with Visual Basic has two big advantages over one created within a VBA program like Access, Word, or Excel. First, it's always a lot faster, because Visual Basic applications are compiled rather than interpreted when you run them. Second, you can freely distribute the application to others — they don't need a copy of the host VBA application. The only real drawback is that you have to buy Visual Basic.

Why Access still may have a role

Even if you decide to forego Access as your development environment, Access is still a great tool for the database application developer. Using its comfortable commands, you can quickly build the tables and queries that constitute the database. You can write and test your VBA code in Access and move it to the final environment when everything is working right. And you can quickly prototype the application's forms.

Caution   You can't export Access forms to the final application: Access forms are incompatible with both standard VBA UserForms and the forms used by Visual Basic.

Applications by Magic: Using the Database Wizards

The easiest way to create a working application is to let Access do it for you. The wizards supplied with Access demonstrate the power and benefits of applications, but the applications they create for you are useful in their own right, too. Included in the collection that comes with Access are wizards for common business database tasks, such as contact management and inventory control, and wizards for keeping track of personal information, such as your video collection or your fitness workouts.

To use the wizards, choose File ➪ New. In the resulting New File task pane, click General Templates in the New from template section. Choose Blank Database to create a new Jet-based database, or click Project (New Database) to create an SQL Server project.

Cross-Reference   For a comparison of the Jet-based and SQL Server-based approaches, see Chapter 46.

You can also use the wizards on the Databases tab of the Templates dialog box to create new Jet databases (see Figure 48-3).

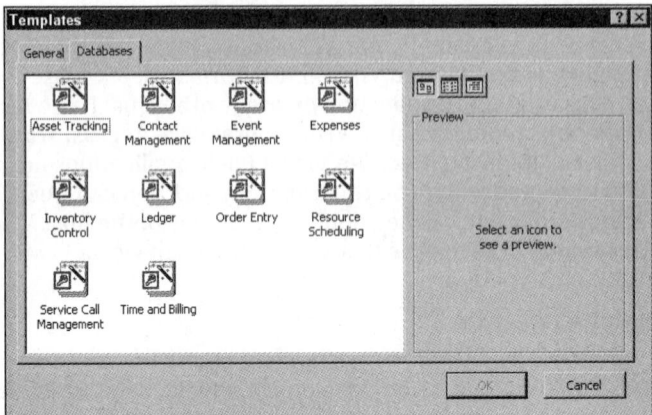

Figure 48-3: Access provides several wizards to help you set up some commonly used types of databases.

When you open a wizard, it walks you through a series of panels in which you can choose which fields to include in the application and set basic formatting options for your forms and reports. Based on your choices, the wizard creates the database objects your application needs, plugging in Visual Basic procedures where necessary. All the objects and the code are available for you to play with, so you can study how Access put the application together. You can customize or add to the existing objects as you see fit.

Realistically, of course, even the most wonder-working wizard can't anticipate your specific information-management needs. After you've generated a few sample applications with the wizards, you're going to want to dig in and create your own.

Building Custom Applications in Access

In outline, the process of constructing an application in Access is really pretty simple. You start by creating a set of basic database building blocks, and then you connect them together to form the application.

Designing the user interface

As an Access application developer, one of your important tasks is to craft a customized user interface that looks inviting and unique and (at the same time) serves its function efficiently. Fortunately, you can devote most of your attention to aesthetics and the behind-the-scenes functionality of your application — the mechanics of building a customized user interface are straightforward. By taking advantage of the drag-and-drop customization features of Office, you can put together your forms, toolbars, and menus with a minimum of hassle.

Setting up switchboards

Chapter 50 discusses the basics of creating forms in Access. The layout techniques described there also apply when you're building switchboards and other forms used not to display data, but to activate other features of the application.

The only thing special about such forms is that they aren't associated with any table or query in the database. When you create a form of this type in the New Form dialog box, just leave blank the line that asks you to select a table or query for the form. You can now use the form as a primary element in your custom user interface without worrying about its connection to your data.

Using the Switchboard Manager

Choose Tools ➪ Database Utilities ➪ Switchboard Manager to start the Switchboard Manager, a utility that creates functioning switchboard forms and enables you to edit existing forms. Click New to create a new switchboard form, and then click Edit to open the Edit Switchboard Page dialog box (see Figure 48-4), which enables you to add and arrange the commands on the switchboard. The forms you wind up with look much like those built by the wizards for the sample applications that come with Access. They're nice, and perfectly serviceable, but not very distinctive.

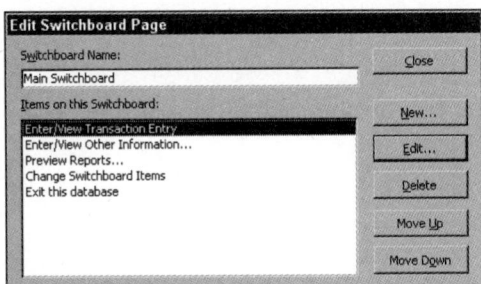

Figure 48-4: The Switchboard Manager creates generic switchboards and lets you edit them in the Edit Switchboard Page dialog box.

 **Cross-Reference** To edit a garden-variety Access form, use the form design tools discussed in Chapter 50.

Setting your startup form

The switchboard or other form that you want users to see when they first run your application is the startup form. Specify the startup form in the Display Form/Page drop-down list of the Tools ➪ Startup dialog box.

Customizing command bars for your application

The basic techniques for creating custom toolbars, menu bars, and buttons in Access are the same ones you can use in any Office application (see Chapter 5). However, Access gives you more direct control over technical settings for these items than do the other Office applications.

Creating new menu bars, toolbars, and shortcut menus

When you're constructing a custom application, you should create custom toolbars from scratch rather than modify the existing toolbars.

Although you can create custom toolbars in the other Office applications, Access alone lets you change a toolbar's properties without VBA code. To do this, go to the Toolbars tab of the Tools ➪ Customize dialog box and choose Properties. A secondary dialog box, Toolbar Properties, appears. Here, selecting a toolbar from the drop-down list lets you modify its settings (see Figure 48-5).

Figure 48-5: You can view and alter basic toolbar properties from this dialog box.

The Toolbar Properties dialog box gives you control over whether the toolbars in your application can be customized, moved, docked, hidden, and so forth. If you're working on a custom toolbar, rather than one that's built in, you can also control the type of toolbar you're building.

Attaching custom toolbars and menu bars to forms and reports

You can designate any of your custom toolbars as a menu bar by using the Type drop-down list in the Toolbar Properties dialog box. You can then attach it — loosely speaking — to a form or report, or make it the default menu bar for the whole database.

To set up a menu bar for a form or report, assign it to the Menu Bar property in the Properties sheet for that object, working in Design view. From then on, every time the object is activated in your application, the specified menu bar appears at the top of the screen, just below the title bar, replacing the global one.

Tip   Speaking of global menu bars, you can set up a custom menu bar for the whole database in the Tools ⇨ Startup dialog box. The menu bar you select there is visible (instead of the Access default bar), except when the current form or report has been assigned a different menu bar.

Regular, non-menu toolbars can also be attached to a form or report, this time using the object's Toolbar property. When the user of your application switches to that object, the specified toolbar appears, not Access's default for that object type. With a form, for example, the Form View toolbar would no longer be visible; instead, the specified custom toolbar would appear.

Tip   In the Toolbar Properties dialog box, designating a custom toolbar as a Popup Type box converts the toolbar into a shortcut menu, ready to receive new right-click commands. While the Customize dialog box remains open, it appears on the Custom menu of the Shortcut Menus toolbar, where you can add menu items to it. (Why the term *Popup* is used here instead of *shortcut menu* is beyond me.)

Adding custom commands to the toolbars

Just as Word lets you assign individual fonts to toolbar buttons, Access is set up so you can easily fill your toolbars with buttons that display specific tables, queries, forms, and reports. Click one of these custom buttons, and the associated object opens immediately. Just as in Word, you can place your macros on toolbar buttons, too.

Using the Tools ⇨ Customize dialog box, switch to the Commands tab and locate the items labeled All Tables, All Queries, and so on, on the menu. Then just drag one of those objects up to its resting point on the toolbar.

Note   Opening a database object by clicking a toolbar button amounts to the same thing as opening it in the Database window. You can't control which view it opens in, or carry out any other actions in the process. To get the results you want, create an appropriate macro and assign *it* to the toolbar.

Working with properties for command bar controls

Access gives you direct, dialog box-style control over a number of settings pertaining to individual controls on the command bars, including menu items and toolbar buttons. In the other Office applications, you would need VBA code to modify these options. With the Customize dialog box open, right-click a button or menu item and then choose Properties at the bottom of the shortcut menu. The Database Control Properties dialog box shown in Figure 48-6 appears.

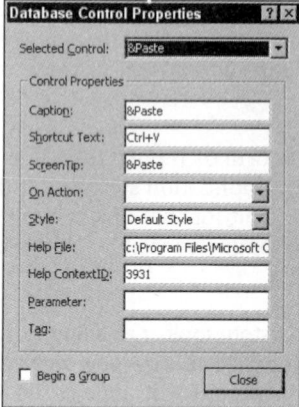

Figure 48-6: Use this Database Control Properties dialog box to specify settings for toolbar buttons and menu items in your custom applications.

Access is the only Office application that doesn't force you to use VBA to specify the text displayed alongside a control when it's used as a menu item. This text is usually used to list the corresponding keyboard shortcut for the control. In Access, type the text of your choice into the Shortcut Text. Similarly, the ToolTip item lets you enter custom text that appears when the user rests the mouse pointer over the control.

Assigning VBA functions to toolbar buttons

Combined with the Database Control Properties dialog box (Figure 48-6), a special toolbar item called Custom Command gives you one-click access to any Visual Basic function procedure. To set this up, start by writing the function using the Visual Basic Editor.

This technique works only with functions, not with Sub procedures, so be sure you use the correct syntax.

After the function is complete, open the Customize dialog box. At the very top of the Commands list, you should see Custom command (if not, be sure File is selected in the Categories list). Drag the Custom command onto a toolbar. Right-click it and choose Properties to bring up the Database Control Properties dialog box.

Now you can type in an expression that runs the function in the On Action field. If your function is called StayAlert, for example, you would enter =StayAlert( ).

Setting startup options and securing your custom interface

Use the Tools ➪ Startup dialog box to take full control of what users see when they run your application and what tools they have access to. To ensure a fully customized environment, clear all checkboxes in the Startup dialog box and specify your own menu bar, shortcut menu bar, and display form/page.

Clearing the Display Database Window box, for example, prevents the appearance of the generic Access main window—hardly an appropriate focus of attention when you're trying to grab attention for your own screens. To prevent users from activating the Database window by way of the keyboard, you must also clear the box labeled Use Access Special Keys.

Even with these measures in place, anyone with a little experience can open up your application and get at Access itself. For example, users could make changes to the toolbars, just as you can when you run Access without special customizations. They could display or hide custom toolbars, position them on the screen where they wanted them, and freely customize them by adding or deleting buttons—or entire toolbars, for that matter.

To lock the user interface so it can't be changed, follow these three steps:

1. Position each of the application's toolbars where they belong. Now use the settings in the Toolbar Properties dialog box (earlier Figure 48-5) to allow or prevent users from moving, resizing, or docking each toolbar.

2. Open the Tools ➪ Startup dialog box and uncheck Allow Toolbar/Menu changes.

   This prevents access to the Customize menu bar and to the View ➪ Toolbars menu and keeps the current toolbars on the screen no matter what. It doesn't prevent users from moving, resizing, or docking the toolbars.

3. So far, so good. Now you need a way to keep users from changing that setting you just made in the Startup dialog box. That requires password protection via user-level security. Consult Chapter 14 and set that up.

Maximum efficiency with minimum VBA code

Although it's often necessary and desirable to write VBA code, you can sometimes get by without it—and there are good reasons to minimize your use of code in an Access application. One reason, of course, is to protect your free time. (VBA, powerful as it is, demands a lot from the programmer.) In addition, though, VBA imposes a performance penalty on your application and increases its size.

Most of the work in a typical application involves setting up simple connections between user interface elements, such as buttons, and ordinary database objects, such as forms or queries. Much of the time, all you want a control to do is take you to another object in the database. In this situation, lightweight forms suffice—you don't need VBA. Likewise, VBA code may not be necessary for large-scale updates and deletions of records in the database. Instead, you can construct an action query as one of the objects in your database and then call it from a lightweight form.

Using lightweight objects

A lightweight form or report is simply one that has no attached VBA module. That doesn't mean the form is crippled. As Chapter 50 makes clear, it can still display field data by way of controls that are bound to fields in the database. In addition, controls can be assigned hyperlinks that navigate to and open other database objects without the aid of VBA. Alternatively, you can use macros to perform actions such as hiding or displaying custom toolbars when the form is opened or just about any other event occurs.

Compared to an object that includes a VBA module, a lightweight form or report takes up less room on a disk and loads into memory faster. Unless you really need the advanced features of VBA, *not* adding a module to the object makes sense.

You can tell whether a form or report has an attached module by looking at the `HasModule` property in the object's `Properties` sheet. The `HasModule` property is near the bottom of the Other tab.

Caution   Don't use the View ⇨ Code command to find out whether the object has an attached module. This command creates a module if one didn't exist already. Even an empty module is a drag on performance and consumes an additional chunk of memory.

When a form or report has an attached module, it remains in place until you explicitly set the `HasModule` property back to `No`. When you do, the module and all the code it contains are permanently deleted.

Using action queries to minimize VBA coding

Many situations require operations on a number of records as a group. At the beginning of each month, for example, you may want to place all the records entered the previous month in a separate archive table for safekeeping. Instead of coding this task in VBA, where it would require a substantial chunk of code, you should use an action query.

As the name implies, action queries don't just retrieve data, they perform some action on the data they find. There are four types: a Delete query, an Update query, an Append query, and a Make-table query, whose names are pretty much self-explanatory.

In this case, you would use query Design view to set up a query that filters records by entry date, using the previous month as the criterion. Instead of hard-coding the month, you would enter in the query's Criteria row an expression such as

```
Month([DateField])= If(Month(Now())=1,12,Month(Now())-1)
```

where `DateField` is the name of the field containing the dates you want to screen the records by. You would then choose Query ➪ Make-Table Query. Enter the name of the archive table you wish to create, and you're ready to run the query. It culls the previous month's records from the complete database, exporting them to a new table.

After the query is ready, you can assign it to a control on your application's switch-board or another similar form. In the macro window, use the `OpenQuery` action to activate the query, specifying its name as the `Query Name` property. You may want to precede the `OpenQuery` action with the `SetWarnings` action to turn off the cautionary message that Access otherwise displays when executing an action query. After the macro is saved, you can use the Properties dialog box to assign it to any of the events recognized by a form, a report, or one of their controls.

Writing VBA code in Access

The techniques described in this chapter so far are adequate for many simple applications; Visual Basic code, however, is always available if you need its power. (Part XI covers the basic concepts and skills you need to write VBA modules for every Office application.) Although the core elements of Visual Basic hold throughout Office, all VBA applications, including Access, have their own set of objects. In Access, the most important of these are its form, report, and data access page objects, and the objects for the individual controls on these items.

Cross-Reference   See Chapter 50 to review techniques for working with database objects in Access VBA.

Distributing the Application

After you've completed the construction of the application building blocks, added the connecting code, and tested all its components thoroughly, you're ready to distribute your magnum opus to an eager public. The following sections cover issues to consider when preparing the completed application for distribution.

Splitting a Jet database for network use

In most organizations, the typical database application is intended for use by multiple individuals and on a number of different PCs. If you're sending out your project to more than one person, and if the group has a reliable network, your best bet is usually to set up the application in two parts — one on each person's computer, the other on a network server. In this scenario, each person has a separate copy of the user interface portions of the application — all the custom forms and toolbars — as well as functional items such as queries, macros, and modules. The database itself — the tables and the data they contain — are stored on a network server where they're accessible to everyone.

Breaking up an application this way makes sense for several reasons. For one, network data are usually more secure, and the backup schedule can be supervised more closely. In addition, because everyone is working with the same copy of the database, you don't have to worry about maintaining, and keeping synchronized, several separate sets of data.

Another advantage in splitting up a database is that the application becomes easier to distribute. Those big tables need to be placed on the server only once. Updating and upgrading the rest of the application should be relatively easy, because in a database of any size, the user interface portion makes up a relatively small amount of the total bulk of the software.

Access supports this split-database configuration by design. In the case of Access projects based on SQL Server databases, data are always stored separately from the project itself. For its part, a Jet-based Access application can be readily linked to tables located on any accessible disk drive, server, or Internet site. If you're linking to external tables that already exist, use the File ⇨ Get External Data ⇨ Link Tables command to open a wizard that helps you locate and link the outside tables to the current database. On the other hand, if you want to place tables from the current database into a different file, use Access's Database Splitter.

Before you break up your completed application, you should decide where on the network your data tables should go. Then, with a good network connection, choose Tools ⇨ Database Utilities ⇨ Database Splitter. The Database Splitter Wizard steps you through the procedure, asking you where it should store the new back-end database. Soon, it starts the process of dividing the raw data tables from the rest of the current database (the front-end portion of the application) and placing them in the new database. If everything goes well, it updates the front-end database with links to the tables in their new location. The application now consists of two separate database files, but it works exactly as it did as a single file.

Database replication

When it's not possible or practical to connect all your users to the same server, Access provides database replication as a way to keep everyone on the same page. A *replicated database* is simply a set of two or more copies of the same information, set up so they can be kept synchronized as the data in each copy changes.

One of these replicas serves as the Design Master, the only copy in which changes to the overall database design can be made. But everyone with the application can change, add to, or delete records. Each time the databases are synchronized, changes made to any replica database are duplicated in all the others. The process is incremental — only changed data are transferred from one database to the other — so it's relatively quick.

Replication is preferred over splitting a database when connections to the network are slow or intermittent, such as when the company sales force connects its laptops to the main network. If each laptop user has a copy of the entire database, each has access to reasonably current data at all times and can still plug into the network for a quick incremental update anytime.

The replication commands are on the Tools ➪ Replication submenu. After using the Create Replica command to get things started, you convert that new database to a Design Master. The Design Master can then be used to make further replicas for other users.

Securing your files

When your database application is fully tested, consider saving it as an .mde file. This process strips out the Visual Basic source code after first compiling it. Although the application runs the same — better, in fact, because it uses less memory — no one can see your programming work or modify the design of components such as forms and queries.

To save an application as an .mde file, choose Tools ➪ Database Utilities ➪ Make MDE file. You get to name the new .mde file, of course. Access doesn't alter the original file, which you should keep somewhere safe yet accessible for the inevitable day you need to make upgrades.

✦   ✦   ✦

Working with Data Using VBA

Although this chapter resides in the Access section, its scope extends way beyond Access alone. Through VBA, any Office application can make full use of information housed in databases on your own PC, a network server, or the Internet. This chapter covers VBA coding techniques for managing data that work in all Office applications. Refer back to Chapter 30 for a full discussion of the options you have for working with databases, including Access alone, Access supplemented by VBA, VBA in other Office applications, and standalone Visual Basic applications.

An Introduction to VBA Database Programming

Before you can start writing database code, you need a bit of background on the technology and terminology involved. This brief section provides those basics.

Using DoCmd in Access

You should know about one difference between Access and the other Office applications when it comes to VBA. It's this: Access includes an entirely separate system for VBA database programming based on the `DoCmd` object. The `DoCmd` object encapsulates all the commands available from Access's menu system. With it, you can open tables, run queries, run reports, display forms, and fiddle with the user interface ... in other words, anything a user can do sitting in front of the computer.

If you're an Access veteran without much previous programming experience, the `DoCmd` object provides a familiar handhold as you transition to VBA. The problem with DoCmd is that it confines you to Access, while with standard VBA your skills translate directly to all other Visual Basic environments.

Even if you opt for "pure" VBA, you still can't do entirely without the `DoCmd` object for applications you create in Access. Perhaps because Access forms aren't standard VBA forms, the `Show` method doesn't work—instead, to display forms in an Access VBA application, you must use the `OpenForm` method of the `DoCmd` object.

SQL and VBA

The Structured Query Language (SQL) is the reigning standard for database queries—every data management system from Access to Oracle recognizes SQL. SQL is the key to getting things done in a database application. SQL statements enable you to select, modify, or delete specific sets of records that you choose.

So how do SQL and VBA complement one another? It's through VBA—working through one of several database object models—that you execute those SQL commands. And once an SQL command has produced a set of records from the database for use by your application, VBA takes over, enabling you to display and modify the retrieved information.

As befits its fundamental importance, SQL rates a full section of its own later in this chapter. The techniques for incorporating SQL statements into your VBA code are covered both there and before that, in the section "Writing Database Code with ADO."

All about database objects

Choosing VBA for your database work leads directly to yet another decision point: Which database object model are you going to use? VBA alone doesn't provide a means for you to access and manipulate databases. Coupled with a database object model, however, VBA becomes an extremely capable database-programming tool.

The job of a database object model is to turn databases and their components— tables, queries, and reports—into objects that behave just like the other objects you use in VBA. That is, you manipulate them using their properties, methods, and events (see Chapter 54). Because the database is "packaged" as a set of objects, you don't have to muck around with the details of the database's structure. Additionally, you can use the same set of objects to manipulate many different types of databases.

In recent years Microsoft has developed and promoted several of these database object models, resulting in a confusing array of acronyms. The three main options are DAO, RDO, and ADO.

DAO (Data Access Objects)

DAO was the default object model for database programming in Office 95 and 97. It provides a complete set of objects for working with all types of databases, whether they are local (on your own PC) or remote (somewhere else). DAO enables access to different types of databases simultaneously—for example, a custom application might blend together information residing in Access, dBase, and Oracle databases.

One problem with DAO is that it provides slightly different object models for local and network data access. By itself, DAO isn't designed for industrial strength client/server applications, although DAO becomes much more potent in that area with the help of ODBCDirect (described in the next section).

RDO (Remote Data Objects)

The RDO object model was designed for accessing SQL databases located on a server and isn't appropriate for use with desktop-type databases such as Jet, dBase, or Paradox. RDO is provided with the high-end Enterprise versions of Microsoft development tools. Advanced features of RDO include disconnected recordsets (the capability to work with records without maintaining a constant connection to the server) and asynchronous queries (which lets the application regain control while the query is still running).

ADO (ActiveX Data Objects)

ADO is intended to be the object model of choice from here on out, superseding and improving upon both DAO and RDO. ADO provides a single, simpler, and more consistent object model for working with both local and remote data. It includes all the major-league features needed for large-scale networked applications with many simultaneous users, yet it works well for single-user desktop projects as well. And unlike DAO and RDO, ADO also can access non-SQL data — meaning it can easily tap storehouses of data, such as Outlook, that don't recognize SQL.

So which object model do you use?

The simple message here is that you should use ADO for all new database applications. ADO's advantages are clear-cut, and besides, it's the only object model Microsoft plans to develop and fully support (for now, at least — the way these folks work, I won't be surprised if the next release of Office comes with something called DOA).

Some related database technologies

You're going to see several other terms in connection with Office database programming, so you'd better know a little about them. ODBC (Open Database Connectivity) is an older Microsoft programming standard for accessing all kinds of structured data via SQL. ODBC was designed with the programming habits of its day in mind, so it requires you to use C/C++ function calls — not something you want to play around with in VBA. But because ODBC has been around for years, ODBC drivers are available for almost every database type imaginable. I should also mention that RDO relies on ODBC, translating ODBC function calls into objects that Visual Basic programmers can readily use.

ODBCDirect is part of DAO. ODBCDirect is a software layer that converts ODBC function calls into DAO objects, enabling you to use DAO to access any database for which you have an ODBC driver. (Although ODBCDirect is based on RDO, it doesn't provide all the features available via RDO itself.) Prior to the invention of

ODBCDirect, Access developers could connect to ODBC databases through Jet. However, doing so slowed things down and didn't provide the advanced server-related features available via ODBC.

OLE DB is a Microsoft specification for data access roughly comparable to and replacing ODBC. Based on COM rather than SQL, OLE DB should in theory enable simpler and more flexible access to any type of information that can be represented in tabular form. That information might be stored in a desktop database, an SQL-based database on a server, a collection of e-mail messages, or a geographical, map-based data system. ADO relies on OLE DB rather than ODBC to present database objects to the programmer. However, because specific OLE DB Providers (drivers) aren't yet available for all data sources, ADO comes with an additional component called the ODBC Provider that can connect any ODBC database through OLE DB to ADO.

Writing Database Code with ADO

Although designing the right SQL statements can be tough, writing database code with ADO itself isn't all that difficult. You have only three main objects to master — `Connection`, `Recordset`, and `Command` — and their properties and methods are implemented logically.

Error handling

Although I don't spotlight the critical role of error handling code in this chapter, the omission is only because space is limited. Be sure to include an error handler in every database procedure you write. Chapter 55 has details on constructing error handlers in VBA.

Creating a reference to ADO in your project

Before you can use ADO and its objects in a VBA program, you must first establish a reference to the ADO software, or type library, in your project. In the Visual Basic Editor (see Chapter 52 for information on using the Visual Basic Editor), choose Tools ➪ References and check the box for Microsoft ActiveX Data Objects 2.*x* Library. Unless you plan to use both ADO and DAO in the same project — not generally a good idea, but perhaps necessary if you're mixing old code with new — be sure to clear all boxes for Microsoft DAO (you may have several DAO versions on your computer).

Caution If you do combine DAO and ADO in the same project, you must preface all references to ADO objects with the object identifier `ADODB`, as in `ADODB.Connection`. Because similar DAO and ADO objects have the same names, VBA needs to know which object model you mean. You can omit the identifier in projects that don't refer to DAO.

Establishing the connection

Your first order of business in accessing a given *data source* (a database or other repository of data) is to establish a *connection* to that data source. You can think of the Connection object as the communications pipeline between your program and the data.

Connecting to the open database in Access

This is really important! If you're using Access to write ADO code, you don't need to create a new Connection object to work with the Jet database that's already open in Access. That's because Access sets up the necessary Connection object for you automatically. Use the Connection property of Access's CurrentProject object to reference the database as a connection. This code fragment shows how to do it:

```
Dim conADOConnection As Connection
Set conADOConnection = CurrentProject.Connection
```

In similar fashion, you can easily connect to the underlying SQL Server database in an Access project, as long you're writing code in that project in Access. In this case, you need the BaseConnectionString property of the CurrentProject object, as illustrated in the following example:

```
Dim conADO As New Connection
conADO.ConnectionString = CurrentProject.BaseConnectionString
```

Creating Connection objects

Under any other circumstances, you must create the Connection object yourself. To create a Connection object, just declare the variable name for your object and then open the connection. The Open method takes as its argument a *connection string* containing various parameters that specify the OLE DB Provider you're using and the specific data source you're accessing. Alternatively, you can first set properties of the Connection object corresponding to the items in the connection string, and then use the Open method by itself. Check out these two equivalent examples, which both create a Connection object for the same Jet database:

```
' Example 1
Dim conADOConnection As New Connection, strConnect As String
strConnect = "Provider=Microsoft.Jet.OLEDB.4.0;" _
    & "Data Source=C:\Data\Toys"
conADOConnection.Open strConnect

' Example 2
Dim conADOConnection As New Connection
With conADOConnection
    .Provider = "Microsoft.Jet.OLEDB.4.0"
    .Properties("Data Source") = "C:\Data\Toys"
    .Open
End With
```

The parameters required by the Open method vary depending on the Provider you're using — consult the Help system, Microsoft's Web site, and Office Developer documentation for details. The following example is for SQL Server:

```
Dim conADOConnection As New Connection, strConnect As String
strConnect = "Provider=SQLOLEDB;Data Source=Hecate;" & _
    "Initial Catalog=toys;User ID=sa;Password=;"
conADOConnection.Open strConnect
```

If you're working in Access, ADO falls short of a universal data management solution. Access projects can connect only to SQL Server/MSDE databases, and not to other OLE DB Providers. Also, creating a connection to an SQL Server database using Access VBA requires different parameters than those used in other development environments. In Access, the Provider property must be set to MSDataShape, whereas the Data Provider property is the one you set to SQLOLEDB.

Tip

Unlike DAO and RDO, ADO enables you to work with database objects without first creating a Connection object — you can associate those objects with a connection when it's time to fill them with real data. Alternatively, you can create a connection implicitly in the process of defining a Recordset or Command object. However, creating the Connection object explicitly makes your code easier to follow and enables you to associate the same connection with multiple other objects.

Working with Recordset objects

Get closely acquainted with Recordset objects — you use them constantly for fundamental data operations. As the name implies, a Recordset object is a container for records drawn from a data source. As befits a container, the same Recordset object can hold different records at different times.

Creating a recordset

After you've declared a variable for a recordset, you can immediately start working with the object's properties. At this point, however, it only exists in a sort of virtual form. To fill the empty container with actual records, you use any of the following techniques:

✦ The Recordset object's own Open method

✦ The Execute method of a Command object

✦ The Execute method of a Connection object

Creating recordsets using the Open method

The simplest technique for creating a recordset is by way of the Open method of the Recordset object itself. The Open method works well when you're using simple SQL Select statements to request the records of interest. The following code shows how to set up a recordset using the Open method:

```
Dim conMan As New Connection
Dim rstMan As Recordset
Dim strSQL As String
... (Code creating the conMan connection object goes here)
strSQL = "SELECT * FROM Toys" ' select the entire Toys table
Set rstMan.ActiveConnection = conMan
rstMan.Open strSQL, , adOpenForwardOnly, adLockReadOnly,
adCmdText
```

Note how the preceding sample code associates a connection with the recordset by setting the recordset's `ActiveConnection` property. Note, too, how options governing the recordset's behavior are included as arguments to the `Open` method.

Creating recordsets using the Command object

SQL SELECT statements only take you so far — in client/server applications, efficiency often dictates that you obtain recordsets by executing stored procedures (queries). When such procedures require parameters, creating a `Recordset` object using a `Command` object is the way to go.

Set up the `Command` object first, setting its `ActiveConnection` property to the desired connection and feeding it your SQL string. You can then turn your attention to the `Recordset` object. In this case, you must set its options as properties first. You then fill it with records by setting it to the results of the `Command` object's `Execute` method. Here's an example:

```
Dim conTest As New Connection
Dim cmdTest As New Command
Dim rstTest As Recordset
Dim strSQL As String
... (Code creating the conTest connection object
... and defining the strSQL string goes here)
' Create the command object:
   With cmdTest
      Set .ActiveConnection = conTest
      .CommandText = strSQL
      .CommandType = adCmdText
   End With
rstTest.CursorType = adOpenForwardOnly
rstTest.LockType = adLockReadOnly
Set rstTest = cmdTest.Execute()
```

Creating recordsets using the Connection object

The final technique for creating recordsets involves the `Connection` object's `Execute` method. This approach is simpler than using the `Command` object but still enables you to access stored procedures, though if they require parameters you have to include these in your SQL string. The following code is illustrative:

```
Dim conVert As New Connection
Dim rstVert As Recordset
```

```
Dim strSQL As String
... (Code creating the conVert connection object
... and defining the strSQL string goes here)
rstVert.CursorType = adOpenForwardOnly
rstVert.LockType = adLockReadOnly
Set rstVert = conTest.Execute(strSQL)
```

Creating a connection on-the-fly

If you know you're going to need a connection for only one recordset, creating the connection first offers no particular advantage. Instead, you can include the connection string as the second argument of the Recordset object's Open method, as shown in this sample code:

```
Dim rstInPeace As New Recordset
Dim strSQL As String, strConnect As String

strSQL = "SELECT * FROM Bicycles" ' Retrieve all records
' code assigning the connection string to strConnect goes here
rstInPeace.Open strSQL, strConnect, adOpenForwardOnly
```

Setting Recordset options

You have control over the type of recordset you create via various settings that determine the cursor type, lock type, and so on. You specify the settings you want in one of two forms, depending on the technique you use to create the recordset: as arguments to the Recordset object's Open method, or as properties of the Recordset object. The code fragments in the previous sections demonstrate both forms.

Choosing a cursor type

In database parlance, a *cursor* refers to the functionality required to navigate through a set of records. The cursor type you choose for a Recordset object determines how free the user is to work with the records it contains and whether changes made by other users automatically appear in the recordset. Use the CursorType property or the corresponding argument of the Open statement to specify your choice. Table 49-1 lists the available options. The default cursor type is Forward-only.

Table 49-1
Cursor Types Available for ADO Recordset Objects

Cursor Type	Constant for CursorType Property	Definition
Forward-only	adOpenForwardOnly	Allows movement through the recordset only in the forward direction, either by a specified number of records or to the last record. Changes made by other users don't appear until the recordset is closed and reopened. This type offers the fastest performance but is only appropriate when you need to run through the records only once.
Static	adOpenStatic	A fixed recordset that can't be updated and doesn't reflect changes made by other users until it is closed and reopened. It allows free movement. Good for finding data and creating reports, and faster than the Keyset and Dynamic types.
Keyset	adOpenKeyset	A recordset whose records and their values can be changed, in turn changing the corresponding items in the underlying data source. The recordset doesn't reflect changes made by other users, however.
Dynamic	adOpenDynamic	Like a keyset-type recordset, except that it does reflect changes made by other users to the underlying data.

Choosing a cursor location

The Resultset object's CursorLocation property lets you specify whether the cursor resides on the client (user's) computer or on the server. Set it to either adUseClient or adUseServer, respectively. In general, you should use client-side cursors with SQL Server and other networked databases, and server-side cursors with Jet databases. You can set a default cursor location for all the recordsets of a connection via the Connection object's CursorType property.

Locks

The LockType property for a Recordset object determines how your program responds when two or more users try to edit the same record at the same time. The default setting is adLockPessimistic, which prevents you or anyone else from making changes to the records. If you want to be able to edit the recordset, you must set the LockType property to one of the other settings shown in Table 49-2.

Table 49-2
Lock Options for ADO Recordset Objects

Cursor Type	Constant for CursorType Property	Definition
No locks	adLockOptimistic	Multiple users can edit the same record at the same time, but they receive notice that the changes they make may conflict with another user's changes (records are locked only when the Update method is in progress, and then only one at a time). Good for single-user databases, and in multiuser databases when the most recent information is assumed to be always correct and complete.
	adLockBatchOptimistic	Same as the preceding, except that records are locked when they are being updated in batches (groups) instead of individually.
Read only (all records)	adLockReadOnly	All records are locked while the recordset is open — no one can edit them. Other users can still retrieve and view the records.
Read only (edited records)	adLockPessimistic	The page of records containing the one currently being edited is locked and can't be changed until the user moves to another record.

Checking for records

Assuming you encounter no errors as VBA creates your Recordset object, the first action you take with it should be to verify that it contains records. If not, you can let the user know there are none to work with. The trick here is to check the record-set's BOF (beginning of file) and EOF (end of file) properties — if they're both True, the recordset is empty. The best way to do that is with the logical And operator, which returns True only if two Boolean values are both True, as shown here:

```
If rstY.BOF And rstY.EOF Then
    MsgBox "No records in this recordset!"
End If
```

Caution

The promising-sounding RecordCount property is not a reliable way to check for the number of records in a recordset.

Moving through recordsets and locating specific records

ADO lets you navigate through a recordset fairly freely. For simple positioning, use the MoveFirst method to jump to the first record in the recordset, MoveLast to get the final record, and MoveNext and MovePrevious to step through records one at a time. The Move method lets you jump a specified number of records forward or backward in the recordset. For example, the statement rstZ.Move -3 moves three records back.

If you know you're going to want to return to a specific record later, set a bookmark for that record. While you're working with the record, assign the Recordset object's Bookmark property to a variable (use a variant) as in this example:

```
varBookmark1 = rstA.Bookmark
```

You can then jump back to that bookmark later by reversing the assignment:

```
rstA.Bookmark = varBookmark1
```

The Seek method and the four Find methods (FindFirst, FindLast, FindNext, and FindPrevious) enable you to track down a specific record based on its contents. Because Seek locates the target record using an index, it's faster than the Find methods — but the database must be indexed on the field containing the data you're looking for.

Adding and deleting records

Use a Recordset object's AddNew method to tack on a new record to the recordset and move to the new record. If you've already created a Recordset object called rstIng, the statement rstIng.AddNew is all you need to add a new record. You can then go on to fill up the record's fields (see "Changing field data" later in this chapter). If you prefer, however, you can specify field values at the time you create the new record. The AddNew method enables you to specify the fields and the values they are to contain, as shown in this example:

```
With rstIng
    .AddNew Array("Name," "Age,""Gender"), Array("Ann," 42, "F")
End With
```

As the example shows, you supply the arguments to the AddNew method as a pair of arrays, the first containing the field names, the second, their values. In the example, I used the VBA Array function to create an array on the fly from literal strings. You could instead use variables representing arrays you previously created. At any rate, using this technique to supply field values at the time you add a new record means you don't need a separate line of code for each field.

The Delete method, of course, deletes the current record.

Reading field data

Working with the current value of a specific field in your code is as simple as reading the field's Value property. Specify the field either by name or index number, as shown in the examples here. Note that Value is the default property, so it isn't required in your code:

```
If rstYGate.Fields("Service visits").Value > 10
    MsgBox "This unit needs a major overhaul!"
End If

strCurrentFieldData = rstYGate.Fields(3)
```

Because the Fields collection is the default collection of a Recordset object, you actually aren't required to mention it by name. To refer to a field, just precede its name by an exclamation point, using brackets around names that include spaces. Here are two examples:

```
rstYGate!Date = #5/15/2000#

With rstYGate
    intItems = ![Oil cans]
End With
```

Changing field data

Changing (updating) field values in particular records is simpler in ADO than its predecessors. All you have to do is specify the new value and then move to a different record, as in this example (assume the rstBucket Recordset object is already open and filled with records):

```
With rstBucket
    .Fields(0).Value = "Love"
    .MoveNext
End With
```

Alternatively, if you don't want to move off of the current record, you can write changes to the database using the Update method. In the example that follows, I've taken advantage of the default status of the Fields collection and Value property to minimize the code I had to write:

```
With rstBucket
    !Volume = 8.93
    .Update
End With
```

As with the `AddNew` method, `Update` lets you supply a set of new field values with a pair of arrays, as shown here:

```
With rstBucket
    .Update Array("Name," "Rank,""Cereal brand"), _
        Array("Lola," "Lt. Colonel," "Sugar Showers")
End With
```

Repeating operations on multiple records

Use a `Do` loop to perform a test or operation on multiple records in a recordset, as in this example:

```
'Loop through the recordset
    With rstInPeace
        Do Until .EOF
            Debug.Print.Fields(0)
            .MoveNext
        Loop
    End With
    Set rstInPeace = Nothing
End Sub
```

Using the Command object

In ADO, a `Command` object represents a command, such as an SQL statement or stored procedure, that is to be carried out by the data source. You can use `Command` objects to retrieve records as `Recordset` objects, and to have the data source carry out operations such as updates and deletes on multiple records. (The code samples shown in this section demonstrate the latter operations; for an example involving recordsets, see the section "Creating recordsets using the Command object," earlier in this chapter.)

Don't be shocked if you can't use the `Command` object with a particular data source. OLE DB Providers aren't required to implement the `Command` object, and those that do aren't required to handle parameters.

About stored procedures

Stored procedures are queries and other operations that you or someone else define in advance (usually using SQL) and store at the data source. Access queries are examples of stored procedures. Although you can design an Access query visually on a grid, it represents an SQL statement, which you can see by switching to SQL view. The query is stored as part of the `.mdb` database file that it pertains to. Network databases such as SQL Server also permit you to define similar stored procedures.

Because a stored procedure is all ready to go, you only need to know its name — you can forget about the complexities of the query definition in your code. More important, stored procedures run faster and are more reliable over a network than equivalent SQL statements. Stored procedures provide a higher level of security, because the code is encapsulated within them. On the downside, the SQL for a stored procedure isn't part of your program's code, so you can't modify it or even examine it there.

Setting up a Command object

To set up a Command object, start by declaring a variable for it and instantiating the actual object. You can then use its properties to associate it with a connection, to define the command you want to run — in the form of an SQL statement or the name of a stored procedure — and to specify the type of command. With all that out of the way, use the Command object's Execute method to actually run the command. Here's an example demonstrating these steps using an SQL update query. Note the CommandType property, which you must set to adCmdText to pass an SQL statement to the data source:

```
Dim conSecrate As Connection
Dim cmdSecret As Command
Dim prmDate
(code to set up the conSecrate Connection object goes here...)
Set cmdSecret = New Command
With cmdSecret
    .ActiveConnection = conSecrate
    .CommandText = _
        "UPDATE Bicycles SET OnSale = True WHERE Category = 4;"
    .CommandType = adCmdText
    .Execute
End With
```

Using command parameters

If the command requires input *parameters* (values that must be supplied when it runs, such as a date range or search criteria), you must also define individual Parameter objects, appending each to the Command object's Parameters collection. The example shown here illustrates how this works, and shows how to use a Command object to execute a stored procedure rather than an SQL statement:

```
Dim conSecrate As Connection
Dim cmdSecret As Command
Dim prmDate
(code to set up the conSecrate connection goes here...)
Set cmdSecret = New Command
With cmdSecret
    .ActiveConnection = conSecrate
    .CommandText = "qryDeleteOldRecords"
    .CommandType = adCmdStoredProc ' in Jet, adCmdTable
End With
```

```
Set prmDate = New Parameter
With prmDate
    .Name = "Date"
    .Value = InputBox "Enter the cut-off date."
    .Type = adDate
    .Direction = adParamInput
End With
With cmdSecret
    .Parameters.Append prmDate 'Adds the parameter just defined
    .Execute ' Executes the command
End With
```

Tip   If you're running a query stored in a Jet/Access database, use `adCmdTable` as the `CommandType` property for the `Command` object — not `adCmdStoredProc`, which is the choice for SQL Server and many other database servers.

Many data sources — but Jet isn't one of them — also support output parameters for stored procedures. These are named items that hold values returned by the procedure.

Working with SQL

It's easy enough to open a recordset using ADO, but filling it with the right records can be a more daunting project. If you're going to build serious database applications, you have to learn to write SQL code — or how to use tools that write it for you.

Avoiding SQL

Inserting SQL statements in VBA code is something like interrupting a letter with snippets of Greek, or calculus, or music notation. Although SQL is a much smaller and more narrowly focused language than Visual Basic, many VBA programmers find it difficult to use just because it's so different. Given this reality, you may want to rely on development tools that compose SQL based on your picks from lists of fields, criteria for selecting particular records, and actions you want the query to perform.

The Access query designer (described in Chapter 47) is one such tool. When you've designed and tested an Access query, you have two choices for connecting a `Command` object in your VBA code to the query: The `Command` object can run the query as a stored procedure, or you can copy and paste the SQL code generated by the query designer into your code. To use the latter technique, design and test the query in Access; then choose View ➪ SQL View to display the corresponding SQL statement. Copy it to the Clipboard, switch to VBA, and paste it — between a pair of quote marks — into the statement that sets the `CommandText` property for the `Command` object. For details on executing SQL statements or stored procedures, see the section "Using the Command object," earlier in this chapter.

The Access query designer is fine so far as it goes, but it can't handle every situation. It won't build sophisticated query types such as union queries and subqueries. Of course, its stored queries work only with Jet databases (however, other databases come with similar visual query design tools). You can try using the Access query designer to generate SQL for use with a non-Jet database, but keep in mind that different databases use different versions of SQL, so you may have to hand-tweak the code.

Understanding SQL dialects

Although SQL is nearly universal as the query language for database management, many databases speak unique SQL dialects. Jet, for example, provides several nonstandard SQL enhancements but doesn't implement certain other features found in the standard version. For the discussion in this chapter, I'm sticking with Jet's version of SQL simply because it's the one everyone can use with Office. If you use a different database system, you may need to make adjustments to conform to its SQL dialect.

Inserting SQL statements in VBA code

The examples in an earlier section, "Writing Database Code with ADO," should make plain how to place SQL statements into a VBA procedure. The key is to remember that VBA treats SQL statements as text strings, not as part of the code itself. These strings receive special handling when interpreted as arguments to the Open or Execute method of ADO objects, but until then, they're just ordinary strings of text characters.

Which means, then, that you must enclose every SQL statement within a pair of double quote marks. Whether you're setting a Command object's CommandText property or entering an argument to a Recordset object's Open method, use the quote marks. Again, you can find a number of examples in the ADO section earlier in this chapter. And don't miss the related Tip in "Refining the recordset: Setting criteria," later in this section.

Writing SELECT statements

I covered the mechanics of creating ADO Recordset objects earlier in this chapter. Here, the focus is on the SQL code you need to specify which records belong in your recordsets. Because it performs precisely this task, the SELECT statement is the workhorse of SQL.

The simplest form of the SELECT statement retrieves all the records from a single table. The following example returns all the fields and all the records from the Toys table:

```
SELECT * FROM Toys
```

Because this statement contains no additional criteria, all records from the `Toys` table are included in the returned recordset. The asterisk indicates that the record-set is also to contain all fields in the chosen table.

Tip

> `SELECT` statements retrieve records from the database, but don't change the stored data. To make such changes, you must modify the values in the recordset's fields and then save your changes, or use `SQL UPDATE` or `DELETE` statements.

Relating multiple tables in SELECT statements

A single `SELECT` statement can query more than one table. Simply listing the tables from which you want to select records in the `FROM` clause works, as shown here:

```
SELECT * FROM Toys, Clerks
```

However, the recordset returned by this simple listing of tables isn't likely to be very useful. Nothing connects the two tables together, so the database doesn't know which record in the first table belongs with which record in the second. As a result, you get for each record in the first table as many new records as there are records in the second table.

To relate two tables together properly, perform a *join* in the `SELECT` statement. An *inner join*, the most common type, creates a record in the recordset from matching pairs of records in the source tables. The match is based on values in a specified field the two tables have in common. The following statement creates a recordset listing the manufacturer's rep for each toy in the inventory:

```
SELECT Toy, Rep FROM Toys INNER JOIN Reps ON Toys.ID =
Reps.ToyID
```

To create an inner join, place the `INNER JOIN` term between the two tables in the `FROM` clause. Follow this with an `ON` clause, which specifies the fields that should contain values to be compared. Normally, the field names in the `ON` clause are separated by an equal sign, indicating that selected records have to have identical values in the two fields (other comparison operators are permitted).

Choosing fields

To specify a subset of particular fields, name them explicitly as in this example:

```
SELECT Toy, InStock, OnOrder FROM ToyInventory
```

If a field or table name contains spaces or punctuation, place square brackets around the name, as shown here:

```
SELECT Toy, [List Price], [Sale Price] FROM ToyInventory
```

By default, the `Name` property of each `Field` object in the recordset returned by the `SELECT` statement is the name of the corresponding field in the original table. You can assign different field names (*aliases*) in the recordset using an `AS` clause for each field you want to rename:

```
SELECT Toy AS ToyName, InStock AS OnHand, OnOrder FROM
ToyInventory
```

If you're retrieving records from multiple tables and want to select fields that have the same name in more than one table, precede each field name with the source table's name. Here's an example:

```
SELECT ToyInventory.Name, Clerks.Name FROM ToyInventory, Clerks
```

Creating calculated fields and values

You can build a recordset containing new fields whose values are calculated from the underlying values in the underlying database. In your `SELECT` statement, define the calculated fields using expressions based on VBA operators and functions. For example, let's say you want to list what prices would be if you put everything on sale at 10 percent off the regular price.

```
SELECT Toy, (Price * .9) AS SalePrice FROM ToyInventory
```

Note that when you define a calculated field, you must include an `AS` clause to create an alias (name) for the field in the recordset. The parentheses aren't necessary but help to clarify the calculation you're performing. You can use more than one field in the expression that creates a calculated field, as in `(Price * InStock) AS InventoryValue`.

As another example, suppose that for some reason you wanted a recordset listing all your clerks' names in uppercase without changing the way the names are recorded in the database. The following statement would do the trick:

```
SELECT UCase(Name) AS [Clerk's name] FROM Clerks
```

Using SQL aggregate functions, a `SELECT` statement can return a recordset consisting of a single summary value, such as the number of records containing an entry in a given field:

```
SELECT Count(Recyclable) AS [Can recycle] FROM Toys
```

or the average of all values for a field:

```
SELECT Avg(Price) AS [Average Price] FROM Toys
```

You can then transfer the value of this one record's one field to a variable in your code for use in other calculations or to display on a form:

```
intRecylableCount = rstRecyclableToys![Can recycle]
```

Aggregate functions include `Count`, `Avg`, `Sum`, `Min`, `Max`, and a few statistical functions.

Selecting records with the DISTINCT, DISTINCTROW, and TOP predicates

Use the `DISTINCT`, `DISTINCTROW`, and `TOP` SQL predicates in a `SELECT` statement as simple tools for specifying a subset of the underlying database. Place these special words directly after `SELECT`, as shown in Table 49-3.

Table 49-3
SQL Predicates for Selecting Records

Predicate	Use	Example
DISTINCT	Selects only one record when the underlying data has two or more records containing the identical data in the named field(s).	`SELECT DISTINCT Address FROM Members` Returns a recordset containing only one record for each address, even when the Members table contains more than one record per address.
DISTINCTROW	Selects all unique records based on all fields. If two records differ by only one character, both are included; if they're identical in all fields, one is omitted.	`SELECT DISTINCTROW Name, Address FROM Members` Returns a recordset with `Name` and `Address` fields. The recordset may contain duplicate records, but only when other fields in the underlying table differ.
TOP n	Selects a specified number of records at the top or bottom of a range determined by an `ORDER BY` clause.	`SELECT TOP 10 ToyName FROM Toys ORDER BY UnitsSold` Returns a recordset containing the 10 best-selling toys. To identify the 10 worst sellers, you would add ASC (ascending) following the `UnitsSold` field name.

Refining the recordset: Setting criteria

To restrict a recordset to a range of records meeting specific criteria, add a WHERE clause to the SELECT statement, as shown in these examples:

```
SELECT * FROM Toys WHERE Price <= 20
SELECT Customer, Date FROM Sales WHERE Date = #10/24/2000#
SELECT Name, Rank, CerealNumber FROM Kids WHERE Rank = 'Queen'
SELECT Name, Age, [Shoe Size] FROM Kids WHERE Age Between 3 And
6
```

As you can see, a WHERE clause follows the FROM clause and includes an expression specifying the criteria that records have to meet to make it into the recordset. As you can also see, these expressions aren't quite like VBA expressions. For one thing, text strings are enclosed by single quote marks, not double ones. For another, you can specify ranges with the Between...And construct, which doesn't exist in VBA. Also, the Like operator functions differently in SQL from the way it does in VBA.

You can combine multiple expressions using logical operators (And, Or, and so on).

```
SELECT * FROM Toys WHERE Price > 20 And Category = 'Action
Figures'
```

Tip

In VBA code, it's proper form to use single quotes to specify a string within an SQL statement — which in its entirety is a VBA string inside double quotes. For example you might set up a Command object like this:

```
strSQL = "SELECT Name FROM Kids WHERE Hates =
'Brocolli'"
cmdEr.CommandText = strSQL
```

Often, especially in WHERE clauses, you need to base a portion of an SQL statement string on a variable — for example, if you're performing a query based on the user's entry in a text box on a form. Compose the string by concatenating the variable with the rest of the string. If the variable represents a string, remember to tack on the single quotes before and after the string, as in this example:

```
strSQL = "SELECT Name FROM Kids WHERE Hates = ' " _
    & frmInputForm.TextBox1 & "'"
```

Grouping records

The GROUP BY clause enables you to combine records having the same values in specified fields, converting them into a single record in the resulting recordset. Typically, this clause is used when you want a recordset that summarizes the underlying data. For example, you might want to know how many records there are in the database for each value of a given field. Try this example:

```
SELECT Category, Count([Category]) AS [Number of Items] FROM
Toys
    GROUP BY Category;
```

The result of this statement is a recordset that might look something like this:

Category	Number of Items
Action Figures	42
Dolls	37
Games	29
Plush	23
Puzzles	17
Sporting Goods	31

You can use other SQL aggregate functions such as Max or Avg to produce other kinds of summaries.

Further filtering with the HAVING clause

A HAVING clause follows a GROUP BY clause and sets criteria for the grouped records. It works like the WHERE clause and can be used alone, or in combination with WHERE to further limit the returned records. In this example, the HAVING clause includes only categories that have at least 30 records meeting the criteria set by the WHERE clause (a price tag greater than $100):

```
SELECT Category, Count(Category) As [Number of Items] FROM Toys
    WHERE Price > 100 GROUP BY Category
    HAVING Count(Category) > 30
```

The result of this statement is a recordset that might look something like this:

Category	Number of Items
Action Figures	42
Dolls	37
Sporting Goods	31

Sorting with the ORDER BY clause

Use an ORDER BY clause to sort the records returned by a SELECT statement according to the values in one or more fields. It belongs at the end of the statement, as in this example:

```
SELECT Toy, Price, InStock FROM ToyInventory ORDER BY Toy
```

The resulting recordset lists the toys in alphabetical order by their names.

To list them by price instead, sorted alphabetically by name when items have the same price, you'd use the following statement. As it demonstrates, you can sort on multiple fields simply by listing the fields in the order in which you want the sort to happen:

```
SELECT Toy, Price FROM ToyInventory ORDER BY Price DESC, Toy
```

By default, sorts are performed in ascending order. To specify a sort order for a field explicitly, add DESC (for descending) or ASC (for ascending) following the name of the field. The previous example produces a recordset with the highest-priced items listed first.

Performing bulk updates and deletions in SQL

The UPDATE and DELETE statements enable you to change or remove a group of records in the underlying data source with one command. These statements work directly on the source database—you don't have to first retrieve a recordset, modify its records, and then update the database with your changes. Consider the following example, useful if you decide to raise your prices by 10 percent in a particular merchandise category:

```
UPDATE Toys SET Price = Price * 1.1 WHERE Category = 'Trains'
```

The name of the table you're working on follows immediately after the UPDATE term. Then comes the SET clause, in which you assign a new value to one or more fields in the target table. Finally, an optional WHERE clause enables you to specify criteria limiting the change to specified records. The WHERE clause works just as it does in SELECT statements.

The DELETE statement is even simpler than the UPDATE statement, because all it does is remove whole records. The following example deletes records for all toys that aren't in stock and haven't been reordered:

```
DELETE FROM Toys WHERE InStock = 0 And OnOrder = 0
```

Tip

To delete entries for a field rather than an entire record, use an UPDATE statement with a SET clause that sets the value for that field to Null.

Caution

UPDATE and DELETE statements produce irreversible changes in the underlying database—you can't undo their results. Be sure to back up your data before running such a statement.

✦   ✦   ✦

Designing Access Forms

Although you can work directly with the information in your tables and queries, an Access database becomes much more, well, *accessible* when equipped with forms for viewing and editing its information.

If you're designing a full-scale database application, custom forms provide the user interface for your program. Even if you use Access more casually, creating a few forms can help you focus on individual records, break up the monotony of table rows and columns, and give you push-button access to macros and VBA procedures. Equally important, forms are one of the most effective ways to work with data *relationally* — that is, with related data from different tables at the same time.

From the designer's perspective, reports have a lot in common with forms. Of course, their mission is different. Reports only present information — they don't allow the user to fiddle with the data. Also, although you can view a report within Access, the real point is to get the information to other people, either in print or electronic form. Nevertheless, you use essentially the same techniques to lay out reports and hook them up to Access data as you do for forms. (There are a few differences, but I don't have space to cover reports explicitly here.)

Access Forms: A World Apart

As with most other VBA applications, Word, PowerPoint, and Excel rely on UserForms (discussed in Chapter 56) for on-screen interactions with users of your custom programs. Not so Access. True, an Access form works and looks very much like a VBA UserForm from the user's point of view — after all, both are Windows dialog boxes, with the typical buttons, text boxes, and other controls. Behind the scenes, however — and during the design process — Access forms differ significantly from UserForms.

Note   As you may know, VBA UserForms and the forms you can build in the standalone version of Visual Basic are distinct as well. Well, Access forms aren't Visual Basic forms, either.

About bound forms

The most important difference between an Access form and a VBA UserForm is this: An Access form — and the controls it contains — can be bound readily to data, as long as it takes the form of a specific table, query, or SQL statement. When a record on such a *bound form* changes, that change is saved in the database table to which the form is bound, whether it's bound directly or through an intermediary query or SQL statement. Access forms also have the innate capability to navigate through a bound set of records automatically. When the user moves from one record to the next, the form's controls immediately fill with the corresponding values from the new record.

Tip   Ordinary VBA UserForms can't navigate through a bound set of records. (You can add this capability, however, with the data controls that come with Office Developer and in many third-party toolkits.)

Form design tools — Access versus VBA

The Access design tools don't work quite like those for VBA UserForms — contrast the Format menus from the Visual Basic Editor and Access (as shown in Figure 50-1) and note the different Toolbox and Properties windows for the two environments (shown in Figure 50-2). Access is slightly less capable when it comes to laying out controls. For example, you can't center selected controls on an Access form or automatically line up their centers, capabilities you do have with UserForms. However, Access lets you group controls to move or resize them as a unit.

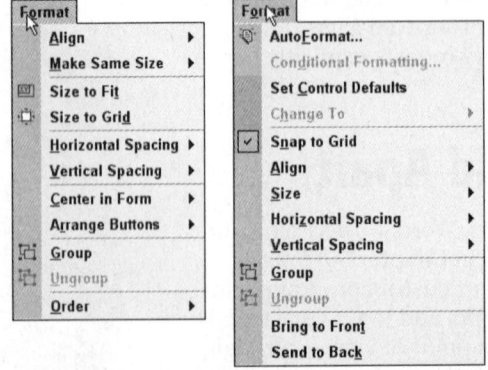

Figure 50-1: On the left is the Format menu of the Visual Basic Editor; on the right, the Format menu in Access.

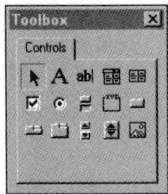

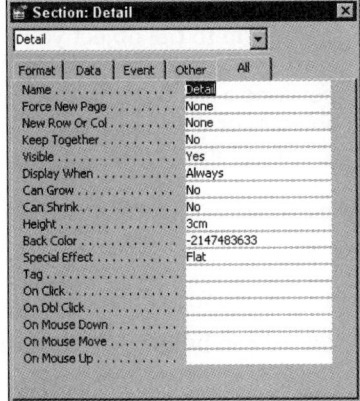

Figure 50-2: The Toolbox and Properties windows
of the Visual Basic Editor (on the top) and Access
(on the bottom)

Access offers different standard controls from those available for VBA UserForms —
as a close look at the Toolbox windows in Figure 50-2 reveals. Even the controls that
the two environments share still differ (rather subtly) in the names and behavior of
the controls' properties. If you're accustomed to working with UserForm controls,
you'll have to make some minor adjustments when you're building Access forms.

Access's unique forms affect your development plans

Before you jump into building a whole set of neat forms in Access, be sure you
understand the implications of the nonstandard forms that come with Access. The

fact that you can't reuse Access forms in Visual Basic or VBA is truly a Big Deal—it may lead you to abandon Access as a development tool for production database applications!

If you're sure that you'll never want to convert your Access application to Visual Basic—even though Visual Basic offers faster performance and easier distribution—then feel free to go hog wild with Access forms. If there's a chance that you might eventually want to convert, be sure to count the cost of reengineering the application's forms. In an application with many complex forms, recreating them from scratch in Visual Basic could take many hours. If you decide to use Access for prototyping purposes only, minimize the time you spend laying out forms. Stick with simple, quick-and-dirty form layouts, even if they're ugly.

Designing Access Forms

To start a new Access form, select Forms in the Objects bar and click New. In the New Form dialog box, pull down the "Choose the table or query where the object's data comes from:" list and select the object (table, query, or view) on which to base the form. This step is important, because it binds the form to the object you select—that is, the fields you can attach to the form and that depend on the underlying table. However, if you're creating a form to serve as a *switchboard* (with buttons that activate other functions and database objects) or if you're going to connect the form to data via VBA code, you can leave this item blank.

The New Form dialog box also asks you to choose from several methods for starting the form:

  ✦ If you want to start laying out a form from scratch, choose Design View.

  ✦ If you don't mind a generic look, the Form Wizard can build fairly complete working forms for you with a minimum of effort on your part.

  ✦ The AutoForm wizards are even less trouble—just double-click the layout you want and you have an instant form.

  ✦ If your form requires a chart or Pivot Table, the appropriate wizards prepare it for you.

Even if you have the wizards do some of the work for you, you're going to wind up in Design view soon enough. That's where you get full control over a form's layout and functionality. When you open a form in Design view (see Figure 50-3), it appears on the screen marked with a grid to assist you in aligning the items you place upon it. The Control Toolbox opens beside the form.

Using form views

You can work with forms in five views, as follows:

✦ **Design view,** illustrated in Figure 50-3, is for laying out the form.

✦ **Form view** displays the working version of the form so you can view, enter, and edit data.

✦ **Datasheet view** doesn't display the form at all, really — instead, it displays the data bound to the form in a plain tabular format, similar to a table or query datasheet. This view isn't particularly pretty, but it's a good way to get at a large number of records at one time.

✦ **Pivot Table View** allows you to dynamically change the layout of a form to analyze data in different ways, by arranging fields in filter, row, column, and detail areas.

✦ **Pivot Chart View** is similar to Pivot Table View, but it allows you to display data visually by selecting a chart type and arranging fields in filter, series, category, and data areas.

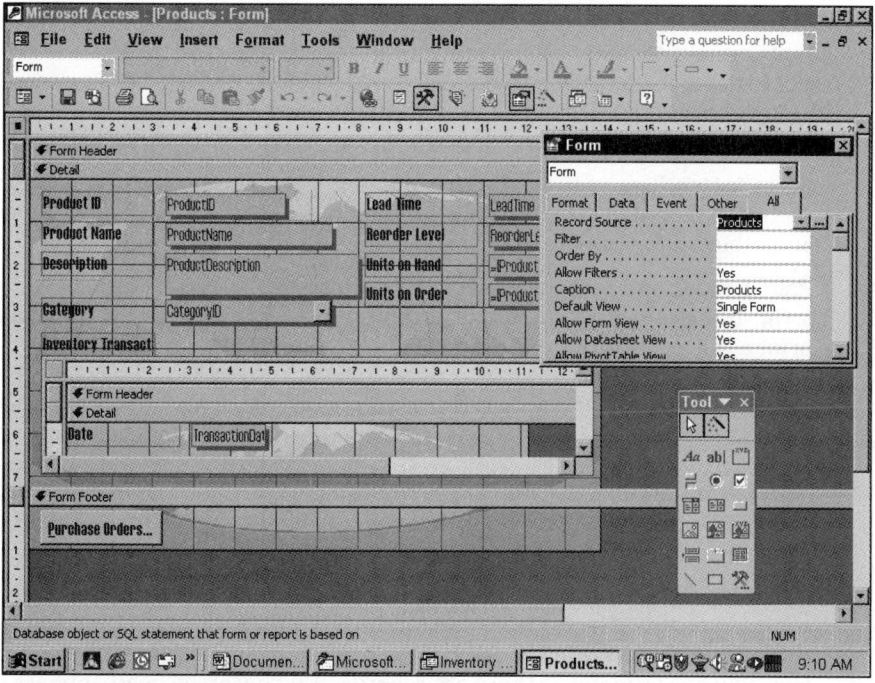

Figure 50-3: Laying out an Access form

Double-clicking an existing form in the database window opens it in Form view. To open a form in Design view, select it and click Design. To switch between views when a form is already open, use the choices at the top of the View menu. Alternatively, you can click the desired choice on the View Split button (if it's visible) or right-click the form's background or title bar and choose an option from the shortcut menu.

Note If you're displaying a popup form in Form view, the only way to return to Design view without closing the form first is via the right-click (shortcut) menu.

Access form anatomy

Access forms have one or more separate sections. These include the following:

✦ **Detail section.** Always present, the detail section is the main part of an Access form — and the only part visible when you create a new form from scratch in Design view. The detail section is usually used to show records from the table, query, or view on which the form is based. It can display a single record at a time (in single form view) or act as a scrollable window showing all the records in the underlying object (in the continuous form or datasheet views).

✦ **Form header.** The form header appears at the top of the form window. Its contents remain constant as you move from record to record in Detail view. Headers are usually used to display items such as the form title, a company logo or other graphic, and column headings for fields in tabular layouts in continuous form or datasheet views.

✦ **Form footer.** Similar to the header, the footer remains static as you flip from record to record. It's a good place to park buttons (such as OK and Cancel) and other action-oriented controls.

✦ **Page header and footer.** These sections appear only on printed copies of the form, at the top and bottom of every printed page, respectively. Use them to print a title or description, the page number, or the date.

Other optional elements present in Access forms but not in VBA UserForms include the following:

✦ **Navigation buttons.** Located at the bottom edge of a form, these buttons enable you to move quickly to other records by typing in a record number or clicking a button.

✦ **Record selectors**. Displayed in a gray bar along the left edge of the form, a separate record selector is visible for each record showing. If the form is set to single form view you see only one record selector, but in continuous form view you see as many as there are records. A heavy arrowhead appears in the record selector of the selected record until you start to edit it, at which point it's replaced by a pencil graphic.

Adding and deleting sections, buttons, and selectors

To add a header or footer to a form, choose View ⇨ Form Header/Footer or View ⇨ Page Header/Footer. Note that Access won't let you add or remove a header or footer individually — it's a both-or-neither proposition.

Tip
> To get the effect of removing a header or a footer without deleting its counterpart, resize the section you want to get rid of to a height of zero. You can do this with the mouse (see the "Sizing forms" section) or by setting the Height property in the Properties window.

Although the header/footer commands are on the View menu, they function to add or delete sections from the form, not just to display or hide them. When you turn off a header/footer, Access irreversibly deletes the affected sections and their controls.

To turn navigation buttons and record selectors on or off, set the corresponding options in the Properties box.

Selecting forms and their sections

As you saw previously in Figure 50-3, each section is set off by a horizontal section bar running across the form.

To select an entire form, click the *form selector*, the box at the top left of the form where the vertical and horizontal rulers intersect. The form is selected when a heavy black square appears in the selector. If the rulers aren't visible and you don't want to display them, choose Edit ⇨ Select Form or press Ctrl+R. To select an individual section, click its section bar so it turns black.

Working with form properties

Many attributes govern the appearance and function of the form and any of its controls. For unfettered access to these attributes, use the Properties dialog box (also called the *Properties sheet*) associated with the form or the control you are working with. To display the Properties dialog box — if it isn't already visible — click the Properties button on the Form Design toolbar. Alternatively, you can right-click any item in the form and choose Properties from the shortcut menu. Although it's visible in earlier screen shots, the Access Properties dialog box is shown again in Figure 50-4 (note that it's not called Properties; it's labeled with the name of the item whose properties it controls).

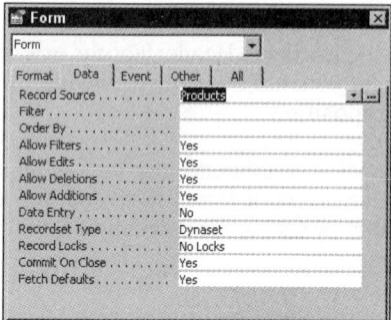

Figure 50-4: Edit properties for a form or control in this dialog box.

When the Properties dialog box is visible, its contents change accordingly as you select different items on the form. Fortunately, you can get help on any property by placing the insertion point in its field and pressing F1. Also, you can select entries for many properties by choosing an option from a drop-down list or clicking the builder button (see "Binding a form to data," later in this chapter).

Sizing forms

Access forms are truly weird, and frustrating, when it comes to the size they occupy on the screen. In Form view, users can resize forms at will with the mouse, assuming you've designed the form to allow this. But if you value a well-proportioned application, at times you'll want to preset and lock a form's size. This section provides an introduction to the peculiar machinations required.

Note   Although Access lets you set a form's dimensions in Design view, the size you set there doesn't control what you see in Form view. Instead, the Design view size determines how much area you have for placing controls. A form often appears larger than that in Form view, but any extra room it occupies is empty. (The size of each section, however, *is* fixed by its size in Design view.)

Sizing a form in Design view

I'll start with the easy part — how to control a form's size settings in Design view. The obvious way to resize a form is with the mouse, but you can also set a form's size in the Properties dialog box. To control width, arrange the form's window so you can see the right border of the form. Point to the right border so the mouse pointer becomes a double-headed arrow, and then drag to the new width. If you want to specify the width with numeric precision, select the form itself and change the value of its Width property on the Format tab of the Properties dialog box.

Changing a form's height is a bit more complicated; the form itself doesn't have a Height property. Instead, the overall height depends on the sum of the heights of each of its sections. To change a section's height with the mouse, point to the bottom border of the section and drag it up or down. Alternatively, you can select a section and type in a value for its Height property in the Properties box.

Controlling the size of a form as it appears in Form view

Here's the key fact to know about the size of forms in Form view: The size of a form, as displayed in Form view, always corresponds to the dimensions of the form's window — not the form itself — in Design view.

The relationship works both ways: You can control the size of a form in Form view by resizing the form's window in Design view. Vice versa also applies: When you resize a form in Form view and switch back to Design view, you'll find that Access has resized the form's window to match.

In Design view, if you leave empty space between the borders of the form itself and its window, Access fills in any empty space when you open the form in Form view. If you make the form window narrower or shorter than the form itself, Access displays the form accordingly, adding scroll bars so you can reach the parts that aren't visible.

You can't make a form appear at the correct height in Form view by visually matching its window to the form's bottom border in Design view; the displayed form is always taller than you expect. The reason: The section bars lower the position of the bottom border in Design view. Those bars aren't visible in Form view, so the form is actually shorter than it appears in Design view.

You've heard all the bad news. Fortunately, you can match the displayed form size to the dimensions of the form itself in a roundabout way (just sneak a peek at the accompanying Tip).

Tip

To display a form at the dimensions specified in Design view, set the Auto Resize property to Yes (the default), close the form, and then reopen it directly from the database window, without opening it in Design view first (double-click the form item in the database window to open it directly). To resize a form already open in Form view, select it and choose Window ⇨ Size to Fit Form. If you then switch back to Design view, you see that Access has resized the form's window accordingly. Click the Save button to be sure that Access stores the window size — and don't change it, or you'll have to repeat the process.

Locking in form size

If you don't want users to be able to resize a form, change the form's Border Style property (on the Format tab of the Properties dialog box) to something other than Sizable. If you don't want them to be able to maximize or minimize the form, choose None or Dialog for the Border Style, or set the Min Max Buttons property to an option other than Both Enabled.

Controlling form appearance with AutoFormat

The AutoFormat command is the easiest and most efficient way to alter a form's look. AutoFormats work much like styles in Excel or Word — they apply a predetermined set of appearance attributes.

You can choose an AutoFormat when you create a form via the Form Wizard. But let's assume you're already working with a form in Design view and decide to change its appearance. Although you can alter the properties that specify fonts, colors, and other characteristics individually, it's quicker to apply an AutoFormat.

To get the ball rolling, select the entire form, one of its sections, or one or more controls (Access applies your AutoFormat choice only to the selected items). Then click the AutoFormat button on the Form Design toolbar, or choose Format ➪ AutoFormat. In the resulting dialog box, select the format you want to use and click OK. Use the Options button to restrict the attributes (properties) you want to alter. Figure 50-5 shows the AutoFormat dialog box with the Options checkboxes turned on.

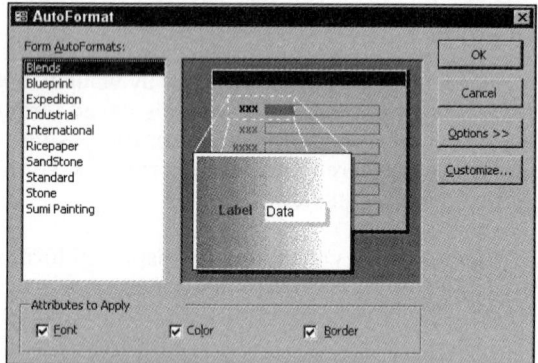

Figure 50-5: Apply a form AutoFormat from this dialog box, using the boxes at the bottom to control which form properties receive AutoFormats.

After you've developed a form design you like, consider saving it as a custom AutoFormat for reuse on other forms. With the form whose properties you want to memorize open in Design view, open the AutoFormat dialog box and click Customize.

Binding a form to data

A form's `RecordSource` property is the key to binding the form to a specific set of records in your database. After the form has been bound to a set of records, and you've fleshed it out with controls bound to individual fields in that record set, the form automatically displays all the records without any programming on your part.

When you specify a table, query, or view at the time you create a form, Access automatically sets the `RecordSource` property accordingly. To set it or change it yourself, select the form, open the Properties dialog box, click on the Data tab, and enter the name of a table, query, or view, or type in an SQL statement directly.

Chapter 49 introduces SQL statement syntax.

If you're creating a full-fledged database application in VBA, you can set the form's `RecordSource` property in your code rather than in the Properties window with a statement such as the following:

```
Forms!frmToyInventory.RecordSource = "Inventory"
```

If you're writing code in the form's own code module, it's easier to use the keyword `Me` to refer to the current form, as in this example (which assumes you've already assigned a valid SQL statement to the `strSQL` variable):

```
Me.RecordSource = strSQL
```

When you're typing a lengthy setting in the `RecordSource` property (or the `ControlSource` property for a control), press Shift+F2 to open the Zoom window, in which you see and edit the entire entry at once. Alternatively, click the builder button to edit the entry in the Expression Builder window, which lets you construct expressions by selecting items from lists of database objects, functions, and keywords.

Remember: For top performance, it's always best to bind a form or control to a narrowly defined query or SQL statement, rather than to an entire table. These performance benefits are especially critical on a network, where connecting to an entire table across the network would slow you way down.

Working with controls

Until you add controls to it, a form is just an empty box. You must add controls to make it come alive with fields from your database, information text, and buttons and other controls to make things happen.

Adding fields and controls to a form

You can place controls on an Access form in two ways: by adding fields from the underlying set of records to which you've bound the form, or by dropping them on the form from the Toolbox.

If your form is bound to data, Access's field list displays the names of the fields in the underlying recordset. All you have to do is drag fields from the field list to the form. If the field list isn't visible, click the Field List button to display it. Upon arrival, a dragged-in field appears in a text box, with a label containing the field's caption or name appearing to its left. The new text box is automatically bound to the data in that field; when you display the form in Form view, the text box shows the data for that field from the current record.

Tip

You can drag multiple fields to the form at once. Select adjacent fields as a group by Shift+clicking, or select individual fields by Ctrl+clicking. Select the whole shooting match by double-clicking the field list's title bar.

To add other types of controls, whether or not you want to bind them to data, drag the controls from the Toolbox to the form. When a control is in place on the form, you can bind it to a field using its `ControlSource` property. Just select the field from the drop-down list in the Properties box (some types of controls can't be bound to data). To display a calculated result, set the `ControlSource` property to an expression. You can include bound field names and controls in such expressions.

For example, suppose the form is bound to a table containing a `CurrentSales` field, and `FantasyMultiplier` is the name of an unbound text-box control. The following expression calculates your hoped-for results each time the user types a new entry in the unbound control:

```
=[CurrentSales] * [FantasyMultiplier]
```

Note

Don't try to set a control's `ControlSource` property to an SQL statement—Access doesn't allow this. If you want to bind a control to data not available in the table or query bound to the form, go back and fix yourself a query that does contain the field you need—along with the other fields needed by the form. Then bind the new or revised query to the form.

Unbound controls can also make nice ornaments on your forms; they're even useful—you can use them to display information under your application's control. They can also function as triggers for macros, hyperlinks, or VBA code.

Formatting controls

To work with a control, click it to select it. After selecting it, you can move it around or resize it by dragging its handles, and you can cut or copy it with the usual Windows techniques. Shift+click two or more controls to select them all. Two or more selected controls can be aligned to one another, matched in size, and spaced evenly by using commands on the Format menu.

One aspect of control layout might throw you initially: Each control has a *label*, a box containing text that tells the form's user what the control is for. The label is considered part of the control, so Access makes it easy to work with both label and control together. For example, if you click the control and then choose Edit ⇨ Cut, both items are placed on the Clipboard. Likewise, Access makes it easy to move both label and control together. However, you can also move them independently, and you can cut or copy the label by itself. After you have selected a control or its label, the mouse pointer changes to an open hand when it's over the perimeter of the selected item, and not over one of the resize handles. Dragging now moves both control and label. To move just one of these items, drag over the heavier move handles at the top-left corner of each item. The mouse pointer becomes a pointing hand when you can drag a label or control by itself. To cut or copy the label independently, click the label to select it first.

Setting default properties for controls

If the defaults for a control's properties don't suit your needs, you're not stuck with them. After you have formatted a control and set up its other properties to suit your project, you can reuse these settings as the default for controls of the same type that you add from now on. To set new default properties, select the control that has the properties you want and then choose Format ➪ Set Control Defaults.

Converting controls

Access lets you convert some types of controls into others, preserving as many of their properties as possible. Text boxes, for example, can become labels, list boxes, or combo boxes, while you can change option buttons into checkboxes or toggles. To convert a control, select it and choose Format ➪ Change To; doing so opens a submenu of the available conversion options.

Making controls responsive without VBA

VBA isn't always necessary to provoke a response from a control — instead, you can assign control events to macros or hyperlinks.

For example, say you design a simple database with two main forms: the EggSales form is for displaying and entering records, and the PriceOfEggs form displays the results of a query. Now you create a third form to serve as the switchboard, placing on it a command button for each of the other forms.

For the sake of variety, you decide to use both the hyperlink and macro techniques to connect the switchboard buttons to their respective forms. In Design view, you would start by placing the two command buttons on the switchboard form. Here's how you would then proceed:

✦ **To assign a hyperlink:** Select the first button. In the Properties dialog box, use the Hyperlink Subaddress property to specify the target for the hyperlink. In this case, type **Form EggSales**. If typing makes you anxious, click the builder button beside either hyperlink property to bring up the Insert Hyperlink dialog box. There you can pick any object in the database by choosing Object in This Database and selecting the object from the graphical list (see Figure 50-6).

✦ **To use the macro technique:** First write and save a macro called See Price of Eggs consisting of one action, OpenForm. After setting the action's Form Name property to PriceOfEggs, close the macro window. Then, back in your switchboard form, select the second button, go to the Event tab on the Properties dialog box, and in the On Click property, choose the name of your macro from the drop-down list (see Figure 50-7).

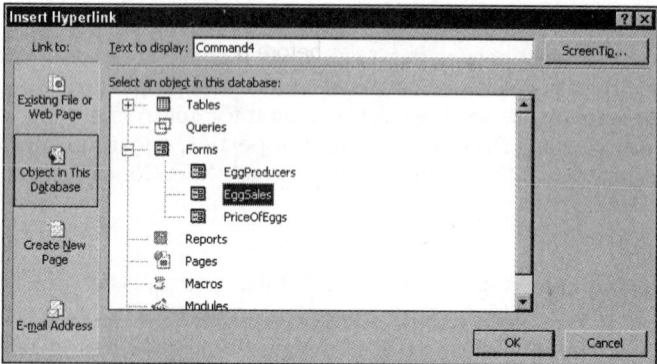

Figure 50-6: Assigning a hyperlink that calls up another form to a command button

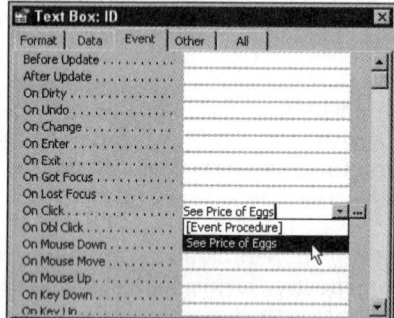

Figure 50-7: Assigning a macro to a button's On Click property

Cross-Reference   Chapter 46 discusses how to write macros in Access.

Working with forms in VBA code

You can use VBA to retrieve or set almost any property available in the Properties dialog box, and some others besides. Some advanced programmers believe you should always set all properties in code, to ensure that your program behaves properly, even if a user makes changes in Design view.

Because most form-related VBA code belongs in event procedures for the form and its controls, you should familiarize yourself with form events. Important form events include Open, Load, Activate, and Current, which occur in that order when you open a form for the first time. At the time you close a form, the Unload, Deactivate, and Close events occur. Look in the Help system to learn how these events differ from one another and when to use each one.

 **Caution** The Access "dialect" of VBA is different from that of other Office applications, so be sure to familiarize yourself with its peculiarities before plunging into code writing.

Writing event code

Access controls and forms respond to events such as mouse-clicks in the same way that standard VBA controls do (see Chapter 56). Here's how to write event code in Access:

1. Open the form in Design view.

2. Select a control (by clicking it) or the form itself (by clicking the form selector or pressing Ctrl+R).

3. Switch to the Event tab of the Properties dialog box for the item you've selected.

4. Click in any of the available events for the item and then click its builder button (the one with three dots to the right of the field).

5. Double-click the Code Builder choice.

6. Access displays the module window for the form with a new procedure started for the event type you chose. You can now add the code for the procedure.

Referring to forms and controls in Access VBA code

One notable contrast in syntax between regular VBA and the Access dialect of VBA is the way you refer to forms and controls in code. In Access, you're supposed to use the exclamation point operator to refer to these objects, as in the following:

```
Forms![An Access Form]!AnAccessButton
```

Note that when you refer to a form or control whose name contains spaces, you must enclose the name in brackets.

When you're working in the Code window for a form, you can refer to any of its controls directly, without mentioning the Forms collection or the form itself by name. For example, to change the Enabled property of a button, the following two statements are equivalent:

```
Forms!UniForm![Big Button].Enabled = False

[Big Button].Enabled = False
```

The preceding code fragment also illustrates the use of the dot operator (.) in Access to refer to properties of forms or controls. In code for standard VBA UserForms, by contrast, you identify objects as well as their properties using the dot operator, as in this example:

```
LittleForm.LittleButton.Enabled = True
```

Use the Me operator to refer to the current form when you write procedures that can be run by more than one form. The statement

```
DoSomethingNow Me
```

runs the DoSomethingNow procedure, passing to that procedure an object reference to the current form.

Working with subforms

A relational database manager earns its title because it can link data stored in one table to related data in another table. When you want to display related data on a form, a subform embedded in the form is very often the best means to that end. Subforms display the "many" side of a one-to-many database relationship.

Take the sample form shown in Figure 50-8. The form is bound to the Purchase Orders table, which records all the details of purchase orders issued by the company. However, because a single shipment for which a purchase order is issued may encompass any number of distinct items, the list of individual items sold is stored in a separate table, Products Ordered. For each record, this table records the date of the order, the name of the item, the quantity sold, the sale price, and what not. The subform, that grid in the middle of the form, is bound to that Products Ordered table.

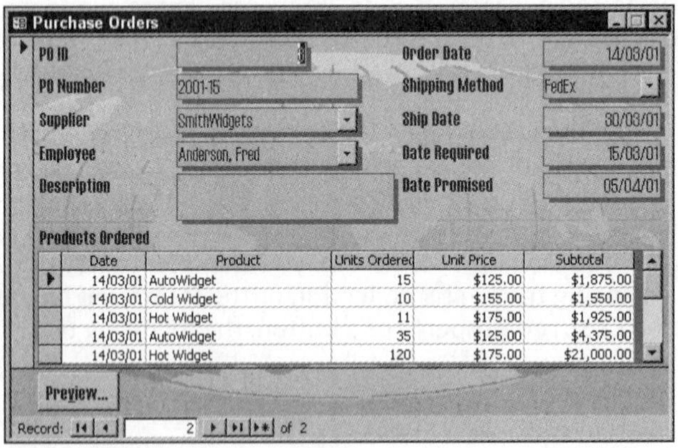

Figure 50-8: A form in the Inventory Control database (one of the templates that come with Access). The grid in the center is a subform.

But what makes a subform really useful is that the main form and the subform can be linked to one another by a common field. That is, by matching a field in the table to which the main form is linked to a field in the table to which the subform is linked, Access can find all the items that meet a particular criterion. And because the subform and the main form are linked in the same way, the subform automatically displays the related line items as you move from one item to another in the main form.

Note In reality, a subform is simply a regular Access form. Subforms appear as separate items on the Forms panel of the database window, and you can open them in their own windows. What makes a subform special is that it's embedded into another form by a subform control.

Adding subforms to forms

Because a form and its subform require a relationship between the tables on which the two forms are based — directly or indirectly through a query — you should specify that relationship in the Tools ➪ Relationships window. This step isn't absolutely necessary, but it ensures that Access can automatically link the two forms by the correct fields.

Note that you don't need to place the fields you use to link the two forms on either form. Often, these fields contain arbitrary ID numbers that are of no interest to the user (and which the user shouldn't change).

Using the Form Wizard to build a new form containing a subform

If you're just starting work on a new form, the Form Wizard can put together a form containing a subform for you. In the New Form dialog box, select the table or query forming either side of the one-to-many relationship. In the first of the wizard's dialog boxes, pick fields from the table to use on the form. Next, remaining in that dialog box, select the table or query forming the other side of the relationship, and pick fields from that object that you want to use. Move to the wizard's next dialog box. Here, you tell Access which table or query belongs on the main part of the form (the one you want to view by). Complete the dialog box by choosing Form with Subform(s), and then work your way through the remaining wizard boxes.

Creating a new subform on an existing form

You can add a subform to an existing form at any time, of course. To create the subform, open the main form in Design view and click the Subform/Subreport control in the Toolbox. Click in the form to place the control where you want it. Assuming the Control Wizards button is pressed, a wizard starts up to guide you through the process of setting up the subform.

Converting an existing form into a subform

If you prefer to do without the wizard's help, follow these steps:

1. Create a form for the subform. Set its Default View property to continuous form or datasheet (so it shows all the records that match the current record on the main form), and then save and close the form.

2. Open the main form and situate it so you can also see the Database window. Drag the subform from the Database window to the main form. If the two forms have matching fields, Access automatically links the subform to the main form.

To redefine a subform, use the following properties on the Data tab for the subform control:

✦ **SourceObject.** The name of the form that you want to function as the subform.

✦ **LinkChildFields** and **LinkMasterFields.** The names of the fields in the subform and main form, respectively, that Access uses to link the two forms together. To select the fields from a list, click the builder button on either of these properties.

Working with subforms in code

There's a simple secret to accessing a subform and its properties and controls from the VBA code for the main form: Use the `Form` property of the subform control that contains the subform. Suppose the subform resides in a control called `LineItemsSubform`. If you're working in the `Code` module for the main form, you can retrieve the number of records shown in the subform with a statement such as this:

```
intRecords = LineItemsSubform.Form.RecordsetClone.RecordCount
```

Note that the object expression begins with the name of the control, not the form that control displays. Then comes the `Form` property, producing a reference to the form object. From that point, you can access any form properties. Don't refer directly to the form on which the subform is based.

If you need to write code for the subform itself or its controls, open the form in its own window (select it in the Database window and choose Design). Add the event code there. If you want events on the subform to trigger changes on the main form, refer to the main form in full. The following sample event procedure activates the `SaleItem` control on the main form as soon as the value in a subform control changes:

```
Private Sub Price_AfterUpdate()
    Forms!Sales!SaleItem.SetFocus
End Sub
```

✦　　✦　　✦

Tapping the Programming Power of VBA

Visual Basic for Applications is a powerful programming language, a tool that enables users to tap into the hidden resources of the Office suite. This part offers a crash course in VBA — beginning with an introduction to VBA (and to the Visual Basic Editor that comes with Office) and following up with detailed discussions of the relevant aspects of VBA programming (including modules, object-oriented programming, debugging, error trapping, and custom dialog boxes).

Basic Visual Basic for Applications

As feature-rich as the Office applications may be, they can't meet every software need. If the point-and-click customizing techniques laid out in Chapter 5 don't go far enough, Office includes a full-fledged software development toolkit called VBA. Visual Basic for Applications — that's what VBA stands for — lets you cook up everything from simple yet intelligent customizations for any Office XP application all the way to complete custom software solutions that can tap the features of the entire Office suite. I don't claim that programming in VBA is as easy as clicking buttons on a toolbar, but it's something anyone can undertake successfully.

A First Look at the Visual Basic Editor

Figure 51-1 shows the Visual Basic for Applications Editor. Get used to this window, because you're going to be spending lots of time here if you use VBA. As an added bonus, you won't have to relearn all the commands and shortcut keys if you also plan to develop in Visual Basic.

Chapter 52 discusses using the Visual Basic Editor in detail. For now, just keep in mind that you must start the Editor from within an Office application (or other VBA app) — you can't run the Visual Basic Editor all by itself. On the screen, the Visual Basic Editor acts as a separate application, in a completely separate window from that of the host application. However, because the Editor operates within the same memory space as its host application, any changes you make in your VBA code are immediately available when you run the code in the host application.

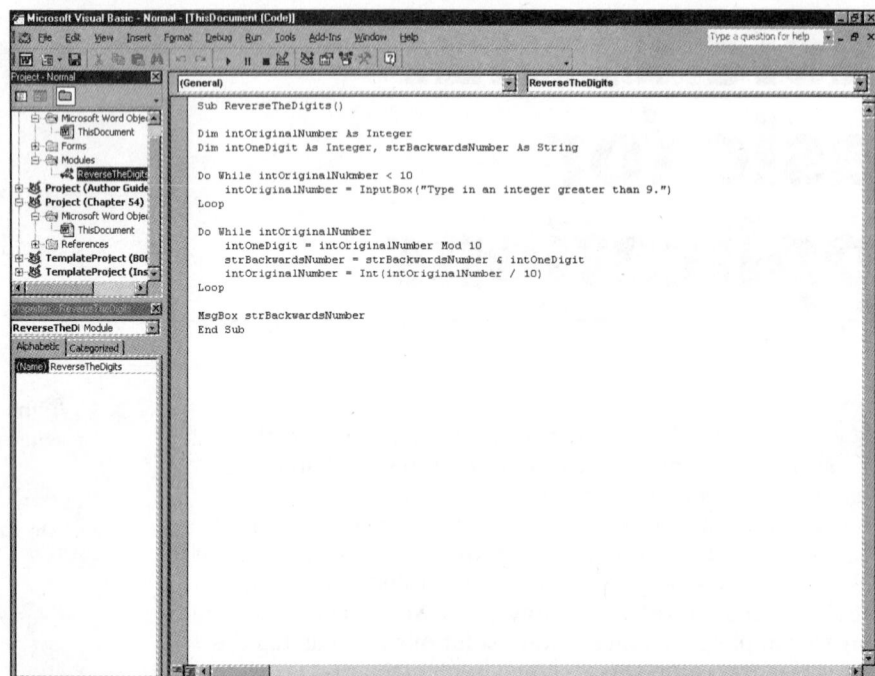

Figure 51-1: The Visual Basic Editor, showing Project, Properties, and Code windows; the Quick Info pop-up help window; and the VBA toolbar

Writing a Simple Module

Just to familiarize yourself with VBA, try writing this very simple one-line module. (Simple as it may be, it actually does something modestly useful.) Follow these steps:

1. Start Word.

2. Press Alt+F11 to start the Visual Basic Editor.

3. Click the Normal item (corresponding to Word's Normal template) in the Project Explorer window.

4. Choose Insert ➾ Module to insert a module into the Normal template. This module will most likely be named Module1.

5. In the Module1 code window, type **Sub DisplayAppVersion** and press Enter. This tells VBA you're writing a Sub procedure.

6. Notice that the editor has provided parentheses following your typing and also has added an `End Sub` statement on a separate line. The blinking insertion point appears between the two lines. Now type the following two additional lines of code exactly as written, including the underscore at the end of the first line:

```
MsgBox "Version/Build: " & application.version & _
    "/" & application.build
```

7. Press Enter. Notice that after you do, VBA automatically capitalizes the first letter of the words *application*, *version*, and *build*.

8. Press F5, the keyboard shortcut for running modules in the Visual Basic Editor. As shown in Figure 51-2, you should see a message box displaying the Build and Version numbers of the copy of Word you're running.

9. Save your work in the Normal template file by choosing File ⇨ Save Normal. You can then choose File ⇨ Close and Return to Microsoft Word.

With this macro in place in your Normal template in Word, you can run the `DisplayAppVersion` macro at any time you like by choosing Tools ⇨ Macro and clicking Run.

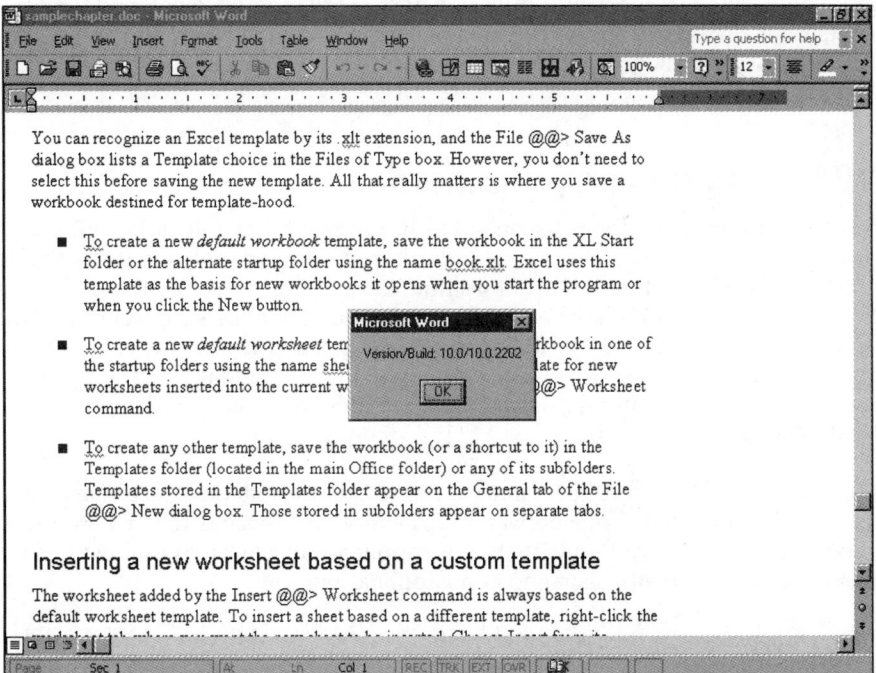

Figure 51-2: Here's how the sample VBA program looks when it runs (it's that small dialog box in the middle of the Word window).

A VBA Backgrounder

VBA shares most of its programming language, window-design features, and other technology with Microsoft's Visual Basic, which has long been one of the most popular software development tools on the planet. In fact, VBA is a subset of Visual Basic. But VBA has a different niche — its main mission is to enable anyone to extend the functionality of existing applications.

A brief history of VBA

VBA, the "for applications" version of Visual Basic, made its debut in Excel 5.0. In previous versions of Excel you could add customizations only by writing routines directly in the cells of a special worksheet (these programs, too, were called "macros," but they didn't resemble the macros of today's Office). The programming environment was cramped, you couldn't organize complex programs into separate chunks of code, and the debugging tools were crude.

All of that changed radically with the advent of VBA. VBA offered the ability to organize code into logical chunks (procedures and functions) accessible in a separate software "environment" tailor-made for the software development process. VBA gradually gained momentum, appearing next in Microsoft Project, and then in Access. Finally — with the arrival of Office 97 — VBA arrived in Word and PowerPoint, replacing the older, application-specific Access Basic and WordBasic languages.

VBA as an industry standard

But the VBA universe doesn't stop at the borders of Microsoft Office. VBA was always envisioned as an industry-standard programming tool, and it has finally started to live up to that billing. More than 200 other software developers have licensed the VBA technology from Microsoft, and VBA appears in such well-known applications as Visio and AutoCAD. Although each application provides a unique set of programming resources with which you must acquaint yourself, the core VBA tools — the language and the Visual Basic Editor — are identical in nearly all VBA applications.

For that matter, VBA and the standalone version of Visual Basic are nearly identical as well. The main difference between VBA and Visual Basic is that a VBA program can run only in conjunction with its host application; programs built with Visual Basic run independently as standalone applications.

Caution   Disappointingly, the forms and controls that come with VBA aren't the same as those you get with Visual Basic, so you can't convert a VBA application to Visual Basic without redesigning its windows and dialog boxes. On the plus side, all your VBA development *skills* transfer directly to Visual Basic.

Some VBA highlights

Here's a quick listing of some major VBA features in Office XP:

✦ **All Office applications host VBA.** This handy bit of design helps make your VBA code portable from one Office application to another.

✦ **All Office applications share a (reasonably) consistent object model.** Thus, most of them can act as either Automation servers or Automation controllers (object models, servers, and controllers are discussed later in this chapter). Some objects, such as the `CommandBar` and `Assistant` objects, are common across all Office applications. VBA itself acts as an Automation server, encouraging the development of add-ins for its own programming environment.

✦ **The Visual Basic Editor provides an integrated development environment (IDE).** This is the environment in which you develop and test your VBA modules and forms in separate windows. The Visual Basic Editor is almost identical to the IDE found in Visual Basic.

✦ **Window-design tools are consistent.** All full-fledged VBA applications — including all Office applications except Access — support a common system for designing custom dialog boxes and windows (called *forms* or `UserForms` in VBA). The benefits to you include a standard set of design tools, and standard controls that work the same way in every Office application. In addition, you can design a form in, say, Word and reuse it in Excel *without any changes*. The controls that come with VBA applications are powerful enough to produce sophisticated, great-looking forms (see Figure 51-3). If these aren't enough, VBA enables you to plug in ActiveX controls from other sources (see the section on ActiveX controls later in this chapter).

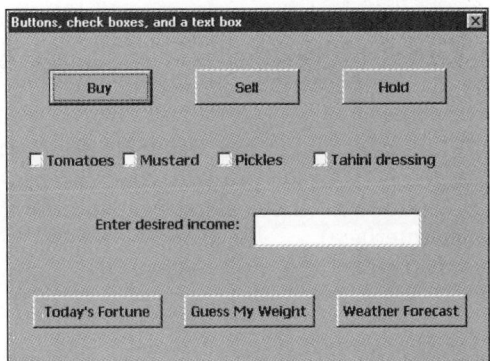

Figure 51-3: A sample dialog box (VBA form) loaded with the ActiveX controls that come with VBA

VBA consistent? Well, reasonably . . .

Although I have described VBA as "reasonably consistent" in all Office applications, the operant word here is *reasonably*. For all the effort Microsoft has made to bring harmony into the VBA universe, some tasks still require coding variations, depending on which application you want them to run in. As a simple example, if you're coding a Word application, you refer to Word's built-in File ➪ Save As dialog box as `wdDialogFileSaveAs`. If you want to refer to the corresponding dialog box in Excel, you have to call it `xlDialogSaveAs`. (Note that the Excel version doesn't mention the File menu.) More problematic is that, compared to Word, the other applications allow significantly less control over their built-in commands via VBA. Be prepared to cope with such differences.

✦ **You can create your own objects in VBA by using class modules.** This feature promotes code reuse and shrinks the time required for developing a project.

✦ **ADO (ActiveX Data Objects) give your Office documents access to data stored in a variety of sources.** The ADO programming standard enables you to retrieve and store information regardless of whether it resides on your PC's hard disk, a workgroup server, relational database, or the corporate mainframe. Besides providing a uniform method for accessing data wherever it's located, ADO is easier to use, faster, and more compact than the data-access tools available in earlier versions of Office — which included Data Access Objects (DAO) and Open Database Connectivity (ODBC) Direct.

Cross-Reference See Chapter 49 to learn more about ADO.

✦ **Conditional code compilation increases the versatility of your code.** This feature enables you to develop (for example) applications localized for different human languages. You can also use conditional code compilation to run selective blocks of code during debugging.

✦ **Direct access to the Windows API enables you to use Windows itself as a programming tool.** If you need features VBA can't provide, your VBA programs can access the features of Windows itself by calling the Win32 API (the Windows application programming interface).

Getting Started with VBA

VBA is a rich enough programming environment to appeal to the professional developer. However, even if you don't have a programming background, VBA can give you a big boost by helping you automate repetitive tasks in your daily work.

Recorded macros are VBA programs

The easy way to get your feet wet with VBA is by using the *macro recorder*—a tool available in Word, PowerPoint, and Excel.

For details on the mechanics of macro recording, see Chapter 5.

The point to make here is that the macros you record are stored as VBA code, just like the kind you type in yourself. To examine the code corresponding to a recorded macro, choose Tools ⇨ Macros, select the macro by name, and choose Edit.

Note that each recorded macro is a single VBA procedure. (To get technical, a macro is a Sub procedure that takes no arguments.) By default, Office stores all recorded macros as separate procedures in a single module (a unit of code that can contain one or more procedures) within the current document.

Procedures and modules are discussed fully in Chapter 54.

Moving beyond macros

Macros are fine for speeding up a set of commands that you use repeatedly in exactly the same order. The problem with a recorded macro, though, is that it's dumb—it always does the same things in the same sequence. To create a software routine that can modify its behavior to suit current conditions, you have to "hand-code" it in VBA.

Here are some other reasons to graduate from the macro recorder to VBA:

✦ **To create custom dialog boxes and windows.** VBA lets you design anything from simple Yes-No-Cancel message boxes to complex interactive windows containing multiple tabbed pages—all without any programming. VBA is a visual software tool expressly because you lay out forms on the screen by drawing them with the mouse.

To make your forms do useful work, you do have to write code.

✦ **To retrieve data from file-based databases such as Access, Dbase, or FoxPro, or from a back-end relational database management system accessible via OLE DB or ODBC.** While you can use Microsoft Query to view data from these sources, you have to write VBA code if you want to manipulate those data in your own custom routines.

✦ **To add error handling to your VBA routines.** Even a recorded macro can benefit from a little code that steps in when errors occur, allowing the routine to make a soft landing instead of crashing violently. Error-handling code is especially vital if you distribute your VBA programs to other people; they will be running your software under conditions you can't control. VBA offers robust error trapping, comparable to that available in Visual Basic.

✦ **To create custom Help messages.** With VBA, you can add context-sensitive help to your program and display appropriate error messages when the user makes a mistake. You can even program the Office Assistant to coach your users through a complex process.

✦ **To protect your programs from unauthorized tampering or copying.** Password-protecting your VBA code encrypts it securely so no one can view the code without the password.

VBA: An Object-Based Development Tool

Although VBA doesn't meet all criteria for a true object-oriented programming language, objects still play a fundamental role in VBA—so you need to understand how they work before you can use VBA effectively. This section can get you started.

Cross-Reference   Chapter 54 discusses VBA objects in detail.

Understanding objects

If you're new to object-based programming, the easiest way to think about objects is as parts of the host application and the documents you create with it. In Excel, for instance, each worksheet cell is an object, each named range of cells is an object, a chart is an object, an entire worksheet is an object, and so is a complete workbook.

But objects can be more abstract. Sticking with Excel, the CustomView object represents a workbook custom view. A custom view isn't something you can see on the screen but instead is a group of settings that define the look of the workbook and its print options. In all VBA applications, a Collection object represents any group of variables or other objects that you want to work with as a unit, regardless of their type.

Working with object models

Each VBA object fits into a hierarchy of other objects, defined by the host application and VBA itself. The object at the top of the hierarchy has its own properties, methods, and events; it also acts as a container for other object types (those beneath it in the hierarchy). These objects contain other subsidiary ones, and so on. The *object model* of a VBA application encompasses the specifics of these hierarchical relationships between objects, along with the characteristics of the individual objects.

Because VBA itself has objects available in all VBA applications, VBA has its own object model, too. Figure 51-4 illustrates a portion of the Word object model.

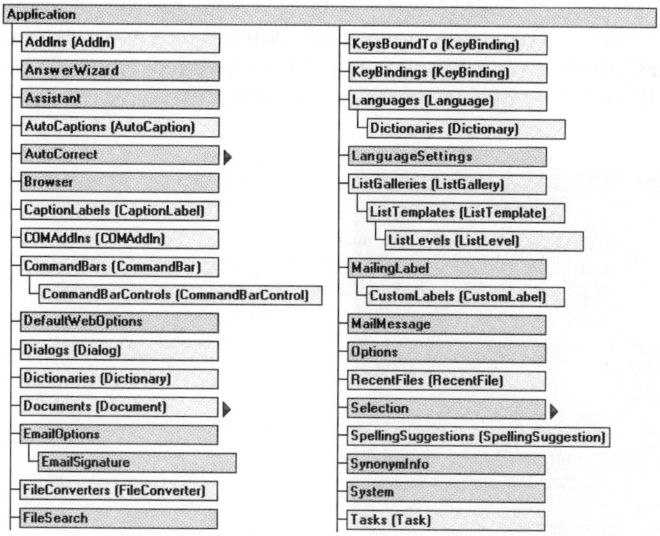

Application	
AddIns (AddIn)	KeysBoundTo (KeyBinding)
AnswerWizard	KeyBindings (KeyBinding)
Assistant	Languages (Language)
AutoCaptions (AutoCaption)	Dictionaries (Dictionary)
AutoCorrect	LanguageSettings
Browser	ListGalleries (ListGallery)
CaptionLabels (CaptionLabel)	ListTemplates (ListTemplate)
COMAddIns (COMAddIn)	ListLevels (ListLevel)
CommandBars (CommandBar)	MailingLabel
CommandBarControls (CommandBarControl)	CustomLabels (CustomLabel)
DefaultWebOptions	MailMessage
Dialogs (Dialog)	Options
Dictionaries (Dictionary)	RecentFiles (RecentFile)
Documents (Document)	Selection
EmailOptions	SpellingSuggestions (SpellingSuggestion)
EmailSignature	SynonymInfo
FileConverters (FileConverter)	System
FileSearch	Tasks (Task)

Figure 51-4: The picture represents part of Word's object model diagrammatically.

At the top of the object hierarchy is the `Application` object. Below the `Application` object come derivative object collections such as `Documents`, `Paragraphs`, `Characters`, `Bookmarks`, `Dialogs`, and so on.

ActiveX Technology and VBA

ActiveX is a Microsoft marketing term for a variety of technologies all having to do with interchangeable software components. The individual ActiveX technologies are actually quite distinct, but you can think of them together as a set of standards for software building blocks. These building blocks can be linked on a mix-and-match basis to produce powerful customized applications.

ActiveX controls

Controls are the individual doodads on dialog boxes and toolbars that a software user can click or type text into to produce a response from the software. Examples of controls include buttons (the push-button type), radio buttons for picking one of several predetermined options, and text boxes in which you can type or edit entries.

The Microsoft standard for *ActiveX controls* means that you're not limited to the controls that come with VBA. ActiveX controls are interchangeable software widgets that you can plug into your programs as you see fit, and they work in Visual Basic, C++, and Java, as well as VBA. If you need a control that doesn't come with VBA, hundreds of other ActiveX controls are available as shareware and from commercial software vendors. You can even create your own ActiveX controls (using the Control Creation Edition of Visual Basic), if you're so inclined. Figure 51-5 illustrates a VBA form with a variety of third-party ActiveX controls.

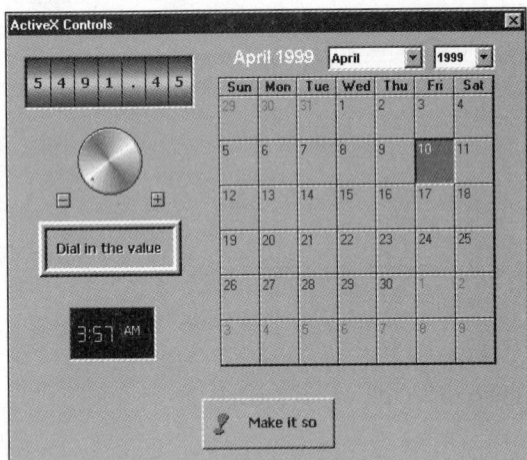

Figure 51-5: A dialog box studded with ActiveX controls that don't come with VBA

Although controls are usually thought of as items you can see on a dialog box or toolbar, some ActiveX controls have no visual presence. Instead, they provide plug-in units of software functionality, performing specialized services such as financial calculations on demand.

Cross-Reference   ActiveX controls are also portable across computers and operating systems when used in Web documents; for details, see Chapter 56.

From within an Internet browser that supports the ActiveX standard, users can see and interact with any ActiveX control that appears on the page. Consequently, ActiveX technology extends the component software model across boundaries imposed by different operating systems and network topologies.

ActiveX automation

Your VBA programs aren't limited to the objects in the host application. Instead, you have access to the objects of any application or software component that adheres to Microsoft's Component Object Model (COM) standard. The COM specification details how objects should be defined within applications and how those objects are exposed so they can be used by other applications. The term *automation* refers to a COM-based application's capability of activating and controlling the objects of other applications.

Automation and COM open up fantastic possibilities for custom VBA applications of tremendous scope and power. If you're really ambitious, you could put together a single application that combines and processes information from Word documents, Excel worksheets, Access and Outlook databases, PowerPoint presentations, Visio diagrams, AutoCAD technical diagrams, and so on. A custom software solution can display all this information on your own custom forms and also in the windows of the individual applications automated by your program. Using DCOM (Distributed Component Object Model) technology, ActiveX components can be maintained and distributed across networks — no matter whether those networks are LANs or enterprise-wide intranets.

About ActiveX automation servers and controllers

Applications that expose their objects to manipulation by other programs are called *ActiveX automation servers*. Conversely, an application that can control another application's objects is called an *ActiveX automation controller*. Every application in Office can function as both an automation server and an automation controller.

VBA Resources

If this book's introduction to VBA whets your appetite for more, one good place to start is *VBA For Dummies*, Second Edition (Hungry Minds, Inc.) by Steve Cummings. Although the material is presented at the introductory level, it offers significant detail.

Resources for VBA programmers abound on the Internet. Begin at the beginning, with Microsoft's VBA and Visual Basic Web pages:

- ✦ msdn.microsoft.com/vba
- ✦ msdn.microsoft.com/vbasic

You can also find lots of VBA-related info at www.microsoft.com in the areas for the individual Office applications and in the Microsoft Knowledge Base.

Other Web sites to explore include the following:

- ✦ www.download.com/PC/Activex/
- ✦ www.geocities.com/WallStreet/9245/
- ✦ www.cgvb.com/

✦ `www.mvps.org/vbnet/`

✦ `www.vbip.com`

✦ `http://searchvb.techtarget.com/`

✦ `www.codehound.com/vb/`

Print periodicals that cover VBA include the following:

✦ *Microsoft Developers Network (MSDN),* Web site `http://msdn.microsoft.com`

✦ *Element K Journals,* phone 800-223-8720, Web site `www.elementkjournals.com`

✦ *Microsoft Office & Visual Basic for Applications Developer,* Informant Communications Group, Inc., 10519 E. Stockton Blvd., Suite 100, Elk Grove, CA 95624-9703; phone 916-686-6610, Web site `www.informant.com`

✦ *Visual Basic Programmer's Journal,* Fawcette Technical Publications, Inc., 913 Emerson Ave., Palo Alto, CA 94301; phone 650-566-2000, Web site `www.windx.com`

✦   ✦   ✦

Using the Visual Basic Editor

A carpenter has her workshop, a baker his kitchen, and you, well . . . now you have the Visual Basic Editor. The Visual Basic Editor is the official term for VBA's integrated development environment, the digital studio in which you sculpt your own software creations. It's an integral part of all five major Office applications.

In this chapter, you get a handle on taming the resources of the Visual Basic Editor—I sometimes refer to it simply as the Editor. First, you get an orientation to the components of the Visual Basic Editor including its toolbars, menus, and windows. Then comes a tour of the individual windows and the unique contributions each one can make to your programming projects.

Working with the Visual Basic Editor User Interface

The Visual Basic Editor's user interface is standard Microsoft fare—the menus, toolbars, and keyboard shortcuts look and work just like those in other parts of Office. You should feel right at home.

Out to lunch with Editor menus

I realize you already know how to use menus. What you might be interested in, though, is where to find certain commands on the Visual Basic Editor's menus.

For the most part, the Editor's commands are organized logically. When you want to display a particular window, for example, you shouldn't have trouble locating the necessary command—it's on the View menu, of course. A few items aren't so obvious, however. The following little table clues you in on some of the Editor's hidden menu commands:

When You Want to Do This	Use this Menu Command	Comments
Control the settings for an entire project.	Tools ⇨ Project Properties	This is an odd location for a command pertaining to the VBA project you're working with (I expected to find it on the File menu).
Customize the Visual Basic Editor itself.	View ⇨ Toolbars ⇨ Customize or Tools ⇨ Options	
Turn on Design mode.	Run ⇨ Design Mode	The Design Mode command sounds like it's intended for laying out forms, so why is it on the Run menu? Because it stops any running program. (What exactly it's good for, I still haven't figured out.)

Tuning the toolbars

If you're familiar with Word, Excel, or PowerPoint, you're probably plenty comfortable with the way toolbars work in the Visual Basic Editor. If not, a few brief comments should suffice.

The included toolbars

The Editor comes with four prefab toolbars. They are as follows:

- ✦ **Debug:** This toolbar contains buttons for commands you're likely to need while tracking down errors in your programs.

- ✦ **Edit:** The buttons on this toolbar are handy when you're editing code. They duplicate commands on the Edit menu.

- ✦ **Standard:** This is the only toolbar visible when you first run the Editor. It includes buttons for a broad range of functions, including saving your work, inserting new forms and modules, editing, and running your programs.

- ✦ **UserForm:** Use this toolbar for forms design. Most of the buttons duplicate commands on the Format menu for aligning, ordering, and grouping controls on forms.

Monkeying with the menus, toolbars, and buttons

As with other Office toolbars, those in the Editor can exist in one of three states: hidden, docked, or floating. You use the same techniques covered in Chapter 4 to display, hide, or move the toolbars, and to convert them from floating to docked and vice versa. Likewise, you can customize the Editor's menus (including the shortcut menus), the toolbars, and their individual buttons using the standard Office procedures covered in Chapter 5.

Keyboard shortcuts

Table 52-1 summarizes keyboard shortcuts available in the Visual Basic Editor. You can also use the standard Windows keyboard commands for cursor control and text editing. Remember also that Shift+F10 pops up the shortcut menu for the window or other item that's currently active—just as if you had right-clicked the item.

Table 52-1 Keyboard Shortcuts in the Visual Basic Editor	
To Do This	**Press**
Displaying Windows	
Display the Code window for the selected form or control	F7
Display the form or control corresponding to the active Code window	Shift+F7
Move to next Code or UserForm window	Ctrl+Tab
Activate the Object Browser window	F2
Activate the Properties window	F4
Activate the Immediate window	Ctrl+G
Activate the Call Stack window	Ctrl+L
Working with Code	
Jump to the definition of the item at the insertion point	Shift+F2
Display the Find dialog box	Ctrl+F
Find Next (find next occurrence of Find text)	F3
Find Previous	Shift+F3
Replace	Ctrl+H
Jump to the line previously edited	Ctrl+Shift+F2
Undo	Ctrl+Z

Continued

Table 52-1 *(continued)*

To Do This	Press
Working with Code	
List properties/methods	Ctrl+J
List constants	Ctrl+Shift+J
Display Quick Info about the variable or object at the insertion point	Ctrl+I
Display parameter information for the function at the insertion point	Ctrl+Shift+I
Complete the word you're typing automatically	Ctrl+Spacebar
Working with Properties	
In the Property window, move to the next property in the list that begins with a particular letter	Ctrl+Shift+*<letter>*
Running Programs	
Run the procedure or UserForm in the active window	F5
Pause code execution and enter Break mode	Ctrl+Break
Debugging	
Execute code one line at a time (step)	F8
Execute statements one line at a time without stepping into procedure calls	Shift+F8
Run, stopping at line containing the insertion point	Ctrl+F8
Specify (set) the next statement to be executed	Ctrl+F9
Run the error handler code or return the error to the calling procedure	Alt+F5
Step into the error handler or return the error to the calling procedure	Alt+F8
Toggle breakpoint in code line with insertion point	F9
Clear all breakpoints	Ctrl+Shift+F9
Add watch for the item at the insertion point	Shift+F9

Managing the Windows

Unless you have a really gargantuan monitor, plan to spend lots of time moving windows around in the Visual Basic Editor. None of those windows are there just for looks — each has something very valuable to contribute to your programming effort. The problem is, it's not practical to keep them all open at once — you won't have enough space left for your VBA code and forms.

By the way, this chapter discusses only the mechanics of working with windows, not the functions of the windows themselves. Later in this chapter, individual windows are discussed in some depth.

Some windows are loners, some run in crowds

One basic fact to understand about Visual Basic Editor windows: You can have as many Code and UserForm windows as you need, but only one each of the other window types. This may make perfect sense to you already, but it took me a while to figure out how the system works.

You need multiple Code and UserForm windows because you're likely to create more than one form and one VBA module. With a window for each, you can keep all your forms and modules in memory and available for quick access.

Some of the remaining windows — the Properties and Locals windows, to name names — change their contents automatically when you switch to a different Code or UserForm window. It's like getting multiple windows for the price of one. Others, such as the Object Browser, the Project Explorer, and the Immediate window, apply to everything you do in the Editor, so only one of each is necessary.

Viewing and hiding windows

Most Editor windows have their own keyboard shortcuts, which means you can pop up a window that isn't currently visible without taking your fingers off the keyboard. Table 52-1 lists the shortcuts you need. If you can't remember the shortcut, though, you can display any window via the View menu.

Perhaps unfortunately, the keyboard shortcuts *aren't* toggle switches. If a window is already open, pressing its key combination doesn't hide it. To put a window back to bed, you have to click the window's little Close button (at the far right on the title bar).

Tip   To display a specific window that is open but buried, you can choose it by name from the Window menu. Only nondockable windows are listed there.

As in many Windows applications, two keyboard shortcuts exist for switching from one window to the next: Ctrl+Tab and Ctrl+F6. In the Visual Basic Editor, however, only nondockable windows become active in sequence as you press the shortcut keys repeatedly. So what is a nondockable window? That's the topic of the next section.

Docking and floating windows

As with the toolbars, most of the Editor's windows are *dockable* — you can attach them along any of the four edges of the main workspace where they can't cover up other windows. Of course, docking a window makes the workspace smaller. Figure 52-1 shows the Editor with all visible windows docked.

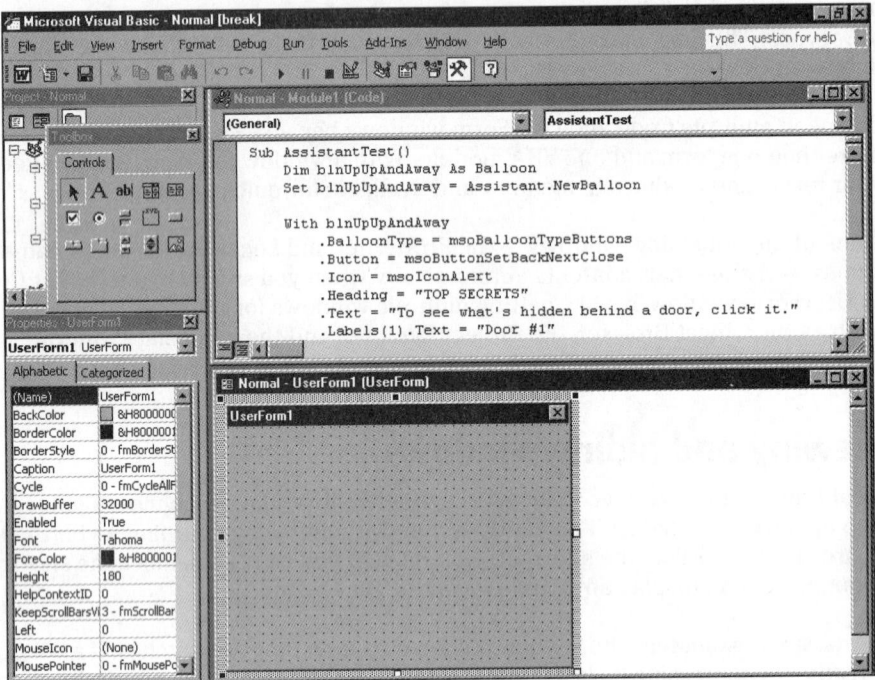

Figure 52-1: As you dock windows along the edges of the Visual Basic Editor window, the space available for editing code and designing forms grows smaller.

Alternatively, you can let your windows float freely in the breeze. Floating windows leave you more room for writing code and designing forms, but they often cover up other windows. If you have a big monitor, you might prefer to display the Visual Basic Editor at less than maximum size and then move individual floating windows outside the Editor altogether.

No docking allowed . . .

Certain windows can't be docked — for example, the Code and UserForm windows — and you can make any other window "nondockable." To check (or set) docking status for all window types (except the Code and UserForm windows, of course), choose Tools ➪ Options and click the Docking tab.

> **Tip** You can also make a dockable window nondockable, or vice versa, by right-clicking the main part of the window and choosing Dockable from the shortcut menu.

More docking factoids

Here are some hidden docking truths to ponder:

✦ A Code, UserForm, or any other nondockable window can be maximized, minimized, or *restored* (Microsoft jargon for "returned to a user-determined size"). Nondockable windows have the standard buttons for these functions at the right side of the title bar.

✦ You can tell whether a window is currently dockable by looking at the title bar. Dockable windows have only a Close button there; nondockable windows have the Minimize and Maximize (or Restore) buttons.

✦ When you maximize any nondockable window, it fills whatever space is left over from any other windows currently docked in the work area.

✦ To move a floating window to the edge of the work area without docking it, you must first make the window nondockable.

✦ All open, nondockable windows are accessible in sequence via the Ctrl+Tab keyboard shortcut. (They're also listed on the Window menu.)

Saving the screen layout

The Visual Basic Editor automatically preserves the layout that's in effect at the time you exit. The locations of your windows, menus, and toolbars don't change from one Visual Basic Editor session to the next. The layout remains the same even if you switch from one Office application to another. This only holds true, however, when you close one application before starting the next.

Managing Your Projects with Project Explorer

In VBA, a *project* is all the code and forms that belong to one document, along with the document itself. In the Visual Basic Editor, you use the Project Explorer window for a bird's-eye view of all projects currently open in your application—and more important, to navigate quickly to the Code or UserForm window you want to work with.

To save the project you're currently working with—the one selected in the Project Explorer, as described later in this section—click the Save button on the Visual Basic Editor's Standard toolbar. You don't have to go back to your VBA application to save the document with its associated code.

Opening the Project Explorer window

The Project Explorer should already be visible when you first open the Visual Basic Editor. If it isn't, you can make it appear with any of the following techniques:

✦ Press Ctrl+R.

✦ Click the Project Explorer button on the Standard toolbar.

✦ Select View ⇨ Project Explorer.

Exploring the Explorer

If you've ever used the Windows Explorer to manage your disks and files (oops, *documents*), you'll be right at home in the Project Explorer. The Project Explorer gives you a branching hierarchical look at your open projects. Figure 52-2 shows an example.

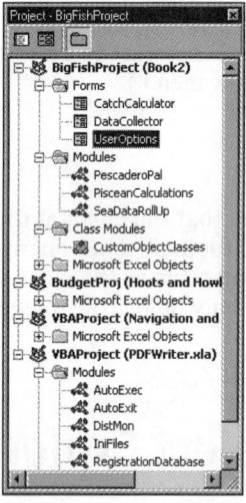

Figure 52-2: Here's the Project Explorer in Excel, showing several active projects open simultaneously.

At the top of the hierarchy are the individual projects themselves. They're listed farthest to the left in the Project Explorer window.

Each document that's open in your application automatically has a project. That's true even if you haven't written any code or created any forms for its project so far. By default, a project takes on the name of its associated document, but you can change the name via the Project Properties dialog box or in the Properties window (see "Renaming a project or module in the Properties window," later in this chapter).

The next level in the hierarchy is groups of related objects: forms, code modules, *references* to other object libraries, and objects from the underlying application. Normally, the Project Explorer displays a folder for each of these groups. At the bottom of the hierarchy come the individual objects themselves.

Navigating the Project Explorer window

The Project Explorer gives you the fastest way to find and activate the modules, forms, and other objects you want to work with. Just like the Windows Explorer, the Project Explorer displays a little box beside each item, or *node*, in its list. When only the project itself is visible, and its contents are hidden, this box, the *expand indicator*, contains a plus sign. If the nodes at lower levels of the hierarchy are visible, the expand indicator displays a minus sign instead.

Here are the techniques you use to work with the Project Explorer:

✦ **To expand a node and display items lower in the hierarchy:** Click the Expand indicator when it contains a plus sign, or highlight the node and press the right-arrow key.

✦ **To collapse a node and hide subsidiary items:** Click the Expand indicator when it contains a minus sign, or press the left-arrow key.

✦ **To open the UserForm or Code window corresponding to a module, form, or class module item in Project Explorer:** Double-click the item or highlight it in the list and press Enter.

✦ **To activate a form's Code window:** Highlight the form in the list and press Shift+Enter.

✦ **To use the buttons at the top of the Project Explorer window:** Place your mouse pointer over one of them, just below the title bar. They work like this:

• The View Code button displays the Code window for the highlighted item.

• The View Object button shows you the highlighted item itself. If the item is a form, you see it in its UserForm window. If the item is a document, you're switched back to the underlying VBA application with that document active.

• The Toggle Folders button turns on or off the middle level of the project hierarchy. Normally, the Project Explorer separates the forms, code modules, and document objects into separate folders. If you click this button, those folders disappear and you see all the individual objects in each project in one alphabetical list. Click the button again to turn the folders back on.

Using the Project Explorer shortcut menu

The Project Explorer's shortcut menu, shown in Figure 52-3, gives you yet more ways to get up close and personal with the elements of your project. These commands are all available via the menus, but the shortcut menu provides faster access when you're already working with the Project Explorer.

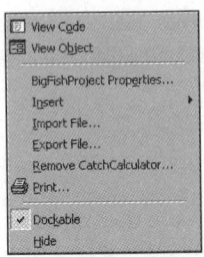

Figure 52-3: The Project Explorer shortcut menu

Setting project properties

The Project Properties dialog box lets you change the name of your project, add a brief description, attach a custom Help file, and protect the project from unauthorized snooping or changes. Until you're a fairly advanced VBA developer, though, most of these options aren't terribly useful.

But anyway, at least now you know this dialog box exists. To display it, choose Tools ➪ *Project Name* Properties, or right-click the Project Explorer window and select *Project Name* Properties from the shortcut menu. Figure 52-4 shows the General tab on the Project Properties dialog box.

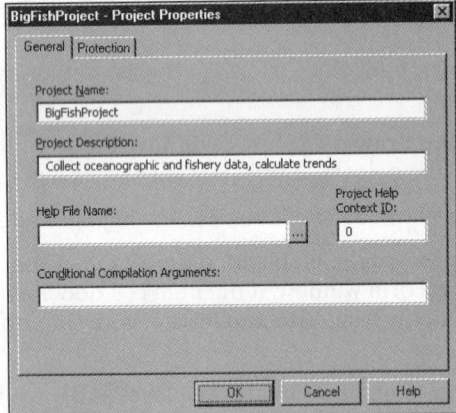

Figure 52-4: The General tab of the Project Properties dialog box

Renaming a project

The Project Explorer and the Object Browser list projects alphabetically by name. This means you can move a project in either window by changing its name. (Of course, you may also want to change a project's name for purely artistic reasons.)

The easiest way to change the VBA-supplied generic project name is in the Properties window. When you highlight the project in Project Explorer, the

Properties window displays its name. You can edit the name right there in the Properties window. You can also change the project's name on the General tab of the Project Properties dialog box, if you have it open for other reasons.

Protecting your project

If there's any chance someone else might get onto your computer and mess around with your programs, consider protecting your VBA projects with a password. To raise your security fence, display the Project Properties dialog box and switch to the Protection tab, shown in Figure 52-5.

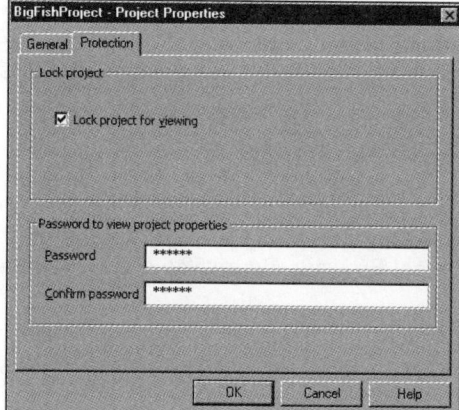

Figure 52-5: The Protection tab of the Project Properties dialog box

Here's how the settings on this tab work:

✦ **Lock Project for Viewing:** Checking this box completely locks out anyone who doesn't have the password. They can't even view the project without the password. If you don't check this box, your password prevents anyone else from opening the Project Properties dialog box — and this prevents them from locking *you* out of your own work.

✦ **Password:** Type in the password you've chosen for your project.

✦ **Confirm password:** Type it again — this guarantees that you entered the password.

Unless your memory is infallible, write down the password and put it somewhere that only you can find it. VBA encrypts the project quite stoutly. Forget the password and you will have to recreate the project from scratch.

Tip To save yourself time, grief, and self-recrimination, save a copy of your project to a safe place before you password-protect it.

Using the Object Browser

Although it looks different and has more bells and whistles, the Object Browser has a lot in common with the Project Manager. As with the Project Manager, it lets you navigate quickly through the hierarchy of objects available to your VBA programs.

Cosmetics aside, a fundamental difference is that the Object Browser displays only one project at a time but lets you access *all* objects available to that project, not just the ones that belong to the project itself. In other words, besides your project's code modules and forms, you can also view the objects provided by your application, by VBA itself, and in other object libraries you may have opened.

The Object Browser's other great advantage is that it can track down the procedures, methods, events, properties, and so on from *any* of these object libraries.

Starting the Object Browser

The F2 key is your quick trigger command for displaying the Object Browser. Slower routes to the same destination include clicking the Object Browser button on the Standard toolbar, or choosing View ➪ Object Browser. Figure 52-6 shows the Object Browser window.

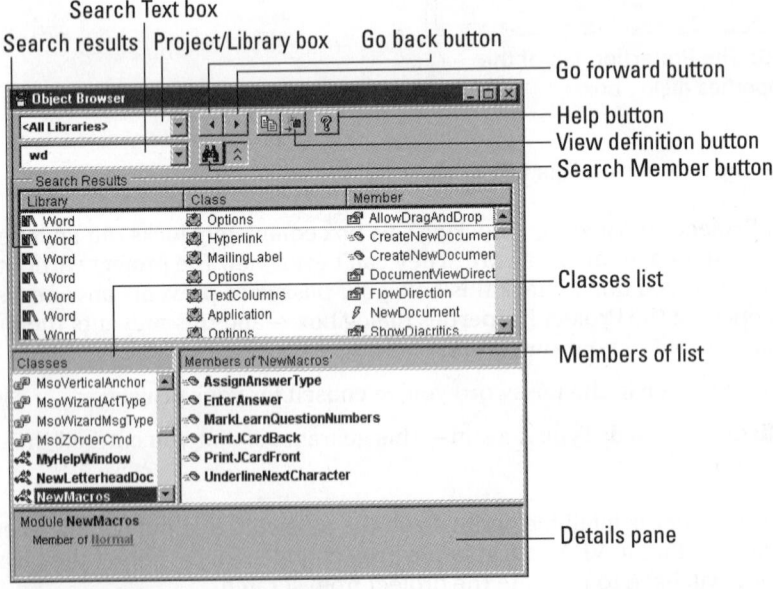

Figure 52-6: The Object Browser

Browsing objects

Before you do any serious work with the Object Browser, be sure you're browsing the right project. All you have to do is select the project you want to work with in the Project Explorer.

With that precaution out of the way, clicking the Project/Library list box at the top left displays the libraries available in the chosen project. (Your project should be there in the list — if it's not, go back to the Project Explorer and make sure it's selected.) By choosing <All Libraries> in the Project/Library box, you can browse all the objects available to your project (that is, the objects of all libraries that are referenced in your project). To hone in on a particular library, just select it in the list. To cruise the objects of other libraries, add a reference to them by using the Tools ⇨ References dialog box.

Browsing panes

The Classes list occupies the left pane in the middle of the Object Browser window. It displays all the objects, collections, modules, forms, and constants available in the selected library or project. Clicking any one of these items displays its members in the pane on the right, the Members Of list. The members may be procedures, methods, properties, events, or individual constants.

Want to know where your VBA code lives? Just look for items displayed in bold in either the Classes list or the Members Of list.

In the bottom pane of the Object Browser window — the Details pane — information about the currently selected object appears. The display lists the item's type and the object it belongs to (if you can't see all this information, drag the separator at the top of the pane upward or use the scroll bar at the right). Clicking the object the item belongs to displays that object in the Browser.

The Object Browser is pretty accommodating when it comes to your layout preferences. You can resize any of the panes (or the columns in the Search Results pane, which I'll cover in a bit) by dragging them into place.

Surfing the projects

The Object Browser works a lot like a Web browser. As in a Web browser you can follow hyperlinks to related items — clicking the underlined object in the Details pane (at the bottom) displays it in the Object Browser.

And as in a Web browser, you can retrace your steps. To revisit objects you've previously examined, click the Go Back button at the top of the Object Browser window. Of course, there's also a Go Forward button, which reverses direction again, eventually returning you to the object you were looking at when you first clicked Go Back.

Instant access to your code

If the item you've selected in the Object Browser is a module or procedure from your own code, just press Enter to bring up its Code window. (Mouse lovers can click the Show Definition button for the same service.)

Help in the Object Browser

Pressing F1, clicking the Help button, or choosing Help from the shortcut menu is supposed to bring up a Help topic on the object, method, property, or event you've selected in the Object Browser. In fact, it usually works this way. If your thinking style is more freeform than regimented, randomly nosing around with the Object Browser and displaying Help for any item that catches your eye is a great way to learn VBA (relatively) painlessly.

Searching for members

Suppose you're not sure which of your code modules contains a particular procedure, or which object "owns" a particular method or event. Rather than comb through your modules in Project Explorer, or rummage through the Help system, you can get the Object Browser to locate the item for you. Here's the drill:

1. Set the Project/Library drop-down list to <All Libraries> if you need to search the entire project, or to a specific library.

Caution   If you select the wrong library, you might find something, but it won't be what you were looking for.

2. Enter the text you want to search for in the Search Text box.

   You can repeat any of your last four searches by reusing it from the Search box's drop-down list of items.

3. Press Enter or click the Search button (the binoculars).

   After the obligatory hard-disk rattle, matching items appear in a new Search Results pane above the list panes. You can resize any column that's too small for the item displayed.

4. To close the Search Results pane, click the double up-arrow button next to the Search button.

   Click the same button (which now displays a double down-arrow) to redisplay the Search Results pane.

Using browsed items in your code

The Object Browser does more than satisfy your curiosity about the objects in your project — it can be a modestly practical coding aid. Once you locate an item that you actually want to use in your own code, you can press Ctrl+C or hit the Copy to

Clipboard button to place the term on the Clipboard. Then (after switching to the appropriate Code window), paste the Clipboard contents into your program. This technique ensures correct spelling—otherwise any little typo can make your code run amok or refuse to run in the first place.

Coding Secrets

Code windows are the heart of the Visual Basic Editor. It's here that you construct the VBA statements that actually perform useful work. In this chapter, the actual content of those VBA statements takes a back seat. Instead, I focus on how to get the most out of the Code window when you're entering code.

Opening Code windows

The Visual Basic Editor gives you lots of different ways to open the Code window of an existing module, class module, or UserForm. First, you have to locate and select the item in the Project Explorer. Once you have it in your sights, any of the following techniques brings up the corresponding Code window:

✦ Press F7.

✦ Click the View Code button at the top of the Project Explorer window.

✦ Right-click the object and select View Code from the shortcut menu.

✦ Open the View menu and choose Code.

✦ For modules, double-click the item or just press Enter (this doesn't work for forms).

If you're currently viewing a UserForm window, pressing F7 or choosing View ➪ Code displays that form's Code window.

Creating new Code windows

Inserting a new module into your project automatically opens a new Code window for that module. When you create a new form, a Code window is automatically created for it (you won't see it until you use one of the techniques just listed).

 Chapter 53 walks you through the process of starting new modules.

Typing (or dragging and dropping) code

VBA Code windows are, in essence, simple text editors, but they include loads of special features designed for writing VBA code. You type your VBA statements just as you would in a word processor, using the same cursor control and editing keys that are standard in Windows (you know, pressing Home takes you to the beginning of a line, whereas Ctrl+Home takes you to the top of the window — just like that). You can select text with the mouse or by holding down the Shift key while you move the cursor.

Note Like every self-respecting text editor of the late twentieth century, the Code window supports drag-and-drop editing.

After you select the text you want to work with, you can

✦ Move it by dragging it into position and dropping it there.

✦ Copy it by holding down the Ctrl key as you drag and drop.

You can drag text to another location in the same Code window, to a different Code window, or to the Immediate window or Watch window (the latter are covered in Chapter 55). If the destination is in a different Code window, you must arrange the two windows so both the original text and the destination are visible before you start.

The Code window also lets you undo previous changes you made to your code. Each time you press Ctrl+Z (or choose Undo from the Edit menu), another change is reversed. The Edit menu does provide a Redo command as well — to undo the effects of the Undo command — but Redo has no keyboard shortcut in the Visual Basic Editor.

The ideal coach

Like that perfect servant you always wished for, the Visual Basic Editor is constantly but unobtrusively checking and correcting your work in these ways:

✦ If you indent one line of code, the following lines are automatically indented to match (you can shut off this feature in the Tools ➪ Options dialog box within the Editor tab by removing the check from the Auto Indent box).

✦ If the editor recognizes a VBA keyword, it automatically capitalizes it according to VBA conventions (if you type an *if...then...else* statement, for example, the Editor changes it to `If...Then...Else`). In addition, keywords are automatically colored blue so they stand out from the other items you type (you can change the Editor's color scheme in the Tools ➪ Options dialog box within the Editor Format tab).

✦ In Code windows, you create a new procedure by typing `Sub` or `Function` followed by parentheses and an argument list, if required. When you do, the Visual Basic Editor automatically supplies the required closing statement for you, either `End Sub` or `End Function`.

✦ Most importantly, typing a VBA statement that is obviously incomplete (or otherwise at odds with proper coding syntax) provokes a warning message from the Editor (see Figure 52-7). With this immediate notification, you can correct the problem while you still remember what you were trying to accomplish with the statement in question. Even if you dismiss the warning for now, the Editor displays the statement in red to remind you that something serious is wrong.

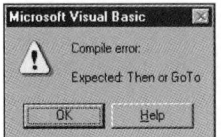

Figure 52-7: You get a warning message like this one when a line of VBA code doesn't follow correct syntax.

Navigating in a Code window

When you create a program of any complexity, a single Code window can contain pages and pages of code. Scrolling up and down randomly to find the section you're looking for would be much too primitive in such elegant surroundings.

Instead, take advantage of those two drop-down list boxes at the top of the Code window. They zoom you directly to the procedure you want to see or edit, as follows:

✦ **Object box:** This is the list box on the left. In a module window, this contains only (General), and you don't need to worry about it. But when you're working with the Code window for a form, this box lets you pick out a specific control on the form (or the form itself). When you do, the Code window displays the default procedure for that object.

✦ **Procedures/Events box:** Here, selecting the Declarations section (for the entire window) or a specific procedure displays the code for the selected item. If you're working in a form's Code window, this box lists only the events available for the item you chose in the Object box. When you select an event, the Code window displays the corresponding procedure for that event.

Bookmarking your code

It's 3:00 a.m. Your eyelids are so heavy they're falling on your typing fingers, but the deadline looms and you keep on knocking out line after line of fairly routine code. Suddenly, inspiration strikes — you've just realized how to solve a major programming problem you were working on yesterday morning.

Before you jump to that other module to implement your brilliant idea, drop a *bookmark* where you're now working. That way, when it's time to get back to this module you can make like Hansel and Gretel and find your way home in a flash. To place a bookmark on a line of code (well actually, alongside the code — see Figure 52-8), click the Toggle Bookmark button.

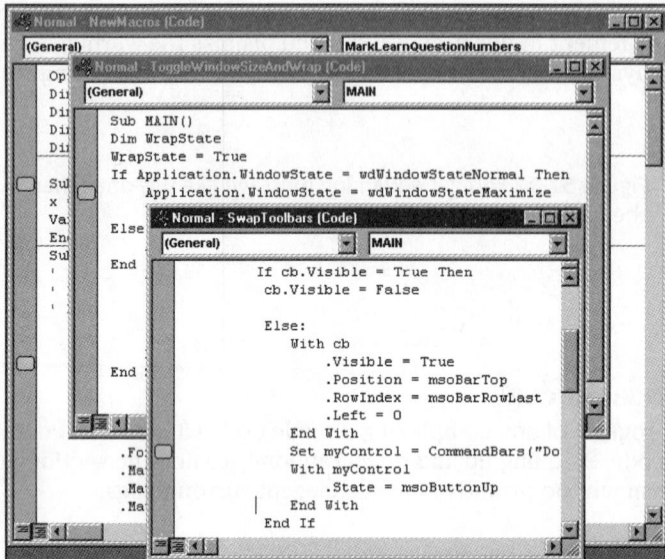

Figure 52-8: Those light ovals along the left side of the Code windows represent bookmarks. They appear in light blue on a color monitor.

All the bookmark-related buttons appear on the Edit toolbar, so you have to display this toolbar if you want access to them. Alternatively, you can use the corresponding menu command (Edit ⇨ Bookmarks ⇨ Toggle Bookmark), but it's much slower. (Cruelly, Microsoft omitted keyboard shortcuts for the bookmark commands.) Rather than displaying the Edit toolbar to get to the Bookmark button, you may right click within the Code window and go to Toggle ⇨ Bookmark. You can lay down as many bookmarks as you want.

Of course, a bookmark does you no good by itself. Click the Next Bookmark or Previous Bookmark button to jump in sequence from one bookmark to the next until you arrive at your destination.

To remove a single bookmark, place the insertion point on the line containing the mark and again click the Toggle Bookmark button. If you've accumulated so many bookmarks that the Next and Previous Bookmark commands work as slowly as scrollbar buttons, you can wipe them out by clicking the Clear All Bookmarks button.

Splitting a Code window

You can split any Code window into two separate panes (see Figure 52-9). This enables you to see code in different parts of the same module at the same time. It also gives you an easy way to cut and paste between sections of your code.

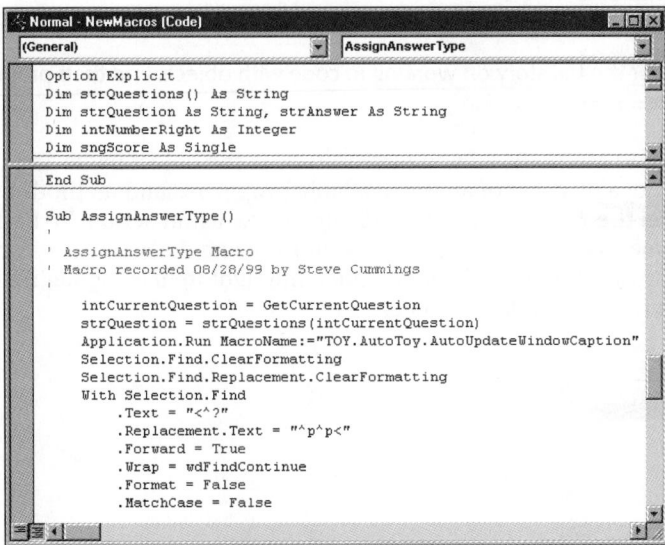

Figure 52-9: This Code window has been split.

To split a Code window, use the split bar — it's that little gray bar just above the top right scrollbar arrow. Drag the split bar downward until the panes are sized to suit you. To reunite them, remove the split bar by double-clicking it, or by dragging it back to the top of the window.

More Code window creature comforts

Why write code when you can have someone else type it for you? The Visual Basic Editor pampers you by automatically entering those wacky VBA terms for you at just the right time. Not only does this minimize your typing, it guarantees accurate spelling.

Several related Editor features, all found on the Edit menu, provide these amenities. They are as follows:

✦ The List Properties and Methods feature

✦ The List Constants feature

✦ The Complete Word feature

Using the List Properties and Methods feature

Of all Editor features, List Properties and Methods sees the most use. Here's how it works: To do anything useful with a VBA object, either you change the setting of one of the object's properties or you activate one of its methods. To identify the property or method you want to work with, you type the object's name, then a period (the *dot* operator), and then the property or method name, like this:

```
ActiveWindow.Selection.Group
```

Cross-Reference   See Chapter 54 for the full story on working in code with objects and their properties and methods.

With List Properties and Methods, all you have to type is the object name and the dot. As soon as you do, a little list of all the available properties and methods for that object pops up in the window. Figure 52-10 shows this list in action. To find the correct property or method, you can scroll the window using the arrow keys or type the first letter or two of the item's name. Once the right item is highlighted, press Tab key to insert it into your document.

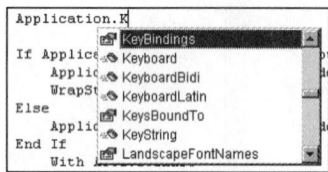

Figure 52-10: The List Properties and Methods feature gives you a power assist when entering properties and methods in code.

The List Properties and Methods feature performs similar service when you're declaring a variable (defining its type). When you start typing a statement such as

```
Dim Muesli As CerealObject
```

a list of all the available data and object types pops up just when you finish typing the word As. Just as before, you pick from this list by scrolling or typing a letter or two and pressing Tab.

Cross-Reference   For more about declaring variables, see Chapter 53.

List Properties and Methods works not only with built-in VBA objects, but also your own object variables — *unless you haven't explicitly declared them as such*. This gives you a good reason to explicitly define variables.

Tip   Oh, one other point. The Properties and Methods list pops up automatically only if the proper setting is turned on in the Options dialog box. If you don't get the list, choose Tools ➪ Options and be sure the box labeled Auto List Members is checked. You can pop up the list manually with the appropriate command on the Edit menu or by using the Ctrl+J keyboard shortcut.

Listing constants automatically

The List Constants feature works just like the List Properties and Methods feature, except that it displays the names of the predefined constants for the property you're working with. This list pops up just after you type the = in a statement such as this one:

```
Muesli.Crispness = Mushy
```

The keyboard shortcut is the same as before: Ctrl+J.

Completing words automatically

The Visual Basic Editor's Complete Word feature can enter just about any valid VBA term for you. To activate it, press Ctrl+Spacebar. This shortcut pops up a list that looks and works just like the one provided by the List Properties and Methods feature described previously. The difference is that this list includes just about everything you might want to type: objects, functions, procedures, constants, methods, properties, and your own variables. One exception is the keywords for built-in data types, such as Integer and Variant.

 **Tip**   Typing a letter or two before you press Ctrl+Spacebar limits the list to items starting with those characters. Better yet, if you've typed enough letters to match only one item, the Editor inserts it for you as soon as you press Ctrl+Spacebar — the list itself never actually appears.

Getting into arguments

Many VBA procedures require you to specify one or more *arguments* when you execute the procedure in your code. Such a procedure bases its calculations (or does whatever else it does) on the information you supply in these arguments. Many object methods require arguments just as procedures do.

The Visual Basic Editor won't type the arguments for you — it can't, because it doesn't know which specific values you want the arguments to have. However, it will pop up a little window containing a kind of cheat sheet — it tells you which arguments the function requires, which are optional, and the type of information each argument represents. Figure 52-11 shows an example.

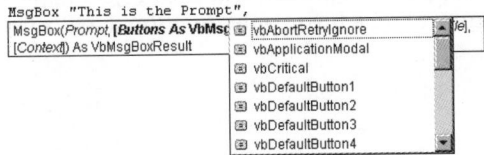

Figure 52-11: The Quick Info window in action

Quick Info versus Parameter Info

The Parameter Info feature complements Quick Info when you get into heavy VBA coding. It often happens that you want to use one function to determine the value of an argument required by another function, as in this simple example:

```
MsgBox(Str(AnIntegerVariable))
```

Here, the Str function converts the integer value stored in the variable AnIntegerVariable into a text string. This string is then used as the argument to the MsgBox function (it becomes the prompt you see when VBA displays the message box on your screen).

But because you can *nest* functions within functions within functions in this way, the Quick Info window isn't enough. It always shows you the argument list for the function containing the insertion point. An extra helper, the Parameter Info feature displays the argument list for the "outermost" function, the one within which all the other functions are nested. The keyboard shortcut for the Parameter Info feature is Ctrl+Shift+I.

This is the Quick Info feature. If the Auto Quick Info box is checked in the Tools ⇨ Options dialog box, the Quick Info window will appear automatically as soon as you type the name of a function, method, or procedure that requires arguments. If you shut off this automatic response, you can still display the Quick Info window by pressing Ctrl+I.

Many functions and procedures require multiple arguments. To help you keep track of where you are in the list of arguments, the Quick Info window displays in bold the argument you're currently typing. As soon as you type the comma that indicates the end of one argument, the next argument turns bold in the Quick Info window.

Using the Properties Window

The Properties window enables you to view and edit the properties of whatever object (project, module, form, or control) is currently active in the Visual Basic Editor. In Figure 52-12, for example, the title bar of the Properties window shows the name of the active object, which also appears highlighted in the Project Explorer. (If the selected object is an individual control on a form, only the form itself is listed in the Project Explorer.)

Figure 52-12: The Properties window for a form

When a project or module is the selected object, the only property listed in the Properties window is the project name. With form and control objects, however, the window gives you access to a myriad of properties governing the appearance and behavior of the selected object.

Cross-Reference For a full discussion of how the Properties window works, see Chapter 56.

The Properties window is primarily useful for designing forms. For that reason, here's a crash course in how to display the window and use it to rename projects and modules.

Invoking the Properties window

You can do any of the following tricks to display the Properties window:

✦ Press F4.

✦ Click the Properties button on the Standard toolbar.

✦ Open the View menu and choose Properties Window.

When the Properties window is visible, you can display the item's properties by switching to a Code or UserForm window or clicking an item in Project Explorer.

Renaming a project or module in the Properties window

Projects and modules have only one property each — a name — but regardless, you still use the Properties window if you want to change that one property. To rename a project or module, follow these steps:

1. Select the project or module in the Project Explorer.

2. Display the Properties window, if it isn't already visible.

3. Activate the Properties window if it isn't already active.

   (Clicking it will do the trick, or you can press F4.)

4. Type the new name.

   Because this is the only property, you don't have to click the row for the (Name) property before you start typing.

The Debugging Windows

Four windows are designed for debugging your code: the Immediate, Locals, Watch, and Call Stack windows.

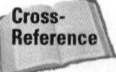

Cross-Reference For a discussion of which windows you use to detect and correct errors in your code, see Chapter 55.

✦ ✦ ✦

Writing Great VBA Modules

After you've been exposed to some fundamental VBA concepts and have struck up a good working relationship with the Visual Basic Editor, it's time to roll up your sleeves and start writing code. This chapter introduces essential programming and testing techniques for all VBA programmers.

Program Building Blocks

A VBA program isn't just a random collection of instructions to the computer; it's a highly *organized* random collection of instructions. Lines of code are collected into *procedures,* which reside in *modules,* which, in turn, are housed within *projects*.

A sample program

To make the discussion of this hierarchy of VBA elements a little less abstract, you can refer to the module of code found within this section. It contains all the elements I mention (except for projects — modules go inside projects, rather than the other way around). The sample module of code presented here searches the selected cells in an Excel worksheet, formatting those containing values greater than 1000 so they stand out in boxed, bold, red type. It then tells you how many cells it changed (see Figure 53-1).

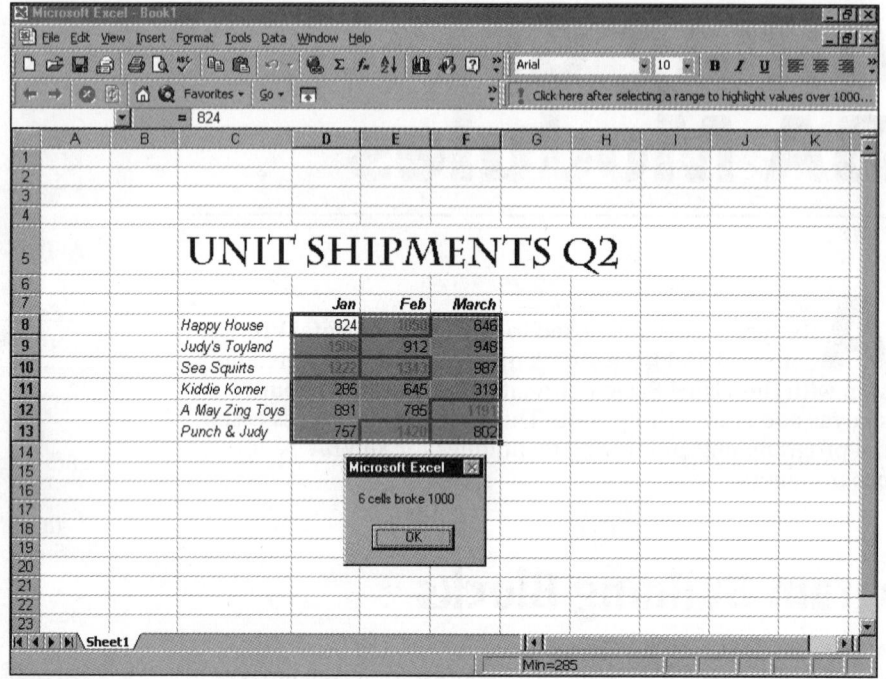

Figure 53-1: Here's what an Excel worksheet looks like when the sample module runs.

If you want a satisfying hands-on experience with the sample, start in Excel, open a new worksheet, and type in numbers in a block of cells — some values should be less than 1000 and some greater. Select the cells with the numbers. Then press Alt+F11 or choose Tools ➪ Macros ➪ Visual Basic Editor to enter the Editor. Display the Project Explorer and Properties windows by pressing Ctrl+R and F4, respectively. Choose Insert ➪ Module to open an empty code window, your blank canvas for the new module.

Note   A generic name for the module appears in the code window's title bar, in the Name field of the Properties window, and in Project Explorer's tree list. To change the module's name, select the current name in the Properties window and type in one of your own. I suggest `HighlightBigNumbers` for the sample, but use any name you like as long as it starts with a letter and contains no spaces — see the information on naming rules and conventions later in this chapter.

Back in the Code window, type the following code:

```
Option Explicit
Const Cutoff As Integer = 1000
Dim objCell As Object
```

```
Sub HighlightBigNumbers()
    Dim intCellCounter As Integer
    intCellCounter = CountAndDoHighlights
    MsgBox (intCellCounter & " cells broke " & Cutoff)
End Sub

Function CountAndDoHighlights() As Integer

On Error GoTo BYE
    Dim z As Integer
    For Each objCell In Selection
      If objCell.Value > Cutoff Then
        With objCell.Font
            .Bold = True
            .Color = RGB(255, 0, 0)
        End With
        objCell.BorderAround ColorIndex:=3, _
            Weight:=xlThick
        z = z + 1
      End If
    Next objCell
    CountAndDoHighlights = z

BYE:
End Function
```

Navigating the VBA hierarchy

With the sample program in mind, you should be better able to understand the following definitions and descriptions of VBA code building blocks.

A *statement* is the smallest unit of VBA code that can accomplish anything. A statement can declare or define a variable, set an option of the VBA compiler, or carry out an action in your program. A valid statement is a lot like a complete sentence; it has to include the proper "parts of speech" or it isn't really a statement at all.

A *procedure* is the smallest unit of code that you refer to by name. It's also the smallest unit of code that you can run independently. VBA recognizes two main types of procedures: Sub procedures and Function procedures. A procedure of either type consists of one or more statements, sandwiched inside two special statements: the procedure's declaration at the top, and the End Sub or End Function statement at the end.

A *module* is a named unit consisting of one or more procedures, plus declarations common to all procedures in the module. Although VBA allows you to place all your procedures in a single module, it makes sense to divide related procedures into separate modules to make it easier to keep track of them.

Two types of modules are available in VBA. By far the most common is the *standard module*, the kind you use for the code you want to run. Use the other type of module, the *class module*, to define custom objects and their properties and methods.

A *project* consists of all the modules, forms, and application-related objects associated with a particular document, plus the document itself.

Programs defined

So what's a *program*? Conceptually, a program is a complete, functioning (or malfunctioning) software totality. A program consists of one or more statements that execute in the order defined by the programmer.

But a program isn't an official VBA entity. VBA recognizes by name procedures, modules, and projects, but not programs as such. A VBA program requires at least one procedure — because VBA executes statements only within procedures — but it can encompass two or more procedures, within one or more modules, spanning one or more projects.

More about projects

You never have to do anything to create a project. Every document from a VBA application is a project automatically. Of course, a document's project doesn't contain any code or forms until you create them in the Visual Basic Editor or record macros in the application. The section on the Project Explorer in Chapter 52 covers the techniques you need for working with projects as a whole.

Working with modules

The module comes just below the project in the hierarchy of VBA code elements. A module provides storage for one or more VBA procedures, along with a Declarations section containing statements that apply to the entire module.

Planning your modules

Deciding how your modules should be organized doesn't have to be a big deal. It does make sense to think about how many modules you should create and which procedures each one should contain. The basic points to remember are these:

✦ Your procedures can *call,* or run, procedures stored in other modules. You can use variables declared in another module too.

✦ However, it's slightly more complicated to use procedures and variables from other modules. For example, to call a procedure in another module, you enter it with the module's name, as in `OtherModule.DoSomethingNow`.

In general, you should place related procedures together in a single module. Typically, a module contains all the procedures for one complete VBA program — and no extraneous procedures. That simplifies your programming, because you don't have to deal with the little complications involved in accessing procedures or variables in other modules.

However, if you create procedures that you plan to use in more than one program, you can organize them in modules according to type, as in `MyMathProcedures` or `TextHandlingRoutines`. You might also create modules called `BrandNewProcedures` or `OldProceduresIMightNeedSomeday`.

Adding a new module to a VBA project

To create a new module in the Visual Basic Editor, start by making sure you're working with the correct project. In the Project Explorer, select the project itself or any of the objects it already contains (this can be a form, an application object, or an existing module — it doesn't matter). You can then use any of the following techniques to insert the new module:

✦ **Click the Insert Module button.** This is a split (multifunction) button for inserting various items. If the module icon isn't visible, click the narrow bar with the arrow to the right of the main part of the button and choose from the menu.

✦ **Right-click the Project Explorer window.** Make sure you do it over the correct project — and choose Insert ➪ Module from the shortcut menu. If you prefer the main menu bar, choose Insert ➪ Module.

The Visual Basic Editor automatically opens the new module's Code window. It also christens the module with a generic name. To change it, type a new name in the Properties window (see Chapter 52).

What goes where in a new module

The Code window for a brand-new module has only one section, the Declarations section. You can tell which section you're in by looking at the list box at the top right of the Code window.

You can enter two types of statements in a module's Declarations section:

✦ **Declarations of variables, constants, and user-defined data types.** These tell the compiler the name and type of each item (but not its value). Variables and constants declared in a module's Declarations section can be used in any procedure in that module.

✦ **Compiler options that control the way VBA compiler operates.** For example, you may specify the `OPTION EXPLICIT` directive. This directive forces you, as a programmer, to declare all variables.

What you can't place in the Declarations section are assignment or executable statements — statements that actually do something when the code runs. For example, you can't specify the *value* of a variable in the Declarations section. That requires an assignment statement, which must go inside a procedure elsewhere in the module. (The differences between executable statements, assignment statements, declarations, and compiler options are clarified in the section "Making statements," later in this chapter).

Tip   Statements in the Declarations section are also referred to as *module-level code*. Each procedure you add to the module is considered a separate section. After you've added a procedure, its name appears in the list box at the top right of the Code window, enabling you to jump directly to that procedure by selecting its name in the list.

Standard modules and modules with class

The garden variety VBA module is a standard module (standard modules were known as code modules in older versions of VBA and Visual Basic). They contain statements that declare variables and constants, define custom (user-defined) data types, and set compiler options, as well as executable statements that actually get things done. You can make use of any existing objects you have access to in a standard module, but you can't create new object types in this type of module.

You use class modules, by contrast, to define your own custom objects. To define a class module, choose Class Module from the Insert menu. After creating a class module for the custom object, you fill it with the code for the object's properties and methods. This done, code in other modules can access the object's properties and methods, just as if it were a built-in VBA object.

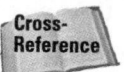

Cross-Reference   Writing your own classes is a powerful VBA programming technique; it's covered in Chapter 54.

Writing procedures

Procedures are critical functional units of your VBA code, because code must be stored within a procedure or you can't run it. VBA procedures fall into two everyday types, Sub procedures and Function procedures (see the "Procedure Types" sidebar). Here are two simple procedures, one of each type:

```
Public Sub SubMarine()
    MsgBox "Up Periscope!"
End Sub
Public Function FunkShun (Birthdate As Date)
    FunkShun = DateDiff("yyyy", Birthdate, Date)
End Function
```

Procedure Types

Here's a summary of the various function types:

✦ A `Sub` procedure is a general-purpose procedure for getting things done in VBA. `Sub` procedures are the only type you can run independently. However, one `Sub` procedure can also run (or *call*) another.

✦ A `Function` procedure can execute any VBA statements you like. However, it differs from a `Sub` procedure in that it calculates a value and then *returns* that value to the procedure that activated the `Function` in the first place.

✦ An `Event` procedure is a special type of `Sub` procedure used to respond to events that occur to forms and to application objects such as documents and the application itself. Chapter 56 covers the particulars on event procedures.

✦ A `Property` procedure determines or assigns the value of a custom object's property. `Property` procedures are covered in Chapter 54.

✦ A VBA macro is, technically speaking, a `Sub` procedure that *takes* (requires) no arguments. Macros are the only kind of `Sub` procedures you can run directly, by name, in the Visual Basic Editor or your VBA application. To run a `Sub` procedure that does take arguments, you must call it from another procedure.

As you can see, each procedure comprises an opening declaration statement, one or more lines of code, and a terminating `End` statement. I'll go into these elements fully in the sections "Sub procedures in detail" and "Function procedures in detail."

Creating a new procedure

Before you can start a new procedure, you have to first open the Code window for the module in which you're going to store the procedure. Create a new module with the steps laid out earlier in this chapter, or open an existing module by double-clicking it in the Project Explorer.

After the module's Code window is open and active, you're ready to begin the new procedure. Your initial task is simply to insert into the module the procedure's declaration statement and its complement, the `End` statement that signals the end of the procedure. You can accomplish this in two ways: via the Insert ➪ Procedure dialog box or by typing the statements yourself.

If you choose the Insert ➪ Procedure dialog box, you may specify the name of the procedure, choose the type of procedure (Subroutine, Function, or Property), and define the scope of the procedure (Public or Private). Optionally, you may choose to define all local variables as static.

Typing versus the dialog box

I recommend typing in the procedure's "shell" yourself, simply because the dialog box method doesn't save any time unless you're a *really* slow typist. The do-it-yourself approach also lets you control where in the module to place the procedure, which you can't do with the dialog box. All you have to do is click where you want the procedure to go, type the procedure's declaration statement, and hit Enter. You don't have to type the parentheses or the closing End Sub or End Function statement — the Visual Basic Editor adds them for you.

Completing the procedure

The real work in writing a procedure is in typing a series of VBA statements between the declaration and End statements. This isn't the place for details on what to type. Suffice to say that statements within a procedure are executed in the order in which they appear, except when your code instructs VBA to jump to another location.

Sub procedures in detail

In some programming languages, the main procedures call smaller, subsidiary procedures called *subprocedures* or *subroutines*. They're also known as Sub procedures because they begin with Sub and end with End Sub. Although (in VBA) a Sub procedure can be called by another procedure, the main procedure of a program is itself *always* a Sub procedure. Here's a sample Sub procedure, with the declaration at the top, the terminating End statement at the bottom, and a few statements in between:

```
Public Sub ASweetProcedure()
    Dim ANiceMessage As String
    ANiceMessage = "Have a nice day!"
    Msgbox ANiceMessage
    (more statements)
    ...
End Sub
```

Items in a Sub procedure declaration

In the declaration statement that begins ASweetProcedure (), the first term, Public, specifies the procedure's scope, which can be either Public or Private. Public is the default, so you don't need to include this keyword — doing so, however, makes the scope obvious so you don't have to wonder. I discuss scope in "Scoping out the scope," later in this chapter.

Next comes the Sub keyword, which simply indicates you're declaring a Sub procedure. After that is the procedure's name, which can be anything you like, as long as it conforms to the standards given in "VBA naming rules," later in this chapter.

About arguments

Closing out the declaration is a pair of parentheses. They are there to hold *arguments*, if the procedure has any. In this case, the procedure has no arguments, so nothing appears inside the parentheses. Arguments are discussed in "Winning arguments," which follows the section on Function procedures.

Built-in VBA Functions

VBA comes with numerous built-in *functions*. As with a Function procedure, a VBA function returns a value to a calling procedure. Also, you use the same technique to call both functions and Function procedures. The names vary, but the only difference between Function procedures and functions to the person using them is that you don't have to write code for functions. The section "Built-In Functions and Statements" offers an overview of the functions available in VBA.

Calling Sub procedures

You can run, or *call*, any Sub procedure — whether or not it takes arguments — from another procedure. To call a Sub procedure, just include a statement consisting of the name of the Sub procedure you want to call, as in this code fragment. The line reading WashMyOldCar calls the WashMyOldCar Sub procedure:

```
...
MyOldCar = "Valiant"
WashMyOldCar
NumberOfCarwashTrips = NumberOfCarwashTrips + 1
...
```

Function procedures in detail

A Function procedure can conduct general business just like a Sub procedure, but its main *raison d'être* is to calculate a value. When the Function completes its work, it returns that value to the calling procedure, which can use it in further computations.

Here's a sample Function procedure:

```
Public Function DeFunct(x As Integer, y As Integer)
    Dim z As Integer
    z = x + y
    DeFunct = x ^ z
End Function
```

Obviously, the basic form of a Function procedure is much like that of a Sub procedure. The declaration begins with an optional keyword defining the procedure's scope (in this case, Public). Next comes the Function keyword, then the procedure's name, and finally its arguments. (Note: The fourth line of code in this example Function procedure raises x to the zth power.) A function ends with a terminating statement, End Function.

The difference between Function and Sub procedures

There is one critical difference between Sub and Function procedures: Somewhere in a Function procedure, at least one statement specifies the value of the function itself. It does so by using the name of the procedure as if it were a variable. In the preceding example, this occurs in the line DeFunct = x ^ z. After this line executes, DeFunct holds the value that will be returned to the calling procedure.

Calling Function procedures

Normally, you call a Function procedure by setting a variable equal to the name of the function. In the first executable statement in the following example, the variable ZPower receives the value returned by the DeFunct procedure. Note that the arguments required by the DeFunct procedure are passed in parentheses following the procedure name:

```
Sub DoDeFunct()
    ZPower = DeFunct(3, 4)
    MsgBox Zpower
End Sub
```

Winning arguments

Arguments represent values that VBA is to transfer, or *pass,* from one procedure to another. The second procedure is said to *take* the arguments. You build arguments into a procedure when you want the procedure to modify its behavior based on values you supply at the time you call the procedure.

Refer to the sample Function procedure DeFunct shown in the earlier section "Function procedures in detail." It takes two arguments, x and y. As the DeFunct illustrates, a procedure's arguments are declared as part of the declaration of the procedure itself. They always appear in parentheses following the name of the procedure. In this *argument list*, you declare individual arguments just as you would variables of the same type except that you leave out the Dim or similar keyword (see "Working with Variables" for details on declaring individual variables).

A procedure that takes arguments requires those arguments to do its job. Within the procedure, arguments serve exactly the same role as variables that you declare in the usual way. Look again at the DeFunct procedure. After declaring a variable z for its own use, the procedure calculates z's value as the sum of the two arguments, x and y. Then, to calculate the procedure's own return value, the next line of code raises the x argument to the power of z. As you can see, x, y, and z all have similar roles. If you wanted, you could have raised z to the power of x instead of the other way around.

So why argue?

So if arguments are so much like variables, why use arguments at all? Actually, you don't have to — you can use ordinary variables to accomplish everything you can do with arguments. But arguments have the following advantages:

✦ When you're reading through your code, arguments make it clear which outside values a procedure requires to do its job.

✦ When you're writing code, arguments help you minimize the number of variables you need to create outside of procedures (in the Declarations section of the module).

✦ When you call a procedure that takes arguments, VBA *forces* you to state values for those arguments. This helps ensure that the procedure gets the correct values it needs.

Calling procedures that take arguments

The way you call a procedure that takes arguments depends on the situation:

✦ When you use a `Function` procedure to return a value, you place the arguments in parentheses separated by commas:

```
ProceedsFromOldCar = SellOldCar ("Rambler Classic",1962)
```

✦ When you call a `Function` procedure by itself, ignoring its return value, and whenever you call a `Sub` procedure, state the arguments without parentheses:

```
SellOldCar "Studebaker", 1957
```

Scoping out the scope

Each VBA procedure has a defined *scope*. The scope determines the parts of your program from which you can call that procedure. If you have a visual imagination, think of it this way: A procedure's scope decides which parts of your program can "see" the procedure. Procedures can have three different scopes:

✦ By default, VBA procedures (except event procedures) are *public* in scope. That means that you can call them from any part of your program — from the same module, from another module, or even (if your program includes multiple projects as discussed in Chapter 51) from a different project.

✦ When it suits your programming needs, you can create procedures that are *private* in scope. Private procedures are visible, if you will, only within the same module. In other words, you can call a private procedure from another procedure in the same module, but not from procedures in any other modules.

✦ In a VBA program that includes more than one project, you can create procedures that are accessible to all the modules within a given project but off limits to other projects.

Variables have scope, too, and scope works in a similar way for them. See the section "Specifying a variable's scope," later in this chapter.

Specifying a procedure's scope

To specify the scope of a procedure, all you have to do is place the `Public` or `Private` keyword at the beginning of the procedure's declaration. Look at these examples:

```
Public Sub IKneadYou()
... (procedure statements)
End Sub

Private Function IKneedYou()
... (procedure statements)
End Function
```

Because ordinary (nonevent) procedures are public by default, you don't have to include the `Public` keyword to give a procedure public scope. If a program contains any private procedures, however, I recommend that you explicitly declare the public procedures so you can tell at a glance which is which.

To restrict the scope of a public procedure to its project only (so it is inaccessible to other projects), place the statement `Option Private Module` in the Declarations section of the module in which you declare the procedure. (See the "Declarations" and "Compiler options" sections later in this chapter for details on working with such statements.)

Using private procedures

Making a procedure private helps prevent errors. Because you can call the procedure only from within the same module, you can more easily control the conditions in effect at the time the procedure gets called (conditions such as the values of variables that the procedure uses).

Making a procedure private in scope is easy enough, but why bother? After all, VBA doesn't *demand* that you call a procedure from another module, just because that procedure is public.

Well, the reason is self-protection. You may forget that you designed a procedure so it should be called only from within the same module. If the procedure is private, VBA won't let you call it from another module even if you try to. As a bonus, in programs of substantial size and complexity, limiting the number of access points to a given procedure helps you keep better track of the program's organization.

Making statements

Procedures are made up of *statements,* the smallest viable units of code. Most statements occupy only one line of code, and normally a line of code has only one statement — but not always, as you'll see later in this section. VBA distinguishes four different statement types: declarations, assignment statements, executable statements, and compiler options. Statements may contain keywords, expressions, constants, operators, and variables.

Declarations

A *declaration statement* announces to the VBA compiler your intention to use a named item — a variable, constant, user-defined data type, an array, or a procedure — in your program. The declaration goes further, specifying which type of item it is and providing any additional information the compiler will need to make use of the item. After you've declared an item, you can use it elsewhere in your program.

The following statement declares the variable named `MyLittleNumber` as an integer variable:

```
Dim MyLittleNumber As Integer
```

This statement creates a string (text) constant named `UnchangingText` that consists of the characters `"Eternity"`:

```
Constant UnchangingText = "Eternity"
```

The following statement declares a `Sub` procedure named `HiddenProcedure`:

```
Private Sub HiddenProcedure()
```

Assignment statements

Assignment statements set a variable, or a property of an object, to some specific value. These statements always have three parts: the name of the variable or property, an equal sign, and an *expression* specifying the new value (see "Expressionism" for a discussion of expressions).

The following statement sets the value of the `MyLittleNumber` variable to the sum of the `SomeOtherNumber` variable and 12:

```
MyLittleNumber = SomeOtherNumber + 12
```

This statement sets the `Color` property of the `AGraphicShape` object to `Blue`, which has presumably been defined as a constant:

```
AGraphicShape.Color = Blue
```

Executable statements

Executable statements don't just sit there; they do things. For example, the following statement executes the `Rotate` method of the `AGraphicShape` object:

```
AGraphicShape.Rotate(90)
```

This statement performs the `Sqr` function — which calculates a square root — on the current value of the `MyLittleNumber` variable, placing the result into the `SquareRoot` variable:

```
SquareRoot = Sqr(MyLittleNumber)
```

Compiler options

Instructions that control the VBA compiler's behavior constitute the last class of statements. Of the four compiler options statements, the main one to learn is

```
Option Explicit
```

See the section "Choosing and using data types" for information on the `Option Explicit` directive.

Manners, Please! VBA Etiquette

In the service of readable, understandable, working code, this section covers rules and conventions for naming VBA items, formatting your code for legibility, and adding comments.

VBA naming rules

VBA enforces rules for naming *program elements* (which include variables, constants, data types, procedures, modules, forms, controls, and projects). If you try to enter a name that violates any of these rules, the Visual Basic Editor warns you as soon as you move the insertion point off that line of code. Here are the rules:

✦ Names must begin with a letter, not a numeral. After the first character, however, you can use numerals and the underscore character, as in the following:

```
Hidden_Variable3
```

✦ Aside from the underscore character, punctuation marks are off limits altogether in VBA names. Off-limits characters include the following:

```
! @ & ' $ # ? , * . { } ( ) [ ] = + - ^ % / ~ < > : ;
```

✦ Names can't include spaces.

✦ You're limited to a maximum of 255 characters (40 characters for forms and controls).

✦ A name can't duplicate a VBA keyword, function, statement, or method.

✦ You can't use the same name more than once in the same scope. For example, all procedures in the same module must have different names. A procedure and a module-level variable — one declared in the Declarations section of a module — can't share the same name. However, you can use duplicate names for variables declared inside different procedures. The section "Specifying a variable's scope" tries to clarify the muddy issue of scope.

VBA ignores the capitalization of names but preserves the capitalization you use.

Naming conventions

As long as you live by the rules listed earlier, you can give any name you like to any item in your program. Nevertheless, you can make your programming life a lot easier by sticking to a logical naming scheme. One method that many people use is to start each name with a short prefix that indicates the type of item and follow that with a capitalized brief descriptive name. Table 53-1 lists commonly applied prefixes for the most commonly used VBA items. You can make up your own or use them as suffixes if you prefer. The important thing is to use them consistently.

Table 53-1
Suggested Prefixes for Naming VBA Items

Use This Prefix	To Name This Type of Item	Example
Variables		
byte	Byte	byteDaysInMonth
bool	Boolean	boolClearedStatus
int	Integer	intWeeksOnChart
lng	Long integer	lngPopulation
sng	Single	sngRadius
dbl	Double	dblParsecs
cur	Currency	curUnitPrice
str	String	strLastName
dat	Date/Time	datBirthdate
var	Variant	varSerialNumber
obj	Object	objStampCollection
Controls on form		
txt	Text box	txtEnterName
lbl	Label	lblAnswerMessage
cmd	Command button	cmdCalculateInterestRate
mnu	Menu	mnuTools
cmb	Combo box	cmbToyCategory
fra	Frame	fraHabitat
opt	Option button	optGasolineGrade
chk	Checkbox	chkCaseSensitive

Continued

	Table 53-1 *(continued)*	
Use This Prefix	**To Name This Type of Item**	**Example**
Other items		
bas	Module	basTextFormatFunctions
frm	UserForm	frmOptionsDialog

Making your code legible

This section offers a few simple suggestions for writing code that you can decipher when you come back to it tomorrow, next week, or next year.

Judicious indenting helps organize your code

Develop and practice a consistent indenting style. The VBA compiler ignores blank space at the beginning of a line. This means you're free to use indentation to set off related lines of code. So which lines of code should you indent, and by how much? Your indenting goal is to indent related statements by the same amount, so the relationship between them is visually obvious. More specifically, statements that are executed only when some condition is in effect should all be indented together.

For example, VBA executes the statements within an If...Then...Else construction or inside Do...Loop and For...Next loops as a group, so they should have the same indentation. Here's an example:

```
Do While intC <> 20
    intA = intA + 1
    If intA = intB Then
        intA = 5
        intB = 10
    Else
        intA = intB
        intC = 20
    End If
Loop
```

Note that *control structures* like Do...Loop and If...Then...Else always consist of at least two statements: one that starts the structure, the other that terminates it. For Do...Loop, the terminating statement is Loop; for If...Then...Else, it's End If. Statements that are part of a given control structure itself should all be indented by the same amount. This enables you to see clearly the outline of the structure, and which other statements fall inside it.

Tip

To cut your workload to a minimum, the Visual Basic Editor automatically indents each new line of code to match the previous one. When you get to a line that requires a smaller indentation, just press the Backspace key to back up. If you don't like the assistance, you can shut off automatic indenting in the Editor tab of the Tools ⇨ Options dialog box.

No scrolling! Use the line continuation character

Although shorter statements are easier to understand and debug, it's perfectly acceptable to extend a single statement over multiple lines in the Visual Basic Editor. Obviously, each line is much easier to read if it all fits into the visible portion of the Code window, so you don't have to scroll sideways.

To continue a statement onto another line, place an underscore, _, at the end of the line. For example, the following three lines together constitute one statement:

```
sngWackyNumber = Cos(12 * 57.5 / Sqr(intMyTinyNumber + _
intMyBigNumber) + CustomDataMassage(sngrawinfo, 12) + _
(bytFirstTuesdayInAugust * curLastPayCheck) + 1)
```

Caution

Be sure you remember to type a space before the underscore (also called the *line continuation character*) on every line where you use it. Otherwise, VBA gives you an `invalid character` error message. Another cautionary note: Don't place the underscore within a pair of quotation marks that enclose a string of text. Otherwise, VBA gives you a compile error message.

Remarks about comments

As with all serious programming languages, VBA lets you add explanations to your code. Comments enable you to record the purpose of each statement or group of statements. Please be lavish with comments. Comments are particularly useful for beginning programmers. When you visit your code later, comments will remind you what various statements are for. The comments you type are totally ignored by the VBA compiler. They live only in the text file representing the contents of the Code window, not in the compiled program. They don't make the compiled program any longer, nor do they slow it down in any way. Comments cost you nothing except a minuscule amount of disk space, so use them freely.

How to make comments

A comment begins when you type an apostrophe. Everything you type to the right of the apostrophe on that line of code is part of the comment. You can place comments on lines all by themselves, or you can add comments after a line of active code. Figure 53-2 shows a Code window with lots of comments interspersed among the active code statements.

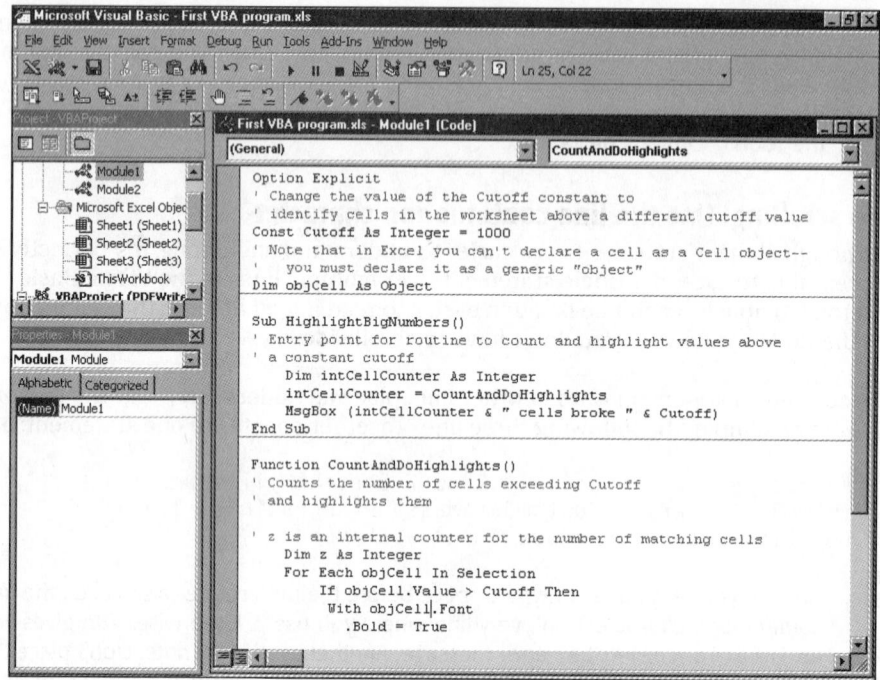

Figure 53-2: Comments, please?

Tip

Commenting is a good way to take real code statements out of active duty without deleting them for good. This can come in handy when you want to try two alternative approaches to the same coding problem, or to shut off code that you know contains an error while you test another part of the same module.

Long-winded comments

To include a long comment spanning two or more lines in your code, you must place an apostrophe at the beginning of each line. But fortunately, VBA provides a one-button command for commenting blocks of lines in bulk. You can also *uncomment* a block of lines that currently begin with apostrophes. Select the block and click the Uncomment Block button. Using the Comment Block and Uncomment Block buttons, you can quickly deactivate and reactivate any code block.

Tip

One little note about the way these buttons work is in order. If a line already starts with an apostrophe, the Comment Block button adds a second apostrophe to it, and so on. Likewise, each time you click the Uncomment Block button, only one apostrophe is removed. This means that when you comment and then uncomment a block of active code, you don't lose any "real" comments that it contained.

Working with Variables

To tap the full potential of VBA, programs require *variables* to store information that can change. Variables are the key to writing programs that alter their own behavior based on up-to-date information or other changes in prevailing conditions. In essence, a variable is an ID tag for a chunk of information stored by your program. It's like when you go to the theater and leave your hat at the hatcheck. The attendant puts your hat away somewhere in a back room — you couldn't care less where, as long as it's safe. In return, you get a slip with a number on it. When you leave, you give the attendant the number and you get your hat back. At the next performance, the staff uses that same number for somebody else's hat.

Declaring variables

One of the most common uses of declaration statements is to declare variables. Variable declarations look like this:

```
Dim varAnyOldVariable
Private intIntegerVariable As Integer
Static strNewYearsResolution As String
```

Most variable declarations are `Dim` statements. The `Dim` keyword is short for dimension, used as a verb. The idea is that the `Dim` statement gives VBA the dimensions for the storage area the variable refers to. You can also use the `Private`, `Public`, and `Static` keywords to declare variables and at the same time specify their scope. Read about scope in "Specifying a variable's scope."

Where to declare variables

You can declare a variable in either of two places in your program:

✦ The Declarations section of the module (at the module level)

✦ Anywhere within a procedure (at the procedure level)

The choice of this location helps determine which procedures can access the variable, or in other words, the variable's scope. In general, if you declare the variable at the module level, any procedure in the module can use the variable. If you declare it in a particular procedure, it can be used only in that procedure. You can also use the `Public`, `Private`, and `Static` keywords to specify a variable's scope. For additional info on scope, see "Specifying a variable's scope," later in this chapter.

Although VBA won't object if you interleave variable declarations with executable statements within a procedure, your code can be clearer if you declare all the procedure's variables at the very beginning. Note how the following procedure follows this practice:

```
Public Sub VariableProcedures ()
Dim strChildsName As String
Dim intToyCount As Integer
Dim curAllowance As Currency
strChildsName = InputBox ("Enter the child's name:")

' in the next two lines, CountToys and NewAllowance
' are Function procedures presumably defined elsewhere
' in your code
intToyCount = CountToys(strChildsName)
curAllowance = NewAllowance(strChildsName, intToyCount)
End Sub
```

When to declare variables

One of the best practices in programming includes declaring variables ahead of time, before you use them in your program. One simple reason for doing so is to make your code easier to understand. Other advantages come into play when you use the Option Explicit compiler directive, covered in "Force yourself to use explicit declarations," later in this chapter.

By default, however, VBA permits you to use variables without declaring them first. If you type **A = 7** anywhere in your code, VBA dutifully creates a variable named A and stores the value 7 in that variable. Variables you create without declaring them are automatically defined as variant variables, which are discussed in the next section.

Choosing and using data types

When you write a variable declaration, you can simply name the variable. The following statement tells VBA to set aside storage space for a variable named varIable but does not say what sort of information that variable should hold:

```
Dim varIable
```

Alternatively, you declare the variable's *data type* explicitly. The statement

```
Dim sngMyOldSocks As Single
```

declares the variable sngMyOldSocks as of the *single* data type, meaning that it holds a relatively small *floating-point number* (the kind written in scientific notation with a decimal point and an exponent, as in $6.02 \infty 10^{23}$).

VBA recognizes a variety of other distinct data types for your variables, including helpful types like Date and Currency. Familiarize yourself with the available types because collectively they are an important key to writing code that works right. Table 53-2 summarizes key facts about the data types. A later section of this chapter offers tips on working with many of the specific types.

Table 53-2
VBA Data Types

Data Type	Explained	Range of Permitted Values
Boolean	Logical true or false	True (–1) or False (0)
Byte	Small whole number	0 to 255
Integer	Smallish whole number	–32,768 to 32,767
Long	Large whole number	–2,147,483,648 to 2,147,483,647
Single	Single-precision floating-point value	–3.402823E38 to –1.401298E45 for negative values; 1.401298E45 to 3.402823E38 for positive values
Double	Double-precision floating-point value	–1.79769313486232E308 to –4.94065645841247E324 for negative values; 4.94065645841247E324 to 1.79769313486232E308 for positive values
Currency	Large, precise number; 19 significant digits, including four fixed decimal places	–922,337,203,685,477.5808 to 922,337,203,685,477.5807
Decimal	Even larger, more precise number with 29 significant digits and up to 28 decimal places	+/–79,228,162,514,264,337,593, 543,950,335 with no decimal point; +/–7.9228162514264337 593543950335 with 28 places to the right of the decimal
Date	Dates and times	January 1, 100 to December 31, 9999; 00:00:00 to 23:59:59
Object	VBA object	Any object reference
String (Variable)	Sequence of text characters of variable length	0 to approximately 2 billion (variable-length)
String (Fixed-length)	Sequence of specified number of text characters	1 to approximately 65,400 (fixed-length)
Variant	Anything goes	Any numeric value up to the range of a Double; same range as for variable-length String
User-defined (requires the Type statement)	Group of variables used together as a unit	The range of each variable in the group corresponds to its data type (see preceding entries)

Pros and cons of using specific data types

Depending on whom you talk to, declaring a variable as a specific data type — that is, as a type other than *Variant* — is either a great idea or a bad one. The practice definitely makes for smaller and faster programs, but in most cases, the speed and size improvements probably aren't significant.

Here's the background: When you declare a variable's data type carefully, you can select the type requiring the smallest amount of storage space needed to hold the information you plan to keep there. The alternative is to declare it as Variant, a catchall type that can hold any kind of data. (If you don't declare the type, you get a Variant variable by default.)

Variants consume more memory than variables of other types, and accessing their information slows down your program. However, these effects are trivial, unless you work with very large numbers of variables. By declaring all variables as Variants, you can reduce errors and make your code easier to write, more flexible, and less complicated to modify. I don't have room to explore this issue in detail, but you should be aware that some very good programmers recommend coding exclusively with Variants.

Tip   You can declare Variants just as you would variables of other types, as in this example:

```
Dim varTootSuite As Variant
```

However, because Variant is the default data type, you can get by with simply listing the variable name in your Dim statement, as shown here:

```
Dim TootSuite
```

Force yourself to use explicit declarations

Whether you decide to declare each variable as a specific data type or use Variant for all your variables, you should set VBA to force you to declare them. When you place the statement

```
Option Explicit
```

in the Declarations section of a module, VBA displays an error message every time you try to use a variable that you haven't declared. Duly reminded, you can go back and add the necessary declaration.

Requiring explicit declarations in this way produces an even more important benefit: It prevents spelling errors from introducing major problems in your code. Imagine this scenario: You decide to wing it without the Option Explicit statement in your module. Still, good little programmer that you are, you declare a variable explicitly. Somewhere in the body of a procedure, however, a random finger spasm strikes while you're typing the variable name. When the VBA compiler encounters this line, it thinks you've just designated a new variable and cheerfully creates it for you. Your program may still run, but don't be surprised if it turns all your text purple or tells you that the world's population just hit 12.

Tip Rather than typing the `Option Explicit` directive in every module, you can have VBA insert it automatically. Go to the Tools➪Options dialog box. On the Editor tab, check the box labeled Require Variable Declaration.

Specifying a variable's scope

A variable's *scope* — that is, where in your program the variable is accessible — depends on two interacting factors:

✦ The location where you declare the variable (either inside a procedure or in the Declarations section of a module — see "Where to declare variables," earlier in this chapter)

✦ The keyword you use to declare the variable (`Dim`, `Public`, `Private`, or `Static`)

If you declare a variable inside a procedure using `Dim`, you can use that variable only inside that procedure. Elsewhere in your program, VBA won't recognize the variable. Variables declared with `Dim` in the module's Declarations section are accessible throughout the module — but not from other modules.

Private variables

The `Private` keyword works exactly like Dim. The two declaration statements shown here function identically:

```
Private strLouie As String
Dim strLouie As String
```

Tip Because `Private` and `Dim` work the same way, you can forget about `Private` if you like. You may want to use `Private` instead of `Dim`, however, to remind yourself when you read the code that the variable is accessible only in the current module or procedure.

Public variables

Declaring a variable with `Public` makes the variable accessible throughout your entire project. Here's an example:

```
Public intBeulah As Integer
```

However, `Public` has its special power only if you declare the variable in the Declarations section of a module. Although VBA accepts `Public` declarations within procedures, the variables so declared are still inaccessible outside the procedure where you declare them.

The Static advantage

Use Static to declare a variable within a procedure when you want the variable to remain in memory—and even more important, to retain its value—even when the procedure isn't running.

In the following example, the variable intLastingVariable acts as a counter, recording the number of times the procedure runs:

```
Sub TransientProcedure()
    Dim strTransientVariable As String
    Static intLastingVariable As Integer
    strTransientVariable = Format(Now(), "Medium Time")
    intLastingVariable = intLastingVariable + 1
    MsgBox "The time is " & strTransientVariable & _
        ". " & "You have executed this procedure " & _
        intLastingVariable & " times."
End Sub
```

In the example, the statement intLastingVariable = intLastingVariable + 1 adds 1 to the value of the variable each time the procedure runs. If you declare intLastingVariable with Dim instead of Static, the variable always starts with the same value (zero) with every pass through the procedure—which means the procedure is essentially worthless.

You can only declare Static variables within a procedure. If you want *all* the variables in a procedure to remain intact even when the procedure isn't running, declare the whole procedure as Static. In the procedure declaration, place the keyword Static immediately before the Sub or Function keyword that defines the type of procedure you're declaring. Here are a couple of examples of this technique:

```
Private Static Sub DoItAll ()
Static Function DontDoVeryMuch(intTimeToWaste as Integer)
```

Note that Static comes after Private or Public in the procedure declaration, if you include either of these optional scope-related keywords.

Declaring multiple variables on the same line

To conserve space, you're free to declare more than one variable on the same line of code. You need only type the Dim keyword once per line; commas should separate the variables. Remember to specify the data type for *each* variable you declare—even if all the variables on the line are of the same type. Here's an example of the right way to do it:

```
Dim intA As Integer, intD As Integer, intL As Integer
```

Mixing data types on the same line works, too:

```
Dim curNetWorth As Currency, datSecondTuesday As Date
```

Caution Declaring multiple variables on the same line increases the likelihood you'll accidentally fail to specify a data type. Any variables on the line for which you don't supply a data type are automatically registered as variants. If your declaration reads

```
Dim strX, strY, strZ As String
```

`strX` and `strY` are treated as variants, not string variables.

After you've declared a variable, the next thing you do with it, usually, is fill it with information (putting known information into a variable for the first time is called *initializing* the variable). To place information in a variable, you *assign* the value of the information to the variable. Whenever it suits your purposes, you can store different data in the variable by assigning a different value to it.

Giving assignments

To assign a value to a variable, all it takes is one little equal sign. For instance, to store the number 3 in a variable named `intC`, just type

```
intC = 3
```

In VBA, an *assignment statement* consists of an equal sign between a variable on the left and an *expression* specifying the variable's value on the right. In the example, the expression is simply the number value 3. Values you specify directly like this are called *literal* values. (See "Expression-ism" for the definition of expressions.)

Take a look at another assignment statement:

```
strQuote = "Ask not what your country can do for you," _
    & " ask what you can do for your country."
```

In this case, the statement assigns all the text to the right of the equal sign to the variable `strQuote`. As before, the information in this statement's expression consists entirely of literal values — the actual text you want to place in the variable. However, the statement is broken up over two lines, so the text expression has to be divided into two separate strings. That & sign tells VBA to join them together. No matter how many parts an expression has, VBA computes its overall value and *then* assigns that value to the variable.

Tip Understand that until an assignment statement actually executes, it isn't a statement of fact. In math, when you write an equation such as 2 + 2 = 4, you're proclaiming that the values on either side of the equal sign are actually equal. By contrast, a VBA assignment statement *compels* the variable to become equal to the expression's value. Another assignment statement can change the variable's value at any time.

Using variables in assignment statements

You can assign a variable a value based on other variables as well as on literal values.

The statement `curSalePrice = curCost * sngMargin` multiplies the `curCost` and `sngMargin` variables together and assigns that result to the `curSalePrice` variable. VBA makes the necessary calculation based on the current values stored in those variables.

Using functions in assignment statements

Functions and `Function` procedures can also be used in assignment statements, as in this example:

```
strFavorite = InputBox("What's your favorite flavor?")
```

Each function or `Function` procedure returns a value. In this example, the `InputBox` function displays a little dialog box with the specified message and provides space for the user of your program to type in a response. That response is the value returned by the function, in the form of a string (more on the `InputBox` function in Chapter 56).

Expression-ism

An *expression* is a portion of a VBA statement that can be evaluated to give a value, such as a number, a text string, or a reference to an object. It can consist of one or more of the following, in any combination:

✦ Variables, such as `bytMonth` or `boolWinter`

✦ Literal values such as 1234 or "This is only a test."

✦ Constants, which stand in for literal values and are covered later in this chapter

✦ VBA functions such as `InputBox()` or `Sqr()`

✦ Function procedures in your code

If the expression has more than one of these elements, they are joined with *operators* such as the + sign, or in some cases, by nesting functions and `Function` procedures inside other functions and `Function` procedures. Note that if an expression has more than one component, each component is itself an expression—it has a value.

What's in a variable before you assign it a value?

When VBA runs a procedure, it creates storage space for each variable and assigns an initial "nothing in here" value to the variable. Most of the time you assign your own information to a variable before using it in any other statements. But it's quite possible, and sometimes useful, to access a variable before you know for sure whether it contains any of your own data.

Suppose that your program has a procedure that runs only under certain conditions. Suppose also that this procedure assigns a value to one of the program's variables. In this situation, another procedure might check to see whether the variable contains a value as a way to see whether the first procedure has already been executed. Table 53-3 lists the values that your variables contain before you assign any values to them yourself.

Table 53-3
Default Values of Data Types

Data Type	Initial Value
All numeric data types	0
String (variable-length)	A string of zero length ("")
String (fixed-length)	A string of the specified length consisting of ASCII character code 0 — which isn't a visible character
Variant	Empty (a special value indicating a variant with no contents)
Object	Nothing (a special value indicating that no object reference has been assigned to the variable)

Working with Constants

When your program uses a value that *doesn't* change, you don't need a variable to represent that value. Although you can always place literal values in the meat of your procedures, declaring *constants* to represent these values is usually better.

Declaring constants

Use a `Const` statement to declare constants:

```
Const cstrPetsName As String = "Foo-foo"
Const cdtmTargetDate As Date = #6/23/01#
Const cblnUp As Boolean = True
```

Note that this technique is quite similar to the way you declare variables. The difference is that you specify the value of the constant when you declare it. You can declare constants as any of the same data types you use for variables except object, user-defined, and, for now, decimal (refer to Table 53-2).

Notice also that I declared the name of each constant with an initial lowercase *c* (standing for "constant," of course). This method is the simplest way and is the common practice used to indicate that a declared name is a constant rather than a variable. However, you can choose another meaningful prefix if you prefer.

You might follow the example of VBA itself and choose a prefix based on your name, or on the name of your VBA project. VBA and Visual Basic identify constants with the prefix vb, as in `vbBlue` (representing the code number for the color blue, 16711680) or `vbKeyTab` (representing the code for the Tab key, 9). VBA applications often name the constants they define using an application-specific prefix, as in the Excel constant `xlBarStacked` (representing the code for a stacked bar chart, 58).

 Tip   By the way, you're free to use the constants defined by VBA or your VBA application in your own programs. You can use the Help system or the Object Browser to locate information on these predefined constants (see Chapter 52 for a discussion of the Object Browser).

The benefits of a constant approach

After you declare a constant, you can use it by name in your program wherever you would have entered the corresponding literal values. For instance, suppose that you write a program that determines an employee's salary based on his shoe size. One way to code a part of the program would be

```
If bytShoeSize > 12 Then
    curJoesSalary = 75000
End If
```

One problem with this approach is that it "hard-codes" the exact salary amount in your program. If a rising cost of living increases salaries across the board, you have to dig through your code to find the amount that needs changing. And if you use the same value more than once in the program, you have to change each occurrence — and you run a bigger risk that typing errors can creep in and gum up the works.

Here's the same code written with a constant:

```
Const CcurTopSalaryStep As Currency = 75000
...
If bytShoeSize > 12 Then
    curJoesSalary = CcurTopSalaryStep
End If
```

With this solution, it's easy to locate the constant declaration at the top of the module or procedure. Change the constant's value there, and you instantly alter your code to match at every place the constant appears. As a bonus, the code is much easier to understand. Instead of asking, "What does this number 75000 represent?" you know at a glance that Joe is due the top step of the salary scale if he wears size 12 shoes.

You *could* use a variable to gain the advantages of a constant. However, variables take up space in memory, and more important, you run the risk of accidentally changing the variable's "constant" value in your program.

Using constants to represent attributes

Constants are handy for working with a group of named elements or characteristics such as days of the week (Monday, Tuesday, and so on) or tastes (sweet, salty, sour, and bitter). Instead of manipulating the names of these items as text strings in your program, an easier approach is to pick a number to represent each item and then declare a constant equal to that number based on the item's name. From then on, you can refer to the items by name rather than number. Here's code that uses this technique:

```
Const cbytSweet = 1, cbytSalty = 2
Const cbytSour = 3, cbytBitter = 4
Do While intTaste = cbytSour
    AddSweetener
    intTaste = CheckTaste()
Loop
```

Hello, Operators

In VBA, an *operator* is a special symbol or keyword in an expression that combines two values (subexpressions, if you will) to give a new result. The two values are listed on either side of the operator. In the following expression, the + (addition) operator adds 3 to the value of the intA variable.

```
intA + 3
```

VBA includes operators in three main categories, arithmetic, comparison, and logical, plus a few miscellaneous operators such as the ones for string *concatenation*.

Caution   When used with text strings, the + operator performs concatenation, not addition — it joins the two strings together. But it's better to use the "real" concatenation operator, the & symbol. VBA interprets the expression

```
"My name is " & "Ellie."
```

as "My name is Ellie."

Here's a comparison operator at work:

```
Tan(sngAngleA) <> 1.4
```

The <> symbol is the "not equal to" operator. It tests to see whether the two values in the expression are unequal, returning a result of True or False. If the tangent of sngAngleA is *not* equal to 1.4, the result of this expression is True. Otherwise, the result is False.

Taking precedence

In fancier expressions that include more than one operator, VBA has to figure out which operation to perform first, second, and third. Take the expression

```
intA + intB * intC
```

It contains two operators, + (the addition operator) and * (the multiplication operator). In English, you would read the entire thing as "intA plus intB times intC."

Although the * symbol is the second operator in the expression, it has *precedence* over the addition operator. VBA first multiplies intB times intC and then adds this result to intA. As this example illustrates, VBA follows a fixed sequence in evaluating the parts of an expression when it contains more than one operator.

You can use parentheses to override the predetermined precedence order by which operators are processed. If you type

```
(intA + intB) * intC
```

VBA first adds the first two variables and then multiplies intC's value by that number.

Without parentheses to guide it, what rules does VBA follow when deciding which operator to process first? If the expression includes two or more categories of operators, VBA evaluates all the operators in each category in the following order:

1. Arithmetic and concatenation operators come first.

2. Comparison operators follow.

3. Logical operators are processed last.

Within a category, VBA applies preset rules to determine which operator comes first. Arithmetic, comparison, and logical operators are processed according to the order shown in Table 53-4. VBA takes comparison operators as they come, working from left to right. If two or more operators at the same level of precedence appear in an expression, VBA processes them from left to right as well.

Table 53-4
VBA Operators and Their Precedence Order *

Operator	Operation Performed	Details, Comments
Arithmetic		
^	Exponentiation	Raises the preceding value in the expression to the power of the value that follows.
-	Negation	Reverses the sign of the next value.
* or /	Multiplication and division	
\	Integer division	Divides but discards any fractional part of the answer rather than rounding it up or down.
Mod	Modulus arithmetic	Divides but returns only the *remainder* of the division as the result.
+ or -	Addition and subtraction	
Concatenation		
&	String concatenation	
Comparison		
=	Equality	
<>	Inequality (not equal to)	
<	Less than	
>	Greater than	
<=	Less than or equal to	
>=	Greater than or equal to	
Like	String comparison to pattern	
Is	Test if two items refer to the same object	
Logical		
Not	Logical not	See "When to use Boolean variables" later in this chapter.
And	Logical and	
Or	Logical or	
Xor	Logical exclusive or	
Eqv	Logical equivalence	
Imp	Logical implication	

* Within each category, operators are processed in the order listed.

Comparing values

VBA has six all-around comparison operators for comparing numeric and string values, plus two special-purpose comparison operators, `Like` (for strings) and `Is` (for objects). (The comparison operators are summarized in Table 53-4.) Note that VBA uses the equal sign, =, as a comparison operator as well as to assign values to variables in declarations.

Tip   The result of an expression based on any of these operators is always either `True` or `False`. For example, here's an expression based on the `<=` (less than or equal to) operator:

```
intX <= 11
```

If the value of `intX` is 12, the result of the expression is `False`, because 12 is not less than 11.

Comparing strings

You can use the comparison operators to compare strings of text as well as numbers. The expression `"Sweetpea" = "Daffodil"` gives `False` as a result — obviously, these two strings are not equal. But in other cases the results of a string comparison aren't so easy to predict. To get the results you want when comparing strings, you have to understand the rules VBA uses to decide whether one string is "greater than" another one.

Unless you specify otherwise, VBA uses a "binary" comparison method. The two strings are compared on the basis of the numeric codes in which the characters are actually stored in your program. In this coding system, common punctuation marks have the lowest numbers, followed by numerals, uppercase letters, lowercase letters, and then accented characters. Because the code numbers for lowercase letters are larger than those for uppercase letters, the expressions `"a" > "A"` and `"a" > "Z"` both give `True` results.

Tip   To use a different, more intuitive method for comparing strings, include the statement `Option Compare Text` in your module's Declarations section. With `Option Compare Text` in force, the strings are compared alphabetically, ignoring case (accented letters are still treated as higher in value than the corresponding unaccented versions). Under these conditions, the following are all `True` expressions:

```
"a" = "A"
"a" < "Z"
"Aunt Hill" < "Žunt Hill"
```

When comparing two strings, VBA starts by comparing the first characters in each string. If these characters differ, the "greater" string is the one with the greater character. If the first characters in each string are the same, VBA then compares the next, and so on.

The Like operator compares a string to a wildcard pattern rather than a specific set of characters. Use it to see whether a string falls within, or outside, a given range. I don't have room here to explain the many details involved in using this operator, but you should know that it exists — it's a powerful tool for handling text.

Using comparison operators in code

The results of a comparison operation can be stored in a variable, typically one of the Boolean data type, using a standard assignment statement:

```
boolTheAnswerIs = 5 > 4
```

Because 5 *is* greater than 4, the result of the greater than operation is True, and in turn VBA assigns True as the value of the boolTheAnwerIs variable.

Tip   The True and False keywords are actually built-in VBA numeric constants, representing the values –1 and 0, respectively. You can assign the result of a comparison to any numeric variable.

Comparison operators are frequently used in conditional statements to decide whether or not to execute a particular branch of code:

```
If intP <= intQ Then
    SomethingWentWrong 'call error-handling procedure
End If
```

Stringing text together

The concatenation operator, &, joins strings together. You can use it with literal strings, string variables, or any function that returns a string value. You can use it repeatedly to construct a long string from multiple string values, as in this example:

```
strA = "You answered " & InputBox("Type an answer:") & _
    " . The correct answer was " & strAnswer & "."
```

After this statement executes, strA might contain "You answered Portugal. The correct answer was Spain."

Note   When assembling large strings from smaller ones, don't forget to build in the spaces and punctuation marks needed in the final string.

Details on Data Types

This section offers tips on when and how to use the garden-variety VBA data types. The object data type is crucial but quite complex, so it rates special treatment in Chapter 54.

Converting between data types

Data types are a convenience for human beings — VBA actually stores all information in numeric form. That being the case, conversions between different data types aren't a big challenge for VBA. VBA comes with many functions for converting one data type to another under your control. Realize, however, that whenever possible, VBA automatically converts between different types of data as the context suggests. For example, the + operator adds the number in a string to a numeric value, as long as the string contains only numerals. Similarly, if you assign a decimal value to an Integer variable, VBA automatically rounds off the value for you.

Understanding variants

The Variant data type provides a one-size-fits-all container for your data storage needs. Variants can hold any kind of data you can use in VBA, including numeric values, strings, dates and times, and objects. What's more, the same variable can store different types of data at different times within a single program. The following code is perfectly acceptable, though hardly very productive:

```
Dim varAnythingGoes As Variant
varAnythingGoes = 3
varAnythingGoes = "I suppose."
varAnythingGoes = #12/31/99 11:59:59 PM#
```

Not only does VBA permit such statements, it also figures out and keeps track of the type of data you're placing in the Variant. After that last statement in the preceding series, for example, varAnythingGoes is cataloged as a Variant/Date variable. You can find out the type of data VBA is currently storing in a Variant by using the TypeName function:

```
strVariantType = TypeName(varAnythingGoes)
```

After this statement executes, the value of strVariantType is "Date".

Because they're so flexible, Variant variables are very convenient. Instead of worrying about which data types to use, all your variables can be Variants, and you can stash any type of data in them as the need arises. However, conventional wisdom has it that Variants cost too much in terms of storage space and speed. For a discussion on this point, see "Choosing and using data types," earlier in this chapter.

Choosing a numeric data type

If you declare data types explicitly, you should choose the smallest possible data type for each variable — your programs can become faster, smaller, and more likely to work properly. Of course, the variable should have enough storage capacity to accommodate the range of values that it may contain. However, any extra room is just wasted space. Table 53-2, shown earlier in the chapter, summarizes the value ranges for each numeric data type.

 **Caution** If your program does calculations with the numbers in a variable, it may be necessary to choose a data type large enough to hold the *result* of those calculations. This can be so even if you don't assign the calculation results to the variable itself.

Here are some tips on specific data types:

✦ Use the Boolean, Byte, Integer, or Long data types to hold whole numbers (the kind without decimals).

✦ Use the Single and Double data types to store floating-point numbers of up to 15 significant digits and their exponents. Though the range of values is huge, be aware that rounding may introduce errors — and these may be significant in operations on values of very different sizes. To assign a floating-point value such as $4.72 \_ 10^{-22}$ to a Single or Double variable, use the following format (VBA assumes the exponent is positive if you leave out a + or – sign after the letter E):

```
sngFloating = 4.72E-22
```

✦ If you need more precise calculations, the Currency data type gives you up to 19 significant digits, and with the Decimal type you can have as many as 29 (neither type provides exponents). In the current version of VBA, however, Decimal isn't a standalone data type — in other words, you can't declare a Decimal variable. Instead, Decimal is only available as a subtype of the Variant data type. To ensure that a number is stored as a decimal variant rather than one of the floating-point types, use the CDec function in the assignment statement.

When to use Boolean variables

Variables of the Boolean data type can hold only one of two values: True (stored as –1) or False (0). Declare a Boolean variable whenever you need to know which of two alternative conditions currently prevails. For example, you might have a variable called boolIsOn, whose value would be True if whatever it is, is on, and False if it's off.

Another way to use Boolean variables is to define other constants with the same values as True and False. Your variable names can then be neutral and the constants can explicitly refer to the two alternative conditions. This is definitely easier to show than to explain:

```
Dim boolBellyButtonStyle as Boolean
Const Innie As Boolean = True
Const Outie As Boolean = False
If boolBellyButtonStyle = Outie Then
    TickleLightly
End If
```

Tip

To toggle the value of a Boolean variable or object property to its opposite, use the `Not` operator. In Word, for example, you can turn on the document map if it's off, or turn it off if it's on, with this line of code:

```
ActiveWindow.DocumentMap = Not ActiveWindow.DocumentMap
```

Working with currency values

The main reason to use the Currency data type for financial work is to ensure accurate results. True, the floating-point data types `Single` and `Double` can store numbers with decimal points (which is what currency values are). However, calculations involving floating-point values often produce small errors, and these drive the bean counters crazy.

Regardless of whether you're working with money, you can use variables of the Currency type any time you need to store larger numbers than you can fit in a Long integer variable, or make calculations on them with more precision than you could get from the floating-point data types. Currency values can have up to 19 significant digits, 15 to the left of the decimal point and 4 to the right (the decimal point is fixed).

Tip

You don't need to declare a variable as Currency to display it as a properly formatted money amount. Use VBA's `Format` function with the "Currency" format to automatically dress up any numeric value as dollars, francs, or whatever is appropriate locally.

Working with dates

Use the Date data type to work conveniently with dates, times, or both. Behind the scenes, VBA encodes a date or time as a number such as 35692.9201273148 — apparently meaningless to mere mortals. But you can ignore this detail and work with dates and times in your programming as you would on paper or in a word processor.

The one trick you have to remember is that you must always type date and time values — date literals — between paired number sign characters. For example, the following statements declare two `Date` variables and assign them values:

```
Dim datWeddingDay As Date, datTimeOfCeremony As Date
datWeddingDay = #4/20/99#
datTimeOfCeremony = #3:15:00 PM#
```

As with currency, VBA automatically outputs dates according to local formatting customs. The expression `Format (#10/24/89#, "Long date")` gives the string `"Tuesday, October 24, 1989"` in the United States, `"Terça-feira, 24 de Outubro de 1989"` in Brazil.

Entering date values

You can type date literals in just about any format that appeals to you. The following are all acceptable:

```
#09/1/2001#
#Sep 25, 93#
#Janua 9 1905#
```

If the Visual Basic Editor recognizes your entry as a valid date, it converts it into the "short form" date format specified in the Windows Control Panel. If you omit the year, VBA adds the current year for you. The conversion happens as soon as the insertion point moves off the line, before you run your program.

Time has value

Enter time literals in the format #*hours:minutes:seconds symbol*#, where *symbol* is AM or PM. Examples include the following:

```
#10:45:00 PM#
#2:3:30 AM#
```

You don't have to type in leading zeros, as in #01:02:03 PM#; VBA adds them for you when you move the cursor to another line of code. Similarly, you can omit portions of the time value you don't need, but VBA fills in the blanks. For example, you can enter seconds alone by typing something like #0:0:23#, but VBA changes such an entry into a complete time value, in this case #12:00:23 AM#.

Date and time math

Adding or subtracting dates with the standard VBA arithmetic operators is *possible*, but unfortunately, it doesn't work the way you would expect. For example, #3/19/2005# - #3/19/2004 does not equal "1 year," but #12/30/1900#. The explanation has to do with the way VBA stores date data, which I won't trouble you with here. All you really need to know is that VBA has two functions, DateAdd() and DateDiff(), that handle all your needs for date math. For details, look them up in Help.

In contrast, you *can* do time calculations fairly easily with the regular arithmetic operators. Take a gander at the following expressions:

```
#07:15 AM# + #12:00# ' = #07:15:00 PM#
#07:15:00 AM# - #0:15 AM# ' = #07:00:00 AM#
#07:15:15 AM# + #0:0:30 AM# ' = #07:15:45 AM#
```

The examples show the minimum entries you can type. As always, VBA converts your entries into complete time literals — 0:0:30 AM# becomes #12:00:30 AM#, for example.

Stringing you along

Because VBA so freely converts between different data types, you may need string variables less often than you think. If all you need to do is display a nonstring value in a form that humans can read, you don't need to convert it into a string first. Instead, you can use a number or date — or a variable containing one — as the argument to a function or as the value of an object property that by rights should be a string.

What you *really* need string variables for is to work with nonnumeric characters, that is, letters and punctuation marks. You can't get these out of number values, no way, nohow.

Tip Careful programming practice dictates that you explicitly convert numeric values into strings before manipulating them as such. If you follow this advice, you're likely to make fewer errors and produce code that's more understandable. Still, it's nice to know you can output variables with so little work.

Along the same lines, you don't really have to use those quote marks when you assign values to a string. Ever the pampering parent, VBA makes its best effort to convert numeric, date, or currency values into strings. If your program executes this code:

```
Dim strGString As String
strGString = #July 22, 1904#
```

the strGString variable will contain the string 7/22/1904 until some other statement changes it. But it's better to assign the actual text in quotation marks to make sure that the variable contains exactly what you intend.

Tip Use VBA's Chr and Asc functions to convert a numeric value (representing an ANSI character code) to the corresponding text character, and vice versa. Chr lets you place characters you can't type (such as quotation marks) in your strings. Asc returns the numeric code of the *first* character in a string.

Working with Arrays

Frequently, you need to work with similar chunks of information together as a group. That situation calls for an *array*, a structured storage compartment for multiple data elements of the same type.

Cross-Reference If you're working with a set of items, one alternative to an array is a Collection object, discussed in Chapter 54.

Suppose you have a list of numbers representing prices, test scores, or the distances of certain astronomical objects from Earth. Imagine typing that list on a piece of paper, with each item on separate rows. What you wind up with is a simple array. Here is an example:

Surefire winning lottery numbers

214236

891982

545273

000000

371453

941241

In this list of very similar items, the individual items have unique values but otherwise lack special identifying characteristics. If you want someone else to ponder an item, you say something like "it's the third item in the lottery-number list." VBA arrays work exactly this way.

About the items in an array

Each VBA array has a name, corresponding to the title of the paper list. To work with an individual item in the array, you refer to it by the array name and an *index*, a positive integer number specifying its "slot" in the array. For example, the expression `intLottoArray (3)` refers to the third item (or fourth, depending on the numbering system in effect) in the array called `intLottoArray`. As you can guess, the `int` at the beginning of the array name lets you know that this is supposed to be an array of integer values. Therefore, it's a safe bet that the data stored in `intLottoArray(3)` is an integer.

You should be clear about two key points regarding arrays:

✦ **You can create arrays of any data type.** VBA will happily store strings, dates, currency values, and any numeric data type in arrays.

✦ **Any one array can hold only one data type.** You can't build an array with separate slots for both `Date` and `String` data-type values. However, the `Variant` data type can store any kind of VBA data; arrays of `Variant`s are perfectly okay.

Array dimensions

An important concept concerning arrays is that they can have multiple *dimensions*. The simple list in the preceding example is a one-dimensional array. A table or spreadsheet with rows and columns corresponds to a two-dimensional array. VBA arrays can have up to 60 dimensions.

Declaring arrays

As with ordinary variables, arrays must be declared before you can use them to store data. Fortunately, declaring an array is just like declaring a variable, with one addition to the declaration statement: You add parentheses following the variable name. The parentheses can be empty, if you want to define the array's dimension later. Alternatively, they can contain values specifying the size of each dimension in the array.

This example declares an array of Currency data but doesn't set its size or dimensions:

```
Public curPriceQuotes () As Currency
```

The next statement declares a one-dimensional array of 12 items of Date data:

```
Dim datTimeOfImpact (12) As Date
```

This statement declares a four-dimensional array of Integer data:

```
Dim intArrayOfIntegers (34, 13, 29, 4) As Integer
```

The total number of individual data elements in an array is equal to the product of the sizes of each dimension, of course. Multiple-dimension arrays can be very large data sets.

Numbering array elements and determining the size of your array

Unless you specify otherwise, the elements in an array are numbered beginning with 0 — or to put it slightly differently, element 0 is the first one in the array. Because this is so, the value you enter when sizing an array should be one less than the number of elements you want to store. If the array is supposed to hold 10 elements, enter **9** as the size.

When you later access the individual data elements in the array, you must keep in mind this numbering system. A reference to intArray (1) is actually a reference to the second element in the array. If you don't like counting from 0, you can start numbering your array from a different number — which would usually be 1. To set things up so VBA numbers all arrays in the current module starting from 1, place the statement Option Base 1 in the module's Declarations section (before any procedures). This statement affects only arrays in the same module, so you must include it in every module if that's how you want to number all your arrays.

Declaring fixed and dynamic arrays

If you specify the size of the array when you declare it, its size remains fixed — your program can't make the array smaller or larger later. To declare a *fixed array*, include the size of each of the array's dimensions in the parentheses in the declaration statement.

Tip   Fixing the size of an array when you declare it can be good practice if you know for sure the array size won't change.

To declare a *dynamic* array, just leave out the array's size when you declare it. Declare your array as a *dynamic array* if you

✦ Don't or can't know the size of your array before your program runs.

✦ Know the array's size will change during the course of your program.

✦ Want to free up the memory it occupies for other variables after you're through using the array. A large array can use lots of memory, which you can liberate if the array is dynamic.

Tip   A dynamic array can't hold any data until you actually create the array by specifying its size. Use the `ReDim` ("redimension") statement to do so, as in this example of a one-dimensional array:

```
Redim datBirthdays (intNumberOfBirthdays - 1)
```

You can (so to speak) re-`Redim` a dynamic array as many times as you like, completely redefining the number of dimensions it has and their sizes.

Caution   In most cases, resizing an array destroys its current contents.

Addressing elements in an array

To work with a particular element in an array in your code, list the array name followed by the element's *index* in parentheses. The index contains an integer value for each array dimension. For example, the expression `strSayings (4,6)` uniquely identifies the string data at row 4, column 6 in a two-dimensional array of strings.

With this system, you can use array data elements just as you would variables. You can

✦ Assign a value to an array element. In this example a value is assigned to a single storage slot in a 3-D array of `Currency` values:

```
curBigDough (5,8,19) = 27.99
```

✦ Assign a value stored in an array to another variable:

```
datThatDate = datTheseDates (25, 10)
```

✦ Use the value of an array element in an expression:

```
intA = 35 * (intB + intCounts (3,2))
```

You're not restricted to literal values in the index. It's often crucial to code the index with variables, and let your program decide which array element you need at the moment. The last line of the following program shows this method in action:

```
Dim strTodaysFortune (29)
Dim intUserChoice As Integer
... ' Code assigning strings to the array goes here
intUserChoice = InputBox ("To see your fortune, enter" _
    & " a number between 1 and 30")
msgBox (strTodaysFortune (intUserChoice - 1))
```

Built-in Functions and Statements

Before you get rolling on writing your own procedures from scratch, be sure you're not reinventing the wheel. VBA comes equipped with a little arsenal of built-in commands that can blast through many common tasks. Covering these functions and statements would take space I don't have. About all I can do is point you in the direction of the VBA help files and reference books on VBA or Visual Basic.

 **Tip** By the way, although Excel's built-in worksheet functions are not VBA functions, you *can* use them in any VBA program if you first add to the project a reference to the Excel object library. Chapter 57 tells how to add object references, and Chapter 30 gives techniques for working with Excel functions in VBA code.

Where to find built-in commands

Keeping in mind that an action may fall into an unexpected category, VBA gives you three types of built-in commands for doing useful work:

✦ **Statements.** Although the term "statement" usually encompasses a complete programming directive, VBA also refers to individual keywords for specific chores as statements. Some of these statement keywords function as complete statements in themselves. For example, the statement

```
Beep
```

sounds the computer speaker. (Please, don't go overboard with that one.) Other statement keywords must be used as part of a complete statement. For example, the ChDir (change directory) "statement" is useless unless you include with it an argument specifying the directory, or folder, you want to change to

```
ChDir("\Documents about Dreams")
```

✦ **Functions.** The built-in functions act just like the Function procedures — that is, they return a value. Often, you use a function by assigning its value to a variable, as in this example with the Tan (tangent) function:

```
dblTangent = Tan(dblAnyOldAngle)
```

Functions are also used to provide values in more complex expressions, or in conditional statements, such as the following:

```
If Tan (dblAcuteAngle) < 45 Then
```

✦ **Methods** of built-in objects. The curious one in this group is the `Print` method, the `Debug` object's only one. You use it to direct output to the Immediate window in the Visual Basic Editor with a statement such as the following:

```
Debug.Print(strMessageFromMars)
```

Table 53-5 lists examples of built-in VBA commands, drawn from all three categories (statements, functions, and methods).

Table 53-5
Examples of Built-in Functions, Statements, and Methods

Command	Type	What It Does
Randomize	Statement	Initializes the random number generator.
Sqr (number)	Function	Returns the square root of *number*.
Format (string)	Function	Formats string according to your specifications.
Date	Statement	Sets the system date.
Date	Function	Returns the current system date.
Err.Raise	Method of Err object	Generates a run-time error by ID number.

Categories of built-in commands

VBA's built-in commands fall into the following categories:

✦ **Formatting data.** VBA's `Format` function formats any of the built-in data types for display or print purposes according to a pattern you specify. Via the `Format` function, you can easily output a date variable—which VBA actually stores as an unintelligible number—in any of many different typical formats such as 11/09/99, or Friday, July 9, 2001. If none of the built-in formats will do, you can create your own formats for reuse with the `Format` function.

✦ **Converting data.** Although VBA converts data types on the fly—and automatically—VBA also includes many explicit conversion functions. They're useful for ensuring that VBA performs the correct conversion, performing conversions that VBA won't do automatically, and making your code self-explanatory. Examples of these conversion functions: `CByte`, `Fix`, `Hex`, and `Val`.

✦ **Manipulating strings.** VBA offers a rich collection of statements and functions for formatting text strings and extracting portions of them that you may find especially mesmerizing.

✦ **Working with dates and times.** VBA offers a panoply of statements and functions for finding out what day or time it is now, making date-related calculations, and extracting from a date variable the component of interest, be it the year, the day of the week, or the hour.

✦ **Interacting with the user.** The MsgBox and InputBox functions display simple dialog boxes that let you talk to the program's users, and let them talk back.

✦ **Performing mathematical and financial calculations.** VBA comes chock full of prefab functions for manipulating numbers. These perform chores ranging from the very simple (such as returning an absolute value or a number's sign) through the staple computations of algebra and trigonometry. If the bottom line is sinking, VBA's healthy dose of financial functions may be just what you need to float the business boat again.

✦ **Handling miscellaneous chores.** You can tap a wide array of commands for working with files on disk, inserting and examining entries in the Windows Registry, manipulating variables, and other chores.

Controlling the Flow

Control structures are code statements that determine what the procedure does next, based on a condition that is in effect at the time the code runs. VBA offers a healthy assortment of powerful control structures falling into three main groups: conditional statements, loops, and the With statement:

✦ **A conditional statement** determines which branch of code to execute based on whether a condition is True or False. VBA conditional statements include If...Then (in several permutations) and Select Case.

✦ **A loop** repeatedly executes a block of code, either a fixed number of times or until some condition becomes True or False. When you know in advance how many times to execute a loop, use a For...Next loop. If your code must test some condition to see whether to continue running a loop, use the Do...Loop statement (available in multiple flavors). And to repeat actions on the objects in a collection, use a For Each...Next loop.

✦ **The With statement** enables you to perform multiple actions using the same object without having to name the object in each action.

Control structures lend clarity, organization, and, well, *structure* to your program. They make it relatively easy to trace the branches of the path your program follows as it runs.

Control structure anatomy

What makes a control structure a "structure" is that it's not just a single statement, but rather a whole block of them. A basic If...Then statement can serve as a model for all control structures:

```
If a < b Then      ' If a is less than b, then
     b = a         '    set b equal to a
     a = c         '    and then set a equal to c.
End If             ' That's all—proceed with the program.
```

The skeleton of this structure is an opening statement that identifies its type and sets up a condition, and a statement that tells VBA where the structure ends. Sandwiched in between is the meat of the structure, the statements that actually *do* something.

All control structures have this general outline, except that in some of them, the structure's condition comes in the last statement rather than the first.

Nesting control structures

When you're talking about control structures, *nesting* means to place one structure inside another, above (that is, preceding) the statement that marks the end of the first structure. VBA enters the second structure before it finishes executing the first. Nesting is a necessity for solving many complex, real-life programming problems. You can nest control structures to as many levels as you think necessary.

In the following example, a Do While...Loop structure is *nested* inside an If...Then structure, and another If...Then structure is nested inside the Do While...Loop:

```
If a < b Then
    Do While b > c
        b = b - 1
        If c > d Then
            d = a
        End If    ' End of inner If...Then
    Loop          ' End of Do While
End If             ' End of outer If...Then
```

The road taken: Using condition expressions

Making choices is as fundamental in software as in life. Although simple in concept, decision-making control structures are some of the most powerful programming tools at your disposal. They choose which of two or more different blocks of code to execute. But after one block executes and the other does not, you will say (with Robert Frost), "And that has made all the difference."

To decide whether to execute a block of code, three of VBA's control structures evaluate a *condition expression* that you write. These include the Do...Loop looping structure as well as the two explicitly named conditional statements, If...Then and Select Case. I devote the rest of this section to discussion of the condition expressions used in all three of these structures. Two other decision-making controls structures, For...Next and For Each...Next, don't use condition expressions.

How condition expressions work

If...Then, Select Case, and Do...Loop structures all decide what to do based on one simple test: Is the condition True, or is it False? The condition in question can be any VBA expression. (And remember, 0 is equal to False in VBA. All other values are considered True.) Most often, condition expressions are built around a comparison operator that compares the values of two subexpressions. VBA's set of comparison operators are listed and discussed earlier in this chapter. However, you can get the basic idea by looking at the sample statements in the Table 53-6.

Table 53-6
Sample Condition Expressions

Expression	Translation in English
a < b	Item a is less than b.
b = c	Item b is equal to c.
colTBears("Henry") Is objCurrentBear	The object stored in the colTBears collection under the "Henry" is the same one now referred to by the ojbCurrentBear variable.
sqr (1/x * 29.3234) >= CDbl (strNumber) + 12	The square root of the quantity 1 divided by x times 29.3234 is greater than or equal to the numeric value of the string variable strNumber plus 12.

Using logical operators in conditions

A logical operator evaluates two subexpressions separately as True or False and then combines them according to a set of rules to produce a final value — also True or False — based on a set of rules. The most important logical operators — or at least the ones that are easiest to figure out how to use — are And, Or, and Xor. Table 53-7 shows how they work.

Table 53-7
Logical Operators

Operator	Returns True	Examples	Result
And	Only if *both* subexpressions are True	3 * 2 = 6 And 12 > 11 2 + 2 = 4 And 4 - 2 = 1	True False
Or	If *either* subexpression is True	10 > 20 Or 20 > 10 5 < 4 Or 6 < 5	True False
Xor	If only one subexpression is True (returns False if both expressions are True or both are False)	5 + 5 < 9 Xor 5 + 5 = 10 5 + 5 > 9 Xor 5 + 5 = 10 5 + 5 < 9 Xor 5 + 5 <> 10	True False False

Using If...Then Statements

By far the most commonly used conditional statements are If...Then and its variations, If...Then...Else and If...ElseIf.

The basic form: If...Then

At its most basic, an If...Then statement executes a special block of code if the condition you feed it is True, but simply does nothing if the condition is False. The syntax is

```
If condition Then
(statements to execute if condition is True)
End If
```

When VBA executes an If...Then statement, if *condition* is True, it plows through the statements between If and End If. If *condition* is False, it skips over them, continuing with the next statement in your program. Note that the Then keyword goes on the same line as If and the condition expression. Be sure to include the End If statement or you get an error message.

One-liners with If...Then

When an If...Then structure has to execute only a single statement if the condition is True, you can put the entire thing on one line. In that situation (and only that one), an End If statement isn't required — in fact, it's illegal. The following statement is an example:

```
If curPrice > 20 Then MsgBox "Warning! Price too high!"
```

It functions identically to this structure:

```
If curPrice > 20 Then
    MsgBox "Warning! Price too high!"
End If
```

Using If...Then...Else statements

If you want your program to choose between two alternative blocks of code based on a condition, you need an If...Then...Else statement. In this case, one block is executed if the condition is True, and a completely different block is executed if the condition is False. Here's the syntax:

```
If condition Then
(statements to execute if condition is True)
Else
(statements to execute if condition is False)
End If
```

If condition is True, VBA executes the first block of statements and then skips over the rest of the structure to the line of code following the End If statement. On the other hand, if condition is False, only the statements in the block following Else get executed.

In the following example, the condition expression checks to see whether the control on a VBA form is a command button. If so, it paints the button's background color red. All other controls are painted cyan (sky blue).

```
If TypeOf ctlCurrentControl Is CommandButton Then
    ctlCurrentControl.BackColor = &HFF& 'Red
Else
    ctlCurrentControl.BackColor = &HFFFF00  'Cyan
End If
```

In the example, you can assume that the ctlCurrentControl variable already holds an object reference to a particular control on the form. The TypeOf keyword enables you to check whether the object referred to by a variable or other object reference is of a specific type, in this case a CommandButton object.

Cross-Reference For more about forms and controls, see Chapter 56.

If...Then complexities

Frequently you need to test two or more conditions before you know what path your program should take. It's a lot like real life: If you were writing a book (to use a purely random example), you might be thinking something like, "If I finish by the deadline and if I don't run out of money before then and if the dollar holds its value against the peso, then I can go to Mexico for two weeks in October. But if the dollar falls, I'll have to settle for Turlock." Depending on the specific tests involved, you may need to include `ElseIf` clauses in your `If...Then` structure, or to nest one or more levels of `If...Then` statements.

Complexities part I: Using If...ElseIf statements

Use the `ElseIf` keyword to test a new condition when you want to execute certain statements only if the first condition *isn't* `True`. The syntax is as follows:

```
If condition1 Then
(statements to execute if condition1 is True)
ElseIf condition2
(statements to execute if condition1 is False but condition2 is
True)
ElseIf condition3
(statements to execute if condition1 and condition2 are both
False but condition3 is True)
... (additional ElseIf clauses)
Else ' optional clause
(statements to execute if all of the conditions are False)
End If
```

Only one `ElseIf` clause is required, but you can have as many as you like. The `Else` clause is optional.

Tip

In an `If...ElseIf` structure, only the statements associated with the first true condition are executed. After they run, any remaining `ElseIf` and `Else` clauses are skipped over. The `Else` clause is optional, but if included, it must be the last one in the structure—which makes sense, if you think about it logically.

Complexities part II: Nesting If...Then statements

Nested `If...Then` statements are sort of the opposite of `If...ElseIf` statements. Use them when you want to test a second condition to decide whether to execute a block of code, but only if the first condition is `True`. Nesting two `If...Then` statements is like saying, "If X is true *and* Y is true, then I'm going to do A, B, and C."

You can nest `If...Then` statements of any variety—`If...Then...Else`, `If...ElseIf`, or garden variety `If...Then`—in any combination. In schematic form, here's a pair of nested `If...Then` statements:

```
If condition1 Then
    If condition2 Then
    (statements that execute if both condition 1 and
      condition2 are True)
    ElseIf condition3 Then
```

```
    (statements that execute if condition1 and condition3
        are True but condition2 is False)
    End If    ' Ends the inner If...Then block
  (other statements that execute if condition1 is True,
      regardless of condition2)
Else
  (statements that only execute if condition1 is False
End If
```

The following simple example of nested `If...Then` statements displays a congratulatory message box for high grades achieved with at least a nominally full-time schedule:

```
If sngGPA > 3.5 Then
    If sngUnits > 10 Then
        MsgBox "You're on the Dean's list!"
    End If
End If
```

Complexities part III: Using logical operators in conditions

Using logical operators in condition expressions can be a more elegant alternative to `ElseIf` clauses and nested `If...Then` structures — but only when just one branch of a multiple-condition path has the statements you want to execute. For example, look at the code fragment just before the heading of this section. You could accomplish exactly the same goal with a single `If...Then` statement, as follows:

```
If sngGPA > 3.5 And sngUnits > 10 Then
        MsgBox "You're on the Dean's list!"
    End If
```

Using Select Case Statements

`If...ElseIf` and nested `If...Then` statements are ideal for testing different expressions before deciding which block of code to execute. If, however, you need to test the *same* value against different conditions, a `Select Case` statement is the way to go. Here's the syntax:

```
Select Case value
Case test1
(statements to be executed if value meets test1
    criteria)
Case test2
(statements to be executed if value meets test2
    criteria)
... ' additional Case clauses
```

```
Case Else  ' optional
(statements to be executed if value meets none of the
    above criteria)
End Case
```

Testing conditions in Select Case statements

The Select Case structure doesn't directly use complete condition expressions of the type outlined earlier. Instead, you have to break up each condition into two parts, represented by *value* and *test*n in the preceding syntax. If the equivalent condition expression is

```
a + b > c
```

you can think of *value* as the part to the left of the comparison operator (a + b) and *test*n as everything to the right, including the operator (> c).

A sample Select Case statement

You definitely need an example to illustrate how a "real" Select Case structure might look. In the code that follows, objRollOfFilm is an object representing a roll of film and has a Type property corresponding to the type of film. Here's the listing:

```
Select Case objRollOfFilm.Type
Case "Slide"
    intCountSlide = intCountSlide + 1
Case "ColorPrint"
    intCountColorPrint = intCountColorPrint + 1
Case "BWPrint"
    intCountBWPrint = intCountBWPrint + 1
Case Else
    MsgBox "Not a known type."
End Case
```

At this point in your program you're only concerned about one value, that returned by the Type property, but it must be compared to several possible alternatives. The Select Case statement is perfect for this situation. The example's first Case clause is equivalent to writing If objRollOfFilm.Type = "Slide" Then. That is, if the object's Type property is Slide, then the program executes the next statement; if not, it moves on to Case clause number 2. Notice, though, that the = operator you'd expect is missing from the tests in all three Case clauses. That's because in Select Case statements, equality is assumed to be the comparison you're making.

The Case Else clause

If the value of the Type property isn't equal to the tests in any of the Case clauses, control falls to the Case Else clause, always the last one in a Select Case structure—in this case, the Case Else clause displays an error message. A Case Else clause is optional, because you may not want anything to happen if none of the criteria are satisfied. As in the example, though, it's often wise to include the Case Else clause if only to alert you to unexpected values stored by your program.

More about Case clause tests

The tests performed by the Case clauses in the preceding example are sweet, simple tests of a single equality, as in "Is the Type property equal to such and so?" But you can do much more sophisticated testing with each Case clause. This is easiest to illustrate with a numeric example. Suppose your Select Case statement opens with this line of code:

```
Select Case intPatientAge
```

In this case, the value being tested is an integer variable that represents the age of a patient at a medical clinic. This is the value being tested in the examples shown here:

✦ You can test the value against a range:

```
Case 18 To 35
    Messages("YoungAdult").Print
```

Note that you place the To keyword between the values defining the bounds of the range. The range includes both values as well as everything in between.

✦ You can test the value using a comparison operator other than =:

```
Case Is > 65
    Messages("OlderAdult").Print
```

Here, you're supposed to use the Is keyword before the comparison operator. Actually, you don't have to type *Is*—VBA puts it in for you if you omit it.

✦ You can perform multiple tests in the same Case clause:

```
Case 0 To 5, 15, Is > 55
    Messages("ImmunizationReminder").Print
```

Be sure to separate the tests with commas. By the way, a Case clause with multiple tests is equivalent to an expression built on a series of Or expressions—if the value passes *any* of the tests, the following statements get executed.

Repeating Yourself with Loops

Use a loop control structure to execute the same block of code more than once. This is a fundamental chore when performing many mathematical computations, extracting smaller data items from larger ones, and repeating an action on multiple items in a group.

VBA offers three main types of loop structures. Table 53-8 shows them, and what they're for.

Table 53-8 Loop Structures	
Loop Type	**How It Loops**
Do...Loop	While or until a condition is True
For...Next	A specified number of times
For Each...Next	For each object in a collection

Tip   When working with nested loops, remember this simple truth: the inner loop finishes looping before the outer loop.

Do-ing loops

The various versions of the Do...Loop statement all are designed to repeat a block of code indefinitely, until a condition is met. To determine whether to continue looping, a Do...Loop statement evaluates a condition expression of the same type described earlier in this chapter and used in If...Then statements. Uses for Do...Loop structures are legion; they include the following:

✦ Displaying an error message repeatedly until the user makes a valid entry in a dialog box

✦ Reading data from a disk file until the end of the file is reached

✦ Searching for and counting the number of times a shorter string occurs within a longer one

✦ Idling your program for a set period

✦ Performing actions on all items in an array

✦ With If...Then statements, performing actions with multiple items that meet criteria in an array or collection

Types of Do...Loop statements

VBA offers the Do...Loop in five flavors, but all of them work very much alike. Table 53-9 explains the different types.

Table 53-9 Do...Loop Statements	
Statement	**What It Does**
Do...Loop	Repeat the block indefinitely, exiting when a conditional statement within the loop executes an End Do statement.
Do While...Loop	Begin and repeat the block only if the condition is True.
Do...Loop While	Execute the block once and then repeat it as long as the condition is True.
Do Until...Loop	Begin and repeat the block only if the condition is False.
Do...Loop Until	Execute the block once and then repeat it as long as the condition is False.

Using the Do While...Loop statement

The prototypical Do structure is Do While...Loop. The syntax is as follows:

```
Do While condition
(statements that execute while condition is True)
Loop
```

When it encounters a Do While statement, VBA begins by evaluating *condition*. If it turns out that this expression is False, it ignores the rest of the loop, skipping to the program statement following Loop. But if *condition* is True, VBA executes the statements in the block. When it reaches the Loop statement, it jumps back up to the Do While statement to test the condition again.

Typically, one or more statements in the body of the loop can change the value of *condition*, so it may now be False. If so, VBA terminates the loop and skips over it. But if *condition* is still True, the loop statements again get executed.

The whole process repeats until at some point, *condition* becomes False. In other words, there is no set limit on how many times the block of statements in the loop get executed. Assuming an infinite power supply and a computer that never breaks down, the loop will repeat forever if *condition* never becomes False.

A Do While...Loop example (Two examples, actually)

The following example relies on two `Do While...Loop` statements to reverse the digits in a number selected by the user. It has no practical value but illustrates how `Do` loops work:

```
Sub ReverseTheDigits()
Dim intOriginalNumber As Integer
Dim intOneDigit As Integer, strBackwardsNumber As String

Do While intOriginalNumber < 10
    intOriginalNumber = _
        InputBox("Type in an integer greater than 9.")
Loop

Do While intOriginalNumber
    intOneDigit = intOriginalNumber Mod 10
    strBackwardsNumber = strBackwardsNumber & intOneDigit
    intOriginalNumber = int(intOriginalNumber / 10)
Loop

MsgBox strBackwardsNumber
End Sub
```

The example explained

The first `Do` loop checks the value of the number typed in by the user of the program to make sure that it's not a negative number, and that it has at least two digits — otherwise, why bother reversing them? The first time the program encounters this loop, the value of the `intOriginalNumber` variable is zero, because nothing has been assigned to it so far. Zero is less than 10, so the condition is `True` and VBA enters the loop.

The loop contains one statement, an input box asking the user to type in a suitable number. After this is done, the `Loop` statement sends VBA back to the top of the loop, where the number entered is checked. The loop terminates only after a valid number is entered. (Note that this example omits important validity checks, such as whether the number is an integer and whether it exceeds the maximum value for an `Integer` variable.)

After VBA confirms a valid entry, it's on to the next loop. The condition for executing this loop is that the variable containing the number must be greater than zero. Because a nonzero value is `True`, you can simply write `Do While intOriginalNumber` instead of `Do While intOriginalNumber > 0` — either version works identically.

In the loop proper, a simple three-step procedure takes apart the digits of the original number, working from right to left, using them in reverse order to build a new string. You don't have to know how this code works to figure out the loop, but consider a few tips:

✦ The first line uses the `Mod` operator to divide the number by 10 and assign only the remainder to the `intOneDigit` variable. Because you're dividing by 10, the remainder is the last (rightmost) digit of the original number.

✦ The second line takes the digit obtained by the first line and adds it to the end of the string under construction.

✦ The third line again divides the number by 10, this time keeping the result of the division in the original variable. This effectively lops off the right-most digit. Note, however, that before the result is assigned to the variable, it is processed by the `Int` function. This is necessary because otherwise, VBA would round off the result — which might change the digits originally entered.

✦ As the loop loops, `intOriginalNumber` will be 0 after all its digits have been processed (any one digit divided by 10 is less than 1, and the `Int` function drops the fractional part of the result). In VBA-land, zero is `False`, so the loop ends and the program displays the reversed number.

Other Do statements

Variations on the `Do While...Loop` are easy to understand once you get the basic form. This section discusses three of the alternative `Do` loops. (See "When to use Do without While or Until" for the fourth.)

Do...Loop While

The difference between the `Do While...Loop` and `Do...Loop While` statements is simple: `Do While...Loop` has the condition at the top of the loop, whereas in `Do...Loop While` the condition comes at the end.

In a `Do While...Loop` structure, the loop is only entered if the condition is `True` the first time the program reaches it. If the condition is `False` to start with, the statements in the loop never execute. In a `Do...Loop While` structure, by contrast, the loop always executes at least once, the first time the program runs through the code. Only then is the condition tested, with the loop repeating as long as it remains `True`. Use a `Do...Loop While` structure when the loop block contains a statement that sets a value in the condition before the condition gets tested.

Another situation that calls for a `Do...Loop While` structure is when you're performing an action on an item (such as a string or an array) that may have more than one element. If you already know it has at least one element, you want the loop statements to execute at least once and then repeat as many times as needed for the remaining components.

Do Until loops

The `Do While...Loop` and `Do Until...Loop` statements are functionally equivalent. That is, you can execute exactly the same statements with either one by modifying the condition expression to perform the opposite test. If the condition for a `Do While` statement is `A = B`, a `Do Until` statement with `A <> B` would function identically. The `Do...Loop While` and `Do...Loop Until` pair are similarly complementary.

Quitting a loop early with Exit Do

At their most elegant, `Do` loops provide all the information VBA needs to decide whether to execute the loop in the condition expression. Unfortunately, things aren't always so tidy in real-world programming. Sometimes a change in a condition occurring in the body of the loop demands a hasty exit. That's why VBA has an `Exit Do` statement. Valid only in a `Do` structure, `Exit Do` summarily terminates the loop, passing program execution to the statement that comes after the loop. This example concatenates a string variable to an existing string, but if the variable contains more than one character the loop terminates:

```
Do While strA <= "Z"
    If len (strA) > 1 Then
        Exit Do
    End If
    strB = strB & strA
    strA = GetNextCharacter
Loop
```

 Tip   Normally, the `Exit Do` statement should appear in an `If...Then` or `Select Case` statement nested in the loop. That way, the loop runs normally unless some special or aberrant value occurs. However, you can also use `Exit Do` as a debugging device to bypass the loop temporarily, without having to "comment out" the code.

When to use Do without While or Until

Standard `Do...While/Until...Loop` statements can test a condition at the beginning or end of a loop. But what if you want to test the condition somewhere *within* the loop?

In this situation, use a `Do...Loop` statement — without `While` or `Until`. This technique requires an `If` or `Select Case` statement nested inside the loop. One or more branches of the nested conditional statement include an `Exit Do` statement, allowing the program to terminate the loop when a specified condition is met.

Here's how a Do...Loop statement looks in schematic form:

```
Do
(statements to be executed with each pass of the loop)
    If condition Then
        Exit Do
    End If
(more statements to be executed only if loop continues)
Loop
```

As you can see, this technique is appropriate when you want to execute some of the loop statements regardless of whether the condition is met. It's also useful if the loop should terminate under several different conditions. Frequently, for example, you must use several criteria to validate a user entry—as in the following code, in which a Do...Loop structure repeats the loop until the user enters a valid letter answer:

```
Sub GetAnAnswer()

strAnswer = InputBox("Enter your answer (A-E)")

Do
    If strAnswer = "" Then
        strAnswer = InputBox("You made no entry." _
            & " Please type a letter from A to E.")
    ElseIf Len(strAnswer) > 1 Then
        strAnswer = InputBox("Your answer should be" _
            & " only one letter long. Please try " _
            & "again.")
    ElseIf strAnswer < "A" Or strAnswer > "E" Then
        strAnswer = InputBox("You typed an invalid" _
        & " character. Type a letter from A to E.")
    Else
        Exit Do
    End If
Loop

End Sub
```

The program executes the Exit Do statement only when all three validation criteria—expressed in the If and ElseIf clauses—have been met.

Repeating on Count with For...Next loops

When you know how many times a loop should execute before the loop runs, use a For...Next loop. You specify how many passes VBA should make through the loop by supplying *start* and *end* values, which can be literal integers, variables, or even complex expressions. As the loop executes, a *counter* variable keeps track of the number of completed cycles. When the counter's value equals that of *end*, the loop is finished.

Simplified, the syntax of a `For...Next` structure is as follows:

```
For counter = start To end
(statements to be executed during each pass of the loop)
Next counter
```

Keeping it simple for starters, the following example procedure uses the Immediate window to display a message for each repetition of the loop (in the Visual Basic Editor, open the Immediate window by pressing Ctrl+G):

```
Sub CountToTen ()
Dim j As Integer
    For  j = 1 To 10
        Debug.Print "This is pass " & j
    Next j
End Sub
```

In the preceding example, the *start* and *end* values are both literal numbers. When the loop begins, j is set to 1 — in other words, the value of `start` is assigned to the `counter` variable. Each time a loop cycle completes, the `Next j` statement increments j (raises its value by one), and control shifts back to the beginning of the loop. When j finally equals 10, the loop terminates.

Important Tips about For...Next loops

Keep your code easy to understand. You should use 1 as the start value for a `For...Next` loop unless you have good reason to choose another number. Such good reasons do exist. One is when the value of the counter is used in the loop itself (not changed in the loop, mind you). If the loop takes an action according to consecutively numbered items (such as part numbers), you can use the actual values of the items as the start and end values. More commonly, Start is set to 0 when working with arrays, as illustrated in the next section.

Tip

In the `Next` counter statement that ends a `For...Next` loop, the counter variable's name isn't actually required — the keyword `Next` by itself automatically calculates the next counter value and sends VBA back to the top of the structure. However, you should definitely train yourself to include the counter in the `Next` statement. That way, when you nest two or more `For...Next` loops, you can see at a glance which one a given `Next` statement belongs to.

Caution

Do not change the value of the counter variable within a `For...Next` loop. Because the counter is just another variable, it's possible, and sometimes tempting, to write code that changes the counter value. Resist the urge — if you fool with the counter, the loop is likely to skip important steps or go on infinitely.

For...Next loops and Arrays

For...Next loops are perhaps most useful for working with arrays, which are named storage bins for sets of data items. A discussion of For...Next loops would be incomplete without a look at their use with these important data baskets. For example, you can use a For...Next loop to fill an array with a set of calculated values:

```
Dim intArrayOfSquares (14) As Integer
For a = 0 to 14
    intArrayOfSquares (a) = a * a
Next a
```

The example code begins by declaring an array of 15 integer values (15, not 14, because VBA normally numbers the first item in an array as 0). It then uses a For...Next loop to assign a value to each item in the array, counting from 0 to 14. The variable a serves not only as the counter but also as the array *index*, pointing to a numbered slot in the array.

Nesting For...Next loops

As with other VBA control structures, For...Next loops can be nested within one another — or within other control structures — as "deeply" as you need to nest them. The following useless fragment of code illustrates the concept:

```
Dim sngR  ' R stands for random number
Randomize ' initialize the random number generator
For A = 1 To 5
    sngR = Rnd ()
    For B = 1 To 5
        Debug.Print sngR * Rnd ( )
    Next B
Next A
```

Tracing the steps VBA follows to execute this code, the code starts by declaring a variable and initializing VBA's random number generator. Next, the outer For...Next loop starts. Here, VBA calls the Rnd function to assign a random number to the sngR variable. Then comes the inner For...Next loop. This loop calculates five other numbers. The results appear in the Immediate window. The inner loop terminates after it completes all five calculations. Now the outer loop takes over again. Obeying the Next A statement, VBA jumps back to the top of the outer loop, which repeats the inner loop four times.

The example I gave may seem relatively trivial, but it could be extended to perform genuinely useful work. Suppose (for example) you wanted to write a multimedia program that selects five CDs at random, playing five random selections from each one. Assuming you have the know-how to write the code that selects CDs and plays individual selections, the preceding example should get you started.

Tip Nested `For...Next` loops are also the key to working systematically with multi-dimensional arrays. Each loop corresponds to one dimension of the array.

Get out now with an Exit For

The `Exit For` statement provides a quick way to terminate a `For...Next` loop before the end of the loop has actually been reached. It's typically used within a conditional statement (`If...Then` or `Select Case`) nested within the main `For...Next` loop.

One use of the `Exit For` escape hatch is to test an array for invalid data, halting whatever process is underway if an aberrant value is detected. As an example, suppose you have learned that a malevolent genius has been able to insert an array containing false information into your price list data. You happen to know he has left behind his trademark. As you update the price information to reflect inflationary price hikes in each array, you want to be sure the price data hasn't been tampered with. The following code does both jobs at once:

```
For p = 1 To varArraySize
    If varPriceArray (p) = "Kilroy was here!" Then
        MsgBox "Infested data in this array!"
        Exit For
    End If
    varPriceArray (p) = varPriceArray (p) * sngCOLA
Next p
```

For Each...Next

A variation on the `For...Next` idea, VBA's `For Each...Next` statement performs a set of statements for each object stored in a *collection*.

Cross-Reference You can read about `For Each...Next` loops in Chapter 54.

Interrupting the Flow with GoTo

If your program is behaving in an unruly fashion, tell it where to go — by transferring execution to another location in the procedure. A `GoTo` statement, combined with a special *label* statement at the destination, enables you to hop at will from place to place within a procedure. A *label* is a statement that simply marks a location in your code. To enter a label, type in its name (VBA naming rules apply) followed by a colon.

A GoTo example

In this example, a GoTo statement jumps out of the main part of the function to the SpecialValue label when an unusual value is encountered:

```
Function GoToExample (ItemNumber As Integer)
    Dim intR As Integer
    Select Case ItemNumber
        Case 2412
            GoTo SpecialValue
        Case Is < CutOffValue
            DoSomething
        Case >= CutOffValue
            DoHardlyAnything
    End Select
    (statements that execute no matter what)
    GoToExample = intR
    Exit Function
SpecialValue:
    DoSomethingSpecial
    GoToExample = -intR
End Function
```

GoTo caveats

Use of the GoTo statement is considered inferior programming form. The problem is that it creates "spaghetti code," with the path of execution wandering all over the place. Code containing more than an occasional GoTo quickly becomes impossible to read. Whenever possible, you should use control structures to direct program execution.

Occasionally, however, a GoTo statement is the most practical way to get your program to do what you want it to. Your brain may be just too tired to come up with the intricate set of nested loops and conditionals required to implement a complex set of criteria. At times like these, GoTo can sometimes cut through the maze. Just don't use it too often.

✦   ✦   ✦

Object-Oriented Programming with VBA

✦ ✦ ✦ ✦

In This Chapter

Exploring objects

Getting the most from objects in your VBA coding

Using methods to make your objects perform

Creating new classes of object

✦ ✦ ✦ ✦

A core aspect of VBA's identity is that it's an object-based software development tool. An understanding of objects is fundamental to VBA programming, especially when you want to create custom dialog boxes or put the features of the host application under your control.

So What's an Object?

Although it's possible to come up with a formal definition of a VBA object, it's a lot easier to understand objects by way of examples and in terms of their functions.

Objects can be components of a VBA application

The easiest way to start thinking about objects is to see them as parts of your VBA application and its documents. A cell in an Excel worksheet is an object, as are named ranges of cells. And so are individual worksheets and complete workbooks, to which all the cells, ranges, and sheets belong. In all Office VBA applications, the toolbars and menus, and the buttons and menu choices they contain, are objects as well.

As is already obvious, VBA objects exist in a hierarchy in which one type of object contains objects of other types. These object hierarchies are the topic of the section "What's an object model?" later in this chapter. For the time being, though, I want to concentrate on understanding individual objects.

Conceptualizing objects can be hard

You may not be able to touch a drawing shape, a worksheet cell, or a toolbar button, but it's fairly easy to think of them as things. In your imagination, at least, you could cut out a circle shape and paste it on another piece of paper. You could write numbers into that worksheet cell or push that button. In addition to fairly concrete items like these, however, VBA applications offer all kinds of more abstract objects. Here are some examples:

✦ Word has a `Style` object, which represents a combination of formatting characteristics for paragraphs.

✦ Word's `FileSearch` object "represents the functionality of the Open dialog box," to quote the relevant Help topic. Note that this object doesn't represent the dialog box itself, but its functionality.

✦ Excel has a `CustomView` object, representing a workbook custom view (in Excel, a custom view defines the look of the workbook and its print settings).

✦ VBA itself has a few objects, which are available in all VBA applications. A `Collection` object, for example, represents a grab-bag set of variables or other objects that you want to work with as a unit, regardless of their data types.

A practical definition

As you can tell, it's often difficult to imagine a VBA object as a material thing. But that's okay—the more you can let go of such mental models, the more freely you can work with the whole range of available objects. The programmer's pragmatic definition of an object is simple, really. An object is a named item that has the following:

✦ **Properties.** Settings you can check and change.

✦ **Methods.** Actions the object can perform when your program asks it to.

And in some cases:

✦ **Events.** Things that happen to the object, to which it can respond by taking a predetermined action automatically.

If you have any poetic sensibility, the term *objects* may not seem fitting for such richly endowed creatures. Indeed, objects are more like animals than inert lumps. Where a tiger or a whale has characteristic features such as eyes, limbs, and a tail, an object has *properties*. Where a horse or a dog can do tricks on command or run away from danger, an object has *methods* and *events*.

Do you still want a technical definition? Try this one: An object is a named unit within a program that possesses both data and the code that acts on that data. An object is said to *encapsulate* the data and the related code.

Object classes versus specific objects

Here's yet another technicality to keep in mind: There's a distinction between a specific object and the pattern on which the object is based. A particular object represents one specific document, shape, worksheet cell, or other organized unit of information. A document object, for example, includes the text of that one document.

An *object class*, on the other hand, can be compared to a set of building plans. You can build many houses from one set of plans, but nobody can live in the plans themselves. In the same way, a class lays down the types of data that can be stored in an object and defines the object's methods, properties, and events. Based on this description, you construct an *instance* of the class — an object — in which you actually store some data. You can create, or *instantiate*, as many objects of a class as you like, each with a separate existence, and each containing different data.

What's an object model?

As you've seen, VBA objects exist in a hierarchical relationship to one another. In addition to having properties, methods, and events of its own, an object at the top of the hierarchy serves as a *container* for one or more other types. These objects in turn each contain other objects, and so on.

For a given VBA application, the specifics of these hierarchical relationships are referred to as the application's *object model*. Often presented graphically, the object model specifies which object contains which other objects. Figure 54-1 shows one such representation of an object model.

As Figure 54-1 makes plain, the `Application` object is at the top of a VBA application's object model. It is the container for all the other objects from the application that you can manipulate. Your own VBA programming project is also a container object. It contains all the code modules you write and the forms you design, as well as the project's document (Chapter 53 defines and discusses VBA projects in more detail).

Why the object model is important

Because you need to tell VBA which specific object you're working with, a good grasp on the object model of your VBA application is critical to efficient work. Following a chart of the object model such as the one shown in Figure 54-1, you can quickly locate the branch that contains the object you're after. In this example, for instance, you can see that a `Selection` object is contained in a `DocumentWindow` object, itself a member of the `DocumentWindows` collection. Later in this chapter I tell how to use the relationships between objects described by the object model to identify in your code each specific object you want to work with.

Microsoft PowerPoint Objects

Application
- Addins (Addin)
- AnswerWizard
- Assistant
- COMAddins (COMAddin)
- CommandBars (CommandBar)
- DefaultWebOptions
- DocumentWindows (DocumentWindow)
  - Panes (Pane)
  - Presentation
  - Selection
    - ShapeRange (Shape)
      - Table
        - Columns (Column)
          - CellRange (Cell)
            - Borders (LineFormat)
            - Shape
        - Rows (Row)
          - CellRange (Cell)
- FileSearch
- LanguageSettings
- Presentations (Presentation) ▶
- SlideShowWindows (SlideShowWindow)
  - Presentation
  - SlideShowView
- VBE

Legend
- ☐ Object and collection
- ☐ Object only
- ▶ Click red arrow to expand chart

Figure 54-1: A portion of PowerPoint's object model

Extending the object model

In the programs you write with VBA, you aren't limited to using the objects in only one VBA application. In fact, you're not even limited to VBA applications per se. Other applications and specialized "components" are fair game, as long as they adhere to Microsoft's Component Object Model (COM) standard.

Tip

COM is the technical specification detailing how objects are defined within applications and other software elements, and how those objects are exposed so they can be used by other applications. The jargon word *automation* refers specifically to the ability of a COM-based application to be controlled by another program. And by the way, COM isn't specific to VBA or even Visual Basic. Several software development tools such as C++ compilers understand COM and can access COM objects.

Anyway, all this opens up fantastic possibilities for powerful, customized VBA applications. You can readily (I didn't say "easily") build an application that processes information from Word documents, Excel worksheets, and even non-Office VBA applications such as Visio. Your custom application can show all this information in windows that you have designed, but that use the display capabilities of the individual component applications. Custom application development on this scale is introduced in Chapter 57.

VBA forms are objects

A form is the generic term for any custom window or dialog box you build with VBA. A key understanding to seal into your brain is that VBA forms are themselves objects. That is, they constitute entities that contain both information — representing the layout of the form — and a set of tools for doing things with that information. The official term for a form is UserForm object.

Likewise, a form's controls — each button, checkbox, and other things you can see and play with on the form — are also objects. VBA offers a different object type for each type of control.

Forms have properties, methods, and events

Because VBA is a visual design tool, you don't have to write code to create and lay out a form and its controls. But because forms and controls are full-fledged VBA objects, you work with them in your program just as you would with any other object. You use the following:

✦ **Properties** to change the appearance or behavior of a form or control while your program is running

✦ **Methods** to make the form or control do something, such as become visible or move to a new location

✦ **Events** to tell the form or control what to do when the user of your program clicks the mouse or presses a key, or when other events occur

The techniques you use in your code to access a particular form and use its properties and methods are exactly the same as you use for other objects. Chapter 56 delves deeply into the application of these techniques to forms and controls.

Forms have their place in the object model

As self-respecting VBA objects, forms fit comfortably into the object model paradigm. Each UserForm object can belong simultaneously to two collection objects, the VBA project in which the form is stored and the UserForms collection, which holds all the forms currently loaded by your program. For its part, a UserForm object is a container for a Controls collection object, which in turn contains all the individual controls you have added to the form. The diagram in Figure 54-2 illustrates these relationships.

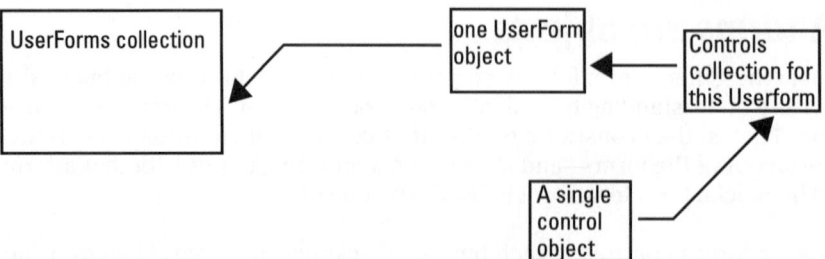

Figure 54-2: This diagram illustrates how control objects reside in control collections, which belong to a UserForm object, which in turn is part of the UserForms collection, and so on.

Using Objects in Code

Now that the theoretical groundwork has been laid, practical directions for programming with VBA objects are in order. Although the object concept itself can be tough to wrap your mind around, using objects is easy. Because objects have names, you always know which one you're working with. In your code, all it takes to identify one of the object's properties or methods is to type the object name, a period, and then the property or method name. For example, `MyWorksheet.Calculate` identifies the `Calculate` method of an Excel worksheet object called `MyWorksheet`.

At this point, though, you may be asking yourself, "But how do I know what the object's name is in the first place?" An excellent question, indeed. For now, though, just assume that it's possible to call an object by name.

What's your object?

Each VBA application has its own different object model (hierarchical set of objects), and each of its objects has its own set of properties, methods, and events. You need a working familiarity with the details of the application's object model to put these objects to work in your programs.

The VBA Help file for each Office application includes a topic devoted to a map of the application's object model (refer back to Figure 54-1 for an example). This graphical outline of the object model is the default topic, but if you don't see it when you open Help, look for it in the VBA Help system's Contents tab under titles such as Microsoft Outlook Objects, Microsoft Excel Objects, and so on.

In the object model map, light blue bars represent single objects; yellow bars represent collection objects. You can jump to the help topics for any object or collection by clicking the corresponding bar in the object model map. Typically, the topic for each object has links to other topics detailing the object's properties, methods, and events.

The Visual Basic Editor's Object Browser is another vital tool for viewing the relationships between the different objects of the application and exploring their properties, methods, and events. Chapter 52 describes the Object Browser in full.

Getting and changing object properties

An object property is a named characteristic of the object. It describes some aspect of the object's appearance, behavior, contents, or "pedigree," if you will. A Document object might have a Pages property that tells how many pages are in the document. A Shape object might have a Fill property that specifies the shape's color. CommandButton objects (representing buttons on dialog boxes) always have a Caption property that contains the text displayed on the button.

Behavior-related properties define the way the object reacts to various stimuli. Controls on forms are objects, and they have properties such as Enabled, which specifies whether the control responds to events such as mouse clicks. Some properties can take on an infinite range of different values. Others are limited to a list of predefined choices, such as Mauve, Teal, and Chartreuse. Many properties can take only two possible settings, such as True or False, Hot or Cold, or Wet or Dry. In any case, you can use simple VBA statements to retrieve the current setting of a given property, and to change the setting to one you prefer.

A VBA program can retrieve the current settings stored in most properties. This allows the program to decide whether or not to take some action, or simply to display the current setting in a window. Conversely, a program can change a property's setting to alter an object's appearance or behavior — but only if the property permits this (many properties can be retrieved but not modified).

What you can't do with some properties

Just knowing how to access a property's value doesn't mean you can. By design, some properties allow you to retrieve their values, but not to change them. These are *read-only* properties. Less commonly, a property is *write-only* — you can set its value, but not retrieve the current setting. However, most properties, are the *read/write* kind — you can both retrieve and change their values.

Property settings are data

Although a property functions metaphorically to describe some characteristic of the object, you should realize that the setting it contains consists of data — no different in kind from the data you stuff into VBA variables. As such, you can think of a property simply as a more-or-less permanent variable that you don't have to declare.

When you understand properties this way, it makes sense that each property stores a particular data type, exactly as variables do. Properties that can take only two alternative settings are of the Boolean type. Some properties are strings, some are integers, some are floating-point or decimal numbers, and so on. Properties can even be objects. (See Chapter 53 for information on VBA's available data types.)

Retrieving a property's current setting

To find out, or get, the current setting of a given property, use the property as if it were a function or `Function` procedure. That is, assign the property to a variable in your code. The variable should be of the same or a compatible data type as the property.

In the sample shown here, the object in question represents, for example, a question on a computerized test for graduate school admission. The property you're interested in checking is the one that describes how hard the question is on a scale of 1–10.

```
Dim intHowTough As Integer
intHowTough = objTestQuestion.DifficultyLevel
```

The first statement declares a variable to hold the property's current value; the second statement assigns the property to that variable.

So why bother retrieving a property's current value? Often, you use it in a conditional statement to decide whether or not to take some other action, based on the value. (In this case, something like, "If the question's `DifficultyLevel` is above 8, and if the answer is correct, award double credit" might be in order.) You might also store a property value in a variable so you can assign the value to the same property of other similar objects.

If you're going to use the property's value only once, you don't need to assign it to a variable—you can access it directly in an expression. The example illustrates this practice:

```
If objTestQuestion.DifficultyLevel > 8 Then
    intTestScore = intTestScore + (intPoints * 2)
End If
```

Caution   This is convenient, but remember that your program slows down if you repeatedly retrieve a property's value. If you need the value more than once or twice, it's better to store it in a variable—VBA can access the value of an ordinary variable more quickly than it can retrieve a property's value.

Changing a property's setting

Remember, properties are just glorified variables. Therefore, you can assign values to them just as you would any other variable—by placing the property name on the left side of an equals sign and the new value on the right. The statement

```
objMetalTune.GrungeFactor = 999
```

sets the `objMetalTune`'s `GrungeFactor` property—presumably, a measure of distortion, feedback, and extraneous noise—to 999.

```
objMetalTune.Ballad = False
objMetalTune.Title = "I have fleas. Bad."
```

Default properties

Many objects have a default property. You can retrieve or set its value using the object only, without mentioning the property itself by name. Sticking with the last example, suppose the default property for the `objMetalTune` object is `Title`. In that case, you could simplify the last statement to read

```
objMetalTune = "I have fleas. Bad."
```

Default properties are convenient, as long as you're sure you know which property is the default. If you have any doubt, or if you think you might forget later, it's better to go ahead and type out the property name.

Objects as properties

As I mentioned earlier, a property of one object can identify another object. This arrangement lets your code access the subsidiary objects that belong to a given container object, just as you would the container's other properties. For example, in the expression

```
Workbook.ActiveWorksheet
```

`ActiveWorksheet` is a property of the `Toolbar` object, but its value is a worksheet object. Using object properties in this way is the critical technique for identifying the specific objects you want to work with. See "Identifying the object you want to work with" later in this chapter for details.

Climbing the family tree

Just as an object's properties can identify other objects that belong to it, they can also tell you which container objects it belongs to. In Excel, if you have a `Chart` object stored in a variable and you want to know which document it belongs to, the expression

```
Chart.Parent
```

returns a reference to the correct document. If you need to know which application an object belongs to, you can often skip up to the top of the object hierarchy by getting an object's `Application` property:

```
Chart.Application
```

Methods

A *method* is a named action that an object performs when the method is called. Actually, methods are nothing more than procedures that are tied directly to specific objects. Because the code for each method is part of the object, the object itself knows what to do when you trigger the method.

Office drawing shape objects, for example, have a `ScaleHeight` method (to change their size in the vertical dimension) and an `IncrementRotation` method (that adjusts their rotation on the page), among others. A worksheet cell object might have a `Calculate` method (that recalculates the cell value) and a `Clear` method (that removes its contents). A `Document` object (representing an entire document) usually has `Print` and `Save` methods.

Calling methods

To call a method, you type the object's name, a period, and then the method name. Suppose an object named `objJazzTune` represents a digital jazz recording in a multimedia program. Most likely, the object has a method called `Play`. Here's how to call the method:

```
objJazzTune.Play
```

The techniques for calling methods are consistent with the ones you use to call procedures and VBA functions, as described in Chapter 53.

Tip

As with properties, many different object classes may have methods with the same names. Objects that contain groups of items or other objects typically have an `Add` method, for instance. This method is discussed in further detail later within this chapter.

Changing properties with methods

Just so it doesn't surprise you, I should mention that a method can change the value of one or more properties. For example, the `objJazzTune` object might have a read-only property called `TimesPlayed`, which can be altered only by the `Play` method, but which you can retrieve via a property statement such as `intPlaybacks = objJazzTune.TimesPlayed`. Some objects even have special methods whose sole purpose in life is to set property values.

Events

An event is something that happens to the object, and to which it can respond with some predetermined action (in VBA lingo, when you say an object "has" events, you mean the object can detect and recognize those events). Events include the following:

✦ Physical actions the user of your program does, such as clicking, just moving the mouse, or pressing a key.

✦ Things that happen to the object under software control. If you're talking about a document object, events might include the opening or closing of the document, or the addition or removal of a page.

Your VBA application specifies which events, if any, a given object can recognize. It's your job to write the code that determines what the object does when the event occurs.

The events that you'll most often write code for are the ones that happen to forms, and the controls on them (like buttons and text boxes). When the user of your program clicks the mouse on a certain button, that action has an effect only if you have written code for the button's Click event. Event programming for forms is the subject of Chapter 57.

However, it's often useful to write code for events that occur to other types of objects. In Word, the `Application` and `Document` objects recognize events. You can write code that runs automatically when these events occur. The techniques required vary from application to application and sometimes even within the same application, so consult your application's documentation or Help files for details.

 **Caution** One point may bear clarification: You don't call an event from your own code. Instead, the object automatically takes action when the event occurs.

Identifying the object you want to work with

To do anything useful with an object, you have to tell VBA which object you want to work with. You use an *object expression* for this purpose. This is a special kind of VBA expression that uniquely identifies the specific object you're excited about. Behind the scenes, the value that VBA calculates based on an object expression is an *object reference*, a value that you can think of as a street address for the object.

Figuring out the correct object expression you need is most of the battle. After you've done that, you can make future tasks much easier by creating a named variable for the object, using the expression to assign the corresponding object reference to the variable. From then on, you can refer to the object by the variable's name in your code.

An object expression is a code fragment — an expression — that "points" at a particular object. Using a valid object expression, you can set the object's properties, activate its methods, or assign the object to a variable.

The ideas covered here are critical to daily work with VBA, yet they're not easy to grasp at first. Because your program can work with many different objects of the same type, a complete object expression must specify all the objects that contain the one you have in mind. It's something like this: Suppose you were told to go get "the boy." You'd immediately ask, "Well, which boy?" If you were told instead to get the oldest boy who lives in the third house on Mayflower Street in the town of Arhoolie in the state of Nebraska in the United States of America, you wouldn't need to ask that question. (Of course, you might ask "Why?")

However, if you're already in the third house on Mayflower Street, and if only one boy lives there, a command such as "feed the boy" is quite adequate. In the same way, if the context is clear, VBA doesn't need the entire list of objects.

Properties can be objects

As I mentioned earlier, a property of one object can be another object. As I've also said, objects exist in a hierarchy, with one object, such as a document, serving as a container for other subsidiary objects such as pages or worksheets.

The connection between these ideas is probably obvious: If an object contains subsidiary objects, you can identify a subsidiary object via a property of the first object. The expression you use to specify this property is the object expression. For example, consider the following expression, which identifies a specific object in a Word document:

```
ThisDocument.Sections(2).Range
```

Notice that this object expression contains two periods, not just one. What this means is that Range is a property of the second Section object, which is in turn a property of the ThisDocument object.

Getting objects

The diagram shown in Figure 54-3 illustrates the relationship between objects referred to in the preceding object expression.

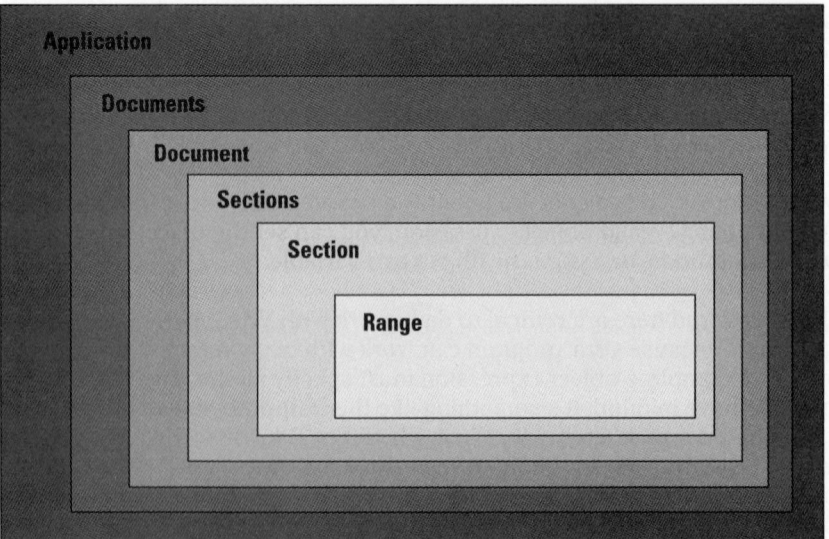

Figure 54-3: This illustration depicts the hierarchical relationship between objects.

The Application object occupies the very top of the object hierarchy in most VBA object models. However, you usually don't need to include it in object expressions—VBA is smart enough to assume you're working with objects from the current application, unless you specify otherwise.

The Application object contains a Documents object, which is a collection representing all the open documents. If you wanted to work with a specific document, you would identify it as a member of the Documents object. For example, Documents(5) would represent Document object 5 in the Documents collection. The expression ThisDocument.Sections(2).Range, however, starts with the special keyword ThisDocument. In many VBA applications, ThisDocument stands for the Document object associated with your project.

In Word, each Document object has a Sections property. This in turn refers to a Sections collection, an object that represents the set of all the pages in the document. So the first part of the preceding expression—ThisDocument.Sections— identifies the particular Sections collection that belongs to the ThisDocument object. When you've identified the Sections object, you can select a single member of its collection. Thus, Sections(2) refers to the second section in the document.

As for the final part of the expression, the tricky part here is that although .Range specifies a property of the Section object, the value of that property is a Range object. The entire expression, then, supplies an object reference to that Range object. Using an expression that threads its way through the object hierarchy like this to a specific object is called "getting an object" in VBA lingo.

Creating object variables

Nobody likes to type a long, complex object expression like the one discussed in the previous section. If your program uses the same object more than once, you should create a named variable to hold a reference to that object. Then, wherever you would have typed the complete object expression, you can enter the variable name instead.

Besides being shorter, easier to remember, and easier to type than the original object expression, an object variable has two other plusses. First, it makes your code run faster. VBA can locate the object directly, rather than having to look up a series of properties in a series of objects. Second, you can use the same object variable to store references to different objects. That way, you can write flexible code that decides which specific object to store in the variable when the program runs.

In outline, the technique for creating an object variable requires two steps:

1. Declare a variable you intend to use to refer to the object.

2. Assign the object you want to work with to that variable.

The next two sections cover the details on each of these steps.

Declaring an object variable

You declare object variables just as you do variables of other data types. The standard method is with a `Dim` statement (just as with other types of variables, though, you can also use the `Public`, `Private`, or `Static` keywords instead of `Dim` to declare object variables). Here are two examples of object declarations:

```
Dim objGreatBigObject As Object ' A generic object
Dim objShapeObject As Shape ' A drawing Shape object
```

Note   The difference between these two declarations is important. The first statement declares an object variable but doesn't specify the type of object it contains. You can use this variable to hold different types of objects as the need arises. The second statement declares the particular type, or class, of object that you want the variable to store. VBA won't allow you to place other object classes in the variable.

These two types of object declarations are referred to as *late binding*, in which no specific class is specified, and *early binding*, in which you do declare the variable as a definite object class. Whenever possible, you should use early binding, declaring the object variable as a specific class. The benefits of early binding include the following:

✦ **Fewer mistakes.** As I mentioned, VBA won't let you assign incorrect objects to the variable. Just as important, by knowing which class of object you're working with, the compiler can check the rest of your code to make sure you use properties and methods that are valid for that class. If you use late binding, the compiler can't perform this check. If your program attempts to use invalid properties or methods, an error occurs while it's trying to run.

✦ **Faster performance.** Because the compiler can determine whether the object has the methods and properties you use in your program, the program doesn't need to pause to check this when it runs.

✦ **More understandable code.** You can tell by looking at the declaration what class of object the variable is supposed to contain.

In spite of these advantages, there are two situations when it's better to use late binding:

✦ You may intend to use the same variable for different classes of objects. This can be a good idea when the different classes share methods or properties that you need to access in your code. With a variable, you don't need to rewrite code that does the same things using different objects.

✦ Some objects can't be declared via early binding when they are accessed from another application. Using objects from other applications is an advanced VBA technique that is introduced in Chapter 57.

Caution   As you know, a variable of the variant type can hold any type of information, including an object reference. If you declare a variable without explicitly stating its data type, VBA sets it up as a variant. Your program still works, but it slows down a bit.

Assigning an object reference to a variable

After you've declared an object variable, you must fill it with a reference to a specific object before you can use the variable. To do this, assign an object expression to the variable using the Set keyword, as in this example:

```
Set objShapeObject = ThisDocument.Pages(1).Shapes(4)
```

Note that this syntax differs a bit from the way you assign other types of data to variables (see Chapter 53). As with other data types, you place an equal sign between the variable name and the object to be assigned. The only difference is you must start the statement with the Set keyword.

Emptying an object variable

When you no longer need to access an object, it's good form to break the tie between the object and the variable with which it's associated. This way, you can be sure your code won't mistakenly make changes to the object. The technique is simple. Using a Set statement, just assign the Nothing keyword to the variable as in this example:

```
Set objPriceIsNoObject = Nothing
```

Creating new objects

If the object you want to work with doesn't yet exist, you have to create it. In simple VBA programs, you use the Add method for this purpose. The Add method should work if you're trying to create one of the built-in objects available in your VBA application (the one with which your project is associated).

Using the Add method

The trick is knowing which object's Add method you should use. What you're looking for is the container object in which the object you want to create resides.

For example, suppose you want to create a new Slide object in PowerPoint. Each Slide object is contained in a Slides object, which represents a collection of (one or more) slides. With this in mind, you would choose the Slides.Add method to create a new individual shape. Of course, because you have to identify the specific Shapes object in which VBA should create the new Shape object, the complete statement required would look something like this:

```
ActivePresentation.Slides.Add 1, ppLayoutTextAndClipart
```

Caution Even if a Slide (singular) object had an Add method (which it doesn't), you wouldn't want to use it. It would create a subsidiary object within the Slide, not another Slide.

When you create an object, create a variable for it

You've gone to the trouble to type out a long object reference—that's what an Add statement amounts to—so you might as well create a variable for the new object at the same time. That way, you can use the variable instead of another lengthy object reference whenever you want to access the object in your code. The two statements here illustrate this technique:

```
Dim objMyBaby As Slide
objMyBaby = ActivePresentation.Slides.Add 1, _
    ppLayoutTextAndClipart
```

Creating objects with New and CreateObject

In other situations, different techniques for creating new objects are required. These alternatives apply when you're creating the following:

✦ New copies of an existing form in your own project

✦ Objects from a different application or ActiveX (COM) component

✦ Specific objects based on classes you write in class modules

Depending on the details of the situation, you may use the New keyword in variable declaration or Set statements, or the CreateObject function to create these objects. Steer clear of the New keyword and the CreateObject function when you're trying to create ordinary objects.

The following example demonstrates the use of a Set statement for creating a new object:

```
Set objCustomThermostat = New Thermostat
```

Efficient object coding using With statements

Whether you refer to an object with a short, mnemonic variable or with a lengthy, inscrutable object expression, typing it over and over again gets old in a hurry. But you may not have to. If your program uses the same object in two or more consecutive statements, the With statement allows you to name the object only once. Not only is this easier than retyping the object in each statement, but it also makes your code easier to understand and faster, too. Here's an example:

```
With objIHaveNoObjection
    .Name = "The Last Straw" ' Set the Name property
    .DisplayName ' Call the DisplayName method
    sngArea = .Area ' Get the Area property's value
    intStretchFactor = .Rotate (60) ' Call the Rotate
    ' method, assigning its return value to a variable
End With
```

As you can see, within the `With...End With` structure you can mix statements that get and set properties with statements that call methods. Note also that the `With` structure is not a loop—the statements it contains are executed only once.

Tip `With` structures can be nested. This is perfect when you must perform multiple actions on both an object and one of the objects it contains.

Comparing object references

If you use variables to store object references, there may come a time when you want to know if the object a variable refers to is the same object referred to by another variable, or by an object expression. Use the `Is` operator in an expression to check whether two object references refer to the same object. The expression's value is `True` if they do, `False` if they refer to different objects. Here's some sample code to illustrate how `Is` works:

```
Dim objObject1 As Object, objObject2 As Object
...
If objObject1 Is objObject2 Then
    MsgBox "It's the same object!"
Else
    MsgBox "They're different objects."
End If
```

Of course, you could also compare an object variable against an object expression with the `Is` operator, as in the expression used in this line:

```
If objObject3 Is ThisDocument.Pages(2).Shapes(3) Then
```

Caution Note that you can't use `Is` (or any other operator) to compare the contents of two different objects.

Managing sets of data with Collection objects

A collection is a special type of VBA object. As the name suggests, its role is to simplify working with a set of objects as a group. In the typical collection, all the objects it contains are of the same type. A `Shapes` collection in an Office document, for example, contains multiple `Shape` objects, and a `Sections` collection in Word contains multiple `Section` objects.

Some collections, however, are less discriminating about which objects they allow in. VBA proper comes with a generic `Collection` class. From it, you can create your own collection objects, using them to store data and objects of any type in any combination as appropriate. Within some limitations, collections can have significant advantages over arrays.

Tip   A collection can store only a simple list of items, comparable to a one-dimensional array. However, because this is the most common type of array, collections can do real service.

Working with Collection objects

What you need to know about `Collection` objects is how to access the individual objects they contain. You have two options:

✦ Refer to the object by its "slot" or *index number* in the collection. In Word VBA, `Documents(2)` designates the second `Document` object in the `Documents` collection.

✦ Refer to the object by name. Many objects have names, and if you know the name of the object you want, you can use it in the object expression. For instance, Office command bars (toolbars) have names so an expression such as `CommandBars("Debug")` identifies a specific command bar in the CommandBars collection.

Caution   Although you can access the item stored in a collection slot with these techniques, you can't use them to place a new value in an existing collection item. The following assignment statement does not work:

```
colInventory(1465) = 119
```

The only way to change a value in a generic VBA collection you create yourself is to remove the existing item and add a new one containing the new value. Many built-in collections provided by VBA and Office applications don't have this limitation.

The trade-offs

When you're comfortable working with VBA objects, you may find that `Collection` objects are handier than arrays for tweaking sets of items. The `Add` and `Remove` methods make resizing the collection effortless. They are also much less likely to result in errors than repeatedly using `ReDim` statements in different parts of your program. (These advantages are especially significant when you must frequently add or remove individual items from the group.)

As a bonus, you can name individual items in the collection so you can retrieve them by name later. This not only gives you an easy-to-remember handle for each element, but it also makes accessing the data much quicker once your collection contains over about a hundred elements.

Creating Collection objects

Set up a `Collection` object in your program as you would any other object, using an `As` clause to specify the type of object. As with other objects, you can use either of two variations of the basic technique:

✦ You can declare a variable name for the object and then use a `Set` statement to create it. Note that you must use the `New` keyword in the `Set` statement to create the new collection:

```
Dim colMixedBag As Collection
...
Set colMixedBag = New Collection ' Create collection
colMixedBag.Add "Howard and Ethel" ' Add a data element
```

✦ To have VBA create the object automatically the first time you use the variable in your code, you can declare it with the `New` keyword.

```
Dim colSetOfStuff As New Collection
...
' The next statement creates the Collection while
' adding an integer to it.
colSetOfStuff.Add intStuffing
```

Adding data to a collection

After you've created your collection, use its `Add` method to fill it with data, just as you would to add objects to your VBA application's built-in collections. The preceding examples show the `Add` method in action. The complete syntax for the `Add` method is as follows:

```
Add (item[, key][, before index][, after index])
```

The item expression is required. It can be a literal value, a variable, an object reference, or a complex expression involving two or more of these components — anything that returns a value VBA recognizes. The remaining terms in the `Add` method are optional. I won't cover the before and after terms here, but the key term deserves mention.

Although you can refer to an item in a collection by its "slot number," giving the item a meaningful name is important. To do this, supply the name as a string when you add the item to the collection:

```
colFinancials.Add 14323.44, "February sales"
```

The preceding statement adds the value 14323.44 to the `colFinancials` collection. At the same time, it creates a *key*, a name, for the item.

The next example boldly adds the built-in Word object `ThisDocument` (referring to the document containing your VBA project) to a collection and assigns it a key:

```
colGrabBag.Add ThisDocument, "DocKey"
```

Caution
A key isn't just easier to remember than a numeric index—it's the only reliable "key" for quick access to an individual item in a collection. Because of the way the `Add` and `Remove` methods work, the positions of specific data items in a collection can change. If item 63 becomes item 29, you can still pull out its value if you know its key name.

With collections based on the generic VBA Collection class, the only way to assign a key is with the Add method. To assign a key to an item that doesn't have one, or to change the existing key, you must Add the item all over again and Remove the original copy.

Removing items

To state the obvious, the Remove method deletes an item from the collection. You can identify the object you want to excise by its index number or by its key:

```
colMineral.Remove 2123
colMineral.Remove "Bauxite"
```

Remember that when you remove an item, VBA fills in the gap, so to speak — the index numbers of all the other items further down in the list decrease by one.

Count-ing your collection

It's easy to lose track of the size of your collection, especially once you Add or Remove a few items. VBA's generic Collection object has only one property, but it's vital — that's the Count property. You can assign it to a variable:

```
intCollectionSize = col20Questions.Count
```

or test it in a conditional expression:

```
If colPrices.Count > 1000
    MsgBox "We have too many entries!"
End If
```

Using For Each...Next loops to work with collections

Use For Each...Next loops to work all of the items in a collection, one at a time. Here's the syntax:

```
For Each objectvariable In collection
(statements to be executed during each pass of the loop)
Next objectvariable
```

One key difference between For Each...Next and the standard For...Next structure is that you don't have to specify the number of times the loop should execute — VBA figures that out for you. Instead of a counter variable, the For Each structure requires an element variable that corresponds to the type of object stored in the collection. Of course, you must also indicate which collection you want to work with.

The following simple example of a For Each...Next structure works in Word, PowerPoint, or Excel, where the Shapes collection is, of course, a collection of Shape (drawing) objects. The first For Each...Next structure simply displays the name of each Shape in the Shapes collection in the immediate window. The second loop looks for a shape named WidgetA and if it finds it, deletes it:

```
' First, place a reference to a document object
' in the someDocument variable.
Dim objS As Shape
For Each objS In someDocument.Shapes
    Debug.Print objS.Name
Next objS
For Each objS In someDocument.Shapes
    If objS.Name = "WidgetA" Then
        objS.Delete
        Exit For
    End If
Next objS
```

The Exit For statement lets you leave the loop as soon as you've found the correct item in the collection. If you want to perform some action on every item in the collection, don't include an Exit For statement.

Do-It-Yourself Objects: Class Modules

When you're comfortable using the built-in objects available in VBA, you should eventually begin building your own. Although you can perform great feats of legerdemain using standard Sub and Function procedures, compartmentalizing your code into objects can have real advantages. These include the following:

✦ By keeping all the code that manipulates a set of data inside a single object, you reduce the opportunities for bugs to creep into your program when you make modifications.

✦ Your programs are easier to read and understand.

✦ You can create as many independent copies of an object as you like by writing two quick statements for each copy.

✦ It can definitely be handy to use the same properties and methods with different object classes. The technical term for this is *polymorphism*.

As you know by now, an object consists of some data (the object's properties) and code that alters that data (its methods). Given that properties are just variables and methods are just procedures, writing the actual code that defines an object is no big deal. But you do have to follow some rules so VBA can figure out what you're trying to do.

Creating class modules

In VBA, a class is the pattern upon which an object is based. The class determines which properties, methods, and events the object has, and how each of those components behave. To create a class, you start by inserting a new class module in your VBA project (choose Insert ➪ Class Module or right-click within the Project window and choose Insert). A class module window looks and works exactly like a code window.

Components of a class definition

The typical class has three main components:

✦ Private declarations for the variables used internally by the object

✦ Public property procedures that allow procedures in your standard modules to retrieve or alter current property settings

✦ Public method procedures that define the actions that the object's methods perform

The simple class definition shown here for a make-believe Thermostat class has all three of these elements. This example does nothing useful, but it does work and you should try it out:

```
Private sngDegrees As Single ' property variable

'Code for the Let Temperature property procedure:
Public Property Let Temperature(ByVal sngInput As _
    Single)
    sngDegrees = sngInput
End Property

'Code for the Get Temperature property procedure:
Public Property Get Temperature() As Single
    Temperature = sngDegrees
End Property

'Code for the CalculateEnergyUse method:
Public Sub CalculateEnergyUse()
    Const cstConversionFactor = 2.45
    Dim dblResult
    dblResult = sngDegrees * 365 * cstConversionFactor
    MsgBox "Annual energy use for this thermostat" & _
        " setting is estimated at " & dblResult & _
        " watts."
End Sub
```

Declaring class variables

Use the Declarations section at the top of the class module to declare any variables you plan to access in more than one property or method. Always declare them as Private. After all, the whole point of objects is to ensure that your program can't access the data directly. Variables that you use in only one property or method should be declared there.

At a minimum, you need to declare a variable for each of the object's properties. The variable name should not be the name of the property (I'll show you how to define the property's name in a moment). But you can also declare other data that the object uses internally and that won't be accessible to other parts of your program.

Writing property procedures

The secret to endowing an object with a property is to write a pair of special procedures, the Let and Get property procedures. Both procedures in each pair should have the same name.

Tip

The name of a property is the name you choose for the property's Let and Get procedures. The name should describe the content or function of the property, of course.

One other point: If you're creating a property representing an object reference, you substitute a Property Set procedure for a Property Let procedure as half of the property procedure pair. Otherwise, such properties work the same as properties of other data types.

Setting object properties with Property Let procedures

A Property Let procedure sets the value of a property. In its simplest form, a Property Let procedure takes a value supplied as an argument, assigning that value to a variable that represents the property. To repeat the previous example:

```
Public Property Let Temperature (ByVal sngInput As _
    Single)
    sngDegrees = sngInput
End Property
```

When in the main part of your program you write a statement that sets the property, such as Thermostat.Temperature = 75, VBA calls the Let Temperature procedure with 75 as the argument.

Of course, your property procedures aren't limited to one line of code. You can add statements that check the argument to ensure it falls in a valid range before you assign it to the property. You can also perform other actions depending on the particular argument.

Retrieving object properties with Property Get procedures

A Property Get procedure works like a Function procedure; it returns a value — the value of the property, of course. As in a Function procedure, you assign the value you want it to return to the procedure name — which also happens to be the property name. Here's the example code again:

```
Public Property Get Temperature() As Single
    Temperature = sngDegrees
End Property
```

Other parts of your program can call the Get Temperature procedure to assign its return value to a variable, or test the return value in conditional statements:

```
sngCurrentSetting = Thermostat.Temperature
```

or

```
If Thermostat.Temperature > 80
    MsgBox "Consider turning down the heater!"
EndIf
```

Writing methods

Methods are simply ordinary `Sub` and `Function` procedures that you happen to store in a class module. In most cases, of course, a method should do something directly related to the object itself, by manipulating the data stored in the object. VBA automatically associates the methods with their class, so you can call them from other parts of the program just as you would the methods of built-in objects.

Using your custom objects

You use an object based on one of your own classes in just the same way you would work with the built-in objects of VBA and your application. The steps are as follows:

1. Declare a variable for the object, as in the following:

   ```
   objCustomThermostat = Thermostat
   ```

2. Use a `Set` statement to create the actual object you'll be working with:

   ```
   Set objCustomThermostat = New Thermostat
   ```

3. Access the object's properties or trigger its methods using the standard VBA dot syntax, as in the following:

   ```
   objCustomThermostat.Temperature = 65
   objCustomThermostat.Calcu2lateEnergyCosts
   ```

4. Release memory when finished using the object:

   ```
   Set objCustomThermostat = Nothing
   ```

✦   ✦   ✦

Unbreakable Code: Debugging and Error Trapping

Writing VBA code is the easy part. It's getting that code to run—and then to produce the expected results—that takes real work. Hunting down and stamping out bugs is a crucial part of the coding process, and in this chapter you can learn how it's done in VBA. I also cover error trapping, which allows a program to respond gracefully when something goes wrong while it's running.

What Can Go Wrong, Will Go Wrong

Three main kinds of problems can beset the programs you write in VBA or most any language. They are as follows:

◆ **Syntax errors.** Syntax and other errors that prevent the program from running in the first place.

◆ **Logic errors.** Flaws in the program's design that cause it to do something you don't want it to do, or not to do something you do want it to—the program runs, but it doesn't run correctly.

◆ **Run-time errors.** These bring the program to a halt while it is running. Run-time errors can result from big-time logic errors or from encountering unexpected conditions.

Of the three, syntax errors are definitely the easiest to uncover and correct. I mention them only briefly, spending most of my time in this chapter on detecting and eliminating the other two types, the true bugs.

Fixing syntax errors

When you make the first type of mistake, a syntax error, the Visual Basic Editor helps you figure out what you did wrong before you try to run the program. As soon as you type something that the Editor can't figure out, it displays the line in red. Then if you've checked the box labeled Auto Syntax Check in the Editor tab of the Tools ➪ Options dialog box, you get a message clarifying the problem as soon as you move the insertion point off the line. For example, if you type **If x = 3** but forget to type **Then**, the message is "Compile error: Expected: Then or GoTo". (VBA doesn't catch some syntax errors until you try to run the program.)

When you know you made a mistake, correcting a syntax error is relatively easy. If you have any doubt about the right way to code what you're trying to accomplish, consult the relevant section here or look up the item in the VBA Help system.

Debugging for VBA programmers

After you get past all the compile errors and your program starts running, it's natural to feel an immediate wave of pride and relief. But when the program reports that 2 + 2 = 22 or all the text in your document turns chartreuse, you know that there's a mistake in your code somewhere.

These are examples of errors in program logic. The program is running; in fact it is doing exactly what you told it to do. The problem is what you told it to do with the code you wrote isn't what you actually wanted it to do. Your job is to track down exactly which statements led to the wrong outcome. This process is called *debugging* your program. The tools and techniques you can use in your debugging campaigns are all cataloged in this section.

Of course, the same debugging techniques you use to stamp out logic errors are vital in preventing the many run-time errors that result from logic errors. But because no program can anticipate every possible circumstance it might face, you should still incorporate code to handle run-time errors in any program destined for others' use.

Test, test, test

It's handy when errors announce themselves by displaying obviously wrong answers or turning things on the screen weird colors. Unfortunately, many logic errors are subtler, and many run-time errors occur only intermittently. Instead of assuming that your program is going to work properly when freshly hatched, budget plenty of time for testing it under different conditions.

If the program is supposed to work with different documents, test it by running it with different documents. Try running the program when two or three documents are open in your VBA application—and when no document at all is open. See what happens if you run the program when the document window is in different states (minimized, maximized, or restored). Start the program when different items or groups of items are selected in the document window.

If the program requires input from the user via an input box or custom form, make all kinds of test entries, both typical and outlandish, to see what happens. If the required value is supposed to be an integer, try floating-point, date, and string entries to see how the program responds. Likewise, if the program works with date or time values, see what it does with different dates—including February 29—and different times of day—including midnight.

If you do find any mistakes, it's time to start debugging in earnest. But if you don't find mistakes, don't assume they aren't there—assume instead that they are.

Tip   Perform code review periodically throughout your project. Generate unit test checklists and test scripts to perform testing of modules. Use unit test checklists to perform unit testing of code modules. Use test scripts to perform functional testing of the application.

Using break mode for debugging

The key to debugging a program is to use VBA's *break mode*. In break mode, your program has begun running but is suspended at a particular statement in the code. Because the program is still live, you can inspect the current values of all the variables. Beginning from that point, you can use the Step commands to run the program one statement at a time, watching the variables change to see whether you're getting the expected results at each step in the process. Later sections have the details on working with variables and the Step commands.

Figure 55-1 shows a VBA procedure in break mode. With the exception of a yellow highlight and arrow marking the next statement to be executed, the Visual Basic Editor looks almost exactly as it does when you're writing or editing code.

Tip   In fact, in break mode, you can actually edit the code while your program is running, making changes or adding brand new lines as whim or necessity dictates. This isn't at all a frill, but a key debugging feature that you should train yourself to take advantage of—more on this later.

Entering break mode

You can use a variety of techniques to put a program into break mode, the computer equivalent of suspended animation. Here's the full list:

✦ Start the program in break mode from the outset using the Step Into command (see "Stepping through code").

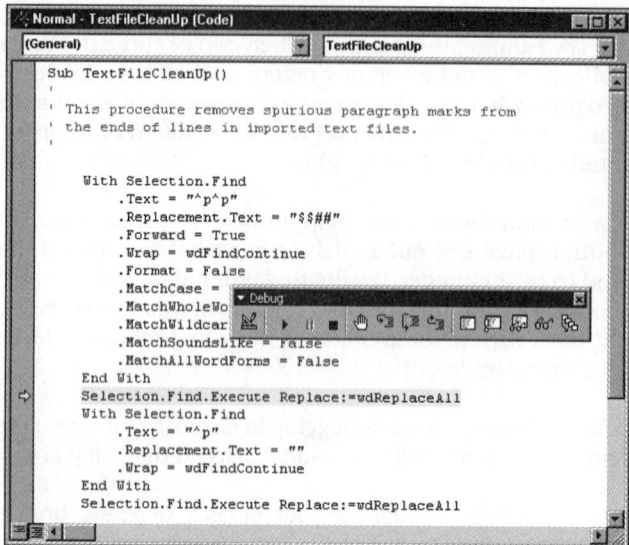

Figure 55-1: A VBA procedure in break mode

✦ Set a *breakpoint* on a line of code. When a running program reaches the statement at the breakpoint, it suspends execution and enters break mode.

✦ Place a `Stop` statement in your code. When the program runs, it enters break mode ready to execute the statement following the `Stop` statement.

✦ Click the Break button, choose Run ⇨ Break, or press Ctrl+Break while the program is running. This is the technique to use to get back control of a runaway program that won't stop on its own. Where you end up when the program enters break mode is anyone's guess, but at least you can see what's going on when you get there.

✦ Create a Break When True or Break When Changed watch. The program enters break mode when the value of the watch expression becomes `True` or undergoes any change.

One other way a program can enter break mode is when a run-time error occurs. VBA displays a dialog box describing the error (see Figure 55-2). Clicking the End button stops the program altogether, but clicking Debug puts it into break mode. You have some control over which run-time errors trigger break mode in the General tab of the Tools ⇨ Options dialog box.

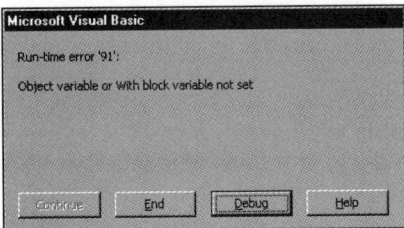

Figure 55-2: A run-time error dialog box

Setting breakpoints

When you suspect a section of code contains a logical error, place a breakpoint just before the miscreant statements. In Figure 55-3, that highlight and the big dot in the margin of the code window show how the Visual Basic Editor represents a breakpoint on the screen.

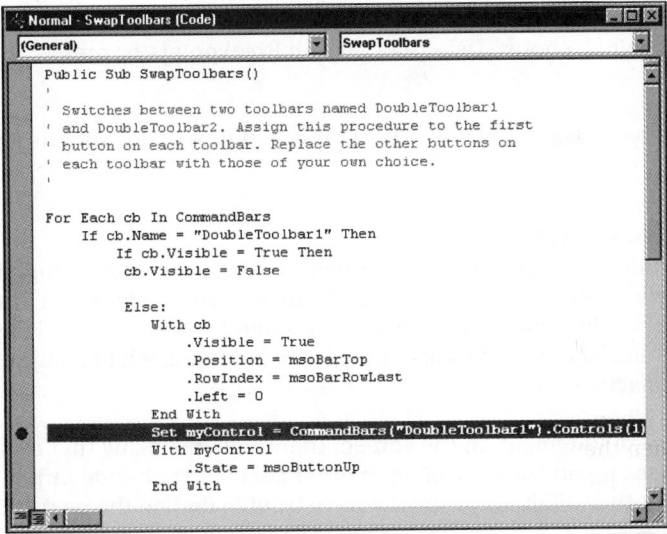

Figure 55-3: When you set a breakpoint, the Visual Basic Editor highlights the line of code before which program execution should stop.

With a breakpoint in place, you can run the program at full speed up to that point, bypassing code that (you hope) works properly. When VBA gets to the statement with the breakpoint, it suspends the program. After break mode is active, you can examine the variables and then use the Step commands to see how they change as VBA executes each dubious statement one at a time.

To set a breakpoint, all you have to do is click in the margin of the code window next to the target line of code. With the keyboard, put the insertion point on the correct line and press F9.

You can set breakpoints on as many executable statements as you like. However, you can't set breakpoints on comments, of course, nor on statements that VBA doesn't actually execute, such as variable declarations.

Tip   Keep in mind that VBA stops the program and switches into break mode after executing the statement just prior to the breakpoint. In other words, the statement at the breakpoint hasn't been executed yet and will be the next to run when the program continues.

Clearing breakpoints

After you correct the errant code, or give up on fixing it for now, clear the breakpoint to remove it. This allows VBA to execute the program normally the next time you run it. The same techniques you used to set a breakpoint — clicking in the Code window margin, or pressing F9 — also clear an existing one.

To deep-six all breakpoints, choose Debug ➪ Clear All Breakpoints or press Ctrl+Shift+F9.

Caution   Be careful. After you clear all breakpoints, they're history — Undo won't restore them.

Knowing where you are in break mode

When a program is running in break mode, the Visual Basic Editor always highlights the statement that will be executed next. To make sure you get the message, there's an arrow in the Code window margin pointing to the same "next statement." Figure 55-4 provides a reminder of how this looks, though the black-and-white image leaves much to the imagination.

When you have the next statement on the screen, there's no mistaking that highlight. But what happens if you start scrolling to other parts of your code or jump to the Code windows of other modules? You may have trouble finding the next statement again.

Tip   That's where the suitably named Show Next Statement command comes in. When you choose Debug ➪ Show Next Statement, the Visual Basic Editor whisks you straight to the statement in question. Another command lets you select a different statement as the next statement, but I cover that later, in the section "Choosing a different next statement."

A breakpoint alternative: The Stop statement

Breakpoints are super easy to use, but they have one drawback — they're only temporary. When you're debugging a complex program, you may not be able to set things right in a single session. Because breakpoints aren't stored with your code, they'll be gone the next time you open the project in the Visual Basic Editor.

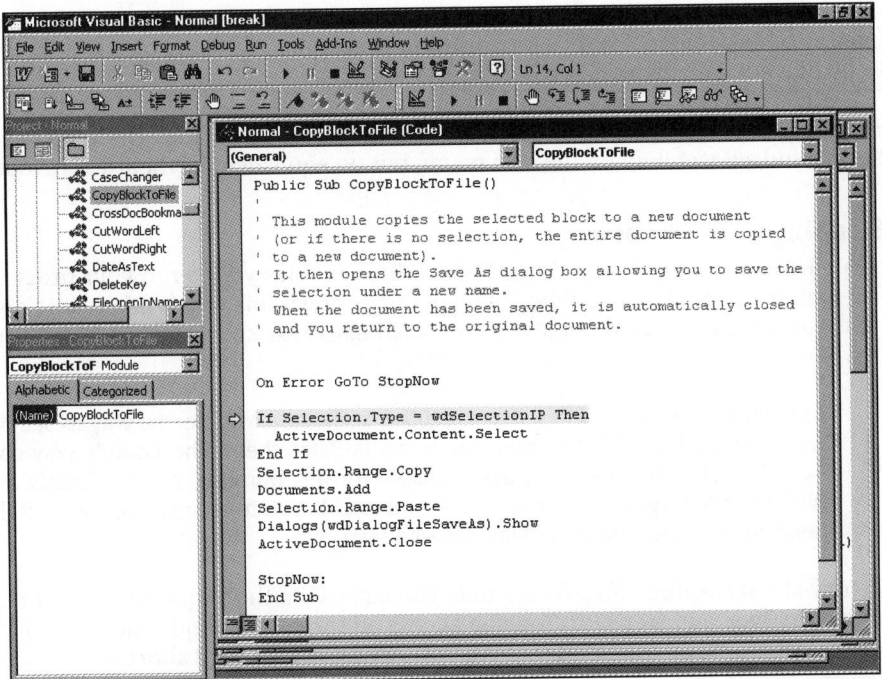

Figure 55-4: You can't miss the statement that's next in line for execution, as long as it's visible on the screen anyway.

The Stop statement is the solution to this problem. Add it to your code wherever you want the program to switch to break mode. Like any other code you type, Stop statements are saved when you save the project. Here's an example:

```
...
intDataFromMars = GetDataFromMars(1.5454)
Stop
MsgBox "The result is " & intDataFromMars / Z
...
```

You can guess that the Stop statement is being used to probe suspect results displayed in the message box. After it has been added, the Stop statement forces the program into break mode just after a function procedure has set the value of a variable. You can now look at the values of both variables involved in the next calculation to see which of them seems out of line.

Getting out of break mode

When you're through with break mode, at least for the time being, you can tell VBA to resume normal program execution. Any command you can use to run a program in the first place will work. In break mode, the Run menu item and toolbar button look the same and are in the same places, but their names are changed — both are now called Continue. F5 is still the keyboard shortcut. A Continued program pops back into break mode if it runs into another breakpoint, or if any of the other conditions that activate break mode occur.

To stop running the program altogether, use the Reset command. There's a Reset button and a Reset item on the Run menu, but no equivalent keyboard shortcut.

Stepping through code

Like all good debuggers, the Visual Basic Editor enables you to run your program one statement, or step, at a time. Slowing things down this way is a fantastic opportunity to catch the very point at which some logic error knocks a critical value out of whack. It's fun, too.

Tip   To make the best use of this *step execution* technique, you need a way to see the values of your variables as your program modifies them. The Editor's way cool Auto Data Tips feature is always available for this purpose, but the Locals and Watch windows give you more details and enable you to change the values if the need arises. I cover all these features a bit later.

So now about the three Step commands you can use in the Visual Basic Editor: Step Into, Step Over, and Step Out. You can access all three commands via the Debug menu, as buttons on the Debug toolbar, or by way of keyboard shortcuts.

Stepping into code

The Step Into command is the one to use when you want to execute each and every statement in your program in proper sequence. Each time you invoke this command, VBA runs the next statement in your program and then returns to break mode, where you can see what changes have been wrought. Pressing F8 is the most efficient way to invoke the Step Into command.

This command gets its name because it steps into other procedures that your program calls as it runs. When the next statement calls a Sub or Function procedure, invoking the Step Into command opens the called procedure in the Code window, where you can step through it to see what it's doing. This is different from the way the Step Over command works, as you'll see shortly.

Tip   The Step Into command is available even when you're not already in break mode. If you want to step through the program from the beginning, just give the Step Into command to run the first statement and enter break mode. Used in this way, Step Into runs the procedure containing the insertion point, always starting from the procedure's first line.

Stepping over and out

Pressing Shift+F8 is the most efficient way to invoke the Step Over command. The Step Over command works just like Step Into, with two exceptions:

✦ Most important, Step Over doesn't step though the individual statements in a called procedure.

✦ You can't start running a program in break mode with Step Over.

When the next statement calls another procedure, Step Over runs the whole procedure in one gulp, going on to the following statement in the current procedure. This is great when you just want to see whether the procedure as a whole does anything goofy before bothering to check it out in detail. Obviously, stepping over a procedure is also a big timesaver when you're already fairly sure that the procedure works as it's supposed to.

The Step Out command is a handy complement to Step Into. Pressing Ctrl+Shift+F8 is the most efficient way to invoke the Step Out command. After you have the chance to examine the inner workings of a called procedure, you may decide that everything is okay, or you may locate the error and fix it. More embarrassingly, you may just have clicked the Step Into button when you meant to click Step Over (this is the most common scenario in my case).

In any event, there's no point in hanging around to step through the procedure's remaining statements. Use the Step Out command to run the rest of the procedure at top speed. VBA returns you to the procedure from where you came, highlighting the statement following the procedure call.

Major manipulations during debugging

In break mode, just because you're running your program doesn't mean the program's course is fixed in stone. VBA is sophisticated enough to allow midcourse corrections. Specifically, you can edit the existing code and alter the sequence in which statements get executed.

Adding and editing code in break mode

The Code window's editing features are fully operational during break mode. You can type in new statements, modify existing ones, or delete them altogether. But what's really special is that most of your changes work immediately, becoming part of the running program. For example, you can declare new variables and use them right away in calculations, perhaps in combination with existing variables. Some edits do bring the program to a halt, such as changing a variable to a different type in its declaration.

Choosing a different next statement

Suppose you're stepping through your code in break mode when you realize that the next statement contains a big mistake. Rather than execute the statement and send your program into a tailspin, you can choose to bypass it altogether until you've had a chance to make it right.

Other Ways to Skip Over Code

You have other options for skipping over code that you know is broken. These methods work whether you're step-executing a program in break mode or editing the code before you run it. One approach is to type in an apostrophe at the beginning of each line you want to skip, turning it into a comment. You can use the Comment Block toolbar button to comment the current line, if you haven't selected anything, or all lines of a selected block of code (see Chapter 53).

Sometimes an even better way to skip over code is by using line labels in conjunction with temporary GoTo statements. When the following code runs, VBA completely skips all the statements between GoTo AfterTheSkip and the statement following the AfterTheSkip: label. When you're ready to run the skipped code again, just remove the GoTo statement or turn it into a comment ("comment it out").

```
. . .
GoTo AfterTheSkip
    A = B + C
    D = A + E/F
    G = B + D
AfterTheSkip:
    MsgBox "Today is " & Format(Now, "dddd")
. . .
```

The Visual Basic Editor lets you select a different statement almost anywhere in your code as the next statement, using either the keyboard or the mouse. You can jump forward or backward in the code. In addition to letting you skip over foul code, this also lets you repeat statements until you're sure you understand how they work.

Just realize that variables retain the values they have before you make the change. These values may well be very different than what they are when the program reaches the code running normally. If necessary, you can give the variables any value you like using the Immediate, Watch, or Locals windows, described later.

If you can keep all that in mind, here's how to select a different next statement:

✦ With the keyboard, move the insertion point onto the line containing the statement. Then press Ctrl+F9 or choose Debug ➪ Set Next Statement.

✦ With the mouse, drag the yellow arrow pointer in the Code window margin to the new next statement (see Figure 55-5).

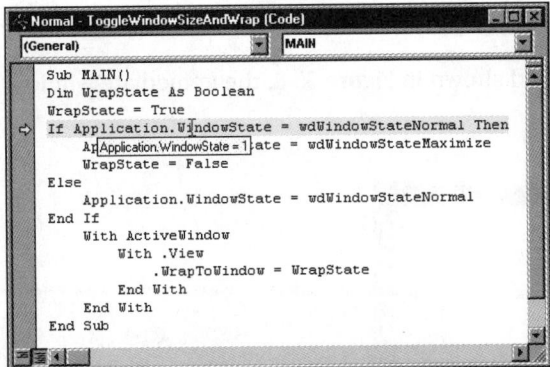

```
Normal - ToggleWindowSizeAndWrap (Code)
(General)                              MAIN

Sub MAIN()
Dim WrapState As Boolean
WrapState = True
If Application.WindowState = wdWindowStateNormal Then
     Application.WindowState = wdWindowStateMaximize
     WrapState = False
Else
     Application.WindowState = wdWindowStateNormal
End If
     With ActiveWindow
         With .View
             .WrapToWindow = WrapState
         End With
     End With
End Sub
```

Figure 55-5: Selecting a different next statement
lets you repeat blocks of code whose functioning
you want to study.

Seeing Data Tips

VBA's Auto Data Tips feature enables you to see the current value of any variable
wherever it appears in your code. While you're in break mode, hovering the mouse
pointer over any variable pops up the Data Tips window, a little box containing the
name and current value of that variable. Figure 55-6 shows Auto Data Tips in action.

```
Normal - ToggleWindowSizeAndWrap (Code)
(General)                              MAIN

Sub MAIN()
Dim WrapState As Boolean
WrapState = True
If Application.WindowState = wdWindowStateNormal Then
     Ap[Application.WindowState = 1]ate = wdWindowStateMaximize
     WrapState = False
Else
     Application.WindowState = wdWindowStateNormal
End If
     With ActiveWindow
         With .View
             .WrapToWindow = WrapState
         End With
     End With
End Sub
```

Figure 55-6: The little Auto Data Tips box shows
the value of the variable beneath the mouse pointer.

In case you don't see the Auto Data Tips box when you should, check to be sure its
box is checked in the Editor tab of the Tools ➪ Options dialog box.

You can use a different Editor feature to display the type and scope of a variable, though not so automatically. Place the insertion point in or beside the variable name and press Ctrl+I to pop up a Quick Info box containing that information. You don't have to be in break mode to use this feature, which is especially helpful when you're working in the middle of a long program whose variables were declared at the top. Figure 55-7 shows the sort of information you get.

```
Normal - BookshelfLookupLongVersion [Code]
(General)                                    MAIN

        strAppPath = GetKeyValue(HKEY_LOCAL_MACHINE, "Software\Microsoft\
        strAppPathLen = Len(strAppPath)
        strAppPath = Left(strAppPath, strAppPathLen - 1) + " /b /I:roget"
        varID = Shell(strAppPath, vbNormalFocus)


        MyLookUp.SetText (MyWord)
        Local MyLookUp As DataObject
        AppActivate "Microsoft Bookshelf Basics - Thesaurus", True

'  4.
        SendKeys "(ESC)", True
        SendKeys "^V", True        ' Copy in selection.
        SendKeys "(TAB)", True
        SendKeys " ", True
    End Sub
```

Figure 55-7: Displaying a Quick Info box for a variable

The Immediate Window

Displayed by pressing Ctrl+G, and shown in Figure 55-8, the Immediate window lets you do two things:

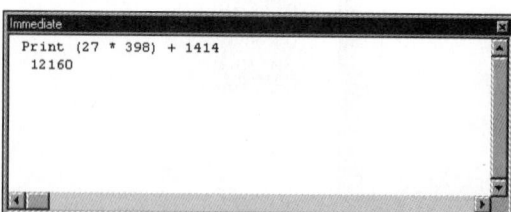

```
Immediate
Print (27 * 398) + 1414
  12160
```

Figure 55-8: The Immediate window in action

✦ See the values of calculations and variables using the `Debug.Print` method.

✦ Execute individual code statements directly, without running them inside a procedure. To execute a statement in the Immediate window, just type it in and press Enter.

So what good are these talents, you ask? Allow me to list the benefits:

✦ You can use the Immediate window as a crude calculator. If you type an expression such as

```
Print (27 * 398) + 1414
```

and press Enter, you get the result, well, *immediately*. When you work in the Immediate window, you don't have to specify the Debug object.

✦ You can route intermediate values of variables and expressions at various points in a running program to the Immediate window by placing the `Debug.Print` method in the program's code (not the Immediate window itself). After the program terminates, you can quickly check to see whether it produced the correct results, without displaying a message box for each value. Figure 55-9 shows an example of this technique.

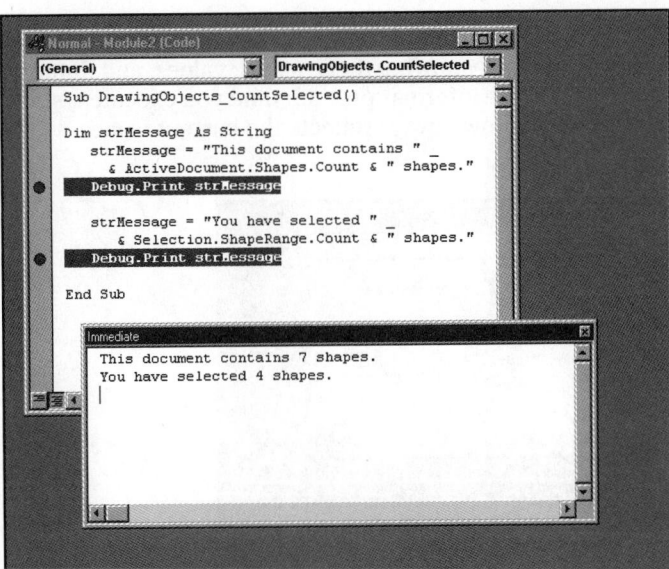

Figure 55-9: Output from a program that uses the Debug.Print method

✦ During break mode, you can display the value of any variable or object property in the Immediate window with a print statement, or change the value by typing a standard assignment such as

```
intTheirNumber = 25
```

✦ You can also call `Sub` and `Function` procedures just as you normally would. Note that during break mode, statements you execute in the Immediate window can access only those variables, objects, and procedures within the scope of the procedure that's currently executing in the program. In other words, executing a statement in the Immediate window produces the same effect as typing it into the running procedure and executing it there.

From the interesting facts department: You can Ctrl-drag selected text from the Code window to the Immediate window, which means you don't have to retype long expressions or variable names if you want to use them there (if you don't hold down Ctrl as you drag, the code is moved, not copied, to the Immediate window). The F1 key works in the Immediate window as it does in Code windows, displaying Help on whatever keyword the insertion point lies within. However, Auto Data Tips does not function there.

The Locals Window

If you have room to display it, the Locals window should be on your screen at all times when you're debugging a program in break mode. Bring this window into view by clicking its button on the Debug toolbar, or by selecting the corresponding item on the View menu.

Shown in Figure 55-10, the Locals window automatically displays all the variables accessible in the current procedure, showing their names, values, and data types. The Visual Basic Editor updates the information each time you execute a statement, so what you see in the Locals window always reflects the current values.

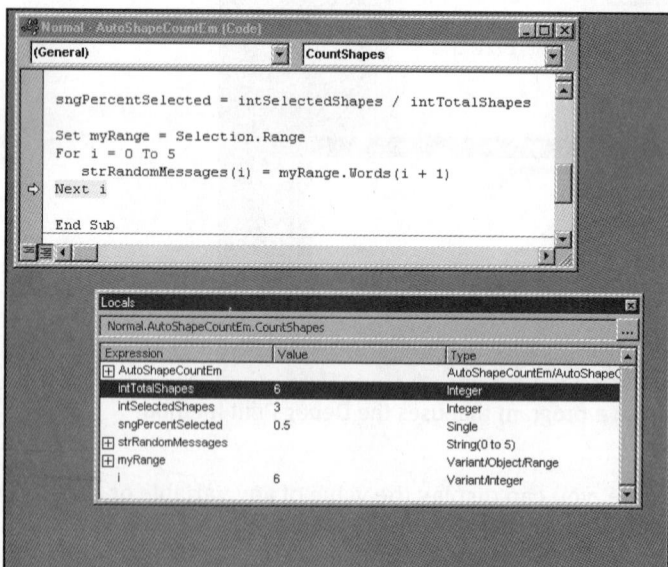

Figure 55-10: The Locals window during break mode

Local mechanics

Like most Visual Basic Editor windows, the Locals window is dockable by default but can also be displayed as a free-floating separate window. Chapter 52 covers the basics of working with Editor windows.

If you can't see all the information in a column, remember that you can resize the columns. Position the mouse pointer over a column separator in the gray column header just above the main part of the window. When the pointer becomes a double-headed arrow, drag to the left or right to change the widths of the adjacent columns.

If you look back to Figure 55-10, you can see that some rows list individual variables; others show items such as arrays, variables of user-defined types, and objects. Such items have no values of their own but instead, hold variables and other "container" items. When you begin running a procedure, the Locals window lists them in collapsed form — you can't see the subsidiary items they contain. To expand a collapsed item, click the boxed plus sign to its left.

Tip   Only variables declared (implicitly or explicitly) in the currently running procedure appear already expanded at the top level of the Locals window hierarchy. To see module-level variables accessible to all procedures in the current module, expand the very first item in the Locals window. This item always pertains to the module in which the current procedure is running. You can't work with global variables or those in other projects in the Locals windows.

Why edit variable values?

Before I tell you how to change a variable's value, you should probably know why you might want to. Here are some good reasons:

✦ A previous line of code has an error in it that assigned an incorrect value to the variable. You've caught the mistake, but you want to continue stepping through the program. Before you go on, change the variable's value to what it should have been, so the mistake won't affect subsequent statements.

✦ You want to test various alternative values for the variable without changing your code. You can use the Set Next Statement command to repeatedly pass through the same stretch of code, entering different values in the Locals window each time.

✦ The values that the program uses when it runs in real life aren't currently available to it. For example, the program may read information from a database or the Internet. In this case, you can supply simulated values via the Locals window.

How to edit variable values

To change the value of a variable in the Locals window, follow these steps:

1. Click twice (don't double-click) directly over the variable's current value in the window so only the value is highlighted. Clicking elsewhere on the same row simply selects the whole line.

2. Type in the new value. If you're typing a string value, you must include beginning and ending quotation marks. Similarly, enclose date literals with # characters.

3. If you change your mind, you can cancel your entry and restore the previous one by pressing Esc. Otherwise, press Enter to confirm it. The Editor won't accept an invalid value, and you may get an error message telling you what was wrong with your entry.

You can edit any variable's values, including those of individual members of arrays and user-defined types. Just realize that you have to expand the array or user-defined type variable before you can get to its member data elements. With an object variable, you can't change the object that's assigned to it, but you can edit the object's properties (except the read-only ones). Again, you must expand the object to see the editable items. Figure 55-11 shows expanded array, user-defined type, and object variables.

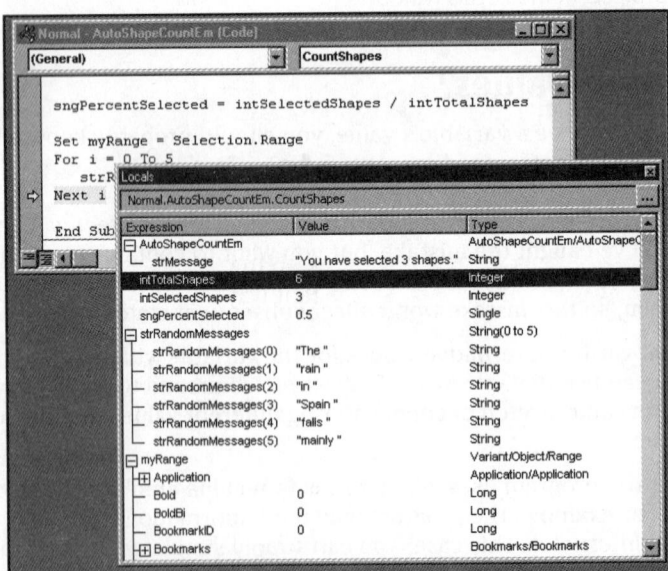

Figure 55-11: The Locals window displays the same procedure shown in Figure 55-10, but items that were collapsed are now expanded.

The Watch Window: A Key Debugging Tool

After you've mastered the Locals window, working with the Watch window is easy. It works in essentially the same way, the obvious difference being that you get to pick out which values it displays. Figure 55-12 shows the Watch window in action. To view the Watch window, select Watch Window from the View menu.

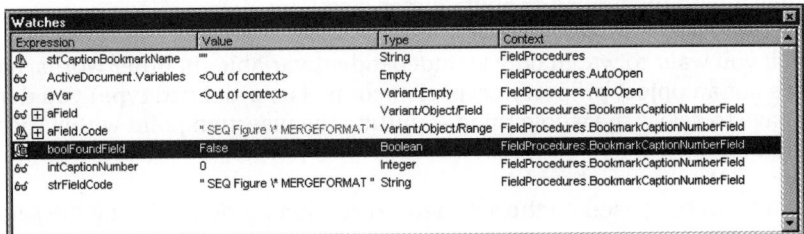

Figure 55-12: The Visual Basic Editor's Watch window

 **Tip**   Use the Watch window when you're debugging larger programs in which many different procedures manipulate global variables. By adding these global variables to the Watch window, you can track their current value no matter what part of the program you're currently stepping through.

The Watch window appears automatically as soon as you define a watch expression. If you want more room on the screen, however, you can put it away by clicking the Close button at the upper right.

What else is different compared to the Locals window

Besides the fact that what appears in the window is up to you, the Watch window differs from the Locals window in two other important ways:

✦ Each line in the Watch window lets you track the value of any valid VBA expression, not just an individual variable. Expressions such as (X - Y) > 15, "The color is " & strColor, or even 2 + 2 are perfectly acceptable. That's why entries are called watch expressions.

✦ Because the Watch window can track variables from any module or procedure in the project, it adds a fourth column labeled Context. This column describes the scope in which the window displays a value for the variable or expression. When you're executing a procedure outside the defined context, all you see is <Out of context>.

Adding watch expressions

If you like having options, you'll love the Watch window—prepare to be over-whelmed by how many different ways you can add watch expressions.

No matter which technique you eventually use, you should start in the Code win-dow by selecting the variable or expression you want to watch. When I say *selecting*, I mean selecting the entire item as you would in a word processor, by highlighting it with the mouse or Shift+cursor keys.

However, if you want to watch only an independent variable (in other words, an item that's not an object property or an element in a user-defined type) you don't actually have to select the whole thing—putting the insertion point within the vari-able name will do.

You can add a watch based on the selected expression by right-clicking the selec-tion and

> ✦ Choosing Add Watch to bring up the Add Watch window
>
> ✦ Choosing Debug ➪ Add Watch, which also displays the Add Watch dialog box
>
> ✦ Clicking the Quick Watch button on the Debug toolbar, or choosing Debug ➪ Quick Watch. The Editor shows you a confirmatory message describing the watch expression you're about to add, but you can't change anything.
>
> ✦ Dragging the selection to the Watch window. This creates the watch without any intermediate steps.

If you're a diehard do-it-yourselfer, you don't actually need to select anything in the Code window. You can just click the Add Watch button and then type in the expres-sion of interest from scratch in the Add Watch dialog box.

Working with the Add Watch window

Figure 55-13 shows the Add Watch window, which appears when you select Add Watch on the Debug menu, or on the Code window's shortcut menu. Here, you define the details of your watch expression.

The Expression field is, of course, where you specify the expression you want to watch. If you selected the correct variable or expression before you started, you shouldn't have to change anything here. But you can if you want to.

The Context section of the dialog box lets you define the procedures in which the Visual Basic Editor actually calculates and displays the value of the watch expres-sion. The values for the Procedure and Module choices are initially set to the proce-dure in which the variable appeared when you added the watch. If you want to see the value when a different procedure is running, select it by name. If that procedure is in a different module, you must first select its module and then choose the procedure.

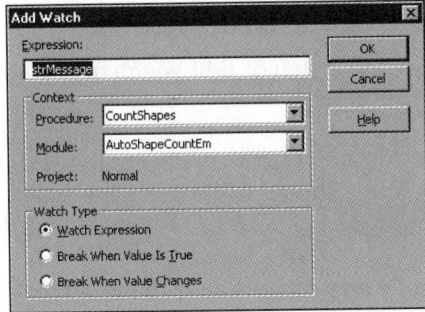

Figure 55-13: The Add Watch dialog box

Tip

If you want the variable value to remain visible no matter which procedure in a given module is executing, select "(All procedures)," the very first item in the Procedures list. And if you want to see it always—throughout the whole program—select "(All modules)" in the Modules list. The broader the scope you select, the longer it takes for VBA to calculate and report the value. Still, being able to track a variable wherever you are in the program is often worth the short wait.

For a normal watch expression, leave the Watch Type set to watch expression. I explain the other choices a bit in "Using watch expressions to define breakpoints," later in the chapter.

Editing watch expressions

As in the Locals window, you can also change the value of a variable while the program is running. However, you can't change the Context setting for a watch expression in the Watch window.

Instead, you have to bring up the Edit Watch dialog box, a spitting image of the Add Watch box shown back in Figure 55-13. To display the Edit Watch dialog box, press Ctrl+W. Edit Watch is a choice on the Debug window and on the shortcut menu for the Watch window. When the dialog box is open, you can make changes to the expression's context or to the expression itself, just as when you originally defined the watch.

Tip

The easiest way to modify an existing watch expression is to type changes in the Expression column of the Watch window. Click once on the line containing the expression to select it, and then click again directly on the expression itself to highlight it. You can then edit the expression to taste. The shortcut menu on the Watches window also offers Edit Watch as a choice.

Using watch expressions to define breakpoints

Using the Watch Type option buttons in the Add Watch or Edit Watch dialog box, you can set up two different types of these automatic breaks:

✦ You can have your program automatically enter break mode as soon as it executes any statement that changes an expression to a nonzero value — in VBA, remember, 0 is False and everything else is True. Select "Break When Value Is True" for this type of breakpoint.

✦ You can automatically enter break mode immediately after the program executes any statement that changes the value of an expression. "Select Break When Value Changes" for this type of breakpoint.

Their special talents notwithstanding, these "breaking" watch expressions still function as ordinary watches in the Watch window. You can distinguish watches of different types, though, by differences in the little icons at the far left of each item. You can sort of see them if you squint real hard at Figure 55-14, but on the screen they're easy to pick out. When a watch-based breakpoint is triggered by a value change, VBA suspends program execution and enters break mode. In the Code window, the statement that caused the change is the one just before the highlighted Exit For statement. The watch expression that triggered the break is highlighted in the Watch window so you'll know which one did it (see Figure 55-14).

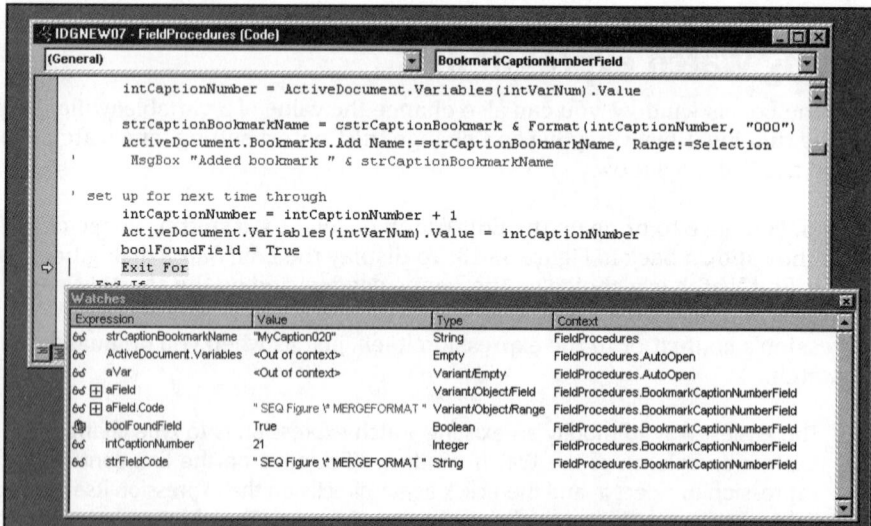

Figure 55-14: A "Break When Value Changes" watch expression on variable boolFoundField has just dropped the program into break mode.

Tip

The larger a program gets, the harder it is to keep track of which procedures and statements are changing which variables. Often, you suspect that a variable's final value is incorrect, but you're not sure where to look for the code that caused the problem. In this situation, a breakpoint based on a watch expression can be a lifesaver—or at least a codesaver.

Trapping Wild Bugs with On Error and the Error Object

When something goes unexpectedly wrong while a program is running, the result is often catastrophic. VBA brings the program to a grinding halt, popping up a run-time error dialog box to give you the bad news about what went wrong, tersely. The choices in the dialog box are End (to terminate the program), Debug (enter break mode), and Help (to display a Help topic about the specific error you've run into).

None of these options is particularly appealing, especially if you're running the program for real, rather than testing it. It would be far less jarring if your program could detect the error and correct it—or at least sidestep it—before VBA muscles in with that ominous run-time error message. Failing that, you might at least present the user with a more congenial message. All this is possible, but it requires you to add your own error-handling code. This section tells you how.

Where run-time errors come from

As I previously mentioned, run-time errors can occur for two reasons:

✦ A serious error in your program's logic produces a situation that VBA can't deal with. Suppose you have written a statement in which a value gets divided by a variable. If your code assigns that variable a value of zero, you're sunk—dividing by zero is strictly forbidden and trying to will give your computer a seizure, so VBA stops the program.

✦ Some unforeseen circumstance has sideswiped your program. For example, a required connection to a database file or Internet set may be cut off, so your program can't retrieve values it needs to do its work.

Either way, the outcome is the same. Protect your program and your users by writing your own error-handling code.

How error-handling code works

To prevent VBA from dealing with run-time errors and to take care of them yourself, you must adorn each procedure with an *error handler*—a block of code whose sole purpose is to step in when an error occurs. If something goes wrong as the procedure runs, VBA transfers program execution to the error handler. The code in the error handler can figure out what type of error has occurred and take whatever steps you think the situation warrants.

How to write error-handling code

To add error-handling code to a procedure, you must do three things:

✦ Add an `On Error` statement at the beginning of the procedure to tell VBA where the error handler code is.

✦ Type in an `Exit Sub` or `Exit Function` statement following the body of the procedure, just before the error handler code.

✦ Write the code for the error handler itself.

All the steps are vital—without the initial `On Error` statement, VBA doesn't know the error handler exists. Also, without an `On Error` statement, errors will cause the program to stop executing.

Writing On Error statements

The `On Error` statement enables the error handler by telling VBA where to find the error handler in the procedure code. The full statement has the syntax `On Error GoTo label`, where *label* is a label elsewhere in the procedure identifying the first line of the error handler's code.

Here's how it looks in a procedure:

```
Sub ErrorHandlerDemo()
On Error GoTo ErrorHandler
    MamaVariable = DoThisFunction (X,Y,Z)
    PapaVariable = DoThatProcedure
    BabyVariable = MamaVariable + PapaVariable
Exit Sub ' Stop the procedure here if no error has occurred
ErrorHandler:
(error-handling code goes here)
End Sub
```

You should know about two other forms of the `On Error` statement. They work as follows:

✦ `On Error GoTo 0` disables error handling from this point forward in the procedure and clears the Err object.

✦ `On Error Resume Next` causes VBA to ignore the line causing the error, continuing execution with the following line of code. This arrangement is useful if you want to check the Err object just after an error-prone line runs to handle any errors in the body of the procedure.

Adding an Exit statement to the procedure

An error handler is part of the procedure in which it appears. That means VBA executes the code in the error handler every time the procedure runs — unless you explicitly tell it not to. Obviously, this isn't right. You want the error handler to run only when an error occurs, and at no other time.

To make this happen, all you need to do is add an `Exit` statement immediately before the error handler code, as shown in the example in the preceding section, "Writing On Error statements." If you're writing a `Sub` procedure, the exit statement should be `Exit Sub`; for a `Function` procedure, it should be `Exit Function`.

Writing the error handler

The error handler itself requires several components, described over the next several subsections.

Adding a label

To identify the start of your error-handling code, enter a standard VBA label as the first line of the error handler. As I explained before, the `On Error` statement for the procedure directs execution to this label if an error occurs. In this example, `ThisIsTheErrorHandler` is the required label.

```
...
ThisIsTheErrorHandler:
...
     (Error handling statements)
...
End Sub
```

Getting information about and dealing with the error

The body of your error handler has two main tasks: checking to see what type of error has occurred and doing something about it. Although these chores differ conceptually, they go on almost simultaneously in practice.

The standard method for learning what has gone wrong is to use VBA's `Err` object. If you know that a particular variable has a tendency to go haywire, you might want to check it directly to see whether its value is out of bounds before looking at the `Err` object. Otherwise, however, the `Err` object is the ticket.

The `Err` object is always available in every VBA program. You can use it directly, without creating an instance of it first. VBA automatically stores information about the most recent error in the `Err` object. All your code has to do is retrieve the `Err` object's properties, which include `Number` and `Description`.

The Number property simply tells you the number of the current error. You can assign it to a variable or use it directly in a conditional statement, as in this example:

```
Sub YetAnotherFineMess()
On Error GoTo ImTryinToThingButNothingHappens
...
(error prone statements)
...
Exit Sub

ImTryinToThingButNothingHappens:
Select Case Err.Number
    Case 7 ' Out of memory error
        (code for handling error number 1)
    Case 11 ' Division by zero error
        (code for handling error number 2)
    ... (and so on)
    Case Else
        (code for handling all other errors)
End Select
End Sub
```

Here, the Select Case statement checks the Number property against a series of values for which you've written specific error-handling statements. Such statements might do the following:

✦ Inform the user that something is wrong and ask for instructions via an input box or custom form.

✦ Try again to get valid data from a source that was unavailable earlier, or try an alternative source.

✦ Change an errant value to a valid one, recording in a file or via a message box that data had to be changed by brute force to make the thing go.

Obviously, effective use of the Number property requires that you know what each error number means. I don't have space to catalog the possibilities, but you can find information about the most common errors in the Trappable Errors topic of VBA Help (you can locate this topic by starting to type **trappable errors** in the Help window's Index tab).

If your code can't deal with an error — or if you don't want to take the trouble — you can still avoid the standard VBA run-time error message using the Err object's Description property. The following example displays a genteel message:

```
strMyErrMessage = "I'm sorry to inform you that " _
    & "something has gone amiss in this lovely " _
    & "program. According to VBA, the cause of the " _
    & "trouble is "
MsgBox strMyErrMessage & Err.Description
```

Some VBA applications provide additional objects and functions that provide information about application-specific problems. Microsoft Access, for example, offers a separate Error object.

Resuming program execution

When your error handler has completed its work, you have a choice: Do you want the procedure to pick up where it left off when the error occurred, or do you want to transfer program execution back to the procedure that called the one where the error occurred?

Place the Resume statement in your error handler if you want to jump back into the current procedure. The Resume statement comes in several flavors:

✦ Simply typing Resume on its own line transfers control back to the procedure at the statement that caused the error. You should use this version of the statement if you have corrected values used in that statement so you know an error won't occur again.

✦ To skip over the statement that caused the error, add a Resume Next statement to your error-handling code instead. Execution continues at the statement immediately following the one that caused the error.

✦ To jump to a particular point in the procedure, enter a Resume *label* statement after the error-handling code. Here, *label* refers to a label somewhere in your procedure, but not the label that identifies your error handler. Of course, if you use this version, you must also add the label to the procedure.

✦ ✦ ✦

Getting Interactive: Custom Dialog Boxes

In programming languages other than VBA, windows and dialog boxes are the only access points for interaction between user and program while a program runs. These features tend to be less critical in VBA programming; you can tack your VBA programs onto the user interface of the underlying VBA application. Even so, plenty of situations in VBA programs call for custom dialog boxes. This chapter covers all the skills you need to construct them.

First, though, I discuss VBA's simpler alternatives: message boxes and input boxes. When these lack the muscle you need, you must design your own forms, homegrown dialog boxes that can be as sophisticated as you want to make them. After an introduction covering the basics of form design, the focus shifts to the details of individual controls (gadgets on the form that the user clicks to make things happen). Finally, I explore the all-important topic of writing code to make your forms and their controls do what you want.

Simple Interactions with the World

VBA's rich form-design tools give you the power to create genuine Windows-style dialog boxes and other windows for your users. But when less will do the job, less is better. Two VBA functions, MsgBox and InputBox, provide the basic tools you need to talk to the program's users and to let them talk back. Their basic duties are as follows:

✦ MsgBox displays a message, of course, but it also lets you know which of two or more buttons the user clicked.

✦ InputBox displays a message and a text box where the user can type a response.

Displaying message boxes

The formal syntax for the MsgBox function is as follows:

```
MsgBox(prompt[, buttons] [, title] [, helpfile, context])
```

As the brackets indicate, only the prompt argument — which specifies the message you want to display — is required.

Specifying the prompt

In its simplest form, the MsgBox function acts like a statement. All you do is type it on its own line, supplying the text you want displayed as the single argument, as in

```
MsgBox "This is a test MsgBox."
```

You can type parentheses around the message, or prompt, but they aren't required when a function is used as a statement — that is, when you don't use the value it returns. The prompt can be literal text, a variable, or any expression, as in the following example:

```
Sub WishCountdown()
    intWishCount = 3
    datWhen = Format(Now, "Short date")
    strInfo1 = "As of "
    strInfo2 = " wishes left."
    MsgBox strInfo1 & datWhen & ", " & intWishCount _
        & strInfo2
End Sub
```

Tip
To display a message on more than one line, separate the lines by adding a carriage-return character (ASCII value 13) to your prompt string, using the Chr function. Likewise, you can line up text on two or more lines in columns with Tab characters (ASCII value 9) inserted with Chr.

```
Sub LinesAndColumns()
    MsgBox "Here is line one." & Chr(9) & _
        "Column two." & Chr(13) & _
        "Here is line two." & Chr(9) & "Column too."
End Sub
```

Fancier message boxes

Besides displaying text, a message box can show one of several icons and include buttons of several different types. You wrap up your choices for all of these options as a single numeric value, the optional buttons argument. By adding an icon, you can make your message box look a little spiffier than the unadorned box. The example in Figure 56-1 carries the critical message icon, which should generate a bit more excitement in the user. The default message box has only an OK button, but you can add buttons labeled OK, Cancel, Yes, No, Abort, Retry, and Ignore in various combinations. (A sample of these wares can also be seen in Figure 56-1.)

Figure 56-1: A relatively spiffy message box, gussied up with an icon and some buttons

Calculating a value for the buttons argument

You calculate the value for buttons by adding together constants representing the various available choices of icons and buttons. You can calculate the number yourself, but it's easier to create an expression using the named constants that VBA has defined for this purpose. Table 56-1 lists each constant with its numeric value and purpose in life. Based on the table, the buttons argument in the function call for Figure 56-1's message box should be 531. Instead, you can type the following statement:

```
intA = MsgBox("Pick a button", VbYesNoCancel + _
    VbCritical + VbDefaultButton3, "Office XP Bible")
```

In this example, MsgBox is used as a true function, returning the value of the button clicked by the user into the variable intA — see the next section, "Who has the button?" Note that VbDefaultButton3, the third of the three constants in the expression for the buttons argument, sets up the third button as the default choice (counting from left to right). In this case, that third button is Cancel. If you look closely at Figure 56-1, you can see that the Cancel button "has the focus" — it's highlighted by a dotted line, indicating that you can activate it by pressing Spacebar or Enter.

Table 56-1
VBA Constants for Message and Input Box
Appearance and Behavior

Numeric Constant	Value	What It Does
VbOKOnly	0	Displays OK button only.
VbOKCancel	1	Displays OK and Cancel buttons.
VbAbortRetryIgnore	2	Displays Abort, Retry, and Ignore buttons.
VbYesNoCancel	3	Displays Yes, No, and Cancel buttons.
VbYesNo	4	Displays Yes and No buttons.
VbRetryCancel	5	Displays Retry and Cancel buttons.
VbCritical	16	Displays Critical Message icon.
VbQuestion	32	Displays Warning Query icon.
VbExclamation	48	Displays Warning Message icon.
VbInformation	64	Displays Information Message icon.
VbDefaultButton1	0	Specifies first button as the default.
VbDefaultButton2	256	Specifies second button as the default.
VbDefaultButton3	512	Specifies third button as the default.
VbDefaultButton4	768	Specifies fourth button as the default.

Who has the button?

The point of buttons in a message box is to give the user some choice. Of course, you need a way to figure out which button that is. That's easy, because the MsgBox function returns an integer value that corresponds to the button the user clicks. To minimize the strain on your memory, you can test the returned value against predefined, named constants rather than arbitrary numbers. Here's a list of the constants and their "real" values:

Constant	Value
vbOK	1
vbCancel	2
vbAbort	3
vbRetry	4
vbIgnore	5
vbYes	6
vbNo	7

An `If...Then` statement works well to figure out which button was clicked—provided your message box has only two buttons, as in this example:

```
If MsgBox ("Go on?", VbYesNo) = VbYes Then
    DoSomething
Else
    DontDoAnything
End If
```

If you had three buttons to test, you would need an `If...Then...Else If...` statement.

Adding a title

By default, a message box displays the name of the VBA application you're using in its title bar. You can substitute any title you like by supplying a string for the `title` argument when you call the `MsgBox` function—refer to Figure 56-1.

Obtaining user input

If you need to know more from the user than which of three options to pursue, then you don't necessarily need a form—getting user input with the `InputBox` function may be adequate. Here's its formal syntax, minus the more advanced optional arguments:

```
InputBox(prompt[, title] [, default])
```

As illustrated in Figure 56-2, a dialog box displayed by this function provides a text box where the user is asked to type in some piece of presumably crucial information. To bring that information into your program, just assign the return value of the `InputBox` function to a string variable:

```
strB = InputBox ("Seat preference?", "NYAir", "Aisle")
```

Figure 56-2: Use an input box to obtain information from the user and feed it to your program.

Although an `InputBox` can collect a much wider range of information than a `MsgBox`, its basic operations are actually simpler—there are no buttons and icons to fiddle with. The `prompt` and `title` arguments work just as they do in the `MsgBox` function. You can make it easier for your users by supplying a default response—if they like it, they just hit Enter.

Designing Forms

When message and input boxes aren't capable or glitzy enough, create a VBA form instead. Compared to writing code—or even to writing decent English sentences—laying out a VBA form is a piece of cake. Still, some work is involved, and there are a few places where you can get into trouble if you're not forewarned.

Running forms

As you lay out a form, you can "run" it (by pressing F5 or clicking the Run toolbar button) whenever you like. When you run a form, it appears on the screen over your VBA application (that is, the Visual Basic Editor disappears for the moment). You can then test it by clicking its controls to see what happens. Just keep in mind that if the form is part of a larger program, it may not work right if you run it in isolation.

Caution   You must fully select a form before it can run. In the Visual Basic Editor, it's possible to select a form part way—selection handles appear around its perimeter, but it doesn't run automatically when you press F5. If the Macros dialog box unexpectedly pops up, cancel it and then click anywhere on the form before you try to run the form again.

To stop a running form that you haven't equipped with a cancel button, you can click the Close button at the far right side of the form's title bar. Alternatively, press Alt+Tab to get back to the Visual Basic Editor and click the Reset toolbar button.

Note   Forms and controls are full-fledged VBA objects. That means they have properties, methods, and events. What's special about the properties of forms and controls is that you don't have to set them in code, as this chapter makes plain.

Caution   Keep in mind, too, that you must write code for every control you add to your program, with the exception of some label and frame controls. Forms themselves often require code, too. Be sure to account for this in your thinking about what needs to be done to complete your project.

Planning forms for your program

Laying out forms in VBA is fun and easy, but designing those forms requires some thoughtful planning when you're constructing real programs. Remember that your forms are part of a larger software entity that has a practical mission to accomplish.

So before you start fiddling with the forms, spend some time defining a mission statement for the program as a whole and listing tasks the forms have to perform to support that mission. Give some thought to how to group those tasks logically on different forms.

Printing forms during the design process

As you work on laying out forms, it sometimes helps to have paper copies that you can carry around with you as you think about the project. Printed forms are great for scribbling tentative design revisions, and you can pass them around to potential users or other programmers for their reactions.

To print a project's forms in the Visual Basic Editor, follow these steps:

1. Select the form or forms in question. If you want to print only one form, select it in the Project Explorer. If you want to print all the forms in a project, select any form, module, or other component for that project.

2. Choose File ➪ Print or press Ctrl+P. A dialog box appears.

3. Check the Form Image box; uncheck the Code box (unless you also want a printout of the form's code).

4. Select Current Module (if you want just the current form printed), or Current Project (if you want to see all the forms on paper).

5. Click OK.

Laying Out Forms

As Figure 56-3 illustrates, a new form provides a blank canvas for your dabblings in user interface design. You can alter its size and position on the screen, give it a different color, and fill it up with the controls that make it do productive tricks.

Before you create a new form, be sure the correct project — the one in which you want the form to live — is active. Use the Project Explorer window to select the project.

Creating the form

Create a new form by choosing Insert ➪ UserForm from the Visual Basic Editor's main menu system or from the Project Explorer's shortcut menu. The new UserForm appears in its own window. VBA refers to custom dialog boxes as UserForms. To change the default name and title of the UserForm, use the Properties window.

Adding controls from the Toolbox

With the empty canvas of a new UserForm on your screen, it's time to start adding *controls,* the little on-screen doodads that people use to interact with the form. Controls come from the Toolbox, which should appear automatically when you create a new UserForm (the Toolbox is also shown in Figure 56-3). It graciously hides itself when you click any other window but pops up again when you click the UserForm window.

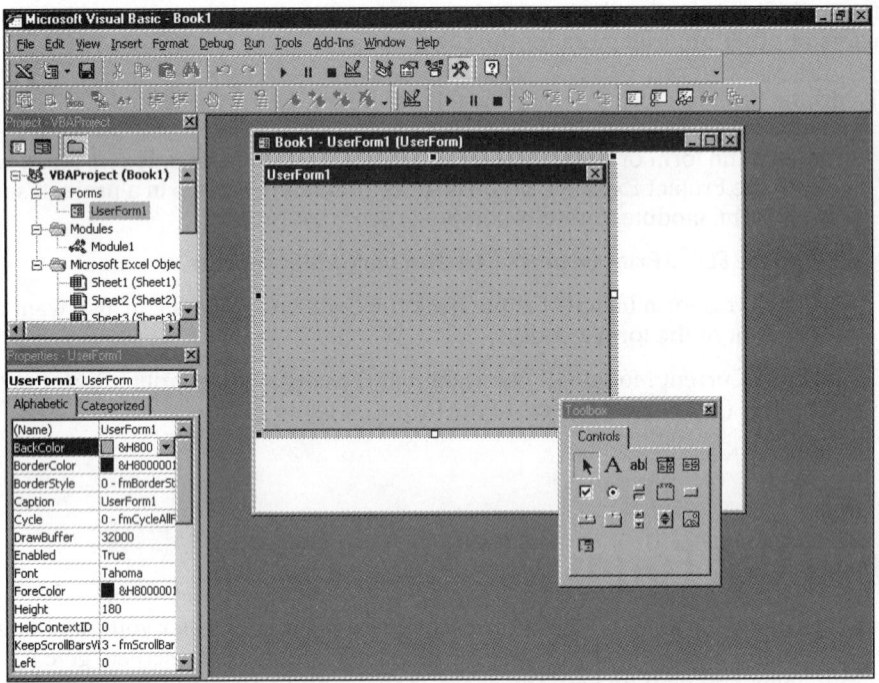

Figure 56-3: A brand-new UserForm. Note the toolbox and its controls.

Tip   If the Toolbox isn't visible when you need it, choose View ➪ Toolbox to call it forth.

To add a control to your form, click the Toolbox icon for the control you want to add and then drag the mouse over the part of the form you want the control to occupy (Figure 56-4). When you let up on the mouse button, the control appears on the form.

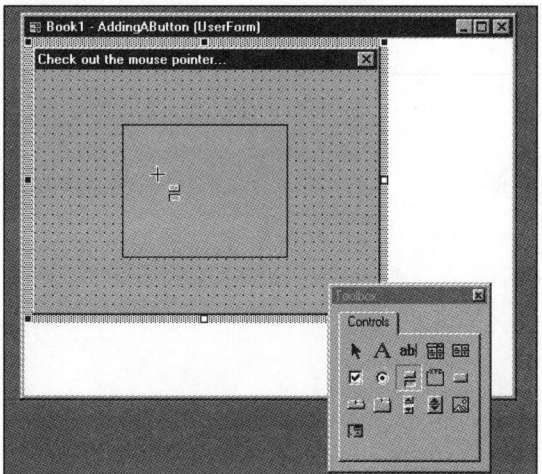

Figure 56-4: Adding a new toggle button control to a form

Tip Normally, VBA reverts to the arrow pointer for selecting objects as soon as you've finished adding a new control. If you want to add two or more of the same type of control to a form, double-click the icon for that control in the Toolbox. When you're through, click the arrow icon to stop adding controls.

Working with Form and Control Properties

Because VBA forms and controls are objects, they have properties that determine their appearance and behavior. And as with all object properties, you can examine and change the properties of forms and controls in your code.

For these objects, however, you don't have to write code. Instead, the Visual Basic Editor's Properties window lets you easily control many critical characteristics of forms and controls without programming per se. As your programs get more sophisticated, you'll want, you'll beg to set properties in code. Even then, though, the Properties window can be the easiest way to control the initial settings for form and control properties. The Properties window is shown in Figure 56-5.

Tip If the Properties window isn't already on your screen, display it by choosing View ➪ Properties Window or by pressing F4.

Figure 56-5: The Properties window for a VBA form

A tour of the Properties window

The Properties window has two outstanding properties of its own:

✦ It automatically shows the properties of whatever you've selected by clicking it in the UserForm window (a particular control or the form itself).

✦ You can still work with the properties for any item on the form by selecting the item from the drop-down list at the top of the Properties window. Figure 56-6 shows the drop-down list in action.

Figure 56-6: The drop-down list at the top of the Properties dialog box gives you immediate access to the properties of any item on a form (or the form itself).

Note that the display at the top of the window always shows the name and type of the item whose properties you're currently working with. The bulk of the Properties window is divided into two tabs. Both display exactly the same set of properties, but the Alphabetic tab lists them in alphabetical order; the Categorized tab divides them into related groups. Whichever tab you choose, the window works the same way. To the right of the property names, each individual property has a field where you can change the property's setting.

Getting help on properties

If you can't figure out what a given property is for (or what settings work), just ask for Help. Click the property's field and press F1 to display the relevant topic from the VBA Forms Help file.

Changing property settings

Depending on the property, you change the setting in its field in one of three ways:

✦ By typing in a new setting

✦ By selecting the new setting from a drop-down list

✦ By selecting the new setting from a dialog box

Some properties enable you to either type in a setting or select it from a list.

Tip

You can't tell that a property has a drop-down list or a dialog box until you click in the property field. When you do, a button appears in the field, which you can then click. (The button has a downward-pointing arrow for drop-down lists and three little dots for dialog boxes.)

Don't forget to select the right item

Before you add controls to a form, the form itself is the only item listed in the Properties window. As soon as you've added one or more controls, however, you need to start paying attention to which item (the form or one of its controls) is selected, as indicated by square handles on the border of the item.

Caution

One way to select an item in the first place, of course, is just to click it. I suggest you make it a habit to select form items a different way, via the drop-down list at the top of the Properties window. The selection handles appear around its perimeter just as if you had clicked it. If you prefer the direct click method, at least practice glancing up at the display at the top of Properties to make sure you've selected the right item.

Key form and control properties

Many properties of forms and controls work identically across different objects and specific properties. For example, you use very similar techniques to change the size of a form and its controls, and all the color-related properties work the same way whether you're setting the color of the form itself, a button control, or some text. This section covers the most important properties common to forms and controls.

The Name is not the Caption

Every object in a VBA program has a name, and forms and controls are no exception. But an object's name doesn't appear anywhere on the form. Instead, you use the name to refer to the object in your code — if, for example, your program needs to activate one of the object's methods or change one of its other properties.

And yes, forms and controls do have a Name property. Like the name you assign to any object, a form or control's Name property is the name you use in your code. A form or control name must be a valid VBA name (no spaces or punctuation characters allowed — see Chapter 53).

The Caption property of a form or control is something else again. A form's caption specifies the text that appears in the title bar; a control's caption — if the control has one — specifies the text on the surface of a control. You can change the Caption property by typing a new text string into the corresponding field in the Properties window. In the case of controls, you can click once to select the control and then click again to edit the caption directly on the control.

Sizing and positioning forms and controls

Before you do any serious design work on a form, be aware the Visual Basic Editor (like any self-respecting graphics program) has a *grid*. The grid defines imaginary "magnetic" lines, vertical and horizontal. When you move or resize any item on a form, the edges automatically snap into place along the nearest grid line. (For more details, see "Working with the Grid," later in this chapter.)

The easiest property to change on a form or control is its size. Although you can set the Height and Width properties in the Properties window, it's easier to just grab the item by one of its handles. Dragging a bottom or right-side handle sizes the form in one dimension; dragging the corner handle changes the size in both dimensions simultaneously.

 **Note**   Note that only white handles work for sizing — and most of the handles for a form are black. The black ones don't do anything except set off the form smartly. Forms are always pushed up against the top-left corner of their windows.

Controlling a form's position on the screen

You have full control over where the form initially appears on the screen when you run your program (or when you run the form alone, if you're just testing it). The StartUpPosition property is the key.

The default value for this property is 1 - CenterOwner. This means that the form appears in the center of the VBA application's window, regardless of how big it is or where it shows up on the screen. If you want your form to appear in the very middle of the screen, no matter what the VBA application is doing, set the StartUpPosition property to 2 - CenterScreen instead. And to set its position yourself, choose 0 - Manual and then type in values for the Left and Top properties.

More important appearance-related properties

Other properties that deserve your attention include the following:

✦ Left and Top. When you change a control's position within a form (usually by dragging the control to where you want it to go), you change these properties — and vice versa. If you're a stickler for details, you can type in numeric position values for the Left and Top properties.

✦ ForeColor and BackColor. These properties set the colors for a form or control.

✦ Font. This property lets you select a font from those installed on your system. To set a default font for all controls on a form, set the form's Font property before you add any controls. That way, you don't need to change the Font properties of every control individually.

✦ SpecialEffect. This property imparts a subtle but definite impression of depth to the target object in a number of variations.

✦ ToolTip. This property specifies the text that appears when the mouse hovers over a control for a second or two.

✦ Picture. This property lets you add a graphic to a form or control (see Figure 56-7). After a picture is in place, use the PictureAlignment, PictureSizeMode, and PictureTiling properties (if they're available for the object you're working with) to adjust the picture to taste.

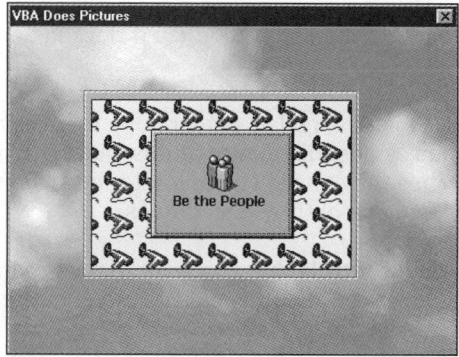

Figure 56-7: Pictures added to a VBA form and several of its controls

Using the Enabled and Locked properties

Two properties, Enabled and Locked, govern whether a control or an entire form is accessible to the user. Obviously, controls are there so people can use them. There are times, however, when a control should be visible to let the user know it exists, but "grayed out," or *dimmed,* to show that it can't be used at the moment.

The Enabled property determines whether the control or form can receive the *focus*, meaning the capability to react to mouse and keyboard actions from the user. Only one object at a time ever has the focus in Windows. To keep you in the know about where the focus goes, Windows places a dotted border around the control that currently has the focus. When Enabled is True, the control appears normally and can receive the focus. When Enabled is False, Windows displays a dimmed version of the control, which can't take the focus.

If the Locked property is False, the control won't respond to mouse-clicks or key presses, regardless of the Enabled setting. However, if Enabled is True, the control can still receive the focus, and it still looks normal on the screen.

Basic Control Editing

The Visual Basic Editor lets you cut, copy, and paste controls individually or in groups. The standard Windows menu commands and keyboard shortcuts apply. In addition, the standard Office buttons for the Cut, Copy, and Paste commands provide one-click access to these functions. When you paste a control from the Clipboard within the VBA environment, VBA deposits it in the center of the form, even if that part of the form isn't currently visible. However, if you select a frame or multipage control before doing the paste, the control appears at the center of that item.

You can delete one or more selected controls (without placing them on the Clipboard) by pressing the Del key or choosing Edit ➪ Delete.

Note   The Backspace key does not work as a deletion technique (as it does in some other programs).

You can select a group of controls and then move, resize, cut, or copy them as a unit, or apply other formatting commands as described later in this chapter. This is also a great way to efficiently set properties they have in common to the same values. To select multiple controls you can use one of three techniques:

- ✦ Draw a selection rectangle around the controls that you want in the group by using the Toolbox arrow pointer. If any part of a control is included in the rectangle, that control is included in the selection.

- ✦ Click the first control in the group and then Shift+Click a control at the other side of the selection area. All controls between the two are included in the selection.

- ✦ Ctrl+Click individual controls to add or remove them to or from the selection.

You can usually reverse the effects of the last formatting change involving controls using the Undo command (Ctrl+Z). Undo doesn't work after you resize a form, nor does it reverse changes you make in the Properties window.

Working with the Grid

The *grid* is an array of horizontal and vertical lines that crisscross your forms. The grid has two functions:

✦ **To visually guide you as you place controls with the mouse.** The visual grid comprises those dotted lines that you've probably seen on your forms.

✦ **To automatically align controls to the grid as you move or resize controls.** No matter how you move the mouse, the edges of your controls always snap into alignment along one of the grid lines. This ensures reasonable consistency in your form layout, though it limits your flexibility.

The two functions work independently — you can turn off the visible grid and leave automatic alignment on, or vice versa.

To control the way the grid works, choose Tools ➪ Options. When the Options dialog box appears, click the General tab to reveal the panel of choices shown in Figure 56-8.

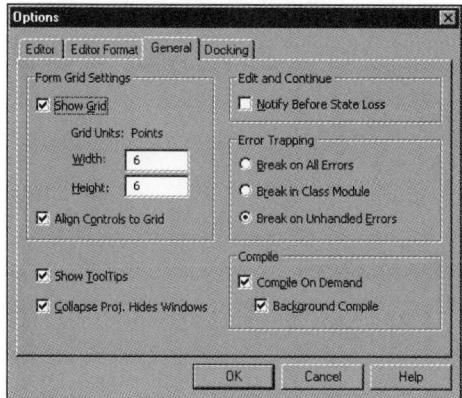

Figure 56-8: Change grid settings on the General tab of the Options dialog box.

Confining your attention to the upper-left part of the dialog box, you can see the few simple grid-related options. They are as follows:

✦ **Show Grid.** Clear this checkbox to turn off the visual grid, those dotted lines on your forms. This doesn't affect automatic alignment to the grid.

✦ **Width and Height.** These two boxes let you can control the size of your grid in the horizontal and vertical dimensions independently. The Width setting controls the distance between each pair of vertical grid lines, which in turn affects the horizontal position of controls. Similarly, the Height setting is for the horizontal grid lines but pertains to vertical position.

✦ **Align Controls to Grid.** When this box is checked, the "snap to grid" feature is in force. Clear this box to give yourself complete freedom to position and size controls to any measurements you please. Again, the visual grid can be on when this function is off.

Formatting Controls

Fortunately, VBA provides a stable of tools that help you achieve the goals of symmetry, consistency, and general neatness easily. Although laying out a well-organized form still takes some manual labor, the Visual Basic Editor's automatic formatting features can handle much of the work.

Using the Format menu

The Visual Basic Editor's Format menu (see Figure 56-9) is the control center for commands that affect the layout of controls on a form. Getting on intimate terms with the menu and its multiple submenus will serve you well during the process of forms design.

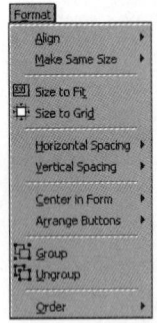

Figure 56-9: The Format menu in the Visual Basic Editor

The UserForm toolbar

When you're working with a form window in the Visual Basic Editor, the UserForm toolbar comes in handy. If it's not already visible, display it by right-clicking any toolbar and choosing UserForm. Figure 56-10 shows how the UserForm toolbar looks in its floating configuration.

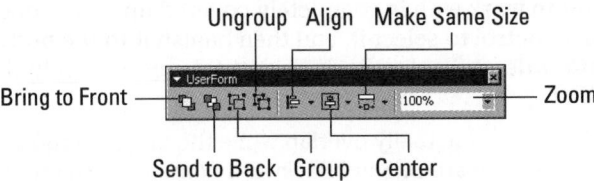

Figure 56-10: The Visual Basic Editor's UserForm toolbar

Most of the buttons on the UserForm toolbar correspond to items on the Format menu. Some of them are split buttons allowing multiple options. If you click the main part of one of these buttons, VBA immediately activates the option that was last used. To select a different option, click the little arrow and pick it from the list.

Grouping multiple controls

Although it's fairly easy to use the mouse to select multiple controls on the fly, this isn't ideal when you want to work repeatedly with the same set of controls as a unit. By combining all the controls into a *group*, you don't have to reselect the same controls every time you do something to them, and you eliminate the possibility of selection mistakes.

Creating a group is simple. Just select all the controls you want in the group and then click the Group button on the UserForm toolbar, or choose Format ➪ Group.

Tip

Grouping lets you apply formatting commands that normally work on single controls to groups as a whole. If you want to even out the spacing between three rows of buttons, for example, you could convert each row into a group, select all three groups simultaneously, and then use the Horizontal Spacing ➪ Make Equal command (which you can read about later, by the way).

Arranging controls on top of each other

Although it's usually best to avoid overlapping controls, such a design can be vital when you need to change the contents of a form while your program runs. By setting each control's Visible property to True or False as necessary, the program can keep all but one of the overlapping controls invisible at any one time. In the Visual Basic Editor, however, every control is always visible—unless, that is, it's buried underneath other controls on the form. When this happens, you can use the Order commands on the Format menu to rearrange the controls.

Here are suggestions for the use of the Order commands:

✦ If you can get to a tiny piece of a buried control, click there to select it and then choose Format ➪ Order ➪ Bring to Front to place the control on the very top of the pile.

✦ If the control you want to work with is completely covered up by the ones on top, click the top-most control to select it, and then banish it to the bottom of the pile with Format ➪ Order ➪ Send to Back. Repeat this process until the control you want is on top.

✦ If you're arranging controls that actually overlap while the program runs, you may need to use the Bring Forward or Send Backward commands to order them just so. These commands move the selected control by one position in the pile.

Formatting multiple controls

Many of the more advanced commands on the Format menu work only on multiple controls, or on selections that include two or more groups. This section describes each of these commands, after an important digression about which selected item has the power in the relationship.

Designating the dominant control

In some formatting commands involving multiple controls, one control serves as the reference point for the command. This is the *dominant control*, in VBA lingo. For example, when you use one of the Format ➪ Make Same Size commands to make uniform a set of selected controls, VBA copies the chosen dimension (height, width, or both) from the dominant control to all the other controls in the set. Likewise for the Align command — the other controls in the set line up with the dominant control, which doesn't move. The effects of the Horizontal and Vertical Spacing commands also depend on which control is dominant.

Look at Figure 56-11, where you can see that only one of the selected controls is outlined in white sizing handles. That's the dominant control, whose handles are always white. Other controls in the selection have black handles around their margins.

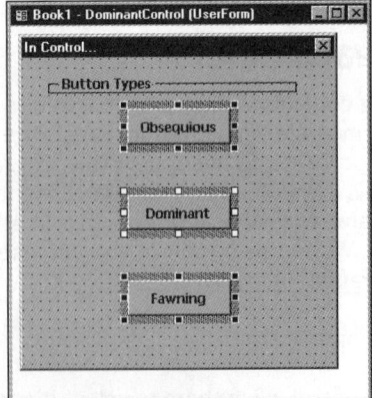

Figure 56-11: The control surrounded by white sizing handles is the dominant control.

Here's how to designate the dominant control while selecting a group:

To	Use This Technique to Select Controls
Choose the dominant control by dragging a selection rectangle	Begin dragging the selection rectangle with the mouse pointer closer to the target control than any other.
Choose the first control you click as the dominant control	Shift+Click to select each control in the set.
Choose the last control you click as the dominant control	Ctrl+Click to select each control in the set.
Choose a different dominant control for an existing selection	Ctrl+Click twice on the chosen control.

Aligning controls to one another

Even with the grid on, it's common to find that controls that ought to be in a straight line or column actually are staggered. Instead of laboriously lining them up by hand, enlist the Format ➪ Align commands or their equivalent buttons to do the work for you. You can bring the midline or any edge (top, bottom, left, or right) of each selected control into alignment along either a vertical or horizontal axis.

Making controls the same size

The three Make Same Size commands automatically adjust all selected controls to match the size of the dominant control in the selection. You can bring instant conformity in width, height, or both dimensions.

Adjusting horizontal and vertical spacing

The Horizontal Spacing and Vertical Spacing commands can each change the space between two or more controls in four different ways. Three of these options are most useful (and one is only available) when the selection includes at least three controls. Here's how the choices work:

✦ **Make Equal.** Evens out the space between three or more selected controls. The controls at either end of the selection stay in place; the controls in between move. This command isn't available if only two controls are selected.

✦ **Increase** and **Decrease.** These commands add or remove space between the selected controls by an amount equal to one grid unit for the dimension you're working with. The dominant control stays in place while the other ones move.

✦ **Remove.** Moves controls so there is no space between them, and their edges touch. The dominant control stays in place.

Other formatting choices

For the most part, the other options on the Format menu work on individual controls as well as groups. After selecting one or more controls, you can use the following:

✦ **Center in Form** to center the items either vertically or horizontally. Note that if you've selected two or more controls, this command brings all the controls to the midline rather than centering the set as a unit (group the controls first if you want the latter result).

✦ **Arrange Buttons** to place one or more selected command buttons at the bottom or right edge of the form. Although Arrange Buttons operates when other controls are included in the selection, only the command buttons move.

✦ **Size to Fit** to have VBA resize the control(s) to fit whatever text they currently contain. This command is a one-shot affair (it does not set the AutoSize property to True); the size remains constant if you later change the text in the control.

✦ **Size to Grid** to move the edges of the selected control(s) to the nearest grid line.

The Visual Basic Editor lacks a command to distribute controls evenly along a row or column. However, you can approximate this easily enough with the following steps:

1. Eyeball the controls to arrange them so they're about where you want them.

2. Select the controls and activate the Align Tops command (or any other horizontal alignment option).

3. With all the controls still selected, activate the Horizontal Spacing Make Equal command.

4. Group the selected controls (activate the Group command).

5. Activate the Center in Form Horizontally command.

The preceding steps assume you're distributing the controls along a row. To distribute them vertically instead, substitute the vertical versions of each command in Steps 2, 3, and 5.

Working with Controls

The controls included with VBA offer everything you need for building dialog boxes that look and act like great professional software. This section explores properties common to many controls (but not available for forms) and then covers most of the types of controls individually. Remember that to get a control to do something useful, you must write code for its event procedures (as discussed in the "Form Programming" section later in this chapter).

Setting the tab order for controls

A Windows convention is that pressing the Tab key moves the focus from one control to another on a dialog box. By default, every control you add to a VBA form takes its proper place in the *tab order*, the sequence in which controls are selected when the Tab key is pressed. (By the way, Shift+Tab walks through the tab order in reverse.)

Tip

You don't need to run a form to check out its tab order. Pressing the Tab key in the UserForm window selects one control after the next in the same order. Initially, tab order is based on the sequence in which the controls were originally added to the form. What usually happens is that you add controls as you think of them, not in the proper tab order. But you can take direct control of the tab order and even remove controls from the sequence if you like.

The easiest way to change the tab order for a form is with the View ➪ Tab Order dialog box. To reshuffle the controls listed there, click a control you want to move and then click the Move Up or Move Down button as appropriate. The tab order is actually controlled by each control's `TabIndex` property. The value of `TabIndex` is 0 for the first control in the sequence, 1 for the second control, and so on. If you change one control's `TabIndex` setting, VBA automatically adjusts all the others. To remove a control from the tab order, set its `TabStop` property to `False`. This doesn't change its position in the tab order, so if you make `TabStop` true again, the control rejoins the sequence right where it was before.

Assigning accelerator keys

Although many people are happy selecting controls with the mouse, some much prefer the keyboard. Be polite — give your users a keyboard shortcut, or *accelerator key*, for each control. When the form is running, pressing Alt followed by the accelerator key moves the focus to the control and may trigger an event (such as the `Click` event).

To make the assignment, type a single character into the `Accelerator` field in the Properties dialog box. The character should be one found in the control's caption, and it should not duplicate the accelerator of any other control on the same form. VBA automatically underlines the accelerator character for you.

To add an accelerator to a control that doesn't have a `Caption` property — such as a text box or scroll bar — follow these steps:

1. Create a label for the control (labels are the subject of the next section).

2. Adjust the tab order so the label comes immediately before the other control.

3. Assign an accelerator to the label.

Secrets of Specific Controls

Each VBA control type is designed for a different task, and each requires a little different handling on your part.

Sending messages with label controls

A *label control* provides a rectangular area on a form where you can display messages. From the viewpoint of a user of your program, a label control isn't much of a control — it doesn't let the user control anything. All it does is display some text, or optionally, a picture. The user can't type over the existing text and can't even copy it to the clipboard.

Still, label controls are vital from the programmer's standpoint because they let you communicate messages to your users. Generally, you use labels to identify controls and their functions, as the example form in Figure 56-12 demonstrates. This is especially useful for controls that don't have their own captions, such as scroll bars, spinner controls, and the like.

The text displayed by a label control is its caption. So to place your own text on the label, change the text in the Caption property in the Properties window.

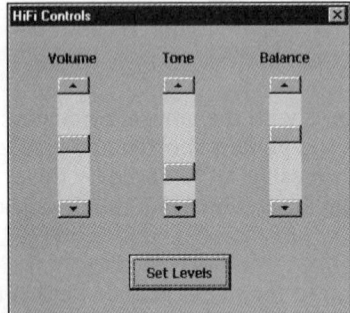

Figure 56-12: Three scroll bar controls, each with an accompanying label

Automatic label adjustments

Via settings you can make in the Properties window, label controls are capable of adjusting themselves automatically to the text they contain. Options include:

✦ Leave the WordWrap property set to True, the default, if you want VBA to automatically break the text into separate lines to fit in the available space, much like a word processor does. If you set WordWrap to False, all the caption text remains on one line, even if there isn't enough room to see it all.

✦ Set the `AutoSize` property to `True` if you want the size of the label itself to change so it can fit all the text. If `WordWrap` is also set to `True`, the label expands vertically. If you change `WordWrap` to `False`, the label widens to accommodate the single line of text.

✦ Use the `TextAlign` property to control how text is justified inside the label: on the left, in the center, or on the right.

Changing label text in code

Although users can't change the text in a label control while your program runs, you can. Using the label's `Caption` property, you need only add a single line of code to modify the text to suit what's currently going on in the program:

```
lblInspirationalMessage.Caption = "Laugh and be happy!"
```

Text boxes let you hear from the user

Use a *text box control* when you want to collect information from the user. Your code can retrieve anything the user types into the text box. Figure 56-13 shows a text box doing its duty.

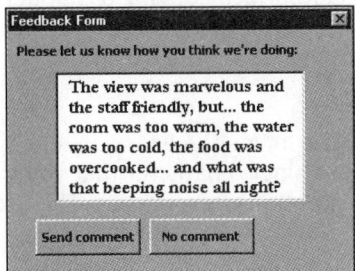

Figure 56-13: Text boxes give users a place to send messages to you.

Use text box controls instead of an `InputBox` when:

✦ You want a prettier dialog box than the standard `InputBox` function can display.

✦ You need at least one more control besides the text box in the same dialog box.

✦ You want to check entries for validity while they are being typed. With a text box, you can program an event procedure that gets triggered each time the user presses a key to see whether the key they pressed meets whatever criteria you set up. With an `InputBox`, you can check only the entire entry, and only after the user has closed the box.

Using text boxes as labels

Like labels, text boxes can also display messages from you to the user. Normally, however, the user can edit text in a text box. If you don't want the user to alter your message, you can ensure they don't by setting the text box control's `Locked` property to `True`. Just be aware that users can still copy the text to the Clipboard within the VBA environment, which they can't do with a label. You can prevent this by setting the `Enabled` property to `False`, but then the text appears dimmed (see the discussion of the `Locked` and `Enabled` properties at the beginning of this chapter).

Default text for a text box

You can place a default entry in a text box so the user doesn't have to type anything if the default is acceptable. To enter the default text, click the text box once to select and then a second time to enter text entry mode, and start typing (don't double-click). Or you can type the text into the `Value` property field in the Properties window.

Note   Text boxes don't have captions. The text string that appears inside a text box is its `Value` property.

What's the secret password?

Passwords are used to protect vital data from unauthorized copying or tampering, and to make people feel that they must be getting something really special if they have to type a password first. Whichever reason appeals to you, it's easy to set up a VBA text box as a password entry field.

With the text box selected in the Visual Basic Editor, locate the `PasswordChar` property in the Properties window. There, type in a single character that you want the text box to display to disguise the actual characters the user types. The text box still records the actual entry, but no one can see it except your program.

Caution   By itself, of course, requiring a password doesn't protect your data. The data themselves and the list of correct passwords must all be encrypted, and your program needs a way to decrypt the data if the user types a valid password.

Retrieving the user's entry

To find out what text the user has entered in a text box, your program should retrieve the box's `Value` property. Typically you would assign the `Value` property to a string variable with a statement such as the following:

```
strTextBoxText = txtMessageFromUser.Value
```

Text box adjustments

Text boxes have the same `AutoSize`, `WordWrap`, and `TextAlign` properties that labels do, and they work mostly the same way. See the information on these properties in the section on label controls earlier in this chapter. However, the `WordWrap` property doesn't do anything except in multiline text boxes. Read on . . .

Multiline text boxes

Text that VBA wraps for you is actually stored behind the scenes as a single line. However, multiline text boxes also permit the user to start a "real" new line, by pressing either Ctrl+Enter, or — if the `EnterKeyBehavior` property is also set to `True` — Enter alone. That way, a line break can come before the one VBA would have automatically generated. You can also control where lines break using code, as discussed in the section on labels earlier in the chapter.

 **Tip**   To get a text box to display text properly, broken up into separate lines to fit in the box, you must set the `MultiLine` property to `True`. Otherwise, even if `WordWrap` is `True`, all the text stays on one line, disappearing beyond the edge of the text box.

Adding scroll bars

Whatever the settings of the `MultiLine`, `WordWrap`, and `EnterKeyBehavior` properties, a text box can display only so much text. Although a user can always scroll with the arrow keys to see the entire contents, you should add scroll bars to all your text boxes via the `ScrollBars` property. VBA is smart enough to display the scroll bars only when the text box doesn't have enough room to show all its contents.

Get things done with command buttons

When you want something done and you want it done now, nothing gives you the feeling that you're in control like pressing a button and getting an immediate response. The standard issue command button is just a gray blob with a bit of explanatory text, such as OK, Cancel, or "Guess Again, Friend." If plain text is too drab for your taste, it's easy to add a little icon graphic to any button. Figure 56-14 demonstrates a variety of command button controls.

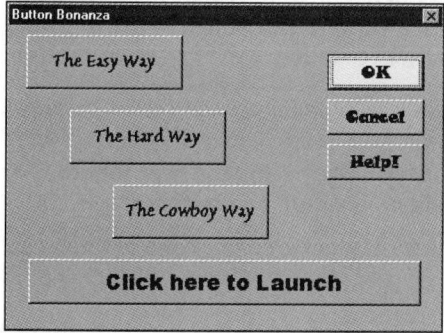

Figure 56-14: Command buttons galore

Unfortunately, command buttons don't *do* anything to speak of until you program them. Clicking a command button generates a `Click` event, but you have to write code to tell VBA what actions to take when the event occurs.

Selecting a default button

In most dialog boxes, pressing Enter triggers a particular button. This is the *default button*, the one that responds when the user presses Enter, unless the focus has been moved to a different control. To designate a command button as the default button for your form, set the button's `Default` property to `True`. Of course, only one button on each form can be the default button.

Creating a Cancel button

If your dialog box can change data or program settings, it's always wise to give users an opportunity to back out before those changes become final. By convention, a button labeled Cancel is this escape hatch. If you're a nonconformist, you might label the button "Never mind" or "Forget it," but concern for the helpless user dictates that you provide a way out, no matter what you call the button.

Also by convention, pressing the Esc key cancels the dialog box, just as if the user had clicked the button in question. Setting a command button's `Cancel` property to `True` simply means that when the user presses Esc, your program reacts as if the button had been clicked. It's up to your code to decide what actually happens when this event occurs.

Caution

To put it more bluntly, setting the `Cancel` property to `True` does not automatically mean that when the user clicks the button, the dialog box is canceled. All it does is connect the Esc key with the button's `Click` event.

Frame controls group other controls

Frame controls are modest but vital components of your VBA forms tool chest. To the eye, a frame is a simple rectangle with a caption embedded in the top side. You place other controls in a frame to group them together.

Frames serve two purposes:

✦ To set off a group of related controls visually, cueing the user that they are in fact related and lending variety and organization to a large form

✦ To define a group of option buttons functionally, so only one of them can be selected at a time

I take up the details on the latter use of frames in a section on option buttons, later in this chapter. Here I stick with the basics on using frames to organize all types of controls.

Placing controls on frames

After you've added a frame to a form, placing any other control on the frame binds the control and frame together. Now, if you move the frame, the control goes with it, always remaining in the same relative location within the frame.

You can add a control to a frame in two ways:

✦ **By drawing a new control on the frame.** Create the new control as you normally would, by clicking the appropriate icon in the Toolbox and then dragging over the target location on your form. In this case, that target location is inside the frame.

✦ **By moving an existing control into the frame.** Drag the control with the mouse until the mouse pointer is within the frame boundary. When you let go of the mouse pointer, the frame takes ownership.

When you successfully stick a control into a frame, the frame border appears selected whenever you select the control. See Figure 56-15.

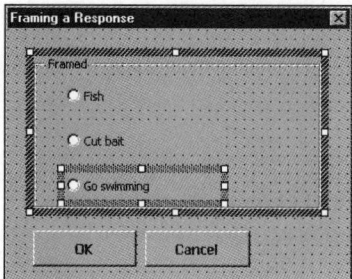

Figure 56-15: Selecting the button inside the frame has selected the frame itself, too.

Removing controls from frames

Breaking the link between a control and its frame is as simple as dragging the control to another spot on the form. As soon as the mouse pointer is outside the frame's border, releasing the button cuts the connection and drops the control into place. Now the two objects (form and control) move independently.

Multipage controls

A *multipage control* reproduces that notebook-tab look found in the dialog boxes used in most commercial Windows software these days. Each page of the control acts like a separate frame. Controls you place on a page become bound to that page and are visible only when the page is displayed. To display a different page, the user clicks the corresponding tab at the top.

Draw a multipage control just as you would any other control. By the way, VBA provides a similar control called a *tab strip*. Tab strips are good when you want the
same controls to display different information, depending on which tab is selected.
They require more programming work than multipage controls and, consequently,
are beyond the scope of this book.

Working with properties of multipage controls and their pages

A multipage control has properties, and so does each page within the multipage.
When you want to fiddle with these properties, you have to be sure you're working
with the right item. Immediately after you place a multipage control on a form, the
multipage as a whole is selected and its properties appear in the Properties window. Later, though, clicking the multipage control selects one of the pages, not the
multipage control. You can select a different page by clicking the corresponding
tab. To select the entire multipage, you must either click the border of the control
or use the drop-down list at the top of the Properties window.

Adding controls to a page

To add buttons, frames, and other controls to a page of a multipage control, just
draw them on the page as you would on a frame. A key first step, though, is to
select the right page before you start plopping down the controls. Again, all you
have to do is click the tab for the page you want — the tab controls work even when
the form isn't running.

Adding and deleting pages

To add another page to a multipage control, right-click over the tab area and
choose New Page from the shortcut menu that pops up. Deleting an existing page is
just as easy, except that you have to be very sure to delete the correct page — the
Visual Basic Editor deletes the page immediately, without asking for confirmation,
and Undo does not work.

Changing the tab text for an individual page

To change the title displayed on a tab, change the caption for that page. One way to
recaption a page is by typing the new text in the Caption field in the Properties window. Alternatively, right-click the page's tab in the control and choose Rename from
the little shortcut menu to display the Rename dialog box. You can type in the new
caption there.

Tip   Don't be confused by the word "Rename" — you really are changing the page's
caption, *not* its name (you need the Properties dialog box to truly rename a page).
Anyway, the Rename dialog box also lets you select an accelerator key and enter
control-tip text; both these options can also be set in the Properties window.

Reshuffling page order

To change the order in which pages of a multipage control are displayed, select Move from the shortcut menu that appears when you right-click over the tab area. In the dialog box shown, click the page you want to move, and then use the Move Up and Move Down buttons to change its position in the lineup.

Picking one item from a group with option buttons

Many choices in life, and in software, are mutually exclusive. When you order a scoop of ice cream, you can pick spumoni or rum raisin or licorice, but not all three at once. When you buy a dress or a pair of slacks, you specify only one out of all the available sizes. And when you marry Ed, you give up on Fred, Ned, and Ted.

In Windows, the most common way to represent mutually exclusive choices like these is with a set of *radio buttons*, the little circular buttons named after the push buttons on car radios. After all, you can listen to only one radio station at a time (unless you're really radical). In VBA, radio buttons are called *option buttons*. Figure 56-16 demonstrates a typical set.

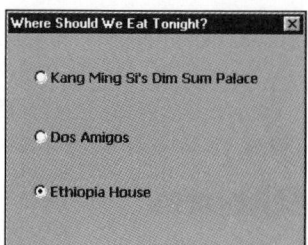

Figure 56-16: Option buttons, also called radio buttons

And option buttons should always come in sets — after all, the point is to represent one choice among several. Only one button in a set can ever be selected. Clicking one option button turns off the previously selected button automatically.

Grouping option buttons

Don't worry about straining yourself to create a group of option buttons. All you have to do is plop down the buttons on the same part of the form. VBA automatically treats them as a group, and they behave as expected — when one is on, the rest are off — when the program runs.

But what did I mean by "the same part of the form?" Well, this isn't official VBA jargon, but here's the idea: One part of the form is the form itself — the background canvas, if you will. Each frame control you add creates another part. And each page of a multipage control is also a separate part. You can even place frames within other frames, or on pages of a multipage control — if you do, each subframe constitutes its own part.

Tip   In a form with one or more frames, VBA treats the option buttons that aren't inside any frame as one group, and each frame's buttons as a separate group. If you want to get tricky, the `GroupName` property lets you define more than one option button group in the same part of a form. All you have to do is use the same `GroupName` for all buttons in the group.

Which option button got clicked?

Clicking an option button selects that button but typically causes no other immediate changes. Instead, the dialog box just sits there, allowing the user to think twice and perhaps pick a different option button. Only when the user clicks the OK button is the selection confirmed.

For you as the programmer, the task is to figure out which option button was selected when the confirming event occurred. To do this, you must check the `Value` property for each button in the group. Though there are trickier ways to do this, an `If...ElseIf` statement is a decent solution, as in the following:

```
If OptionButton1.Value = True Then
    ChosenOption = "Bill"
ElseIf OptionButton2.Value = True Then
    ChosenOption = "Bob"
ElseIf OptionButton3.Value = True Then
    ChosenOption = "Barney"
Else
    ChosenOption = ""
```

Turning options on or off with checkboxes and toggle buttons

Option buttons are great when you're working with multiple, mutually exclusive choices. However, when the number of choices collapses to just two, you should use a checkbox or a toggle button to let the user pick. *Checkboxes* and *toggle buttons* are indicated for any choice involving paired opposites such as Yes or No, On or Off, True or False, and Stay or Leave. In practice, the big difference between checkboxes and toggle buttons is just that they look different.

Grouped checkboxes

Checkboxes are often grouped together to present a list of choices that aren't mutually exclusive. It's like when you go to the store to buy breakfast cereal and come home with one box of Toastie-O's, one of Healthy Cardboard Crunch, and one of Sugar Coated White Flour Kibbles. Figure 56-17 offers several additional examples. Note that each individual checkbox still represents a yes or no choice for the item it pertains to.

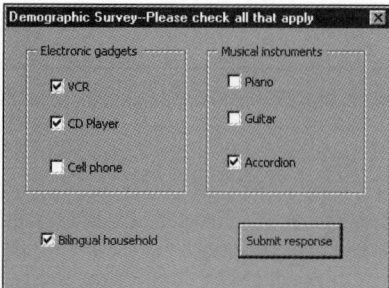

Figure 56-17: Grouped checkboxes let you select multiple items for the same overall option.

For the sake of the user's sanity, you should arrange all the checkboxes in a group together on a form, so the user can see at a glance that they're all related. Frames can help to distinguish these groups.

> **Tip** Because each checkbox functions independently, you don't need to worry about grouping them together in any other way. If you like, though, you can identify them as members of a group by entering the same GroupName property for each checkbox in the group. This mainly helps you keep track of which checkboxes belong together in case you reorganize the form.

How to tell whether a checkbox is checked or a toggle button is toggled

As usual, the Value property holds the crucial information concerning the user's interaction with these controls. If a checkbox is checked, its Value property is True; if it's cleared, Value is False. Likewise for toggle buttons: Value is True if the button is pushed in, False if not. So code like the following retrieves and acts on the current setting:

```
If tglLightSwitch.Value = True
    TurnLightsOn
Else
    TurnLightsOff
End If
```

Selecting options with list and combo boxes

If you establish more than four or five mutually exclusive choices for an item, your dialog box becomes confusingly cluttered if you present all the choices as option buttons. When the choices aren't mutually exclusive, you can get away with maybe 10 or 12 checkboxes, because the user can consider each checkbox on its own merits. Still, a forest of checkboxes won't do.

Now That You Know What List Boxes Are, Don't Use Them

My advice is to use combo box controls for all options you present in lists, whether or not the user is allowed to type in entries that aren't on the list. Forget about list boxes.

Here's why: A VBA list box can't display items in a drop-down list. Instead, it's just a rectangular area on the form where the choices are listed. This doesn't really solve the space and clutter problem — if the list contains any significant number of items, it takes up too much room on your form and distracts attention when it's not in use. If the choices are few enough to make an unobtrusive list, a set of option buttons or checkboxes would work just as well and look more appealing.

In contrast, combo boxes are much more compact, because they always display only a single choice from those on the list. And when you need it to, a combo box can act just like a list box, not accepting typed entries. All you have to do is set the combo box's `Style` property to 2 (`fmStyleDropDownList`). So why bother with list boxes?

List boxes

The *list box* is Windows' solution to such problems. A list box presents a compact list of named options, allowing the user to select them individually in the list. Obvious examples would be list boxes for picking a salad dressing choice or selecting one of the 50 states.

VBA's list box control lets you set up list boxes with relative ease, although programming is required to add items to the list. A VBA list box can stand in for a framed group of option buttons, allowing the user to choose only one of the listed items. Alternatively, it can function like a set of checkboxes, letting the user pick as many of the options as desired. What a list box can't do is accept entries that aren't in the list. Also, you can't present a VBA list box as a drop-down list on a single line. To overcome these limitations, you need a combo box.

Combo boxes

A *combo box* combines the virtues of a list box with those of a text box. The user can pick a supplied item from the list, but if none of these is appropriate, the user can type in an entry from scratch.

From a user's point of view, combo boxes are usually cooler, because they give you free reign to make your wishes known. From the programmer's standpoint, however, many situations call for limiting user choices to prevent invalid entries. Given that there are only 50 states in the United States, it wouldn't make sense to allow users to make up their own state entries in an address database.

Putting items into a list or combo box

Now for the harder part. You can't use the Properties window to type in the choices that should appear in a list or combo box. Instead, you either have to write code for the control's AddItem method or bind the control to a *data source*, meaning a list in an Excel worksheet or an Access database.

To create the list directly in code requires an event procedure for the form's Activate event. It should contain a series of statements like the ones in this example:

```
Private Sub UserForm_Activate()
    cmbOpinionPoll.AddItem "Overpopulation"
    cmbOpinionPoll.AddItem "Global warming"
    cmbOpinionPoll.AddItem "No time to smell the roses"
    cmbOpinionPoll.AddItem "No roses to smell"
    cmbOpinionPoll.AddItem "Taxes on the rich too high"
    cmbOpinionPoll.AddItem "Too many social services"
    cmbOpinionPoll.AddItem "Inadequate social services"
    cmbOpinionPoll.AddItem "HMOs"
End Sub
```

Cross-Reference

Chapter 50 (on Access forms) covers techniques for binding a list or combo box to a data source.

Retrieving options selected by users

To retrieve the item that the user has selected or typed in a list or combo box, use the object's Value property in your code. This works just like it does in a text box. Just assign the property to a suitable variable (whether a string, numeric, or variant), as in

```
strOpinion = cmbOpinionPoll.Value
```

Selecting values with scroll bars and spin buttons

When you turn up the volume on your stereo or turn down the thermostat on your heater, you're using a real-life control to select a value from a range of possible values. The job of emulating this kind of choice on a form falls to two controls, *scroll bars* and *spin buttons*. Figure 56-18 shows examples.

Of course, scroll bars are most commonly used in Windows for scrolling the visible area of a document or dialog box, when all the information won't fit at one time. But you can think of a scroll bar more generically as a slider control that slides through any range of numeric values. To select a value, the user can drag the *scroll box*, that squarish thing on the scroll bar itself, or click the arrow controls at either end.

Spin buttons are just scroll bars with the bar removed — only the arrows remain. A spin button doesn't actually spin anything except the numbers it controls.

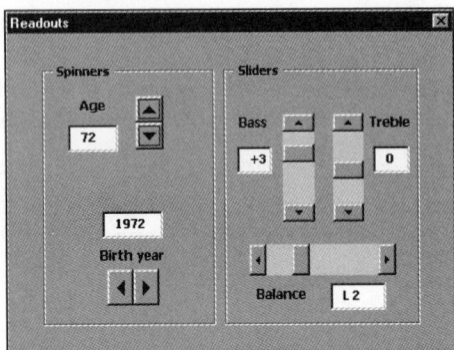

Figure 56-18: Sample scroll bars and spin buttons

Drawing the controls

You place scroll bars and spin buttons on your forms just as you do other controls, by clicking the correct icon on the Toolbox and then dragging on the form to place the control. Both scroll bars and spin buttons can be oriented either vertically (with the arrows pointing up and down) or horizontally (left and right). By default, VBA determines the orientation automatically, based on how you draw the control. You can fix the orientation using the Orientation property.

Setting up the controls

After you place a scroll bar or spin button on a form, you have two main tasks to complete (in the following order) to get the control working properly:

1. You must specify the range of values that can be selected with the control.

2. You should provide users with visual feedback about which value they've selected.

Selecting a range of values

Use the Max and Min properties of a scroll bar or spin button to specify the range of values for the control. Only integer values are acceptable.

Note   Despite their names, these properties refer to locations on the control, not a numeric maximum or minimum. In other words, the Max property can take a smaller number than the Min property. The Max property determines the extreme value by clicking the top arrow on a vertical scroll bar or spin button or the right arrow on a horizontal one. Min corresponds to the bottom or left arrow. Setting the Min property less than Max reverses the polarity of the control, you might say — pressing the down arrow would increase the value.

Giving feedback

Spin buttons and scroll bars aren't very useful unless users know what value they're selecting. Unfortunately, neither control comes with a default gauge. You're stuck with using code to connect the value selected with the spin button or scroll bar to another control's text display. This isn't actually all that tough—you can do it with a single line of code. This example passes the value of a scroll bar to the caption of a label control when the scroll bar control is double-clicked:

```
Private Sub sclWarpFactor_DblClick
    lblScrollBarReadout.Caption = sclWarpFactor.Value
End Sub
```

Note that to provide immediate feedback, the code that displays the selected value in another control should be placed in the Click event procedure for the spin button or scroll bar, as in the example (sclWarpFactor is the name of the scroll bar control). The next section discusses event programming in detail.

Form Programming

Adding controls to a form is a piece of cake, but getting them to do your bidding takes a little more brain power and programming work. This section cuts through the complexities.

Loading and showing forms

After you've decided to include custom forms in a VBA program, the first and most fundamental programming problem is how to get your forms on the screen to begin with. Because a VBA program can fall back on the user interface of the underlying application, the program doesn't automatically display a form when it runs. In this respect VBA is different from its cousin Visual Basic, in which the program is the form, unless you take extraordinary measures. At any rate, in a VBA program, you must add code to display a form so it becomes accessible to users.

Displaying a VBA form is a two-step process. You must first load the form into memory and then show the form on the screen. As a programmer, you can use a single VBA statement to perform both steps. However, as the next few sections discuss, it can sometimes be useful to split them up.

Show-ing windows

The ticket to displaying any form is to execute its Show method. If the form is named FormICa, all you need to type is the following:

```
FormICa.Show
```

Note that Show is a method of the UserForm object, so you append it to the form name following a period. If the form in question isn't already loaded into memory, the Show method loads it and then displays it. If the form is loaded but hidden, the Show method just makes it visible.

Loading a form without displaying it

Use the Load statement to load the form into memory before you actually display it on the screen. Load is not a method, so the syntax is backward compared to Show, as in the following:

```
Load FormAlDeHyde
```

Why load a form without displaying it? Well, if your program uses numerous or complicated forms, this can make your program seem faster to the user. Because a program of any complexity performs lots of miscellaneous initialization procedures (such as reading data from files, calculating initial variables, and creating objects), a waiting period is typical when the program starts up. If you load your forms at that time too, users won't notice the wait as much as they might later on.

Making changes in your form before you display it

You can also load a form — without the Load statement — by entering code statements that manipulate a property or method of the form, or of one of its controls. This technique allows your program to make changes in a form before displaying it on the screen. After all, you may not know how the form (or its controls) should look or act until your program is running.

As a simple example, suppose you want the form's caption to display the date and time. Because you can't predict when someone is going to run your program — and because you probably expect it to run more than once — you need to let VBA figure out the current date and time for you. This simple sample does the trick:

```
Sub DisplayDateCaptionedForm ()
    DateCaptionedForm.Caption = Now
    DateCaptionedForm.Show
End Sub
```

Using a similar approach, you could have the form use a label or text box control to display information about whatever is currently selected in your VBA application. Figure 56-19 shows what you get by running the following PowerPoint procedure, coupled with an appropriate form:

```
Sub DisplayShowSelectionForm()
    Dim ItemCount As Integer, Message As String
    Items = ActiveWindow.Selection.ShapeRange.Count
    Message = CStr(Items) & " objects are selected."
    ShowSelectionForm.lblCountOfItems.Caption = Message
    ShowSelectionForm.Show
End Sub
```

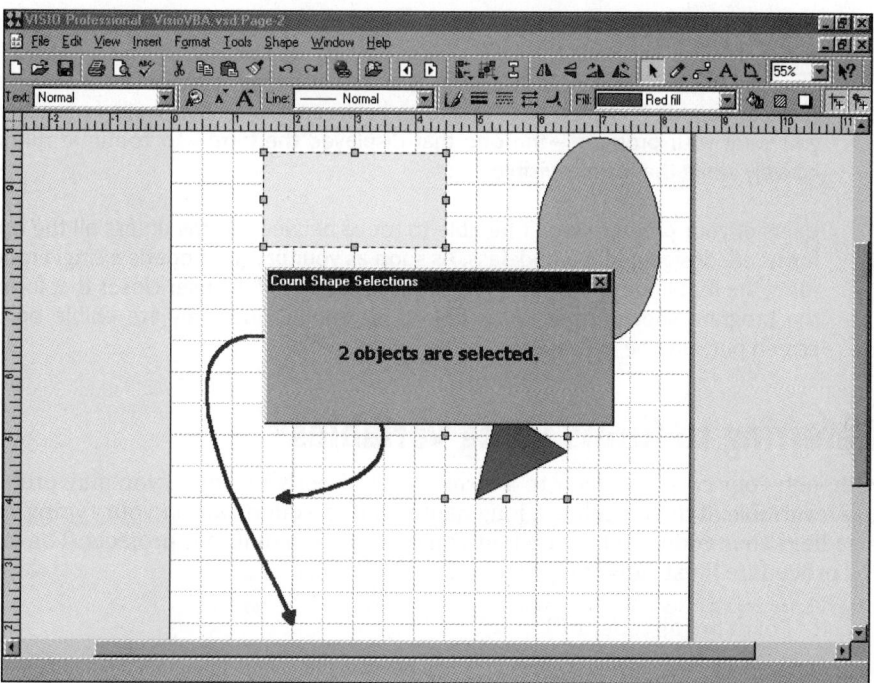

Figure 56-19: This program figures out what to display in the label caption just before you show the form.

Altering a form with the Initialize and Activate events

Another way to make changes in a form before displaying it is to use the form's own `Initialize` or `Activate` event. Code you place in these event procedures runs automatically when the corresponding event occurs. Use the `Initialize` event for code that should run only when VBA first loads the form, and use the `Activate` event for code that should run every time the form is displayed (including the first time). Writing code for event procedures is discussed in the section "Event Programming for Forms and Controls," later in this chapter.

Modal versus modeless forms

The classic example of a *modal form* is the typical dialog box: When the dialog box is active, you can't work with any other part of the program. You have to close the dialog box in order to work with a different dialog box or directly with a document. When a modal form is active, the only parts of your VBA program that can run are the procedures belonging to the form itself. The form can respond to events, but the rest of your program is suspended, and the underlying application itself is off limits to the user — until the form is closed. For example, when a user closes a form, you may want to prompt the user to save changes. A modal form may be used to display this prompt. This type of form will force the user to respond by clicking the Yes or No button.

Tip   The version of VBA that comes with Office XP gives you a choice between modal and modeless behavior for each dialog box. By default, the form's `ShowModal` property is `True`, meaning the form is modal. Change it to `False` if you want users to be able to switch back and forth between it and other open forms, and if you want your program—the one that displayed the form—to continue running actively while the form is visible.

Note   Users of your program won't be able to move between forms unless all the open forms are designated as modeless. As soon as your program opens a single modal form, the remainder of the program is suspended until the user closes that form. If the program shows other forms before the modal one, they are visible on the screen but can't be activated.

Referring to forms using variables

Although your code can refer to a form object directly by name, you may prefer to use a variable. If the form has a long name, this can cut down on your typing. It can also help your code run faster when you use forms in different projects. The following procedure illustrates the process:

```
Sub FormVariableDemo()

Dim frm1 As FormAnOpinion
Set frm1 = FormAnOpinion

' Alter properties and invoke methods via the variable:
With frm1
 .Caption = "All of the above"
 .Show
End With
End Sub
```

Note   You must declare a form variable based on a specific form, not as a generic `UserForm`.

Hiding a visible form

Use a form's `Hide` method to close the form so your program can return to the VBA application's document or activate another form. A statement such as

```
FormErly.Hide
```

does the trick. But you can't use the `Hide` method just anywhere in your program. You must place it in an event procedure belonging to the form. Most often, a `Hide` statement comes at the end of the event procedures for command buttons captioned OK and Cancel. Hiding the form does not remove it from memory. You can redisplay the form at top speed any time you need it with the Show method.

Removing a form from memory

If you know your program won't be needing a form again, you can destroy the form altogether, removing it from memory. Just as when you load a form, you use a statement, not a method, to unload a form from memory, as in the following:

```
Unload FormAtion
```

Unloading a form also removes it from the screen, if it was visible.

If you know that a form won't be needed again, you can substitute the Unload statement for the Hide method in event procedures that close the form (see the previous section).

Event Programming for Forms and Controls

When you activate a Sub procedure that doesn't display forms, your code has full control of what the program does and when it does it. After a form is on the screen, though, your program enters a much more passive state, watchfully waiting for instructions from the user. As the user presses keys or moves or clicks the mouse, each such action generates a software event. In turn, your program registers each event, checking to see whether the form's code contains an event procedure tied to that event. If not, the event passes through your program without a trace. But if the form does have a corresponding event procedure, then the program springs to life, faithfully running the procedure.

An event procedure can do anything that any ordinary procedure can. It can calculate variables, manipulate object properties and methods, and even load and display other forms. After the event procedure finishes running, control returns to the form. The program goes back to waiting for the next event to occur.

Common events

VBA forms and their controls are capable of detecting and recognizing a wide variety of different events. Table 56-2 lists commonly useful ones.

Table 56-2
Selected Events for Form and Control Objects

Event(s)	Objects It Applies To	When It Occurs
Activate	Forms	Each time the form is activated (receives the focus)
AddControl	Forms, frames, and multipage controls	When a control is added to the object at runtime
AfterUpdate	All action controls except command buttons (not labels, pictures, frames, or multipage controls)	After VBA has registered a new value for the control, just before exiting the control to move to another one
Change	All action controls except labels and command buttons; also multipage and tab strip controls	When the Value property of the control changes
Click	Forms and all control types	When the user clicks the mouse over the object
DblClick	Forms and all control types	When the user double-clicks the mouse over the object
DropButtonClick	Combo and text boxes	When the drop-down list drops down (when the user either clicks the drop-down button or presses F4)
Enter	All control types	Just before the control receives the focus from another control on the same form
Error	Forms and all control types	When an error occurs and error information can't be returned to the program
Exit	All control types	Just before the focus moves from the current control to another one on the same form
KeyUp, KeyDown, KeyPress	Forms and all control types	When the user presses or releases a key
Layout	Forms, frames, and multipage controls	When the object's size changes
RemoveControl	Forms, frames, and multipage controls	When a control is removed from the object while the form is running

Event(s)	Objects It Applies To	When It Occurs
Scroll	Forms, frames, multipage controls; and text, combo, and list boxes	When the scroll box is repositioned
Zoom	Forms, frames, and multipage controls	When the object's magnification (Zoom property) changes

Writing and editing event procedures

A form or control can respond to lots of different events. But when does it actually respond to a specific event? Answer: Only when the form or control in question has an event procedure for that event. Writing an event procedure is called *trapping* the event.

Working in Code windows for forms and controls

Writing an event procedure is just like writing any other VBA code. You simply have to know where to put the statements. Code for an event procedure — and any other code associated with a specific form — belongs in that form's code window in the Visual Basic Editor. Event procedures for all the controls on the form, as well as for the form itself, go in the form's code window.

To write an event procedure for a form or one of its controls, begin by displaying the Code window for the form. Double-clicking the form or control is the quickest way to do so. Alternatively, you can choose View Code from the item's shortcut (right-click) menu.

Next, select the object you're writing the event procedure for — pick it from the Object drop-down list at the top left of the form's Code window (see Figure 56-20). Now select the event you want to write code for. This time, use the Procedure drop-down list at the top right of the Code window.

Beginning work on an event procedure

As soon as you select an event in the Procedure drop-down list, VBA whisks you directly to the event procedure for that event in the Code window. If no code has been previously written for this event procedure, VBA creates a new procedure skeleton for you, placing the insertion point on a blank line between the declaration and the closing statement. If the event procedure already contains code, you're simply placed at the top line of the existing code.

Object drop-down   Procedure drop-down

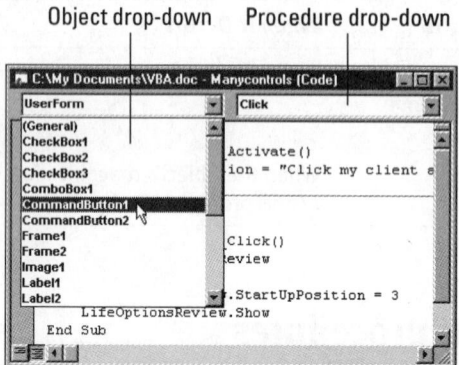

Figure 56-20: Selecting a control in a form's Code window in preparation for writing an event procedure

Event procedure syntax

The basic syntax for an event procedure is exactly the same as for ordinary Sub procedures you write in VBA modules (see Chapter 53). The only thing unique about an event procedure is its name. For the event procedure to function at all, its name must consist of the name of the object (the form or control), followed by an underscore, followed by the official VBA name for the event. If you have a button named cmdCalculateSquareRoot, the Click event procedure for that button should be named cmdCalculateSquareRoot_Click. You don't usually have to worry about naming an event procedure, because VBA creates the procedure declaration for you when you select the event in the form's Code window.

Caution

The one time you can get into trouble with an event procedure's name is when you change the name of its associated object. Suppose (for example) you've written an event procedure for the Click event of a button automatically named CommandButton1 by VBA. At this point, the procedure name is CommandButton1_Click. Now you belatedly give the button a more descriptive name, such as cmdTakeOutTheTrash. Unless and until you change the name of the event procedure to cmdTakeOutTheTrash_Click, the button just sits there mute and unresponsive when the form runs, no matter how many times you click it.

Working with the Click event

Because clicking is so integral an activity in the Windows user interface, you definitely want your VBA forms to respond to mouse-clicks. For most controls, however, you don't have to write any code to make this happen—I'll explain why in a bit. But this is not so for the most important control of all, the command button.

Every command button control definitely must have a `Click` event procedure, if you want the button to do anything when someone clicks it. This event procedure simply counts the number of times the user clicks the `cmdCountClicks` button:

```
Private Sub cmdCountClicks_Click()
' Declaring the intCount variable as Static preserves
'    its value between calls to the procedure
Static intCount As Integer
intCount = intCount + 1
cmdCountClicks.Caption = "You clicked this button " _
    & intCount & " times."
End Sub
```

This code is pretty straightforward. Each time the event procedure runs — which should occur only when the user clicks the button — the value of the `intCount` variable is increased by one. This value is then used in a string that sets the button's `Caption` property. By the way, declaring the `intCount` variable as `Static` tells VBA to retain the variable's value between passes through the event procedure. If you declared it with a `Dim` statement, VBA would reinitialize the variable to 0 each time.

Obviously, this example is trivial. Still, it illustrates the way event procedure code looks and acts like any other code.

Often, you don't need to write Click event procedures

Most VBA controls you can place on a form have (that is, recognize) the `Click` event. However, except in the case of command buttons, it's usually neither necessary nor wise to write event procedure code for the `Click` event. The reason: These controls respond to clicks automatically, and in the way you want them to.

For example, say you place some option buttons on a VBA form. When you run the form, clicking an option button selects the one you clicked — no programming is required to make this happen. In like fashion, VBA handles clicks on a toggle button or checkbox automatically, and text box controls automatically respond to clicks by positioning the insertion point at the spot where you click.

Note   What VBA can't do — and what you have to do by writing code — is transfer the setting of the control, after the user has clicked it, to your program. See the sections "Responding to control changes" and "Validating entries" for details on how to do this.

Click events on UserForms

Even forms themselves have `Click` events. If you want it to, an entire form can act as one big button; then clicking it anywhere makes something happen in your program. When the program is running, VBA triggers the procedure only if the user clicks over the part of the form that isn't covered by any controls.

Responding to control changes

When users click the up arrow button at the top of a scroll bar or spinner, they deserve some sort of feedback. How much has the value increased by virtue of this click? For that matter, did they actually manage to click the button? Trapping the `Change` event enables you to write code to provide that feedback. The `Change` event occurs whenever there's a change in the value of the control (that is, when the control's `Value` property changes). It's most often useful with option buttons, checkboxes, and toggle buttons, as well as with spin buttons and scroll bars.

The simplest response to a `Change` event is simply to display the changed `Value` property as the caption of a label. Of course, a `Change` event procedure can do more with a control's new value than just display it. It can do the following:

✦ Check to see whether the value meets certain criteria (see "Validating entries," later in this chapter).

✦ Make calculations based on the value, taking other actions depending on the calculated results.

✦ Use the control's value to manipulate some other setting, such as the volume on your computer's speaker.

The `Change` event occurs every time the control's value changes — with every mouse click or key press. Sometimes it makes more sense to let the user finish making changes before doing something about those changes. You can use the `BeforeUpdate` and `AfterUpdate` events in this situation. The `BeforeUpdate` event is best used for validating the user's entry in the control and is discussed in "Validating entries" later in this chapter. The `AfterUpdate` event occurs when the user finishes working with the control and has moved to another control. It's appropriate for performing calculations with the changed value of the original control, or using that value to alter some other setting.

Note One caveat: The `AfterUpdate` event occurs only when the control's setting is changed by the user. If you alter the text in a text box via an assignment statement such as

```
txtHerTextBox = strNewsFlashScl
```

you must use the `Change` event if you want the arrival of the new text to trigger other actions.

Detecting keystrokes

Use the `KeyPress`, `KeyDown`, and `KeyUp` events to respond to the user whacking away at the keyboard. The `KeyPress` event is good for reading ordinary "typeable" keys when you're processing entries in a text box or combo box. It can also recognize many Ctrl+key combinations and the Backspace key. The `KeyDown` and `KeyUp` events, by contrast, detect just about any key combination you throw at them, including convolutions, such as Alt+Shift+Ctrl+F9. Although they're harder to work with than `KeyPress`, these events give you more flexibility for creating keyboard shortcuts. For example, you could write a `KeyDown` event procedure to have the Ctrl+Left Arrow and Ctrl+Right Arrow combinations lower and raise the value of a scroll bar or spin button control by 10.

Handling Common Form Programming Tasks

Armed with an understanding of how event procedures work, you can put your knowledge to work in building dialog boxes that work the way you want them to and users expect them to. In this section, I've collected a set of tips covering many of the common scenarios in dialog box construction.

Adding a Close or Cancel button

At a minimum, most dialog boxes have one all-important command button: the one that removes the dialog box from the screen. Depending on the way the rest of the dialog box works, this button is typically captioned Close or Cancel, but captions such as Exit, Finish, All Done, or Give Up would also be appropriate. Every form you make needs such a button.

By convention, both Close and Cancel buttons simply hide or unload the form, without doing much else. Here's how to tell which of them your form should have:

✦ Use a Close button for a form that just displays information or performs tasks immediately, without changing program settings or modifying variables to be used later in the program.

✦ Use a Cancel button on a form that does change variables or program settings. When the user clicks the Cancel button, the dialog box closes without recording those changes — everything stays the way it was before the dialog box was displayed. The form should also have an OK button that confirms the changes made.

Easy event procedures for Close and Cancel buttons

Like any other command button, a Close or Cancel button needs a `Click` event procedure to do its job in response to a mouse-click. In most situations, this event procedure requires only a single statement, as in these two examples:

```
Private Sub cmdClose_Click()
    Hide ' Object reference to current form implied
End Sub

Private Sub cmdCancel_Click()
    Unload frmOptions
End Sub
```

Of course, event procedures tied to Close or Cancel buttons can do other tasks before closing the form. One simple example would be a statement displaying a message box asking whether the user really wants to close (or cancel) the dialog box:

```
Private Sub cmdCancel_Click()
    Message = "Do you really want to close the " _
        & "dialog box and cancel all the changes " _
        & "you've made?"
    If MsgBox(Message, vbYesNo) = vbYes Then
        Hide   ' Hide only if the user clicked Yes
    End If   ' Otherwise do nothing
End Sub
```

The keyboard alternative

Remember to tie the Close or Cancel button to the Esc key. People are used to pressing Esc to back out of a dialog box, and you shouldn't disappoint them. You don't need to add a KeyPress event procedure—simply setting the button's Cancel property to True in the Property window does the trick.

Programming the OK button

Suppose someone clicks a dialog box's OK button. The person expects your program to accept the current entries in the form as final, making the specified changes in the program's appearance, behavior, or data. After that, the form should remove itself from the screen.

Gratify these expectations by writing a Click event procedure for the OK button. All the code has to do is transfer values from the form's controls to variables in your program, or use the controls' values in conditional statements. The final statement in the procedure should contain the form's Hide method or an Unload statement. In the following examples, txtCName and txtCAddress are text boxes. The first two statements transfer their contents to corresponding program variables. Next, the program checks the status of the tglSend toggle button and, if it's on, runs a procedure called SendBillToCustomer. Finally it Hides the form.

```
Private Sub cmdOK_Click()
    strCustomerName = txtCName.Value
    strCustomerAddress = txtCAddress.Value
    'check toggle button status
    If tglSend.Value = True Then
        SendBillToCustomer
    End If
    Hide
End Sub
```

Validating entries

One of the most common tasks performed in event procedures is validation of entries the user makes via a control. Often, a program can accept only certain values. However, the user is free to enter any text in a text or combo box and to pick almost any number via a slider or spinner. The solution is to add validation code to an event procedure for the control. The code looks at the user's entry, evaluating it to see whether it meets your criteria. If so, the code can store the value or pass it along to another part of your program. If not, you can display a message informing the user of the problem (see Figure 56-21). Alternatively, the code might convert the entry into an acceptable one, say by capitalizing lowercase letters.

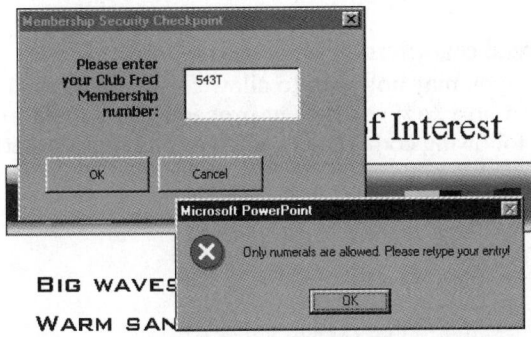

Figure 56-21: I used a Change event procedure to check the entry in the text box and display this error message to the user.

Code for validation routines

Validating the value of a control requires you to write `If...Then` statements, `Select Case` statements, or both. This simple example checks a spin button for an unacceptable value:

```
Private Sub spnVolumeControl_Change
    If spnVolumeControl.Value = 11 Then
        MsgBox "11 is not an acceptable setting."
    End If
End Sub
```

Events you can use to validate user entries

It can make sense to perform validation at several different points in the cycle of user and form interactions. Each of these validation points corresponds to a different event procedure on the current control or the form as a whole, as shown here:

When Validation Takes Place	Event Procedure to Use
Each time the value of the control changes	Change event for the control (evaluates the entire value)
Each time a key is pressed	KeyPress event for the control (evaluates the one key just pressed)
When the user finishes working with the control but before moving to another	BeforeUpdate (allows the update to be canceled, returning the user to the control)
When the user closes the form	Click event for the form's OK or Close button

Screening out or changing individual characters

In text box or combo box entries, you may not want to allow certain individual characters anywhere in an entry. Use a KeyPress event procedure to screen them out as the user types them. The following code rejects all characters except letters and numerals:

```
Private Sub txtSerialNumber_KeyPress(ByVal KeyAscii _
    As MSForms.ReturnInteger)
' this whole block is the condition:
If      Chr(KeyAscii) < "0" Or _
    (Chr(KeyAscii) > "9" And Chr(KeyAscii) < "A") Or _
    (Chr(KeyAscii) > "Z" And Chr(KeyAscii) < "a") Or _
    Chr(KeyAscii) > "z" _ Then

    MsgBox "Invalid character!"
    KeyAscii = 0 ' Throw out the character

End If
End Sub
```

After the If...Then statement detects an invalid character, it displays a message to that effect. Then comes the statement, KeyAscii = 0. KeyAscii is an argument to the KeyPress event procedure, so it works like a local variable in the procedure. Changing its value changes the character code sent to the text box. Because the text box itself won't accept a character code of 0, the character typed by the user vanishes without a trace.

Changing the KeyAscii value also lets you change an invalid entry into a correct one. For example, you could use the following event procedure to display and store all letters typed by the user in uppercase:

```
Private Sub txtSerialNumber_KeyPress(ByVal KeyAscii _
    As MSForms.ReturnInteger)
KeyAscii = Asc(UCase(Chr(KeyAscii)))
End Sub
```

The conversion statement requires three nested functions. Because KeyAscii is a numeric character code, you must first convert it to a string with Chr, then make it uppercase with UCase, and finally convert it back to an integer with Asc.

Delayed validation with the BeforeUpdate event

Sometimes it's preferable to postpone validating the entry until after the user is finished working with it. Some people appreciate being allowed to correct their own mistakes before passing an entry off to the program for a final check — it makes them feel like you're giving them some credit in the intelligence department. Another reason to put off validating an entry is because the validation code takes a long time to run.

To check a control's value after the user indicates that work is complete, write a BeforeUpdate event procedure. These events occur when the user clicks a different control, presses Tab, or presses the keyboard shortcut for another control. VBA detects the BeforeUpdate event just before leaving the original control, which gives you an opportunity to cancel the update and remain there, forcing the user to fix the problem. This example shows how to use the Cancel statement:

```
Private Sub txtSerialNumber_Change
    If len(txtSerialNumber.Value) > 5 Then
        MsgBox "Your entry is too long. Try again."
      Cancel
    End If
End Sub
```

Waiting until the form closes

Sometimes it makes sense to postpone validation for a control until the user clicks the OK button to close the entire form. You could do this if the validation criteria depend on the values of other controls. If you go this route, place the validation code in the OK button's Click event procedure.

Morphing forms and controls

With event procedures to enliven it, a form can become a dynamic entity that responds to events by changing its own appearance, not just the data in your program. These are key techniques for creating professional-looking forms.

Morphing method 1: Altering control properties

An easy way to change the appearance of a form is by modifying the properties of the form or its controls in your event procedure code. As you've seen in several previous examples, a basic but very useful application of this idea is to change a label's caption. This lets you send messages to your users based on current conditions.

In the example here, a form has a command button named cmdClickMe and a label named lblLittleMessage. Clicking the button changes the label's caption. The button's Click event procedure looks like this:

```
Private Sub cmdClickMe_Click()

' Declare static integer to count the times
'     the procedure runs
Static X as Integer

X = X + 1
Select Case X Mod 3
    Case 0
        lblLittleMessage.Caption = Now
    Case 1
        lblLittleMessage.Caption = CStr (X/2 * X)
    Case 2
        lblLittleMessage.Caption = _
            "Life is a series of interruptions."
    End Select
End Sub
```

Of course, you're not limited to changing text on labels. You can modify any property on any of the form's objects, except for read-only properties that are always off limits. Set the Enabled property to False when conditions dictate that a control should be unavailable to the user. You can even change the Value displayed in a control.

Morphing method 2: Multiple sets of controls

Although it's easy to change the appearance of your form in response to events, changing what those controls do takes more work. Suppose your program is supposed to display test questions, get an answer from the user, and then show a message discussing why the chosen answer was right or wrong. You could handle this problem by alternating between two different forms, one for the question and user's answer, the other giving the answer from the program. But consider a slicker method. You could use a single form, displaying one set of controls when the asking the question and another set when providing the answer. This approach involves a little more work, but no rocket science.

An easy way to make one form act as two (or more) is to add a distinct control to the form for every function. You can then use the Visible property of each control to hide or display it at your will and pleasure.

Installing and Using ActiveX Controls

Despite its reputation for software imperialism, Microsoft has taken pains to make its development tools "open." Based on the ActiveX spec, anyone can create new controls that work with just about every Windows-based programming language — including C++, HTML, Visual Basic, and VBA. The benefit to you is that you can add new features by plugging in ActiveX controls that don't come with VBA.

Adding new controls to the Toolbox

Before you can use an ActiveX control in your VBA programs, you must install the software for the control onto your computer's hard disk and register the control in Windows. You can register controls in various ways, and the installation step often does it for you. But if you have to do it yourself, the easiest way is in the Visual Basic Editor.

Registering a control

To register a new control, make sure you know the name of the file that contains the control and where it's located on your hard disk. Then you can follow these steps:

1. Choose Tools ➪ References. The ActiveX references available to your project appear.

2. In the dialog box, click Browse. A standard-issue Windows dialog box for opening files appears.

3. Select ActiveX controls in the Files of Type combo box.

4. When you locate the file for the control, double-click it to open it. You're returned to the References dialog box.

5. Scroll to the item for the control and make sure that its little checkbox is checked.

6. Close the dialog box.

Next, putting the tool in your Toolbox

After a new control has been registered, the next step is to activate it by placing its icon on the Toolbox. Here's how:

1. Display the Toolbox by selecting any UserForm window or choosing View ➪ Toolbox.

2. Either right-click the Toolbox and select Additional Controls or choose Tools ➪ Additional Controls. This brings up the dialog box shown in Figure 56-22.

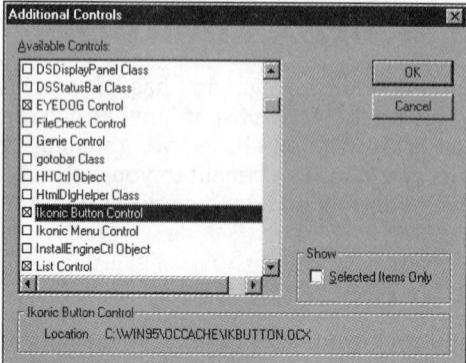

Figure 56-22: Activate new ActiveX controls
in this dialog box.

3. Scroll through the list of available controls to locate the one you want to activate. When you find it, check its little checkbox.

4. Close the dialog box. The icon for the newly activated control appears on the Toolbox. Figure 56-23 shows the Toolbox with a bunch of new controls.

If you use lots of third-party controls, you can organize them on separate pages of the Toolbox. To add new pages to the Toolbox, right-click over the tabbed area at the top and choose New Page (just like you would with a multipage control on a form). The page that's showing when you activate a control is the one that receives the control's icon.

Figure 56-23: A customized Toolbox with lots of additional ActiveX controls

Using ActiveX controls in your programs

As soon as you have an ActiveX control on the Toolbox, you can add it to your forms just like the stock controls that come with VBA. However, to make the control do something useful, you need to know how its properties and methods work. For that you need the documentation and Help files that come with the control. If the control was properly designed and installed, you should be able to get Help on any of its properties by pressing F1 from when that property is selected in the VBA Properties window.

Some controls are invisible

Lots of really great ActiveX controls are invisible when your program runs. Rather than directly interacting with the user, such controls perform various actions for you so you don't have to write your own procedures or create your own objects to get these jobs done (for example, a counter or a control that performs calculations in the background). Even though these invisible controls don't show up when your form is actually running, they do appear on the form during the design process.

To use an invisible control in your program, then, you have to add it to a form just as you would any other control. Because the control is never visible to the user, where you stick it on the form doesn't really matter. Just put it someplace where it doesn't overlap other controls.

✦   ✦   ✦

Building Power Applications

◆ ◆ ◆ ◆

In This Chapter

Building applications
with COM objects

Creating add-ins for
specific applications

Increasing versatility
by setting document
properties as
variables

Securing and locking
your finished code

Fleshing out your
custom-built
applications with
Office Developer

Distributing your
completed
application

◆ ◆ ◆ ◆

If all you ever do with VBA is write individual modules to make your work in Office more efficient, well and good. But VBA is a full-blown software development tool. You can use VBA to create complete custom applications that solve nearly any computing challenges. Your custom VBA software can draw on the power of any combination of the Office applications.

Building Custom Applications with COM Objects

For many custom VBA applications, the goal is to enhance or concentrate the functionality of one of the standard Office applications. For example, you can add a collection of special-purpose financial and reporting functions to an Excel spreadsheet that helps you perform your month-end accounting tasks. You might further enhance such an application by modifying Excel's user interface with new command bars and toolbars. Perhaps you would want to implement a switchboard interface with simple command buttons for inexperienced users who don't want to learn how to navigate the Excel's menu structure. Figure 57-1 illustrates a custom application based on Excel.

But a software world of dazzling variety lies just outside the confines of any particular VBA application — and you're free to travel there with VBA. All the Office applications and accessory components incorporate the Component Object Model (COM), brazenly exposing their objects so you can access them in your own programs. That means you can readily build custom applications that tap the combined firepower of, say, Word, Excel, and Access. For that matter, your VBA apps can draw on the capabilities of any COM-based application, whether it's part of the Office suite or not. If you want to create a Visio organization chart based on personnel data stored in your Outlook folders, you can. Figure 57-2 illustrates a custom Outlook form based on an Excel spreadsheet.

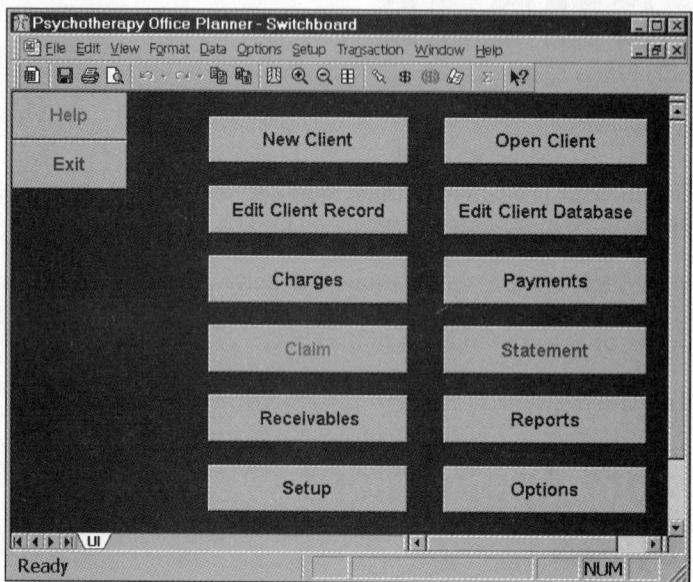

Figure 57-1: A VBA application using a switchboard user interface for less advanced users. Notice the custom command bars at the top of the application window.

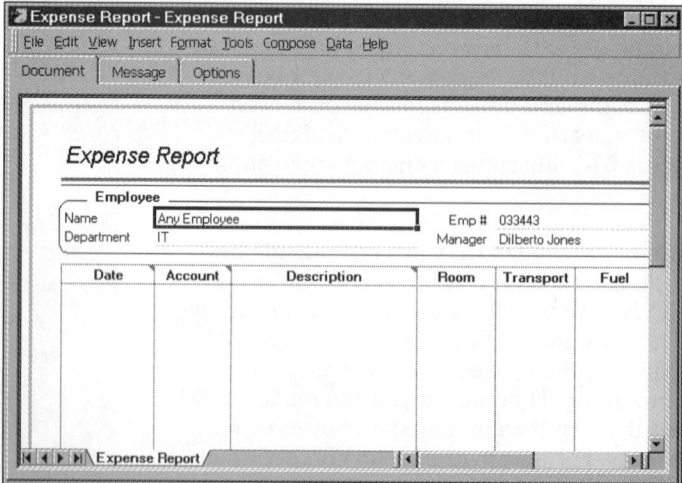

Figure 57-2: A custom Outlook form based on Excel worksheet data

The Component Object Model teaches a developer that great software is built from reusable parts — reinventing the wheel for each application isn't smart, and it's a waste of your time and productivity. Think about the vast array of software functionality Office makes available. Access performs well as a database for large record sets with primary keys and multiple indexes on a table. Excel supports complex statistical and financial formulas that would be hard to duplicate in Access. Word provides text editing and formatting capabilities far beyond those in either Access or Excel. And so it goes. With COM, you can mesh any of these software components to achieve your exact design goals.

In the sample code presented in this section, data stored in Outlook are retrieved and passed for analysis to Excel. The sample code demonstrates many of the concepts you must master to build custom VBA applications.

The assignment

You're dreaming of that vacation in Hawaii that you've had planned for over a year. You and your team just completed a software project that required several months of 12-hour days and you're really looking forward to a rest. In only a week, you'll be relaxing in the warm waters of the Pacific Ocean! At 4:30 P.M., your boss requests that you drop by for a chat. She informs you that an urgent request has come down from top management that requires an immediate solution.

It seems that management has sponsored a Groupware application in the public folders of your Exchange server that tracks customer contacts, marketing efforts, and sales results in terms of total sales dollars. The bonuses of certain individuals in marketing depend on numbers that have to be extracted from the Customer Contacts public folder, analyzed in Excel, and then presented to management for a final decision by the day on which you're leaving for vacation.

No one else on your team has the time to complete this project. The responsibility has fallen on your shoulders and you don't want to disappoint your boss. All you know about Outlook is that it's your e-mail program. You certainly have no idea about how you're going to move information from an Outlook folder to an Excel spreadsheet. Looks like you're going to endure many more long workdays before you bask in the warmth of the Hawaiian sun.

Defining the problem

Before you start to write a line of code, it's important to define as concretely as possible the problem you need to solve. Unless you understand the problem clearly, you'll thrash around accomplishing little. Taking this advice to heart, you dash off a quick e-mail to your boss requesting additional information on the task. Reading her reply, you feel the challenge comes into focus — they're not requesting the impossible; they just want you to extract information so the spreadsheet gurus in accounting can work their magic on the numbers. Your task becomes one of moving data from one container application into another.

When you can summarize the project's overall goal in concrete terms, your next step is to break it up into a series of specific tasks that your application must perform to meet that goal. Using diagramming software such as Visio — or pencil and paper, if you prefer — sketch out the structure of the application.

Assume that your application asks the user, a financial analyst, for a date range and a customer category and then extracts the data from a public Outlook folder to a worksheet. The overall goal is to move the data from one object collection container (an Outlook folder) to a different object collection container (an Excel worksheet).

Fortunately, both of the applications involved are components of Office. Office is built upon ActiveX technology, which has at its foundation the concept of reusable software components defined as objects with properties, events, and methods. Outlook makes available, or exposes, an object model to VBA controller applications such as Excel, where the code will reside.

So in more detail, this problem comes down to determining how to define the objects of Outlook, access those object's properties (their data), and place the retrieved properties into the objects of Excel (sheets, rows, and columns). When you start thinking in this ActiveX object frame of mind, solving your assignment starts to sound like an exciting adventure rather than a direct path to insomnia.

Getting started

Start a new VBA project by running the Office application you want to host the project and opening a new document (to hold the project) in that application. (In the example code presented a little later in this chapter, the host application is Excel.) Then kick-start the Visual Basic Editor by pressing Alt+F11.

Cross-application programming

Maybe it's obvious, but you can only use the objects of another application if that application has been installed on your system. If that requirement is met, working with objects from another COM-based application requires three preliminary steps:

1. In the Visual Basic Editor, add a reference to the external application's object library.

2. Declare variables for the objects you plan to use in the program.

3. Create (instantiate) the objects using the `CreateObject` function.

I have more to say about each of these steps in the next three sections. Please refer to Chapter 49 for the basic techniques you need for working with objects in VBA code.

Adding a reference to the foreign object model

To inform the Visual Basic Editor about an external application's object model, you add and activate a reference to the application's object library. In the Visual Basic Editor, choose Tools ➪ References to open the References dialog box (see Figure 57-3).

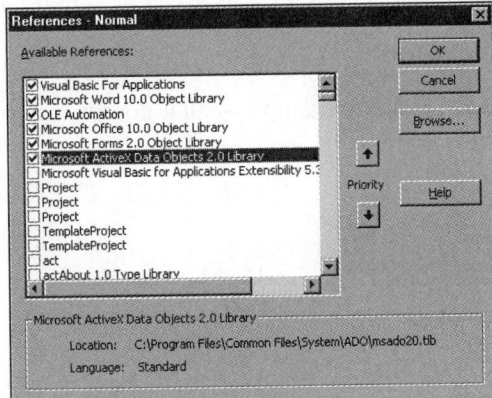

Figure 57-3: Add and activate references to object libraries here.

Outlook's object library should already be listed in the dialog box, assuming you've already installed Outlook on your computer. All you have to do is find it in the Available References list and check its box to activate it and make its objects accessible. If the object library you want to use isn't listed, add the reference to the list yourself using the Browse button.

Declaring external objects

Use standard VBA syntax to declare variables for objects from external applications. Use the Object Browser or the external application's Help file to learn what objects it makes available. The following statements from the Declarations section of your module declare variables for the Outlook objects required in the example program:

```
Dim objOutlook As Outlook.Application
Dim objOLNamespace As Outlook.NameSpace
Dim colFolders As Outlook.Folders ' collection of folders
Dim objPeopleFolder As Outlook.MAPIFolder
Dim colPeople As Outlook.Items ' collection of contacts
Dim objPerson As Object ' one individual contact
Dim strName As String
```

Creating the external object

Declaring the objects just announces your intention to use them. You must then actually create the objects you need with Set statements inside a VBA procedure.

The key to creating an object belonging to an external application is the CreateObject function. CreateObject starts the application, which in turn creates the object. The function's return value is a reference to the object, which you can assign to the appropriate variable. To start the application with a specific file or document, use the GetObject function instead.

Here's a sample procedure for the Excel-Outlook example — all it does is instantiate the needed objects:

```
Sub PeopleWorksheet()

' start Outlook, create an object reference to the application
Set objOutlook = CreateObject("Outlook.Application.10")

' create references to subsidiary Outlook objects
Set objOLNamespace = objOutlook.GetNamespace("MAPI")
Set colFolders = objOLNamespace.Folders ' all folders
Set objPeopleFolder = colFolders.Item("Personal Folders")

' drill down into folder hierarchy
' reuse some variable names—previous objects no longer needed
Set colFolders = objPeopleFolder.Folders
Set objPeopleFolder = colFolders.Item("Customer Contacts")
Set colPeople = objPeopleFolder.Items

' Call a Sub procedure that puts the Outlook data to work:
OutlookToExcel
End Sub
```

Caution Since the OutlookToExcel subprocedure has not been defined yet, executing the PeopleWorksheet () example will generate an error message. Additionally, the folders hierarchy within Outlook installed on your system should include "Personal Folders" and "Customer Contacts" folders.

Note that in many situations — including this example — you only need the CreateObject function once. After you create the external application's object, you can access any of its properties and methods. In this case, as is common, those properties include other objects (here, the Folders collection, the Personal folders and Contacts folders, and the collection of items within the Contacts folders).

Applications you run from within your code via the CreateObject function start up in hidden form — you can't see them on the screen. This is great when you want to use an application's data in your own program without distracting the user.

However, sometimes you'll want to see the application in its usual form. Depending on the application, you may have to activate a `Display` method or set a `Visible` property to `True`, with a line of code such as this:

```
objPeopleFolder.Display
```

Using the external objects

At last, you're ready to roll — you can now use the external application's objects in your code, just as if they came from your VBA application:

```
Sub OutlookToExcel()
For each objPerson in colPeople
    With objPerson
' retrieve data from a contact item into variables
        strName = .FullName
        curSales = .SalesTotal
    ... (here's where to put the code that inserts this data
                into your worksheet and analyzes it there)
    End With
Next
End Sub
```

Hawaii, here you come!

Note that this example uses Outlook objects simply to retrieve data from Outlook's data store. However, once you have access to another program's objects in your code, you can trigger any actions they're capable of. You can open, edit, and save documents in the "foreign" application. You can use its data analysis tools, even on data that comes from your VBA code, not the other application.

Building Add-Ins

VBA code running in an ordinary document is fine for personal use, but it's not a very attractive solution for distributing custom applications. By building your own add-ins, you can seamlessly blend your VBA customizations with the underlying Office application, making it appear to the user that your enhancements are part and parcel of the original program.

In Office, an add-in is simply a software component that adds functionality to one or more of the Office applications. But add-ins differ from ordinary documents that contain VBA code in two important ways:

✦ The features provided by an add-in are available to all documents.

✦ When an add-in is loaded, no document associated with the add-in is accessible to the user. The add-in may make changes to the application's user interface, but the only other way to tell that it's running is to look in the relevant dialog box (usually Tools ➪ Add-Ins).

Creating application-specific add-ins

In versions prior to Office 2000, an individual add-in could work only with one Office application, and in most cases it consisted of ordinary VBA code that had to be compiled every time the add-in was loaded. You can still create such application-specific add-ins, and fairly easily. Here are the basic steps:

1. Create a new document for the add-in.

2. In the new document, add VBA modules and forms, write your code, and test the program. In Access, you need also to add a special table containing Registry information that allows the add-in to be installed.

3. Save the document as an add-in as appropriate for the application (in Word, as a .dot template, in Excel, as an .xla add-in, in PowerPoint, as both a .ppt presentation and a .ppa add-in, and in Access, as an .mda add-in or an .mde database).

4. Install the add-in using the Tools ⇨ Add-Ins dialog box. (In Word, choose Tools ⇨ Templates and Add-Ins and click Add to load the template as an add-in. In Access, choose Tools ⇨ Add-Ins ⇨ Add-In Manager.)

Creating COM add-ins

Office 2000 introduced COM add-ins, a new and more powerful add-in type. A COM add-in is a compiled dynamic link library (DLL) containing special "hooks" that allow it to be loaded by Office. As its name implies, such an add-in works by manipulating the object model of the target Office application through COM technology. COM add-ins have these advantages:

✦ Because COM add-ins are already compiled, they load and run faster than comparable old-style add-ins.

✦ A single COM add-in can be shared by more than one Office application when that's appropriate.

✦ COM add-ins work in Outlook and FrontPage, which don't support application-specific add-ins.

You can create COM add-ins with many different Microsoft programming tools. VBA works, of course, but only if you have Office XP Developer (see "Using Office Developer," later in this chapter). Developer includes special software for compiling the add-in code as a DLL and registering the DLL with Windows, and it comes with full instructions for creating COM add-ins using Visual Basic as well as VBA. You can even use Visual C++ or Visual J++ to build COM add-ins.

Using Custom Properties as Document Variables

Plenty of programming situations call for a way to store variable values, even when the program isn't running. Take a simple counter, for example. Suppose you want to know how many times one of Excel's toolbar buttons gets clicked over the course of a month. Unless you want to keep Excel running constantly for the entire month, you need to store the current count each time you exit the program, and read it back in the next time you start Excel.

Among the Office applications, only Word includes in its object model the tools needed to directly manage persistent variables (via its Variable object). However, custom document properties provide a workaround that fits the bill in Excel and PowerPoint. You can use VBA to create custom document properties, fill them with data, and retrieve that data on demand. And because these properties are part and parcel of the document they're associated with, you don't have to worry about keeping track of them in a separate file—when you save a document, its properties are automatically saved to disk along with the rest of the document.

Cross-Reference See Chapter 12 if you need background on document properties and how to work with them in the Properties dialog box.

To create a new custom document property in Word, Excel, or PowerPoint, use the Add method of the document's CustomDocumentProperties collection. The following example works in Excel, where the ActiveWorkbook object refers to whatever workbook is currently active when the procedure runs (the comparable objects in Word and PowerPoint are ActiveDocument and ActivePresentation, respectively):

```
ActiveWorkbook.CustomDocumentProperties.Add _
    Name:="Button Count", LinkToContent:=False, _
    Type:=msoPropertyTypeNumber, Value:=0
```

The LinkToContent parameter should be False unless you want the value of the property to be based on a range or bookmark. The Type parameter determines the data type of the property; valid constants aside from the one shown in valid constants include msoPropertyTypeBoolean, msoPropertyTypeDate, msoPropertyTypeFloat, and msoPropertyTypeString.

To retrieve the information stored in a document property, get the Property object's Value property with a statement such as:

```
intCurrentCount = _
    ActiveWorkbook.CustomDocumentProperties("Button
Count").Value
```

At least two alternative solutions to this problem are available. You can write and read values to the Windows Registry using the `SaveSetting` and `GetSetting` statements, or you can save and read data to separate disk files using the `Put` and `Get` statements.

Securing Your Code with Digital Certificates

As with anything powerful, VBA can be used for good or ill. VBA procedures can carry viruses that wreak havoc with your system. For that matter, code from a well-intentioned but unskilled programmer sometimes causes serious problems.

To help mitigate these dangers, VBA can identify VBA projects using digital certificates. Using Microsoft's analogy, a digital certificate has a function similar to that of a wax seal on an envelope, allowing the recipient to know who sent the project and that its contents haven't been modified, either intentionally or unintentionally. Unlike a seal, however, a digital certificate doesn't assure the recipient that no one else has viewed the project. (To prevent others from seeing your code, follow the steps discussed in "Locking Your Code" later in the chapter.)

A user who opens a file or loads an add-in signed with a digital certificate sees the digital signature, which displays the name of the person who signed it with other identifying information. If everything looks okay, the user approves the code and it becomes active on her system. If the digital signature is missing, however, or if the identifying information is incorrect, the user may choose not to open or load the item.

Note Digital signatures are recognized only if Internet Explorer 4 or later is present on the user's system.

As a developer, signing your work digitally requires that you first obtain and install one or more digital certificates on your computer. Digital certificates are issued by commercial certification authorities, such as VeriSign, to whom you can apply as an individual or organization. If you're a staff programmer, you probably don't have the authority to apply for a digital certificate for your company. Instead, your organization obtains the certificates and sets up a system for administering them, and you request a certificate from whoever is responsible for security in your group.

Anyway, once the digital certificate is in place on your computer, digitally signing the current project is a straightforward process. In the Visual Basic Editor, choose Tools ➪ Digital Signature. In the resulting Digital Signature dialog box, click Choose to display a list of the certificates in place on your system. Make a selection and click OK in both dialog boxes to activate the signature.

When a project carries a digital signature, any change made to the project in the absence of the original certificate invalidates and removes the signature. If you plan to pass on the project in its signed form to someone else, don't modify the project unless you have a copy of the digital certificate on your computer.

Caution In many organizations, only project leaders or other administrative types actually *sign* VBA projects. As a team developer in this scenario, you would complete a project and forward it to the person with signing authority for final testing, approval, and a signature. Only then would the project be distributed to users. (It never hurts, however, to know how to sign a project—just in case the administrative officer has the authority, but not the knowledge, needed to do so.)

Locking Your Code

If you are developing custom applications for resale and you want to keep others from unauthorized use of all your hard work, you need to protect the code that you've created, hiding it so no one can see or modify it. Protecting your code often makes sense when you distribute your application in a corporate environment to keep it from inadvertent or malicious changes. After your project is debugged and tested, take these steps to protect the code that you've written:

1. Select the Tools ➪ <*ProjectName*> Properties command and, in the Project Properties dialog box, switch to the Protection tab.

2. Check the Lock Project for Viewing box to ensure that your code cannot be viewed.

3. Enter a password twice to confirm you've typed it correctly.

Caution Don't misplace the password or you will be unable to modify your code at a later date.

4. Click OK.

After a project is locked, only its name appears in the Project window. Anyone trying to see the project's contents must type in the password to proceed.

You can enter a password without checking the Lock Project for Viewing box. In this case, the password is required to open the Project Properties dialog box, but not to view or modify the project's code or forms.

Using Office Developer

For anyone doing serious VBA development work, Office XP Developer is a must. It's a special edition of Office intended for VBA programmers. Table 57-1 lists the tools and other components provided with Office XP Developer.

Table 57-1 Tools in Office XP Developer	
Tool	*Function*
Package and Deployment Wizard	Creates setup disks for distribution of your application.
Visual Source Safe	Keeps track of versions.
COM Add-In Designer and templates	Converts VBA code into COM add-in DLLs; templates enable you to create COM add-ins using Visual Basic, Java, or C++.
Code Librarian	Allows storage and reuse of code in a searchable database, and includes loads of prefab code in various Microsoft languages.
Error Handler	Automates the addition of standardized custom error-handling routines to your code.
Code Commenter	Adds automatic comment blocks to your code according to your specifications.
String Editor	Assists in writing SQL statements for database access and manipulation.
Data Environment Designer	Provides easier database connections in host applications other than Access.
Data Report Designer	Enables you to design database reports visually without Access.
Additional ActiveX controls	Includes controls such as a data-aware grid and the Common Dialog control.
HTML Help Workshop	Enables you to create complete HTML Help systems for your custom applications.
Access Run-time	Allows royalty-free distribution of Access applications to users who don't have Access.
Replication Manager	Displays and manages replicated Jet databases on networks or the Internet.

Distributing Your Solution

To prepare your solution for distribution to other users, use the Package and Deployment Wizard included in Office Developer. This wizard builds the distribution files needed for installing and running the application. A full discussion of the Package and Deployment Wizard is beyond the scope of this chapter, but the following points summarize the steps it walks you through:

✦ Specifies the files required for your application, including your main application file containing the objects and code that make up your application; data files used by your application; icon, bitmap, sound, or multimedia files; and custom Help files (including ActiveX controls, DLLs, and run-time files).

✦ Creates shortcuts and Start menu items for Windows.

✦ Writes the Windows Registry keys (or modifications to existing keys) necessary for your application.

✦ Identifies redistributable components for your application, such as ODBC drivers.

✦ Specifies options for a typical, custom, or compact installation.

✦ Sets options for distribution media (floppy disk, network share point, or CD-ROM).

Building Standalone Access Applications

When you develop custom applications using Excel, Word, PowerPoint, or Outlook, the users of your applications must have Office installed to run them. The situation is different for custom Access apps, if you have Office Developer. By distributing with your application the Access Run Time module (a component of Office Developer), you ensure that your apps can run on anyone's computer, regardless of whether Access already resides there. You can freely distribute the database engine provided with either Access, Jet, or MSDE.

✦   ✦   ✦

Finding Office Information on the Web

The following sites may provide additional useful information about using Office XP, as well as additional macros, templates, themes, and other useful add-ons.

The Microsoft Office Home Page

Following is the official Microsoft Office Home Page, run (naturally enough) by Microsoft. Here you'll find the latest Office news, plus product information, demos, and more:

http://www.microsoft.com/office

Microsoft Office Tools on the Web

Another site run by Microsoft focuses on updates to the Office suite. Office XP Help sends you to this site if it can't answer your question:

http://office.microsoft.com

Element K Journals

Look for a monthly journal about Office here:

http://www.elementkjournals.com

CNET.com Office Suites

CNET is an excellent source for information about all aspects of computers, including Microsoft Office:

```
http://www.cnet.com
```

FileMine

CMPNet's FileMine and similar huge compendiums of downloadable software are great places to find templates, themes, ActiveX controls, macros, and other add-ons to increase your Office productivity:

```
http://www.filemine.com
```

Emazing Tip of the Day

To receive a daily tip on Office by e-mail, consider subscribing to one of Emazing.com's Office-related tip service at:

```
http://www.emazing.com/office.jsp
```

Woody's Office Watch

Another source of Office tips and trivia is Woody's Office Watch, a free weekly newsletter that Woody Leonard distributes via e-mail. Subscribe at:

```
http://www.mcc.com.au/wow/
```

Web Site with Office XP Bible Code Samples

The longer, more involved code samples in this book can be found at the following Web site: `http://catalog.hungryminds.com/extras/0764535927/`. At that site and at your leisure, you can access and copy these longer code samples for your own trial purposes.

✦   ✦   ✦

Index

Continued

Continued

Continued